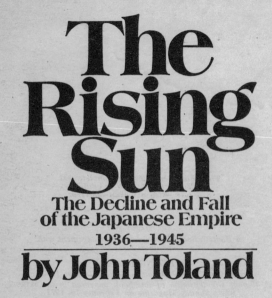

The Rising Sun

The Decline and Fall of the Japanese Empire

1936—1945

by John Toland

BANTAM BOOKS
TORONTO · NEW YORK · LONDON · SYDNEY · AUCKLAND

*This edition contains the complete text
of the original hardcover edition.*
NOT ONE WORD HAS BEEN OMITTED.

THE RISING SUN

*A Bantam Book / published by arrangement with
Random House, Inc.*

PRINTING HISTORY

Random House edition published October 1970
A 40-page Condensation of this book appeared in the DETROIT
NEWS *Sunday Magazine on February 14, 1971.*
Literary Guild selection March 1971
Playboy Book Club selection March 1971
History Book Club alternate selection April 1971
Bantam edition / November 1971
14 printings through April 1988

Bantam Books are published by Bantam Books, a division of
Bantam Doubleday Dell Publishing Group, Inc. Its trademark,
consisting of the words "Bantam Books" and the portrayal of
a rooster, is Registered in U.S. Patent and Trademark Office
and in other countries. Marca Registrada. Bantam Books,
666 Fifth Avenue, New York, New York 10103.

PRINTED IN THE UNITED STATES OF AMERICA

KR   23 22 21 20 19 18 17 16 15 14

To
Orie
and
Tokiji Matsumura
and
Paul R. Reynolds

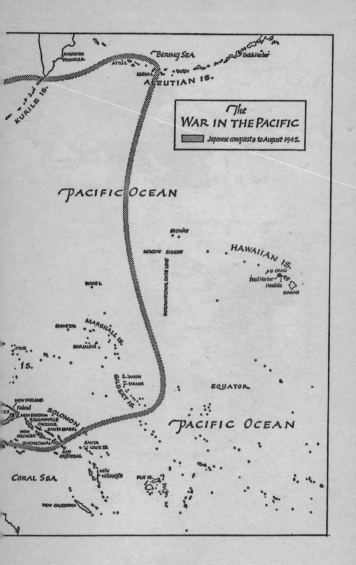

KAMCHATKA PENINSULA

BERING SEA

ATTU I.

KISKA I.

Dutch Harbor

ALEUTIAN IS.

KURILE IS.

The
WAR IN THE PACIFIC
Japanese conquests to August 1942

PACIFIC OCEAN

MIDWAY

MONDAY   SUNDAY

HAWAIIAN IS.

OAHU
Pearl Harbor
Honolulu

HAWAII

WAKE I.

INTERNATIONAL DATE LINE

ENIWETOK

MARSHALL IS.

TRUK

KWAJALEIN

IS.

S. MAKIN
TARAWA

GILBERT IS.

EQUATOR

NEW IRELAND
Rabaul
SEA   NEW BRITAIN
BOUGAINVILLE
CHOISEUL
NEW   SANTA ISABEL
GEORGIA
GUADALCANAL
SAN
CRISTOBAL

SOLOMON

PACIFIC OCEAN

SANTA
CRUZ IS.

CORAL SEA

NEW HEBRIDES

FIJI IS.

NEW CALEDONIA

Contents

Part Four—Isle of Death

Part Five—The Gathering Forces

Part Six—The Decisive Battle

Part Seven—Beyond the Bitter End

Part Eight—"One Hundred Million Die Together"

Maps

Foreword

After World War II most Westerners felt that General Tojo and other Japanese leaders—indeed the mass of Japanese—were no better than Hitler and his Nazi cohorts, and deserved all the punishment and misfortune that befell them.

Twenty-five years have passed and Japan has recovered from almost total moral and economic disaster to resume a respected place among nations of the world. Still, the question remains: How could we have come to admire and respect a people who often acted like barbarians during the war?

This book, which is largely seen from the Japanese point of view, is an attempt to answer that question as well as others about the war that changed the face of Asia. Why did a country the size of California launch the suicidal attack on Pearl Harbor which involved it in a death struggle with an enemy ten times stronger? Was war between the two nations, which today find so much in common, inevitable and essential? Did the winning of that war perpetuate American involvement in Asian affairs?

I would not have attempted to write this book—even with the assistance of a Japanese wife and her family—but for two things: a drastic change in Japanese attitudes toward their own immediate past and the appearance of significant new documents. In addition to the mountain of material already available in the Japanese Ministry of Foreign Affairs and the Military History Archives of the Japan Defense Agency, valuable documents that had been hidden or lost were recently discovered, such as records of the imperial and liaison conferences, the supposedly burned portions of the Konoye Diary, and the thousand-page "Notes" of Field Marshal Gen Sugiyama, Chief of the Army General Staff from 1940 to February 21, 1944.

Even more important has been the willingness of Japan's former military and civilian leaders—including Marquis Koichi Kido, the Emperor's chief adviser; Prince Mikasa, the Emperor's youngest brother; Admiral Ryunosuke Kusaka, de facto commander at Pearl Harbor and Midway; and General Kenryo Sato, perhaps Tojo's most trusted confidant—to talk freely and at length about the unhappy past. Gone is the reluctance, apparent only a few years ago during research for *But Not in Shame*, to discuss certain sensitive subjects. Moreover, they are convinced that Westerners, after their postwar experiences in Asia, will have more understanding of the blunders they made in Manchuria and China. Those who fought the war, from generals to privates, have also been more willing to talk of their mistakes, and speak of the unspeakable: cowardice, murder, cannibalism, surrender—and desertion.

In the interest of accuracy these men, as well as everyone else interviewed whose story is included in the book, read the passages about themselves and often added illuminating comments. The dialogue in the book is not fictional. It comes from transcripts, records and stenographic notes, and the memory of the participants. The extensive debates during the various imperial and liaison conferences, for example, are based on the Sugiyama "Notes"; the recently assembled official records; diaries; and interviews with Marquis Kido, who was given an immediate report of each conference the Emperor attended, and participants including General Teiichi Suzuki, Naoki Hoshino and Okinori Kaya. The *Notes* (at the end of the book) list sources for all material used, chapter by chapter.

America's greatest mistake in World War II, I believe, was in failing to recognize that she was fighting two different kinds of war simultaneously: one in Europe against another Western people and philosophy, Nazism, and one in Asia which was not only a struggle against an aggressive nation fighting for survival as a modern power but an ideological contest against an entire continent. Millions of Orientals saw Japan's battle as their own, as a confrontation of race and color; they also saw in Japan's victories their own liberation from Western domination.

"Each nation, the United States not excepted, has made its contribution to the welter of evil which now comprises the Far East question." Tyler Dennett, an authority on the Far East, wrote in 1922: "We shall all do well to drop for all time the pose of self-righteousness and injured innocence an penitently face the facts."

If we had done so, it is very probable that our negotiation with Japan in 1941 would have ended in peace, not war, an America would not have been forced to become the mora policeman of Asia for many years. And a moral policeman's lot is not a happy one, particularly when his own morality is in question.

What follows is a factual saga of people caught up in the flood of the most overwhelming war of mankind, told as it happened—muddled, ennobling, disgraceful, frustrating, full of contradiction and paradox. I have done my utmost to let the events speak for themselves, and if any conclusion was reached, it was that there are no simple lessons in history, that it is human nature that repeats itself, not history. We often learn more about the past from the present, in fact, than the reverse. The lessons of our own brutalities in post-war Asia, for example, have undoubtedly given Americans insight into the actions of the Japanese a generation ago.

J. T.

PART ONE

The Roots
of War

1   Gekokujo

1.

The sky over Tokyo on the afternoon of February 25, 1936, was dark and foreboding. A thick blanket of snow already covered the city and there was threat of more to come. Three nights earlier more than a foot had fallen, breaking a record of fifty-four years, and causing such a traffic snarl that some theaters had to be turned into temporary hotels for audiences unable to get home.

Even under its white cloak of snow, Tokyo looked almost as Western as Oriental. Japan had left much of its feudal past behind to become by far the most progressive, westernized nation of Asia. A few hundred yards from the Imperial Palace with its traditional tile roof was a modern four-story concrete building, the Imperial Household Ministry, where all court business was conducted and the Emperor's offices were located. Just outside the ancient stone walls and moat surrounding the spacious Palace grounds was the same mélange of East and West: a long line of modern structures, including the Imperial Theater and the Dai Ichi Building, as Occidental as the skyline of Chicago, while a few blocks away, in narrow cobblestone streets, were row upon row of geisha houses, *sushi* stands and kimono stores, and assorted little ramshackle shops, gay even on that cloudy day with their flapping doorway curtains and colorful lanterns.

Next to the Palace on a small hill was the not quite completed Diet Building, constructed mainly of stone from Okinawa and looking quasi-Egyptian. Behind this commanding edifice was a cluster of spacious houses, the official residence of government leaders. The largest was that of the Prime Minister. It was two buildings in one, the business part Western in the early Frank Lloyd Wright style, the living

1

quarters Japanese with paper-thin walls, tatami floors an
sliding doors.

But beneath the peaceful exterior of Tokyo seethed a
unrest which would soon spill violently into the snow-covere
streets. At one end of the Palace grounds were the barrack
of the 1st (Gem) Division. Here authorities were alread
prepared for trouble after a tip about a military insurrectio
from a major in the War Ministry: he had learned from
young officer that a group of radicals planned to assassina
several advisers to the Emperor that day. Suspects had bee
put under surveillance, and important public figures we
given emergency bodyguards. The doors of the Prime Mini
ter's official residence were reinforced with steel, iron ba
installed in the windows, and a warning system connecte
directly to police headquarters. But the *kempeitai* (militar
police organization)* and the regular police felt they cou
easily handle the situation. After all, what real damage cou
a handful of rebels do, however strongly motivated? And b
now they were wondering how reliable the information w
that the uprising was at hand. The day was almost over.

It seems strange that they were so complacent, since th
spirit of rebellion was high among elite troops charged wi
defense of the Palace grounds. Their defiance was so appa
ent that they were on orders to be shipped out to Manchuri
in a few days, and their contempt for authority so open th
one unit, ostensibly on maneuvers, had urinated in cadence
metropolitan police headquarters. Fourteen hundred of the
unruly officers and men were preparing to revolt. Just befo
dawn the next morning, attack groups would strike simu
taneously at six Tokyo targets: the homes of several gover
ment leaders, as well as metropolitan police headquarters.

While intricate preparations for these attacks were pr
ceeding, pleasure seekers roamed the darkening streets
search of entertainment. Already the Ginza, Tokyo's Broa
way–Fifth Avenue, was teeming. To young Japanese it h
long been a romantic symbol of the outside world, a fair
land of neon lights, boutiques, coffee shops, American a
European movies, Western-style dance halls and restaurants.
few blocks away, in the Akasaka section, where the kimo
was common for both men and women, the old Japan al
anticipated a night of pleasure. Geishas looking like som

Kempei were soldiers acting as armed policemen, with some auth
ity over civilians. (In Japanese, one form serves for both singular a
plural; there is no suffix to indicate number.)

thing out of antiquity in their theatrical make-up and resplendent costumes were pulled in rickshaws through the winding, willow-lined streets. Here the lights were more muted, and the traditional red lanterns carried by the police gave off a soft, nostalgic glow. It was a charming woodcut come alive.

These insurrectionists were not motivated by personal ambition. Like half a dozen groups before them—all of which had failed—they were about to try once again to redress the social injustices in Japan through force and assassination. Tradition had legitimized such criminal action, and the Japanese had given it a special name, *gekokujo* (insubordination), a term first used in the fifteenth century when rebellion was rampant on every level, with provincial lords refusing to obey the shogun,* who in turn ignored the orders of the emperor.

The crumbling of autocracy in Europe after World War I, followed by the tide of democracy, socialism and Communism, had had dramatic impact on the young people of Japan, and they too set up a cry for change. Political parties emerged and a universal manhood suffrage bill was enacted in 1924. But it all happened too fast. Too many Japanese looked upon politics as a game or a source of easy money and there was a series of exposés—the Matsushima Red-Light District Scandal, the Railway Scandal, the Korean Scandal. Charges of bribery and corruption resulted in mob brawls on the floor of the Diet.

The population explosion which accompanied Japan's westernization added to the confusion. Hokkaido, Honshu, Kyushu and Shikoku (her four main islands, comprising an area scarcely the size of California) already burst with eighty million people. The national economy could not absorb a population increase of almost one million a year; farmers who were close to starvation following the plunge of produce prices began to organize in protest for the first time in Japanese history; hundreds of thousands of city workers were thrown out of work. Out of all this came a wave of left-wing parties and unions.

These movements were counteracted by nationalist organizations, whose most popular leader was Ikki Kita,** a na-

---

*De facto ruler in feudal Japan; a sort of generalissimo. Until the reign of Meiji, the present ruler's grandfather, the emperor had for centuries been little more than a figurehead, a puppet of the shogun.
**In Japan the family name comes first but is reversed in this book for easier reading.

3

tionalist as well as a fiery revolutionary who managed t
combine a program of socialism with imperialism. His trac
on reform, "A General Outline of Measures for the Recor
struction of Japan," was devoured by radicals and worshiper
of the Emperor alike. His words appealed to all who yearne
for reform. "The Japanese are following destructive example
of the Western nations," he wrote. "The possessors of finar
cial, political and military power are striving to maintai
their unjust interests under cover of the imperial power. . . .

"Seven hundred million brethren in India and China ca
not gain their independence without our protection and leac
ership.

"The history of East and West is a record of the unifica
tion of feudal states after an era of civil wars. The onl
possible international peace, which will come after the prese
age of international wars, must be a feudal peace. This will b
achieved through the emergence of the strongest country
which will dominate all other nations of the world."

He called for the "removal of the barriers between natio
and Emperor"—that is, the Diet and the Cabinet. Votir
should be restricted to heads of families and no one would b
allowed to accumulate more than 1,000,000 yen (abor
$500,000 at the time). Important industries should be natior
alized, a dictatorship established, and women restricted 1
activities in the home "cultivating the ancient Japanese arts o
flower arrangement and the tea ceremony."

It was no wonder that millions of impressionable, idealist
young men, already disgusted by corruption in governmei
and business and poverty at home, were enthralled.* Th
could battle all these wicked forces as well as Communisr
free the Orient of Occidental domination and make Japan tl
leading country in the world.

In the West these young men could have found an outl
for action as unionists or political agitators, but in Japa
many, particularly those from small landowning and sho

---

*The song of Nikkyo (the All-Japan Council for the Joint Strugg
of Patriots) indicated the peculiarly Japanese spirit of such you
rebels:

> Daily we submit to hypocrisy and lies,
> While national honor lingering dies.
> Arise ye! O patriots, arise!
> Onward we march, defying death!
> Come prison bars! Come gory death!

4

keeping families, found they could serve best as Army and Navy officers. Once in the service, they gained an even more profound understanding of poverty from their men, who would be weeping over letters from home—with their sons away, the families were on the verge of starvation. The young officers blamed their own superiors, politicians, court officials. They joined secret organizations of which some, like Tenkento, called for direct action and assassination, while others, like Sakurakai (the Cherry Society), demanded territorial expansion as well as internal reforms.

By 1928 this ferment came to a head, but it took two extraordinary men operating within the military framework to put it into action. One was a lieutenant colonel, Kanji Ishihara, and the other a colonel, Seishiro Itagaki. The first was brilliant, inspired, flamboyant, a fountain of ideas; the second was cool, thoughtful, a master organizer. They made a perfect team. What Ishihara envisioned, Itagaki could bring to pass. Both were staff officers in the Kwantung Army, which had originally, in 1905, been sent to Manchuria to guard Japanese interests in a wild territory larger than California, Oregon and Washington combined.

The two officers felt that Manchuria was the only answer to poverty in Japan. It could be transformed from a wilderness into a civilized, prosperous area, alleviating unemployment at home and providing an outlet for the overpopulated homeland, where more than two thirds of all farms were smaller than two and a quarter acres. Manchuria could also supply Japan with what she so desperately needed to remain an industrial state—a guaranteed source of raw materials and a market for finished goods. But all this could not come about, Ishihara and Itagaki reasoned, until the Japanese gained complete control of Manchuria, which was loosely governed by a Chinese war lord, Marshal Chang Tso-lin. At the time, Japan had only the right to station troops along railroads and to engage in mining, farming and business activities.

There had been a struggle over the vast territory north of China for several hundred years, with the Chinese occupying Manchuria and Korea, and the Russians taking over Maritime Province, the coastal region of Siberia from Bering Strait to Vladivostok. For centuries Japan had cut herself off from the outside world and did not join this scramble for territory until 1853. In that year an American commodore, Matthew C. Perry, sailed into Edo (Tokyo) Bay and, at cannon point, opened up a medieval Japan to modern life.

5

The Japanese took to it with a will. They assiduously copied the latest techniques of mass production and even added original procedures—girls in textile factories, for example worked on roller skates to handle more spindles. They built a strong army and navy and began imitating the European game of forceful diplomacy, by sending out punitive expeditions. Within a few decades Japan controlled most of Korea and in 1894 fought a war with China for this country. Japan won easily, and also gained possession of Formosa, the southern tip of Manchuria and the Liaotung Peninsula with the important seaports of Port Arthur and Dairen.

Alarmed that an interloper was taking a piece of their "Chinese Melon," Russia, Germany and France joined forces and compelled Japan to give up the peninsula she had just won in battle. Russia then appropriated Liaotung for herself but could keep it less than ten years. In 1904 the Japanese their national pride stung, struck back at the Czar, whose empire covered one sixth of the earth's land surface, and astonished the world by winning overwhelming victories Once more Japan had Port Arthur and Dairen.

She also had all the railways built by Russia in southern Manchuria. Japan could have seized the rest of the country but wanted to be recognized by the Europeans as a respected member of the imperialist community. Accordingly, she poured a billion dollars into the bandit-infested, sparsely populated territory, and maintained such law and order along the railroads that hundreds of thousands of Japanese, Chinese and Korean traders and settlers flooded into the area.

It was this mass influx that had inspired Ishihara and Itagaki to envision a Manchuria free of its Chinese war-lord ruler. Ishihara dreamed of making it an autonomous state, haven for all of its ethnic groups—Japanese, Chinese, Manchurians, Koreans and White Russians. Here genuine democracy and eventual socialism would be practiced and buffer set up against Soviet Russia.*

All this was to be effected by the Kwantung Army, with the blessing of Tokyo. But the Emperor and the War Ministry refused to sanction a plan that appeared to be masked aggression. Undeterred, Ishihara, Itagaki and their followers

---

*Itagaki wrote: "Manchuria is, of course, important from the point of view of Japanese capitalism. From the standpoint of the proletariat which finds it necessary to demand equalization of national wealth, a fundamental solution can be found within the boundaries of natural poor Japan that will ensure a livelihood for the people at large."

decided to act on their own—to commit *gekokujo*. The first step was to eliminate Marshal Chang, the aging Chinese war lord. On June 4, 1928, a Kwantung Army staff officer commanding men from an Engineer regiment dynamited Chang's special train and he was fatally injured. From then on, and despite numerous warnings from Tokyo, Ishihara and Itagaki used the Kwantung Army as if it were their private legion. At last, in the summer of 1931, they were ready for the final step and secretly massed troops to take Manchuria from the Chinese by force. Hearing rumors of this, the Foreign Minister persuaded the War Minister to send an officer from Tokyo to bring the Kwantung Army under control. The man selected, a major general, arrived in Mukden on the evening of September 18. A few miles away a charge of dynamite was being planted on the tracks of the South Manchurian Railway near the barracks of the 7th Chinese Brigade. The explosion would be the excuse "to bring order" by sending in troops and seizing Mukden.

The general was easily diverted by Colonel Itagaki to the Kikubumi, a Japanese inn, for an evening with the geishas. About ten o'clock there was a detonation, but the damage to the track was so slight that a southbound train passed by safely a few minutes later. A Japanese consular officer wanted to adjust the matter with the Chinese, but a Kwantung Army staff major drew his sword and threatened to run him through. At ten-thirty Japanese troops fired on the Chinese barracks while other detachments converged on the walls of Mukden. At the Kikubumi, the general was too drunk to notice the fusillade. If he had, it would have made no difference. He had known about the plot from the beginning—and approved of it.

By morning Mukden was in Japanese hands, to the dismay of not only the world but Tokyo itself. At the request of the Cabinet, the Army General Staff ordered the Kwantung Army to limit the expanse of hostilities. This group of individualists simply ignored the command and continued to sweep over the rest of Manchuria. It was *gekokujo* on a grand scale.

In Tokyo, members of the Cherry Society were already secretly conspiring to support the rebel action in Manchuria with a coup d'état of their own. Their primary purpose was to impose radical internal reforms. These reforms, together with the conquest of Manchuria, would lead to the new Japan. The plot (the Brocade Flag Revolution) involved 120 officers and their troops, augmented by followers of the firebrand Ikki Kita. The rebels planned to assassinate government and court officials, then assemble in front of the Palace, and by way of apologizing to the Emperor, commit hara-kiri.

But so many groups with so many differing opinions were involved in the coup that someone turned informer, in pique or for pay, and the plotters were arrested on October 17, 1931. The leader of the conspiracy was sentenced to twenty days' confinement and his assistant got half that. Their accomplices were merely reprimanded. It was the old story: amnesty for any actual or planned violence if it was done for the glory of the nation.

That evening the War Minister radioed the Kwantung Army a limp reproach:

1. THE KWANTUNG ARMY IS TO REFRAIN FROM ANY NEW PROJECT SUCH AS BECOMING INDEPENDENT FROM THE IMPERIAL ARMY AND SEIZING CONTROL OF MANCHURIA AND MONGOLIA.

2. THE GENERAL SITUATION IS DEVELOPING ACCORDING TO THE INTENTIONS OF THE ARMY, SO YOU MAY BE COMPLETELY REASSURED.

As if this wasn't enough, the War Vice Minister added these conciliatory words:

WE HAVE BEEN UNITED IN MAKING DESPERATE EFFORTS TO SOLVE THE EXISTING DIFFICULTY . . . TRUST OUR ZEAL, ACT WITH GREAT PRUDENCE. . . . GUARD AGAINST IMPETUOUS ACTS, SUCH AS DECLARING THE INDEPENDENCE OF THE KWANTUNG ARMY, AND WAIT FOR A FAVORABLE TURN OF EVENTS ON OUR SIDE.

Rather than being appeased, the Kwantung commande indignantly denied that his army was seeking independence and though admitting it had "tended to act overpositively an arbitrarily," claimed it had done so "for the country."

The abortive Brocade Flag Revolution did achieve one o its purposes: in the next few years it assured the success o the Manchurian adventure. It also convinced many Japanes that politics and business were so corrupt that a military-le reform had to be supported. At the same time it engendere such bitterness that the two wings of the reform movemer began to split. One, nicknamed "the Control" clique b newsmen, believed it was not enough to take Manchuri since security against a possible attack by the Soviet Unic ould be forestalled only by control of China itself. The Kita ollowers, known as "the Imperial Way" clique, were convinced this new expansion would be folly; an industrialized Manchuria would be a sturdy enough fortress against Communism.

The younger, more idealistic officers belonged to the latter faction, while field-grade officers as well as key men in the War Ministry supported the Control clique. The more radical nationalists turned immediately to assassination. Each member of the Blood Brotherhood, for example, was pledged to kill at least one "corrupt" political or financial leader on or about February 11, 1932, the 2,592nd celebration of the ascension to the throne of Jinmu, the first human emperor of Japan, the fifth in line of descent from the Sun Goddess, according to legend. Those marked for death included Finance Minister Junnosuke Inoue, a forthright man who often opposed the mounting Army appropriation. The conspirator assigned to kill Inoue practiced shooting on a deserted beach, and four days ahead of schedule put three bullets into Inoue right on the sidewalk. Less than a month later, the second murder took place under similar circumstances. As Baron Takuma Dan, president of Mitsui, stepped out of his car, a young assassin jabbed a pistol in his back and pulled the trigger.

Once again the trials provided the citizens of Japan with melodrama and propaganda. The assassin in Japanese history had often been a more sympathetic figure than the victim. Wasn't there some lack of virtue in a man who let himself be killed, and wasn't an assassin who murdered for lofty purposes merely defending the common people against tyranny? Overwhelming evidence of guilt notwithstanding, the two killers were not executed but given life imprisonment, from which it was obvious they would be paroled in a few years.

On Sunday, May 15, only two months after the death of Dan, a pair of taxis pulled up at the side entrance to the Yasukuni Shrine in Tokyo, a Shinto temple dedicated to all who have died in Japan's wars. Nine Navy and Army officers alighted from the cabs and bowed toward the Sun Goddess; then, armed with charms bought from a priest, returned to the taxis and headed for the Prime Minister's official residence. Here they forced their way past a police sergeant and into the room of Prime Minister Tsuyoshi Inukai, a diminutive man of seventy-five with a goatee. The old man calmly led the would-be assassins to a Japanese-style room, where they politely removed their shoes and sat down. At that moment a

comrade who had got lost in the corridors entered, dagger i
hand, and cried out, "No use talking! Fire!" Everyone bega
shooting at the courageous little man who had opposed th
conquest of Manchuria and steadfastly refused to recogniz
the puppet government of the province now going under th
manufactured name of Manchukuo ("State of Manchu"
The assassins left by taxi for police headquarters to launch a
attack, but it was Sunday, and except for a few duty office:
there was no one to fight. Before surrendering they heave
a grenade at the Bank of Japan. Other conspirators scattere
handbills in the streets, and threw bombs which shattered
few windows.

The coup itself—named the 5/15 (May 15) Incident—ha
fizzled out, but it brought forth even more sensational trial
There were three in all—one for civilians, one each for Arm
and Navy personnel. As usual a large segment of the publ
sympathized with the assassins, and there was general a
plause when one defendant declared that he and his con
rades only wanted to sound an alarm to awaken the natio
The people had heard so much about "corruption" that litt
sympathy was shown the memory of gallant little Inukai. H
death was a warning to politicians.

Feeling ran so high that 110,000 petitions for clemenc
signed or written entirely in blood, inundated officials of t
trial. Nine young men from Niigata asked to take the pla
of those on trial and to show their good faith enclosed the
own nine little fingers pickled in a jar of alcohol.

One of Inukai's assassins did express regret but said th
the Prime Minister had to be "sacrificed on the altar
national reformation." Another declared, "Life or death do
not count with me. I say to those who bemoan my death, 'I
not shed tears for me but sacrifice yourselves on the altars
reform.' "

The results of the trials could have been predicted. No o
was sentenced to death, and of the forty to receive sentenc
almost all were free in a few years. To the people they we
martyrs, their own champions. Who else called for su
drastic methods to end the crippling depression?* Who el
would lead the farmers and workers out of poverty? Who el
dared publicly assail leading politicians, court officials a
financial barons for corruption? And since so many peo

---

*Poverty in Japan had increased in the wake of America's depr
sion. The price of raw silk, Japan's main export, had dropped mc
than 50 percent.

believed in this so implicitly, the power of the militarists and rightists continued to grow.

For three years the idealistic young officers, chafed by the corruption surrounding them, bided their time. Only their reverence for the Emperor prevented them from supporting a Communist revolution. But one of them, driven by "an impulse from on high," took matters into his own hands. It was a bloody and bizarre action even for a country with one foot planted in feudalism. One morning in August 1935, Lieutenant Colonel Saburo Aizawa, after visiting the Meiji Shrine for advice, entered the back door of Army General Staff headquarters, a decrepit two-story wooden building just outside the Palace grounds. Like so many other idealistic, radical officers of the day, he had become incensed when their idol, General Jinsaburo Mazaki, was dismissed from his post as Inspector General of Military Education.*

Aizawa strode unannounced into the office of another general, Tetsuzan Nagata, chief of the Military Affairs Bureau and one of Mazaki's most outspoken foes. "I feel an impulse to assassinate Nagata," Aizawa had recently told the Sun Goddess at the Ise Shrine. "If I am right, please help me succeed. If I am wrong, please make me fail." Nagata, at his desk, did not even look up as Aizawa pulled his sword, lunged and missed. Slightly wounded on the second thrust, the general lurched for an exit but Aizawa stabbed him through the back, pinning him momentarily to the door. Aizawa slashed his neck twice, then walked to the office of a friend to say he had just carried out Heaven's judgment and went off to buy a cap—he'd lost his in the fracas. When a military policeman arrested him, Aizawa thought he'd be examined briefly and allowed to return to duty. Instead he found himself the star of a sensational trial that was shaking the foundations of the Army and became the rallying point of all the young superpatriots who wanted to reform the nation overnight.

At his trial Aizawa was treated gingerly by the five judges and was allowed to use the witness stand to attack statesmen, politicians and the *zaibatsu* (family business combines such as Mitsui and Mitsubishi) for corruption. Pleading

---

*The three most important posts in the Japanese Army were the chief of the General Staff, the War Minister and the Inspector General Military Education (referred to as "the Big Three"). This triangular system dating from 1878 had been recommended by a Prussian major, Jacob Meckel, on loan to Japan from the Kaiser.

11

guilty to the charge of murder, he claimed he had only do[ne]
his duty as an honorable soldier of the Emperor. "Th[e]
country was in a deplorable state: the farmers were impove[r]
ished, officials were involved in scandals, diplomacy w[as]
weak, and the prerogative of the Supreme Command ha[d]
been violated by the naval-limitation agreements," he d[e]
clared in the stilted prose of reform.* "I came to realize th[at]
the senior statesmen, those close to the Throne, powerf[ul]
financiers and bureaucrats, were attempting gradually to co[r]
rupt the government and the Army for their own selfish inte[r]
ests." These conditions had inspired him to murder—to com[m]
mit *gekokujo*.

"If the court fails to understand the spirit which guide[s]
Colonel Aizawa," his defense counsel said ominously, "[a]
second Aizawa, and even a third, will appear."

2.

These prophetic words were uttered on February 2[5,]
1936, in snowbound Tokyo, even as the leaders of the mo[st]
ambitious coup in the history of modern Japan were ready [to]
strike. Their principal target the following morning would [be]
Prime Minister Keisuke Okada, a retired admiral. Okada w[as]
hosting a banquet at his official residence on the evening [of]
the twenty-fifth, in celebration of the victory of the gover[n]
ment party (Minseito) in the general election for the Hou[se]
of Representatives five days earlier. He was a politician [by]
request, not choice. The previous fall the Emperor had ask[ed]
him to form a new cabinet after a scandal involving Finan[ce]
Ministry officials forced the resignation of his predecesso[r,]
Viscount Makoto Saito, also a retired admiral.

While Okada's guests toasted the election results as [a]
resounding triumph for the admiral's policies and a blow [to]
fascism and militarism, his private wish was that he cou[ld]
resign. He was weary from the struggle, and it seemed to hi[m]
that despite the victory at the polls, the militarists a[nd]
chauvinists were as strong as ever.

Two other men marked for assassination were at a par[ty]

---

*His last charge referred to the naval disarmament conference h[eld]
in Washington (1922), which adopted a 5-5-3 ratio as to capital sh[ips]
belonging to America, Britain and Japan. The Japanese (particula[rly]
the young radicals) were still incensed at the big-power curtailm[ent of]
their naval strength. The lower ratio for Japan implied a stigma [of]
national inferiority.

12

veral blocks away at the American embassy, where Ambas-
dor Joseph C. Grew was giving a dinner for thirty-six in
onor of the recently cashiered prime minister, who had
en made Lord Keeper of the Privy Seal. Among the guests
as still another retired admiral, Kantaro Suzuki, Grand
hamberlain to the Emperor.

Grew was a tall, courtly man with black bushy eyebrows,
ustache and gray-white hair. Born in Boston's Back Bay, as
as his great-grandfather, he had attended Groton and Har-
rd with Franklin D. Roosevelt. An aristocrat with dem-
ratic instincts, he had already distinguished himself as a
plomat in Europe. He was particularly qualified to serve in
okyo, since he had a rare understanding and affection for
pan and all things Japanese, as well as a wife who had
eviously lived in the country, spoke the language and was a
scendant of Commodore Perry.

That evening Grew had gone to the trouble of providing
ecial entertainment for his guest of honor: a private
owing of *Naughty Marietta*, starring Jeanette MacDonald
d Nelson Eddy. He had chosen the film because "it was
ll of lovely old Victor Herbert music, beautiful scenes, a
etty, romantic story and no vulgarity whatever. . . ." After
nner he escorted former Prime Minister Saito to a com-
rtable armchair in the salon. Grew knew the old gentleman
d never attended a sound movie and if he was bored he
uld take a nap. But Viscount Saito was too enraptured to
ep; and though it was his custom to leave parties promptly
ten o'clock, not only did he stay for refreshments at the
d of the first half of the film but remained until the end.
e other guests must also have been moved by the romantic
ry, for when the lights went on, the eyes of all the
panese ladies "were distinctly red."

It was half past eleven when the Privy Seal and his wife
t up to leave. The Grews saw them to the door, pleased
at the admiral had enjoyed himself so much. Scattered
kes of snow drifted down gently as the Saito car drove off.

At four o'clock in the morning on February 26, Captain
yosada Koda and the other rebel leaders routed out their
listed men, who still knew nothing of the plot; they thought
ey were going out on another night maneuver. A few were
d there would be killing that night.

"I want you to die with me," Lieutenant Kurihara told
c. Kuratomo.

Completely taken by surprise, Kuratomo nevertheless an-

swered immediately, "Yes, sir. I'll die." A superior office
order was absolute, never to be disobeyed. "This," Kuraton
later recalled, "was the first time I realized something ve
serious was taking place."

Snow was now falling steadily in huge flakes, and it
minded several of the insurgent officers of the incident
"the forty-seven *ronin*." In the seventeenth century a pr
vincial lord was so disgraced by Kira, the chief minister of t
shogun, that he committed suicide. Oishi, a samurai warri
serving the dishonored man, vowed to avenge his death, a
for the next seven years he pretended, in the tradition
samurai sacrifice, to be a dissolute drunk while secre
planning revenge. Early one morning in a snowstorm, t
forty-seven *ronin* (samurai who had lost their master a
were forced to become wanderers; they might be compar
to America's drifting cowboy heroes) raided the Kira hom
not far from the Imperial Palace. They assassinated the chi
minister, cut off his head and brought it to the temple whe
their master's ashes were enshrined. Then, in true *bushi*
style, all forty-seven committed hara-kiri. A factual story,
represented an ideal of samurai behavior and was a favor
theme in Japanese movies and the kabuki theater.

The groups headed for their various destinations: one, l
by Koda himself, would seize the War Minister's offic
residence and force high-ranking officers to support the
another would occupy police headquarters; four other grou
would assassinate the Prime Minister, the Finance Minist
the Lord Keeper of the Privy Seal and the Grand Chamb
lain. The killers of the Privy Seal would then proceed to t
suburban home of the Inspector General of Military Edu
tion and murder him while two other units raced out of to
as well, to kill Count Nobuaki Makino, former Privy Seal a
counselor to the Emperor, and eighty-seven-year-old Prit
Kinmochi Saionji, the Emperor's closest adviser, the natio
most honored elder statesman, the last *genro*.*

Lieutenant Kurihara and a military police officer
proached the front gate to the Prime Minister's offic
residence. A police officer on guard inside the gate ask
what was going on. The *kempei* said, "Open the gate quic
The guard didn't think anything of it because they were

---

*The *genro* were important statesmen who had helped Empe
Meiji draw up the Imperial Constitution in 1889 and afterward bec
advisers to the Emperor. In 1916 Saionji had been added to the gro
and by 1936 he was the only surviving *genro*.

olleague and an Army officer. As the guard came closer to he gate Lieutenant Kurihara's hand grabbed the police uard, and poking his pistol at him with the other hand, rdered, "Open up!"

Kurihara and other officers broke in ahead of their men nd disarmed the sleeping policemen in the guardhouse by the ate. Kurihara pushed past them into the residence, which as in total darkness. He turned on the hall light, got his earings and snapped it off. Suddenly the corridors reverber- ted with deafening gunfire. This was the signal the rebels utside had been waiting for; they opened up with heavy achine guns. The chandelier in the hall shattered and plum- eted to the floor.

Just before five o'clock young Hisatsune Sakomizu, one of rime Minister Okada's secretaries, had been wakened by a uffled commotion outside his house, which was across the reet from the rear gate of the official residence. They have nally come! he thought, for he had long anticipated an ttack on his employer, and jumped out of bed. His ties to te old man were close; he was married to Okada's daughter, nd his father's younger sister was Okada's wife.

Sakomizu softly opened the window and in the whirling now saw the policemen who were guarding the rear gate mill ound in confusion. He phoned police headquarters.

"We just heard the minister's alarm bell ring," replied a ice. "One platoon is already on the way. Reinforcement nits are just leaving." Reassured, Sakomizu started to go ck upstairs, when he heard the clop of boots in the street. e looked out expecting to see either the police reinforce- ents or the special Army troops detailed to protect the rime Minister, but a rifle shot cracked and he saw one oliceman fall and others retreat before a group of soldiers ith glittering bayonets. There was a shattering burst of e—it sounded like rifles and machine guns—and the secre- ry finally realized that Army troops were attacking the sidence. He hastily dressed so he could help the admiral. As rushed into the street he could hear shots inside the panese section of the ministry. Soldiers at the gate came rward brandishing their rifles. They forced Sakomizu back to his own house and followed him without taking off their t boots. Frustrated, Sakomizu paced up and down. What d happened to the special Army troops or the police inforcements? The police had already come and been driv- off; the troops were among the rebels.

Sakomizu again called police headquarters. "This is the

insurgent unit," said a voice. About five hundred rebels we
occupying the building. Sakomizu hung up and called tl
Kojimachi *kempeitai* station nearby. "The situation is out
control" was the sheepish answer. "What can we do?"

A few blocks from the Prime Minister's official residen
170 men, commanded by a first cousin of Sakomizu
stormed into the official residence of War Minister Yoshiy
ki Kawashima. With them was Captain Koda. He routed o
Kawashima and began to read off a list of demands: politic
and social reforms; the arrest of leaders of the Contr
clique; the assignment of Imperial Way clique officers to k
positions (the insurgents were against expansion into China
the assignment of General Araki* as commander of tl
Kwantung Army "for the purpose of coercing Red Russia
Koda also insisted that martial law be proclaimed and th
the War Minister visit the Palace at once to convey tl
rebels' intentions to the Emperor.

While the argument was going on, Captain Teruzo An
and 150 men were bursting into the official residence
Grand Chamberlain Kantaro Suzuki, who, like Viscount S
to, had so enjoyed the private showing of *Naughty Marie*
a few hours earlier. The elderly admiral, wakened by a ma
rushed to a storage room for a sword. He couldn't find
Hearing footsteps in the corridor, he stepped into the ne
room—it would have been a disgrace to die in a closet.
moments he was hemmed in by a score of bayonets. O
soldier stepped forward and asked politely, "Are you F
Excellency?"

Suzuki said he was and raised his hands for quiet. "Y
must have some reason for doing this. Tell me what it i
Nobody answered and Suzuki repeated the question. Silen
The third time he asked, a man with a pistol (he looked
the Grand Chamberlain like a noncom) said impatient
"There's no more time. We're going to shoot."

Suzuki supposed they were acting under orders from
superior and didn't know why. "Then it can't be helped,"
said stoically. "Go ahead and shoot." He drew himself er
as if facing a firing squad. Just behind him hung the pictu
of his parents. Three pistols erupted. One bullet missed, o
hit him in the crotch, and the third went through his heart.

---

*General Sadao Araki had long been the idol of the reformists
had figured prominently in the 1932 insurrection, when he was
minister. He was known throughout the world for his outspo
remarks and ferocious handlebar mustache.

he fell, still conscious, bullets struck him in the head and shoulder.

"*Todome* [*Coup de grâce*]!" someone shouted repeatedly. Suzuki felt the muzzle of a pistol pressed against his throat, then heard his wife say, "Don't do it!" At that moment Captain Ando entered. "*Todome?*" asked the man with the pistol.

Two years earlier Captain Ando had come to Suzuki with a program for reform; the admiral had refuted his arguments so forthrightly that Ando still secretly admired him. Now he said that *todome* would be "too cruel," and ordered the men to salute His Excellency. They all knelt by the fallen admiral and presented arms.

"Get up! Leave!" Captain Ando told his men. He turned to Mrs. Suzuki. "Are you *okusan* [madam]?" She nodded. "I have heard about you. I am particularly sorry about this." He said they had no ill feeling toward the admiral. "But our views on how to bring about reformation in Japan differ from His Excellency's, and so we had to come to this."

The captain left, burdened by a sense of guilt and certain Suzuki was dying (one of the maids heard him say that he was going to commit suicide). But miraculously Suzuki would survive to play a leading role in Japan's last days as an empire.

A lieutenant led his men to the large sprawling home of Finance Minister Korekiyo Takahashi. They broke down the door of the inner entrance, and while one group seized half a dozen police guards and servants, the rest roamed through the house, kicking down the doors of room after room looking for their victim.

Minister Takahashi was alone in a spacious ten-mat bedroom. He was a remarkable man who had started as a footman, turned Christian and become president of the Bank of Japan and a member of the House of Peers. The young officers loathed him for having fought the previous year's huge military budget.

Finally the lieutenant entered the minister's room brandishing a pistol. He kicked the quilt off Takahashi, crying *Tenchu!* (Punishment of Heaven!). Takahashi looked up unafraid and shouted "Idiot!" at the lieutenant, who hesitated before emptying his pistol into the old man. Another rebel officer leaped forward and with a shout swung his sword with such force that it cut through the padded coat Takahashi was wearing for extra warmth and severed his right arm; he then

17

stabbed the minister through the belly and slashed him viciously right and left.

Mrs. Takahashi burst from her room in the attached Western-style section, and at the sight of her disemboweled husband, cried out in anguish. As the lieutenant shouldered through the crowd of servants gathered horrified in the corridors, he said, "Excuse me for the annoyance I have caused."

Prime Minister Okada had been awakened by the sound of the alarm bell just before five o'clock and moments later his brother-in-law, Denzo Matsuo, a retired colonel, pushed into the bedroom with two police officers.

"They've finally come," said Okada, adding fatalistically that there was nothing anyone could do about it.

"It's no time to talk like that!" shouted the sixty-one-year-old Matsuo. An energetic, dogmatic man, he had insisted on serving his brother-in-law, whether Okada liked it or not, as unofficial factotum without pay. He pulled the reluctant Okada, clad in a thin nightgown, across the corridor toward a secret exit, but on hearing the rebels break down doors, one of the policemen shoved Okada and Matsuo into a bathroom which was used primarily as a storeroom, and closed the door. A moment later they heard shouts from the corridor several shots, a scuffle, then silence.

"Stay here," said the impetuous Matsuo and left. The Prime Minister tried to follow but in the darkness bumped into a shelf, knocking down several *sake* bottles. He stiffened with fear. Silence, Okada moved again, this time stumbling noisily over the *sake* bottles.

"Don't come out yet!" one of the policemen called weakly from the corridor, so Okada quickly returned to the bathroom. When he heard a voice shouting, "There's someone in the courtyard!" he looked through the window and saw his brother-in-law standing pressed against the building and a half a dozen soldiers watching him from inside.

"Shoot him!" yelled their leader, but the soldiers hesitated "You men will be in Manchuria soon! What are you going to do, if you can't kill a man or two now?"

Reluctantly the men stuck their rifles through the window and fired into the courtyard.

"*Tenno Heika banzai* [Long live His Majesty the Emperor]!" cried Matsuo and slumped down on a doorstep, bleeding profusely. Painfully, he straightened his shoulders, as on parade, but could not keep from groaning.

18

Lieutenant Kurihara, followed by Pfc. Kuratomo, pushed his way through a wall of soldiers, rigid with shock. They told Kurihara that it was Prime Minister Okada. The lieutenant hesitated, then turned to Kuratomo and ordered, *"Todome!"*

Kuratomo was reluctant; all he had was a pistol. "Use it!" said Kurihara impatiently.

Against his will Kuratomo leveled the weapon and fired one bullet into Matsuo's chest, another between his eyes. The colonel toppled forward, dyeing the snow red.

Kurihara, who had taken the Prime Minister's photograph from his bedroom, knelt beside the body and compared it with Matsuo's face. "Okada!" he said without hesitation. *"Banzai!"* shouted the soldiers and carried the body to the Prime Minister's bedroom, laying it on a thin mattress.

To find out what had happened, Okada crept out of the bathroom into the corridor. One of the police guards was lying there unconscious, his left arm slashed off; a few yards away the other was jackknifed over a chair, dead. Okada bowed his head in tribute and continued on to his bedroom. Seeing Matsuo's body on the mattress, he sobbed and flung himself down. Finally he rose and began putting on a kimono. As he was tying the strings on an outer garment he heard footsteps and went out to the corridor.

"What's that?" a soldier called out and Okada lurched to a dark corner.

"I just saw something strange," the soldier told several comrades. "It was an old man. But he disappeared like a ghost."

Death seemed to be everywhere and yet by a miracle Okada was alive. Until that moment he had been sure he would die. For the first time he began to think of the future. Had the rebels seized the Palace? Were the *jushin** assassinated? He decided it was his responsibility to stay alive, and once the uprising was suppressed, enforce discipline on the Army. But where could he hide in a house overrun with rebels? The answer was solved for him when he suddenly came upon two maids in the corridor. They hustled him to their room, pushed him into a large closet and covered him with a pile of soiled laundry.

---

*Former prime ministers were referred to as *jushin* (senior statesmen); their main duty was to recommend prime ministers to His Majesty.

By now two of the attack groups assigned to out-of-town missions had reached their destinations. Lieutenant Taro Takahashi and thirty men broke into the suburban home of Mazaki's successor, Inspector General Jotaro Watanabe. Mrs Watanabe and a maid tried to stop Takahashi, but he pulled free and broke into the bedroom where the general lay on a *futon* with his young daughter. Takahashi fired a pistol at Watanabe, then drew his sword and slashed at his head.

The other group was ranging through a resort in the mountains in search of Count Nobuaki Makino, whom Saito had succeeded as Privy Seal and who still was one of the Emperor's closest advisers. Unable to find him, the rebels set fire to the hotel to drive him into the open. The old man was led out through the rear of the hotel by his twenty-year-old granddaughter, Kazuko. They struggled up a steep hill, but the soldiers were at their heels and loosed a fusillade. Ignoring the bullets, Kazuko stepped in front of her grandfather and spread out her kimono sleeves. One of the rebels, perhaps moved by the girl's heroism, shouted "Success!" and persuaded his mates to leave.

The third group, the one assigned to kill Prince Saionji, never left Tokyo. At the last moment the officer in charge refused to go; he could not bring himself to do any violence to the last *genro*.

At his home in Okitsu, the aged prince had just wakened from a horrifying dream—he was surrounded by decapitated heads and a heap of bloody bodies. Once news of the uprising was received from the capital, the local police arrived in force and took Saionji to a nearby cottage. Then came a telegram announcing that a large automobile filled with young men in khaki uniform was heading for Okitsu. The prince was wrapped up like a mummy and transferred from place to place to fool the assassins—who turned out to be patent-medicine salesmen.

At the War Minister's official residence, Captain Koda found continued vacillation among the hierarchy. The generals were still reluctant to either join the uprising or confront the rebels. Major Tadashi Katakura, a brilliant, impetuous career officer, was one of the few showing any resolve. The rebels infuriated him. He was not so much against their aims as against disorder and insubordination. The Army, he believed, could only exist through stern discipline and absolute loyalty to the Emperor.

Katakura was in the courtyard of War Minister Ka

washima's residence assailing a group of rebels for misusing the power of His Majesty's Army. The Emperor alone had the right to mobilize troops, he shouted, and demanded to see the minister, General Kawashima.

"The Showa Restoration* is what we are all thinking of," he told a crowd that gathered around him. "I feel as you do about the reforms. But we must continue to revere the Emperor and honor the Supreme Command. Don't make private use of the troops."

A rebel commander emerged from the building. "We cannot let you in to see the minister," he said.

"Did the minister himself tell you that?"

"No, Captain Koda gave the order. The minister is just getting ready to go to the Imperial Palace. Please wait awhile. The situation will soon clear up."

Katakura assumed the rebels were using violence to force the War Minister to help them set up a military government. He started toward the entrance, where General Mazaki was standing aggressively with his legs apart, like one of the *deva* kings that guard Buddhist temples. Katakura had an impulse to rush at Mazaki and stab him—Mazaki must be behind all this; he probably wanted to be prime minister. Katakura controlled himself; first he would find out more what was going on. Just then the Vice Minister came out of the building. Katakura accosted him and asked to have a few words. As the other put him off, the War Minister himself came out of the door buckling on his sword.

Something crashed against Katakura's head and he noticed a peculiar odor. He instantly put his left hand to his head. "You don't have to shoot," he yelled. A pale-faced captain (it was Senichi Isobe, another of the leaders of the uprising) advanced with drawn sword.

"We can talk! Sheathe your sword!" Katakura cried out. Isobe slid it back in its scabbard, then changed his mind and pulled it out again.

"You must be Captain Koda," Katakura continued. "You

---

*The present ruler, Hirohito, had named his reign Showa (Enlightned Peace). On Japanese calendars the current year, 1936, was Showa 1, the eleventh year of his reign. Only after his death, however, will he e referred to as Emperor Showa. His father, Yoshihito, took the name f Taisho (Great Righteousness). His grandfather, Mutsuhito, chose Meiji (Enlightened Rule); his era saw the greatest reforms and evelopment in Japanese history and was known as the Meiji Restora-ion. The young reformers of the moment wanted to emulate the chievements of their fathers with the Showa Restoration.

can't mobilize troops unless you get an imperial order." Faintly he heard someone, perhaps Mazaki, say, "We must not shed blood like this."

He staggered, and several officers helped him to the War Minister's car. As it was passing through the main gate, he dimly saw several *kempei*. "Get the *kempei* in the car," he exclaimed. They did. Someone suggested they take him to the Army Hospital or the Army Medical College, and again he forced himself to speak: "No . . . some private hospital in the city." He didn't want to be assassinated in bed.

3.

William Henry Chamberlin, chief Far Eastern correspondent for the *Christian Science Monitor*, first heard of the rebellion from a Japanese news agency. In town he encountered a rash of conflicting rumors. The Ministry of Foreign Affairs was open and unoccupied by rebels, but no one was there to tell the foreign correspondents what was going on. Troops were posted at the main crossings in the center of Tokyo. Chamberlin didn't know whose side they were on. Was any government in existence?

The office workers throughout the city had no idea this was anything but an ordinary day until police detoured their buses around the Imperial Palace and government offices. By now the violence was over. The rebels occupied a square mile of central Tokyo—the Diet Building and the entire area around the Prime Minister's residence—and were using the Sanno Hotel as a temporary headquarters. They commandeered tablecloths from the Peers Club dining room, paid for them, and made them into banners reading in black ink, "Revere the Emperor—Restoration Army," and hoisted them over the Prime Minister's residence.

When General Rokuro Iwasa, head of the *kempeitai*, learned of the revolt he got out of bed, half paralyzed from palsy, and drove to the rebel area. Here he was stopped by guards. "Is this the Emperor's Army?" he asked and wept in mortification.

The rebels were distributing their "manifesto" to all newspapers and news agencies. The police impounded almost every copy, but correspondent Chamberlin managed to get one. To most Westerners it seemed further proof of the inscrutability of the Orient, but to Chamberlin, a student of Japanese history, it made frightening sense.

22

The national essence [*kokutai*] of Japan, as a land of the gods, exists in the fact that the Emperor reigns with undiminished power from time immemorial into the farthest future in order that the natural beauty of the country may be propagated throughout the universe, so that all men under the sun may be able to enjoy their lives to the fullest extent. . . .

In recent years, however, there have appeared many persons whose chief aim and purpose have been to amass personal material wealth, disregarding the general welfare and prosperity of the Japanese people, with the result that the sovereignty of the Emperor has been greatly impaired. The people of Japan have suffered deeply as a result of this tendency and many vexing issues now confronting Japan are attributable to this fact.

The *genro*, the senior statesmen, military cliques, plutocrats, bureaucrats and political parties are all traitors who are destroying the national essence. . . .

It is our duty to remove the evil retainers from around the Throne and to smash the group of senior statesmen. It is our duty as subjects of His Majesty the Emperor.

May the gods bless and help us in our endeavor to save the land of our ancestors from the worst that confronts it.

Near the edge of the rebel zone at the American Embassy, Ambassador Grew cabled the first news of the revolt to the State Department:

THE MILITARY TOOK PARTIAL POSSESSION OF THE GOVERNMENT AND CITY EARLY THIS MORNING AND IT IS REPORTED HAVE ASSASSINATED SEVERAL PROMINENT MEN. IT IS IMPOSSIBLE AS YET TO CONFIRM ANYTHING. THE NEWS CORRESPONDENTS ARE NOT PERMITTED TO SEND TELEGRAMS OR TO TELEPHONE ABROAD. THIS TELEGRAM IS BEING SENT PRIMARILY AS A TEST MESSAGE, TO ASCERTAIN IF OUR CODE TELEGRAMS WILL BE TRANSMITTED. CODE ROOM PLEASE ACKNOWLEDGE IMMEDIATELY UPON RECEIPT.

The German embassy was also in range of rebel fire. Here the unofficial correspondent for the *Frankfurter Zeitung* and secretary to the military attaché was writing his preliminary report on the revolt—one copy for the German Foreign Ministry and a duplicate for the Red Army's Fourth Bureau, Intelligence. This was Dr. Richard Sorge, born in Russia of a German father and Russian mother and raised in Germany. Sorge was flamboyant and resourceful. He had managed to gain the complete confidence of the German ambassador, General Eugen Ott (who unwittingly supplied Sorge with some of the most devastating intelligence material which he sent to Moscow), and their business relationship had grown

23

into a warm personal friendship. He was irresistible to women and was at the time writing love letters to his first wife in Russia, living with a second in Tokyo and carrying on several love affairs. He could not resist alcohol in any form and often shocked his fellow countrymen by drunken bouts which were sometimes staged. He was a Communist of bohemian bent (his great-uncle had been friends with Marx and Engels) who had joined the Nazi party as a cover for his role as head of the Red Army spy ring in the Far East. It had taken him almost two years to set up his organization in Japan, and this rebellion was his first genuine test.

The coup, he later wrote, had "a very typical Japanese character and hence its motivations required particular study. A discerning study of it, and, in particular, a study of the social strains and internal crisis it revealed, was of much greater value to an understanding of Japan's internal structure than mere records of troop strength or secret documents." Once the report was dispatched to Moscow, Sorge ordered his ring to find out all possible details of the uprising. Then he induced the German ambassador and the military and naval attachés to make independent investigations and share their findings with him.

At the Palace the War Minister had just informed the Emperor about the rebellion. Ordinarily, if His Majesty spoke at all, it would be in vague terms, but today he was so distressed that he replied directly. "This event is extremely regrettable regardless of the question of spirit. In my judgment this action mars the glory of our national essence." Later he confided to his chief aide-de-camp that he felt the Army was going "to tie its own neck with floss silk"—that is, no more than gently admonish the rebels.

The role the Emperor played was difficult if not impossible for foreigners to understand. His powers and duties were unlike those of any of the monarch in the world. His grandfather, Meiji, a man of strong will and conviction, had led the nation from semifeudalism to modern times under the slogans "Rich Country, Strong Army" and "Civilization and Enlightenment"; in his reign the welfare of the nation took precedence over that of the individual. Meiji's heir, Taisho, was an eccentric who once rolled up a speech he was to make to the Diet and used it as a telescope; his antics and tantrums became so exaggerated that his heir, the crown prince, was named regent in 1921. Five years later, on Christmas Day, Taisho died and his twenty-five-year-old son became emperor.

Since childhood Hirohito had been trained for this role principally by Prince Saionji, who himself had been influenced by the French Revolution and English liberalism. Time and again the last *genro* would tell the young man that Japan needed a father figure, not a despot, and that he should therefore assume a position of responsibility in all affairs of state, yet never issue any positive order on his own volition. He should be objective and selfless.

Theoretically the Emperor had plenary power; all state decisions needed his sanction. But according to tradition, once the Cabinet and military leaders had agreed on a policy, he could not withhold his approval. He was to remain above politics and transcend party considerations and feuds, for he represented the entire nation.

All these restrictions notwithstanding, he exercised prodigious influence since he was in the unique position of being able to warn or approve without getting involved. More important, every Japanese was pledged to serve him unto death. This moral power was so potent that he used it sparingly and then only in vague terms. Those reporting to the Throne had to divine his wishes, since he almost always spoke cryptically without expression.

A more positive emperor, like his grandfather, might have consolidated his power; by the Meiji Constitution he was Commander in Chief of the Armed Forces. But Hirohito was a studious man who would rather be a scientist than a monarch. His happiest days were Monday and Saturday when he could retire to his modest laboratory and study marine biology. Neither did he have the slightest wish to be a despot. From his trip to Europe as crown prince he had brought back a taste for whiskey, Occidental music and golf, along with an abiding respect for the English version of constitutional monarchy. He could also defy tradition and court pressure when principle was involved. After the Empress Nagako had given birth to four daughters he refused to take a concubine or two so he could sire a male heir—and within a few years was rewarded with two sons by Nagako.

He was an unlikely-looking emperor, slouching around the Palace in frayed, baggy trousers and crooked tie, dreamily peering through glasses as thick as portholes, so oblivious of his appearance that occasionally his jacket would be fastened with the wrong button. He disliked buying new clothes, on the grounds that he couldn't "afford" them. He was so frugal that he even refrained from buying books he wanted, and he wore down every pencil to a stub. He was completely without vanity, a natural and unaffected individual who looked and acted like a village mayor. Yet this small round-shouldered man had some of the qualifications of a great one: he was pure, free of pride, ambition and selfishness. He wanted what was best for the nation.

His subjects regarded him as a god, and children were warned that they would be struck blind if they dared look at his face. If a public speaker mentioned the word "Emperor" the entire audience would sit at attention. If a reporter had the temerity to ask a personal question about the Emperor, he was icily told one should not pose such queries about a deity.

But "god" did not mean in Japan what it meant in the West. To a Japanese the emperor was a god, just as his own mother, father and teacher were lesser gods. His reverence for the monarch was not only a feeling of awe but also of affection and obligation, and no matter how low his station, each subject felt a family kinship to the emperor, who was the father of them all. As Meiji lay on his deathbed, all Japan prayed for his recovery and multitudes remained in the Palace plaza day and night; the entire nation grieved his death as a single family. For Japan *was* one great family, a modernized clan which had evolved from a number of warring tribes.

Every child was taught *kodo*, the Imperial Way: that the basis for Japanese morality was *on* (obligation) to the emperor and one's parents. Without the emperor one would be without country; without parents, homeless. For centuries the Japanese ruler had been benevolent, never attempting to exert his authority. Just as a parent loved and guided his children, he loved and guided his people with compassion. The imperial line had once gone 346 years without sanctioning a single execution throughout the land.

Out of the present Emperor's vague status evolved an almost autocratic power for the Army and Navy Chiefs of Staff. They had become, in essence, responsible to themselves alone. Only once had the Emperor challenged the military and that was in 1928 upon learning of the assassination of old Marshal Chang Tso-lin by the Ishihara-Itagaki group. His fury was such that he forgot his rigid training and sharply criticized the Prime Minister. Prince Saionji, who was the influence behind the Emperor's distrust of the military, was just as angry—but his target was the Emperor. He spoke out as a teacher, not as a subject, and accused Hirohito of acting like a tyrant. The old man's rebuke so shook the Emperor

26

that with three exceptions, he would never again fail to follow the last *genro*'s primary rule: "Reign, not rule."*

4.

Okada's secretary, Hisatsune Sakomizu, had returned to the Prime Minister's official residence with the rebels' permission, and when he found his father-in-law safe in the closet he whispered, "I'll come back; keep up your spirits," and returned to his own home to plan a rescue. Shortly before ten o'clock an official of the Imperial Household Ministry phoned, with polite condolences on the Prime Minister's demise. He said the Emperor wished to send an imperial messenger to the family; should the messenger go to the ministry or to Okada's home?

Fearing the phone was tapped, Sakomizu put him off; the truth had to be reported in person to the Emperor, and Sakomizu changed into a morning suit, with a bulletproof vest underneath. Armed with an umbrella, he walked across the street to the official residence, and after an argument got authorization from the rebels to pass through their lines. He took a taxi to the Hirakawa Gate of the Imperial Palace grounds, and struggled on foot through the deep snow to the concrete headquarters of the Imperial Household Ministry.

Household Minister Kurahei Yuasa began to express his condolences, but Sakomizu interrupted to tell him Okada was still alive. Startled, Yuasa dropped something, said he must relay the good news to His Majesty and disappeared. He must have run all the way to the Emperor's wing of the rambling building and back, for he returned in minutes to tell Sakomizu in a solemn voice, "When I reported that Prime Minister Okada was alive, His Majesty was most pleased. He said, 'That is excellent,' and told me to bring Okada to safety as soon as possible."

Sakomizu suggested that they get help from the commander of the 1st Division, who could send troops to rescue Okada. Yuasa disagreed; it would be too risky because the commander would have to get clearance from his superiors. "And you never know which way *they* are looking."

---

*Prince Mikasa, the Emperor's youngest brother, was convinced that the assassination of Chang was the basic cause of war with America. It not only actuated the Manchurian Incident but was the turning point in his brother's role as emperor. Prince Mikasa revealed this in an interview on December 27, 1966.

This made sense and Sakomizu decided to seek help from a more independent source. He went into a room filled with high-ranking officers. They all looked worried, as if they were about to be reprimanded. Many expressed regrets at Okada's death, but a few rudely remarked that something like this was bound to happen, since the Prime Minister ignored the Army's suggestions.

The rebels' manifesto was being passed around and hotly debated but nobody seemed to be in charge. War Minister Kawashima appeared to be completely perplexed; he certainly couldn't be depended on. Sakomizu surveyed the gathering in dismay. This was the hierarchy of the Army and it was a mob—vacillating, undependable, opportunistic. There was not one he felt he could trust with his secret, so he elbowed his way out of the crowd. He went into another room where the Cabinet was convening and found just as chaotic a scene. The ministers were apprehensive and truculent and doing nothing until the arrival of their senior member, Minister of the Interior Fumio Goto. They descended on Sakomizu, deluging him with questions about the Prime Minister. How had he died? Where was the body? Who killed him? While Sakomizu gave evasive answers, he caught sight of someone he could trust—the Navy Minister, who was an old friend of Okada's and a fellow admiral. Picking his words carefully in case someone was eavesdropping, Sakomizu said, "Mr. Minister, we'd like to claim the body of a senior member of the Navy. Will you send a landing force unit to the Prime Minister's residence to give us protection?"

The admiral failed to see through this charade and said, "Impossible. What if it ends in a skirmish between the Army and Navy?"

Sakomizu lowered his voice. "I'm going to tell you something important. Now, if you don't accept my proposal, I would like you to forget everything I say." Sakomizu informed the puzzled minister that Okada was still alive and should be rescued by naval troops.

"I haven't heard a thing," said the embarrassed admiral and drifted away.

There didn't seem to be anyone else to turn to and Sakomizu began to dream up wild schemes. He thought of imitating the dramatic balloon escape from Paris of French President Gambetta during the Franco-Prussian War, until he realized there were only advertising balloons in Tokyo. What about spiriting Okada and Matsuo's body out of the residence in one coffin? No, that would take a suspiciously large coffin. It was

28

already past noon and every moment counted. Desperate, he wandered restlessly from room to room, at a loss as to what to do.

By midafternoon there was a semblance of normalcy in the streets outside the square mile held by the rebels. Boys on bicycles pedaled through the snow with groceries. Shopkeepers near the edge of the action came out in their aprons and quizzed the young soldiers manning the barricades. Nobody seemed to know much about anything.

The Army leaders still vacillated. Though they were all repelled by the seditious actions of the rebels, so many agreed in principle with their aims that no decision could be reached. They couldn't even agree on an appeal to Captain Koda and his comrades, not until it was watered down and hopelessly vague. Labeled an "admonition," it failed to call them what they were—rebels:

1. The purpose of the uprising has reached the Emperor's ears.
2. Your action has been recognized as motivated by your sincere feelings to seek manifestation of the national essence.
3. The present state of manifestation of *kokutai* is such that we feel unbearably awed.
4. The War Councilors unanimously agree to endeavor to attain the above purposes.
5. Anything else will be subject to the Emperor's wishes.

This was published at three o'clock in the afternoon, along with a ridiculous emergency defense order placing the center of Tokyo under the jurisdiction of the 1st Division, the unit that had revolted. It was an attempt at expediency; with orders to guard the area they had seized, the rebels supposedly would regard themselves as loyal government troops.

Neither the conciliatory "admonition" nor the emergency order had the desired effect; they merely convinced Koda's group that a large segment of the military hierarchy was on their side. Koda's answer was: "If our original demands are granted, we will obey your orders. Otherwise we cannot evacuate the territory we have occupied."

That night reinforcements arrived from Kofu and Sakura to take up positions opposite the barricades. At the American embassy, observers on the roof could see the rebel banner waving from the Prime Minister's residence and the Sanno Hotel. Mrs. Grew was so nervous that she insisted on sleeping in a different room, even though the ambassador assured her that the last thing the insurgents wanted was trouble with the United States.

A few blocks away a car drove up to *kempeitai* headquarters and three spruce military figures stepped out—Captain Koda and two other rebel leaders. As they marched through the entrance to continue negotiations with the Army, two sentries smartly presented arms.

"*Bakayaro* [Idiot]!" shouted a noncom leaning out of a window. "Saluting rebel officers! They aren't the Imperial Army!"

The three spent the next thirty minutes listening to Generals Mazaki and Araki urge them to end the rebellion, but again conciliation only made them more steadfast.

At the Imperial Household Ministry, Interior Minister Goto had finally arrived after a curious six-hour delay to get himself appointed "temporary and concurrent prime minister." A few minutes later he was listening to demands for martial law by War Minister Kawashima. Goto and the other civilians in the Cabinet feared this might degenerate into a military dictatorship and argued that since this was strictly an Army insurrection which had nothing to do with the public, it should be settled within the Army itself.

Kawashima replied that there must have been instigators from the outside and it was therefore necessary to take extraordinary measures to ensure the nation's safety. Feeble as this retort was, it swayed the undecided members and at a meeting held at midnight in the presence of the Emperor it was agreed that martial law should be declared at once.

By this time a *kempei* sergeant had been told of Okada's whereabouts: one of his men, permitted to bring out the dead and wounded police officers, had chanced to open the closet where the Prime Minister was sitting resigned like a Buddha. The startling news about Okada was reported to their commander, who decided not to relay the information to his own superiors—if it was a mistake, he'd be ridiculed, and if true, some *kempei* sympathetic to the rebels would tell them and Okada would be killed. But to the sergeant, Keisuke Kosaka, this was dereliction of duty. On his own initiative he and two volunteers stole through the rebel lines late that night and just before dawn of February 27 boldly marched into the Prime Minister's residence. Kosaka went directly to the maid's room, opened the closet, assured Okada he would soon be rescued, and crossed the street to get help from a secretary of the Prime Minister's named Ko Fukuda who lived next door to Sakomizu.

The secretary and the sergeant cautiously sounded each other out as they sipped black tea until Kosaka finally revealed that Okada was alive. Only then did Fukuda admit that he and Sakomizu also knew and hoped to smuggle Okada out of the ministry in a crowd of mourners that would soon arrive to pay their respects.

In the next half-hour the resourceful sergeant and his two men spirited a suit of Western clothes for Okada from the bedroom and commandeered a car in the courtyard. They were just in time. Two black sedans pulled up and a dozen condolence callers filed into the ministry. Fukuda led them to the bedroom, where one of the sergeant's men was waiting to make sure they wouldn't get close enough to the corpse to realize it wasn't the Prime Minister.

While the callers burned incense and honored the dead, Fukuda and Kosaka practically carried the cramped Okada, his face half hidden behind a germ mask, to the rear. A group of rebels stood at the door and Kosaka called out authoritatively, "Emergency patient! He shouldn't have taken a look at the corpse."

The rebels stepped aside and the trio was in the courtyard. But there was no car waiting, and curious to see what was going on, the commander of the guard approached. Suddenly the commandeered car drew up. Fukuda opened the door, pushed the exhausted Okada into the 1935 Ford and climbed in after him. Kosaka watched with pounding heart as the car drove slowly through the gates and disappeared. Tears flowed down his face and he remained standing there as if in a trance.

So Okada had escaped, but there was still the problem of getting rid of Matsuo's body before someone discovered the deception. This was Sakomizu's task but he felt it would be best to do nothing until Okada was in a secure hiding place. Hour after hour he sat in lonely vigil next to the corpse. At last the phone rang. His wife reported that her father was safe in a Buddhist temple. Now Sakomizu could act. First he phoned the Imperial Household Ministry to tell of Okada's escape, then called the Okada home to ask that a coffin be sent to the official residence as soon as possible. The answer was that a ready-made coffin wasn't proper for a Prime Minister, and it would take several hours to make one.

The delay began to unnerve Sakomizu: he'd be found out

and murdered. As his terror grew he recalled that in his father's day boys used to hold a contest of courage called *shibedate* (standing a rice stalk on end). One boy would put some object on a grave; the next would retrieve it; a third would stick a rice stalk on the grave. This went on and on until someone lost his nerve. The boys believed that fear came only if their testicles shrank, so when they walked toward the grave they would pluck at them to stretch them out. Sakomizu discovered that, sure enough, his testicles had contracted to almost nothing. He managed to stretch them and to his amazement found his own fear disappearing. People in the old days were clever.

It was dark by the time the coffin finally arrived. Sakomizu dismissed the pallbearers, wrapped Matsuo's body completely in a blanket and got it in the coffin. As the cortege slowly left the ministry, the rebel in charge saluted and said a few courteous words of farewell. The funeral carriage moved quietly through the gate, and after a harrowing trip, safely reached the home of the Prime Minister. A crowd had already collected for services. A tombstone was placed on the coffin along with a large photograph of Okada, framed in black ribbon.

Sakomizu gave strict orders not to open the coffin and was off for the Imperial Household Ministry, where Cabinet members had again gathered. Now he told them that Okada was still alive, and while they were recovering from the shock, proposed that the Prime Minister see the Emperor as soon as possible. To Sakomizu's amazement, Acting Prime Minister Goto protested: Okada was responsible for the rebellion and should resign on the spot. Goto refused to listen to any explanations—apparently he liked being prime minister—and Sakomizu was compelled to phone influential men for support.

He found none. The consensus was that if the rebel troops learned that Okada was on the Palace grounds they might fire toward the Palace. And that would be "too appalling." In resignation Sakomizu phoned Fukuda not to bring Okada there and returned to the Okada home to see that the prefuneral ceremonies went off without discovery of the deception—otherwise the rebels would start a manhunt.

Mrs. Matsuo sat silently in front of the coffin. As the hours passed and she asked no questions about her husband, Sakomizu felt such pity that he could no longer hold back the truth. He gathered the Prime Minister's close relatives, including three of his four children and three of Matsuo's four children, and controlling his emotions, told how Colonel Matsuo had sacrificed his life so that the Prime Minister could escape.

"I am very pleased if my husband could be of service," said the widow softly. She was the daughter of a samurai.

5.

By now the mutiny had a name, the 2/26 (February 26) Incident, and though the attitude of the military leaders was beginning to harden, it took the Emperor himself to get them into action. Exasperated by their dallying, he stepped out of his role for the first time since the murder of Marshal Chang and spoke out clearly: "If the Army cannot subdue the rebels, I will go out and dissuade them myself."

This forced the Army to issue an edict at 5:06 A.M., February 28. It ordered the rebels, in the Emperor's name, to "speedily withdraw" from their present positions and return to their respective units. Inhabitants in the danger zones would be evacuated; if the rebels had not withdrawn by 8 A.M., the following day, they would be fired on.

This order split the rebels into two camps: one wanted to obey the Emperor; the other insisted it was not truly the wish of the Emperor but the result of pressure from the Control clique.

During the day Sakomizu met with more disappointment. Goto still opposed Okada's visit to the Emperor, and in any case, the police refused to provide an escort for the Prime Minister to the Palace—it was "too grave a responsibility." Fearing that Okada might commit hara-kiri, Sakomizu ignored Goto and the police and brought the Prime Minister to the Imperial Household Ministry.

Shortly before seven o'clock in the evening the old man was escorted to the Emperor's wing of the building. In the corridors they passed Household officials who stared in terror at the grim-faced Okada, imagining they were seeing a ghost. A few ran off as the rest crouched in fright.

Once in the imperial presence, the Prime Minister humbly apologized for the mutiny, as if it had been his fault, and offered his resignation. "Carry on your duty for as long as you live," the Emperor replied and added that he was very pleased.

Okada was too awed to speak or stop the flow of tears but

finally managed to say, "I am going to behave myself from now on." This time the Emperor did not reply.

Okada slept that night in the Household Ministry but Sakomizu returned to the Prime Minister's home, which was still crowded with mourners. A group of irate admirals hemmed him in. "As a samurai, how dared you surrender the castle?" one shouted. "Even with the Prime Minister dead, you should have stayed to protect his body and defend the official residence to the death. How can you be so irresponsible as to run off to the Imperial Household Ministry for what business I don't know!"

They were disgusted with the way Sakomizu was handling the funeral arrangements and said they were taking the body to the Navy Officers Club the next day for a proper service. Sakomizu begged them to be patient, but was immediately set upon by yet another admiral: "Your father was a fine military man. I arranged your marriage for you because, since you are his son, I thought you'd be a reliable man. But you've proven by this case to be a miserable fellow, a weak-kneed man unable even to manage a funeral. Okada must be weeping for having given his daughter to such a fellow. Your father is weeping too. Pull yourself together!"

Despite the Emperor's edict, all but a few of the rebels refused to withdraw. As more Army reinforcements invested Tokyo from outlying cities, the Combined Fleet steamed into Tokyo Bay and landing forces took positions outside the Navy Ministry and other naval installations. The younger men were itching for action and revenge: three of their senior officers—Admirals Saito, Suzuki and Okada—had been assassinated or gravely wounded by the Army. One young officer, whose ship's main guns were trained on the Diet Building, was "tempted by an impulse" to blow off the tower but controlled himself.

At six o'clock in the morning on February 29—it was leap year—the Army announced: "We are positively going to suppress the rebels who caused disturbances in the neighborhood of Kojimachi in the imperial capital." For the first time the word "rebels" was officially used. It was a cloudy day with a threat of more snow. Except for soldiers, it was a dead city. Schools were closed; there were no streetcars or trains. It was impossible to make a phone call or send a telegram. Tokyo was isolated. All civilian traffic in the city was suspended while the Army marshaled its forces for the attack, but even as tanks were brought to assault positions other tanks clanked up to rebel barricades, their sides placarded with messages invoking the insurgents to "respectfully follow the Emperor's order" and withdraw at once. Fully loaded bombers droned overhead while other planes dropped leaflets addressed to noncommissioned officers:

1. Return to your units. It is not yet too late.
2. All those who résist are rebels; therefore, we will shoot them.
3. Your parents and brothers are weeping to see you become traitors.

An advertising balloon was raised above the Aviation Building, its long trailer in large characters reading: IMPERIAL ORDER ISSUED. DON'T RESIST THE ARMY FLAG. Loudspeakers were brought up to strategic places, and Chokugen Wada, the noted announcer of radio station NHK, began reading a plea to the rebel enlisted men in a choked voice: "You faithfully and sincerely obeyed your officers, trusting their orders to be just. But the Emperor now orders you to return to your units. If you continue to resist, you will be traitors for disobeying the Emperor's order. You believed you were doing the right thing but now that you realize you were wrong, you must not continue to revolt against His Majesty and inflict upon yourself eternal disgrace as traitors. It is not too late. Your past crime will be forgiven. Your fathers and brothers, as well as the entire nation, sincerely pray that you do this. Immediately leave your present positions and come back."

The rebellious soldiers began to look at one another questioningly. Still each waited for the other to act first. By midmorning the solidarity of the ranks began to crack. Thirty noncoms and soldiers walked away from their positions with rifles and machine guns. By noon almost all enlisted men had returned to their units except for small detachments at the Prime Minister's official residence and the Sanno Hotel. At two o'clock the banner flying over the Prime Minister's residence came down and an hour later Army headquarters announced by radio that the rebels had surrendered without a shot being fired.

The leaders of the insurrection were still at the War Ministry and the Sanno Hotel, but the loyal troops made no attempt to capture them; they were giving the rebels a chance to act like samurai. General Araki, who admired their spirit and sympathized with their motives, asked them to commit hara-kiri, since they had performed an outrageous, reckless act that grieved the Emperor. The young officers considered mass suicide, but finally decided to submit to a court-martial where, like Aizawa, they could alert the nation to the corruption besetting Japan.

One officer, however, refused to surrender. Captain Shiro Nonaka went off by himself and wrote a final statement regretting that his division hadn't seen action for over thirty years while other units were shedding their blood in glory. "In recent years the sins of the traitors at home have been redeemed by the blood of our comrades in Manchuria and Shanghai. What answer can I give to the souls of these men if I spend the rest of my days in vain here in the capital? Am I insane or am I a fool? There is but one road for me to take." He signed the declaration, then took the road: hara-kiri.

At four-thirty that afternoon the weary Sakomizu assembled the mourners at Okada's home to read a prepared statement revealing the details of Matsuo's death and Okada's escape. The listeners were stunned to silence. Finally someone shouted *"Banzai!"* All the others joined and the news was spread throughout the neighborhood.

The 2/26 Incident was over. What violence there was had been incredibly bloody; yet only seven people had been killed and the mutineers had surrendered peacefully. The most outstanding feats of courage had been performed by women, and the vacillation by generals. To most foreigners the mutiny was no more than another ultranationalist bloodbath, and few realized its significance. The Soviets did, largely because of Richard Sorge, who correctly guessed that this would lead to expansion into China.*

---

* Dr. Sorge's detailed report to Moscow included an analysis of the deep social unrest that had inspired the rebellion. Sorge also sent photographs of the cream of the material gathered by the German military attachés, including a secret pamphlet written the previous year by two of the rebel leaders, entitled "Views on the Housecleaning of the Army." The Fourth Bureau was pleased with its new secret agent and requested additional information: Would it affect Japanese foreign policy? Would it make Japan more anti-Soviet or less?

With the help of a highly connected journalist and an artist turned Communist, Sorge answered all these questions, as well as observing that the 2/26 Incident would result in either social reforms or a policy of permanent expansion. And expansion would go in the direction of China. He was careful to be circumspect and objective, since he was aware that unlike Berlin and Washington, "Moscow knew China and Japan too well to be fooled easily."

36

It was over, but like a stone tossed in a millpond, its ripples were already spreading across the Pacific.

2   To the Marco Polo Bridge

1.

Uneasy relief hung over the five million people of Tokyo, as it had after the great earthquake of 1923. During the mutiny they had shown little sympathy for the young rebels. For the first time public condemnation of mutineers was almost unanimous and there was criticism of the unruly streak running throughout the Army.

At the time of the 5/15 Incident the people had been confident that the militarists and nationalists would smash corrupt party politics and right social wrongs by direct acts of force. But corruption and social injustice had persisted and now, after the past four wild days, the public had lost its blind faith in force and wanted a return to orderly ways—at almost any cost.

And although every performance at the Kabuki Theater of that paean to revenge, violence and bloody self-sacrifice, *The Forty-seven Ronin*, was still packed, there was increasing support for the group in the Army that seemed the answer to chaos—the Control clique. Its very name stood for the need of the hour, discipline, even though what it really advocated was control of China. Civilian leaders, swayed by this same desire for law and order, began a move to crush the Imperial

---

To this day a number of informed Japanese believe the mutiny was inspired by Communist agents. They claim that General Mazaki secretly conferred with left-wing leaders prior to the rebellion, and point out that not only the young officers but Ikki Kita and other civilian nationalists were unwitting tools of the Communists, whose plan it was to communize Japan through the action of idealists who preached socialism and the Imperial Way simultaneously. Realizing the power of emperor worship, the Communists intended to utilize the imperial system, not do away with it. This theory was somewhat shared by Sorge himself, who later told a friend that Japanese Communists may have had some connection with the uprising and that it was possible to have a Communist Japan ruled by an emperor.

Way clique; and inadvertently jarred open the door to the gradual weakening of their own power by the military.

On the surface it looked as if the civilians had won new power when a new cabinet was formed by Foreign Minister Koki Hirota. Ambassador Grew informed the State Department that Hirota would "curb the dangerous tendencies of the Army in China and Manchuria," and wrote in his diary that he was pleased at the choice "because I believe that Hirota is a strong, safe man and that while he will have to play ball with the Army to a certain extent, I think that he will handle foreign affairs as wisely as they can be handled ..."

Hirota made a promising start by selecting the openly pro-American diplomat Shigeru Yoshida as his foreign minister, but the Army's protest was so violent that Hirota dropped him. This was only the first of a series of conciliatory moves, climaxed by the new Prime Minister's acceptance of a demand that all future war ministers be approved by the Big Three of the Army. Apparently an innocent move, this return to the old system meant that the policies of the country were now at the mercy of the Army. If the military disapproved of a cabinet, the war minister could resign and the Big Three would simply refuse to approve anyone else, thereby bringing about the fall of the cabinet. The Army could then refuse to provide a minister until a cabinet to their liking was selected. It meant the voluntary abandonment of one of the last civilian controls over the affairs of state.

Although the Army leaders were gaining political control, this was not their primary goal. They were striving above all to prevent another "2/26." They realized that no amount of discipline could control idealistic young officers passionately dedicated to wiping out poverty and corruption. The solution was to eradicate the causes of discontent, which could only be done by correcting what the insurgents considered to be the evils of free economy. Already the settlers of Manchuria were demanding that their planned economy, which had brought such rapid material progress, be applied to the homeland. But who would carry out such a sweeping economic reform? The capitalists were busy defending their interests, and their servants—the politicians—were not only unsuited for the job but had lost the confidence of the public. And since the Army could not openly enter into politics without being corrupted itself, there was but one course left: to "propel reform" without too much involvement.

To forestall public hostility, the Army leaders placed

Araki, Mazaki and a dozen other generals sympathetic to the Imperial Way clique on the inactive list and transferred many of the younger officers to unimportant posts.*

Martial law, invoked during the rebellion, continued month after month, with the press rigidly controlled and voices of dissent silenced. The mutineers were tried swiftly and in private. Thirteen officers and four civilians, including Ikki Kita, were sentenced to death. On July 12 they were bound to racks, blindfolded, and their foreheads marked with bull's-eyes. Lieutenant Takahashi, who had helped assassinate General Watanabe, sang a song before remarking, "Indeed, indeed, I hope the privileged classes will reflect upon their conduct and be more prudent." One embittered young officer cried out, "O, people of Japan, don't trust the Imperial Army!" Another shouted, "The people trust the Army! Don't let the Russians beat us!" Almost all gave three *banzai* for His Majesty just before the shots rang out.

Even with the purge of Imperial Way officers, there was a small but influential group in Tokyo dedicated to their main principle—the end of expansion. Their leader was the man who had engineered the seizure of Manchuria, Kanji Ishihara. Now on the General Staff, he had become appalled by the results of his own deed. He had dreamed of a democratic Manchuria comprised of five nationalities, all living in harmony as well as providing a bulwark against Russian aggression. But this idealistic goal had degenerated into a determination by the Army leadership to use Manchuria as a base for a takeover of North China.

Soon after the execution of the mutineers, Ishihara secretly met with eleven other key officers from the War Ministry and Army General Staff at the Takara-tei restaurant in Tokyo. These men shared his fear of expansion into China and had convened to discuss what should be done.

Ishihara opened with a question: Why risk war with China when the most dangerous enemy was their traditional foe, Russia? Two wars at once would be suicidal to a Japan weak in heavy industries, he continued. Instead the nation should concentrate all its energies on expanding its productive power

---

*In an interview a few weeks before his death in 1966 General Araki said, "We [Imperial Way] were idealists, they [Control] were pragmatists. We thought force was necessary at times but it was more important to set the nation in a proper course according to Meiji's five principles. Therefore it was not right simply to crush China." He then added wryly, "But those who speak of ideals lose. The realists always get their own way in the end."

until it could compete with that of the Soviet Union. To attain self-sufficiency in heavy industry, Japan would have to develop the resources of Manchuria in a series of five-year programs, avoiding all conflicts with Russia and China. When Japanese industry reached its peak in 1952, then an all-out war could be waged with Russia—and won. This alone could save Japan, not the expansion policy of the Control clique which called for a push into China and perhaps Southeast Asia that had to result in war with Britain and America. If this happened, the only one to profit would be the real enemy, Russia. Ishihara added that the greatest danger to the nation lay not in Tokyo, with the hierarchy comprised of men open to reason and persuasion, but in Manchuria.

In that country, influential radicals in the Kwantung Army were already organizing unauthorized forays into North China. Their leader was Major General Kenji Doihara, much like Ishihara with the same brilliance, flamboyance and talent for intrigue. He had already been nicknamed "The Lawrence of Manchuria" by Western newsmen. The previous year he had gone alone into North China inveigling the war lords and officials of the northernmost five provinces to break away from China and form an autonomous government under the wing of the Imperial Japanese Army. Once Prime Minister Okada learned this, he had sent out word to check the impetuous Doihara. But he ignored Tokyo—as had Ishihara—and continued to plot so successfully that an autonomous government of sorts was set up. Opportunistic Japanese merchants flooded into North China under their slogan "Follow the Japanese Flag," irritating Chinese merchants and stirring up anti-Japanese feeling all over China. Doihara claimed he had established the puppet regime merely as a buffer between Manchuria and China, but a few weeks later he brought in five thousand Japanese troops on the grounds that Japanese merchants needed protection from bandits.

Now Ishihara charged that this influx of troops was but the beginning of a mass raid into China and that Doihara's buffer area was "a poisonous flower" which should be destroyed before it involved Japan in total war with Nationalist forces under Chiang Kai-shek. Both the Russians and the Chinese Communists were plotting to this end so they could step in once both sides were exhausted and establish a Red China.

Ishihara concluded that the best way to curb Doihara was to get back to their offices and advise their chiefs to remove Japanese troops from trouble spots in North China. One such was the ancient Marco Polo Bridge fifteen miles southwest of Peking.

Japanese troops had been stationed in the Peking area ever since an international expeditionary force—including European, American and Japanese troops—suppressed the bloody, xenophobic Boxer Rebellion in 1900. The next year the chastened Chinese signed the so-called Boxer Protocol allowing certain foreign powers to occupy key points near Peking "for the maintenance of open communications between the capital and the sea."

With the Boxers crushed, China became even more of a plundering ground for Western imperialism, but the continued depredation of her resources at last stirred her people to revolt. Long ago Napoleon had sounded the warning that China was but a sleeping giant: "Let him sleep! For when he wakes he will move the world."

In 1911 the collapse of the decadent Manchu Empire under the attacks of Dr. Sun Yat-sen, China's first genuine nationalist, finally awakened the sleeping giant. At once the fledgling republic was besieged on all sides by local war lords hungry for spoils, and although Dr. Sun's Kuomintang (National People's Party) continued to gain support throughout the country, China was torn to pieces. Finally, after a dozen frustrating years of bloody conflict, Dr. Sun called for help from a country which was glad to oblige—the Soviet Union. Soon Canton was swarming with Communists offering advice on everything from mass propaganda to military tactics. The moving spirit behind the Kuomintang armies called himself Galen but was in truth a Soviet general named Bluecher; and the chief political adviser was a colorful man who had taught in a Chicago business college and was one of the Kremlin's top political agitators, Michael Borodin. With their help the republic grew in power, and its armies, under an able young general, Chiang Kai-shek, crushed its war-lord foes and pushed north, capturing Shanghai and Nanking. But success brought a much greater problem, the rising power of Communism within the ranks of the Kuomintang itself. In 1927 Chiang, now Sun's successor, concluded that continued help from Russia would lead to a Red China; he outlawed the Communists.* From that day until the 2/26 Incident a triple

---

*After he had been forced to leave China, Borodin reportedly said, "When the next Chinese general comes to Moscow and shouts, 'Hail to the world revolution!,' better send at once for the OGPU. All that any of them want is rifles."

war raged through China. On Monday, Kuomintang troops fought war lords; on Tuesday, the two would unite to fight one of the growing Red armies; and on Wednesday, war lords and Communists would jointly fall upon Chiang Kai-shek.

This constant turmoil, along with the relentless surge of international Communism, alarmed Japanese military leaders. They were threatened from the north by Stalin's bombers in Vladivostok, less than seven hundred miles from Tokyo, and from the west by the bourgeoning legions of the Chinese Communists under a determined peasant named Mao Tse-tung.*

To the militarists, there was no choice but to consolidate Manchuria, which lay between the two threats, as a break-water against Communism. Those in the Control clique further argued that Manchuria was not enough and North China should also be seized. A state of anarchy existed throughout that area, and the considerable Japanese interests were needed protection. The claim of anarchy was somewhat justified. According to the *Survey by the Royal Institute of International Affairs,* banditry was rampant but Communism itself had become "an organized and effective political power exercising exclusive administrative authority over large stretches of territory." There were also indications that the Chinese Communists were in league with the Soviets. "The possibility that Chinese and Russian Communism might join hands was

---

*On their part, the Soviets accused America and Britain of plotting against them in Asia. *A Short History of the U.S.S.R.,* Part II, put out by the Academy of Sciences of the U.S.S.R. Institute of History, states: "In April 1927, political circles in Britain and the U.S.A. tried to provoke a military conflict between the Soviet Union and China. Police and troops broke into the Soviet Embassy in Peking, arrested members of the staff and searched and ransacked the premises. This provocation was instigated by representatives of the Western powers, a fact which was confirmed by the Chinese chargé d'affaires in the U.S.S.R. in his reply to the Soviet protest note. He stated quite clearly that the action of the Chinese military authorities and police had been prearranged with Western diplomats." This same work further declares: "In the summer of 1927 . . . ruling circles in the U.S.A., Japan, Britain and France made another attempt to provoke a Sino-Soviet clash and involve the U.S.S.R. in war in the Far East. On May 27, 1929, bandits attacked the Soviet consulate in Harbin, and on July 10, Chinese militarists tried to seize the Chinese Eastern Railway, which was administered jointly by the U.S.S.R. and China . . . In September an October 1929, detachments of Chinese militarists and Russian white guards invaded Soviet territory." No corroborating evidence could be found to these accusations.

thus to be reckoned with if Chinese Communism were Communism in the Russian sense."

Most of the world lived in terror of Communism, and it was not remarkable that the Control clique regarded its spread in China as Japan's principal danger. For the Chinese Communists, unlike those in America and Europe, were not merely members of a party but actual rivals of the national government, with their own laws and sphere of action. Already large sections of China had been Sovietized, and Shanghai itself was a fount of Communist propaganda.

At this time Mao was declaring that his Red troops alone were fighting the Japanese, while Chiang was simply waging a "war of extermination" against Communism. "I solemnly declare here, in the name of the Chinese Soviet government," he told Western newsmen, "that if Chiang Kai-shek's army or any other army ceases hostilities against the Red Army, then the Chinese Soviet government will immediately order the Red Army to stop military action against them. . . . If Chiang Kai-shek really means to take up the struggle against Japan, then obviously the Chinese Soviet government will extend to him the hand of friendship on the field of battle against Japan."

This call for a united front, which had originated in Moscow, failed to move Chiang, but one of his most important field commanders, Chang Hsueh-liang, was not so adamant and Mao decided to work through him. Chang was known as "the Young Marshal," since his father was Old Marshal Chang Tso-lin, whose assassination had led to the Japanese occupation of Manchuria. Though the Young Marshal commanded the Northeastern Army, which had been ordered by the Kuomintang to wipe out all Red forces in North China, he had serious reservations about Chiang's course; he had come to believe that those he was fighting were also patriots and perhaps both sides should unite against the Japanese.

In the fall of 1936 Mao sent his most able negotiator, Chou En-lai, to work out a truce with the Young Marshal. Chou was mild-mannered, soft-spoken, almost effeminate-looking, but it was he who had directed the gory massacres of anti-Communists in Shanghai in 1927. Like all good diplomats, he was blessed with endless patience. "No matter how angry I get," said an old school friend named Han, "he always smiles and goes back over the same ground covered in our argument, only in a different way—different enough to make you feel as though he were presenting a new point."

He met with Chang in a Catholic mission in Sian, a remote

43

city in North China, and after admitting that Chiang Kai-shek was the logical leader against the Japanese, promised that the Red generals would serve under him. In return Chang would have to assure him that the Red troops get equal treatment with the Nationalists. In addition, Communists held in Nationalist prisons would be released, and the Communist party allowed to operate legally once Japan was defeated.

They signed a document listing these conditions and shook hands to seal the bargain. "Young Marshal, now that it is all settled," said Chou, "I am ready to take orders from you this very moment."

Chang replied coldly that they would both have to wait and take orders from Chiang Kai-shek.

"If you still have any doubt about the determination of my party to join in a united front against Japan," said Chou, "I will gladly stay here in Sian with you as a hostage."

Chang said this wouldn't be necessary and that he was as determined as anyone to fight the Japanese—after all, he had a personal account to settle with them. Nevertheless, he was a soldier and must first attempt to persuade his superior, the Generalissimo, to accept the terms of the truce just signed.

But before such a meeting could take place, another of Chiang's field commanders, General Yang Hu-cheng, an ex bandit chief, convinced the Young Marshal that the Generalissimo could only be made to co-operate with the Reds if he were kidnapped. Chiang was already on his way to Sian to confront Chang with evidence that the Young Marshal was being influenced by leftists and to warn him that "unless timely measures were taken, the situation could lead to rebellion."

Although he had agreed to the kidnapping, the presence of Chiang Kai-shek in Sian weakened Chang's resolve; he continued to vacillate until General Yang took matters in his own hands on the morning of December 12. He seized the Generalissimo and all troops in the area loyal to him. Chiang had been badly injured in a fall while trying to escape, but he was more composed than the Young Marshal when they came face to face. "Both for your own sake and for the sake of the nation, the only thing for you to do is to repent at once and send me back to Nanking," he said. "You must not fall into the trap set by the Communists. Repent before it is too late."

It took the sheepish Chang two days to get up his nerve to show his superior a proposed eight-point agreement similar to the one made with Chou. Once it was signed, Chang prom-

44

ised, the Generalissimo would be escorted back to the Nationalist capital.

"So long as I am a captive, there can be no discussion," said Chiang. He dared the other to shoot him and went back to the Bible.

The distressed Chang turned to the Reds for help. When Chou arrived he praised Chang for his courage, scolded him for bungling the kidnapping and went in to see the prisoner. They knew each other well. Chou had once served under the Generalissimo at the Whampoa Military Academy, China's West Point; here, with Chiang's approval, he had set up a political-commissar system. What Chiang didn't realize until too late was that most of the commissars selected were Communists.

Chiang had since offered $80,000 for Chou's head and was understandably pale and apprehensive. But Chou was all affability. He swore that the Communists would not exploit the situation if Chiang joined them. All they wanted was an end to civil war, and a joint effort against the Japanese.

Hostile at first, Chiang listened with growing interest but still refused to commit himself. Within a week, however—according to the Communist version—Chou persuaded him to lead the fight against the Japanese on his own terms. In any case, he was flown back to Nanking on Christmas Day. Surprisingly, the Young Marshal went along with him and once there the two went through a typically Oriental face-saving game. It was like a stylized duel in Chinese opera. First Chang abased himself, confessing that he was "surly and unpolished" and had acted impudently and illegally: "Blushing with shame, I have followed you to the capital in order to receive from you appropriate punishment. Whatever is best for the state I will not evade, if I have to die ten thousand deaths." Then it was Chiang's turn: "Due to my lack of virtue and defects in my training of subordinates, an unprecedented revolt broke out." Chang was tried, sentenced to ten years' imprisonment, and pardoned within twenty-four hours.

At the same time Chiang was publicly proclaiming that despite stories from Sian, he had been freed "without having to accept any conditions." It was undoubtedly a version contrived to appease those in Nanking much more violently opposed to any dealing with the Reds than he, because within weeks he was dickering with Mao. The negotiations went so well that early in 1937 the Chinese Communist Party Central Committee wired the Kuomintang that they would abandon their policy of armed uprising against the Nationalist government and place the Red Army under Chiang's full control. The terms were informally accepted and once more, as in the honeymoon days of Borodin, the Kuomintang and Communists were united.

This brought China her first semblance of tranquillity in more than ten years. "Peace is achieved," declared Chou En-lai in an interview. "There is now no fighting between us. We have the opportunity to participate in the actual preparations for the defensive war against Japan. As to the problem of achieving democracy, this aim has only begun to be realized. . . . One must consider the anti-Japanese war preparations and democracy like the two wheels of a rickshaw, for example. That is to say, the preparation for the anti-Japanese war comes first, and following it, the movement for democracy—which can push the former forward."

A few months later, on July 5, 1937, a formal Kuomintang-Communist agreement was signed and both sides made preparations to drive the Japanese out of Peking and the rest of North China.

2.

In Japan, the increasing influence of the military over the government had become an issue. In the name of law and order, Prime Minister Hirota was now so obviously subservient to the generals that liberal members of the Diet denounced them. One aroused deputy told the War Minister he should commit hara-kiri. This was greeted by such enthusiastic shouts and applause that the minister resigned in anger. And of course, with his resignation, in February 1937, came the end of the Hirota Cabinet.

Without hesitation Prince Saionji advised the Emperor to name another general, Kazushige Ugaki, to succeed Hirota. This choice infuriated almost everyone in the Army, since Ugaki was a moderate who had once reduced their number by four divisions. Consequently the Big Three said they simply couldn't find anyone who would serve with Ugaki. He was compelled to report to the Emperor that he was unable to form a cabinet and gave vent to his indignation in a statement to the newspapers: "What I see is that only a few men in authoritative positions in the Army have formed a group [the Control clique] and are forcing their views on the authorities, propagandizing as if their action represents the general will of the Army. The Army belongs to the Emperor. Whether their action during the last few days represents the general will of the Army of the Emperor or not is not too clear. The selection of a war minister by the Big Three of the Army is too formal and lacks sincerity. . . . I believe that Japan stands at the crossroads between fascism and parliamentary politics. I am partly responsible for the present condition in the Army, which has become a political organization. I feel sorry for the Emperor because of this state of affairs. Moreover, I greatly regret that the Army, which I have loved so long, has been brought to such a pass. . . ."

A general named Senjuro Hayashi who was sympathetic to the Control clique was selected as prime minister, but he ran into such opposition from the Diet that his government, nicknamed the "eat-and-run cabinet," lasted just four months. Hayashi was succeeded by a civilian, Prince Fumimaro Konoye, a descendant of the Fujiwara family, which had ruled the land for several centuries. A disciple of Saionji's, he had long resisted the last *genro*'s efforts to get him involved in politics. In the harrowing days following the 2/26 Incident, the old prince had concluded that Konoye alone could lead the new government and recommended him formally to the Emperor. Konoye had refused—he preferred to remain as President of the House of Peers and besides was in poor health—causing Saionji's "most embarrassing moment."

But Konoye considered the present crisis so critical that he was persuaded to accept the position hitherto reserved for old men. At forty-six years of age he was a popular choice to lead the country, since the people had little confidence in politicians and feared a continuance of military rule. For their part, most military men trusted him because he was above political greed. The *zaibatsu* counted on him to bring stability, the intellectuals to stem the tide of fascism. Ordinary people were impressed by his comparative youth and good looks and his very reluctance to be prime minister. Any man with such an utter lack of ambition had to be sincere.

"Evolutionary reforms and progress within the Constitution must be our watchdogs," he promised upon assuming the premiership in June, "but the country demands national reform, and the government, while neither socialist nor fascist, must listen to its call. The impetus of the great [Meiji] Restoration has carried us thus far with honor and success;

but now it is for the young men to take up the task and carry the country forward into a new age."

The new age came sooner than he expected and was not at all what he had envisaged. It was ushered in on the night of July 7 at the ancient stone bridge named after Marco Polo. A Japanese company stationed near this historic landmark was holding night maneuvers about a mile from a large Chinese unit. Just as a bugle signaled the end of the operation, bullets came whistling from the Chinese lines. The Japanese returned fire, but within minutes the skirmish was over. There was a single Japanese casualty—one man was missing. The company commander reported the incident to his battalion commander, who phoned regimental headquarters in nearby Peking. A second company was sent to the bridge, as well as a staff officer who began arranging a truce with the Chinese. Both sides had just agreed it was an unfortunate mistake when a second fusillade poured into the two Japanese companies.

The first shots had probably been accidental. The second volley was suspicious, particularly since relations between the Chinese and Japanese troops in the area were so good. This had come about through a close friendship between General Sung Chi-yuen, commander of all Chinese troops in North China, and General Gun Hashimoto, chief of staff of the North China Garrison. The question was who had fired the second volley, if not the Chinese troops. Cohorts of Doihara trying to aggravate the incident into an excuse to invade China in force? Or Communists hoping to start a full-scale war between Chiang Kai-shek and the Japanese that would probably end in the communization of China?*

---

*It was not until after the war that the Japanese officers involved in the Marco Polo Bridge incident generally concluded that Mao's agents had sparked the incident. "We were then too simple to realize this was all a Communist plot," General Akio Doi, a Russian expert, said in 1967. General Ho Ying-chin, Chiang's minister of war at the time, still believes, like most Chinese, that the incident was plotted by Japanese radical militarists, although he did admit in a recent interview that after Chou En-lai read Chiang's diary in Sian and realized the Generalissimo was strongly anti-Japanese, he began conspiring to get the Kuomintang involved in an all-out war with Japan.

Without doubt, both the Russians and the Chinese Communists were doing their best to foster a long, enervating conflict between Chiang and the Japanese. That fall Mao Tse-tung told his troops in Yenan: "The Sino-Japanese conflict gives us, the Chinese Communists, an excellent opportunity for expansion. Our policy is to devote seventy percent of our effort to this end, twenty percent to coping with the Government, and ten percent to fighting the Japanese. This policy is to

48

Whoever it was, the Japanese counterattacked, and it wasn't until the next morning that the negotiators agreed that both sides should peacefully withdraw. While the Japanese were pulling out, they again drew fire, retaliated and the fight was resumed.

Though it should have seemed obvious by now that a third party was trying to keep the skirmish going, each side accused the other of breaking the truce and the negotiations floundered. When the news arrived in Tokyo, the Army Chief of Staff cabled a routine order to settle the trouble locally. Later in the day representatives of the War, Navy and Foreign ministries agreed on a policy of "nonexpansion" and "local settlement." This was approved by Prince Konoye and his cabinet, but at a special meeting of the Army General Staff, the expansionists argued that more troops should be sent into China to teach Chiang a lesson, otherwise he might use this incident as an excuse to retake Manchuria; this would endanger Japanese-controlled Korea and eventually put Japan at the mercy of Russian and Chinese Communists. They promised to make the military action brief and come to a quick agreement with Chiang. Then all Japanese troops would be withdrawn into North China, which would be used purely as a buffer against Russia.

The greatest opposition came from Kanji Ishihara, now a general and head of Operations. He argued for hours but finally had to admit that the poorly disciplined Chinese troops in North China were bound to start massacring the Japanese traders and settlers in the area. This would arouse the Japanese public and bring about what he feared and abhorred the most, an endless war of retribution.

That was why the man who once said, "The first soldier marching into China will only do so over my dead body," approved the reinforcement of North China with two brigades from the Kwantung Army, one division from Korea and three from the homeland. And on July 11 Prince Konoye, who had so recently pledged international integrity, gave his consent to the flood of troops into another country. But there was little else he could have done, according to his private secretary, Tomohiko Ushiba, "in the face of the War

be carried out in three stages. During the first stage, we are to work with the Kuomintang in order to ensure our existence and growth. During the second stage, we are to achieve parity in strength with the Kuomintang. During the third stage, we are to penetrate deep into parts of Central China to establish bases for counterattacks against the Kuomintang."

49

Minister's assurance that it was merely a troop movement to stop local fighting."

At the Marco Polo Bridge, after hours of wrangling, the negotiators had just arranged another truce. But as both sides pulled back, a loud crackling like machine-gun fire broke out (it turned out to be firecrackers) and the battle was on again. This time the two friendly generals, Sung Chi-yuen and Gen Hashimoto, personally stepped in and before the day was over a firm local agreement had been signed. In it Sung apologized for the entire incident. He promised to punish the officers responsible, rigidly control any Red elements in his forces and withdraw troops from the bridge area. On his part Hashimoto, acting for his dying commander, agreed to bring no more reinforcements into North China.

Chiang Kai-shek ignored the truce and sent Sung orders to concentrate more forces in the troubled area. Instead Sung kept his promise and began withdrawing troops. It looked as if the crisis was over, but unfortunately communications were so bad that Tokyo had no idea the problem was being solved and on July 17 peremptorily demanded that the Chinese stop sending troops into North China and recognize the puppet government Doihara had helped set up. This so incensed Chiang that he issued a defiant proclamation from Nanking. "If we allow one more inch of our territory to be lost or sovereign rights to be encroached upon, then we shall be guilty of committing an unpardonable crime against our Chinese race. . . . China's sovereign rights cannot be sacrificed, even at the expense of war, and once war has begun there is no looking back."

The Japanese military attaché in Nanking, General Seiich Kita, told his old friend, Chinese War Minister General Ho Ying-chin, himself a graduate of the Japanese Military Academy, that if Chinese troops were not withdrawn at once from North China, the "situation might get out of hand." He was not averse to some co-operation with the Japanese but said, "If war breaks out, both Japan and the Chinese Republic will be defeated and only the Russian and Chinese Communists will benefit. If you don't believe it now, you will in ten years." He asked Kita to pass this warning on to his government with a promise that the Chinese would "fight to the last man."

Already concerned by exaggerated reports of the large number of Chinese troops flowing up into North China, the Japanese public was indignant at Chiang's proclamation; and one paper, the *Nichi Nichi*, declared editorially that the Chinese reply left Japan no choice but "to cross the Rubicon."

Only then did the long-delayed information from Hashimoto reach Tokyo that all was quiet at the Marco Polo Bridge and that it was not necessary to send any reinforcements to North China. The transfer orders were canceled and even the expansionists in the Army high command were relieved that a crisis had been averted. It was assumed that Chiang would agree to the terms signed by Sung, and peace return to China.

Sung continued to do his part by removing all sandbag barricades from the streets of Peking and relaxing martial law. Passenger trains from the south at last began entering the ancient capital. But there was still no word of reconciliation from Chiang Kai-shek, and what the negotiators on both sides feared came about: Japanese and Chinese troops, at trigger's edge for almost three weeks, began firing at one another in earnest. It happened on the night of July 25 at the railroad station of Langfang, some fifty miles below Peking. Within an hour a skirmish turned into a major conflict. Heavy Japanese reinforcements were dispatched to Langfang and at dawn seventeen planes bombed a Chinese barracks. A few hours later the city was occupied.

The friendship between Sung and Hashimoto was now of little avail. The latter's commander had died and a new one, Lieutenant General Kiyoshi Katsuki, had arrived. He was strictly a military man who felt he had been sent "to chastise the outrageous Chinese." He cabled Tokyo that he had done everything to bring about a peaceful settlement and asked for persmission to "use force" wherever necessary to protect Japanese lives and property. The Army leaders approved and one division was ordered to Shanghai and another to Tsingtao.

Again Prime Minister Konoye, assured by the military that the Chinese problem could be "solved in three months," felt constrained to go along lest his cabinet fall. The following day, July 27, he announced in the Diet that the government must now achieve a "new order" in East Asia. To patriotic Japanese it seemed proper and equitable. Japanese lives and property had to be protected and Communism contained; it was time for firmness, not weakness. Nobody realized that it was a declaration of total war with China. The Army leaders were truly convinced they could force Chiang to negotiate before fall.*

It bore no resemblance to the Manchurian coup. In 1931 the Kwantung Army had deliberately provoked the incident at Mukden, but in 1937 the North China Army neither sought nor organized the confrontation at the Marco Polo Bridge. In 1931 the Army General Staff sanctioned the seizure of Manchuria; in 1937 they did their utmost to forestall operations in North China. In 1931 Prime Minister Reijiro Wakatsuki's failure to execute a diplomatic settlement satisfactory to the Control clique brought about the fall of his government; in 1937 there would be no change of cabinet.

With approval from Tokyo in hand, General Katsuki issued a proclamation that he was going to "launch a punitive expedition against the Chinese troops, who have been taking acts derogatory to the prestige of the Empire of Japan." Copies of this proclamation were dropped from planes at dawn on July 28. Bombers struck at three cities and shelled others as ground troops attacked Chinese forces all over the Peking area except in the city itself.

The Rubicon had, in truth, been crossed. The rhetoric of the China conflict had evolved into action without benefit of credible strategic calculations, and Japan had taken the first giant step to war with America.

3.

"Crush the Chinese in three months and they will sue for peace," War Minister Sugiyama predicted. As city after city fell, patriotic fervor swept through Japan, but almost the entire Western world condemned Japan's aggression, and even Germany (because she feared for her interests in China) was critical. China appealed to the League of Nations and while the world awaited its report, a bold attack came

---

*James B. Crowley, assistant professor of history at Amherst College, wrote in the May 1963 issue of *Journal of Asian Studies* that "it would be safe to conclude that this incident was not caused by any 'conspiracy' of Japanese army officers and that the Japanese military was not primarily responsible for the steady drift towards war." More likely, he believes, it was the Chinese—and they had plenty of provocation—who raised Marco Polo into a major crisis. "The tragedy is that the interaction of conflicting national policies and aspirations transformed an incident into a war from which neither government was to derive substantial benefit."

from another quarter. On October 5, 1937, President Franklin D. Roosevelt made a forceful speech in Chicago condemning all aggressors and equating the Japanese, by inference, with the Nazis and Fascists.* "When an epidemic of physical disease starts to spread, the community approves and joins in a quarantine of the patients in order to protect the health of the community," he said and explained that war was a contagion, whether declared or undeclared. "We are adopting such measures as will minimize our risk of involvement, but we cannot have complete protection in a world of disorder in which confidence and security have broken down." There was no mistaking Roosevelt's meaning when on the following day, after the League of Nations had censured Japan, the United States, although not a member, quickly concurred.

At home, Roosevelt's action was largely applauded but Secretary of State Cordell Hull was unhappy about the "quarantine" clause, feeling that it set back "for at least six months our constant educational campaign intended to create and strengthen public opinion towards international cooperation." Ambassador Joseph Grew also felt it was a grievous mistake. No American interest in China justified risking a war with Japan and it was futile to hurl "moral thunderbolts" at a country which respected force above all; it would create bitterness between the two countries and destroy the good will he had been building. Aware that his staff members shared his shock and resentment, he warned them two days later not to express their opinions outside the embassy. That night he wrote in his diary:

This was the day that I felt my carefully built castle tumbling about my ears and we all wandered about the chancery, depressed, gloomy, and with not a smile in sight. That afternoon Alice, Elsie and I went to the cinema to see *Captains Coura-*

---

*Ever since his school days at Groton, Roosevelt had been convinced of Japan's long-range plans of conquest. He pored over Admiral Alfred Mahan's *The Influence of Sea Power Upon History* until, according to his mother, he had "practically memorized the book." Later he corresponded with Mahan and learned that the admiral shared with him a strong concern over Japan as a major threat in the Pacific.

At Harvard, in 1920, a Japanese student told Roosevelt in confidence about his nation's hundred-year plan for conquest, drafted in 1889. It allegedly covered the annexation of Manchuria, the establishment of a protectorate in North China, the acquisition of American and British possessions in the Pacific, including Hawaii, as well as bases in Mexico and Peru. In 1934 Roosevelt informed his Secretary of State, Henry L. Stimson, of this "plot," pointing out to him that many of its particulars had already been verified.

geous. . . . And then I sunk myself in *Gone with the Wind*—which is precisely the way I felt.

Japanese reaction, of course, was quick and bitter. "Japan is expanding," retorted Yosuke Matsuoka, a diplomat whose sharp tongue and ready wit was winning him many followers. "And what country in its expansion era has ever failed to be trying to its neighbors? Ask the American Indian or the Mexican how excruciatingly trying the young United States used to be once upon a time." Japan's expansion, like that of America's, was as natural as the growth of a child. "Only one thing stops a child from growing—death." He declared that Japan was fighting for two goals: to prevent Asia from falling completely under the white man's domination, as in Africa, and to save China from Communism. "No treasure trove is in her eyes—only sacrifices upon sacrifices. No one realizes this more than she does. But her very life depends on it, as do those of her neighbors as well. The all-absorbing question before Japan today . . . is: Can she bear the cross?"*

A few weeks later, on November 16, Koki Hirota, now foreign minister, officially accused America of initiating an anti-Japanese front. An economic boycott against Japan, he told Grew, would not stop the fighting in China, but encouraged the Chinese to prolong the hostilities. Hirota said that until now the Japanese had felt America was the only country with genuine impartiality and would help bring about peace, as Theodore Roosevelt had done in the Russo-Japanese War.

Three days later Japan took Soochow, and the roads to Nanking and Shanghai were open. On December 12, the eve of the fall of Nanking, relations with America and Great Britain were almost shattered when Japanese naval aviators sank the gunboat *Panay* on the Yangtze River, though its American flag was clearly visible. A week earlier an artillery regiment commanded by Colonel Kingoro Hashimoto (founder of the Cherry Society) had fired on the British gunboat *Ladybird*, then seized it.

---

*In interviews in 1966-67 a number of former Japanese leaders including Generals Teiichi Suzuki, Sadao Araki and Kenryo Sato pointed to this and similar speeches regarding Japan's increasing involvement in China as parallels to America's accelerating war in Vietnam. Both countries, they agreed, were fighting a sacrificial war despite the world's censure—and both had gone about wiping out Communism the wrong way.

These incidents revived President Roosevelt's hope of quarantining the aggressor. He summoned the British ambassador in Washington, Sir Ronald Lindsay, and suggested their two nations join in a naval blockade which would cut Japan off from raw materials. Lindsay protested that such a quarantine would lead to war. He cabled London that his "horrified criticisms" had "made little impression upon the President." The next day, December 17, Roosevelt sketched out his quarantine plan to the Cabinet. His resolve was strengthened by a report from the Navy's official Court of Inquiry in Shanghai that the attack on *Panay* had been wanton and ruthless; more important, a message to Combined Fleet had been intercepted and decoded by the U.S. Naval intelligence indicating that the raid had been deliberately planned by an officer on the carrier *Kaga*.

In Tokyo the Konoye government was as aggrieved by the destruction of *Panay* and *Ladybird* as the Americans and the British. Foreign Minister Hirota brought a note to Ambassador Grew expressing regrets and offering full restitution for the sinking of the *Panay*. Abjectly apologetic, Hirota said, "I am having a very difficult time. Things happen unexpectedly." The Japanese Navy high command also showed its disapproval by dismissing the *Kaga* commander, who was responsible for the *Panay* bombing. "We have done this to suggest that the Army do likewise and remove Hashimoto from his command," said Admiral Isoroku Yamamoto, the Navy Vice Minister, who had no relish for doing battle with the U.S. fleet, since he had spent considerable time in America and was cognizant of her potentialities.

The Japanese apology was officially accepted in Washington on Christmas Day (Grew observed that its arrival on Christmas Eve was a "masterly" arrangement) and the incident was apparently closed.* Great Britain also gracefully

---

*Roosevelt was still intent on his quarantine. He sent Captain Royal Ingersoll, chief of the Navy's War Plans Division, to London with instructions to explore the implementation of a long-range naval blockade of Japan. The proposal that had "horrified" Ambassador Lindsay found approval in the British Admiralty. They told Ingersoll that they were "prepared to stop all Japanese traffic crossing a line roughly from Singapore through the Dutch East Indies, New Guinea, New Hebrides and around to the east of Australia and New Zealand." They considered "that the United State could prevent all westbound trade to Japan by controlling by embargo or ships the entire Pacific east from Alaska to Cape Horn." But eight days later, on January 13, 1938, Prime Minister Neville Chamberlain abruptly rejected another proposal of Roosevelt's calling for Britain to join an international

55

accepted an apology for the attack on the *Ladybird*, despite the refusal of the Japanese Army to follow Yamamoto's advice. Hashimoto was not even reprimanded. He had been allowed to proceed to Nanking with his troops.

By the time the Japanese entered the city in December, all resistance had ended, and their commander, General Iwane Matsui—who had left Japan with the announcement: "I am going to the front not to fight an enemy, but in the state of mind of one who sets out to pacify his brother"—ordered them "to exhibit the honor and glory of Japan and augment the trust of the Chinese people" and to "protect and patronize Chinese officials and people, as far as possible."

Instead they roamed the city, looting, burning, raping, murdering. According to one witness, men, women and children were "hunted like rabbits; everyone seen to move was shot." Even the friendly Germans in an official report condemned the Japanese Army as "bestial machinery."

It was not until General Matsui triumphantly entered the city that he learned there had been "breaches of military discipline and morality." He ordered strict compliance with his former orders to "insure that no act whatsoever, which tends to disgrace honor, be perpetrated." He declared: "Now the flag of the Rising Sun is floating over Nanking, and the Imperial Way is shining forth in the area south of the Yangtze. The dawn of the renaissance is about to take place. On this occasion, it is my earnest hope that the four hundred million people of China will reconsider." Matsui returned to Shanghai, only to hear rumors a week later that "illegal acts" were still being committed. "Anyone guilty of misconduct

---

conference to discuss essential principles of international law that would, incidentally, awaken American public opinion to the true nature of the "bandit nations," as Roosevelt was privately calling them. At first the President did not grasp the full implication of Chamberlain's unanticipated rejection, but within a week it was clear that the Prime Minister's refusal to join an international conference meant that his government would take no part in a quarantine of the aggressor, either in the Orient or in Europe.

The above information (much of it based on notes of the Ingersoll talks recently uncovered in the archives of the United States Navy) indicates beyond argument that as early as 1938, President Roosevelt was prepared to do more than assail the "bandit nations" by words. If Chamberlain had joined him in the naval quarantine, further aggression in both Asia and Europe might have been stemmed. But Chamberlain's rebuff forced Roosevelt to abandon his vigorous foreign policy and allow his country to revert to isolation. Within two months it was too late. On March 12 Hitler's seizure of Austria started the world on the road to its most devastating war.

must be severely punished," he wrote the Nanking commander.

But the atrocities continued for another month. About one third of the city was gutted by fire; more than 20,000 Chinese male civilians of military age were marched out of the city and massacred by bayoneting or machine-gun fire. As many women and young girls were raped, murdered and then mutilated. Numerous older civilians were robbed and shot. By the end of the month at least 200,000, perhaps as many as 300,000 civilians had been slaughtered.

Why was such savagery inflicted on a nation the Japanese regarded as their main source of cultural inspiration, their Rome and Greece? It is axiomatic that soldiers of any army get out of hand in a foreign land and act with a brutality they would never dare exhibit at home, but this could hardly account for the extent and intensity of the atrocities. They could only have been incited by some of the more radical officers, in the belief that the Chinese should be taught a lesson.

Back home, Prime Minister Konoye knew less about the atrocities in Nanking than the Germans. He was aware, however, that with all the conquest of vast areas, the Japanese were no nearer to victory but were sinking more deeply into a quagmire. Konoye was a unique individual—a prince by birth and a socialist at heart. He seemed soft, shy and effete, if not weak. To those who knew him best, he was a man of almost painfully discriminating taste, of such wide interests and objectivity that he could listen with sympathy to those of all political beliefs. In fact, he listened with such sympathy that each in turn thought the prince agreed with him. It always took him an interminable time to make up his mind, since he first wanted to know all sides of a question, but once decision was made, almost nothing could make him change it. "He was simply impregnable," his private secretary, Tomohiko Ushiba, recalled. Konoye had few idols and one was Lord Balfour, considered not quite qualified for the job of prime minister but decisive and effective once he took office. Undoubtedly Konoye hoped to be the Japanese Balfour.

Prince Konoye was the eldest son of Prince Atsumaro Konoye and the first heir in 250 years in the Konoye family to be born of a lawful wife—an occasion which prompted his great-grandfather to write numerous poems expressing his joy. Eight days after his birth, his mother died of puerperal fever, but until he was an adolescent he believed that his father's second wife, his mother's sister, was his real mother.

"When I learned that she wasn't," he later said, "I began to think that life was a tissue of lies."

When he was still a young man he was stricken with tuberculosis and spent two years doing little but staring at a ceiling and thinking. From this time he had a feeling for the underdog. He disliked money, millionaires and politicians and wrote many radical essays. Some of the socialistic convictions clung to him as he matured and even now he was against the privileged classes. To outsiders he gave the appearance of being democratic and treated all alike with courtesy. "Even beggars are guests," he once told Ushiba. But his innermost self remained aristocratic—"far more so," Ushiba recently recalled, "than you can possibly imagine."

Almost everything about him seemed contradictory but made sense. He felt ill at ease with Americans, yet sent his eldest son, Fumitaka, to Lawrenceville and Princeton. He was fond of kimonos and wore them with fastidious care, yet he was equally at ease in Western clothes. His marriage was a love match but he treated his mistress, a geisha, with great affection. He had upset family tradition twice: first, by abolishing the system of having rooms in the main house for second, third and fourth "wives" ("It's pardonable to have just one mistress, don't you agree?"); and second, by discontinuing the family diary ("How could I possibly write the truth if it were unfavorable to me?").

Only once did he seriously scold any of his five children, this in a stern letter to Fumitaka at Princeton chastising him for drinking and neglecting his studies. Fumitaka replied that he was just following the American way of life and the subject was closed.

His own father, who died when Konoye was thirteen, was so overprotective that Konoye spent his childhood with a leash around his waist to keep him from falling. Konoye showed affection to all his children, including the youngest, a daughter by his mistress. He would eat with them, singing and cavorting for their amusement more like an American father than a Japanese.

Product of an elegant society, with one foot in the past and one in the future, Prince Konoye's considerable personal charm and polish hid to all but the discerning his profound sense of obligation to his country and a cynicism so deep that he trusted no man, including himself. He seemed to be what he was not, and even his family rarely saw the man behind the façade. Ushiba, probably as close to him as anyone, did see beyond the overly fond father, the loving husband, the charming dilettante, the considerate employer, to a strange, cold man; he was self-restrained and refined, and sophisticated to such a degree "that it was sometimes quite difficult to make out his real thinking."

Once Ushiba asked him which Japanese historical figures he respected. "None," was the answer. "Not even General Nogi or Admiral Togo [heroes of the Russo-Japanese War]?" "Certainly not!"

He treated the Emperor, for whom he had a warm personal feeling, rather intimately. While others sat on the edge of their chairs like ramrods in His Majesty's presence, Konoye would sprawl comfortably. He didn't do this as an insult, but because he felt so close to Hirohito. When he told someone on his way to an audience, "Oh, do remember me to the Emperor," he was not being facetious, merely natural. He felt he came from just as good a family.

As hope of a solution in China had faded with every month, Prince Konoye looked desperately in another direction—a negotiated peace. He preferred England as mediator but the Army persuaded him to use the good offices of Germany, which was friendly with both parties. Hitler had sent Chiang Kai-shek arms and military advisers and was bound, if tenuously, to Japan by the year-old Anti-Comintern Pact. The terms were so reasonable that when the strongly pro-Chinese German ambassador to China, Oskar Trautmann, presented them, Chiang Kai-shek seemed about to accept them.

But those two banes of stability in Japan—*gekokujo* and opportunism—again appeared. First, news came of another great triumph in China, and War Minister Sugiyama raised the price of negotiation; then the commander of the North China Garrison unexpectedly set up a puppet regime in Peking, against the specific orders of Konoye and the General Staff. Though the latter, under the urging of Ishihara, still called for negotiations with Chiang Kai-shek, Trautmann labored in vain. After conversations in Washington between their ambassador and President Roosevelt, China insisted that the Japanese terms were too broad. The Japanese saw this as evasion, and being inflexible negotiators themselves, lost their patience. Concluding that Chiang Kai-shek really didn't want to negotiate, Konoye decided to take a shortcut to peace and deal with those Chinese who "shared Japan's ideals." On January 16, 1938, he announced that "the Imperial Government shall cease to deal with the National Government of China, and shall rely upon the establishment and growth of a new Chinese regime for co-operation."

This brought sharp rebukes from intellectuals and a number of liberal Diet members. Ishihara also warned Konoye that it was a policy which would inevitably lead to endless trouble. Such criticism forced the Prime Minister to review his position and he began to realize that his hasty act might have committed Japan to a rigid, do-or-die policy—a settlement by full-scale war, the last thing he wanted. Assailed by self-doubts, he wondered if he should resign. But court officials persuaded him to remain in office, otherwise the Chinese would quite properly assume that failure to settle the China question had caused his resignation and it would be more difficult than ever to achieve the solution they wanted.

It was at last apparent to Konoye that the Army itself didn't have a fixed policy on China and was drifting with the tide of events, but unable to get reliable information about Supreme Command matters, he could only watch in frustration as the situation in China worsened.

In the name of national defense the Army proposed a national mobilization law, designed to take away the Diet's last vestiges of control over war measures and direct every aspect of national life toward an efficient war economy. Army spokesmen argued persuasively and not unreasonably that Japan was a small, overpopulated country with almost no natural resources; surrounded as it was by enemies— Russians, Chinese, Americans and British—total mobilization of the nation's strength was the sole solution. The law was passed in March 1938—the Diet, in effect, voting for its own capitulation to the Army. "Liberties lost to the Japanese Army," commented Sir Robert Craigie, the British ambassador in Tokyo, "were lost for good."

The people were also being prepared psychologically for the crusade in East Asia with two slogans borrowed from the past. One was *"kokutai,"* the national essence, and the other was *"kodo,"* connected, ironically, with the recently crushed clique. The original meaning of *kodo,* the Imperial Way, was twisted now into signifying world order and peace to be achieved by Japanese control of East Asia.

Both *kokutai* and *kodo* underlined the father relationship of the Emperor to the people as well as his divinity and were already rousing millions with ardor for a holy war to free Asia from both colonialism and Communism.

"Then the War Will
Be a Desperate One"

1.

The Japanese continued to win. They took Hankow and Canton, forcing Chiang Kai-shek to move his government far inland to Chungking. But they were conquering territory, not people, and by the beginning of 1939 were still far from final victory. They had lost thousands of men, millions of yen and incurred the wrath of the Western world, and Americans in particular.

The relations between the two countries had begun precariously the day Commodore Perry's ships steamed into Tokyo Bay with a letter from President Millard Fillmore inviting Japan to open doors long closed to the outside world. The Americans were inspired by three motives: a desire to trade, spread the Gospel to the yellow pagans and export the ideals of 1776. The Japanese reluctantly, resentfully complied, but the ensuing years brought improved relations as American officials and private citizens materially helped Japan make the transition from feudalism to modern times in the fields of education, science, medicine and production. American obtrusion into the Pacific late in the nineteenth century with acquisitions of Hawaii, Guam, Wake Island and the Philippines perturbed the Japanese, but in 1900 the Boxer Rebellion brought the two nations together again in a common cause.

These fraternal bonds were strengthened four years later by Japan's war with Czarist Russia. American sympathies were overwhelmingly for the underdog. The New York *Journal of Commerce* declared that Japan stood as "the champion of commercial rights," and cartoonists pictured the Japanese soldier as a heroic figure—a noble samurai confronting the Russian Bear. Jacob Schiff, president of Kuhn, Loeb & Company, distressed by reports of Russian anti-Semitism, felt that the effort of Japan was "not only her own cause, but the cause of the entire civilized world." Practicing what he preached, he made the resources of his company available to the Japanese war effort. Despite spectacular victories, Japan could not terminate the war and turned to President Theodore Roosevelt for help. He accomplished this with the Treaty of Portsmouth, New Hampshire, in 1905, achieving for Japan the best possible terms. In one of the perverse twists of history, this act of friendship ended the good will between the two nations: the Japanese, who were unaware that their country was close to bankruptcy, were incensed at a treaty which gave them no indemnity. Anti-American riots erupted throughout the land, and martial law had to be established in Tokyo. Still not a word came from the Japanese government explaining that Roosevelt had saved the empire from embarrassment, perhaps disaster.

The next year the situation deteriorated. This time America was to blame. An unreasonable fear that a resurgent Asia under Japanese leadership would engulf Western civilization gained force in the United States, particularly on the Pacific coast. The San Francisco *Chronicle* averred that it was "a pressing world-wide issue as to whether the high-standard Caucasian races or the low-standard Oriental races would dominate the world." Caught up in the "yellow peril"* hysteria, the San Francisco school board ordered all Nisei children to attend a school in Chinatown.

The Japanese government responded hotly that this was "an act of discrimination carrying with it a stigma and odium which is impossible to overlook." There was talk of war, and Roosevelt secretly warned his commander in the Philippines to prepare for a Japanese attack.

The crisis passed, but not the resentment, and antagonism reached a climax during World War I, even though the two countries were allies. Already President Woodrow Wilson was calling for "territorial integrity and political independence throughout the world" and a return to China of land and rights lost to conquerors. This idealistic stance was a direct threat to the empire Japan had won in the past few decades and it seemed inevitable to her military leaders that they were destined to fight America for supremacy of the western Pacific and Asia. They gained popular support in 1924 when Congress passed the Exclusion Act barring Japanese from immigration to the United States. It seemed like a deliberate

---

*The phrase originated with Kaiser Wilhelm in 1895. He had a revelation of Oriental hordes overwhelming Europe and made a sketch of his vision: a Buddha riding upon a dragon above ruined cities. The caption read: *"Die gelbe Gefahr!"*—"The Yellow Peril." Several copies were made and presented to royal relatives all over Europe as well as every embassy in Berlin.

challenge to the proud, sensitive Japanese, and even those with pro-American sympathies were discomposed. "Japan felt as if her best friend had, of a sudden and without provocation, slapped her on the cheek," wrote a well-known Japanese scholar. "Each year that passes without amendment or abrogation only strengthens our sense of injury, which is destined to show itself, in one form or another, in personal and public intercourse."

With the seizure of Manchuria and the invasion of North China, the gulf widened as America denounced Japanese aggression with increasingly forceful words. This moral denunciation only hardened the resolve of the average Japanese. Why should there be a Monroe Doctrine in the Americas and an Open Door principle in Asia? The Japanese takeover in bandit-infested Manchuria was no different from American armed intervention in the Caribbean.* Moreover, how could a vast country like the United States even begin to understand the problems that had beset Japan since World War I? Why was it perfectly acceptable for England and Holland to occupy India, Hong Kong, Singapore and the East Indies, but a crime for Japan to follow their example? Why should America, which had grabbed its lands from Indians by trickery, liquor and massacre, be so outraged when Japan did the same in China?**

Superpatriots plotted to assassinate pro-Western leaders and blow up the American and British embassies. Mass meetings were held denouncing both countries for giving help to China, and calling for acceptance of Hitler's invitation to join Germany and Italy in a tripartite pact. Westerners were refused rooms in some hotels, insulted publicly and occasionally beaten in sight of police.

---

*Arnold Toynbee saw some logic in their point of view. He later wrote that Japan's "economic interests in Manchuria were not superfluities but vital necessities of her international life. . . . The international position of Japan—with Nationalist China, Soviet Russia, and the race-conscious English-speaking peoples of the Pacific closing in upon her—had suddenly become precarious again."

**In this connection, Ambassador Grew once told the State Department: "We should not lose sight of the fact, deplorable but true, that no practical and effective code of international morality upon which the world can rely has yet been discovered, and that the standards of morality of one nation in given circumstances have little or no relation to the standards of the individuals of the nations in question. To shape our foreign policy on the unsound theory that other nations are guided and bound by our present standards of international ethics would be to court sure disaster."

All this emotional turmoil was worsened by marked differences between East and West in morality, religion and even patterns of thinking. Western logic was precise, with axioms, definitions, and proofs leading to a logical conclusion. Born dialecticians, the Japanese held that any existence was a contradiction. In everyday life they instinctively practiced the concept of the contradiction of opposites, and the means of harmonizing them. Right and wrong, spirit and matter, God and man—all these opposing elements were harmoniously united. That was why a thing could be good and bad at the same time.

Unlike Westerners, who tended to think in terms of black and white, the Japanese had vaguer distinctions, which in international relations often resulted in "policies" and not "principles," and seemed to Westerners to be conscienceless. Western logic was like a suitcase, defined and limited. Eastern logic was like the *furoshiki*, the cloth Japanese carry for wrapping objects. It could be large or small according to circumstances and could be folded and put in the pocket when not needed.

To Westerners, the Japanese were an incomprehensible contradiction: polite and barbarous, honest and treacherous, brave and cowardly, industrious and lazy—all at the same time. To the Japanese, these were not anomalies at all but one united whole, and they could not understand why Westerners didn't comprehend it. To the Japanese, a man without contradictions could not be respected; he was just a simple person. The more numerous the contradictions in a man, the deeper he was. His existence was richer the more acutely he struggled with himself.

This philosophy was derived mainly from Buddhism, a doctrine wherein all is absorbed in the spaceless, timeless abyss of nondifference.* All is vanity and nothing can be differentiated because nothing has entity or identity. "I" has no entity and is an illusion appearing transitorily and momentarily on constantly floating relations of fallacious phenomena which come and go as the Almighty Wheel of Causality moves on. Nobody knows or is responsible for the movements of change, since there is no Creator or Heavenly Father or Fate.

---

*Almost every Japanese household had two shrines—one Buddhist, one Shinto. Shinto ("the way of the gods") was the national religion. It was based on awe inspired by any phenomenon of nature. More of a cult of ancestor worship and communion with the past than a religion per se, it had been revived in the nineteenth century and transformed into a nationalistic ideology.

Among the reasons for Japan's plunge into military adventure in Manchuria and China, this Wheel of Causality loomed significantly. Out of cowardice, or in some cases out of self-interest or simple indecision, a number of military and political leaders failed to curb the fanatic group of young officers who engineered these aggressions. But many on all levels just moved along with the tide, caught up in the Wheel of Causality. They lay down obediently and quietly, as it were, on the road of Blind Change, following the Buddhist belief that the Wheel of Causality went on eternally and absolutely nonteleologically. With characteristic flexibility, some sects believed that everyone could become a Buddha, or "blessed one," after death; others that the individual was nothing and salvation lay only in the negation of self, that man was a bubble on the Ocean of Nothingness who would eventually vanish in the boundless water where there was no birth, no death, no beginning, no end. Buddha himself was nothing more than a finger pointing at the moon.

This was all expressed in the word *sayonara* (*sayo*—so, *nara*—if), that is, "So be it." The Japanese said *sayonara* every moment to everything, for he felt each moment was a dream. Life was *sayonara*. Empires could rise or fall, the greatest heroes and philosophers crumble to dust, planets come and go, but Change never changed, including Change itself.

This strong recognition of death gave the Japanese not only the strength to face disaster stoically but an intense appreciation of each moment, which could be the last. This was not pessimism but a calm determination to let nothing discourage or disappoint or elate, to accept the inevitable. The most admirable fish was the carp. He swam gallantly upstream, leaping the sheerest falls, but once caught and put on the cutting board, lay quiet, accepting serenely what must be. So be it. *Sayonara*.

Understanding little or nothing of either the Wheel of Causality or the power wielded by the dedicated young rebels, informed Americans mistakenly assumed that the takeover in Manchuria and the foray into China were steps plotted by military leaders who, like Hitler, wished to seize the world for themselves.

Within the Japanese, metaphysical intuition and animalistic, instinctive urges lay side by side. Thus philosophy was brutalized and brutality was philosophized. The assassinations and other bloody acts committed by the rebels were inspired by idealism; and the soldiers who sailed to China to save the

Orient for the Orient ended by slaughtering thousands of fellow Orientals in Nanking.

There was no buffer zone in their thinking between the transcendental and the empirical—between the chrysanthemum and the sword. They were religious but had no God in the Western sense—that is, a single Divine Being. They were sincere but had no concept of sin; they had sympathy but little humanity; they had clans but no society; they had a rigid family system which gave security but took away individuality. They were, in short, a great and energetic people often driven by opposing forces and often trying to go in opposite directions at the same time.

There were also numerous petty differences between East and West that needlessly aggravated matters. If a Westerner asked, "This isn't the road to Tokyo, is it?" the Japanese would reply yes, meaning, "What you say is correct; it is not the road to Tokyo." Confusion also resulted when the Japanese agreed with the Westerner just to be agreeable or to avoid embarrassment, or gave wrong information rather than admit his ignorance.

To most Westerners, the Japanese was utterly inscrutable. The way he handled his tools was all wrong: he squatted at an anvil; he pulled rather than pushed a saw or plane; he built his house from the roof down. To open a lock, he turned a key to the left, the wrong direction. Everything the Japanese did was backwards. He spoke backwards, read backwards, wrote backwards. He sat on the floor instead of in chairs; ate raw fish and live, wriggling shrimp. He would tell of the most tragic personal events and then laugh; fall in the mud in his best suit and come up with a grin; convey ideas by misdirection; discuss matters in a devious, tortuous manner; treat you with exaggerated politeness in his home and rudely shove you aside in a train; even assassinate a man and apologize to the servants for messing up the house.

What Westerners did not realize was that underneath the veneer of modernity and westernization, Japan was still Oriental and that her plunge from feudalism to imperialism had come so precipitously that her leaders, who were interested solely in Western methods, not Western values, had neither the time nor inclination to develop liberalism and humanitarianism.

2.

Hostility between the Russians and the Japanese also continued, but this was less a misunderstanding of cultures than a struggle for territory. In the summer of 1938 their troops battled for possession of a barren hill on the Manchurian-Soviet border, and the Red Army and air force gave the Japanese such a drubbing that within two weeks they agreed to a settlement. Some ten months later another squabble started near Nomonhan on the Manchurian–Outer Mongolian border, relatively close to Peking. In a few weeks it turned into full-fledged warfare, with the first large-scale tank battles in history. Once again the Russians crushed the Japanese, who suffered more than fifty thousand casualties. This embarrassing rehearsal for war not only caused a revolution in Japanese weaponry and military tactics but drove Japan closer to an alliance with Germany and Italy, since she felt that the Soviet Union, England, China and America might combine against her at any moment.*

Before this border war could be settled, Stalin threw both the Chinese and the Japanese into turmoil by signing, on August 23, 1939, a pact with his bitterest enemy, Hitler. Prime Minister Kiichiro Hiranuma, who had succeeded Prince Konoye in January, and whose cabinet had held more than seventy meetings in a futile effort to reach agreement on a Tripartite Pact, was so embarrassed and dismayed that he announced, "The Cabinet herewith resigns because of complicated and inscrutable situations recently arising in Europe."

Both Hitler and Stalin trumpeted to the world the clauses of their historic treaty—except for a secret protocol dividing

---

*This was not mere paranoia. Shortly before, Stalin had written to Chiang Kai-shek: "If our negotiations with the European countries should produce satisfactory results—which is not impossible—this may be an important step toward the creation of a bloc of peace-loving nations in the Far East as well. Time is working favorably toward the formation of such a bloc.

"As a result of the now two-year-old war with China, Japan has lost her balance, begun to get nervous, and is hurling herself recklessly, now against Britain, and now against Soviet Russia and the Republic of Outer Mongolia. This is a sign of Japanese weakness and her conduct may unite all others against her. From Soviet Russia, Japan has already received the counterblows she deserves. Britain and the United States are waiting for an opportune moment to harm Japan. And we have no doubt that before long she will receive another counterblow from China, one that will be a hundred times mightier."

up eastern Europe—and nine days later, on September 1, one and a half million German troops invaded Poland. World War II had begun. Though Poland, crushed between two massive forces, disintegrated in a few weeks, the western front remained so quiet that newsmen sardonically labeled the conflict "the phony war."

As the fighting in China dragged on into 1940, the Japanese Army General Staff decided in secret that unless total victory was achieved within the year, forces would be gradually withdrawn, leaving only troops in the northern part of China as defense against Communism. However, six weeks later, on May 10, Hitler again charged the course of Japan by launching a blitzkrieg against the western front. At dusk, four days later, the Dutch commander surrendered. The next morning at seven-thirty Britain's brand-new Prime Minister, Winston Churchill, was wakened by a phone call from Paris. "We have been defeated!" exclaimed Premier Paul Reynaud. "We are beaten!" Two weeks later King Leopold III surrendered, ignoring the advice of his government, and refused to seek refuge in England. "I have decided to stay," he said. "The cause of the Allies is lost." Within a month France capitulated and England herself appeared doomed.

The Japanese military leaders, intoxicated by Hitler's easy victories, changed their minds about the war in China and adopted the slogan "Don't miss the bus!" With France defeated and Britain fighting for survival, the time had come to strike into Southeast Asia for oil and other sorely needed resources. On the morning of June 22 the Army General Staff and the War Ministry held a joint meeting, and those who had recently advocated a withdrawal from China recommended an immediate surprise attack on Singapore. Conservatives squashed this scheme, but the spirit of chance lingered in the air and the virus of opportunism spread with each passing day. Reconciled to defeat in China a few months earlier, the Japanese were tempted by Hitler's sudden fortune in Europe to make a bid for the resources of Southeast Asia.

Before the end of July, Prince Konoye was persuaded to re-enter politics and form his second cabinet. Two of the key posts were filled by rising men—one a diplomat, the talkative, brilliant, quixotic Yosuke Matsuoka, who became foreign minister, and the other a soldier, Lieutenant General Hideki Tojo, who became war minister. Hard-working, hardheaded and dedicated, Tojo had already earned the nickname "the Razor." As simple as Konoye was complicated, he enjoyed great prestige within the Army, having ably executed a number of difficult assignments, including command of the *kempeitai* in the Kwantung Army. He was incorruptible, a rigid disciplinarian who demanded and got absolute discipline, and he selected subordinates for their ability and experience alone. Unlike other generals who wavered during the 2/26 Incident, he had acted with dispatch proclaiming a state of emergency in Manchuria, thus crushing any sympathetic revolt. To his legalistic mind, *gekokujo* was "absolutely unpardonable," not to be tolerated. This brought him respect from conservative military circles as well as from civilians who dreaded another bloody revolt, and it was undoubtedly the main reason Konoye selected him.

Foreign Minister Matsuoka, president of the South Manchurian Railway and a close associate of Tojo's while the general was in the Kwantung Army, was almost his opposite. He was equally strong-minded but far more flamboyant, venturesome and intuitive. Whereas Tojo was a man of few words, Matsuoka was an orator of extraordinary eloquence who deserved his nicknames "Mr. 50,000 Words" and "the Talking Machine." He good-naturedly denied he was loquacious. "Being verbose means trying to cancel out or excuse what one has just said. I'd never do that. Therefore I'm not verbose." "I have never known anyone talk so much to say so little," observed Ambassador Craigie, who judged him also to be a stubborn and determined man with an acute mind.

Matsuoka was small and swarthy, and his clipped bullet head, mustache, big tortoise-shell glasses and flare for the dramatic had brought him world attention when he precipitously stalked out of the League of Nations Assembly during the debate on Manchuria. At the age of thirteen he had gone to sea, and was dumped ashore in America by the captain, his uncle, and told to fend for himself. An American family in Portland, Oregon, gave him refuge and he spent the next formative years working diligently as a laborer, in a law office, and even as a substitute minister while getting himself an education. After graduation from the University of Oregon he worked for three more years before returning to Japan, where he rose to fame by brilliance and energy alone.

Prince Konoye listened to practically everybody, Matsuoka to practically nobody. He was too busy expounding the ideas that kept leaping to his agile mind. His mystifying statements confused many, and some thought he was insane, but subordinates in the Foreign Ministry, like Dr. Yoshie Saito and Toshikazu Kase, felt it was merely his paradoxical nature in action. An intellectual gymnast, he would often say something contrary to what he believed and propose something he opposed in order to get his own way by default. A man of broad visions, he seldom explained these visions, or if he did, talked at such cross-purposes that it was no wonder he left a wake of confusion behind him; even those who thought him one of the most brilliant men in Japan watched anxiously as he nimbly played his dangerous diplomatic games. He assured his associates over and over again that he was pro-American, yet talked insultingly about America; he distrusted Germany, yet courted Hitler; he was against the rise of militarism, yet sprouted his arguments for war.

In his home he also played the paradox. He shouted at his seven children, and let them ride on his back; he was autocratic, yet gave unstintingly of his love and attention. Kiwamu Ogiwara, who worked for Matsuoka as *shosei* (a combination secretary and personal servant) became so terrified at his temper tantrums that he could never look directly at him. One day after taking a bath, Matsuoka shouted *"Oi!"* (Hey!) from his room, and when Ogiwara peered in, gestured impatiently at his middle. The *shosei* brought in an *obi* and this set Matsuoka off on a furious pantomime. Ogiwara had to find out from the maid that this particular gesture meant the master wanted his loincloth. On days when he was "not at home," a visitor would sometimes insist on seeing the master and the *shosei* would announce him to Matsuoka. "How can a man who isn't here see anyone!" he would yell. Almost constantly in a nervous state, Ogiwara left Matsuoka's employ detesting him. Yet a few years later, when he wrote asking for a job on the South Manchurian Railway, Matsuoka saw to it that he got a position. Under the fierce, arrogant, impatient exterior was a different person which few ever glimpsed.

The Cabinet was just four days old when it unanimously approved a new national policy to cope with "a great ordeal without precedence" in Japan's past. The basic aim of this policy was world peace, and to bring it about, a "new order in Greater East Asia" would have to be established by uniting Japan with Manchukuo and China—under the leadership, of course, of Japan. The entire nation was to be mobilized, with every citizen devoting himself to the state. Planned economy would be established, the Diet reformed and the China Incident brought to a satisfactory conclusion.

Moreover, a tripartite pact would be signed with Germany and Italy, and a nonaggression treaty arranged with the Soviet Union. Although America had placed an embargo on strategic materials to Japan, attempts would be made to placate her as long as she went along with Japan's "just claims." In addition, Japan would move into Indochina and perhaps farther, seizing an empire by force of arms if necessary while Europe was involved in its own war.

This policy was the brainchild of the military leaders, but they had convinced Prime Minister Konoye and the civilians in the Cabinet that it was Japan's last hope for survival in the chaotic modern world. What it means was that the "Don't miss the bus" fever had become national policy, escalating the China Incident into war and pushing Japan to further aggressions. While the supremacy of civilian leaders over the military was a fundamental aspect of American democracy, the reverse was true in Japan. The Meiji Constitution had divided the power of decision between the Cabinet and the Supreme Command, but the military leaders, who had little understanding of political and diplomatic affairs, could almost always override the civilians in the Cabinet; their resignation would bring down the government. Their influence, however, went beyond the threat of resignation. Military monopoly had become a tradition and was rarely questioned. Consequently, it was the policies of well-meaning but ill-equipped generals and admirals, based on narrow military thinking, which dominated Japan.

The militarists who had formed this "Don't miss the bus" policy did not want to foresee the possibility of war. With France defeated, and England battling for its own existence, Indochina with its rubber, tin, tungsten, coal and rice was to them "a treasure lying in the street just waiting to be picked up." Within two months Japan forced the impotent Vichy government to sign a convention in Hanoi allowing Japan to set up air bases in northern Indochina* and use that area as a jumping-off place for attacks on China.

All this was not done without protests from Matsuoka and more thoughtful men in the Supreme Command who foresaw a collision course with the Anglo-Saxons in the making. The Army Chief of Staff, Prince Kanin, resigned in tears.

The United States reacted violently to the Japanese move; it meant a potential threat to the Burma Road, through which America was sending supplies into China. Prime Minister Churchill, however, felt quite sanguine about the Japanese garrisons in northern Indochina and suggested that two Indian brigades be removed from Singapore. Foreign Secretary

---

*Now North Vietnam.

Anthony Eden disagreed. "It seems to me difficult to maintain now that the Japanese threat to Malaya is not serious," he wrote in a minute to the Prime Minister. "There is every indication that Germany has made some deal with Japan within these last few days, and it seems, therefore, wise to make some provision for the land defense of Singapore."

Eden had guessed right. The long-discussed Tripartite Pact with Germany and Italy was near conclusion even though the Navy still objected, fearing that such an agreement would require Japan's automatic entry into war under certain circumstances. Matsuoka countered this with persuasive and interminable rebuttals. The pact, he declared, "would force the United States to act more prudently in carrying out her plans against Japan" and would prevent war between the two countries. Furthermore, if Germany did get into a fight with America, Japan would not be automatically obliged to come to her aid.

Unable to withstand the onslaught of Matsuoka's arguments—and, incidentally, vociferous popular support for the alliance—the dissidents were won over. Konoye gave his grudging approval because he well knew he would again be forced to resign if he opposed the Army. "My idea is to ride on the military *away* from war," he told his son-in-law. Like the Navy, the Emperor opposed the pact, and before affixing the official seal, he warned Konoye that he feared it would eventually lead to war with America and Britain. "You must, therefore," he added ominously, "share with me the joys and sorrows that will follow." On September 27, 1940, the pact was signed in Berlin.* To British and Americans this was further evidence that Japan was no better than Nazi Germany and Fascist Italy, and that the three "gangster" nations had joined forces to conquer the world. The United States retaliated immediately by adding scrap metal of every kind to the list of embargoes, such as strategic materials and aviation fuel, which had been announced in July.

Not only the Anglo-Saxons were dismayed by the treaty.

---

*At this time Hitler did not want war with Japan *and* the Anglo Saxons and felt, like Matsuoka, that the pact obviated such a conflict He wrote Mussolini that "a close co-operation with Japan is the bes way either to keep America entirely out of the picture or to render he entry into the war ineffective." Almost as soon as the pact was signe the Führer changed his mind about keeping peace in the Far East. H decided that Japan had to become involved in the war as soon a possible, and the German ambassador in Tokyo was ordered to inveigl Japan into attacking Singapore at the risk of provoking the Unite States.

Pravda called it a "further aggravation of the war and an expansion of its realm." German Foreign Minister Joachim von Ribbentrop assured Vyacheslav Molotov, his Russian counterpart, that it was directed exclusively against the American warmongers. "The treaty, of course, does not pursue any aggressive aims against America. Its exclusive purpose is rather to bring the elements pressing for America's entry into the war to their senses, by conclusively demonstrating to them that if they enter the present struggle, they will automatically have to deal with the three great powers as adversaries." Why not join the pact, he suggested, and wrote a long letter to Stalin saying that it was

the historical mission of the four powers—the Soviet Union, Italy, Japan, and Germany—to adopt a long-range policy and to direct the future developments of their people into the right channel by delimitation of their interests on a world-wide scale. . . .

Matsuoka was positive he had engineered a plan for world peace. To confused intimates who considered him friendly toward America, he said it was the best way to prevent war with the United States. "If you stand firm and start hitting back," he told his eldest son, "the American will know he's talking to a man, and you two can then talk man to man." He thought he, and he alone, knew the real America. "It is my America and my American people that really exist," he once said. "There is no other America; there are no other American people."

"I admit people will call all this a tricky business," he told Dr. Saito; but he had allied with Hitler "to check the Army's aggressive policy . . . and to keep American warmongers from joining the war in Europe. And after that we can shake hands with the United States. This would keep peace in the Pacific while forming a great combine of capitalistic nations around the world against Communism."

The Tripartite Pact was also a means of settling the China Incident, he said. "The solution of the incident should rest on mutual assistance and prosperity, not on the hope of getting outside help to threaten China. To do this we should use the good offices of a third nation. I think the United States would do admirably for this purpose. But here the question is, What concessions will Japan (or rather, the Army) make? Japan should agree to a complete withdrawal of her troops from China."

The devious Matsuoka concluded that his aims could best

be accomplished by supporting Ribbentrop's plan for a grand quadruple alliance uniting Germany, Italy and Japan with their common enemy, Russia, and requested permission to go to Europe so he could personally bring this to pass. After lengthy debate the military chiefs approved the trip but rejected his request to bring along a gift for Hitler—promise of a Japanese attack on Singapore.

On March 12, 1941, a large crowd gathered at Tokyo Station to bid Matsuoka farewell. As the bell rang announcing the train's departure, he rushed up to General Sugiyama and pestered him once more about Singapore. When was he going to take the city?

"I cannot tell you now," the general replied stiffly, thinking to himself, What a troublesome fellow this Matsuoka is!

That he was became evident when, on the long trip across Siberia, he said privately to Colonel Yatsuji Nagai, sent along by the Army to see that he would make no rash promises about Singapore. "Nagai-*san*, you try to stir up some trouble along the border; I'm going to try to close a Japanese-Soviet neutrality pact."

In Berlin he first saw Hitler and even in these discussions it was Matsuoka who, as usual, dominated the conversation. In fact, Hitler rarely talked, and when he did he usually railed against England, exclaiming, "She must be beaten!"

Both Ribbentrop and Hitler, as well as high officials of the Reich, did their best to convince Matsuoka that seizure of Singapore would be advantageous to Japan. Ribbentrop argued that it would "perhaps be most likely to keep America out of war," because then Roosevelt couldn't risk sending his fleet into Japanese waters, while Hitler assured him that if Japan *did* get into war, Germany would come to her aid and "would be more than a match for America, entirely apart from the fact that the German soldiers were, obviously, far superior to the Americans."

But Matsuoka became evasive at every mention of Singapore. For example, when Hermann Göring, after accepting a scroll of Mount Fuji, jokingly promised to come and see the real thing only "if Japan takes Singapore," Matsuoka nodded toward the edgy Nagai and said, "You'll have to ask him."

Matsuoka was not at all reticent about the treaty he hoped to make with Stalin and was surprised to hear Ribbentrop, who had given him the idea of a grand quadruple pact, say, "How can you conclude such a pact at this time? Just remember, the U.S.S.R. never gives anything for nothing." Nagai took this to be a warning, but Matsuoka's enthusiasm

74

could not be damped even when the ambassador to Germany, General Hiroshi Oshima, told him in confidence that there was a good likelihood Germany and Russia would soon go to war.

On April 6 the party left Berlin. At the Soviet border they learned that Germany had invaded Yugoslavia. Nagai and the other advisers were disturbed—just the previous day Russia had signed a neutrality pact with Yugoslavia—but Matsuoka himself was effervescent. "Now I have the agreement with Stalin in my pocket!" he told his private secretary, Toshikazu Kase.

He was right. A week after arriving in Moscow, he signed a neutrality pact in the Kremlin. At the extravagant celebration party, Stalin was so obviously delighted at the turn of events that he personally brought plates of food to the Japanese, embraced them, kissed them, and danced around like a performing bear. The treaty was a coup for his diplomacy, convincing proof that he could disregard rumors about a German attack on Russia. After all, if Hitler had any such plans, would he have allowed Japan to conclude this agreement? *"Banzai* for His Majesty the Emperor!" was his opening toast. He averred that diplomatic pledges should never be broken, even if ideologies differed.

Matsuoka toasted him in turn and then added something no other Japanese diplomat would have said. "The treaty has been made," he blurted out. "I do not lie. If I lie, my head shall be yours. If you lie, be sure I will come for your head."

"My head is important to my country," Stalin retorted coldly. "So is yours to your country. Let's take care to keep both our heads on our shoulders." It was an embarrassing moment made worse when Matsuoka, in an attempt to be funny, remarked that Nagai and his naval counterpart "were always talking of how to beat the devil out of you."

Stalin wasn't joking when he replied that while Japan was very strong, the Soviet Union was not the Czarist Russia of 1904. But an instant later he had regained his good humor. "You are an Asiatic," he said. "And so am I."

"We're all Asiatics. Let us drink to the Asiatics!"

The innumerable toasts made it necessary to delay the eastbound train for an hour. At the station platform the Japanese were taken aback to see Stalin and Molotov tipsily converging on them from a side door for a final good-bye. Stalin kissed Nagai. "The reason England's in trouble today," he bellowed, "is because she has a low opinion of soldiers." Beaming, Stalin then encompassed the diminutive Matsuoka in a bear hug and gave him several affectionate smacks. "There is nothing to fear in Europe," he said, "now that there is a Japan-Soviet neutrality pact!"

Matsuoka should have heeded Corneille's character who said, "I embrace my rival, but only to choke him." Instead, he blithely exclaimed, "There is nothing to fear in the whole world!" and like a conqueror, climbed aboard the train. (Stalin was already embracing another ambassador—Hitler's envoy, Count Friedrich Werner von der Schulenburg—and telling him, "We must remain friends, and you must do everything to that end.") As the train carrying Matsuoka traversed Siberia, he told Kase that just before leaving Moscow he had talked freely with his old friend Laurence Steinhardt, the American ambassador, and they had agreed to try to restore good relations between their two countries. "Now the stage is set," he said. "Next I will go to Washington."

3.

On the other side of the world Matsuoka's ambassador in Washington, the good-natured, one-eyed Kichisaburo Nomura, a retired admiral, was already endeavoring to patch up the differences between Japan and America with Secretary of State Cordell Hull. Their talks had been inspired by two energetic Catholic priests, Bishop James E. Walsh, Superior General of the Maryknoll Society, and his assistant, Father James M. Drought. Some six months earlier, armed with an introductory letter from Lewis L. Strauss of Kuhn, Loeb & Company, the two priests had gone to Tokyo, where they visited Tadao Ikawa, a director of the Central Agricultural and Forestry Bank. They persuaded him that men of good will in both Japan and America could help bring about a peaceful settlement, and showed Ikawa a memorandum calling for a Japanese "Far Eastern Monroe Doctrine" and a stand against Communism, "which is not a political form of government but a corroding social disease that becomes epidemic." Ikawa was impressed by the memorandum and felt sure any reasonable Japanese would agree to its terms. During several years' service in the United States as an official of the Finance Ministry, he had made numerous friends in New York banking circles and acquired an American wife. He assumed that the proposal had the backing of President Roosevelt, since Father Drought had mentioned he was acting with the approval of "top personnel" in the U. S. government and, fired with enthusiasm, introduced the clergymen to Prime Minister Konoye and Matsuoka. The former suggested that Ikawa sound out the Army in the person of an influential colonel in the War Ministry named Hideo Iwakuro. He was a unique combination of idealism and intrigue and was just the man to put the priests' project into action: he ardently believed that peace with America was Japan's salvation, and plotting was a way of life with him. Behind his impish smile was one of the most agile brains in the Army. An espionage and intelligence expert, he had founded the prestigious Nakano School for spies, which was at the time sending out groups of well-trained agents throughout Asia imbued with his own idealistic views of a free amalgamation of Asian nations. It was he, too, who had dreamed up the idea for wrecking the Chinese economy by flooding that country with a billion and a half dollars' worth of counterfeit yen. He had also succeeded in getting refuge in Manchuria for some five thousand wandering Jews who had fled Hitler, by persuading the Kwantung Army leaders on grounds that no true Japanese could deny: a debt was owed the Jews; the Jewish firm of Kuhn, Loeb & Company had helped finance the Russo-Japanese War.

Colonel Iwakuro arranged an interview for the two Americans with General Akira Muto, chief of the Military Affairs Bureau, and the latter was equally impressed by their proposal; he gave it his blessing. Around New Year's the two priests returned to America, where they made an ally out of Postmaster General Frank C. Walker, a prominent Catholic. He set up an interview with President Roosevelt. The President met Bishop Walsh, read his long, enthusiastic memorandum and passed it on to Hull with the notation: ". . . What do you think we should do? FDR."

"In general, I am skeptical whether the plan offered is a practical one at this time," Hull replied in a note drafted largely by Dr. Stanley Hornbeck, his senior adviser on Far Eastern affairs, well known for his sympathy toward China and hostility toward Japan.* "It seems to me that there is

---

*Hornbeck's views on China were shared by an America which had made Pearl Buck's novel *The Good Earth* a best seller. For three decades Americans had held a highly idealized picture of the Chinese, looking upon them as childlike innocents who needed protection against the imperialism of Britain and Japan. China was a helpless, deserving nation whose virtues America alone understood.

"In this highly subjective picture of the Chinese," wrote George F. Kennan, "there was no room for a whole series of historical and psychological realities. There was no room for the physical ruthlessness that had characterized Chinese political life generally in recent decades;

little or no likelihood that the Japanese Government and the Japanese people would in good faith accept any such arrangement at this stage."

But the President was so intrigued by the idea that he asked Postmaster General Walker to turn over his duties to an assistant and give Bishop Walsh whatever assistance he could. As a "presidential agent," Walker was empowered to set up secret headquarters on the eighteenth floor of the Berkshire Hotel in New York City, and was given a code name, "John Doe."

Late in January, Bishop Walsh cabled Ikawa: AS A RESULT OF MEETING WITH THE PRESIDENT, HOPEFUL OF PROGRESS, AWAITING DEVELOPMENTS. Ikawa wondered if he should go to Washington as well, to help the priests and Ambassador Nomura, who was about to sail for the United States, find a formula for coexistence. The admiral was a straightforward, honest man of good will and good nature, with many American friends, including President Roosevelt, but unfortunately had no foreign office experience and little aptitude for diplomacy.

Ikawa went to Colonel Iwakuro for advice. The colonel encouraged him to go and, moreover, wangled a commercial passport for him, as well as money for the trip from two industrialists who were willing to make a contribution toward peace. Ikawa would assist Nomura on the pretext of negotiating with American businessmen. When word of the trip leaked out, Matsuoka (just before his trip to Europe) accused the Army of "taking upon itself negotiations with America" and of "putting up the money." War Minister Hideki Tojo knew nothing of the arrangement and summoned Iwakuro to his office. Iwakuro was so persuasive that Tojo categorically, and in good faith, informed the Foreign

---

for the formidable psychological and political powers of the Chinese people themselves; for the strong streak of xenophobia in their nature; for the lessons of the Boxer Rebellion; for the extraordinary exploitative talent shown by Chinese factions, of all times, in turning outside aid to domestic political advantage."

The so-called China Lobby did much to further China's cause in America. It was created by T. V. Soong, a clever and charming member of China's most omnipotent family. One sister had married Sun Yat-sen; another, a descendant of Confucius, H. H. Kung; and third, Chiang Kai-shek. Educated at Harvard and Columbia, Soong became close friends with influential Americans such as Henry Morgenthau, Harry Hopkins, Roy Howard, Henry Luce, Joseph Alsop and Thomas Corcoran. With their help, and that of a Pole, Ludwig Rajchman, Soong set up the lobby in 1940 and found he now had direct access to President Roosevelt without having to go through Hull

Ministry that the Army had no knowledge whatsoever of the Ikawa mission.

It was a dangerous game but Iwakuro felt that friendly relations with America were well worth it, and playing dangerous games was his hobby. He thought this ended his part in the matter but it had just begun, for Tojo had become so impressed with Iwakuro's grasp of the situation that he was ordered to proceed to America to help Nomura in his mission.

To prepare himself for the assignment, Iwakuro consulted with those who called for war as well as those who wanted peace. One night at a party in the Ginza, Nissho Inoue, leader of the Blood Brotherhood, urged him to become a spty: "We are going to fight against Britain and the United States, since they are blockading us, and your duty in America is to find out when we should start the war." But these saber rattlers were far outnumbered by those who urged Iwakuro to arrange any kind of honorable settlement.

Exuding an air of conspiracy, he arrived in New York City on March 30 to find an America widely split on the issue of war or peace. The interventionists, convinced their country's future and ultimate safety depended on helping the democracies crush the aggressor nations, had just pushed through Congress the Lend-Lease Act committing America to unlimited aid, "short of war," to the enemies of the Axis. She was to be the Arsenal of Democracy. Supporting this measure, and war itself, were such groups as "Bundles for Britain," as well as national minorities whose European relatives had suffered at the hands of Hitler and Mussolini. Their antiwar opponents included strange bedfellows: the right-wing "America Firsters" of Charles Lindbergh, Senator Borah and the German-American Bund; the "American Peace Mobilization" of the American Communist and Labor parties; and the traditionally isolationist Midwest which, though sympathetic to Britain and China, wanted no part of a shooting war.

Iwakuro was taken from the airport to St. Patrick's Cathedral to confer with Bishop Walsh and Father Drought. "Because of the Tripartite Pact, Japan cannot do anything to betray its co-signers," he said. "The thirteenth disciple, Judas, betrayed Christ, and every Christian despises him. It is the same with us Japanese. So if you insist that we withdraw from the pact, it will be hopeless to go on." The priests said they understood, and Iwakuro proceeded to Washington. He got a room at the Wardman Park Hotel, where Cordell Hull had recently taken an apartment. The next morning he reported to Admiral Nomura and found him affable and eager to utilize the unofficial channel opened up by the two priests and Ikawa. Most of the professional diplomats at the embassy, however, were hostile to this approach and were already treating Ikawa with open contempt. To them the new arrival was even more of an enigma. Iwakuro appeared to be "engagingly frank" but they felt he had come to camouflage the aggressive intents of the Army, and were wary.

On April 2 Father Drought began helping the two unofficial Japanese diplomats draw up a Draft Understanding between Japan and the United States. In three days it was completed. It was a broad agreement, conciliatory in tone, touching on problems ranging from the Tripartite Pact to economic activity in the southwest Pacific. Its most significant points concerned China, with Japan promising to withdraw troops and renounce all claims to any Chinese territory, provided China recognized Manchukuo and provided the government of Chiang Kai-shek was merged with that of a rival regime in Nanking under a former premier of the Republic of China, Wang Ching-wei.*

Drought took one copy to Postmaster General Walker, who called it "a revolution in Japanese 'ideology' and policy as well as a proof of the complete success of American statesmanship," and passed it along to Roosevelt, with the recommendation that he sign it immediately before "the Japanese leaders [were] assassinated." At the Japanese embassy Nomura, Minister Kaname Wakasugi, the military

---

*Several months earlier, on November 30, 1940, Japan had signed a treaty with the Wang government. The son of a scholar, Wang had studied political science in Tokyo and became Sun Yat-sen's chief disciple. It was he who wrote down Sun's last wishes at his deathbed. He served twice as premier of the Republic of China before becoming vice president of the Nationalist party. From the beginning he had been a rival of Chiang Kai-shek's, and their relations became so strained that at a private luncheon late in 1938 he suggested they both resign their offices and "redeem the sins they had committed against China." This infuriated Chiang and a few days later Wang thought it best to escape by plane to Hanoi. On March 30, 1940, he established his own splinter government in Nanking, although he had little popular support and not much money.

What he wanted primarily was peace with Japan for the good of the Chinese people, and if he had succeeded he would have become a national hero. But the treaty, which, by recognizing Wang's government, purportedly gave Japan a legal basis for fighting in China, was turning out badly for both Wang and the Japanese. It ruined any chance there was for Japan to make peace with Chiang Kai-shek and made the Nanking government a puppet of Japan. As a result, Wang had already become the symbol of treachery in China.

and naval attachés and a man from the Treaties Section, after some changes in wording, unanimously approved it.

The Draft Understanding was carefully examined at the State Department by the Far Eastern experts. They concluded that "most of its provisions were all that the ardent Japanese imperialists could want." Hull concurred but felt that "however objectionable some of the points might be, there were others that could be accepted as they stood and still others that could be agreed to if modified." On April 14 Ikawa told Nomura that he had arranged a private meeting with Hull at the Wardman Park Hotel that evening. Nomura was to go to Hull's apartment by a rear corridor and knock on the door at eight o'clock. Nomura did this, but he was afraid it was a practical joke. To his surprise, Hull opened the door. His was a sad, thoughtful face and he spoke slowly and gently except—as Nomura was to learn—when aroused. He came from Tennessee, land of mountain feuds, and was himself a man of implacable hatreds.

Nomura announced cryptically that he knew all about a certain "Draft Understanding," and though he hadn't yet forwarded it to Tokyo, thought his government "would be favorably disposed toward it." Hull raised objections to some of the points in the agreement but said that once these had been worked out, Nomura could send the revised document to Tokyo to ascertain whether the imperial government would take it as a "basis for negotiations." The inexperienced Nomura inferred from this that a revised Draft Understanding would be acceptable to the United States.

But the admiral was seriously mistaken. Hull had unwittingly misled Nomura, since he did *not* regard the proposals as a solid basis for negotiations. Perhaps the misunderstanding was a result of Nomura's faulty English. Or perhaps Nomura's great desire for a settlement had influenced his interpretation of Hull's vague phraseology. Nevertheless, it was largely Hull's fault. He should have known he was giving some encouragement to Nomura, when he had no such intentions. He had committed a tactical error.

The two diplomats met again two days later at Hull's apartment. "The one paramount preliminary question about which my Government is concerned," Hull began in his slow, circuitous manner, "is a definite assurance in advance that the Japanese Government has the willingness and ability to go forward with a plan . . . in relation to the problems of a settlement; to abandon its present doctrine of military conquest by force and . . . adopt the principles which this Government has been proclaiming and practicing as embodying the foundation on which all relations between nations should properly rest." He handed over a piece of paper listing these four principles:

1. Respect for the territorial integrity and the sovereignty of each and all nations.
2. Support of the principle of noninterference in the internal affairs of other countries.
3. Support of the principle of equality, including equality of commercial opportunity.
4. Nondisturbance of the status quo in the Pacific except as the status quo may be altered by peaceful means.

Wondering if his earlier optimism had been well founded, Nomura asked if Hull "would to a fairly full extent approve the proposals contained" in the Draft Understanding. Some would be readily approved, Hull replied, while others would have to be changed or eliminated. ". . . But if [your] Government is in real earnest about changing its course," he continued, "I [can] see no good reason why ways could not be found to reach a fairly mutually satisfactory settlement of all the essential questions and problems presented." This reassured Nomura and he remained optimistic even when Hull pointed out that they had "in no sense reached the stage of negotiations" and were "only exploring in a purely preliminary and unofficial way what action might pave the way for negotiations later."

Nomura transmitted Hull's suggestions and objections to the unofficial diplomats and most of his comments were incorporated in a revised Draft Understanding. The document was enciphered and dispatched to Tokyo, accompanied by a strong recommendation from Nomura for a favorable response. He added that Hull had "on the whole no objections" to the Draft Understanding (which Hull had said, in so many words) and was willing to use it as a basis for negotiation (which he had no intention of doing).

It was now Nomura's turn to commit a diplomatic blunder—as serious as Hull's. He failed to relay the Secretary of State's four basic principles to Tokyo. Certainly this information would have cooled some of Prime Minister Konoye's enthusiasm for the Draft Understanding. As it was, the Prime Minister was so encouraged by the way things seemed to be working out that he convened an emergency meeting of government and military leaders. They were just as enthused, including the military, and agreed that the American proposals

82

al—for that is what they thought the Draft Understanding was—should be promptly accepted in principle.*

Matsuoka's deputy protested. They should wait for a few days, until the Foreign Minister returned from Moscow. Konoye wanted no collision with the troublesome Matsuoka and acquiesced. On April 21 he learned that Matsuoka had at last arrived at Dairen, not far from the battlefields of the Russo-Japanese War, and told him over the phone to come home at once to consider an important proposal from Washington. Matsuoka assumed this was a result of his talk in Moscow with U. S. Ambassador Laurence Steinhardt and triumphantly told his secretary that he would soon be heading for America to complete his plan for world peace.

The next afternoon Matsuoka's plane landed at Tachikawa Air Base and he stepped out warmed by the cheers of the waiting crowd. Prime Minister Konoye was on hand, even though he was suffering so intensely from piles that he had to sit on an inflated circular tube. He offered to take Matsuoka to the Prime Minister's official residence, where other Cabinet ministers were waiting; he would brief the Foreign Minister on the negotiations with America en route. Matsuoka mentioned that he wanted to stop briefly at the plaza outside the Palace moat to pay his respects to the Emperor. To Konoye it was pretentious and in bad taste to bow deeply while newsmen took pictures, and he could not stand to the side while Matsuoka went through the ceremony or he'd be accused of insolence to the Emperor.

Since Matsuoka insisted on having his own way and Konoye was too proud to join him, the two left the airport in separate cars.** On the drive to the Palace, Matsuoka learned from his Vice Minister that the proposal for a peaceful

---

*The Army General Staff had already received an optimistic report from the military attaché in Washington: IMPROVEMENT OF DIPLOMATIC RELATIONS BETWEEN JAPAN AND THE UNITED STATES CAN BE ESTABLISHED. PLEASE EXERT ALL EFFORTS TO SEND INSTRUCTIONS IMMEDIATELY.

One of War Minister Tojo's most trusted advisers, Colonel Kenryo Sato, was astounded that America would make such concessions. It was all "too good to be true," he felt, and passed along his suspicions to Tojo. But the War Minister was willing to do almost anything to settle the war in China honorably and went along with the rest of the Cabinet.

**Later Konoye repeatedly said, "If only I had ridden that day with Matsuoka!" His secretary, Ushiba, believes pain from piles was probably a contributing factor. If so, it was not the first time this relatively minor ailment changed history. Napoleon suffered intensely from hemorrhoids at Waterloo.

"Konoye may not have succeeded in placating Matsuoka," Ushiba

83

settlement was not his own doing but the work of a couple of amateur diplomats. He was mortified, and that night was late for a conference at the Prime Minister's official residence, convened to discuss the Draft Understanding. He avoided not only Konoye but the subject of the meeting as well, talking incessantly of Hitler-*san* and Stalin-*san* as if they were his closest friends. Piqued at first, he became spirited and expansive as he boasted of how he had told Steinhardt that Roosevelt was "quite a gambler" and that the United States was keeping both the China Incident and the war going with her aid. "I told him the peace-loving President of the United States should co-operate with Japan, which is also peace-loving, and that she could inveigle Chiang to make peace with us." He also related that Ribbentrop had told him that Germany had signed the pact with Russia only because of "unavoidable circumstances" and that if it came to war, Germany would probably be able to defeat Stalin in three or four months.

But the business of the conference could not be avoided indefinitely. When the Draft Understanding was finally brought up, Matsuoka burst out stridently, "I cannot agree to this, whatever you Army and Navy people say! First of all, what about our treaty with Germany and Italy? In the last war the United States made use of Japan through the Ishii-Lansing agreement,* and when the war was over, the United States broke it. This is an old trick of theirs." Suddenly he announced that he felt very tired and needed "a month's rest" to think things over, and went home.

His arrogant manner had not been of a kind to bring reassurance, and as the meeting continued far into the night, both Tojo and General Muto recommended that the Draft Understanding be approved without further delay. The following day Konoye summoned his Foreign Minister. Matsuoka had calmed down, but about all he would say was, "I wish you would give me time to forget all about my European trip; then I'll consider the present case."

A week passed without any action from Matsuoka, and

---

commented further, "but his failure to ride with Matsuoka as he had planned may have been a turning point of history. It was really a great pity inasmuch as Konoye had been very keen on personally explaining to Matsuoka, and even restrained other Cabinet ministers from going to meet him. This incident throws much light on Konoye's character: he lacked persistence; he easily cooled off."

*In 1917 the United States consented to Japan's request that her "special interests" in China be recognized, but terminated the ambiguous agreement after the Armistice.

pressure began to build in the Army and Navy for his removal. Whether he was so offended that negotiations had been initiated without him that he was deliberately sabotaging them or was merely being properly cautious for fear that an amateur attempt at peace might lead to disaster, it was difficult to tell.

The reason Matsuoka himself gave was that the Draft Understanding was merely a plot of the Army, and Colonel Iwakuro was making a cat's-paw out of him. So he did nothing, while the Army and Navy fumed and the negotiators in Washington wondered what had gone wrong. It was hardest on the impetuous Iwakuro. Finally, on April 29, the Emperor's birthday, he could restrain himself no longer and suggested telephoning Matsuoka. It was indiscreet, but indiscretion was Iwakuro's creed and his associates were persuaded by his enthusiasm. It was decided that he and Ikawa should make the call from Postmaster General Walker's secret headquarters in New York City. By the evening they were in Room 1812 at the Berkshire Hotel, and began toasting the Emperor in port. The colonel had a small tolerance for wine and after two glasses he was feeling light-headed. At eight o'clock (it was ten o'clock the next morning in Japan) he put in the call to Matsuoka's home in Sendagaya.

"Congratulations on your trip to Europe," Iwakuro began. "About the fish I sent you the other day, how did you find it? Please have it cooked as soon as possible. Otherwise it will go bad. Nomura and all the others are expecting to have your reply soon."

"I know, I know," said Matsuoka curtly. "Tell him not to be so active."

Iwakuro wished he could have slapped Matsuoka for answering so rudely. "Please find out how others think about it. If you keep the fish around too long, it will surely go bad. Please be careful. Otherwise people will hold you responsible for everything."

"I know," was the blunt answer. Iwakuro hung up, muttered something incomprehensible, and to Ikawa's consternation, abruptly passed out.

The following day the two men called on former President Herbert Hoover, who welcomed them warmly but observed that since the Republicans were not in power, they could be of little help in the negotiations. "If war comes, civilization will be set back five hundred years," he said and added somberly, "The negotiations should be completed before summer or they will fail."

In Tokyo, Matsuoka was still delaying the reply to Hull. He had informed Hitler of the Draft Understanding and was waiting for his comments.* To those who pressed for action, he repeated that before approving the Draft Understanding, Japan should ask America to sign a neutrality treaty which would be in effect even if Japan and Britain went to war. Nomura was told to sound out Hull on such a treaty. Naturally, Hull rejected the proposal peremptorily. This irritated Matsuoka no end; he told the Emperor on May 8 that if the United States entered the war in Europe, Japan should back their Axis allies and attack Singapore. He predicted that the talks in Washington would come to nothing, and that if they did succeed it would only mean that America had been placated at the expense of Germany and Italy. "If that happens, I am afraid I cannot remain in the Cabinet."

When Prince Konoye heard this—from the Emperor himself, who expressed his "astonishment and grave concern"—he secretly met with his War and Navy ministers, General Tojo and Admiral Koshiro Oikawa, and they agreed to force the fractious Foreign Minister to act. A reply accepting the main conditions of the Draft Understanding was drawn up, and Matsuoka was instructed to send it without delay.

On May 12 Nomura brought this document to Hull's apartment. Hull read it with disappointment. It "offered little basis for an agreement, unless we were willing to sacrifice some of our most basic principles, which we were not." Still, it was a formal proposition and he decided "to go forward on the basis of the Japanese proposals and seek to argue Japan into modifying here, eliminating there, and inserting elsewhere, until we might reach an accord we both could sign with mutual good will."

The problem—already beset by language difficulties, stubbornness, rigidity and confusion—was further aggravated by American intercepts of Japanese messages. Diplomatic codes, supposedly unbreakable, had been cracked by American ex-

---

*Matsuoka also promised the German ambassador, General Eugen Ott, who expressed fears that the negotiations in Washington would negate the Tripartite Pact, that if the United States entered the war, Japan would definitely get in it. Notwithstanding, Hitler was suspicious of Matsuoka, and told Mussolini that Matsuoka was a Catholic who also sacrificed to pagan gods and "one must conclude that he was combining the hypocrisy of an American Bible missionary with the craftiness of a Japanese Asiatic."

perts, and messages from the Japanese government to its diplomats overseas were being intercepted and deciphered under the cover name of Operation Magic. Consequently, Hull usually knew what was on Nomura's mind before he walked into a conference.* But since many of the decoded messages were not considered worthy of Hull's attention—a naval officer made this decision on his own—and since messages were translated by men not fluent in the stylized and difficult language of Japanese diplomacy, Hull was occasionally misled.

The judge from Tennessee, moreover, was constantly annoyed at the perpetual, "frozen" smiles of the Japanese, and either ridiculed or made fun of their bowing and "hissing."** As a result, it was easy for his chief adviser, Dr. Hornbeck, to persuade him that the Japanese were not to be trusted and that any compromise with Japan would be a betrayal of American democratic principles.

Hornbeck, a highly ethical man like his superior, who had been brought up in China, was by nature antagonistic to the Japanese and looked on their expansion from a purely moralistic standpoint. Hornbeck's associate in the State Department, J. Pierrepont Moffat, described him as regarding "Japan as the sun around which her satellites, Germany and Italy, were revolving." A proponent for economic warfare since the fall of 1938, he stood for "a diplomatic 'war plan.'" Stubborn and sensitive, he was convinced that Japan was a "predatory" power run by arrogant militarists who were encouraged by world timidity to go from aggression to aggression. He had always felt they could only be blocked by a series of retaliations, ending, if need be, in economic sanctions. This program should be put into effect even if it ended

---

*About two weeks earlier Ambassador Hiroshi Oshima had cabled from Berlin that he had just been told by Dr. Heinrich Stahmer, a Foreign Ministry official in charge of Japanese-German affairs, that German intelligence was fairly certain the American government was reading Nomura's coded messages. "There are at least two circumstances to substantiate the suspicion," said Oshima. "One is that Germany is also reading our coded messages. And the other is that the Americans once before succeeded in compromising our codes, in 1922, during the Washington Conference." But Kazuji Kameyama, chief of the Cable Section, assured Matsuoka that it was humanly impossible to break the diplomatic code, and it was assumed that any secret information America obtained had come through security leaks.

**Snakes and cats hiss by expelling breath. Japanese do just the opposite, *sucking* in at times of cogitation, uncertainty or embarrassment.

in war; bowing to the militarists' demands would eventually end in war, anyway. Like so many intellectuals—and he was one of the most brilliant men in the foreign service—he was opinionated.* He was also dictatorial and could easily override more objective subordinates, such as the modest Joseph W. Ballantine, the department's leading Japan expert.

During these trying days Hull and Nomura often met at the Wardman Park Hotel in an effort to work out their differences, but made little progress. Part of their trouble came from Tokyo, where Matsuoka was making provocative announcements both privately and publicly. On May 14 he told Ambassador Grew that Hitler had shown great "patience and generosity" in not declaring war on the United States, and that American attacks on German submarines would doubtless lead to war between Japan and America. The "manly, decent and reasonable" thing for the United States to do, he said, was "to declare war openly on Germany instead of engaging in acts of war under cover of neutrality." Grew with all his sympathies could not bear such an insult, and he rebutted Matsuoka's assertions point for point. Matsuoka realized he had gone too far and after the meeting wrote a conciliatory note:

. . . I was wondering, to be frank, why you appeared so disturbed when I referred to the American attitude and actions. After Your Excellency's departure, it all suddenly dawned on me that I misused a word. . . . Of course, I didn't mean to say "indecent." No! I wanted to say "indiscretion."

I write you the above in order to remove any misapprehension; I'd feel very sorry if I caused any.

Three days later Matsuoka wrote Grew again. In a long, disjointed letter marked "Entirely Private" he said he knew how to be "correct" as a foreign minister but often forgot that he was foreign minister. Furthermore, he hated the so-called correct attitudes of many diplomats which "hardly get us anywhere" and then admitted that he thought in terms of one, two and even three thousand years, and if that sounded like insanity he couldn't help it because he was made that way.

Indeed, more than one thought this last was the case. At a

---

*"I am still convinced," Ushiba wrote in 1970, "that *on the U. S. side*, Hull's formalism and orthodox diplomacy and Hornbeck's stubbornness proved the undoing of Konoye's efforts (granted there was much more stubbornness on the Japanese side!)"

recent liaison conference Navy Minister Oikawa had re-marked, "The Foreign Minister is insane, isn't he?" And President Roosevelt, after reading a MAGIC translation of instructions sent by Matsuoka to Nomura, thought they were "the product of a mind which is deeply disturbed and unable to think quietly or logically."

Prince Konoye, however, believed Matsuoka's provocative, inflammatory and sometimes erratic statements were pur-posely made to frighten opponents; perhaps that was why he kept aiming so many barbs at America. But if this had started as a tactic and he sincerely wanted peace, it ended in disaster. Because of his insults and delays, the talks in Wash-ington had about reached an impasse. Matsuoka knew this was happening, yet he continued insulting and delaying and look-ing to Hitler for advice. He was deliberately wrecking the negotiations probably out of his egomaniacal conviction that he and he alone knew the real America and could resolve the controversy.

He remained belligerent while Nomura and Iwakuro talked peace, and Hull understandably concluded that he was being misled. On June 21 the Secretary of State at last answered the Japanese proposal: Japan would have to abandon the Tripartite Pact, and he rejected the Japanese plan to retain troops in certain areas of North China to help the Chinese combat the Communists.

Konoye and his cabinet were dismayed. It wasn't even as acceptable an offer as the Draft Understanding. Why had the Americans changed from their "original" proposal? wondered Konoye, still unaware that Hull had never regarded the Draft Understanding as a basis for negotiations.

What infuriated Matsuoka was an Oral Statement that accompanied Hull's answer to the effect that recent public statements by certain Japanese officials—and it was obvious he meant Matsuoka—seemed to be an unsurmountable road-block to the negotiations. The Foreign Minister took this as a personal insult, and cause for breaking off the talks in Wash-ington altogether.

This concern and confusion was eclipsed the next day, Sunday, June 22, when Hitler invaded Russia. The Japanese were taken by surprise, although Ambassador Oshima, after talks with Hitler and Ribbentrop, had cabled sixteen days earlier that war between Germany and Russia was imminent.

It also came as a blow to Stalin, despite 180 German violations of Soviet air space (including penetrations as deep as four hundred miles) in the previous two months. There were also unheeded warnings of an impending attack from official Washington and London—and Stalin's own secret agent in Tokyo, Richard Sorge, who had correctly predicted in the spring of 1939 that Germany would march into Poland on September 1. Sorge not only dispatched photocopies of telegrams from Ribbentrop informing his ambassador in Tokyo, General Eugen Ott, that the Wehrmacht would invade the Soviet Union in the second half of June, he also sent a last-minute message on June 14: "War begins June 22." In the first few hours the Luftwaffe wiped out 66 Soviet airfields and destroyed 1,200 planes while ground forces swept forward capturing almost 2,000 big guns, 3,000 tanks and 2,000 truckloads of ammunition.*

The news of the attack reached Tokyo a little before four o'clock on Sunday afternoon. Within minutes Matsuoka phoned the Lord Privy Seal, Marquis Koichi Kido, and asked for an audience with the Emperor. Kido was a small, neatly compact man of fifty-two, with a trimmed mustache, and had, like Konoye, been a protégé of Prince Saionji's. The liberal political philosophy and logical reasoning which characterized the last *genro* (he had died the previous year at the age of ninety-one) had always made a deep impression on him, particularly Saionji's repeated warnings that Japan's policy must be based on co-operation with Britain and America. Accordingly, Kido had actively opposed the seizure of Manchuria, the push into China and the Tripartite Pact. His grandfather by marriage, as it were, was Koin Kido, one of

---

*According to *A Short History of the U.S.S.R.*: "The country's poor preparedness was due to grave errors of judgement made by Stalin in evaluating the general strategic situation and in his estimates of the probable time the war would break out. . . . Hitler hoped that his surprise attack would knock out the Red Army, and to be sure, Stalin's errors of judgement, and his outright mistakes, went a long way to further his designs."

Early in 1969, however, the Soviet Communist party's most authoritative journal, *Kommunist*, declared that Stalin was an "outstanding military leader," and that Nikita Khrushchev's dramatic attack on Stalin at the 20th Party Congress in 1956 was completely unfounded. "Not a stone remains of the irresponsible statements about his military incompetence, of his direction of the war 'on a globe,' of his supposedly absolute intolerance of other views, and of other similar inventions grasped and spread by foreign falsifiers of history." This reappraisal was echoed a few days later by the Red Army newspaper *Krasnaya Zvezda* in a lengthy attack on "revisionists" in such countries as Czechoslovakia, Yugoslavia and France.

the four most illustrious leaders of the Meiji Restoration,*
but the young man had earned every advancement by his
own industry and ability. As Lord Keeper of the Privy Seal,
Kido was the permanent confidential adviser to the Emperor
on all matters ("I was to the Emperor what Harry Hopkins
was to President Roosevelt") and Hirohito had grown to lean
on his counsel. Konoye and Kido were probably the two
most influential civilians in Japan, and though close friends,
were almost exact opposites in character as well as appearance. Already highly respected as a hard-headed, practical
man, the Privy Seal was direct and decisive, a pragmatist. He
was an able administrator and every detail of his life was
carefully planned, precisely executed. In golf, which he played
with zealous regularity, he was such a model of precision
with his modulated swing that his partners called him "Kido
the Clock."

After arranging a five-thirty audience for Matsuoka, Kido
informed the Emperor that the Foreign Minister's views
probably differed from Konoye's. "I would like His Majesty
to ask him if he has consulted with the Prime Minister
regarding the question, and tell him that this question is
extremely important," said Kido. "Therefore he should confer closely with the Prime Minister and tell him that the
Emperor is basically in agreement with the Prime Minister.
Please excuse my impertinence for daring to give His Majesty
this advice."

When Matsuoka spoke to the Emperor, within the hour, it
was evident he had not yet talked with Konoye. He was sure
Germany would quickly defeat Russia,** and recommended

---

*In going over this portion of the manuscript for corrections,
Marquis Kido wrote: "My grandfather is generally called Koin, but the
proper pronunciation of the Japanese characters is Takayoshi."
Takayoshi had no son to carry on the family name, and his nephew
Takamasa (his younger sister's son) was legally made a Kido after he
married Takayoshi's only daugher. She died and Takamasa married
again; Koichi Kodo was the eldest son of that union.
**The U. S. military agreed. Secretary of the Navy Frank Knox
prognosticated that "it would take anywhere from six weeks to two
months for Hitler to clean up in Russia." Secretary of War Henry
Stimson wrote in his diary: "I cannot help feeling that it offers to us
and Great Britain a great chance, provided we use it promptly," and
then told Roosevelt that in his opinion it would take Germany from
one to three months to whip the Soviet Union. Ambassador Grew
thought only good could come of the attack and wrote in his diary:
"Let the Nazis and the Communists so weaken each other that
the democracies will soon gain the upper hand or at least be released
from this dire peril."

an immediate attack on Siberia and a postponement of the push to the south. Astonished, since this policy meant expansion in two directions, the Emperor asked Matsuoka to consult with Konoye and indicated that the audience was over.

Matsuoka did see Konoye but listened to no advice, and continued to call for an attack on Russia in private as well as at liaison conferences. These were ordinarily held at the Prime Minister's official residence. They were informal gatherings of the Big Four of the Cabinet—the Prime Minister, Foreign Minister, War Minister and Navy Minister— with the Army and Navy Chiefs and Vice Chiefs of Staff. Other Cabinet ministers and experts occasionally attended to give counsel and information. The Prime Minister sat in an armchair near the center of a medium-sized conference room surrounded by the others. Three secretaries—the Chief Secretary of the Cabinet, the chief of the Military Affairs Bureau of the War Ministry and the chief of the Naval Affairs Bureau of the Navy Ministry—sat near the entrance.

The conferences were lively. There was no presiding officer, no strict protocol, and arguments were common. The meetings had been started in late 1937, to co-ordinate activities of the government and the military, discontinued for some time, then resumed in late 1940 when the situation became more critical.

Three days after Matsuoka's audience with the Emperor, he met direct opposition from the military, who were not eager for a simultaneous fight with the Soviet Union and America. Naval operations against both these countries, said Navy Minister Oikawa, would be too difficult. "To avoid this kind of situation, don't tell us to attack the U.S.S.R. and at the same time push south. The Navy doesn't want the Soviet Union provoked."

"When Germany wipes out the Soviet Union, we can't simply share in the spoils of victory unless we've done something," said Matsuoka and then uttered words which were strange coming from a foreign minister. "We must either shed our blood or embark on diplomacy. And it's better to shed blood." The following day he pressed his argument. What was more important, the north or the south? he asked.

Of equal import, replied Army Chief of Staff Sugiyama. "We're waiting to see how the situation develops." He did not reveal that if Moscow fell before the end of August, the Army would attack Siberia.

"It all depends on the situation," said Army Vice Chief of

Staff Ko Tsukada, a bright, short-tempered man. "We can't go both ways simultaneously."

After the conference Colonel Kenryo Sato continued the debate with Tojo, who felt Matsuoka had made several good points. "We gain nothing in the north," said Sato. "At least we get oil and other resources in the south." He was as brilliant and impulsive as General Ishihara and Colonel Iwakuro, and often served as the official spokesman for Army policy. He was already notorious throughout the country for having yelled "Shut up!" at a Diet member who kept interrupting his speech.

Wary as he was of Sato's quixotic behavior, Tojo had come to depend on advice from the "Shut up" colonel. Sato's logic made him wonder, "If we declare war on the Russians, would the United States back them up and declare war on us?"

"It's not impossible. America and the Soviet Union have different systems, but you never can tell in war."

The following day Tojo gave Matsuoka no support at all. But the Foreign Minister was undaunted. He argued that reports from Ambassador Oshima indicated that the war in Russia would soon be over and that England would capitulate before the end of the year. "If we start discussing the Soviet problem *after* the Germans beat the Soviets, we'll get nowhere diplomatically. If we hit the Soviets without delay, the United States won't enter the war." He was confident, he said, that he could hold off the United States for three or four months with his diplomacy. "But if we just wait around to see how things will turn out, as the Supreme Command suggests, we'll be encircled by Britain, the United States and Russia. We must first strike north, then south." He went on and on almost compulsively until he saw that his words were having no effect. Then, in an attempt to force the issue, he said, "I would like a decision to attack the Soviet Union."

"No," said Sugiyama, who spoke for all the military.

Matsuoka's strongest ally was in Berlin, but Hitler himself had yet to come out with a flat request to attack Russia. He did this three days later, in the form of a telegram from Ribbentrop to his ambassador in Tokyo. On the morning of June 30 General Ott transmitted this request to Matsuoka, who used it as a principal argument at the liaison conference that afternoon. Germany, he announced, was now formally asking Japan to come into the war. He became so fervent in his appeal for an attack on Russia that one listener likened it to "a vomit of fire." "My predictions have always come true," Matsuoka boasted. "Now I predict that if war starts in the south, America and Britain will join it!" He suggested postponing the drive south and was so persuasive that Oikawa turned to Sugiyama and said, "Well, how about postponing it for six months?"

It looked as if Matsuoka had abruptly turned things around by his oratory. A Navy man leaned over and whispered to Army Vice Chief of Staff Tsukada that perhaps they should consider the postponement, but Tsukada could not be swayed; with a few impassioned words of his own, he brought Oikawa and Sugiyama back to their original position. At this point Prince Konoye, who had been almost silent until then, said that he would have to go along with the Supreme Command. There was no more to say. The long debate was over and the decision was made to go south.

The final step was to get formal approval from the Emperor. This would come automatically at a ceremony held at the Imperial Palace, an imperial conference. At these meetings the Emperor traditionally did nothing but sit silent and listen to explanations of the policy in question. Afterward he would indicate his approval with a stamp of his seal. The members were comprised of those who attended liaison conferences, an expert or two, and the President of the Privy Council, a civilian who represented the Throne in a sense by occasionally asking questions the Emperor himself could not.

The conference to approve the move south was convened on July 2. The members sat stiffly on both sides of two long tables covered with brocade, but the minute the Emperor entered the room they shot to their feet. His skin, like that of his three brothers, was smooth as porcelain and of unique coloring. His army uniform did not make him look a bit martial. He stepped up to the dais and sat down before a gold screen, facing south, the direction to be honored according to court etiquette. He seemed detached, as if above worldly affairs.

Below, the members sat down at right angles to His Majesty and stared woodenly at each other, hands on knees. Then the ceremony began. All but the President of the Privy Council, Yoshimichi Hara, had rehearsed what they would say. First Prince Konoye rose, bowed to the Emperor and read a document entitled "Outline of National Policies in View of Present Developments." It was the plan to go south; the first step would be occupation of French Indochina. This, hopefully, would come without bloodshed by exerting diplomatic pressure on the Vichy government; but if persuasion failed, military force was to be used, even at the risk of provoking war with America and Britain.

Sugiyama bowed and said he agreed that Japan should push south. "However, if the German-Soviet war develops favorably for our empire, I believe we should also use force to settle this problem and so secure our northern borders."

Admiral Osami Nagano, Chief of the Navy General Staff, also felt it was necessary to go south despite the risks. When he finished, the President of the Privy Council began asking questions, some of them more embarrassing than expected at such a formalized meeting. What were the realistic chances of taking Indochina by diplomatic means? he wondered.

"The odds are that diplomatic measures won't succeed," replied Matsuoka. Still against going south, he had to argue the majority decision.

Hara was a small, mild-looking man but he was not at all intimidated by the stern faces of the generals and admirals. He emphasized that military action was "a serious thing." And wasn't sending troops into Indochina while attempting to ratify a treaty between Japan and France inconsistent with the Imperial Way of conducting diplomacy? "I do not think it wise for Japan to resort to direct, unilateral military action and thus be branded an aggressor."

"I will see to it that we won't seem to be involved in an act of betrayal in the eyes of the world," Matsuoka assured him.

Hara remained dubious. Why not go north? he suggested and began using some of Matsuoka's own arguments. Hitler's attack on Russia presented the chance of a lifetime. "The Soviet Union is spreading Communism all over the world and we will have to fight her sooner or later. . . . The people are really eager to fight *her*." What was supposed to be a formality threatened to turn into a debate. "I want to avoid war with the United States. I don't think they would retaliate if we attacked the Soviet Union." On the other hand, Hara feared a move into Indochina would bring war with the Anglo-Saxons.

Matsuoka had used the same words the day before. "There is that possibility," he agreed.

Sugiyama privately thought that Hara's questions were "sharp as a knife," but curtly pointed out that the occupation of Indochina was "absolutely necessary to crush the intrigues of Britain and America. Moreover, with Germany's military situation so favorable, I don't believe Japan's advance into

French Indochina will provoke America to war." He warned, however, of counting out the Soviet Union prematurely. They should wait "from fifty to sixty days," to make certain that Germany would win. The finality of his statement shut off further discussion, and any hopes that Matsuoka might have had about resuming the debate vanished. A vote was taken and the policy document unanimously approved. Japan would go south.

Throughout the proceedings the Emperor had been sitting silent and impassive, as custom decreed, his mere presence making any decision legal and binding. The document was taken to the Cabinet secretariat, where a copy was made on official stationery. It was signed by Konoye and the Army and Navy Chiefs of Staff, brought to the Emperor and finally to the Privy Seal's office, where the imperial seal was affixed. It was national policy, and another step had been taken toward total war.

4.

Now Hull's counterproposal had to be dealt with. Matsuoka, predictably, was still in a rage over the Oral Statement, which criticized unnamed Japanese officials for inflammatory public remarks. This rather innocuous rebuke was, to Matsuoka, a personal insult as well as an unforgivable affront to Japan, and at a liaison conference on July 12 he said, with anger bordering on paranoia, "I've thought about it for the last ten days, and I believe America looks on Japan as a protectorate or a dependency! While I'm foreign minister, I can't accept it. I'll consider anything else, but I reject the Oral Statement. It is typically American to ride roughshod over the weak. The statement treats Japan as a weak and dependent country. Some Japanese are against me, and some even say the Prime Minister is against me." His words tumbled out, revealing as much resentment for his personal enemies as for Hull. "Little wonder then that the United States thinks Japan is exhausted and therefore sends us such a statement. I propose right now that we reject the statement out of hand and break off negotiations with the United States!" He called Roosevelt "a real demagogue" and accused him of trying to lead America into war. As for himself, it had been his cherished hope since his youth to preserve peace between Japan and America. "I think there is no hope, but," he concluded irrationally, "let us try until the very end."

At last he had said something the military liked. Even if there seemed to be no hope, Tojo repeated, they should keep negotiating with America. "Can't we at least keep the United States from formally going to war by means of the Tripartite Pact? Naturally, the Oral Statement is an insult to our *kokutai* and we must reject it, as the Foreign Minister advises. But what if we sincerely tell the Americans what we Japanese hold to be right? Won't this move them?"

Navy Minister Oikawa was also for coming to some agreement with the Americans. According to reports, they weren't in any position to instigate a war in the Pacific. "Since we don't want a Pacific war either, isn't there room for negotiation?"

"Room?" Matsuoka retorted with some sarcasm. "They'll probably listen only if we tell them we won't use force in the south. What else would they accept?" He was in no mood for compromise. "They sent a message like this because they're convinced we submit easily."

It was obvious to Prince Konoye that Matsuoka was making this a personal issue and that it would be necessary to by-pass him. But the Foreign Minister's influence was still so great that the Prime Minister had to meet surreptitiously with key Cabinet members to draft their own conciliatory reply to Hull. This was presented to Matsuoka, but it took him several days just to read it—he claimed he was sick—and even after he had, he tried to delay matters. First, the Oral Statement should be rejected, then there should be a wait of several days before dispatching the answer.

Prime Minister Konoye agreed to reject the statement but insisted that both the rejection and the reply be sent simultaneously to Hull, to save time. Konoye gave these instructions to Matsuoka's associate Dr. Yoshie Saito, who promised to follow orders. He disobeyed—another act of *gekokujo*—and without consulting anyone, cabled a single message to Washington: the rejection of the Oral Statement. He held back the proposal for a few days, as Matsuoka had wanted, and Hull first saw it in an intercepted cable to Germany.

To the legal-minded Tojo such action was insupportable, and he told Konoye that Matsuoka should be dismissed at once. But the prince did not want open conflict with Matsuoka, who was still a public hero after his meetings with Hitler and Stalin. Konoye decided to get rid of him by subterfuge: he would ask the entire Cabinet to resign and then form a new one with a different foreign minister. He called an extraordinary session of the Cabinet at six-thirty on

July 16, and when he made his proposal, no one objected; Matsuoka was home ill in bed.

This terminated the stormy career of the most controversial figure in Japanese diplomacy. The end had come through an act of insubordination committed for Matsuoka's sake by a faithful subordinate, but without his knowledge.

The following day the Emperor asked Konoye to form a new cabinet. He did so within twenty-four hours, which was possible only because there were so few changes. Matsuoka was replaced by an admiral who got along well with Americans, Teijiro Toyoda. One of his first acts was to cable his ambassador in Vichy that the Japanese Army would push into Indochina on July 24 no matter what the Vichy government decided to do. But on the day before the deadline, Vichy agreed to the peaceful entry of Japanese troops in southern Indochina. The ambassador in Vichy triumphantly wired Tokyo:

THE REASON WHY THE FRENCH SO READILY ACCEPTED THE JAPANESE DEMANDS WAS THAT THEY SAW HOW RESOLUTE WAS OUR DETERMINATION AND HOW SWIFT OUR WILL. IN SHORT, THEY HAD NO CHOICE BUT TO YIELD.

When Hull read this, courtesy of MAGIC, he was as indignant, and perhaps rightly so, as if Indochina had been taken by force. He pressed Roosevelt to retaliate by imposing a new embargo on Japan, despite a recent warning from the War Plans Division of the Navy that such action "would probably result in a fairly early attack by Japan on Malaya and the Netherlands East Indies, and possibly involve the United States in early war in the Pacific."

This time Roosevelt listened to those who, like Ickes, had long been urging him to act forcefully against all aggressors.* On the night of July 26 he ordered all Japanese assets in America frozen, and Britain and the Netherlands soon followed suit. In consequence, not only did all trade with the United States cease, but the fact that America had been Japan's major source of oil imports now left Japan in an

---

*On the day after Hitler's invasion of Russia, Secretary of the Interior Harold Ickes wrote Roosevelt: "To embargo oil to Japan would be as popular a move in all parts of the country as you could make. There might develop from the embargoing of oil to Japan such a situation as would make it, not only possible but easy, to get into this war in an effective way. And if we should thus indirectly be brought in, we would avoid the criticism that we had gone in as an ally of communistic Russia."

untenable situation. To *The New York Times* it was "the most drastic blow short of war." To Japan's leaders it was much more. They had secured the bases in Indochina by negotiation with Vichy France, a country recognized if not approved by America, and international law was on their side; the freezing was the last step in the encirclement of the empire by the ABCD (American, British, Chinese, Dutch) powers, a denial to Japan of her rightful place as leader of Asia and a challenge to her very existence.

The frustration, near-hysteria and anger could be expected but not the confusion among the Supreme Command. Five days later Naval Chief of Staff Nagano, a cautious and sensible man, still had not recovered from an event that should have been foreseen. In an audience with the Emperor, he first said he wanted to avoid war and that this could be done by revoking the Tripartite Pact, which the Navy had always maintained was a stumbling block to peace with America. Then he warned that Japan's oil stock would only last for two years, and once war came, eighteen months, and concluded, "Under such circumstances, we had better take the initiative. We will win."

It was a curious performance. In one paragraph Nagano had put in a word for peace, cleared the Navy of responsibility for any diplomatic disaster, prophesied an oil famine, suggested a desperate attack and predicted victory.

The Emperor cut through the tangle with one question: "Will you win a great victory? Like the Battle of Tsushima?"

"I am sorry, but that will not be possible."

"Then," said the Emperor grimly, "the war will be a desperate one."

The Leering Clouds

The Lowering Clouds

4   "Go Back
to Blank Paper"

1.

Konoye's actions over the past few years had baffled those who sympathized with the tremendous problems he faced. Why had a liberal allowed the Army to gain ascendancy? Why had he subordinated himself to his own Foreign Minister, permitted him to endanger the negotiations in Washington? Ambassador Craigie was impressed by Konoye's numerous acts of statesmanship "only to be irritated just as often by his apparent lack of firmness in leadership and his failure at times of crisis to use his strong personal position to curb the extremists."*

In the opinion of Lieutenant General Teiichi Suzuki, director of the Cabinet Planning Board and an Army intellectual, Konoye wavered at critical moments not from weakness, but from intellectual doubts, and his objectivity rendered him almost incapable of making a clear-cut decision and taking action on it.

But both Suzuki and Craigie agreed on one thing—Konoye

---

*Ushiba, who was privy to Konoye's thoughts, comments: "A Churchill or a Kennedy might have succeeded in controlling the Army, but given the Japanese constitutional system, by which the Supreme Command was independent of the Prime Minister, and confronted with such a huge organization determined to control national destiny, it is doubtful if even Churchill could have succeeded. Konoye was no leader, was not a strong-man type, was not the kind of man whose outstanding feature is courage, resoluteness, dedication to a cause. He was, however, informed of what the Japanese Army was like, better perhaps than any other outsider, and concerned about taming it as much as anybody else. His philosophy was basically negative; that is, not to offend or provoke, and to defer the showdown as long as possible. If you stood in the Army's way, it would simply remove you and proceed to find another convenient blind or cover behind which it could do whatever it wanted."

was another Hamlet. And like Hamlet he was finally spurred to decisive action—he would meet privately with President Roosevelt to settle once and for all the question of China.* On August 4 he summoned War Minister Tojo and Navy Minister Oikawa and told them of his decision. "If the President still does not see reason I shall, of course, be fully prepared to break off the talks and return home." Both Japan and America would have to make concessions, but he felt agreement could be reached if the high-level talks were "carried out with broad-mindedness." He promised that he would neither be "too anxious or hasty to come to terms, nor assume a supercilious manner or act submissively."

Tojo and Oikawa refused to commit themselves without consulting their colleagues. Within hours the admiral reported back that the Navy was in "complete accord and, moreover, anticipated the success of the conference." But Tojo found Army opinion divided. He wrote the Prime Minister that it was feared the summit meeting would weaken Japan's current policy, which was based on the Tripartite Pact, as well as cause repercussions at home. Nevertheless, the Army had no objections to the meeting so long as Konoye promised to lead the war against America if Roosevelt refused to appreciate Japan's position. He concluded the letter with the pessimistic observation that "the probability of failure of this meeting is eight to ten."

Konoye himself had no doubts, and over lunch told his close friend Shigeharu Matsumoto, editor in chief of the Domei News Agency, about the proposed meeting with Roosevelt. On the morning of August 6 the prince advised the Emperor of his intentions. "You had better see Roosevelt at once," said His Majesty, recalling what Admiral Nagano had told him about the dwindling oil stockpile. The following morning a message was sent to Secretary of State Hull suggesting that Konoye and Roosevelt meet in Honolulu to discuss means of adjusting the differences between the two countries.

But Hull was dubious of Konoye's proposal. It had the same "hand-to-heart touch" used by Hitler on Chamberlain at Munich. Secretary of War Stimson was in accord and

---

*About this time Konoye called Admiral Isoroku Yamamoto, commander in chief of the Combined Fleet, to his private home and asked what chances there were in an attack on America. Yamamoto foresaw success for a year or so. "But after that I am not at all sure." This confirmed Konoye's own suspicions and his conviction that a meeting with Roosevelt was the only solution.

wrote in his diary: "The invitation to the President is merely a blind to try to keep us from taking definite action." After two days the Secretary of State saw Ambassador Nomura, who wanted a definite reply. But Hull, mixing accusations with moral observations, contended that it was now clear that those in Japan who favored peace "had lost control." The Japanese press "was being constantly stimulated to speak of encirclement of Japan by the United States." That very day, he continued, he had told correspondents "there is no occasion for any nation in the world that is law-abiding and peaceful to become encircled by anybody except itself." The frustrated Nomura finally asked if this was the reply to the suggested summit meeting and Hull reiterated everything he had just uttered, concluding that "it remained with the Japanese Government to decide whether it could find means of shaping its policies accordingly and then endeavor to evolve some satisfactory plan."

Since the Japanese military leaders felt they had bent a good deal to approve the meeting, its cool reception in Washington sharpened a growing suspicion. Did the Americans really want peace or were they playing for time? Each day twelve thousand tons of irreplaceable oil were being consumed and soon the armed forces would be as helpless as a whale thrown up on the beach.

Roosevelt was not on hand to discuss the situation. The cruiser *Augusta* was taking him to a rendezvous in Argentia Bay, Newfoundland, with Winston Churchill. On Sunday, August 10, the President attended church services on the deck of the British battleship *Prince of Wales*, in the shadows of its big guns. The lesson, appropriately, was from Joshua: "There shall not any man be able to stand before thee all the days of thy life: as I was with Moses, so will I be with thee: I will not fail thee, nor forsake thee."

After the service Roosevelt, in his wheelchair, was taken on a tour of the ship by Churchill. Belowdecks, Acting Secretary of State Sumner Welles was being shown two messages to Japan drafted by Churchill, to be sent simultaneously from Washington and London, warning of severe countermeasures if Japan continued her aggression in the southwest Pacific.

As Welles was leaving *Prince of Wales*, Churchill said he didn't think "there was much hope left unless the United States made such a clear-cut declaration of preventing Japan from expanding further to the south, in which event the prevention of war between Great Britain and Japan appeared to be hopeless."

The next day Roosevelt and Churchill conferred on *Augusta*. Roosevelt felt "very strongly that every effort should be made to prevent the outbreak of war with Japan." The problem was what line to take—tough, medium or soft? Tough, said Churchill; the proposals from Tokyo were no more than "smoothly worded offers by which Japan would take all she could for the moment and give nothing for the future."

Roosevelt suggested that he negotiate "about these unacceptable conditions" and win a delay of some thirty days while Britain secured its position in the Singapore area. The month gained would be valuable. "Leave that to me," he observed. "I think I can baby them along for three months."

Confident that he had swayed Roosevelt to take the "tough" line, Churchill telegraphed Foreign Secretary Anthony Eden:

. . . AT THE END OF THE NOTE WHICH THE PRESIDENT WILL HAND TO THE JAPANESE AMBASSADOR WHEN HE RETURNS FROM HIS CRUISE IN ABOUT A WEEK'S TIME HE WILL ADD THE FOLLOWING PASSAGE, WHICH IS TAKEN FROM MY DRAFT: "ANY FURTHER ENCROACHMENT BY JAPAN IN THE SOUTHWEST PACIFIC WOULD PRODUCE A SITUATION IN WHICH THE UNITED STATES GOVERNMENT WOULD BE COMPELLED TO TAKE COUNTERMEASURES, EVEN THOUGH THESE MIGHT LEAD TO WAR BETWEEN THE UNITED STATES AND JAPAN." HE WOULD ALSO ADD SOMETHING TO THE EFFECT THAT IT WAS OBVIOUS THAT THE SOVIET BEING A FRIENDLY POWER, UNITED STATES GOVERNMENT WOULD BE SIMILARLY INTERESTED IN ANY SIMILAR CONFLICT IN THE NORTHWEST PACIFIC.

Perhaps Churchill was right, but once at home Hull, who was himself convinced that nothing would stop the Japanese except force (recently, he had told Welles over the phone, "I just don't want us to take for granted a single word they say, but to appear to do so to whatever extent it may satisfy our purpose to delay further action by them"), convinced the President to reconsider and take a more moderate course. On August 17, though it was Sunday, he sent for Ambassador Nomura. Roosevelt was in high spirits and said that if Japan halted her expansion activities and decided "to embark upon a program of peace in the Pacific," the United States would be "prepared to reopen the unofficial preparatory discussions which were broken off in July, and every effort will then be made to select a time and place to exchange views." He was intrigued by the idea of a secret meeting and even suggested that it take place in Juneau, Alaska, "around the middle of October."

Nomura immediately cabled Tokyo: A REPLY SHOULD BE MADE BEFORE THIS OPPORTUNITY IS LOST.

The following afternoon, August 18, Ambassador Grew was summoned by Foreign Minister Teijiro Toyoda. The admiral ("a sympathetic and very human type," according to Grew) said he wanted to speak frankly, as a naval officer and not as a diplomat. Japan had gone into Indochina to solve the China affair and not because of pressure from Germany. The freezing of funds which followed had left "a big black spot on the long history of peaceful relations" between Japan and America, and future historians would be unable to understand if the negotiations broke down. The solution was a meeting between the two leaders of both countries in which the problems could be settled "in a calm and friendly atmosphere on an equal basis."

Grew, who had not been informed by the State Department of the proposed Konoye-Roosevelt meeting, was taken by the novel idea. Both leaders were gentlemen from distinguished families and they could reach an honorable settlement. Moreover, he would be in attendance and it could be the crowning moment of his own career.

With the heat so oppressive in the ministry, the admiral ordered iced drinks and cold wet towels, and suggested that they remove their coats. As they swabbed themselves with the towels, Grew said, "Admiral, you have often stood on the bridge of a battleship and have seen bad storms which lasted for several days, but ever since you took over the bridge of the Foreign Office you have undergone one long, continuous storm without any rest. You and I will have to pour some oil on those angry waves."

The meeting lasted for an hour and a half, and as soon as Grew returned to the embassy he sent an extraordinary message to Hull:

. . . THE AMBASSADOR [Grew] URGES . . . WITH ALL THE FORCE AT HIS COMMAND, FOR THE SAKE OF AVOIDING THE OBVIOUSLY GROWING POSSIBILITY OF AN UTTERLY FUTILE WAR BETWEEN JAPAN AND THE UNITED STATES, THAT THIS JAPANESE PROPOSAL NOT BE TURNED ASIDE WITHOUT VERY PRAYERFUL CONSIDERATION. NOT ONLY IS THE PROPOSAL UNPRECEDENTED IN JAPANESE HISTORY, BUT

IT IS AN INDICATION THAT JAPANESE INTRANSIGENCE IS
NOT CRYSTALLIZED COMPLETELY OWING TO THE FACT
THAT THE PROPOSAL HAS THE APPROVAL OF THE EMPEROR
AND THE HIGHEST AUTHORITIES IN THE LAND. THE GOOD
WHICH MAY FLOW FROM A MEETING BETWEEN PRINCE
KONOYE AND PRESIDENT ROOSEVELT IS INCALCULABLE.
THE OPPORTUNITY IS HERE PRESENTED, THE AMBASSADOR
VENTURES TO BELIEVE, FOR AN ACT OF THE HIGHEST
STATESMANSHIP, SUCH AS THE RECENT MEETING OF PRES-
IDENT ROOSEVELT WITH PRIME MINISTER CHURCHILL AT
SEA, WITH THE POSSIBLE OVERCOMING THEREBY OF AP-
PARENTLY INSURMOUNTABLE OBSTACLES TO PEACE HERE-
AFTER IN THE PACIFIC.

A few weeks before, Colonel Iwakuro and Ikawa, who had
labored so diligently on the Draft Understanding, realized
that their attempt at independent diplomacy had failed. On
the last day of July they had left Washington, arriving home
two weeks later. Iwakuro was struck by the warlike atmosphere in Tokyo on all levels. There was growing hatred of
America and Britain and a general feeling that the ABCD
encirclement was strangling the nation. In America the pre-
dominant mood, though anti-Axis, seemed one of peace.
Antiwar groups were picketing the White House, and the
isolationists' opposition to Roosevelt's aid to China and Britain was widespread and vocal. A bill extending the service of
draftees had passed with a margin of one vote, and in Army
camps the word Ohio was given a cryptic meaning—Over the
Hill In October.

Iwakuro made dozens of speeches to top-level military,
political and industrial groups urging that the negotiations be
continued; America's potential was far superior to Japan's
and a conflict would end in disaster. But the staff officers
were far more interested in talking about an advance to the
south, and at naval headquarters one said, "Japan is blockaded by the ABCD line. We cannot afford to lose time. We
have only one course now—to fight." Iwakuro remembered
that several months before, the Navy had been almost solidly
aligned for a peaceful settlement with America, and sadly
concluded that "the die was cast."

Nevertheless, he refused to give up and went pleading
from ministry to ministry. But his words had no more effect
than "hitting a nail into rice bran." During the last week in
August he attended a liaison conference, where he contrasted
the alarming differences between American and Japanese war
potential. In steel, he said, the ratio was 20 to 1; oil more

106

han 100 to 1; coal 10 to 1; planes 5 to 1; shipping 2 to 1; labor force 5 to 1. The overall potential was 10 to 1. At such odds, Japan could not possibly win, despite *Yamato yamashii*—the spirit of Japan. For once his listeners were impressed and Tojo ordered Iwakuro to make a written report of everything he had just said.

The following day Iwakuro arrived at the War Minister's office to discuss the report but was summarily told by Tojo that he was being transferred to a unit in Cambodia. "You need not submit the notes in writing I requested yesterday."

As Iwakuro was boarding the train for the first leg of the trip south, he told his friends, "So many of you have come to bid me farewell, but when I return to Tokyo—if I survive—I'm afraid I shall find myself alone in the ruins of Tokyo station."

Iwakuro's missionary zeal may have caused his banishment but he was not alone in his views, and they brought about a dramatic policy reversal. The military leaders had finally agreed, after long arguments, to avoid war with the United States even at the cost of major concessions. On the day of Iwakuro's departure—it was August 28—two messages were on their way to Franklin Roosevelt. One was a letter from Konoye again requesting a meeting, and the other an official proposal to withdraw all Japanese troops from Indochina once the China Incident was settled or a "just peace" was established in East Asia. Japan further promised to make no military advances into neighboring countries and to take no military action against the Soviet Union as long as Russia remained "faithful to the Soviet-Japanese neutrality treaty" and did not "menace Japan or Manchukuo." Far more important, the Japanese consented to abide by Hull's basic four principles—which had by now arrived in an official U. S. missive.

. . . Regarding the principles and directives set forth in detail by the American Government and envisaged in the informal conversations as constituting a program for the Pacific area, the Japanese Government wishes to state that it considers that these principles and the practical application thereof, in the friendliest manner possible, are the prime requisites of a true peace and should be applied not only in the Pacific area but throughout the world. . . .

The proposal was a negation of policies championed for months—and, though limited, gave promise of more concessions to come. Roosevelt's first reaction to it was one of optimism and he made tentative plans to spend three days or so with Konoye. But Dr. Stanley Hornbeck didn't believe the offer was sincere and when Hull read MAGIC intercepts of a military buildup in Southeast Asia, it was not surprising that he, too, became suspicious of the Japanese. Nor was it any wonder that Roosevelt, who still "relished a meeting with Konoye," was easily persuaded that it should not be held "without first arriving at a satisfactory agreement." In other words, the Americans, who didn't believe what they were offered in the first place, would not bargain unless they were previously assured that their own conditions would be generally met.

In Tokyo, Grew and his staff were more than willing to take the new proposal at face value and were convinced that Konoye would agree "to the eventual withdrawal of Japanese forces from all of Indochina and from all of China with the face-saving expedient of being permitted to retain a limited number of troops in North China and Inner Mongolia temporarily." Accordingly, Grew pleaded that the Konoye-Roosevelt meeting be approved before time ran out. For months he had warned Washington that the Japanese Army was "capable of sudden and surprise action" and that traditionally in Japan "a national psychology of desperation develops into a determination to risk all."

This psychology of desperation overshadowed the session of the liaison conference which started at eleven o'clock on September 3, next door to the Palace in the Imperial Household Ministry.* As yet no official word had come from Roosevelt, and the members were filled with misgivings. Had it been a mistake to make such a conciliatory offer? Were the Americans simply playing for time?

"With each day we will get weaker and weaker, until finally we won't be able to stand on our feet," said Navy Chief of Staff Nagano. "Although I feel sure that we have a chance to win a war right now, I'm afraid this chance will vanish with the passage of time." There was no way to "checkmate the enemy's king"—industrial potential—and a decisive initial victory was essential. "Thus our only recourse is to forge ahead!"

---

*It was assumed that security leaks, such as those reported by Ambassador Oshima in Berlin, had come from Cabinet civilians, and to seal these off, all liaison conferences, after July 21, were held on the Palace grounds. MAGIC, of course, continued to keep U. S. officials informed of most political decisions.

These words brought the Army to the point of panic, and Chief of Staff Gen Sugiyama introduced a new element—a deadline. "We must try to achieve our diplomatic objectives by October 10," he said. "If this fails we must dash forward. Things cannot be allowed to drag out."

It was a perilous suggestion and might mean war. Yet the two who wanted peace the most, Prince Konoye and Foreign Minister Toyoda, raised no objections. Perhaps they secretly felt that the negotiations would be successfully concluded within the five weeks of grace, and the only substantial argument was over phraseology. After seven hours they all finally fixed the following policy: "For the self-defense and self-preservation of our empire, we will complete preparations for war, with the first ten days of October as a tentative deadline, determined, if necessary, to wage war against the United States, Great Britain and the Netherlands." Concurrently they would negotiate in a sincere attempt to attain minimum objectives, but if it appeared that these were not met by October 10—war.

The operational plans for war had already been completed. Assaults by the Navy and Army would be launched simultaneously at Pearl Harbor, Hong Kong, Malaya and the Philippines.* The Army General Staff had learned about Pearl Harbor only a few days before. Several in the War Ministry also knew but, curiously, Tojo was not one of them.

The slim hope that this hastily conceived deadline would be reconsidered by the Cabinet before presentation to the Throne disappeared with the arrival, a few hours later, of a reply from Roosevelt to Japan's conciliatory proposal. It was in two parts: one was a polite refusal of Konoye's reiterated invitation to meet until they first came to agreement on the "fundamental and essential questions"; the other, an Oral Statement, was as vague and more disappointing. It was the kind of clever riposte so many diplomats seemed to delight in: it politely avoided promising anything of import while side-stepping the main issues. It noted "with satisfaction" Japan's willingness to abide by Hull's four principles but seemed to ask the question, "Do you really mean it?" and never mentioned Japan's offer to withdraw all troops from Indochina.

Since it seemed to be a deliberate rebuff (which it was not), as well as a belittling of concessions made by the Army

---

*Chapter 7 is devoted to the detailed development of plans for these attacks.

at agonizing cost (which it was), the Cabinet approved the deadline policy without argument. On September 5 Konoye went to the Palace to request an imperial conference to make the policy official. First he stopped off at the office of the Privy Seal.

"How can you suddenly present such a proposal to the Emperor!" Marquis Kido exclaimed. It sounded to him like out-and-out preparations for war. "He won't even have time to consider it." Konoye's excuse was weak.

"Couldn't you make it vague?" Kido asked. "It's too dangerous to set the limit at mid-October."

Konoye shifted uncomfortably. "You must do something!" Kido persisted. Konoye muttered that the matter had been decided at the liaison conference, and what could he do now?

At four-thirty a chamberlain announced that the Emperor was ready to see the Prime Minister. His Majesty looked up from the proposed policy. "I notice you first speak of war and then of diplomacy. I must question the Chiefs of the General Staff about this tomorrow at the conference."

"The order in which the items are listed doesn't necessarily indicate importance," Konoye replied with embarrassment. He suggested that the Chiefs of Staff come at once and give a fuller explanation of the Supreme Command's position, and at six o'clock he returned with General Sugiyama and Admiral Nagano.

The Emperor asked if the operations in the south would succeed as planned and was given a detailed presentation of the operational plans for the Malay and Philippine campaigns. But these details didn't relieve his concern. "Is there a possibility that the operations will not proceed on schedule? You say five months, but isn't it possible it won't work out that way?"

"The Army and Navy have studied the whole matter a number of times," Sugiyama explained. "Therefore, I imagine we'll be able to carry out the operations as planned."

"Do you think the landing operations can be carried out so easily?"

"I do not believe it will be easy, but since both the Army and the Navy are constantly training, I feel confident we'll be able to do it successfully."

"In the landing maneuvers on Kyushu a considerable number of ships were 'sunk.' What would you do if the same thing happened in reality?"

Sugiyama was disconcerted. "That was because the convoy

had started cruising before enemy planes were shot down. I don't believe that will happen."

"Are you sure it will work out as planned?" the Emperor persisted. "When you were War Minister you said Chiang Kai-shek would be defeated quickly, but you still haven't been able to do it."

"The interior of China is so vast," said the chagrined Sugiyama.

"I know, but the South Seas are much wider." The Emperor was agitated and showed it. "How can you possibly say you can end the war in five months?"

Sugiyama tried to answer. He said Japan's strength was gradually diminishing and that it was necessary to strengthen national prosperity while the empire still had its resiliency.

This was no answer and the Emperor interrupted him. "Can we absolutely win?"

"I couldn't say 'absolutely.' However, I will say that we can probably win; I don't dare say we can absolutely win. It won't help Japan to gain peace for half a year or a year if this were followed by a national crisis. I believe we should seek peace that will last twenty years or fifty years."

"Ah so, I understand!" the Emperor exclaimed in an unnaturally loud voice.

Sugiyama saw that he was still troubled. "We'd rather not fight at all. We think we should try our best to negotiate, and only when we're pushed to the edge shall we fight."

Nagano immediately came to his colleague's assistance. "It is, I think, like a critically ill patient awaiting a surgical operation." The decision to operate had to be made quickly. No operation meant the gradual decline of the patient. Operation, though an extreme measure, might save his life. But a quick decision was essential. "The Supreme Command hopes for successful negotiations, but if they fail, an operation is necessary." He quickly added that diplomacy was, of course, of "primary importance."

"Am I to understand that the Supreme Command now gives first preference to diplomacy?" Both Chiefs said yes and the Emperor seemed to be reassured.

But the next morning at nine-forty—it was September 6—he sent for Kido, just before the imperial conference was to start. Could Japan win a war against America? he asked. What about the negotiations in Washington?

Kido advised the Emperor to remain silent at first and leave the questions to Privy Council President Hara; he had already instructed Hara what these should be. But once the

111

discussion was over, the Emperor should break precedent. He should cease to reign, that is, and momentarily rule: "Instruct the Chiefs of Staff to co-operate with the government in making the negotiations successful." Only through such a dramatic break in tradition could the disastrous dead-line policy be reversed.

As members filed into the conference room, Konoye took aside General Teiichi Suzuki, who had been brought in as an expert on resources, and showed him the new policy. A glance convinced Suzuki that it should not be presented to the Emperor. Konoye was in accord but said that the Supreme Command, and Tojo in particular, insisted on speed and if the imperial conference was put off even for twenty-four hours, the Cabinet would probably have to resign. "Whether we go to war or not will be decided later. This is merely a decision to prepare for battle while negotiating. Therefore I'm going to let this go through."

Promptly at ten o'clock the crucial meeting opened. "With your permission, I will take the chair so we may proceed," Konoye began, and reviewed the tense international situation. Everyone sat stiffly, hands on knees, as Navy Chief of Staff Nagano urged that every effort be made to negotiate. But if Japan's minimum demands were not met, the problem could only be solved by "aggressive military operations," despite America's "unassailable position, her vaster industrial power and her abundant resources."

The Army Chief of Staff reiterated the same hope for successful negotiations, and General Suzuki spoke about the grim state of national resources. Even with strict wartime control, the liquid-fuel stockpile would be exhausted in ten months. "If the negotiations in Washington succeed, fine; but if not and we wait too long, it would be disastrous." There were three alternatives: start war preparations at once; continue the negotiations; or just sit and starve. "The third is unthinkable. Therefore we must choose between the first two."

The practical Hara stood up. The time had passed for conventional diplomacy, he said, and praised Konoye for his resolution to meet Roosevelt and come to some agreement. He held aloft a draft of the new policy. "This draft seems to imply that war comes first and diplomacy second, but can't I interpret this to mean that we'll do our utmost in diplomacy and go to war only when there is no other recourse?"

"President Hara's interpretation and my intentions when I

composed the draft are exactly the same," said Navy Minister Oikawa.

But the more the military explained, the more it bothered Hara. "This draft still gives me the impression that we will turn to belligerency rather than diplomacy. Or are you actually going to place emphasis on diplomacy? I should like to have the views of the government as well as of the Supreme Command."

In the embarrassing silence the Emperor stared at the conferees, then did the unheard-of. He said in his loud, high-pitched voice, "Why don't you answer?"

Not since the 2/26 Incident had he abandoned his role as passive emperor. His listeners were stunned at the sound of his voice and it was a long moment before a member of the Cabinet finally rose. It was Navy Minister Oikawa. "We will start war preparations but, of course, we'll also exert every effort to negotiate."

There was another pause as the others waited for one of the Chiefs of Staff to speak. But both Nagano and Sugiyama sat paralyzed.

"I am sorry the Supreme Command has nothing to say," the Emperor remarked. He took a piece of paper from his pocket and began reading a poem written by his grandfather, Emperor Meiji:

> "All the seas, everywhere,
>   are brothers one to another
> Why then do the winds and waves of strife
>   rage so violently through the world?"

The listeners sat awed by the Emperor's censure. There wasn't a sound or movement until the Emperor spoke again. I make it a rule to read this poem from time to time to remind me of Emperor Meiji's love of peace. How do you feel about all this?"

Finally Nagano forced himself to stand up. "Representing the Supreme Command," he said humbly, head bowed, "I express our deep regret for not replying to His Majesty's request but—" He floundered in apology. "I think exactly the same as President Hara. I made two mentions on this point in the text. Since President Hara said he understood my intentions, I didn't feel there was any need to re-emphasize the point."

Sugiyama got to his feet. "It was exactly the same with me. I was about to rise from my seat to answer President

Hara's question when Navy Minister Oikawa answered it for me." This made it unnecessary for the two Chiefs of Staff to speak. "However, I am overawed to hear His Majesty tell us directly that His Majesty regrets our silence. Allow me to assume that His Majesty feels we should make every effort to accomplish our goals by diplomatic means. I also gather His Majesty suspects that the Supreme Command may be giving first consideration to war, not to diplomacy." He assured the Emperor that this was not true.

2.

The decision to start war preparations at once while attempting to negotiate was much more than that. It meant, in fact, that hostilities would commence unless the negotiations were successfully concluded by October 10. The decision was made and approved with the Emperor's seal, but His Majesty's displeasure left a sense of doubt even among the military. He had put the accent on diplomacy, and Prime Minister Konoye realized that this gave him a last chance to achieve peace. The problem was not so much the Tojo group as the public. The controlled press had led the people to believe that the Anglo-Saxons were intent on reducing Japan to a third-rate nation, and out of all this came a rash of indignation meetings calling for action. The situation was so ominous that Ambassador Grew took to wearing a pistol although it made him feel silly and "wild west."

The danger was real: two secret organizations, which had learned of the proposed Konoye-Roosevelt meeting, were plotting to murder the Prime Minister. One had decided to make a daring, gangland-style assault in Tokyo; the other, to emulate the bombing of Marshal Chang. The latter plan was devised by a lieutenant colonel named Masanobu Tsuji, already an idol of the most radical young officers. A chauvinist of the first water, he was determined to thwart a summit meeting that was destined to end in a disgraceful peace.

As his instrument of murder he chose a civilian who had already spent two terms in prison: once for something he had done—handing the Emperor a rightist petition demanding relief for the unemployed, and once for something he had not done—throwing a stick of dynamite into the Finance Minister's home. Yoshio Kodama, leader of the most active nationalist society, shared Tsuji's convictions and approved his plan. Konoye would have to go to the meeting by ship and since there wasn't a good highway to the naval base at Yokosuka, would travel by train. As it passed over the Rokugo Bridge outside the capital, Kodama would set off an explosion.

Several hours after the imperial conference, Konoye called his mistress at the hairdresser's. There was a note of urgency in his voice as he told her to get ready at once; a car would call for her. A few minutes later she was driven to the home of Count Bunkichi Ito, son of Prince Hirobumi Ito, one of the four great men of the Meiji Restoration. There wasn't a servant in the house.

Two other cars arrived, one with Konoye and his private secretary, Tomohiko Ushiba; the other, diplomatic tags removed, carried Ambassador Grew and Embassy Counselor Eugene H. Dooman. Never before had either diplomat been invited to such a meeting. Traditionally, prime ministers had no social or official contact with foreign envoys except on state occasions.

Konoye introduced his mistress as "the daughter of the house"; she alone would serve them dinner and they could converse freely. For the next three hours Konoye and Grew talked "with the utmost frankness," with Ushiba and Dooman interpreting. Konoye assured Grew that both General Tojo and Admiral Oikawa wanted a peaceful settlement.

What about Hull's four principles? Grew asked.

Konoye said they were generally acceptable. "However, when it comes to applying them practically, various problems will arise, and to solve them I must have a meeting [with the President]." He admitted that he was to blame for the "regrettable state of relations" between America and Japan— he took the responsibility for the China Incident and the Tripartite Pact—and therefore was determined to take any personal risk to settle the differences between the two countries.

He and Roosevelt, face to face, could surely come to an agreement, but only such a meeting in the near future could accomplish this. Negotiations using the ordinary diplomatic channels would take a year. Konoye couldn't reveal, of course, that he had less than five weeks before the October 10 deadline. "A year from now," he said, "I'm not sure that anything can be done to solve our differences. But I can do it now. I promise that some agreement can be reached if I can only see him [Roosevelt]. I'll offer him a proposal which he can't afford to reject." After this cryptic remark he turned to Dooman, who was born in Osaka of missionary parents and who had already spent almost twenty-three years in Japan: "You know the conditions in this country. I want to tell you something you must not repeat to Mr. Grew. You should know so you can impress him with your belief in my sincerity. You realize that we cannot involve the Emperor in this controversy, but as soon as I have reached a settlement with the President I will communicate with His Majesty, who will immediately order the Army to cease hostile operations."

This was a bold plan, something never before attempted in Japan's history. Although impelled to tell Grew, Dooman promised to keep it a secret.

Konoye reiterated that Generals Tojo and Sugiyama had already given their consent to the proposal he could make to the United States, and the former had promised to let a full general accompany him to the summit meeting. "I will talk to the President with two generals and two admirals standing behind me." Admittedly, a certain group in the armed forces opposed peace negotiations, but with the full support of the responsible Chiefs of the Army and Navy, he was confident he could put down any opposition. He might be assassinated later, but if peace came, it would be worth it. "I do not care that much about my life."

Grew, deeply impressed by Konoye's obvious earnestness and willingness to abide by Hull's four principles, said that he was going back to the embassy and send immediately "the most important cable" of his diplomatic career.*

Though it was true that General Tojo had approved the summit meeting, he wasn't giving it his full support, so Konoye asked Prince Higashikuni, uncle-in-law of the Emperor, to use his influence on the War Minister. The next morning Higashikuni summoned Tojo: "I hear the Emperor

---

*At one point in the message Grew either embellished Konoye's remarks or had not clearly understood the Prime Minister via Dooman's translation when he declared that the Japanese "conclusively and wholeheartedly agree with the four principles enunciated by the Secretary of State ..." In his memoirs, Konoye recalled he had said "*Gensokuteki ni wa kekko de aru ga ...*"—"They are agreeable in principle." In a recent interview Ushiba confirmed the Konoye version and explained that several times during the meeting he had to correct Dooman's translations. Robert Butow translates the phrase "splendid as a matter of principle." Although "splendid" is listed in dictionaries as one translation for *kekko,* conversationally in this context it merely means "agreement without accent"—that is, "I'll go along with that."

The Grew interpretation later gave the Hornbeck group an excuse for labeling Konoye a liar.

116

is very concerned over the Washington negotiations and is putting high hopes on the Konoye-Roosevelt meeting." As war minister, Tojo should respect His Majesty's feelings and take a more positive view of this meeting as well as of Japan's problems with America.

"I am sorry indeed for the inadequate explanation given to the Throne," said Tojo tightly. "In the future I will certainly see to it that the Army explains so His Majesty fully understands. I am quite aware of the Emperor's views on the Japan-U. S. negotiations and the Konoye-Roosevelt meeting." He promised to do his best as war minister to bring about the meeting, although he personally didn't think it had more than a 30 percent chance of success. "Nevertheless, if there is the slightest hope of success, I believe we should conduct the negotiations." He became more agitated and vowed that if the diplomatic settlement turned out to Japan's future disadvantage he would have to "remonstrate with His Majesty," and if the Emperor refused to heed this advice, he would be forced to resign. "That is the only way I can fulfill my loyalty to His Majesty."

Higashikuni let Tojo speak without interruption. Now he said reminiscently, "While I was in France, Pétain and Clemenceau told me, 'Germany was an eyesore to the United States in Europe and it did away with her in the Great War. In the next war it will try to get rid of another eyesore, this one in the Orient, Japan. America knows how inept Japan is diplomatically, so she'll make moves to abuse you inch by inch until you start a fight. But if you lose your temper and start a war you will surely be defeated, because America has great strength. So you must bear anything and not play into her hands.' The present situation is exactly as Pétain and Clemenceau predicted. At this time we must persevere so that we won't get into war with America. You're a member of the Konoye Cabinet. In the Army, an order must be obeyed. Now the Emperor and the Prime Minister want to bring about the negotiations. As war minister, you should either follow their line of policy or resign."

The desperation of the Japanese should have been obvious to the Americans when Hull's cool reception of their offer to get out of Indochina and abide by his four principles was followed by two more Japanese proposals the very next day. One, submitted to Grew, promised to resort to no military action against any regions lying south of Japan and to withdraw troops from China once peace was achieved. In return

117

America would rescind the freezing act and suspend her own military measures in the Far East and southwest Pacific.

This was an official offer, but the second was not. Without informing Tokyo, Nomura handed Hull a long statement drafted months earlier, during the days of Colonel Iwakuro; apparently the admiral thought the old formula would appeal to Hull. All it did was confuse him. With two proposals in hand, covering entirely different points, he quite rightly wondered just where Japan stood.

It took about a week to straighten out the tangle and answer the official proposal. Hull told Nomura it "narrowed down the spirit and scope of the proposed understandings," and handed over half a dozen pages of objections.

The delay and the apparent reluctance to come to a quick agreement convinced the militarists in Tokya that Hull was playing for time. They turned on Konoye in public as well as in private. Widespread vocal criticism was climaxed by a physical attack on the Prime Minister on September 18. As he was leaving his quiet, rural refuge in Ogikubo, a suburb about forty-five minutes' drive from the center of Tokyo, four men, armed with daggers and swords, leaped up on the runningboards of his car. But the doors were locked and before the would-be assassins could break the glass they were seized by plain-clothes men.

Konoye was less concerned with violence than with the approaching deadline—he had less than three weeks to make a peaceful settlement and Roosevelt still declined to set a date for their meeting. Grew knew nothing about the deadline but sensed the urgency, four days after the assassination attempt, when he was summoned to the office of the Foreign Minister. Toyoda said he couldn't understand Hull's remark that the latest proposal narrowed the scope of the negotiations—on the contrary, it was widened. Toyoda was willing to go further, and set forth the peace terms Japan was now prepared to offer China: fusion of the Chiang Kai-shek and Wang Ching-wei governments; no annexations; no indemnities; economic cooperation; and withdrawal of all Japanese troops except those needed in certain areas to help the Chinese fight the Reds.

Grew dispatched this new offer to Hull, and in view of the critical situation decided to make a special appeal of his own. Presuming on his long friendship with Roosevelt (they had served together on the staff of the Harvard *Crimson*), he wrote directly to the President:

I have not bothered you with personal letters for some time for the good reason that letters are now subject to long delays owing to the infrequent sailings of ships carrying our diplomatic pouches, and because developments in American-Japanese relations are moving so comparatively rapidly that my comments would generally be too much out-of-date to be helpful when they reach you. But I have tried and am constantly trying in my telegrams to the Secretary of State to paint an accurate picture of the moving scene from day to day. I hope that you see them regularly.

As you know from my telegrams, I am in close touch with Prince Konoye who in the face of bitter antagonism from extremist and pro-Axis elements in the country is courageously working for an improvement in Japan's relations with the United States. He bears the heavy responsibility for having allowed our relations to come to such a pass and he no doubt now sees the handwriting on the wall and realizes that Japan has nothing to hope for from the Tripartite Pact and must shift her orientation of policy if she is to avoid disaster; but whatever the incentive that has led to his present efforts, I am convinced that he now means business and will go as far as is possible, without incurring open rebellion in Japan, to reach a reasonable understanding with us. In spite of all the evidence of Japan's bad faith in times past in failing to live up to her commitments, I believe that there is a better chance of the present Government implementing whatever commitments it may now undertake than has been the case in recent years. It seems to me highly unlikely that this chance will come again or that any Japanese statesman other than Prince Konoye could succeed in controlling the military extremists in carrying through a policy which they, in their ignorance of international affairs and economic laws, resent and oppose. The alternative to reaching a settlement now would be the greatly increased probability of war,—*Facilis descensus Averno est*—and while we would undoubtedly win in the end, I question whether it is in our own interest to see an impoverished Japan reduced to the position of a third-rate Power. I therefore most earnestly hope that we can come to terms, even if we must take on trust, at least to some degree, the continued good faith and ability of the present Government fully to implement those terms. . . .

The letter had as little effect as earlier recommendations (in fact, it merely provoked a bland acknowledgment five weeks later) and Konoye felt so desperate at the finish of the September 25 liaison conference, where the Supreme Command demanded an irrevocable deadline of October 15, that he refused to eat the lunch prepared at Imperial Headquarters and instead invited the Cabinet to accompany him to his official residence. Here, he applied pressure on Tojo. Was the

October 15 deadline a demand or a request on the part of the Supreme Command?

"It was a definitely set opinion but not a demand," replied the War Minister. It was just putting into effect what had been previously decided at the imperial conference of September 6. "And that decision cannot be easily changed now."

Against such resolve Konoye felt helpless and he told Marquis Kido that with the Army insisting on the deadline, all he could do was resign. Kido chastised him as if he were a child. Between Konoye and Kido, according to Ushiba, existed a unique informality. With the Privy Seal, Konoye showed a rare side of himself—he discarded all pretense. Now, since Konoye was responsible for the decision of September 6, it would be "irresponsible to step out by leaving things as they are." Be "prudent," Kido cautioned.

Konoye didn't answer. Despondent, his mood aggravated by another intense attack of piles, he left and told his private secretary he had to think things over in peace and tranquillity. And so, on September 27, he quit the capital for the nearby seaside resort of Kamakura.

3.

To the people in the State Department, nine thousand miles away, Japan's Prime Minister was an aggressor. Hull could not forget that Konoye had been prime minister when China was overrun and the Tripartite Pact consummated. And although Konoye expressed support for the four principles, did he mean it? For all these reasons any meeting with Roosevelt, without first working out the details, would be a fiasco.

Hull's apprehensions chilled Roosevelt's initial enthusiasm for the meeting, and on September 28 the President sent his Secretary of State a memo from Hyde Park:

I wholly agree with your pencilled note—to recite the more liberal original attitude of the Japanese when they first sought the meeting, point out their much narrowed position now, earnestly ask if they cannot go back to their original attitude, start discussions again on agreement in principle, and reemphasize my hope for a meeting.

In Tokyo, however, Ambassador Grew had not yet given up hope, and he was so certain that those in Washington

120

lacked insight into the problems faced by Konoye that the following day he sent another report to Hull. It was as much a warning as an appeal:

> . . . THE AMBASSADOR [Grew] RECALLS HIS STATEMENTS IN THE PAST THAT IN JAPAN THE PENDULUM ALWAYS SWINGS BETWEEN MODERATE AND EXTREMIST POLICIES; THAT IT WAS NOT THEN POSSIBLE UNDER THE EXISTING CIRCUMSTANCES FOR ANY JAPANESE LEADER OR GROUP TO REVERSE THE PROGRAM OF EXPANSION AND EXPECT TO SURVIVE; THAT THE PERMANENT DIGGING IN BY JAPANESE IN CHINA AND THE PUSHING OF THE JAPANESE ADVANCE TO THE SOUTH COULD BE PREVENTED ONLY BY INSUPERABLE OBSTACLES. . . .
>
> THE AMBASSADOR STRESSES THE IMPORTANCE OF UNDERSTANDING JAPANESE PSYCHOLOGY, FUNDAMENTALLY UNLIKE THAT OF ANY WESTERN NATION. JAPANESE REACTIONS TO ANY PARTICULAR SET OF CIRCUMSTANCES CANNOT BE MEASURED, NOR CAN JAPANESE ACTIONS BE PREDICTED BY ANY WESTERN MEASURING ROD. . . .
>
> SHOULD THE UNITED STATES EXPECT OR AWAIT AGREEMENT BY THE JAPANESE GOVERNMENT, IN THE PRESENT PRELIMINARY CONVERSATIONS, TO CLEAR-CUT COMMITMENTS WHICH WILL SATISFY THE UNITED STATES GOVERNMENT BOTH AS TO PRINCIPLE AND AS TO CONCRETE DETAIL, ALMOST CERTAINLY THE CONVERSATIONS WILL DRAG ALONG INDEFINITELY AND UNPRODUCTIVELY UNTIL THE KONOYE CABINET AND ITS SUPPORTING ELEMENTS DESIRING RAPPROCHEMENT WITH THE UNITED STATES WILL COME TO THE CONCLUSION THAT THE OUTLOOK FOR AN AGREEMENT IS HOPELESS AND THAT THE UNITED STATES GOVERNMENT IS ONLY PLAYING FOR TIME. . . . THIS WILL RESULT IN THE KONOYE GOVERNMENT'S BEING DISCREDITED AND IN A REVULSION OF ANTI-AMERICAN FEELING, AND THIS MAY AND PROBABLY WILL LEAD TO UNBRIDLED ACTS. . . .

He ended with the observation that unless America placed a "reasonable amount of confidence" in Konoye and his supporters to remold Japan, it was the end "to the hope that ultimate war may be avoided in the Pacific."

The next day Grew wrote in his diary that he had done his "level best to paint to our Government an accurate picture of the situation in Japan." He was upset by receipt from Hornbeck of a batch of recommendations he himself had earlier made to be firm with Japan.

I don't quite know just what was in Stanley Hornbeck's mind in sending me those excerpts, unless it was in the belief, and with the purpose of calling attention to that belief, that I am now advocating so-called "appeasement" in contra-distinction to my former recommendations for a strong policy. In the first place, "appeasement," through association with Munich and umbrellas, has become an unfortunate, ill-used and misinterpreted term. It is not appeasement that I now advocate, but "constructive conciliation." That word "constructive" is important. It connotes building, and no one is going to be foolish enough to try to build any structure, if it is to be a permanent structure, on an insecure foundation. . . . What the eventual outcome will be, I do not know; nobody knows; but defeatism is not within my philosophy.

Hornbeck was right about Grew to a certain extent. Perhaps he *was* too trustful of the Japanese. Nor was he intellectual or even particularly keen. He did have three great assets: a sensitive wife with a rare sympathy for Japan; an adviser (Dooman) born in Japan with an equally rare understanding of that country's flaws and virtues; and finally, his own overriding sense of honor and duty. Moreover, his beliefs and convictions were shared by a canny British colleague, Ambassador Craigie. At four-twenty the next morning he telegraphed Foreign Secretary Anthony Eden:

. . . I DO NOT QUESTION THE VIEW THAT JAPAN'S MOTIVES MAY BE MIXED, BUT IS THIS IN ITSELF A REASON FOR DOING NOTHING TO ENCOURAGE JAPAN ALONG THE NEW PATH ON WHICH THE PRESENT GOVERNMENT HAVE NOW ENTERED? EVEN ASSUMING JAPANESE POLICY TO BE ACTUATED SOLELY BY THE IDEA THAT IDENTICAL AMBITIONS CAN FOR THE MOMENT BEST BE SERVED BY A CHANGE OF TECHNIQUE (A VIEW TO WHICH I DO NOT ALTOGETHER SUBSCRIBE), THERE IS NO CHANCE OF JAPAN'S EXPANSIONIST AIMS BEING REALIZED IN THE IMMEDIATE POSTWAR FUTURE, ONCE GERMANY HAS BEEN DEFEATED. FOR THIS REASON AND BECAUSE TO KEEP JAPAN NEUTRAL WILL CONTRIBUTE TO THE DEFEAT OF GERMANY, I VENTURE THE OPINION THAT POST-MORTEM ON OUR HORIZON [This telegram was in code and a few words in the copy made available to the author were not decoded. HORIZON probably meant "part"] MAY LEGITIMATELY BE BOUNDED BY LIMITS OF WAR. . . .

Since Matsuoka's departure a radical change had occurred in the political situation and there was now a steady swing from the Axis.

THE ALL-IMPORTANT QUESTION AT THE MOMENT IS THE DISCUSSION NOW PROCEEDING BETWEEN THE UNITED STATES AND THE JAPANESE GOVERNMENT. THE MAIN DIFFICULTY APPEARS TO BE THAT, WHILE THE JAPANESE WANT SPEED AND CANNOT YET AFFORD TO GO BEYOND GENERALIZATIONS, THE AMERICANS SEEM TO BE PLAYING FOR TIME AND TO DEMAND THE UTMOST PRECISION IN DEFINITION BEFORE AGREEING TO ANY CONTRACT FOR A STEP OF RAPPROCHEMENT . . . IF PERSISTED IN, IT BIDS FAIR TO WRECK THE BEST CHANCE OF BRINGING ABOUT A JUST SETTLEMENT OF FAR EASTERN ISSUES, WHICH HAS OCCURRED SINCE MY ARRIVAL IN JAPAN.

MY UNITED STATES COLLEAGUE AND I CONSIDER THAT PRINCE KONOYE IS TELEPHONE [probably "most"] SINCERE IN HIS DESIRE TO AVERT THE DANGERS TOWARDS WHICH HE NOW SEES THE TRIPARTITE PACT AND THE AXIS' CONNECTION (FOR WHICH HE NATURALLY ACCEPTS HIS SHARE OF RESPONSIBILITY) ARE RAPIDLY LEADING JAPAN . . . DESPITE THE EMPEROR'S STRONG BACKING. I DOUBT IF HE AND HIS GOVERNMENT BRITISH CONSULAR OFFICER [probably "can"] SURVIVE IF THE DISCUSSIONS PROVE ABORTIVE OR DRAG ON UNDULY.

He admitted that any agreement might make Chiang Kaishek suspicious and discouraged, and that America's interest in the Far East was not wholly identical with Britain's.

. . . BUT THE RISKS MUST BE FACED EITHER REPAIRED [probably "in any case"], AND MY UNITED STATES COLLEAGUE AND I ARE FIRMLY OF THE OPINION THAT ON BALANCE THIS IS A CHANCE WHICH IT WOULD BE ILLEGIBLE [probably "inexcusable"] FOLLY TO LET SLIP. CAUTION MUST BE EXERCISED, BUT AN EXCESSIVE CYNICISM BRINGS STAGNATION . . .

It was not until October 2 that Hull finally gave some definite answers to the questions the Japanese had long been awaiting. He "welcomed" a summit meeting and found Konoye's acceptance of the four principles "gratifying," but the proposals themselves were unacceptable, particularly those on China—all Japanese troops had to be withdrawn without delay. Therefore the meeting would have to be postponed until there was "a meeting of minds on essential points."

"We have no desire whatever to cause any delay," he hastened to assure Nomura. It was a deception that must have been repugnant to such an honorable man; surely Hull had not forgotten the reiterated pleas of General George C.

Marshall, the Army Chief of Staff, and Admiral Harold R. Stark, Chief of Naval Operations, for more time to reinforce the Pacific. Ironically, it was giving them less by accelerating Japan's necessity to make a decision for war. At eleven o'clock on October 5, the Army division and bureau chiefs met in Tojo's office and concluded: "There is no possibility to settle the matter by diplomatic negotiations. We must therefore petition the Emperor to hold an imperial conference and decide upon war."

Konoye returned from his holiday more discouraged than ever. His associates were just as disheartened. Marquis Kido alone had not given up hope for peace. "Judging the situation both at home and abroad, it is difficult to predict the outcome of a war between Japan and America," he told the prince. "We should, therefore, re-examine the situation. Instead of making an immediate decision to declare war on the United States, the government should make clear that its first consideration is to bring the China Incident to a successful conclusion. The people should be told flatly that we now face ten to fifteen years of *gashin-shotan*."*

It was a disagreeable solution, but realistic, and Konoye decided to pursue it. On the morning of October 12 he summoned the War, Navy and Foreign ministers and General Suzuki of the Cabinet Planning Board to his villa in Ogikubo. It was a fine Sunday, his fiftieth birthday.

Konoye's private home was a comfortable but far from ostentatious Japanese structure located on spacious grounds at the edge of the suburb. Just before the conference was to start, Chief Cabinet Secretary Kanji Tomita arrived with a note for Konoye from the chief of the Naval Affairs Bureau, Admiral Takasumi Oka: "The Navy does not want the Japanese-American negotiations stopped and wishes to avoid war if at all possible. But we cannot see our way to expressing this openly at the meeting."

Tojo somehow learned of the note and by the time he

---

*Literally, "sleep on kindling and lick gall." "This phrase is Chinese in origin," Marquis Kido explained in a personal letter. "In the dictionary it says: 'to suffer hardships and privations repeatedly in order to take revenge'; however, here it means to ask the people to endure a life of patience and austerity in order to accomplish our purposes. Not too long ago, after the Sino-Japanese War, when Japan was forced to return the Liaotung Peninsula by the Triple Intervention [of Germany, Russia and France], this phrase was first used in Japan to mean that we were to endure a life of patience and austerity until someday our national strength burgeoned and we would rise again."

reached Ogikubo he had resolved to make Navy Minister Oikawa speak out plainly. It was cowardly of the Navy to *sekinin o nasuri-tsukeru* ("transfer their responsibility"). Tojo was so nettled that he was scarcely civil to Oikawa as they sat down at a table to begin the conference. Then he blurted out impetuously, "There is no point in continuing the talks in Washington." His adamant stand forced the Navy to do what Oka had written they could not do: speak with candor. "We are now at the crossroads—war or peace," said Oikawa. "If we are to continue with diplomacy, we must give up war preparations and go in completely for talks—to negotiate for months and then suddenly change our tack won't do. . . . The Navy is willing to leave the decision entirely up to the Prime Minister . . ."

Whatever the choice, it had to be made at once, said Konoye. "It's risky either way. The question is, Which is riskier? If we have to make a decision here and now, I will be in favor of negotiations."

Tojo turned to Admiral Toyoda. "Mr. Foreign Minister, have you any confidence in negotiations?" he asked with more than a touch of sarcasm. "I'm afraid you can't persuade the Army General Staff, judging from what you've already said. I would like to hear if you have any confidence."

"Weighing both sides," Konoye replied in his stead, "I still choose negotiations."

"That's only from your own subjective point of view," said Tojo sharply. "You can't prevail on the Army General Staff." Oikawa said he concurred, but this only irked Tojo. He asked Konoye not to reach a hasty conclusion. "I want to hear the opinion of the Foreign Minister."

"That depends on the conditions," said Toyoda. "I think the thorniest issue today is the presence of troops in China, and if the Army won't concede a thing to the United States, then there's no point in continuing the talks. But if the Army can see its way clear to making some slight compromise, it may not be impossible."

"The stationing of troops is a matter of life and death to the Army!" Tojo burst out. "No concession in that direction!" Japan had already agreed in principle to the withdrawal of all troops from China, he continued. That, in itself, was a tremendous concession. Now it was obvious that America was demanding that Japan withdraw *all* troops *at once*. This was impossible. A million Japanese were still locked in battle in China. Japan could not withdraw completely until order was restored in China. The interior was a hotbed of Communists and bandits, and only the presence of Japanese troops in certain areas could guarantee law and order and the successful economic growth of that whole part of the continent. Total withdrawal before the aims of war had been accomplished "would not be in keeping with the dignity of the Army," and the entire General Staff "as well as the troops abroad" agreed with him.

"Don't you think now is the time to forget the glory and reap the fruits?" Konoye remarked. Why not give in to America in form? That is, agree in principle to withdraw all troops, yet make an arrangement with China to retain some troops in unstable areas?

Unthinkable, said Tojo. If they made a pledge they would have to honor it scrupulously; and once they bowed to the American demand, the Chinese would show contempt. They were always most to be feared when contemptuous; withdrawal would lead to a complete loss of face and the rise of Communism. It would be like a run on the bank, and Korea as well as North China would be lost.

It was Tojo against the other four, but he stuck obstinately to his opinion. "The Army has no intention of changing the decision of the imperial conference which was held the other day [September 6]. If there is hope of success in negotiation before the deadline set by the Supreme Command, then the talks should continue. The Navy Minister said the decision for war or peace rests with the Prime Minister. I don't agree at all. The decision for war should be made jointly by the government and the Supreme Command. And I don't think there is any possible way to settle the problem by diplomacy at this stage."

"I'm not confident of victory in war," Konoye retorted. "I think there is no way to overcome the present difficulties except by diplomatic negotiations. As for war, I will leave that to a person who is confident of victory." He turned to Tojo. "If you keep insisting on war, I cannot hold myself responsible for that."

"Haven't we decided to go to war if diplomacy fails?" Tojo was exasperated. "Of course, you were present at that conference. I don't see why you can't assume responsibility for that."

"That decision was really *nai-nai*," said Konoye, meaning "only among ourselves"—that is, it was a secret decision and, with the Emperor's approval, could be reconsidered. Tojo took this literally to mean "of an unofficial nature"—an insult to the Emperor—and he was so visibly agitated that

126

Konoye tried to elaborate. "Since I have greater confidence in negotiations, why should I hold myself responsible? That's all I meant. We must consider the decision for war as final only when there is no prospect of carrying on negotiations. And there is still a chance for success."

"Just suppose we do abandon war preparations," said Suzuki, envisaging another 2/26 Incident, "how can we control the Army?"

"If that is the case," said Tojo, "controlling the Army won't be difficult."

The argument continued through the afternoon, and finally ended in compromise: they would continue negotiations until October 15, or later if Imperial Headquarters approved it, but concede nothing on the stationing of troops in China to fight Communism.

Compromise or not, the meeting did have one good effect. Tojo had argued stubbornly, but on the way back to Tokyo he began to realize that the September 6 decision had been too hasty, since the Navy seemed to lack confidence. War under such circumstances could be a great mistake. Once back at the War Ministry, he summoned Kenryo Sato, who was now chief of the Military Affairs Section, and told him the Navy still seemed to be wavering.

"Mr. Minister," said Colonel Sato, "I will arrange a conference for you with the Navy Minister and the two Chiefs of Staff. Why don't you make it a private meeting over *sake* at a *machiai* [restaurant where geisha girls entertain]? You can say, 'Is the Navy confident or not about this war? The main role in such a war would be played by the Navy. If you men really don't believe in it, we must not fight this war. In that case, I promise never to say we're not fighting because the Navy lacks confidence. Instead I will take full responsibility and say, "I, the War Minister, will not fight." ' "

Tojo's face flushed and he began to sputter. "Do you mean to tell me that responsible men like the Navy Minister and the Chiefs of Staff would say at a *machiai* what they won't talk about at an imperial conference?" He refused to be party to such shameful subterfuge.

Out of the inconclusive meeting at Ogikubo came rumors of a Cabinet crisis and a possible declaration of war. Konoye was already regretting the compromise. With no further concessions on China, it would be impossible to conclude a settlement with America. He wondered what he could possibly do before time ran out, then decided to speak to Tojo informally. He phoned the War Minister early in the morning of October

14 and arranged to see him just before the ten o'clock Cabinet meeting.

"I can go along with you except for your stand on our troops in China," Konoye said and suggested they withdraw all troops at once "for formality's sake."

Tojo bristled; Konoye was already going back on his word. "If once we give in, the United States will assume a high-handed attitude and keep on acting that way. Your solution is really not a solution. War will crop up again in a few years. I respect you, Mr. Prime Minister, but your view is too pessimistic. You know our weak points too well . . . America has her weaknesses too."

"That's a matter of opinion." Konoye reminded him that on February 4, 1904, Emperor Meiji summoned Prince Ito and asked if Japan could defeat Russia. Ito replied that the enemy could be checked at the Korean border for a year. In the meantime America would be asked to mediate a peace. Relieved, Emperor Meiji had sanctioned a declaration of war. In the present case, however, there was no third party to mediate. Therefore, they must proceed with great caution, particularly since America had such tremendous superiority in material resources.

Tojo stiffened at the word "caution." "There are times when we must have the courage to do extraordinary things— like jumping, with eyes closed, off the veranda of the Kiyomizu Temple!"*

Konoye said that was possible only for a private individual. "People in responsible positions should not think that way."

Tojo looked at him with scorn and said, "All this is a matter of difference in our personalities, isn't it?" He thought, This man is too weak to be prime minister at such a critical time; he can't even keep a promise.

Tojo went into the Cabinet meeting determined to repudiate his own promise, and take such a strong stand that Konoye would be forced to resign. By the time the meeting started he had purposely worked himself into a state of excitement. Flicking a piece of paper, he said, "The Army will continue its preparations. I don't mean this will necessarily interfere with the negotiations, but I will not consider another day's delay!" He swung on Foreign Minister Toyoda and

---

*A Buddhist temple located on a hill at the edge of a ravine in Kyoto.

asked if he thought the talks with America would be successful.

"The point of dispute," reiterated the admiral, "is the withdrawal of troops. The United States is not satisfied with Japan's reply. If we are to answer again on this matter, we must do so in a straightforward manner. . . . America is becoming more and more suspicious of our attitude, so we can't satisfy them unless we give them facts. They cannot understand Japan's way of carrying on peace talks while preparing for war."

"I make no concessions regarding withdrawal!" shouted Tojo as if he had lost his temper—and perhaps by now he had. "It means defeat of Japan by the United States—a stain on the history of the Japanese Empire! The way of diplomacy isn't always a matter of concession; sometimes it is oppression. If we concede, Manchuria and Korea will be lost." He repeated all his old arguments, but this time with a fervor that moved the listeners. Then he turned his wrath on the Navy, and Oikawa in particular, for failing to declare openly and frankly if they could beat America. Konoye and the Cabinet sat in silence, petrified by Tojo's "bomb speech."

Tojo's outburst did what he had hoped. Several hours after the meeting, General Suzuki came to his office to say that he was acting as Konoye's go-between: he could not continue as prime minister since the War Minister had publicly expressed such a forceful opinion.

Tojo refused to retract his statement and said Konoye could only continue in office if he was willing to go along. But others in the Army were alarmed at the thought of a Konoye resignation. General Muto conceded to Suzuki that although the Prime Minister was a coward, he alone could maintain the unity of the nation. "If he resigns, Japan cannot fight a war." Muto paced around and half jokingly said, "How about carrying out a big maneuver in Manchuria so the troops can let off steam?"

Later that afternoon Muto called on Konoye's cabinet secretary, Kanji Tomita, and said, "Somehow or other it seems that the reason the Prime Minister can't make up his mind is because the Navy can't make up its mind." The Army would have to reconsider the entire matter if it was sure the Navy really didn't want war. "But the Navy just says it will 'leave the decision entirely up to the Prime Minister.' Saying that isn't enough to control the inner circle of the Army. That can only be done if the Navy openly states, 'We don't wish war.' I wonder if you can arrange it so that the Navy says something along that line."

But the Navy still refused to make an official statement. "The most we can do," Admiral Oka told Tomita, "is ask the Prime Minister to deal with the matter at his own discretion."

All that day Suzuki, Tomita, Oka and Muto shuttled from office to office. Use of such go-betweens was common in critical times, since telephones might be tapped; moreover, ideas could be expressed through a middleman which would have been difficult to bring up face to face; and if things didn't go well, the go-between could simply be repudiated.

That night Suzuki returned to the War Ministry. He blamed the Navy for the impasse, then asked Tojo who should be the next prime minister. "I'd say it can be nobody but Prince Higashikuni," Tojo replied. "Even Konoye could not solve this problem, so we must call upon a member of the royal family." If the decision was for peace, the uncle-in-law of the Emperor was one of the few Japanese who could bring it about without a revolt within the Army. He could summon both Chiefs of Staff and tell them he'd decided against war. The Emperor could not do this—it was against custom and Constitution. But a prince of the royal family could, and his wishes would have to be followed by the military. Thus peace could come without civil disorder. Before they parted, Tojo said he didn't think he ought to meet again with Konoye or he might lose his temper.

Suzuki went directly to Konoye's villa in the suburbs and told him about Higashikuni as the War Minister's choice. Konoye was in accord. "Prince Higashikuni is a very good man. I know him well. He is against war. I will tell this to the Emperor when I see him tomorrow."

The next day was October 15, the deadline for peace, and Suzuki was busier than usual. In the morning he told Marquis Kido about the recommendation of Higashikuni for prime minister, but the Privy Seal showed no enthusiasm. The prince was "talented" but lacked political experience and training. More important, a member of the imperial family should not bear the responsibility in case war broke out.

At noon Suzuki heard from Konoye. He'd spoken to the Emperor, who, unlike Kido, considered Higashikuni a suitable candidate for prime minister. Konoye asked Suzuki to sound out the prince himself for his reaction.

"We in the Army are not all for war," Suzuki told Higashikuni. "I too believe you can control the situation." He added

130

that Tojo himself felt Higashikuni alone could go directly to the Emperor and find out exactly what he wanted, and then control the Army, whatever the decision—war or peace.

"This is a grave matter," said the prince. "I want some time to think it over. I'd like to talk with the War and Navy ministers before making up my mind."

That evening Konoye phoned Kido for advice. Should he talk to Prince Higashikuni informally? Too soon, said Kido. "But as long as the government takes the responsibility, I have no objection." Despite this lukewarm endorsement, Konoye secretly went at once to Higashikuni and said the negotiations could not succeed unless the Army agreed to withdraw all troops from China, and only a new cabinet led by the prince could resolve the matter and unite the Army and the Navy.

"This is too sudden and too difficult a question to decide on the spur of the moment," said the prince. "I'm against a prime minister from the royal family, but in case you organize a new cabinet and still can't come to an agreement with the Army, I might take office as a last resort, even at the risk of my life." He was far more enthusiastic about Konoye as prime minister and suggested that he form the new cabinet with a war minister who would be more open to peace than Tojo. He promised to use his considerable influence to bring this about. Konoye left the man he had come to proselyte, determined to succeed himself as prime minister.

His chief antagonist, Tojo, had also made a resolution. He was impatient for action: the deadline had come and none was being taken. Though torn by doubts, he made up his mind to force the issue by placing the question before the Emperor, and the following afternoon went to the man who could arrange an interview, Privy Seal Kido. "The time has come to act upon the decision of September 6," he demanded.

Kido said that decision had been made too abruptly, without sufficient deliberation. "It must be reconsidered."

There was reason in this reply, but Tojo brushed it off with a "Yes, I know" and took a new tack. "How about a cabinet formed by a member of the royal family?"

Kido said it would not do to pick Higashikuni. "The royal family should join the government only in times of peace."

There was also reason in this reply, but it wasn't what Tojo wanted to hear. He paused to find a rejoinder, and finding none, reverted to the September 6 decision. It had to be carried out, he said stubbornly.

131

"If we do, what will happen to Japan?"

"What do you think?"

"I think," said Kido, "that Japan will become a third- or fourth-class nation."

It was a conversation that left Tojo dejected and Kido hopeful. He sensed Tojo's doubts and was satisfied that he could be dealt with once Konoye could be persuaded to "exert himself a little harder" in the quest for peace. By coincidence he was called to the phone; it was Konoye. "I am going to resign," he said abruptly.

What Kido had feared had come with unsettling suddenness, and now he faced a task made more difficult by the times. The new cabinet would be Japan's most critical, and the burden of choice was his own. Since the death of Prince Saionji in 1940, he, as privy seal, had taken over the last *genro*'s major task because the vacuum had to be filled and because he was one who never shirked responsibility, nor made a show of it. The very anonymity of his personality had left this assumption of power unchallenged.

The new cabinet would lead the nation to war or peace and it was up to him to see that it was peace. The man who would help make the choice was the one who had made it necessary. Just before dusk Prince Konoye appeared, worn by weeks of anxiety.

"The September 6 decision should be canceled; it is a cancer," said Kido. "It should then be reconsidered under someone who is familiar with the situation." The new prime minister could not be an outsider. He must be someone of stature who had participated in the arguments of the past few months. This limited the choice to two men—Admiral Oikawa and Tojo. Since Tojo had precipitated the present crisis, perhaps Oikawa, who had expressed some doubts about the outcome of a war, should be chosen. But Oikawa might not be acceptable to the young officers, who actually ran the Army; they might resist or even revolt.

The quiet, scholarly Oikawa would of course give a better impression on the international scene. "But if we appoint him," Kido told Konoye, "the Army wouldn't select a war minister." Therefore Tojo was the sole choice. He could control the fiery elements in the military in case the decision was peace; he was a man of character with no political ambitions. He was too direct to scheme and had shown, since his appointment as war minister, that he would do whatever His Majesty wished.

It was typical of Konoye that his immediate reaction was

132

positive. Perhaps he was overreacting to his own antipathy to Tojo. They had reached the point where they could no longer meet face to face, yet Konoye began listing arguments (or were these rationalizations?) in his favor: not only could he control the Army but he had recently assumed a "rather humble" manner; he appeared to be reconciled to renewed negotiations with America. "Tojo told me the other day that since the Navy's attitude still wasn't clear, we should look into the matter thoroughly and reconsider the whole situation. So I don't think he will push for war on assuming the premiership. And he will be still more cautious if he gets words of counsel from the Throne."

Kido assured Konoye that the Emperor would surely ask Tojo to reconsider the decision. It was a scheme that no one but a pragmatist could have devised: to select a cabinet primarily because it could control the situation, and then force it to think in terms of peace by an extraordinary act of the Emperor.

Konoye left the Palace engrossed by the idea. But as he drove home with his son-in-law, he began to have doubts about Tojo, and did what few in the land would have dared—vocally blame the Emperor for the crisis. His Majesty had recently remarked, "How stupid the Army people are!" If he felt that way, why hadn't he expressed his views candidly, firmly? In normal times it was proper for an emperor to remain silent, but when the question of war or peace was at stake, he should unhesitatingly point the way.

Both Konoye and the Emperor were examples of what was most admirable in Japan, and what might lead to national disaster. Both were unselfish and without personal ambition, putting the welfare of the people ahead of everything else. Each showed he could step out of character and act decisively, but these times were too rare. This was the tragedy of Hirohito and Konoye—and Japan. That day—October 16—a new patriotic song recently broadcast over radio station JOAK appeared in the *Japan Times & Advertiser*, the nation's leading English-language newspaper:

> Siren, siren, air raid, air raid!
> What is that to us?
> Preparations are well done,
> Neighborhood associations are solid,
> Determination for defense is firm.
> Enemy planes are only mosquitoes or dragonflies.

We will win, we must win.
What of air raid?
We know no defeat.
Come to this land to be shot down.

Eugene Dooman was still dressing the next morning when the phone rang. It was Ushiba, Konoye's secretary, asking if he could come over right away. Ushiba arrived "nervous and excited" while Dooman was at breakfast, and said he had been up all night helping Konoye make arrangements for a new prime minister. He had a letter from the prince to Ambassador Grew expressing "regret and disappointment" over his resignation. It had been drafted by Ushiba after a full explanation from Konoye of why Tojo had to be his successor. Only he would be able to revoke the decision for war—"to let the Navy do it would be too provocative."

... I feel certain, however, that the cabinet which is to succeed mine will exert its utmost in continuing to a successful conclusion the conversations which we have been carrying on up till today. It is my earnest hope, therefore, that you and your Government will not be too disappointed or discouraged either by the change of cabinet or by the mere appearance or impression of the new cabinet. I assure you that I will do all in my power in assisting the new cabinet to attain the high purpose which mine has endeavored to accomplish so hard without success. ...

Shortly after one o'clock the *jushin*—the seven ex-premiers—met in the West Antechamber of the Palace to help select a prime minister. Kido was there, still determined to recommend Tojo; Konoye was not, since he was the outgoing premier.

Someone suggested that they choose a prince of the blood. Kido opposed this. If war came, "the imperial family might be faced with a storm of denunciation from the people." He suggested Tojo; he was "fully acquainted with the development of the situation" and could "effect real co-operation between the Army and the Navy." He also understood the need of reexamining the September 6 decision.

One Navy man, Admiral Okada—who as prime minister had so miraculously escaped assassination by the "2/26" rebels—disapproved someone like the War Minister. Hadn't the Army hierarchy Tojo represented proved it was tough and uncompromising? "To quote the Privy Seal: 'In the past the Army used to shoot rifles at us from the rear; I hope they don't start using cannon.' "

The man just quoted agreed that this was certainly a matter of concern; yet who but Tojo had the position, prestige and strength to control the young officers and rightists? Some Navy man?

"In my opinion, the Navy should absolutely not step in at this time," said Okada and recommended his liberal friend General Ugaki, who had favored a reduction of the armed forces back in the twenties.

Resistance to Tojo continued until three-thirty. Then Yoshimichi Hara, present in his capacity as President of the Privy Council, agreed to go along, provided Tojo would follow the policy laid down by the Emperor—that is, reconsider the September 6 decision. Koki Hirota—the civilian prime minister who had succumbed to Army pressure after the 2/26 Incident—asked if Tojo was also to retain his position as war minister.

"Yes," Kido replied.

"In that case, fine." That would give Tojo control of the Army radicals.

The other *jushin* gave their consent, but Hara spoke for all of them when he remarked, "I don't think the Privy Seal's choice is very satisfactory, but since it's the only specific one, we have nothing to do but give it a try."

Kido had got his way.

Tojo was packing. He was concerned about a possible reprimand from the Emperor for his part in the fall of Konoye and wondered where he would be assigned. At about three-thirty the Grand Chamberlain phoned and asked him to report to the Palace at once. Tojo hastily stuffed into a briefcase some papers which might support his position.

He had gone to the Palace to be admonished, and was confounded to hear the Emperor say, "We order you to form a cabinet. Observe the provisions of the Constitution. We believe that the nation is facing an extremely grave situation. Bear in mind that the Army and Navy should, at this time, work in even closer co-operation. We will later summon the Navy Minister to tell him the same."

Tojo requested time to consider and went into the waiting room. He was joined a few minutes later by Admiral Oikawa, who had just been instructed by the Emperor to work "in closer co-operation" with the Army. Kido approached them. "I assume the Emperor has just talked to you both about Army-Navy co-operation," he said and explained what His Majesty could only imply. "With regard to the decision on our *kokutai* [national essence], it is the Emperor's wish that you make an exhaustive study of domestic and foreign conditions—without regard to the decision of the September 6 imperial conference. I convey this to you as an order of the Emperor."

It was unprecedented in Japanese history. No Emperor had ever before rescinded a decision of the imperial conference. Tojo was ordered to "go back to blank paper," that is, start with a clean slate and negotiate with America for peace.

Tojo could not fully comprehend what had occurred. He managed to tell Kido that he accepted the responsibility thrust on him by the Emperor. At the Yasukuni Shrine, where the souls of Japan's war dead were enshrined, he bowed his head in prayer. Appropriately a thousand dead warriors were just being enrolled in a mass ceremony. Tojo realized that he faced a completely new life. From now on he had to think as a civilian, not as a soldier. It was a disruptive turnabout, but he forced himself to examine the problems ahead: he must at once form a cabinet based solely on merit and experience and embracing all segments of Japanese life. His would not be a military but a national cabinet and he should, above all, scrupulously follow the wishes of the Emperor. He vowed to live by a new motto: "To Have the Emperor as the Mirror of my Judgment." He would take every decision to the Emperor. If His Majesty's mirror was clean, Tojo would go ahead; if it was even slightly clouded, he would reconsider. What better criterion was there? The Emperor was born to be fair, belonged to no class and reflected the interests of the people exclusively.

He returned to find the War Ministry in ferment. Two excited generals intercepted him in the hall with their cabinet nominations. Tojo turned on his heel, muttered something about the military "meddling too much," and strode into his office to summon Naoki Hoshino, a close civilian associate from Manchuria. He was finally located at the Kabuki Theater, and when he arrived at the ministry, Tojo was sitting on the floor surrounded by papers. "I'd like you to be my secretary-general," said Tojo.

Together they began picking the new cabinet. "The Army should have no part in the selection," Tojo explained but suggested Hidehiko Ishiguro, a favorite of military men, as minister of education. Hoshino thought this might create troublesome opposition; why not keep the present minister, a professor?

"Good idea," said Tojo and crossed Ishiguro's name off his

list. "Which do you think would be better as finance minister, Aoki or Kaya?"

"They're both fine men of character and experience," said Hoshino, but since the former was in Nanking and the latter in Tokyo, Tojo put a check opposite Okinori Kaya's name. "What do you think of Togo for foreign minister?"

Hoshino said he knew him well. They had worked together when buying the Chinese Eastern Railway from the Russians. "He's quite tenacious. I think he's a good man." Tojo made another check mark.

Hoshino began phoning those selected, asking for a quick decision. Seven accepted on the spot but four, including Kaya and Togo, had doubts and insisted on speaking to Tojo first. Kaya came at once. "There are many rumors of war between Japan and America," he said. "I hear the Army is advocating this. Are you for war or not?"

"I intend to bring a peaceful solution if possible. I have no desire for war.

"It's fine that you don't want to start war, but the Supreme Command is independent," Kaya retorted and reminded Tojo of Manchuria and China.

"I will never allow the Army to start war against the wishes of the Cabinet," said Tojo.

His candor impressed Kaya, but before accepting, he decided to phone Konoye despite the late hour. The prince advised him to accept the post and do what he could to work toward peace.

Shigenori Togo,* who came from a samurai family but was no relation of the famous admiral, arrived soon after Kaya. He was a heavyset, thoughtful man who talked deliberately in a heavy Kyushu accent that was harsh to Tokyo ears. To Grew he was grim and "ultra-reserved." An experienced career diplomat, he had an understanding of European ways and had scandalized his family by marrying a German. Unlike most diplomats, however, he was in the habit of saying what he meant with a bluntness that some construed as rudeness. He wanted to make sure he could negotiate in good faith. Why had Konoye failed in the negotiations with America?

Tojo was frank. Konoye had been dismissed because the Army had insisted on stationing troops in China. The Army would have to agree "to make genuine concessions" re-

---

*Pronounced approximately like Tohngo. In Japanese the sound of g, except when it is the first letter of a word, is somewhat similar to ng.

garding the troops in China and other problems so a settlement could be reached "on a reasonable basis." Tojo added that he had no objection to reviewing any of the issues but insisted on an immediate answer so he could submit the list of ministers to the Emperor in the morning.

Togo accepted.

The next day the fifty-seven-year-old Tojo was promoted to full general, a rank commensurate with his new post. After the investiture ceremony of the Cabinet, he took the train for the Ise Shrine, the most sacred of all Shinto shrines, to pay homage, according to custom, to the Sun Goddess.

Publicly the selection of Tojo was greeted with enthusiasm. One newspaper, the *Yomiuri*, declared it should inspire the nation "to rise to the occasion and administer a great shock to the anti-Axis powers." But privately a few like Higashikuni were concerned. The prince wondered how Kido could possibly have recommended Tojo, since he was so "war-minded." And how could the Emperor have accepted him?

American opinion was divided as well. Otto Tolischus, the Tokyo correspondent of the *New York Times*, after discussing the matter with Embassy Counselor Dooman, wrote: "It would be premature to assume that the new Government will necessarily be dominated by the extremists whose belligerent pronouncements heralded the fall of Konoye. Tojo himself is a certain guarantee against this. . . . In some respects, the negotiations might even be facilitated by the change. . . . Now the United States knows that it is dealing with the Army directly."

But the one whose opinions would carry the most weight in the negotiations, Cordell Hull, characterized the new Prime Minister as a "typical Japanese officer, with a small-bore, straight-laced, one-track mind" who was "rather stupid." He had expected little good from Konoye; from Tojo he expected "even less."

5 The Fatal Note

1.

Even though the Russians didn't yet know the results of the imperial conference of July 2, one of their agents, Hotsumi Ozaki, had just heard a rumor of the decision to go south instead of attacking Siberia. For confirmation his chief, Richard Sorge, sent him to Manchuria, where he discovered that the Kwantung Army's secret order for three thousand railroad workers to help mount an attack on the Red Army had inexplicably been reduced to practically nothing. On October 4 Sorge radioed this information to Moscow, along with the latest diplomatic developments:

ACCORDING TO INFORMATION OBTAINED FROM VARIOUS JAPANESE OFFICIAL SOURCES, IF NO SATISFACTORY REPLY IS RECEIVED FROM THE U.S. TO JAPAN'S REQUEST FOR NEGOTIATIONS BY THE 15TH OR 16TH OF THIS MONTH, THERE WILL EITHER BE A GENERAL RESIGNATION OR A DRASTIC REORGANIZATION OF THE JAPANESE GOVERNMENT. IN EITHER EVENT . . . THERE WILL BE WAR WITH THE U. S. THIS MONTH OR NEXT MONTH. THE SOLE HOPE OF THE JAPANESE AUTHORITIES IS THAT AMBASSADOR GREW WILL PRESENT SOME SORT OF ELEVENTH-HOUR PROPOSAL THROUGH WHICH NEGOTIATIONS CAN BE OPENED. WITH RESPECT TO THE SOVIET UNION, TOP-RANKING ELEMENTS ARE GENERALLY AGREED THAT, IF GERMANY WINS, JAPAN CAN TAKE OVER HER GAINS IN THE FAR EAST IN THE FUTURE AND THAT THEREFORE IT IS UNNECESSARY FOR JAPAN TO FIGHT RUSSIA. THEY FEEL THAT IF GERMANY PROVES UNABLE TO DESTROY THE SOVIET GOVERNMENT AND FORCE IT OUT OF MOSCOW, JAPAN SHOULD BIDE HER TIME UNTIL NEXT SPRING. IN ANY EVENT, THE AMERICAN ISSUE AND THE QUESTION OF THE ADVANCE TO THE SOUTH ARE FAR MORE IMPORTANT THAN THE NORTHERN PROBLEM.

This remarkably accurate information, which helped influence the Red Army to transfer most of its troops from Manchuria to the western front, was the last sent by Sorge. A week later a member of his ring, Yotoku Miyagi, a thirty-eight-year-old artist with tuberculosis, was arrested by chance when a woman who had been picked up in a general anti-Communist drive by the *tokko* ("Thought" police) revealed that she had known him in America, where both had been members of the Communist party. Miyagi had become a Communist out of resentment for "the inhuman discrimination practiced against the Asiatic races" in the United States. He had in his possession a study of Japan's oil-stock level in Manchuria and other top-secret material, but refused to talk for a day. During a lunch break, in a unique try at suicide for a Japanese, Miyagi suddenly dived out a third-story window. A detective instinctively plunged after him. Both landed in a tree and Miyagi suffered a broken leg. After that he told everything he knew about Sorge's setup.

This resulted in Ozaki's arrest three days later. Both he and Miyagi were supposed to rendezvous with their chief that night, and when they failed to appear, Sorge suspected that they had been caught. As he gloomily drank cup after cup of *sake*, he became more certain than ever that his mission in Japan was over; recently he had drafted a message to Moscow requesting that he be sent to Russia or Germany "to embark on new activities."

As it happened, Sorge himself was safe for the moment. The Minister of the Interior was alarmed lest the resulting publicity reveal that Ozaki was "a close friend" of Konoye's (the connection was tenuous; he was merely an acquaintance and had gained access to the prince's celebrated discussion group, the Breakfast Club, through his classmate Ushiba), thus causing the government to fall. But since Konoye resigned the following day, this was no longer a consideration. Permission was granted to pick up Sorge.

Before dawn the next morning—the day Tojo was to be installed formally as prime minister—Sorge was arrested in bed and taken in pajamas and slippers to the Toriizaka police station. Ambassador Ott protested to the Foreign Ministry and demanded to see Sorge. When they met, Sorge seemed embarrassed. They talked of trivialities for a few moments, then Ott asked if Sorge had anything else on his mind. After a pause he said, "Mr. Ambassador, this is our final farewell. Give my regards to your wife and family."

At last Ott realized he had been betrayed by his friend. The two stared at each other silently, and once Sorge was taken away, the shaken Ott told the official in charge, "For the good of our two countries, investigate this case thoroughly. Get to the bottom of it."

At the liaison conference of October 23, Navy Chief of Staff Nagano observed somberly, "We were supposed to have reached a decision in October and yet here we are." The Navy was consuming four hundred tons of oil per hour. "The situation is urgent. We must have a decision at once, one way or the other."

The Army was in agreement. "There's already been a month's delay," Sugiyama said. "We can't waste four or five days in study. We must rush forward!"

Prime Minister Tojo's answer could have come from Konoye. "I can understand why the Supreme Command is urging haste, but the government prefers to study the matter carefully and responsibly, since we have new ministers of Navy, Finance and Foreign Affairs. We should make up our minds whether to accept the September 6 decision or look at it from a different point of view. Does the Supreme Command object?"

No, said Sugiyama and Nagano.

Tojo had met his first formal test with authority. Kido's instinct had been correct; Tojo had proved he could cope with a disgruntled military.

Subsequent liaison conferences during the next ten days were devoted to the negotiations in Washington and the chances of success in case of war. The members agreed to maintain their stand on the Tripartite Pact and to honor Konoye's promise to adhere to Hull's four principles. The only discord was on the withdrawal of troops from China. Tojo, so adamant with Konoye, suggested that "as a diplomatic gesture" they should offer to withdraw all troops in about twenty-five years. Now it was Sugiyama who argued Tojo's former position. He adamantly refused time and again to make any concession. The Prime Minister found stronger support than he wanted from Foreign Minister Shigenori Togo, who said "it would be better to withdraw troops right away," and then that "everything would turn out for the better" if the American proposals were accepted, almost intact.

These suggestions were so disruptive—in fact, several thought Togo had lost his mind—that a motion was made for an adjournment until the next day. This was agreeable to Togo, who welcomed the chance "to get my mind in order."

It was Tojo who insisted that they continue. Every minute counted and a decision must be made, if they had to stay up all night. He urged them to study three courses: avoid war even at the expense of great hardship, or as Kido had put it,

141

gashin-shotan—"to sleep on kindling and lick gall"; decide on war at once; or continue negotiations but be ready to go to war if necessary. Personally, he added, he was hoping that diplomacy would bring peace.

Sugiyama and Tsukada left the prolonged meeting, bewildered and distressed by Tojo's change in attitude; he was talking more like a civilian than a general. Tojo returned to his office and discussed the three alternatives with his favorite sounding board, Kenryo Sato, now a major general, who said an immediate declaration of war was folly. The Kido solution, *gashin-shotan*, would solve neither the China Incident nor the basic differences between America and Japan; nevertheless, this course would have to be taken if the Navy officially admitted lack of confidence. "If there is any real prospect of winning, I am of course for war. But if there's no chance of victory, it would be nonsense to start it."

Tojo needed little persuasion. He told Sato to induce Chief of Staff Sugiyama privately not to insist on immediate war at the crucial liaison conference the next morning. But Sugiyama answered with some sarcasm, "Tell the *War Minister* the only possible answer is war."

The conference was set for nine o'clock, but Tojo asked Sugiyama to see him earlier; he was hoping that a personal confrontation would lead to a compromise. At seven-thirty Sugiyama and his deputy, the outspoken Tsukada, arrived at the official residence.

"The Emperor," Tojo began, "is strongly opposed to abandoning diplomacy and starting a war in the south." He doubted that Sugiyama's views would change the Emperor's mind. "If you feel confident, please see him yourself. I have no objection."

The General Staff felt that the negotiations with America were at a dead end, Sugiyama replied, and as long as the United States remained stubborn there was neither opportunity nor need to continue the talks. There was but one solution—war! Then he berated Tojo, a military man, for siding with the civilians. Tojo made no reply; he was the Prime Minister, and secondarily War Minister.

The conference—it was the sixty-sixth since their inception in 1937—started on November 1 at the Palace in the Imperial Courtroom amidst an atmosphere of apprehension. With the fate of the nation in the balance, a prime minister was again at odds with the Army, which still held the voting majority. Tojo said he would like to discuss the three alternatives. What about the first—*gashin-shotan?*

One of his civilian supporters, Finance Minister Kaya, answered with two questions: "What if we go along as now, without war, and in three years the American fleet attacks us? Would the Navy have any prospect of winning then or not?"

"Who knows?" said Admiral Nagano.

"*Will* the U. S. fleet come and attack us or not?" pressed Kaya.

"I think the chances are fifty-fifty," said Nagano.

If it came, Kaya insisted, could the Navy win?

Nagano still refused to commit the Navy. "We can either avoid war now and go to war in three years; or go to war immediately and plan for it to continue for the next three years." It would be better, he said, to start war at once while Japan held the advantage.

Kaya reminded him that Nagano himself had admitted that victory was not certain if the war lasted for three years. "What's more, I firmly believe there is little chance of the United States attacking us and I must conclude it would not be a good idea for us to go to war at the present."

Another civilian, Foreign Minister Togo, supported him on both counts.

"Remember the old saying, 'Don't count on what won't happen,'" said Nagano. "The future is a question mark and anything can happen." Within three years America would be strong in Southeast Asia.

"All right, so when can we go to war and win it?" Kaya goaded him.

"At once," Nagano replied emphatically. "An opportune time for war will not come later!"

The conflict should be started at the begining of December, said Sugiyama, but negotiations with America should be carried on to give Japan a military advantage. To Kaya, this was totally repugnant. "We have come to a great turning point in our 2,600-year history. The fate of our country hangs in the balance. It's simply outrageous for us to resort to diplomatic trickery!"

"We can't do such a thing!" Togo protested.

The Navy Vice Chief of Staff ignored their outbursts. "Speaking for the Navy, you can negotiate until November 20 [Tokyo time]."

The Army was not willing to wait that long—their deadline was November 13.

Togo was indignant. "I can't carry on diplomacy as foreign minister unless there is a chance of success. I simply cannot accept deadlines or conditions that will hinder hope of success. It's obvious you'll have to give up the idea of starting a war."

Prime Minister Tojo somehow remained calm, backing Togo and Kaya as often as he did the military. Gradually the Army began concentrating on Togo, and even tried to pressure him during the breaks. He was told, "If the Foreign Minister opposes war, all we have to do is replace him." After lunch, which was served at the conference table, Togo continued to berate the Army. "November 13 is too outrageous," he said. "The Navy puts it at November 20."

"Until November 13 at the latest!" said Tsukada. A delay would create confusion among operational units.

It was an admiral who objected to such rigid thinking. Navy Minister Shigetaro Shimada didn't see why negotiations couldn't continue until November 29.

"Keep quiet, please!" exclaimed General Tsukada. "Your suggestion is out of order." He turned to Togo. "What deadline would you like?"

The discussion got out of hand. Tojo called a break. During the twenty-minute recess the Army conferred and concluded that negotiations *could* continue, if necessary, until November 30.

When the meeting reconvened, Prime Minister Tojo tried for one more concession. "Can't we make the deadline December 1?" he said. Psychologically it might give the diplomats much more time. "Can't you let negotiations go on just one more day?"

"Absolutely not," said Tsukada. "We absolutely cannot go beyond November 30."

"Tsukada-*san*," Admiral Shimada asked, "until exactly what time on November 30? Till midnight?" This would, in effect, put the deadline where Tojo wanted it—December 1.

"All right," Tsukada conceded, "until midnight."

With the deadline for negotiations tentatively agreed upon, the burden of convincing the Americans to come to agreement would rest on Foreign Minister Togo. He said he had drawn up two proposals to be sent to America. Proposal A was a somewhat watered-down version of their previous offers. In it the Army agreed to withdraw all troops from China, including those left as defense against Communism, by 1966. Proposal B was to be used in case Secretary of State Hull turned down the first, and constituted a *modus vivendi*, a temporary arrangement pending a final settlement, to be used as a last resort. It was designed to allay Hull's suspicions about the drive into Indochina and assure him that Japan was abandoning any idea of a military conquest of Southeast Asia.

In Proposal B, Japan promised not to make any more aggressive moves south, and once peace was restored with China or a general peace in the Pacific established, all troops would be pulled out of Indochina. In the meantime Japan would at once move all troops in south Indochina to the north of that country. In return, America was to sell Japan one million tons of aviation gasoline.

Proposal B was unacceptable. "Stationing troops in French Indochina keeps China under control, and also enables us to get raw materials in the south on a fifty-fifty basis," said Sugiyama. "Moreover, it places us in a stronger position strategically toward the United States as well as in settling the China Incident. Coming to an agreement with the United States doesn't mean they will give us materials. We're against Proposal B." Such stubborn opposition forced Togo to come out in the open and say he really didn't think "A" would have much chance in Washington with such a short time left to negotiate. The only realistic hope of salvaging peace was to narrow the negotiations to the south. "You're putting me in a difficult position if you tell me to do something that can't be done."

A few—including Secretary-General Hoshino and Finance Minister Kaya—realized that he was right, but the Army remained adamant. "We absolutely cannot pull out our troops from southern Indochina!" Tsukada exclaimed and repeated Sugiyama's arguments. "Besides, withdrawal of these troops would place our supply routes for all materials from the south at the mercy of the Americans, who could cut them off whenever they wanted." It would merely delay the crisis for another six months and by then—because of the weather—Japan's chances to win a decision by arms would have come and gone. "Therefore, Proposal B is out. Just present Proposal A."

For hours the Army refused to accede to any suggestion of withdrawal from Indochina, while insisting that Hull be asked to unfreeze Japanese assets and cease his sabotage of a peaceful settlement of the China Incident.* It was a ridicu-

---

*In addition to sending considerable supplies to China, America was now providing manpower. Claire Chennault, a former U. S. Army Air Corps colonel, and his Flying Tigers were openly training in Burma for air battle with the Japanese. On April 15, 1941, President Roosevelt had signed an unpublicized executive order authorizing Reserve officers and enlisted men to resign from the Army Air Corps, the Naval and

lous proposition and Togo thought he could not possibly negotiate on such terms. In desperation he burst out, "We can't carry on diplomacy—but we still shouldn't start a war!"

"That's why we should go ahead with Proposal A!" Tsukada shouted back.

"Yes," said Nagano, "we should just go ahead and negotiate with Proposal A."

Confronted as he was by combined Army-Navy opposition, Foreign Minister Togo still refused to back down on Indochina. How could he negotiate without any ammunition? The shouting reached such a peak that one of the secretaries—it was General Muto—proposed a ten-minute recess, then helped Tojo herd the three other Army men into an anteroom to reason with them. "If the negotiations fail on account of the Army's resistance to the Foreign Minister's proposal," Muto asked, "can the Army take the responsibility?" Tojo reminded them that the Emperor had called for "blank paper" and they should bow to his wishes. Finally Sugiyama reluctantly acquiesced, but only if Proposal A failed. He was still concerned about how the radicals in the Army might be kept from rebelling when they learned that Japan had made such a humiliating concession.

"I can handle that," said Tojo. The discussion simply could not go on and on. It was already after midnight.

The rest of the group was out in the imperial garden recovering from the smoke and the heat of the argument. Admiral Nagano tapped Togo on the shoulder: "Can't the Foreign Ministry take over this task and straighten everything out by diplomacy? As far as the Navy is concerned you can settle the problem at your own discretion."

Togo was startled. A few minutes earlier this man had been an adversary. Encouraged by such unexpected support he went back to the meeting more determined than ever. But once the discussion resumed, Nagano was back recommending war. It was another example of the Navy talking peace in private and war in public—to save face and get their share of military appropriations. "Of course, we may lose," he said

Marine Air services so they could join Chennault's American Volunteer Group. Since the United States was not at war with Japan and could not deal openly with China, all arrangements had to be made with an unofficial agency to ensure secrecy. The Central Aircraft Manufacturing Company of China was set up and authorized to hire a hundred American pilots and several hundred ground crewmen to "operate, service and manufacture aircraft in China." The Japanese considered this a hostile, provocative act.

"but if we don't fight, we'd just have to bow to the United States. If we fight, there's a chance we can win. If we don't fight, wouldn't that be the same as losing the war?"

Nagano's words irked Tsukada, who found them cautious and vague. It seemed as if Nagano was set on going to war; why didn't he speak out, like Sugiyama? "All of us wonder if there isn't some way to achieve peace," he said urgently. "But no one is willing to say, 'Don't worry, I'll assume all responsibility even if the war is a long one.' However, we just can't maintain the status quo, so there is only one conclusion: we must go to war. I, Tsukada, believe we cannot avoid war. This is the moment. If we don't go to war now, we'll have to next year or the year after. This is the moment! The moral spirit of Japan, the Land of the Gods, will shine on our enterprise!" Japan's drive south would probably help Germany and Italy beat Russia and force China to surrender. The capture of Southeast Asia would be a mighty blow to America's resources. "We will build an iron wall, and inside it we will crush, one by one, our Asian enemies. We will also crush America and Britain!"

Tsukada's urgent call for battle was rebutted from an unlikely source—his own commander. Sugiyama said, "with extreme reluctance," that he would have to acquiesce to Togo's proposal to withdraw troops from southern Indochina. The abrupt shift came like an electric shock to all except Sugiyama's Army colleagues who had heard his concession in private. It was a considerable compromise, one that everyone knew would cause tremendous resentment throughout the ranks of the Army.

In return the military expected an end to civilian resistance and called for an immediate formal adoption of the deadline proposal. But Finance Minister Kaya refused to be rushed. "I cannot agree to a decision involving the destiny of Japan so suddenly," he said. He proposed they wait another day "to sleep on it," and the exhausted conferees filed into the garden at two o'clock in the morning.

As Kaya started home through the silent city he debated with himself. What if he persisted in opposing war? This would compel Tojo to dissolve the entire Cabinet, and the new one would undoubtedly bow to the militarists. On the other hand, there was still a possibility that the negotiations in Washington could be concluded successfully. Therefore, wouldn't it be wiser to go along with the proposal? Besides, if war did erupt, who was better equipped as finance minister to prevent inflation? His conclusions were logical but war with

147

America was still unthinkable and he could not bring himself to phone Tojo and give his approval.

Togo was also debating with himself on the lonely trip home. He had won his fight for Proposal B but he wasn't sure it would be enough to satisfy America. Perhaps more concessions could be wrung out of the Army if he resigned? After a few hours' sleep he called on an old friend, Koki Hirota, and asked for his opinion. The former prime minister thought he should stay in office and "work for the success of the negotiations." A new foreign minister would back the war party. It made sense.

Togo's next stop was Tojo's office. The Prime Minister had shown such reasonableness the day before that it encouraged Togo to ask for support in "persuading those concerned to make further concessions" if Hull reacted favorably to either "A" or "B."

Tojo did not disappoint him. He was more than willing to make further compromises if the Americans also came partway, and would soon tell an associate, "I'm praying to the gods that some way we'll come to an agreement with America." There was, he felt, a 50-50 chance that "B" would be accepted. Now only Kaya's resistance remained. All morning Tojo had pressed the Finance Minister by phone for a decision. Worn down by this persistency and unable to ignore the logic of this own arguments, Kaya drove to the Prime Minister's official residence, and about two o'clock informed General Tojo that he was reluctantly bowing to the majority opinion.

At last unanimity had been achieved. Now it was Foreign Minister Togo's well-nigh hopeless task to engineer peace before the deadline. The only chance for success in Washington, he decided, was to send assistance to Ambassador Nomura, who had already made several diplomatic blunders. Months before, the admiral himself had put in a request for Saburo Kurusu, an extremely able diplomat. He had signed the Tripartite Pact for Japan, but he also had strong ties with the United States. His wife was an American, Alice Jay, born of British parents on Washington Square, New York City.

Kurusu was hesitant but finally accepted the assignment. The difficulty was to get him to Washington as soon as possible and in utmost secrecy. If the war-minded staff officers or ultranationalists learned of the trip, his assassination was likely. A Pan American Clipper was scheduled to leave Hong Kong in forty-eight hours, but it would take several days to make arrangements to spirit Kurusu there by naval plane. The problem was solved by Ambassador Grew, who phoned Maxwell Hamilton, chief of the Far Eastern Affairs Division in Washington. He persuaded Pan American to delay its flight for two days.

On the afternoon of November 4, Kurusu bade good-bye to Tojo, who said, "The American people are against war, and their supply of rubber and tin is dwindling," and added that he had thought the chances of Kurusu's success were 30 percent. In two days he had grown 20 percent more dubious. "Please do your best to reach an agreement."

Late that night Kurusu tiptoed into the bedroom and sat on his wife's bed. "Where are you going?" she asked. "Probably to the United States," he told her. She wrapped a steamer blanket around him and made him coffee. Since there was "every possibility" he might be assassinated she suggested that their twenty-two-year-old son, an Army aviation engineer, accompany him on the first leg of the journey from Tokyo Station to Yokosuka. The reporters would assume Kurusu was merely seeing his son off on an assignment. Kurusu agreed. As he left he said, "I may never return."

The next morning at ten-thritry, thirteen men filed solemnly into the conference room set up for the imperial conference. When the fourteenth man, the Emperor appeared, the ceremony proceeded according to custom. There was a general feeling of anxiety as General Tojo explained that the September 6 decision had been reconsidered. "As a result of this, we have concluded that we must be prepared to go to war, with the time for military action tentatively set at December 1 [it sounded better than the actual date, midnight of November 30] while at the same time doing our best to solve the problem by diplomacy."

Foreign Minister Togo reviewed the diplomatic prospects. There was "little room left to maneuver diplomatically" and the chances of success were "we most deeply regret, dim."

General Suzuki reiterated the crucial problem of Japan's resources. "Briefly, we will have no easy task to fight a long war against Britain, America and the Netherlands, while still at war with China." However, the chances of victory in the first months were so bright that he felt war was the answer. It would be better than merely "waiting until the enemy applied the pressure."

Admiral Nagano called for secrecy of battle plans, since the fate of Japan depended on a decisive victory in the early moments of the war, and Sugiyama advised them to consider the importance of timing. "As far as operations, if the start of hostilities is delayed," he said, "the armament ratio between Japan and the United States will become increasingly unfavorable to us with the passage of time." He was fully confident of success in the early stages. "Nevertheless, we must face the fact that it will probably be a long-drawn-out war." Even so, he felt Japan could "establish a strategically impregnable position" and thus frustrate the enemy.

With all the brave talk, an air of growing despair hung over the room; and General Sugiyama himself called for a "stepping up" in diplomacy. In response to a question on the negotiations from Privy Council President Hara, Tojo said the American had answered with "flowery words." "The United States hasn't conceded a single point; all it does is make strong demands on Japan." The most serious point of argument was the stationing of troops in China, he said, and as he spoke about that frustrating war, became emotional "We dispatched a million men at the cost of over one hundred thousand dead and wounded, bereavement of families, four years of hardship, and several tens of billions of yen." And if the troops were pulled out, China would rise up against Japan. "She would try to take over Manchuria, Korea and Formosa as well!"

Hara asked how America would react to Proposals A and B. Togo's answer was that Proposal A would not bring quick results. "I'm afraid we can't even settle things with Proposal B." There were only two weeks left to negotiate. "Therefore I think chances of success are small. As foreign minister I will do my utmost but, I regret to say, I see little hope of success in the negotiations ... about a ten percent chance of success."

"Forty percent!" said Tojo. He had apparently regained 10 percent of his optimism overnight.

Hara feared war was inevitable and warned of its racial implications. America, Britain and Germany all were Caucasian. "So I'm afraid that if Japan attacks America she will come to terms with Germany, leaving Japan all alone. We must face the possibility that hatred of the yellow race could shift the hatred now directed against Germany to Japan, and as a result the German-British war would be turned against us."

Tojo also sounded a warning—the dangers of a prolonged war with a foe like the United States. "When I think about the increasing American strength in the southwest Pacific, the still-unfinished China Incident, and other things, I see no en-to our troubles. We all can talk about *gashin-shotan* at home, but how many years and months will our people be able to endure it?" His answer implied the affirmative: despite his show of optimism for peace a few minutes earlier, he too agreed that they would have to go to war. "I am afraid we would become a third-class nation in two or three years if we just sat tight." Morally there were grounds for war, since Britain and America threatened Japan's very existence. "Also, if we govern occupied areas with justice, the hostile attitude toward us will probably soften. America will be outraged at first but then she'll come to understand [why we waged war]. Anyway, I will carefully avoid making this a racial war. Do you have anything more to say? If not, I take it the proposals have been approved in their original form." There were no further comments. This time, unlike the last conference, the Emperor remained silent.

2.

Grew understood how frustrated the Japanese leaders were and to what that frustration might lead. Several days before the historic imperial conference of November 5, he had written in his diary: "Japan is obviously preparing a program of war, to be carried out if her alternative program of peace should fail. Resort to the former may come with dramatic and dangerous suddenness." In this mood he sent Hull an ominous cable once more recommending a reconciliation:

... IF THESE EFFORTS FAIL, THE AMBASSADOR [Grew] FORESEES A PROBABLE SWING OF THE PENDULUM IN JAPAN ONCE MORE BACK TO THE FORMER JAPANESE PO-SITION OR EVEN FARTHER. THIS WOULD LEAD TO WHAT HE HAS DESCRIBED AS AN ALL-OUT, DO-OR-DIE ATTEMPT, ACTUALLY RISKING NATIONAL HARA-KIRI, TO MAKE JAPAN IMPERVIOUS TO ECONOMIC EMBARGOES ABROAD RATHER THAN TO YIELD TO FOREIGN PRESSURE. IT IS REALIZED BY OBSERVERS WHO FEEL JAPANESE NATIONAL TEMPER AND PSYCHOLOGY FROM DAY TO DAY THAT, BEYOND PERAD-VENTURE, THIS CONTINGENCY NOT ONLY IS POSSIBLE BUT IS PROBABLE. ...

This wasn't advocacy of appeasement or a compromise with principles.

. . . THE AMBASSADOR'S PURPOSE IS ONLY TO ENSURE AGAINST THE UNITED STATES BECOMING INVOLVED IN WAR WITH JAPAN BECAUSE OF ANY POSSIBLE MISCONCEPTION OF JAPAN'S CAPACITY TO RUSH HEADLONG INTO A SUICIDAL STRUGGLE WITH THE UNITED STATES. WHILE NATIONAL SANITY DICTATES AGAINST SUCH ACTION, JAPANESE SANITY CANNOT BE MEASURED BY AMERICAN STANDARDS OF LOGIC. . . . ACTION BY JAPAN WHICH MIGHT RENDER UNAVOIDABLE AN ARMED CONFLICT WITH THE UNITED STATES MAY COME WITH DANGEROUS AND DRAMATIC SUDDENNESS.

He prayed for understanding in Washington. "The trouble with you Anglo-Saxons," a Japanese friend had told him, "is that you regard and deal with the Japanese as grown-up people, whereas the Japanese are but children and should be treated as children."

Grew's message, however, was as usual ignored in the State Department. Stanley Hornbeck regarded the ambassador as old-fashioned and honorable but gullible. Grew was, he thought, too influenced by Doorman, who had lived too long in the Orient to deal with the Japanese objectively; his pro-Japanese sympathy obviously colored every dispatch from Tokyo.

The MAGIC intercepts had convinced Hornbeck of Japanese duplicity. How could you trust a nation that played the two-faced game of talking peace while preparing for war? Moreover, he was so convinced that Japan was bluffing and would not dare fight America that he advised Hull to ignore Grew's latest warning.

Ironically, it was the two military Chiefs—General Marshall and Admiral Stark—who were making a joint appeal to Roosevelt to do nothing that might force a crisis. The defeat of Germany, after all, was the major strategic objective. "If Japan be defeated and Germany remains undefeated, decision will still not have been reached," they said and warned the President that war with Japan could cripple the Allied struggle against "the most dangerous enemy," Germany. They wanted no ultimatum issued to the Japanese for three or four months, until the Philippines and Singapore were strengthened.

Roosevelt began searching for a way that would, as he told Stimson, "give us further time," but even as he looked received information that the crisis could not be avoided. It came in an intercepted message from Foreign Minister Togo to Ambassador Nomura, a long cable containing Proposals A and B, along with secret instructions. The cable was decoded translated and rushed to Hull. The opening sentence of the instructions gave the impression that the Japanese had given up on the negotiations:

> WELL, THE RELATIONS BETWEEN JAPAN AND THE UNITED STATES HAVE REACHED THE EDGE, AND OUR PEOPLE ARE LOSING CONFIDENCE IN THE POSSIBILITY OF EVER ADJUSTING THEM.

Such pessimism was not in the original, for Togo had written:

> STRENUOUS EFFORTS ARE BEING MADE DAY AND NIGHT TO ADJUST JAPANESE-AMERICAN RELATIONS, WHICH ARE ON THE VERGE OF RUPTURE.

The translation of the second paragraph was even more misleading:*

> CONDITIONS BOTH WITHIN AND WITHOUT OUR EMPIRE ARE SO TENSE THAT NO LONGER IS PROCRASTINATION POSSIBLE, YET IN OUR SINCERITY TO MAINTAIN PACIFIC RELATIONSHIPS BETWEEN THE EMPIRE OF JAPAN AND THE UNITED STATES OF AMERICA, WE HAVE DECIDED AS A RESULT OF THESE DELIBERATIONS, TO GAMBLE ONCE MORE ON THE CONTINUANCE OF THE PARLEYS, BUT THIS IS OUR LAST EFFORT. . . .

The original was responsible in tone:

> THE SITUATION BOTH WITHIN AND OUTSIDE THE COUNTRY IS EXTREMELY PRESSING AND WE CANNOT AFFORD ANY PROCRASTINATION. OUT OF THE SINCERE INTENTION TO MAINTAIN PEACEFUL RELATIONS WITH THE UNITED STATES, THE IMPERIAL GOVERNMENT CONTINUES THE NEGOTIATIONS AFTER THOROUGH DELIBERATIONS. THE PRESENT NEGOTIATIONS ARE OUR FINAL EFFORT. . . .

The translation then stated that unless these proposals succeeded, relations between the two nations would be ruptured.

---

*Many Japanese are convinced that this and other diplomatic messages were purposely mistranslated. No evidence could be found of this. It is far more likely that the inaccuracies came from ignorance of the stylized Japanese used by diplomats. It is also possible that the hastily trained translators wanted to make their copy more readable and interesting.

> ... IN FACT, WE GAMBLED THE FATE
> OF OUR LAND ON THE THROW OF THIS DIE.

Togo's actual words were:

> ... AND THE SECURITY OF THE EMPIRE DEPENDS ON IT.

Where Hull read—

> ... THIS TIME WE ARE SHOWING THE LIMIT OF OUR
> FRIENDSHIP: THIS TIME WE ARE MAKING OUR LAST POS-
> SIBLE BARGAIN, AND I HOPE THAT WE CAN THUS SETTLE
> ALL OUR TROUBLES WITH THE UNITED STATES PEACEABLY,

Togo had written:

> ... NOW THAT WE MAKE THE UTMOST CONCESSION IN
> THE SPIRIT OF COMPLETE FRIENDLINESS FOR THE SAKE OF
> PEACEFUL SOLUTION, WE HOPE EARNESTLY THAT THE
> UNITED STATES WILL, ON ENTERING THE FINAL STAGE OF
> THE NEGOTIATIONS, RECONSIDER THE MATTER AND AP-
> PROACH THIS CRISIS IN A PROPER SPIRIT WITH A VIEW TO
> PRESERVING JAPANESE-AMERICAN RELATIONS.

Hull got just as inaccurate a version of Togo's specific
instructions regarding Proposal A, as the following excerpts
show:

What Hull Read	*What Togo Wrote*
THIS PROPOSAL IS OUR RE-VISED ULTIMATUM.	THIS IS OUR PROPOSAL SET-TING FORTH WHAT ARE VIR-TUALLY OUR FINAL CONCES-SIONS.
(NOTE: SHOULD THE AMER-ICAN AUTHORITIES QUESTION YOU IN REGARD TO "THE SUITABLE PERIOD [for re-taining Japanese troops in China]," ANSWER VAGUELY THAT SUCH A PERIOD SHOULD ENCOMPASS 25 YEARS.)	(NOTE) IN CASE THE UNITED STATES INQUIRES INTO THE LENGTH OF THE NECESSARY DURATION, REPLY IS TO BE MADE TO THE EFFECT THAT THE APPROXIMATE GOAL IS 25 YEARS.

... IN VIEW OF THE FACT THAT THE UNITED STATES IS SO MUCH OPPOSED TO OUR STATIONING SOLDIERS IN UNDEFINED AREA OUR PURPOSE IS TO SHIFT THE REGIONS OF OCCUPATION AND OUR OFFICIALS, THUS ATTEMPTING TO DISPEL THEIR SUSPICIONS. ...

IN VIEW OF THE STRONG AMERICAN OPPOSITION TO THE STATIONING FOR AN INDEFINITE PERIOD, IT IS PROPOSED TO DISMISS HER SUSPICION BY DEFINING THE AREA AND DURATION OF THE STATIONING ...

... WE HAVE HITHERTO COUCHED OUR ANSWERS IN VAGUE TERMS. I WANT YOU IN AS INDECISIVE YET AS PLEASANT LANGUAGE AS POSSIBLE TO EUPHEMIZE AND TRY TO IMPART TO THEM TO THE EFFECT THAT UNLIMITED OCCUPATION DOES NOT MEAN PERPETUAL OCCUPATION ...

... YOU ARE DIRECTED TO ABIDE, AT THIS MOMENT, BY THE ABSTRACT TERM "NECESSARY DURATION," AND TO MAKE EFFORTS TO IMPRESS THE UNITED STATES WITH THE FACT THAT THE TROOPS ARE NOT TO BE STATIONED EITHER PERMANENTLY OR FOR ANY DEFINITE PERIOD.

(4) AS A MATTER OF PRINCIPLE, WE ARE ANXIOUS TO AVOID HAVING THIS INSERTED IN THE DRAFT OF THE FORMAL PROPOSAL REACHED BETWEEN JAPAN AND THE UNITED STATES ...

WITH REGARD TO THE FOUR PRINCIPLES [of Hull], EVERY EFFORT IS TO BE MADE TO AVOID INCLUDING THEM IN THE TERMS OF A FORMAL AGREEMENT BETWEEN JAPAN AND THE UNITED STATES ...

To Hull, this last example alone was convincing-enough proof of Japan's deceitful intentions to underline his old suspicions. Actually, it was a colossal blunder. The translator had taken the "FOUR" of "FOUR PRINCIPLES" and made it point (4), concluding part of the instructions following "(1) NON-DISCRIMINATION AND TRADE," "(2) INTERPRETATION AND APPLICATION OF THE TRIPARTITE PACT" and "(3) WITHDRAWAL OF TROOPS." By making this excerpt appear to be one of the main divisions of the message and changing "WITH REGARD TO THE FOUR PRINCIPLES" into "(4) AS A MATTER OF PRINCIPLE" and arbitrarily inserting the word "ANXIOUS," the translator had misled Hull into believing that the Japanese were trying to avoid committing themselves to a formal agreement on *any* of the proposed points.

155

On the evening of November 7 Nomura arrived at Hull's apartment with Proposal A. Hull glanced through it rapidly; he already knew all about it—or thought he did—and was convinced that it contained no real concessions. His attitude was so obvious that Nomura asked for an appointment with the President. Every day was precious and the admiral was desperate. He was being pressed for a quick decision at the urging of the Japanese Chiefs of Staff; Hull was holding up the decision because the American Chiefs of Staff wanted time. This maneuvering at cross-purposes unfortunately was contributing to the deterioration of the negotiations.

When Nomura finally got to see the President three days later he pointed out the "considerable concessions" made by Japan and reiterated the need for haste. Roosevelt must also have been mindful of Marshall and Stark's plea for time in his reply that "nations must think one hundred years ahead, especially during the age through which the world is passing." A mere six months had been spent in the negotiations. It was necessary to be patient; he didn't want a temporary agreement. Nomura cabled Togo that the United States "was not entirely unreceptive" to Proposal A. The wishful-thinking admiral was ready to grab at any straw of hope.

So was Bishop James Walsh. Just back from another trip to the Far East, he made one more attempt to bring Japan and America together in the form of a long memorandum delivered to Hull on November 15. In reading it, Hornbeck added a number of sarcastic notes for Hull which revealed his own strong bias.

Where the bishop explained that the Emperor's sanction of any policy was regarded by all Japanese as "the final seal that makes it the irrevocable policy of the nation," Hornbeck noted in pencil: "If a policy sanctioned by the Emperor is 'irrevocable,' then the alliance with the Axis is *irrevocable*." And to a long plea for understanding between the two countries, he put down: "Naive."

"It is perhaps worthwhile to recall," Walsh observed, "that the Chinese were well on the way to actual collaboration with Japan when the Manchurian Incident rudely arrested the movement and turned the Chinese radically in the other direction." Opposite this, Hornbeck penciled: "He speaks as though the *Chinese* had started the 'Manchurian Incident.' " And when Walsh noted that "There is no real peace anywhere in the Far East today," Hornbeck wrote down: "And for that *fact* who are responsible?—the Japanses (& the Germans)."

That very day Special Envoy Saburo Kurusu arrived in Washington after a tiring trip across the country, and two days later Ambassador Nomura brought him to Hull's office. One glance at the diminutive, bespectacled man with the neat mustache who had signed the Tripartite Pact was enough for the Secretary of State to conclude that he was not to be trusted. "Neither his appearance nor his attitude commanded confidence or respect," Hull wrote in his memoirs. "I felt from the start that he was deceitful. . . . His only recommendation in my eyes was that he spoke excellent English, having married his American secretary."

Convinced that Kurusu was privy to his government's trickery and would try "to lull us with talk until the moment Japan got ready to strike," Hull escorted the two Japanese the few hundred yards to the White House. Roosevelt put himself out to be affable: "As Bryan said, there is no last word between friends."

Kurusu replied that a way must be found to avoid war. The Pacific was "like a powder keg." Roosevelt agreed that a broad understanding should be reached.

As for the Tripartite Pact, Kurusu said he didn't see why America, "which has been a strong advocate of observance of international commitments, would request Japan to violate one." Japanese leaders had already assured the Americans that the pact would not automatically lead to war; that would require an independent decision. Moreover, an understanding between Japan and America "would naturally 'outshine' the Tripartite Pact, and American apprehension over the problem of application of the pact would consequently be dissipated." It was a step toward actual abrogation of the treaty, but Hull didn't believe a word Kurusu said; it was merely "some specious attempt to explain away" the pact.

Roosevelt remained friendly, and reaffirmed that there was "no difference of interest between our two countries and no occasion, therefore, for serious differences," and even offered to act as "introducer" between China and Japan.

3.

That same day Prime Minister Tojo made a speech in the Diet which was also broadcast to the nation. It dealt with the negotiations in Washington and he pointed out that their success would depend on three things: America must not interfere with Japan's solution of the China Incident; she must "refrain from presenting a direct military menace to our empire" and call off the economic blockade; and exert efforts to "prevent the extension of the European war" to East Asia.

There was thunderous applause, whereas excellent speeches ordinarily failed to get much of a response. In the diplomatic box of the U. S. embassy, the naval attaché leaned over and whispered to his companions. An *Asahi Shimbun* reporter noticed this and wrote:

. . . The four staff members of the American embassy suddenly went into a huddle and conversed with each other, and then all vigorously shook their heads, although no one knows what they meant by this. All others in the visitors' gallery looked at them with fixed attention.

What the naval attaché whispered was: "Well, he didn't declare war, anyway."

Among the leaders of Japan hope dwindled as each day passed with no definite word from Washington on Proposal A. America's attitude seemed to be stiffening on the major issues. All that remained was the last resort, and Togo cabled Nomura to present "B." On November 20 the admiral read it to Hull, who took it as an ultimatum and in his memoirs described the conditions as "of so preposterous a character that no American official could ever have dreamed of accepting them." But he hid his feelings to "avoid giving the Japanese any pretext to walk out of the conversations" and said he would give the proposal "sympathetic study."

His reaction was unfortunate and uncalled-for. Only one of Proposal B's five conditions—the one to stop giving aid to China—was unreasonable. This paragraph aroused him so much that he made it the most vital issue. In a fit of temper he burst out, "In the minds of the American people there is a partnership between Hitler and Japan aimed at enabling Hitler to take charge of one-half the world and Japan the other half." The Tripartite Pact strengthened the public in this belief, he added, and began to assail it vigorously.

Nomura turned to Kurusu helplessly. Little more than a week before, Hull had admitted that the pact was not a major problem. Yet three times in the past few days he had declared that as long as Japan clung to it, a peace settlement could not be taken seriously. Why was the pact being elevated again to importance? It was almost as if nothing had changed in Japanese-American relations since the days of Matsuoka.*

Hull's subordinates also had a similarly curious reaction to Proposal B. The man most sympathetic to Japan, Joseph Ballantine, feared its acceptance would mean "condonement by the United States of Japan's aggressions, assent by the United States to unlimited courses of conquest by Japan in the future . . . betrayal by the United States of China . . ." and "a most serious threat to American national security."

Such talk of aggression made little sense. The proposal adequately covered Southeast Asia and the southwest Pacific and offered peace in China. Japan could not have committed further aggression without breaking her own proposal, and if the Americans had wanted a definite pledge to stop military expansion they probably could have gotten it.

It was not really a question of Proposal B itself, but of State Department refusal to accept it at face value. What the Japanese Army considered a major concession and had accepted only after bitter arguments—withdrawal of troops from southern Indochina to the north—was scorned by Ballantine. It was a "meaningless" offer, since the Japanese could easily return the same troops to southern Indochina "within a day or two."

Roosevelt, on the other hand, must have been impressed by "B" because he responded with his own *modus vivendi*. He wrote it out in pencil and sent it on to Hull.

6 months

1. U. S. to resume economic relations—some oil and rice now—more later.
2. Japan to send no more troops to Indochina or Manchurian border or any place South—(Dutch, Brit. or Siam).
3. Japan to agree not to invoke tripartite pact even if U. S. gets into European war.
4. U. S. to introduce Japs to Chinese to talk things over but U. S. to take no part in their conversations.

Later on Pacific agreements.

---

*There were several possible reasons why Hull revived this dead issue: out of moral indignation; out of fear of denunciation from the American public, which generally equated Japan with Nazi Germany, if any agreement was reached with Japan; to prepare the public for a war with Japan by raising the specter of a Hitler-Tojo joint attack.

This *modus vivendi* was further evidence that Roosevelt, unlike Hull, was a practitioner of *Realpolitik*, and brought about the first genuine relaxation of American rigidity, the first realistic hope for a peaceful settlement. Though it must have offended Hull's purist nature, he dutifully began putting it into diplomatic form. Despite personal reservations about Kurusu and suspicions of his superiors back in Tokyo, he was still willing to negotiate.

Since the talk with Hull had revealed the great importance he still attached to the Tripartite Pact, Kurusu called the following day at the State Department with a draft letter declaring that Japan was not obligated by that agreement to collaborate or co-operate in any aggression by any third power.

... My Government would never project the people of Japan into war at the behest of any foreign power: it will accept warfare only as the ultimate, inescapable necessity for the maintenance of its security and the preservation of national life against inactive justice.

I hope that the above statement will assist you in removing entirely the popular suspicion which Your Excellency has repeatedly referred to. I have to add that, when a complete understanding is reached between us, Your Excellency may feel perfectly free to publish the present communication.

Neither the indirect negation of the Tripartite Pact nor the offer to publish it allayed Hull's suspicions, which were "confirmed" a day later in an intercept from Tokyo to Nomura extending the deadline of negotiations to November 29 (Washington time).

... THIS TIME WE MEAN IT, THAT THE DEADLINE ABSOLUTELY CANNOT BE CHANGED. AFTER THAT THINGS ARE AUTOMATICALLY GOING TO HAPPEN.

That evening—it was Saturday, November 22—Kurusu and Nomura called at Hull's apartment to urge a prompt reply to Proposal B. They were smiling and courteous. It was a "strain" for Hull to respond amiably, knowing what he did "of Japan's nefarious plans" from MAGIC. "There they sat, bowing agreeably, Nomura sometimes giggling, Kurusu often showing his teeth in a grin, while through their minds must have raced again and again the thought that, if we did not say Yes to Japan's demands, their government in a few days would launch new aggressions that sooner or later would inevitably bring war with the United States and death to thousand or millions of men."

Hull said, "It's a pity that Japan cannot do just a few peaceful things to help tide over the situation."

Nomura was just as ill at ease. He reiterated the need for haste and pressed for an item-by-item answer.

"There is no reason why any demand should be made on us" was the testy reply. "I am quite disappointed that despite all my efforts you are still trying to railroad through your demand for our reply." Hull could see no reason why Tokyo couldn't wait for a few days, but did promise to get an answer as soon as possible. This would be Monday at the earliest, since he had to consult several friendly governments with interests in the Far East. The answer Hull had in mind was his version of Roosevelt's hastily scribbled *modus vivendi*.

On Monday, November 24, Hull invited representatives of England, China, Australia and Holland to his office and passed around copies of the latest draft of the Roosevelt plan. Dr. Hu Shih, the Chinese ambassador, was troubled. Why should five thousand Japanese be allowed to remain in Indochina? Hull replied that in General Marshall's opinion, even twenty-five thousand troops wouldn't be a menace. "While my government does not recognize the right of Japan to keep a single soldier in Indochina," he explained, "we are striving to reach this proposed temporary agreement primarily because the heads of our Army and Navy often emphasize to me that time is the all-important question for them, and that they must be fully prepared to deal effectively with a possible outbreak by Japan."

The Dutch minister, Dr. Alexander Loudon, forthrightly declared that his country would support the *modus vivendi*, but the other three had to wait for instructions. Irked and impatient, Hull said, "Each of your governments has a more direct interest in the defense of that area of the world than this country. But your governments, through some preoccupation in other directions, do not seem to know anything about this matter under discussion. I am definitely disappointed at this unexpected development, at their lack of interest and lack of disposition to ço-operate."

The next day Dr. Hu apologetically handed Hull a note from his Foreign Minister stating that Chiang Kai-shek had had a "rather strong reaction" to the *modus vivendi* and felt that America was "inclined to appease Japan at the expense of China."

Exasperated, Hull said America could of course kill the *modus vivendi,* but if so, she was "not to be charged with failure to send our fleet into the area near Indochina and into Japanese waters, if by any chance Japan makes a military drive southward."

Although it was dark by the time Dr. Hu left, Hull called together his staff for further discussion. He himself was strongly in favor of sending the *modus vivendi* to the Japanese despite the slender chance of acceptance. If nothing else, it would underline "for all time to come that we were doing everything we could to avoid war, and a Japanese rejection would serve more fully to expose their predetermined plan for conquest of the Orient."

Later that night a cable for Roosevelt arrived from Churchill:

... OF COURSE, IT IS FOR YOU TO HANDLE THIS BUSINESS AND WE CERTAINLY DO NOT WANT AN ADDITIONAL WAR. THERE IS ONLY ONE POINT THAT DISQUIETS US. WHAT ABOUT CHIANG KAI-SHEK? IS HE NOT HAVING A VERY THIN DIET? OUR ANXIETY IS ABOUT CHINA. IF THEY COLLAPSE, OUR JOINT DANGERS WOULD ENORMOUSLY INCREASE. ...

Obviously Chiang Kai-shek had carried his complaints to London and this subtle rebuff wore out Hull's last patience, MAGIC had assured him that Proposal B was the last offer Japan would make and that the negotiations would definitely be terminated at the end of the month. That Tojo was prepared to make still further concessions in a sincere attempt for peace he did not know, nor would he have believed it if he had. Ever since midsummer he had been "well-satisfied that the Japanese were determined to continue with their course of expansion by force."

That was why Chiang's objection and Churchill's half-hearted endorsement, coupled with his own doubts and exhaustion from months of negotiating, caused him at this moment to shelve the *modus vivendi.* Instead he would offer the Japanese "a suggested program of collaboration along peaceful and mutually beneficial, progressive lines." His assistants began putting this new proposal into draft form.*

---

*At Sugamo Prison, after the war, Tojo told Kenryo Sato that if he had received the Roosevelt *modus vivendi,* the course of history would probably have changed. "I didn't tell you at the time, but I had already prepared a proposal with new compromises in it. I wanted somehow to carry out the Emperor's wishes and avoid war." Then he heaved a big sigh. "If we had only received that *modus vivendi!*"

Stimson was making an entry in his diary. He described a meeting that noon of the so-called War Cabinet at the White House:

... [Roosevelt] brought up the event that we were likely to be attacked perhaps next Monday [December 1], for the Japanese are notorious for making an attack without warning, and the question was ... what we should do. The question was how we should maneuver them into the position of firing the first shot without allowing too much danger to ourselves. It was a difficult proposition. Hull laid out his general broad propositions on which the thing should be rested—the freedom of the seas and the fact that Japan was in alliance with Hitler and was carrying out his policy of world aggression. The others brought out the fact that any such expedition to the south as the Japanese were likely to take would be an encirclement of our interests in the Philippines and cutting into our vital supply of rubber from Malaysia. I pointed out to the President that he had already taken the first steps towards an ultimatum in notifying Japan way back last summer that if she crossed the border into Thailand she was violating our safety and that therefore he had only to point out [to Japan] that to follow any such expedition was a violation of a warning we had already given.*

The following day, November 26, Secretary of the Treasury Henry Morgenthau, Jr., arrived at the White House just as Roosevelt was starting his breakfast. The phone rang

---

*This entry was later used by revisionist historians such as Charles Beard to bolster their claim that President Roosevelt purposely maneuvered Japan into an attack on American territory. A superficial reading of the controversial diary entry and subsequent remarks by Stimson seem to indicate that the anti-Roosevelt group is correct, but a study of the records of the discussions between the President and his advisers in the last days of November make it evident that they were expecting an onslaught on Singapore, Thailand or some other part of the Southeast Asian continent. They certainly did not appear to anticipate an initial attack on any American territory such as the Philippines or Guam, much less Hawaii. Thus, when Roosevelt said "we were likely to be attacked" he probably used "we" meaning the ABCD powers. It was a "difficult proposition" just because he did not expect a direct assault on the United States, and the problem was to make an attack on Singapore or Thailand seem to be a "first shot" against America. There were two ways to carry on this "maneuvering"—with a diplomatic warning to Japan or with a message to Congress so phrased that if Japan made a move south, even without directly menacing American territory, we would take it to be an assault on our vital interests—and, as it were, an assault on the United States.
In the absence of positive proof this assumption, and it can only be an assumption, seems much more logical and fair than the wishful reasoning of those who disapproved of almost everything Roosevelt did.

before the President could eat his kippered herring. It was Hull, who told of the Chinese protests to the *modus vivendi*. "I will quiet them down," Roosevelt said and went back to his breakfast. By now it was cold, so he pushed it aside, inspiring Morgenthau to jot down in his notes: "I don't think the President ought to see me or anybody else until he has finished his breakfast."

Hull was already on the phone with Stimson, telling him that he had "about made up his mind not to give ... the proposition [the *modus vivendi*] ... to the Japanese but to kick the whole thing over—to tell them that he has no other proposition at all."

This prompted Stimson to check with Roosevelt by phone to find out if the paper he had sent the night before about the new Japanese expedition from Shanghai into Indochina had been received. Roosevelt reacted so violently that Stimson commented in his diary that he "fairly blew up—jumped up into the air, so to speak"—and said no, he hadn't seen it and it "changed the whole situation because it was an evidence of bad faith on the part of the Japanese that while they were negotiating for an entire truce—and entire withdrawal [from China]—they should be sending this expedition down there to Indochina."

Not much later Hull appeared in person. He recommended that in view of the opposition of the Chinese they drop the *modus vivendi* and offer the Japanese a brand-new "comprehensive basic proposal for a general peaceful settlement."

Still angry at the news of the Japanese convoy, Roosevelt approved, and that afternoon Kurusu and Nomura were summoned to the State Department. At five o'clock Hull handed them two documents, "with the forlorn hope that even at this ultimate minute a little common sense might filter into the military minds of Tokyo."

Kurusu and Nomura expectantly began reading the first paper, an Oral Statement which set forth that the United States "most earnestly" desires to work for peace in the Pacific but that it believed Proposal B "would not be likely to contribute to the ultimate objectives of ensuring peace under law, order and justice in the Pacific area ..." In place of Proposal B, Hull offered a new solution and it was embodied in the second paper, marked "Strictly Confidential, Tentative and Without Commitment." Kurusu read its ten conditions with dismay. It peremptorily called for Japan to "withdraw all military, naval, air and police forces from China and Indochina"; to support no other government or regime in

China except Chiang Kai-shek's; and, in effect, to abrogate the Tripartite Pact.

It was far harsher than the American proposal made on June 21 and Hull had drawn it up without consulting General Marshall or Admiral Stark, who happened to be in the act of drafting still another memorandum to Roosevelt begging for more time to reinforce the Philippines. Hull's proposal again raised the dead issue of the Tripartite Pact, though Kurusu had already given written assurance it had little significance, and introduced a new proposal calling for "a multilateral nonaggression pact among the British Empire, China, Japan, the Netherlands, the Soviet Union and Thailand and the United States." Kurusu knew this would complicate an already complicated situation and cause more delay. When Nomura sat down, too stunned to talk, Kurusu asked if this was the American reply to Proposal B.

It was, said Hull, and pointed out the economic advantages to Japan if she accepted: an offer to unfreeze Japanese funds, make a trade agreement based upon reciprocal most-favored-nation treatment, stabilize the dollar-yen rate, reduce trade barriers and grant other considerable economic concessions.

Kurusu foresaw that in Tokyo this would be regarded as an insult, as a bribe, and began taking exception to the conditions. He didn't see how his government could possibly agree to the immediate and unconditional withdrawal of all troops from China and Indochina, and if the United States expected Japan "to take off its hat to Chiang Kai-shek and apologize to him," no agreement was possible. He requested that they informally discuss the proposal at greater length before sending it on to Tokyo.

"It's as far as we can go," said Hull. Public feeling was running so high that he "might almost be lynched" if he let oil go freely into Japan.

Kurusu observed with mordant humor that at times all "statesmen of firm conviction" failed to find public sympathy. Wise men alone could see far ahead and they sometimes became martyrs, but life was short and one could only do his duty. Dejected, he added that Hull's note just about meant the end, and asked if they were not interested in a *modus vivendi*.

The phrase had become an unpleasant one to Hull. We explored that, he said curtly.

Was it because the other powers wouldn't agree? Kurusu asked.

It was uncomfortably close to the truth. "I did my best in the way of exploration," said Hull.

4.

The first news of Hull's reply reached Tokyo late in the morning on November 27. It came in a message from the military attaché in Washington to Imperial Headquarters which began by announcing that the United States had replied in writing to Proposal B but that "there was no gleam of hope in negotiations." Staff officers huddled around the communications room, anxiously waiting while the rest of the message, containing the gist of Hull's proposal, was being decoded.

The message was sent at once to the Palace, where a liaison conference was in session. It arrived just as the meeting adjourned for lunch and Tojo read it aloud. There was dumfounded silence until someone said, "This is an ultimatum!" Even Togo, who had held forth slight hope of success, never expected this. "Overpowered" by despair, he said something in such a stutter that no one could understand him; the Hull note "stuck in the craw." His distress was intensified when he saw that several Army men were pleased, "as if to say, 'Didn't we tell you so?'"

But to one Navy man, Admiral Shimada, it was "a jarring blow." Hull's reply was "unyielding and unbending" and didn't so much as recognize the fact that Japan had made significant concessions.

The demands were equally outrageous to a peacemaker like Kaya. Hull obviously knew that Japan would have to refuse them. He was rejecting an immediate accommodation and seemed to be wanting endless discussions instead. It was just a stall for time. America had made up her mind to go to war—to attack Japan! That Japan had already offered to withdraw troops from southern Indochina at once wasn't enough; Hull wanted all troops withdrawn at once from Indochina and China. An impossibility.

What particularly infuriated every man in the room was the categoric demand to quit *all* of China. Manchuria had been won at the cost of considerable sweat and blood. Its loss would mean economic disaster. What right did the wealthy Americans have to make such a demand? What nation with any honor would submit?

Hull's proposal was the result of impatience and indigna
166

tion, but the passage that most incensed the Japanese had been tragically misunderstood. To Hull, the word "China" did not include Manchuria and he had no intention of demanding that the Japanese pull out of that territory. Back in April he had assured Nomura that there was no need to discuss recognition of Manchukuo until a basic agreement had been reached, and he imagined that the issue was disposed of. To the Japanese, however, the Hull note had to be taken at face value. After all, the Americans had hardened their position on a number of issues since the days of the Draft Understanding.

The American reply should have been clear on this point; at the very least, the Japanese reaction would have been far less bitter. The exception of Manchuria would not have made the Hull note acceptable as it stood, but it might have enabled Togo to persuade the militarists that negotiations should be continued; it could very well have forced a postponement of the November 30 deadline.*

Thus it was that two great nations who shared a fear of a Communist-dominated Asia were set on a collision course. Who was to blame—the United States or Japan? The latter was almost solely responsible for bringing herself to the road of war with America through the seizure of Manchuria, the invasion of China, the atrocities committed against the Chinese people, and the drive to the south. But this course of aggression had been the inevitable result of the West's efforts to eliminate Japan as an economic rival after World War I, the Great Depression, her population explosion, and the necessity to find new resources and markets to continue as a first-rate power. Added to all this were the unique and undefined position of the Emperor, the explosive role of

---

*All of the men at the liaison conference, from Tojo to Togo, believed that Hull's reference to "China" included Manchuria. In 1967 a number of Tojo's close associates were asked what might have happened *if* Hull had clarified that point. Kenryo Sato, learning the truth for the first time, slapped his forehead and said, "If we had only known!" Very excitedly he added, "If you had said you recognized Manchukuo, we'd have accepted!" Suzuki, Kaya and Hoshino would not go that far. Kaya, now a leading politician, said, "If the note had excluded Manchukuo, the decision to wage war or not would have been rediscussed at great length. There'd have been heated arguments at liaison conferences over whether we should withdraw at once from North China in spite of the threat of Communism." At least, said Suzuki, Pearl Harbor would have been prevented. "There might have been a change of government."

gekokujo, and the threat of Communism from both Russia and Mao Tse-tung which had developed into paranoiac fear.

Americans, too, suffered from paranoiac fear, theirs of the "yellow peril," and yet, oddly, they had no apprehensions about Japan as a military foe and reveled in stories of Nipponese ineptitude. According to one story going around Washington, the British had built warships for Japan so top-heavy that they would capsize in the first battle. The Japanese air force was also generally ridiculed, its pilots regarded as bespectacled bunglers, more to be laughed at than dreaded. Perhaps this sense of superiority subconsciously tempted some American leaders, including Roosevelt, to drive the Japanese to the limit of their forbearance.

How could a nation rich in resources and land, and free from fear of attack, understand the position of a tiny, crowded island empire with almost no natural resources, which was constantly in danger of attack from a ruthless neighbor, the Soviet Union? America herself had, moreover, contributed to the atmosphere of hate and distrust by excluding the Japanese from immigration and, in effect, flaunting a racial and color prejudice that justifiably infuriated the proud Nipponese. America should also have perceived and admitted the hypocrisy of taking such a moral stand on the four principles.* Her ally, Britain, certainly did not observe them in India or Burma, nor did she herself in Central America where "gunboat diplomacy" was still upholding the Monroe Doctrine. Her self-righteousness was also self-serving; what was morality at the top became self-interest at the bottom.

Finally, America made a grave diplomatic blunder by allowing an issue not vital to her basic interests—the welfare of China—to become, at the last moment, the keystone of her foreign policy. Until that summer America had had two limited aims in the Far East: to drive a wedge between Japan and Hitler, and to thwart Japan's southward thrust. She could easily have attained both these objectives but instead made an issue out of no issue at all, the Tripartite

---

*Morality is an unstable commodity in international relations. The same America that took a no-compromise stand on behalf of the sanctity of agreements, maintenance of the status quo in the Orient, and the territorial integrity of China, reversed herself a few years later at Yalta by promising Russia territory in the Far East as an inducement to join the war in the Pacific. A rapprochement with Japan in 1941 would admittedly have meant American abandonment and betrayal of Nationalist China. Yet it might have led to a more stable non-Communist China in the long run.

168

Pact, and insisted on the liberation of China. For this last unattainable goal America's diplomats were forcing an early war that her own militarists were hoping to avoid—a war, paradoxically, she was in no position to wage. America could not throw the weight of her strength against Japan to liberate China, nor had she ever intended to do so. Her major enemy was Hitler. Instead of frankly informing Chiang Kai-shek of this, she had yielded to his urgings and pressed the policy that led to war in the Far East—and the virtual abandonment of China. More important, by equating Japan with Nazi Germany, her diplomats had maneuvered their nation into two completely different wars, one in Europe against Fascism, and one in the Orient that was linked with the aspirations of all Asians for freedom from the white man's bondage.

There were no heroes or villains on either side. Roosevelt, for all his shortcomings, was a man of broad vision and humanity; the Emperor was a man of honor and peace. Both were limited—one by the bulky machinery of a great democracy and the other by training, custom and the restrictions of his rule. Caught up in a medieval system, the Japanese militarists were driven primarily by dedication to their country.* They wanted power for it, not war profits for themselves; Tojo himself lived on a modest scale. Prince Konoye's weaknesses came largely from the vulnerable position of a premier in Japan, but by the end of his second cabinet he had transformed his natural tendency for indecisiveness into a show of purpose and courage which continued until his downfall. Even Matsuoka was no villain. Despite his vanity and eccentricities this man of ability sincerely thought he was working for the peace of the world when he saddled Japan with the Tripartite Pact; and he wrecked the negotiations in Washington out of egotism, not malice.

Nor were Stimson and Hull villains, though the latter, with his all-or-nothing attitude, had committed one of the most fatal mistakes a diplomat could make—driven his opponents into a corner with no chance to save face and given them no option to capitulation but war.

The villain was the times. Japan and America would never have come to the brink of war except for the social and economic eruption of Europe after World War I and the rise

---

*After his trial Tojo admitted the independence of the Supreme Command had led to Japan's ruin. "We should have risen above the system we inherited, but we did not. It was the men who were to blame. ... Especially myself."

of two great revolutionary ideologies—Communism and Fascism. These two sweeping forces, working sometimes in tandem and sometimes at odds, ultimately brought about the tragedy of November 26. America certainly would never have risked going to war solely for the sake of China. It was the fear that Japan in partnership with Hitler and Mussolini would conquer the world that drove America to risk all. And the ultimate tragedy was that Japan had joined up with Hitler mainly because she feared the Anglo-Saxon nations were isolating her; hers was a marriage in name only.

A war that need not have been fought was about to be fought because of mutual misunderstanding, language difficulties, and mistranslations as well as Japanese opportunism, *gekokujo*, irrationality, honor, pride and fear—and American racial prejudice, distrust, ignorance of the Orient, rigidity, self-righteousness, honor, national pride and fear.

Perhaps these were essentially the answers to Händel's question: "Why do the nations so furiously rage together?" In any case, American had made a grave mistake that would cost her dearly for decades to come. If Hull had sent a conciliatory answer to Proposal B, the Japanese (according to surviving Cabinet members) would have either come to some agreement with America or, at the least, been forced to spend several weeks in debate. And this hiatus would in turn have compelled postponement of their deadline for attack until the spring of 1942 because of weather conditions. By this time it would have been obvious that Moscow would stand, and the Japanese would have been eager to make almost any concessions to avoid going into a desperate war with an ally which now faced inevitable defeat. If no agreement had been reached, America would have gained precious time to strengthen the Philippines with more bombers and reinforcements. Nor would there have been such a debacle at Pearl Harbor. There is little likelihood that the implausible series of chances and coincidences that brought about the December 7 disaster could have been repeated.

Operation Z

1.

In early summer of 1939 when the Army was urging closer ties with Germany and Italy, Navy Minister Mitsumasa Yonai and his deputy had opposed any pact. The Army was sure that by conquering all Europe, Hitler would be in a position to help Japan settle the China Incident. But Admiral Yonai and his deputy were convinced that a war between England and Germany would be a prolonged affair. Eventually America would get into it, Germany would wind up the loser, and if Japan had a treaty with Hitler, she would find herself fighting the United States all alone.

The Navy Vice Minister was even more outspoken than his chief, publicly predicting that Japan would be defeated in any war with the United States. He was only five feet three inches tall (the exact height of the legendary Admiral Togo), but gave an impression of size with his broad shoulders and barrel chest. He was Admiral Yamamoto and his first name, Isoroku (meaning "fifty-six"), was the age of his schoolmaster father at the time he was born. He had enlisted in the Navy "so I could return Admiral Perry's visit," and subsequently lived in America—at Harvard as a student and in Washington as naval attaché. Consequently he had sounded the warning of her industrial strength so often and so persuasively that Yonai, fearing that Yamamoto might be assassinated by ultranationalists, sent him to sea in August 1939 as commander of Combined Fleet.

The basic strategical plans of Japan's admirals in the thirties had been to let her enemy, America, sortie from Pearl Harbor to make the initial attack: as the Americans proceeded they would be harassed by submarines while the Japanese fleet simply waited in their own territory. By the time the forces met in Japanese waters, the Americans would be so weakened by losses that they could be defeated in one great surface battle somewhere west of Iwo Jima and Saipan.

Once Yamamoto assumed command of the fleet, however, he extended the theoretical battle line to the Marshall Islands, which, together with the Carolines, had been turned over to

Japan as mandates after World War I and constituted her possessions farthest east in the Pacific. Then in 1940, while witnessing the remarkable achievements of carrier-based planes in the spring fleet maneuvers, he turned to his chief of staff, Rear Admiral Shigeru Fukudome, as they paced the deck of the flagship *Nagato* and said, "I think an attack on Hawaii may be possible now that our air training has turned out so successfully." In one sudden crushing blow the American fleet at Pearl Harbor would be crippled, and before it could be rebuilt Japan would have seized Southeast Asia with all its resources.*

The idea for a surprise attack was based on the tactics of his hero, Admiral Togo, who had, without any declaration of war, assaulted the Second Russian Pacific Squadron at Port Arthur in 1904 with torpedo boats while its commander, an Admiral Stark, was at a party. The Russians never recovered from this loss—two battleships and a number of cruisers—and the following year almost their entire fleet was destroyed in the Battle of Tsushima during which, incidentally, young Ensign Yamamoto lost two fingers on his left hand.

(The concept of achieving decisive victory by one surprise blow lay deep in the Japanese character. Their favorite literary form was the *haiku*, a poem combining sensual imagery and intuitive evocation in a brief seventeen syllables; a rapier thrust that expressed, with discipline, the illumination sought in the Japanese form of Buddhism. Similarly, the outcome in judo, *sumo* [wrestling] and *kendo* [fencing with bamboo staves], after long preliminaries, was settled by a sudden stroke.)

Yamamoto was not the only one thinking seriously of an

---

*It is intriguing to speculate on the inspiration for Yamamoto's plan for an attack on Pearl Harbor. In 1921 a book entitled *Sea Power in the Pacific* was published in the United States, written by Hector C. Bywater, naval correspondent for the London *Daily Telegraph*. Four years later, part of this book was expanded into a novel under the title *The Great Pacific War*. In it, Bywater described a Japanese surprise attack on the U. S. Asiatic Fleet in Pearl Harbor, with simultaneous assaults on Guam and the Philippines, and with landings on Luzon at Lingayen Gulf and Lamon Bay. The Navy General Staff in Tokyo, which had had *Sea Power in the Pacific* translated and distributed among top naval officers, also adopted *The Great Pacific War* for the curriculum at the Naval War College.

At the time *The Great Pacific War* was published, Yamamoto was serving as naval attaché in Washington. In September 1925 the New York *Times Book Review* featured the book on page one, under the headline IF WAR COMES IN THE PACIFIC. Undoubtedly Yamamoto, an obsessive student of naval affairs, had the book called to his attention.

air attack on Pearl Harbor. In Tokyo, Commander Kazunari Miyo, the aviation operations officer of the Navy General Staff, was trying to convince his chiefs that the way to beat a powerful enemy like America was to force her into a decisive battle as soon as possible. This could be done by using giant six- to eight-engine aircraft in a number of bombing raids on the U.S. fleet at Pearl Harbor. The Americans would either have to flee to the mainland or come out and fight near the Marshalls on Japanese terms.

Although the idea was never seriously considered by Miyo's superiors, the discussion at naval headquarters might have been overheard. On January 27, 1941, Dr. Ricardo Rivera Schreiber, the Peruvian envoy in Tokyo, told a friend, First Secretary Edward S. Crocker of the American embassy, of a rumor that the Japanese intended to make a "surprise mass attack on Pearl Harbor" with all their strength. Crocker passed this on to Ambassador Grew, who cabled Washington. The message was routed to Naval Intelligence, which reported that "based on known data regarding the present disposition and employment of Japanese Naval and Army forces, no move against Pearl Harbor appears imminent or planned for the foreseeable future."

At that moment Yamamoto was already moving forward. On February 1 he wrote an unofficial letter to Rear Admiral Takijiro Onishi, chief of staff of the Eleventh Air Fleet, outlining his plan and asking Onishi to carry out a secret study of its feasibility. Onishi turned to his friend and subordinate, Commander Minoru Genda, one of the Navy's most promising officers, whose influence extended far beyond his rank—in China his brilliant innovations in mass long-range fighter operations had won him fame. Now he was asked to study the Yamamoto plan. After ten days he presented his conclusions: the attack on Pearl Harbor would be difficult to mount, and risky, but contained "a reasonable chance of success."* Onishi forwarded this report to Yamamoto, along with his own deductions. The admiral was by then discussing

---

*The main source of this information is Minoru Genda, whose testimony was inconsistent. He was questioned on November 28, 1945, by Captain Payton Harrison, USNR, with Douglas Wada interpreting. Captain Harrison conducted several more interrogations, and Genda also made a deposition for the defense in the Tokyo trials. Each time the facts varied: the Pearl Harbor attack was conceived in February 1 in a conversation with Admiral Onishi; then, it was outlined in a letter from Yamamoto to Onishi, but he gave three different dates—January 27, February 1 and February 10.

the attack with his own operations officer, Captain Kameto Kuroshima, a brilliant eccentric who would absentmindedly roam the flagship in kimono leaving a trail of cigarette ashes behind him. Orderlies referred to him as "the foggy staff officer." Kuroshima closeted himself in his cabin for several days and finally emerged in a cloud of garlic, incense and cigarette smoke with a detailed plan entitled Operation Kuroshima.*

Success rested on two precarious assumptions: that the Pacific Fleet (the United States Fleet had been so renamed on February 1) would be anchored at Pearl Harbor at the time of attack; and that a great carrier force could be moved halfway across the Pacific Ocean without being detected. Only a gambler would embark on such a venture and Yamamoto was certainly this. He was an expert at bridge and poker, as well as at *shogi* (Japanese chess). Once an American asked him how he had learned bridge so quickly. "If I can keep five thousand ideographs in my mind," he explained, "it is not hard to keep in mind fifty-two cards." He often told Commander Yasuji Watanabe, perhaps his favorite staff officer, that gambling—half calculation, half luck—played a major role in his thinking. As for the Hawaii attack, it was dangerous but the odds were too good not to take. "If we fail," he said fatalistically, "we'd better give up the war."

Two days after sending the letter to Onishi, Yamamoto outlined the plan to Captain Kanji Ogawa of Naval Intelligence, requesting that he collect as much data as possible about Hawaii. Although Ogawa already had a small group of spies in the islands—a timid German named Otto Kühn who needed money, a Buddhist priest and two Nisei—they merely provided unimportant bits of information. He decided to send in a naval intelligence expert who had already been selected and prepared for such a mission, even though an amputated finger made him readily identifiable. Takeo Yoshikawa was a twenty-nine-year-old ensign from Section 5, the American desk. He was slender, good-looking and appeared younger than his years.

Yoshikawa had attended the Naval Academy at Etajima, where he was a swimming champion (before graduating, every cadet was required to swim the ten miles of cold, jellyfish-ridden waters from the famed shrine at Miyajima to Etajima) and won fourth rank at *kendo*. He was a unique

---

*After the war, shortly before his death, Kuroshima told Miyo, "The Pearl Harbor attack was my idea."

scholar. While hs mates crammed for exams, he studied Zen Buddhism to attain spiritual discipline. Even so, he graduated on schedule and after a term as code officer on a cruiser, attended torpedo, gunnery and aviation schools. Heavy drinking, however, led to stomach trouble and temporary retirement from the service. He returned as a Reserve officer in Naval Intelligence. At first he served in the British section, then was transferred to the American section, where he sifted through a mountain of material that had accumulated, familiarized himself with ship movements and memorized various types of naval equipment.

In the spring of 1940 he was asked by his section chief, Captain Takeuchi, if he would volunteer to serve in Hawaii as a secret agent. He would get no espionage training, not even a single manual, and would in effect be on his own. Yoshikawa accepted and turned into a civilian, assuming the cover name of Tadashi Morimura. In preparation for his role as consular official, he let his hair grow and began to study international law and English at Nippon University. He passed the diplomatic exams and divided his time between the Foreign Ministry, where he did research on American politics and economy, and Section 5.

By the time Admiral Yamamoto made his request for additional Hawaiian intelligence it was spring of 1941, and Yoshikawa was ready. On March 20 he boarded the liner *Nitta-maru* at Yokohama. A week later he arrived in Honolulu, keyed up at the thought of pitting himself against the U. S. Navy. Consul General Nagao Kita greeted him cordially and the following night took him to the Shunchoro, a Japanese restaurant located on a hill overlooking Pearl Harbor. The proprietress, Namiko Fujiwara, came from Yoshikawa's own prefecture, Ehime. She told him she had five geishas, trained in Japan. The assignment would not be a dull one.

Yoshikawa got a salary of $150 a month, as well as $600 for six months' expenses. He began operations, improvising his own methods. First he made a grand tour of all the main islands, followed by two auto trips around Oahu, and then an air junket over Oahu wearing a loud aloha shirt like any other tourist and accompanied by a pretty geisha. After a second tour of the islands he was sure there were no naval ships except at Pearl Harbor and decided to concentrate on Oahu. Twice a week he took a six-hour drive around the island and visited the Pearl Harbor area every day. As a rule, he would simply gaze at it from the crest of a hill, but several times he got inside the gates. Once, armed with a lunch box, he followed a group of laborers and spent the day wandering around without being questioned; he tapped a big oil tank to see how much was inside and discovered that full tanks usually leaked and could easily be detected from outside the fence. Another time he persuaded a hostess at an officers club to hire him as a kitchen helper at a big party, but all he learned was how Americans wash dishes.

The large Japanese community was no help at all. Yoshikawa sounded out many individuals, usually over drinks at the consulate, but discovered that almost all considered themselves loyal Americans; to Yoshikawa it didn't make sense to be American while worshiping at Buddhist temples and Shinto shrines and contributing generously to the Imperial Army's relief fund. One old man did promise to set fire to a sugarcane field in case of war and talked freely of all the guns he'd seen, but Yoshikawa discounted the man's reports when he began describing one on top of Diamond Head as "big as a temple bell."

Gossiping with American sailors was just as fruitless. They talked a lot without saying a thing. What information he got was by simple, unexciting methods. He sat on a tatami in the Shunchoro with the geishas—sometimes Shimeko, sometimes Marichiyo—and drew diagrams of the ships in the sprawling harbor below. On his regular drives he usually took a girl—a geisha or one of the maids at the consulate—because guards stopped him if he was alone.

Once he taxied up to Hickam Field, the big Army Air Corps bomber base near Pearl Harbor. At the gate he told the guard he was meeting an American officer and was waved on. As the cab slowly cruised around the base, Yoshikawa made mental notes of the number of hangars and planes, and the length of the two main runways. He also attended an air show at Wheeler Field, a fighter air base in the center of Oahu. He sat on the grass with other spectators watching P-40 fighter pilots do aerobatics; several swooped through an open hangar. He made no notes, but memorized the number of planes and pilots, hangars, barracks and soldiers. He never photographed anything, depending instead on his "camera eyes."

Once a week he submitted a report to Kita, who sent his chauffeur with the coded messages to the Mackay cable office in Honolulu. Within a month Yoshikawa was sure he was being "tailed" by the FBI in a black car with radio antenna. Kita warned him to be more careful but Yoshikawa

176

stubbornly continued his routine; before long the two men found themselves quarreling almost every day.

2.

By April the Pearl Harbor plan had a new name—Operation Z, in honor of the famed Z signal given by Admiral Togo at Tsushima: ON THIS ONE BATTLE RESTS THE FATE OF OUR NATION. LET EVERY MAN DO HIS UTMOST. Now it was time to turn it over to those who would have to put it into effect—the First Air Fleet.

On April 10 Rear Admiral Ryunosuke Kusaka was made chief of staff of the First Air Fleet. He was sturdy and energetic, with a candid face. His father had been a business executive, but young Kusaka's calling was the sea. After graduation from the Naval Academy in 1913 he spent most of his time in naval aviation, once crossing the Pacific in the *Graf Zeppelin* as an observer. He captained two carriers, *Hosho* and *Akagi*, and before coming to Tokyo, commanded the 24th Air Squadron in Palau.

After reporting to the Navy General Staff, the forty-eight-year-old admiral was brought to the office of a former classmate at the Naval War College, Admiral Shigeru Fukudome, the then chief of the Operations Bureau. "Take a look at this," Fukudome told his colleague and held out a sheaf of papers written in pen. A glance through the pages made it clear to Kusaka that the writing was Onishi's. "This is supposed to be an operational plan," he said, "but we can't use it in a real fight."

"This is merely a proposal. Nothing has been decided yet. In case of war, we need a practicable plan from you. Make it work."

Kusaka took a train south to Hiroshima, where he reported to his new chief, Vice Admiral Chuichi Nagumo, on board the flagship *Akagi*. Nagumo was short, slight. A torpedo expert, he knew little of aviation, and told Kusaka he would have to be responsible for Operation Z. Kusaka was no flier, either; he considered himself "an aviation broker." The details would have to be drawn up by men with intimate knowledge of flying, so he summoned the senior staff officer, Commander Tamotsu Oishi, and the aviation staff officer, Commander Minoru Genda. The latter, of course, knew all about Pearl Harbor, but kept it to himself when Kusaka told the two to draw up a complete, workable plan.

The more Kusaka studied the project the more he doubted its feasibilities: it was too risky, and defeat in such an initial battle would mean losing the war. As Operation Z developed, so did Kusaka's concern. He visited Admiral Onishi late in June and pointed out the flaws in the plan so persuasively that Onishi finally conceded it was too much of a gamble.

Kusaka suggested that they go to Yamamoto.

"You were the one who started this argument," said Onishi. "You tell him."

Kusaka returned to *Akagi*, got permission from his commander to see Yamamoto, and took a launch to *Nagato*, the flagship of the Combined Fleet. The plan was too speculative, he said, and summed up all his arguments.

Yamamoto took Kusaka's criticisms good-naturedly. "You just call it speculative because I play poker and mah-jong, but actually it isn't." These words ended the interview, but not Kusaka's anxiety. Downcast, he was walking toward the gangway when he felt a tap on his shoulder. It was Yamamoto. "I understand why you object, but the Pearl Harbor attack is a decision I made as commander in chief. Therefore I'd appreciate it if you will stop arguing and from now on make every effort to carry out my decision. If in the future you should have any objections from other people, I'll back you up."

Oishi worked out the overall plan and Genda studied the techniques of air attack—he had been thinking of a concentrated carrier strike since watching an American newsreel in 1940—while Kusaka himself devoted his energies to the aspect he felt was the most vulnerable: bringing the Striking Force within air range of Pearl Harbor without being discovered. It seemed an impossible task. Japanese ships were faster than American, but at the expense of armor and cruising range. The ships in the Striking Force, except the new carriers *Shokaku* and *Zuikaku*, simply did not have the fuel capacity to approach Pearl Harbor. How would he be able to refuel on the run?

There was also the element of surprise. What course would ensure it? He called in Lieutenant Commander Toshisaburo Sasabe, the staff navigation expert, and told him to study the nationalities and types of ships which had crossed the Pacific during the past ten years. Sasabe reported that no ships traveled at latitude 40 degrees north during November and December because of rough seas. The first thing that came to Kusaka's mind when he read Sasabe's report was the surprise attack made by Yoshitsune Minamoto in the twelfth century upon the enemy's supposedly impregnable castle; Minamoto had gained access by launching an assault from a completely unexpected quarter.* Kusaka could do the same thing by striking at Pearl Harbor from the north; the U. S. fleet usually held maneuvers southwest of Hawaii, on the assumption that any attack would come from the Japanese base on the Marshall Islands. The one drawback—and it was a considerable one—was the problem of refueling his ships in the rough seas, but Kusaka dismissed it at once; he would overcome that problem by discipline and training.

The precise course to the launching site now had to be worked out. On the basis of information from Hawaii, Kusaka expected U. S. Navy flying boats to patrol an area five hundred miles out of Pearl Harbor while other PBY's covered five hundred miles south of Dutch Harbor in the Aleutians. The Striking Force, he concluded, would have to navigate undetected through this neglected part of the ocean by heading almost due east to a point approximately eight hundred miles north of Pearl Harbor. Here, the day before the attack, the ships would refuel for the last time and at dark steam south toward their target. At first light the planes would take off.

Ordinarily the training and operation of planes was the responsibility of each carrier's captain or squadron commander, but this attack had to be co-ordinated by a single flight commander. The man selected was the squadron leader on *Akagi*, Commander Mitsuo Fuchida, whose flying skill was exceeded by his ability to lead. A thirty-nine-year-old veteran of the China War, he had already logged 3,000 hours in the air. Not all of the carrier captains could accept Fuchida's commanding their planes, however, and it took Kusaka himself to bring them into line.

The primary target, according to Genda's plan, was Battleship Row, the two lines of battleships moored off Ford Island in the middle of Pearl Harbor. First, torpedo planes would swoop down and launch their cargo at the outside row, then the inside line would be attacked by high-level (horizontal) and dive bombers.

Kusaka didn't believe this second assault could succeed without an accurate bombsight—the Japanese knew of America's Norden bombsight but had been unable to acquire

---

*This battle, fought on February 7, 1184, followed by a sea victory a year later, decided the struggle between the Minamoto and Taira clans for domination of Japan.

the plans—or a bomb capable of piercing a battleship's thick armor without detonating. The answer to the first problem was constant practice with the erratic Type 97 bombsight, a copy of a German model; for the second, Genda, Fuchida and the engineers finally hit upon a simple solution: reconstruct battleship shells into bombs, with their outer faces so reinforced that they would not explode on impact.

Not until the outbreak of hostilities in Europe had the Japanese Army General Staff thought in terms of a major war. Previously their operations had been limited to the Asian continent, but once England became one of the belligerents, they made preparations for action against her and possibly America. They dispatched one of their shrewdest officers, Major Kumao Imoto, to investigate the strategic feasibilities of Southeast Asia. He worked his way from Hong Kong to Hanoi, Saigon and on to Singapore. Upon his return he drafted invasion plans for both Hong Kong and Singapore.

The following year other officers went farther south to probe possible invasions of Java, Sumatra and the Philippines. But the plans that evolved were vague and no practical spy network was ever established. A scattering of Japanese nationals and retired officers was willing to serve on a volunteer basis, and there was some help from natives. Many Filipinos still carried bitter memories of Emilio Aguinaldo's unsuccessful but heroic attempt to overthrow American rule around the turn of the century, and in British and Dutch territories the vast majority was in favor of an overthrow of white domination.

In December 1940—about the same time Yamamoto was seriously pondering the attack on Pearl Harbor—three divisions in China were ordered to start training for operations in the tropics. A special unit, the Formosan Army Research Department, was established to collect all data on tropical warfare in Southeast Asia within a period of six months. It was a small group, commanded by a Colonel Yoshihide Hayashi, but the driving force was provided by the controversial Colonel Masanobu Tsuji, who made a commonplace of eccentricity; once he had burned down a geisha house filled with fellow officers in a fit of moral indignation. With his roundish face, bald head and small, blinking eyes, he looked like the typical staff officer, but his brilliant maverick spirit inspired fanatic devotion in the younger staff officers. They revered him as Japan's "God of Operations," the hope of the Orient. Some of his superiors, however, had grave reservations. General Hitoshi Imamura, one of the most respected figures in the Army, saw the genius in Tsuji—but also the madman. A number of his peers, such as Colonel Takeo Imai, regarded him as a clever, fanatic idealist with a one-track mind who thought, like the legendary Kanji Ishihara, that he alone was right, Tsuji was, in fact, a protégé of Ishihara's. He, too, was determined to make Manchuria into a Buddhist paradise of five nationalities living in harmony, but he wanted to go much further; he dreamed of making Asia one great brotherhood, an Asia for the Asians.

Yoshio Kodama (who would be inveigled by Tsuji to plan to assassinate Prince Konoye by dynamite) first met him at the Nanking Army headquarters. He had a letter to Tsuji from Ishihara, and was told by Colonel Imai, "Oh, that crazy man lives in a filthy little room behind the stable." Kodama asked Tsuji why he lived alone in such squalor.

"These headquarters officers are all rotten," Tsuji answered with disgust. "They are only working for their medals. Every night they go to parties and play with geishas. Since the China Incident, all the military have gone bad. They hate me because I know all this and speak out." He did more than speak. He turned one fellow staff officer over to the *kempeitai* for "corruption," who then committed suicide.

On January 1, 1941, this colorful figure found himself in Formosa—exiled there, according to rumor, by Tojo, who had always opposed Ishihara—and involved in a seemingly useless project. Instead of feeling sorry for himself, he threw himself wholeheartedly into his personal assignment, the Malayan campaign. Within two months, through various sources, he learned that the island of Singapore, connected to the tip end of the Malay Peninsula by a 1,100-yard-long causeway, was a fortress impregnable from the sea but practically defenseless from an attack in the rear.

One of Tsuji's chief assistants was a fellow eccentric, Captain Shigeharu Asaeda, an agile, muscular six-footer of twenty-nine. He had always wanted to be an engineer, but since his father was poor, he had drifted into the Military Academy because it was free. After graduating from the War College, he fought in China so recklessly that Tsuji sought him out. The two took to each other at once, for both burned with the same idealism and spirit of adventure. When Asaeda was transferred to a desk job in the War Ministry he became so bored that he abandoned not only the Army but his wife and family as well. He disguised himself in civilian clothes, took a new name, wrote a letter informing his wife and parents that he was "going to commit suicide in the

Inland Sea," and left Tokyo. He was actually off to join the Indonesian fight against Dutch colonialism.

On his way south he asked Tsuji for help. Though Tsuji promised to keep his friend's whereabouts a secret, within hours a disgruntled Asaeda was on his way back to Japan under guard. He expected to be court-martialed, but the Army, which did not want the public treated to a scandal, simply retired him from the service; perhaps his heroism in China tempered a harsher sentence. In any case, he again left his family and returned to Formosa to confront the man who had betrayed him. Such was the force of Tsuji's personality that Asaeda found himself volunteering as a secret agent. He was to assemble firsthand information on Burma, Malaya and Thailand. With fanatic intensity Asaeda immersed himself in round-the-clock studies of the language and geography of each country he was to infiltrate.

About the time Yoshikawa began operations in Hawaii, Asaeda set off for Thailand pretending to be an agricultural engineer. Judicious bribes enabled him to photograph key areas; and talks with hundreds of natives, some of high rank, convinced him that Thailand was the best springboard for operations against Burma, and could be taken over bloodlessly.

The Burman border was closely guarded by the British, but after several months he managed to slip through and collect the material Tsuji wanted. By the time he returned to Formosa he had discovered terrain and climate peculiarities that changed the accepted theories of tropical warfare.

In June, secret maneuvers were held on Japanese-controlled Hainan—a large island just off southern China in the Gulf of Tonkin—under the supervision of Hayashi and Tsuji. New concepts, based on information from Asaeda and research in Formosa, were tested. It had been regarded as suicidal to send transports jammed with men and horses through the suffocating heat of the tropics. Tsuji was certain it was solely a matter of training and discipline. His method of proof was uniquely his own. He packed thousands of fully equipped soldiers into the sweltering holds of ships, three to a tatami (a mat about six by three feet), and kept them there for a week in temperatures up to 120 degrees with little water. These wilted men, along with horses and heavy equipment, were successfully landed on open beaches under the worst (simulated) circumstances. A final mock landing was made under combat conditions by a battalion of infantry, a battery of artillery and a company of engineers.

Now all that was needed was accurate information about the terrain and tides of the invasion beaches. To get this, Tsuji sent his one-man spy ring, the ubiquitous Asaeda, into Malaya itself.

Though the Navy had always opposed a drive to the south on the grounds that it would lead to a clash with America, Admiral Nagano had submitted an official proposal in mid-June advocating an advance into southern Indochina whether it would take force or not. As it happened, no force was needed against the Vichy government, but the act led to the freezing of Japan's assets in the United States and made war against the West appear inevitable. At first Army Chief of Staff Sugiyama disapproved plans to prepare operations at once to seize Southeast Asia but on August 23 he succumbed to pressure.

There was similar resistance in the Navy high command to Operation Z, led by the chief of the Operations Section, Captain Sadatoshi Tomioka. Late that summer he debated the risks involved with Yamamoto's "foggy staff officer," Captain Kuroshima. Tomioka charged that the southern campaign was being short-changed; too much was being thrown into Operation Z, which might be a totally wasted effort. What if the attack planes found Pearl Harbor empty? His blood was as hot as Kuroshima's and their differences almost led to a fistfight but they parted friends, with the latter beginning to doubt his own arguments.

Yamamoto had no doubts whatsoever and the opposition from Tokyo made him more steadfast. One day he remarked to his chess partner, Watanabe, "I will just have to resign." Watanabe grinned. But this was not a passing mood. The admiral had made up his mind to use the threat of resignation as a last resort.

Training for the air attack on Pearl Harbor continued at an accelerated pace on Kyushu, the southernmost of Japan's four major islands, famed for its active volcanoes, men of warlike spirit, and pornography. Except for those involved in the planning, no one, not even the captains of the carriers, knew what the target would be. The fighter pilots at Saeki Air Base only knew they were being prepared for some great air assault involving all the fighter planes of four carriers. The dive bombers were located some 150 miles down the coast at Tominaka Air Base. Here the men were specializing in night attacks and accuracy, using as targets towed rafts which made a heavy wake.

The other fliers were near the mouth of Kagoshima Bay in the south. They had to double as high-level and torpedo bombers. Torpedo practice was more exhilarating, for they had instructions to do what almost every pilot longed to do—buzz civilians and stunt around buildings. Each plane had a crew of three: pilot, observer (who also acted as bombardier) and radioman (who doubled as gunner). It would fly over a mountain some 5,000 feet high behind Kagoshima City, then zoom down, playing tag with the Yamagataya Department Store and the railroad station and dodging between telephone poles and smokestacks before suddenly dropping to an altitude of 25 feet when it reached the piers. Here the observer pulled a toggle which supposedly launched a torpedo at a breakwater (Battleship Row) about three hundred yards away. Then the plane made a sharp right turn to avoid slamming into Mount Sakurajima, an active volcano on a little island in the bay, and continued, skimming the water, scaring the wits out of every fishing-boat skipper who had the misfortune to be nearby. It was great fun and it was legal. But the people of Kagoshima made numerous complaints. Couldn't the Navy control its young hotheads who were practically tearing the roof off the Hirano restaurant just to impress the geishas?

Genda had picked Kagoshima City—home of the lusty hero, Saigo*—because it presented most of the problems the torpedo bombers would have to face at Pearl Harbor. They would have to fly over a number of smokestacks and buildings, just as at Kagoshima City, and then drop down at suddenly reduced speed to launch their torpedoes at Battleship Row from an extremely low altitude. The reason why Genda insisted that they practice at such a suicidal height was that the waters of Pearl Harbor were shallow, and if dropped from the usual height, a torpedo would plow straight into the bottom. But even a drop from 25 feet would not solve the problem and Genda was deviling the experts at Yokosuka Naval Base to come up with a shallow-running torpedo.

Several hundred miles to the northeast on the rugged, spectacularly beautiful coast of Shikoku Island, a detachment

---

*Takamori Saigo, the prototype of the Japanese man of action, led the Satsuma Rebellion in 1877 against the Meiji government. Though one of Japan's great heroes, the people failed to respond to his call for revolt. His statue, standing in Kagoshima, is still a shrine of Japanese *seishin* (spirit).

of Navy men was carrying out another phase of Operation Z that completely mystified the inhabitants of Mitsukue. Every morning a dozen spirited young ensigns sailed out into Mitsukue Bay in fishing boats towing canvas-covered cigar-shaped objects about eighty feet long. Late in the afternoon the boats, mysterious canvas-covered objects and all, would return and the ensigns congregate at the Iwamiya Inn for dinner.

The canvas-draped objects were two midget submarines which their pilots were slipping through the mouth of Mitsukue Bay in a mock torpedo attack on American warships, but even their instructors did not know this was supposed to be Pearl Harbor.

On September 2 all fleet commanders and their key staff officers, as well as important personnel from Combined Fleet, the Navy General Staff and the Naval Ministry (about forty in all), gathered at the Naval War College in Meguro, a suburb of Tokyo, to conduct final tabletop maneuvers in the presence of several Army observers who had just been advised of Pearl Harbor. There were two general problems to be solved: first, to work out final details for a successful surprise attack on Pearl Harbor; and, second, to make a detailed schedule, from the naval point of view, for occupying Malaya, Burma, the Dutch East Indies, the Philippines, the Solomons and the central Pacific islands, including ultimately Hawaii.

Umpires were selected from the Navy General Staff and Navy Ministry and the rest were divided into three teams. Yamamoto himself led the N-team (Nippon); Vice Admiral Nobutake Kondo of the Second Fleet led the E-team (England); and Vice Admiral Ibo Takahashi the A-team (America). On September 5—the day before the Emperor recited his grandfather's poem—the war games got under way. Yamamoto set his Striking Force on its way to Hawaii over the huge game board, but before the carriers reached launching position, Takahashi's "American" search planes from Pearl Harbor had discovered them. With the surprise element gone, a third of Yamamoto's planes were shot down and two carriers sunk. Despite these "losses," Yamamoto's plan was not dropped lest he make good his threat to resign and because Hitler's attack on Russia had made the Japanese position in Manchuria more secure.

Within a week the Navy planners completed a staff study setting November 16 as X-Day (their D-Day). An officer handed over about a hundred mimeographed copies of the forty-page study to Yeoman Second Class Mitsuharu Noda, a staff clerk on *Nagato*, and simply told him to take them to the flagship anchored off Kure. Each copy was in a black manila folder; curious, Noda glanced through one. It opened with the words: "Japan is declaring war on the United States, Great Britain (and the Netherlands)." Fascinated, he read the details of an attack on Pearl Harbor, complete with charts and codes.

Noda and an assistant wrapped the studies into four bundles and clambered aboard a train at Tokyo station. They spent that night on a third-class sleeper to Kure, using the bundles as head and foot rests.

The study called for four carriers and thus brought protests from every staff officer in Combined Fleet and the Striking Force. At least six carriers were needed. Kusaka alone, however, was willing to do more than register a formal request for another two ships. He flew to Tokyo to fight for his convictions. After a day of frustrating argument with the Navy General Staff, he sent a telegram direct to Yamamoto, without consulting anyone, complaining about the lack of support from Combined Fleet.

Kusaka's efforts were in vain and, moreover, his was the painful task of deciding which two carriers to leave behind. He selected the two smallest—*Soryu* and *Hiryu*. Their commander was an old friend, Tamon Yamaguchi, whose temper was only matched by his courage. Kusaka asked Genda to transmit the unwelcome information in person, but he showed such reluctance that the admiral summoned Yamaguchi to *Akagi*.

The volatile Yamaguchi, a Princeton man, seemed to accept the decision, and sought solace in *sake*. He downed half a dozen shots and then, before Kusaka could stop him, charged into Admiral Nagumo's private office with a bellow. Such behavior was not unique in the Japanese Navy on this level, and Nagumo tried to calm him by saying that although *Soryu* and *Hiryu* had to be left behind, their well-trained crews could be switched to *Shokaku* and *Zuikaku*. This still left Yamaguchi out of the battle and he shouted, "I insist on taking *Hiryu* and *Soryu!*" The burly Yamaguchi lunged at Nagumo from behind and hooked the little admiral in a headlock.

Kusaka appeared in the doorway. "What's going on?" He tugged at Yamaguchi's arm.

Nagumo, face red but composed, said, "I'm good at judo

so I can handle a drunk like this. Don't worry." He struggled to get free. Yamaguchi squeezed tighter. Nagumo got redder. Finally Kusaka got a headlock on Yamaguchi, pried him loose, pushed him into the next room and said, "Do what you like in here."

Yamaguchi's anger dissipated. A cherubic smile appeared on his round face and he began prancing around the room singing "Tokyo Ondo," a popular song.

The wrestling match brought no repercussions—or results—but a few days later Yamamoto himself got the two carriers reinstated with a phone call to Tokyo.

Several weeks later Kusaka summoned all carrier captains and their chief aviation officers to *Akagi*. He told them about Pearl Harbor and ordered targets changed from moving to stationary. At Tominaka Air Base a large rock fifteen feet in diameter was painted white, replacing the towed raft as a target. Lieutenant Heijiro Abe, who commanded ten high-level bombers, made an outline in lime of a battleship on a beach at Kagoshima Bay and told his men to drop their dummy bombs on it. Only he knew it was the outline of the battleship *California*.

Thanks to all the weeks of arduous practice, the bombing results were remarkable, with scores as high as eighty percent. But they had been achieved at a price; chickens were refusing to lay eggs because of the almost constant roar of planes.

3.

On the evening of September 24 the Mackay cable office delivered a coded radiogram to Consul General Kita in Honolulu. It was a message from Captain Ogawa ordering future reports on Pearl Harbor to be keyed to five subareas:

... AREA A: THE WATERS BETWEEN FORD ISLAND AND THE ARSENAL. AREA B: WATERS ADJACENT TO BUT SOUTH AND WEST OF FORD ISLAND. AREA C: EAST LOCH. AREA D: MIDDLE LOCH. AREA E: WEST LOCH AND THE CHANNEL.

Kita passed this on to Yoshikawa, who made several tours of all areas and four days later cabled back a list of warships at anchor. It included a battleship, heavy and light cruisers, destroyers, and submarines—but no carriers.

Another Navy agent was at work in Mexico City, but his cover was in grave danger of being exposed. Commander

Tsunezo Wachi had been posing for the past year as assistant naval attaché. He was the chief of "L," Japan's largest overseas espionage ring, and his primary mission was to intercept messages of the U. S. fleet in the Atlantic. He soon broke the simple American code and was sending accurate reports to Tokyo on all naval movements in the Atlantic.

As a sideline he was buying mercury—he had already picked up some two thousand 90-lb. bottles—through a Mexican general. Since mercury was on the embargo list, these bottles had to be secreted in big drums, the top half containing bronze scrap. Late in September, however, one bottle was broken while its drum was being loaded onto a Japanese ship, and the mercury spilled out. Wachi's espionage career would have ended but he had smuggled in a big bundle of $1,000 bills for just such an emergency. His contact, an influential Mexican banker, promised to suppress the story and gave him a list of officials to be paid off—$100,000 was written opposite the name of the President of Mexico.

Wachi paid willingly, for he was on the verge of a major espionage breakthrough. A cashiered American Army major was already on his payroll at $2,000 a month. The disgruntled major, using the code name of Sutton, had given Wachi detailed reports of all naval shipping through the Panama Canal which he knew were accurate from his own intercepts. Once war broke out, Wachi planned to send Sutton to Washington, where he still had a number of friends in high places, as well as access to the Army-Navy Club.

On October 22—five days after the Emperor had ordered Tojo to form a new cabinet—Colonel Tsuji himself went on an espionage mission. Captain Asaeda had brought him information about the beaches and tides of Malaya, but he wanted to take a look for himself and persuaded Captain Ikeda, commander of a reconnaissance squadron, to fly him over the peninsula. At dawn the two men took off from Saigon, the new headquarters of the invasion forces, in an unmarked, unarmed twin-engine plane with fuel for five hours. Tsuji was wearing an air force uniform in case they were forced down in British territory.

They traversed the Gulf of Siam and two hours later could see the eastern coastline of Malaya stretched out clearly in front of them. On the left was Kota Bharu, the northernmost town of British-held Malaya, and on the right, Pattani and Singora, two Thai coastal towns. They flew directly over Singora and its pitiful airstrip. There were rubber plantations on either side of the main road. One good battalion, Tsuji figured, could seize the airfield and use it as a base of operations. He excitedly took a picture.

Next they turned toward the west coast of Malaya. Rain had lowered the visibility, so Tsuji told Ikeda to drop to 6,500 feet. Suddenly they saw a large air base through the haze. Tsuji shouted that it was Alor Star, a British base, and Ikeda pulled up into the storm and headed south. They flew over two equally impressive British aerodromes, turned back north and saw clearly two more fields, just as large. Tsuji was stunned. A small Japanese base at Singora would be helpless in the face of air attacks from such modern installations. Alor Star itself, as well as Kota Bharu, would have to be seized at "any sacrifice" within hours after the first landings.

They landed at Saigon with ten minutes of fuel left. "I saw all I wanted to see," Tsuji told the pilot, "and now I know we will win."

Still in air force uniform, Tsuji reported his findings to the Army commander and his staff, and new operations were devised which called for simultaneous landings of the 5th Division (at Singora and Pattani) and part of the 18th (at Kota Bharu); the 5th Division would seize the strategic bridge over the Perak River and occupy the Alor Star air base while the men of the 18th Division, after taking Kota Bharu and its field, would push south down the east coast.

Tsuji knew that it would be almost impossible to get the Army General Staff to accept such a radically different plan without loss of face, so he flew to Tokyo in order to present it in person. But even the remarkable Tsuji could not have succeeded without the help of an old friend, Colonel Takushiro Hattori, recently promoted to chief of the Operations Section of the Army General Staff. Hattori was not only stirred by Tsuji's daring flight but convinced his solution alone would work. Against considerable opposition, Hattori persuaded Army Chief of Staff Sugiyama to approve the Tsuji proposal.

In Hawaii, the regular diplomatic courier had just arrived with a package of $100 bills and instructions to deliver the money to a German on the payroll, Otto Kühn. An acquaintance of Himmler, who didn't like him, he had quit the Nazi party and come to Hawaii. Here he had lost his capital in a furniture venture and was now living off espionage and the profits from his wife's beauty salon. As yet he had done little for the Japanese except boast of his contacts.

Consul General Kita wrote "Kalama" on a sheet of paper, tore it in half through the word and sent one of the pieces to Kühn. Then he summoned Yoshikawa, gave him the other half, and asked him to take it "to a German-American who will carry on espionage when we all leave Hawaii."

Yoshikawa was reluctant—he knew nothing about any German and didn't want to act as a messenger boy—but Kita insisted. He went over to the safe and brought out the package, wrapped in newspapers, which contained $14,000 and a message. "Show your half of the paper to the German; if he has the other half, give him the money." Yoshikawa was also to get an answer to the message.

Not long before sunset on October 28 Yoshikawa, wearing green pants and an aloha shirt, strode out the front gate of the consulate and into a waiting taxicab. After climbing Diamond Head, it proceeded up the east coast for several minutes. About a mile from Kühn's house Yoshikawa dismissed the cab and sauntered down the road until he came to the right address, a large house with a spacious courtyard. Yoshikawa knocked at the kitchen door, but no one answered. He went inside, calling, "Hello . . . hello?" He waited for ten minutes; then, out of nowhere, a man appeared. He was in his early forties.

"Otto Kühn?"

The man nodded, but in case it was an FBI agent, Yoshikawa inconspicuously slid his half of the paper onto the edge of a table. The other turned pale and started to tremble but drew out a piece of paper. Still without saying a word, Yoshikawa matched the two pieces—"Kalama." He followed the equally silent Kühn out the back door to an open-air summer house, a Hawaiian-style gazebo. Here he handed over the bundle and told Kühn there was a message inside. Kühn fumbled with the package until he found unsigned instructions requesting a test with a shortwave transmitter. Using the call letter EXEX on frequency 11980, Kühn was to get in touch with station JHP at 0100 Pacific standard time on November 3 and at 0530 on November 5.

Yoshikawa asked for a reply and for the first time Kühn spoke. "I'll give the consul general an answer in two or three days," he said in a high, shaky, almost inaudible voice, then wrote down on a piece of paper that he could not make the test. He sealed the note in an envelope and handed it to Yoshikawa.

It was dusk by the time Yoshikawa reached the highway,

half expecting some FBI man to jump out at him. He caught a taxi and, with relief, headed back for the consulate.

Two more secret agents were on their way to Oahu aboard the liner *Taiyo-maru*. One was Commander Toshihide Maejima, a submarine expert, disguised as a ship doctor. The other was the assistant purser, Takao Suzuki. Only the ship's captain and purser knew he was Suguru Suzuki, the youngest lieutenant commander in the Navy and an aviation expert. He was the son of a general and nephew of a famous admiral, the Grand Chamberlain Kantaro Suzuki, who had escaped assassination so narrowly during the 2/26 Incident. His primary mission was to determine the exact positions of the targets, what types of bombs should be used, a possible emergency landing site and—most important—whether the Lahaina harbor on the island of Maui was still a base for U. S. naval ships. If so, a large number of planes would have to be diverted from the attack on Pearl Harbor. And he had been told to study sea and weather conditions on the trip to Honolulu. *Taiyo-maru* was going out of its way to track the exact course that Nagumo's Striking Force was scheduled to take.

The American passengers aboard were comfortable in spite of the heavy seas, but most of them, like Carl Sipple and his wife, felt ill at ease. The Sipples had left Japan with their two small children because of the growing international tension. Their uneasiness increased as day after day passed without an announcement of the ship's position. Considering how windy and cold it was and how low the sun stood above the horizon, they guessed they were far north of the usual shipping lane, and there was no trace of other vessels. Were they being taken to another port? The Sipples tried to send a radiogram to friends in Honolulu, but no messages could be dispatched. *Taiyo-maru* was on radio silence.

Before dawn of November 1 the ship finally approached Oahu. Sipple went up on deck to get a glimpse of Diamond Head and at first light saw a small white launch in the ship's wake. Fighter planes circled above, then swooped so low that the passengers could exchange waves with the pilots.

Suzuki was on the bridge, scanning the mouth of Pearl Harbor with binoculars. It was barely wide enough for one big ship to slip through. Just after six o'clock a launchload of U. S. Marines boarded and stonily stood guard at the bridge and engine room. Suzuki guessed they were there to prevent any attempt to sink the ship at the entrance to Pearl Harbor.

He accosted the group of port officials, including several

U. S. Navy officers, who came aboard to pilot the ship into Honolulu, and offhandedly asked how deep the water was, and if there were any mines. The answers came readily. Over drinks at the ship's bar he also learned there was a steel net across the mouth of the harbor which opened and closed automatically, and that the whirling gadget on the mast of a nearby British warship was something called radar.

But the rest of his mission could not be carried out. Kita sent a staff member with a warning that it would be wiser if the two agents stayed aboard the ship. Suzuki industriously made up a list of ninety-seven questions. He was told the answers would be brought back before the ship left.

The questionnaire was turned over to Yoshikawa. "On what day of the week are the greatest number of ships in the harbor?" That was easy—Sunday. "Are there any large flying boats on patrol?" That too was easy—the big PBY's went out every morning and evening. "Where do the ships that leave the harbor go, and why?" He had no idea, but surmised from the ships' speed and the time they were gone that they traveled some five hundred miles for maneuvers. "Is there an antisubmarine net at the mouth of Pearl Harbor? If so, describe." He had only heard there was but decided to find out for himself. Wearing his sporty outfit of the usual green trousers and aloha shirt and carrying a bamboo fishing pole, he walked down the highway past Hickam Field, then crossed a barren area toward the mouth of Pearl Harbor, ready to pose as a Filipino if caught. He walked into a small woods next to some naval buildings and almost blundered into sailors hanging up wet laundry. He hid in the brush until sunset. He thought briefly of committing suicide if he was apprehended, but decided to just say, "I give up," and to hell with it.

At dusk he crept to the entrance of the harbor. He heard voices and froze until there was silence. Then he lowered himself gently into the water, and quietly fluttering his legs, swam fifty yards into the channel. He groped with his feet. Nothing. He dived for the net but was so excited that he had only enough breath to go down a few yards. Five more times he dived. Still nothing. He swam back to shore. These were his most anxious moments as an agent, and in the end he had nothing positive to report.

On *Taiyo-maru*, Suzuki spent hours observing and taking pictures of the Pearl Harbor entrance and the adjoining Hickam Field. During the next few days various consular employees carrying newspapers walked past the Marines guarding *Taiyo-maru*. Inside the newspapers was the information Suzuki wanted.

By November 5, the day of departure, he knew the thickness of both the concrete roofs of the hangars at Hickam Field and the armor of the battleships, and had pictures of Pearl Harbor taken from surrounding hills, as well as recent aerial photographs. He summarized all he could on a single sheet of paper and hid it. His mission was completed at three o'clock in the afternoon, when the final courier came aboard ship just prior to sailing time with a locked diplomatic pouch containing Yoshikawa's latest findings and the most accurate maps.

4.

Off Kyushu a large crate was brought aboard Nagumo's flagship, *Akagi,* and carried to Kusaka's office. Inside was a seven-foot square mock-up of Oahu. For the next few days Genda, the planner, and Fuchida, the leader, memorized every feature of the terrain.

The Combined Fleet moved from its regular base off Sakurajima, the beautiful little island two hours' sail south of Hiroshima, into Bungo Strait, where it posed as the U. S. Pacific Fleet. Nagumo's carriers moved to within two hundred miles of the "Americans" and launched dive bombers and their fighter escort, followed by high-level and torpedo bombers. The planes assembled without an intercom system, by means of signals chalked on slates and held up in the cockpits.

The ultimate technical problem—a suitable torpedo—had finally been solved by Captain Fumio Aiko, a torpedo expert at Yokosuka. He made wooden fins from aerial stabilizers and fitted them on torpedoes. After scores of tests in Kagoshima Bay, 80 percent of the torpedoes ran shallow enough for the Pearl Harbor waters. Now the problem was to manufacture the improvised fins in time for the attack.

All objections within the Navy to Operation Z ended on November 3 when Yamamoto and his key staff officers flew to Tokyo to see Nagano. At the end of the discussion the Chief of Staff sighed and said, "As for the Pearl Harbor attack, my judgment is not always good, because I'm old. So I will have to trust yours."

Two days later Yamamoto issued "Combined Fleet Top Secret Operation Order No. 1," a bulky 151-page document.

It outlined naval strategy for the first phase of hostilities covering not only Pearl Harbor but more or less simultaneous assaults on Malaya, the Philippines, Guam, Wake, Hong Kong and the South Seas.

Yamamoto then assembled all squadron leaders to his flagship and told them about Pearl Harbor.* "This time," he said, "you must not think lightly of your enemy. America is not an ordinary foe and will never fall short as one."

On November 6 General Count Hisaichi Terauchi took command of Southern Army, which was made up of four armies. He was to seize all American, Dutch and British possessions in the "southern area" as soon as possible. After simultaneous attacks on Malaya and the Philippines, Lieutenant General Tomoyuki Yamashita (pronounced Ya-*mash*-ta) would take Malaya and Singapore with the 25th Army. Lieutenant General Masaharu Homma, an amateur playwright and leader of the pro–British-American minority in the Army, was to conquer the Philippines with the 14th Army. General Tsukada, who had represented the Army at so many stormy liaison conferences, was made Terauchi's chief of staff. Many officers at Army General Staff headquarters watched him leave Tokyo with foreboding. Now who could control the tempestuous younger officers?

Within twenty-four hours Yamamoto issued his second secret order setting the tentative date to start hostilities as December 8. Two factors had determined the choice: there would be a full moon, which would facilitate launching from the carriers, and it would be Sunday (December 7) in Hawaii. From Yoshikawa's reports it had been established that the Pacific Fleet usually entered Pearl Harbor on a Friday and left the following Monday.

On November 10 Admiral Nagumo put Yamamoto's plan into effect by issuing his first operational order. There was an understanding that if diplomatic negotiations with America were successfully concluded even at the very last moment, the attack on Pearl Harbor would be called off and the Striking Force returned to a rendezvous point at latitude 42 degrees north by longitude 170 degrees east, where it would stay in a state of readiness until further instructions.

The six carriers were stripped of personal belongings and

---

*Lieutenant Commander Shigeru Itaya, who would command all the fighter squadrons, was the only fighter squadron leader present. The others had already been informed of Pearl Harbor by Genda. He told them it would have to be a one-way mission but when they vowed to kill the men who had made such a plan, he promised to get it changed.

unnecessary equipment and loaded with extra jerricans and drums of oil. All ships were under tight security. Usually when a fleet left Japan it was stocked with tropical clothing and special food for southern climates. This time the sailors would need foul-weather clothing, antifreeze grease, special weatherproof gun tarpaulins and other equipment for the cold, and Kusaka hoped it could all be collected without arousing suspicions.

On November 16 the Pearl Harbor Carrier Striking Force (*Kido Butai*) gathered at the mouth of the Inland Sea. It was a formidable armada: six carriers; two fast battleships with 14-inch guns, *Hiei* and *Kirishima;* two heavy cruisers, *Tone* and *Chikuma;* a light cruiser; eight destroyers; and a train of three oilers and a supply ship. Two of the carriers, *Akagi* (Red Castle) and *Kaga* (Increased Joy), had been converted from a battle cruiser and a battleship and displaced more than 30,000 tons. *Hirya* (Flying Dragon) and *Soryu* (Green Dragon) were only 18,000 tons, but of more modern design. *Shokaku* (Soaring Crane) and *Zuikaku* (Happy Crane) were the newest and largest, 826 feet long, almost exactly the same size as America's most formidable carrier, *Enterprise*. The six carriers held 360 planes: 81 fighters, 135 dive bombers, 104 high-level (horizontal) bombers and 40 torpedo bombers, which had only thirty-torpedoes fitted with the new fins. The remaining hundred would not be ready for more than a week and *Kido Butai* would have to start without them.

Late the following afternoon Yamamoto visited *Akagi* to wish Nagumo and key personnel good luck. Fuchida thought the admiral looked grim as he warned of the strongest foe in their history, but later at a farewell party in the wardroom Yamamoto's confidence was infectious. He said, "I think this operation will be successful," and a rousing toast was drunk to the Emperor.

Soon after dark *Akagi* slowly steamed out of Saeki Bay flanked by two destroyers. Her lights were out and crystals had been temporarily removed from the communications equipment to ensure radio silence. But the ships left behind in the Inland Sea were ready to set up a large volume of radio communication to mislead enemy listeners.

On the quarterdeck of *Nagato*, hands behind his back, Yamamoto paced back and forth, stopping every so often to stare at the dim shape of the departing carrier. Confident as he was of Operation Z, he still dreaded war with America. "What a strange position I find myself in now," he had recently written an Academy classmate, "having to make a decision diametrically opposed to my personal opinion, with no choice but to push full speed in pursuance of that decision. Is that, too, fate? And what a bad start we've made. . . ."

One by one, at irregular intervals, other ships in the Striking Force weighed anchor and headed on separate courses for a rendezvous some thousand miles north of Tokyo. It would have been too obvious to set sail directly en masse for Oahu. Instead *Kido Butai* would reassemble at Etorofu Island in the Kuriles which possessed a large deep bay, rough in summer but strangely calm in winter. The island was an ideal clandestine rallying point. Its single village comprised three dwellings, a small concrete pier, a post office and a wireless station. To be on the safe side, the gunboat *Kunajiri* was already impounding outgoing mail and telegrams, while patrol boats rounded up any fisherman in Hitokappu Bay.

Kaga was the last carrier still left in the Inland Sea. It was being loaded with the final modified torpedoes. Once the ship got under way the captain gathered the entire crew on deck to announce that they were heading for Hitokappu Bay and then Pearl Harbor—where Yoshikawa was watching a large battleship enter the harbor along with eight destroyers. Already at anchor were five heavy cruisers and one *Enterprise*-class carrier.

Taiyo-maru was docking in Yokohama. The vital information Suguru Suzuki needed was still locked in the diplomatic pouch. And now he had to turn it over to a Foreign Ministry representative. Empty-handed, he took the train to Tokyo, where Admiral Nagano ordered him to leave at once for Hitokappu Bay with the latest information from Hawaii. But the pouch had been lost in transit. The Foreign Ministry officials knew nothing about it, neither could they locate it, and Suzuki was forced to head north on the battleship *Hiei*, bringing only a single sheet of paper which contained his own summary of the missing information and a sketch of Pearl Harbor made from memory.

Urgent though his mission was, it took him four days to reach *Kido Butai*. He learned that the missing diplomatic pouch had finally been found in Tokyo, only to disappear again. The courier plane with the pouch aboard, sent out two days earlier, had not yet arrived and Suzuki had to brief Genda, Kusaka and other staff officers on the basis of his page of notes. He described Hickam and Wheeler fields in detail and said there were 350 Army planes on Oahu.* No one at the Japanese consulate had seen any ships at Lahaina and he had confirmed this on the voyage back to Japan over drinks from half a dozen returning Nisei.

On *Akagi*, ship captains and their executive officers were given the course. One of the captains wanted to know what to do if he ran into a Soviet merchant ship out of Vladivostok. "Sink it," was the answer. "Sink anything flying any flag."

In the late afternoon on November 25 more than five hundred flying officers from all the carriers jammed into *Akagi*'s aviation-crew quarters, which had been stripped of bunks and tables. Nagumo outlined the attack. It was the first time most of them had heard the words Pearl Harbor. As the admiral spoke, excitement mounted and when he ended with a "Good fight and good luck!" there was a deafening cheer.

When the noise died down, Genda and Fuchida detailed the attack on the Pearl Harbor mock-up. Each flier was given pictures of American warships and islands near Oahu which could be used for forced landings; friendly submarines would be at marked positions to pick them up.

It had grown so dark and the seas were so rough that many of the fliers could not get back to their own ships. That night, the eve of departure, there was a giant *sake* party aboard *Akagi*. But the commander in chief was in no mood for celebration. For a man of courage, Nagumo was a compulsive worrier and the past week he had been telling his chief of staff over and over, "I wonder if it will go well," and Kusaka would invariably reply, *"Daijobu"*—"Don't worry."

But Nagumo could not be reassured. Long after midnight he got out of bed and ordered his aide to rouse Lieutenant Commander Suguru Suzuki. Still in sleeping kimono, he apologized for waking Suzuki, but something bothered him. "You're absolutely certain no one sighted the Pacific Fleet in Lahaina?"

"Yes, Admiral."

"Is there any possibility the Pacific Fleet might assemble in Lahaina?"

---

*Most of his information was fairly correct except for this figure. There were 231 (Army) planes in all the Hawaiian islands.

The courier plane with the vital information arrived several hours after the Striking Force departed. Suzuki had remained behind and he ordered the pilot to give chase and drop the material on *Akagi*. But the plane ran into a local snowstorm and had to turn back.

"None."

Nagumo seemed to relax. He nodded his thanks. Suzuki retired, grateful and moved that he had been able to calm his commander's fears.

The morning of the twenty-sixth dawned bright and clear with unusually high pressure for this time of year. The seas had calmed. It seemed a good omen; but just as the fleet was weighing anchor, one of the giant screws of *Akagi* got fouled in wire, and a sailor fell into the icy waters of Hitokappu Bay.

Half an hour late, the armada finally got under way, except for the man overboard who could not be found. There was a feeling of excitement and purpose on every ship and as they filed past Etorofu, fringed with its usual veil of mist, the heavy cruisers and battleships test-fired their guns by throwing live rounds into a hillside of the island. The sound of the guns and the splashes of snow bursting on the hill like huge white flowers stirred the men.

In Washington, Hull's uncompromising note was being typed out for Ambassadors Kurusu and Nomura.

7   "This War May Come Quicker Than Anyone Dreams"

1.

On the morning after Hull sent the note, Secretary of War Henry Stimson phoned him to ask whether he had dispatched the *modus vivendi* to Japan. The Secretary of State replied, "I have washed my hands of it and it is now in the hands of you and Knox—the Army and the Navy."

Stimson called Roosevelt and expressed concern about reports that a large Japanese expeditionary force was moving out of Shanghai for the south. Shouldn't a final alert be sent to Lieutenant General Douglas MacArthur, commander of the United States Army Forces in the Far East (USAFFE), in the Philippines advising him to be "on the *qui vive* for any attack"? The President thought it was a good idea, and at nine-thirty Stimson summoned to his office Brigadier General Leonard T. Gerow, chief of the General Staff Operations

Division, as well as Secretary of the Navy Frank Knox and Admiral Harold ("Betty") Stark, the Chief of Naval Operations.

Once more the military urged that a crisis be postponed as long as possible. Stimson said that he also would be "glad to have time," and thought Stark was being "as usual, a little bit timid and cautious" when it came to a real crisis, but he "didn't want it at any cost of humility on the part of the United States or of reopening the thing which would show a weakness on our part."

The war warning they finally radioed to MacArthur read:

NEGOTIATIONS WITH THE JAPANESE APPEAR TO BE TER-
MINATED TO ALL PRACTICAL PURPOSES WITH ONLY THE
BAREST POSSIBILITIES THAT THE JAPANESE GOVERNMENT
MIGHT COME BACK AND OFFER TO CONTINUE PERIOD
JAPANESE FUTURE ACTION UNPREDICTABLE BUT HOSTILE
ACTION POSSIBLE AT ANY MOMENT PERIOD IF HOSTILITIES
CANNOT, REPEAT CANNOT, BE AVOIDED THE UNITED STATES
DESIRES THAT JAPAN COMMIT THE FIRST OVERT ACT
PERIOD THIS POLICY SHOULD NOT, REPEAT NOT, BE CON-
STRUED AS RESTRICTING YOU TO A COURSE OF ACTION THAT
MIGHT JEOPARDIZE YOUR DEFENSE . . .

A similar message was sent to General Walter C. Short, commander of the Hawaiian Department of the Army, but it also ordered him to do nothing "to alarm civil population or disclose intent."* General Short took the entire warning to mean he should institute a sabotage alert. He informed Washington of this but apparently nobody there read his reply carefully. He was never told he had missed the import of the instructions.

Admiral Stark wrote his own message to the naval commanders in the Pacific—Admiral Thomas C. Hart in the Philippines and Admiral Husband E. Kimmel in Hawaii. It was clear and to the point:

THIS DISPATCH IS TO BE CONSIDERED A WAR WARNING X
NEGOTIATIONS WITH JAPAN LOOKING TOWARD STABILIZA-
TION OF CONDITIONS IN THE PACIFIC HAVE CEASED AND AN
AGGRESSIVE MOVE BY JAPAN IS EXPECTED IN THE NEXT
FEW DAYS X THE NUMBER AND EQUIPMENT OF JAPANESE
TROOPS AND THE ORGANIZATION OF NAVAL TASK FORCES
INDICATES AN AMPHIBIOUS EXPEDITION AGAINST EITHER

---

*The Army Pearl Harbor Board later sarcastically referred to this as the "Do or Don't Message."

Despite these alerts, the negotiations continued in name. That same day Kurusu and Nomura called on the President. Roosevelt said he still hadn't given up hope for a peaceful settlement. But the recent occupation of Indochina, troop movements to the south and hostile talk from Japan all had had "the effect of a cold bath on the United States Government and people."

Just before midnight Kurusu phoned Tokyo, using a clumsy voice code that wouldn't have deceived a layman. The negotiations, for example, were "marriage proposal"; Roosevelt was "Miss Kimiko"; a critical turn was the "birth of a child." For seven minutes Kurusu talked to Kumaichi Yamamoto, chief of the American Bureau in the Foreign Ministry, as American intelligence recorded every word.* He asked how things were in Japan. "Does it seem as if a child might be born?"

"Yes," Yamamoto replied firmly, "the birth of the child seems imminent."

". . . In which direction . . ." Kurusu hesitated, realizing he was not using the code. "Is it to be a boy or a girl?"

Yamamoto laughed, then caught on. "Oh, it's to be a strong healthy boy. . . . The matrimonial question, that is, the matter pertaining to arranging a marriage—don't break them off."

"Not break them? You mean talks?" asked the befuddled Kurusu. "Oh, my," he said helplessly and added with a resigned laugh, "Well, I'll do what I can." He paused. "Please read carefully what Miss Kimiko had to say as contained in today's telegram. . . . They want to keep carrying on the matrimonial question. They do. In the meantime we're faced with the excitement of having a child born. On top of that Tokugawa [the Japanese Army] is really champing at the bit, isn't he? Tokugawa is, isn't he?" He laughed nervously. "That's why I doubt if anything can be done."

Yamamoto said he didn't think it was as bad as all that. "Well, we can't sell a mountain [Well, we can't yield]."

---

*The U.S. translation is the only source available. No Japanese record could be found, and both Yamamoto and Kurusu are dead.

"Oh, sure, I know that. That isn't even a debatable question any more."

"Well, then, although we can't yield, we'll give you some kind of a reply to that telegram."

"In any event," Kurusu went on, "Miss Kimiko is leaving town tomorrow, and will remain in the country until Wednesday."

"Will you please continue to do your best?"

"Oh, yes. I'll do my best. And Nomura's doing everything too." Yamamoto asked if the talks that day with Miss Kimiko contained anything of interest. "No, nothing of particular interest, except that it is quite clear now that southward—ah ..."—Kurusu began to flounder again—"the south—the south matter is having considerable effect."

"I see. Well, then, good-bye."

"Good-bye," said the relieved Kurusu.

The next day MAGIC uncovered even more important information from an intercepted message to Consul General Kita sent from Tokyo nine days earlier:

. . . In case of emergency (danger of cutting off our diplomatic relations), and the cutting off of international communications, the following warning will be added in the middle of the daily Japanese-language shortwave news broadcast:

(1) In case of Japan-U. S. relations in danger: HIGASHI NO KAZE AME [east wind, rain]
(2) Japan-U.S.S.R. relations: KITA NO KAZE KUMORI [north wind, cloudy]
(3) Japan-British relations: NISHI NO KAZE HARE [west wind, clear]

This signal will be given in the middle and at the end as a weather forecast and each sentence will be repeated twice. When this is heard, please destroy all code papers, etc. This is as yet to be a completely secret arrangement.

This "winds" message created a turmoil in Washington. Alarmed intelligence officers made arrangements to monitor around the clock all future Japanese newscasts for the key phrases, unaware that a packet of untranslated intercepts could instantly have unmasked the attack on Pearl Harbor. Yoshikawa's espionage reports were piling up in the busy translators' "Incoming" baskets—too low on the priority list for even a cursory examination.

That same morning—it was November 28—Stimson burst into Roosevelt's bedroom, finding the President still in bed but in conference, with more news of the southbound Japanese expedition. Stimson wanted to attack it with Philippine-based B-17's but Roosevelt would not be panicked, and when he met a few hours later with the War Council it was agreed that there should be no precipitous countermeasures. Japan would only be warned that "we should have to fight" once her troops reached a certain point. It was also decided to have the President send a personal message to the Emperor expressing a desire for peace and a warning that war was bound to come if Japan persisted in her aggression.

It was a good idea and the Emperor would have been receptive. He had just requested the *jushin* to re-examine the entire situation and report back to him. The former prime ministers—Prince Konoye was the eighth—had not been involved in the previous decisions and would have a more objective viewpoint. Marquis Kido, the Privy Seal, had wanted the meeting conducted in the presence of His Majesty, but Prime Minister Tojo refused on the grounds that the *jushin* had no legal function. A compromise was reached: after the meeting the senior statesmen would lunch with the Emperor and express their opinions.

The next morning at nine-thirty, November 29, they met in the Imperial Court Room with Tojo, four of his Cabinet ministers and Privy Council President Hara. It was more of an informal discussion than a conference; there was no presiding officer and no decision was to be made. Baron Reijiro Wakatsuki, long an opponent of militarism, wanted to know more about the deadline for negotiations. "Does this mean there is no room for further talk?"

Foreign Minister Togo said there was "no use going any further," and Tojo felt there was "no hope for diplomatic dealings." From now on diplomacy should solely be used "to facilitate operations."

"Are we to go to war upon abandoning negotiations?" insisted Wakatsuki.

"Until today we have tried our best to reach a diplomatic solution," Tojo said, "conducting ourselves with extreme prudence. But now we don't have to be ashamed of mobilizing military force as a dignified and just action."

This did not satisfy the baron. Like Kido, he thought that *gashin-shotan* (enduring hard times) would be better for Japan than war.

What if we resorted to *gashin-shotan* and still ended up in war? asked General Suzuki. "Then we wouldn't have a chance in the world of winning it."

This prompted so many questions from Wakatsuki that Tojo impatiently interrupted. "Please trust what we say. We can occupy the sphere [Southeast Asia] and get enough oil. In three years we can gradually expand our sphere. As for aircraft oil, we can somehow manage; as for iron and steel, last year's production was four million seven hundred and sixty thousand tons. We can increase this after three years."

"I don't understand what I've heard so far," Admiral Keisuke Okada interjected, taking up the questioning. What about the European war, for example?

"We are going hand in hand with Italy and Germany, with whom we have a treaty," Tojo replied. This was a strategic necessity that would enable Japan to move west and join up with Hitler's forces. "We must crush England." India would be an objective on the way. "Then we'll carry out Near East joint operations in line with the German-Soviet war."

Okada didn't think this grandiose plan would work, nor would expansion to Southeast Asia bring any increase in production. "Shipping of materials back home will get tight. After three years, I couldn't even dream of production. What are you going to do about raw materials?"

These were realistic fears but Tojo's response was brusque. "The question of resources is precarious, but we can manage. All other things being equal, I think we can get along. Please trust us."

"Very doubtful," Okada remarked. "You can go on building up armament plants, but how are you going to get hold of raw materials? It is not an easy task. We'll soon run out of natural resources."

"We will go on a priority principle."

Okada turned his attack in a new direction and asked if the Navy was good enough to beat America.

Tojo, who had still to get a positive answer from the Navy, said that Japan, by taking strategic points one by one, was preparing for a long war and would emerge victorious.

"So far so good," Okada said wryly. "But there are many xyz's. With the U. S. building program as it is at present, don't you think there is some danger?"

"Everything is being taken into consideration," said the exasperated Tojo and lost his composure. "Suppose we don't fight. What would be the result? We just can't bow to England and the United States. We've lost one hundred and sixty thousand lives so far in the China Incident. Now more than two million people are suffering. No more suffering! If we go on like this for a few years, we'll lose our chance to fight. We're already losing valuable time for operations!"

But Okada was not to be cowed and became openly

sarcastic. "We're trying to come to an amicable settlement with America so we can redeem the blood being shed every moment! We're building up the Greater East Asia Co-prosperity Sphere just for this purpose. We import great quantities of rice from these countries, yet they are still poverty-stricken! We want to take care of these people. Labor and shipping is short, and to make them happy we must make sacrifices. Buying materials there by Army scrip is simple injustice."

Tojo ignored the mockery. "That all depends on how we appeal to the people's feelings," he said. "We must make good use of native organizations. At first the people will find life difficult but very soon they will get on well."

It was past noon and the meeting was adjourned for lunch with the Emperor. Afterward everyone, including His Majesty and Kido, moved to the Imperial Chamber. The Emperor said, "We're going through very difficult times, aren't we?" It was a polite invitation to speak out.

"We don't have to worry about the spiritual strength of our people," said Baron Wakatsuki, "but we must carefully study whether or not we have the material resources to carry out a long war. This morning we listened to the government explanations, but I'm still concerned."

Tojo reminded the Emperor that what had been said was based on the unanimous views of the Cabinet and the Supreme Command.

"I've also been listening to the government explanations, and I too am not yet convinced," said Okada.

Neither was Prince Konoye. "I wonder if it is necessary to resort immediately to war even if the negotiations have broken down. I feel we might find a solution and still keep the status quo. In other words, to remain in the condition of *gashin-shotan*."

Nor was Admiral Mitsumasa Yonai. "I'm not able to express a concrete opinion, since I don't have the background. But if you'll forgive the slang, I'm afraid that by trying to avoid *jiri-hin* [slow poverty] we'll end up in *doka-hin* [instant poverty]."

Only two *jushin* generals, Nobuyuki Abe and Senjuro Hayashi, put their complete trust in the Tojo government. It appeared the session was over, but Wakatsuki wanted to bring up still another point. Tojo tried to stop him but the baron would not be silenced. "If our very existence is at stake, we should go to war even in the face of possible defeat and a scorching of our land, but to push a national policy for an ideal—for instance, the establishment of the Greater East Asia Co-prosperity Sphere or the stabilization of East Asia—and to spend our national strength shackled by such ideals, that is indeed dangerous. And I'd like you all to think it over."

Stubbornly, Tojo reiterated that the whole matter had been discussed for hours on end at liaison conferences. They had explored in detail whether Japan could get the necessary supplies for a long war, and when and how the war, once started, could be brought to an end. The first aspect depended on the outcome of the initial stage of the conflict, and the second might be resolved through the mediation of the Soviet Union or the Vatican.

In the face of almost universal disapproval Tojo had not wavered, and Kido—who had not uttered a word, but taken voluminous notes—realized the situation was "beyond control." The influence of the Throne had failed. War was inevitable and the rise or fall of Japan was in the hands of the gods.

It was already four o'clock but Tojo's day was by no means over. He immediately convened the 74th Liaison Conference, and it was agreed to warn Hitler and Mussolini that the Japanese-American negotiations were certain to be broken off and that there was imminent danger of war.

Foreign Minister Togo asked Navy Chief of Staff Nagano what the zero hour was. Finance Minister Kaya also had to know; once hostilities started, the stock market would drop precipitously. Only with the knowledge of the exact hour could he prevent a crash.

"Well, then," said the reluctant Nagano, "I'll tell you. The zero hour is . . ."—he lowered his voice—". . . December 8." This was news even to General Tojo.* "There is still time, so you'd better come up with the kind of diplomacy that will help us win the war."

"I understand," said Togo. "But can't we tell our representatives [Kurusu and Nomura] that we've made up our minds? We've told the attachés [in Washington], haven't we?"

"We haven't told the naval attaché," Nagano answered.

Togo wondered why Nagano was acting so suspiciously.

---

*He knew about the combined Army and Navy operations in the Philippines and Malaya, but it was not until the following day that he learned of Pearl Harbor, and even then he was given no operational details. None of the civilian members of the Cabinet or high court officials, like Kido, yet had an inkling of the main target—nor would they be told.

"We can't go on keeping our diplomats in the dark, can we?"

Nagano finally had to answer. "We're going to make a surprise attack," he said. His deputy, Vice Admiral Seiichi Ito, explained that the Navy wanted the negotiations with America left hanging until hostilities had begun so the initial attack would be a complete surprise.

Togo restrained himself. He was quite calm when he said that Japan would lose international good faith unless she made a proper notification of her intent. But his self-control gave way, and he began to stutter that the Navy plan was "entirely unpermissible, being in contravention of accepted procedure." It was unthinkable for Japan "to commit irresponsible acts which would be hurtful to the national honor and prestige."

Someone remarked, "This is one occasion when the entire population of Japan will have to be like Kuranosuke Oishi." Oishi was the leader of the forty-seven *ronin* who pretended to be a dissolute drunk.

Togo said he had a previous engagement, suggested the meeting adjourn and shot back his chair. As he was rising, Ito asked a favor for the Navy; if prior notification had to be given, couldn't it go to Ambassador Grew rather than to Hull?

Togo answered with a brusque "No!" and shouldered his way out of the room. He went directly to his office and composed cables to Berlin and Rome which were dispatched late that night. The one to Ambassador Hiroshi Oshima revealed that the negotiations had failed.

... IN THE FACE OF THIS, OUR EMPIRE FACES A GRAVE SITUATION AND MUST ACT WITH DETERMINATION. WILL YOUR EXCELLENCY, THEREFORE, IMMEDIATELY INTERVIEW CHANCELLOR HITLER AND FOREIGN MINISTER RIBBENTROP AND CONFIDENTIALLY COMMUNICATE TO THEM A SUMMARY OF THE DEVELOPMENTS. SAY TO THEM THAT LATELY ENGLAND AND THE UNITED STATES HAVE TAKEN A PROVOCATIVE ATTITUDE, BOTH OF THEM. SAY THAT THEY ARE PLANNING TO MOVE MILITARY FORCES INTO VARIOUS PLACES IN EAST ASIA AND THAT WE WILL INEVITABLY HAVE TO COUNTER BY ALSO MOVING TROOPS. SAY VERY SECRETLY TO THEM THAT THERE IS EXTREME DANGER THAT WAR MAY SUDDENLY BREAK OUT BETWEEN THE ANGLO-SAXON NATIONS AND JAPAN THROUGH SOME CLASH OF ARMS AND ADD THAT THE TIME OF THE BREAKING OUT OF THIS WAR MAY COME QUICKER THAN ANYONE DREAMS.

Curiously, Togo did not order Oshima to ask for a German declaration of war in case Japan and America fought. He did summon Ambassador Ott. If worse came to worst, would Germany come to Japan's assistance? Ott answered without hesitation: We will give you all possible help.

The message to Oshima was intercepted by MAGIC and passed on to Roosevelt. Equally alarming was a United Press dispatch in the *New York Times* from Tokyo that Sunday morning, November 30: Prime Minister Tojo had just made a provocative speech declaring that Chiang Kai-shek was "dancing to the tune of American and British Communism because the United States and Britain desire to fish in troubled waters" and stir up Asians one against the other. "This is the stock in trade of Britain and the United States and therefore we must purge this sort of action with a vengeance." Japan was determined to co-ordinate all Asians "so that a chorus of victory may go up in the camp of justice as speedily as possible," and nothing be allowed "to interfere with this sphere because this sphere was decreed by Providence."

It was a speech that Togo had never made, or even read, let alone approved. Someone else had written it and it had been read at a meeting commemorating the first anniversary of the Sino-Japanese Basic Treaty. Its belligerency had been exaggerated by poor translation. The expression "we must purge this sort of action with a vengeance," for example, should have read, "this sort of practice must be stopped."

There was also an item in the *Times* indicating that the President might curtail his Thanksgiving holiday at Warm Springs, Georgia; and late that night Kurusu again phoned Kumaichi Yamamoto in Tokyo. "The President is returning tomorrow!" he said. "He is hurrying home."*

"Is there any special significance to this?"

"The newspapers have made much of the Premier's speech, and it is having strong repercussions here."

"Is that so?" Yamamoto didn't know what Kurusu was talking about.

"Yes, it was a drastic statement he made. The newspapers carried large headlines over it; and the President seems to be returning because of it. There no doubt are other reasons, but this is the reason the newspapers are giving." Kurusu was

---

*This dialogue is taken from the MAGIC translation, "a preliminary condensed version" of the eight-minute conversation.

disturbed and showed it. "Unless greater caution is exercised in speeches by the Premier and others, it puts us in a very difficult position . . ."

"We *are* being careful."

"We here are doing our best, but these reports are seized upon by the correspondents and the worst features enlarged upon. Please caution the Premier, the Foreign Minister, and others. Tell the Foreign Minister that we had expected to hear something different, some good work, but instead we get this [the "Tojo" speech]." Kurusu paused, then asked, "Are the Japanese-American negotiations to continue?"

"Yes."

Irritated, Kurusu said, "You were very urgent about them before, weren't you; but now you want them to stretch out." He did not know that the negotiations were now to be used solely to mask the Pearl Harbor raid but he was getting suspicious and just recently had mused to Masuo Kato of the Domei News Agency, "Am I being used as a smoke screen?" He began to scold Yamamoto. "Both the Premier and the Foreign Minister will need to change the tone of their speeches! Do you understand? Please, all, use more discretion."

The Emperor's official sanction was the last formal step before war. At five minutes after two on Monday, December 1, the imperial conference was opened in Room One East of the Palace in the usual formal style. Face stern and voice clipped, Prime Minister Tojo announced that Japan could not submit to American demands to quit China and nullify the Tripartite Pact, or her very existence would be in jeopardy. "Matters have reached the point where Japan must begin war with the United States, Great Britain and the Netherlands to preserve her empire."

After Tojo detailed the long, tedious history of the American-Japanese negotiations, Admiral Nagano rose and spiritedly declared that the officers and men of the Army and Navy were "burning with a desire to serve their Emperor and their country even at the cost of their lives." This was followed by dissertations on problems ranging from public morale, emergency precautions and food supplies to the nation's economy and finance.

The Emperor, on his dais, sat passive and silent. Occasionally he nodded and seemed to be in an excellent mood. Sugiyama was "awed and deeply moved by His Majesty's graceful humor," but Finance Minister Kaya thought it was obvious he did not want war.

Privy Council President Hara began to ask questions and the last were the most unsettling. "What will happen in case of air raids? . . . What will we do if a great fire should break out in Tokyo? Do you have a plan for this?"

General Teiichi Suzuki said that there would be simple shelters for those who remained in the city. The reply was unsatisfactory, but even Hara found this no reason to make any more concessions to America. "The United States is acting in a conceited, stubborn and disrespectful manner," he said. "If we give in, we'd surrender in one stroke what we won in the Sino-Japanese and Russo-Japanese wars as well as the Manchurian Incident. We cannot do this."

Tojo himself summed up what they all felt. The Japanese Empire stood at the threshold of glory or collapse. "We tremble with awe in the presence of His Majesty. . . . If his Majesty decides on war, we will all do our best to repay our obligations to him by bringing the government and the military closer than ever together, resolving that a united nation will go on to victory, making every effort to achieve our national purposes and thereby putting at ease His Majesty's mind."

There was nothing else to do but bow to the Emperor, who then, silent, without expression, left the room. Those remaining signed the documents proposing war, which were delivered to the Emperor. For some time he pondered the matter until he felt assured that the decision to initiate hostilities was not being pushed through by a few aggressive military men. He told Kido that Hull's demands were too humiliating. He had already defied tradition and training by insisting on a return to "blank paper," and could do no more. He affixed his seal to the historic papers. The decision for war was formally sanctioned.*

---

*In January 1946 the Emperor broke his silence about these events in a rare display of confidence to his Grand Chamberlain, Hisanori Fujita: "Naturally, war should never be allowed. In this case, too, I tried to think of everything, some way to avoid it. I exhausted every means within my power. However, my utmost endeavor was to no avail, and we plunged into war at the end. It was truly regrettable. . . .

"The Emperor of a constitutional state is not permitted to express himself freely in speech and action and is not allowed to willfully interfere with a minister's authority invested in him by the Constitution.

"Consequently, when a certain decision is brought to me for approval, whether it concerns internal affairs, diplomacy or military matters, there is nothing I can do but give my approval as long as it has been

In one week the simultaneous attacks would begin, and their success depended entirely on the element of surprise. But late that night a cable arrived from China with news that the secret was in jeopardy. It was from General Tsutomu Sakai, commander of the 23rd Army, which was poised near Canton to seize Hong Kong. A transport plane bound for Canton had crashed in Chinese-held territory, and one of its passengers was Major Tomozuki Sugisaka, a courier carrying the secret orders concerning the surprise attacks.

There was alarm at Army General Staff headquarters. The Navy was summoned to an emergency meeting. Had Major Sugisaka had time to destroy the secret documents before the crash? Had the papers burned in the crash itself? Or were they already being rushed to Chiang Kai-shek, who would undoubtedly pass them on to Roosevelt? Should Operation Z be canceled?

The next morning these apprehensions seemed to be confirmed: a reconnaissance plane had sighted the wreckage of a big Army transport in a Nationalist stronghold about fifty miles northeast of Canton. According to the pilot, "the scene of the crash was already surrounded by the Chinese who were swarming like ants."

Still in suspense, Nagano and Sugiyama drove to the Palace to inform the Emperor of the exact date of attack. They told him that December 8 would be December 7 in Hawaii, a day of rest with most of the warships at anchor. The moon would also be in the right phase for launching the attack, since it would shine "from midnight to about sunrise." Nagano respectfully requested the Emperor to give his sanction to issuance of orders fixing December 8 as X-Day. His Majesty, without hesitation, approved.*

---

reached by lawful procedure, even if I consider the decision extremely undesirable. . . .

"If I turned down a decision on my own accord, what would happen? The Emperor could not maintain his position of responsibility if a decision which had been reached by due process based on the Constitution could be either approved or rejected by the Emperor at his discretion. It would be the same thing as if the Emperor had destroyed the Constitution. Such an attitude is taboo for the Emperor of a constitutional state." ("I believe," Fujita observed, "that His Majesty was talking abstractly about the prewar imperial conferences and so forth.")

*After the Tokyo trial U. S. Chief Prosecutor Joseph Keenan met the Emperor, who reportedly told him he didn't know Pearl Harbor was going to be bombed. From available evidence, however, it is evident he

At two o'clock that afternoon Sugiyama sent a cable of two words to General Terauchi, commander of Southern Army: HINODE YAMAGATA. This was code for "The date for commencing operations [HINODE] will be December 8 [YAMAGATA]."

Three and a half hours later Yamamoto sent a slightly longer cable in a new code to the Pearl Harbor Striking Force: NIITAKA-YAMA NOBORE [Climb Mount Niitaka*] 1208. This meant: "Attack as planned on December 8."

Kido Butai was cruising eastward at a modest 14 knots to conserve fuel, advancing in ring formation with three submarines ahead scouting for neutral merchant ships which, if found, were to be boarded and seized. A chance encounter with the U. S. Pacific Fleet, however, could not be handled so easily. This awkward possibility was discussed time and again, and once the irrepressible Yamaguchi half jokingly suggested, "Fire a salute, shout *'Sayonara!'* and go back home." The remark brought laughter, but Kusaka thought, What else could we do? We're not yet at war.

The "Climb Mount Niitaka" message gave Kusaka a welcome sense of commitment. He felt as if a tremendous burden had been lifted from his back. They would launch one overwhelming attack and disappear. It was like *mamono* (devil), a tactic in *kendo:* one surprise thrust, then fall back like the wind. Still, there was always the chance that as they neared Pearl Harbor some American patrol plane would spot *Kido Butai* before the launching. In that case Kusaka was prepared to change tactics—to attack in full strength even though surprise had been lost.

The weather was the calmest it had been in the past ten years and refueling was no problem. Nagumo ordered all ship captains to travel without lights—and to inform their entire crews of Operation Z. That night a spirit of intense, subdued excitement swept from ship to ship.**

---

did know and approve of Operation Z. It is also well documented that he issued explicit directives to give America due notice before the attack.

*Mount Niitaka on Formosa was, at 13,599 feet (1,211 feet higher than Mount Fuji), the highest peak in the Japanese Empire.

**Commander Naohiro Sata, *Kaga*'s Chief Aviation Officer, however, was openly critical of the entire operation. He told a group of pilots, "Here we are heading out into the North Pacific where not even a bird flies." What Japan needed was oil and that was far to the south. "Therefore, it is the height of stupidity to attack Pearl Harbor."

Back home that evening, the headline of the *Japan Times & Advertiser* read:

JAPAN WILL RENEW EFFORTS TO REACH
U. S. UNDERSTANDING.

2.

Hours after *Kido Butai* had left the icy waters of Hitokappu Bay, Lieutenant Commander Wilfred J. Holmes, whose job it was to plot Japanese ship movements, reported to his superior in the Navy's Communications Intelligence Unit in Pearl Harbor that the six enemy carriers were "in home waters." After that, however, Holmes admitted he had lost track of them. Day after day there was "no information" about the carriers.

Lieutenant Commander Edward T. Layton, Admiral Kimmel's fleet intelligence officer, relayed this information to his chief on December 2. If it disturbed Kimmel he didn't show it; in fact, he jokingly asked, "Do you mean to say that they could be rounding Diamond Head this minute and you wouldn't know?"

"I hope they would be sighted by now, sir."

A few miles away, in Honolulu, Consul General Kita had just received a message from Tokyo:

IN VIEW OF THE PRESENT SITUATION, THE PRESENCE IN PORT OF WARSHIPS, AIRPLANE CARRIERS, AND CRUISERS IS OF UTMOST IMPORTANCE. HEREAFTER, TO THE UTMOST OF YOUR ABILITY, LET ME KNOW DAY BY DAY. WIRE ME IN EACH CASE WHETHER OR NOT THERE ARE ANY BARRAGE BALLOONS ABOVE PEARL HARBOR OR IF THERE ARE ANY INDICATIONS THAT THEY WILL BE SENT UP. ALSO ADVISE ME WHETHER OR NOT THE WARSHIPS ARE PROVIDED WITH ANTITORPEDO NETS.

This message, which would have meant a warning of attack on Pearl Harbor to anybody reading it, was intercepted in Hawaii and passed on the cryptographers in Washington for decoding, but since it concerned Hawaii and had nothing to do with diplomacy, its low priority sent it to the bottom of somebody's basket. Another important intercept consigned to a similar fate back in September—the one dividing Pearl Harbor into five subareas—had finally been translated, but Brigadier General Sherman Miles, chief of Military Intelligence, regarded it as a naval message of no

212

concern to the Army while Lieutenant Commander Alvin D. Kramer, chief of the Naval Intelligence Translation Branch, marked it with a single asterisk, for "Interesting," rather than two, for "Urgent." As far as Kramer was concerned, it was merely "an attempt on the part of the Japanese diplomatic service to simplify communications."

Bernard Baruch, Roosevelt's unofficial adviser and Churchill's close friend, was in his Washington hotel room talking with Raoul Desvernine, an attorney representing the Mitsui combine. The lawyer said that Special Envoy Saburo Kurusu wanted to get a message directly to the President without going through Hull. Would Baruch help? Baruch passed on the request to Major General Edwin ("Pa") Watson, one of Roosevelt's secretaries. Watson phoned back to say the President refused to meet Kurusu without Hull but saw no objection to Baruch's finding out what the message was.

The next day, December 3, Baruch met Desvernine and Kurusu at the Mayflower Hotel. The Japanese ambassador vowed that he, the people of Japan and the Emperor all wanted peace but that the military leaders "were sitting with a loaded gun in each hand ... determined to shoot." War could be averted if he could talk to the President, without the "hostile and untrusting" Hull, and tell him he could thwart the Japanese military by appealing directly and personally to the Emperor, who would then ask Roosevelt to mediate a settlement between Japan and China. The important thing, said Kurusu, was to keep the conversations going and this could best be done if Roosevelt sent a personal representative such as Harry Hopkins to Japan.

Although Baruch didn't think the proposals were "anything into which anybody could put their teeth," he promised to relay the information to the White House.

Another emissary of peace—Dr. E. Stanley Jones, a prominent Methodist missionary—was trying to present a similar suggestion to the President. He phoned his secretary, Marvin McIntyre, with a request to see the President on a matter he could not put on paper: a plan (inspired by Hidenari Terasaki, an offical at the Japanese embassy) to avert war by a personal cable from Roosevelt to the Emperor. McIntyre told him to be at the East Gate of the White House in twenty minutes. A guide would take him through a secret entrance to the President's office so he wouldn't have "to run a barrage of reporters."

Roosevelt told Jones he'd already been considering a letter

to the Emperor. "But I've hesitated to do it, for I don't want to hurt the Japanese envoys here at Washington by going over their heads to the Emperor."

"That is the point on which I have come," said Jones. The idea had originated with Kurusu and Nomura themselves. "They asked me to ask you to send the cable. But they also said there could be no record, for if it were known that they had gone over the heads of the Japanese government to the Emperor, their own heads wouldn't be worth much."

"Well, that cleans my slate," said the President. "I can do it."

Jones cautioned him not to send it through the Foreign Ministry but directly to the Emperor, otherwise it would never reach him. "I don't know the mechanics of it, but this is what they told me."

"I'm thinking out loud," Roosevelt mused. "I can't go down to the cable office and say I want to send a cable from the President of the United States to the Emperor of Japan. But I could sent it to Grew." He could take it directly to His Majesty. "And if I don't hear within twenty-four hours—I have learned how to do some things—I'll give it to the newspapers and force a reply."

As Jones was leaving he asked the President never to mention Mr. Terasaki, who had come up with the idea.

"His secret is safe," Roosevelt promised.

The message would probably have been sent that day if it hadn't been for Hull. Still suspicious, he argued that an appeal to the Emperor should be a last-minute resort; besides, His Majesty was a mere figurehead under the thumb of Tojo's Cabinet, and a message by-passing its members would not only be resented but would be regarded as a sign of weakness.

Hull's suspicions were borne out by an intercepted dispatch from Tokyo. It ordered the embassy on Massachusetts Avenue to burn all but three codes and to destroy one of the two "B" code machines. An Army intelligence officer, sent to reconnoiter the embassy, found employees burning papers in the backyard. Chief of Military Intelligence Sherman Miles and his Far Eastern Section chief, Colonel Rufus S. Bratton, concluded that "at the least a break in diplomatic relations and probably war" was imminent.

On the other side of the world General Tomoyuki Yamashita was reading the attack order to division and detachment commanders and staff officers. They listened attentively, aware that Japan's destiny was at stake. There were tears on almost every face.

Three landings would be made at dawn of December 8 on the east coast of the Malay Peninsula near the border. Two were in Thai territory, Pattani and Singora, and one in Malaya, Kota Bharu. Inspired by a dream, Colonel Tsuji intended to take over neutral Thailand with a modern version of the Trojan Horse. A thousand Japanese in Thai uniforms would come ashore near Singora and round up café and dance-hall girls as a cover. They would then commandeer twenty or thirty buses, get aboard with the girls, and drive merrily down to the Malay border. Waving Thai flags with one hand and Union Jacks with the other, they would shout in English, "Japanese soldier is frightful!" and "Hurrah for the English!" In the boisterous confusion, Tsuji was sure the border guards would let his soldiers cross into Malaya.

At dawn the next morning, December 4, a convoy of twenty-six transport ships left the island of Hainan, off the southernmost coast of China, and bore south toward the Malay Peninsula. Colonel Tsuji stood on the bridge of the Army transport *Ryujo-maru* and watched a deep-red sun rise in the east as the moon, looking like a tray, vanished in the west. Tsuji visualized the faces of his mother, wife and children. Except for the reassuring throb of engines, there wasn't a sound on the ship. All was peaceful.

Early that afternoon a liaison conference was convened to discuss the delivery date of the final note to Hull. Vice Admiral Seiichi Ito had no objections if it was handed over at 12:30 P.M., December 7, Washington time. Both Tojo and Togo were concerned that the note be presented *before* the attack. Ito assured them on that score, and the time was approved.

There was to be no simple declaration of war, as Togo wanted, merely a notice terminating the negotiations; the draft he presented reflected the common bitterness and righteous indignation felt after receipt of the Hull note and declared that Japan had been patient in its attempt to conciliate. "On the other hand, the American Government, always holding fast to theories in disregard of realities, and refusing to yield an inch on its impractical principles, caused undue delay in the negotiations." It concluded that Japan regretfully was forced to announce "that in view of the attitude of the American Government it must be concluded that it is impossible to reach an agreement through further negotiations."

Someone expressed the unrealistic hope that room be left for further negotiations. But the others realized this was, in truth, a declaration of war and that time had run out.

That day the Japanese fleet code was changed as a last-minute precaution. It blinded American naval intelligence, which no longer had any idea where the six carriers were and would need some time to break the new code. *Kido Butai* was already more than a third of the way to Hawaii, leaving behind it no telltale path of refuse. All garbage was stored away, and empty oil cans were crushed and piled on the decks. By late morning the final major reservicing point was reached—42 degrees north and 170 degrees east—and all ships were refueled. Earlier this could be accomplished at a maximum speed of 9 knots, but by now everyone was so adept it was done at 12. With the Striking Force loaded to capacity, all supply ships turned back except for three, which would make the final refueling in forty-eight hours.

That afternoon came the first alarm, a cable in the new code from Yamamoto: a radio message had been intercepted which had probably originated from an enemy submarine in their vicinity. Kusaka queried all his ship captains but no one had intercepted any unexplained message. Undeterred, the Striking Force turned southeast, maintaining speed despite heavy fog. For the fliers belowdecks the waiting seemed interminable. They busied themselves with painting, drawing and *kendo*, and at least one began writing a book. Fighter pilot Yoshio Shiga had produced eight watercolors of a temple and invited the officers on *Kaga* to a private showing. He felt sheepish displaying "such unserious work at such a serious time," but was certain that he would not be alive to exhibit them later. It had been weeks since the last maneuvers and many fliers feared they would lose their touch. Pilots sat in their planes to keep the feel of the controls; bombardiers gazed intently through bombsights. Only gunners had actual practice; they shot at kites.

The next day, December 5, Vice Admiral Ito called on Togo at the Foreign Ministry and said the notification should be presented to Hull at 1 P.M., Washington time, a half-hour later than previously requested. Why the delay? Togo asked. I miscalculated, was the reply. Togo asked how much time there would be between notification and attack. Ito refused to give the exact moment of attack on the grounds of "operational secrecy," but assured the Foreign Minister that there would be sufficient time. As he was leaving, Ito reiterated his warning not to cable the notification too early.

It was raining in Oahu. A small Piper Cub dawdled over Pearl Harbor with Yoshikawa on his last "sightseeing" flight. He had received an urgent cable that morning from Tokyo requesting "a comprehensive report on the American fleet." After landing, he made a final tour of Pearl City, confirming what he had seen from the air, and then cabled Tokyo:

> . . . THE FOLLOWING SHIPS WERE IN PORT ON THE AFTERNOON OF THE 5TH: 8 BATTLESHIPS, 3 LIGHT CRUISERS, 16 DESTROYERS.

The message was intercepted by MAGIC but the Yamamoto luck held. Once again, it was placed in a "Hold" basket.

3.

Tokyo newspapers such as the *Asahi Shimbun* continued to accuse the West of preparing for war. On December 6 the headlines read:

U. S. USELESSLY EXTENDING TALKS.
HAS NO INTENTION OF COMPROMISE WITH JAPAN

U. S. LEADERS DISCUSS POLICY FOR JAPAN
BUT NO CHANGE SEEN IN THEIR DOGMATIC VIEWS

THAILAND IN AGONY FOR NEUTRALITY

SCANDALOUS ENCIRCLEMENT OF JAPAN,
TRAMPLING ON JAPAN'S PEACEFUL INTENTIONS.
FOUR NATIONS SIMULTANEOUSLY START MILITARY
PREPARATIONS

Otto Tolischus cabled the *New York Times* his impressions of the approaching crisis. Most Japanese, he wrote, refused to believe they were facing war with four nations simultaneously,

. . . but their instinctive hopes are daily contradicted by the evidence of their senses. They listen to alarming statements by the highest Government officials about the greatest crisis Japan has ever faced in her 2,600-year history. They are called to mass meetings to hear denunciations of the enemy, and they read a steady war clamor in the press. They see air shelters and water reservoirs being built everywhere in preparation for aid raids. They are being drilled in air raid defense, especially in fighting fires, the greatest dread of Japanese cities. Finally, they see taxes and prices rising. They know that all these things are not done for fun, and that war, real war, which only a short time ago seemed so far away, is rapidly stretching out its fiery arms toward Nippon, land of the gods.

The people do not want war, but neither do they want to give up he fruits of the war they have been fighting, which has cost them such a lot of blood and treasure. They have been told that this war is war of self-defense, to obtain elbow-room for the Japanese people, crowded into a few small islands with few national resources, and to liberate one thousand million of Oriental peoples from exploitation by the white races. . . .

It would be a great mistake to assume that the Japanese are so war-weary that they would be reluctant to fight if war really came to their land, or that their war potential is as small or as straitened as the outward picture might suggest. As members of a divine family state, in which patriotism and religion merge, they not merely say, "My country, right or wrong!" but they are convinced with all the fervor of religious faith that their country is right, whatever mistakes in tactics individual statesmen may take.

In Manila, Admiral Thomas Hart, commander of the Asiatic Fleet, predicted hostilities might begin at any moment. His inadequate fleet—one heavy cruiser, one light cruiser, thirteen World War I four-stack destroyers and twenty-nine submarines—was as ready for battle as it ever could be; ammunition was in the racks and warheads were on the torpedoes.

Unidentified aircraft had been reported the past three nights over nearby Clark Field, the main bomber base, but General MacArthur refused to be panicked. That afternoon he and Hart conferred with a visitor from Singapore, Vice-Admiral Sir Tom Phillips, commander of the British Far Eastern Fleet. A Japanese convoy sighted off Indochina near the Gulf of Siam was subsequently lost in a fog. Was it heading for a direct attack on Malaya and Singapore or merely landing in Thailand?

MacArthur reassuringly remarked that by April he would have a trained army of 200,000 men, and a powerful air force of 256 bombers and 195 fighter planes.

"Doug, that is just dandy," Hart interposed. "But how defensible are we right now?" The answer was painfully obvious. While MacArthur had about 130,000 men in uniform, almost 100,000 of these were poorly equipped Philippine Army divisions with a few months' training in close-order drill. About the only thing they could do well was salute. His air force was also inadequate. There were 35 Flying Fortresses and 107 P-40's.

After the conference Phillips—nicknamed "Tom Thumb" because of his stature; he was an inch shorter than Napoleon—made one specific request of Hart. He wanted four destroyers to accompany his fleet, which included the battle cruiser *Repulse* and the battleship *Prince of Wales*, on a sortie from Singapore up the east coast of Malaya as a countermove to the advancing convoy. No sooner had Hart agreed to send four of his own overage destroyers than a messenger arrived with a dispatch for Phillips: Singapore-based planes had again spotted the Japanese armada off the Thai coast.

"Admiral," Hart said to Phillips, "when did you say you were flying back to Singapore?"

"I'm taking off tomorrow morning."

"If you want to be there when the war starts, I suggest you take off right now."

That afternoon the final draft of the notification to Hull, together with general instructions for the Japanese embassy in Washington, was turned over to Kazuji Kameyama, chief of the Foreign Ministry's Cable Section. He was told to cable the instructions so they would arrive about 8 A.M., December 6, Washington time. This would be followed an hour later by the first thirteen parts of the notification—in English to prevent mistranslation. For security purposes the final part, the fourteenth, which would break off diplomatic negotiations, should not arrive until 4 or 5 A.M. on December 7.

Communications to Washington were generally good and never took more than an hour. Allowing additional time for further messages of correction and unforeseen difficulties, Kameyama sent the instructions and the first thirteen parts to the Central Telegraph Office at 8:30 P.M. Forty minutes later the instructions were cabled to Washington, and an hour after that, the first thirteen parts were on their way.

Kameyama went home well satisfied that the messages would surely arrive long before the deadline. The next afternoon he would send the crucial fourteenth part, followed half an hour later by a final cable instructing Kurusu and Nomura to deliver all fourteen parts to Hull at 1 P.M. on December 7, Washington time.

Kido Butai, completely blacked out, was speeding southeast at 20 knots through gales and high seas. Several of the exhausted lookouts had already been swept overboard and the fog was so thick that it was often impossible to see the ship ahead. But in spite of this and constant changes in course, the warships were still maintaining good formation.

Never before had the Japanese military custom of using Tokyo, not local, time been much of a problem, since cruises had invariably been to north or south in approximately the same time zone. Now it was disconcerting to find light at night and darkness in the day. The clock had to be forgotten and meals served according to the sun.

Alarms were keeping Nagumo in a state of anxiety that day. First came a report from Tokyo that a Russian ship was in the area. Six fighter planes on the decks of *Kaga* were warmed up and their pilots given orders to stand by, but nothing was sighted and the planes never took off. After dark a general alarm sounded on the flagship when someone noticed a light soaring overhead. Men ran to their battle stations and antiaircraft batteries of several ships zeroed in on the mysterious light. It was an illuminated balloon sent up by *Kaga* itself to determine wind direction.

Before retiring, Kusaka tried to reassure his commander with another *"Daijobu."*

"I envy your optimism," said Nagumo with a sigh.

4.

In Washington it was still Saturday, December 6, and there was concern among officials over a detailed British Admiralty report that a Japanese fleet of thirty-five transports, eight cruisers and twenty destroyers was moving directly toward the Malay Peninsula.* At his daily top-level naval meeting, Secretary of the Navy Frank Knox asked, "Gentlemen, are they going to hit us?"

Rear Admiral Richmond Kelly Turner, regarded as Admi-

---

*Some attention was diverted by a bitter political controversy involving treason. Several anti-Roosevelt Army officers had stolen top-secret documents revealing America's war plans and turned them over to three isolationist newspapers—the Chicago *Tribune,* the New York *Daily News* and the Washington *Times-Herald*—which simultaneously published these secrets on December 4 in an effort to prove that Roosevelt was a warmonger.

ral Stark's spokesman, said, "No, Mr. Secretary. They are going to hit the British. They are not ready for us yet."

There was no dissenting voice.

The Navy's Cryptographic Section was getting ready to relax for the weekend. Most of the staff would leave at noon. One translator, Mrs. Dorothy Edgers, with time on her hands, began sifting through untranslated MAGIC intercepts of low priority—those involving Hawaii that had been piling up. She'd only been on the job a few weeks and was still fascinated by everything around her. One message from Tokyo to Consul General Kita in Honolulu, dated December 2, asked about ship movements, antitorpedo nets and barrage balloons at Pearl Harbor. Intrigued, she picked up another, dated December 3, from Kita to Tokyo. She became excited as she read a lengthy report from Yoshikawa describing in detail how Otto Kühn would transmit information about the fleet in Pearl Harbor to Japanese ships lying off Oahu by putting lights in windows, burning garbage as a smoke signal or placing want ads on the radio.

Suspicions aroused, she passed on the messages to Chief Ship's Clerk H. L. Bryant, but he said she could never translate the long intercept by noon and to let it ride until Monday. Mrs. Edgers refused to be put off and worked overtime, finishing the translation at 3 P.M. Just then Lieutenant Commander Alvin Kramer, chief of the Translation Branch, checked in for duty but instead of sharing her excitement, he merely criticized her work and began editing it. Finally he put it aside, telling her to run along; they could finish editing the long message sometime the next week. When Mrs. Edgers protested, Kramer said, "We'll get back to this piece on Monday," and once more discovery of Operation Z was narrowly averted.*

At the Japanese embassy on Massachusetts Avenue the telegram of instructions (in Japanese) and the first thirteen parts of the long message to Hull (in English) had both come in. Late in the afternoon the cipher staff quit work to attend a farewell party for an embassy official who was being transferred to South America. They had only completed about eight parts.

First Secretary Katsuzo Okumura was personally typing out the deciphered parts which were too secret for any office

---

*After the war Colonel Rufus Bratton of Army Intelligence declared: "If we had gotten that message [on December 6] ... the whole picture might have been different."

typist to handle. When he finished he went to the basement playroom to relax. Two correspondents were playing ping-pong and one, Masuo Kato, came over to query Okumura about the liner *Tatsuta-maru*, which had left Yokohama five days earlier and was due to reach Los Angeles on the fourteenth.

"I'll bet you a dollar the liner never gets here," said Okumura enigmatically.

President Roosevelt—perhaps influenced by Dr. Jones or Baruch or both—had finally made up his mind to send a personal message to the Emperor. Drafted by the White House, it reminded the Emperor that almost a century previously another President of the United States, Millard Fillmore, had sent a personal message to the Emperor of Japan offering friendship. After years of peace, war threatened because of the Japanese occupation of southern Indochina, and the people of the Philippines, Malaya, Thailand and the Dutch Indies now feared they too would be taken over.

None of the peoples whom I have spoken of above can sit either indefinitely or permanently on a keg of dynamite.

There is absolutely no thought on the part of the United States of invading Indochina if every Japanese soldier or sailor were to be withdrawn therefrom.

I think that we can obtain the same assurance from the Governments of the East Indies, the Governments of Malaya and the Government of Thailand. I would even undertake to ask for the same assurance on the part of the Government of China. Thus a withdrawal of the Japanese forces from Indo-China would result in the assurance of peace throughout the whole of the South Pacific area.

I address myself to Your Majesty at this moment in the fervent hope that Your Majesty may, as I am doing, give thought in this definite emergency to ways of dispelling the dark clouds. I am confident that both of us, for the sake of the peoples not only of our own great countries but for the sake of humanity in neighboring territories, have a sacred duty to restore traditional amity and prevent further death and destruction in the world.

He signed the letter "Franklin D. Roosevelt" and sent it to Hull along with a handwritten note:

Dear Cordell: Shoot this to Grew—I think can go in gray code—saves time—I don't mind if it gets picked up.

F.D.R.

At about 7:40 P.M. the State Department announced to the press that the President was sending a personal message to the Emperor, and the message itself was dispatched.

Secretary of War Henry Stimson was still in town at Woodley, his estate above Rock Creek Valley. He had decided not to go to Long Island for the weekend, since, as he wrote in his diary, the "atmosphere indicated that something was going to happen."

The U. S. Navy cryptographers were more industrious than the cipher staff at the Japanese embassy and by 8:30 P.M. all thirteen parts of the Togo message were typed and ready for distribution. Realizing how important it was, Commander Kramer began phoning those who should get copies. "I have something important that I believe you should see at once," he told Navy Secretary Knox; he also called the Director of Naval Intelligence, the Director of the War Plans Division and the White House. One man on his list couldn't be reached—Admiral "Betty" Stark was not at his quarters on Observatory Circle.

A little after 9 P.M. Kramer left his office and was driven by his wife to the White House grounds. In the mailroom of the office building near the White House he handed over a locked letter pouch containing a copy of the message to the man on duty, Lieutenant Robert Lester Schulz.

Schulz brought the pouch to the President's study, where Roosevelt was sitting at his desk talking to Harry Hopkins. After Roosevelt read the thirteen parts he silently handed the papers to his adviser. When Hopkins finished reading, Roosevelt said, "This means war."

While Schulz waited they talked about the crisis. "Since war is undoubtedly going to come at the convenience of the Japanese," said Hopkins, "it's too bad we can't strike the first blow."

"No, we can't do that. We are a democracy and a peaceful people." Roosevelt raised his voice. "But we have a good record." He reached for the phone to call Stark, but when told he was at the National Theater, hung up and said, "I'll call Betty later; I don't want to cause public alarm by having him paged in a theater."

Stark was taking a rare night off. He was watching the perennial *Student Prince*, but it made so little impression on him that later he couldn't even remember where he'd been on the night of December 6. War was imminent but what puzzled him was where the Japanese would strike. The troop convoy heading into the Gulf of Siam suggested Singapore, but it could be the Philippines or the Panama Canal. In any case he didn't have to worry about Hawaii. The Joint Army-Navy Hawaiian Defense Plan for protection of Pearl Harbor against a surprise air attack was so good that he had sent it to all his district commanders as a model.

General Sherman Miles, chief of Military Intelligence, happened to be at a dinner party given by Captain Theodore S. Wilkinson, the Director of Naval Intelligence, and he too read the thirteen parts. But to Miles they had "little military significance" and he was not particularly apprehensive. He phoned Colonel Bratton, his Far Eastern expert, and told him there was "no reason for alerting or waking up" General Marshall, who was spending a quiet evening at his quarters in Fort Myers with his wife. Miles went off to bed so unconcerned he didn't plan to go to his office the next morning.

It was past midnight, the first minutes of December 7. Some high officials were still awake, wondering when the Japanese would jump—and where. Not one—Roosevelt, Hull, Stimson, Knox, Marshall or Stark—expected it could be Pearl Harbor.

In Oahu it was still early Saturday evening. Like Marshall and Stark, the Army and Navy commanders of Hawaii had no worry of an air attack on Pearl Harbor. General Walter Short was on the *lanai* of his home at Fort Shafter holding an emergency meeting with his intelligence and counterintelligence officers. They were discussing the transcript of a telephone conversation monitored by the FBI from a local Japanese dentist to a Tokyo paper. Its editor had a strange curiosity about Hawaii: planes, searchlights, weather, even the flowers. Had the dentist-correspondent's remark that the hibiscus and poinsettia were in bloom any significance? Was it some code?

For almost an hour the general's wife had been waiting impatiently outside in a car, and at last Short told his visitors that nothing could be done until morning and joined his wife. It was fifteen miles to the Schofield Barracks Officers Club, which was putting on a special benefit show that Saturday night. They would have to hurry.

Admiral Kimmel was trying to relax at a private dinner party at Honolulu's "House Without a Key," but he was a dynamic, dedicated man who was only content when working. At nine-thirty he excused himself after drinking his usual single cocktail. He wanted to get to bed. He was to play golf in the morning with General Short, which belied the gossip that they were not on speaking terms. It would be one of the rare Sundays the admiral didn't spend at his desk.

Both Kimmel and Short were of the opinion that constant alerts were unnecessary. Warnings from Washington had not specifically implied any air attack on Pearl Harbor even as a remote possibility. Kimmel was prepared for submarine attacks; Short was ready for saboteurs. Neither had been significantly concerned by reports that the Japanese consulate in Honolulu had been burning papers the past two days and the Joint Army-Navy Hawaiian Defense Plan—the one so admired by "Betty" Stark—was not in effect on the night of December 6. In fact, normal peace-time liberty had been granted to men and officers that evening.

Only routine and limited air patrols were planned for the next morning; and aircraft batteries in the Pearl Harbor area were lightly manned. Most of the men aboard the ninety-four ships moored in the harbor, except the watch crews, were getting ready for bed. It was just another lazy, uneventful tropical evening.

The FBI agents who had so assiduously been tracking the innocent dentist still had no suspicion that a minor official at the Japanese consulate, Tadashi Morimura, was actually an Imperial Navy secret agent named Yoshikawa. That night he was working late at the consulate on his final report. He had already cabled Tokyo a few hours earlier that he did not believe the battleships had antitorpedo nets and there was no barrage-balloon equipment near Pearl Harbor.

... IN ADDITION, IT IS DIFFICULT TO IMAGINE THAT THEY HAVE ACTUALLY ANY. HOWEVER, EVEN THOUGH THEY HAVE ACTUALLY MADE PREPARATIONS, BECAUSE THEY MUST CONTROL THE AIR OVER THE WATER AND LAND RUNWAYS OF THE AIRPORTS IN THE VICINITY OF PEARL HARBOR, HICKAM, FORD AND EWA, THERE ARE LIMITS TO THE BALLOON DEFENSE OF PEARL HARBOR. I IMAGINE THAT IN ALL PROBABILITY THERE IS CONSIDERABLE OPPORTUNITY LEFT TO TAKE ADVANTAGE OF A SURPRISE ATTACK AGAINST THESE PLACES. ...

Now he was at his desk writing that the following ships had just been observed at anchor: nine battleships, three light cruisers, three submarine tenders and seventeen destroyers, as well as four light cruisers and two destroyers at docks. Then he added that the heavy cruiser and carriers had left port and that it appeared "no air reconnaissance is being conducted by the fleet arm."

He buzzed for the radio-room code clerk, gave him the message and went for a stroll around the spacious consulate grounds. In the distance he could see a bright haze over Pearl Harbor but could hear no patrol planes. He went off to bed.

Tatsuta-maru, the passenger ship en route to Los Angeles, was still steaming on its course northwest of Hawaii. In the morning, to the puzzlement and concern of its passengers, it would swing around and head back home. First Secretary Okumura was going to win his dollar bet with correspondent Kato.

In Manila, it was late afternoon of December 7. It had been a hot, clear day. Here apprehension was greater than in either Washington or Hawaii, for the Philippines could be a battlefront any minute. Unidentified aircraft were again reported over Clark Field.

That night the 27th Bombardment Group was giving a mammoth welcome party at the Manila Hotel in honor of Major General Lewis H. Brereton, commander of MacArthur's recently established Far East Air Force. It was a gala affair long to be remembered as "the best entertainment this side of Minsky's." But the guest of honor's mind was on war and his sadly inadequate air force. During the party Admiral Hart's chief of staff told him, "It's only a question of days or perhaps hours until the shooting starts," and a moment later MacArthur's chief of staff said the War Department believed hostilities might begin at any time.

As a precaution Brereton phoned his own chief of staff and told him to put all airfields on combat alert. Fortunately heavy air reinforcements were on the way. One convoy, carrying fifty-two dive bombers and two regiments of artillery as well as ammunition, was due January 4. In addition, thirty Flying Fortresses would arrive in a few days and almost double his puny force. Twelve had already taken off from California and would land at Hickam Field, next door to Pearl Harbor, soon after dawn.

At Clark Field, fifty air miles to the northwest, sixteen Flying Fortresses were lined up ready for flight. The wide field, rimmed by a few trees and waist-high cogon grass, was honeycombed with revetments, foxholes and slit trenches. To the northeast, cone-shaped Mount Ararat, named after the final resting place of Noah's Ark, rose dramatically out of the plains, weird and unworldly in the moonlight.

In a nearby barracks Staff Sergeant Frank Trammell was trying to contact his wife Norma in San Bernardino, California, by ham radio. It was queer. The air was dead. All he could raise was a city he was forbidden to talk to—Singapore.

This 220-square-mile island was sixteen hundred miles to the the southwest, about the same distance and direction as a flight from New York to New Orleans. It was the keystone of the Allied defense system in Asia and if it fell, not only Malaya but all of the rich Dutch East Indies with its oil, tin and rubber would be lost.

That night the probing fingers of searchlights lit the sky above Singapore. Great 15-inch guns protected its sea approaches. And in the sprawling naval base—a labor of twenty years at the cost of £60,000,000—were moored the two mighty warships so feared by Council President Hara—*Repulse* and *Prince of Wales*.

The code warning "Raffles" had just been signaled throughout the Malayan Command, and British, Australian and Indian soldiers were standing to arms, prepared and confident. Singapore was an impregnable fortress.

About 1,650 miles to the north-northeast was Great Britain's other fortress in Southeast Asia, Hong Kong. This island was just a few minutes' ride by ferry from the mainland of southern China. Its 11,319 defenders were on the alert.

By midnight the spacious harbor—except for its usual patchy regatta of ketches, proas, junks and sampans—was almost empty. The previous night, pages had ranged the bars and ballrooms of hotels telling all officers and men of the merchant marine to report to their ships. The announcement about the Japanese convoy in the Gulf of Siam signified one thing alone in Hong Kong: the balloon had gone up. But, like Singapore, Hong Kong was ready and confident.

From Washington to Hong Kong it was expected that Japan would probably strike in hours. But in many places "readiness" was merely a word. Few were actually prepared for the brutal reality of war. And not one was yet aware of the detailed, ingenious Japanese plan of attack which was about to be loosed from Pearl Harbor to Singapore.

It had been a bright, warm, pleasant Sunday in Tokyo, but to Otto Tolischus it was "ominously quiet" and everyone in Japan "seemed to be waiting for something." He spent most of the day at his typewriter working on an article about Ambassador Grew for the *New York Times Magazine*. The old cry against "foreign barbarians," he wrote, was being revived now that the Japanese had learned all they could from the Occident about warfare.

... As a result the long-predicted war between the white and yellow races in general, and war between Japan and the United States in particular, has become an imminent possibility, and whether it shall become a grim reality is now the great issue being decided in Tokyo and Washington.

Tolischus read over what he had written. It sounded a little strong, but he decided to let it stand and sent it by messenger to Grew for approval.

It was not the imminence of war but the possible discovery of the secret attacks which concerned Japan's leaders that Sunday. Just before noon a cable reported that the convoy heading for the Malay Peninsula across the Gulf of Siam had been sighted by a British flying boat. A few minutes later it was learned that an Army fighter pilot had shot down the British plane. But had the flying boat had time to radio back the information?*

Roosevelt's personal bid for peace—his letter to the Emperor—reached Tokyo at noon; however, a recent general directive would automatically hold it up for ten hours. The previous day Lieutenant Colonel Morio Tomura of the Army General Staff had phoned his friend Tateki Shirao, the censor of the Ministry of Communications, instructing him to delay all foreign cables on an alternating schedule of ten hours one day, five hours the next. Sunday, December 7, happened to be the day scheduled for ten hours.

Ambassador Grew first heard of the message from the daily San Francisco news broadcast but didn't receive it until ten-thirty in the evening despite its TRIPLE PRIORITY stamp. He was justifiably annoyed. It was fifteen minutes past midnight when Grew, decoded message in hand, arrived at Togo's official residence. He told the Foreign Minister that he had a personal message from Roosevelt to the Emperor and read it aloud.

Togo promised "to study the document" and "present the

---

*They must also have been jolted by an article by a retired admiral in Saturday night's edition of the *Japan Times & Advertiser*. The author boasted that U. S. naval authorities were "apparently talking in delirium when they say it is improbable for Japan to extend its activities to Hawaii, and that such an attempt is bound to end in failure."

matter to the Throne." As soon as Grew left, Togo phoned Imperial Household Minister Tsuneo Matsudaira and asked if the Emperor could be disturbed at such a late hour. He was told to call Kido, since a message from the President was political, not ceremonial. Togo phoned the Privy Seal at his home in Alaska. Kido said that under these circumstances His Majesty could be roused "even in the dead of night," and promised to leave for the Palace at once.

Togo drove to the Prime Minister's official residence. Does the message contain any concessions? was Tojo's first question. The answer was no. "Well, then, nothing can be done, can it?" Tojo remarked, but had no objection to Togo taking the letter to the Emperor. Together the two worked out a reply, which amounted to a polite refusal, and Togo got up to leave. "It's a pity to run around disturbing people in the middle of the night," he joked.

"It's a good thing the telegram arrived late," said Tojo, and he was probably being facetious. "If it had come a day or two earlier we would have had more of a to-do."

Togo found Kido waiting for him at the Palace. "There's no use, is there?" said the privy Seal upon learning what was in the message. "What's Tojo's opinion?"

"The same as yours."

5.

About the time Grew received the Roosevelt telegram, Commander Kramer was at his office in the Navy Department reading the fourteenth part of the message to Hull breaking off negotiations. It was 8 A.M., December 7, in Washington.

The entire fourteen parts were assembled, put in folders, and once more Kramer began his delivery rounds. By 10:20 he was back in his own office. Another important message was on the desk. It was the telegram from Togo to Nomura marked URGENT—VERY IMPORTANT, ordering the admiral to submit the entire message to Hull at 1 P.M.

While it was being put in folders Kramer hastily made a time-zone circle and discovered that 1 P.M. would be 7:30 A.M. in Hawaii. Having spent two years at Pearl Harbor, he knew this was the normal time for the piping of the crew to Sunday breakfast—a very quiet time indeed. Disturbed, he headed down the corridors of the sprawling Navy Building for Admiral Stark's office.

On Massachusetts Avenue the Japanese were in a state approaching disorder. The cipher staff had returned to work after the farewell party and numerous *sake* toasts to finish the thirteen parts before midnight, then waited impatiently hour after hour for the final part. Finally at dawn everybody but a duty officer went home. About an hour later a bundle of cables arrived. One was Part Fourteen, sent from Tokyo by both Mackay and RCA and marked VERY IMPORTANT in plain English.

The duty officer called his colleague, but it was almost 10 A.M. before the cipher crew was back on the job, grumbling about lost sleep. In the meantime First Secretary Okumura was slowly, laboriously tapping away at a typewriter in an attempt to get a clean copy of the message. But he was an amateur typist, and though he had been laboring for two hours, he was far from finished.

It wasn't until 10:30 that Nomura was reading the decoded instructions to hand the entire message to Hull at 1 P.M. He hadn't yet read the fourteenth part, which had arrived three and a half hours earlier but was yet to be deciphered. He hastily phoned Hull's office to set up the appointment. Sorry, was the reply, Secretary Hull had a luncheon engagement. "It is a matter of extreme importance," the admiral said urgently—and if not Hull, how about his undersecretary? After a pause he was told that Hull himself would be available.

A few minutes later Okumura finally finished his bumbling typing of the first thirteen parts, but the eleven pages of typescript were so full of erasures that he decided it would never do as an official Japanese document. He started to redo the whole thing, this time with the assistance of another amateur typist, a junior interpreter. Despite everything, Okumura felt sure that he could finish the entire document in time for the one o'clock appointment.

When Nomura was calling Hull, young Kramer stepped into Stark's office. The admiral, who had just returned from a leisurely walk around the grounds and greenhouses of his quarters, was engrossed in the fourteen-part message. While waiting in the outer office, Kramer pointed out to a colleague the possible significance of the one o'clock time with reference to Hawaii.

At last Stark finished the long message and then read the "one o'clock" note. "Why don't you pick up the telephone and call Admiral Kimmel?" an intelligence man suggested. Stark reached for the phone but decided his "war warning" of November 27 was enough to keep everyone on his toes. Besides, a raid on Pearl Harbor seemed most unlikely. He said he'd rather call the President and dialed the White House. The President's line was busy.

Even the fourteenth part had failed to alarm Colonel Bratton, but a glance at the "one o'clock" note sent him into "frenzied" action. Convinced that "the Japanese were going to attack some American installation," he literally ran to his chief's office. General Miles was at home. So was Marshall. Without going through channels, Bratton phoned Marshall's quarters just across the Potomac. An orderly, Sergeant Aquirre, said the Chief of Staff had just left for his Sunday horseback ride.

Marshall had risen as usual at 6:30 A.M. but dawdled over breakfast with his wife, their first together in a week. They lived a restful, rather monastic life, since he had already collapsed twice from ill health. "I cannot allow myself to get angry, that would be fatal—it is too exhausting," he had recently told Mrs. Marshall. "My brain must be kept clear."

Unaware of the message which had meant "war" to the President the night before, he was heading at a lively gait toward the government experimental farm, the site of the future Pentagon Building. Ordinarily he rode for about an hour, but this time he took longer while Aquirre was searching for him in vain. By the time Marshall returned home to get the sergeant's message, it was 10:25. He phoned Bratton, but the latter was so circumspect in explaining the "most important message" that the Chief of Staff didn't realize its urgency. Marshall showered, sent for his limousine parked across the river at the Munitions Building and wasn't at his desk until a few minutes after 11 o'clock. He methodically read through the entire message, as unimpressed as Bratton. But, like Bratton, he was jolted by the implications of the "one o'clock" note. Using a yellow pad, he hastily jotted down a dispatch to his Pacific commanders:

The Japanese are presenting at 1 p.m. Eastern Standard Time today what amounts to an ultimatum. Also they are under orders to destroy their code machine immediately.

Just what significance the hour set may have we do not know, but be on the alert accordingly.

He phoned Stark. "What do you think about sending the information concerning the time of presentation to the Pacific commanders?"

"We've sent them so much already, I hesitate to send any more. A new one will be merely confusing."

Marshall hung up. Moments later the phone rang.

"George," Stark began in a concerned voice, "there might be some peculiar significance in the Japanese ambassador calling on Hull at one P.M. I'll go along with you in sending that information to the Pacific." He offered the Navy's transmission facilities, which he said, were very fast in emergencies.

"No, thanks, Betty, I feel I can get it through quickly enough."

"George, will you include instructions to your people to inform their naval opposites?"

Marshall said he would, and added a sentence to that effect on the yellow sheet. He marked it "First Priority—Secret," and ordered it rushed to the Message Center for transmission to the Panama Canal, the Philippines, Hawaii and San Francisco, in that order of priority. Concerned about time, he sent an officer several times to find out how long it would take to deliver the message. "It's already in the works. Will take maybe thirty to forty minutes to be delivered" was the reassuring answer from Colonel Edward French, chief of Traffic Operations. Marshall didn't consider using the direct scrambler telephone, since it could be easily tapped and the Japanese might deduce that their "unbreakable" code had been broken.

The message was enciphered and a few minutes after 12 noon in Washington, the commanders in San Francisco, the Panama Canal and the Philippines were warned. But Hawaii could not be raised because of atmospheric conditions. There was still, of course, the Navy's direct radio communications to Hawaii, but for some reason Colonel French eschewed the "very fast" facilities of the rival service for Western Union, which didn't have a direct line to Honolulu. The message wasn't even marked "Urgent."

The Combined Fleet, at anchor off the beautiful little islet Hashirajima, was on the alert, ready to sail from the Inland Sea to the aid of *Kido Butai* if necessary. Yamamoto had already issued his final order, an exact duplicate of Admiral Togo's message at Tsushima.

On *Nagato* there was a calm sense of watchful waiting. The earlier concern about the discovery of the Malay convoy was obviously groundless. As usual Yamamoto played Japanese chess with Commander Yasuji Watanabe. His mind was on the match and he won three of the five games. Afterward both men bathed and returned to the staff room. Then Yamamoto retired to his own cabin, where he composed a *waka*, a thirty-one-syllable poem:

> *It is my sole wish to serve the Emperor as His shield*
> *I will not spare my honor or my life.*

There were, in fact, two Japanese forces approaching Pearl Harbor. The second was a fleet of submarines. Eleven boats had taken the great-circle route and were converging on Oahu—four northeast of the island and seven in the channel between Oahu and Molokai. Nine others had come from the Marshalls and seven of these were lying just south of Oahu while the other two were nearing Maui to discover if the American fleet could possibly be at Lahaina.

Five other submarines, the Special Attack Unit, had surfaced under cover of darkness and had silently approached Pearl Harbor from the southwest. Each carried piggyback a midget two-man submarine seventy-nine feet long, which could travel at the remarkable speed of 20 knots submerged. The midgets were to steal into the channel, lie in wait off Battleship Row until the air attack started, then surface and launch their twin torpedoes at some capital ship. At first Yamamoto had canceled the raid on the grounds that it was suicidal. He finally relented when assured that every attempt would be made to recover the crews.

Just before 11 P.M., December 6, local time, the mother ships had stopped about eight miles off Pearl Harbor, and the tricky launching process began. Those on the decks of the submarines could see bright lights along the shore and even pick out neon signs on Waikiki Beach. Across the water came faint sounds of jazz. Minutes later four of the midgets were launched, but the fifth's gyrocompass would not work. It could not be repaired, but the two-man crew insisted on carrying out their mission. They climbed into their tiny boat. The mother ship dived, the securing clamps were cast off, and the midget started slowly for Pearl Harbor.

Kido Butai was racing full steam at 24 knots toward the launching point, two hundred miles north of Pearl Harbor. The men were at general quarters; the gun crews ready to fire at anything in sight. The pilots and crews had been routed from their bunks at 3:30 A.M., December 7, Hawaiian time. They had already written last letters and left in their

233

lockers fingernail clippings and snips of hair for their families. They put on clean *mawashi* (loincloths) and "thousand-stitch" belts.* For breakfast they were served an extra treat, red rice and *tai*, a red snapper eaten at times of celebration.

The ships were rolling so badly that some waves swept onto the decks of the carriers. Because of this, the torpedo pilots were told they could not go in the first attack but must wait for the second, when it would be completely light. To no avail the pilots grumbled that after all their hard training they could take off in the predawn murk, no matter how rough the seas were.

Nagumo was still concerned about Lahaina, despite reassurance from a submarine on the spot and a message from Combined Fleet that the Pacific Fleet, except for the carriers, was at Pearl Harbor. He ordered search planes to make a last-minute reconnaissance. An hour before first light *Chikuma* and *Tone*—the two heavy cruisers leading the fleet, and only 150 miles from Pearl Harbor—each catapulted a pair of seaplanes into the light wind. Two of the planes started for Lahaina, two for Pearl Harbor. Their instructions were to get to their destinations half an hour before the attack and radio back reports on clouds, the speed and direction of the wind, and most important, where the Pacific Fleet really was.

Some 6,600 miles to the west, a large convoy was closing in on the Malay Peninsula in three sections. The main force, fourteen ships, headed for Singora. To its left, three ships approached Pattani. Farther to the left, another three transports were bound for Kota Bharu; they were the first to reach their destination, and at midnight, Tokyo time, they dropped anchor just off the city. There was a moon, but fortunately for the invaders it was covered by clouds. There was little pitch and roll, and everything augured well for an easy landing. Then, at 1:15 A.M., the transports' naval escort began bombarding the coast, the signal for the landing.

The war in the Pacific had started by mistake. It was only 5:45 A.M. in Hawaii. Originally Genda and Commander Miyo of the Navy General Staff had agreed to hit Pearl

---

*A bellyband worn as a good-luck charm. Mothers, wives or sister would stand on street corners and ask passers-by to add their stitch to the belt until it had one thousand. This meant each belt contained a thousand prayers for good luck and a good fight.

Harbor just before dawn. But so many pilots complained of the hazard in taking off in the pitch-dark that at the last moment Genda delayed the first strike by about two hours. Miyo had not learned of this until several days after *Kido Butai* left Hitokappu Bay and took it upon himself to remain silent because a change in schedule at that stage might not reach all commands. He accepted the entire responsibility for his decision and did not even tell Vice Admiral Ito that an attack might very well come in the Malay Peninsula ahead of time. "I was resigned to leave our fate to Heaven."

And so the Kota Bharu force began the war between East and West, between white and yellow, two hours and fifteen minutes before the first bombs were scheduled to drop on Hawaii. The question was: Would the British report the attack in time to alert Pearl Harbor?

At the first shot of war the carriers of *Kido Butai* had just slipped across the launching point and were not quite two hundred miles north of Pearl Harbor. The first faint light of day glimmered in the east. Pilots and flight crews strapped themselves into their planes; motors roared. In the sky were patches of clouds. Long heavy swells rolled the ships from 12 to 15 degrees. Maneuvers were usually canceled when swells exceeded 5 degrees, but today there could be no postponement.

Admiral Kusaka ordered the Z flag raised above *Akagi*. This was an exact copy of the one Togo had used at Tsushima, but in the intervening years it had become an ordinary tactical signal. Kusaka was sure that every man in the Striking Force would realize its symbolic significance, but several staff officers, including Genda, protested when they saw it go up. It would cause confusion. Reluctantly Kusaka revoked the command and ordered another flag raised that vaguely resembled Togo's signal.

The minute the sailors of *Kaga* saw the Z flag they excitedly hoisted their own. It was going to be another Tsushima! Then, inexplicably, *Akagi*'s flag fluttered down, and with it some of their enthusiasm.

On the decks of the six carriers, the planes of the first wave were lined up, with forty-three fighter planes in the van, followed by forty-nine high-level and fifty-one dive bombers, and forty torpedo planes in the rear—at the last moment it was decided to let them risk takeoff in the predawn gloom.

At the head of *Kaga*'s fighters was Lieutenant (s.g.) Yoshio Shiga, the amateur painter. He was champing, hoping to be the first to take off. He beckoned to one of his ground-crew men and told him to yank out the chocks at his own command—not to wait, as usual, for the flagman's signal.

On the bridge Chief Aviation Officer Naohiro Sata told the carrier captain, "Planes are ready," and the skipper turned *Kaga* into the wind. A triangular pennant with a white circle on a red background was run halfway up the mast of the command ship, *Akagi*. In this position, the aviation flag meant "Get ready for takeoff." Then it was hoisted to the top of the mast. Commander Sata was watching it from *Kaga;* when it was lowered he would give a hand signal to drop *Kaga*'s aviation flag.

Lieutenant Shiga was not watching his own carrier's flag. He had his eyes glued on *Akagi*'s. It dropped. He shouted, "Remove chocks!" and roared down the runway. *Kaga*'s captain was leaning out a window, expecting to see the usual courtesy salute, but Shiga was too intent on getting into the air before anyone else. His Type Zero* plunged off the deck, dropped precipitously to within 15 feet of the sea. He turned left and climbed, noticing with dismay that the first fighter pilot on *Akagi*, Lieutenant Commander Shigeru Itaya, had beaten him by a few seconds. He had not waited for his flagman either. Shiga took his time in the turn so that his squadron could catch up, then joined Itaya, who was commanding all the fighters. They streaked south in loose formation like a flock of swallows.

Behind them the high-level medium bombers were taking off. Squadron leader Heijiro Abe was in the first Mitsubishi to leave *Soryu*. Contrary to American practice, he was not the pilot but the navigator-bombardier. Concerned about the roll and pitch of the carrier, he looked back anxiously into the dimness as the others followed. To his relief all his planes were soon in a precise V formation behind the fighters. Next the Aichi Type 99 dive bombers got off the runway and joined up.

The takeoff of the Nakajima Type 97 torpedo bombers was the most hazardous, and putting them in the initial wave while it was still partially dark was a gamble. The first off *Hiryu* was squadron leader Hirata Matsumura. When he plunged from the deck it was like being sucked into a dark pit. He fought his way up to 500 feet and was immediately engulfed in dense clouds. He broke through into the open,

---

*The name came from the date of the plane's origin, 1940, the 2,600th year of Japanese recorded history.

then veered left. Once his men had collected, he met the *Soryu* torpedo planes, and together they tagged after the *Akagi* and *Kaga* planes at 13,000 feet. The entire launching had taken no more than fifteen minutes—a record—and a single aircraft, a Zero fighter, had crashed.

Up ahead, Shiga looked back upon a great straggling formation. Never before had he seen so many planes. Half an hour after the takeoff a huge, brilliant sun rose to the left. It was the first time Juzo Mori, a young torpedo pilot—son of a farmer—had ever seen a sunrise from the air. The planes ahead were etched in black silhouette against the red, and it was such a romantic, incongruous sight that he could not believe he was heading for Japan's most important battle. To Lieutenant Matsumura, the sunrise was a sacred sight; it marked the dawn of a new century.

In Pearl Harbor it was 6:30 A.M. The antitorpedo net across the entrance to Pearl Harbor was open for an approaching vessel, the target ship *Antares*. Outside the entrance to the harbor Lieutenant William Outerbridge, the young skipper of the destroyer *Ward*, had just been roused from his bunk, and wearing glasses and a Japanese kimono, was peering off the port bow at *Antares* in the murky light. It was towing a raft into Pearl Harbor. Outerbridge saw something else following. It looked like a submarine's conning tower. "Go to general quarters," he shouted. Just then *Antares* blinkered confirmation: "Small sub 1,500 yards off starboard quarter."

Ward closed to a hundred yards and fired Number 1 gun at point-blank range. It missed. Number 3 gun fired, hit the conning tower and the midget began to sink. While the crew was still cheering, Outerbridge shouted, "Drop depth charges!" The destroyer's whistle blasted four times and four charges rolled off the stern.

At 6:51 A.M. Outerbridge radioed the 14th Naval District: WE HAVE DROPPED DEPTH CHARGES ON SUB OPERATING IN DEFENSIVE AREA. Then, deciding this message wasn't strong enough, sent another two minutes later: WE HAVE ATTACKED FIRED UPON AND DROPPED DEPTH CHARGES UPON SUBMARINE OPERATING IN DEFENSIVE SEA AREA.

Because of delay in decoding, the second message didn't reach Admiral Kimmel's chief of staff, Captain John B. Earle, until 7:12 A.M. A few minutes later Admiral Claude C. Bloch read it and said, "What do you know about it?"

237

Earle was dubious. "We get so many of these false sightings. We can't go off half-cocked."

Block saw his point. In the past few months there'd been a dozen such sub warnings—all false. "Ask this to be verified."

At almost this same moment another warning was being reported to the Army—and also discounted—from the Opana outpost at Kahuku Point on the northern tip of Oahu. Private George Elliott, Jr., of the 515th Signal Aircraft Warning Service, a recent transfer from the Air Corps, had seen a large blip on his radar unit at 7:06 A.M. He called over Private Joseph Lockard, who had much more experience. It was the largest group Lockard had ever seen on the oscilloscope and looked like two main pulses. He figured something had gone wrong with the machine, but after a check agreed with Elliott that it was really a large flight of planes.

By now Elliott had located the blip on the plotting board: 137 miles to the north, 3 degrees east. He was so excited that he suggested they call the Information Center at Fort Shafter. At first Lockard was reluctant but finally let his assistant make the call. The switchboard operator at the Information Center could find no one on duty except a pilot named Kermit Tyler. When told that the blips were getting bigger and that the planes were now only ninety miles from Oahu, Tyler said, "Don't worry about it," and hung up—the blips must represent the flight of Flying Fortresses coming in from the mainland or planes from a carrier.

In Washington it was 12:30 P.M. and Nomura was frantic. In thirty minutes he was to see Hull, and the fourteenth part of the note had just been deciphered and turned over to Okumura for typing. This harried man and his inept assistant were still punching away at the first thirteen parts. The confusion had been compounded when two "correction" messages were received: one amending a single word, and the other announcing that a sentence had been dropped in transmission. The first meant the retyping of one page, and the second, two pages.

As the minutes ticked away, Nomura returned to the doorway again and again, pleading with Okumura and his helper to hurry. The pressure created more mistakes. Already it was obvious that the envoys would be at least an hour late.

A Japanese floatplane from *Tone* was above Lahaina Roads and another from *Chikuma* was almost directly over

Pearl Harbor. No one on the ground noticed either plane. Nor was any communications man listening when the plane over Lahaina radioed back to *Kido Butai* in simple code at exactly 7:35 A.M.:

ENEMY'S FLEET NOT AT LAHAINA 0305.

A moment later came another:

ENEMY'S FLEET IN PEARL HARBOR.

This was about "the most delightful message" Kusaka had ever received. Right on its heels came a third report: there were some clouds over Oahu, but the sky over Pearl Harbor was "absolutely clear."

Togo had just arrived at the Palace grounds. Stars shone brilliantly. It was going to be a fine day. The Foreign Minister was immediately ushered into the Emperor's presence. It was almost at the exact moment Nomura and Kurusu were supposed to see Hull. Togo read Roosevelt's message and the proposed draft of the Emperor's reply. The Emperor approved the reply, and his countenance, Togo thought, reflected "a noble feeling of brotherhood with all peoples."

The spacious plaza outside the Sakashita Gate was deserted, and as Togo drove away, the sole noise in the city was the crunching of gravel under the car tires. His mind was far away: in a few minutes one of the most momentous days in the history of the world would begin.

PART THREE

Banzai!

8   **"I Shall
Never Look Back"**

1.

The first Zeros approached the northern tip of Oahu, Kahuku Point, at 7:48 A.M. Through clouds below him Lieutenant Yoshio Shiga, leader of the *Kaga* fighters, could barely make out a jut of land and a rim of white surf. A moment later he saw Fuchida's high-level command bomber and awaited a blue flare, the attack signal for the fighter planes, which were without radios. Those in the bombers were tuned in to a local Honolulu station. They heard the haunting strains of a Japanese song.

Banks of cumulus clouds clung to the peaks of the mountain ranges east and west of Pearl Harbor, but over the great naval base, lying in a valley between, the clouds were scattered. The sun shone brightly, its slanting rays giving the cane fields a deep-green hue. The waters of Pearl Harbor—originally named Wai Momi, "water of pearl"—glimmered a brilliant blue. Several civilian planes were lazily circling over the area, but of all the Oahu-based Army planes, not one was airborne. They were tightly bunched together, wing to wing, for security against saboteurs at Hickam, Bellows and Wheeler fields. So were the Marines planes at Ewa Field. The only American military planes in the air were seven Navy PBY's on patrol many miles to the southwest.

Antiaircraft defense was also off-guard. Three quarters of the 780 AA guns on the ships in Pearl Harbor were unmanned, and only four of the Army's 31 AA batteries were in position—and their ready ammunition had been returned to depots after practice, since it was "apt to disintegrate and get dusty."

Upon reaching Kahuku Point, Fuchida's plane—he was the observer—began circling around the west coast of Oahu to approach Pearl Harbor. At exactly 7:49 A.M. Fuchida radioed back to *Kido Butai* in Morse code: TO . . . TO . . . TO . . . This represented the first syllable of *Totsugeki!* (Charge!) and meant: "First wave attacking." As Fuchida neared the target, he was faced with a tactical decision. If in his judgment the Americans were completely surprised, the torpedo planes would streak directly for Battleship Row; if not, the fighters would first have to eliminate any interceptors. The sky ahead was empty and peaceful. Before long, Pearl Harbor—legendary abode of the shark goddess Kaahupahau—was spread out below like a huge relief map. It looked exactly as he had imagined. Still not a single fighter climbed up to challenge, neither was there one mushroom puff of AA fire. It was incredible.

At 7:53 A.M. he radioed to Nagumo TORA, TORA, TORA! The repeated code word, meaning "tiger," stood for "We have succeeded in surprise attack." He set off one blue flare to signal that surprise had been achieved. The nearest fighter squadron leader failed to waggle his wings in acknowledgment and Fuchida fired a second flare. Shiga, who was some distance to the rear, thought this was the two-flare signal indicating that surprise had *not* been achieved and that he was to head directly for Hickam Field to clear the skies there of enemy interceptors. He shot through Kola Kola Pass, signaling the others with his right hand to get into attack formation. The leader of the fifty-one dive bombers, Lieutenant Commander Kakuichi Takahashi, also misinterpreted the second flare and veered off to knock out the AA guns protecting Pearl Harbor.

But the torpedo bombers were heading straight for their targets. Lieutenant Commander Shigeharu Murata had not been confused by the second flare, and radioed his forty bombers to proceed as planned. By the time he saw the mix-up, so many torpedo planes were in attack formation that he decided to go ahead with the strike on Battleship Row.

The torpedo planes from *Soryu* were cutting directly across the island through Kola Kola Pass behind Shiga's fighters, and Lieutenant Mori could make out slit trenches in the mountain slopes. They're ready for us! he thought with a start. As he emerged from the pass he swooped down at 130 knots, just clearing the barracks and hangars of Wheeler Field. Scanning the runway, he guessed there were two hundred fighters packed in neat rows. He was stunned. He hastily calculated that with at least five airfields on Oahu, there would be a thousand enemy fighters.* His machine-gunner began strafing the parked planes—probably the first shots fired that morning—and then Mori made for Pearl Harbor.

Royal Vitousek, a Honolulu lawyer, and his seventeen-year-old son Martin were circling the island in the family Aeronca when they saw two Japanese fighter planes—undoubtedly Shiga's—approaching. Vitousek dived under the raiders and headed for his home field to make a report. He prayed the Japanese would ignore his little plane. Shiga kept zigzagging toward Pearl Harbor. It reminded him of a Japanese box garden. The American ships looked bluish white, unlike the gloomy gray of Japanese warships. How beautiful, he thought, like peace itself. In seconds he was past Pearl Harbor and over his target, Hickam Field. There wasn't a single enemy fighter in the air or taking off. The attack *was* a surprise! He looked around. Where were the torpedo bombers? Now was the time to strike.

Just then a dive bomber roared down on Ford Island, loosed a bomb and zoomed up. A cloud of heavy black smoke billowed out of a hangar. It would obscure nearby Battleship Row by the time the torpedo bombers got there, and Shiga thought angrily, What is that crazy helldiver doing?** To the west he saw a lazy line of torpedo planes. Why were they coming in so slowly? Like children trotting to school. They approached the big battleships moored along the southeast side of Ford Island. This was Battleship Row, seven warships anchored together in two rows—five on the inside, two on the outside. The line of planes dumped their torpedoes like "dragonflies dropping their eggs" and arced away. There was a pause. Then a jarring explosion. The battleship *Oklahoma* shuddered. In seconds two more torpedoes tore into her side and she took a list of about 30 degrees.

The next group of torpedo planes was Lieutenant Matsumura's, from *Hiryu*. His first view of Pearl Harbor was a forest of masts against the garish rising sun. They'd made it! "Look for carriers!" he called through the voice tube to his observer. He dropped to 150 feet over a field of waving

---

*To Lieutenant Mori, "all planes looked like fighters." There were 231 Army planes of all types on Oahu, and 88 of these were under repair.

**The Japanese Navy pilots were so impressed by an American movie, *Hell Divers,* starring Clark Gable, that they had adopted the name.

sugar cane. Helldivers were plunging down on Ford Island through clouds of smoke. *"Bakayaro!"* he muttered. How could they make such a mistake and obscure the main targets! Half a dozen planes converged on a big ship that looked like a carrier on the northwest side of Ford Island. "Damn fools," he repeated. "Who can they be?" Before takeoff he had warned his men to leave this one alone. It was merely the thirty-three-year-old target ship *Utah,* her stripped decks covered with planks.

He circled out above the sea and turned back over Hickam at 500 feet so he could come in on Battleship Row. His path cut across a long line of torpedo planes from *Kaga* and *Akagi*—several were ablaze from enemy fire but continued on to ram their targets. He'd have done the same thing, he thought, as he skimmed through towering fountains of water. He went down to less than 100 feet and started a run on one of the ships in the outside row—it was *West Virginia.* Usually the pilot alone released the torpedo, but today, to make doubly sure, most navigator-bombardiers were also pushing their release buttons. *"Yoi* [Ready]," he called over the tube. Then: *"Te!"* (Fire!) As the torpedo was launched, he pulled the stick back sharply. "Is the torpedo running straight?" he called to the navigator. He was afraid it might dig into the mud.

Matsumura pushed in the throttle, but instead of making the standard left turn, climbed to the right. He kept looking back to keep his torpedo in view. In the oily water he saw American sailors; they seemed to be crawling in glue. He banked further and saw a column of water geyser from *West Virginia.*

This one moment was worth all the hard months of training. "Take a picture!" he shouted to the navigator, who thought he said "Fire!" and ordered the machine-gunner to open up. "Did you get the picture?" asked Matsumura. Without comment the navigator took a picture—of someone else's column of water.

Lieutenant Mori, who had swept directly across Oahu, was still looking for a target. He hedgehopped over Ford Island, but finding only a cruiser on the other side, made a semicircle and came back just above the waves toward *California* at the southern end of Battleship Row. At the last moment a breakwater loomed between him and the target. He climbed, circling over *Utah,* which looked as if it had been twisted in two, again went down to 15 feet and came at *California* from a different angle. His radioman-gunner took a picture of the torpedo explosion as Mori prepared to make his left circle to the assembly point. But his path was barred by a heavy pillar of smoke at the end of Ford Island and he was forced to bank right directly into the oncoming torpedo planes from *Akagi* and *Kaga*; he narrowly missed collision and his plane rocked from the turbulence. Bullets ripped through Mori's plane "like hornets." One set the navigator's cushion on fire, another grazed the hand of the machine-gunner, but none hit the fuel tanks.

The high-level bombers were going after the inner row of battleships and anything else that looked tempting. The battleships were obscured by smoke at first, but on the second pass the first five *Soryu* planes were able to unload their 1,760-lb. bombs on the badly listing *Oklahoma*. Squadron leader Heijiro Abe snapped a picture as his bomb smashed between two gun turrets, penetrated into an ammunition room and exploded. Great tongues of flame blasted out of half a dozen holes in the ship. A flood of tears obscured Abe's vision. He was ready to die.

2.

Vitousek landed his Aeronca a quarter of an hour after the encounter with the two Zeros and phoned Army and Air Corps duty officers that he had seen Japs over Oahu. Nobody would believe him or even send out an alert.

The first bombs had already hit Wheeler Field a few minutes earlier, shortly after 7:50 A.M. Second Lieutenant Robert Overstreet of the 696th Aviation Ordnance Company, asleep in the two-story wooden BOQ (bachelor officers quarters), was awakened by a deep rumble. He thought it was an earthquake until he heard a voice shouting, "Looks like Jap planes!" and someone else saying, "Hell, no, it's just a Navy maneuver."

Then Overstreet's door opened and a friend looked in, face white and lips trembling: "I think Japs are attacking!" Overstreet peered out the window and saw olive-drab planes overhead. One roared by so close that he could see the pilot and a rear gunner. On the fuselage and wing tips were flaming-red suns. He finished dressing on the run and outside the barracks came upon a group of fighter pilots.

"We've got to get down to the line and tag some of those bastards," Lieutenant Harry Brown shouted. But the closely grouped planes on the ramp were already on fire. "Let's go to Haleiwa," he said. This was an auxiliary sod field on the north coast, where a few P-40's and P-36's were kept. Brown and several other fighter pilots piled into his new Ford convertible and careened off. Lieutenants George Welch and Kenneth Taylor were right behind in another car.

As bombs continued to fall, Overstreet pushed his way through a crowd milling in confusion toward the permanent quarters area. Brigadier General Howard C. Davidson, the fighter commandant, and Colonel William Flood, the base commander, were standing in pajamas by their front doors, staring up in the sky, faces aghast.

"Where's our Navy?" Flood muttered. "Where're our fighters?"

"General, we'd better get out of here!" Overstreet shouted. "Those planes have tail gunners." At that moment Davidson noticed to his horror that his ten-year-old twin daughters were roaming the lawn, picking up empty Japanese cartridges as if it were an Easter egg hunt. Davidson and his wife rounded up their children; then he set off for the ramp to get some of his planes in the air. But those salvaged from the flames had no ammunition and the ordnance building, containing a million rounds of machine-gun ammunition, was ablaze. All at once the big hangar was racked by salvos that sounded like an endless string of giant firecrackers.

Fifteen miles to the south, at Hickam Field, two aircraft mechanics were walking toward the flight line. Jesse Gaines and Ted Conway had gotten up early to get a look at the B-17's due from the States. They'd never seen a Flying Fortress. At 7:55 a V formation of planes appeared in the west. As they began to peel off, Conway said, "We're going to have an air show." Then Gaines noticed something fall from the first plane and guessed it was a wheel. "Wheel, hell—they're Japs!" cried Conway.

As Gaines said, "You're crazy," a bomb exploded among the closely packed planes. The two started for the three-storied barracks, "Hickam Hotel." Gaines saw some gas drums and ducked behind them for protection. He felt something kick him in the rear. "Don't you know better than that?" a grizzled sergeant barked. "Those damn drums are full!" Gaines headed for the ramp. Looking up, he saw bombs wobble down, each one aimed directly at him. He scrambled in terror, first one way, then another.

Colonel James Mollison, chief of staff of the Hawaiian Air Force, was shaving when he heard the first bombs fall. He dashed to his office and phoned Colonel Walter C. Phillips, General Short's chief of staff, that the Japanese were attacking.

"Jimmy, you're out of your mind," said Phillips. "Are you drunk? Wake up!" Mollison held up the receiver so that Phillips could hear the explosions. Phillips was convinced, in fact dumfounded. "I'll tell you what," he shouted. "I will send you over a liaison officer immediately." Then the ceiling crashed all around Mollison.

Two miles to the north, in the center of Pearl Harbor, the first bomb was falling on the naval air station at Ford Island. From his seat in a parked PBY, Ordnanceman Third Class Donald Briggs decided a plane from the carrier *Enterprise* had spun in. Then the ground erupted all around him as a dozen more explosions followed in rapid succession.

In the first few minutes the Navy bases at Kaneohe and Ford Island, and the Army bases at Wheeler, Bellows and Hickam, as well as the lone Marine base, Ewa, were crippled. Not a single Navy fighter and only some thirty Army Air Corps fighters managed to get into the air.

A moment after the first bomb fell, the Pearl Harbor signal tower alerted Kimmel's headquarters by phone. Three minutes later Rear Admiral Patrick Bellinger broadcast from Ford Island:

AIR RAID, PEARL HARBOR—THIS IS NO DRILL.

At 8 A.M. Kimmel radioed Washington, Admiral Hart and all forces at sea: AIR RAID ON PEARL HARBOR. THIS IS NO DRILL. Even as these messages were going out, flames and billows of black smoke were rising from Pearl Harbor.

Not far from Battleship Row, Boatswain's Mate Graff of the oil tanker *Ramapo* scrambled down the ladder into the crew's quarters and yelled, "The Japs are bombing Pearl Harbor!" His shipmates looked at him as if he were joking as usual, and when he said, "No fooling," someone gave a Bronx cheer. "No crap. Get your asses up on deck!" Yeoman C. O. Lines clambered topside to the fantail just in time to hear a dull explosion and see a plane dive toward *California*, the first of the seven big vessels in Battleship Row.

Above her, in tandem formation, were *Maryland* and *Oklahoma*. A torpedo couldn't hit *Maryland* because she was berthed inboard, next to Ford Island. But the outboard ship, *Oklahoma*, was hit by four torpedoes within a minute. As she listed to port, Commander Jesse Kenworthy, senior officer aboard, ordered the ship abandoned over the starboard side. Inexorably the ship settled, its starboard propeller out of the water. Below, more than four hundred officers and men were trapped alive in the rapidly filling compartments. Next in Battleship Row came *Tennessee* and *West Virginia.* Like *Maryland, Tennessee* was inboard and protected from torpedo attack. On *West Virginia*'s battle conning tower, Captain Mervyn Bennion doubled up. A fragment, probably from an armor-piercing bomb that had just hit the nearby *Tennessee,* had torn into his stomach. Lieutenant Commander T. T. Beattie, the ship's navigator, loosened the skipper's collar and sent for a pharmacist's mate. Bennion knew he was dying, but his concern was how the ship was being fought. Fires swept toward the bridge.

Next in line came *Arizona* and the repair ship *Vestal.* The torpedo planes had missed *Arizona,* but a few minutes later high-level bombers found her with five bombs. One of these plunged through the forecastle into the fuel-storage areas, starting a fire. About sixteen hundred pounds of black powder, the most dangerous of all explosives, were stored here, against regulations. Suddenly the volatile stuff exploded, igniting hundreds of tons of smokeless powder in the forward magazines.

Arizona erupted like a volcano. Those on nearby ships saw her leap halfway out of the water and break in two. Within nine minutes the two fragments of the great 32,600-ton ship settled in the mud as sheets of flame and clouds of black smoke boiled above her wreckage. It didn't seem possible that a single one of the more than fifteen hundred men aboard could have survived. Ahead was the last ship in Battleship Row, *Nevada.* She was down several feet by the head from a torpedo in her port bow and a bomb in the quarterdeck.

All along Battleship Row, men were jumping overboard and trying to swim the short distance to Ford Island. But the surface was coated with a layer of oil, six inches deep in some places, and this finally burst into flames, killing most of those in the water.

On the other side of Ford Island, torpedo bombers were still assaulting one of the least important ships in the harbor— the ancient target ship *Utah.* At 8:12 A.M. she rolled over, keel sticking out of the water. Men on Ford Island could hear a faint knocking inside the hull.

Only one ship in the entire harbor was under way. This was the destroyer *Helm,* scurrying at 27 knots through the channel toward the mouth of the harbor and the relative safety of open water. The antitorpedo net, opened hours earlier for *Condor,* was still unaccountably agape, and the Japanese midget submarine with the faulty gyrocompass was trying to stab its way blindly into this opening and go after a battleship. The commander, Ensign Kazuo Sakamaki, surfaced to get his bearings. Ahead were columns of black smoke. "The air raid!" he called to his aide. "Wonderful! Look at that smoke. Enemy ships burning. We must do our best too, and we will."

At 8:15 he saw *Helm* knife out of the harbor, but he held his fire. His two torpedoes were marked for bigger game. He submerged and again aimed blindly at the harbor mouth. He hit a reef, backed away, tried again. This time he ran up so far on the reef that his conning tower struck out of the water. An explosion shook the little boat violently. Something hit his head and he blacked out. When he came to, the tiny inner chamber was filled with acrid white smoke. He felt dizzy, sick. He reversed his engine. The boat refused to budge. On his stomach, he wormed his way up the narrow forward passage to begin the agonizing job of transferring 11-lb. ballast weights to the stern. At last he felt the submarine stir.

Helm continued to fire at the midget as it slid off the coral and vanished beneath the surface. SMALL JAP SUB TRYING TO PENETRATE CHANNEL, radioed the destroyer.

Inside the harbor, another midget was slowly rising to the surface just west of Ford Island. It was sighted at 8:30 and several ships opened fire. The midget launched her two torpedoes, one detonating against a dock, the other against the shore. Then the destroyer *Monaghan* rammed into the midget and dropped depth charges over the spot where it had disappeared.

Fighter pilot Shiga and his squadron of Zeros were lagging 8,000 feet above Hickam, waiting for enemy fighters to come up, but the only American plane in sight was a little yellow ship flying over the sea just east of the field. Shiga ignored it. Moments later he saw six huge four-engine planes coming in for a landing at Hickam.

They were the first of the dozen Flying Fortresses from California. At the sight of the high-flying Zeros, Major Truman Landon, the squadron commander, thought, Here comes the U. S. Air Corps out to greet us. Then came the distant blinking of machine guns, and a voice shouted over the intercom, "Damn it, those are Japs!" Landon's planes scattered. One started north for Bellows while the rest hastily made for Hickam. Four of them landed safely, but one was shot in half by ground troops as it touched down.

Shiga and his men strafed Hickam in single file, raking a long line of parked planes, then hedgehopped for the sea to avoid AA fire. They turned and swept back. To Shiga's surprise, not one of the planes just strafed was burning. If they had been Japanese they would all be on fire. After three passes at Hickam, Shiga decided to hit Ford Island, but since it was covered with smoke, he led his men to the Marine field near Barbers Point, to the southwest. They left most of the parked fighters in flames.

The torpedo bombers were already droning away from Pearl Harbor. Lieutenant Mori had been driven off course by AA fire after hitting *California* and found himself over Honolulu. He banked away from this forbidden civilian area and headed for the assembly point. Just off the mouth of Pearl Harbor, his navigator said, "Mori-*san*, some strange-looking plane is on our tail." He turned and saw a little yellow biplane tagging along behind. "Scare it away," he told the radioman-gunner, who loosed a warning burst.

After Lieutenant Matsumura hit *West Virginia* he too flew south just in time to see *Helm* fire at Sakamaki's midget sub. He started for the destroyer, then remembered he had no torpedo. He saw a big passenger plane (it was one of the Flying Fortresses) and bore in so his machine-gunner could knock it down. It was too fast and Matsumura gave up the chase. He told the radioman-gunner to report the attack and got the sheepish answer, "I can't. I shot off our antenna."

One plane alone circled above Pearl Harbor. It was Fuchida assessing the damage. Battleship Row was a holocaust; every battleship still afloat was burning.

Now from the east a second wave of raiders—eighty dive bombers, fifty-four high-level bombers and thirty-six fighters—approached Oahu. At 8:55 A.M. Lieutenant Commander Shigekazu Shimazaki gave the signal for attack and the 170 planes shot over the mountains east of Honolulu and headed for Battleship Row and Drydock No. 1, where the eighth battleship, *Pennsylvania*, was berthed.

A principal target was *Nevada*, moving slowly past *Arizona*, which still belched huge tongues of flame. Gun crews shielded ammo from the intense heat with their own bodies. Already suffering from one torpedo hit, *Nevada* drew up to the toppled *Oklahoma*. Several men stood up on the sides of that ship and cheered as *Nevada* made for open water. But the attackers were finding the range, and six bombs hit within a few minutes. The bridge and forestructure of the battleship erupted in flames. *Nevada* turned to port, and with the help of two tugs, was beached not far from *Pennsylvania*'s drydock.

To the southeast the second group of six Flying Fortresses approached Waikiki Beach, and Captain Richard Carmichael, the squadron commander, began pointing out the sights to his co-pilot. He thought the planes ahead were part of some Navy maneuver until he saw flames and smoke at Hickam. Anxiously he called the tower for permission to land.

"Land from west to east," said Major Gordon Blake. "Use caution. The field is under attack."

As Carmichael lowered his wheels he became the target of violent AA fire from below. He broke off his approach and turned north to Wheeler. This field, too, was under heavy attack, and he had to make for Haleiwa. It was twelve hundred feet long, and by the time the mammoth B-17 skidded to a stop he had used every foot of it. All six of his planes landed safely: two at Haleiwa, one at Kahuku Golf Course and three at Hickam. When his first Flying Fortress touched down at Hickam, two sprucely dressed captains stepped out. "Get your ammo, load up and get ready to go!" shouted someone. The captains stammered that they were in no shape for battle. All their guns were packed in cosmolene and would take hours to clean.

At Wheeler the men were still groggy from the first attack when the second hit. Lieutenant Overstreet began arguing with a sergeant from the Base Ordnance Office about rifles and pistols.

"I doubt if I'm authorized to give you any without a hand receipt," said the reluctant sergeant above the din of exploding bombs.

"Hell, man, this is war!" Overstreet yelled. He got the guns.

At Ford Island all the Navy planes had been destroyed or were inoperable. With little else to do, six pilots hid behind palm trees to take pot shots at the invaders with their pistols.

The Army fighter pilots had some success; they shot down eleven Japanese. The two lieutenants from Wheeler—Kenneth Taylor and George Welch—accounted for seven of these.

The citizens of Honolulu were more reluctant than the military to believe that war had come to Hawaii. They ignored the noise; it was either maneuvers or practice firing of the giant coastal defense batteries at Fort DeRussy near Waikiki Beach. Edgar Rice Burroughs, author of he Tarzan stories, did not interrupt breakfast with his son at the Niumalu Hotel. Afterward they played tennis with two Navy wives, still unaware that the war had started a few miles away.

At his Waikiki apartment Robert Trumbull, city editor of the Honolulu *Advertiser*, was awakened by the telephone. His wife, Jean, answered it and came back half puzzled, half amused. A friend had called to say that from his vantage point on a hill it looked as if Pearl Harbor was being bombed "for real," and Trumbull as a newspaperman might know something about it.

"It's just another maneuver," said Trumbull. No sooner had he hung up than Ray Coll, his editor, called to say there was a reported raid on Pearl Harbor and to get down to the office at once. Incredulous, Trumbull hung up and phoned one of the best-informed reporters in town, who said, "What's the boss been drinking?"

Trumbull wasn't convinced until he heard Webley Edwards of station KGMB say, "The island is under attack! I repeat, the island is under attack! This is the real McCoy!" At his office Trumbull checked the flood of reports (all false) of sabotage by local Japanese: an arrow was cut out of a sugar-cane field pointing to Pearl Harbor; a high-powered radio transmitter was found in a gym owned by a Japanese.

Trumbull dialed the number of the residence of the governor of Hawaii. To his amazement Joseph Poindexter, the seventy-two-year-old governor, answered himself. He didn't know a thing about any attack, and in a skeptical but polite tone asked for details.

At 9:45 A.M. the skies above the smokebound harbor were all at once empty. The stench of burning oil was overwhelming. *Arizona*, *Oklahoma* and *California* were sunk at their berths. *West Virginia*, aboil with flames, was sinking. *Nevada* was aground. The other three battleships—*Maryland*, *Tennessee* and drydocked *Pennsylvania*—were all damaged.

In Honolulu the secret agent Takeo Yoshikawa had been eating breakfast when the windows started to rattle and several pictures dropped to the floor. He went into his backyard and looked up in the sky. There was a plane with Japanese markings. They did it! he told himself. This is just about perfect with so many ships in the harbor.

He clapped his hands and rushed to the back door of Consul General Kita's official residence. "Mr. Kita!" he called.

"They've done it!" Kita came out and said, "I just heard 'East wind, rain' on the shortwave!"* This meant, of course, that Japanese-American diplomatic relations were in danger of rupture. "There's no mistake."

The two stood looking up at the dense black clouds rising over Pearl Harbor. Tears in their eyes, they clasped hands. Finally Kita said, "They've done it at last. Good job, Morimura."

Yoshikawa locked himself and a clerk in the code room and set about burning code books in a washtub. Within ten minutes there was a loud knocking. Someone shouted, "Open the door!" It was the FBI, alerted by the smoke.

The door caved in and half a dozen armed men burst in and began stamping on the burning code books. "Good-bye to the days of my youth—forever," whispered Yoshikawa. He walked out into the yard to watch the tiny planes above Pearl Harbor. The other members of the consulate were being rounded up and kept in the office, but nobody paid any attention to the secret agent. He returned to the office, found it locked and suggested to an FBI man that he be incarcerated with the others.

"Who are you?"

"Morimura, an official."

"Get in," said the FBI man.

In Honolulu, few doubted any longer that it was war. Sixty-eight civilians lay dead. A single Japanese bomb had hit the city. The forty-nine other explosions were caused by

---

*Although both U. S. Army and naval intelligence were supposed to be monitoring Japanese shortwave newscasts around the clock for just such a "winds" message, this one was not intercepted. Neither was an RCA telegram that Kita had received from Tokyo at 3:20 that morning which, decoded, read: RELATIONS STRAINED BETWEEN JAPAN AND THE UNITED STATES AND BRITAIN.

The so-called "winds" code is still shrouded in mystery. Commander Laurence F. Safford, chief of the Communication Security Section, testified that he had received an intercepted "execute" of the "winds" code on December 4 or 5 in a Japanese weather broadcast indicating "War with the United States, war with Great Britain, peace with Russia." He showed the intercept to Kramer, who also believed it was a genuine execute but changed his mind when he testified because of evidence from MacArthur interrogations of Japanese who denied sending out any execute message. Their testimony must be discounted, however, since they also denied even setting up the "winds" code. Neither the original nor any copy of the "execute" teletype could be found in Navy files, and some critics of the Roosevelt Administration still maintain they were purposely destroyed to discredit the possibility that an execute was ever sent.

spent AA shells improperly fused. Still, there was no panic. At the height of the attack Hawaiian girls in hula skirts appeared as usual at the Pan American dock, arms loaded with leis to bid aloha to departing Clipper passengers. They had to be told it was the end of traditional ceremony for a long, long time.

3.

Yamamoto and his staff aboard the flagship *Nagato*, anchored off Hashirajima, had all been awake since 2 A.M., an hour before the scheduled attack. They set around in silence, time and again getting up to examine a large chart. Chief Steward Omi passed around tea and cakes to relieve the tension. All at once a voice called excitedly over the voice tube, "We have succeeded in surprise attack!" It was the chief code officer in the message room and by a "skip" due to atmospheric conditions, he had just heard Fuchida signal, "TORA, TORA, TORA!"

The staff officers shook hands, bursting with elation and relief after their prolonged anxiety. Yamamoto tried to hide his emotions, but Watanabe could see that he, too, was excited. Omi brought out *sake* and *surume* (dried squid) to celebrate, and numerous toasts were tossed down. Every few minutes the voice tube would repeat triumphant reports from the attacking planes and frantic American messages: "All ships clear Pearl Harbor"; "This is no drill"; "This is the real McCoy."

Yamamoto gave orders to leave for Hawaii after dawn so that the Combined Fleet could support *Kido Butai* in case of a U. S. attack.

In Tokyo a relay of Fuchida's first signal, the tactical order to attack, was picked up at the message room of Navy General Staff headquarters. The code officer phoned the operations room and said, "The commander of *Akagi* is repeating 'TO' over and over." It wasn't in the code book and he had no idea what it meant. Commander Miyo spoke up and said he had originated that code long ago as squadron leader on *Kaga*. "They're doing fine," he said. "It means 'charge.'" It was the first good moment Miyo had had since hearing the report that the Malay invasion had jumped the schedule. A few minutes later the second message came in—this one in the code book: TORA, TORA, TORA.

The first planes found their way back to the carriers at 10 A.M. The weather worsened and a number of planes crashed on the pitching decks. As Matsumura's tail hook caught the landing wire on *Hiryu* he felt a surge of joy. He'd never expected to come back and there he was, alive!

Fuchida returned about an hour later and was greeted by an exultant Genda; then he went to the bridge and reported to Nagumo and Kusaka that at least two battleships had been sunk and four seriously damaged. He begged the admirals to launch another attack at once and this time concentrate on the oil tanks. American air power had been smashed, he assured them, and the second attack would just have antiaircraft fire to contend with.

Kusaka considered Fuchida's suggestion. His volatile friend Admiral Yamaguchi had already signaled that *Soryu* and *Hiryu* were prepared to launch another attack, and *Kaga*'s captain, at the urging of Commander Sata, also recommended a strike against installations and fuel tanks. The oil was an alluring target, but Kusaka believed a commander should not be obsessed by such temptations. The second attack would surely be no surprise; and no matter what Fuchida thought, the bulk of their planes would probably be shot down by AA fire. More important, the task force itself would be placed in jeopardy. *Kido Butai* was the heart of the Japanese Navy and should not be risked. From the beginning he had wanted to deliver a swift thrust and return like the wind.

"We should retire as planned," Kusaka advised Nagumo, who nodded.

A staff officer suggested that they try to locate and sink the American carriers. Opinion on the bridge was divided. "There will be no more attacks of any kind," said Kusaka. "We will withdraw."*

Secretary of the Navy Frank Knox was at his office in the Navy Department on Constitution Avenue. It was long past noon, and he was getting hungry. He was about to order lunch when Admiral Stark burst in with Kimmel's "This is no drill" message.

"My God, this can't be true!" Knox exclauimed. "This must mean the Philippines."

*Some accounts state that Fuchida and Genda repeatedly pleaded with Nagumo to return. In an interview in 1966, Admiral Kusaka recalled that they merely suggested a second attack and that his words "We will withdraw" ended the discussion; thereafter no one expressed a forceful opinion.

Stark assured him grimly it did mean Pearl Harbor, and Knox picked up the phone with a direct connection to the White House. It was 1:47 P.M. Roosevelt was lunching at his desk in the Oval Office with Harry Hopkins. Knox read the dispatch.

"There must be some mistake," said Hopkins. He was sure "Japan would not attack in Honolulu" but Roosevelt thought the report was probably true and said, "It's just the kind of unexpected thing the Japanese would do." He talked at some length of his efforts to complete his administration without war, finally remarked somberly, "If this report is true, it takes the matter entirely out of my hands."

At 2:05 P.M. Roosevelt phoned Hull and in steady but clipped tones passed on the news. Hull told him that Ambassadors Nomura and Kurusu had just arrived and were in the Diplomatic Reception Room. Roosevelt advised him to receive them, but not to mention that he knew about Pearl Harbor. He should be formal, cool and "bow them out." Then the President called Secretary of War Henry Stimson, who was lunching at home, and excitedly asked if he had heard what had happened.

"Well," Stimson replied, "I have heard the telegrams which have been coming in about the Japanese advances in the Gulf of Siam."

"Oh, no, I don't mean that," said Roosevelt. "They have attacked Hawaii! They are now bombing Hawaii!"

Stimson replaced the receiver. Well, that was an excitement indeed, he told himself. His immediate feeling was one of "relief that the indecision was over and that a crisis had come in a way which would unite all our people."

At the State Department, Hull turned to Joseph Ballantine and said, "The President has an unconfirmed report that the Japanese have attacked Pearl Harbor. The Japanese ambassadors are waiting to see me. I know what they want. They are going to turn us down on our note of November 26. Perhaps they want to tell us that war has been declared. I am rather inclined not to see them." Finally he decided to take Roosevelt's advice and admit the envoys. Besides, there was "one chance out of a hundred" that the report wasn't true.

In the waiting room the anxious Nomura was still breathing heavily after the race from the embassy. He was already more than an hour late and knew the fourteen-part message contained several minor typographical errors. Okumura had wanted to retype the entire message but Nomura had impatiently snatched it away from him. He still hadn't had time to read it carefully.

At 2:20 P.M. Kurusu and Nomura were finally ushered into Hull's office. The Secretary of State greeted them coolly, refusing to shake hands. He didn't invite them to sit down.

"I was instructed to hand this reply to you at one P.M.," said the admiral apologetically, holding out the note.

Hull's face was stern. "Why should it be handed to me at one P.M.?"

"I do not know the reason," Nomura replied truthfully, puzzled that his friend should be so upset just because he and Kurusu were late.

Hull seized the note and pretended to glance through it. Ordinarily his speech was slow and gentle, but now the words tumbled out headlong as he assailed them bitterly, "I must say that in all my conversations with you during the last nine months I have never uttered one word of untruth. This is borne out absolutely by the record. In all my fifty years of public service I have never seen a document that was more crowded with infamous falsehoods and distortions—infamous falsehoods and distortions on a scale so huge that I never imagined until today that any government on this planet was capable of uttering them."

Nomura started to say something, but Hull raised his hand and dismissed them by a curt nod toward the door. Still bewildered, the admiral approached Hull, said farewell and held out his hand. This time the Secretary of State shook it, but as the two Japanese turned and walked out, heads down, Hull, reverting to his Tennessee vocabulary, was heard to mutter, "Scoundrels and piss-ants!"

At the embassy Okumura told them, "Our planes have bombed Pearl Harbor!" Military Attaché Isoda, eyes filled with tears, approached Nomura and sadly said it was regrettable that things "had come to such a pass" despite the admiral's efforts. "But, alas, this is Fate." Nomura was too deeply moved to be consoled, particularly by an Army man.

At the Navy Department, Admiral Stark had already sent a message to all commanders in the Pacific area and Panama: EXECUTE UNRESTRICTED AIR AND SUBMARINE WARFARE AGAINST JAPAN. A few doors away, Knox was on the phone with Pearl Harbor, talking to the commandant of the 14th Naval District, Admiral Claude C. Bloch, who described the damage he could see through his window. *Oklahoma*'s badly hit. Also *Arizona*. But *Pennsylvania* and *Tennessee* are only superficially damaged, and we can raise *California* without too much trouble. Fortunately, there's no damage to the Navy Yard and oil reserves."

The Giants-Dodgers football fans at their radios were the first of the American public to learn of the attack. At 2:26 P.M. station WOR interrupted its broadcast of the game with the initial news flash. There was no announcement at the Polo Grounds itself, where Brooklyn had just scored the game's first touchdown, but there was a stir of curiosity when Colonel William J. Donovan was paged by Washington over the PA system. He headed the Office of the Coordination of Information, an intelligence organization.

Another announcement came just before the 3 o'clock broadcast of the New York Philharmonic concert. In Washington, Rear Admiral Chester W. Nimitz, chief of the Bureau of Navigation, was settling down to enjoy the Artur Rodzinski concert over CBS. When the broadcast was interrupted, he shot out of his chair and was on his way to the Navy Building.

A few blocks away Masuo Kato of Domei heard the news over a taxicab radio. "God damn Japan," said the driver. "We'll lick the hell out of those bastards now." In New York, radio station WQXR hastily switched its Gilbert and Sullivan program from *The Mikado* to *H.M.S. Pinafore* "in honor of the Royal Navy." And on the banks of the Potomac someone cut down one of the cherry trees donated years before by Japan. This sense of outrage was shared by a large group of Nisei living in the Manhattan area. Without delay the Tozai (East-West) Club of New York dispatched a telegram to Roosevelt:

WE THE AMERICAN CITIZENS OF JAPANESE DESCENT OF NEW YORK CITY AND VICINITY JOIN ALL AMERICANS IN CONDEMNING JAPAN'S AGGRESSIONS AGAINST OUR COUNTRY AND SUPPORT ALL MEASURES TAKEN FOR THE DEFENSE OF THE NATION.

A restive crowd had gathered outside the Japanese embassy on Massachusetts Avenue. Kurusu was summoned to the phone. It was Ferdinand Mayer, until recently an American diplomat; the two had become good friends in Berlin. Mayer said he would be glad to see Kurusu—without mentioning that he had called at the suggestion of Colonel Donovan, whose intelligence organization would soon become the Office of Strategic Services, America's first genuine espionage system.

His voice breaking, Kurusu thanked "Ferdinand" for phoning but said he "would hate to inconvenience" him, since there was a surly crowd outside the embassy. From the tone of his voice Mayer guessed Kurusu was "quite overwhelmed and in the deepest sort of despair."

Crushed as he was, Kurusu still had no feeling of bitterness toward Hull, who had despised him on sight—and shown it. That old man, he thought, had worked to the best of his ability to preserve peace. The trouble was that both America and Japan were like children. Diplomatically, neither was mature. Now the two children were playing foolish war games.

By evening the envoys were confined under guard in a luxury hotel by Assistant Secretary of State Adolf A. Berle, Jr. The admiral asked for a samurai sword but Berle rejected the request; Nomura's suicide might endanger Ambassador Grew.

That evening the Cabinet met in the Red Room on the second floor of the White House at eight-thirty. The members formed a semicircle facing Roosevelt, who sat behind his desk. This was the most serious meeting of a cabinet since the outbreak of the Civil War, the President solemnly announced. He enumerated the losses at Pearl Harbor, then slowly read a message he planned to make to Congress the following noon.

It was effective, Stimson thought, but didn't cover Japan's "lawless conduct in the past. Neither did it connect in any way with Germany." Hull, too, wanted Germany included, but Roosevelt said the message would be "more effective ... and certain to be read if it was short." He could not be budged, even in the face of Hull's insistence that Congress and the nation would listen to "anything" the President had to say.

Stimson wanted to go further than Hull, and at the end of the meeting went up to Roosevelt and urged him to declare war against Germany before the indignation of the people subsided. The President refused but did promise to present the full matter to the people in two days.

Just before nine-thirty the leaders of Congress were ushered into the room: Vice President Henry Wallace and six senators, including Alben Barkley, Speaker of the House of Representatives Sam Rayburn and two congressmen. Roosevelt told them frankly what had happened in Hawaii. His listeners sat riveted in dead silence. When Roosevelt finished,

Senator Tom Connally wondered why the fleet was "caught napping," but the others were still tongue-tied.

A little later in the evening Marine Captain James Roosevelt, the President's eldest son, came upon his father thumbing through his beloved stamp collection "with no expression on his face, very calm and quiet." He didn't look up, only said, "It's bad, it's pretty bad."

Mrs. Roosevelt found her husband more serene than she'd seen him for a long time and thought to herself that "it was steadying to know finally that the die was cast" and that the future "presented a clearer challenge than the long uncertainty of the past."

4.

Japan had started the war but had yet to declare it. At a hurriedly assembled Cabinet meeting an hour before dawn, Navy Minister Shigetaro Shimada calmly described the results of Pearl Harbor, cautioning his listeners to make allowances for the exaggerations of bomber pilots. Hastily an imperial rescript declaring war was composed, signed and sent on to the Privy Council.

The sun was rising as Privy Seal Kido, who had opposed the war, approached the Palace by car. Still staggered by Pearl Harbor, he closed his eyes, and bowing toward the sun, offered a prayer to the gods. He was profoundly grateful for the divine assistance that marked the beginning of Japan's desperate course. As a patriotic Japanese he fervently hoped for victory.

Several blocks away at the NHK (Japanese Broadcasting Corporation) Building, announcer Morio Tateno checked the script of the first news program of the day. Curbing his agitation, he began to broadcast at exactly 7 A.M.: "We now present you urgent news. Here is the news. The Army and Navy divisions of Imperial Headquarters jointly announced at six o'clock this morning, December 8, that the Imperial Army and Navy forces have begun hostilities against the American and British forces in the Pacific at dawn today."

The news was blared through hundreds of loudspeakers in the streets. People stopped in their tracks, startled; then, as martial music blared out, many began clapping as if it were a ball game. The enthusiasm was general, but some of the older citizens started toward the Palace gates to pray for victory, not with jubilation but with solemnity.* In the plaza, newsvendors with "extras" trotted by, the bells around their waists jingling so loudly that they could be heard in Number Three East reception hall of the Imperial Palace.

In the spacious room the Privy Council was in session. The longest discussion was on a problem of little note: why the Netherlands was not included in the imperial rescript. There was another lengthy argument about use of the terms "America" and "England." One councillor protested that this would cause confusion and, moreover, would be impolite. Togo stubbornly refused to make the change; everyone in the world knew that America meant the United States of America.

Before noon the Emperor put his seal on the rescript and war was officially declared. He added one line expressing his personal regrets that the empire had been brought to war with Britain and America and toned down the closing phrase, "raising and enhancing thereby the glory of the Imperial Way within and outside our homeland," to "preserving thereby the glory of our empire."

Marquis Kido found the Emperor apparently undisturbed. Then His Majesty confessed that it had been a heartrending decision to declare war on the United States and Britain, and particularly unbearable to make an enemy of such close friends as the British royal family. Kido made no reply. What could he say?

Prime Minister Tojo was already talking to the nation by radio, soberly, without any oratorical flourishes. The West, he said, was trying to dominate the world. "To annihilate this enemy and to establish a stable new order in East Asia, the nation must necessarily anticipate a long war. . . ." The fate of Japan and East Asia was at stake and the hundred million

---

*Finance Minister Kaya feared that the news might cause a disastrous decline in the stock market and ordered his secretary, Hisatsune Sakomizu, to somehow control the situation. He advised two men of the problem: the president of the exchange and the head of the brokers' union, Aizawa by name. They decided that the opening prices could be raised if they bought heavily in Shinto, which, because of its name, had become something of a symbol in the market. When the stock exchange opened, Aizawa bought forty thousand shares. This pushed the price some 30 sen above the previous day's closing quotation. But almost immediately there was a general downward trend on the big board; the public was reacting to Tateno's announcement on the radio. Within an hour, however, an "extra" was distributed on the floor telling of great successes in the Pacific and on the Asian continent. In minutes the prices on the big board began climbing.

people of the empire must now pledge all energies—their lives—to the state.

There followed a recording of "Umi Yukaba," a martial song:

> *Across the sea, corpses in the water;*
> *Across the mountain, corpses in the field.*
> *I shall die only for the Emperor,*
> *I shall never look back.*

That afternoon as Prime Minister Tojo was leaving the official residence in riding clothes, his secretary, Colonel Susumu Nishiura, stopped him. "How can you go riding today? What would happen if you were injured?" Tojo went back inside without a word.

Japanese fears that the premature Malayan attack might compromise the Pearl Harbor strike were groundless. Surprisingly, London was not alerted. More surprising, word of Pearl Harbor itself did not reach Churchill until two and a half hours after the first bombs fell. And he had to learn it from a newscast. He was spending the weekend at his country residence, Chequers, with two American house guests— W. Averell Harriman, who was the U. S. Lend-Lease coordinator, and Ambassador John Winant. At 9 P.M. they all heard a BBC announcer go on and on about fighting everywhere but the Far East, before announcing matter-of-factly that the Japanese had attacked Hawaii.

The two Americans straightened in their chairs.

"It's quite true," said the butler, Sawyer. "We heard it ourselves outside. The Japanese have attacked the Americans."

After a moment's silence Churchill left for his office. Winant took for granted that he was going to declare war on Japan, as he had recently promised "within the moment." "Good God," Winant said, "you can't declare war on a radio announcement!"

"What shall I do?"

"I will call up the President and ask him what the facts are."

When the ambassador had Roosevelt on the line he said, "I have a friend who wants to talk to you. You will know who it is as soon as you hear his voice."

Churchill picked up the phone. "Mr. President, what's this about Japan?"

"It's quite true. They have attacked us at Pearl Harbor. We are all in the same boat."

"This actually simplifies things. God be with you." Churchill couldn't help feeling great elation, now that the United States was officially at his side. He recalled Sir Edward Grey's telling him more than thirty years earlier that America was like a gigantic boiler: "Once the fire is lighted under it, there is no limit to the power it can generate."

Saturated with emotion, he went to bed and slept soundly.

5.

During the plotting of the Malay campaign the perpetrators had counted on only an even chance that it could be launched in complete secrecy and drew up plans for the men making the initial landings to live off the land in case they were isolated by the British fleet. For a time the planners seriously considered having them plant seeds so they would survive a long siege, but this scheme was discarded as bad for morale.

The invasion of the Malay Peninsula that preceded Pearl Harbor evolved smoothly despite six-foot waves, and by the end of the day the Kota Bharu airport was in Japanese hands. But the other two landings to the north, across the border in Thailand, were impeded by faulty execution of orders. Major Shigeharu Asaeda was assigned to lead the way at Pattani. He had personally picked that beach on one of his secret missions as suitable for landing because its white sand at high tide indicated firm footing. The launches of the Pattani force churned toward the shore an hour before dawn. When the water was chest-high the troops, burdened by full field equipment, began leaping overboard. To his horror Asaeda found himself sinking in mud; the beautiful white sand did not extend into the water at low tide. Some of the men carrying machine guns were dragged down and drowned. It took the others almost three harrowing hours to slog the three hundred yards to solid ground, where they were raked by Thai fire.

At Singora the sand was solid and it looked as if Colonel Tsuji would make a reality of his imaginative scheme to crash the Malayan border in buses. Tsuji assumed that a major, who was posing as a clerk at the Singora consulate, had already persuaded the Thai Army and police not to interfere. But Major Osone was not on the beach waiting for the invaders. Tsuji went into town and finally managed to rouse the Japanese consulate by pounding at the gate. It was the portly consul himself who sleepily greeted them with a surprised "Ah so, the Japanese Army!" Behind him was the equally sleepy Major Osone. He had burned his secret code too soon and had been unable to decode the last-minute telegram with the exact time of the landing.

The exasperated Tsuji ordered the consul to drive him to the police station. In case persuasion failed, he had brought a large *furoshiki* containing 100,000 ticals of Thai money. They were not far from the station when a bullet smashed a headlight. "Don't shoot!" Tsuji's interpreter called out. "This is the Japanese Army. Join us and attack the British Army!" The answer was a volley of shots which seemed to be directed at the fat consul, whose gleaming white suit made him an inviting target. The Japanese returned the fire. It was the end of Tsuji's fanciful plan.

Off the tip end of the Malay Peninsula the citizens on the island of Singapore first learned of the war when bombs exploded at four o'clock in the morning. Half an hour earlier the fighter control operations room had received a report of unidentified aircraft 140 miles from Singapore, but no one at the Civil Air Raid Headquarters answered its repeated phone calls. Consequently, the lights of the city guided the invaders to their target; in fact, they stayed brightly lit during the entire raid. The custodian of the keys to the master switch could not be found.

Sixty-three people were killed and another 133 were injured, but there was still no sign of alarm in Singapore. The great majority was reassured by an order of the day issued by Air Chief Marshal Sir Robert Brooke-Popham, commander in chief in the Far East.

We are ready. We have had plenty of warning and our preparations are made and tested. . . . We are confident. Our defences are strong and our weapons efficient. . . . What of the enemy? We see before us a Japan drained for years by the exhausting claims of her wanton onslaught on China. . . . Confidence, resolution, enterprise and devotion to the cause must and will inspire every one of us in the fighting services, while from the civilian population, Malay, Chinese, Indian or Burmese, we expect that patience, endurance and serenity which is the great virtue of the East and which will go far to assist the fighting men to gain final and complete victory.

Not everyone was assuaged by such rhetoric. Yates McDaniel, the American representative of the Associated Press, knew that the Brewster Buffalo fighter planes protecting Singapore were slow and cumbersome. He also knew there wasn't a single tank in Malaya; that almost every one of the great fixed guns of Singapore was pointing out to sea, useless in case of land attack down the peninsula; that the troops in Malaya had no jungle training; that the native groups had been excluded from any participation in the defense of their homes and that most of them hated the British more than they did the Japanese.

Late that morning McDaniel's good friend Vice-Admiral Sir Geoffrey Layton told him on the phone, "We're sending out two capital ships under 'Tom Thumb' Phillips." By his tone McDaniel guessed Layton strongly disapproved. "Would you like to go along?"

"How long will they be out?" McDaniel admired Phillips and had been struck by the strangely heroic figure of the little admiral standing on a box so he could look over the bridge.

"Five or six days." Layton explained that Phillips was determined to sail north, up the east coast of Malaya, and attack the invasion convoy which was still landing Japanese troops at two points.

McDaniel was tempted. It sounded like a good show, but since he was the only AP man in town, he had to refuse. He was concerned by Layton's obvious opposition to the plan. And he remembered the black cat of *Prince of Wales* sitting in President Roosevelt's lap at the signing of the Atlantic Charter. It gave him a feeling of foreboding.

Just before sailing that afternoon, Phillips asked Air Vice-Marshal C. W. Pulford what air cover the fleet would get on its sortie. Pulford, a former Navy man, was eager to cooperate, but his airfields in northern Malaya were already reportedly knocked out. He promised to give Phillips air reconnaissance the next day, December 9, but didn't think he could spare any planes at all on December 10.

As Phillips boarded the 35,000-ton *Prince of Wales,* Captain L. H. Bell noticed his uneasiness. "I'm not sure," Phillips said, "that Pulford realizes the importance I attach to fighter cover over Singora on the tenth." He said he would ask him in a letter what he could do for certain.

The sun was setting as the fleet, under the code name of Force Z, steamed out of the sprawling Singapore base. *Prince of Wales* led, followed by *Repulse* and the destroyers. As they passed Changi Signal Station at the eastern end of the island, Phillips was handed a radiogram from Pulford: REGRET FIGHTER PROTECTION IMPOSSIBLE.

"Well," said Phillips, "we must get on with it." After the publicity about the two warships since their arrival in Singapore, it would have been unthinkable to retire. Force Z continued on its northern course.

In Manila, Major General Lewis Brereton, commander of MacArthur's Far East Air Force, requested permission to bomb Formosa, some six hundred miles north, with his Flying Fortresses. It was 7:30 A.M., five and a half hours after the first attack on Hawaii.

"I'll ask the general," replied Major General Richard K. Sutherland, MacArthur's chief of staff, and a moment later reported, "The general says no. Don't make the first overt act." Wasn't the bombing of Pearl Harbor an overt act? Brereton wanted to know. He was told there had been little reconnaissance on Formosa and such a raid would be pointless.

On western Formosa, Japanese naval officers of the Eleventh Air Fleet were equally frustrated. Fog had prevented them from taking off before dawn for strikes at Clark Field and its adjoining fighter bases. Now they feared that the Clark-based B-17's would suddenly appear overhead and smash their own planes lined up on the runways.

The only aircraft to leave Formosa were from an Army field and all they did was drop their bombs far north of Manila on unimportant targets. Reports of these nuisance raids reached Brereton's headquarters at Nielson Field, on the outskirts of Manila, at 9:25 A.M. Brereton phoned Sutherland again begging permission to bomb Formosa. Again he was turned down, and when MacArthur finally changed his mind after forty minutes it was so late that Brereton had to make new plans hastily.

His bombers were cruising aimlessly above Mount Arayat in order not to be caught on the ground, and for half an hour were not informed that it was a false alarm. They returned to Clark for refueling, followed by fighters flying cover.

Back at Nielson Field, new alarms were coming in to the Interceptor Command by phone and telegraph from towns all along the northwest coast of Luzon. Some spoke of twenty-seven planes that looked like fighters, other of fifty-four heavy bombers. The fog had lifted in Formosa, and 196 Japanese naval planes in several groups were nearing their targets on Luzon. The bulk was bound for Clark Field. Colonel Alexander H. Campbell, Brereton's aircraft warning officer, tried to make sense of the conflicting reports and concluded that one group was heading for Manila and several for Clark Field. At 11:45 A.M. he sent a teletype to Clark that failed to get through. Nor could anyone be raised on radio; apparently the operator was having lunch. Finally Campbell got a faint phone connection with Clark and was assured by a junior officer that he would immediately give the information to the base commander or operations officer.

By 12:10 P.M., all fighter pilots on Luzon were either in the air or on alert—except for those at Clark Field. The junior officer had not yet passed on Campbell's warning. Not a single fighter plane was flying cover over the parked Flying Fortresses.

At 12:25, twenty-seven new Mitsubishi high-level bombers roared over Tarlac, just twenty miles to the north. Their goal was Clark, where many of the ground crew were walking unconcernedly from the mess halls to the flight line. Ordnance men were loading bombs on the huge unpainted Flying Fortresses. Pilots of the eighteen P-40B fighters, under Lieutenant Joseph H. Moore, were lolling in their planes at the edge of the field near empty fuel-drum revetments.

At the 30th Squadron mess hall, mechanics and bomber crewmen were listening to a Don Bell broadcast over KMZH. "There is an unconfirmed report," said Bell, "that they're bombing Clark Field." This elicited laughter and catcalls. Indeed, there were those who refused to believe that Pearl Harbor had been attacked; it was probably some "eager beaver's" idea to put everyone on the alert.

The Japanese in the twenty-seven Mitsubishis could already see a mass of large American bombers glittering in the bright sun. Their target was ridiculously visible, parked out in the vast open plain with Mount Arayat rising up like a huge traffic marker fifteen miles east of the field. Just behind came twenty-seven more bombers, and hovering high above were thirty-five Zero fighters. It was 12:35 P.M. Ten hours after Pearl Harbor, every plane at Clark Field was a sitting duck.

At the edge of the field, New Mexico national guardsmen of the 200th Coast Artillery were eating lunch around their 37-mm. and 3-inch antiaircraft guns. At the cry "Here comes the Navy!" Sergeant Dwaine Davis of Carlsbad grabbed a movie camera bought with company funds and began taking pictures.

"Why are they dropping tinfoil?" someone asked.

"That's not tinfoil, and those are goddamn Japs!" Then there was a roar like the sound of rushing freight trains.

At the other end of the field a crew chief of the 20th Pursuit Squadron shouted, "Good God Almighty, yonder they come!" Lieutenant Joe Moore raced for his P-40B. Followed by six of his squadron, he taxied into position. He lifted into the air, swung wide and started a maximum power climb. Two others got off, but the last four planes were hit by bombs.

The air-raid siren shrieked, but the ground crews seemed transfixed by the great V formation overhead—until strings of bombs fishtailed toward them.

For the first time the national guardsmen at the AA guns fired live ammunition; much of their training had been with broomsticks and boxes or wooden models. Their bursts exploded far below the targets, but it was satisfying and somehow exhilarating to let loose at something in earnest.

All at once there was nothing to shoot at. The sudden silence came like a jolt. Corporal Durwood Brooks walked toward the flight line in a daze. The idea of war was new and terrifying. Bodies and limbs were scattered around. He saw a friend, a Polish boy of nineteen, in a slit trench. By some freak an explosive bullet had blown him up like a balloon; he looked almost transparent.

Men began emerging from the trenches like sleepwalkers, momentarily numb to the groans of the wounded. Buildings blazed and dark rolls of smoke churned from the oil dump across the field. But by a miracle only a few Flying Fortresses had been damaged.

Lieutenant Moore and his two companions were trying to give chase. They found to their amazement that the Zeros were faster and more maneuverable, climbing at an astounding rate. They had been assured there was no such thing as a good Japanese fighter plane, although exact data on these Zeros had been sent to the War Department by the brilliant and unorthodox Colonel Claire Chennault in the fall of 1940. The chief of the Flying Tigers had also elaborated in detail on ways whereby the heavier P-40 should be able to shoot down the faster Zero, but this information, which could have saved the lives of bewildered American pilots dying that moment, had been filed away. Chennault was too much of a maverick to be taken seriously by his superiors.

Almost unopposed, the Zeros began strafing the parked Flying Fortresses and P-40B's. They were joined by forty-four Zeros which had just raked a nearby fighter base and were after new blood. One by one the big Fortresses exploded as tracers ignited their gas tanks. Once again the attack was abruptly over. Black clouds of smoke drifted across the field. All of the fighter planes and thirty medium bombers and observation planes were on fire. All but three of the Flying Fortresses were destroyed. In one raid the Japanese naval fliers had crippled MacArthur's Far East Air Force. Every one of the Japanese bombers returned safely, as did all but seven fighters.

It was a second Pearl Harbor. In one day two of the three most powerful deterrents to quick Japanese success in Southeast Asia had been canceled: the Pacific Fleet and MacArthur's air force. The third was British Admiral "Tom Thumb" Phillips' powerful Force Z. According to the latest Japanese reconnaissance report, *Prince of Wales* and *Repulse* were still in Singapore harbor—too shallow for their conventional aerial torpedoes and well protected by antiaircraft.

If only the two big ships could be lured into the open sea.

At that moment they were steaming north toward the Japanese convoy.

At Pearl Harbor it was confirmed that 18 ships had been sunk or badly damaged; 188 planes destroyed and 159 damaged; 2,403 Americans killed. It was a disaster, but it could have been a catastrophe. Luckily, the carriers were at sea and the enemy had neglected to bomb the oil storage tanks at the Navy Yard and the submarine pens. Moreover, almost all of the sunk or damaged ships would eventually return to battle. The Japanese lost 29 planes and 5 midget submarines; 45 airmen had died, and 9 submariners. One, Ensign Sakamaki, was captured when his boat went aground on the other side of Oahu.

At dusk, smoke still spewed from the shattered fleet. Through a drizzling rain the stench of oil, fire and death was thick and nauseating. Rumor fed on rumor: eight Japanese transports were seen rounding Barbers Point . . . gliders and paratroopers had dropped at Kaneohe . . . other paratroopers were coming down in sugar-cane fields southwest of Ford Island, still others in Manoa Valley.

One official Navy report even claimed that paratroopers in blue coveralls with Rising Sun emblems were landing on the north shore. Fifth columnists, saboteurs and spies were reported everywhere—driving taxis, waiting on tables, tending gardens, selling groceries. They had ringed Oahu with sampans to direct the Japanese to their targets; they had driven milk trucks down airstrips, methodically knocking off the tails of American planes; they had poisoned reservoirs—in other words, there was no end to their mischief. Actually they had done nothing at all, but the man most responsible for guiding the raiders to their proper targets, Takeo Yoshikawa, was still hiding behind the identity of a minor consular official.*

It was unsafe to be abroad in the dark. Every moving object was a target for some edgy rifleman. At Wheeler someone heard a pilot mention poison gas, and the alarm was sounded. At Hickam a guard saw a dim form—it was a friend returning from the latrine—and fired several wild rounds, setting off a wild barrage of AA fire which created more casualties.

At Ford Island six planes from the carrier *Enterprise* were returning from a fruitless search for Nagumo's carriers. Despite a contrary radar report, they had searched to the southwest. This time Pearl Harbor was not caught napping and the planes were raked by antiaircraft fire. The score was almost perfect: of six planes, four were destroyed and one damaged.

Pearl City was blacked out, but the harbor glowed from burning ships. Flares dotted the overturned *Oklahoma*. Men with acetylene torches were trying to cut into the hull to rescue their suffocating comrades inside.

There were men trapped inside *West Virginia*, lying flat on her keel at the bottom of the harbor. A huge pocket of air was keeping some sixty survivors alive. They were vainly tapping on the sides of the ship to attract attention.

The reasons for the disaster would be debated bitterly for years. Stripped of politics and personalities, they were simple. The American military leaders had been assured that the Japanese could not mount an independent carrier striking force (after the fact they were still convinced that Nagumo had come from the Marshalls), and could not imagine that the Japanese would be "stupid enough" to attack Pearl Harbor. They were not alone in this. The Japanese Navy General Staff itself had branded Operation Z reckless.

In a deeper sense, every American would have to accept a share of the blame. The disaster was caused by a national unwillingness to face the facts of a world torn from its stable course after World War I by economic and social revolution, fostered by nationalism and racism, and the inevitable realignment of power in both hemispheres.

---

*His true identity and mission were discovered only after the war.

9

"The Formidable Years
That Lie Before Us"

1.

On Monday morning Americans were still staggered by the worst military disaster in their history. There were no scenes of panic or even excitement, but strangers on the streets looked at one another with a new awareness. Personal problems were overshadowed by national catastrophe. The bitter wrangles between the interventionists and the "American Firsters" suddenly had no meaning.

The War Department feared a Japanese carrier attack on the locks of the Panama Canal or the aircraft factories on the California coast. Many eminent government officials were caught up in hysteria and one phoned the White House claiming that the West Coast was no longer defensible and demanded that battle lines be established in the Rocky Mountains.

Pearl Harbor had temporarily crippled American naval power in the Pacific, but it had another and more lasting effect. Telegrams and letters from the public flooded the White House pledging full aid and co-operation. Americans would never forget Pearl Harbor.

A little after noon on Monday, senators, congressmen and Supreme Court Justices filed into the House chamber. In the packed gallery was Mrs. Roosevelt. She was "deeply unhappy," recalling her anxieties about her husband and brother when World War I broke out. Now she had four sons of military age. Near her, at the President's request, was Mrs. Woodrow Wilson, the widow of another war President.

Just before one o'clock the Cabinet entered. Speaker Sam Rayburn rapped his gavel for silence and announced, "The President of the United States!" Roosevelt slowly walked in on the arm of his son James. The President opened a black loose-leaf notebook and began to read: "Yesterday, December 7, 1941—a date which will live in infamy—the United States of America was suddenly and deliberately attacked by naval and air forces of the Empire of Japan. . . ."

The speech, often interrupted by bursts of applause, continued for several minutes. In conclusion the President said, "I ask that the Congress declare that since the unprovoked and dastardly attack by Japan on Sunday, December 7, 1941, a state of war has existed between the United States and the Japanese Empire."

Roosevelt closed his notebook to a thunder of clapping, cheers and rebel yells. He raised his hand in acknowledgment, took his son's arm and left the dais. For the first time since he became President, Roosevelt had spoken for all Americans. People of every political conviction were welded into a single angry voice. Partisan politics, for the moment at least, were forgotten. America had declared total war.

2.

Shrouded by rain and clouds, *Prince of Wales* and *Repulse* were deep in the Gulf of Siam when they were sighted by the Japanese submarine *I-56* at 1:45 P.M. on December 9. The radioman on *I-56* tapped out the report, but the static was so bad that although he tried again and again, he couldn't make himself understood. Across the gulf, in Saigon, Rear Admiral Sadaichi Matsunaga of the Navy's 22nd Air Flotilla was sure that the two warships were at their home base. Two reconnaissance planes had just returned from Singapore with pictures of what looked like one of the big ships (it was actually a massive floating dock).

At 3 P.M. a message from *I-56* was at last heard in Saigon: two enemy men-of-war and four destroyers were heading north at 14 knots near Procondor Island. This seemed more logical than the reconnaissance report, and the admiral ordered planes to prepare for attack at sea. While torpedoes were hastily being loaded and unpinned, a large group of curious Army officers arrived. Somehow they had learned that the Navy had tracked down he two British ships. Each plane lifted off to enthusiastic cheers.

Thirty minutes later Vice Admiral Phillips aboard *Prince of Wales* signaled *Repulse* and the destroyer escort:

WE HAVE MADE A WIDE CIRCUIT TO AVOID AIR RECONNAISSANCE AND HOPE TO SURPRISE THE ENEMY SHORTLY AFTER SUNRISE TOMORROW, WEDNESDAY. WE MAY HAVE THE LUCK TO TRY OUR METAL AGAINST SOME JAPANESE CRUISERS OR SOME DESTROYERS IN THE GULF OF SIAM. WE ARE SURE TO GET SOME USEFUL PRACTICE WITH HIGH-ANGLE ARMAMENT, BUT WHATEVER WE MEET I WANT TO

FINISH QUICKLY AND GET WELL CLEAR TO THE EASTWARD BEFORE THE JAPANESE CAN MASS TOO FORMIDABLE A SCALE OF AIR ATTACK AGAINST US. SO, SHOOT TO SINK.

For the next few hours every ship in Force Z was alive with quiet anticipation until it was announced at about 9 P.M. that they had been discovered by three enemy aircraft and would be returning to Singapore. There was open disappointment and sarcasm.

The three planes which had forced "Tom Thumb" Phillips to turn back were Allied and they either did not see the British fleet or neglected to report it. The admiral was reading a message from his chief of staff in Singapore: ENEMY REPORTED LANDING AT KUANTAN—a point on the east coast of Malaya midway between Singapore and Kota Bharu. Almost an hour after midnight Force Z changed course for Kuantan, where not a single invader was landing. Another Japanese submarine, *I-58*, sighted the British fleet at 2:10 A.M., December 10, and after maneuvering around, fired six torpedoes at *Repulse*. All missed. No one aboard the battle cruiser was aware of the narrow escape.

Soon after dawn Phillips came upon a suspicious-looking tug and four barges about a hundred miles off Kuantan. *Prince of Wales* and *Repulse*—escorted by only three destroyers, since one, *Tenedos*, was already on its way home to refuel—headed toward the tug at 9 A.M.

By this time three Japanese groups, totaling ninety-six high-level and torpedo bombers, and ten search planes sent out from Saigon before dawn had about given up hope of locating the British. The search planes were in fact on their way home when, through the clouds, one of them sighted two battleships and three destroyers seventy miles southeast of Kuantan. Fifteen minutes later, at 10:30 A.M., radio contact was finally made with the twenty-seven torpedo planes of Kanoya Air Group. Its three squadrons altered course. Lieutenant Haruki Iki, leader of the 3rd Squadron, forgot exhaustion and hunger. His nine-plane squadron held the title of "Champions of the Navy" and he was eager to prove himself in action. In moments he saw, from 10,000 feet, what looked like a British observation plane dodging behind a cloud. The enemy fleet had to be near.

Genzan Air Group got the same message. Lieutenant Sadao Takai, leader of the 2nd Squadron, radioed his men and they all banked north-northwest, followed by the 1st Squadron. Clouds began to pile up but occasionally Takai could see patches of sea. His hands trembled. He had a strange impulse to urinate. He remembered what his commander had told him at takeoff: "Calm down and put your strength in your stomach."

On the 26,500-ton *Repulse*, CBS correspondent Cecil Brown was taking pictures of a gun crew playing cards. As the ship zigzagged, he snapped *Prince of Wales* half a mile ahead. At 11:07 A.M. he heard the loudspeaker announce: "Enemy aircraft approaching. Action stations!" Suddenly a file of nine planes loomed to the south. Rooted to the flag deck in fascination, he watched a cloud of fluttering bombs grow larger and larger. There was a dull thud and the ship shuddered. "Fire on the boat deck!" blared the loudspeaker. "Fire below!"

The two squadrons of Genzan Air Group approached and Lieutenant Takai heard his commander order "Assault formation," then, "Go on!" The 1st Squadron swept ahead of Takai in a gradual dive. Takai followed. Where were the enemy fighters? Antiaircraft fire engulfed the 1st Squadron but none was near Takai. Through binoculars he studied a large ship giving off a narrow plume of white smoke. It looked exactly like the battleship *Kongo* and his blood ran cold. He called the observer over the voice tube, who answered shakily, "It looks like our *Kongo* to me, too."

Takai was down to 1,500 feet before he was certain it was not *Kongo*. He turned into the clouds to confuse the enemy and when he darted into the open again he was less than two miles from his target.

A bugle blew on *Repulse*. "Stand by for barrage!" roared the loudspeaker. Every gun blasted as Takai's nine torpedo planes swooped in. "Look at those yellow bastards come," Brown heard someone mutter. Torpedoes slapped into the sea one by one and swam toward the battle cruiser as if they had eyes, but *Repulse*, despite her twenty-five years, dodged each one with elephantine grace. "Plucky blokes, these Japs," someone else said. "That was as beautiful an attack as ever I expect to see."

On the bridge Captain William Tennant had just noticed "Not under control" balls hoisted above *Prince of Wales*. He asked the flagship what damage she had suffered but got no answer. She was listing 13 degrees to port and weaving uncertainly at 15 knots. Both port shafts had been knocked out in the first attack and her steering gear wouldn't respond. Tennant signaled Admiral Phillips, "We have dodged nineteen torpedoes thus far, thanks to Providence," adding that all damage from one bomb hit was under control. No answer. Tennant took it on himself to radio Singapore: ENEMY AIRCRAFT BOMBING. The message was received at 12:04 P.M., and in eleven minutes six clumsy Brewster Buffalo fighters plodded off to the rescue.

Tennant again signaled Phillips. Again no answer. He reduced *Repulse*'s speed to 20 knots and moved toward the flagship to offer any assistance. Just then another ominous line of torpedo planes appeared on the horizon.

It was a squadron from the third section, Mihoro Air Group, led by Lieutenant (s.g.) Katsusaku Takahashi. Like Takai, he thought the ships ahead were Japanese—until they fired at him. He dived at the admiral's flag on *Prince of Wales*, but since the ship was turning away, he swung toward *Repulse*, a mile or so to the north. As he lowered to less than 200 feet, followed by his squadron, he estimated the speed of *Repulse* by its wake. He adjusted a simple aiming device in front of him. How could he possibly miss such a long target?

His plane was 2,500 feet from *Repulse*. "Ready," he said. The navigator-bombardier gripped the release. "Fire!" The navigator pulled up. The plane skimmed so low over the battle cruiser that Takahashi could see sailors in white scrambling from his machine-gunners' spray. Once Takahashi began a climbing turn he asked, "Did it drop?"

"No, sir."

"I'll come in again." Takahashi banked to the right and came in from the other side of *Repulse*, but once more the torpedo failed to drop. Doggedly Takahashi circled around for a third try. This time he began jerking up on his own release a mile from the target. As the plane swept over *Repulse*, he and the navigator were still struggling with their releases but to no avail. Their disappointment was bitter. However, the squadron had scored at least one hit. *Repulse* was listing to port.

Lieutenant Iki's nine planes drew near. Iki dropped below the clouds to 1,300 feet. Pompom bursts blossomed on both sides. His instinct was to pull up but he had to get in much closer. He skimmed 125 feet above the water into a wall of fire from *Repulse*. Eighteen hundred feet from the ship he yanked his release. He had her broadside!

Flak peppered his wings as he banked sharply to the left. Momentarily parallel with the ship, he could distinguish sailors in raincoats lying flat on the deck. The plane behind him, piloted by Chief Petty Officer Toshimitsu Momoi, became a ball of fire. The next, First Class Petty Officer Yoshikazu Taue's, exploded and the wreckage pinwheeled clumsily into the sea. At the bow of the battle cruiser, there were two rapid explosions. As Iki climbed to wait for his six remaining planes, he watched another torpedo drive home.

Repulse veered crazily. One torpedo had smashed into the starboard, two into the port. The fourth, Iki's, did the most immediate damage; it hit near the gun room, jamming the rudder. The battle cruiser was doomed and Captain Tennant coolly announced over the loudspeaker, "Prepare to abandon ship." He congratulated the men for fighting the ship so well and added, "God be with you." The list increased to 70 degrees. "Well, gentlemen, you had better get out of it now," he told his staff, but he himself remained rooted to the bridge. Several officers laid hands on him. He struggled but was bodily carried off.

The men formed orderly lines to abandon ship. One young sailor tried to push ahead until a second lieutenant calmly remarked, "Now, now, we are all going the same way too." As the ship took on more and more water, her bow lifted and those still in the superstructure felt giddy from the sway. A man dived from the defense control tower into the sea 170 feet below, but the next one smashed into the deck and a third hurtled into the funnel. At the stern a group of marines jumped off—and were sucked into the churning propellers.

At 12:33 P.M. the battle cruiser rolled over, then with ponderous majesty slid stern first, her bow sticking up "like a church steeple," underplates a gruesome red. From 5,000 feet, Iki looked down incredulous at the bow pointing straight at him. *Repulse* plunged out of sight. It was not possible. Planes couldn't sink a battleship so easily. "*Banzai, banzai!*" he shouted and threw up his hands. The bomber, with no hands on the controls, dipped.

The crew was also shouting in frenzy. They drank a *sake* toast. Below, Iki could make out hundreds of dots in the water. Two destroyers were picking up the survivors. It never occurred to Iki to strafe them. The British had fought gallantly, in the tradition of *bushido*. He had yet to learn that an enemy spared today may kill you tomorrow.

Mortally wounded by five torpedoes, *Prince of Wales* was barely under way as nine high-level bombers approached. At 12:44 P.M. bombs careened down. Only one struck home but it staggered the 35,000-ton battleship and she began to founder. Her beams were almost awash. Captain Leach ordered all hands to abandon ship, while he and Admiral Phillips stood together on the bridge and waved to their departing men. "Good-bye," Leach called to them. "Thank you. Good luck. God bless you." At 1:19 the battleship—nicknamed *"H.M.S. Unsinkable"*—keeled heavily over to port like a stricken hippopotamus and within a minute sank from sight, taking with her the little admiral and Captain Leach.

The six lumbering Buffalos from Singapore arrived to find a sky empty of Japanese planes. Flight Lieutenant T. A. Vigors peered down in shock at masses of men struggling in the water. They waved and held up their thumbs.

Takahashi, who had failed to release his torpedo, was halfway home. Upon hearing that *Prince of Wales* and *Repulse* were doomed he felt a strange sympathy—the British Navy was like a big brother. He fought the impulse, but tears blurred his goggles. Lieutenant Iki thought with sadness of Momoi and Taue. He knew his own torpedo had hit *Repulse* but reported that the initial two hits had been made by his two dead comrades. It was the least thing, the last thing he could do for them. As Iki's squadron landed, exuberant mechanics crowded around each plane. The crews were dragged out, tossed into the air. After he escaped the friendly pummeling, one of Iki's pilots told him, "As we dived for the attack, I didn't want to launch my torpedo. It was such a beautiful ship, such a beautiful ship."

At naval headquarters in Tokyo, the senior officers found it difficult to accept that battleships in the open sea could have been sunk by planes. It meant the end of their concept of naval warfare. The airmen were exultant. What they had been preaching for the past decade was proved. The third and final deterrent to victory in Southeast Asia had been eliminated at the cost of four planes.

The next dawn Iki flew over the graves of *Repulse* and *Prince of Wales*. As he skimmed over the sunken ships he dropped bunches of flowers.

3.

About the time Force Z turned back toward Singapore, Adolf Hitler finally arrived in Berlin from the eastern front. He was doubly concerned—by a mammoth Soviet counteroffensive in front of Moscow and the news from the Pacific. In a flash Pearl Harbor had freed his chief adversary from worry over attack from the east; Stalin could now transfer almost all his strength in Asia against Germany. For months the Führer had been urging Japan to fight Russia and avoid war with America; at the same time Tokyo pressed Ambassador Hiroshi Oshima to get written assurances that Hitler would attack America if war started, while withholding any promise to assault Russia in return.

Foreign Minister Joachim von Ribbentrop told Hitler that General Oshima was demanding an immediate declaration of war against America but reminded him that according to the terms of the Tripartite Pact, Germany was bound to assist Japan only in case she was directly attacked.

"If we don't stand on the side of Japan, the pact is politically dead," Hitler said. "But that is not the main reason. The chief reason is that the United States already is shooting at our ships. They have been a forceful factor in this war and through their actions have already created a situation of war."

Ribbentrop must have been confounded. This was a startling reversal of Hitler's own insistence on keeping America out of the European war at all costs, and for months the Führer had shown remarkable restraint in view of the U. S. Navy's provocative actions against U-boats in the Atlantic. Now all at once Hitler seemed to welcome a clean break. Perhaps it was a result of his frustration over the reversals in Russia and his wish to ride the crest of Japanese victories, or perhaps his almost psychotic hatred of Roosevelt had taken over. Whatever the reason, it would be folly, a major psychological blunder, and would only solve another of Roosevelt's domestic problems. The President would not have to declare war on Germany and risk opposition from a substantial segment of America. National unity, so unexpectedly won at Pearl Harbor, would remain intact.

Hitler began to indulge in a frenzy of wishful thinking. How could a country like America—"half Judaized, half Negrified" and "built on the dollar"—hope to hold together? Besides, Pearl Harbor couldn't have come at a more opportune moment. Russia was counterattacking and "everybody in Germany was oppressed by the certainty that sooner or later the United States would enter the conflict."

Later in the day, after ordering Hans Thomsen, the chargé d'affaires in Washington, to burn his codes and confidential papers, Ribbentrop received an estimate from Thomsen that "within twenty-four hours the United States will declare war on Germany or at least break off diplomatic relations."

Ribbentrop knew Hitler was set on getting in his own declaration first "for the sake of prestige," and warned

Thomsen to have no dealings with the State Department. "We wish to avoid under all circumstances that the Government there beats us to such a step."

On December 11 Hitler convoked the Reichstag. "We will always strike first!" he thundered. "We will always deal the first blow!" Roosevelt was as "mad" as Woodrow Wilson. "First he incited war, then falsifies the causes, then odiously wraps himself in a cloak of Christian hypocrisy and slowly but surely leads mankind to war, not without calling God to witness the honesty of his attack. . . .

"I think you have all found it a relief now that, at last, one nation has been the first to take the step of protesting against this historically unique and shameless ill treatment of truth and of right. . . . The fact that the Japanese government, which has been negotiating for years with this man, has at last become tired of being mocked by him in such an unworthy way, fills us all, the German people, and I think, all other decent people in the world, with deep satisfaction. . . .

"I have therefore arranged for passports to be handed to the American chargé d'affaires today, and the following—" His words were drowned in a bedlam of cheers.

"The Reich Government therefore breaks off all diplomatic relations with the United States and declares that under these circumstances, brought about by President Roosevelt, Germany too considers herself to be at war with the United States, as from today." Later that day Germany, Italy and Japan signed another tripartite pact asserting their "unshakable determination not to lay down arms until the joint war against the United States and England reaches a successful conclusion," and pledging under no circumstances to conclude a separate peace.

Three days later, at the presentation to Oshima of the Grand Cross of the Order of Merit, Hitler said, "You gave the right declaration of war." It was certainly proper to negotiate as long as possible, but "if one sees that the antagonist is interested only in putting one off, in shaming and humiliating one, and is not willing to come to an agreement, then one should strike—indeed, as hard as possible—and not waste time declaring war." Japan had shown "angelical patience toward that ruffian Roosevelt," he said and quoted a German proverb: "The most amicable man can't live in peace if his quarrelsome neighbor wants to fight."

Oshima spread out a map to brief Hitler on the war situation throughout the Pacific. "After the capture of Singapore, Japan must turn toward India," he said and suggested that Germany synchronize operations with Japan. "When Japan attacks India from the east, it will be most advantageous if German troops threaten India from the west." Hitler refused to commit himself but did promise to drive over the Caucasus as far as Iraq and Iran. He wanted their oil.

The day Hitler declared war on America, reports reached Manila of a tremendous Allied victory in Lingayen Gulf the previous night. The 21st Division of the Philippine Army had repelled a major Japanese landing. Most of the invasion vessels had been sunk and the beaches were strewn with Japanese bodies.

Life photographer Carl Mydans couldn't find one casualty along Lingayen Gulf. Except for Filipino soldiers lolling beside their weapons, the beaches were empty. An amused American major explained that a single unidentified boat at the mouth of the Agno River had touched off a furious barrage of every gun in the area, from 155-mm. guns to pistols. (Their target, a Japanese motorboat on reconnaissance, escaped unharmed to report that the main landing, to come eleven days hence, should be made at the northern end of the gulf, some thirty miles away, where there were almost no beach defenses.)

Major LeGrande A. Diller, MacArthur's press chief, released a statement of how the enemy landing had been thwarted. While other reporters were wiring their papers and magazines, Mydans buttonholed Diller. "Pic," he said, "I've just been to Lingayen and there's no battle there."

Diller jabbed a finger at his communiqué. "It says so here."

The story of "the Battle of Lingayen Gulf" brought a welcome surge of pride and relief to Americans. The *New York Times* banner headline that Sunday read: JAPANESE FORCES WIPED OUT IN WESTERN LUZON. Lingayen Gulf had been retaken from the Japanese in sensational fashion. United Press went further: there had been a fierce three-day fight at Lingayen Beach; 154 enemy boats were sunk without, miracle of miracles, a single enemy reaching shore alive.

The morning after the Lingayen Gulf communiqué another announced a second triumph in the Philippines: Captain Colin P. Kelly, Jr., had "successfully attacked the battleship *Haruna*, putting that ship out of commission." The crew of Kelly's Flying Fortress had sighted a large warship just off the north coast of Luzon and the bombardier, Corporal

Meyer Levin, released three 600-lb. bombs. Two missed but one appeared to go down the smokestack and when dark clouds of smoke erupted, the crew of the B-17 was certain the ship had been mortally damaged.

On the way back to Clark Field, Kelly's plane was pounced on by a Zero—its pilot was Saburo Sakai, already an ace. The Fortress burst into flames and Kelly ordered his men to bail out. The ship exploded with Kelly aboard and plummeted into a dirt road at the foot of Mount Arayat. Kelly had sacrificed his life so his crew could live, and America had her first super hero of World War II. Kelly's gallantry deserved the posthumous D.S.C. he was awarded, but he had not sunk *Haruna*, which was fifteen hundred miles away in the Gulf of Siam. There had not been a battleship near the Philippines. Nothing in the area had been sunk or, for that matter, badly damaged, but the facts became even more distorted with each telling. The most popular version, the one many Americans still retain, was that Kelly won the Medal of Honor (which he did not) by diving his plane into *Haruna*'s smokestack to become the first suicide pilot of the war.

At the same time the public was being lulled into over-confidence by dispatches from Clark Lee, the Associated Press correspondent in Manila, which derided the ability of the Japanese fighting man and the quality of his equipment. A competent newsman, Lee was merely repeating what he had been told by American military men: "The Japanese Army is an ill-uniformed, untrained mass of young boys between fifteen and eighteen years old, equipped with small-caliber guns and driven forward by desperate determination to advance or die." Their .25-caliber rifle and machine-gun bullets could not even kill a man. "They're no damned good on the ground," he quoted one cavalry colonel. "We licked the pants off them three times and were beaten only by their tanks and planes. When our tanks and planes go into action we'll chase them back to the sea. These Charlies—we call them Charlies—can't shoot. Somebody gets hit about every 5,000 shots."

MacArthur himself knew this was ridiculous. In 1905 he had studied voluminous reports of the Russo-Japanese War by American military observers, including General John J. Pershing: "Intelligence, patriotism, abstemiousness, obedience to, and inborn respect for, legally constituted authority go far toward achieving victory. When to these we add physical strength, a love of nature and of manly sports, modern organization, armament, equipment, and careful military training we have an army that will give a good account of itself. All of these were found in the Japanese army."

One observer noted that Japanese casualties were "curiously active in spite of their wounds, men shot through the head, neck, body, arms and legs being observed walking around or hopping around, as the case might be, cheerful and lively and indifferent to their wounds. They showed extraordinary vitality, with a noticeably less amount of nervous shock from wounds than I have observed in American soldiers whom I have seen similarly wounded in the Spanish war and the Philippine insurrection."

The initial phase of the Japanese master plan was working as neatly in the field as it had in tabletop maneuvers. The confusion in Malaya was short-lived and General Yamashita was driving steadily down the peninsula toward Singapore. Far to the north, at Hong Kong, the last Indian, Scotch and Canadian troops on the mainland of China were evacuated across the narrow bay to the island itself. The arrival of these defeated soldiers caused a near-panic, for it emphasized how desperate the British military position was in reality.

Out in the Pacific, the American island of Guam had fallen after a brief struggle in which seventeen American and Guamanians and one Japanese were killed. But at Wake Island, two thousand miles from Honolulu, American resistance was savage. Rear Admiral Sadamichi Kajioka's Wake Island Invasion Force—a light cruiser, six destroyers, two transports and a landing party of 560 infantry-trained sailors—was thrown back on the morning of December 11 by the small garrison under Marine Major James Devereux. Kajioka regrouped, got surface reinforcements from *Kido Butai* returning to Japan, and made a second assault early on the morning of December 23 with 830 men.

On the beach Devereux had 250 Marines, 100 civilian volunteers and no more than a few rounds of ammunition. The defenders fought desperately to the last bullet, but at eight-thirty Devereux was forced to walk out of his battered command post with a white rag on a swab handle and surrender to a Japanese officer who offered Devereux a cigarette and said he had attended the San Francisco Fair in 1939. That afternoon Admiral Kajioka, wearing spotless whites, medals and dress sword, came ashore to take formal possession of the two and a half square miles of coral rubble. It was renamed Bird Island.

Japan welcomed home the heroes of Pearl Harbor with celebrations and flowery congratulatory speeches but Yamamoto sounded a note of caution, warning his men to beware of smugness: "There are many more battles ahead."

Vice Admiral Nagumo was ordered to Tokyo along with the commanders of the two waves, Mitsuo Fuchida and Shigekazu Shimazaki, to report to the Throne. The Imperial Household had submitted a series of questions the Emperor would ask, and Kusaka had written down word for word the answers so Nagumo would not slip into the earthy phrases of his native Aizu. All went well at the audience until the Emperor began asking impromptu questions. While his two junior officers sweated in embarrassment, blunt little Nagumo reverted to colloquial terms, referring to American admirals as *aitsu* (that guy) and *koitsu* (this guy). The replies so fascinated the Emperor that the fifteen-minute audience stretched on for another half-hour. He asked Fuchida if any hospital ships had been hit or civilian or training planes knocked down. Instead of answering through an imperial aide, Fuchida became so flustered that he replied directly that no noncombatants had been attacked. It was a miserable moment for Fuchida—a worse ordeal, he thought, than the raid itself.

Roosevelt, Churchill and Stalin were united against Hitler, but at the moment the first two were desperately in need of help on the other side of the world. In Moscow, Foreign Secretary Anthony Eden put the question politely to Stalin in mid-December: would he join his allies and declare war on Japan? Stalin explained that he had been forced to withdraw troops from the Far East to hold back Hitler and didn't think he could replace them in less than four months. He couldn't declare war on Japan or provoke her until these forces were back to strength. Perhaps before then Japan would herself solve the problem by attacking Russia: he was inclined to hope that would happen, since it would be difficult to get much popular support for another war thousands of miles to the east.

Curiously, he was convinced that Japanese air successes would not have been possible without the Germans, who—according to one secret report—had contributed fifteen hundred aircraft and hundreds of pilots.

"Certainly the Japanese have shown more skill in the air than we expected," Eden remarked politely.

"We have had experience fighting the Japanese in the air

and we have also carefully observed them in China for a very long time, and I have come to the conclusion that this is not really a Japanese war. I think some of the Japanese pilots were trained in Germany, and others are German."

"How do you think the airplanes got there?"

"Probably through South America."

Eden apologized for not sending ten squadrons to the Russian front; they would have to go to Singapore.

"I fully understand and have no objection," Stalin said.

"It is a great disappointment to us."

"I fully realize the position and that the situation has changed. We, too, have had our difficult periods."

"I very much appreciate the spirit of your answer," Eden said, "and if the wheel goes round again we shall be very glad to help."

On his part, Stalin was sorry he could not help in the Far East. "We can do nothing now, but in the spring we shall be ready, and will then help."

Eden made another effort to get a more definite commitment and used the deteriorating situation in Malaya as the excuse.

"If the Soviet Union were to declare war on Japan," Stalin replied, "we should have to wage a real war by land, on sea and in the air. It would not be like the declarations of war on Japan by Belgium and Poland. Consequently we have to make a careful estimate of the forces involved. At present we are not ready. . . . We would prefer that Japan should attack us, and I think it very probable that she will do so—not just yet, but later. If the Germans are hard pressed it is likely that they will urge the Japanese to attack us, in which case the attack may be expected about the middle of next year."

This did not satisfy Eden. "I fear that the Japanese may meanwhile adopt a policy of dealing with their opponents one by one, and may try to finish with us before attacking the Soviet Union."

"Great Britain is not fighting Japan alone. She has allies in China, the Dutch East Indies and the United States of America."

"The main attack at the moment is on Malaya, where our allies cannot help us much," said Eden. The next six months were going to be most difficult. "We have got to stick it out, and we shall do so. But it is a very uncomfortable situation." Even so, the Libyan campaign would not be called off just to increase the strength in Malaya. "The Far East must hold until we can afford to send reinforcements."

"I think that is quite sound. The weakest link of the Axis is Italy, and if this link is broken the whole Axis will collapse." Stalin couldn't help adding that if the British had attacked Italy in 1939, "they would now be masters of the situation in the Mediterranean."

Dinner that evening went on until dawn and several officers—notably the colorful Commissar for Defense, Marshal Semën Timoshenko—became intoxicated. Stalin turned to Eden in embarrassment. "Do your generals ever get drunk?"

"They don't often get the chance" was the diplomatic answer.

Churchill was aboard *Duke of York*, a day's sail from Chesapeake Bay, when he received a cable from Eden announcing that the talks with Stalin had "ended on a friendly note." He was bound for "Arcadia," code name of the first wartime conference between Britain and America and named after the region in Greece so famed for its pastoral innocence and contentment that it has become a universal symbol. The conference, designed to bring about the best means of fighting the Axis, was to belie its name from the beginning.

Churchill and his Chiefs of Staff expected to dominate "Arcadia," and by the time they arrived in Washington on the evening of December 22, they had formulated a detailed program: Germany was the prime enemy and her defeat was the key to victory. Italy and Japan would then speedily collapse. "In our considered opinion, therefore, it should be a cardinal principal of A-B [American-British] strategy that only the minimum of force necessary for the safeguarding of vital interests in other theatres should be diverted from operations against Germany."

But at the first meeting the following afternoon it was immediately apparent that the Americans had not come merely to listen and approve. They made it clear that only a frontal attack on Germany would bring victory and that the British concept of maneuver was nothing but a pecking away at the edges. It was an understandable conflict between a nation whose limited forces had already been strained by more than two years of war and one new to battle with almost unlimited resources and manpower. To the Americans, war was something like an athletic contest and little was thought of what would happen when peace came. The more sophisticated British regarded battle as flexible, a continuation of policy that could take surprising turns. Even the best friend the United States had among the British military leaders, Sir John Dill, privately felt that America had not—"repeat not—the slightest conception of what the war means, and their armed forces are more unready for war than it is possible to imagine."

4.

On the day Churchill arrived in Washington a large invasion force of eighty-five transports approached the Philippines. The submarine *Stingray* had sighted the convoy in time to alert General MacArthur, who expected the Japanese to land at the southern end of Lingayen Gulf where the bulk of his artillery was emplaced. The Japanese knew all about this concentration from "the Battle of Lingayen Gulf" and were about to land the 14th Army miles up the coast.

The Army commander, General Masaharu Homma, the amateur playwright, had long opposed the road to war. He had spent eight years with the British, including service in France in 1918 with the British Expeditionary Force and had deep respect for and some understanding of the West. Following the fall of Nanking, he had publicly declared that "unless peace is achieved immediately it will be disastrous," and then confided to General Muto that Tojo would make a poor minister of war.

Few of his men knew where they were. They had been secretly loaded five days earlier at Formosa and the Pescadores, and even those officers who knew their destination had the vaguest of instructions. The first of Homma's 43,110 men began going overside at two o'clock in the morning on December 22. The high seas almost swamped the first boats, and it took two and a half hours to load two battalions of infantry and a battalion of mountain artillery. Forty-seven minutes later the first boat ground onto a beach near the town of Agoo, but many of the landing craft which followed were overturned by the roaring breakers. On the beach the soldiers met no resistance.

By midmorning the entire first wave had landed and the beachhead was consolidated with spirited opposition from a lone Filipino battalion. Late that afternoon all the infantry and half the tanks were ashore and moving south down Route 3, the paved highway running along the coast to Manila.

In the capital MacArthur anxiously awaited news from

Lingayen Gulf. He radioed Marshall a suggestion that carriers bring pursuit planes within range of the Philippines: CAN I EXPECT ANYTHING ALONG THAT LINE? Marshall replied that according to the Navy, this was impossible and MacArthur would have to rely on the planes already ferried as far as Brisbane in Australia.

At dawn General Brereton's remaining bombers—four Fortresses—attacked the Japanese convoy in Lingayen Gulf. They dropped 100-lb. bombs and then turned south for Australia. Homma was steadily pushing toward Manila and early in the afternoon attacked the unit blockading the main road. With scarcely ten weeks' training, few of these Filipino soldiers knew how to operate their antiquated Enfield rifles. They broke and fled, leaving the supporting artillery unprotected. Major General Jonathan M. ("Skinny") Wainwright, commander of all forces in northern Luzon, phoned MacArthur for permission to withdraw behind the Agno River.

With no air force or navy, MacArthur had to abandon his dream of holding the enemy at the beaches and was obliged to fall back on a plan drawn up by his predecessors. This was known as War Plan Orange-3 and provided for withdrawal of Fil-American forces to the Bataan Peninsula if enemy landings could not be contained. Here, within sight of Manila, the defenders would hold out for as long as six months until the Navy could bring in reinforcements. MacArthur had long since shelved this operation as defeatist. All he could do now was call in his staff and say, "Put WPO-3 into effect."

The situation was worse than MacArthur had feared. The next morning he discovered that his forces were caught in a giant pincers. Twenty-four Japanese transports had landed during the night at Lamon Bay, sixty air miles southeast of Manila, and almost ten thousand men of the 16th Division were advancing on Manila in three columns. At ten o'clock MacArthur ordered his South Luzon Force, two divisions, to retreat to Bataan. The battle in the south was over before it started and MacArthur was forced to give instructions to transfer his headquarters to Corregidor Island at dark.

Nearby in the Marsman Building, Admiral Hart told Rear Admiral Francis W. Rockwell, commandant of the 16th Naval District, that he was moving his headquarters south to Borneo so he could be with the operating fleet. Rockwell would assume command of all naval remnants. Their conversation was drowned out by the roar of planes and thunder of bombs exploding in the Walled City. They could see flames all over the port area. Dust from pulverized cement and stone mixed with black billows of smoke and engulfed the entire Pasig River section.

At Malacañan Palace, President Manuel Quezon was exhorting his executive secretary, Jorge Vargas, and José Laurel to make a sacrifice without parallel for the good of the people: "You two will remain here and deal with the Japanese." He and Vice President Sergio Osmeña would join MacArthur on Corregidor.

All four of them must pledge never to reveal his order to Vargas and Laurel. But people will call me a collaborator, protested Laurel. He broke down and begged for permission to accompany Quezon to Corregidor. It was Laurel's duty, insisted Quezon, who was dying of tuberculosis. "Someone has to protect the people from the Japanese."

Outside, the streets swarmed with Army trucks and squat Pambusco buses overflowing with soldiers and supplies. Every vehicle was going north—toward Bataan, on the other side of the bay. As darkness came on, the steamer *Don Esteban,* with MacArthur and most of his staff aboard, plowed across the inlet toward Corregidor, less than thirty miles away. It was balmy and the moon was shining. In the distance, flames leaped up from Cavite Navy Yard's oil dump. Almost all of the men of USAFFE headquarters were in short sleeves. It was a strange Christmas Eve for Americans.

Seven hundred miles to the north another island bastion was about to fall. The Japanese held most of Hong Kong's mountainous thirty-two square miles. The British forces were split in two and their final lines were crumpling. There was little ammunition left and only enough water for another day or so. Though the resistance on the mainland had been disappointing, the stand on the island was stubborn, primarily because of the determination of the 1,759 men of the Hong Kong Volunteer Defence Corps. Dubbed "playboy soldiers" by the Regulars, this mixture of local British, Eurasian, Chinese and Portuguese civilian recruits had fought as well as any of the other troops and better than most.

By Christmas morning those defenders were overrun who were cut off at the narrow Stanley Peninsula on the southern end of the island, and uncontrolled groups of Japanese began butchering the wounded and raping Chinese and British nurses. The main force at Victoria, the capital of Hong Kong, was also close to being overwhelmed. At nine o'clock two prisoners of the Japanese—a retired British major and a civilian—were released with a message for Major-General

C. M. Maltby, military commander of the colony: it would be useless to continue the fight and the Japanese had promised to hold fire for three hours while the British made up their minds.

Maltby held off until three-fifteen before reluctantly ordering his commanders to surrender. It was a humiliating end to British rule in China—and even with surrender the atrocities continued throughout Christmas night.

It was also a dark Christmas in the Philippines. That morning MacArthur reviewed the gloomy situation at his new headquarters on Corregidor, a small tadpole-shaped island three miles south of Bataan Peninsula in the mouth of Manila Bay. Whoever held it controlled the bay, for it stuck in its throat like a bone. The coastal-gun, mortar and antiaircraft batteries were formidable, and the labyrinthine tunnel system in the solid rock under Malinta Hill provided bombproof shelter for a hospital, headquarters, shops and storehouses.

The flow of American traffic was moving toward Bataan from every direction. Route 3 out of Manila was clogged with trucks, 155's on their carriages, naval guns on trucks, buses, cars, *calesas* and oxcarts. A couple of well-placed bombs on the two bridges at Calumpit, thirty miles north of Manila, over the wide, unfordable Pampanga River, would have cut off all forces from the south.

Ten miles above the bridges the line of vehicles turned left at San Fernando toward the peninsula. Here they met the van of Wainwright's main body flowing in from the north. The result was a monumental traffic jam and the road from San Fernando leading into Bataan was so narrow that traffic had backed up into town before noon.

The peninsula itself was bedlam. As thousands of frightened civilian refugees fleeing ahead of Homma's army streamed into Bataan on foot, in oxcarts and ramshackle cars, fragments of units arrived to find few road signs or markers and wandered about in confusion. The trenches and fortifications specified by WPO-3 existed on paper alone. The villagers should have been evacuated but someone had apparently forgotten to give the order; they stared in wonder as an endless parade of trucks, cars and guns rumbled past, coating their bamboo houses with thick layers of dust.

WPO-3 called for a six-month food supply, but there was not enough for a month. More provisions were on the way by water, rail and highway, but for how many more hours would the roads to Bataan be kept open? The one hope was that Wainwright's men could delay the enemy drive from the north another two weeks. This would give the troops on Bataan time to dig defenses while the South Luzon Force retreated up through Manila and into Bataan. At best it was a slim chance. Then came an official report that the Japanese had penetrated the Agno River line, the last formidable natural fortification between them and Bataan. It seemed unlikely that the poorly trained and exhausted defenders could hold back the Japanese long enough. Could they resist even until New Year's Day?

On Christmas Day a flying boat brought an admiral to Hawaii from the mainland. It was Chester Nimitz, the man chosen to relieve Admiral Kimmel and command all naval forces in the Pacific. His hair was turning white but he was trim-looking and his blue eyes were piercing. He had hoped for a sea command.

In a few hours Nimitz found what he had feared—too much pessimism. Morale was at "rock bottom" and he noticed that the shock of Pearl Harbor had turned several senior officers' hair white. He summoned the staff he had inherited, some of whom were taking sedatives on surgeon's orders. "There will be no changes," he said. "I have complete confidence in you men. We've taken a terrific wallop but I have no doubts as to the ultimate outcome."

In his Academy classbook he was described as a man "of cheerful and confident tomorrows," and true to form his calm serenity was infectious. But he knew the complete rehabilitation of spirit would take time. The Pacific Fleet would not be ready to strike back in force for several months.

The last survivors of those trapped inside the sunken battleship *West Virginia* finally lay lifeless on the lower shelf of storeroom A-111. On a bulkhead was a calendar with X's marked from December 7 through 23.

5.

"This is a strange Christmas Eve," Winston Churchill said emotionally. He was standing next to Roosevelt on the south portico of the White House addressing a crowd of thirty thousand gathered on the south lawn for the traditional lighting of the municipal Christmas tree. "Almost the whole world is locked in deadly struggle, and with the most terrible weapons which science can devise, the nations advance upon each other. . . . Here, in the midst of war, raging and roaring over all the lands and seas, creeping nearer to our hearths and homes, here, amid all the tumult, we have tonight the peace of the spirit in each cottage home and in every generous heart. . . . Let the children have their night of fun and laughter. Let the gifts of Father Christmas delight their play. Let us grown-ups share to the full in their unstinted pleasures before we turn again to the stern task and the formidable years that lie before us, resolved that, by our sacrifices and daring, these same children shall not be robbed of their inheritance or denied their right to live in a free and decent world."

He told his personal physician, Lord Moran, that he'd had palpitations during the ceremony and wanted his pulse taken. "It has all been very moving," he lisped excitedly. "This is a new war, with Russia victorious, Japan in, and America in up to the neck."

On Christmas morning Roosevelt took his guest to church, remarking, "It is good for Winston to sing hymns with the Methodies." He sang one he had never heard of before—"O Little Town of Bethlehem." After the service he spent hours preparing a speech for Congress. What mood would he find his listeners in the next morning? Some were not at all friendly to the British.

They were captivated from the moment he said, "I feel greatly honored that you should have invited me to enter the United States Senate Chamber and address the representatives of both branches of Congress. I cannot help reflecting that if my father had been American and my mother British, instead of the other way round, I might have got here on my own." A loud shout erupted when, speaking of the Japanese, he cried, "What sort of people do they think we are?" He continued, his voice rising above the din, to speak movingly and effectively of the task that lay ahead. "It is not given to us to peer into the mysteries of the future. Still, I avow my hope and faith, sure and inviolate, that in the days to come the British and American peoples will for their own safety and for the good of all walk together side by side in majesty, in justice, and in peace."

There was a spontaneous and unreserved burst of applause.

The American military leaders, however, were in no such mood. They had just been informed that their impulsive President had had himself wheeled into Churchill's room the previous night for an impromptu meeting—and agreed to consider giving the British the reinforcements promised to MacArthur if the line of supply to the Philippines was cut. The outraged American Chiefs appealed to Stimson, who became so "extremely angry" that he immediately phoned Hopkins to say the President would have to get a new Secretary of War if he kept on making such quixotic personal decisions. Roosevelt hastened to deny that "any such proposition had actually been made," and swore he had never considered siphoning off any supplies from MacArthur.

The first plenary session of "Arcadia" met that afternoon in an edgy, uneasy atmosphere, and it was Roosevelt himself who jolted the British by saying he was not satisfied that available resources were being put to their best use. Had the Chiefs of Staff discussed the possibility of a unified command in the Far East? He was echoing the suggestion of General Marshall, who the day before had told the British and American Chiefs of Staff that "there must be one man in command of the entire theater—air, ground, and ships."

Churchill violently disagreed. Unity of command was fine if there was one continuous front, as in World War I, but in the Far East some Allied units were a thousand miles apart. "The situation out there is that certain particular strategic points have to be held, and the commander in each locality is quite clear as to what he should do," he contended. "The difficult question is the application of resources arriving in the area. This is a matter which can only be settled by the Governments concerned."

Lord Beaverbrook, the Minister of Supply, passed a note to Hopkins:

You should work on Churchill. He is being advised. He is open minded and needs discussion.

Encouraged by this, Hopkins told Churchill, "Don't be in a hurry to turn down the proposal the President is going to make to you before you know who is the man we have in mind." It was General Archibald Wavell.

The next evening the British Chiefs of Staff called on Churchill to say they were ready to accept a unified command in principle. They suggested that an American officer be chosen to head the ABDA (American, British, Dutch, Australian) command. Churchill imagined his Chiefs would be as delighted as he to hear that the Americans were willing to accept Wavell. But they interpreted this suggestion as a

Roosevelt trick—the Far East was crumbling and Wavell would be blamed for the defeat.* Let some American take the post.

Their attitude did not set well with Churchill. He could not believe Roosevelt was "attempting to shift disaster onto our shoulders," nor did he want to surrender responsibility for Singapore to the Americans. Think what the Australians would make of that! Prime Minister John Curtin had recently stated in an article: "Australia looks to America, free from any pangs as to traditional links or kinship with the United Kingdom."

As he argued, his indignation grew. The Chiefs' suspicions were insulting to the President—whose offer had been a friendly, generous gesture—and he would not stand for it. Argument ended, but not resentment. The British Chiefs felt they were becoming minor partners under the polite but forceful domination of their juniors.

Ironically, out of this squall came one of the most significant developments of the war—reaffirmation of a previous decision, the creation of a unified command system, a Combined Chiefs of Staff with headquarters in Washington, the new capital of Western democracy. This remarkable achievement, fathered by Marshall and fostered by Roosevelt, was made possible by the open-mindedness of Winston Churchill. He saw beyond the objections and suspicions of his own Chiefs, to solidify Anglo-Saxon unity and achieve what he had come for: confirmation that Hitler was the main enemy and realization that the war in the Pacific would have to be, for the time being, a holding action.

On New Year's morning Roosevelt turned his mind from the military to global politics. He was wheeled into Churchill's room with a draft of a joint declaration by twenty-six nations fighting the Axis powers "to defend life, liberty, independence and religious freedom, and to preserve human rights and justice in their own lands as well as other lands" by waging common war against "savage and brutal forces seeking to subjugate the world." According to Hopkins, Churchill burst out of the shower stark naked. ("I never received the President without at least a bath towel wrapped around me," said Churchill.) Roosevelt apologetically made as if to leave but Churchill said, "The Prime Minister of

---

*Informed of his appointment, Wavell wryly said, "I have heard of men having to hold the baby, but this is twins."

Great Britain has nothing to conceal from the President of the United States."

The two men agreed on the draft, which was the genesis of the United Nations, and later in the day both signed it in the President's study, along with Soviet Ambassador Maxim Litvinov and Chinese Foreign Minister T. V. Soong.

"Arcadia" lasted for another two weeks. Much had been accomplished, but some of the British left disgruntled. "The Americans have got their way and the war will be run from Washington," Lord Moran wrote in his diary, "but they will not be wise to push us so unceremoniously in the future. Our people are very unhappy about the decision, and the most they will agree to is to try it out for a month."

Churchill himself went home in great good humor, exulting over the final joint production estimates reached at the conference: 45,000 tanks and 43,000 planes in 1942, and 75,000 tanks and 100,000 planes the following year. "He is drunk with the figures," commented Moran.

The decisions at "Arcadia" were picked up by a Japanese secret agent almost as soon as they were made. "Sutton," the cashiered American major, pumped this information from friends at the Army-Navy Club on Farragut Square and passed it along to Commander Wachi, the spy master in Mexico City. Sutton revealed that America's initial intentions to wage all-out war against Japan had been drastically altered and that the Allies would concentrate on defeating Hitler while holding Japan as best they could. He even had details of the final plan to defeat Japan by co-ordinated attacks of submarine packs and fleets of huge bombers; the latter would hit Kyushu from bases in China while the submarines cut all sea lanes to the homeland.

It was a major coup, as significant as any of Sorge's. Wachi sent it to Japan through two channels: a local German agent who dispatched reports to Berlin almost every night in code; and by ordinary airmail (the message was written in invisible ink bought from another German agent for $2,000) to the Japanese naval attaché in neutral Buenos Aires.

The information industriously gleaned by Major Sutton reached Tokyo from both sources, but naval headquarters was so intoxicated by recent victories that the report was merely glanced at, and forgotten.

10

"For a Wasted Hope and Sure Defeat"

1.

New Year's, the favorite Japanese holiday, was celebrated as usual in Tokyo. Debts were paid up; an endless parade thronged into the Meiji Shrine to throw coins at a donation chest on the stroke of midnight and, for good luck, buy red *daruma* dolls with weighted bottoms. The gaiety was not dampened by the war; on the contrary, it fostered a mood of expectancy. When would the next triumph come?

General Muto, chief of the Military Affairs Bureau, called on Shigenori Togo at the Foreign Ministry and after several cups of *toso* (New Year's wine) said, "The people are enjoying the victories too much. It won't do." It was going to be an arduous war. "Your policy, therefore, should be to end it as soon as possible." The first step was to replace Tojo as prime minister, said Muto, and left to tell the same things to a former premier who had long opposed military aggression, Admiral Okada.

The Japanese in the Philippines celebrated the day by converging on Manila from two directions. General Homma was just seventeen miles from the capital with little in front to stop him. The troops in the south had been slowed up some forty miles away because dynamiters had destroyed so many highway and railroad bridges, but they too faced almost no opposition. Homma halted his columns, ordering his men to clean themselves and tighten their formations. Unkempt troops, he knew, did not parade with pride and were more likely to loot and rape.

Stores were boarded up in the city. Near the dock area Carl Mydans of *Life* magazine watched looters rifle warehouses of everything from automobiles to unexposed movie film. When he returned to the Bayview Hotel his wife, Shelley, handed him a cable from *Life*. It requested: ANOTHER FIRST-PERSON EYEWITNESS STORY BUT THIS WEEK WE PREFER AMERICANS ON THE OFFENSIVE.

She showed her answer: BITTERLY REGRET YOUR REQUEST UNAVAILABLE HERE.

Smoke seemed to permeate Manila. The Pandacan oil fields as well as all Army and Navy installations were ablaze. At five forty-five Major General Koichi Abe led three battalions of his 48th Division into Manila from the north. They were greeted with silence by lines of sullen Filipinos. The cheers came from a handful of Japanese freed from internment.

From their hotel room the Mydanses watched three companies of Japanese soldiers and sailors form ragged lines on the lawn in front of High Commissioner Francis B. Sayre's residence across the boulevard. The American flag was lowered from a pole and three small cannon boomed as it fluttered to the ground. A sailor stamped on it and fastened in its place the emblem of the Rising Sun. As the new flag rose, the band spiritedly played the Japanese national anthem, "Kimigayo."

> The Emperor's reign will last
> For a thousand and then eight thousand generations
> Until pebbles become mighty rocks
> Covered with moss.

Across Manila Bay, General MacArthur's troops streamed into Bataan for the final battle, but Homma and most of his staff concluded that this mass migration to the peninsula was merely a disorganized flight. He was confident, as were his superiors in Saigon and Tokyo, that Manila was the key to total victory. The Philippine campaign was over even if MacArthur did hold out on Corregidor and the tip end of Bataan for several weeks.

From Saigon, General Hisaichi Terauchi sent word to transfer the 48th Division to the Java invasion force. The successes in the Philippines and Malaya had exceeded all expectations and Terauchi could invade Java a month ahead of schedule.

Despite his easy victory, Homma was disturbed. Mopping-up operations would be difficult and the loss of the 48th, his best division, would place an unwarranted burden on the remaining troops. He asked to keep the division another month but was refused.

The 48th was on the front line in Bataan. Its replacement was the 65th "Summer" Brigade from Formosa, an occupation force of seventy-five hundred, comprised mostly of older men almost totally unprepared and unequipped for front-line duty. The unexpected assignment dismayed its commander,

Lieutenant General Akira Nara, who had spent many years in the United States, where he attended Amherst College as a classmate of President Coolidge's son and graduated from the Fort Benning Infantry School.

On the night of January 5 Nara—a stocky, middle-aged man—led his troops toward the front on foot. Behind him, stretching halfway back to Lingayen Gulf, straggled his weary men, already delayed for days by American engineers who had left 184 destroyed bridges behind them.

The tropical evening was beautiful, the air fragrant with the exotic scent of frangipani. Bushes clustered with fireflies reminded Nara of Christmas trees, but those who trudged behind were too miserable to savor the beauties of the tropics.

They approached a Bataan crammed with some 15,000 Americans and 65,000 Filipino troops. Ten thousand of the latter were professional soldiers, the elite Philippine Division; the rest was a conglomerate ill-equipped group almost totally untrained. With this force and barely enough unbalanced field rations for 100,000 men for thirty days, MacArthur was supposed to hold out for six months. His greatest asset was the terrain. The peninsula, fifteen miles wide and twice as long, was almost completely occupied by the ancient remnants of two great extinct volcanoes, one in the north, one in the south. In between was thick jungle. There were but two roads. One was a semibelt highway coursing down the flat, swampy east coast, around the tip and two thirds of the way back up the other side of the peninsula. The other was a cobblestone road cutting across the midriff of Bataan through the valley between the two volcanoes.

MacArthur intended to make his first stand at a line about ten miles down the peninsula, running from Manila Bay across the northern volcano, whose mouth, after thousands of years, had been eroded into four jagged peaks. The eastern and highest peak was the precipitous Mount Natib.

By the morning of January 9 MacArthur's men were in position, and morale was high though they were already on half rations. They were tired of retreat and wanted to stand and fight. MacArthur split his battle line in two, assigning the left (the western half) to Wainwright, whose men were in no shape for immediate combat after their chaotic flight from Lingayen Gulf. It was obvious that the Japanese would first attack on the right side, down the east coastal highway. This sector was turned over to Major General George Parker, commander of the twenty-five thousand men who had escaped from the south with relative ease.

His right flank, the east coast, was flat and swampy, with fish ponds and rice paddies extending inland for about two miles. Then came gradually rising cane fields and little bamboo groves for another five miles. At this point Mount Natib began to rise dramatically. Since no military force on earth could possibly march across the complex of crags, ravines and cliffs, all matted with dense jungle growth, Parker's left flank ended abruptly at the foot of the rugged mountain.

This was the Abucay line, named after a cluster of nipa shacks for sugar-cane workers. The Filipinos were anxious to show MacArthur they deserved his faith and to prove that the rout on the humiliating retreat had been no fair test. Their American instructors were not as sanguine. But there was one advantage to the Abucay line—retreat would be difficult. It was fight or die.

A few miles to the north, General Nara's overaged and underarmed troops had just moved into position, relieving the cocky veterans of the 48th Division. At the War College, Nara had warned his pupils never to attack without accurate maps. Here he had a road map and several large-scale maps. Nor did he have a plan of attack; his instructions from 14th Army had merely been to "pursue the enemy in column down the highway," with the help of two artillery regiments and the 9th Infantry Regiment of the 16th Division.

He had been assured that there were no more than twenty-five thousand disorganized enemy troops on Bataan and that they would retreat pell-mell to the little town of Mariveles on the tip end of the peninsula at the first rattle of gunfire. Here they would make a brief stand before trying to escape to the island of Corregidor. All the same, Nara asked for time to make a survey. He was ordered to attack immediately. He hastily drew up a plan. It was perforce simple, with only a day for organization. He instructed his own 141st Infantry, under Colonel Takeo Imai, to attack straight down the coastal highway while the 9th Infantry, commanded by an old and trusted friend, Colonel Susumu Takechi, headed down the peninsula toward the slopes of Mount Natib. He would cross the supposedly impassable mountain and cut back to the coastal highway, thus encircling the enemy.

That afternoon, after an hour-long artillery barrage, Imai started down the highway while Takechi struck off into the tangled jungle. Imai had scarcely gone a hundred yards before the road ahead erupted with a series of thunderous

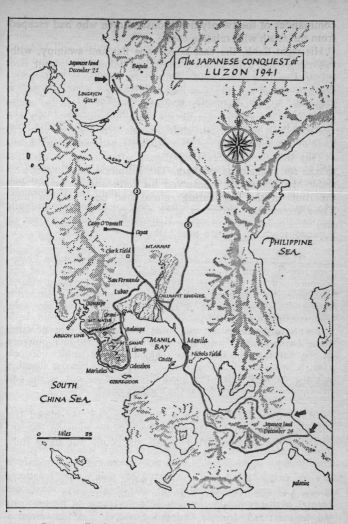

The Japanese Conquest of LUZON 1941

roars. It was Parker's artillery. The Americans were not going to cut and run at the first volley.

The Filipinos weren't either. They fell upon the Japanese dispersed by the artillery bombardment and in the next forty-eight hours cut Imai's regiment to a third. Accordingly, Nara was forced to replace the remnants with a reserve unit.

His troubles were just beginning. Not a word had come from Takechi; he should already have crossed Mount Natib and circled behind the enemy. Darkness came and he still had not appeared. The jungle had swallowed him up. Nara did not report this to Homma, neither did he record it in his war diary or brigade report; it was the least he could do for a classmate at the Academy. It meant the end of Nara's bold plan. Now he turned his efforts to rebuilding his lines. He shuttled Imai's exhausted troops to the west to fill in the hole vacated by Takechi and sent out orders to begin probing for a weak spot in the Abucay line.

That same day, January 13, Quezon sent a radiogram to Roosevelt through MacArthur complaining that the President had failed to keep his pledge to send aid to the Philippines. He urged him to direct the full force of American strength against the Japanese at once. His indignation carried over in an accompanying note to MacArthur:

... Has it already been decided in Washington that the Philippine front is of no importance as far as the final result of the war is concerned and that, therefore, no help can be expected here in the immediate future, or at least before the power of resistance is exhausted? If so, I want to know, because I have my own responsibility to my countrymen. ...

I want to decide in my own mind whether there is justification for allowing all these men to be killed when for the final outcome of the war the shedding of their blood may be wholly unnecessary. It seems that Washington does not fully realize our situation nor the feelings which the apparent neglect of our safety and determined defense will defeat the enemy's attack. ...

MacArthur did not have to be persuaded. He hoped the message would stir up Marshall. To his own men on Bataan, however, he sent inspiring words he could not have fully believed:

Help is on the way from the United States. Thousands of troops and hundreds of planes are being dispatched. . . . No further retreat is possible. We have more troops in Bataan than the Japanese have thrown against us; our supplies are ample; a determined defense will defeat the enemy's attack. ...

I call upon every soldier in Bataan to fight in his assigned position, resisting every attack. This is the only road to salvation. If we fight, we will win; if we retreat, we will be destroyed.

Most of the Americans on Bataan didn't believe it either. The Filipinos alone found inspiration in MacArthur's words, which made them more determined than ever to prove themselves worthy to fight under the Stars and Stripes. On the morning of January 16 the 51st Philippine Army Division launched a determined counterattack. In fact, they were so eager that one regiment far outran units on its flanks.

It was the opportunity Colonel Imai had been looking for. The Filipinos had formed a salient more dangerous to themselves than to him and he promptly struck at the eastern end of the bulge. At that moment, too, Colonel Takechi's lost regiment burst out of the jungled slopes directly into the other side of the bulge. Assaulted from both sides the Filipino salient crumpled and by noon collapsed. It left a two-mile hole in the Abucay line.

It was late afternoon by the time Takechi—face lined with fatigue and hunger, uniform in tatters—reported to Nara how he had become hopelessly lost on Mount Natib. The general was sympathetic and ordered him to go into reserve. Takechi saluted crisply, and without pausing for supplies or rest, led his troops off—not north into reserve but back to the south. He thought Nara was punishing him for getting lost; he was going to lead his men back over Mount Natib this time or die in the attempt.

The other side of Bataan, from Mount Natib to the South China Sea, was so inaccessible that as yet Homma had been unable to mount any appreciable offensive. But late the following afternoon five thousand Japanese moved opposite Wainwright's positions. Their commander, Major General Naoki Kimura, discovered that the American defense line extended only halfway up the western slope of Mount Silanganan, a peak two miles west of Mount Natib. He decided to do what Takechi had failed to do on the other side. Led by Lieutenant Colonel Hiroshi Nakanishi, seven hundred infantrymen secretly circled Wainwright's right flank and turned sharply west. By dawn of January 21 they reached the South China Sea, cutting off all of Wainwright's front-line troops.

To the east, the Abucay line was at the point of collapse. Troops sent in to boost the punctured front had become bogged down in the dense vegetation and rugged crevasses and never reached their positions. Along the front itself the troops were exhausted from constant fighting during the day and harassing attacks at night from infiltrators who terrorized the defenders with firecrackers and taunts over loudspeakers.

After a quick tour of Bataan, General Sutherland advised his chief to withdraw immediately to another defense line behind the cobblestone road bisecting Bataan. MacArthur ordered a general retreat, starting at darkness the following evening. At seven o'clock on January 24, trucks and men began pouring back from the Abucay line. By midnight the trail to the rear was jammed with battered buses full of gaunt-faced Filipinos in blue denims and coconut helmets, command cars packed with fatigued officers in filthy uniforms, and marching troops. There were no military police to regulate the flow to the rear, and units became separated in the nightmare chaos. Officers could do nothing but keep men and vehicles moving south and pray that no shells would fall.

Just before dawn the handful of troops holding the front lines began leapfrogging to the rear. They looked like walking dead. Unwashed and unshaven for nine days, their gaunt faces were blank. The withdrawal continued all through the next day, harried by Japanese planes which freely strafed and bombed the trails and the coastal road. Retreat turned into rout when the indomitable Colonel Takechi and his starved men burst out of nowhere. They had done the impossible, crossed Mount Natib.

By January 26 the new Fil-American line, connected by an ingenious network of communication and supply trails hacked out of the jungle, was almost completely manned. It lay in the valley between the two dead volcanoes, just behind the cobblestone road, and extended uninterruptedly from Manila Bay to the South China Sea. It was divided into two sectors, with Wainwright again commanding the western half and Parker the eastern. The troops rested in foxholes and dugouts, thanking God they had survived the arduous retreat from Abucay. In his position Lieutenant Henry G. Lee, of the Philippine Division, was composing a poem about the withdrawal. Bataan, he wrote, had been

> . . . saved for another day
> Saved for hunger and wounds and heat
> For slow exhaustion and grim retreat
> For a wasted hope and sure defeat. . . .

Like the Americans, the Japanese were in no condition to continue the battle. Nara's "Summer" Brigade was riddled with more than two thousand casualties. The survivors were exhausted and still stupefied by their first taste of battle.

The resumed fighting brought on even more confusion than at Abucay. Here the jungle was so dense that one Japanese force of a thousand men slipped through Wainwright's lines without being detected for three days. It took almost three weeks of desperate, deadly hand-to-hand combat to wipe them out. The Japanese also tried to outflank Wainwright by sea, landing in barges on the rugged west coast far behind the front. They planned to drive south to Mariveles and cut off supplies from Corregidor. Five separate landings were attempted over the next two weeks, and it wasn't until February 8 that the last pocket of infiltrators was eliminated. That same day Homma held an important conference at his command post in the sugar center of San Fernando. It was muggy, above 95 degrees. The general was tormented. He had already lost seven thousand men in combat on Bataan, and another ten thousand had been stricken with malaria, beriberi and dysentery. He had twice asked for reinforcements and been rejected twice.

There were only three Japanese infantry battalions strung across Bataan, and Lieutenant General Masami Maeda, Homma's chief of staff, warned that if MacArthur discovered this he could break through. The senior operations officer, Colonel Motoo Nakayama, still insisted the attack should be prosecuted vigorously. "The main effort, however, should be made along the east coast, not the west."

Maeda wanted Bataan merely blockaded while the rest of the archipelago was occupied. "By that time the men of General Matsukuasa [MacArthur] will be starved and ready to surrender."

Maeda was right, but to Homma it was unthinkable not to press for a quicker victory. Tokyo would never permit such face-losing strategy. He said a new and much more powerful offense had to be launched, To do this he would have to bear the unbearable—swallow his pride and once more ask for heavy reinforcements. Tears coursed down his face. As the staff started to file out he was handed a telegram from Tokyo. Tojo was displeased; there were victories everywhere except in the Philippines. A look of agony came over Homma's face and he slumped heavily onto the table. The unconscious commander was carried to the next room.

On Corregidor, Quizon in his wheelchair listened in mounting fury as Roosevelt told a radio audience how thousands of aircraft would soon be on their way to the battlefront— Europe. Quezon pointed to smoke rising from the mainland. "For thirty years I have worked and hoped for my people. Now they burn and die for a flag that could not protect them. *Por Dios y todos los santos!* I cannot stand this constant reference to England, to Europe. Where are the planes this *sinvergüenza* [scoundrel] is boasting of? How American to writhe in anguish at the fate of a distant cousin while a daughter is being raped in the back room!"

He summoned MacArthur and said, "Perhaps my presence on Corregidor is not of value. Why don't I go to Manila and become a prisoner of war?" MacArthur thought such a surrender would be misinterpreted abroad. "I don't care what outsiders think," Quezon snapped, but agreed to think it over.

That night a young Filipino second lieutenant crawled up a rocky beach on Corregidor with a bag of ping-pong balls tied around him as a life preserver. He had swum from Bataan to warn Quezon of the increasing hostility between Filipinos and Americans at the front. "We feel we should have the same rations as the Americans," Antonio Aquino told the President. He was the elder son of Benigno Aquino, the sugar-cane king and speaker of the Philippine Assembly. "We eat only salmon and sardines. One can per day for thirty men, twice a day."

Quezon was enraged. He summoned his cabinet and said he would ask Roosevelt to let him issue a manifesto requesting the United States to grant at once absolute independence to the Philippines. Then he would demobilize the Philippine Army and declare the Philippines neutral. Consequently both America and Japan would have to withdraw their armies.

Vice President Sergio Osmeña tried to point out the consequences of such an action in Washington, but Quezon continued to rage. He was stilled by hacking coughs. To calm him, Osmeña reluctantly approved sending the message to Roosevelt. As usual, it would have to go through MacArthur. He not only let it pass but—rankled by the suspicion that Washington, and Marshall in particular, had let him down—supported it with his own grim assessment of the situation.*

---

*MacArthur's staff was fiercely loyal and even more outspoken in their criticism of those back home. Like their chief, they believed that the man primarily responsible for their abandonment was George Marshall, who had presumably never forgiven MacArthur for not promoting him to general when MacArthur was Chief of Staff. Those close to Marshall insist he was too objective to let personal differences ever sway his military judgment. He knew and loved the Philippines (as a young lieutenant he had put up NO TRESPASSING signs on the three little islands near Corregidor), but he had long been convinced that a massive U. S. commitment in the Pacific would be playing into Hitler's hands.

"There is no denying that we are nearly done," he wrote; Quezon's plan "might offer the best possible solution of what is about to be a disastrous debacle." MacArthur was risking his military career but felt it was worth the gamble. Perhaps Quezon's desperate proposal would shock Washington into action.

It dismayed Marshall, as did the fact that MacArthur "went more than halfway toward supporting Quezon's position." Roosevelt's reaction was unequivocal. "We can't do this at all," he tersely told Marshall and Stimson. Until that moment the Chief of Staff had entertained some doubts about Roosevelt's leadership. The President's firm decision convinced him that he was, after all, "a great man."

Roosevelt had enough insight not to expect Quezon and MacArthur to agree with the policy determined by "Arcadia" that Hitler should be defeated first. He must somehow persuade them that everything possible was being sent to the southwest Pacific. By the middle of March seventy-nine thousand troops would have left for the Pacific front, almost four times the number heading for Europe. Most of the available planes were also bound for the Orient.*

It was vital that Quezon understand that there were two fronts—almost 200,000 tons of American shipping had already been sunk off the North Atlantic coast and Rommel was threatening to push the British back to Alexandria. Roosevelt had to find the right words to get all these facts to Quezon without a hint of threat or accusation.

He succeeded in masterful fashion: while rejecting Quezon's proposal as unacceptable to America, he gave his word that no matter what Quezon did, the United States would never abandon the Philippines.

SO LONG AS THE FLAG OF THE U. S. FLIES ON FILIPINO SOIL . . . IT WILL BE DEFENDED BY OUR OWN MEN TO THE DEATH. WHATEVER HAPPENS TO PRESENT AMERICAN GARRISON WE SHALL NOT RELAX OUR EFFORTS UNTIL THE FORCES WHICH ARE NOW MARSHALLING OUTSIDE THE PHILIPPINES RETURN TO THE PHILIPPINES AND DRIVE OUT THE LAST REMNANT OF THE INVADERS FROM YOUR SOIL.

*It seems evident that Roosevelt wanted to do everything possible for MacArthur. On December 30, 1941, he wrote this memorandum to Secretary of the Navy Knox: "I wish that War Plans would explore every possible means of relieving the Philippines. I realize great risks are involved but the objective is important."

These words overwhelmed Quezon. He swore to himself and God that as long as he lived he would stand by America regardless of the consequences to his people or himself.

. . . THE DUTY AND THE NECESSITY OF RESISTING JAPANESE AGGRESSION TO THE LAST TRANSCENDS IN IMPORTANCE ANY OTHER OBLIGATION NOW FACING US IN THE PHILIPPINES. . . . I PARTICULARLY REQUEST THAT YOU PROCEED RAPIDLY TO THE ORGANIZATION OF YOUR FORCES AND YOUR DEFENSES SO AS TO MAKE YOUR RESISTANCE AS EFFECTIVE AS CIRCUMSTANCES WILL PERMIT AND AS PROLONGED AS HUMANLY POSSIBLE.

This meant that the Philippines had been irrevocably written off, and MacArthur's own value was reduced to a symbol of resistance. He replied that he would fight to destruction on Bataan and then Corregidor, making them names for Americans to remember forever.

I HAVE NOT THE SLIGHTEST INTENTION IN THE WORLD OF SURRENDERING OR CAPITULATING THE FILIPINO ELEMENT OF MY COMMAND. . . . THERE HAS NEVER BEEN THE SLIGHTEST WAVERING AMONG THE TROOPS.

While this was an exaggeration, it was truer than it had been a few weeks earlier. Riddled as they were by dysentery and malaria, their uniforms in tatters, the half-starved men of Bataan were full of fight and confidence. The Japanese had been held, and Filipino recruits who had fled in panic from Lingayen Gulf had become tough and dependable.

2.

On the Malay Peninsula the Japanese rolled relentlessly toward the keystone of the British Empire in Asia, Singapore Island. On January 7 General Wavell, chosen at "Arcadia" to command the entire area, flew from his headquarters in Bandung on Java to Singapore on a brief inspection tour. The previous night fifteen Japanese tanks had burst through the front lines of the 11th Indian Division to cross the strategic Slim River bridge, less than 250 air miles from Singapore itself. There wasn't a single Allied tank in all Malaya to stop them; British experts had decreed that armor was unsuited for jungle warfare.

Wavell drove north to find III Corps disorganized and the

11th Indian Division completely shattered. He ordered a general withdrawal of almost 150 miles to Johore Province, where Major-General Gordon Bennett and his Australians would make the final attempt to stop the invaders.

Wavell returned to Singapore to inspect the defenses on the north side of the great fortress island. He found nothing, not even detailed plans for resistance against land attack. To his consternation, he also learned that almost all of the island's great guns facing the sea could not be turned around to fire at the advancing Japanese.

Churchill was dumfounded by Wavell's report that Singapore, far from being impregnable, was almost naked. He blamed himself for putting his faith in Fortress Singapore and hastily penned this note for his Chiefs of Staff:

I must admit to being staggered by Wavell's telegram of the 16th. . . . It never occurred to me for a moment . . . that the gorge of the fortress of Singapore, with its splendid moat half a mile to a mile wide, was not entirely fortified against an attack from the northward. What is the use of having an island for a fortress if it is not to be made into a citadel? . . . How is it that not one of you pointed this out to me at any time when these matters have been under discussion? More especially this should have been done because . . . I have repeatedly shown that I relied upon this defence of Singapore Island against a formal siege, and never relied upon the Kra Isthmus plan. . . .

Not only must the defence of Singapore Island be maintained by every means, but the whole island must be fought for until every single unit and every single strong point has been separately destroyed.

Finally, the city of Singapore must be converted into a citadel and defended to the death. No surrender can be comtemplated.

From the first the enemy had kept the British off balance in Malaya. Outnumbered more than 2 to 1, the Japanese never stopped to consolidate a gain, to regroup or wait for supplies; they surged down the main roads on thousands of bicycles and in hundreds of abandoned British cars and trucks. Whenever they came to a destroyed bridge, the cyclists waded across the river holding aloft their bikes or crossed on log bridges supported on the shoulders of engineers.*

---

*At first tires blown out by the intense heat slowed the advance, but the Japanese soon learned to ride down the paved highways on the rims. The resulting clatter sounded like tanks and at night the defenders, particularly the Indians who were terrified of any kind of armor, would shout "Tanks!" and break for the rear.

The accelerating Japanese success was unforeseen on both sides. A captured British Engineer officer told Colonel Tsuji he had expected the defenses in northern Malaya to hold out for at least three months. "As the Japanese Army had not beaten the weak Chinese Army after four years' fighting in China we did not consider it a very formidable enemy."

Tsuji himself was often up front giving advice and pushing the troops forward. At one roadblock halfway down the peninsula he impatiently devised a frontal attack on the spot and phoned back to Army headquarters for reinforcements and cannon. The answer was no—make a flank attack. This tactic was successful, but at midnight Tsuji stormed into headquarters and wakened everyone with a shower of insults. "What are you doing sleeping while a battle is going on!" he roared and broke into the bedroom of Lieutenant General Sosaku Suzuki, Yamashita's chief of staff. The gentlemanly Suzuki greeted Tsuji with his usual courtesy. This only infuriated Tsuji more. "What do you mean wearing *nemaki* [nightwear] when I'm reporting from the front line!"

Cowed by such righteous indignation, as other generals before him, Suzuki drowsily changed into his dress uniform and buckled on a sword. "I am the chief operational staff officer responsible for the operations of the entire army," Tsuji raved on. "I submitted my idea based on actual front-line conditions and your rejection of my request means you no longer have confidence in me!" He shouted and swore and repeated the same accusations over and over until dawn. Finally he stamped out, wrote his resignation and handed it to Yamashita.

He was so petulant that he refused to eat and sequestered himself in his bedroom. A week later he emerged. His actions were ignored by Yamashita and Suzuki, and he returned to his duties as if nothing had happened—as arrogant, inexorable and brilliant as ever.

Yamashita himself was under emotional stress. The son of a simple country doctor, he had not chosen the Army as a career. "My father suggested the idea," he said, "because I was big and healthy, and my mother did not seriously object because she believed, bless her soul, that I would never pass the highly competitive entrance examination." He was a heavyset man with bull neck and large head. His face was expressionless and he appeared insensitive, but inside he seethed with resentment. He felt his promotion to lieutenant general had been delayed for years because back in 1929 he had supported General Ugaki's plan to reduce the Army by several divisions, and his suspicions of superiors in both Saigon and Tokyo were beginning to verge on paranoia: General Terauchi was purposely holding back air support, and Tojo planned to have him assassinated once Singapore fell. Yamashita wrote in his diary: "It's a crime that there is no one in high places in Japan who can be relied upon," and "That damn Terauchi lives in luxury in Saigon, sleeps in a comfortable bed, eats good food and plays *shogi.*"

His feelings of persecution reached a climax on January 23 when Terauchi's chief of staff arrived from Saigon with a packet of notes on how to capture the island of Singapore. Yamashita tore up the suggestions and confided to his diary: "If there are two ways of doing something, trust Southern Army to pick the wrong one."

In the meantime his troops methodically kept breaking through the static British lines of defense. It was clear that even Bennett's Australians could not hold them back and a general retreat from Malaya began. By midnight of January 31 almost all British troops had crossed the seventy-foot-wide causeway that connected the peninsula with the island of Singapore. Just after dawn a skirl of bagpipes could be heard, and to the tune of "A Hundred Pipers" the battered remnants of the Argyll Battalion, a mere ninety men, marched briskly onto the bridge. Bringing up the rear was their commander, the last man off Malaya.

Demolition squads laid final charges on the causeway and at eight o'clock there was a dull roar. When the smoke drifted away, onlookers could see water rushing through a wide gap. They figured their fortress was safely cut off from the Japanese; but the water in the gap was scarcely four feet deep at low tide.

Singapore, ten times the size of Manhattan, extended twenty-six miles from east to west, fourteen miles from north to south. Most of its population was crowded in the city in the south. Except for scattered towns and settlements, the rest of the island was covered with rubber plantations and jungle growth. The commander in chief was Lieutenant-General A. E. Percival, a tall, thin man with two protruding, rabbitlike teeth. He was a man of quiet charm and ability, but some felt he lacked the forcefulness to inspire the assorted units under him.

There were two ways to defend the island: hold at the beaches or fight the enemy inland with massed reserves. Even with a coastline of more than seventy miles, Percival decided to make his stand on the beaches. The situation seemed to favor him. His intelligence unit estimated he would have to face 60,000 Japanese troops, and he had 85,000 men. Of course, 15,000 of these were noncombatants and many of the others were untrained and poorly armed, but the enemy would suffer heavy casualties in the attempt to storm across Johore Strait.

In fact, he would only have to do battle with 30,000 Japanese. Their intelligence was as far off as Percival's. Tsuji, who had been given the responsibility of planning the invasion, was told there were merely 30,000 defenders. He sat up all that night drawing a plan that would throw the British off balance. The main attack would be made to the right of the causeway and at night by the 5th and 18th divisions. However, the Konoye Division would make a demonstration attack the previous day on the other side of the causeway to deceive the British. To ensure secrecy, all inhabitants within a dozen miles of the strait were to be evacuated while the two attack divisions moved steathily into position, with orders not to build any cooking fires.

The following morning Yamashita assembled forty division commanders and senior officers in a rubber plantation and with flushed face read out the attack orders. *Kikumasamune* (ceremonial wine) was poured into each man's canteen cap and a traditional toast was drunk: "It is a good place to die; surely we shall conquer."

Yamashita set up headquarters in the Green Palace, built by the Sultan of Johore on a hill overlooking the causeway. It was a striking building of red brick and green tile surmounted by a five-story observation tower. The command post was set up at the top of the tower in a room with large windows, which gave Yamashita a panoramic view of the north coast of Singapore. It was the most vulnerable spot he could have chosen, but he reasoned that the British would never imagine he was foolhardy enough to use it. Moreover, he was certain it ran against British policy to bombard such a fine building.

During the following days, trains and three thousand trucks moved up big guns, ammunition and supplies. Hundreds of folding boats and landing craft were transported under cover of darkness and hidden in the bushes a mile or so from the shoreline.

On the evening of February 7 the demonstration by the Konoye Division began. With considerable commotion twenty motor launches landed four hundred men and two mountain guns on a small island in the strait overlooking Seletar

Naval Base and Changi Fortress. The next morning at first light, artillery began pounding the fortress. As expected, the British rushed reinforcements above the causeway. After dark the 5th and 18th divisions hoisted their boats to their shoulders and carried them more than a mile to the strait. As they neared the shore a concentrated artillery barrage of 440 guns opened up. The first targets were the huge tanks at the naval base to prevent the British from dumping oil into the strait and igniting it. Next, the guns were trained on the pillboxes, trenches and wire entanglements below the causeway where the landings would take place.

At ten-thirty the first wave, almost four thousand men, boarded three hundred collapsible boats, landing craft and pontoons. The bombardment drowned out the sound of the motors as the little armada neared the northwest coast of Singapore. It was defended by twenty-five hundred Australians.

From the glassed-in tower Yamashita and his staff could see little of what was happening. It looked as if all of Singapore Island was engulfed in fire and explosions. Ten minutes later blue flares rocketed up from the island. The 5th Division had landed on schedule.

The first invaders had hit the beach at the end of Lim Chu Kang Road to be racked with heavy fire from Australians of the 24th Machine-Gun Battalion. Other landing craft beached on a nearby mangrove swamp area which was lightly defended. The outnumbered Australians fought hard all night but were unable to hold back the Japanese, and in the early-morning hours scores of tanks landed and strong infantry-tank teams moved inshore. By dawn there were fifteen thousand infantrymen and several artillery units on the island.

From the Green Palace tower Yamashita watched his men stream past rubber trees toward Tengah Airfield. Advance elements were already within ten air miles of the city of Singapore. By the end of the day Yamashita left the tower with his staff to cross Johore Strait in a raft made of three boats.

On Java, General Wavell decided to make a personal inspection of the embattled island. The Japanese controlled the air, but the following day the ABDA commander managed to break through. From the corridors at Percival's headquarters, staff officers could hear angry voices. Wavell was criticizing Percival for allowing the Japanese to establish a bridgehead so easily, and he got so exasperated with Bennett that he told the Australian commander to "get the hell out" and take his "bloody Aussies" with him.

Wavell ordered an immediate counterattack. Its utter failure did not inhibit him from issuing an order of the day that could have come from Churchill himself:

It is certain that our troops on Singapore Island greatly outnumber any Japanese that have crossed the Straits. We must defeat them. Our whole fighting reputation is at stake and the honour of the British Empire. The Americans have held out on the Bataan Peninsula against far greater odds, the Russians are turning back the picked strength of the Germans, the Chinese with almost complete lack of modern equipment have held the Japanese for 4½ years. It will be disgraceful if we yield our boasted fortress of Singapore to inferior enemy forces.

There must be no thought of sparing troops or the civil population and no mercy must be shown to weakness in any shape or form. Commanders and senior officers must lead their troops and if necessary die with them.

There must be no question or thought of surrender. Every unit must fight it out to the end and in close contact with the enemy. ... I look to you and your men to fight to the end to prove that the fighting spirit that won our Empire still exists to enable us to defend it.

This done, he flew back to Java. In the dark he fell off a dock and broke two small bones in his back. From the hospital he signaled Churchill:

BATTLE FOR SINGAPORE IS NOT GOING WELL ... MORALE OF SOME TROOPS IS NOT GOOD, AND NONE IS AS HIGH AS I SHOULD LIKE TO SEE. .... EVERYTHING POSSIBLE IS BEING DONE TO PRODUCE MORE OFFENSIVE SPIRIT AND OPTIMISTIC OUTLOOK, BUT I CANNOT PRETEND THAT THESE EFFORTS HAVE BEEN ENTIRELY SUCCESSFUL UP TO DATE. I HAVE GIVEN THE MOST CATEGORICAL ORDERS THAT THERE IS TO BE NO THOUGHT OF SURRENDER AND THAT ALL TROOPS ARE TO CONTINUE FIGHTING TO THE END.

By sunrise the Japanese had taken almost half the island, including strategic Bukit Timah (Mountain of Tin), the highest point on the island. Advance units were approaching the racetrack at the edge of Singapore City. Nevertheless, Tsuji was dismayed by the increasingly stiff resistance, particularly from effective British artillery fire. The enemy seemed to have an endless supply of shells, while Japanese ammunition was already dangerously low. Moreover, it was now obvious that intelligence had grossly underestimated British strength at thirty thousand troops; there must be at least twice that many.

And so it was with covert desperation that Yamashita sent Percival a demand for surrender. Late that morning a reconnaissance plane dropped a tube marked by red and white streamers on the outskirts of the city. It contained a message signed by Yamashita but composed by Lieutenant Colonel Ichiji Sugita. The words were inspired by the surrender of the forty-seven *ronin*.

In the spirit of chivalry we have the honour of advising your surrender. Your army, founded on the traditional spirit of Great Britain, is defending Singapore, which is completely isolated, and raising the fame of Great Britain by the utmost exertions and heroic feelings. . . . From now on resistance is futile and merely increases the danger to the million civilian inhabitants without good reason, exposing them to infliction of pain by fire and sword. But the development of the general war situation has already sealed the fate of Singapore, and the continuation of futile resistance would only serve to inflict direct harm and injuries to thousands of non-combatants living in the city, throwing them into further miseries and horrors of war. Furthermore we do not feel you will increase the fame of the British Army by further resistance.

Percival did not send Yamashita a reply. He had been told to "fight to the end." As yet there was no panic in Singapore despite bombs and shells. Civilians were standing in line outside the cinema in the Cathay skyscraper to see *The Philadelphia Story,* and the Raffles Hotel was crowded with staff officers with nothing to do but drink and carp. Someone scrawled in chalk on a wall: ENGLAND FOR THE ENGLISH, AUSTRALIA FOR THE AUSTRALIANS, BUT MALAYA FOR ANY SON OF A BITCH WHO WANTS IT.

Stragglers streamed down the main roads toward the city. An intelligence officer, David James, stopped a formation of Indians and asked their commander why they were going in the wrong direction. He said an Australian officer had advised them "to beat it because the Nips were coming over the hill." You're supposed to find the Japanese, not run a foot race with them, said James. "Quite so, but you don't remain where you are not wanted, do you?" answered the commander and led off his men at a jog.

Even several Australian units which had fought well in Malaya pushed aside MP's attempting to block their way to the city. "Chum, to hell with Malaya and Singapore," said one. "Navy let us down, air force let us down. If the 'bungs' [natives] won't fight for their bloody country, why pick on me?"

Sensing complete collapse, Percival formed a tight defense arc in front of the city, but by Friday the thirteenth it was apparent to every one of his commanders that Singapore was doomed. Wavell was asked to approve an immediate surrender, but his stiff answer from Bandung ordered the defenders to "continue to inflict maximum damage on enemy for as long as possible by house-to-house fighting if necessary." Percival replied that the Japanese controlled most of the reservoirs and there was little water left. Wavell replied:

YOUR GALLANT STAND IS SERVING A PURPOSE AND MUST BE CONTINUED TO THE LIMIT OF ENDURANCE.

Ironically, Japanese concern over Singapore was growing on all levels. "I hope it won't turn out to be another Bataan," Admiral Matome Ugaki, Yamamoto's chief of staff, wrote in his diary. On the island itself Captain Asaeda prophesied that if the British held out for another week, "they'll beat us." Each field gun had a hundred rounds at most, and the big guns fewer than that. There was pressure on Yamashita to call off the attack and even to withdraw to the peninsula. He ordered the assault continued.

On the morning of February 15 Percival called a conference of area commanders and told them that there was almost no gasoline or field-gun and Bofors ammunition. In twenty-four hours there wouldn't be a drop of water. He said he would ask the Japanese to cease fire at four o'clock. Before the day was out, he got permission for what he had already planned to do. Wavell told him he was free to surrender once it was evident that he could do no more.

... WHATEVER HAPPENS I THANK YOU AND ALL TROOPS FOR YOUR GALLANT EFFORTS OF LAST FEW DAYS.

From the heights at Bukit Timah, Yamashita watched a Union Jack still fluttering atop Fort Canning in the city of Singapore. It would take a week of hard fighting to take that hill alone, and many more days to break through the final defense lines. The field phone rang. A front-line commander reported that the British were sending out a flag of truce.

Colonel Ichiji Sugita, his neck encased in a plaster cast after a motorcycle crash, drove forward to meet the British parliamentaries. "We will have a truce if the British Army agrees to surrender," he said in Japanese. "Do you wish to surrender?"

The British interpreter, Captain Cyril H. D. Wild, said, "We do." He was tall, blue-eyed, the son of the Bishop of Newcastle. Sugita told him to return with Percival and his staff. They met again at four forty-five and proceeded in two cars toward the Ford factory near the village of Bukit Timah. Next to Percival sat Sugita. He turned painfully to the general and said in halting English, "We fought for more than two months. Now we come to the end. I compliment you on the British stand." Percival politely mumbled a few amenities. His thin face was red, his eyes bloodshot.

The surrender party dismounted in front of the factory. They seemed arrogant to the Japanese, although it was Percival himself who carried the white flag. Inside the big rambling building they were surrounded by clamoring reporters, photographers and newsreel men. Five minutes later, at seven o'clock, Yamashita appeared, and the commotion increased as more than forty men crowded into one small room. The surrender had come so unexpectedly that Yamashita had not glanced at the surrender terms, which Sugita had typed out in English days earlier. "The Japanese Army will consider nothing but surrender," said Yamashita. He knew the British outnumbered him by far and his greatest concern was to prevent Percival from finding this out.

"I fear that we shall not be able to submit our final reply before ten-thirty P.M.," Percival replied. He had no intention of continuing the battle. He merely wanted to work out specific details before signing any surrender.

But Yamashita was sure the Englishman was stalling. Terms had to be settled before the enemy realized that the Japanese were numerically inferior. Street fighting in the city would be disastrous.* "Reply to us only whether our terms are acceptable or not," he said tersely. "Things must be settled swiftly. We are prepared to resume firing." Through a window came the glare of fires in Singapore.

Sugita saw that misunderstanding was threatening the surrender and took over from Yamashita's incompetent interpreter. He did little better. The disjointed argument contin-

---

*After the war Yamashita said, "I felt that if we had to fight in the city we would be beaten." He described his strategy at Singapore as "a bluff, a bluff that worked."

ued, aggravated by Wild's poor command of Japanese and Percival's reluctance to submit on the spot.

Yamashita lost his patience. "Unless you do surrender," he burst out, "we will have to carry out our night attack as scheduled."

"Cannot the Japanese Army remain in its present position?" the stunned Percival asked. "We can resume negotiations again tomorrow at five-thirty A.M."

"*Nani!*" Yamashita pretended indignation to hide his concern. "I want the hostilities to cease tonight and I want to remind you there can be no arguments."

It was not the gentlemanly surrender Percival wanted. "We shall discontinue firing by eight-thirty P.M.," he mumbled. "Had we better remain in our present positions tonight?"

Yamashita told him to do so. Firing would cease at eight-thirty and a thousand men could keep arms to maintain order in the city. Percival's vague manner made Yamashita suspicious. "You have agreed to the terms but you have not yet made yourself clear as to whether you agree to surrender or not." Percival could not speak. It was the worst military disaster in British history, the bitterest moment of his life. He cleared his throat but all he could do was nod.

In exasperation Yamashita told Sugita he wanted the British to give a simple answer. The interpreter, however, got involved in another lengthy discourse with Wild. Yamashita restlessly kept looking at his watch and finally shook a finger at Sugita. "There's no need for all this talk. It is a simple question and I want a simple answer." He turned to Percival and shouted, "We want to hear 'Yes' or 'No' from you! Surrender or fight!"

"Yes, I agree," said Percival faintly. He paused. "I have a request to make. Will the Imperial Army protect the women and children and British civilians?"

"We shall see to it. Please sign this truce agreement."

At seven-fifty Percival signed. Forty minutes later, as agreed, the roar of battle ceased abruptly. Singapore, the City of the Lion, the most famous fortress in the world, was Japanese. In seventy days Yamashita, at the cost of 9,824 battle casualties, had rolled 650 miles down the Malay Peninsula and across Singapore. The British had slightly fewer casualties, but surrendered more than 130,000 troops.

It was the greatest land victory in Japanese history. They had again proved dramatically to all their Asian brothers that the white man could be defeated. In Japan a jubilant government announced it was distributing two bottles of beer and a packet of red beans to every family, as well as three *go* of *sake*. Each child under thirteen got a box of caramel drops, cakes and assorted candies.

The *Asahi Shimbun* headlined its story of the battle: GENERAL SITUATION OF PACIFIC WAR DECIDED. "To seize Singapore Island in as little time as three days could only have been done by our Imperial Army," declared Colonel Hideo Ohira, chief of the Press Division. "Japan is the sun that shines for world peace. Those who bathe in the sun will grow and those who resist it shall have no alternative but ruin. Both the United States and Britain should contemplate the 3,000 years of scorching Japanese history. I solemnly declare that with the fall of Singapore the general situation of war has been determined. The ultimate victory will be ours."

Prime Minister Tojo told the Diet that Burma and the Philippines would be granted independence but that it would be necessary to retain Hong Kong and Malaya as vital bases in defense of Greater East Asia. "The objective in the Greater East Asia war," he said, "is founded on the exalted ideals of the founding of the empire and it will enable all the nations and peoples of Greater East Asia to enjoy life and to establish a new order of coexistence and co-prosperity on the basis of justice with Japan as the nucleus."

3.

Java had been almost isolated for a month. To the west, Sumatra was under attack by paratroopers and men from a recently landed convoy. To the east, another invasion convoy had just anchored off the exotic island of Bali.

At his headquarters in Bandung, high in the mountains of central Java, ABDA Commander Archibald Wavell was certain Java itself would be the next target. He was right. Two powerful invasion forces, each protected by strong cruiser and destroyer units, were already bound for that strategic island. The commander of the Netherlands Naval Forces—a short, rotund, balding vice admiral named C. E. L. Helfrich—was still of the opinion that the Japanese could be defeated at sea. He rejected the assumption of U. S. Admiral Hart, commander of the ABDA Navy, that the defense of the Dutch East Indies was a lost cause. The Dutch fleet had already sunk more Japanese tonnage than the combined American air, surface and underwater forces.

In fact, it was Admiral Helfrich's prodding that inspired the Americans to make their first surface attack since Pearl Harbor. On January 24 a quartet of four-stack destroyers dating from World War I slipped into Makassar Strait, between Borneo and Celebes, and sent three enemy transports to the bottom. It was a daring raid, brilliantly executed, and it forcefully proved Helfrich's point. He now pressed his belief that the place to stop the Japanese was at sea, not on the beaches of Java.

American reluctance to engage in surface combat was as puzzling to the Japanese as it was to Helfrich. Below the Philippines they had met almost no resistance and now held all of Borneo and the Celebes islands, and had secured strong footholds on New Guinea. Once Java was conquered, Southeast Asia's treasures of oil, tin and tungsten would be in their hands.

Wavell's evaluation of the threat to Java, where he was, was markedly different from his assessment of the problems faced by the defenders of Singapore. On February 22 he signaled Churchill:

I AM AFRAID THAT THE DEFENCE OF A.B.D.A. AREA HAS BEEN BROKEN DOWN AND THAT DEFENCE OF JAVA CANNOT NOW LAST LONG. . . . ANYTHING PUT INTO JAVA NOW CAN DO LITTLE TO PROLONG STRUGGLE: IT IS MORE QUESTION OF WHAT YOU WILL CHOOSE TO SAVE. . . . I SEE LITTLE FURTHER USEFULNESS FOR THIS H.Q. . . . LAST ABOUT MYSELF. I AM, AS EVER, ENTIRELY WILLING TO DO MY BEST WHERE YOU THINK BEST TO SEND ME. I HAVE FAILED YOU AND PRESIDENT HERE, WHERE A BETTER MAN MIGHT PERHAPS HAVE SUCCEEDED . . . I HATE THE IDEA OF LEAVING THESE STOUT-HEARTED DUTCHMEN, AND WILL REMAIN HERE AND FIGHT IT OUT WITH THEM AS LONG AS POSSIBLE IF YOU CONSIDER THIS WOULD HELP AT ALL.
GOOD WISHES. I AM AFRAID YOU ARE HAVING VERY DIFFICULT PERIOD, BUT I KNOW YOUR COURAGE WILL SHINE THROUGH IT.

The Allied air defense could no longer offer effective resistance. There were few British planes left after the disaster in Malaya; the Dutch were reduced to a handful of dilapidated aircraft; and of the 111 planes which America had rushed to Java, 23 heavy bombers and a few fighters remained.

Three days later Wavell turned over the final defense of the East Indies to the Dutch governor general and left Java. Helfrich's fleet was the only force that stood between Java and the two approaching Japanese invasion convoys. He no longer hoped to stop them but was determined to kill as many Japanese soldiers at sea as possible.

By dawn—it was February 26—the Western Assault Convoy of fifty-six transports was 250 miles from the western end of Java. It was escorted by one carrier, three light cruisers, two flotillas of destroyers and covered by four heavy cruisers. The Eastern Assault Convoy of forty transports was less than 200 miles from its goal, eastern Java. It was escorted by a light cruiser and seven destroyers. Near at hand were two heavy cruisers, a light cruiser and seven destroyers. Overall commander of these eighteen ships was Rear Admiral Takeo Takagi, able but cautious.

Just before noon the eastern convoy was sighted by two Allied planes. Helfrich, who had taken over command of the ABDA Navy from Hart, radioed Rear Admiral Karel W. F. M. Doorman, a fellow countryman, to leave port at dark with the main force of fifteen ships and attack. A few hours later Helfrich learned about the convoy coming from the west. He ordered a smaller force—the light cruiser *Hobart*, two old cruisers and two equally aged destroyers—to meet this new threat as best it could.

At six-thirty Doorman sailed out of Surabaya. The shadowy column nosed north into the Java Sea through the violet light of early dusk. Though an inspiring sight, it was a patchwork fleet sharing no common doctrine or technique, with each of the four national groups of distinct and separate task force. It reminded a young lieutenant on the American heavy cruiser *Houston* of eleven all-stars playing Notre Dame without a single practice session.

All through the night Doorman's force swept along the coast but found nothing and turned back at daylight. It had no sooner nosed into Surabaya harbor around two-thirty in the afternoon than Doorman received a new order to engage an enemy force some ninety miles to the north.

Since the fleet had no common code of tactical signals, Doorman's first order was relayed by radio, signal flags and flashing light in plain English: FOLLOW ME, THE ENEMY IS 90 MILES AWAY.

There was rising excitement as the fleet turned and headed out to sea again. The three British destroyers, screening abreast, led the way followed by the light cruiser *De Ruyter*. Behind in column came the famed British heavy cruiser *Exeter; Houston,* host of President Roosevelt on four cruises; the Australian light cruiser *Perth;* and bringing up the rear, the Dutch light cruiser *Java.* To the left was a second column

—two Dutch destroyers trailed by four antique American destroyers. But the fleet was blind. Doorman had no search planes to catapult from his cruisers; they had been left ashore the night before.

Admiral Takagi, however, knew Doorman's position. Three float planes had already sighted the ABDA column. He ordered the thirty-eight vessels of the eastern ship convoy to turn away and placed his own ships in battle position. Doorman had an extra light cruiser but Takagi had almost twice as many destroyers and this gave him a numerical advantage —eighteen warships to fifteen.

It was a clear, bright day and the Japanese imagined they could smell the fragrance of nearby Java. Sailors, wearing white fatigues and steel helmets, crowded into shrines and tied *hachimaki* tightly around their foreheads. Officers in trim white dress uniforms and baseball caps strained to see the enemy. Japan had not engaged in a major naval battle since Tsushima.

At four o'clock the cruiser *Jintsu* sighted mastheads seventeen miles to the southeast. Then lookouts on the two big cruisers, *Nachi* and *Haguro*, made out the lofty masts of *De Ruyter*. As it came closer, its towering, odd-shaped superstructure took on the alarming shape of some prehistoric monster.

Aboard *Nachi*, Takagi and his chief of staff, Captain Ko Nagasawa, were not sure they should become involved in a running sea battle. Their primary mission was to protect the transports, but Takagi gave orders to close in. At 28,000 yards Nagasawa asked for permission to fire. Takagi nodded, and at four-fifteen the eight-inch guns of *Nachi* and *Haguro* roared. A minute later the two Allied cruisers opened fire but it was an unequal duel with twelve big guns against Takagi's twenty.

The Japanese were approaching so fast that it soon became obvious they would pass across the head of the Allied column, "crossing the T." By this classic maneuver Takagi would bring his broadsides to bear on Doorman's cruisers, which could only retaliate with their forward guns. But the Dutch admiral perceived the trap and swung his cruisers 20 degrees to the left, away from the Japanese.

Takagi also turned, putting the two fleets almost parallel, heading west, with Doorman hemmed in between the Japanese and Java. Ten minutes later Nagasawa informed Takagi it was time to move in for the attack. "Proceed," said the admiral, who was a submarine expert. At 16,000 yards the

Japanese destroyers loosed their torpedoes. Newly designed, they had the astounding range of 30,000 yards and their oxygen propulsion system left no telltale trail of bubbles.

Doorman had no idea they were coming until he saw columns of water spout high in the air. The new torpedoes had been set wrong and were exploding prematurely in midrun. Their sudden appearance caused mounting panic; they must have come from a wolf pack of submarines.

The spouts also alarmed Nagasawa. He decided they must be enemy mines detonated from nearby Bawean Island. He warned Takagi it would be suicide to proceed farther, and orders to move to within 6,000 yards were canceled. Doorman had been given a respite. It was short-lived. At five o'clock, shells from *Haguro* crashed through an antiaircraft mount on *Exeter* and exploded in the boiler. The big cruiser, speed halved, lurched and turned hard left so *Houston* just behind wouldn't pile into its stern.

De Ruyter saw the melee behind and also turned left just as another school of torpedoes sliced toward the Allies. At five-fifteen the Dutch destroyer *Kortenaer* exploded and broke in two like a jackknife. Doorman signaled ALL SHIPS FOLLOW ME and turned southeast. He lost one more destroyer, *Electra*, but the wounded *Exeter* escaped in the smoke and confusion.

Now Doorman had only *Houston*'s six 8-inch guns to match Takagi's twenty. Behind dark clouds of smoke Doorman formed a new line, but within moments two big shells plowed into *Houston*. This time luck was with the Allies; both shells were duds. Doorman swung his line in an evasive counterclockwise circle, but *Nachi* and *Haguro* drew nearer. So did a destroyer flotilla.

Doorman called for smoke from the four American destroyers. Their commander, T. H. Binford, obliged and then on his own launched a torpedo attack on *Nachi* and *Haguro* from 10,000 yards. The cruisers managed to elude the torpedoes, but the daring of the attack forced Takagi to retire northward. He decided to wait until dark, the time the Japanese traditionally preferred to attack.

Though severely hurt, Doorman had no intention of withdrawing. Instead he began probing blindly for the Japanese transports. At nine o'clock his flagship reached shoal water and swung right to parallel the Java coast. The other cruisers followed, as did two British destroyers, *Encounter* and *Jupiter*. Twenty-five minutes later there was an explosion at the end of the line and *Jupiter* was enveloped in flames. She had most likely hit a drifting Dutch mine.

The other ships plunged uneasily into the dark. Nothing happened until nine-fifty. Then a parachute flare floated down, lighting up the column. The stalker was being stalked by one of Takagi's search planes. In rapid succession half a dozen more ghostly flares straddled the Allied line.

Takagi moved in, and just before eleven o'clock a lookout on *Nachi* sighted the enemy column through the special night glasses fixed on the bridge. Someone on *De Ruyter* finally saw the two Japanese cruisers on the port beam and mistakenly reported they were heading in the opposite direction. The Dutch cruiser fired. So did *Perth, Houston* and *Java*. The sky was bright with bursting star shells.

All at once the firing stopped. In the sudden blackness the Allies were unaware that *Haguro* and *Nachi* were silently closing in from behind. Nagasawa waited until he was within 10,000 yards of the enemy before he turned to Takagi and said it was time to launch torpedoes. The admiral approved and around eleven-twenty *Nachi* unleashed eight torpedoes and *Haguro* four. For several minutes the torpedoes slithered toward the oblivious Allied column, which held its course. Then *De Ruyter* erupted with a terrifying abruptness inexplicable to those aboard. As flames spread across her decks, rockets shot up from the stricken ship. Fire had touched off her pyrotechnic locker.

Four minutes later there was another deafening explosion, this time just behind *Houston*. It was *Java*. Burning furiously, her bow reared high into the air. Hundreds of crewmen dropped off like ants as the ship slid backwards into the dark sea. Then *De Ruyter* too vanished, hissing furiously as water enveloped her flames. With her went Doorman and 366 shipmates. One of his last orders was to leave any survivors "to the mercy of the enemy," and the new senior officer of the fleet, the captain of *Perth,* ordered *Houston* to follow as he speeded away to the southeast.

The Battle of the Java Sea, the greatest surface engagement since the Battle of Jutland in 1916, was over. Even in the daylight Takagi had been able to severely damage the Allied fleet, and in the darkness Doorman had had no chance at all against the specialized training of the Japanese. They had hardly been hit, but Doorman lost three destroyers, two light cruisers and his life.

Ten Allied ships survived the battle, and by first light they had managed to make their way back to either Batavia (soon to be renamed Djakarta) or Surabaya. The four American destroyers received permission to escape to Australia, and at five o'clock slipped out of Surabaya harbor past the moored *Exeter*. In the gloom they dashed safely through the narrow Bali Strait.

That same night *Perth* and *Houston* left Batavia to try to escape through Sunda Strait, which was scarcely fourteen miles wide. They plunged full steam into a Japanese armada: the four heavy cruisers, three light cruisers, about ten destroyers and the aircraft carrier *Ryujo* protecting the fifty-six transports of the Western Assault Convoy, which were dropping anchor at the western tip of Java in Bantam Bay.

Perth fought back valiantly on all quarters, but just before midnight a shell smashed into the ordinary-seamen's mess from the starboard side near the water line. Then a torpedo ripped into the same side near the forward boiler room. As the ship rapidly began to lose life, torpedoes and shells struck home in quick succession and she finally rolled over and sank.

Now it was *Houston*'s turn. She had already been damaged by a torpedo, and the big guns of the cruiser *Mikuma* were finding their target. Fifteen minutes after midnight a salvo ripped into the American cruiser's after engine room, scalding everyone to death. Steam geysered through jagged holes in the deck and the ship slowed. As the bugle sounded Abandon Ship a 5-inch shell exploded on the bridge, killing the captain.

Houston lay dead in the water, her guns sticking out at eccentric angles. Slowly she rolled to one side and paused. The Stars and Stripes waved—defiantly, it seemed—from the mainmast. Finally, at twelve forty-five, the ship shuddered and dived out of sight.

Of *Houston*'s 1,000 men, and *Perth*'s crew of 680, fewer than half were still alive, and many of those would perish in the oily waters. The Japanese had also been hurt, but not by *Houston* or *Perth*. Eight torpedoes aimed by *Mikuma* at *Houston* had missed and continued on toward the transports massed in Bantam Bay. Four were sent to the bottom, including *Ryujomaru*, headquarters ship of General Hitoshi Imamura, commander of the 16th Army. Imamura and hundreds of soldiers leaped into the warm waters. The general and his aide grabbed pieces of wood, for neither wore a life jacket. Ashore the aide found his chief, face black from oil, seated on a pile of bamboo. "Congratulations," he said, "on the successful landing."*

The landings at Bantam Bay and on the north coast brought the final disintegration of Allied command on Java. In Bandung a British admiral told Helfrich, "I have instructions from the Admiralty to withdraw His Majesty's ships from Java when resistance will serve no further useful purpose. This time, in my judgment, has come."

"Do you realize you're still under my orders?" Helfrich retorted.

"I do, of course. But in this vital matter I cannot do other than my duty as I see it."

The American senior officer, Rear Admiral W. A. Glassford, sympathized with his British colleague but assured Helfrich he still remained under his command. "Any order you give me will be obeyed at once."

But there were no meaningful orders to give. Helfrich sighed heavily. "You will order your ships to Australia," he said and thanked the American effusively for his help. As for the British admiral, he could give his ships any orders he wished.

The last British ships—*Exeter* and two destroyer escorts—were already heading northwest in hopes of escaping through Sunda Strait at dark. But Takagi sighted them at nine thirty-five in the morning, and with the help of dive bombers from the *Ryujo,* sank all three.

A little after midnight the last American plane took off from the dying island of Java with thirty-five passengers, and at dawn a flying boat lifted ponderously off a lake near Bandung for Ceylon. In it was Admiral Helfrich. He felt like a raw ensign.

Almost completely unopposed, Japanese land forces converged on Batavia and Bandung from two sides. The Dutch commander of the scattered and disorganized Allied forces knew that guerrilla warfare was impossible because the natives were too hostile to their Dutch masters. On March 8 he ordered everyone to lay down arms. The last message to the outside world came from a dispatcher at Bandung's commer-

---

*Commander Shukichi Toshikawa of the 5th Destroyer Flotilla was sent to apologize to Imamura for torpedoing the four transports and dumping the general into the bay. But Imamura's chief of staff advised Toshikawa to keep quiet; Imamura imagined a *Houston* torpedo had sunk him. "Let her have the credit," the chief of staff told Toshikawa. To this day official records on both sides have been crediting *Houston* with the hit.

cial station. "We are shutting down," he said. "Good-bye till better times. Long live the Queen!"

Like Singapore, Java was gone. Despite the devastating defeat and bitter arguments and recriminations, the Americans, British, Dutch and Australians had achieved momentary unity in a gallant but hopeless battle at sea. Now there was only one remaining pocket of resistance inside the Japanese Empire—Bataan and Corregidor.

11   "To Show Them Mercy Is to Prolong the War"

1.

Bataan was quiet. The defenders set out patrols, and tried to strengthen the line across the peninsula. Food had become an obsession. Front-line troops got a third of a ration a day. The efforts to bring supplies to Corregidor and Bataan through the Japanese sea blockade had failed. There was so little fodder for the remaining cavalry horses and mules that General Wainwright, with tears in his eyes, ordered them all, including his own prize jumper, Joseph Conrad, to be destroyed.

By mid-February the sickness rate rose alarmingly. Bataan was one of the most malaria-infested areas in the world and the supply of quinine was almost gone. Weakened by hunger and dysentery, over five hundred men were hospitalized for malaria in the first week of March and doctors feared an epidemic. There was still talk of the "mile-long" convoy filled with supplies and reinforcements, but Filipinos as well as Americans repeated with relish the verse just written by correspondent Frank Hewlett, a frequent front-line visitor:

> *We're the battlings bastards of Bataan:*
> *No mama, no papa, no Uncle Sam,*
> *No aunts, no uncles, no cousins, no nieces,*
> *No pills, no planes or artillery pieces,*
> *And nobody gives a damn.*

On March 10 Wainwright was summoned to Corregidor, where Sutherland informed him that MacArthur was leaving the next evening by torpedo boat for Mindanao, the southernmost island of the Philippines. A Flying Fortress would take him from there to Australia. Sutherland told Wainwright he would command all troops of Luzon as head of the newly established Luzon force. "If it's agreeable to you, General Jones will get another star and take over your I Corps."

MacArthur came out of a small gray house at the eastern end of Malinta Tunnel and said to Wainwright, "I want you to make it known throughout all elements of your command that I'm leaving over my repeated protests." He had considered disobeying direct orders from Washington so he could lead his troops to the end, but his advisers had persuaded him that he could do more in Australia for his beleaguered troops.

"Of course, I will, Douglas," said Wainwright.

"If I get to Australia, you know I'll come back as soon as I can with as much as I can."

"You'll get through."

"And back." MacArthur gave Wainwright a box of cigars and two large jars of shaving cream. "Good-bye, Jonathan." They shook hands. "If you're still on Bataan when I get back, I'll make you a lieutenant general."

The next evening, March 11, at about eight o'clock, *PT-41*, commanded by a colorful bearded lieutenant, John Bulkeley, pulled away from "The Rock" with General MacArthur, his wife, his four-year-old son, Arthur, General Sutherland and several other officers. MacArthur removed his familiar field marshal's cap, raising it in farewell to the small group on the pier.

For thirty-five hectic hours Bulkeley navigated *PT-41* through the enemy-controlled waters, and a little after dawn on March 13, made a landfall on the north coast of Mindanao near the Del Monte pineapple factory. MacArthur's face was pale, his eyes dark-circled as he stepped off the boat. He told Bulkeley he was recommending him and his crew for the Silver Star. "You've taken me out of the jaws of death and I won't forget it."

Waiting for MacArthur on an airstrip hacked out of long lines of pineapples was a worn-out B-17 flown from Australia. The general was infuriated that a single dilapidated plane had been sent and refused to let anyone get aboard. It wasn't until the evening of March 16 that three new Flying Fortresses touched down. MacArthur and his party took off soon after ten o'clock with each passenger, regardless of rank, allowed thirty-five pounds for luggage.*

The next morning MacArthur landed at Batchelor Field, thirty-five miles south of Darwin. "It was close," he told those anxiously awaiting him on the runway. "But that's the way it is in war. You win or lose, live or die—and the difference is just an eyelash."

Then came another eyelash escape. Two fighters appeared out of the blue just as MacArthur's plane took off. The MacArthur luck held and three hours later he landed softly at Alice Springs in the middle of Australia. Reporters clustered around for a statement and he scribbled a few lines on the back of a used envelope:

The President of the United States ordered me to break through the Japanese lines and proceed from Corregidor to Australia for the purpose, as I understand it, of organizing the American offensive against Japan, a primary object of which is the relief of the Philippines.

I came through and I shall return.

Tojo's chagrin at the stalemate in Bataan was aggravated by MacArthur's daring escape. He was no longer certain of Homma's ability to achieve quick success without help. The Prime Minister was reluctant to speak directly to Army Chief of Staff Sugiyama; instead he delegated his secretary, Colonel Susumu Nishiura, to convey his concern about Bataan.

Nishiura took the problem to the Chief of Operations, Colonel Takushiro Hattori, a long-time friend—as boys they had attended the same military school. Study convinced Hattori that what appeared to be the strongest feature in the Bataan defense system was the weakest. This was Mount Samat, a rugged hill rising 1,920 feet just behind the center of the American front lines. Once in Japanese hands, Wainwright's entire line would fold. First should come a concentrated air and artillery bombardment on a two-and-a-half-

---

*Someone overheard an enlisted man remark that the mattress he'd put aboard the MacArthur plane was heavy and started a rumor that it was filled with gold pesos. The following day a few men were willing to swear that they had seen chests of drawers as well as a large refrigerator loaded. This fiction was built into a whispering campaign against MacArthur that still persists. Of a score of people interviewed, one alone maintained that he helped load the refrigerator and mattress full of pesos. The other declared categorically that the MacArthurs took the prescribed thirty-five pounds of luggage.

mile sector in front of Mount Samat, followed by a full-scale infantry drive through the hole.

Hattori had no trouble in persuading General Sugiyama to approve the plan. Now, he thought, it would have to be presented to 14th Army so subtly that they would think it was their own idea and wouldn't lose face. He need not have worried. One glance at the proposal satisfied Homma that this was the solution of the problem that had been harassing him.

Wainwright was established in new headquarters on Corregidor. The War Department had promoted him to lieutenant general and made him commander in chief of all forces in the Philippines. MacArthur had not been consulted, perhaps because Washington knew he would never approve; he wanted to control the islands from Australia. Privately MacArthur did not feel Wainwright was qualified to assume overall command, and he reacted sharply when the new commander cabled Washington that his troops would be "starved into submission," unless he got food by April 15. MacArthur curtly radioed Marshall:

IT IS OF COURSE POSSIBLE THAT WITH MY DEPARTURE THE VIGOR OF APPLICATION OF CONSERVATION MAY HAVE BEEN RELAXED.

The Filipinos on Bataan still regarded MacArthur as the greatest man alive, and his pledge to return was a personal guarantee that their country would be freed. But an increasing number of Americans on Bataan felt he had abandoned them and passed around a parody of "The Battle Hymn of the Republic."

Dugout Doug's not timid, he's just cautious, not afraid,
He's protecting carefully the stars that Franklin made.
Four-star generals are rare as good food on Bataan.
And his troops go starving on.

April 2 was the eve of Good Friday. More significant, it was also the eve of the birthday of Japan's first emperor, the legendary Jinmu. By nightfall 50,000 Japanese, including 15,000 fresh troops from the homeland, were massed for the all-out attack. Behind them 150 guns, howitzers and mortars—many sent from Hong Kong—were ready to lay down the heaviest barrage of the campaign.

328

"Our four groups have been brought into line, and on a front of twenty-five kilometers ten flags are lined up," Homma wrote in his operational diary that evening. "Artillery is plentiful. . . . There is no reason why this attack should not succeed." It should take, he estimated, about a month.

Across the line waited 78,000 starving Americans and Filipinos, but only 27,000 were listed as "combat effective" and three fourths of these were weak from malaria. Dawn was clear. At ten o'clock the firing started. The Filipinos had never experienced anything so devastating. Shells seemed to explode on top of each other. It reminded American veterans of the heaviest German barrages in World War I.

Bombers of the 22nd Air Brigade approached unmolested in perfect formation and dropped tons of explosives on the two and a half miles in front of Mount Samat. Bamboo groves burst into flame. The phenomenon was treated lightly at first; men lit cigarettes on the burning trees. Then brush, dry as tinder, ignited and the heat became intolerable. Americans and Filipinos alike leaped from their foxholes and scrambled back to the second line of defense. Here foliage had been blasted away, leaving the ground almost barren, and the defenders thought they were safe. But a wind sprang up and flames leaped over the cleared area to the lush jungle growth beyond. The men were trapped in a circle of fire; hundreds were cremated. Those who escaped fled to the rear like frenzied animals, spreading panic.

Masked by smoke and flame, the Japanese infantry and tank attack began rolling south almost unimpeded at three o'clock in the afternoon. Within an hour they had ripped open a three-mile gap. General George Parker, commander of II Philippine Corps which defended the eastern half of Bataan, didn't learn this until dusk. He ordered his reserve, six hundred men, to plug up the hole. It was too late. By the end of the next day General Akira Nara swept west of Mount Samat while fresh troops from Shanghai circled around the other side of the craggy hill.

April 5 dawned hot. It was Easter Sunday. While many Americans and Filipinos, entrenched on by-passed Mount Samat, worshiped at sunrise services, shells began screeching overhead. Once the barrage lifted, Japanese troops started up the little mountain, and after lunch planted the Rising Sun on its summit. As Hattori had predicted, its seizure threatened the collapse of the entire defense system across Bataan. In desperation Parker ordered a counterattack, which failed, and by the following noon the entire left half of his corps had disintegrated. There was nothing to keep Nara from sweeping all the way to the end of the peninsula.

The lines still held on the right. East of Mount Samat, Brigadier General Clifford Bluemel, a peppery man who had terrorized his junior officers before Pearl Harbor, tried to counterattack with the 31st Division, but the collapse on his left forced him to pull back. Without orders he began forming a new defense line along the little San Vicente River. He confronted the demoralized stragglers with his Garand rifle. By threat and insult he herded them into new positions.

From the heights of Mount Samat, Colonel Hattori watched the plan he had conceived in Tokyo develop beyond his hopes. Close by, to the west, he could see Nara's troops stream relentlessly past scattered American units. To the east the assault by the Shanghai troops was beginning on Bluemel's hastily improvised line. By nightfall this alone stood between Homma and a complete rout—and it could not hold for long. On his inspection tour at daylight Bluemel confronted a truck column rumbling toward the rear. "The San Vicente line has broken!" shouted a GI from the first vehicle.

This time even Bluemel could not stop the stampede. It was appalling to see American soldiers running again and again from a fight. A mass of Filipinos surged toward him. Brandishing his rifle, he ordered them to form a line on either side of the trail. A shell burst along the road, then another and another. The men pushed past him, scattering in terror to the south. The irate general tried to grab and hold on to several, but they wrenched themselves loose.

2.

Major General Edward P. King, Jr., who had taken over command of the Luzon Forces after Wainwright's promotion, was a modest man, courteous to all ranks, an intellectual with the air of a professor. An artilleryman of wide experience, he was an extremely able soldier, reasonable and realistic, who gave out orders in a quiet, undramatic way. On April 7, a few hours after Bluemel's line broke, he received a phone call from Corregidor. Wainwright said that since the troops on the western half of the peninsula were intact, why shouldn't they turn right and attack toward Manila Bay, cutting Homma's line in two?

It was true that the entire left half of the line was still in position, but King was sure they were in no physical condition to attack. Nevertheless, he reluctantly agreed to give it a try. The recently promoted Major General Albert M. Jones, commander of I Philippine Corps, was not so easily persuaded. The outspoken General Jones thought any attack was senseless and told Wainwright so directly in a three-way telephone conversation with King. With some exasperation Wainwright said he would leave the decision to King and hung up. King ordered Jones to pull back his men in four phases, then sent his chief of staff, Brigadier General Arnold J. Funk, to Corregidor to impress upon Wainwright the fact that surrender might come at any minute.

The gaunt Wainwright knew what the men on Bataan were going through but he was under constant pressure from MacArthur, down in Australia, to hold out. Recently MacArthur had radioed that he was "utterly opposed under any circumstances or conditions to the ultimate capitulation of this command," and that Wainwright should "prepare and execute an attack upon the enemy" once food supplies were exhausted.

Wainwright could not accept Funk's talk of capitulation. "General," he said in his slow drawl, "you will go back and tell General King he will *not* surrender. Tell him he will attack. Those are my orders."

"General, you know, of course, what the situation is over there." Funk's eyes brimmed with tears. "You know what the outcome will be."

"I do."

The next afternoon Colonel Takeo Imai planted a large flag on top of Mount Limay, one of the peaks of the southern volcano. He could see Japanese steadily pouring down the eastern half of Bataan. After dark he returned to the summit. Flashes of light came from the southern tip of Bataan where the enemy was blowing up equipment and munitions. Beyond he could make out the dark polliwog outline of Corregidor. Every so often angry spits of fire erupted from its heights; giant cannon were trying to stop the advance by interdicting the eastern road.

Fleeing before the Japanese columns, Americans and Filipinos poured out of the jungles into the toe of the peninsula. They came by trail, across rugged mountains, by the coast road. There was no order anywhere. Terror alone kept the exhausted men moving.

At the end of Bataan in the town of Mariveles a few boats

were evacuating the last refugees to Corregidor while the remaining vessels were towed out into the bay and sunk. Mobs of disorganized soldiers bitterly watched the privileged few pull away from the docks: *they were going to join those draft dodgers on Corregidor where life was soft—with plenty of drinking water, canned food and romantic nurses; they would sit safely in Malinta Tunnel until the mile-long convoy arrived to relieve them; they would be the heroes while those left to rot on Bataan would be disgraced for throwing in the towel.*

Suddenly, the ground began to shake violently. It was an earthquake, but some of the dazed men thought it was the end of the world.

At his office in Malinta Tunnel the distraught Wainwright phoned King at eleven-thirty in the evening on April 8 and told him to launch an attack northward with Jones's I Corps. King passed on the order to Jones, who characteristically replied, "Any attack is ridiculous, out of the question."

Forget the attack, said King. He knew Jones was right and that any more fighting at all would mean needless casualties. At midnight King summoned his chief of staff and operations officer. There was no debate; the situation was hopeless. Wainwright was hamstrung by MacArthur's explicit order to attack until the end, and King decided to take the burden on his own shoulders. He knew full well he would have to disobey orders and that if he ever got back to the States, he would be court-martialed. But the lives of his 78,000 soldiers were more important than his honor. "I have decided to surrender Bataan," he said. "I have not communicated with General Wainwright because I do not want him to assume any part of the responsibility."

Just before two o'clock in the morning his phone rang. It was Jones. Before either could say a word there was a deafening roar. The door of King's command post blew off and rubble showered down. The sky lit up fantastically. Then came other explosions, and roaring flames lit the sky.

"For crying out loud, Ned," Jones shouted. "What's going on?"

"The ammunition dump is blowing up," King replied calmly above the din.

"Hell, I can feel the ground shaking all the way up here. It must be an earthquake."

"I hate to tell you this, Honus, but I'm surrendering at six

A.M." He told Jones to put white flags all along his line and destroy his artillery and machine guns.

"I don't see what else you can do," said Jones.

It wasn't until four hours later that the night duty officer in Malinta Tunnel informed Wainwright of King's surrender. "Tell him not to do it!" the general shouted. It was too late. "They can't do it! They can't do it!" he muttered. Finally he regained control of himself. He radioed MacArthur:

AT 6 O'CLOCK THIS MORNING GENERAL KING . . . WITHOUT MY KNOWLEDGE OR APPROVAL SENT A FLAG OF TRUCE TO THE JAPANESE COMMANDER. THE MINUTE I HEARD OF IT I DISAPPROVED OF HIS ACTION AND DIRECTED THAT THERE WOULD BE NO SURRENDER. I WAS INFORMED IT WAS TOO LATE TO MAKE ANY CHANGE, THAT THE ACTION HAD ALREADY BEEN TAKEN. . . .

At nine o'clock the stocky King, wearing his last clean uniform, headed up front in a jeep with his two aides, Majors Achille Tisdelle and Wade Cothran. As Japanese guides escorted them to the Experimental Farm Station at Lamao, it occurred to King that Lee had surrendered to Grant at Appomattox on that same day, April 9. He remembered what Lee had said just before the ceremony: "Then there is nothing left to do but to go and see General Grant, and I would rather die a thousand deaths."

A shiny black Cadillac drove up with Colonel Motoo Nakayama. Through an interpreter, Homma's senior operations officer asked King if he was General Wainwright.

"No, I am General King, commander of all forces on Bataan."

Puzzled, Nakayama told him to get Wainwright; the Japanese could not accept surrender without him. King said he could not communicate with Wainwright. "My forces are no longer fighting units. I want to stop further bloodshed."

"Surrender must be unconditional."

"Will our troops be well treated?"

"We are not barbarians. Will you surrender unconditionally?"

King nodded. He said he had left his saber in Manila, and instead placed his pistol on the table.

Americans and Filipino soldiers huddled in disconsolate groups. There were tears of humiliation, but many wept from the relief of knowing their ordeal was over. They waited uneasily for the conquerors.

The first ones Air Corps Captain Mark Wohlfeld saw were packing a mountain gun. They had big smiles on their faces and spoke in gentle tones. These couldn't be such bad chaps after all, he thought with relief. Wohlfeld was from a dive-bomber group but had been fighting as an infantryman since January. Next came the Japanese infantry. Grim-faced, they immediately began stripping the prisoners of blankets, watches, jewelry, razor blades, mess equipment, food and even toothbrushes. One also found twenty rounds of .45-caliber pistol ammunition on Wohlfeld and, with shouts, began beating him on the head with his rifle barrel. Someone behind Wohlfeld muttered, "For Christ's sake, don't fall down!" Then the guard glimpsed a gold ring on Lieutenant Colonel Jack Sewell's finger and yanked at it. "It's my wedding ring," Sewell protested and withdrew his hand. The Japanese snapped the bayonet off his rifle and was going for the colonel when Wohlfeld came between. He tried to spit on the ring to loosen it but his throat was too dry. So was the colonel's. Wohlfeld smeared blood from his head on the finger. The ring came off.

Another Japanese enlisted man stole a ring just as his commanding officer passed by. The officer noticed that the ring bore the University of Notre Dame insignia. He hit the looter in the face and returned the ring to its owner. "When did you graduate?"

"1935."

A faraway look came over the Japanese officer's face when he said, "I graduated from Southern California in '35."

Wainwright's intolerable burden was somewhat lightened by a message from Roosevelt:

AM KEENLY AWARE OF THE TREMENDOUS DIFFICULTIES UNDER WHICH YOU ARE WAGING YOUR GREAT BATTLE. THE PHYSICAL EXHAUSTION OF YOUR TROOPS OBVIOUSLY PRECLUDES THE POSSIBILITY OF A MAJOR COUNTERATTACK UNLESS OUR EFFORTS TO RUSH FOOD TO YOU SHOULD QUICKLY PROVE SUCCESSFUL. BECAUSE OF THE STATE [over] WHICH YOUR FORCES HAVE NO CONTROL I AM MODIFYING MY ORDERS TO YOU. . . . MY PURPOSE IS TO LEAVE TO YOUR BEST JUDGMENT ANY DECISIONS AFFECTING THE FUTURE OF THE BATAAN GARRISON. . . . I FEEL IT PROPER AND NECESSARY THAT YOU SHOULD BE ASSURED OF COMPLETE FREEDOM OF ACTION AND OF MY FULL

CONFIDENCE IN THE WISDOM OF WHATEVER DECISION YOU
MAY BE FORCED TO MAKE.

And in Australia, MacArthur was reading a prepared
statement to reporters: "The Bataan Force went out as it
would have wished, fighting to the end its flickering, forlorn
hope. No army has done so much with so little, and nothing
became it more than its last hour of trial and agony. To the
weeping mothers of its dead, I can only say that the sacrifice
and halo of Jesus of Nazareth has descended upon their sons,
and that God will take them unto Himself."

3.

Estimating that he would capture twenty-five thousand
prisoners, Homma had turned over the logistics planning to
his transportation officer, Major General Yoshikata Kawane.
Kawane had divided the operation into two phases, and ten
days before the final attack, presented the plan to Homma
for approval. Colonel Toshimitsu Takatsu would be responsible for the first phase—bringing all the prisoners to Balanga,
halfway up the peninsula. The distance for those who were at
Mariveles, at the southern tip, would be nineteen miles—an
easy day's march to any Japanese soldier—so there would be
no need for transportation; nor would there be any need to
issue food that day, since the prisoners could use their own
rations. Kawane would personally supervise the second
phase: the trip from Balaga to the prison camp. No more
than two hundred trucks could be spared for the operation,
but these would surely be sufficient to shuttle the prisoners
the thirty-three miles from Balanga to the rail center of San
Fernando. Freight trains would take the men north for thirty
miles to Capas, a village just above Clark Field. From there
they would be marched eight miles to their new home, Camp
O'Donnell.

Kawane explained to Homma that the prisoners would eat
the same rations as Japanese troops, and field hospitals were
being established at Balanga and San Fernando; there would
also be medical units, aid stations and "resting places" set up
every few miles along the route.

Homma approved the plan. Tragically, it was based on
fallacies. Wainwright's men were already starving and weak
with malaria. And there would be seventy-six thousand prisoners, not twenty-five thousand.

335

At Mariveles, groups of three hundred were started up the road. Some had no guards; others had as many as four. The ditches along the zigzag route leading north were littered with abandoned equipment: burned trucks, self-propelled mounts and rifles. The prisoners trudged by King's former headquarters, where a side road led to Hospital No. 2. There a rumor had just spread through the sprawling open-air wards that the Japanese were freeing all Filipinos. The chief of surgery went from ward to ward trying to convince the wounded Filipinos it was a hoax. But Japanese hospital guards, apparently eager to rid themselves of responsibility, encouraged the patients to join the line of prisoners. Infected by mass hysteria, five thousand of them scrambled along the dusty trail; amputees, using tree limbs for crutches, hobbled off, their dressings unraveling. Within a mile the hysteria dissipated but by then the ditches were lined with dead and dying.

The marchers from Mariveles continued straight up the coast of Bataan. On the left was towering Mount Bataan, its peaks shrouded by clouds as usual. On the right were the blue-green waters of Manila Bay. Ordinarily it was a scene of lush tropical beauty—banana trees, nipa palms with long leaves, coconut trees gracefully bent. Today there was no beauty. The foliage was covered with a heavy coat of chalk from months of heavy American traffic, and the road itself was hardly visible through the choking dust clouds churned up by the Japanese howitzers, tanks, ammunition and supply vehicles and trailers loaded with strange-looking boats. They were streaming south in preparation for the assault on Corregidor. Infantrymen in trucks jeered at the marchers, and a few knocked off their hats and helmets with long bamboo poles. Occasionally a Japanese would stop the sport, apologize to the captives. Once a Japanese officer rushed up to an American tank commander and embraced him. They had been classmates at UCLA.

There was no consistency to the actions of the Japanese. One truckload of troops would toss down canteens to the prisoners, while the next swung "liberated" golf clubs at their heads. One thing, however, was becoming clear to the marchers: the situation grew worse as they moved up the peninsula.

The brutalities of that first day were spontaneous but they would not remain so. Colonel Tsuji had arrived in Manila several days earlier from Singapore, where five thousand Chinese had been murdered largely at his instigation for "supporting" British colonialism. He had already—unknown to Homma—convinced several admiring officers on the general's staff that this was a racial war and that all prisoners in the Philippines should be executed: Americans because they were white colonialists and Filipinos because they had betrayed their fellow Asians.

A division staff officer phoned Colonel Imai, conqueror of Mount Limay, and told him, "Kill all prisoners and those offering to surrender."

"How can I possibly obey such an order?" asked Imai. He demanded a copy in writing.

The staff officer informed him that it was an order "from Imperial Headquarters" and had to be obeyed.* Imai said he would not comply unless he received a written order, and hung up. He refused to carry out the decree and, incensed at this violation of the samurai code, ordered his staff to set all the prisoners free with directions on the best way to escape from Bataan.

His staff stared at him. Imai yelled at them to execute his command and not stand around "like so many wooden-headed dolls." More than a thousand prisoners were released. As Imai watched them go into the jungle he argued with himself that no Japanese general would have issued such an inhuman order. But it if was true, he would have to pretend that the prisoners had escaped on their own.

A similar order to kill prisoners was relayed verbally to Major General Torao Ikuta, commander of a recently arrived garrison unit, by a staff officer of a neighboring division. Like Imai, Ikuta and his chief of staff, Lieutenant Colonel Nobuhiko Jimbo, doubted that the order came from Imperial Headquarters. The staff officer said that his own division was already executing prisoners and advised Ikuta to do the same. The general refused to act without a written order.

Even in repose the marchers from Mariveles suffered all through the sultry night. They were so jammed together in enclosures that it was difficult to turn over. Captain Mark Wohlfeld finally got to sleep despite the drone of mosquitoes in his ears. He was wakened by spasmodic kicks from the soldier behind him and muttered to him to lie still. The usual stench grew worse and Wohlfeld opened his eyes inquisitive-

---

*Homma remained ignorant of this order to his death. His chief of staff learned about it only after the war.

ly. His face was lying on filthy rags. He jumped up, and in the bright tropical moonlight examined the rags. They were the trousers of the man behind him and were dripping with feces and blood. "That rotten son of a bitch!" Wohlfeld shouted. He crammed the trousers in the soldier's face. "Get up!" When the man didn't move, Wohlfeld dragged him to a narrow aisle. He was dead.

Suddenly Wohlfeld felt himself flung head over heels by Japanese guards. This was repeated several times, and whenever he fell among the prisoners they would curse and throw him back to the Japanese. Finally Wohlfeld landed on his feet, and waving his arms in abject surrender, pointed to the dead American. He pantomimed for permission to carry him back to the "sick-rows." He didn't have the strength to pick up the emaciated corpse. When neither the guards nor his fellow prisoners offered to help, he grasped the dead soldier under the arms and hauled him off.

He was allowed to rinse himself in a creek. He crawled back to his place and told his neighbors exactly what had happened and how terrible he felt about having abused a fellow American soldier who had shit himself to death. He didn't know how he would be able to live with himself and said he would remember the incident ever after with remorse. He warned them to be quiet lest they get another visit from the Japanese MP's.

4.

According to General Kawane's calculations, it would take the prisoners a single day to march to Balanga, but some of them were on the road for three days. With each mile the guards became more confused and irritated, and consequently more brutal. The sun was blistering and there was little shade for the marchers on the long stretches between towns. Thick dust from the road clung to their sweating bodies, stung their eyes and turned their damp beards to a dirty white. Near Balanga the jungle still smoldered from the cataclysmic Good Friday bombardment. The rolling hills, stripped of trees and foliage, were a bleak desert of blackened stumps. As the long lines of prisoners filed into the outskirts of town they instinctively broke for the cool-looking waters of the Talisay River. Perhaps half made it; the rest were callously driven back to the road.

By daylight of April 11, Balanga was swollen with milling

captives and shouting guards, constantly fed by two streams of humanity, one from Mariveles, one—Jones's men—from the west. It was already obvious that the estimated total would be drastically exceeded. An attempt was made to feed the prisoners their first meal but the unmanageable numbers led to aggravating inequities. Some were given rice, salt and water; many got nothing.

From Balanga on, Kawane had planned to transport all the prisoners in trucks to San Fernando, but it was evident that more than half would have to continue marching; for the first time in history, numbers of American generals were walking toward a prison camp.

General Jones led his column past a burned-out village, its charred ruins still giving off a faint, acrid odor. To the left was the torn battlefield of the Abucay line, and beyond towered Mount Natib. It was past midnight by the time the Jones party reached Orani, eight miles above Balanga. They were shoved into a rice paddy enclosed by barbed wire. The foul odor was overpowering; feces crawling with maggots covered the area. It was, thought Jones, another Andersonville.

With dark came another nightmare. The air was oppressive; vicious mosquitoes swarmed in. It took an hour to get permission to visit the latrine pits, which were open morasses of excrement. Anyone who slipped in had to be pulled out by a comrade willing to take the risk, and those who lost consciousness after falling in were doomed to drown in the sea of feces. In the morning Mark Wohlfeld noticed several bodies floating in one pit. He gestured to a guard that he was willing to drag out the bodies, and several other Americans offered to help. The guard shouted for two companions, who seized Wohlfeld as if to toss him in the latrine. Instead they flung him to the ground. They kicked him and beat him with truncheons. Wohlfeld struggled to his feet as quickly as possible, and covered with filth from rolling near the latrine, staggered back to his place.

In an adjoining field a Japanese officer shouted a command; his men clapped hands three times—to simulate the flapping of a rooster's wings at dawn—and prayed out loud to the Sun Goddess. The prisoners were fed *lugao*, a rice mush that tasted like paste. No one left a particle. It was sixteen miles to the next station, Lubao, but it seemed twice that under the tropical sun. Again good treatment was a matter of luck. One set of guards would permit their charges to rest at proper intervals under shade trees and drink from the numerous roadside artesian wells. The next set would kick over cans of water placed on the highway by civilians, and "rest" their groups by forcing them to squat for an hour in the blazing sun.

Corpses, swollen to monstrous size by the heat, lined the ditches. Crows tore open the cadavers with their beaks; buzzing hordes of fat greenbottle flies clustered at every open wound. Scores of the bodies were beheaded. After counting twenty-seven, Lieutenant Colonel Allen Stowell told himself, "You've got to cut this out," and began marching with eyes fixed straight ahead.

Lieutenant Tony Aquino, the young Filipino who had swum to Corregidor to see President Quezon, had been walking without rest or water. He had lost more than fifty pounds since he came to Bataan, but his legs were swollen. In front of him an American staggered and crumpled to the road. A guard kept kicking him in the ribs. The American tried painfully to rise and extended a pleading hand to the Japanese. The guard deliberately placed the tip of his bayonet on the prisoner's neck and drove it home. He yanked it free and plunged it again into the American's body as Aquino and the other watched helplessly.

Farther back the pugnacious General Bluemel marched next to Brigadier General Luther Stevens. A Japanese soldier in a passing truck swung viciously at Stevens' head with a bamboo pole. Bluemel grabbed his staggering colleague and the two stumbled toward the ditch. A guard pointed a revolver at Bluemel, motioning him to move off, but he ignored the order. He helped the dazed Stevens to his feet, but his legs gave way and Bluemel had to drag him to the middle of a rice paddy. Another guard thought they were escaping and charged at them with fixed bayonet. He saw Stevens' bloody head just in time; he prodded Bluemel back to the highway. Stevens crawled behind some undergrowth and watched motionless as the column disappeared. But for Bluemel's courage he would probably be dead. His respite didn't last long, however; he was discovered and taken prisoner by another Japanese unit.

At a resting place a few miles to the north, Corporal Roy Castleberry watched two civilians dig a hole and lay a delirious American captain in it. The captain suddenly began a desperate struggle to escape his grave. A guard ordered the Filipinos to hit the American with their shovels. They refused until the Japanese raised his rifle menacingly. Faces twisted in agony, they beat the captain back into the hole and buried him alive. Horrified, Castleberry saw a hand feebly, hopelessly, claw in the air above the grave.

As the prisoners finally left Bataan and turned east toward Lubao, they faced a brutal stretch of completely unshaded road. Thirst had become intolerable for some and they risked their lives to sneak into adjoining fields for the meager moisture in sugar cane. Those unwilling to take the chance scrambled for the chewed cane dropped by their bolder comrades. Most of them were so dehydrated that they could not urinate, and those who did winced in agony as if hot irons had been shoved up their penises. Even so, it brought unspeakable relief.

At Lubao, a sprawling city of thirty thousand, the streets were lined with weeping people. They tried to throw the prisoners boiled eggs, fried chicken wrapped in banana leaves or pieces of *panocha* (hard brown sugar), but the surlier guards kept the crowds back with swinging rifle butts. Every so often an old woman swathed from crown to ankle would pull some staggering prisoner from the line and stand over him with her long skirts.

At the far edge of town the Japanese began herding the vanguard of marchers into a large corrugated-tin building, a rice mill, until several thousand men were packed inside. There was a single water spigot. The remaining prisoners were grouped outside the mill. They too had only one faucet. At the rice mill brutality was routine. Prisoners were slashed with sabers for minor insubordinations and beaten to death for no apparent reason.

The final lap to San Fernando, the rail center, was the second shortest, only nine miles, but the cruelest. The asphalt road, churned by tanks and trucks, was molten from the sun's rays, and to barefoot marchers whose soles were already raw it was like walking over hot coals. The last mile seemed endless to the dehydrated, starving men. At the outskirts of town they passed between parked lines of trucks, which formed a gantlet, and soldiers in the trucks swung their rifle butts at the Filipinos and Americans floundering through. In the town itself hordes of civilians from all over Luzon were looking for loved ones. The crowd moaned and wept as the skeleton army dragged by.

Here at last part of Kawane's plan was carried out with some measure of efficiency: the prisoners got rice balls, water and medical treatment. They were imprisoned in makeshift places—a pottery shed, the Blue Moon dance hall,

341

empty lots, old factories, school buildings and yards, and the large circular cockfight arena near the railroad station.

Lieutenant Aquino's group was locked up in a decrepit vinegar factory. He dropped exhausted on a straw mat. Fourteen hours later he was wakened and escorted to a Japanese barracks where he found his father with a Japanese colonel. Father and son embraced.

"Mr. Aquino is a good friend of Japan," said the colonel, a *kempei* commander, in a British accent, and told young Aquino he could go home. But the lieutenant could not desert his men. He requested more food and medicine for all the prisoners.

"Your father was right," the colonel remarked. "He said you would refuse. Please accept my apologies for the way you all have been treated."

Once alone with his son, Benigno Aquino revealed that President Quezon had ordered Laurel and himself to pretend to collaborate with the Japanese: the first step would be to press for the early release of all Filipinos from prison camp.

"Hurry, Papa, we are dying like flies."

The men were herded into boxcars, similar to the French 40 and 8 of World War I. Over one hundred were jammed into each small car. Those with dysentery were unable to control themselves; others vomited on their comrades. The stench became almost unbearable as the trains slowly headed north on the three-hour trip to Capas. Some of the men died in the crush but were held erect by the pressing mob. There was momentary relief at the few stops; each time friendly guards opened the locked doors. The fresh air was like elixir. Filipinos were always on hand to pass out bottles of water, tomatoes, bananas, rice, eggs, coffee, sugar cane. Americans with a low opinion of Filipinos began to appreciate their courage and humanity.

At Capas the trains were unloaded. There was still an eight-mile march over a shadeless, dusty road to Camp O'Donnell, but anything was better than the cramped boxcars. At last the prisoners came to a maze of tumbledown buildings spread out on a vast plain. Guards herded them through a gate flanked by towers spiked with machine guns and up a hill to a building flying the Japanese flag. They sat in the sun for an hour before an officer, the commandant of the camp, strode out the door. He faced the prisoners and announced in a belligerent voice, through an interpreter, that the United States was his greatest enemy and that the Japanese were going to whip the Americans if it took a hundred years.

"Captain, he say you are not prisoners of war," the interpreter told Captain Ed Dyess's group. "You will be treated like captives. He say you do not act like soldiers. You got no discipline. You do not stand to attention while he talk. Captain, he say you will have trouble from him."

Two days after the first group plodded into Camp O'Donnell, the Manila Sunday *Tribune* published pictures of the march, along with a Japanese-inspired story:

The task of making observations upon the tragic aspect of marching war prisoners from the Bataan front, where they surrendered on April 9, to San Fernando, Pampanga, previous to their entrainment to their permanent concentration camp is a sad one; hence, our effort to avoid details about the whole episode.

So the public would not get the wrong impression from such an enigmatic remark, however, we make it plain that the Imperial Japanese Forces, whose business is clearly to prosecute the present war to its successful termination, are going well out of their way to feed and help 50,000 men who once were their enemies beyond most reasonable men's expectations.

If, in spite of the humane treatment the Japanese are giving these prisoners, the latter are too weak to reach their destinations, we have only the high command of the American forces to blame for surrendering when many of their men had already been terribly weakened by lack of food and by diseases.

Homma was so absorbed with mounting the assault on Corregidor that it was two months before he learned that more Fil-Americans had died on the march than on the battlefields of Bataan. Only 54,000 men reached Camp O'Donnell, but many escaped and no one will ever know the exact death toll. Between 7,000 and 10,000 died on the march from malaria, starvation, beatings or execution. Of these, approximately 2,330 were Americans.

Most of the survivors were certain that the march was a cruel plan of the Japanese high command. But the cruelty was not systematic. The prisoners lucky enough to ride in trucks from Balanga to San Fernando suffered little, and a number of those who marched were adequately fed and encountered not a single brutality. Yet comrades a mile behind were starved, beaten and murdered.

Brutality to the Japanese soldier was a way of life. He took the slaps and beatings of his officers as a normal kind of reprimand, and in turn slapped and beat those under him. When prisoners failed to understand his orders or were too weak to follow them, he often, out of impulse or frustration at their apparent disobedience, resorted to violence and even murder. To the Japanese soldier, moreover, there was no such thing as surrender. He fought to the death. If taken prisoner while wounded or unconscious, he was forever disgraced. He was dead to his own family and his name was removed from the village or ward register. His soldier's manual read: "Bear in mind the fact that to be captured means not only disgracing the Army but your parents and family will never be able to hold up their heads again. Always save the last round for yourself."

Such training and background were responsible for much of the brutality but additional murders resulted directly from the unauthorized, oral order emanating from Colonel Tsuji. General Ikuta and Colonel Imai undoubtedly were not alone in refusing to follow this order; but others had obeyed it in full or in part, since they had been conditioned from childhood to carry out a command swiftly, without question. The average Japanese found it easier to follow than take the initiative and, in the Army particularly, was a slave to conformity in every aspect of life—he accepted without question, for example, that at inspections his penis had to be on the left side.

Nor was Colonel Tsuji the only one calling for vengeance against the whites and their dark-skinned collaborators. On April 24 the *Japan Times & Advertiser* printed an article which publicly echoed Tsuji's demands that no mercy be shown to prisoners of war.

... They [the Allies] surrender after sacrificing all the lives they can, except their own, for a cause which they know well is futile; they surrender merely to save their own skins ...

They have shown themselves to be utterly selfish throughout all the campaigns, and they cannot be treated as ordinary prisoners of war. They have broken the commandments of God, and their defeat is their punishment.

To show them mercy is to prolong the war. Their motto has been, "Absolute unscrupulousness." They have not cared what means they employed in their operations. An eye for an eye, a tooth for a tooth. The Japanese Forces are crusaders in a holy war. Hesitation is uncalled for, and the wrongdoers must be wiped out.

The atrocities unleashed by such fanaticism inevitably became a focal point of hate and revenge to the Allies.

1.

The succession of brilliant and unexpectedly easy victories in the Pacific had brought dissension rather than unity to the Japanese Supreme Command. The original war plan called for the seizure of raw materials in Southeast Asia; the conquered territory would be fortified into a strategic web of bases for long-range naval operations. The Army still felt the only sensible course was to make the web so strong that America would be forced eventually to make some sort of peace. But the Navy had experienced such exhilarating triumphs that it was no longer willing to accept such a limited, defensive role. Why not operations against Australia, Hawaii and India? These would generate great naval battles, and as in the Battle of the Java Sea, the enemy would be destroyed. So far less than 25,000 tons of shipping had been lost in conquering all of Southeast Asia, and the biggest warship sunk had been a destroyer.

The Navy began pressing upon the Army a series of plans reaching far beyond the original goals. One was to destroy the British fleet in the Indian Ocean and join up with the Germans. There was a more ambitious plan, aimed at America—cut the supply line between the United States and Australia. If the American fleet dared sortie to break this blockade, the result would be the long-dreamed-of Decisive Battle for the supremacy of the Pacific.

The Navy envisaged invasion of Australia itself with five Army divisions. This daring operation was drawn up by Captain Sadatoshi Tomioka of the Navy General Staff. At a joint operational meeting his opposite number in the Army, Colonel Takushiro Hattori, ridiculed the idea. Australia was twice the area of occupied China and its conquest would require not only the main body of the Combined Fleet but a dozen infantry divisions as well. The shipping for the Army alone would run to 1,500,000 tons. Tomioka suggested that they use the Kwantung Army in Manchuria, which was on garrison duty along the Soviet border. Hattori was against using so many troops on what would essentially be a diversionary effort; every man in uniform would be needed in the protracted struggle with the West. Seeing that Tomioka remained unshaken, Hattori picked up a cup. "The tea in this cup represents our total strength," he said and spilled it on the floor. "You see it goes just so far. If your plan is approved I will resign."

On March 7 a liaison conference brought their differences into the open. Echoing Hattori, General Moritake Tanabe argued that the Army's main objective was to build "a political and military structure capable of withstanding a long war." Neutralization forays in certain areas were practical, but only as long as they were on a modest scale. From now on the enemy should be forced into fighting far from his own bases on Japanese terms. Before Pearl Harbor they had all agreed on this strategic concept. Why improvise now? It would lead to catastrophe.

The Navy insisted that it was vital to keep the enemy on the defensive—anything else would invite disaster. Admiral Takasumi Oka wanted to destroy enemy sea power and wipe out any key bases that might be used for a counterattack "by the positive employment of forces in the Australian and Hawaiian areas."

The unresolved debate carried over into heated meetings at the Army and Navy Club which at times came close to physical violence. It was two weeks before a compromise could be reached: the Australian invasion was scrapped but the Army agreed to less enterprising projects such as an amphibious assault on Port Moresby, a town four hundred miles north of Australia, on the east coast of New Guinea, the second largest island in the world.

Hattori and Tomioka met informally and came to further accord. The latter agreed to abandon the plan to meet Hitler in the Indian Ocean, while Hattori approved the conquest of three island groups off the northeast coast of Australia— Samoa, Fiji and New Caledonia. This would cut the supply line between Australia and America at minimum cost.

On March 13 Tojo and the two Chiefs of Staff went to the Palace to submit a joint report to the Emperor on the new war policy: "It will not only be most difficult to defeat the United States and Britain in a short period, but the war cannot be brought to an end through surrender. It is essential to further expand the political and military advantages achieved through glorious victories since the opening of hostilities, by utilizing the present war situation to establish a political and strategic structure capable of withstanding a protracted war. We must take every possible step, within the limits of our national capabilities, to force the United States and Britain to remain on the defensive. Any definite measure of vital significance to be effected in this connection will be given thorough study and will be presented to His Majesty for approval each time."

The hard-won compromise was accepted by everyone but the most influential man in the Navy. Spurred by his gambler's instinct, Admiral Yamamoto was set upon launching another audacious attack on American territory—an invasion of Midway, an atoll comprising two small islands, less than thirteen hundred miles northwest of Pearl Harbor. This alone would protect the homeland from a direct surprise attack by the Pacific Fleet.

Yamamoto's plan found few adherents in the Navy General Staff, and he sent his favorite chess partner, Commander Yasuji Watanabe, to Tokyo to win support. But Captain Tomioka and Commander Kazunari Miyo, the aviation operations officer, were not impressed by his advocacy. How could Midway be held, let alone supplied, assuming it was taken? Moreover, it offered few rewards. On the other hand, seizure of the three island groups near Australia would surely lure the U. S. fleet to the Decisive Battle in an area where Japan could get support from the neighboring Solomon Islands.

The argument was settled not by reason but by threat. Watanabe took Yamamoto's case to their superior, Admiral Shigeru Fukudome. Miyo persisted in his arguments, and Watanabe went off to telephone Yamamoto. He brought back an ultimatum: it was either the Midway operation or Yamamoto's resignation. Navy Chief of Staff Nagano ruled: "In that case, we might as well let him try his plan."

This was April 5. Eleven days later a directive was issued to invade Midway and the Aleutians. Tomioka and Miyo were "mortified," but had no choice but to end all resistance. No specific date, however, was set by Tokyo, despite Yamamoto's insistent requests. The Navy General Staff saw no need for haste. It took an American named Doolittle to spur them into action.

2.

Shortly after Pearl Harbor, President Roosevelt had remarked that he would like to bomb the enemy mainland as soon as possible to avenge in small part the "sneak" attack. The distance involved made it seem like wishful thinking until it occurred to the operations officer on Admiral King's staff that long-range Army bombers might be launched from a carrier's deck. The idea intrigued King and the Army Air Corps, and by the beginning of March, twenty-four crews were at Eglin Field, Florida, learning how to lift off a modified twin-engine B-25 bomber from a 500-foot runway. Their commander was a remarkable combination—an aeronautical scientist and a daring pilot with several speed records to his credit. Lieutenant Colonel James H. Doolittle was the first man to fly across the United States in twelve hours; the first to do the impossible, the outside loop; and the first to land a plane blind.

On April 1 the sixteen crews finally selected for the mission boarded the carrier *Hornet* at Alameda Air Station in California while the other eight crews looked on with envy. The next day after breakfast Doolittle collected the men in an empty mess hall and began, "For the benefit of those who have not already been told or have been guessing, we are going to bomb Japan." Thirteen planes would drop their four bombs apiece on Tokyo; three single planes would hit Nagoya, Osaka and Kobe. "The Navy will get us in as close as possible and launch us off the deck." They would not return to the carrier but would overfly Japan and make for small fields in China. Did anyone want to back out? No one did.

Just before noon, accompanied by one heavy and one light cruiser, four destroyers and an oiler, *Hornet*, with the sixteen B-25's lashed to her decks, passed under the Golden Gate Bridge. The departure of the bombers on their secret mission was witnessed by thousands of onlookers.

On April 8 Admiral William Halsey—"Bull" to reporters, but Bill to his intimates—steamed out of Pearl Harbor on the carrier *Enterprise* with two heavy cruisers, four destroyers and an oiler. He was to rendezvous with *Hornet* and her escort and accompany them to the launching point.

The Japanese knew nothing of the double sortie until two days later when Combined Fleet radio intelligence men intercepted messages between the two forces and Pearl Harbor. They deduced that if the Americans continued to proceed westward, Tokyo would be bombed. Because of the limited range of a carrier plane, the American ships would have to approach within four hundred miles before reaching the launching point. Since a surveillance net extended seven hundred miles offshore, there would be ample time to attack the enemy before the planes could take off. The assessment was accurate except for one thing—these were no ordinary carrier planes and they were scheduled to take off five hundred miles from the target.

On April 13 the two American units merged into one formidable group, Task Force 16, and steamed directly for Tokyo. The crews' confidence in the secrecy of their mission was shaken three days later when they heard a propaganda broadcast from Radio Tokyo: "Reuters, British news agency, has announced that three American bombers have dropped bombs on Tokyo. This is a most laughable story. They know it is absolutely impossible for enemy bombers to get within five hundred miles of Tokyo. Instead of worrying about such foolish things, the Japanese people are enjoying the fine spring sunshine and the fragrance of cherry blossoms."

The following day the fliers reported to the flight deck for a special ceremony. Captain Marc A. Mitscher handed over to Doolittle five Japanese medals awarded to Americans. The recipients had all asked that they be attached to a bomb and returned to Japan. While the medals were fixed to a bomb, fliers chalked on derisive slogans like "*I don't want to set the world on fire, just Tokyo,*" and "*You'll get a BANG out of this!*"

Doolittle ended the horseplay by announcing that they would take off the next day. Task Force 16 would arrive at the launching point a day ahead of time. This was their last briefing. Doolittle would leave first, timed to reach Tokyo at dusk. "The rest of you will take off two or three hours later and can use my fires as a homing beacon."

There was one last-minute question that no one had put before: what to do in case of a crash-landing in Japan. That was up to each pilot. Doolittle didn't intend to be taken prisoner. "I'm going to bail my crew out and then dive it, full throttle, into any target I can find where the crash will do the most good. I'm forty-six years old and have lived a full life."

The next morning at three o'clock, while they were still more than seven hundred miles from Tokyo, the secrecy of the mission—and therefore its success—was directly threatened. The radar of *Enterprise* detected two enemy ships off the port bow some twelve miles away. Several minutes later a light flickered on the horizon. Task Force 16 changed course and General Quarters was sounded on every ship. For half an hour the men waited uneasily. Then the All Clear sounded and the fleet resumed its westerly course as if nothing had happened.

The weather was foul and the ships pitched and rolled. Just before dawn three search bombers left *Enterprise* to probe two hundred miles ahead. One of the pilots sighted a small patrol boat through the murky gray overcast; he turned back and dropped a bean-bag on the carrier's deck. In it was a scrawled message:

Enemy surface ship—latitude 36-04N, Long. 153-10E, bearing 276° true—42 miles. Believed seen by enemy.

As a precaution Halsey swung all his ships to port. Within an hour, lookouts on *Hornet* herself sighted a small patrol vessel—it was No. 23 *Nitto-maru*—which began sending a message in the clear that three enemy aircraft carriers had been sighted seven hundred miles from Tokyo. Then another patrol boat was sighted little more than six miles away. Halsey ordered them both sunk and flashed a message to *Hornet:*

LAUNCH PLANES X TO COL. DOOLITTLE AND GALLANT COMMAND GOOD LUCK AND GOD BLESS YOU.

On the bridge of *Hornet*, Doolittle pumped Mitscher's hand and scurried down the ladder to his cabin, shouting, "Okay, fellas, this is it! Let's go!" The klaxon screeched. The bullhorn boomed: "Army pilots, man your planes!"

No one realized as keenly as the pilots how seriously this abrupt change jeopardized their chances for success—and survival. Everything had been planned precisely to the last gallon of gas, and now 150 miles had been added to their flight. Moreover, the surprise element was gone and they would have to bomb in daylight. All the same, they were eager to go and one refused an offer of $150 from a relief crewman to take his place.

As Commander John Ford, the noted movie director, and his crew took pictures, a mechanical donkey began pulling the twin-ruddered bombers into position. The first plane, Doolittle's, had 467 feet of runway. Ten extra 5-gallon cans of gasoline were loaded into each plane; the main tanks were topped.

Doolittle gave his engines full throttle and they roared so that some of the pilots feared he'd burn them up. The wheel blocks were yanked away and the plane lunged ahead, the left tire following a white line running down the port side of the deck. The port wing of the B-25 hung over the side of the carrier as the bomber clumsily wobbled forward, flaps down, into the teeth of the gale sweeping down the deck.

The other pilots watched tensely, wondering if the stiff wind would be enough to help lift Doolittle in time. If he didn't make it, they surely wouldn't. The B-25 gained speed. To some pilots Doolittle's acceleration seemed agonizingly slow, but just as the bow of the carrier was lifted high by the heavy sea, he pulled up the bomber with yards of deck to spare. It was 7:20 A.M.

There were spontaneous cheers as the Doolittle plane circled, passed low over *Hornet* and took a direct course for Tokyo. The remaining bombers began rolling heavily down the deck one at a time, each "sweated" into the air by the onlookers. All went well until the last plane slowly taxied toward the starting line. Suddenly one of the deck crew— Seaman Robert W. Wall—lost his footing and was blown like a tumbleweed by the preceding plane's blast into the spinning left propeller. It mangled his left arm but knocked him free.

Feeling the jar, the pilot glanced back to see Wall sprawled on the deck. Rattled, he put his flap control lever back in retract instead of neutral. The plane struggled off the end of the deck and abruptly dropped out of sight under the bow. The deck crews were certain it was going to plunge into the sea; then, to their relief, they saw it skimming just above the waves. Ponderously it lifted, turned and followed the other planes. It was 8:20 A.M.

Naval headquarters in Tokyo were aware that an aerial attack was imminent, but the position given by *Nitto-maru* made them equally certain it would not come for another day. All available planes—90 fighters and 116 bombers— were alerted and Vice Admiral Nobutake Kondo was ordered to leave Yokosuka Naval Base at once and intercept the Americans with six heavy cruisers and ten destroyers.

At 9:45 A.M. a patrol plane reported it had come across a two-engine bomber flying westward some six hundred miles from land. But no one believed the report; the Americans didn't have twin-engine planes on carriers. The bombing attack could not possibly come until the next morning at the earliest, when the enemy carriers would be within three hundred miles of the coast.

By coincidence, just as the last planes were leaving *Hornet* an air-raid drill began in Tokyo. It was a tame affair, without as much as the shriek of a siren, and civilians ignored orders of officious air wardens to seek shelter. Instead they watched fire-fighting brigades show off their equipment. By noon it was all over. Most of the barrage balloons had been hauled down and three fighter planes circled lazily above the city. It was a warm, pleasant Saturday and the streets were again busy with shoppers and pleasure seekers.

A few minutes later Doolittle reached the coast of Japan eighty miles off course to the north. He banked left. In the plane behind, Navigator Carl Wildner began looking for fighter interceptors but all he saw were trainers rolling and looping. As the B-25 skimmed over the countryside he noticed people going about unconcerned. He passed over a military camp low enough to make out a group of officers, their swords flashing in the sunlight.

The most important officer in Japan was in a plane trying to land through the line of oncoming American bombers. That morning Prime Minister Tojo had learned that an enemy task force was somewhere off the coast but had been assured it would be safe to take an inspection trip by air to Mito Aviation School. As his American-made passenger plane approached the landing field, a two-engine craft came up on the right. Tojo's secretary, Colonel Nishiura, thought it was a "queer-looking plane." It came so close that the pilot's face was visible, and it occurred to Nishiura—it's American! It flashed by without firing a shot.

At exactly 12:30 P.M. Doolittle was over his target. Using a twenty-cent "Mark Twain" bombing device, which was more accurate for a low-altitude attack than the overrated Norden bombsight, Fred Braemer released the first bomb. There was no effective opposition from fighters or antiaircraft as plane after plane swept over the city dumping their explosives. One of the pilots, Captain Edward York, discovered that he didn't have enough gas to get sufficiently deep into China and turned northwest for Vladivostok, though it meant probable internment. "I'll bet we're the first B-25 crew of five to bomb Tokyo and cross Japan at noon on a Saturday," joked the co-pilot to ease the tension.

Except for those near the impact areas, the citizens of Tokyo assumed the American attack was just a realistic climax to the air-raid drill. Nor did the truth come from radio station JOAK, which had abruptly gone off the air with the first explosions. Children in schoolyards and people in the crowded streets waved at the passing planes, mistaking their circular red, white and blue markings—similar to those used by the Allies in World War I—for the Rising Sun. Not a plane was shot down.

Planes passed over the Imperial Palace but nothing was dropped. The crews had cut cards to see who would go after the Emperor's residence, but Doolittle had issued explicit orders to avoid the Palace grounds as well as hospitals and schools.

At the Army and Navy Club, Captain Tomioka was having lunch with Colonel Hattori. Their discussion of the Midway invasion, which both continued to oppose, was interrupted by the crump of bombs. "Wonderful!" Tomioka exclaimed, guessing that they came from enemy carrier planes. If the American fleet moved in closer, the Navy could have its Decisive Battle in homeland waters.

This possibility never occurred to the man most eager about Midway. Instead Admiral Yamamoto was so stricken by shame at the attack on the capital that he left the pursuit of the Americans to Matome Ugaki, his chief of staff, retired to his room and refused to come out. Chief Steward Heijiro Omi had never seen him so pale or depressed.

Admiral Ugaki was unable to locate the enemy fleet and that evening wrote in his diary: "We must improve counter-measures against future enemy attacks by checking the types and numbers of planes. At any rate, today the victory belonged to the enemy." He wondered if the American task force had reversed course and run or was preparing another air assault on Tokyo.

Halsey had long since turned back toward Pearl Harbor; there were no more bombers to launch. Captain York's plane arrived safely in Vladivostok, where the crew of five was interned by the Russians. The other fifteen bombers came down in Japanese-occupied China. Three men were killed in crash-landings or bailouts; eight were captured and brought to Tokyo for trial.* The rest, including Doolittle, were alive and heading by various routes for Chiang Kai-shek's lines.

The feat lifted the morale of Americans still shaken by the fall of Bataan. It seemed to be a pledge that America would soon go over to the attack, and Allies on every battlefield and

---

*The captured fliers gave their interrogators such confusing accounts (some said they came from the Aleutians, some from a special carrier no one had ever heard of, some from a mysterious island in the Pacific on no map) that Ugaki issued an order to somehow "solve the riddle of the enemy attack." The prisoners were, according to Ugaki's diary, "forced to tell the truth," and finally revealed most of the facts of the attack, but by that time Halsey was halfway to Pearl Harbor.

in every prison camp found fresh hope. Newspapers in the United States headlined the story with exuberance. DOOLITTLE DID IT, crowed the Los Angeles *Times*. Roosevelt added to the public's delight over the surprise raid by announcing, with his flair for the dramatic, that the bombers had taken off from Shangri-La.

The foray caused no outward panic in Japan, but was a psychological shock to a nation brought up to believe for centuries that somehow the homeland would always be safe from assault. The newspapers belittled it as a "complete failure," yet pictured Doolittle's men as demons who "carried out an inhuman, insatiable, indiscriminate bombing attack on the sly," and demonstrated "their fiendish behavior" by ruthlessly strafing civilians and noncombatants. As testimony of the effective Japanese air defense of Tokyo, a wing and a landing-gear tubing of a B-25 (secretly brought over from China) were exhibited at the Yasukuni Shrine Provisional Festival; a parachute was effectively draped over a ginkgo tree in full bloom.

The raid itself *was* a failure as far as physical damage was concerned, but the fact that it had happened forced the Supreme Command to over-react. Four fighter groups were reassigned to protect Japan from assaults that were not even being planned by the enemy. The China Expeditionary Army was ordered to cease other operations and rout out enemy air bases in the Chekiang area.

More important, it finally brought an end to opposition within the Navy to the Midway campaign. Yamamoto came out of his one-day retirement to renew demands that the invasion be executed promptly. Unless Midway—which had probably been the base of the air attack—was captured shortly, air and sea patrols in front of the homeland would have to be strengthened at the expense of battle area. Those who had been hoping to sabotage the project by a series of delaying actions capitulated, and on April 20 at a joint Army-Navy meeting, the Navy General Staff proposed that the plan to cut the Australian life line by seizing Samoa, Fiji and New Caledonia be postponed so the Midway invasion could proceed as soon as possible. The Army still considered it a risky venture, but with Nagano openly supporting Yamamoto, reluctantly approved the operation. It was no time to create antagonistic feelings between the two services. Besides, the Navy would go ahead with the invasion no matter what the Army said.

General Homma's guns began to churn Corregidor into a no man's land. Though morale was fairly high among the defenders, there was little hope that the island could be held long. A favorite song was "I'm Waiting for Ships That Never Come In," and some of the men sarcastically wondered if the V's for Victory chalked on so many helmets stood for Victim.

On April 29 Japanese artillery fire and bombing reached a crescendo. It was the Emperor's birthday. Two ammunition dumps exploded, solid rock cliffs were disintegrated and uncontrollable grass fires swept the little island, covering it with thick clouds of smoke and dust. The next day, and the next, there was no respite. The bombardment concentrated on the big mortars of Batteries Geary and Way which covered the approach from Bataan. By the morning of May 2 Battery Geary was still intact, but not for long. At noon an explosion rocked Corregidor like an earthquake. Battery Geary erupted. The barrels of its eight 10-ton mortars were tossed into the air like match sticks, one landing 150 yards away on the pockmarked golf course.

Corregidor now had little except its beach-defense troops to hold off the landings. Of the 4,000 in number at the fall of Bataan, there were little more than 3,000 effectives left because of extensive bombardment casualties. Of these, about 1,300 were well-trained fighters from the 4th Marine Regiment. The rest was a conglomerate force of Filipino fliers and artillerymen and American refugees from Bataan.

Life outside Malinta Tunnel was dangerous, but at least there was fresh air and light. The 10,000 people who lived safely in the rambling underground system suffered from an intolerable tension nicknamed "tunnelitis." The dust made breathing difficult, and the smell of death from the hospital pervaded every lateral. When the blowers were off during bombings, the air became fetid, the heat almost unbearable. Huge black flies, roaches and other insects overran the place. Tempers grew short: arguments sprang up over trifles.

On May 3 General Wainwright was told that the water supply was dangerously low and radioed MacArthur:

SITUATION HERE IS FAST BECOMING DESPERATE.

The following day sixteen shells burst on the island. The terrified beach defenders crouched in their shallow foxholes, filled with an overpowering hatred for the "tunnel rats." But those inside were not comforted by the protection Malinta offered. The almost continuous drumfire of explosions drove many to the point of hysteria. In his little whitewashed office Wainwright wrote Marshall an estimate of the situation:

IN MY OPINION THE ENEMY IS CAPABLE OF MAKING ASSAULT ON CORREGIDOR AT ANY TIME.
SUCCESS OR FAILURE OF SUCH ASSAULT WILL DEPEND ENTIRELY ON THE STEADFASTNESS OF BEACH DEFENSE TROOPS. CONSIDERING THE PRESENT LEVEL OF MORALE, I ESTIMATE THAT WE HAVE SOMETHING LESS THAN AN EVEN CHANCE TO BEAT OFF AN ASSAULT. I HAVE GIVEN YOU, IN ACCORDANCE WITH YOUR REQUEST, A VERY FRANK AND HONEST OPINION ON THE SITUATION AS I SEE IT.

Homma was again behind schedule. Corregidor should have fallen two weeks earlier but the invasion had been delayed by a malaria epidemic in the infested river valleys of southern Bataan which was finally brought under control by quinine tablets flown in from Japan.

On the evening of May 4 Homma stood above the little harbor of Lamao and anxiously watched landing craft carrying two thousand men and several tanks disappear in the dusk toward Corregidor. The odds were chilling; the assault troops faced at least seven times their number on the fortress island. They were to land in two waves on the north beach of Corregidor's polliwog tail and push west toward Malinta Hill, where they would wait for reinforcements the following night. But in the darkness the erratic tides and currents pushed the small invasion fleet a mile off its course, and as the first boats approached shore they met devastating fire from two 75-mm. guns, saved for just such an emergency. Boat after boat was blown out of the water. The barrage became so intense that many of the invaders leaped from their boats too soon and were dragged under water by almost a hundred pounds of equipment. Less than one third of the entire assault force survived. They were led by their commander, Colonel Gempachi Sato, toward the east mouth of Malinta Tunnel.

At midnight a Marine messenger raced into the tunnel. Six hundred Japs had landed! For three hours Wainwright remained in suspense. Then came news that a Marine AA gun pit, one mile from the tunnel, had been seized. The next message, moments later, was a radiogram from Roosevelt. He praised the defenders as "living symbols of our war aims and the guarantee of victory."

Just before dawn, five hundred untrained sailors—the last reserves—left the mouth of the tunnel and crawled up toward the fighting. Together with the Marines of Headquarters and Service Company, they launched an attack that completely surprised the Japanese, who were waiting for plane and tank support, and forced them to fall back on both flanks. But at ten o'clock the Americans could hear the ominous rumble of tanks.

Once Wainwright learned that armor was moving against men with no antitank defenses, a nightmare flashed through his mind—a tank nosing into the tunnel and spraying lead at the wounded and nurses.

"We can't hold out much longer," he told his staff. At ten-fifteen he ordered Brigadier General Lewis C. Beebe to broadcast a previously prepared surrender message. In a choked voice Wainwright said, "Tell the Nips that we'll cease firing at noon."

To limit his own surrender to the four little islands in Manila Bay, he radioed Major General William F. Sharp, commander of all troops in the southern islands, releasing to him the rest of the Philippines.

Guns were spiked, codes burned and radio equipment smashed. Wainwright wrote out his last message to Roosevelt.

WITH BROKEN HEART AND HEAD BOWED IN SADNESS BUT NOT IN SHAME I REPORT TO YOUR EXCELLENCY THAT TODAY I MUST ARRANGE TERMS FOR THE SURRENDER OF THE FORTIFIED ISLANDS OF MANILA BAY. . . . THERE IS A LIMIT OF HUMAN ENDURANCE AND THAT LIMIT HAS LONG SINCE BEEN PASSED. WITHOUT PROSPECT OF RELIEF I FEEL IT IS MY DUTY TO MY COUNTRY AND TO MY GALLANT TROOPS TO END THIS USELESS EFFUSION OF BLOOD AND HUMAN SACRIFICE.
IF YOU AGREE, MR. PRESIDENT, PLEASE SAY TO THE NATION THAT MY TROOPS AND I HAVE ACCOMPLISHED ALL THAT IS HUMANLY POSSIBLE AND THAT WE HAVE UPHELD THE BEST TRADITIONS OF THE UNITED STATES AND ITS ARMY.
MAY GOD BLESS AND PRESERVE YOU AND GUIDE YOU AND THE NATION IN THE EFFORT TO ULTIMATE VICTORY.

WITH PROFOUND REGRET AND WITH CONTINUED PRIDE IN MY GALLANT TROOPS I GO TO MEET THE JAPANESE COMMANDER. GOODBYE, MR. PRESIDENT.

All American guns ceased firing. Wainwright waited for two hours, then drove east in a Chevrolet with five others to Denver Hill. They continued on foot past the dead and dying and were met near the top of the hill by a Japanese group. An arrogant lieutenant said surrender must include all American and Filipino troops in the archipelago.

"I do not choose to discuss surrender terms with you," said Wainwright. "Take me to your senior officer."

Colonel Motoo Nakayama, who had accepted King's surrender, stepped forward. Wainwright told him he would surrender the four islands in Manila Bay. Nakayama replied angrily that he had explicit orders from Homma to bring Wainwright to Bataan for the capitulation ceremony only if he agreed to relinquish all his troops.

As yet General Homma had no idea that Corregidor wanted to give up. A report had come in that thirty-one boats had been sunk the night before, and the reinforcement wave would have to be canceled, since there were just twenty-one landing craft left. He knew he faced disgrace. Suddenly a staff officer burst in with the news that a white flag was fluttering over Corregidor. Homma was so relieved that he radioed Nakayama to disregard former orders and bring Wainwright to Bataan at once.

At four o'clock in the afternoon Wainwright, leaning heavily on his cane, thin body bent, once more stepped on Bataan soil at Cabcaben. Two cars brought the party to a small house, painted blue, surrounded by a luxuriant growth of mangrove. The Americans waited on the open porch; to the south out in Manila Bay they could see Corregidor still erupting with shell bursts—the battle had apparently not ended as far as the Japanese were concerned. The general and his companions were given cold water and lined up for pictures by Japanese newsmen.

Finally, at five o'clock, a Cadillac drew up and the barrel-chested General Homma, looking crisp and vigorous in his olive-drab uniform, stepped out. He welcomed the Americans. "You must be very tired and weary."

Wainwright thanked him and they all sat on the porch around a long table. Wainwright handed over a signed note surrendering Corregidor and Forts Hughes, Drum and Frank, the four islands in Manila Bay. Homma had some command of English but wanted his staff to understand the proceedings and asked an interpreter to read it aloud. His face was stony; he said he could only accept the surrender of all troops in the Philippines.

"The troops in the Visayan Islands and Mindanao are no longer under my command," Wainwright explained. "They are commanded by General Sharp, who in turn is under General MacArthur's high command."

Homma flushed. Did Wainwright take him for a fool? He ordered his interpreter to tell Wainwright the Japanese had intercepted messages from Washington confirming Wainwright's position as commander in chief of all Philippine forces.

But Wainwright insisted that he had no authority over Sharp. Losing all patience, Homma banged the table with both fists. He faced his new chief of staff. "What should we do, Wachi?" Major General Takaji Wachi said he was sure Wainwright was lying. "In that case, we cannot negotiate," said Homma curtly. "Let us continue the battle." He turned back to Wainwright and informed him in a controlled voice that he could only negotiate with his equal, the commander in chief of all forces in the Philippines. "Since you are not in supreme command, I see no further necessity for my presence here." He started to rise.

One of Wainwright's companions called out in alarm, "Wait!" There was a quick conference among the Americans. Pale, Wainwright turned to Homma and forced himself to say, "In face of the fact that further bloodshed in the Philippines is unnecessary and futile, I will assume command of the entire American forces in the Philippines at the risk of serious reprimand by my government following the war."

But Homma was too offended to accept the abrupt turnabout. He doubted Wainwright's sincerity. Stiffly he told the American commander to go back to Corregidor and think the matter over. "If you see fit to surrender, then do so to the commanding officer of the regiment on Corregidor. He in turn will bring you to me in Manila. I call this meeting over. Good day." He nodded and walked to his Cadillac.

The distraught Wainwright had chewed the cigarette in his mouth to shreds. "What do you want us to do now?" he asked Nakayama.

"We will take you and your party back to Corregidor, and you can do what you damn please."

The entire emotional exchange had taken place through interpreters whose translations had been vague. No one knew exactly what had been said except a completely bilingual newsman named Kazumaro Uno who had been raised in Utah. He sympathized with the plight of the Americans and explained to Nakayama that Wainwright was quite ready to surrender all the Philippines.

Somewhat mollified. Nakayama said he would accompany Wainwright to Corregidor and added, "First thing tomorrow morning you will go to General Homma with a new surrender and a promise to contact the other American forces in the Philippines."

Wainwright saw many campfires all over Corregidor and guessed that the Japanese had already landed reinforcements. He was led around Malinta Hill and introduced to the island commander, Colonel Sato. The tunnel had been cleared except for those in the hospital. Now Sato was preparing to attack the main part of the island, Topside. Immediate unconditional surrender to Sato was the only way Wainwright could save his men from slaughter, and in the feeble light he signed a document accepting all of Homma's original demands. He felt drained of energy.

It was midnight. Wainwright was escorted to the west entrance of Malinta Tunnel, past solemn groups of Americans and Filipinos. Some of the men reached out to touch his hand or pat his shoulder. "It's all right, General," said one. "You did your best."

His eyes filled with tears.

Wainwright's humiliation was just beginning. The following morning he summoned his operations officer, Colonel Jesse T. Traywick, Jr. The Japanese would fly the colonel to Mindanao so he could personally deliver a letter to General Sharp explaining the situation.

. . . You will therefore be guided accordingly, and *will* repeat *will* surrender all troops under your command both in the Visayan Islands and Mindanao to the proper Japanese officer. This decision on my part, you will realize, was forced upon me by means beyond my control. . . .

Traywick was empowered to place Sharp under arrest if he failed to follow instructions implicitly. Wainwright broke down. "Jesse." he said, "I'm depending on you to carry out these orders."

Wainwright and five of his officers were taken by assault boat to Bataan late that afternoon. At Lamao they were kept waiting for two hours but did receive their first food in two days, rice and bony fish. At dusk they started the tedious trip to Manila by car. Around eleven o'clock the party arrived at radio station KZRH and was met by Lieutenant Hisamichi Kano of the Propaganda Corps, who had been educated in New York and New Jersey. Hhe greeted Wainwright affably and offered the Americans some fruit.

Wainwright had difficulty reading the prepared speech, which was a combination of his letter to Sharp and Japanese interpolations, until Kano reworded it into more colloquial English. Shortly before midnight Wainwright, so gaunt that he looked almost like a skeleton, sat down at a small round bamboo table and began speaking into a microphone in a voice husky with suppressed emotion. He addressed Sharp directly, ordering him to surrender all forces. "You will repeat the complete text of this letter and such other instructions as Colonel Traywick will give you by radio to General MacArthur. However, let me emphasize that there must be on your part no thought of disregarding these instructions. Failure to fully and honestly carry them out can have only the most disastrous results." He almost choked as he warned that the Japanese would continue operations unless the orders were carried out scrupulously and accurately. "If and when such faithfulness of execution is recognized, the commander in chief of the Japanese forces in the Philippine Islands will order that all firing be ceased." He coughed and paused. "Taking all circumstances into consideration, and—"

There was another longer pause. Wainwright seemed unable to continue. The Filipino announcer, Marcela Victor Young, broke in and signed off. It was 12:20 A.M., May 8.

Kano led the emotionally drained Wainwright and his companions to his office. He poured them drinks from a bottle of Scotch while the Americans tried to comfort their stricken commander.

The speech was heard by Americans and Filipinos all through the islands. Was it really Wainwright talking? If so, did he have a pistol at his head? General Sharp didn't know what to do. That morning he'd received a message from Wainwright relinquishing his command and now he was taking it back. He requested instructions from MacArthur. MacArthur in turn radioed Washington that he placed "no credence in the alleged broadcast by Wainwright." His reply to Sharp went out at 4:45 A.M.:

ORDERS EMANATING FROM GENERAL WAINWRIGHT HAVE NO VALIDITY. IF POSSIBLE SEPARATE YOUR FORCE INTO SMALL ELEMENTS AND INITIATE GUERRILLA OPERATIONS. YOU, OF COURSE, HAVE FULL AUTHORITY TO MAKE ANY DECISION THAT IMMEDIATE EMERGENCY MAY DEMAND. KEEP IN COMMUNICATION WITH ME AS MUCH AS POSSIBLE. YOU ARE A GALLANT AND RESOURCEFUL COMMANDER AND I AM PROUD OF WHAT YOU HAVE DONE.*

This message neither reassured Sharp nor clarified the situation. But it did leave the decision up to him, and he decided to wait for Wainwright's emissary. Two days later, upon Traywick's arrival after a harrowing trip, Sharp read Wainwright's letter and concluded there was no alternative. He immediately ordered the commanders of the various islands to "cease all operations against the Japanese Army at once" to save further bloodshed, then radioed MacArthur:

. . . DIRE NECESSITY ALONE HAS PROMPTED THIS ACTION.

In Washington, General Marshall was reading a message from MacArthur:

I HAVE JUST RECEIVED WORD FROM MAJOR GENERAL SHARP THAT GENERAL WAINWRIGHT IN TWO BROADCASTS ON THE NIGHT OF THE 7/8 ANNOUNCED HE WAS REASSUMING COMMAND OF ALL FORCES IN THE PHILIPPINES AND DIRECTED THEIR SURRENDER GIVING IN DETAIL THE METHOD OF ACCOMPLISHMENT. I BELIEVE WAINWRIGHT HAS TEMPORARILY BECOME UNBALANCED AND HIS CONDITION RENDERS HIM SUSCEPTIBLE OF ENEMY USE.

But it was too late to prevent the surrender of all the Philippines.

Their conqueror was in no triumphant mood. He was in disfavor with the Army General Staff; it had taken him too long to achieve victory. Moreover, General Count Hisaichi Terauchi, commander of Southern Army, was displeased with Homma's lenient treatment of Filipino civilians. Homma had

---

*When Marshall subsequently attempted to get Wainwright a Medal of Honor, MacArthur refused to approve on the grounds that his actions did not warrant this great distinction and it would be an injustice to others who had done far more. It was not until after the war that Wainwright at last received the decoration from President Truman. Bitterness toward MacArthur over this and similar matters still exists among the surviving group of officers close to Wainwright, nicknamed the Wainwright Travelers.

forbidden pillage and rape and ordered his troops not to regard the Filipinos as enemies but to respect their customs, traditions and religion. His defense was that he had been scrupulously following the Emperor's instructions to bring enlightenment to Southeast Asia.

But what exercised Terauchi most was Homma's suppression of a propaganda pamphlet describing the exploitation of the Islands by the Americans. Homma told Terauchi to his face that the Americans had never exploited the Philippines and that it was wrong to make such false statements. "They administered a very benevolent supervision over the Philippines. Japan should establish an even better and more enlightened supervision."

Homma's insistent tolerance left Terauchi more resolved than ever to send an adverse report to Tokyo from his headquarters in Saigon. It also provoked a small but influential group of his own subordinates, those under the influence of Colonel Tsuji, into secret retaliation. In Homma's name, they sent out orders countermanding his liberal policy.

Homma had no knowledge of this until two days after Wainwright's surrender. Major General Kiyotake Kawaguchi, commander of Japanese forces in the Visayans, burst into Homma's office, his ten-inch Kaiser mustache bristling. He accused Homma of having authorized the execution of Chief Justice José Abad Santos and wanted to know the reason why. Santos had been captured on Negros Island with his son and brought to Kawaguchi's headquarters on Cebu in April, on the evening Bataan fell. Santos was willing to work with the Japanese, and Kawaguchi had radioed Manila a recommendation that he be given a position in the Laurel "Quising" government. The answer was unexpected: HIS GUILT IS OBVIOUS. DISPOSE OF HIM IMMEDIATELY.

THIS WAS an outrageous betrayal of *bushido* and the Emperor, and Kawaguchi had thrown a staff officer from Manila named Inuzuka out of his office for insisting on the execution of Santos' son as well. Then he wrote a letter to an old friend, Major General Yoshihide Hayashi, Military Administrator of 14th Army, reiterating why the two Santos should be spared. Two weeks later Kawaguchi received another dispatch from Manila. It ordered him to deliver the two Santos to the Davao garrison commander on Mindanao for immediate execution. The indignant Kawaguchi responded by crumpling up the message.

But it was followed by the persistent Inuzuka, who had

come to make sure that the executions take place. Kawaguchi summoned the two prisoners and told them he had done his utmost to save their lives but was now forced to execute the elder Santos in the name of the 14th Army. "I promise to protect your son, so don't worry," he told the father.

Santos said he had never been anti-Japanese. "I appreciate your kindness toward me and my son and wish glory for your country." He stilled his son's pleas for mercy; they could only embarrass the general. "When you see Mother, give her my love. I will soon die. Be a man of honor and work for the Philippines." Santos was taken to a nearby coconut plantation. He declined to be blindfolded and crossed himself just before the shots of the firing squad rang out.

Homma was dumbfounded to learn of Santos' execution from Kawaguchi. He, too, had had high regard for Chief Justice Santos and appreciated his friendship for Japan. He remembered approving Kawaguchi's original request for clemency and had ordered Hayashi to take care of the matter. Mortified, he told Kawaguchi, "I regret very much what has happened."

The following day Kawaguchi confronted Hayashi. "What a *keshikaran* [shameful] thing you did!" he burst out. "I trusted you as my classmate."

Hayashi was defensive; Homma had already admonished him. "But," he excused himself, "Imperial Headquarters was so insistent about the execution of Santos."

"Whom do you mean by 'Imperial Headquarters'?"

"It was Tsuji."

Homma's reprimand had little effect on those staff officers determined to carry out Tsuji's policy of revenge. Several weeks later when General Manuel Roxas, former Speaker of the House of Representatives, was captured on Mindanao, a message came from Manila ordering the local commander, General Torao Ikuta, to execute Roxas "secretly and immediately." It was authorized in the name of Homma and stamped by Hayashi and three staff officers.

On Bataan, Ikuta had refused to shoot prisoners without a written order, but even though he had one this time, he found himself incapable to act, and turned over the responsibility to his chief of staff, Colonel Nobuhiko Jimbo, a balding man with glasses and a Tojo mustache. As a Catholic, Jimbo was tormented while he drove Roxas and another high-ranking captive, a governor, toward the execution grounds. Throughout the hour-long trip past hemp fields and coconut groves the governor begged for his life. He was an administrator, not a soldier; he had always co-operated with the Japanese and should be treated differently from General Roxas. His voice became so hysterical that Roxas patted his shoulder and said, "Look at the *sampaguita*." He pointed at clusters of delicate white blossoms, the national flower of the Philippines. "Aren't they beautiful?"

No samurai could have acted more nobly and Jimbo decided to try to save Roxas no matter what the consequences. He left his two charges under guard in a small town and returned to Davao; somehow he had to persuade General Ikuta to ignore the execution order.

Jimbo's arguments were all that Ikuta needed. The two men decided to use Roxas to help restore law and order, but for a while he would have to be kept hidden. What they did could not be kept secret for long. An officer arrived from Manila; Jimbo was to be court-martialed for his "high-handed" actions.

Jimbo flew up to Manila to confront Homma himself, but since the general was out of his office, he had to speak instead of his chief of staff. General Wachi couldn't believe such an order had gone out, particularly after Homma's violent reaction to the execution of Santos.

Jimbo showed him the original document. Although Wachi was not able to cancel any order stamped with Homma's name, he wrote out another, temporarily suspending the execution. He told Jimbo to wait and pushed his way into Hayashi's office, where the general and four staff officers were in conference. Jimbo could hear Wachi's angry voice: "Did you men issue the order to execute General Roxas?" Hayashi and the others denied it; it would be violation of a specific order by General Homma. How could Wachi ask such a question?

"Colonel Jimbo, come in!" Wachi hollered.

The staff officers glared at Jimbo as he pulled out the execution order—but were forced to confess that they had stamped it "without giving it too much thought." There was an awkward pause. Hayashi wheeled on Jimbo and shouted, "You have done a terrible thing to us!"

Later that night Wachi came to Jimbo's room at the Manila Hotel. Homma was pleased with Jimbo's initiative and had already issued an order countermanding the Roxas execution.

Moreover, he would report the matter, including Jimbo's part in it, to the Emperor.*

So Roxas was saved, but the episode emphasized the subversion in Homma's own command. It also further undermined a career already in jeopardy. As a commander in the field Homma had not been as aggressive as Tokyo wanted, and in peace he was far too lenient toward the Philippine people. Even after Terauchi's admonition he continued to treat the Filipinos as potential friends rather than a conquered enemy. Against advice from his staff he ordered the release of all Filipino soldiers in the prison camps.

He was relieved of his command, ordered to Japan and forced to retire in semidisgrace without making the traditional report of a returning commander to the Emperor.**

---

*Roxas survived the war to become the first President of the Republic. When he learned in August 1946 that the man who had saved his life was still a prisoner in North China awaiting trial as a war criminal, he wrote a personal letter to Chiang Kai-shek requesting amnesty for Jimbo. He was released and returned to Japan the following year and is now living in Tokyo. As Vice President of the Order of the Knights of Rizal [Dr. José Rizal], Tokyo Chapter, he is authorized to use the title Sir Nobuhiko.

**After the war Homma was tried, convicted and executed as a war criminal by the man he defeated, MacArthur. Homma's chief defense counsel, John H. Skeen, Jr., called it "a highly irregular trial, conducted in an atmosphere that left no doubt as to what the ultimate outcome would be." The others on the defense staff signed a letter to Homma stating that he had been unjustly convicted. Associate Justice Frank Murphy of the U. S. Supreme Court protested the verdict. "This nation's very honor, as well as its hope for the future, is at stake," he wrote. "Either we conduct such a trial as this in the noble spirit and atmosphere of our Constitution or we abandon all pretense to justice, let the ages slip away and descend to the level of revengeful blood purges. . . . A nation must not perish, because in the natural frenzy of the aftermath of war, it abandoned the central theme of the dignity of the human personality and due process of law."

While Homma was awaiting sentence he wrote his wife, Fujiko: "In the twenty years of our married life we've had many differences of opinion and even violent quarrels. Those quarrels have now become sweet memories. . . . Now as I am about to part from you, I particularly see your good qualities, and I have completely forgotten any defects. I have no worry about leaving the children in your hands because I know you will raise them to be right and strong. . . . Twenty years feel short but they are long. I am content that we have lived a happy life together. If there is what is called the other world, we'll be married again. I'll go first and wait for you there but you mustn't hurry. Live as long as you can for the children and do those things for me I haven't been able to do. You will see our grandchildren and even great-grandchildren and tell me all about them when we meet again in the other world. Thank you very much for everything."

The last words from Homma came in a letter to his children just

1.

By the end of April Captain Kameto Kuroshima, the "foggy staff officer," had transformed Yamamoto's basic idea into an intricate war plan that involved almost two hundred ships maneuvering in close co-operation over a battlefield stretching two thousand miles from the Aleutians to Midway, which was 2,300 miles east of Japan. On the face of it, the objective was to capture Midway and the western Aleutians. These islands would then become key points in a new outer perimeter stretching all the way from Kiska in the north, through Midway and Wake to Port Moresby in the south, just three hundred miles from Australia. Patrol planes based on these three islands could detect any enemy task force attempting to pierce the empire's inner defense. In fact, however, the seizure of Midway was of secondary importance to Yamamoto; it was merely bait in the trap designed to lure the remnants of Nimitz' fleet out of Pearl Harbor so it could be destroyed. That would mean the end, or at least postponement, of American efforts to dislodge the Japanese from their recent conquests in Southeast Asia.

The commanders who would have to fight the battle—including Admiral Nagumo's chief of staff, Ryunosuke Kusaka—were summoned to the recently completed 63,000-ton battleship *Yamato*, the new flagship of the Combined Fleet which bore the ancient name for "Japan," to be briefed by Yamamoto personally. In the past five months Nagumo's Striking Force had devastated Pearl Harbor, battered Darwin harbor, sunk two British heavy cruisers off Colombo, and the carrier *Hermes* and other ships off Trincomalee, on Ceylon, without a single surface loss. Nevertheless, Kusaka had seri-

---

before the execution: "There are six men here who have been sentenced for life. It will be better to be shot to death—like dying an honorable death on the battlefield—than spending a disgraceful life in such a cage the rest of one's life. Don't lose courage, children! Don't give in to temptation! Walk straight on the road of justice. The spirit of your father will long watch over you. Your father will be pleased if you will make your way in the right direction rather than bring flowers to his grave. Do not miss the right course. This is my very last letter."

ous reservations. Another major operation, he said, would be foolhardy. *Kido Butai* had steamed fifty thousand miles since Pearl Harbor and the ships needed reconditioning. The crews, too, needed a rest; exhaustion was so prevalent that some men were actually seeing ghosts. Yamamoto overrode the objections. He ordered preparations accelerated.

At the same time another important plan was set in motion. This was Operation Mo, the invasion of Port Moresby on the Coral Sea. Its fall would lead to easy conquest of the rest of New Guinea and place Australia itself in peril. As a preliminary, a force seized Tulagi, a small island some twenty miles north of Guadalcanal in the Solomon Islands, and began constructing a seaplane base. The next day, May 4, the Port Moresby Invasion Force left Rabaul, since January the staging area for operations in the South Pacific at the upper tip of New Britain in the Bismarck Archipelago. There were fourteen transports escorted by a light cruiser and six destroyers, and covered by the light carrier *Shoho*, four heavy cruisers and a destroyer.

Most of this was known to Admiral Nimitz; his cryptanalysts had broken the Japanese fleet code. He had already dispatched Task Force 17—two carriers, six heavy cruisers, two light cruisers and eleven destroyers—under Rear Admiral Frank Jack Fletcher to intercept the Japanese.

Fletcher had reached the Coral Sea off northeastern Australia by the time he learned of the Tulagi landing. He immediately launched an air attack of ninety-nine planes on Tulagi from his flagship, the carrier *Yorktown*. To counteract this unexpected threat Vice Admiral Takeo Takagi, victor of the Battle of the Java Sea, was sent south from Bougainville with two heavy carriers, *Zuikaku* and *Shokaku*, two heavy cruisers and six destroyers.

The two opposing forces drew closer, and it was Takagi who made the first contact. On the morning of May 7 one of his search pilots who spotted the oiler *Neosho* and a destroyer became overly excited and he reported them as an enemy carrier and cruiser. Two waves of high-level bombers and thirty-six dive bombers sank the destroyer and left the oiler helplessly adrift. While Takagi was concentrating his force on these minor targets, ninety-three planes from *Yorktown* and *Lexington* found the light carrier *Shoho* and began an aggressive bomb and torpedo attack. About 160 miles away comrades on the mother ships strained to hear this action on their radios, but the static made it difficult. Suddenly the voice of Lieutenant Commander Robert Dixon, leader of a scout bomber squadron, came in strong and clear: "Scratch one flattop! Dixon to carrier. Scratch one flattop!" At last, after five months, a Japanese ship larger than a destroyer had been sunk.

In Rabaul the overall commander of Operation Mo, Vice Admiral Shigeyoshi Inoue, radioed the transports to turn back and wait until the seas were cleared of Americans. That afternoon visibility decreased and squalls limited aerial observation. By midnight the two enemy fleets had lost contact.

Takagi, aboard a heavy cruiser, signaled Rear Admiral Tadaichi Hara, commander of the two carriers: CAN YOU LAUNCH A NIGHT AIR ATTACK? Hara signaled back from *Zuikaku* that he was prepared to send twenty-seven planes. They took off just before dusk but found nothing. On the way back, however, they were set upon by a group of Fletcher's fighters. Nine Japanese were shot down; the others dispersed and tried to make their way home in the dark. One cluster of six eventually found a carrier and let down to join the other planes in the landing pattern. As the first Japanese skimmed the deck, landing hook extended, he was blasted over the side with a hail of gunfire. The carrier was *Yorktown*.

After the fiasco, Takagi decided to retire temporarily to the north. Several hours later he doubled back toward the American carriers at 26 knots, and just before dawn on May 8, he dispatched twenty-seven search planes. The first carrier battle in history was imminent. Fletcher had radar but his carriers had operated together less than a week. Takagi had no radar but his two carriers had been working as a division for more than six months. Fletcher had 122 planes, Takagi one less. They were well matched, with Takagi having the slight advantage of cover from an overcast.

But the first break went to Fletcher. At eight-fifteen one of his search pilots sighted the Japanese Striking Force. He circled, counting the ships, and radioed:

TWO CARRIERS, FOUR HEAVY CRUISERS, MANY DESTROYERS, STEERING 120 DEGREES, 20 KNOTS. THEIR POSITION 175 MILES, ROUGHLY NORTHEAST.

Fletcher ordered both carriers to launch air strikes, and around eleven o'clock thirty-nine planes from *Yorktown* came upon *Shokaku*, screened by heavy cruisers and destroyers. *Zuikaku*, just ten miles away, was hidden by a dense squall. *Shokaku* avoided torpedoes, but dive bombers made two direct hits which started fires. Another wave, twenty-four planes from *Lexington*, found the carriers. *Shokaku* escaped with one more bomb hit. Her fires were brought under control and she headed for home.

Simultaneously the Japanese also found the Americans. Seventy planes converged on Fletcher's two carriers. One bomb pierced the flight deck of *Yorktown*, but fires were skillfully brought under control. *Lexington* was not so lucky; two torpedoes ripped into her port side, while small bombs struck the main deck forward and the smokestack structure.

The air attacks had been costly to both sides and by noon the battle was over. It was the first naval engagement in which opposing ships never saw each other or exchanged gunfire. It appeared as if Fletcher had emerged the victor. He had sunk a light carrier, a destroyer and three small vessels while losing one destroyer and an oiler. Then two explosions rocked the wounded *Lexington* and set off uncontrollable fires. Shortly after five o'clock Rear Admiral Aubrey Fitch, commander of the Carrier Group, leaned over the flag bridge and called down to *Lexington*'s skipper, Captain Frederick C. Sherman, "Well, Ted, let's get the men off."

They lined up their shoes on the flight deck and calmly began going over the sides, as unconcerned as if it were a drill. One group went below to the ship's service store; they filled their helmets with ice cream and ate it while waiting in line on the flight deck. As the last man, Captain Sherman, started down the life line, he told himself, Wouldn't I look silly if I left this ship and the fires went out? But he clambered down the line, and once the survivors were clear, four torpedoes from the destroyer *Phelps* drove into the carrier's starboard side. She shuddered and steam rose in billowing clouds.

"There she goes," said an officer watching from a nearby cruiser. "She didn't turn over. She is going down with her head up. Dear old *Lex*. A lady to the last."

With the sinking of *Lexington* the battle became a tactical victory for Takagi, but the more important strategic triumph still was Fletcher's. Admiral Inoue was forced to postpone the Port Moresby operation. Fletcher had accomplished his mission, and for the first time since Pearl Harbor a Japanese invasion had been thwarted.

Takagi, however, was reluctant to give up. He was getting set to engage the Americans in a night battle when he learned that his own destroyers were almost out of fuel. Grudgingly he turned back for Rabaul. Far to the north, at his homeland anchorage Yamamoto was still resolved to pursue the Americans. Through Rabaul he ordered Takagi to attack in spite of the fuel shortage. Takagi obediently reversed course, but it was too late. Fletcher had vanished.

Both sides claimed victory. The *New York Times* of May 9 announced:

JAPANESE REPULSED IN GREAT PACIFIC BATTLE, WITH 17 TO 22 OF THEIR SHIPS SUNK OR CRIPPLED: ENEMY IN FLIGHT, PURSUED BY ALLIED WARSHIPS

The *Japan Times & Advertiser* proclaimed that the enemy was panic-stricken. The source was a correspondent in Buenos Aires who wrote: "The effect of the terrible setback in the Coral Sea is indeed beyond description. A state of mania is prevalent in the American munitions fields."

Hitler was exultant. "After this new defeat the United States warships will hardly dare to face the Japanese fleet again, since any United States warship which accepts action with the Japanese naval forces is as good as lost."

2.

Japanese newspaper accounts accurately reflected the jubilation at Imperial Headquarters—both *Lexington* and *Yorktown* had been sunk, a crushing blow to American power in the Pacific. The "triumph" stilled the objections of those who regarded the Midway operation as too hazardous. Coral Sea had been won by the 5th Air Squadron, the least experienced in the fleet. What chance would the Americans have against the veterans of the 1st and 2nd Air Squadrons? *Zuikaku* and *Shokaku* arrived home a few days later. The "inferior" American pilots had inflicted more damage than first reported. Both would have to be scratched from the Midway invasion. *Zuikaku* had lost too many planes and pilots, and it would take a month to repair *Shokaku*.

But nothing could undermine the supreme optimism that swept through Combined Fleet, and even Kusaka, recently so pessimistic, was sure *Kido Butai* could "beat the hell out of the Yankees." The result was a relaxation of security measures. In contrast to preparations for Pearl Harbor, there was little attempt to disguise the flow of messages that marked the final stages, and staff officers openly discussed Operation Midway in restaurants and teahouses.

On the evening of May 25 Yamamoto invited several

hundred officers, including Nagumo and Kusaka, to a party on *Yamato*, which lay off Hashirajima in the Inland Sea. Too late Yamamoto's steward, Heijiro Omi, discovered that the cook had made a grievous mistake. The *tai*, a fish cooked from head to tail, had been broiled in *miso* (salted bean paste) instead of salt; and the saying "to put *miso* on food" was a metaphor meaning "to make a mess of things." Omi scolded the chef and in turn was scolded by the admiral's flag secretary, but Yamamoto himself ignored the blunder and endless *kampai* (toasts) were drunk in heated *sake* to the Emperor and victory.

The following day at the final briefing Kusaka asked a question which, surprisingly, had not been posed before: "If we sight the American fleet, should we attack it or take Midway first?" Admiral Matome Ugaki, who had prepared for the battle by getting a haircut and a new set of false teeth, turned to Nagumo and said it would be his decision. "You are in the front line and can assess the situation better than we can."

Kusaka refused to accept the responsibility; only Combined Fleet could make the proper decision, since the operation was so complicated and involved so many units. Besides, *Akagi* had a short mast and was not equipped to intercept enemy messages, whereas Yamamoto's flagship had a very high mast and the latest facilities. Ugaki said this was immaterial; radio silence would have to be maintained, since the whole plan depended on surprise.

On *Akagi* there was such a feeling of confidence that many fliers had brought aboard personal belongings and a plentiful supply of beer and *sake*. One man, Lieutenant Heijiro Abe, did not share their faith. At the last moment he advised Commander Minoru Genda to call off the operation. Abe, who had dropped a bomb on *Oklahoma*, had just received a letter from a friend in China wishing him luck on the attack of "M." Everyone seemed to know about Midway, said Abe, and he predicted that they would be "beaten in a bag." But Genda said it was too late to cancel the operation; other units were already on the move.

At six o'clock in the morning on May 27, Nagumo's Carrier Striking Force—a light cruiser, eleven destroyers, two battleships (including *Haruna*, supposedly sunk by Colin Kelly) and four carriers—filed slowly through the Inland Sea toward Bungo Strait as the sailors on the other ships of the Combined Fleet cheered them on. The following day the force scheduled to invade the Aleutians left its port at the northern tip of Kyushu; on June 3, the day before the raid on Midway, planes from two light carriers would bomb Dutch Harbor to divert Nimitz' attention to the north. Far to the south, on Saipan in the Marianas, a dozen transports filled with the five thousand men who would take Midway set off, accompanied by a light cruiser, a tanker and a covering force of four heavy cruisers.

Early on the morning of May 29, the rest of the Combined Fleet moved out of the Inland Sea—first Vice Admiral Nobutake Kondo's Midway Invasion Force, then the Main Force of thirty-four ships led by Yamamoto's flagship, *Yamato*. In all, eleven battleships, eight carriers, twenty-three cruisers, sixty-five destroyers and almost ninety auxiliary ships plowed eastward in the most ambitious naval operation ever conceived by man. More oil would be used in this single operation than the peacetime Navy consumed in a year.

As before, Japanese success depended on secrecy, but as at the Coral Sea, Nimitz knew a massive attack was being mounted thanks to his Combat Intelligence Unit, some 120 men, including the sunken *California*'s entire band (musicians were eminently suited for such work), under Lieutenant Commander Joseph John Rochefort. They were on duty practically around the clock in a windowless basement in the Navy Yard, protected by vaultlike doors, steel-barred gates and constant guards—and they were reading 90 percent of the code messages sent out by Combined Fleet. The scattered information about Midway was, in a sense, a gift from the Japanese Navy. On May 1 it had scheduled one of the periodic revisions of its main code which always blacked out information until Rochefort's men broke it. But the old code was still in effect because of the rush of work. Besides, Japanese naval intelligence experts were positive their codes could not be broken.

On May 20 the bits and pieces about the invasion fell into place with the interception of a lengthy order issued by Yamamoto. Fifteen percent of the message was missing, but the magnitude of the operation was evident. All that was left in doubt was the target, which was referred to simply as "AF." Rochefort felt reasonably sure it was Midway, but Washington experts were just as positive it stood for Oahu.

Nimitz agreed with Rochefort, and flew to Midway to determine what additional equipment and how many more men were needed to stem a large-scale amphibious attack. Every plane he could spare was dispatched to Midway. Nimitz also enlarged the tiny island's garrison to two thousand, set up three submarine patrol arcs and ordered installation of additional antiaircraft batteries. To confirm the location of "AF," Nimitz had Midway transmit a fake message in the clear complaining of the breakdown of its distillation plant. The Japanese took the bait and two days later radioed Tokyo that "AF" was low on fresh water.

With this corroboration Nimitz decided to meet the Japanese head-on. They would be lying in wait for him, but Nimitz knew he had to meet the challenge of Yamamoto's armada, even though he had only eight cruisers, seventeen destroyers and two carriers. The third, *Yorktown*, had not yet reached Pearl Harbor after the damage it had absorbed at Coral Sea. Repairs would take about ninety days.

Nimitz called in his two commanders, Fletcher and Rear Admiral Raymond A. Spruance—a last-minute substitute for Halsey, who was suffering from a skin disease. He ordered them "to inflict maximum damage on enemy by employing strong attrition attacks." They were to strike again and again from the air and "be governed by the principle of calculated risk, which you shall interpret to mean the avoidance of exposure of your force to attack by superior enemy forces without good prospect of inflicting, as a result of such exposure, greater damage on the enemy."

The day after Nagumo's four carriers had left the Inland Sea, Spruance sailed out of Pearl Harbor on the carrier *Enterprise*, with *Hornet*, six cruisers and eleven destroyers making up the rest of Task Force 16. Two days later Fletcher followed, with two cruisers and six destroyers, on *Yorktown*. Thanks to the almost superhuman efforts of fourteen hundred workmen, the estimated three months' repair of the damaged carrier had been accomplished in two days.

That same day Yamamoto, trailing Nagumo by six hundred miles, received three distressing messages. First, he learned that aerial reconnaissance of Pearl Harbor would be impossible; by chance an American seaplane tender had anchored at the exact point where the reconnaissance planes from Kwajalein Atoll in the Marshalls were to have been refueled by submarines. Second, the seven submarines which were to form a picket line between Oahu and Midway and intercept American carriers heading toward *Kido Butai* could not, for some reason, get into position in time.* Finally, and

---

*Rear Admiral (Captain at the time) Keizo Komura, skipper of the cruiser *Chikuma* at Midway, revealed in 1967 that a typographical

most disturbing, from a submarine patrolling the waters around Midway came a report that the island seemed to be on a strict alert with intensive air patrols; many construction cranes were visible, indicating a probable expansion of defenses. Yamamoto was going to relay this information to the man who most needed it—Nagumo—but his operations officer, Captain Kuroshima, insisted on continued radio silence.

Unaided by radar, the Striking Force steamed ahead shrouded in a thick mist. The following day, June 2, was worse. Nagumo and Kusaka peered anxiously from the bridge of *Akagi* at a blanket of heavy fog. It kept them hidden from enemy observation, but made navigation at close quarters hazardous. Kusaka still fretted about the dual tactical mission: to attack Midway on June 4 in preparation for the landing two days later and to find and destroy Nimitz' fleet. How could they do both? The second mission required freedom of movement and secrecy, but if they bombed Midway, both mobility and secrecy were gone. It was "like a hunter chasing two hares at once."

In Nagumo's presence he put the question to the staff. Captain Tamotsu Oishi gave the most succinct answer: "The Combined Fleet operation order gives first priority to the destruction of enemy forces. Co-operation with the landing operation is secondary. But if we do not neutralize the Midway-based air forces as planned, our landing operations two days later will be strongly opposed and the entire invasion schedule will be upset."

Where is the enemy fleet? Nagumo wondered. Nobody knows, Oishi confessed. "Even if they are already aware of our movements and have sortied to meet us, they can't be far out from base at this moment and certainly can't be near us." Therefore the Midway attack should take place as scheduled. The others agreed.

That day the new edition of the fleet code finally went into effect and the cryptanalysts in the Pearl Harbor basement were temporarily in the dark. But it made no difference. Nimitz already knew enough. The next morning Midway received the first visual report that an invasion was imminent. Ensign Jack Reid, on patrol in a Catalina out of Midway, came upon what looked like a cluster of "miniature ships in a backyard pool" about thirty miles ahead. "Do you

---

error in the orders had sent the submarines to the wrong positions. Combined Fleet attempted to conceal the blunder, but Komura learned of it soon after the battle from an officer on Yamamoto's staff.

see what I see?" he asked co-pilot Hardeman. Hardeman took the glasses. "You're damn right I do."

MAIN BODY, Reid flashed to his base on Midway.

It was, however, the invasion transports, and they in turn sighted the Catalina and alerted Yamamoto. *Akagi* intercepted the message, but Nagumo was unconcerned. The Striking Force was still undetected. His complacency was not shared by those on the bridge of *Yamato*. Never had Yamamoto or his staff imagined that the transports would be discovered before the first air assault on Midway.

By nightfall the Japanese were rapidly converging on Midway from the northwest and by dawn would be at the launching point, two hundred miles from the target. Fletcher and Spruance had positioned themselves three hundred miles east-northeast of the island. Fletcher, who was in overall command of the two task forces, guessed correctly that Reid had only seen transports, but it did indicate that carriers were not far behind. At 7:50 P.M. he headed southwest, with the conviction that tomorrow could be "the most important day in the history of the U. S. Navy." By daybreak he would be north of Midway, in perfect position to attack the enemy striking force. It was a remarkable deduction; the American carriers would be about a hundred miles from *Kido Butai*.

By visual signal Spruance informed his men they would probably encounter a superior force, four or five carriers, and that success in the battle would be "of great value to our country." Somehow, by that mysterious grapevine prevalent on every American ship, word spread that the Japanese code had been broken and that a trap was being set. There was a feeling of excitement in the wardrooms and mess halls.

3.

At 2:45 A.M. on June 4, *Akagi*'s loudspeakers blared and aircrews tumbled out of bunks. All over the ship there was a spirit of celebration, almost gaiety, as if the battle had already been won. Mitsuo Fuchida had led the attack on Pearl Harbor and was supposed to do the same at Midway. He was in sick bay, stricken by appendicitis the first night at sea. In a nearby cot was his friend Minoru Genda. He had a bad cold and his eyes looked feverish. Still in pajamas, Genda shuffled up to the bridge and apologized to Nagumo for being so late. He assured his chief that he was fit enough to direct and take personal charge of the attack. The admiral affectionately put an arm around his shoulder, and everyone on the bridge was buoyed to see him. Belowdecks the aircrews were eating the traditional breakfast served for decades to Japanese setting off to battle: rice, soybean soup, dry chestnuts and *sake.*

The four carriers were now 240 miles northwest of Midway, steaming full into the wind. Genda ordered preparations for the first wave against the tiny atoll. At 4:30 A.M. Kusaka gave the word to commence launching. Suddenly Fuchida appeared. He could not stay below and had staggered out of sick bay to watch his substitute, First Lieutenant Joichi Tomonaga on *Hiryu,* lead the raiders. The air officer waved his green lantern and the first Zero fighter skimmed down the illuminated flight deck and flung itself into the black sky. A chorus of spontaneous cheers was swept off the deck by the wind. Eight Zeros followed, then eighteen dive bombers.

Within fifteen minutes all four carriers had cleared their decks of planes; 108 were in the air, but the people below could only make out a long chain of red and blue lights strung toward Midway. At the same time Genda ordered seven reconnaissance planes to fan out to the east and southeast in search of American carriers. Five hurtled off, but one from the heavy cruiser *Tone* was delayed by catapult trouble. Kusaka thought a stronger reconnaissance should be made but said nothing. It was Genda's show (on practically any subject Nagumo accepted Genda's recommendations without question. Indeed, cynics referred to the Striking Force as "Genda's fleet") and it was not at all likely that the enemy carriers were anywhere in the area. They shouldn't arrive from Pearl Harbor for forty-eight hours, but just in case they appeared unexpectedly, Kusaka ordered thirty-six planes armed with torpedoes brought up to the flight decks of *Akagi* and *Kaga.*

Not only was the American fleet closer than the Japanese thought but their own carriers were about to be discovered. At 5:25 A.M. a Catalina search plane from Midway, piloted by Lieutenant Howard Ady, burst out of the clouds near *Kido Butai* and he stared in awe at a mass of ships. It was "like watching a curtain rising on the Biggest Show on Earth." ENEMY CARRIERS, Ady radioed. He slipped the clumsy PBY behind the clouds, and circled. He came up on Nagumo's ships from the rear and identified two carriers and several battleships.

Ady's reports indicated that he had found the Japanese

Striking Force, but Admiral Fletcher decided to wait for more explicit information. He radioed Spruance:

> PROCEED SOUTHWESTERLY AND ATTACK ENEMY CARRIERS WHEN DEFINITELY LOCATED. I WILL FOLLOW AS SOON AS PLANES RECOVERED.

On Midway, radar picked up the first wave of oncoming Japanese around 5:50. Air-raid sirens shrieked as planes took off pell-mell. While six Navy Avenger torpedo planes and four Army Marauders, also armed with torpedoes, headed north toward the enemy carriers, twenty-five Marine fighter pilots in obsolete Brewster Buffalos and Grumman Wildcats climbed northwest. Within minutes they encountered the raiders. They flung themselves into battle, but they were outnumbered and outclassed by the Zeros. Fifteen Marines were shot down and the Japanese swept unopposed to their target. Dive bombers plummeted through heavy antiaircraft fire and blasted buildings, oil tanks and the seaplane hangar. John Ford, who had filmed the takeoff of the Doolittle fliers, was high up in a powerhouse with his movie camera. There came a blast, and shrapnel tore into his shoulder. He picked himself up, put the camera to his eye and continued to follow the action.

For twenty minutes the Japanese had their own way and when the last had turned out to sea, Midway's two islands appeared to be a mass of smoke and flames. But Lieutenant Tomonaga stayed long enough to see that he had failed to destroy American capabilities. Enemy planes (they were dive bombers) were still taking off from the airstrip and heading out toward *Kido Butai*. He radioed at 7 A.M.: THERE IS NEED FOR A SECOND ATTACK.

For more than an hour there had been a state of consternation on Nagumo's flagship, *Akagi*. Ady's Catalina had been sighted and an air raid from Midway was expected. The heavy clouds began to clear, uncovering *Kido Butai*. At 7:10 a destroyer out front hoisted a flag signal: "Enemy planes in sight."

The four Marauders and six Avengers from Midway came boring in with their torpedoes. Zero fighters screening the carriers dived and spun three into the ocean. Antiaircraft fire from destroyers, cruisers and the battleship *Kirishima* picked off two more. But three of the attackers penetrated far enough to launch torpedoes at *Akagi*. The flagship swerved and the torpedoes churned harmlessly by. This raid, together

378

with Tomonaga's request for another strike, prompted Nagumo to order a second attack on Midway, whose planes were a greater present threat to his carriers than the possibility of meeting the American fleet.

The decision had, in truth, been made by Nagumo's chief of staff. As at Pearl Harbor, Kusaka was the de facto commander; he never failed to consult Nagumo before taking action, but as yet none of his decisions had been countermanded. The latest one meant that the torpedo planes on *Akagi* and her sister ship, *Kaga,* had to be rearmed with bombs, and there was chaotic activity as these planes were lowered from the flight decks to their hangars. In the midst of this hubbub a message came in at 7:28 from one of *Tone*'s search planes that "ten ships, apparently enemy" were 240 miles north of Midway. There was agitation on *Akagi*'s bridge—this put the American fleet two hundred miles to the east!

For the first time since Pearl Harbor, luck had deserted the Japanese in battle. If the plane from *Tone* that had been delayed for thirty minutes on its catapult had gone off on schedule, it would have discovered the Americans before the Japanese torpedo planes were lowered for rearming, and they could now be winging toward *Enterprise, Hornet* and *Yorktown.* As it was, crucial time was lost while crews again went through the arduous task of refitting the planes with torpedoes.

At 7:47 A.M. Kusaka asked the *Tone* plane pilot to ascertain the ship types, but before the answer came, sixteen enemy planes appeared in the distance. These were the Marine dive bombers which, by-passing Tomonaga's planes, had left Midway minutes after the air-raid alarm and headed for the carriers. Now their commander, Major Lofton Henderson, ordered a glide-bombing attack, since his inexperienced pilots knew little about dive bombing. They bore down on *Hiryu.* Kusaka saw the light carrier enveloped in a smoke screen and towering waterspouts. Zeros managed to cut down half the Marines but the rest kept resolutely on course, released their bombs and returned to Midway. *Hiryu* emerged unscathed.

Then, at 8:09, came good news. The *Tone* search plane reported that the enemy ships were "five cruisers and five destroyers." However, there was no time for congratulations; 20,000 feet overhead fifteen Flying Fortresses were dropping bombs. Having left Midway before dawn to attack the transports, they had found carriers instead. The B-17 crews watched their bombs fall among the swerving carriers and radioed erroneously that they had scored four hits; there were none.

Kusaka was impressed by the variety of attacks: with torpedo planes, in a glide-bombing approach, with dive bombers and high-level bombers. The Americans were like Hiru-Daikokuten, the legendary demon with three heads and six arms. In ten minutes he learned of another—and more dangerous—threat. The *Tone* plane radioed:

ENEMY FORCE ACCOMPANIED BY WHAT APPEARS TO BE AIRCRAFT CARRIER BRINGING UP THE REAR.

Kusaka believed the report; his staff did not. If there was a carrier in the area, why hadn't it already launched an attack? Besides, the three ineffectual raids from Midway had proved that the enemy was not to be feared.

At 8:30 A.M., just as the first of Tomonaga's planes began returning from Midway, the *Tone* plane sent still another report: two enemy ships, probably cruisers. It was obvious that the American force was so big that it had to include at least one carrier. Kusaka wanted to attack but was in a quandary. The fighter planes which would escort the carrier strike were circling overhead to intercept any attackers and were running low on fuel. And what about Tomonaga's planes? If they weren't recovered, scores of the Navy's best pilots would be lost and future operations jeopardized.

He turned to Nagumo and suggested that they delay the strike, then asked Genda for his opinion. Genda was anxiously watching the clusters of Tomonaga's planes hovering over their carriers, many nursing the last gallons of fuel in their tanks. Almost every pilot was a personal friend. "I believe all our aircraft should first land and refuel," he said.

The planes on the decks of *Akagi* and *Kaga* were again lowered, this time to clear the way for the fighters and the exhausted Midway raiders. It was 9:18 A.M. by the time the last plane was recovered. Then *Kido Butai* raised speed to 30 knots and turned sharply from southeast to north-northeast to head in the general direction of the American fleet.

Crews worked feverishly on all four carriers to prepare thirty-six dive bombers, fifty-four torpedo bombers and their fighter escort for the assault. The Decisive Battle for the Pacific they had dreamed of for years was at hand.

Fletcher had ordered Task Force 16 to attack the enemy carriers as soon as they were definitely located. Spruance had planned to hold off his strike until *Enterprise* and *Hornet* were as close as a hundred miles from the target, but the report of the raid on Midway inspired his chief of staff, Captain Miles Browning, to urge an earlier attack—it might catch the Japanese in the act of refueling their planes.

Spruance was a studious, brainy commander who was aggressive only when he thought it worth the risk. He was the antithesis of the man he had relieved—the ebullient, explosive Halsey—and avoided any publicity ("A shy young thing with a rather sober, earnest face and the innocent disposition of an ingenue"—according to his class book at Annapolis—who would "never hurt anything or anybody except in Line of Duty"). Even on *Enterprise* he was an enigma, a quiet, solitary man who paced the deck interminably for exercise and spent hours alone in his cabin studying charts.

The extra distance added a hazard he ordinarily would not have accepted, but the possibility of catching the Japanese off-guard outweighed the risk. His first important decision was to heed Browning. His second, just as important, was to order every operational plane, except patrol craft, to join in the attack. Sixty-seven dive bombers, twenty fighters and twenty-nine torpedo planes began leaving his two carriers at 7:02 A.M. They would have barely enough fuel to return home. It was no time for caution.

Fletcher, some fifteen miles behind Spruance, didn't start launching from his single carrier for an hour and a half, and it was 9:06 A.M. by the time seventeen dive bombers, six fighters and twelve torpedo planes had left the flight deck of *Yorktown*.

Twelve minutes later Nagumo made his abrupt turn to the north-northeast. While consciously avoiding another Midway-based air strike, he had inadvertently turned away from the 151 American carrier planes trying to find him.

Minutes after the turn, *Hornet*'s dive bombers and fighters reached the point where they were to intercept the Japanese carriers. The leader, Commander Stanhope Ring, saw clouds to his right (Nagumo was behind them) and veered southeast toward Midway—away from *Kido Butai*.

But three groups of lumbering torpedo planes—one from each of the American carriers—were almost directly on target. The first were fifteen unescorted Douglas Devastators from *Hornet*. Their leader, Lieutenant Commander John Waldron, had not followed the dive bombers on to Midway; he had a hunch the Japanese would turn to the east. Waldron was seamy-faced, square-jawed, part Sioux Indian. The night before he had written to his wife: "If I do not come back—well, you and the little girls can know that this squadron struck for the highest objective in naval warfare—'To Sink the Enemy.'" At the end of a message to his men he wrote: "If there is only one plane left to make a final run in, I want that man to go in and get a hit."

He banked east and for several minutes could see nothing. Then in the distance, eight miles away, he made out four carriers in boxlike formation. Twenty-five or thirty Zeros began diving at the Devastators, their cannon exploding. Waldron ignored them. He waggled his wings and slanted down at a carrier full speed, his men trailing behind. A plane tumbled like a bird shot by a hunter.

"Was that a Zero?" asked Waldron above the racket of machine-gun fire from the rear seat. His gunner-radioman, Horace Dobbs, didn't hear. It was a Devastator. Another one plunged down. Still Waldron bore in. As the attackers neared the carrier they were confronted by a wall of harmless-looking black puffs and strings of bright tracers. Another Devastator splashed into the sea. Waldron's left gas tank erupted in flames. Ensign George "Tex" Gay, who was flying at the tail of the formation, saw him stand up and try to get out of the cockpit as the burning plane skimmed the water. All at once a wave caught the undercarriage. It was the end of Waldron and Dobbs.

Still another torpedo plane pinwheeled into the sea—and another—and another. That left Gay and two others. Two explosions. Only Gay was left. He remembered Waldron's instructions for the last plane "to go in and get a hit."

"They got me." It was his radioman, Bob Huntington. Gay turned and saw Huntington's head limp. A bullet dug into Gay's right arm. He had the carrier straight ahead. It turned to starboard and he also swung right. He released a white-nosed torpedo and executed a flipover, skimming ten feet above the carrier's bow. As he started a turning climb he was riddled by Zeros. His Devastator pancaked into the sea. He pulled at the canopy. It was stuck. He tugged. No good. The plane was rapidly filling with water. He gave a yank. The canopy opened and he squirmed out. As he surfaced he thought he heard an explosion—his "pickle" must have got the hit! But like the torpedoes from all the other planes, this one had missed and was settling harmlessly far beyond the carrier.

Within minutes, torpedo planes from *Enterprise* and *Yorktown* also found Nagumo. Fourteen Douglas Devastators from the first carrier attacked without fighter escort. Ten were shot down; four managed to launch their missiles. Then the twelve torpedo planes from *Yorktown* appeared. Their six escorting fighters were swamped by Japanese interceptors, but five torpedoes were released.

One American headed straight for *Akagi*'s bridge. Kusaka ducked as the Devastator roared a few feet over his head and plunged into the sea. Kusaka was shaken by the realization that the American was as determined as any samurai. He silently prayed for him.

In all, nine torpedoes were launched but not a single one found its mark. All that was left of the American air strike was the dive bombers and it looked as if they would not even find the Japanese; already those from *Hornet* had gone on to Midway, and the seventeen from *Yorktown*, under Lieutenant Commander Maxwell Leslie, were miles southeast of the target.

The other thirty-seven dive bombers—they were led by Lieutenant Commander Clarence W. McClusky and came from *Enterprise*—had taken off more than an hour before Leslie. McClusky, like others before him, had missed Nagumo's Striking Force and gone on toward Midway, but finding nothing, turned back north.

At 9:55 A.M. he sighted the white wake of a Japanese destroyer scudding northeast. He hoped it was joining up with the carriers and followed. He heard Captain Browning shout excitedly over the radio telephone, "Attack! Attack!"

"Wilco," McClusky replied, "as soon as I find the bastards." He kept on course for another twenty minutes, found nothing. His fuel was dangerously low but he decided to continue on for another minute. It was 10:20 A.M.

At last all the Japanese torpedo planes were back on the flight decks, along with their refueled fighter escorts. The four carriers turned into the wind in preparation for launching. In a quarter of an hour every plane would be in the air.

At that moment McClusky's thirty-seven Douglas Dauntless dive bombers appeared from the southwest. In addition to his own squadron, McClusky commanded those of Lieutenants Wilmer Earl Gallaher and Richard H. Best. Two carriers were turning into the wind to launch and he ordered Best to attack what looked like the smaller one—it was *Akagi*.

"Earl," he told Gallaher, "you follow me down." They nosed over toward *Kaga*.

Gallaher aimed at a huge Rising Sun, about fifty feet across, painted in blood-red on the flight deck. Ever since the day he saw *Arizona* lie smashed and smoldering in Pearl Harbor he had vowed to go after an enemy carrier. At about 1,800 feet he released his bomb, then pulled up into a steep climb and kicked the Dauntless around. He kept watching his bomb—something he had warned his pilots never to do—tumble closer and closer to the target. It exploded on the after part of the flight deck, and he thought exultantly, *Arizona,* I remember you!

The crew of *Kaga* looked up startled as Dauntlesses began plunging out of the sun. Bombs fell into the sea on both sides. *Kaga* could not be hit; she was charmed. Then in rapid succession four bombs slammed into the after, forward and middle sections of the flight deck. *Kaga* erupted with fires.

On the flagship, Kusaka was so transfixed by *Kaga*'s fate that he didn't notice dive bombers streaking for his own ship. He heard an eerie whistle and looked up. Three bombs, dropping so close and straight that they seemed to be connected by a wire, were coming at him. All three hit the line of planes preparing to take off, and erupted in a single shattering explosion. The ship trembled as in an earthquake. The amidship elevator was twisted grotesquely. Planes upended rakishly and burst into flames. Their bombs and torpedoes began to explode one by one, driving away fire-control parties. The blaze spread to fuel and munition reserves carelessly stacked on deck. These too exploded. Huge chunks were torn out of the flight deck. The bridge shook like a tree house in a hurricane.

Akagi was helpless. Flames licked the glass windows of the bridge. Above the din, Kusaka shouted to Nagumo, "We must move to another ship!" Nagumo refused. Kusaka said the ship could no longer steer and had no communications.

Nagumo kept saying, "We are all right," over and over again.

Thousands of gallons of burning fuel cascaded into the lower decks, and torpedoes stored in the hangars began detonating. Blasts of fire shot out through the sides of the ship like a huge blowtorch. Nagumo still refused to leave his position at the compass. Captain Taijiro Aoki, skipper of the carrier, shouted that he alone would be responsible for the ship. "You and your staff can do nothing, so please transfer to another ship!"

Nagumo ignored him. Kusaka began reprimanding his superior; he was commander of the entire Striking Force, not the captain of a single ship. Finally Nagumo nodded but it seemed to be too late. The bridge was almost surrounded by fire. "Break the window!" Kusaka hollered to the youthful flag secretary. Glass shattered. Two ropes were lowered forty-five feet to the deck. Kusaka pushed Nagumo out first and the little admiral clambered down nimbly. The heavyset Kusaka went next, but he could not control his descent. The rope burned through his hands as he dropped to the deck. He landed in a heap, stunned. He had no left shoe. His hands were raw and both ankles were badly sprained but he felt no pain. He looked for a path through the flames. Machine-gun bullets, ignited by the heat, ricocheted off the carrier's island. Far away he heard staff officers calling to hurry and he hobbled over the hot deck through flames toward the voices.

Moments after McClusky discovered *Kido Butai*, so did Leslie, the commander of the seventeen dive bombers from *Yorktown*. He had noticed smoke smudges on the horizon and banked northwest. Through clouds he caught a glimpse of *Hiryu* and *Soryu*. He patted his head in signal and pushed over in a steep dive on the latter.

Within half an hour *Soryu* was engulfed in flames. At 10:45 A.M. her skipper, Captain Ryusaku Yanagimoto, ordered Abandon Ship but refused to leave himself. A Navy wrestling champion, Chief Petty Officer Abe, climbed up to the bridge. "I have come on behalf of all your men to take you to safety," he said. The captain turned away. Sword in hand, he began singing "Kimigayo," the national anthem.

In minutes, fifty-four American planes had fatally damaged three carriers. Only *Hiryu* was left. The last chance for victory depended on Rear Admiral Tamon Yamaguchi, the Princeton man who not long before had wrestled with Nagumo. At 10:40 A.M. six fighters and eighteen dive bombers had left *Hiryu* to search out an enemy carrier. They would not have found it by themselves. Their guides were Leslie's dive bombers, who unwittingly led them all the way to Fletcher's flagship. *Yorktown* fighters ripped into the attacking Japanese, but half a dozen managed to break free and drop their

385

bombs. Three of these tore into the carrier, which still showed scars from the Battle of the Coral Sea. Two boilers were knocked out, bringing the burning ship to a standstill at 12:30 P.M. Within an hour, however, damage-control parties had subdued the flames and got the carrier under way. By that time another wave from *Hiryu* was forty miles away. Ten Nakajima torpedo planes came at *Yorktown*. While their six-fighter escort tied up the carrier's interceptors, the Nakajimas slipped under the fighter defense, and despite heavy antiaircraft fire sent two torpedoes into *Yorktown*. The damage was severe and the ship listed so badly by 3 P.M. that Captain Elliott Buckmaster ordered Abandon Ship.

This left only two American carriers, both commanded by Spruance. At 3:30 he ordered dive bombers to make their second strike. Under Lieutenant Gallaher—McClusky had been wounded—twenty-four unescorted dive bombers headed for *Hiryu*. Spruance radioed Fletcher, who had transferred to the cruiser *Astoria*, for further instructions. The answer was: "None." From now on the battle was in Spruance's hands.

5.

Aboard *Yamato*, Yamamoto was still four hundred miles to the west when he received word at 10:30 A.M. that *Akagi* was on fire. He didn't appear troubled by the news. Twenty minutes later the radio room sent up a full report from Nagumo:

> FIRES RAGING ABOARD KAGA, SORYU AND AKAGI RESULTING FROM ATTACKS BY ENEMY CARRIERS AND LAND-BASED PLANES. WE PLAN TO HAVE HIRYU ENGAGE ENEMY CARRIERS. WE ARE TEMPORARILY WITHDRAWING TO THE NORTH TO ASSEMBLE OUR FORCES.

Yamamoto still seemed unperturbed. As if nothing had happened, he started a game of chess with Watanabe. Further information elicited a noncommittal "Ah so." Finally, ninety minutes after getting the first report, he ordered the invasion transports to retire, and the two light carirers which had launched a diversionary bomb attack on Dutch Harbor the previous day to head toward Midway and assist Nagumo. His own powerful Main Force was to continue steaming east full speed while Vice Admiral Kondo, who was covering the transports, brought his powerful fleet, including the carrier

Zuiho, up from the south. From three directions formidable new forces were converging on Midway. The Decisive Battle was still to be fought.

The surviving crews returning to *Hiryu* from the second attack on *Yorktown* reported that they had destroyed two carriers, and Yamaguchi ordered a third strike. But before the first plane could be rolled into position, a lookout shouted, "Enemy dive bombers!" To the southwest a string of planes struck out of the sinking sun like a snake. It was terrifying. The crew looked up helplessly as Gallaher's twenty-four dive bombers swooped in. Four bombs smashed around the bridge. Fires spread rapidly from plane to plane until the flight deck was a holocaust.

"Look at that bastard burn!" Gallaher muttered over his radio.

Nagumo and Kusaka were aboard a new flagship, the light cruiser *Nagara*. With all four carriers on fire and out of action, Kusaka still wanted to attack. He couldn't put any weight on his injured ankles and ordered a sailor to carry him piggyback up to the bridge. He urged Nagumo to mount a night attack with destroyers, cruisers and battleships.

This was Nagumo's element—a surface fight. "Now it will be my battle," he said. The remnants of the once powerful *Kido Butai* began to stalk the Americans.

Spruance guessed the Japanese intentions, and cautious though he was, was tempted to accept the challenge, then remembered Nimitz' "calculated risk" instructions. This time the risk was too great. The Japanese commander was probably hoping for a showdown, and his crews were trained night fighters. Spruance turned back east.

The sea northwest of Midway was a flaming graveyard. *Soryu* tilted. On nearby destroyers her agonized survivors watched the ungainly carrier disappear at 7:13 P.M. with a furious hissing as water enveloped the flames. With her went 718 trapped or dead men and one who had lashed himself to the bridge, Captain Yanagimoto. A muffled underwater explosion shook the surrounding ships. Forty miles to the south *Kaga*, a mass of flames, was racked by two explosions. In minutes the battered carrier and eight hundred of her crew were swallowed up by the sea.

For several hours Nagumo searched the dark sea but could not locate the enemy. It was obvious there would be no night battle. He summoned his staff and ordered a general withdrawal to the northwest. Captain Oishi, who had helped plan the Pearl Harbor attack, was in a state bordering hysteria. He searched out Kusaka in the officers' infirmary. "We started the war and we are responsible for this disaster," he said. "We should all commit hara-kiri!" He added that the entire staff agreed with him and he wanted Kusaka to tell Nagumo.

"*Bakayaro!*" said Kusaka. "Assemble all the other idiots in the staff room." He was carried down the passageway in his white hospital gown to confront the staff. "You men cheer when the battle is successful. When it isn't, you threaten hara-kiri. You're acting like hysterical women." They faced a long war and he forbade "such nonsense."

Kusaka had himself transferred to Nagumo's cabin. "Are you too planning suicide?" he asked and began lecturing the little admiral on his duty to Emperor and nation. Nagumo admitted that he could see his point but questioned its application to "the commander of a fleet." Kusaka reacted so vehemently at this that Nagumo relented and assured him he would do nothing rash, adding characteristically, *"Daijobu"*— "Don't worry."

On *Yamato,* Yamamoto's staff was desperately looking for some way to inflict serious damage on the enemy and compensate for the loss of four carriers. Spruance had not risen to the bait and the most impractical schemes were considered. Captain Kuroshima, for example, suggested that they shell Midway with all battleships.

Chief of Staff Ugaki coldly remarked that this was "stupidity." The battleships would be sunk by air and submarine attacks before they could move in close enough to use their guns. Furthermore, another air strike should be postponed until the Aleutian force joined them. "But even if that proves impossible and we must accept defeat, we will not have lost the war. There are still eight carriers in the Combined Fleet. We should not lose heart. In battle as in chess, it is the fool who lets himself be led into a reckless move out of desperation."

"How can we apologize to the Emperor for this defeat?" asked one staff officer.

Yamamoto had been listening quietly. "I am the only one who must apologize to His Majesty," he said and instructed Watanabe to send orders to Kondo and Nagumo to withdraw. Choked with emotion, Watanabe sat down to write out the distasteful orders and managed to compose them without using the word "withdraw."

The remnants of *Kido Butai* began to turn back, but the

fires on both *Hiryu* and *Akagi* were raging out of control. *Akagi*'s captain requested permission to scuttle her. The idea was unthinkable to most of Yamamoto's staff. Ugaki called them "old women," but Kuroshima argued that the Americans would seize the ship and "exhibit it in San Francisco as a museum." There were tears in Yamamoto's eyes. Years before, he had skippered the carrier. He said evenly, "Have destroyers torpedo *Akagi*."

The pragmatic Ugaki went off and wrote in his diary: "Emotion must not be mixed with reason." He was more concerned with the fact that the enemy had somehow been forewarned about the Midway operation. Perhaps an American submarine had discovered Nagumo en route or a Russian ship had sighted the Aleutian force. Either that or the fleet code itself had been broken.

Hiryu's skipper, Captain Tomeo Kaku, didn't have to radio Combined Fleet for permission to scuttle. Admiral Yamaguchi, who had commanded the two light carriers from *Hiryu,* took on the responsibility and ordered the destroyer *Kazagumo* to sink the flaming wreck. At 2:30 A.M., on June 5, Yamaguchi summoned the crew topside and told the eight hundred survivors that he alone was responsible for the loss of both *Hiryu* and *Soryu*. "I shall remain on board to the end. I command all of you to leave the ship and continue your loyal service to His Majesty." They all faced the Imperial Palace. The admiral led them in three cheers for the Emperor.

Yamaguchi gave his senior staff officer, Commander Seiroku Ito, his last message. It was to Nagumo, his wrestling antagonist, and typically, called for "a stronger Japanese Navy—and revenge." The staff drank a silent toast in water. Yamaguchi handed Ito his black deck cap and asked him to give it to Mrs. Yamaguchi. Then he turned to Captain Kaku, who would share his fate, and said, "There is such a beautiful moon tonight. Shall we watch it as we sink?"

Even Admiral Kondo's fleet was not to escape intact. Two heavy cruisers, *Mogami* and *Mikuma,* victims of a night collision, lagged so far behind the retiring forces that Spruance's planes were able to catch up with them early on June 6. *Mikuma* was sunk but *Mogami,* though hit six times, limped safely off.

The only real success won by the Japanese came too late to influence the battle. That same day Lieutenant Commander Yahachi Tanabe sighted the crippled *Yorktown* from the bridge of *I-168*. The submarine slipped under the ring of covering destroyers and launched two torpedoes into the carrier and one into the destroyer *Hammann*. The destroyer went down in four minutes, but *Yorktown,* veteran of the first two carrier battles in history, died hard. She sank the following day just after dawn with all battle flags flying.

It was small compensation for the loss of four carriers and the flower of the Japanese naval air force. One of the greatest sea battles of all time was at last over and America had gained control of the Pacific. The outcome had been determined by Japanese overconfidence, a code broken by a few men in a basement, and the resolution of men like Waldron, McClusky and Gallaher. In every battle luck plays a part. At Midway it went against the Japanese; the half-hour delay of the *Tone,* search plane led to catastrophe. In war there is a time for caution and a time for boldness. Yamamoto conceived the Midway operation too recklessly and his commander fought it too carefully. On the other hand, Spruance was bold at the right time—by launching his strike early and with all available planes—and prudent when he should be—by refusing to accept Nagumo's challenge for a night encounter. Spruance, however, would not have had his chance but for the wisdom of a man more than a thousand miles from the battle area; Chester Nimitz had made all the right decisions before a shot was fired.

"The Navy has made a great mistake," General Moritake Tanabe whispered to Tojo at a party for members of the German and Italian embassies.

"At Midway?" asked the tight-lipped Tojo.

"Yes, they have lost four carriers."

Tojo couldn't resist remarking that the Navy had gone into the operation against the advice of the Army, then said, "The news must not leak out. Keep it a complete secret."

The following day Tojo reported to the Emperor but said not a word about Midway.* Later at a restricted session of

---

*The Emperor was usually apprised of the performance of his fighting forces; in fact, there was a "hot line" to his military aide which was open at all hours in case important news was received by Army Headquarters in the middle of the night. It is safe to say that the Emperor's information about Japanese fortunes of war was as accurate as Roosevelt's or Churchill's about their own, and much better than Hitler's on the German battles. The announcement about the defeat at Midway was probably withheld from His Majesty at this time because of shock and in anticipation of confirmed details.

Imperial Headquarters, the Prime Minister recommended that attention be diverted from the naval debacle by publicizing the Aleutian operation. The force which had steamed toward Midway to help Admiral Nagumo had been ordered to return north; on June 7 the small but strategic islands of Attu and Kiska were occupied without a casualty.

In America, Midway was already a household word and the battle was celebrated as the turning point of the war in the Pacific. Nimitz himself, though some criticized his considered words as premature, said in his communiqué of June 6:

Pearl Harbor has now been partially avenged. Vengeance will not be complete until Japanese sea power is reduced to impotence. We have made substantial progress in that direction. Perhaps we will be forgiven if we claim that we are about midway to that objective.

On June 7 the Chicago *Tribune* jeopardized the secret that had made victory possible—the breaking of the Japanese fleet code. The strength of the Japanese forces at Midway, it revealed, was well known in American naval circles several days before the battle began. The Navy, upon learning of "the gathering of the powerful Japanese units soon after they put forth from their bases," had guessed that "Dutch Harbor and Midway Island might be targets."

The dispatch carried no byline, but it had been sent from the Pacific by war correspondent Stanley Johnston. It went on to describe the composition of the Japanese forces in detail, and named the four carriers of the Striking Force and the four light cruisers supporting the Invasion Force. The Navy feared that the release of such accurate information would alert the Japanese to the fact that their code had been broken.

The fear was groundless; the Japanese Navy, convinced their fleet code was unbreakable, attributed the rout at Midway to overconfidence. Kusaka held himself responsible for the debacle. He should not have allowed Genda to send out so few search planes. On June 9, still in winter uniform, he was rolled up in a bamboo mat, lowered in a cutter and taken alongside *Yamato*. He was picked up like a parcel and set on the deck. He gave Yamamoto and his staff a personal report of the battle, adding a request that the Navy, which occasionally issued false communiqués, tell the people the whole truth, since this was a war involving every citizen.

Once they were alone, Kusaka told Yamamoto that *Kido Butai* would take all the blame for the defeat. "If you want someone to commit hara-kiri as a token of responsibility, let me do it." But he said that he really hoped instead to be Nagumo's chief of staff with a new carrier force that could avenge Midway. "I would like you to give it consideration."

"I understand," Yamamoto answered huskily. Kusaka was excused and Yamamoto took to his bed with severe stomach pains. The chief surgeon diagnosed it as "roundworm" but Steward Omi was sure it had been caused by the disastrous events of June 4.

In Japan, Tojo's orders to conceal the defeat were carried out. Survivors of the sunken ships were isolated, and the truth about Midway was withheld from leading officials as well as the public. Imperial Headquarters announced on June 10 that Japan had at last "secured supreme power in the Pacific" and that the war had been "indeed determined in one battle." To celebrate the victory the enthusiastic people of Tokyo staged a flag procession and a lantern parade.

In Tennessee, Ensign Kazuo Sakamaki, the only survivor of the midget submarine attack on Pearl Harbor and for some time the sole Japanese prisoner of war, saw no reason to celebrate. He believed what he read about Midway in American newspapers. On his long journey to Tennessee he had seen countless factories and endless fields and he knew that tiny Japan had yet to feel the full might of the United States. Midway was just the beginning of the end of Japan's hope of conquest.

PART FOUR

Isle of Death

14   **Operation Shoestring**

1.

Gen Nishino was a slight man of thirty-seven, about five feet tall. He looked frail and sensitive—and was—but had already survived arduous months in China reporting that disjointed war for his newspaper, the *Mainichi*. Several months after Pearl Harbor he was ordered to cover the campaign in the south. His greatest concern was not for his life but for the $25,000 worth of yen he would be carrying for expenses. His city editor wished him bon voyage, gave him an amulet for good luck and said, "Don't get killed."

Nishino, who headed a team of eight newsmen, set sail for Davao, the main port of southern Mindanao, but it was not until June 7, a week after their arrival, that he learned his group was going to ship out with the 17th Army for New Caledonia (this was part of the operation to cut off Australia). However, the Nishino party never got there. Three days later they were caught up in the excitement that swept the Japanese Empire when the victory at Midway was announced. They joined officers in the dining room of their hotel for an impromptu celebration. Even a severe earthquake failed to dampen the enthusiasm. One young officer joked that San Francisco was the center of the quake and all America had collapsed.

Nishino couldn't shake a nagging doubt after reading newspaper accounts of the battle; they were suspiciously vague. He left the party and went up to his room, where there was a shortwave radio. He turned the dial slowly until he heard a Strauss waltz; then a woman's voice announced that this was Radio San Francisco and that America had won a tremendous naval victory. It seemed like the usual propaganda until the newscaster confidently listed details of the various units involved at Midway and named the four Japanese carriers that had been sunk.

Nishino couldn't escape the feeling that this was the truth. Yamamoto had been crushed. Down below he could hear the jubilant clink of beer bottles above the din and felt a wave of pity for the young officers so innocently celebrating a spurious triumph. He thought of telling them what he had heard but knew it would be a mistake. They wouldn't believe him and he'd be arrested by the *kempeitai*.

His suspicions were finally confirmed two months later when the 17th Army and the *Mainichi* group set off—not for New Caledonia but for an island in the Solomons that didn't appear on their maps. Its name was Gadarukanaru.

In English it was called Guadalcanal and American interest in this remote island evolved from a bitter debate between the Army and the Navy over which should have the dominant role in the Pacific. In March two separate commands had been set up by the Joint Chiefs of Staff. From Melbourne, Douglas MacArthur commanded the Southwest Pacific Area, comprising the Philippines, the South China Sea, the Gulf of Siam, most of the Netherlands East Indies, Australia *and* the Solomons. The Pacific Ocean Areas—the rest of the Pacific, including the Marshalls, the Carolines and the Marianas—were under the control of Admiral Nimitz in Pearl Harbor. Out of this divided command, from the very first, came almost as much diffused effort and conflict as those existing in Tokyo.

MacArthur warned time and again that the Japanese were converging most of their power in *his* area and that there would be a disaster unless he got more men and matériel than Nimitz. Then came Midway and MacArthur saw it as an opportunity for quick victories. He radioed Washington an optimistic plan: he would overrun New Ireland and New Britain in a few weeks, "forcing the enemy back to his base at Truk." Besides his own three infantry divisions MacArthur would need "one division trained and completely equipped for amphibious operations and a task force including two carriers."

General Marshall, Army Chief of Staff, was impressed enough to write Fleet Admiral Ernest J. King, his opposite number, an urgent request to lend MacArthur several Marine units and two or three carriers. But before this letter could be delivered, Marshall received one from King curtly disposing of the MacArthur plan. The Navy was already considering operations against the same objectives and they would be "primarily of a naval and amphibious character supported and followed by forces operating from Australia." In other words, the Navy would do the job with MacArthur's assistance.

This, of course, was completely insupportable to MacArthur. He and he alone should lead the assault, since it lay within his domain. The Navy agreed that one man should be in charge, but not a general; a landlubber might place their precious carriers in jeopardy in the dangerous waters around the Solomons.

Marshall backed MacArthur and the argument stretched on until King reached the end of his patience. He warned Marshall that he was going to start an offensive "even if no support of Army forces in the Southwest Pacific is available." The Army Chief of Staff's first impulse was to answer in kind, but he decided to hold off a reply until he regained his composure.

Not so MacArthur. He lost his temper and radioed Washington:

IT IS QUITE EVIDENT IN REVIEWING THE WHOLE SITUATION THAT NAVY CONTEMPLATES ASSUMING GENERAL COMMAND CONTROL OF ALL OPERATIONS IN THE PACIFIC THEATER, THE ROLE OF THE ARMY BEING SUBSIDIARY AND CONSISTING LARGELY OF PLACING ITS FORCES AT THE DISPOSAL AND UNDER THE COMMAND OF NAVY OR MARINE OFFICERS. . . .

It was, he charged, all part of a master plan for "the complete absorption of the national defense function by the Navy" which he had "accidentally" uncovered when he was Chief of Staff.

. . . BY USING ARMY TROOPS TO GARRISON THE ISLANDS OF THE PACIFIC UNDER NAVY COMMAND, THE NAVY RETAINS MARINE FORCES ALWAYS AVAILABLE, GIVING THEM INHERENTLY AN ARMY OF THEIR OWN AND SERVING AS THE REAL BASES OF THEIR PLANS BY VIRTUE OF HAVING THE MOST READILY AVAILABLE UNITS FOR OFFENSIVE ACTION.

While Marshall agreed in spirit with MacArthur, he realized that the best solution was a fair compromise. He asked King to meet him and work out the problem amicably. They sat down face to face, and it was a measure of King's own maturity that the gruff and bleak admiral was equally willing to make concessions. In many respects Marshall found it easier to deal with King than with MacArthur, who was "supersensitive about everything" and "thought everybody had ulterior motives about everything."*

During the next few days the men hammered out a general plan for the ultimate objective—seizure of the New Britain–New Guinea area—by dividing the offensive into three separate parts. Task One, under Nimitz, was the assault about August 1 on the Japanese seaplane base at Tulagi, the tiny Solomon island twenty miles north of Guadalcanal, while MacArthur would be responsible for Tasks Two and Three, the seizure of the rest of the Solomons, the northwest coast of New Guinea, and the key base of Rabaul on New Britain.

The recent fall of Tobruk to Rommel had already brought a sense of impending disaster to Washington. Then on July 2—the same day the operation in the Pacific was approved by the Joint Chiefs of Staff—two alarming bulletins arrived: Sevastopol, in the Crimea, had collapsed, and in North Africa the British Eighth Army had been forced to retreat to the gates of Alexandria. What if the German forces in Russia broke through to the Caucasus and linked up with Rommel? Then it would only be a question of time before an even more ominous link-up with the Japanese. Added to all that was the rising toll of Allied merchant shipping losses in the Atlantic. In June alone, more than 627,000 tons had been sunk and the rate was rising.

It was, thought Marshall, "a very black hour."

The Pacific theater alone gave the Allies grounds for optimism. Hopes centered on the plan to seize Tulagi, which the Japanese had occupied in May. As yet the island of Guadalcanal was of incidental interest to the planners, and the officer Nimitz had placed in charge of Task One, Vice Admiral Robert L. Ghormley, first heard of the possibility of attacking it on July 7 when he was in Melbourne conferring with MacArthur. The information came in a radiogram from Nimitz revealing that the Japanese were building a small airfield on Guadalcanal and suggesting that it be taken simultaneously with Tulagi.

Both MacArthur and Ghormley agreed in principle, but both expressed their objections to the immediate launching of Task One; there was a single amphibious division, not enough

---

*The quotes came from a postwar interview between Marshall and his official biographer, Forrest Pogue. "With Chennault in China and MacArthur in the Southwest Pacific," Marshall reminisced wryly, "I sure had a combination of temperament."

shipping and a dangerous scarcity of planes. Moreover, the carriers of the Amphibious Force would have to remain too long in the Guadalcanal-Tulagi area far beyond the range of Allied land-based air protection and at the mercy of Japanese land-based aircraft. The Joint Chiefs ignored their separate recommendations and ordered the invasion to take place as scheduled; only by taking such prompt action could the Americans capitalize on the victory at Midway and seize the initiative in the Pacific. The operation was given a symbolic name, Watchtower.

Guadalcanal was Japan's southernmost outpost, significant merely as a base for any naval action in the Solomon area. It was a quiet, peaceful island 10 degrees below the equator, ninety-two miles long and thirty-three miles wide, about twice the size of Long Island. From the air it looked like a tropical paradise of lush green mountains, forested shores and colorful coral reefs. In reality it was paradise lost, a study in dramatic contrasts—peaks, barren hills and dense dark-green jungles, white cockatoos and ferocious white ants, myna birds and malarial mosquitoes; bone-chilling torrential rains and insufferably hot, dusty plains. It was an island of bananas, limes, papayas—and crocodiles, giant lizards, fungus infections, poisonous spiders, leeches and scorpions. "If I were a king," author Jack London once said, "the worst punishment I could inflict on my enemies would be to banish them to the Solomons."

A series of blue-green, jagged, quiescent volcanoes towering as high as 8,000 feet ran down the island like a backbone, and the only possible place for military operations was the narrow strip of rolling hills and plains running along the north coast. And even this area was forbidding, cut by many rivers and by ridges with stretches of razor-sharp grass.

In late 1567 a young Spaniard, Don Alvaro de Mendaña, set sail from Peru to find King Solomon's gold mines and after eleven weeks came upon a verdant group of islands. He named them the Solomons but they contained so little gold and were so inaccessible that there were few visitors in the centuries to follow.

The natives—woolly-headed, coal-black Melanesians—paid little attention to those who did come. They preferred to carry on their own bloody wars and headhunting to wiping out the pale-skinned intruders. They listened politely to missionaries, and it wasn't until 1896 that the first important confrontation between East and West occurred. In that year the Albatros Expedition, sponsored by the Geographical Society of Vienna, landed on Guadalcanal and marched across the plains and foothills to mile-high Mount Tatuve. The eighteen Austrians planned to scale it and ignored the natives' warnings that everyone on the island would die if any man "conquered" the mountain of their Great Spirit. The Austrian leader, the eminent geologist Heinrich Foullon von Norbeeck, replied that they had come a long way to climb Tatuve and were going to do it. The next morning while the Austrians breakfasted, a great number of natives quietly surrounded them but felt such pity for those who were about to die that they let them finish their meal before they attacked. The Austrians, however, fought so desperately that they drove off the natives, at a cost of six dead, including their intrepid leader. Thus ended the first battle of Guadalcanal.

At the time of Pearl Harbor the Solomons were an Australian mandate. Its capital on Tulagi consisted of a small hotel, a wireless station, a street of shops and a few neat bungalows for officials. Neighboring Guadalcanal couldn't claim that much civilization—all it had were several Catholic missions, a few coconut plantations and a Burns Philp trading station. A single trail led along the north coast through the plantations, but inland there were only native footpaths and it was the rare white man who dared follow them.

One of these was District Officer Martin Clemens, a former Cambridge athlete of renown, dedicated to keeping peace among the natives, who sometimes reverted to savage customs. Soon after the Japanese invasion he and four other men were stationed at various places on Guadalcanal as coastwatchers for the Royal Australian Navy. Theye were to radio reports on Japanese troop-ship and plane movements to the Directorate of Naval Intelligence in Australia. Like most of the other coastwatchers in the Solomons and Bismarcks, they were planters or civil servants who had lived for years in the area, and it was these intrepid men who had alerted Washington of the enemy build-up on the island. They continued to keep close watch on the enemy: there were 2,230 Japanese on the island, mostly laborers and engineers, and they had almost finished a primitive airfield for the Navy on the north coast.

The overconfidence of the Japanese Navy that had led to Midway was not diminished by the defeat; the Navy high command did not expect a counteroffensive in the Pacific for months. Its false sense of security was not shared by Lieutenant Commander Haruki Itoh of the Naval Intelligence Center in Tokyo. Late in July his unit picked up two new Allied call signs in the southwest Pacific. Since both stations operated on the commander-in-chief circuit (4205 kc series) and both communicated directly with Pearl Harbor, Itoh deduced that either could be headquarters for a new enemy task force. On August 1 radio direction finders located one station in Nouméa, New Caledonia, and the other near Melbourne. The first, guessed Itoh, was the headquarters for Admiral Ghormley and the second the base of a British or Australian force. Consequently, he and his staff concluded that the Allies were about to start an offensive on the Solomons or New Guinea. An urgent warning was radioed to Truk and Rabaul, but it was ignored in both places.

2.

Though Ghormley was in nominal command of Operation Watchtower, he could not exercise tactical control from Nouméa, so he left this to Vice Admiral Frank Jack Fletcher, veteran of Coral Sea and Midway. Fletcher, as well as those who would have to carry out the assault, was not enthusiastic about Watchtower because of the meager forces available and the necessarily hasty preparations. It was nicknamed "Operation Shoestring."

On July 26 Fletcher summoned all unit commanders of the Expeditionary Force to a rendezvous in the South Pacific four hundred miles south of Fiji. The meeting on Fletcher's flagship, *Saratoga,* opened on a note of comedy. A garbage chute inadvertently dumped milk over an admiral climbing aboard. At the conference in the wardroom, Major General Alexander A. ("Archie") Vandegrift, the red-cheeked commander of the seventeen thousand Marines who would take Tulagi and Guadalcanal, found Fletcher lacking in "knowledge of or interest in the forthcoming operation." Fletcher, who looked "nervous and tired," openly discussed his doubt about the successful outcome of Watchtower. He was even more disheartened when he learned that it would take five days to disembark Vandegrift's troops on Guadalcanal. Fletcher was the one flag officer present who had experienced the devastation of Japanese air attacks (he had lost *Lexington* at Coral Sea and *Yorktown* at Midway) and he blanched at the idea of exposing his three flattops (there was but one other heavy carrier in the Pacific) to such peril.

"Gentlemen," he said, "in view of the risks of exposure to land-based air, I cannot keep the carriers in the area for more than forty-eight hours after the [initial] landing."

Vandegrift controlled his temper; five days of air cover was cutting it dangerously thin. Rear Admiral Richmond Kelly Turner, commander of the Amphibious Force, whose tongue was as sharp and whose nature was as crusty as King's, concurred. But Fletcher's sole concern was the possible end of American carriers in the Pacific. They would leave on D-day plus 3—and that was final.

Vandegrift was furious as he left the ship and his mood was not improved by a botched landing rehearsal in the Fijis. It was, he thought dejectedly, a complete bust, and he could only console himself that "a poor rehearsal traditionally meant a good show."

At dusk on August 6 Admiral Turner's Amphibious Force approached the Solomons from the south. Four transports and four destroyer-transports were bound for little Tulagi while fifteen transports and cargo transports headed for Guadalcanal. They were escorted by eight cruisers (three of them Australian) and a destroyer screen. One hundred miles to the south lurked the Air Support Force: three carriers, a battleship, five heavy cruisers, sixteen destroyers and three bombers.

The invasion fleet—a total of eighty-two ships—probed north at 12 knots through a light haze. On the transports, engineers checked engines on landing craft as boatswain's mates tested falls and davits. The air was sticky and it took little movement to bring on streams of sweat. The order Darken Ships went out. In the sleeping quarters men lolled on bunks fully clad, playing cards, reading, or writing letters home. The mess halls were jammed with Marines listening to the roar of jukeboxes and watching buddies jitterbug alone or with partners. On *American Legion* the man who would lead the first unit ashore at Guadalcanal, Colonel Le Roy P. Hunt, was entertaining his officers with a one-man show. A bemedaled veteran of World War I—wounded and gassed—he clogged away to his own vocal accompaniment of "I Want a Girl Just Like the Girl That Married Dear Old Dad."

General Vandegrift was at the rail of Turner's flagship, *McCawley,* a transport known as the "Wacky Mac," trying to see through the darkness. He was in good spirits despite the "bleak" prospects. The invasion could be what Wellington called Waterloo—a "near-run thing." They were going in with little and without knowing how strong the enemy was. He pushed away from the rail and groped his way back to his stifling little cabin to finish a letter home:

Tomorrow morning at dawn we land in the first major offensive of this war. Our plans have been made and God grant that our judgment has been sound. . . . Whatever happens you'll know that I did my best. Let us hope that best will be enough.

By midnight the men who would have to make the first American landing of the war were in their bunks—sleeping or trying to sleep. Two hours later lookouts sighted a black pyramid in the distance. It was Savo, a small volcanic island lying north just off the western end of Guadalcanal. The haze had lifted and the ships of the Amphibious Force, still undetected, slipped into calm waters. At two-forty a message was relayed to the flagship that Cape Esperance, at the tip of Guadalcanal, was thirteen miles away. The transport groups separated, those bound for Tulagi continuing north beyond Savo and the rest making a sharp right turn into the channel between Savo and Cape Esperance. The still waters gave the men on watch "the creeps." The land breeze, usually welcome after weeks at sea, was rank with the stench of swamp and jungle.

At three o'clock reveille sounded on *McCawley*. Vandegrift ate breakfast, and as the eastern horizon grew bright, returned to the deck. There was no sign of the enemy. Was it some trap? The transports edged toward their destinations: Beach Blue on Tulagi, and Beach Red, located near the center of the north coast of Guadalcanal, just three miles from the almost completed airfield.

Around six-fifteen three cruisers and four destroyers belched fire in unison. Standing on the bridge of *American Legion*, correspondent Richard Tregaskis watched "the red pencil-lines of shells arching through the sky" toward Guadalcanal. Two minutes later, through the din, he could distinguish another roar, more distant. A cruiser and two destroyers were flinging shells at Tulagi.

There was still no movement along either Beach Red or Blue. The Japanese apparently had been caught completely off-guard. Within thirty minutes all transports were in position. Dive bombers and fighters from the three carriers appeared overhead and began strafing the beaches and bombing-target areas. They were met with desultory antiaircraft fire.

"Land the landing force!" intoned the loudspeakers.

On the transports Marines lined up at debarkation stations. Men who had been raucous were mute. A few joked and several uttered the usual "Well, this is it." The 36-foot personnel landing craft were let down by hand. Booms gently lowered the 45- and 56-foot cargo craft while Marines in green dungarees—rifles slung over backs, canteens bulging from hips, heavy packs filled with everything from head nets to fend off mosquitoes to personal mementos—clambered down debarkation nets that slammed into the ships' sides with each gentle roll.

At Tulagi, Marines scrambled ashore but saw no one. It was as if the island were uninhabited. At eight-fifteen their commander signaled: LANDING SUCCESSFUL NO OPPOSITION. An hour later the first boat grounded off Beach Red on Guadalcanal and the men dropped into the warm shallow water. Everyone expected a withering blast, but as they crossed the bare beaches and plunged into the jungle, not a shot was fired at them.

From *McCawley*, Vandegrift was scanning 1,500-foot Mount Austen, which reared up behind the airfield. A plantation manager had called it "a hill only a couple of miles from the coast" but it looked like Mount Hood and was much farther inland. Was all the information so inaccurate? His men were held up only by the humid heat and a rain forest. Dripping with perspiration, often with no scouts ahead or flankers on either side, they blundered forward. Fortunately they met no enemy. The bombardment had driven almost all the Japanese back into the hills.

Their superiors in Rabaul had heard about the invasion before the first shell fell. The radio operator at Tulagi signaled: LARGE FORCE OF SHIPS, UNKNOWN NUMBER OR TYPES, ENTERING THE SOUND. WHAT CAN THEY BE? It was obviously a hit-and-run raid, but Rear Admiral Sadayoshi Yamada, commander of the 25th Air Flotilla, sent out long-range search planes to investigate. Before they could report, another message came in from Tulagi—the last: ENEMY FORCES OVERWHELMING. WE WILL DEFEND OUR POSTS TO THE DEATH, PRAYING FOR ETERNAL VICTORY.

Yamada summoned his squadron leaders and informed them that the scheduled attack on New Guinea was canceled; instead they were to hit the Guadalcanal area at once with every medium bomber, dive bomber and fighter that could get into the air. Tadashi Nakajima, commander of the fighters, protested. Guadalcanal was almost six hundred miles to the southeast and he would lose at least half his planes. The most experienced pilots alone could survive a mission of that range. The two men argued vehemently until Nakajima agreed to send eighteen planes.

He told his men they were going to fly the longest fighter operation in history. "Stick to your orders, and above all, don't fly recklessly or waste your fuel." The pilots waited in their Zeros until the twin-engine bombers—twenty-seven in all—roared down the runways. Nakajima signaled his men and guided his own tiny fighter down a narrow strip covered with a layer of dust and ash from the active volcano rising in the background. Some days its violent eruptions threw rocks high into the air threatening the planes on the field, but today all that issued from the cone was a stream of smoke.

The bombers swept low over Bougainville on their way to Guadalcanal. A planter named Mason counted them and radioed Australia on the "X" frequency for emergency traffic: TWENTY-SEVEN BOMBERS HEADED SOUTHEAST. It was picked up by a number of stations, including Port Moresby, which relayed it to Townsville, Australia, and from there to the powerful transoceanic station at Pearl Harbor. Within minutes every American ship off Guadalcanal and Tulagi was ready.

As the bombers neared their targets, the fighters caught up with them. Saburo Sakai, who had already shot down fifty-six planes, including Colin Kelly's Flying Fortress, saw an awesome sight spread out before him—at least seventy enemy ships clustered off the beaches. The bombers swung around for their runs. All at once half a dozen enemy fighters appeared high above in the sun. They were new to Sakai, chubbier than any other American fighter he'd seen: they must be the Grumman Wildcats, a type reportedly in the area.

The carrier-based Wildcats swept toward the bombers which were dumping their loads on ships near Savo Island. Sakai watched in frustration as the bombs fell around the ships throwing up harmless geysers of water. How stupid to expect to hit moving ships from four miles up! Why hadn't they been armed with torpedoes?

The Grummans made one pass through the bomber formation before they were driven off by the Zeros. Sakai was puzzled by the American pilots' lack of aggressiveness—then he noticed a single Wildcat successfully holding off three Zeros. He gaped. Every time a Zero got the Wildcat in his sights, the American would flip his stubby plane away wildly and get behind the Zero—never had Sakai seen such flying. He loosed a burst at the Grumman; it rolled, came around in a tight turn and climbed straight up at Sakai. He snap-rolled but the American clung on. It took a series of tight loops before Sakai could get the Wildcat in his sights again. He sprayed between five and six hundred rounds into the plane.

The Wildcat did not come apart or catch fire. How could it stay in the air? Where had the Americans got such planes and pilots? He opened his cockpit window and stared at his opponent, a big man with a fair complexion. He challenged his adversary with a gesture of "Come on if you dare!" but the pilot must have been seriously wounded, for he did not attack despite his advantageous position. Sakai felt admiration for the dauntless foe and reluctantly turned his 20-mm. cannon on the Grumman. The plane exploded, and far below Sakai could see the pilot drifting toward land in his parachute.

The bombers had done no damage, and the transports headed back to the beaches to unload. But within an hour a second wave of bombers forced the transport to scatter again. In two strikes the Japanese had succeeded merely in delaying the landing operation for several hours. The same number of bombs could have blown up most of the supplies stacked on the beaches and jeopardized the troops on shore.

In Rabaul the import of the landing was not recognized by Lieutenant General Harukichi Hyakutake, commander of the 17th Army. New Guinea was still the main target and his attention was focused on a plan to cross the Owen Stanley Range and take Port Moresby. Not a single soldier could be spared for what was merely a diversion. Vice Admiral Gunichi Mikawa completely disagreed with him. He commanded the recently organized Eighth Fleet and had just arrived in Rabaul with a double mission: to spearhead a new drive south and to protect the Solomons from any Allied counterattack. The first reports of the landings had indicated beyond doubt that it was a major invasion, but he knew it was useless to argue with the Army. If anything was to be done immediately, it was up to the Navy alone. He managed to assemble 410 sailors, some rifles and a few machine guns and dispatched them at once to Guadalcanal in the transport *Meiyomaru*. Then he radioed the Navy General Staff in Tokyo for permission to launch a surface attack the following night on the American transports.

It sounded too audacious to Navy Chief of Staff Nagano— Mikawa would have to break through a formidable ring of warships that far outgunned him—and he passed on the decision to Combined Fleet. Yamamoto knew that Mikawa was not at all reckless and radioed him direct: WISH YOUR FLEET SUCCESS.

Mikawa was advised to command the battle from Rabaul, but being a true samurai, the gentle, soft-spoken admiral boarded the heavy cruiser *Chokai* that afternoon. Ordering his other seven ships—four heavy cruisers, two light crusiers and a destroyer—to follow in column, he headed south through the St. George Channel.

The area was poorly charted and the few maps available were unreliable. It would be humiliating to run aground, and for hours the admiral pored over charts with his staff navigator. Finally he decided to lurk above Bougainville out of range of any American carrier planes until late the next afternoon. Then he would lead his little fleet into that dangerous channel through the Solomons (the Americans would nickname it "The Slot"), trusting to luck that no Allied search plane would sight him in the fading light. It was dangerous, but if he didn't take the chance he would never reach Guadalcanal in time. All depended on surprise.

But he had been discovered. A U. S. submarine, the *S-38*, lying in ambush at the mouth of the St. George Channel, was almost run down by Mikawa's column. Swaying in the wash, *S-38* was too close to fire her torpedoes. Her captain, Lieutenant Commander H. G. Munson, a veteran of the frustrating Java campaign, radioed:

TWO DESTROYERS AND THREE LARGER SHIPS OF UNKNOWN TYPE HEADING ONE FOUR ZERO TRUE AT HIGH SPEED EIGHT MILES WEST OF CAPE ST. GEORGE.

3.

By dusk on D-day, eleven thousand Marines had landed on Guadalcanal without a casualty. The beaches were piled high with supplies and ammunition. The next afternoon a battalion advanced to the airfield against practically no opposition. The Marines found an almost completed 3,600-foot airstrip; it was abandoned. The entire garrison—leaving meals on tables—had fled inland without trying to destroy any installations or supplies or blow up the runway. They left behind stacks of rifles, machine guns, trucks, steam rollers, cement mixers, ammunition, gasoline, oil and two radar scopes as well as large quantities of rice, tea, beer and *sake*. Nearby were two large electric-power generators, machine shops, an elaborate air-compressor factory for torpedoes, and an ice plant, which soon had a fresh sign: TOJO ICE PLANT, UNDER NEW MANAGEMENT.

Mikawa's ships had reached Bougainville at dawn. The admiral sent out four search planes and scattered his fleet to deceive any Allied scout. At ten-twenty an Australian bomber, a Hudson, began circling over his flagship. *Chokai* reversed course as if heading back to Rabaul, but when another Hudson appeared, Mikawa decided to brazen it out. The column re-formed and headed down toward the narrow passage through the Solomons. Before long one of his own search planes reported sighting eighteen transports, six cruisers, nineteen destroyers and a battleship near Savo Island. The enemy seemed to be split in two forces—the main one guarding the Guadalcanal transports, the other Tulagi. The Americans had twenty-six warships to his eight, but perhaps he could destroy one of the forces before it could join up with the other. What concerned Mikawa most was the carrier force. Where was it?

Admiral Turner was still unaware that an enemy fleet was heading toward his Amphibious Force. The report from the submarine was too inconclusive and the Australian search pilot had decided that his information wasn't important enough to break radio silence. Turner was preoccupied most of the day with two bombing raids that caused more confusion than damage; the destroyer *Jarvis* was hit by a torpedo, and the transport *George F. Elliott* set afire.

By late afternoon—just as the Marines were taking over the airfield on Guadalcanal—Mikawa's column at last entered the almost unbelievably blue waters of the Solomons passage and started southeast directly for Guadalcanal. It should reach the enemy about midnight and the battle plan had to be simple, since the eight ships had never before maneuvered as a unit or sailed in formation. At four-forty, orders were sent by blinker from *Chokai* to the other ships: "We will proceed from south of Savo Island and torpedo the enemy main force in front of the Guadalcanal anchorage, after which we will turn toward the Tulagi forward area to shell and torpedo the enemy. We will then withdraw north of Savo." The recognition signal would be white sleeves streamed on both sides of the bridge.

As Mikawa neared Guadalcanal the dangers of being discovered increased and there was little room in the narrow waters to evade bombers. Every minute of daylight seemed interminable. Just before dusk a lookout on *Chokai* shouted, "Mast ahead on the starboard!" Sirens shrilled and bells clanged as the men scrambled to their battle stations and trained guns to starboard. It was a friendly ship, the seaplane tender *Akitsushima* heading for the bulky island sticking out of the water to the right, New Georgia.

Admiral Turner was not blind to the significance of The Slot. Any sailor could see it was the highway between Rabaul and Guadalcanal. He had ordered a Catalina to patrol the upper area where Mikawa had been steaming since dawn, but unknown to Turner, the PBY never took off. As darkness fell on the Amphibious Force, a messenger from the flag coding room handed the admiral a copy of a dispatch from Fletcher to Admiral Ghormley in Nouméa:

FIGHTER PLANE STRENGTH REDUCED FROM NINETY-NINE TO SEVENTY-EIGHT X IN VIEW OF THE LARGE NUMBER OF ENEMY TORPEDO PLANES AND BOMBERS IN THIS AREA I RECOMMEND THE IMMEDIATE WITHDRAWAL OF ALL CARRIERS X REQUEST TANKERS SENT FORWARD IMMEDIATELY AS FUEL RUNNING LOW.

Turner was incensed. He was being left "bare arse" without carrier support and would have to pull out at dawn; he couldn't risk another air strike without carrier-plane protection. He ordered General Vandegrift and Rear Admiral V. A. C. Crutchley, commander of the cruiser-destroyer covering force, to report immediately to his flagship, *McCawley*, anchored off Guadalcanal. Crutchley was a British officer, winner of the Victoria Cross at Jutland, a hearty man with a full red beard. He had already deployed his ships in three protective groups around the transports and freighters. The Southern Force—three cruisers and two destroyers—was stationed between Savo and Cape Esperance. The Northern Force, with the same number of ships, barricaded the line between Savo and Tulagi while the Eastern Force—two light cruisers and two destroyers—stood off to the east.

There was no battle plan, and the good-natured Crutchley had simply ordered the Northern force to operate independently and conform in general to the movements of the Southern Force, which Crutchley himself would command. When Crutchley received Turner's urgent summons, he signaled the captain of the cruiser *Chicago* to take temporary command of the Southern Force and steered down the darkened coast of Guadalcanal in his flagship, *Australia*, in search of *McCawley;* it would be quicker to reach her in a cruiser than in a small boat.

Nobody in the covering force suspected that a surface attack was imminent and ships remained in a second condition of readiness. No one thought to inform the commander of the Northern Force, Captain Frederick L. Riefkohl on the heavy cruiser *Vincennes,* that he was now senior officer of both forces guarding The Slot. Nor did Captain Howard D. Bode of *Chicago* bother to take his proper position as temporary commander of the Southern Force ahead of *Australia's* sister ship *Canberra.*

Australia poked around in the gloom for almost two hours before finding *McCawley.* Turner and Crutchley discussed a message from the Australian search pilot who had discovered Mikawa that morning. It had finally come after eight hours' delay—and was misleading: it said that the Japanese force consisted of three cruisers, three destroyers and two seaplane tenders or gunboats. The key words to both admirals were "seaplane tenders" and they concluded this meant an air attack in the morning. Certainly no one would launch any kind of night surface attack with three cruisers. Besides, there had been no report from the PBY that Turner had ordered sent out that morning.

Aboard a small boat General Vandegrift was still hunting for *McCawley* through the mass of blacked-out ships and it wasn't until after eleven that he finally joined the conference. The night was hot, overcast, oppressive. Vandegrift thought the two admirals "looked ready to pass out," and he himself was worn by his exertions on Guadalcanal.

While they drank coffee Turner showed his subordinates Fletcher's message. Vandegrift was as angry as Turner about Fletcher; he was "running away twelve hours earlier than he had already threatened." Turner believed he should withdraw his transports soon after dawn and asked Vandegrift's opinion.

"We are in fair shape on Guadalcanal," said the general, but he doubted that many supplies had been unloaded at Tulagi. He would like to check in person.

"I thought you would want that," Turner remarked, peering over his glasses. "I have a minesweeper standing by to take you over there."

Crutchley offered to take Vandegrift to the minesweeper on his way back to his flagship. The general declined but

Crutchley insisted. "Your mission is much more urgent than mine."

It was not quite midnight when the two boarded Crutchley's barge. To the left a heavy rain squall had sprung up near Savo, forming a curtain between the Northern and Southern Forces. To the right they could see a red glare—the transport *George F. Elliott* was still burning. As Vandegrift disembarked, Crutchley shook his hand. He knew what the withdrawal of transports meant to the Marines, but said, "Vandegrift, I don't know if I can blame Turner for what he's doing."

Mikawa's column was coming on Savo at 26 knots, trailed by phosphorescent wakes. The flagship *Chokai* led the way, followed at 1,300-yard intervals by the four other heavy cruisers and the two light cruisers, with the lone destroyer bringing up the rear. Decks were cleared for action; topside flammables were jettisoned, and depth charges and unnecessary gear stowed below. Every captain passed on to his men Mikawa's final message, similar to one by his hero, Lord Nelson: "Let us go forward to certain victory in the traditional night attack of the Imperial Navy. May each one of us calmly do his utmost."

Above all, Mikawa feared the enemy carrier force. He knew it was nearby from numerous high-frequency radio messages such as RED 6 TO RED BASE and GREEN 2 TO GREEN BASE. But there was still a good chance of escaping back through the Solomons passage in the daylight hours.

Directly ahead in the darkness, Crutchley's cruiser groups lumbered off Savo on their monotonous patrols, those on watch exhausted from forty-eight hours on constant alert. All the cruiser captains were asleep.

Mikawa saw the volcano of Savo rise out of the sea. No one on the bridge spoke. One, two, three minutes slowly passed. Unlike the Americans the Japanese had no radar, only eyes sharpened by night training. The starboard lookout on *Chokai* saw a dim form. "Ship approaching, thirty degrees starboard!" he called out. It was the U. S. destroyer *Blue*. She and the destroyer *Ralph Talbot*, which was six miles to the northeast, were pickets, the American early-warning system. But their sonar and radar, strangely, gave no indication that a Japanese column was bearing down on them.

"Prepare for action," said Mikawa, and to keep out of sight, ordered, "Left rudder. Slow to twenty-two knots."

The black line of ships silently turned, starboard guns ready to blast *Blue*, but all she did was reverse course and sail off at a leisurely 12 knots toward *Ralph Talbot*, which had also reversed course. The two sentries passed and drew away, leaving an open gate for the oncoming raiders.

Mikawa knifed forward and was in the center of the Amphibious Force, thanks to an unbroken series of Allied mishaps: he had been sighted three times, but to no avail. The B-17's patrolling The Slot had missed him entirely, and the extra search order by Turner had not been carried out. Finally, the two picket destroyers had almost been run down by the column, yet had not been alerted by lookouts or radar or sonar operators; either the blips were not seen or they were presumed to be friendly and ignored. In addition, a float-plane—one of three sent out after dark by Mikawa—had been sighted before midnight and reported by *Ralph Talbot*. It, too, had been assumed to be friendly. As at Pearl Harbor, no one could believe an attack was imminent.

Chokai swung below Savo, unobserved. A lookout saw a cruiser on the port bow. A minute passed. Nothing happened. It was a false alarm. Port lookouts barely discerned what looked like a destroyer moving very deliberately to the west. It was the destroyer *Jarvis*, torpedoed in the daylight air attack, and steaming back to Australia for repairs. Mikawa's incredible luck held. *Jarvis*, too, failed to notice the Japanese column, which was finally swallowed up by a heavy curtain of rain.

Chokai signaled with hooded blinkers visible only to those in the column: "Prepare to fire torpedoes." A port lookout made out a ship almost ten miles away in the glare of the burning *Elliott*. "Cruiser, seven degrees port!" At 1:36 A.M. a starboard lookout called out, "Three cruisers, nine degrees starboard, moving right!" It was the heart of Crutchley's Southern Force, the heavy cruisers *Canberra* and *Chicago* and the destroyer *Patterson*.

"Commence firing," Mikawa said quietly and the order was relayed to the torpedo crews. "All ships attack" was the next command. Schools of long-range torpedoes that could carry a thousand pounds of explosives eleven miles at 49 knots churned toward *Canberra* and *Chicago*.

The two big cruisers were heading slowly to the northwest, guarded by two destroyers, *Bagley* to starboard and *Patterson* to port. Finally, at 1:43 A.M., someone on *Patterson* made out several ships in the distance and the alarm was sounded by radio: WARNING—WARNING—STRANGE SHIPS ENTERING HARBOR!

The warning was unnecessary. Overhead, parachute flares

exploded in the darkness behind the Allied ships, making them as distinct as silhouettes in a shooting gallery. The flares had been dropped by Mikawa's three "friendly" floatplanes.

On the bridge of *Canberra* a lookout called an officer's attention to a vague form ahead in the pounding rain. A ship, a strange ship. It began spitting fire. As the two Australians intuitively flinched, a pair of torpedoes plowed into *Canberra*'s bows. From above, shells hurtled into the cruiser, killing the captain and the gunnery officer. Her main guns useless, the big ship listed, dead in the water. Fire coursed through the companionways, fed by linoleum on the decks. The paint on the bulkheads burst into flame; the upholstered furniture in the wardrooms went up like tinder. Men frantically tried to jettison gasoline and ammunition, but it was too late. Explosions wracked the ship.

The destroyers on either side of *Canberra* fought back blindly, but *Patterson* was promptly pinpointed by searchlights and knocked out of action. *Bagley* rushed at the enemy, got into position to launch torpedoes—there were no firing primers.

With *Canberra* an inferno, Mikawa's fleet turned on *Chicago*. The temporary commander of the Southern Force, Captain Bode, wakened out of a sound sleep, got to the bridge just before a torpedo crunched into the bow. Despite a 16-foot hole and a shell hit, *Chicago* still looked for a target. Sighting something to the west—it was the sole Japanese destroyer—she gave chase. Bode was inadvertently steaming away from the main battle. Worse, he had yet to warn the Northern Force of what was happening.

On *McCawley*, Admiral Turner knew of the battle only from the flash of guns followed by the freight-car rumble of shells. What struck him was that the fate of the Marines on Guadalcanal and Tulagi and the sailors in the helpless transports was at stake. These thin-skinned ships had pulled anchor and were milling around in the darkness.

Admiral Crutchley was far from the action on *Australia*. He ordered seven destroyers to join his flagship at a set rendezvous—if they were not engaged with the Japanese. In the turmoil the order was misunderstood and four destroyers pulled out of the battle.

Mikawa had disposed of the Southern Force in about six minutes without taking a hit. He continued his counterclockwise swing around Savo to find new targets. Three heavy cruisers followed the flagship *Chokai*, but the next in line, *Furutaka*, was so far behind that it mistakenly swung to starboard and the next two ships followed, splitting Mikawa's force in two. The mistake put Mikawa in an enviable tactical position: he had four cruisers west of the Northern Force and three on the other side. The five American ships, three heavy cruisers and two destroyers, were about to be flanked on both sides—simultaneously, and without warning from Captain Bode.

At 1:48 A.M., lookouts on the heavy cruiser *Astoria* saw torpedoes approach—they came from *Chokai* and they all passed by. Wakened by the general alarm, Captain William Greenman rushed to the bridge and wanted to know who the devil had sounded the alarm and why the ship's main battery was blasting away. He was sure whatever they were shooting at was friendly. "Let's not get excited and act too hastily," he said. "Cease firing." He changed his mind quickly enough when he saw splashes falling around the cruiser *Vincennes*. "Commence firing!" he shouted and ordered a slight turn to port. "Our ships or not, we've got to stop them!"

Salvo after salvo from *Chokai* crashed into *Astoria*, knocking out all power and killing everyone in turret No. 2. The cruiser coasted to a stop, her decks aflame—and every fire main was ruptured.

Nearby the heavy cruiser *Quincy* was also on fire from a hit on a scout plane and its store of fuel. The cruiser made a perfect target and was caught in a devastating crossfire. "We're going down between them," Captain S. N. Moore phoned his gunners. "Give them hell!" Shells tore into *Quincy*, and Moore finally ordered the signalman to beach the doomed ship on Savo, four miles to port. A shell exploded on the bridge, flinging bodies like dolls, killing almost everyone. Moore lay near the wheel, mortally wounded. He tried to get up but fell back with a moan. The ship heeled rapidly to port and began sinking by the bow.

The commander of the Northern Force, Captain Riefkohl of *Vincennes*, still didn't know a battle was going on. He had heard *Ralph Talbot*'s report of a plane overhead just before midnight, but assumed like so many others that it was friendly and went to bed. The roar of guns, he surmised, had been set off by some small Japanese ship trying to steal past the Southern Force. From his bridge Riefkohl felt two underwater explosions and saw gun flashes and made another bad guess: the Southern Force was shooting at enemy planes.

He was annoyed—but not perturbed—when searchlights illuminated the three cruisers of the Northern Force at 1:50 A.M. He radioed the Southern Force to shut them off. As if in reply, spouts shot up five hundred yards away. Captain Riefkohl at last realized he was in a fight. *Vincennes'* 8-in. guns bellowed and one salvo hit *Kinugasa*, but the scout planes on *Vincennes'* stern burst into flame and she, like *Quincy*, became an easy target. Riefkohl ordered a zigzag course to avoid the deadly assault, but two, perhaps three torpedoes exploded in a port fire room. Steam pressure dropped steadily. Another torpedo hit the No. 1 fire room. *Vincennes* wallowed in the water. Shell after shell ripped along the decks. Fires broke out in the movie locker and search-light platform. Riefkohl was wondering if he should abandon ship. Then the Japanese searchlights blacked out. The firing ceased as abruptly as it had started. It was 2:15 A.M.

Mikawa signaled: "All ships withdraw." On every side he could see flaming wreckage. It reminded him of the water lantern festival at Lake Hakone. He was tempted to turn back and attack the transports, but his own ship had been hit three times and his fleet was scattered. It would take more than an hour to get back into battle formation; by the time he sank the transports it would be dawn and he would have to make the long run back to Rabaul in broad daylight at the mercy of American carrier-based planes. He remembered what Admiral Nagano had told him before he left Japan: "The Japanese Navy is different from the American Navy. If you lose one ship it will take years to replace." He also remembered how contemptuously the 17th Army in Rabaul had talked of the U. S. Army; how easy it was to beat them in battle. Why then should he risk his precious fleet just to sink Army transports? He gave the order to make for Rabaul.

Mikawa's concern about the carrier planes was logical, but he need not have worried. Fletcher had already turned his back on the Solomons and within an hour would get Ghormley's permission to retire completely from the area. Mikawa had inflicted on the U. S. Navy its most humiliating defeat at sea. Shortly after she started up The Slot, the battered *Quincy* went down, and a quarter of an hour later. *Vincennes* took her final plunge. Then *Astoria* and *Canberra* —burning furiously in the cold driving rain—sank beneath the waters of what would be known as Ironbottom Sound.

At dawn the waters around Savo were heavy with oil, wreckage and half-dead men clinging to bits of flotsam. It was more crushing than the debacle at the Java Sea. The Japanese, who had not lost a ship, had destroyed four modern heavy cruisers, killed 1,023 men and wounded another

709. And though Mikawa had not attacked the transports, he left such terror in his wake that every Allied ship—warships as well as transports, cargo vessels and minesweepers—fled the area toward Nouméa; the abandoned Marines of Guadalcanal and Tulagi were short of ammunition and had enough food for little more than a month.

What happened at Savo was bitterly debated and recollected with rancor and shame by the men of the U. S. Navy. No one was punished as a result of an official investigation, but Captain Riefkohl emerged a broken man who went about like the Ancient Mariner telling his story over and over of how *Vincennes* had kept Mikawa from destroying the transports by putting a shell into *Chokai*'s chart room. Captain Bode committed suicide.

15   Green Hell

1.

In Tokyo the victory at Savo overshadowed the significance of the American seizure of Guadalcanal. All the same, it was an annoyance to the Navy and with reluctance they informally asked Army General Staff operations officers if they would mind clearing the island. The Army asked how many troops would be needed for the operation. Not too many, said the Navy. The American invasion was little more than a nuisance involving a mere 2,000 Marines; the enemy could not possibly mount a major counterattack up through the Solomons for a year.

The Army operations officer agreed to recommend the plan to Tojo, and before the end of the week the Army General Staff radioed General Hyakutake in Rabaul to mop up Guadalcanal with 6,000 men—a Special Naval Landing Force of 500 men; the Kawaguchi Detachment of 3,500, and the Ichiki Detachment, the 2,000 men who had been scheduled to seize Midway and were now back on Guam.

Kiyotake Kawaguchi—the mustached general who had tried in vain to save Chief Justice Santos—was on Koror, one of the Palau island group some six hundred miles east of Mindanao, and from the moment he read his change of orders sending him to the Solomons, he instinctively guessed the import of the American invasion. He showed Nishino, the *Mainichi* reporter, a map of the Solomons and pointed to a tiny speck. "This is our new destination—Gadarukanaru. I know you think this might be small-scale warfare. It's true there will be nothing heroic in it, but I'd say it will be extremely serious business." Kawaguchi somberly predicted that the island would be the focal point in the struggle for the Pacific. "If you decide to continue on with us, you must put your life in my hands. Both of us will probably be killed." Nishino said he would go and they shook hands.

Two nights later, on August 15, Kawaguchi instructed his squad leaders to distribute three months' pay to the troops. They were embarking on "a very important mission" and many would die. "Have the men send most of the money home and spend the rest on eating and drinking so they can enjoy their last night here."

Soon after dawn the 3,500 men of the Kawaguchi Detachment, still feeling the effect of their all-night celebration, began boarding two 10,000-ton transports. The decks of *Sado-maru* were hot from the tropical sun and burned Nishino's feet through his sneakers. He watched the soldiers file into the spacious hold and pack themselves into the bunks. Electric fans brought blasts of warm air, so Nishino returned topside. The decks were steaming from a recent squall.

As the ship weighed anchor, a large black dog paddled from the shore and scrambled up the last loading platform. He darted frantically around until he found his master, a young lieutenant named Ueno. "All right, I was wrong," the lieutenant said apologetically to the dog; he had given him away the night before.

For three days the transports plowed southeast toward Rabaul at 16 knots. The soldiers jogged around the decks singing military songs, lounged, did setting-up exercises. Their spirits were high despite the enervating heat. At supper they were issued warm beer, which put them in an exuberant mood: They had no fear of the Americans, they boasted; all they had to do was attack them at night. Their training manual said: "Westerners—being very haughty, effeminate and cowardly—intensely dislike fighting in the rain or mist or in the dark. They cannot conceive night to be a proper time for battle—though it is excellent for dancing. In these weaknesses lie our great opportunity." They reminisced about their easy conquest of Borneo. "After we got through firing there wasn't a blade of grass," said one youngster. "I'm not going to let any grass grow on Dakarunaru."

"It isn't Dakarunaru, it's Gadarukanaru," a sergeant corrected him. "Remember the name, will you?"

Six destroyers—they carried the first echelon of the Ichiki Detachment—made a landfall off Taivu Point on the north shore, only twenty-five miles east of the Guadalcanal airstrip. Boats were lowered and just before midnight—it was August 18—Colonel Kiyono Ichiki and 915 men came ashore. Like the Marines, they met not a single round of fire.

WE HAVE SUCCEEDED IN INVASION, Ichiki radioed Rabaul. His orders were to wait until the second half of his detachment arrived a week later and then retake the airstrip which the Japanese had almost completed in July. But he was so confident that he left 125 men to guard the beach and struck off up the coast.

His presence on Guadalcanal was known to the Marine commander but only from inconclusive evidence—the wake of the destroyers. However, combined with reports of enemy landings west of the airstrip (this was the 500-man Special Naval Landing Force, which never became significantly involved in the fighting), it was sufficient to convince General Vandegrift that a major counterattack was imminent. He sent out probing patrols to the west, east and southeast. He also asked a native sergeant major named Vouza (he was a scout for Martin Clemens of the Australian Coastwatching Service) to take a patrol south, then circle back north to the coast.

It took the bandy-legged Vouza and his men little more than a day to reach the sea. On August 20 they discovered the Ichiki Detachment. (It was within ten miles of the airstrip and Ichiki's latest message to Rabaul had indicated his optimism: NO ENEMY AT ALL LIKE MARCHING THROUGH A NO MAN'S LAND.) Vouza tried to creep in closer for more information but was captured and brought to Ichiki. When he was stripped a tiny American flag, a souvenir, fell out of his loincloth. Vouza refused to answer questions. He was tied to a tree; his face was beaten almost to a pulp by rifle butts. He stubbornly shook his head. He was bayoneted twice through the chest. Still he said nothing. A soldier thrust a bayonet through his throat.

But Vouza was not dead, and at dusk when Ichiki and his 790 men moved on along the beach, he began chewing through his ropes. Finally he freed himself and with determination managed to crawl back to the Marine lines. He gasped out that "maybe two hundred and fifty, maybe five hundred"

Japanese were approaching their perimeter. He fainted but came to long enough to say, "I did not tell them."

Ichiki was forming his troops in a coconut grove on the east bank of a sluggish stream between him and the airstrip, little more than a mile away. This was the Ilu River (mistaken for the Tenaru by the Marines), which formed a natural defense line, and Ichiki was certain there were Marines on the other side. At the mouth of the Ilu he found a narrow 45-yard-wide sand bar which penned up its green, stagnant water and formed a bridge almost to the other side.

He was sure he had achieved surprise but the Americans were well dug in across the river waiting for him, alerted by Vouza and a Marine patrol which had captured enemy maps. At about one-thirty in the morning Ichiki gave the order to attack. Mortars arched their rounds toward the Americans and machine guns raked the jungle beyond the river. Then several hundred Japanese burst out of the grove and headed for the sand bar with fixed bayonets and cries of "Banzai!" On the run they fired from the hip and lobbed grenades.

A volley of rifle fire met them head-on, followed by a whiplash of machine-gun fire. The first Japanese, officers brandishing sabers, were cut down. Canister shots from a 37-mm. gun toppled scores of men. A few made it across the Ilu but the fusillade forced the survivors to flee back to the coconut grove.

Vandegrift was already mounting a counterattack from the south with his reserve battalion, commanded by Lieutenant Colonel Leonard Cresswell. By dawn Cresswell was across the river and leading his men down the east bank. At two o'clock in the afternoon he approached the coconut grove. Ichiki was cut off.

But the Japanese would not surrender. Wounded men would cry out, and Americans who went forward to help were blown up by grenades or picked off by sharpshooters. The Marines were encountering a new kind of war, one without quarter. Vandegrift decided, therefore, to send in a platoon of light tanks.

Late that afternoon five tanks clanked over piles of Japanese bodies on the sand bar and made for the grove, blasting canister shots from their 37-mm. guns. They butted into palm trees, knocking down snipers, and ran down cornered Japanese until the treads of the tanks looked like "meat grinders." First Lieutenant Sakakibara and an enlisted man barely escaped being crushed by scrambling into the sea and hiding with their noses just above the water level.

By dusk there was only a handful of Japanese left in the grove. They clustered around the wounded Ichiki, who clutched the regimental flag. "Burn the colors," he ordered. The colorbearer poured gasoline on the flag, which was soaked with Ichiki's blood, and set a match to it just as a tank found the little group. Before Ichiki could be mowed down with the others he drew his sword and committed hara-kiri.

Pieces of bodies, blown to bits by Marine howitzers or shredded by canister, littered the grove. The trail of tanks could be followed by tread tracks over mangled bodies. There was not a sign of life in the grove. Almost 800 Japanese had been killed, at the cost of 35 dead and 75 wounded Americans. When it was dark the sole Japanese survivors, Lieutenant Sakakibara and his companion, crept out of the sea and headed back along the coast to their 125 comrades who had been left to guard the supplies.

For the first time both Army and Navy leaders in Tokyo began to take the American presence in Guadalcanal seriously. The Army plan to retake the island now also had Admiral Yamamoto's full support. He saw Guadalcanal as another opportunity for Combined Fleet to lure the Americans into the decisive sea battle.

Four slow transports, already bound for Guadalcanal with the rest of the Ichiki Detachment and five hundred sailors trained as infantrymen, were instructed to turn back and rendezvous with the Guadalcanal Supporting Forces, which had hastily been assembled by Yamamoto and was sailing south toward the Solomons. In the lead were six submarines, followed closely by the overall commander, Vice Admiral Kondo, and a group of six cruisers and a seaplane carrier. Behind steamed the newly formed *Kido Butai,* still led by Nagumo, but with only two big carriers, *Zuikaku* and *Shokaku,* and an escort of two battleships and three heavy cruisers. Accompanying them was the Diversionary Group— the light carrier *Ryujo,* a heavy cruiser, and two destroyers— which was to be sent out at the psychological moment as bait for the American carriers.

It was not long before the Americans learned of the formidable surface force advancing toward them from the north and they were forced to meet this new threat head-on. Admiral Ghormley sent out Admiral Fletcher to do battle with Task Force 61—three large carriers (*Enterprise, Saratoga* and *Wasp*), seven cruisers and eighteen destroyers. By dawn on August 23 Fletcher was less than 150 miles east of Guadalcanal, in perfect position to block the Japanese charge. Several hours later an American patrol plane sighted the four Japanese transports and their immediate escort—a light cruiser and five destroyers under the command of an obstinate rear admiral, Raizo Tanaka—and radioed back that troopships were headed for Guadalcanal. Tanaka was as wily as he was aggressive. He kept bearing south until 1 P.M., then put the transports out of range of aerial attack by reversing course. Five hours later Kondo's large force, which was forty miles to the east and still undiscovered, did the same.

Tanaka's move misled Fletcher into assuming that there wouldn't be a major engagement for several days and he sent the *Wasp* group south to refuel. It was an unfortunate decision that deprived him of one third of his power on the eve of battle.

Just before dawn on August 24, the Diversionary Group swung back south to tempt Task Force 61. Then the rest of the Japanese armada also reversed course, lurking out of sight and waiting for Fletcher to take the bait. At 9:05 A.M. an American patrol plane discovered the little carrier and her three escorts 280 miles northwest of Task Force 61. Fletcher hesitated even after it was reported two and a half hours later that the Diversionary Group was less than 250 miles away. But at 1:30 P.M. his skepticism vanished when his radar blips showed planes heading for Guadalcanal.

They were fifteen fighters and six bombers from *Ryujo* bound for the airfield on Guadalcanal. Recently completed (named Henderson Field after Major Lofton Henderson, who was killed at Midway), it was the base for two Marine squadrons—nineteen Wildcat fighters and a dozen Dauntless dive bombers—and fourteen P-400's from an Army fighter squadron.

Fletcher moved fast, and within fifteen minutes thirty dive bombers and eight torpedo bombers were launched from *Saratoga*. In two hours the Dauntlesses found *Ryujo* and began diving at her from 14,000 feet. In the midst of the attack, six Douglas Devastators swept in and released their torpedoes from 200 feet. At least four bombs and one torpedo smashed into the little carrier. She listed 20 degrees to starboard and came to a dead stop.

Ryujo was doomed but she had accomplished her main purpose; she had diverted Fletcher's attack and allowed *Kido Butai* to locate *Saratoga* and *Enterprise*. Fifty-one Wildcats

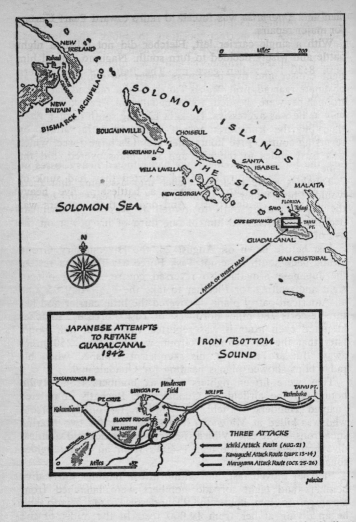

JAPANESE ATTEMPTS
TO RETAKE
GUADALCANAL
1942

IRON BOTTOM
SOUND

THREE ATTACKS

→ Ichiki Attack Route (AUG.-21)
→ Kawaguchi Attack Route (SEPT. 13-14)
→ Maruyama Attack Route (OCT. 25-26)

tried to screen the two carriers, but twenty-five Aichi dive bombers broke through. At exactly 5:14 P.M. a bomb penetrated through five decks of *Enterprise* and exploded in the chief petty officers' quarters. Two more bombs with instantaneous fuses ripped up the flight deck. By the time the raging fires were brought under control, seventy-six men had died and *Enterprise* was forced to retire toward Pearl Harbor for major repairs.

With a single carrier left, Fletcher did not relish a night battle and wisely decided to turn south. Nagumo chased him until 8:30 P.M., then gave up. The Battle of the Eastern Solomons was over. Like Coral Sea, it appeared to be inconclusive. A small Japanese carrier had been sunk, while Fletcher had been deprived of the services of *Enterprise* for at least two months. More important, however, Fletcher lost seventeen planes to Nagumo's seventy, and the Japanese could not afford the loss of so many experienced crews. As at Coral Sea, the Japanese imagined they had inflicted heavy losses on the Americans. Returning pilots reported they had sunk or heavily damaged three carriers, a battleship, five heavy cruisers and four destroyers. And one of these carriers was allegedly *Hornet* (she wasn't in the battle); Doolittle's sneak attack on Tokyo had been avenged.

The Guadalcanal Supporting Forces retired but Tanaka continued doggedly down the Solomons passage, even though the transports could not possibly reach Guadalcanal until daylight. The risk was great but he tried to minimize it by sending five of his destroyers ahead to shell the planes at Henderson Field. All through the night they ranged along the north coast bombarding the airfield, then left to join the transports coming from the north.

The next morning at 9:35 eight Marine dive bombers from Henderson, led by Lieutenant Colonel R. C. Mangrum and out on a quest for enemy carriers, accidentally discovered the transports and their escort. They plummeted down on the light cruiser *Jintsu*, Tanaka's flagship, and *Kinryu-maru*. *Jintsu* was able to limp away, but the burning transport had to be abandoned. As the destroyer *Mutsuki* began picking up survivors she was attacked by eight Flying Fortresses based on Espíritu Santo Island, in the New Hebrides. The captain, Commander Kiyono Hatano, had little regard for American high-level bombers and continued his rescue operations. This time the B-17's had a stationary target, and three bombs ripped into *Mutsuki*. "Even the B-17's can make a hit once in a while," gasped Hatano as he swam to safety.

Tanaka stubbornly kept moving toward Guadalcanal and would have attempted to land the fifteen hundred reinforcements in the daylight. All that stopped him was a message from Rabaul ordering him to return at once to Shortland, the little island off Bougainville that had become the springboard for what the Americans called the "Tokyo Express"—the runs down to Guadalcanal.

The memory of these losses was still vivid in Tanaka's mind when, on the morning of August 29, he met with the officer who would lead the second assault on Henderson Field. General Kawaguchi and his 3,500-man detachment had just arrived in Shortland by way of Rabaul and he wanted to get to Guadalcanal as soon as possible—on barges. Tanaka was glad to provide transportation but insisted on using destroyers. One reason Ichiki had been wiped out, Kawaguchi countered, was because he hadn't been able to take sufficient equipment and food on destroyers. The next day they resumed the argument, but Tanaka's reasoning, based on personal experience, eventually won Kawaguchi over. Late that afternoon the general summoned his commanders to the mess of his transport and told them they were transferring to destroyers for the run to Guadalcanal. Colonel Akinosuke Oka, a regimental commander, thought this would be too dangerous. "I think it would be better to go by motorboat, weaving our way secretly from island to island."

In the stifling heat the two men debated at length the merits of "Rat Express" (destroyers) and "Ant Freight" (motorboats). Kawaguchi finally ended the argument by compromise. "I will lead the main unit directly to Taivu Point by destroyers. Colonel Oka will lead Headquarters and First Battalion by motorboat to the northwest end of Guadalcanal." Kawaguchi made two red marks on a large map, one at Taivu Point (the same place selected by Ichiki), where he would disembark with 2,400 men, and the other at Kokumbona, about ten miles west of the airfield, where Oka and the remaining 1,100 troops would land. From these two points he and Oka would simultaneously head inland to get behind Henderson in position for a joint attack.

The general stepped onto an empty cider box. "Gentlemen," he said, "I think our faith is our strength. Men who fight bravely, never doubting victory, will be the victors in the long run. Before we get to the battlefield we must sail three hundred miles and may very well encounter enemy attacks en route." Advance elements had been attacked but safely landed by destroyers at Taivu Point during the previous two nights. "But we have trained ourselves, haven't we? I swear to all of you that we will smash the enemy. On to Guadalcanal!"

"To Guadalcanal!"

"We solemnly swear to fight to the end," shouted an officer and raised his glass in a toast.

Correspondent Nishino followed Kawaguchi topside. Enlisted men and junior officers were diving into the blue-green water and swimming back to the ship.

"They need constant training, Nishino-*san*," Kawaguchi remarked. A young, fully clad lieutenant leaned on the rail, a cigarette dangling from his lips. "Hey, Lieutenant," Kawaguchi called to him. "Why aren't you in there with the others?"

The lieutenant quickly dropped his cigarette into the water and sprang to attention. While he was mumbling an excuse, Kawaguchi summarily pushed him over the rail. "There are some lazy ones," he observed. "In war when you're thrown into the sea, even a hammer has to swim."

That midnight the detachment transferred to destroyers and motorboats. Kawaguchi, with Nishino, climbed aboard the destroyer *Umikaze*. When they were alone in the general's cabin, Kawaguchi revealed that the Americans were well dug in and had almost endless supplies. "When we come to think of such things it seems extremely difficult for a small unit like ours to retake the airfield. Wouldn't you think the destruction of the Ichiki Detachment would be a lesson to us? But Imperial Headquarters belittles the enemy on Guadalcanal and declares that once we land successfully, the Marines will surrender." He stopped as if alarmed by his own words. "It's not a problem for us to discuss here."

Nishino was wakened by a chilly breeze. At eight twenty-five a bugle, the signal for departure, sounded and the eight slender destroyers, two abreast, began gliding southeast at 26 knots. It was the last day of August. Deep in the hold the roar of the revolving screws, coupled with the suffocating heat, drove Nishino to the open deck. He was almost blown off his feet by the brisk wind. It was cloudy, a good time to start the hazardous trip down the channel. The lashing spray forced him back to the hold just in time to hear a ship's officer tell a group of soldiers that they should reach Guadalcanal several hours before midnight. A petty officer began checking the soldiers' lifebelts. "Don't worry about air attacks," he said cheerfully.

All through the nerve-wracking day sailors urged the soldiers to avenge comrades who had been trapped on Guadalcanal by the invasion. The soldiers promised to "wipe out every last Yankee." After dinner the sailors returned to the hold with beer, cider, tobacco and candy. "We are responsible for the sea!" bellowed one tipsy sailor. "You're responsible for the island. Okay? So good luck!" He began pumping hands with every soldier within reach.

A soldier gave a sailor half of his wrinkled pack of Kinshi cigarettes and said, "Let's celebrate with a smoke if we ever meet again alive." Another pair exchanged fingernail clippings. "Please send them to my son if I die," said the soldier. "The boy is only two years old." "This is my mother's name and address," said the sailor.

The eight ships, rolling violently, drove ahead full speed through the blackness. Their wakes were like an endless display of fireworks; the water was filled with millions of noctilucae—luminescent creatures. A dark shadow of land materialized half a mile away. It was Taivu Point. Launches, cutters and rowboats were lowered and the soldiers piled in silently. The ships' guns leveled on the coconut trees that lined the beach. All Nishino could hear as he dropped into a boat was the muted hubbub of debarkation. His boat ground into the sand and he clambered awkwardly over the side. The surf, brilliant with noctilucae, pushed him ashore. He waited for the crack of fire from the silent line of coconut and palm trees. There was only the sound of his comrades and the crunch of surf.

He staggered up to dry sand and looked at his watch. It was one minute past nine, Tokyo time; here it was an hour later. His body glistened from the waist down with the tiny phosphorescent animals, and the long beach itself, alive with crowds of luminiscent men, was a shiny belt. He stood entranced in a world of fantasy.

"How beautiful," said a voice next to him.

Nishino moved toward the jungle until he was halted by another voice: "What unit are you from?" He saw a silhouette. It was a Japanese soldier in tattered uniform. Several other figures appeared from the jungle like ghosts. They were survivors of the first Ichiki echelon.

"Glad to see you," said the gaunt soldier. "But shake those damn worms off you. The enemy can see them from the air." His voice trembled as he anxiously pointed to the ground. "It's suicide to leave footprints in the sand," he said. "We're always being attacked by U. S. planes." The Ichiki men expertly wiped out footprints with palm leaves as they backed off to the edge of the jungle. They bowed and were gone.

Kawaguchi saluted the destroyers, then led the way into the jungle. It was so dark that each man had to hang on to the shoulder of the one ahead. They came to a narrow river bridged by a fallen tree. Nishino couldn't see the river but could tell it was deep by the rush of water. As he crept across the slippery tree he almost panicked. What if he fell? His 70-lb. pack would drag him under. Compulsively he began cataloguing everything on his back: a movie camera, two still cameras, film equipment, clothing, food and five books—a selection of Chinese poems, a geography of the Solomons, two volumes of French poetry, and an English copy of *The Good Earth*.

By the time he finished the list he was on the other side. He stepped off into something that felt like spongy cushions. Huge rain drops began to penetrate the umbrella of the jungle, then the drops turned into a shower. The trail became blocked with thick tangles of vines studded with long sharp thorns and huge trees with knobby roots. Kawaguchi stopped, and the men curled up on the ground and tried to sleep in the beating rain. Nishino began shivering. Mosquitoes swarmed over his face; their bites stabbed him like inoculating needles.

In the darkness they were roused, and they continued to grope through the jungle, circling back toward the coast. By dawn they reached Tasimboko, a deserted village near the beach, three miles west of Taivu Point. Here they ate their first meal on Guadalcanal. It had been prepared by the Navy and packed in each man's *hango*—a covered metal mess kit about the size and shape of a binocular case. Inside was an unexpected treat: white rice, dried fish (heads and all), fish paste and cooked beef. In thanks each soldier raised his *hango* to his forehead and bowed.

Their breakfast was interrupted by the frantic barking of the large black dog which had swum after Ueno. "Enemy plane!" the lieutenant shouted and dropped to the ground. The drone of engines could be heard faintly in the distance. In moments a dozen planes swept across so low that the leaves rustled, and continued toward Taivu Point.

All during the morning P-400's, Wildcats and dive bombers from Henderson searched along the coast but each time the big dog's warning barks came in time. Then the Americans began to attack the area blindly. Nishino scrambled behind a log, chased by a line of tracers that reminded him of the stitches of a sewing machine. He heard the whistle of falling bombs. Explosions shook the earth and he was showered with branches and dirt. A dozen men were killed.

That night Nishino went to sleep in one of the abandoned

huts of the village but was wakened by a voice shouting, "Guard Company, rally!" A figure looked into the hut. "Newsmen, report to headquarters." Nishino and his five men ran toward the beach through the dark jungle. In his eagerness Nishino slammed into tree after tree before he came to Kawaguchi's command post behind a sand dune overlooking the sea. Over the rumble of surf came the sound of motors.

"Prepare to fire!"

Peering over the edge of the dune, he saw the outline of landing craft not a hundred feet away. Nishino didn't have a helmet and he was afraid he'd die before he could file his first story.

"Fire!"

Bullets ricocheted off the sides of the landing craft. There was no answering volley. A voice cried out in Japanese, "My arm! I've been hit!"

"Cease firing!" shouted an officer behind the dunes. "They're friends."

"Oi!" called a voice from the beach. It was one of the men from part of the second echelon of the Ichiki Detachment; they were to join Kawaguchi in the attack on Henderson. Two men were killed and eight wounded. Worse, the fusillade had alerted the Americans and within minutes the jungle was illuminated by flares. Planes began strafing and bombing the village and the beach. A young soldier near Nishino cried out in pain, "I'm wounded! My shoulder." He writhed and grimaced. Nishino held a towel to the wound. "Please don't make fun of me," said the youngster. "We're going to suffer real pain in battle, aren't we?"

Although the Americans had discovered Kawaguchi's position, he refused to move; he was waiting for a report that Oka had landed on the other side of Henderson Field. Why had he allowed himself to be talked into letting Oka go by Ant Freight? Day after day while Vandegrift's planes strafed and bombed the village Kawaguchi waited in vain. One day Nishino counted seventy-one raids. The entire area was a desolation of bomb craters and smoldering tree trunks. The men were afraid to build fires and subsisted on fruit and raw rice.

At three o'clock on September 4 a report finally came from Colonel Oka: he was "approaching" Guadalcanal in his motorboats. Kawaguchi ordered First Lieutenant Nakayama to take three men and circle behind the airfield; they were to locate Oka and tell him the details of the joint attack, since it was too dangerous to send the information by radio. It was a hazardous mission, said the general, and success in the battle depended on perfect timing. He presented Nakayama with the only personal item of food he had brought from Palau—a can of sardines.

Kawaguchi gave the scouts a two-day start, and just before sunset on September 6 led the way along the beach. He left 300 men and a few artillery pieces behind to guard the supplies but still was far above strength with 3,100 troops; 1,000 were from the second Ichiki group. At Koli Point, ten miles east of Henderson, they would turn south and strike off into the jungle to circle behind the field.

Ships were skirting the shore so closely that Kawaguchi could hear the sound of winches. Across the water came faint voices—speaking English. Orders were passed down the line to crouch in place. Nishino peered out and in the light of the moon saw what looked like a cruiser, five destroyers and five transports. As the cruiser began moving along the coast toward Henderson, followed by the transports and destroyers, Nishino made out the silhouettes of sailors on the decks. It was the first time he had ever seen the enemy.

Kawaguchi guessed the ships had just transported Marines up the beach for a surprise attack on the village he had evacuated. He hoped the guard detail could hold off the enemy but he couldn't afford to send a single man back to help them.

It was not a landing force, but a convoy from Nouméa—two transports and escort—on its way with more supplies for Vandegrift. The following night there *was* a Marine amphibious landing near Tasimboko. The Marines beached just above the village. The Kawaguchi rear guard put up a token defense, killing two Americans, before disappearing into the jungle. The Marines sailed back with captured documents and Kawaguchi's dress uniforms. "The bastard must have been planning to shine in Sydney society," one Marine remarked.

Oka himself had just landed thirty miles on the other side of Henderson, after delays caused by aerial attacks and storms. During the harrowing, week-long trip down the Solomons passage he had lost 650 men, and the 450 survivors, with no food and little ammunition, were in no shape to fight.

Kawaguchi assumed that the Oka group had arrived intact and on September 8 gathered his officers near Koli Point for a final battle briefing. Nishino stood next to the general in the drizzling rain, taking notes. They would continue along the beach to the Tenaru River and follow it upstream for almost two miles. Here the artillery and most of the Ichiki men would make a crossing and head directly west until they were about a mile and a half east of the airfield. The main body would continue south for several miles, then arc around until it was behind Henderson. In the meantime Oka's 1,100 men would get into position west of the airfield. A few minutes before nine in the evening on September 13 the artillery group to the east would start a barrage to make the enemy think the attack was coming from that direction, while the Navy laid down a bombardment from the sea. At exactly nine o'clock Kawaguchi and Oka would attack simultaneously from the south and west.

"We will take the enemy airfield by surprise," said Kawaguchi. Handlebar mustache dripping water, he looked up from his notes at the officers who stood stiffly in silence. "As you know, gentlemen, the Americans have been strongly reinforced with men and supplies. Perhaps they are stronger than we are. Above all, their air force cannot be underestimated. Our troops must also overcome difficult terrain problems before we even reach the enemy lines. We are obviously facing an unprecedented battle. And so, gentlemen, you and I cannot hope to see each other again after the fight. This is the time for us to dedicate our lives to the Emperor."

"Hai!" The officers shouted the resounding "Yes!" in unison.

The rains slackened. There came a cry of *"Hikoki!"* (Planes!). The men were about to scatter when they heard a derisive cackle and saw a parrot fly off clumsily. For the past few days parrots had been mimicking the men by screeching, *"Oi, Jotohei!"* (Hey, Private First Class!). They had added a third Japanese word to their growing vocabulary.

Kawaguchi laughed with the rest of the officers and brought out a small bottle of whiskey. "Now, gentlemen, before we resume the march, shall we drink to success?" He poured a few drops in the cap of each officer's canteen. He turned to Nishino. "You, too."

In the distance were the dull thuds of explosions. Nishino thought it was American artillery. He had been hearing it day and night. But it came from Japanese bombers and was aimed at Henderson Field; and the night explosions were bombardments from Japanese warships.

"To the detachment's good luck in battle forever," said Kawaguchi. *"Kampai!"*

As the officers started back to their units and a detail began burning important papers, the general pointed out the enemy's positions to Nishino on a mimeographed map. "No matter what the War College says, it's extremely difficult to take an enemy position by night assault." He lowered his voice. "There were a few cases in the Russo-Japanese War but they were only small-scale actions. If we succeed here on Guadalcanal, it will be a wonder in the military history of the world."

They turned inland into jungle that seemed impenetrable, hacking their way through stout vines, traversing dark rain forests, clambering up and down precipitous ravines and rugged ridges. They traveled by night, stumbling over roots and falling into holes. Someone discovered phosphorescent moss and this was rubbed on the back of the man ahead. They sloshed through swamps dank with the stench of rotting vegetation and so treacherous that it took hours to go a few hundred yards. Added to this physical hardship was the growing fear that the Americans would suddenly ambush them.

Nishino's assistants had long since thrown away their cameras and supplies, but he himself refused to give up anything and scrambled at the heels of the long-legged Kawaguchi, conscientiously noting down everything the general said or did.

Dysentery from drinking river water was sweeping the ranks and already more than half the men had malaria. They subsisted on small quantities of dried fish, crackers and hard candy; they still had plenty of rice but dared not keep a fire going for more than a few minutes. On September 10 they reached the Tenaru River and the artillery peeled off, along with most of the Ichiki men, and headed directly toward Henderson while Kawaguchi and the main group kept plodding south to get behind the airfield.

For a week Lieutenant Nakayama and his three men—Corporal Abe, Lance Corporal Inenaga and Private First Class Morita—had been pushing ahead of Kawaguchi trying to make contact with Colonel Oka. They were half starved, exhausted. Their uniforms were ripped, their bodies slashed with deep cuts. They had fought off an attack by a native and his pack of ferocious dogs with saber and bayonets, and waded miles down a mountain stream only to find it so deep near the bottom that they had to turn around and struggle all the way back.

On the day Kawaguchi's force separated, they heard the distant rumble of engines. They were approaching the airfield. They turned west and at every clearing expected to come upon Oka. But they met no one and by dark were at the end of their endurance. Nakayama opened their last provision, Kawaguchi's can of sardines. The fish seemed to melt in their mouths. They sucked juice from vines and lay down to sleep. The next morning they were stopped by a wide dark-blue river. (It was the winding Lungga, which, a mile downstream, went past Henderson Field.) They waded toward the sea close to the bank and in the afternoon came to a small barren hill. Nakayama climbed it. On the other side, Americans squatted around a fire. It was the heart of the Marines' western perimeter. The crackle of frying and the smell of meat was almost unbearable.

The four scouts circled the Americans and came to another clearing blasted out of the jungle by bombs. There were a dozen foxholes—all empty except for discarded ammunition boxes and cans of rations. What kind of soldiers were these Americans? The scouts ate ravenously. It was as though they had "a new life." One of the men broke wind.

"It seems you're at last feeling human," said Nakayama.

"Yankee, smell my fart" was the cocky reply.

They crossed the river and kept moving due west into a patch of jungle, finally emerging from the dense growth into another clearing. The sun was painfully dazzling.

"Oi!"

Startled, they turned. A Japanese sailor, bare from the waist up, rifle in hand, stared at them. They embraced the sailor and began pummeling him. The sailor thanked them for coming. His eyes seemed abnormally large and bright. "You are friends in need," he said. His unit had been stationed at the airfield, and since the invasion had eaten nothing except berries which tasted delicious but turned putrid in the mouth. Every day at least one man died without complaint, "only licking his palms" for a last taste of salt. The sailor began weeping and dropped on his knees. "Please, soldiers, avenge us."

For two more days the scouts struggled west through the jungle and finally reached the Mataniko River, seven miles from Henderson. It was the morning of September 13, the date of the general attack. Would they ever find Oka? They turned north and followed the river downstream. At two-fifty Nakayama saw soldiers ahead fording the river. They were small. Japanese. It was the Oka group.

Nakayama found enough strength to relay the battle plan to Oka before collapsing at the colonel's feet. Almost inaudibly he said he was ready to die in battle.

"Let us die together," said Oka. He looked at his watch. In six hours the attack was scheduled to start. For the first time since landing he broke radio silence and informed Kawaguchi that he was moving east.

Kawaguchi had reached his jumping-off point the previous night, a hill three miles south of Henderson. Under deep jungle cover the men were making a final check of their equipment. The general had called in his company and platoon leaders. He told them it was essential to break through the American lines that night and retake the airfield. "You must put the enemy to rout and crush them by daybreak. The time has come for you to give your lives for the Emperor." In Rabaul he had been informed there were 5,000 Americans guarding Henderson, but if all went well his 2,100 men, Oka's 1,100 and the artillery-Ichiki group of more than 1,000 would be victorious.

2.

Earlier that morning General Vandegrift had surveyed the wreckage of Henderson Field caused by the naval bombardment the night before, and told his operations officer, "We're going to defend this airfield until we no longer can. If that happens, we'll take what's left to the hills and fight guerrilla warfare." He now had more than nineteen thousand troops but still felt outnumbered. According to reports, sizable Japanese detachments had landed on both sides of Henderson and were preparing to close in. For two weeks enemy warships had been shelling the Marine positions at night almost at will and his men were becoming increasingly intimidated by these fearsome raids—the Tokyo Express. His little air force was fighting off bomber attacks almost daily, but losses were heavy and he didn't know when replacement crews and planes would arrive.

Vandegrift was certain of one thing: there would be no help from the Navy for some time. Recently Rear Admiral Turner had flown in with a message from Ghormley: a shortage of ships, planes and supplies prevented the Navy from giving further support to the Guadalcanal operation.

The Marines all along the perimeter were instructed to dig in, wire up tight and get some sleep. An attack could come at any time.

At dusk Kawaguchi's 2,100 men stealthily started down the hill toward the airfield. They came to a grassy plain and crossed it in the ghostly light of the new moon. They stopped and readied for the attack. Nishino felt someone grasp his hand. It was a private named Hayashi who had become a close friend since their departure from Palau. He had enlisted three months after graduating from college and was engaged to be married, but had left Japan so unexpectedly that he had not even said good-bye to his fiancee. "Perhaps I'll be killed tonight," he said. "I often used to think of going back home and marrying my girl but now I don't have such dreams. This is my address. When I'm dead, will you write to my . . . mother?"

Nishino squeezed his hand reassuringly, hoping that Hayashi, in turn, would write his wife if he was killed. Quietly the men stacked their knapsacks. Those who had fresh underwear changed; they wanted to be clean when they died. Officers crisscrossed each other's backs with strips of white cloth so their men would be able to follow them in the dark. Lieutenant Kurakake went them one better. In Borneo he had bought a large bottle of Guerlain for his wife. He doused himself with the perfume and said, "Follow your noses."

Kawaguchi had just learned that a winding ridge, running from north to south, lay between him and Henderson. It was a natural barricade, but since there was not enough time to circle it, he gave orders to storm the tip end from the front and sides.

Kawaguchi moved out with Nishino close behind, notebook in hand. He carried an Eastman 8-mm. movie camera and two still cameras, strung across his chest like a Mexican bandit's bandoleer. Someone slipped. There was a light metallic clink. A rifle shot cracked.

Again silence. A twig snapped, followed by two more reports. How could the enemy have discovered them so soon? An officer stumbled across a wire. He whispered to keep quiet and probed on the ground until he found something—a small black object that resembled a microphone. It had to be some kind of listening device. Young Private Hayashi found three more like it and brought them to Kawaguchi. *"Kakka-dono* [Your Excellency, sir]," he said, saluted and stood at rigid attention.

Kawaguchi was amused. He explained to Hayashi that in addressing officers up to a colonel's rank, it was proper to use "*-dono*." "You should simply address me as Your Excellency Kawaguchi."

"But I thought it would be impolite if I didn't add 'sir'!"

Cautiously they moved forward through the dense undergrowth until they reached the southern tip of the ridge. Here they were forced to split into two sections. One of Nishino's shoelaces, rotten from the jungle march, snapped and when he stooped to tie it, someone bumped into him.

"*Yama* [Mountain]," he whispered.

"*Kawa* [River]," came the countersign.

There was a shout from a bush just ahead. A grenade exploded and in the flash Nishino saw an American. A smaller figure lurched with a bayonet and the Marine fell. Again there was eerie silence, then another grenade explosion, a shriek of pain. Nishino noticed the scent of Guerlain and moved toward it.

"Japs!" some American shouted. Silence. "Japs! Front five!"

A few minutes before nine o'clock the quiet was shattered by a series of blunt explosions. It was the artillery unit Kawaguchi had left to make the diversionary attack. Almost immediately these guns were joined by a distant rumble and then the jarring crash of heavy shells. Japanese warships were once more bombarding Henderson.

At nine o'clock shouts of "*Totsugeki!*" (Charge!) echoed along the line. Led by dark figures wearing the unearthly white crosses, Kawaguchi's 2,100 men closed in on the tip of the ridge.

The Marines dug in on the serpentine ridge were under the command of Colonel Merritt ("Red Mike") Edson. They were outnumbered about 3 to 2. The Raider Battalion held the center and right flank, while the left flank was manned by the Parachutists under Harry Torgerson, a burly, pugnacious captain who had had most of his trousers blown off in a dynamite attack on a Tulagi cave.

Red signal flares shot up, followed by a barrage of Japanese mortar fire. The sky seemed full of fireworks. Parachute flares burst overhead, momentarily blinding the Marines. The Parachutists on the left heard a rhythmic slapping of gun butts coming from the foot of the ridge and a chant repeated over and over: "U. S. Marines be dead tomorrow!" Figures filtered through the darkness below, swarmed up the ridge.

One forward company, Captain Justin Duryea's, was almost cut off. He ordered smoke pots. The flash of explosions reflected against the billowing smoke and someone yelled

"Gas!" In the confusion the companies on the advanced slopes began to pull out of their exposed positions. The withdrawal endangered one flank of Major William J. McKennon's company, but he knew the ridge had to be held at all costs or it would be the end of Henderson. He moved his men back slowly, spreading them out to right and left.

Torgerson was all over the left flank rallying his troops with encouragement and insults. He shouted at the men by name and dared them to attack. A few lagged back, were kicked into place, and the entire line started forward.

The Japanese rushed to meet them, supported by desultory light-machine-gun fire. But three of McKennon's machine guns opened up, bowling over the Japanese "like tenpins." A second wave surged forward and was hurled back. It was, thought McKennon, like a rainstorm beating down, subsiding and resuming a moment later with equal fury.

On the crest of the ridge Colonel Edson was talking to one of his captains on the phone. A voice broke in: "Our situation here, Colonel Edson, is excellent. Thank you, sir." It was obviously no Marine. The Enemy had tapped the line somewhere and this meant the Raider company on the right was cut off and had to be pulled back. The line out front was dead, so Torgerson sent a noncom forward; his bull voice could be heard above the din of battle: "Red Mike says it's okay to pull back!"

The entire end of the ridge seemed engulfed by Japanese, and Edson hugged the ground, telephone in hand, until he saw Marines scrambling to the rear. He grabbed two as they went by and yelled, "The only thing the Japs have that you don't is guts!" He picked up his phone and called in artillery. "Closer, closer," he said as he watched fountains of dirt march steadily toward him.

The attack was broken, but within half an hour there was another. It was preceded by smoke bombs and shouts in English of "Gas attack! Marine, you die!" In the smoke and confusion Edson was no longer able to maintain contact with his commanders. He ordered his outnumbered men back to the northern end of the ridge, a half mile from Henderson Field.

The Japanese stumbled over bodies of their own men in a blind rush forward—slowed but not stopped by machine-gun fire and an almost continuous barrage of grenades and mortar shells. In the vanguard on one side of the ridge were the remnants of a battalion led by a captain named Kokusho. Their headlong charge was interrupted by the discovery of a pile of Marine field rations. They wolfed down ham, sausage and beef. Kokusho lit an American cigarette, took a few deep puffs, and ordered his men to move out again against a battery of antiaircraft guns up ahead. "I'm not going to let any of you get in front of me, understand?" He cocked his helmet back, raised his sword and shouted *"Totsugeki!"*

They were caught in a cross fire, but Kokusho reached one of the guns followed by a handful of his own troops and a group of artillery men armed with bamboo spears. Kokusho was wounded in the face, and his uniform was splattered with blood. He gave a cry of *"Banzai!"* and started for the next gun position. He was staggered by a bullet but he leaped onto a gun platform. As he triumphantly raised his sword, a grenade exploded in his face. From the ground he mumbled. *"Totsugeki! Totsugeki!"* and died, sword still in hand.

All along the ridge devastating fire from the Americans was stopping the most fanatical charges. Round after round from 105-mm. howitzers, some fired as close as 1,600 yards, tore into the attackers. At two-thirty in the morning Edson picked up his phone. "We can hold," he told Vandegrift.

Dawn revealed the ridge as a slaughterhouse. From now on it would be known as Bloody Ridge. Six hundred Japanese were sprawled in the grotesque positions of death. There were forty dead Marines. The dazed defenders congratulated one another on being alive and exchanged stories of the enemy: the wounded who called for help—and exploded hidden grenades when an American approached; prisoners who kept pleading "Knife!" and pointing to their bellies.

Survivors were still making suicidal forays. Vandegrift was in front of his command post reading a message. He looked up at the cry of *"Banzai!"* to see three Japanese charging headlong at him; one of them, an officer, was flourishing a sword. Shots cut down all three at Vandegrift's feet.

The Japanese slowly withdrew toward Mount Austen, to reorganize, dragging hundreds of wounded with them. A rough count was taken—only eight hundred effectives remained. Nothing had worked according to plan. They had run into a rugged natural barricade, and the Marine defense had been unexpectedly strong. Moreover, a vital element had been missing; Colonel Oka never joined in the battle.

The colonel's position remained a mystery until that afternoon, when firing was heard from the northwest. Oka was at last attacking! But the crackle of fire died down almost immediately. Obviously he had met more than he could handle and would be of no help. A second assault was doomed before it started. Nevertheless, Kawaguchi was resolved to make a suicidal effort to redeem his failure—at least he would die in battle. At dusk he again led his men toward Henderson Field. After a two-hour march the ridge loomed once more before them. This time they started circling around it.

Kawaguchi gave the order to charge, and eight hundred men loped forward in the dark. Marine artillery had zeroed in on the area, and the Japanese were engulfed in a hell of explosions. It was far worse than the night before. Machine-gun bullets ripped through the brush. The ground shook incessantly like a never-ending earthquake. Trees toppled over; red-hot pieces of shrapnel whistled through the air. Kawaguchi could not turn back. He pressed on toward the airfield, but there was no escape anywhere. Fire followed their advance and eventually pinned them down. All night they hugged the ground. At dawn there were a few pitiful bursts from the last Japanese machine guns, the crump of mortar explosions in return, then silence.

"*Okasan!*" pleaded a soldier, calling for his mother. Another youngster wanted water and clutched at Nishino's leg with one arm; the other was a gushing stump. Nishino shook his canteen. Empty. He put the damp spout to the soldier's dry lips. He gulped, smiled wanly and died.

The sun was blinding and Nishino found it difficult to keep his eyes open. They burned and everything looked milky. What had been jungle was a barren wasteland. A few tree trunks stood like ruined Grecian columns. Nishino saw Yoshino, his liaison man, stagger to his feet and called to him in a croaking voice, "Hit the dirt, you fool!" Yoshino dropped beside him as a mortar round exploded yards away. Nishino covered his eyes and ears. He shivered from a malaria chill. Shells continued to plow into the ground probing for them. He felt his body slowly rise in the air and fall—again and again—as in a slow-motion movie. Overcome by an irresistible drowsiness, he let his head come to rest on the leaves. His body seemed to be sinking into something unknown and he wondered if he was going to sleep or if he was dying. Faces came to his mind: first his city editor, Honda; then his wife, looking very sad. There followed a procession of friends and, strangely, Verlaine and François Villon. He heard distant thunder like the crash of a tidal wave, and his body was again slowly lifted from the ground. He felt his breast pocket; a seashell rosary was still there, and the amulet Honda have given him for luck at the time when he told him not to get killed. He could see a little better. Less than a half a mile away was the end of a runway; they had almost made it to the airfield. As if in a dream, he started to creep back.

3.

The battle of Bloody Ridge had ended but Vandegrift's men, wracked by dysentery, fungus infections and malaria, scarcely resembled victors. The real crisis in the Pacific, however, was one the Marines on Guadalcanal were not even conscious of. Operation Shoestring had opened with three heavy carriers. Then *Enterprise* was so badly damaged in the Battle of the Eastern Solomons that she had to return to Pearl Harbor for extensive repairs. A week later the submarine *I-26* put a torpedo into *Saratoga*. Only twelve men were injured—Admiral Fletcher was one of them—but it would be months before the big ship could return to duty.

This left *Wasp*—and *Hornet*, which had arrived too late for the Battle of the Eastern Solomons. And the day after Bloody Ridge two Japanese submarines, *I-51* and *I-19*, penetrated the destroyer rings around these two flattops and moved into position to fire torpedoes. It was a clear, pleasant day with a brisk 20-knot trade wind. *Wasp* had just slowed down in order to launch twenty-six planes and take aboard eleven others which had been out on patrol. Startled lookouts saw torpedoes—a spread from *I-19*—approaching "hot, straight and normal," and gave the alarm. The skipper, Captain Forrest Sherman, ordered a turn to the right, but two torpedoes plunged into the starboard side of the carrier. Explosions shuddered through *Wasp*, and she began to list heavily.

Five miles away, torpedoes from *I-15* were churning toward *Hornet*. They all missed her but just before three o'clock one struck the battleship *North Carolina*, blasting a hole eighteen by thirty-two feet below the water line. Two minutes later another ripped open the destroyer *O'Brien*. The fires on *Wasp* were already out of control. A monumental explosion rocked the carrier. At three-twenty Sherman was forced to abandon ship. The Navy had one battleship and one carrier to back up the Marines on Guadalcanal.

On the hillside overlooking Bloody Ridge, Kawaguchi, uniform in tatters, faced the battlefield, bowed his head and clasped his hands together in prayer for the dead. Now his task was to get his men back safely to the coast. He decided it was shorter to keep heading west and follow the path of the scouts he had sent to search out Oka.* By the second day hundreds of walking wounded had collapsed, and exhausted litter carriers had to abandon scores of others on the trail. There was no order at all. They traveled in groups of fifteen or twenty, each at its own pace. Nishino's left arm was useless and he was weak from malaria. Weighted down by his heavy money belt of 50,000 yen, he followed the ragged column along the slopes of Mount Austen, through endless jungles. There was nothing to eat but grass, moss and an occasional betel nut. He passed scores of bodies in blood-soaked uniforms. Most had outstretched arms as if reaching for something.

By the sixth day the noncoms had to lash the younger soldiers with switches to keep them moving. Nishino could hardly put one foot in front of the other. Just before noon he emerged from the dark jungle into a palm grove. Ahead was an endless expanse of green sea. They had come out at Point Cruz, seven miles west of the airfield.

"Oi! The sea!" a soldier shouted and led the way into the surf, clothes and all. They gulped down salt water. Nishino called out a warning but one private shouted back, "I don't mind if I die!" Nishino tried a mouthful of water but had to spit it out. He picked several little stones and licked the salt; it tasted almost sweet. He gathered another handful of pebbles and went back to the grove.

All afternoon they lazed around, drinking coconut milk, eating the white meat and discussing the battle. "We say we have Japanese *seishin*, but those Yankees have their own, don't they! On the night of the thirteenth when we attacked the gun position, an American jumped at me but I bayoneted him. He screamed, but just before he died he set off a red signal flare. In a moment mortar shells came in all around us. My comrades all died. Only I escaped."

There was silence. "That's Yankee spirit," murmured another man.

"That's it."

"They love their country too. We're not the only ones."

---

*More than half of the Ichiki men returned on their own to the coast in the other direction, the way they had come.

Guadalcanal already had a new name—Starvation Island. *Ga*, the first syllable of Gadarukanaru, means among other things "hunger." Even during the indescribable ordeal of the march to the sea, one sentence always brought sardonic laughter: "The sky may fall but never Gadarukanaru"—the line supposedly uttered by the Navy commander of the island just before the Americans landed.

On September 18, four days after the Bloody Ridge battle, the Marines were reinforced with 4,200 men of the 7th Marine Regiment. They landed along with trucks, heavy engineer equipment, ammunition and supplies, and for the first time since he had been left stranded by the Navy, Vandegrift felt in control of the situation. He had a total of 23,000 men and an aggressive if dwindling air force that was more than holding its own.

But this confidence was not shared by his superiors. The next day Hanson Baldwin, the military correspondent for the *New York Times*, informed him that Washington was extremely alarmed by the situation on Guadalcanal, and Ghormley's headquarters in Nouméa even more so.

The aggravated Vandegrift said he "could neither understand nor condone such an attitude." It was obvious that the seizure of Guadalcanal "had caught Japan away off guard," and intercepted messages "pointed in certain cases to mass confusion at top command levels."

"Are you going to hold this beachhead?" Baldwin asked. "Are you going to stay here?"

"Hell, yes. Why not?"

Kawaguchi decided to send the reporters back to Rabaul. Nishino wanted to stay, but the general told the *Mainichi* group they had to leave. "After you've gone we shall fight resolutely and I hope to welcome you again on this island, gentlemen."

Nishino grasped his hand. It was bony, hot from fever.

At Shortland Island, Nishino transferred from a destroyer to the transport *Daifuku*, where he ran into an old acquaintance, Major General Yumio Nasu, commander of an "infantry group" of the 2nd Division.* The general failed to recognize him until he introduced himself.

---

*Before Pearl Harbor, a Japanese army division had two infantry brigades, each with two infantry regiments. After Pearl Harbor, a division had one infantry group consisting of three infantry regiments.

"Ah so, Nishino, you seem to be terribly ill," he said. "Gadarukanaru?" He moved his chair nearer. His division was bound for Guadalcanal and he wanted firsthand information. Nishino hesitated, but Nasu said, "I'd like to hear what an amateur thinks about things."

Nishino told about the fate of the Kawaguchi Detachment, of incessant air raids, of the Marines' use of electric warning devices, their endless food supplies, their inexhaustible ammunition and their surprising *seishin*.

"It's very serious," the general muttered. "What should be done?"

"Under such circumstances, I would say that if we keep sending in forces piecemeal, they will be swallowed up one by one. It's the worst thing to do, don't you agree, sir?" Nasu's interest encouraged him to be candid. "If I talked like this to anyone else, I'd probably be sent off to jail." Japanese soldiers were being asked to give their lives without proper equipment and supplies. "The last hope of our soldiers before they die is to see planes marked with the Rising Sun. They tell me they have the spirit to fight without food, but they can do very little on spirit alone."

"I agree," said Nasu. "It's a great pity we don't have enough planes and ships to do what you want."

Nasu was the vanguard of a new offensive to take Henderson Field. In Rabaul, General Hyakutake had decided to go to Guadalcanal and take personal command of the campaign. He was going to bring with him the 17th Army artillery—field pieces, 100-mm. guns and huge 150-mm. howitzers.

A series of joint Army-Navy meetings convened in 17th Army headquarters to co-ordinate the operation. One of the observers was Lieutenant Colonel Tsuji, "God of Operations." He had persuaded his superiors in Tokyo to send him south to find out what was really going on at Guadalcanal.

Tsuji listened without comment as General Hyakutake and the Navy argued endlessly over the means of transporting the 2nd Division to Guadalcanal. The Navy insisted that they be sent by the usual "Rat Express" or "Ant Freight." The general said the risk was too great; the 2nd Division had to be taken as a body in one large convoy under powerful naval escort. Impossible, said the Navy. They couldn't afford to provide more than "rat and ant" transportation: "How can we shake a sleeve we don't have?"

The Navy's refusal to commit important surface units to

the operation enraged Hyakutake and he delivered a reckless threat. "If the Navy lacks the strength to escort the Second Division properly to Guadalcanal, we will go in transports without any escort. And Seventeenth Army Headquarters will lead the way!"

Tsuji knew that if Hyakutake was forced to abide by his rash plan, it meant almost certain destruction of all the transports, and he abandoned his role as observer. He met privately with Hyakutake and offered to fly up to Truk, where he could present the general's arguments direct to Admiral Yamamoto.

Tsuji found Yamamoto on the battleship *Yamato* in the great Truk harbor. The admiral was on the floor of his cabin engrossed in writing bold Japanese characters with a brush—perhaps it was a poem for some admirer or a slogan for a schoolboy. His short, powerful body seemed to be bursting from his uniform.

Yamamoto listened in silence, occasionally nodding his head, as Tsuji dramatized the sacrifices made by the detachments which had previously been sent to Guadalcanal: "Our supply has been cut off for more than a month. Officers and men have to dig grass roots, scrape moss and pick buds from the trees and drink sea water to survive." They were all thinner than Gandhi. The new invasion force must be transported intact, and with supplies, to the island or it too would fail. "I beg you provide it with a strong escort. If the Navy finds it impossible to do this, then Army Commander Hyakutake is determined to lead the convoy himself and is prepared to be wiped out in his attempt to retake the island."

Yamamoto began to speak slowly. He admitted that the mistakes of the Navy had aggravated the hardships of the soldiers on Guadalcanal. "Very well," he said deliberately, "I, Yamamoto, will be personally responsible. If necessary, if we have to bring *Yamato* alongside the island, I promise to escort the transports the way the Army wants. There is only one thing—to save my face, don't let Hyakutake-*san* sail on a transport. Please have him go on a destroyer so he can land safely. His command capabilities are needed on the island."

Tears streaked Yamamoto's impassive face. Tsuji, also in tears, impulsively wished he could die under Yamamoto's command as a Navy staff officer.

There were many officers in the Japanese Army who would not have accepted—as Yamamoto so readily did—the realities of Guadalcanal. Nishino had just arrived in Rabaul by transport from Shortland, intent on making a report in person to 17th Army headquarters. He was taken to the office of the adjutant, a lieutenant colonel named Fukunaga, who asked, "How's the island?"

Nishino disliked him on sight. He was haughty and his well-fed body looked greasy—so unlike the skeletons on Guadalcanal. "Our friends on Gadarukanaru are now surviving on fighting spirit alone. But it won't last much longer. Let me beg you, sir, to supply them with as much food as possible—"

"Are you criticizing the Army?" he accused.

"This is not criticism." Nishino explained that he only wanted to tell the truth about Guadalcanal. He began to feel dizzy and put his hands on the adjutant's desk to steady himself.

"This is the tropics," said the colonel. "Why are you so pale?" It too came out like an accusation.

"I've been in the jungle. There's no sunlight there."

"You just lack *seishin!*"

"My *seishin* saved me from the hell of Gadarukanaru. If you go there, you'll see." It was useless to talk to such a fool. He turned to leave.

"Eat tomatoes, that'll do you good!" Nishino was almost at the door when he heard, "Hey, you!" Fukunaga's voice was ominous. "Just remember, we'll never let you return to Japan. It would be like sending a spy back home."

16   "I Deserve Ten Thousand Deaths"

1.

Before Colonel Tsuji left *Yamato*, Admiral Yamamoto put his verbal promise on paper: the Combined Fleet would escort the 2nd Division transports to Tassafaronga Point, and Henderson Field would be shelled by battleships on the eve of the landing. Yamamoto went further. He saw in Guadalcanal yet another opportunity to force the Decisive Battle that obsessed Japan's military leaders. Once Hyakutake launched his general attack on the airfield and began to make progress, Combined Fleet would compel the U. S. Navy to wage a major engagement. It would be the end of American naval power in the Solomons and the beginning of the end of their authority in the Pacific.

Tsuji returned to Rabaul to work out final plans for the attack on Henderson with General Hyakutake's senior staff officer. Colonel Haruo Konuma—his father ran a small silk-weaving plant—had followed the classic military route: cadet school, Military Academy and War College. Chief of the Strategy and Tactics Section of the General Staff at the time of the American occupation of Guadalcanal (even he had not heard of the island), he was not involved in the operation until September. To dislodge the enemy, he concluded, it would take a full division, heavy guns, tanks and substantial quantities of ammunition and supplies. But these could not be transported to Guadalcanal without wholesale support by the Army air force. The Navy fliers were trained to screen warships rather than transports.

Operations Chief Takushiro Hattori saw the merit of his argument but vetoed it; he was afraid that the Soviet Union might attack the Kwantung Army if so many planes were withdrawn from Manchuria. Although his plan was rejected, his services were not. He was selected to go to Rabaul as Hyakutake's operations officer. Konuma refused at first. He not only doubted the feasibility of retaking Guadalcanal—Ichiki and Kawaguchi had already failed miserably—but had no confidence that the Navy would supply strong enough escorts for convoys.

It took more than the persuasion of his department chief to change his mind. Colonel Tsuji, his close friend and classmate at the War College, offered his services as unofficial adviser, and his reputation for overcoming all obstacles was such that Konuma, albeit reluctantly, took the post.

The first problem he faced in Rabaul did not originate with the Navy but with the Army. Hyakutake's chief of staff, General Akisaburo Futami, was a sick man, which may in part have accounted for his conviction that Guadalcanal was a lost cause. At every meeting—even at the conferences with the Navy—he would repeat over and over again, "We must not try to retake Guadalcanal; we have no chance of winning there!"

By-passing Hyakutake, Konuma radioed the Army General Staff direct, demanding a replacement. Before the day was over, Futami was relieved but there continued to be command problems. Since Kawaguchi had failed, the younger staff officers wanted him taken off Guadalcanal and returned to Tokyo lest his critical attitude toward Imperial Headquarters infect newcomers. But Konuma remembered him as an able and bright officer and arranged to have him brought up to Rabaul for interrogation. Kawaguchi arrived in a torn, filthy uniform. His report of the tribulations of his detachment was irrefutable and Konuma advised Hyakutake to let him command one of the units in the coming attack. Who else knew the conditions and terrain so intimately?

Recently arrived reinforcements and supplies allowed Vandegrift to set up a complete perimeter defense, studded with foxholes and machine-gun emplacements, and following hills and ridges where possible. There was enough barbed wire to surround the entire front with two bands of double-apron fencing.

With more than nineteen thousand men Vandegrift at last felt ready to inaugurate a limited offensive of his own against the concentration of Japanese to the west. On September 23 he sent one battalion southwest; upon reaching the slopes of Mount Austen, it began looping back toward the sea along the east bank of the Mataniko River closely tagged by another battalion. Surprisingly, they met no resistance. As these two forces approached the mouth of the river, they were joined by a third battalion which had come the easy way, along the coast.

The following day, September 27, the Marines tried to push across the river but were unexpectedly pinned down by enemy fire. A message back to Colonel Edson, commander of the joint forces, got so badly scrambled in the heat of action that "Red Mike" took it to mean that his troops had successfully crossed the Mataniko. Consequently he ordered another battalion to make an amphibious landing at Point Cruz and trap the retreating enemy. This battalion landed without opposition and advanced 350 yards inland before the enemy attacked from both flanks. Badly mauled, the Marines fought their way back to the beach and were evacuated under heavy fire to a destroyer. Sixty Americans died.

There were no more than five thousand Japanese scattered on both sides of Henderson and most of them were starving. Probably not more than half that number was capable of bearing arms, but these men were prepared to fight to the death. Their first aggressive reaction at the Mataniko convinced Vandegrift that he was facing a much stronger force. The Navy, which had abandoned the Marines after the Savo debacle, did not agree. Admiral Turner wrote Vandegrift that it was time to press the enemy. "I believe you are in a position to take some chances and go after them hard," he said.

Stung, Vandegrift radioed back that reconnaissance "would tend to show that we may expect an attack in force from additional troops to be landed some time around the first of October when the moon is favorable to such landing and operations." Accordingly, he added, a major Marine push would be dangerous. He was irked that Turner couldn't realize that the Japanese were merely slacking off while they mounted a new offensive.

Two days later Admiral Nimitz flew in and patiently listened to Vandegrift's argument that the principal mission of the Marines was to hold Henderson Field. The admiral was sympathetic but noncommittal. That evening over a drink he said, "You know, Vandegrift, when this war is over we are going to write a new set of *Navy Regulations*. So just keep it in the back of your mind because I will want to know some of the things that ought to be changed."

"I know one right now. Leave out all reference that he who runs his ship aground will face a fate worse than death. Out here too many commanders have been far too leery about risking their ships."

Nimitz smiled, but something about his manner gave Vandegrift the feeling that he understood the problems on Guadalcanal and would send out more air, ground and sea reinforcements. Heartened by Nimitz' visit, Vandegrift decided to launch another limited attack to keep the enemy off balance. This time he ordered a full regiment to move down the coast from the east to the mouth of the Mataniko, and sent three battalions through the jungle about a mile inland to cross the river secretly upstream and catch the Japanese in a pincers.

The regiment reached the east bank of the river and began making obvious preparations for crossing. Men moved about noisily, and amphibious tractors rumbled around just behind the lines. This diversion allowed the three battalions to cross the Mataniko on the morning of October 9 without being discovered. They then wheeled sharply to the right toward the sea, entrapping the Japanese along the west bank. Tons of artillery and mortar shells were dumped onto the Japanese positions. Those who tried to escape over the ridges were caught in the open and cut down by automatic-weapon fire. The Marines reported that more than seven hundred Japanese (almost one third of their entire effective force on the island) lay dead along the Mataniko. The Marines lost sixty-five.

Yamamoto kept his word, and that midnight the transports carrying the 2nd Division, as well as 17th Army Headquarters, safely reached Tassafaronga Point. General Hyakutake—accompanied by Kawaguchi, Konuma and Tsuji—waded ashore. With them was Major General Tadashi Sumiyoshi, commander of 17th Army artillery units.

As bags of rice and other supplies were brought to the shore, ragged figures emerged from the brush and timidly approached. They looked like walking skeletons; their hair was long and dirty and their torn, begrimed clothing no longer resembled uniforms. One man told Tsuji they were survivors of the Ichiki and Kawaguchi detachments and they had come to help unload the supplies.

Kawaguchi led Hyakutake and his party down the beach toward the new headquarters of the 17th Army. It was dawn, October 10, by the time they reached their destination near a small river five miles west of the Mataniko. At breakfast Hyakutake received a report that most of the rice unloaded the night before had been stolen by the volunteer coolies. "It is my fault for having brought such loyal soldiers to such a miserable lot," said Hyakutake. "May they fill their stomachs with our food and be remade into good soldiers."

All along the coast near Hyakutake's headquarters the last survivors of the Battle of Bloody Ridge were stumbling out of the jungle. Their ribs protruded. Their black hair had turned a dirty brown and could be pulled out in patches. Their eyebrows and eyelashes were dropping off and their teeth were loose. For almost three weeks no one had had a bowel movement and their bodies were so starved for salt that the sea water tasted sweet. The water brought on a painful urge to evacuate but they were too weak. They had to help each other with fingers. The relief was indescribable.

The dismay that Hyakutake felt at the sight of such suffering was compounded when he learned the details of the devastating defeat at the Mataniko. He radioed Rabaul: SITUATION OF GUADALCANAL IS FAR MORE SERIOUS THAN ESTIMATED, and asked for reinforcements and supplies at once.

Furthermore, the Marine victory made it necessary for Konuma and Tsuji to draw up another battle plan, to start in about ten days. Instead of attacking straight down the coast across the Mataniko, they would make a surprise night attack on Henderson from the rear. While the 2nd Division pushed through the jungle behind Mount Austen, General Sumiyoshi would keep the Americans occupied by shelling their postions from the west bank of the Mataniko and then, several hours before H-hour, launch an infantry attack of regiment size as a diversion—and draw the Americans to the Mataniko. At H-hour Lieutenant General Masao Maruyama, commander of the 2nd Division, would launch a simultaneous two-pronged attack from the south. The main body—commanded by General Yumio Nasu, who had first learned about Guadalcanal on Shortland from Nishino—would turn left and come up the corridor between Bloody Ridge and the Lungga River while the right flank, under Kawaguchi, advanced to the east of the ridge over almost the same ground he earlier fought. Kawaguchi felt apprehensive about the plan but he was in too precarious a position to argue that this particular terrain was too rugged for an attack, particularly since it was logical to make a flanking attack where the enemy least expected it.

Success depended on the prompt arrival of artillery and ammunition, as well as on the completion of a semicircular trail which led behind Mount Austen and then northward along the Lungga River to a point just below the airfield. Fortunately it had been started a month earlier and was almost finished. It ran fifteen miles through jungle so thick that men could not walk upright for more than a few paces. The Army Engineers had only hand tools with which to cut down large trees and hack through tough vines as thick as a man's arm. The felled trees were placed along either side of the trail; bushes and roots were cut away. Log roads spanned marshes, and camouflage netting hid stretches across grass plains. Ravines as wide as a hundred feet were bridged with thick vines, with smaller vines serving as hand rails up steep inclines.

It was already nicknamed "the Maruyama Trail" after the resolute commander of the 2nd Division. Maruyama was a mild-looking man, imperturbable under fire. He had no illusions about the difficulties of his mission but realized its significance. Before they set out for Guadalcanal he told his troops; "This is the Decisive Battle between Japan and the United States, a battle in which the rise or fall of the Japanese Empire will be decided. If we do not succeed in the occupation of these islands, no one should expect to return to Japan alive."

The first answer to Hyakutake's urgent call for reinforcements was a modest force of two small seaplane carriers and six destroyers. They came down Solomons passage at full speed on October 11, bringing four big howitzers, two field guns, an antiaircraft gun, ammunition, assorted supplies and 728 troops.

They were sighted by a B-17, and at dusk an American task group of two heavy and two light cruisers and five destroyers, commanded by a veteran of World War I, Rear Admiral Norman Scott, speeded at 29 knots from its hiding place less than a hundred miles below Guadalcanal, to catch the enemy convoy before it reached the island. Unlike previous American units, Scott's was ready and eager for night battle; for weeks the crews had been kept at their stations from sunset to dawn. What Scott didn't know was that lurking behind the convoy was a special bombardment force— the three heavy cruisers and two destroyers of Rear Admiral Aritomo Goto.

The sky was slightly overcast and the silver of a new moon gave off almost no light. There was a gentle breeze as Scott approached Cape Esperance from the southwest just before ten-thirty, cruisers in column, one destroyer on either side. Scott planned to turn right at the cape in order to contact the enemy and be in position to hit the transports when they tried to unload on the north coast of Guadalcanal. He signaled his ships to form a single column and prepare for battle.

About forty miles to the northwest Goto was approaching Savo with his three cruisers in column—the first was his flagship, *Aoba*—flanked by the two destroyers. The transport group was ahead, just off Cape Esperance, and starting down the coast toward Tassafaronga Point to land its valuable cargo.

Around eleven o'clock the eight ships were discovered by one of Admiral Scott's planes but reported only as "one large, two small vessels." Friend or foe? Scott wondered. And, if enemy, where were the rest of the transports? He set out to look for them and turned left to pass six miles west of Savo. The light cruiser *Helena* had already picked up the Japanese column with its new SG search radar, but her commander, Captain Gilbert C. Hoover, wanted to make sure before passing on the information to Scott. The flagship *San Francisco* was not yet equipped with SG, and Scott had no idea that Goto was bearing down on him. Upon reaching the north end of the little volcanic island at eleven-thirty, he ordered the entire column to reverse course. Two minutes later the nine ships started heading back to the southwest at 20 knots, patrolling the passage between Savo and Cape Esperance. After ten more minutes Captain Hoover at last signaled Scott that there was definitely an enemy six miles to the northwest and coming fast.

Then the light cruiser *Boise* reported "five bogies." Scott was confused; "bogey" usually meant an unidentified plane. At last *San Francisco's* less efficient radar found Goto's flagship just 5,000 yards away. Before Scott could determine whether it was friend or foe, Captain Hoover got a message from a lookout: "Ships visible to the naked eye." By voice radio Hoover asked permission to open fire. Scott laconically answered "Roger," meaning "Message received," but fortunately Hoover took it for its code meaning, "Commence firing." And so, shortly before midnight, *Helena* opened up on Goto.

With no radar at all, Goto was taken completely by surprise. As other ships joined in the bombardment, he assumed that the transport convoy was firing on him because it had mistaken him for the Americans in the dark. He ordered the column to turn right and almost immediately was knocked to *Aoba's* deck, mortally wounded, by one of the shells exploding the length of the cruiser.

Like Goto, Scott imagined friend was attacking friend and ordered Cease Firing a minute after the first shots. It took him another four minutes to learn the truth, but once Scott was sure it was the enemy out front, he bore in tenaciously to give the Japanese their first real challenge in a night battle. The action was furious and bold, with both sides loosing salvo after salvo on the other and refusing to back off. By the time all firing had ceased, about twenty minutes after midnight, the waters between Cape Esperance and Savo were ablaze with flaming ships. *Aoba,* though hit forty times, escaped up The Slot with the dying Goto, but the cruiser *Furutaka* and the destroyer *Fubuki* were sinking.

The American task group was also hurt. *Boise* was an inferno and the magazines threatened to go up at any moment. Then sea water cascaded in through a shell hole, flooding the magazines. Only one of Scott's ships was in desperate shape, the destroyer *Duncan;* its fires could not be controlled. For the first time the Japanese had been beaten at their own game—night battle—and the Americans were elated. The humiliating Battle of Savo had been avenged. Victory it was, but as at Savo, where Admiral

Mikawa had allowed the American transports to land, the Battle of Cape Esperance had diverted the winners from the Japanese convoy. During the fierce melee, the transports were putting ashore the artillery, ammunition and reinforcements that General Hyakutake needed so desperately.

The seesaw battle of supply, however, went to the Americans the next day, October 13: 2,852 GI's of the Americal Division, along with sixteen British Bren-gun carriers, twelve 37-mm. guns, ammunition, trucks and a mountain of provisions were unloaded at Lungga Point in spite of two bombing raids. Now Vandegrift had 23,088 men to defend his perimeter, and judged by Japanese standards, he was unbelievably rich in all kinds of supplies.

Still, there was no time for complacency. At noon two dozen Japanese planes bombed Henderson from an altitude of 30,000 feet with devastating accuracy, and before Seabees could clear away the worst of the rubble, another fifteen bombers droned over to rip up the airstrips. Combat Engineers swarmed back to work and finished filling in the holes. There was an unearthly shriek followed by an explosion on the main runway. General Sumiyoshi had already moved up the first of his 150-mm. howitzers to the Mataniko River and he continued to pound the field so unerringly that the Marines nicknamed the long-range gun "Pistol Pete."

Nor was this the end of Japanese harassment for the day. At dusk two battleships, *Kongo* and *Haruna*, plowed toward Guadalcanal, along with six destroyers. The big warships hoped to blast Henderson out of existence with their mighty 36-cm. guns.* Together they carried over nine hundred shells. Some were Type 3 incendiaries, but most were the brand-new Type Zero armor-piercing bombardment shells.

Just before midnight the raiders, still undetected by the Americans, approached Guadalcanal at 18 knots, guided by oil drums set afire by Japanese infantrymen. *Kongo* led, with *Haruna* a thousand yards behind, all sixteen of their big guns trained to the south. Shortly after one o'clock, October 14, they began spewing out incendiary shells. In moments Captain Tomiji Koyanagi, skipper of *Kongo*, could see a lake of fire to starboard. It was Henderson! He gave orders to load up with the new armor-piercing shells. The cannonade became even more deafening, and on Guadalcanal spouts of

---

*The diameter of their barrels was slightly over 14 inches.

flame shot up from exploded fuel and ammunition depots. The Marines burrowed into their foxholes or crouched helplessly in shelters as the earth shook. It was the most terrifying experience in their lives and Vandegrift himself was shaken. Finally, after half an hour, the firing stopped. "I don't know how you feel," said his operations officer, "but I think I prefer a good bombing or artillery shelling."

Vandegrift nodded. "I think I do——" His words were cut off by a violent explosion. The concussion bowled over everyone in the shelter. *Kongo* and *Haruna* had resumed the bombardment on the return trip up the coast.

So far, not a plane or ship had gone out to challenge the Japanese, but now four torpedo boats from Tulagi rushed at them, launching torpedoes and spraying the area with machine-gun fire. It was a gallant gesture, but they were driven off by destroyers and their torpedoes skipped past the battleships.

For an hour and a half the bombardment continued. With ammunition almost exhausted—814 armor-piercing shells and 104 incendiaries had been flung at Guadalcanal—the Japanese were ordered to cease fire. *Kongo* and *Haruna* turned north, slipping between Savo and Tulagi at 29 knots.

Henderson Field had been blasted almost beyond recognition. Bits of clothing and equipment dangled from phone wires. Forty-one men lay dead, many others were wounded. Vandegrift's tiny Cactus Air Force ("Cactus" was the code name for Guadalcanal) was a shambles. There was almost no aviation gas; only thirty-five fighters and seven dive bombers were operable. Army fliers eyed the ravaged field and wondered if they could get in the air with their P-400's and Airacobras. "We don't know whether we'll be able to hold the field or not," a Marine colonel told them. "There's a Japanese task force of destroyers, cruisers and troop transports headed our way. We have enough gasoline left for one mission against them." He told them to load up with bombs and go after the enemy. "After the gas is gone we'll have to let the ground troops take over. Then your officers and men will attach yourselves to some infantry outfit. Good luck and good-bye."

Gone were the high hopes of yesterday; a feeling of doom settled over the island. The night bombardment had done more than physical damage; Marines would never forget the primal terror that came when the very earth writhed and exploded in the dark.

The report that another Japanese convoy was heading for the island was true. Six big new high-speed transports loaded with four thousand men, fourteen tanks and a dozen 15-cm. howitzers and assorted supplies were coming down The Slot protected by destroyers and fighter planes.

The Cactus Air Force managed to get eleven planes off the ground, but the best they could do was slightly damage one destroyer. By midnight the transports were unloading off Tassafaronga Point as two heavy cruisers, *Chokai* and *Kinugasa*, ranged up and down the coast lobbing in 8-inch shells. Their captains had been so sure they would be sunk that all men had been told to prepare to swim for shore and join the soldiers as infantrymen. But like the battleships, *Kongo* and *Haruna*, they escaped without damage up The Slot after firing 752 shells.

Three empty transports also managed to withdraw; however, the other three were still unloading at dawn when the remnants of Vandegrift's planes, after a frantic scramble for fuel, took to the air. All three ships were set afire and had to be run aground. Most of the tank fuel went up in flames, detonating countless rounds of ammunition, but the troops aboard did make it to shore along with the tanks and howitzers. Now Hyakutake had more than fifteen thousand able-bodied men and adequate artillery. He was as ready as he ever would be for his offensive.

Vandegrift suspected that most of the supplies had been landed and radioed Nimitz, Ghormley and Turner that at least fifteen thousand Japanese and a considerable amount of equipment and supplies were now on the island.

... OUR FORCE EXCEEDS THAT NUMBER BUT MORE THAN HALF OF IT IS IN NO CONDITION TO UNDERTAKE A PROTRACTED LAND CAMPAIGN DUE TO INCESSANT HOSTILE OPERATIONS ... THE SITUATION DEMANDS TWO URGENT AND IMMEDIATE STEPS: TAKE AND MAINTAIN CONTROL OF SEA AREAS ADJACENT TO CACTUS TO PREVENT FURTHER ENEMY LANDINGS AND ENEMY BOMBARDMENT SUCH AS THIS FORCE HAS TAKEN FOR THE LAST THREE NIGHTS; REINFORCEMENT OF GROUND FORCES BY AT LEAST ONE DIVISION IN ORDER THAT EXTENSIVE OPERATIONS MAY BE INITIATED TO DESTROY HOSTILE FORCE NOW ON CACTUS.

Nimitz' inspection of Guadalcanal and Nouméa had convinced him that Ghormley had to be replaced with a more aggressive commander, a man who would see opportunities rather than difficulties. On October 18 he radioed Halsey:

Halsey got the message moments after his flying boat
touched down on the waters of Nouméa harbor. He read it
twice in wonder and then exclaimed, "Jesus Christ and General
Jackson! This is the hottest potato they ever handed
me!" He went from astonishment to apprehension. He knew
only enough about the situation in the South Pacific to realize
it was desperate; and he regretted having to relieve his
old friend Bob Ghormley, who had played on the same
football team at the Academy.

Halsey ordered Vandegrift to fly down to Nouméa. The
Marine general reported that his men were "practically worn
out" by more than two months of lean diet, disease, bombings,
bombardments and *banzai* attacks, and had to have air
and ground reinforcements.

The stocky Halsey, gray eyebrows bristling, thoughtfully
drummed his fingers on the desk. "Are we going to evacuate
or hold?" he asked.

"Yes, I can hold. But I have to have more active support
than I have been getting."

Admiral Turner protested. The Navy was doing all it could
to send in more supplies, but there were no warships to
protect transports, neither was there a base at Guadalcanal
where they could find shelter. Moreover, enemy submaries
were getting more numerous and increasingly aggressive.

Halsey knew Turner was right, but Guadalcanal *had* to be
held. "All right," he told Vandegrift, "go on back. I'll promise
you everything I've got."

2.

On Guadalcanal 5,600 men of Maruyama's 2nd Division—
not including artillery, engineer and medical troops—had
begun their march toward Mount Austen. They planned to
be in position to attack on the night of October 21. Just
before they left, Hyakutake's senior staff officer, Colonel
Konuma, took Tsuji aside and said he had hoped to direct
operations in person but had to remain at 17th Army headquarters
to act as chief of staff. "Would you go in my
place?" he asked. There was nothing Tsuji wanted better. Besides,
he would have "jumped into fire" for a friend like
Konuma.

Starting off with a compass and a single inaccurate map, General Maruyama led his force down the trail. The first day was an easy walk through coconut groves and over barren ridges, and that night the men settled down as if it were a camping trip. But at midnight a torrent of rain beat down on the sleeping men. They tried to protect themselves with huge umbrella-like leaves. Shivering, soaking wet, miserable, they huddled together for warmth.

The next day the long line was swallowed up by a dark, dense, hilly forest. The white-haired Maruyama led the way, pushing himself forward with his white cane. Beside him General Nasu, a *hachimaki* tied around his forehead, was wracked by malaria, but he continued stolidly without complaint. At a break he called to Tsuji, "I have something good but there's only a spoonful left." The general reached for a round cigarette tin which was attached to his waist by a string, much in the same way his ancestors had carried pillboxes. Tsuji found about a spoonful of sugar at the bottom of the can and poured half into his palm. He gave the rest to his aide. Nothing had ever tasted so sweet.

The Maruyama Trail narrowed, forcing the men to walk single file. The winding column crossed hill after hill, rivers, streams, inching forward slowly, painfully, like a great worm. Each man carried, in addition to his pack, some part of a field gun, a shell or other equipment. Since it was too dangerous to cook, all—from Maruyama to the lowliest private—lived on half rations of rice. They scaled steep cliffs with ropes, hauling up light field pieces and machine guns by sheer muscle. But by the third day the task was too much except for the hardiest, and gun after gun had to be abandoned at the side of the trail.

Since it was obvious that they could never keep their schedule, Maruyama radioed 17th Army headquarters that the attack would have to be postponed one day. On October 22 Maruyama still had not reached his line of departure and he made another postponement of twenty-four hours. By afternoon his men had circled around Mount Austen. Here the 2nd Division split in two, with Nasu and Division Headquarters continuing on the trail directly toward Henderson Field. Kawaguchi, who would command the right flank, turned off to the southeast with three infantry battalions and three machine-gun and trench-mortar battalions.

As Kawaguchi left the main body, he encountered Tsuji. The colonel had no use for Kawaguchi. First, he was a loser and a complainer; second, he was one of the so-called "liberal" officers who, like Homma, had tried to save captured Filipino leaders from their just fate—death. But the general was not aware of his enmity. "I'm glad to find you here," he began and went on to discuss his misgivings about the Tsuji-Konuma plan of attack. It could not possibly work: although Nasu would be attacking over fairly good terrain on the left flank, his own advance on the right would be over much the same ground where his detachment had suffered such a disaster in September. The area around the ridge was just too rough for a frontal type of assault.

"Have you seen the Navy's aerial photographs?" he asked. In his opinion these recent pictures indicated that the Americans had greatly strengthened and enlarged their perimeter defense. "They show clearly that I have no chance of success with a frontal assault. I would like to lead the right column in a circle *behind* the enemy's eastern flank." This was a point southeast of Henderson, with nothing but rolling open hills, fields and sparse woods to traverse. He knew that section well from personal observation. Nasu could advance as planned, and the two forces would catch the Americans in a real pincers.

"I don't need to see the pictures," Tsuji replied. "I'm familiar with the terrain and I agree fully with your proposal." Kawaguchi wanted to take his suggestion to Maruyama, but Tsuji assured him that wouldn't be necessary. "I will explain personally to His Excellency Maruyama. I wish you great success." He extended his hand. "Well, the battle is really getting interesting, isn't it?" he said and laughed. As Kawaguchi was soon to find out, the Machiavellian colonel never told Maruyama about the conversation.

On the morning of October 23, Maruyama was not yet in position and made a third postponement, issuing final orders to launch the general attack the following day at midnight. He added his personal exhortation for every officer and man "to fight desperately and fulfill his duty in repayment of His Majesty's favor."

Kawaguchi didn't get the message until midafternoon, when he was still at least a day and a half's march from his new line of departure. In the emergency he cable-phoned Maruyama that he couldn't get into position in time. Maruyama curtly replied that there could be no further delays, and it suddenly dawned on Kawaguchi that the division commander knew nothing about his verbal agreement with Tsuji of the day before. Controlling himself, Kawaguchi said, "In that case, I will carry out the night assault with my advance unit, the Third Isshiki Battalion."

Maruyama began shouting that Kawaguchi would follow orders to the letter. With that he slammed down the receiver, so angry that his hair seemed to bristle—the stories about Kawaguchi were apparently true. He got Kawaguchi on the phone again. "Major General Kawaguchi," he said stiffly, "report immediately to Division headquarters." He was to turn over command of the right flank to Colonel Toshinari Shoji.

It was Tsuji himself who phoned 17th Army headquarters with the information. "Kawaguchi refused to advance," he told Konuma, "and the division commander relieved him of his command." He gave no details.

On the coast General Sumiyoshi was ready for his diversionary attack. All his heavy artillery and ammunition had been manhandled into position several miles west of the Mataniko River. Early that evening, the twenty-third, he opened his attack, a day ahead of time. He had not received notice of the third postponement.*

After a heavy bombardment he sent nine tanks across a sandbar in the van of his infantry. They were met by a counterbombardment so effective that only one tank managed to reach the other side of the river. It ran into the sea, however, wallowing about in the surf until it stalled and was blasted to pieces by a 75-mm. tank destroyer. Six hundred Japanese infantry men lost their lives.

It was a useless gesture. The diversion had failed and by now the Americans were alerted. The next afternoon they discovered that the enemy was behind Henderson in force: first, a column was detected crossing the foothills of Mount Austen, then someone noticed a Japanese officer studying Bloody Ridge through field glasses, and finally a Marine from the Scout-Sniper Detachment reported seeing "many rice fires" rising out of the jungle two miles south of the ridge.

Tsuji and Konuma had guessed correctly that Vandegrift never expected a major attack from this direction. But unlike the Kawaguchi Detachment, which had arrived behind Hen-

---

*After the war Maruyama and Hyakutake blamed each other for failing to notify Sumiyoshi in time. The latter said it had been Maruyama's responsibility to keep Sumiyoshi informed of the final postponement. The former claimed that Hyakutake had overestimated the progress of the march and had directly ordered the Sumiyoshi attack on the twenty-third.

derson undiscovered, Maruyama's presence was now known. Marine Colonel Lewis "Chesty" Puller, a short man with a pouter-pigeon chest who had survived a hundred combats in the "banana war" of Haiti and Nicaragua, walked along the lines south of the airfield personally checking the positions. He ordered his men to dig in deeper and to set up more sandbags. Shell fragments and other pieces of metal were hung on barbed wire to give audible warning of any surprise assault at night, while men using bayonets as scythes cut fields of fire in the seven-foot-tall grass out front. Lookouts were posted on top of a barren knoll. Puller's Marines were ready.

Maruyama wasn't—but thought he was. Nasu was in position on the left, but Kawaguchi's replacement, Colonel Shoji, had encountered such precipitous ravines and dense jungles after leaving the Maruyama Trail that he had not yet been able to get his main body to the original line of departure.

An hour before midnight huge drops of rain fell slowly, heavily, like blobs of oil. They plummeted faster—and faster, becoming an almost solid sheet of water. Maruyama, his staff and Tsuji scrambled up a disintegrating hill to a small flat ledge. The staff sat in a tight circle, huddling together around Maruyama to keep him warm. A few minutes after midnight they heard small-arms fire from the right. It grew in intensity. Had Shoji broken through or been thrown back?

A report finally came in by phone from Matsumoto, a division operations officer on liaison duty with Shoji. "The right flank attacked the airfield," he cried. "The night attack is a success!"

"*Banzai!*" Maruyama shouted impulsively.

Now they could hear firing on the left—the ping of rifles and the low chuckle of machine guns. It was Nasu. Then a roar of mortar and heavy-artillery fire. The Americans! The response was so immediate and so intense that Tsuji feared something had gone wrong. The others—including Maruyama—were infected by his anxiety and sat rigid.

The phone rang again. "I was mistaken about the success of the right flank," said Matsumoto. "They haven't reached the airfield yet. They crossed a large open field and thought it was the airfield. It was a mistake." Shoji's meager vanguard, forced to attack prematurely at midnight, was already pinned down.

The bombardment on the left continued, louder than ever. An hour passed without a report from Nasu. Tsuji was struck with "an omen of doom" and his bones "felt cold."

457

Nasu's first charge had been forced back by a furious mélange of Marine small-arms, automatic-weapon and artillery fire. Critically ill from malaria, Nasu remained near the front, more afraid of dying from the disease than of the explosions around him. His troops—the 29th Regiment—regrouped, but a second charge in a new direction was stemmed by Puller's men. Again and again Nasu's men tried to penetrate the American defenses, hastily shored up by GI's of the Americal Division, but each attack grew weaker.

In the rear Kawaguchi sloshed disconsolately through the jungle in search of Maruyama's headquarters. To the right he heard the rumble of battle. He slumped against a tree as rain streamed over his head. His career was over. What did life have to offer now? Curling up in the hollow of some tree roots, he dozed off, wondering almost disinterestedly if the rain would wash him away.

By dawn Nasu had lost half of his troops. Practically the entire 29th Regiment, the best in the 2nd Division, had been wiped out. Its commanding officer and the regimental flag were missing.

"*Soka* [That's it]," muttered Maruyama when he heard the report. His staff advised him to withdraw, but he would not listen. He phoned Nasu and said Division was giving him its last reserves for an all-out attack the following night.

It would have been normal for a commander who was called upon to launch a major attack after a crushing defeat to ask for more time to prepare. "Let me carry out the attack *tonight*," Nasu replied in a feverish voice. He gave no reasons and was so insistent that Maruyama acceded; Nasu would know what was best.

Nasu called for another shot to control his temperature, which was already over 40 degrees Celsius (104 degrees Fahrenheit), and prayed that he would live to lead the assault.

The first message to Admiral Yamamoto from his liaison officer on Guadalcanal was "*Banzai.*" It was code for "We have seized airfield." Yamamoto radioed Vice Admiral Kondo to head south with his armada, which included Nagumo's *Kido Butai*, and force the Americans into a battle. Another, much smaller naval group—eight destroyers and the light cruiser *Yura*—was already on its way to back up Maruyama's assault on the airfield with a daylight naval bombardment.

A second message from Guadalcanal about the continued fighting at the airfield failed to deter Yamamoto and his staff, but a third, at 6:23 A.M., announcing that the Americans held Henderson, made Yamamoto hesitate. With the airfield still a threat he ordered Kondo to mark time, so his formidable aggregation of vessels milled around three hundred miles northeast of Guadalcanal.

But the *Yura* force, oblivious of what had taken place, continued down the channel. By the time its commander learned that the airfield had not fallen, planes from Henderson swept down on his ships. A bomb plunged into *Yura*'s central boiler room, killing all occupants. The cruiser sluggishly started back north, but other bombs turned her into a helpless hulk. The skipper, Captain Shiro Sato, gave the order to abandon ship, then tied himself to the bridge with a rope.

Yamamoto was right in thinking that the Americans would come out to challenge any carrier force moving south. In Nouméa, Halsey had already ordered the commander of Task Force 16, Rear Admiral Thomas Kinkaid, to bring his ships—two carriers, *Enterprise* and *Hornet*, nine cruisers and twenty-four destroyers—to a point off the Santa Cruz Islands, about four hundred miles east of Guadalcanal. Kinkaid was to stop any carrier force heading toward the island.

On the afternoon of October 25, American patrol planes discovered two large enemy groups 360 miles from Task Force 16. From his flagship, the *Enterprise* (back in action after around-the-clock repairs in Pearl Harbor), Kinkaid sent out a search and then a strike, but *Kido Butai* had seen one of the enemy patrol planes, a PBY. Nominally Admiral Nagumo was under Kondo but in reality he acted independently, and without asking Kondo's permission, he ordered a turn north, away from a confrontation.

Yamamoto, however, had already decided that there was to be a fight no matter what the outcome of the battle for Henderson Field, and Nagumo's hasty withdrawal brought to a head a disagreement over the use of *Kido Butai*. For weeks Yamamoto had pressed Nagumo, without ever making it a direct order, to take his carriers south and engage the American carriers. But his chief of staff, Kusaka, persuaded Nagumo each time that this would be a foolhardy venture; it would lead to another Midway.

Late that afternoon Yamamoto decided to force Nagumo into action. He dispatched a message, deliberately insulting in tone, "urging" Nagumo to attack "with vigor." Nagumo summoned Kusaka to his little battle room under the bridge. Kusaka could see that his chief was upset. Nagumo said he could not ignore Yamamoto's latest message, and he wanted Kusaka's support this time.

"I admit I've objected to your suggestions, but you are the commander and must make the final decisions," Kusaka replied. "It's your battle. If you really want to head south, I'll go along with your verdict." However, he reminded Nagumo, they had not yet located the enemy fleet and warned him that they themselves would undoubtedly be discovered by B-17's operating from Espíritu Santo. "But now that your mind is made up, I want you to know that we shall not be destroyed without first destroying the enemy."

Kusaka returned to the bridge in the gathering darkness and ordered the carrier striking force—three flattops, a heavy cruiser and eight destroyers—as well as the Vanguard Group of two battleships, four cruisers and seven destroyers, to turn south toward the enemy at 20 knots.

The two enemy carrier forces were closer to each other than either realized. Admiral Kinkaid (described in the *Annapolis Yearbook* of 1908 as a "black-eyed, rosy-cheeked, noisy Irishman who loves a roughhouse") was coming up toward *Kido Butai* on an aggressive zigzag course.

On Guadalcanal, General Nasu had hastily moved into position for attack. On the left was his own reserve regiment, the 16th, and the remnants of the 29th; on the right were the reserves sent by Maruyama. After nightfall the feeble Nasu led the first charge, using his sword as a cane. He managed to hobble across the line of barbed wire before a volley of rifle fire flashed in the dark. A bullet tore into Nasu's chest. All along the line automatic-weapons fire raked the attackers. Within minutes almost every commander down to the company level was dead or wounded. Their men continued to drive forward. Whenever they were stopped, they re-formed and charged again. The GI's and Marines refused to give ground. In the lulls the two sides shouted at each other. "Blood for the Emperor!" yelled a Japanese in English. "Blood for Elea-nor!" retorted a Marine. The shouting turned to insults. "Tojo eat shit!" taunted a GI of the Americal Division. There was a moment's pause, then from the other side: "Babe Ruth eat shit!"

The fighting continued until midnight. The assault was crushed and the survivors filtered back over the bodies of their comrades. In two days Nasu's attacks had left more than three thousand Japanese dead or dying in the uprooted jungle. It was as if a fire storm had swept over the area. The wounded Nasu was carried on a litter back to Division headquarters. As he held out a feeble hand to Maruyama and opened his mouth to speak, he died.

3.

Early in the morning on October 26, Nagumo and Kusaka stood anxiously on the bridge of the carrier *Shokaku*. Kusaka's prediction that they would be discovered was borne out at two-thirty; a communications officer reported that a plane, probably a B-17, was nearby. For twenty minutes Nagumo stood silent, his face "like stone," staring up at the black sky. His vigil was ended by a sudden explosion, and then another. Two huge columns of water geysered near the flagship.*

Nagumo turned to his chief of staff. "What you said before was true. Reverse course, full speed."

Hiding his indignation, Kusaka told the helmsman to head north at 24 knots. He also ordered twenty-four search planes to fan out to the south; he would not be caught as he was at Midway.

The Japanese fleet had been found and it was up to Halsey in Nouméa to determine what to do about it. Obviously a strong enemy force was coming down toward Guadalcanal and it was equally obvious that it was stronger, at least in carriers, then Kinkaid's task force. Just before dawn Halsey made the decision that most Americans in the Pacific were hoping for. He radioed all combat commands: ATTACK RE-PEAT ATTACK. The United States Navy was at last going on the offensive.

Kinkaid headed toward *Kido Butai* and had no sooner sent out search planes than he himself was discovered by one of the aircraft long since dispatched by Kusaka: ONE CARRIER AND 15 OTHER SHIPS BEARING NORTHWEST. For weeks Kusaka had avoided battle, but with the enemy 250 miles away he unhesitatingly ordered an attack wave to take off at once.

At seven o'clock eighteen torpedo bombers, twenty-two dive bombers and twenty-seven fighters began lifting off *Kido Butai*'s three carriers—*Shokaku*, *Zuikaku* and little *Zuiho*—and before the last planes left the decks, Kusaka ordered a second wave to follow as soon as possible. Never

---

*The attack came not from a B-17, but from two lumbering PBY's carrying torpedoes and bombs.

before had he fussed during a battle, but today he was so conscious of the mistakes of Midway that he kept shouting impatiently from the bridge for *Shokaku*'s desk officers to move faster. Through his glasses he could see that things were going even slower on *Zuikaku*. He stamped a foot angrily and told the flagman to signal: "What's the delay?"

He ranged around the bridge until the last of the dozen torpedo bombers, twenty dive bombers and sixteen fighters of the second wave were airborne. From his window he shouted to hose down the decks and prepare for enemy attack. Not a single fighter was left to protect the two big carriers and *Zuiho*, but Kusaka, now that he was committed to battle, was so agitated that he did not care. "Bring spears, enemy," he muttered to himself. "Anything!"

The first American strike group left almost half an hour after the initial Japanese wave, and by eight-fifteen there were seventy-three dive bombers, torpedo bombers and fighters winging toward *Kido Butai*. The Japanese and the American strike forces passed within sight of each other. For some time neither side broke formation and kept driving on to its own destination, but a dozen Japanese fighters could not resist the temptation no longer and swung back. They caught up with a group of nineteen *Enterprise* planes and knocked down three Wildcats and three torpedo bombers at a cost of three of their own planes.

The first Japanese dive bombers were less than fifty miles away when Kinkaid received radar verification. He controlled all fighters from his flagship, *Enterprise,* but until this moment his experience had been confined to battleships and cruisers, and he hesitated momentarily before sending up the Wildcats to intercept. Before they could gain altitude, the Japanese had begun their attack on *Hornet*—*Enterprise* was ten miles away, hidden by a local rain squall. At nine-ten the Aichis nosed over, plummeting down on the carrier. One bomb hit near the flight deck, two barely missed but battered the hull. The squadron commander purposely dived at the stack. His plane caromed off and plunged into the flight deck, where its two bombs exploded.

Nakajimas were already sweeping in low. Two torpedoes ripped into the engineering space, exploded and shook the entire ship. *Hornet* staggered, came to a stop. As she lay helpless in the water, another group of Aichis began boring in, recklessly raking the smoking ship from stem to stern with half a dozen more bombs. Within ten minutes the Japanese were heading back for home, and *Hornet*, listing 8 degrees, was covered with flames.

Hornet's own Dauntless dive bombers were getting some measure of revenge on *Chikuma*, a cruiser running interference for Nagumo's carriers. A bomb plunged into the bridge. Captain Keizo Komura, standing starboard of the compass, was knocked backwards by the blast. Almost everyone else on the bridge was dead. Komura staggered to his feet, his head roaring; his eardrums were broken. Through the voice tube he ordered the ship to change course. Another bomb hit the bridge. "Jettison torpedoes!" he shouted and someone made a hand signal. Seconds after the last one was released, a bomb exploded in the empty torpedo room.

Another group of Dauntlesses sighted *Shokaku*. Ignoring heavy flak, they dived on Nagumo's flagship in single file. Kusaka felt the ship shudder as the first 1,000-lb. bomb struck. There were more explosions—he lost count. The flight deck was in flames. Was this another Midway? He called the engine room by voice tube and was told there was no damage there. "We can go thirty-two knots, sir." But communications were out and Kusaka decided to transfer the flag to a destroyer. He ordered the helmsman to reverse course and head out of danger. She was followed by *Zuikaku*, a 50-foot hole in her flight deck; she had been put out of action by audacious attacks from two passing American search-plane pilots—Lieutenant Stockton Strong and Ensign Charles Irvine.

Several hundred miles away, forty-three Japanese dive bombers and torpedo bombers were heading for Kinkaid. The dive bombers came first and were picked up by radar at a distance of fifty-five miles. But again Kinkaid hesitated to send up fighters from *Enterprise* to intercept them. Completely unopposed, the Aichis started to dive, and it looked as if America's last carrier in the Pacific would go the way of *Hornet*. Then antiaircraft gunners from *Enterprise* and her screen opened up. The fire was concentrated and accurate— particularly from the battleship *South Dakota* and the cruiser *San Juan*—and only two bombs hit the carrier; a third exploded so close to the hull that a main turbine bearing was damaged. Within minutes, however, fires were contained, machinery adjusted and holes patched, and by the time the Japanese torpedo planes appeared, the big flattop was able to dodge everything fired at her.

More Japanese raiders were less than a hundred miles away and fast approaching—a strike force from *Junyo*, the single carrier in Kondo's Advance Force. It was made up of seventeen dive bombers and escorted by a dozen fighters under Lieutenant (s.g.) Yoshio Shiga, the amateur artist who had distinguished himself at Pearl Harbor. The sun was almost directly overhead, and below he could see whitecaps on the blue sea. At eleven-twenty he spotted a large carrier, pushing forward "with a bone in its teeth." It looked alive but the decks seemed to be empty. Then two fighters took off. (There were other Wildcats hidden in the squall clouds above.)

Until that moment Shiga had been repeating to himself, "Leave some for us," but now his anticipation turned into anxiety. Had the first Japanese wave been knocked down without scoring any hits? The bombers were already forming up for the attack. The fighters were ordered to escort them in their dive, one with one. However, there were more Aichis than fighters, so Shiga signaled that he would protect the first two—a job no fighter pilot relished. Just before leaving *Junyo,* Shiga had cautioned his inexperienced young pilots to stay with the bombers and not be drawn off into duels with enemy fighters. "Don't separate. That's an order." But as he got into position behind Lieutenant Masao Yamaguchi, leader of the bombers, he noticed several of his Zeros lured out of line by the Wildcats in the clouds. It was too late to call them off and Shiga followed Yamaguchi, who was diving directly at *Enterprise* through bursts of ack-ack. At 9,000 feet Yamaguchi lowered his flaps to check speed. Shiga's Zero had no flaps, and to keep from passing Yamaguchi, he had to pull the stick to his stomach and go into a tight loop. He was pressed against the back rest and almost blacked out before coming out of the loop. He glanced around to see if there were any enemy fighters near and to make sure he wasn't blocking the next dive bomber.

Flak blossomed on all sides and he went into a second tight loop, and a third, continually losing altitude. He looked around but couldn't find Yamaguchi. His escort duties were over and he searched for enemy interceptors. Two stubby fighter planes were just ahead. They must be Grumman Wildcats! He had heard awesome stories of their fire power and indestructibility. As he approached they split apart and he banked after the leading one. Strangely, it took no evasive action, and just as he was about to shoot, the other Wildcat came in fast on his tail. This was why so many of his comrades had been shot down lately! He tried to isolate one of the Americans time and again, but the other always darted in on the attack.

Enterprise successfully dodged all of Yamaguchi's bombs, but *South Dakota* and *San Juan*, which had helped save the carrier earlier, came in so close to throw up flak that both were hit. One bomb exploded on the battleship's No. 1 turret and another pierced the cruiser, exploding near the ship's bottom.

A second wave of fifteen planes from *Junyo* found *Hornet* in tow behind the cruiser *Northampton*, and six Nakajimas swept across the water toward the crippled carrier. The cruiser captain ordered the towline cut so that his ship could evade torpedoes. This left *Hornet* almost dead in the water, and without fighter cover. The declining efficiency of Japanese pilot replacements was evident: five torpedoes missed the almost stationary target. But the sixth ripped into the starboard side; there was a sickly green flash followed by a hissing, then a dull rumble. The deck on the port side "seemed to crack open" and fuel oil erupted, flinging sailors down the slanted deck. The after engine room began flooding as the starboard list increased to 14 degrees. The word went out to prepare to abandon ship. Six high-level bombers, also Nakajimas, came over in a perfect V formation. One bomb hit the flight deck just as the Americans began scrambling down lines to the water.

By now Shiga and his fighter pilots had returned to *Junyo* with a report that the carrier seemed "very much alive" when they left her. He recommended another strike. An operations officer asked if he could return in the dark.

"It's not a question of returning," said Shiga. He had expected to die at Pearl Harbor and felt he was living on borrowed time. "It has to be done. If possible, send out a homing signal." Some carrier captains didn't like to reveal their positions this way. "If you don't send it out, I'll come back anyway. Then watch out!" It was half joke, half threat.

Only one officer among the dive bombers had survived the first attack, a plump, baby-faced youngster, Shunko Kato. This had been his first mission and when Shiga awakened him and said they were going to attack again, Kato's face drained of color. "This is a battle to avenge your squadron leader," said Shiga. "That's war."

Kato sat up in his bunk. "Let's go."

Shiga summoned the five fighter pilots he felt could make it back in the dark, and the five men who would pilot the dive bombers. "This is the last attack," he said. "You helldivers do everything Yamaguchi taught you. Get in as close as you can to the target before releasing your bombs." He turned on his own pilots. "Don't you fighter planes ever separate from me again. If you do, I'll shoot you down."

With Shiga in the lead, the eleven planes took off. In the setting sun he thought he saw something way down. Several minutes later, he discerned ships through the cloud patches, one a carrier. It was the wrong ship, *Hornet,* and was already dead in the water. Kato and his dive bombers hurtled down. This time Shiga managed to stay with Kato until he saw his bomb plunge into the hangar deck. Shiga banked and swept back over the carrier. To his puzzlement there were few figures on the flight deck. It was a dead ship.

His problem now was to return to *Junyo.* He gathered his planes like a mother hen and headed back under darkening skies. Would there be a homing signal? He located the proper cycle on his radio. At first he heard nothing, then came a welcome series of beeps. *Junyo* was transmitting!

Dinner that night for Shiga and his men was grim. There were empty chairs all around the tables, with plates of food standing uneaten. There was no boasting or elation over the triumphs of the day.

The reports of the fliers were so impressive that Kondo's entire Advance Force, as well as Vanguard Group, was sent out to engage the enemy in a night battle. The two intact carriers, *Zuikaku* and *Junyo,* were to follow in case another strike could be launched. The Vanguard Group came upon *Hornet,* her entire length ablaze. She was still afloat despite nine torpedoes from her screening destroyers, which fled at the sight of the enemy. The Japanese, in turn, sent four torpedoes of their own into the abandoned hulk, and finally, at one thirty-five, October 27, the ship that had launched the first planes to bomb Tokyo plunged out of sight. The rest of the American fleet could not be found. The Battle of the Santa Cruz Islands was over.

An hour before dawn Nagumo and his staff transferred from the destroyer to *Zuikaku.* From reports of pilots and crews Nagumo and Kusaka estimated that at least two cruisers, one destroyer, one battleship and three carriers had been sunk. Midway had been avenged and the Japanese Navy at last ruled the seas around Guadalcanal.

Yamamoto's evaluation was even more favorable. His chief of staff, Admiral Ugaki, radioed Tokyo that four flat-tops and three battleships had been sunk. He could not sleep and strolled in the moonlight along the decks of *Yamato,* reveling in the fact that the great victory had come on America's Navy Day. He retired to his cabin and wrote three *haiku* poems:

> *After the battle I forget the heat*
> *while contemplating*
> *the sixteen-day moon.*
>
> *Contemplating the moon,*
> *I mourn*
> *the enemy's sacrifice.*
>
> *Beneath the moon*
> *stretches a sea at whose bottom*
> *lie many ships.*

The Japanese had won a decided tactical victory without losing a ship, but the Americans had gained valuable time and thwarted the enemy's ambitious combined operations to retake Henderson Field. In addition, sixty-nine Japanese planes had failed to return to their carriers, and another twenty-three were lost in emergency landings. It would take months to replace these planes and crews.

But in Tokyo the victory was considered so momentous that the Emperor wrote an imperial rescript praising Yamamoto for the "brave fight" put up by the Combined Fleet. In it His Majesty did predict that the situation in the Solomons would "become more and more difficult." As he presented the rescript to Navy Chief of Staff Nagano, he said, "I add my personal wish to the latter part of the rescript, that is, regarding the struggle for Guadalcanal. It is a place where a bitter fight is being waged between forces of Japan and the United States and is, moreover, an important base for the Imperial Navy. I hope that the island will be recovered by our forces as soon as possible."

By now, however, Yamamoto and Ugaki had privately concluded that it would be next to impossible to retake Guadalcanal. Three times the Army had failed. With the Americans strengthening their garrison almost daily, how could a fourth attempt possibly succeed?

On Guadalcanal, Hyakutake's chief of staff, Colonel Konuma, had been forced almost to the same conclusion. He was hoping that the Americans would not learn that Maruyama's division had been virtually annihilated; if they did, they might launch an attack of their own that would no doubt wipe out the entire Japanese force on the island.

Colonel Tsuji was on his way back over the Maruyama Trail with a firsthand report of the condition of the 2nd Division. En route he found battalion commander Minamoto lying at the side of the trail, the lower half of his body soaked in blood. "Hold on," Tsuji told him. "We'll have someone come back for you."

"I haven't eaten since day before yesterday," said Minamoto in a weak voice.

From his *hango*, Tsuji put two chopstickfuls of rice in the wounded officer's mouth. Minamoto pointed feebly to a group of men lying nearby. They opened their mouths like baby sparrows as Tsuji went to feed each one of them.

It took Tsuji five days to reach the coast and 17th Army headquarters. He ordered rice sent to the front and dispatched a radiogram to Army Chief of Staff Sugiyama in Tokyo:

I MUST BEAR THE WHOLE RESPONSIBILITY FOR THE FAILURE OF THE 2ND DIVISION WHICH COURAGEOUSLY FOUGHT FOR DAYS AND LOST MORE THAN HALF THEIR MEN IN DESPERATE ATTACKS. THEY FAILED BECAUSE I UNDERESTIMATED THE ENEMY'S FIGHTING POWER AND INSISTED ON MY OWN OPERATIONS PLAN WHICH WAS ERRONEOUS.

He said he deserved "a sentence of ten thousand deaths" and requested permission to stay on Guadalcanal with the 17th Army. The answer came on November 3:

YOUR APPLICATION FOR TRANSFER TO 17TH ARMY IS NOT APPROVED. RETURN HERE TO REPORT ON BATTLE SITUATION.

Late that afternoon Colonel Ichiji Sugita (who had interpreted for General Yamashita at the surrender of Singapore) turned up at 17th Army headquarters exhausted, his uniform scarcely recognizable. He had been supervising the diversionary action of General Sumiyoshi's troops on the Mataniko River. His face was pale, his eyes strangely bright as he reported that the Americans had broken through the 4th Regiment, the infantry unit holding the bulk of the line on the east bank of the river. "The regimental commander is going to make a last attack with the remaining hundred and fifty men and the regimental flag. I am going with them!"

"Don't be so rash, Sugita," said Tsuji. "There will be no attack. Put the regimental colors in the center and have the men dig in around them. The enemy will never charge;

besides, in the jungle out there, artillery and bombing isn't too effective. It's merely a question of holding out another day or two." Reinforcements were already landing. Sugita, leaning on a piece of bamboo, hobbled back toward the Mataniko River.

The reinforcements comprised the advance guard of the 38th Division. With them was another good friend of Tsuji's, Colonel Takushiro Hattori. The newcomer from Tokyo, looking spruce in a brand-new uniform, exuded his usual confidence. As long as this man is alive, Tsuji thought, we don't have to worry. The two shook hands fervently.

The following day General Kawaguchi left the island in disgrace, "feeling as if my intestines were cut." He nursed more hatred for his countryman Tsuji than for the enemy.

17   The End

1.

On the night of November 9, the commander of the 38th Division, Lieutenant General Tadayoshi Sano and his Headquarters detachment arrived at Tassafaronga Point to join the advance guard units. They had come safely down the Solomons passage in five destroyers, but the main body of the division and other reinforcements for General Hyakutake— some 12,000 men and 10,000 tons of supplies—were still at Shortland Island. It was decided to send them all in one convoy—eleven transports and cargo ships escorted by a dozen destroyers. They would be preceded by a Raiding Group—a force of two battleships, one light cruiser and fourteen destroyers—whose mission it was to neutralize Henderson Field by bombardment, after which the convoy could safely make the run to Guadalcanal.

The Raiding Group, under the command of Vice Admiral Hiroaki Abe, started down toward Guadalcanal on the morning of November 12, and by late afternoon was one hundred miles north of Savo Island. The Americans had known of its presence for hours and surmised it was coming either to shell Henderson or to attack an American transport convoy that was anchored off Guadalcanal with 6,000 troops, ammunition, 105-mm. and 115-mm. howitzers, and rations. By dusk the last of these troops had been disembarked, and the transports and cargo ships, with two thirds of the supplies still in their holds, started hastily withdrawing to the south.

They were escorted to the open sea by Task Group 67.4, commanded by Rear Admiral Daniel J. Callaghan, a deeply religious, close-mouthed man. Once the transports were safely on their way to Nouméa, Callaghan turned back and headed along the north coast of Guadalcanal toward Savo. His mission was to stop Abe and he had to do it with two heavy cruisers, three light cruisers and eight destroyers. He would be outgunned by the oncoming Japanese but his was the sole American naval force in the area.

He had recently taken over command from Norman Scott, a classmate at the Academy, and he did what Scott had done at the Battle of Cape Esperance—put his ships in a single line with four destroyers in the lead and four bringing up the rear. It was easier for a column to navigate in such dangerous waters. He rode in the heavy cruiser *San Francisco,* despite its ineffective search radar—perhaps for sentimental reasons, since he had been her skipper and had such a close relationship to the crew that they still called him "Uncle Dan"— though not to his face.

The last thing Admiral Abe expected was any night action. There were no American battleships in the area, and cruisers wouldn't dare attempt to stop him. His two battleships, with *Hiei* in the lead, slipped past the tip of Santa Isabel Island and continued south toward Savo with six destroyers and a light cruiser screening, and with destroyers on either flank to fend off any torpedo boats.

Their course led them into a heavy rainstorm northwest of Savo, but Abe did not reduce speed; the squall would hide them from air, surface and submarine attacks. The storm did not let up, however, and when Abe learned that the weather over Guadalcanal was just as bad, he ordered all ships to make a simultaneous 180-degree turn and reduce speed to 12 knots. Half an hour later the rain stopped, and though Abe had just received a report of Callaghan's presence somewhere in Ironbottom Sound, he ordered another countermarch toward Savo.

It was well past midnight by the time the cone of the little island reared up. The mountains of Guadalcanal beyond were a dim mass. Ground observers on the island radioed they could see no enemy ships off Lungga Point and Abe decided to make his bombardment run. He ordered the thin-skinned Type 3 shells loaded in all main batteries of the two battleships.

It was not until 1:24 A.M., November 13—a Friday—that the Americans discovered Abe. The TBS (Talk Between Ships) on *San Francisco*'s bridge began squawking: "Contacts bearing 312 and 310, distant 27,000 and 32,000 yards." It was *Helena*. She had picked up Abe's horseshoe screen and the two battleships. Callaghan turned his columns north to try to cross the T.

The range between the two forces closed fast. Five minutes passed, then ten, as Callaghan anxiously kept calling over TBS for further information. Radar was not serving him well, for at 1:41 lookouts on his leading destroyer saw two Japanese destroyers unexpectedly materialize out of the darkness. The destroyer *Cushing* swung hard left to avoid collision, and caused a violent chain reaction down the column.

The cruiser *Atlanta* swerved sharply and Callaghan, on the ship behind, demanded, "What are you doing?"

"Avoiding our own destroyers," replied the cruiser's captain.

There was almost as much confusion on Abe's bridge. On sighting the enemy he had ordered the *Hiei* and *Kirishima* gunners to replace the incendiary shells with armor-piercing rounds. In a stampede, every available man on *Hiei* rushed to stack the Type 3 shells on the deck. There was chaos in the dark and each minute seemed interminable. One enemy round landing in the lines of incendiary shells would make a torch of the big ship.

Four more minutes passed. At 1:49 *Hiei*'s searchlight stabbed through the darkness and found the bridge of *Atlanta,* some 5,000 yards ahead. The American ships reacted quickly and a dozen water spouts rose in front of *Hiei*. Her own 14-inch guns blasted. A salvo of one-ton shells crashed down on *Atlanta*. The bridge disintegrated. Admiral Scott and all but one of his staff were dead.

Only then did Callaghan order, "Odd ships commence fire to starboard, even ships to port." But his column had become intermingled with the enemy and each ship began firing at anything in sight. A spread of torpedoes from one of Abe's destroyers slammed into *Atlanta,* almost lifting her from the water. She settled but was helpless, out of the battle.

Hopelessly entangled, the two forces went at each other at close quarters in the most tempestuous melee of the war.

"Cease firing own ships!" Callaghan ordered, and as the shelling momentarily ceased, *Kirishima* commenced pumping her huge shells at the *San Francisco*. At least four other Japanese ships converged on the American flagship.

"We want the big ones!" Callaghan called to all his ships. "Get the big ones first!"

A shell exploded on *San Francisco*'s bridge killing everyone except the captain, who was mortally wounded, and Lieutenant Commander Bruce McCandless. He was appalled by the sight—bodies, limbs, gear littered the deck. A siren moaned as water poured down from the deck above. McCandless conned the wounded ship through the reckless traffic, toward Guadalcanal.

At 2 A.M. Abe's flagship, battered by fifty topside hits, turned to port, and accompanied by *Kirishima*, steamed north. The battle had lasted for less than half an hour, but Ironbottom Sound was ablaze with burning wrecks. Only one American ship escaped injury, and *Atlanta* and two destroyers were going down. One Japanese destroyer had been sunk and another was drifting, and *Hiei* was so slowed that it seemed likely she would be unable to get out of range of American planes before dawn.

Callaghan's headlong plunge into the enemy had saved Henderson Field from a devastating pounding—at the cost of hundreds of lives, including Admiral Scott's and his own.

The rising sun revealed seven crippled ships off Guadalcanal—five American and two Japanese. Some were burning hopelessly, some were abandoned, and one—*Portland*—was so bent that it kept circling. Nor was the ordeal over. As the five surviving American ships left the scene of battle and made for the New Hebrides, just before 11 A.M., the captain of *I-26* sighted one of them, *San Francisco*, and loosed a spread of torpedoes. They skimmed harmlessly by the damaged cruiser, but one crunched into the port side of *Juneau*. From *San Francisco*, McCandless saw the ship blow up "with all the fury of an erupting volcano." A huge brown cloud boiled up, followed by a thunderclap. When the cloud lifted the cruiser was gone. It was awesome.

Captain Gilbert Hoover on *Helena*, who as senior officer was in command of the little American flotilla, feared that other ships would probably be sunk if he stopped to pick up survivors. And so the four intact vessels raced off without leaving lifeboats or rafts, and some seven hundred men—

almost the entire crew of *Juneau,* including the five Sullivan brothers—perished.*

The slow-moving *Hiei* could not escape either. Since dawn she had successfully been fighting off planes until a bomb disabled her steering mechanism and she began to circle helplessly. In the next few hours the big ship was battered by Flying Fortresses and torpedo planes from Henderson Field. Two torpedoes finally left *Hiei* dead in the water. Her crew was transferred to destroyers and moments later she plunged out of sight, stern first.

The loss of a battleship was a serious blow to Yamamoto, but he did not waver in his determination to get the convoy of eleven transports safely to Guadalcanal. And that meant Henderson Field had to be temporarily put out of action. That night there was another run of the fearsome "Tokyo Express"; cruisers and destroyers scudded down The Slot full speed and bombarded the airfield for thirty-seven minutes. It was a terrifying experience for the Marines, but only eighteen planes were destroyed and the runways were operational by the next morning.

The eleven transports, escorted by a dozen destroyers, under the command of the redoubtable Rear Admiral Raizo Tanaka, were already halfway to Guadalcanal, and they continued down the narrows even after two dive-bombers from *Enterprise* discovered them at 8:30 A.M. Three hours later, thirty-seven Marine and Navy planes from Henderson swept in and severely damaged two transports. Still, Tanaka refused to withdraw; Hyakutake had to have the reinforcements and supplies. With destroyers belching out a black smoke screen, convoy and escort continued south on a zigzag course. All through the day the attacks continued and the Henderson fliers were joined by Flying Fortresses from Espíritu Santo and by bombers and fighters from *Enterprise.* Tanaka transferred troops from sinking transports to destroyers which then returned to Shortland, but kept his other ships moving ahead. Before the sun set, six transports had been sunk and one disabled. The last four transports, accompanied by the remaining four destroyers, drew closer to Guadalcanal in the growing darkness.

Yamamoto ordered Admiral Kondo to lead an attack personally down the Solomons passage with the battleship *Kirishima,* two heavy cruisers, two light cruisers and a de-

*The U. S. Navy thereafter never assigned more than one member of a family to a single ship.

stroyer squadron. Such a force under such a commander should be able to blast Henderson Field into oblivion.

This time, however, the Japanese would be opposed by battleships. Task Force 64—two battleships and four destroyers—had been detached from Kinkaid's carriers and rushed ahead to save Henderson. Halsey would have done this earlier had he not been reluctant to leave *Enterprise* (the last operational carrier in the Pacific) unprotected during daylight hours.

Task Force 64 had been hiding all day about a hundred miles southwest of Guadalcanal. Early that evening its commander, Rear Admiral Willis A. ("Ching") Lee, brought it up the west coast of the island. The four destroyers, followed by the battleships *Washington* and *South Dakota*, continued north, past Cape Esperance and Savo. At 10:52 P.M. the column turned to starboard. *Washington*'s radar picked up a ship coming down The Slot. It was Kondo's lead vessel, the light cruiser *Sendai*.

Lee waited for twenty-four minutes before ordering his captains to fire. *Sendai* hurriedly retired, but other Japanese ships moved forward in a resolute attack. By 11:35 all four American destroyers—two of them sinking—were out of action, and *South Dakota*, crippled by power failure, had become the target for *Kirishima* and the two heavy cruisers. The Japanese were so absorbed that they failed to notice *Washington* 8,000 yards off. She rapidly flung seventy-five 16-inch shells at *Kirishima*. Nine smashed home, as did numerous 5-inch shells. The great battlewagon's top structure was aflame and she kept turning in a circle, out of conrol. The captain slowed the ship in an attempt to steer with the engines, but it was useless.

At 12:25 A.M. Kondo, aboard the heavy cruiser *Atago*, ordered a withdrawal. Lee had prevented him from attacking Henderson and had given him a tactical beating as well. Imagining he had won the battle, Kondo retired to the north under cover of smoke, leaving *Kirishima* and a disabled destroyer behind. *Kirishima*'s captain was finally forced to scuttle his ship. He transferred his crew to a destroyer which returned for that purpose, and ordered the Kingston valves opened. The battleship sank northwest of Savo.

Standing off a few miles to the north, Tanaka witnessed the action with concern. He had already sent three of his destroyers to help Kondo, and now decided to make a run for Tassafaronga Point with his last destroyer and the four transports. There was not enough time to unload the troops before dawn by landing craft and he radioed Rabaul for permission to run the transports aground. Rabaul turned down the request but Kondo told him to go ahead. So much time had elapsed that gray light was already showing in the east as the four big transports ploughed into a beach near Tassafaronga Point.

Almost simultaneously eight Marine dive bombers from Henderson, led by Major Joe Sailer, swept in, evaded eight float Zeros and hit the transports with three bombs. They were followed by more Marine Dauntlesses and a succession of Navy torpedo planes. By early afternoon the carnage was so grisly that some American aviators vomited at the sight of the bloody waters covered with fragments of bodies.

Of the 12,000 troops and 10,000 tons of supplies that had left Shortland, only 4,000 shocked men and 5 tons of supplies were safely beached. The three-day naval battle for Guadalcanal was at last over, and it had ended in catastrophe for the Japanese Navy, with 77,609 tons of shipping sunk—two battleships, one heavy cruiser and three destroyers, plus eleven ships of Tanaka's convoy. Hyakutake's hopes for a final great offensive were crushed.

General Vandegrift, who had been the victim of Navy timidity since his landing, for the first time expressed unqualified approval of that branch of the service in an ecstatic message to Halsey:

WE BELIEVE THE ENEMY HAS SUFFERED A CRUSHING DEFEAT—WE THANK LEE FOR HIS STURDY EFFORT OF LAST NIGHT—WE THANK KINKAID FOR HIS INTERVENTION YESTERDAY—OUR OWN AIRCRAFT HAS BEEN GRAND IN ITS RELENTLESS POUNDING OF THE FOE—THOSE EFFORTS WE APPRECIATE BUT OUR GREATEST HOMAGE GOES TO SCOTT, CALLAGHAN AND THEIR MEN WHO WITH MAGNIFICENT COURAGE AGAINST SEEMINGLY HOPELESS ODDS DROVE BACK THE FIRST HOSTILE STROKE AND MADE SUCCESS POSSIBLE—TO THEM THE MEN OF CACTUS LIFT THEIR BATTERED HELMETS IN DEEPEST ADMIRATION.

Roosevelt was just as jubilant. Within a few days the Allies had scored four notable victories: the successful landings in North Africa, Montgomery's triumph over Rommel at El Alamein, the gallant Russian stand at Stalingrad—and now Guadalcanal. "For the past two weeks we have had a great deal of good news," he told the New York *Herald Tribune* Forum, "and it would seem that the turning point in this war has at last been reached."

In Tokyo the Army General Staff was still resolved to retake Guadalcanal and made a drastic realignment of forces. Hereafter Hyakutake's entire 17th Army would concentrate on the Solomons while the 18th Army took over its duties in eastern New Guinea, and both operations would be under the command of Lieutenant General Hitoshi Imamura. One of the most respected men in the military service, Imamura had succeeded in taking Java with dispatch as well as quickly establishing order throughout the Netherlands East Indies with a minimum of force. His liberal methods, however, had brought on his head so much criticism from powerful forces in the General Staff itself that for a time his career was in danger.

Imamura began his occupation by releasing Achmed Sukarno from his prison cell. Sukarno, the most influential revolutionary leader in the Indies, was brought to Imamura's official residence, an elegant structure recently occupied by the Dutch governor. "I know that you're not the kind of man who would just obey my orders," said Imamura. "Therefore I won't give you any. I won't even tell you what to do. All I can promise is that I can make the Indonesians a happier people under our occupation if they learn our language. Anything further will have to be done by the Japanese government. I cannot promise independence."

In addition to promoting the Japanese language, Sukarno helped set up a committee of fifteen Indonesians and five Japanese to listen to local grievances. Complaints of Imamura's liberalism reached his immediate superior in Saigon, General Terauchi. He passed them on to Tokyo, and Generals Akira Muto and Kyoji Tominaga of the War Ministry were sent to Batavia to investigate. Imamura was aggressive in defense of his policy. "I am merely carring out the Emperor's instructions," he said. "If you find that my administration is not successful, relieve me. But first see the results." They were impressed by what they saw. In their report they advised Prime Minister Tojo and Chief of Staff Sugiyama to give Imamura a free hand.

Now Imamura was to command an Army Group, comprising the 17th and 18th Armies, but his assignment was the most difficult facing any Japanese officer. In Tokyo he went to the Imperial Palace to receive his orders from the Emperor. As the general was bowing himself out, His Majesty said, "Imamura! I understand that my soldiers are suffering terribly on Guadalcanal. Go as soon as you can and save them.

Even one day is important." Imamura saw tears glisten on his imperturbable face.

At Army General Staff headquarters, Imamura was told that he and Admiral Yamamoto would work together to intensify air attacks in the Solomons and to reinforce the troops on Guadalcanal. Then the two would mount a joint offensive to retake Henderson Field and Tulagi.

Imamura arrived in Rabaul, New Britain, on November 22. He radioed Hyakutake, who was still on Guadalcanal, that he was sending two fresh divisions within a month; he asked for a complete factual report "without hiding anything."

Hyakutake had just lost a thousand men on the Mataniko front. He radioed Imamura that his troops had been living on grass roots and water for a month.

... AN AVERAGE OF 100 MEN STARVE TO DEATH DAILY. THIS AVERAGE WILL ONLY INCREASE. BY THE TIME WE GET TWO DIVISION REINFORCEMENTS, DOUBTFUL HOW MANY TROOPS HERE WILL BE ALIVE.

The General Staff had not prepared Imamura for this but he was committed to their ambitious plans by his personal vow to the Emperor to retake Guadalcanal. For the moment all the general could do was send a message of sympathy to the men of Guadalcanal calling their bravery "enough to make even the gods weep," and asking them to "set His Majesty's heart at ease" by helping him retake the island.

It was the Army General Staff alone that remained irrevocably committed to the continuation of the Guadalcanal campaign. Their demands for more men, supplies and particularly another 370,000 tons of shipping had finally forced the War Ministry to reassess the situation. The chief aim, at present, said the War Ministry, was to increase the national power and war potential, and the requisition of additional ships would decrease the number of civilian ships, thereby decreasing national power. This could be worse than the loss of Guadalcanal.

The General Staff said it was ridiculous to set up Imamura's new command without giving him ships to transport his troops—he would be "a man without a head."

"Today there is the impression that Japan is on the verge of rise or fall," Colonel Sako Tanemura, who had witnessed most of these arguments, wrote in his unofficial "Imperial

Headquarters [Army] Diary" on November 18. It was like the lull before a great storm. "Does the General Staff have good prospects of success? If not, what should it do to get out of the difficulty? The Supreme Command must reflect carefully to cope with this touchy situation. Advance or withdraw! It is very delicate. No one is confident of victory ... but the fake pride of Imperial Headquarters is forcing us to wage the Decisive Battle of Guadalcanal. If we should be defeated on Guadalcanal, it is certain we will lose the Pacific war itself."

While debate over shipping dragged on, the Navy devised a makeshift operation to resupply Guadalcanal. Large metal drums partially filled with medical supplies or basic victuals with just enough air space for buoyancy were to be strung together with rope and hung from a destroyer's gunwales. Upon arrival at Guadalcanal the string of drums would be cut loose as the destroyer made a sharp turn. A motorboat or a swimmer would pick up the buoyed end of the rope and bring it ashore, where soldiers would haul in the long line of drums.

First test of the new system came on the night of November 29. Admiral Tanaka, on the flagship *Naganami,* led a column of eight destroyers down the Solomons passage at 24 knots. Six of the ships were necklaced with from 200 to 240 drums apiece. The first and last destroyers acted as escort. Just before eleven o'clock the convoy passed west of Savo and swung left toward Tassafaronga. As it approached the point, the six supply destroyers broke off and prepared to loose their drums. There wasn't a breath of wind, and the sea was like black glass.

One of the destroyers discovered ships, bearing 100 degrees, and signaled Tanaka: "Seven enemy destroyers sighted." The admiral gave orders to cease unloading and take battle stations.

Coming toward them was an eleven-ship formation—five cruisers in column with three destroyers on either flank—commanded by Rear Admiral Carleton H. Wright. His flagship, *Minneapolis,* had already made radar contact but the admiral hesitated to send his van destroyers into the attack. Ten minutes later the destroyer *Fletcher*'s radar showed the Japanese on the port bow 7,000 yards away. Her skipper, Commander William M. Cole, asked Wright for permission to fire torpedoes; the admiral again hesitated—he thought the distance was too great—and it took Cole four minutes to convince him it wasn't. At eleven-twenty Cole finally launched ten torpedoes. A moment later Admiral Wright ordered his cruisers to commence firing. "Roger! And I do mean Roger!" Wright said over voice radio. His cruisers opened up with their 5-, 6- and 8-inch guns, and shells began to rain on Tanaka's lead ship, *Takanami*. She was almost ripped to pieces, but the crew continued working their guns until the ship exploded.

The cheering on *Minneapolis* was cut short as the cruiser was jarred twice by Japanese torpedoes. A third ripped into the port bow of *New Orleans;* two magazines exploded, ripping off the forward part of the ship. Almost simultaneously *Pensacola* was staggered by a hit below the mainmast on the port side, which flooded her after engine room.

While *Northampton* was avoiding the three damaged cruisers, *Oyashio* sent two torpedoes into her. The explosions were so cataclysmic that men on the bridge of nearby *Honolulu* broke uncontrollably into tears. *Northampton* listed sharply to port, afterpart in flames, and had to stop to check flooding. But she was beyond help and sank stern first.

Tanaka had already withdrawn. In the half-hour battle he had whipped the much heavier American force. At the cost of a single destroyer and without radar, he had sunk one cruiser and badly damaged three others. But his mission had failed; not a drum was delivered to the starving men of Guadalcanal.

Two nights later Tanaka made a second attempt. This time seven drum-laden destroyers survived an ineffectual Allied air raid, and reached Tassafaronga Point intact. The drums, 1,500 in all, were cut loose, but little more than 300 could be hauled to the beach. Tanaka tried again several days later; air and torpedo-boat attacks, however, were so effective that the entire convoy had to turn back.

On Guadalcanal, starvation and malaria had become the real enemy of Hyakutake's men. Formal battle would have dissipated Japanese resistance in a matter of days and Colonel Konuma had to devise new tactics to cope with the combined Marine-GI attacks. Japanese soldiers dug individual foxholes and were ordered to stay in them even if the Americans overran their positions. Each foxhole would become a little fortress and Konuma gambled that the Americans would not accept the losses to overcome such a guerrilla-type defense.

Those who were too weak from disease and hunger to fight crowded the beaches. The air was putrid from the smell of rotting corpses. Large bluebottle flies feasted on the wounded and sick who were unable to drive them off. The men devised a mortality chart:

He who can rise to his feet	30 days left to live
He who can sit up	20 days left to live
He who must urinate while lying down	3 days left to live
He who cannot speak	2 days left to live
He who cannot blink his eyes	dead at dawn

2.

Colonel Tsuji, who had confessed he deserved "a sentence of ten thousand deaths" for his mistakes on Guadalcanal, was back in Tokyo with a new recommendation for saving the island. He convinced the General Staff that Lieutenant Colonel Kumao Imoto of the Operations Section should be sent, as Tsuji had, to supervise the new offensive on Guadalcanal.

Tsuji's influence was as effective as ever, and early in December Imoto left Tokyo. Imoto had accepted the assignment, but privately he disagreed with his superiors; in his opinion Guadalcanal should be evacuated. He stopped at Truk to report to Combined Fleet, where Admiral Ugaki, one of his instructors at the War College, told him, "This is a most difficult situation. Let's not worry about who should take the initiative in solving the problem. Our sole concern should be to decide what ought to be done at the present moment."

It was an abstruse way—understandable only to one used to Navy subtlety—of advising Imoto that withdrawal from Guadalcanal was the only alternative. "I understand what you mean," said Imoto. He flew on to Rabaul with the conviction that Admiral Yamamoto shared his chief of staff's conclusions—and he was right.

At Imamura's headquarters Imoto encountered vehement criticism of General Staff policy. "The people in Tokyo are insane!" one of Imamura's officers blurted out during the map games held to work out the details of the Guadalcanal offensive. "Do you honestly think there is the slightest chance of success in another attack?"

Nevertheless, Imoto forced the games through to their conclusion. He had to demonstrate the futility of further attacks before revealing his own reservations. The games proved what they all feared: hardly a transport reached the island.

In the corridors of Army headquarters in Tokyo, where the War Ministry and the Army General Staff shared the same building on Ichigaya Heights, there was already talk of withdrawal from Guadalcanal. The first general officer to suggest this course of action openly was Major General Kenryo Sato, Tojo's adviser and chief of the Military Affairs Bureau of the War Ministry. Perturbed by the General Staff's insistence on another 620,000 tons of shipping, he told Tojo they should "give up the idea of retaking Guadalcanal."

"Do you mean withdrawal?" Tojo asked sharply.

"We have no choice. Even now it may be too late. If we go on like this, we have no chance of winning the war." The position on Guadalcanal, moreover, was untenable. The enemy completely controlled the air and sea. "If we continue to hang on, it will end up as a battle of attrition of our transports."

Tojo heard Sato out but remained troubled by the Emperor's order to retake Guadalcanal; also, he was reluctant to interfere with military authority. He still believed, in spite of nagging doubts, that the General Staff should remain independent of the government. "Besides, even if we wanted," he finally said, "we couldn't give the General Staff all the ships they demand. If we did, our steel-production quota of over four million tons would be cut by more than half and we would be unable to continue the war." He was torn by old loyalties. His face became pinched. He asked Sato if a reduction in the number of ships would oblige the General Staff to decide on withdrawal.

"Not immediately," Sato replied. But he brightened at the thought of intrigue. He suggested that they make no mention of withdrawing for the time being, but give the Army only their share of shipping. Tojo nodded grimly.

At the next Cabinet meeting Tojo pushed through a plan to give the Army and Navy a total of but 290,000 tons, with the promise that more would follow, if possible. This resolution brought the continuing argument between the War Ministry and the Army General Staff to a crisis. Sato spoke for Tojo and his reasoning was sound; what infuriated the General Staff most was his implication that the operation on Guadalcanal would have to be "suspended."

Under pressure from the General Staff, Tojo convened a special meeting of his cabinet on the evening of December 5 to reconsider the demands for more shipping. It was agreed to give both services another 95,000 tons. The increase was so small that Sato's assistants warned him to explain the matter to the General Staff in person. But it was already past ten o'clock and Sato said that he would wait until morning. As he entered his quarters the phone was ringing. Lieutenant General Moritake Tanabe, the Vice Chief of Staff, asked Sato to come to his official residence at once and explain the Cabinet's decision.

At the door of Tanabe's house Sato heard angry shouts from inside. He recognized the voice of the Army's Chief of Operations, the impulsive and hot-tempered Lieutenant General Shinichi Tanaka. Inside, Sato was confronted by seven or eight members of the General Staff.

"*Bakayaro!*" Tanaka shouted. He had been drinking.

When Sato turned to leave, Tanaka reached for his sword. Several of his colleagues seized him but he broke away, rushed at Sato and hit him in the face. Sato punched back. The two generals swung at each other as several General Staff officers shouted encouragement to Tanaka, made savage by the "power of *sake.*" Sato broke loose and pushed his way out of the hostile room. It was the first fight he had ever walked away from.

With Sato gone, the impetuous Tanaka still could not be restrained. It was well past midnight when, belligerent with charges and demands, he burst into the home of Tojo's deputy in the ministry. Heitaro Kimura, a quiet man, apologized to Tanaka for the "insufficiency of my efforts" and finally persuaded him to go home. Even when he was sobered up the next morning, Tanaka continued his attacks. This time his victim was General Teiichi Suzuki of the Cabinet Planning Board. This intemperate display hardened Tojo's position. He told Sato to inform the General Staff that "come what may" the Army was to get only what the Cabinet had decreed.

It was clear to the General Staff that Tojo's ultimatum meant eventual suspension of the battle for Guadalcanal. The division chiefs held an emergency meeting and then, uninvited, drove in a body to the Prime Minister's official residence. In the anteroom Sugiyama took aside Colonel Tanemura, the diarist, and whispered, "If there is another quarrel, bring *him* [Tanaka] out at once."

Tanaka was ushered into a Japanese-style room where Sato and two others were sitting on the floor. Sato and Tanaka stared at each other as if ready to resume their fight. The atmosphere grew increasingly embarrassing. Finally, just before midnight, Tojo entered in kimono and lowered himself to the tatami. Tanaka begged him to reconsider the demand of the General Staff. Calmly, without a trace of emotion, Tojo refused. For half an hour the two argued, their voices rising. Tanaka lost all control. "What are you doing about the war?" he shouted. "We'll lose it this way. *Kono bakayaro* [you damn fool]!"

Tojo stiffened. "What abusive language you use!" he said. The room was hushed. Tanemura entered from the anteroom and took Tanaka's arm. "The Chief's orders," he said.

Tanaka, after being officially reprimanded for insulting a superior officer, was dismissed from his position, but as so often was the case in Japan, his crude and violent advocacy won the Army a temporary victory. The following evening Tojo bowed to the General Staff's request for more shipping.

3.

Six hundred miles due west of Henderson Field lay the eastern tip of the second largest island in the world. Ungainly New Guinea, shaped very much like a plucked turkey, sprawled laterally for fifteen hundred miles. It was rugged, savage country, hardly worth fighting for except for its peculiar strategic position as a stepping stone—first by the Japanese to Australia and now by the Allies to New Britain and its vital port, Rabaul.

Thirty thousand American and Australian troops under Lieutenant General Robert Eichelberger had fought their way from Port Moresby—on the south coast of the Papua peninsula, which pointed like a stubby finger at Guadalcanal —to take Buna Village on the opposite side of the promontory.

"Bob, I want you to take Buna or not come back alive," MacArthur had told Eichelberger. "And that goes for your chief of staff too."

It was a victory achieved at high cost in lives and suffering. The troops had been forced to cross the formidable Owen Stanley Range while fighting battles as fierce as those on Guadalcanal under just as miserable conditions. Though Buna had fallen, the ordeal was far from over. As on Guadalcanal, the Japanese refused to admit they were defeated and were making Australians and Americans pay for every yard of territory.

Attention at Imperial Headquarters, however, remained focused on Guadalcanal, where disaster was even more imminent. It was becoming more and more difficult to get supplies through. The drum supply system had proved impractical. Only limited amounts of medicine and food could be brought in by submarines stripped of torpedoes, guns and shells, or dropped from planes.

The Navy was ready to abandon Guadalcanal; and Yamamoto had let it be known in high circles that he favored such action immediately. But the Army General Staff still stood firm—in public. In private, however, informal conversations were going on among its members about how to withdraw without losing face. After all, they *had* promised the Emperor victory on Guadalcanal.

The urgency of the situation was emphasized by a radiogram from General Hyakutake on December 23:

NO FOOD AVAILABLE AND WE CAN NO LONGER SEND OUT SCOUTS. WE CAN DO NOTHING TO WITHSTAND THE ENEMY'S OFFENSIVE. 17TH ARMY NOW REQUESTS PERMISSION TO BREAK INTO THE ENEMY'S POSITIONS AND DIE AN HONORABLE DEATH RATHER THAN DIE OF HUNGER IN OUR OWN DUGOUTS.

On Christmas Day the Army and Navy leaders held a formal emergency meeting at the Imperial Palace to resolve the problem. It was no longer a question of whether withdrawal was necessary, but which service would have the courage to recommend it officially and thereby risk accepting the blame for defeat. Chief of Staff Nagano, his assistant Ito, Admiral Fukudome and Captain Tomioka represented the Navy; Chief of Staff Sugiyama and Colonel Tsuji represented the Army.

Admiral Fukudome, Nagano's Chief of Operations, urged withdrawal but he himself hesitated. "What do you think of joint tactical map games before we decide?" he suggested.

Tsuji erupted. More than anyone else in the room he realized what each day's delay meant to the starving men on Guadalcanal. Waving his arms, he exclaimed that it was the Navy's duty to study general trends *before* an emergency arose. "You are all very well posted on the battle situation and yet you can't even reach a decision. You had better all resign! I've often been on destroyers and undergone heavy air raids. The naval commanders I met there all told me, 'The big shots at the Tokyo Hotel [Navy General Staff] and the *Yamato* Hotel [Combined Fleet] should come out here and see what we have to take and then they might understand!'"

Tomioka agreed with Tsuji on withdrawal but was so

aroused by the insult to the Navy that he shot to his feet. "What are you trying to say? That destroyer commanders are all faint of heart? Take that back!"

"Have you ever been to the fighting front?" Tsuji said accusingly. "Do you understand what's going on out there today?"

Tomioka, who had pleaded again and again for sea duty, plunged toward Tsuji. Fukudome intercepted him and said, "I am sorry, Tsuji-*kun*. What you say is true."

It may have been true, but Nagano still insisted on map games. They demonstrated again what everyone knew—that less than one fourth of any reinforcements and supplies would arrive intact. The argument went on, with each service continuing to blame the other for the situation on the island. The Army wanted to know how it could win without ammunition and food. "You landed the Army without arms and food and then cut off the supply. It's like sending someone on a roof and taking away the ladder."

The Navy sarcastically wanted to know how long this business of reinforcements would go on. The Army replied in kind that it could win if it were given *half* of what the enemy had. "Up till now we've only received one percent."

There was no way out of such a bitter debate—until Colonel Joichiro Sanada arrived on December 29 from Rabaul with a report which was supported by almost every Army and Navy officer he had interviewed in the Solomons, including Imoto and Imamura's operations officer: all troops should be withdrawn from Guadalcanal as soon as possible. The island could be retaken "only by a miracle," and future military operations "must not, out of eagerness to regain Gadarukanaru, be jeopardized by following previous plans and by continuing a campaign in which neither the high command [17th Army] nor the front-line commanders have any confidence."

Sanada's report settled the matter for both the Army and the Navy. Sugiyama seemed "rather relieved" and Nagano, without further argument, agreed to remove Hyakutake's troops from the island by destroyers by the end of January if possible.

The two Chiefs of Staff reviewed the problem for the Emperor at an imperial conference on the last day of the year, then formally recommended the evacuation of both Guadalcanal and Buna in New Guinea. The Emperor turned to Nagano and observed in his expressionless manner that the United States seemed to have won by air power, then asked an embarrassing question: Why was it that it took the Americans just a few days to build an air base and the Japanese more than a month or so? "Isn't there room for improvement?"

"I am very sorry indeed," Nagano acknowledged humbly; the enemy used machines while the Japanese had to rely on manpower.

But it was apparent that His Majesty was not pleased with the answer. For two hours he continued to probe the defeat, to the discomfort of the two Chiefs. Finally he raised his already high-pitched voice: "Well, now the Army and Navy should do their best as they have just explained." He approved withdrawal from Guadalcanal and Buna.*

Aboard *Yamato* that night Admiral Ugaki made the final entry in his diary for 1942:

... How splendid the first stage of our operations was! But how unsuccessfully we have fought since the defeat at Midway!

Our strategy, aimed at invasion of Hawaii, Fiji, Samoa, and New Caledonia as well as domination over India and the destruction of the British Eastern Squadron, has dissipated like a dream. In addition, the occupation of Port Moresby and Guadalcanal has been frustrated. A welter of emotions are awakened in my breast as I look back upon the past. In war things often do not turn out as we wish. Nevertheless, I cannot stem my feeling of mortification. The desperate struggles of our officers and men are too numerous to mention.

I express my heartfelt thanks to them and at the same time offer my condolences to those who died a glorious death at the front.

---

*Contrary to widespread belief, the Emperor took a lively, personal interest in military operations. On January 9, 1943, His Majesty told Sugiyama, "The fall of Buna is regrettable, but the officers and men fought well. I hear the enemy has ten tanks or so; don't we have any tanks in that area? And what is the situation in Lae? . . . I am very pleased with the improvement made by antiaircraft units throughout Burma." When Sugiyama reported to the Throne several weeks later on the failure of transporting reinforcements to Lae, the Emperor said, after offering the Army Chief of Staff a chair—an indication of favor, "Why didn't you change your mind at the last minute and land on Madang [a port northeast of Lae]? We must admit we suffered a setback, but if we take it to heart I believe it will be a good lesson for future operations. Make every effort so I don't have to worry in the future. Increase air support, build roads where our troops can pass safely, and gain firm footholds step by step. Give enough thought to your plans so that Lae and Salamaua don't become another Guadalcanal."

Even in defeat the Japanese had left an indelible impression on the victors of Guadalcanal and New Guinea. Lieutenant General George C. Kenney, chief of the Allied Air Forces in the southwest Pacific, reported to General H. H. ("Hap") Arnold, head of the U. S. Army Air Forces, that those back home, including the War Department, had no conception of the problems in the southwest Pacific.

... The Jap is still being underrated. There is no question of our being able to defeat him, but the time, effort, blood and money required to do the job may run to proportions beyond all conception, particularly if the devil is allowed to develop the resources he is now holding.

Let us look at Buna. There are hundreds of Bunas ahead for us. The Jap there has been in a hopeless position for two months. He has been outnumbered heavily throughout the show. His garrison has been whittled down to a handful by bombing and strafing. He has had no air support, and his own Navy has not been able to get past our air blockade to help him. He has seen lots of Japs sunk off shore a few miles away. He has been short on rations and has had to conserve his ammunition, as his replenishment from submarines and small boats working down from Lae at night, and, once, by parachute from airplanes, has been precarious, to say the least. The Emperor told them to hold, and, believe me, they have held! As to their morale—they still yell out to our troops, "What's the matter, Yanks? Are you yellow? Why don't you come in and fight?" A few snipers, asked to surrender after being surrounded, called back, "If you bastards think you are good enough, come and get us!"

... I'm afraid that a lot of people who think this Jap is a "pushover" as soon as Germany falls, are due for a rude awakening. We will have to call on all our patriotism, stamina, guts, and maybe some crusading spirit or religious fervor thrown in, to beat him. No amateur team will take this boy out. We have got to turn professional. Another thing: there are no quiet sectors in which troops get started off gradually, as in the last war. There are no breathers on this schedule. You take on Notre Dame, every time you play!

4.

On the afternoon of January 13, 1943, ten destroyers carrying a thousand men and supplies left Shortland. In one was Colonel Imoto. He had helped Imamura's staff and several naval officers hastily draw up a plan of evacuation, Operation KE. His present assignment was to transmit the order to Hyakutake and assist him as a member of his staff.

The first thing Imoto saw as he disembarked near Cape Esperance was a dead body; the beach that led to 17th Army headquarters was a trail of corpses. It was midnight when he finally reached Hyakutake's camp—a complex of tents and jerry-built shelters near Tassafaronga Point.

He blundered around in a chilling rain until he found Colonel Haruo Konuma and several staff officers in a leaky tent. They were lying on beds made from coconut leaves and covered with mosquito netting. All, that is, but Major Mitsuo Suginoo, who was shaving by candlelight. He and Imoto had served in the same regiment and he greeted his friend with enthusiasm. "I'm preparing to die tomorrow," he said half in jest.

"That's an admirable attitude," Imoto replied in the same spirit.

Konuma led Imoto to the next tent to meet the new chief of staff—Futami's replacement—Major General Shuichi Miyazaki. Imoto sat down stiffly facing the general and said, "I have brought General Imamura's order for the Seventeenth Army to withdraw from Guadalcanal."

"How could we go home after losing so many men?" Konuma broke in. He had ordered the men to die in their foxholes.

Miyazaki was equally outraged. "In a situation like this, to consider such an operation would be unthinkable even in a dream! We don't mean to disobey the order but we cannot execute it. Therefore we must attack and die, and give everyone an example of Japanese Army tradition."

Imoto's arguments had no effect on the two emotional officers. Konuma doubted that any withdrawal was feasible; the men out front were too entangled with the enemy, and if any of them did manage to get on ships they would end by drowning. "It's impossible, so leave us alone!"

As a last resort Imoto drew out the order from Imamura. "Don't you realize that this is an order of withdrawal from the commander of the Army Group based on the Emperor's order!" They had no right to oppose it.

Miyazaki finally got control of himself. "You are correct," he said. "This is not our decision. The Army commander must make it."

Imoto was brought to General Hyakutake at dawn. His tent was snuggled at the roots of a huge tree. He was sitting Japanese style on a blanket before a table—a biscuit box—meditating. He opened his eyes. Imoto explained why he was there. Hyakutake stared wordlessly at him for a minute and closed his eyes again. Finally he said quietly, "This is a most difficult order to receive. I cannot make up my mind right now. Give me a little time."

The morning lull was broken by a rumble of explosions; the Americans were resuming their daily bombardment. It was almost noon before Imoto was summoned to Hyakutake's tent.

"I will obey the order," the general stated with dignity, "but it is very difficult and I can't say if the operation will succeed. At least I will do my best."

Konuma knew the men in the front lines felt even more strongly about retreat then those at headquarters and would find it unbearable to leave dead comrades behind. He volunteered to go up front. The commanders of the 2nd and 38th divisions accepted the orders but it would be necessary to tell their men it was simply a strategic withdrawal, not that they were being taken off the island.

On the night of January 23 the troops up front began stealing from their foxholes and back through the next line of defense toward Cape Esperance, where they would be evacuated in three sections over a period of one week. Incredibly, the Americans—fifty thousand strong now—did not pursue. The following night the leapfrogging continued. Again there was no pursuit. Finally the rear guard itself started pulling back a little at a time. Still the Americans failed to press forward and within a week Japanese scouts alone, keeping up a deceptive volume of fire, maintained contact with the foe. By the end of January the remnants of the 38th Division had reached Cape Esperance. The following night, February 1, nineteen destroyers would stand less than a thousand yards offshore and flash blue signals to Hyakutake's men hiding in the coconut groves with their landing craft.

By dusk on February 1 the Americans still imagined they faced an enemy in force. They did know a fleet of destroyers was coming full speed down The Slot but assumed it was another troop convoy which had to be stopped. At six-twenty, when the Japanese were halfway to Guadalcanal, twenty-four bombers covered by seventeen Wildcats converged on the destroyers. They were driven off by thirty Japanese fighters after damaging but one ship.

At Cape Esperance the landing craft were brought out of cover and the men lined up to get aboard. Colonel Imoto admired the beautiful evening and wished he could enjoy it in peaceful times. In his pocket he had a letter from Hyakutake addressed to General Imamura. Several PT boats careened in toward the beach, but their pilots saw nothing in the dark and swung off. The minutes passed slowly. It was after ten o'clock. Had the first evacuation been postponed? From the blackness in the direction of Savo Island blue signal lights flashed.

While four destroyers patrolled cautiously, the other fourteen crept silently to within 750 yards of the shore. They stopped their engines but didn't drop anchor. The commander of the little fleet, Tomiji Koyanagi—promoted to rear admiral after his shelling of Henderson from *Kongo*—paced the bridge of his flagship, anxiously watching landing craft emerge from the gloom. One bombing attack, even if it failed, could cause havoc.

A destroyer's gun thundered nearby and there followed a blaze of light. A PT boat had been set afire. Had they been discovered? Other PT boats began boring in. Two were sunk, the rest driven off. But where were the planes from Henderson? By this time the destroyers were loaded; it had taken little more than half an hour to get 5,424 men aboard. Emaciated, eyes sullen, they stared without expression, overcome by the bitterness of defeat and the humiliation of leaving behind comrades who had not been given proper burial rites.

The destroyers pulled out into the night, still unopposed by the Cactus Air Force, leaving the Americans with the belief that their enemy had again been reinforced. Army Major General Alexander M. Patch, who had relieved Vandegrift early in December, feared that a new Japanese offensive was being mounted, and his three divisions continued their unwarranted respect for the thin shell of Hyakutake's rear guard.

In the afternoon on February 4 the second rescue column, nineteen destroyers, came down the Solomons passage to evacuate 4,977 men. A single ship was damaged. Admiral Koyanagi attributed success largely to "heavenly assistance," but feared the third and last rescue mission would meet with disaster. At nine-thirty in the morning on February 7, eighteen destroyers left Shortland. Koyanagi was so apprehensive that he ordered ten of them to provide cover. Once again a destroyer was damaged en route and had to be towed off by another, leaving but six for transportation. Four headed for Guadalcanal and the others for nearby Russell Island.

The last troops, including Hyakutake and his headquarters, were waiting on the beach along with several hundred sick and wounded who had managed to make their way to the evacuation area. Pfc. Tadashi Suzuki, one of the few survivors of the Ichiki Detachment, was unable to climb a rope ladder and had to be boosted aboard a destroyer by two sailors. On the deck he felt safe, as if he were on Japanese soil. But he couldn't forget the hundreds of sick comrades he had left lying along the beaches, too feeble to be saved and equipped only with grenades to blow themselves up at the last moment. Rice balls mixed with green peas were passed out. Although Suzuki couldn't taste the food, he gulped it down, vowing to send his sons and grandsons into the Navy; sailors were well fed until they died.

Not a single American plane attacked the convoy on the long trip back to Shortland; 2,639 more men had been evacuated.* In all, more than 13,000 were saved. It was cold comfort: 25,000 others, dead or within hours of death, had been left behind (1,592 Americans died—1,042 Marines and 550 GI's). Many thousands of tons of shipping had been lost in repeated efforts to supply the island. Moreover, although the Imperial Navy had fought well and gallantly, sinking about as many warships as were sunk, the vessels Japan lost were irreplaceable.

In a Manila hospital a skeletal little man approached the cot of General Kawaguchi, who was slowly recovering from malaria and malnutrition. At first the general did not recognize Nishino, the correspondent. They grasped hands and stared at each other. The general confided that on his arrival in Rabaul from Guadalcanal he had been treated as an incompetent and a coward; his career was over—all because of Tsuji.

"I know how you feel better than anyone else," said Nishino. "But the day is bound to come when the truth about Guadalcanal will be known and people realize you were right."

Bitterly the general blamed Tsuji for the defeat on Guadal-

---

*According to Lieutenant Commander Haruki Itoh (the signal officer who had warned his superiors in vain of the American invasion of the Solomons), it was no miracle but the result of a fake message sent out from Rabaul at 4 A.M., February 8. Pretending it came from a Catalina patrol boat and using American call signs, he radioed: HENDERSON, HENDERSON, URGENT SIGNAL, THIS IS NUMBER 1 SCOUT PLANE CALLING. When Henderson acknowledged the message, Itoh "reported" that he had sighted a Japanese task force of two carriers, two battleships, ten destroyers. A little later Itoh's men heard the fake message being relayed to Nouméa and Pearl Harbor and concluded that they had lured American planes away from the returning destroyers. U. S. naval historians, however, discount the story, pointing out that nothing in their records substantiates such a claim.

canal. "We lost the battle. And Japan lost the war." Tears spilled onto the pillow.

Nishino gripped the general's feeble hand. "You must think of yourself and get well." He gave him a box of *sushi*, a concoction of rice, raw fish and other delicacies.

To be polite Kawaguchi took a mouthful. A smile came over his face. *"Wa!"* he exclaimed. *"Umai!"* (Delicious!).

PART FIVE

The Gathering Forces

18   Of Mice and Men

1.

If 1943 was the Year of the Sheep in Japan, it was the year of the conference to the Allies, with sites ranging from Casablanca to Cairo and from Quebec to Teheran. Before the agonizing battle of Guadalcanal ended, Roosevelt and Churchill had made plans to meet their partner, Stalin, at Casablanca. It seemed the perfect setting for a momentous convocation, the name itself synonymous with mystery and intrigue, but what should have been the first memorable Big Three conference of the war began with a disappointment. A suspicious Stalin politely refused to attend, on the grounds that he was too busy holding back Hitler's legions.

And there was even pressure by American Secret Service agents to keep Roosevelt from the conference. They objected to his presence in an active war theater replete with German spies and saboteurs. But the danger itself must have appealed to the President; he had often remarked how he enjoyed escaping, if only for a few days, from the dreary politics of Washington.

Both Roosevelt and Churchill stayed at the Anfa Hotel, a modern building four miles outside the city, atop a hill, surrounded by tropical gardens and luxurious private villas, a visual paradise with bougainvillea and begonia in bloom and the brilliant blue of the Mediterranean as a background. The entire hotel area was fenced in by barbed wire and protected by an army of military police. Squads of security agents lurked around the grounds, and most of the Moroccan servants had been replaced by GI's and Tommies.

The American military leaders—the Joint Chiefs of Staff—held preliminary discussions at the hotel on January 13. Unexpected triumphs had come in the past two months on both sides of the world, and it was time to take another look at global strategy and make long-range plans for victory in Europe and the Far East. The British wanted a limited war in the Pacific; only after Hitler was defeated should full attention be turned to the Far East. The American Chiefs, spurred by the thorny Admiral King, felt that the British underestimated the Japanese, and decided to call for both offensive and defensive operations in the Pacific and Burma.

The next day they met with their British counterparts. From the first, King took the offensive; only 15 percent of Allied resources was going into the Pacific and this was far too little to keep the Japanese from consolidating their initial victories.

The British Chief of Staff, Sir Alan Brooke, with his habitual air of barely concealed irritation, replied that the Japanese were definitely on the defensive. Moreover, the situation in the West was now so favorable that victory was possible before the end of the year—but not if forces and matériel had to be diverted to places like Burma.

King retorted that Japan was still powerful, and if the Burma campaign was not pressed Chiang Kai-shek might pull out of the war. Seizure of the Philippines would probably have to wait for the defeat of Hitler, but the prompt capture of Truk and the Marianas was mandatory.

King's rugged eloquence had little effect on the British. They had come to Casablanca determined to have their own way, and moreover, had arrived elaborately prepared to get it. Anchored a few miles away was a 6,000-ton liner, their staff headquarters and communications center. It also contained "technical mechanism for presenting every quantitative calculation that might be called for."

In private King urged his compatriots to be firm, and at a meeting of the Combined Chiefs on January 17 Marshall threatened the British: if the Pacific did not get 30 percent of Allied resources it "would necessitate the United States regretfully withdrawing from the commitments in the European theater." The British, somewhat shaken, countered by suggesting that operations in the Far East be limited in 1943 to the seizure of Rabaul and Burma.

King would not give up on the Marianas. There were already enough forces in the area for a campaign and it would be a waste of manpower to let them sit idle. Besides, the operation wouldn't drain off any resources intended for Europe.

The British reaction was lukewarm. Nothing should be

undertaken in the Pacific that might weaken the attack on Germany. King's response was icy; it was up to the Americans alone to decide where and when to attack in the Pacific.

His words left no doubt that the Pacific was closest to the hearts of Americans. The names Pearl Harbor, Bataan and Guadalcanal stirred them more than Rome, Paris and Berlin. A reasonable compromise, taking into account this national pride (and shame) would have to be worked out.

Brooke was dejected. He feared that nothing the British could ever say would have "much effect in weaning King away from the Pacific." The war in Europe was "just a nuisance that kept him from waging his Pacific War undisturbed." At lunch he despairingly told Sir John Dill, "It is no use, we shall never get agreement with them."

The objective Dill had often acted as a buffer between Brooke and the Americans since Christmas 1941, when he became the British representative in Washington of the Combined Chiefs of Staff. "You have already got agreement on most of the points," he placated the general. "It only remains to settle the rest."

"I won't budge an inch," Brooke said.

"Of course you will," Dill coaxed him with a smile. "You know you have to reach an agreement or else put the whole thing up to the Prime Minister and the President. And you know as well as I do the mess that *they* would make of it."

By evening the planners for both sides had worked out an agreement outlining the Allied objectives for 1943 in such general terms that both Brooke and King were satisfied. It stated that "operations in the Pacific shall continue with the object of maintaining pressure on Japan" (which pleased King) but that such operations should not excessively drain resources from Europe (which pleased Brooke) However, it was the American Chiefs of Staff who would decide whether they were a drain. When Harry Hopkins read the agreement he wrote Dill: "I think this is a *very* good paper and damn good plan—so I am feeling much better."

Both Churchill and Roosevelt accepted it almost without question. Churchill was high in his praise of the Combined Chiefs and said, "There never has been, in all of the interallied conferences I have known, anything like the prolonged professional examination of the whole scene of the world war in its military, its armament production and its economic aspects."

But the differences had merely been masked by compromise; it was a bandage over a deep wound.

On the last day of the conference Prime Minister and President, basking in the hot African sun, chatted in generalities with the reporters about the course of the war. Then, without preliminaries, Roosevelt made an announcement. "The elimination of German, Japanese and Italian war power," he said deliberately and thoughtfully, "means the unconditional surrender of Germany, Italy and Japan."

It was a bombshell to everyone but Churchill, who had heard Roosevelt utter the phrase the previous day at a private luncheon attended by Hopkins and Elliott Roosevelt. Churchill had first frowned, then he broke into a grin and said, "Perfect! And I can just see how Goebbels and the rest of 'em'll squeal!"*

But it was soon apparent that Hitler and Tojo had been handed an invaluable piece of propaganda to incite their people to resist to the end. Moreover, many in the Allied camp, particularly the military, were disturbed by the pronouncement. Admiral William O. Leahy, for example, reasoned that now the enemy had to be destroyed; diplomacy had been abandoned and the Allies were set on the rigid course of unlimited war.

2.

In the Pacific, Lieutenant General Hitoshi Imamura decided to use the lull after Guadalcanal to his advantage and reinforce the garrison at Lae, now the capital of New Guinea, with 6,400 troops. This strategic town, some 150 miles west of Buna on the north coast, was important to the defense of Rabaul itself. At midnight, on the last day of February, a convoy of eight transports and eight destroyers under Rear Admiral Masatomi Kimura left Rabaul on a counterclockwise course around New Britain into what would soon be called the Bismarck Sea. As the ships plowed through stormy waters the next afternoon, a B-24 sighted them. The following day they were found again and attacked by twenty-nine heavy bombers. One transport was sunk and two others set afire, but the convoy continued on course.

The U. S. Fifth Air Force (formerly the Allied Air Force)

---

*Churchill later wrote Robert Sherwood that he had not heard Roosevelt use the phrase until the press conference and that he himself wouldn't have used those words. Still later, however, he admitted in a statement to Parliament that the words *had* been mentioned previously, "probably in informal talk, I think at mealtimes."

in New Guinea, however, was stronger than the Japanese knew. There were at the time 207 bombers and 127 fighters in the area and General George Kenney had drastically modified his bombers as part of a revolutionary attack technique against surface vessels. The noses of B-25's had been stripped and outfitted with eight .50-caliber machine guns for strafing from as low as 200 feet. The pilots could also get down almost to sea level and release their bombs just before reaching the target. The bombs, which would either hit the ship or skip into its side, were equipped with five-second delay fuses, allowing the attackers to be at a safe distance before the explosions. Kenney had been waiting for the proper time to try out this skip bombing and Kimura's convoy was the perfect opportunity.

At ten o'clock in the morning on March 3, eighteen B-17 Flying Fortresses and twenty medium bombers made a conventional run on the transports from 7,000 feet, followed by eighteen Australian Beaufighters strafing the line of ships. Kimura was undeterred. Then a dozen B-25 skip bombers swooped in a few yards above the waves. The Japanese captains assumed they were torpedo bombers and had begun to turn their ships away when the multiple machine guns in the noses of the B-25's sprayed the troops crowded on the decks. It was slaughter. At the last minute bombs tumbled down from masthead level. Almost half the bombs, seventeen of them, found their mark.

A dozen more planes came in low. These were light bombers, but instead of launching torpedoes they, too, "skipped" their bombs and raked the decks with machine guns in their noses as they hurdled over the transports. Their bombing score was better, eleven out of twenty. Every ship was hit in the first few minutes, and either sunk or badly damaged. One destroyer went down and three others were left crippled.

The attack continued through the afternoon. The damaged ships were finished off, and the survivors in rafts and lifeboats ruthlessly strafed. The attackers were in no mood to fight a gentleman's war. They had heard too many stories from Australians whose buddies had been bayoneted after capture and left to perish with placards reading: "It took them a long time to die."*

---

*Admiral Morison wrote: "It was a grisly task, but a military necessity since Japanese soldiers do not surrender and, within swimming distance of shore, they could not be allowed to land and join the Lae

The debacle, together with the sinking of four freighters and a tanker by American submarines, discouraged Imamura from sending further reinforcements to New Guinea by convoy. He could not afford to let that island become another Guadalcanal.

Allied troops were already moving in force toward Lae; from there they could leap across the strait between New Guinea and New Britain and launch a ground assault on Rabaul itself. MacArthur's ambitious plan necessitated an additional eighteen hundred planes and five fresh divisions.

His request called for a major reassessment of priorities, and representatives of each of the Pacific commands were summoned to Washington to participate in the Pacific Military Conference. Inevitably it revived the continuing debate over theater priorities. The Army Air Force representative did not support MacArthur; he claimed that the Casablanca agreement gave the bombing offensive against Germany first priority. The Navy just as vigorously called for seizure of Rabaul as well as "adequate forces" to keep the Japanese on the defensive.

Unanimity was impossible and the problem was brought to the Joint Chiefs. Here the debate resumed, with Admiral King predictably championing the Pacific and General Arnold's deputy refusing to let up on the air raids over Germany. Each used the vague Casablanca decisions to support his argument. But settlement had to be reached and it was eventually agreed to limit the drive on Rabaul but prepare for the "ultimate seizure of the Bismarck Archipelago."

MacArthur accepted the compromise with uncharacteristic equanimity and set his planners to work on Operation Cartwheel. It was a complicated, yard-by-yard offensive involving thirteen separate phases. It would begin about the middle of June and conclude in December with a combined Army-Navy assault on Rabaul.

New Guinea was a point of contention at Imperial Headquarters as well. The Army wanted to defend it in force; it would make an excellent stage for massive ground oper-

garrison. . . . Several hundred swam ashore, and for a month there was open season on Nips in Papua; the natives had the time of their lives tracking them down as in the old head-hunting days." Japanese survivors of this massacre still resent reading American stories castigating their aviators for shooting Americans in parachutes while regarding the strafing of helpless Japanese as a "military necessity." Both instances, in their eyes, were military necessities.

ations. To the Navy, the Solomons were far more important. Its islands had many more air bases than New Guinea, and if Bougainville fell, Rabaul—and Truk itself, headquarters of Combined Fleet—would be endangered. The Army insisted that New Guinea was more significant; if it was lost, the Philippines and Java would be cut off. Strategic logic was on the side of the Navy, and it had already been proved how costly it was to send convoys to New Guinea. But the more skillful Army advocates prevailed. On March 25 Admiral Yamamoto and General Imamura each received a directive giving priority to New Guinea.

For both Americans and Japanese it was a time for planning and preparation rather than combat; in the lull each side strengthened bases and brought up reinforcements. The Imperial Navy had lost the argument, but it was Admiral Yamamoto who was ordered to deliver the first strikes against the enemy. His task was to destroy Allied air and sea power in the entire area, and he devised I-Go (Operation I), which would first concentrate on the Solomons, then New Guinea.

Early in April he moved to Rabaul with Ugaki, Kuroshima, Watanabe, and other key members of his staff, to take personal charge of the offensive. On April 7 Guadalcanal was hit with the greatest air concentration since Pearl Harbor—224 fighters and bombers. The pilots returned, as usual, with enthusiastic reports, and as usual, little damage had been done. One destroyer and two smaller ships had been sunk, and seven Marine fighter planes shot down.

Yamamoto then turned his attention to New Guinea and launched three big strikes within four days at Oro Bay, Port Moresby and Milne Bay. Pilots reported that 175 planes had been destroyed and one cruiser, two destroyers and twenty-five transports sunk. No more than five Allied planes had been eliminated, one transport and one merchantman sent to the bottom and another beached, but the reports led Yamamoto to believe that the aims of I-Go had been achieved.

Before returning to Truk, he scheduled a one-day inspection tour of defenses in the Solomons. His first stop would be Ballale, a small island off southern Bougainville, for a brief visit with troops from General Maruyama's division who were recuperating from their ordeal on Guadalcanal. He wanted to thank them in person for their sacrifices.

General Imamura had misgivings about the tour and told Yamamoto of his own narrow escape from an American fighter plane near Bougainville. But Yamamoto was insistent;

even the commander of the Eleventh Air Fleet could not dissuade him. Commander Watanabe wrote out the schedule by hand and personally took it to Eighth Fleet headquarters. He wanted the information delivered by courier, but a communications officer said it had to be sent by radio. Watanabe protested; the Americans would pick up the message and perhaps decode it. Impossible, said the communications officer. "This code only went into effect on April first and cannot be broken."

Watanabe's fears were justified. Moments after the message had been transmitted it was intercepted and delivered to Combat Intelligence headquarters at Pearl Harbor. The men in the cellar, who had helped win the Battle of Midway, labored most of the night and by dawn of April 14 had a decoded plain text in Japanese. Lieutenant Colonel Alva Lasswell, a Marine language officer, and his staff filled in the blanks and identified the code symbols for the place names. RR, for example, meant Rabaul, and RXZ was Ballale.

At 8:02 A.M. Commander Edward Layton, the fleet intelligence officer, was admitted to Admiral Nimitz' office. "Our old friend Yamamoto," said Layton and handed over the message. The admiral read that Yamamoto would leave Rabaul at 6 A.M., April 18, in a medium bomber escorted by six fighters, and would arrive at Ballale Island at 8 A.M. He looked up with a smile. "Do we try to get him?"

"He's unique among their people," Layton replied. Yamamoto was idolized by the younger officers, and by the enlisted men as well. "You know the Japanese psychology; it would stun the nation."

"The one thing that concerns me is whether they could find a more effective fleet commander." The answer was that Yamamoto was "head and shoulders" above all other Japanese admirals. "It's down in Halsey's bailiwick," said Nimitz finally. "If there's a way, he'll find it. All right, we'll try it."

Nimitz wrote out a message for Halsey authorizing him to "initiate preliminary planning." The mission was approved by both Secretary of the Navy Frank Knox and the President, and on April 15 Nimitz radioed Halsey final approval with a "good luck and good hunting."

Sunday, April 18, dawned clear and humid. Exactly one year before, Doolittle had bombed Tokyo. Yamamoto, methodical as ever, was ready. His aides had persuaded him to wear green fatigues rather than his more conspicuous dress whites. As he approached his plane, a Mitsubishi bomber, he turned to the naval commander in Rabaul, Vice Admiral

Jinichi Kusaka (cousin of Nagumo's chief of staff), and handed him two scrolls to give to the new commander of the Eighth Fleet. They were poems by Emperor Meiji, copied out by Yamamoto.

The admiral's plane left Rabaul at exactly 6 A.M., Tokyo time. With him was his secretary, the fleet medical officer and the staff officer for air. A second Mitsubishi took off with Chief of Staff Ugaki and several other staff officers. Commander Watanabe watched both planes disappear, disappointed that he was not in the party.

The two bombers headed south at 5,000 feet, so close that Ugaki feared their wings might collide. Six Zero fighters hovered protectively overhead. It was a pleasant, uneventful trip, and soon after Bougainville appeared on the left the planes began to descend for a landing at the Kahili airfield.

From the south, sixteen tightly grouped P-38 Lightning fighters from Henderson Field were approaching Bougainville at 2,000 feet. Their commander, Major John W. Mitchell, looked at his watch. It was 9:34 (an hour later than Tokyo time). They had flown more than six hundred miles over open water, extra fuel tanks strapped onto the wings, on an indirect course with only a compass and an air-speed indicator to guide them—and, incredibly, had reached the interception point at the right moment. Hopefully, Yamamoto's plane would appear in one minute. It should be about three miles to the west. There wasn't a plane in sight.

"Bogey's eleven o'clock." It was one of Mitchell's pilots breaking radio silence in a low voice. "High."

Mitchell counted eight enemy planes. Two were bombers. There should have been one. Could the four Lightnings in the "killer" group knock down both bombers? The leader of this group, Captain Thomas G. Lanphier, Jr., was also counting the Japanese planes. They looked like bursts of anti-aircraft fire. He switched to internal fuel, dumping his auxiliary tanks. The Japanese came on, unsuspecting. Two miles from the coast Lanphier noticed silvery belly tanks falling from the Zeros. The ambushers had been discovered. The two Japanese bombers began diving toward the jungle.

Zeros came hurtling at Lanphier and he opened fire.

"Leave the Zeros, Tom," Mitchell called from far above. "Bore in on the bombers. Get the bombers. Damn it all, the bombers!"

Ugaki's plane was barely skimming the jungle. "What happened?" he asked the plane commander, who was bracing himself in the aisle.

"I think there is some operational mistake," he said.

Ugaki looked up and saw a tangle of Zeros and Lightnings. Where was Yamamoto? The other bomber abruptly swung off and disappeared.

Two of Lanphier's planes were already out of action; one pilot couldn't release his belly tanks and his wing man had to stay with him. It was up to Lanphier and his own wing man, Lieutenant Rex T. Barber, to shoot down the two bombers. Lamphier fought his way past three Zeros, kicked his plane over on its back. He caught a glimpse of a bomber below. He plunged down and loosed a long, steady burst. The Mitsubishi's right engine and wing flamed up.

Barber closed in on the other Mitsubishi. He opened fire and could see the bomber shudder. He continued raking the plane, and the top of its tail section disintegrated. Barber hurtled by. He looked back and was sure he saw "debris rising from the jungle." Both he and Lanphier were sure they had shot down the first bomber, Yamamoto's.

Ugaki had seen his commander's plane crash into the jungle. "Look at Yamamoto's plane!" Stunned, he pointed to a pillar of black smoke. "It's over!" His own plane shimmied from a hit in the right wing and plunged toward the sea. The pilot held back on the controls but could not stop the dive. The Mitsubishi careened into the water.

"This is the end of Ugaki!" he told himself as water enfolded him. He didn't try to struggle in the darkness. As in a dream he saw light above and felt himself rising to the surface. He gasped for breath. A wing was burning; everything else had disappeared. He was two hundred yards from shore and began swimming, using breaststrokes. Exhausted, he reached for a floatbox but couldn't hang on and only then realized that his right arm was broken. He clung to the box with his left hand and kicked his way to the shore.

The first Lightnings returning to Henderson Field did barrel rolls and those on the ground knew Yamamoto had been shot down. A message went out to Halsey:

POP GOES THE WEASEL. P-38'S LED BY MAJOR JOHN W. MITCHELL USA VISITED KAHILI AREA ABOUT 0930. SHOT DOWN TWO BOMBERS ESCORTED BY ZEROS FLYING CLOSE FORMATION. ONE SHOT BELIEVED TO BE TEST FLIGHT. THREE ZEROS ADDED TO THE SCORE SUM TOTAL SIX. ONE P-38 FAILED RETURN. APRIL 18 SEEMS TO BE OUR DAY.

Halsey read the message the next morning at his regular conference. Admiral Turner "whooped and applauded."

"Hold on, Kelly," said Halsey. "What's so good about it? I'd hoped to lead that scoundrel up Pennsylvania Avenue in chains, with the rest of you kicking him where it would do the most good!" He ordered the story withheld from the press. It might reveal to the Japanese that their code had been broken.*

Commander Watanabe, overwhelmed with grief, supervised the cremation of Yamamoto's body. He put the ashes in a small wooden box lined with papaya leaves. At Truk he boarded *Musashi* for the sad trip home. On May 21 the superbattleship arrived in Tokyo Bay and a radio announcer told the nation in a choked voice that Yamamoto had "met gallant death in a war plane."

His ashes were divided and put into two urns for two ceremonies, one in Nagaoka, Yamamoto's birthplace, and the other for a state funeral. The latter took place on June 5—the anniversary of the funeral of Japan's other great naval hero, Admiral Togo. A million citizens lined the streets of Tokyo to watch the cortege. Commander Watanabe, carrying his former chess partner's sword, walked right behind the artillery caisson on which the ashes were mounted. They were interred in Hibiya Park.

Yamamoto's successor, Admiral Mineichi Koga, said, "There was only one Yamamoto and no one can replace him."

The tragic death of their greatest war hero was "an insupportable blow" to the Japanese people. Moreover, it closely followed the grim announcement that the United States had retaken the Aleutian island of Attu. Propagandists attempted to present the death of 2,351 Japanese on that dreary island off Alaska as an inspirational epic that would be "a tremendous stimulant to the fighting spirit of our nation."

But the Emperor himself was deeply distressed. "In the future, please see to it that you have a reasonable chance of success before launching into an operation," he told Army Chief of Staff Sugiyama—and then unburdened himself at length in the presence of his chief aide-de-camp, General Shigeru Hasunuma. "They [the Army and Navy Chiefs of Staff] should have foreseen that such a situation would develop. Instead it took them a week to prepare countermea-

*Japanese communications officers never suspected their code had been broken. To the end of the war they were convinced it was "unbreakable."

sures after the enemy landed on May twelfth. They mentioned something about 'heavy fog,' but they should have known about the fog. . . . Are the Navy and the Army really frank with each other? It seems as if one makes an impossible demand, and the other irresponsibly promises to fulfill it. Whatever the two agree upon must be carried out. If they can't accomplish what they promise each other, it's worse than making the promises in the first place. If there is friction between the Army and the Navy, this war cannot be concluded successfully. They must be completely open with each other in planning their operations. . . . If we continue getting involved in such operations it will only help raise enemy morale, as in the case of Guadalcanal. Neutral nations will waver; China will be encouraged, and it will have a serious effect on the nations of the Greater East Asia Sphere. Isn't there any way we can confront the United States forces somewhere and beat them? . . . Sugiyama was saying something to the effect that a Decisive Battle by the Navy should 'finish off' this war, but it is an impossible idea."

The fall of Attu also engendered outspoken criticism of Imperial Headquarters by high-ranking Navy officers. "We should have just pounded Attu and withdrawn from there," Vice Admiral Takijiro Onishi told a civilian friend, Yoshio Kodama—the same Kodama who had plotted with Tsuji to assassinate Prince Konoye. "But we took a foolish liking to the place and poured in too much matériel and unnecessary personnel, making it impossible to leave. There are also many islands like that in the south."

Kodama said he thought Japan's strategy was "too much concerned with outward show."

Onishi was in accord. "Just as the Army and Navy are squabbling over every trivial thing, Air Force headquarters and Fleet Administration headquarters are, as you know, at loggerheads with each other. No matter how often we point out the absolute necessity of strengthening the air force, Fleet Administration headquarters sticks to its old ideas of 'Fleet First' and can only view the overall situation in this light. In the final analysis, unless the Navy itself is driven up against the wall, it won't get around to reforming those things which should be reformed. But when that comes it will already be too late."

Onishi's rancor went beyond the general progress of the war. He felt that Fleet Administration headquarters and its outmoded ideas of "Fleet First" were overriding the more important needs of the air force. His, of course, was a parochial point of view but it reflected the growing rivalry between individual departments, civilian as well as military.

The slow but significant drop in production aggravated the situation. Losses of matériel in battle could no longer be replaced and even the minimum requirements of the Army and Navy could not be met. Not only had commanders of occupied areas failed to develop local natural resources but a mere fraction of what was produced reached the homeland because of Japan's limited merchant marine and America's devastating submarine assaults on the ships taking the long trip north.

This crippling lack of raw materials was compounded by controls that often overlapped and were inconsistent. Economic mobilization in the United States, on the other hand, was accelerating. While the output in Japan under the stimulus of war had risen one-fourth, that in America had gone up about two-thirds, and Japan's manufacturing efficiency was but 35 percent that of her enemy's. More significant, Japan's gross national product (using 1940 as an index basis of 100) had gone up a meager 2 points by the beginning of 1943, while America's had climbed to 136. Moreover, it was a well-planned expansion on all levels. The Japanese had failed to diversify. Their output of munitions had soared—but at the expense of nonmilitary items. The ten years before Pearl Harbor had seen such growth in production that the leaders had assumed they could carry on a major war without any substantial enlargement.

Confronted with reality, they made every effort to raise the general level. Within a few months, the gross national product was on the upswing. Total output showed a marked increase and production of military items climbed higher than ever. The prospect was promising, but was it too late?

Shipping remained the most crucial problem. The carefully allotted budget was upset by the fall of Attu and the sercet evacuation of the nearby island of Kiska.* With these two bridgeheads in the Aleutians gone, the Kurile Islands would have to be fortified and manned. All this would divert a vast amount of shipping from the beleaguered areas in the south.

The liaison conference came to grips with this emergency

---

*When the Americans stormed in to take Kiska with almost thirty-fi e thousand troops, they could find nothing but three mongrel dogs. This inspired a GI ballad, "Tales of Kiska," which included these lines:

It took three days before we learnt
That more than dogs there simply weren't.

505

in June, concluding that the Kuriles had to be turned into a fortress even though it meant national power would suffer a loss: the production of iron would have to be lowered 250,-000 tons, aluminum 6,000 tons and coal 650,000 tons.

"We are facing a grave crisis," Colonel Tanemura wrote in his "Diary" that night. It was a crisis made more acrimonious by the debilitating struggle between the Army and the Navy for strategic materials. Admiral Soemu Toyoda began referring to the Army as "horse dung." In public he declared that he would rather his daughter married a beggar than an Army man.

The debate on shipping was abruptly overshadowed a few days later, on June 30, by the announcement that the hiatus in the Solomons was over. Admiral Halsey had leapfrogged his amphibious force halfway up The Slot to the island of New Georgia, the key to the central Solomons. The Japanese garrison was on the alert, and reinforcements soon brought its strength up to five thousand, but the defenders could not repel the Army and Marine divisions that had splashed ashore. It could be no more than a matter of weeks before the island was overrun. Then there would be little between the Americans and strategic Bougainville.

The Emperor summoned the Prime Minister. Tojo left the audience shaken by His Majesty's "grave concern" and sent for the man whose advice he had often relied upon, General Kenryo Sato. His face a mask, Tojo said, "Ask the General Staffs where they plan to stop the enemy."

"We will never get an answer," Sato replied. "Neither the Army nor the Navy can possibly draw up a plan to stop them." Tojo was silent but his face could no longer hide his distress.

"What happened at the Palace?" Sato asked.

"The Emperor is very worried about all this," Tojo muttered and lapsed into silence again.

"What exactly did the Emperor say?" Sato prodded him.

The Prime Minister abruptly straightened up from his slouch and said, "To tell the truth, the Emperor said, 'You keep repeating that the Imperial Army is invulnerable, yet whenever the enemy lands you lose the battle. You've never been able to repulse an enemy landing. Can't you do it *somewhere?* How is this war going to turn out?'"* He shrugged

---

*In the next few weeks the Emperor expressed his displeasure a number of times. On August 5 he upbraided Army Chief of Staff Sugiyama for the series of defeats in New Guinea and the Solomons.

his shoulders as if to make light of what he had just revealed. "Well, he said something to that effect."

But Sato insisted that by uttering such words to his Prime Minister, the Emperor must have concluded that he wouldn't get a direct answer from either the Army or Navy Chief of Staff. "That's probably why he finally put the question to you. And if that's the case, I repeat, it's a grave matter. He must be losing confidence in the military."

Tojo protested that Sato went too far. "What I said now is not exactly the Emperor's words. He didn't express lack of confidence in the military. On the other hand, I do admit he was sorely troubled. I'm going to speak to Sugiyama. You talk to the Operations chief, and then we must come up with some measure. It is extremely urgent. Without saying it's an order of the Emperor, we must insist on a definite strategic plan indicating exactly where we can stem the enemy counteroffensive and where our last defense line should be."

Sato was in agreement and, moreover, added an urgent admonition: "We must also conduct our political strategy with all this in mind."

The central instrument of Japan's political aims was still the Greater East Asia Co-prosperity Sphere, and if Japan was losing the battle of production, she was winning the battle of propaganda throughout a large part of the continent. It was a policy that envisaged an Asia united "in the spirit of universal brotherhood" under the leadership of Japan, with each nation allotted its "proper place" by the Emperor; it would lead to peace and prosperity. Established in November 1938 by the first Konoye government, it had already induced millions of Asians to co-operate in the war against the West.

It had been created by idealists who wanted to free Asia from exploitation by the white man. As with many dreams, it was taken over and exploited by realists. First came those

---

"We can't continue being pushed back inch by inch. Constant setbacks will produce a great effect not only on the enemy but on the third nations. When are you going to wage the Decisive Battle?" "Things have gone wrong for us everywhere," Sugiyama replied. "I am deeply sorry."

Three days later the Navy was the target of His Majesty's displeasure. "What in the world is the Navy doing?" he asked Hasunuma. "Isn't there any way we can get our men to attack the enemy? They are gradually being pushed back and losing their confidence. Couldn't they somehow deal the enemy a heavy blow somewhere?"

who looked upon Southeast Asia with its wealth of natural resources as a solution to economic ills; Japan could not remain a modern state under the humiliating domination of trade by the West. Militarists also saw in its policy the answer to their most pressing need—raw materials for war—and became its most ardent champions. What had gone from idealism to opportunism now developed into an unlikely combination of both. Corrupted as the Co-prosperity Sphere was by the militarists and their nationalist supporters, its call for Pan-Asianism remained relatively undiminished in its appeal to the masses.

Colonialism with its concomitant exploitation had helped raise Asia out of the mire of its past. But by the turn of the century its historical role had been fulfilled and colonialism itself was challenged by the rise of nationalism. Woodrow Wilson's idealistic demand for the self-determination of nations after World War I seemed to apply to Asians as well as Europeans. But the promised democracy never came to the East, where colonies remained colonies; the West had two standards of freedom, one for itself and one for those east of Suez. With each year the gap between East and West widened as the Western masters, particularly the British, offered mere patchwork reforms.

Except for China, a continent that should have been ripe for revolution remained dormant; rebels of each country waited for someone else to revolt first. They no longer looked to democratic leaders; instead, their idols were dictators like Hitler, who had achieved dramatic diplomatic and military victories over England and France. All over Asia the Fascist salute and the worker's clenched fist vied for popularity.

Britain's attempts to win support from Asians in her war against the Axis were met with derision. In 1940 Dr. Ba Maw, who had been educated at Cambridge and became the first premier of Burma, warned his parliament to remember Britain's "idealistic" war aims in World War I. "With the same moral fervour she declared that in fighting Germany she was defending the smaller nationalities; she was making the world safe for democracy; . . . and she had absolutely no territorial ambitions. . . . But what was the result? What happened when the battle and the shouting were done and the victors obtained their victory? The British Empire added to itself roughly a million and a half square miles of new territory as a result of the war. What happened to the doctrine of self-determination? When I, with my usual recklessness, mentioned self-determination before the Joint Select

Committee at the time the Committee was hammering out Burma's constitution, the British representatives were amused." But this seditious speech was not amusing to the British and Ba Maw was thrown in jail.

The next year the signing of the Atlantic Charter by Churchill and Roosevelt again brought a glimmer of hope to some Asian political leaders that the West had at last dropped its double standard of freedom. Hadn't it proclaimed "the right of all people to choose the form of government under which they will live"? Churchill soon made it clear, however, that the Charter did not apply to the British colonies—in other words, only to white nations.

The time, therefore, was more than ripe for wide acceptance of Japan's rallying cry for a Pan-Asia. Since the middle of the previous century, her own independence had been a constant reminder that Asians could be free. Admiral Togo's crushing defeat of the Russian fleet in 1905 had marked the emergence of Asia from Western domination and given all Orientals a sense of pride. The fall of Singapore in 1942 gave more dramatic proof that the white man was not invincible. The sight of the British retreating on all fronts was heady to Asians, and much of the continent was about ready to actively ally itself with the victors.

The glaring exception, of course, was China, where hundreds of thousands of Japanese troops were still entangled in a frustrating, endless battle. Most Japanese could not see why Chiang Kai-shek continued to fight. Wasn't it obvious that he was being used as a tool by Churchill and Roosevelt?* There were some liberal Japanese, however, who had always opposed Japan's occupation of China. One was Mamoru Shigemitsu, the ambassador to the collaborationist puppet government in Nanking. He was now arguing that the success of the

---

*That the average Japanese saw only the idealism in the Co-prosperity Sphere was indicated by the winning slogans in a contest held by the *Japan Times & Advertiser*:

"Japanese Action Spells Construction
Enemy Action Spells Self-Destruction"

"With Firmness We Fight
With Kindness We Build"

"Fight Onward till Asia Is Asia's Own"

"In the Freedom of the East
Lies the Peace of the West"

Co-prosperity Sphere depended on a just solution of the China problem. How could Japan call for the end of colonialism while treating a large part of China like a colony? The unequal treaties that existed with Nanking should be abolished and economic aid offered without restrictions.

Tojo, who had fully supported the war in China as a militarist, saw the issue in a different perspective as prime minister, and welcomed Shigemitsu's proposal. There was stubborn resistance from Army leaders, but by the beginning of 1943 Tojo had persuaded them that the best way to get raw materials from China was to adopt the Shigemitsu plan. Arrangements were made to return the Japanese settlements in Soochow, Hankow, Hangchow and Tientsin to the Nanking government, and new treaties were negotiated. Shigemitsu was recalled to Tokyo to become the new foreign minister and in the Diet he urged again and again that *all* of East Asia be freed from military occupation and given political freedom. "For Japan it means the establishment of the 'good neighbor' policy and the improvement of our international relations."

It was Shigemitsu who had initiated this new phase of the crusade, but Tojo who led it. He announced to the Diet that Burma would be recognized as an independent state before the end of the year. In March a Burmese delegation was invited to Tokyo. It was headed by Dr. Ba Maw, who had escaped from jail just before the British evacuated Burma. The Burmese were greeted warmly. Ba Maw was overwhelmed by the surge of patriotic feeling he found on all sides. Japan was "the very vortex of the whole Asian conflict." Tojo, General Sugiyama, Admiral Shimada and Shigemitsu all struck him as true products of the "exploding Asian age, dynamic, daring, full of the new Asian consciousness underlying the concept of the Greater East Asia Co-prosperity Sphere." Tojo, moreover, was showing "astonishing farsightedness" that "positively amounted to political vision" in his determination to give independence to the occupied countries.

3.

In America the Co-prosperity Sphere was almost universally ridiculed as crude propaganda, but the author Pearl Buck tried to warn her fellow Americans that the spirit of Pan-Asianism did indeed run deep. She wrote Mrs. Roosevelt, a few days after Pearl Harbor, that there was "in all the Oriental peoples a very deep sense that the white man generally is, or may be, their common enemy, and that in the final analysis it remains always a possibility that the point may come when these peoples, even such present enemies as the Chinese and Japanese, may unite as colored against white. They are not now at that point, but the possibility is always in their minds. It may be best expressed by a remark made lately by a Chinese professor. 'Although the Japanese are our enemies just now, if it came to the ultimate choice, we would rather be a dependency of Japan than of the United States, because at least the Japanese do not consider us an inferior race.' The truth is that these peoples of the Orient, even those now allied with us, are secretly watchful of our behavior toward them as peoples of a different race, and if they fear at all that they will not in the long run be treated as our complete equals, they will go with us only so far as their temporary purposes are served, and then turn against us as a white race historically aggressive against them, at least from their point of view, and historically their exploiters."

She warned that an underground colored solidarity was "growing in the world as these politically awakened Asiatic peoples come to a knowledge of themselves, and unless we are exceedingly wise and careful, the result of this awakening is going to be disastrous to us. . . . We white people are for the most part ignorant or oblivious to the fact that there may develop out of all this struggle an entirely new alignment of peoples according to race and color, but the Asiatic peoples never forget the possibility, and all that they do will be done with the reservations necessary for that new alignment. I have found to my horror that there is such a reservation even in the minds of many of our colored Americans, who though they are naturally and wishfully loyal to our country, have yet because of the stubbornness of race prejudice here been led to believe, from their own experience and the propaganda of Japanese here also, that there is no hope of fairness from the white man, and that the colored peoples must unite and conquer the white man before there can be any way of getting rid of the yoke of race prejudice."*

---

*Paradoxically, white skin has been a mark of feminine beauty in Japan since earliest times. There is an old proverb: "White skin makes up for seven defects." Early in the Meiji period writers began expressing their admiration for the white skin of Westerners, and in the 1920's Japan's favorite movie stars were Clara Bow, Gloria Swanson and Greta Garbo. This predilection is illustrated in Junichiro Tanizaki's

511

Mrs. Buck voiced her concern publicly in an article in the *New York Times Magazine*, published a week before Midway.

... This Second World War has taken on a new and dangerous aspect most of all because of Japan. Although we may not be willing to know it, it is possible that we are already embarked upon the bitterest and the longest of human wars, the war between the East and the West, and this means the war between the white man and his world and the colored man and his world. ...

In India it [the racial problem] is the burning question, whose flames leap higher every hour; in Burma it is a raging fire; in Java, yes, and in the Philippines and in China.

The main barrier between East and West today is that the white man is not willing to give up his superiority and the colored man is no longer willing to endure his inferiority. . . . The white man is a century behind the colored man. The white man is still thinking in terms of colonies and colonial government. The colored man knows that colonies and colonial-mindedness are anachronisms. The colonial way of life is over, whether the white man knows it or not, and all that remains is to kick off the shell of the chrysalis. The man of Asia today is not a colonial and he has made up his mind he will never be a colonial again.

. . . In short if the white man does not now save himself by discovering that all men are really born free and equal, he may not be able to save himself at all. For the colored man is going to insist on that human equality and that freedom. . . .

Unfortunately Mrs. Buck's prophetic article had little effect on Washington. No efforts were made to counter

---

novel *The Love of an Idiot*. He compares a Japanese girl, Naomi, with a Russian woman:

The latter's skin color . . . was so extraordinarily white, an almost ghostly beauty of white skin under which the blood vessels of light violet color were faintly visible like the veining of marble. Compared with this skin, that of Naomi's lacked transparency and glow and was rather dull to the eye.

Expression of this preference for fair skin and Occidental features had to be banned while Japan was proclaiming itself the "champion of the colored nations" in the battle against "whites." But the fact remained that the Japanese did not consider themselves to be "yellow." The woman preferred, and still do, to call the color of their skin *komugi-iro* (wheat color); and the word for lighter shades of their own skin was *shiroi* (white). Traditionally, white was always the color of virtue; the hero in the kabuki theater, for example, always wore dazzling white make up, a popular symbol similar to the white hat of the "good" cowboy in American movies.

charges of American color prejudice by Asians. On the contrary, the government was lending weight to these charges by grossly mistreating American citizens of Japanese ancestry. Immediately after Pearl Harbor, fear overran the West Coast and demands followed that all Japanese, citizens as well as aliens, be evacuated to the interior.

"I don't think it's a sensible thing to do," General John L. DeWitt, commander of the Western Defense Command, told the Provost Marshal General over the phone. "An American citizen, after all, is an American citizen. And while they all may not be loyal, I think we can weed the disloyal out of the loyal and lock them up if necessary."

Secretary of War Henry Stimson concurred, but agitation all along the West Coast grew with each Japanese victory. In California, District Attorney Earl Warren warned that unless the Japanese-Americans were evacuated promptly there might be a repetition of Pearl Harbor. Governor Charles Sprague of Oregon wired the U. S. Attorney General demanding "more thorough action for protection against possible alien activity, particularly by Japanese residing on coast." The mayor of Seattle, Earl Millikin, declared that of the city's estimated 8,000 Japanese, "7,900 probably are above question but the other 100 would burn this town down and let the Japanese planes come in and bring on something that would dwarf Pearl Harbor."

Nor was rising anti-Japanese feeling by any means confined to the Pacific Coast. In a national poll 41 percent believed that "the Japanese people will always want to go to war to make themselves as powerful as possible"; 21 percent considered the Germans militaristic by nature. It was understandable, therefore, that a consummate politician like Roosevelt would heed these voices—it was an election year—and against the advice of J. Edgar Hoover, he ordered the War Department to implement a mass Nisei evacuation. The Supreme Court upheld the legality of the act. At first the intention was to settle the Japanese-Americans in the interior, but residents of the areas selected protested so vehemently that it was considered advisable to place the "prisoners" in government camps.

A similar plan to relocate German and Italian aliens aroused such protest that the government canceled it, explaining that it would affect the nation's economic structure and lower morale among citizens of those nationalities. But there was no one to speak for the Nisei, who were citizens but usually referred to as "aliens"—their skin was a different color. Almost 110,000 loyal Americans, whose sole crime was their ancestry, were uprooted from their homes, which they were forced to sell for a pittance. They were interned behind barbed wire in "relocation centers" along the coast which were little better than concentration camps; many were even deprived of their life savings.*

Elmer Davis, Director of the Office of War Information, protested officially to the President:

... Japanese propaganda to the Philippines, Burma, and elsewhere insists that this is a racial war. We can combat this effectively with counter propaganda only if our deeds permit us to tell the truth. Moreover, as citizens ourselves who believe deeply in the things for which we fight, we cannot help but be disturbed by the insistent public misunderstanding of the Nisei; competent authorities, including Naval Intelligence people, say that fully 85 percent of the Nisei are loyal to this country and that it *is* possible to distinguish the sheep from the goats.

But Davis' warning was no more heeded than Pearl Buck's. Washington remained blind to the effect the Nisei evacuation might have on the peoples of Asia. Nor was much thought given to their postwar problems. Asia was solely a battlefield, the importance of which continued to grow in the minds of the Joint Chiefs of Staff even in the face of

---

*These actions are perhaps understandable under the pressure of war hysteria, but the postwar attitude of the government is difficult to equate with democracy. Little indemnity was paid to people who had lost their land and most of their personal possessions through no fault of their own. Damages were estimated at $400,000,000 but only $40,000,-000 were paid in reparations—ten cents to the dollar.

The case of some 4,000 depositors in the California branch of the Yokohama Specie Bank is particularly shameful. The government seized all the bank's assets as "enemy property," thus freezing the life savings of these depositors. It took the Office of Alien Property until 1957 to decide to return this money—at the rate of two cents to the dollar. It was such a miserly sum that only 1,600 depositors applied for the refunds. These people appealed the low rates and a court finally ordered the OAP to pay them the rest of their savings. On learning this the other 2,400 depositors asked for their money but were told by the OAP that they had lost title to it, since they had neglected to accept the original 2 percent offer. It was not until October 24, 1966, almost twenty-five years after Pearl Harbor, that the Supreme Court finally agreed to hear their appeal. On April 10, 1967, the Court reversed the decision and remanded the case to the Court of Appeals for the District of Columbia Circuit "for further proceedings consistent with this opinion." At last, on August 1, 1969, the case was settled in favor of the depositors "approximately at the prewar rate without interest."

persistent British resistance. On May 8, 1943, Churchill cabled Stalin:

I AM IN MID-ATLANTIC ON MY WAY TO WASHINGTON TO SETTLE FURTHER EXPLOITATION IN EUROPE AFTER SICILY, AND FURTHER TO DEAL WITH THE PROBLEM OF THE INDIAN OCEAN AND THE OFFENSIVE AGAINST JAPAN THERE.

He was bound for another conference, this one with the Americans alone, which he had personally christened "Trident." Three days later his ship arrived off Staten Island. The following afternoon at two-thirty he met at the White House with Roosevelt and military leaders of both countries. He said the British had come to Trident "adhering to the Casablanca decisions." The African campaign was about over and the invasion of Sicily was imminent. What should come next? In his opinion, the first objective should be the defeat of Italy. This "would cause a chill of loneliness over the German people, and might be the beginning of their dawn." It would, moreover, dramatically change the situation in the Balkans and permit the shift of many British battleships and carriers to the Bay of Bengal or the Pacific.

The time had also come, he said, to "study the long-term plan for the defeat of Japan." Assuming Germany would be defeated in 1944, the British pledged to "concentrate on the great campaign against Japan in 1945." In any case, the best solution to the war in the Far East was to bring Russia in.

Roosevelt replied that a million tons of Japanese shipping had been sent to the bottom, and if this continued the enemy's field of operations would be seriously restricted. But for America to keep up this devastating naval offensive, it would be necessary to set up air bases in China; and that country, he warned, might collapse unless more aid was sent at once.

For nine days the conferees worked hard to come to a working agreement. The two military staffs held as many as four meetings a day; on the principal war issues six plenaries alone, attended by Churchill and Roosevelt, took place.

But Brooke, with his low threshold of patience, became more and more irritated at the deliberate Admiral King and his incessant "desire to find every loophole he possibly can to divert strength to the Pacific." Their quarrel broke out into the open on May 21 at a Combined Chiefs meeting when King insisted that "unremitting pressure" on Japan not only be maintained but extended. He wanted an air offensive from China bases within the year, as well as operations in Burma, seizure of the Marshall and Gilbert islands, New Guinea and the Solomons-Bismarck archipelago.

The British were outraged. They also refused to set a firm date for the invasion of Europe across the English Channel. The American argument prevailed, however, and at the final meeting both Roosevelt and Churchill gave approval to a channel invasion on May 1, 1944, and to "unremitting pressure" against Japan, with a face-saving proviso that the Combined Chiefs should review operations "before action is taken."

But disagreement over theater priorities was a difficult one to lay to rest. In less than three months Roosevelt and Churchill met again in Quebec at the Hotel Frontenac. Once more the Americans pressed for a major offensive in Burma and once more Churchill tried to side-step the issue by proposing, instead, a supplementary assault on Sumatra. Roosevelt would not be diverted. Such an attack would lead *away* from Japan. They should concentrate all resources on the Burma Road, which was the shortest route to Tokyo.

The debate unresolved, the Combined Chiefs retired to their own conference room, still ruffled with one another. Those waiting outside in the corridor were startled by pistol shots from inside.

"My God, now they've started shooting!" someone cried out.

It was merely a dramatic experiment. Lord Mountbatten, an avid supporter of using a new kind of ice, Pykrete, to create floating airfields, had fired his pistol into a block of ordinary ice, shattering it, and then at a block of Pykrete. The bullet caromed off, nicking King's trousers.

Mountbatten was unsuccessful in his advocacy of Pykrete, but his military capabilities were recognized and he was given the Southeast Asia Command—which included Burma.

4.

That country, which was now the responsibility of Mountbatten, was about to be granted independence by Japan. A constitution was hastily composed, incorporating both democratic and totalitarian theories. It proclaimed that Burma would be a fully independent and sovereign nation, all of whose powers were derived from the people, while asserting that she would be "ruled over by the *Naingandaw Adipadi,* or Head of State, who shall have sovereign status and power." The official slogan of the new nation was also inspired by Hitler: "One Blood, One Voice, One Leader."

Early in July Dr. Ba Maw, the obvious choice for *Adipadi,* met Tojo in Singapore. The Prime Minister had news he thought would please Ba Maw: the Japanese were turning over to the new nation most of the Shan States—located on Burma's eastern border. Two sections, however, would go to Thailand.

Ba Maw's feelings were mixed. "Neither the Burmese nor the Shans will be completely happy about the dismemberment of the Shan territory and its people." Tojo was apologetic, but Japan had promised the two sections to Thailand as a price for becoming an ally.

"But we have come in with you too," said Ba Maw, "and we also have our claims."

Tojo tried to shrug it off and jokingly promised to "pay off Burma some other way." Ba Maw turned aggressive and spoke accusingly of the arrogant and often arbitrary behavior of the Japanese soldiers in Burma.

Tojo was in Singapore for another reason: to confer with Subhas Chandra Bose, the leader of the militant disobedience campaign in India who, unlike Gandhi and Nehru, believed that force alone could lead to India's freedom. A large man—he towered over Tojo and Ba Maw—Bose was a passionate revolutionary with a charismatic personality and a gift for oratory. He had come to Singapore to recruit the thousands of Indian troops who had surrendered in the Malay compaign. They had already endorsed his crusade— the battle of freedom from Great Britain—and had accepted him as leader of the Indian Independence League in East Asia.

At a mass meeting he addressed the recruits with zeal: "When France declared war on Germany in 1939 and the campaign began, there was but one cry which rose from the lips of the German soldiers—'To Paris, to Paris!' When the brave soldiers of Nippon set out on their march in December 1941, there was but one cry which rose from their lips—'To Singapore, to Singapore!' Comrades, let your battle cry be 'To Delhi, to Delhi!' "

Tojo's promise of independence for Burma materialized on August 1. At ten o'clock General Masakazu Kawabe ordered withdrawal of the Japanese military administration. It was a bright morning with occasional spits of rain, and Rangoon was in a holiday mood. One hour and twenty minutes later, at Government House, Burma was decalred to be an independent and sovereign country with Dr. Ba Maw as Head of State, and that afternoon he read a proclamation in Burmese declaring war against the United States and Great Britain. He cautioned his people, however, that there was more to freedom than cheering and celebration. "Many have wept to see this day of liberation which they had almost despaired of seeing within their lifetime," he said. "But we know that there are not only dreams, there are also realities. . . . Now that independence has come to us out of this war, we must defend it in this war. . . . Burma is definitely in the front line in the present war. . . . It is clear we must adopt a front-line policy."

On October 14 the Philippines proclaimed their independence and a week later the Provisional Government of Free India was established, with Chandra Bose as Head of State. The West failed to see the significance of these events. The new governments were puppets of Japan, but through them millions of Asians glimpsed freedom from the white man for the first time. Their enthusiasm reached a culmination when China, Thailand, Manchukuo, the Philippines and Burma sent representatives to Tokyo for the Greater East Asia Conference early in November.* Chandra Bose attended as an observer.

"We were getting together," Ba Maw wrote, "not so much as separate peoples but as members of a single historical family containing all these peoples." José Laurel, President of the Philippines, who had secretly been charged by Quezon to pretend co-operation with the Japanese, now found Pan-Asianism irresistible: "One billion Orientals, one billion people of Greater East Asia," he proclaimed with eyes glistening, at the formal reception on the eve of the initial meeting, "how could they have been dominated, a great portion of them particularly by England and America?"

The austere setting of the conference room in the Diet Building belied the fervor of the conferees on November 5. Tables, covered with blue wool cloth, were laid out in the shape of a squarish horseshoe, flanked by three dwarf trees.

---

*The Indonesian political leader, Sukarno, was not invited. According to Kenryo Sato, Tojo opposed giving Indonesia independence at this time because Japan's war effort depended on her raw materials, and Indonesia was not "quite ready to handle all that treasure."

As chairman, Tojo sat at the head of the horseshoe with his delegation. On his right were Burma, Manchukuo and China, and on the left Thailand, the Philippines and India.

"It is an incontrovertible fact," said Tojo in his concise manner, "that the nations of Greater East Asia are bound in every respect by ties of an inseparable relationship. I firmly believe that such being the case, it is their common mission to secure the stability of Greater East Asia and to construct a new order of common prosperity and well-being."

Wang Ching-wei, head of the Nanking government—the first of the puppets—declared: "In the war of Greater East Asia we want victory, in the construction of Greater East Asia we want common prosperity. All the nations of East Asia should love their own countries, love their neighbors and love East Asia. Our motto for China is resurgence of China and defense of East Asia."

Prince Wan Waithayakon of Thailand took the floor, followed by Chang Chung-hui, Prime Minister of Manchukuo, and then Laurel. The Filipino's emotions were evident in his voice as well as through his words. "United together one and all into a compact and solid organization there can no longer be any power that can stop or delay the acquisition by the one billion Orientals of the free and untrammeled right and opportunity of shaping their own destiny. God in His infinite wisdom will not abandon Japan and will not abandon the peoples of Greater East Asia. God will come and descend from Heaven, weep with us, and glorify the courage and bravery of our people and enable us to liberate ourselves and make our children and our children's children free, happy and prosperous."

Ba Maw was fittingly saved for the last. "It is impossible to exaggerate the feelings which are born out of an occasion like this," he said fervently. "For years in Burma I dreamed my Asiatic dreams. My Asiatic blood has always called to other Asiatics. In my dreams, both sleeping and waking, I have heard the voice of Asia calling to her children.

"Today . . . I hear Asia's voice calling again, but this time not in a dream . . . I have listened with the greatest emotion to all the speeches delivered around this table. All these speeches have been memorable, moving, and—I may be exaggerating, and if so you must forgive me—I seem to hear in them the same voice of Asia gathering her children together. It is the call of our Asiatic blood. This is not the time to think with our minds; this is the time to think with our blood, and it is this thinking with the blood which has brought me all the way from Burma to Japan. . . .

"Only a very few years back the Asiatic people seemed to have lived in another world, even in different worlds, divided, estranged, and not knowing each other or even caring to know. Asia as a homeland did not exist a few years ago. Asia was not one then, but many, as many as the enemies which kept her divided, large parts of her following like a shadow one or another of these enemy powers.

"In the past, which now seems to be a very long time ago, it was inconceivable that the Asiatic peoples should meet together as we are meeting here today. Well, the impossible has happened. It has happened in a way which outstrips the boldest fantasy or dream of the boldest dreamer among us. . . .

"I say that today's meeting is a great symbolic act. As His Excellency the Chairman has said, we are truly creating a new world based upon justice, equality and reciprocity, upon the great principle of live and let live. From every point of view East Asia is a world in itself. . . . We Asiatics forgot this fact for long centuries and paid heavily for it, for as a result the Asiatics lost Asia. Now that we have once more, thanks to Japan, recaptured this truth and acted upon it, the Asiatics shall certainly recover Asia. In the simple truth lies the whole destiny of Asia. . . .

"We have once more discovered that we are Asiatics, discovered our Asiatic blood, and it is this Asiatic blood which will redeem us and give us back Asia. Let us therefore march ahead to the end of our road, a thousand million East Asiatics marching into a new world where East Asiatics will be forever free, prosperous, and will find at last their abiding home."

This was the voice of awakening Asia, and for Tojo these hours were the most satisfying of his career. He dominated the proceedings subtly, beaming paternally upon the representatives. He saw it as more than a military alliance; he too had been caught up in the Pan-Asian spirit—and his military comrades were troubled.

The following afternoon Chandra Bose climaxed the final session with a speech that rivaled Ba Maw's for emotional pitch. ". . . I do not think that it is an accident that this assembly has been convened in the Land of the Rising Sun. This is not the first time that the world has turned to the East for light and guidance. Attempts to create a new order in this world have been made before and are being made elsewhere, but they have failed. . . .

"For India there is no other path but the path of uncompromising struggle against British imperialism. Even if it were possible for other nations to think of compromising with England, for the Indian people at least it is out of the question. Compromising with Britain means to compromise with slavery, and we are determined not to compromise with slavery any more."

Affected by his own oratory, Bose could not continue. The audience waited, transfixed, until the Indian leader composed himself again. "But we have to pay the price of our liberty. . . . I do not know how many members of our national army will survive the coming war, but that is of no consequence to us. Whether we individually live or die, whether we survive the war and live to see India free or not, what is of consequence is the fact that India shall be free."

Toshi Go of the *Nippon Times* (until recently the *Japan Times & Advertiser*) called the conference a "soul-stirring reunion of blood brothers" and one of the most momentous gatherings in the history of the world.

Here, I felt, all were my brothers, not merely in a figurative sense, but literally as sons of the same Mother Asia. Japanese, Chinese, Thai, Manchukuoan, Filipino, Burmese, Indian—Asiatics all, and, therefore, brothers.

He believed, as did Ba Maw, that no matter how polite individual Westerners were to him personally, they could never really understand what it was to be an Asian.

I too have felt that only Asiatics could really understand and work effectively for the welfare of Asiatics, and I too have longed for the day when all Asiatics would be able to push aside the artificial barriers which Western intruders had set up between us and work together hand in hand for the common well-being of Asia. As I looked upon the Assembly Saturday, I felt that that day had at last come, that the ties of blood had prevailed at last, that as long-lost brothers who had found one another again we were about to restore the fortunes of our one Asiatic family.

As I noted the obvious sincerity and fervor with which all the speakers stressed this realization of oneness, which all of them apparently realized with overwhelming force, the conviction became solidly implanted in me that never again would this unity be broken. Whatever the fortunes of war, whatever the strains future problems may create, whatever the form future world organizations might eventually take, the consciousness of blood

521

brotherhood which this Assembly had crystallized could never be dissolved. The oneness of Asia is a fact so fundamental, so elemental, so natural, and hence so inevitable that once realized, it could never again be lost.

The Joint Declaration, unanimously adopted by the conferees, called for an order of common prosperity and well-being based on justice, respect for each other's independence, sovereignty and traditions, efforts to accelerate economic development on a basis of reciprocity, and an end to all racial discrimination.*

It was the Pacific version of the Atlantic Charter, a promise of the dream long held by Asians. Those who came to Tokyo may have been puppets but, born in servitude, they now felt free and had jointly proclaimed for the first time a Brave New World for Asia.

5.

Two weeks later the leader of Asia's largest nation, Chiang Kai-shek, met with Roosevelt and Churchill in Cairo to determine, he hoped, an entirely different kind of continent. Churchill did not welcome Chiang's presence, certain it would increase Roosevelt's interest in the Far East.

Indeed, the China problem was the first item on the agenda—not, as Churchill and Brooke had hoped, the last. But Churchill, who had not met Chiang Kai-shek before, was favorably impressed by the Generalissimo's "calm, reserved and efficient personality." However, the Prime Minister couldn't seriously regard China as a great power and resented the attention Roosevelt gave Chiang. "To the President, China means four hundred million people who are going to count in the world of tomorrow," Churchill's physician, Lord

---

*Tojo's adviser, Kenryo Sato, drafted the original declaration and meant what he wrote. Critics of the draft argued that his strong statement on racial prejudice might backfire, but Sato maintained that oppressive as the Japanese sometimes were in their occupational policies, racial discrimination was never practiced. "Why hesitate to use this article when it is a reality?"

When the Covenant of the League of Nations was drafted at the 1919 Paris Peace Conference, the Japanese had attempted to insert a racial-equality paragraph in the resolution endorsing the "principle of equality of nations." Britain blocked the measure, and Woodrow Wilson, chairman at the time, ruled it should not be instituted "in view of the serious objections of some of us." Only Britain and the United States voted against the resolution.

Moran, wrote in his diary, "but Winston thinks only of the colour of their skin; it is when he talks of India or China that you remember he is a Victorian."

The Chinese delegation left Cairo in a cheerful mood, since Roosevelt, despite Churchill's objections, had promised an amphibious assault across the Bay of Bengal within the next few months and, moreover, left the impression he was going to back up the Generalissimo massively.

The three Allies disagreed not only on military priorities for China but on the political future of Asia. Each waged a separate war for different reasons. Churchill had no thought of dismembering the British Empire; Chiang Kai-shek was primarily interested in eliminating the Communists and setting himself up as the sole leader in his country; and Roosevelt was intent exclusively on bringing about the surrender of Japan as soon as possible.

Roosevelt did realize that Asia could not emerge unchanged from the war but he could not appreciate, except to a limited degree, the admonition of such Americans as Pearl Buck and Wendell Willkie that Asia was determined to free itself from Western domination.

On November 27 Churchill and Roosevelt left Cairo separately, the debate on the Far East still at issue, to fly on to Teheran to meet Josef Stalin. The Prime Minister was apprehensive as he was driven slowly through the streets of the Iranian capital and people began to press up to his car. Assassins with pistols or bombs would have an easy time, he thought, and it was with great relief that he finally entered the British legation, a ramshackle structure very close to the elaborate Soviet embassy.

After the oppressive heat of Cairo, Teheran, lying just below the Caspian Sea, felt colder than it was. The countryside was bleak and dusty, studded with mud huts that had not changed for a thousand years; Teheran itself, though an oasis in the midst of a vast desolation, struck many of the conferees as an artificial, modern and uninteresting city.

The following morning, a Sunday, the Soviets warned Roosevelt that Axis agents might be in the city to assassinate him, and offered to have his headquarters transferred to a building on their own embassy grounds. Here conferences could be held without risky travel back and forth through the streets. Harry Hopkins and Averell Harriman discussed the matter with Churchill's chief of staff, General Hastings Ismay, and though they agreed it was probably a Russian

trick, they all advised Roosevelt to make the move.* A
heavily guarded caravan of cars left the American legation,
followed moments later by a single car carrying the President, Hopkins and Admiral Leahy. The driver, a Secret
Service man, took a roundabout way but drove so fast that
he beat the decoy presidential caravan to the Russian embassy. It was a welcome diversion to Roosevelt, and he was in
an expansive mood when, fifteen minutes later, Stalin called
on him. It was their first meeting. "I am glad to see you,"
Roosevelt said through his interpreter, Charles ("Chip")
Bohlen. "I have tried for a long time to bring this about."

Through his own interpreter, M. Pavlov, Stalin apologized
for not meeting the President sooner; it was his fault but he
had been very busy with military matters. He was a rather
slight, low-slung man who appeared stockier than he was
because of his square-cut, loose tunic; with his discolored
teeth, pockmarked face and yellow eyes, he reminded George
Kennan of "an old, battle-scarred tiger."

They talked of Chiang Kai-shek and the Burma offensive.
Stalin didn't think much of Chinese soldiers or their leadership; Roosevelt said there was a great need to educate the
people of Indochina, Burma, Malaya and the East Indies in
self-government. He boasted about America's good record in
helping prepare the Filipinos for freedom, confidentially adding that India was a sore point with Winston—and cautioned
Stalin not to bring it up.

The Big Three met a few minutes later for the first time at
the initial plenary session of the conference. Roosevelt proposed that Stalin "make a few opening remarks."

"No," Pavlov interpreted, "he would rather listen."

Roosevelt welcomed the Russians as "new members of
the family circle"; the Big Three meetings would be friendly

---

*There *was* a plan to assassinate the Big Three at Teheran. It had
been devised by SS Sturmbannführer (Major) Otto Skorzeny, Hitler's
favorite commando—who had recently rescued the imprisoned Mussolini—with the help of the Führer and Himmler. But Skorzeny could get
little specific information from the lone German agent planted in
Teheran by the *Abwehr* (military intelligence), and informed his
superiors that a successful assassination or kidnap operation was
impossible. According to *Hitler's Plot to Kill the Big Three*, by Laslo
Havas (published in 1969), half a dozen Germans were subsequently
parachuted into Iran but were killed before they could carry out their
mission, largely through the efforts of a double agent, Ernst Merser,
and an adventurous American, Peter Ferguson. In 1970 Skorzeny wrote
that he had never heard of this operation. "I honestly doubt," he
added, "that the action ever took place."

and frank and the co-operation of the three nations would outlast the war by generations. "He beamed on all around the table and looked very much like the kind, rich uncle paying a visit to his poorer relatives," Churchill's interpreter, A. H. Birse, recalled.

The Prime Minister had a feverish cold and his throat was so sore that he could barely talk, but his eloquence was unimpaired. The people around the table, he said, "probably represented the greatest concentration of worldly power that had ever been seen in the history of mankind" and that in their hands "lay perhaps the shortening of the war, almost certainly victory, and, beyond any shadow of doubt, the happiness and fortunes for mankind."

Once more Roosevelt turned to Stalin, suggesting that, as host, he would undoubtedly like to say a few words. Stalin conferred briefly with Pavlov, who rose, looked at his notes and said, "I take pleasure in welcoming those present. I think that history will show that this opportunity which we have, and the power which our people have invested in us, can be used to full advantage within the frame of our potential collaboration." Pavlov hesitated and then added with some embarrassment, "Marshal Stalin says, 'Now let's get down to business!'"

Roosevelt reviewed the war in the Pacific, saving his most dramatic announcement to the end for Stalin's benefit: an immense invasion of Normandy, Operation Overlord, had been set for May 1, 1944.

"We Soviets welcome your successes in the Pacific," Stalin replied. "Unfortunately we have not been able to help because we require too many of our troops on the eastern front and are unable to launch any operations against Japan at this time." But once Germany had been defeated, reinforcements could be sent to eastern Siberia. *"Then,"* he said, "by our common front, we shall win." It was the first promise that the Soviets would join in the fight against Japan.

The meeting ended at seven-twenty—they had been at the large round table for three hours and twenty minutes—and the Russians served tea and cakes. The Americans were reassured by Stalin's quiet and unassuming manner, but not so the British. Admiral Leahy, who had regarded him merely as a bandit leader, admitted he was wrong; Stalin was obviously an intelligent man whose approach was direct, agreeable and considerate, if occasionally brutally frank. General Ismay, on the other hand, still felt he was "completely ruthless and devoid of the milk of human kindness," and was thankful he was "neither his enemy nor dependent on his friendship."

"This conference is over when it has only just begun," Brooke told Lord Moran. "Stalin has got the President in his pocket." Churchill, too, was glum and when Moran asked if anything had gone wrong, he replied curtly, "A bloody lot has gone wrong."

That night at dinner the Big Three talked of many things—of France, Poland, Germany, Hitler—and unconditional surrender. Stalin questioned the wisdom of the vague pronouncement made at Casablanca; leaving it unclarified would unite the German people. "Whereas drawing up specific terms, no matter how harsh, and telling the German people that this is what they have to accept would, in my opinion, hasten the day of German capitulation."

The next day after lunch Stalin again called on Roosevelt and was handed several memoranda. One was a request for establishing bases in Siberia for a thousand American heavy bombers, and another suggested further preliminary co-operation in the war against Japan. Stalin promised to study the requests and summarily closed the subject.

The plenary that afternoon concentrated on Operation Overlord. It was Churchill against Stalin with Roosevelt mediating, cigarette holder clenched between teeth, and often getting in the last word, even if it was irrelevant. It was bad, Brooke thought, from beginning to end. After listening to the arguments of the last two days, he felt "like entering a lunatic asylum or nursing home."

Stalin peered at Churchill across the vast table and said he wanted to pose a very direct question to the Prime Minister. "Do you really believe in Overlord, or are you stalling on it to make us feel better?"

The reply was pure Churchill. "Provided the conditions previously stated for Overlord are established when the time comes, it will be our stern duty to hurl across the Channel against the Germans every sinew of our strength." On this rolling sentence the session ended.

That evening Stalin, the host at dinner, mercilessly teased Churchill. At first the Prime Minister didn't realize his leg was being pulled. "Fifty thousand Germans must be killed," Stalin said with a straight face. Churchill pushed back his chair and stood up. "I will not be a party to any butchery in cold blood. What happens in hot blood is another thing."

"Fifty thousand must be shot!" Stalin repeated.

Churchill flushed. "I would rather be taken out into the

garden here and now and be shot myself than sully my own and my country's honor by such infamy."

Roosevelt tried to smooth Churchill's ruffled feathers. "I have a compromise to propose," he said facetiously. "Not fifty thousand, but only forty-nine thousand should be shot."

Churchill stamped out of the room, with Stalin trailing behind saying it was just a joke. Churchill was persuaded to return to the table but was still suspicious. Stalin, grinning, again began to bait him. "You are pro-German," he said. "The Devil is a Communist, and my friend God a conservative." This time Churchill took it good-naturedly and before the end of the evening Stalin had an arm draped around the Prime Minister's shoulder as if they were fellow revolutionaries.

At midnight Lord Moran went to Churchill's room to see if his services were needed and found the Prime Minister talking to Anthony Eden about the postwar world. "There might be a more bloody war," he was saying in an exhausted voice, eyes closed. "I shall not be there. I shall be asleep. I want to sleep a billion years." He lit a cigar and said he had told Stalin that Britain wanted no new territory. "He rather pressed the point. You see, it would make it easier for Russia if we took something. When I asked what Russia wanted, Stalin said, 'When the time comes we will speak.'"

Churchill's pulse count was one hundred, and Moran warned him it was because of "all the stuff" he drank. "It will soon fall," said Churchill cheerfully but a moment later became gloomier than ever and stared at Moran, eyes popping. "I believe man might destroy man and wipe out civilization. Europe would be desolate and I may be held responsible." He went on in this vein for several minutes, then suddenly asked, "Do you think my strength will last out the war? I fancy sometimes that I am nearly spent."

A night's rest returned the Big Three to the equable relationship of the first day. At lunch Stalin was clearly delighted at Roosevelt's unsolicited suggestion that Russia be granted use of the warm-water port of Dairen in Manchuria. And at dinner Churchill acted as if nothing had happened the night before. Stalin, however, was ill at ease. First he sniffed the cocktails suspiciously and asked Interpreter Birse, who had been placed at his left, what they were made of. Birse's explanation "failed to allay his doubts" and he took whiskey neat. Good, he said, but ordinary vodka was better. He sat uncomfortably on the edge of his chair, dismayed by the array of knives and forks in front of him. "It is a problem which to use," he confided to Birse. "You will have to tell me, and also when I can begin to eat. I am unused to your customs."

Churchill, in a sentimental mood, announced that it was his sixty-ninth birthday party and that, in the Russian manner, anybody could propose a toast at any time. He himself began with a toast to the King, then praised his two comrades in exaggerated terms. He lauded Roosevelt for devoting himself to the weak and helpless and for preventing a revolution in 1933, and declared that the Marshal deserved the title of Stalin the Great.

Stalin's reply diverted the attention of the waiter serving "Persian Lantern," a huge ice cream pudding sitting atop a block of ice with a lighted candle inside. Absently the waiter let the platter tip, and the pudding slid off the ice onto Pavlov's head. With ice cream oozing down his hair and face and onto his shoes, the imperturbable interpreter didn't skip a word: "Mr. Stalin says that the Red Army is worthy of the Soviet people. . . ."

Stalin abruptly turned his sarcasm on the British Chief of Staff. "General Brooke," he said, staring directly at him, "has not been very friendly to the Red Army and has been critical of us. Let him come to Moscow, and I'll show him that Russians aren't bad chaps. It will pay him to be friends."

Brooke rose, locking Stalin's eyes with his own. "I am surprised that you should have found it necessary to raise accusations against me that are entirely unfounded. You will remember that this morning while we were discussing cover plans Mr. Churchill said that 'in war Truth must have an escort of lies.' You will also remember that you yourself told us that in all your great offensives your real intentions were always kept concealed from the outer world. You told us that all your dummy tanks and dummy aeroplanes were always massed on those fronts that were of an immediate interest, while your true intentions were covered by a cloak of complete secrecy. Well, Marshal, you have been misled by dummy tanks and dummy aeroplanes, and you have failed to observe those feelings of true friendship which I have for the Red Army, nor have you seen the feelings of genuine comradeship which I bear towards all its members."

Stalin's face remained inscrutable. He turned to Churchill and said, "I like that man. He rings true. I must have a talk with him afterwards."

It was another tense moment, but it was quickly over and was followed by a succession of toasts. Leahy was bored, but

THE RISING SUN

THE ROAD TO PEARL HARBOR

1 Young officers, opposed to expansion into China take over Tokyo
  in 1936. The failure of their revolt led to war with America.
  —Mainichi

2 Japan joins the Axis—1940. In Germany, Foreign Minister
  Marsuoka announces Tripartite Pact. To his left, wearing glasses,
  is General Eugen Ott, Hitler's envoy in Tokyo.   —Wide World Photos

3 Prime Minister Konoye's persistent efforts to keep peace with
  the United States, including a proposed summit meeting with
  Roosevelt, ended in the fall of his cabinet. —Courtesy Konoye Family

4 In Washington, Ambassador Nomura greets three unofficial peace
  emissaries—Colonel Hideo Iwakuro (far left) and two Maryknoll
  priests, Father Drought and Bishop Walsh. —Courtesy Colonel Iwakuro

2

4

3

5

5 General Hideki Tojo, who succeeded Prince Konoye as prime minister weeks before Pearl Harbor. —Courtesy General Kenryo Sato

6 Ambassador Grew, with Foreign Minister Togo, repeatedly warned that war would come "with dangerous and dramatic suddeness" unless Washington relaxed its rigid policy. —Wide World Photos

7 December 7, 1941. Ambassador Nomura and Special Envoy Kurusu wait in Secretary of State Hull's office to deliver Japan's last note. They were unaware at that moment that bombs were falling on Pearl Harbor. —National Archives

6

7

PEARL HARBOR

8 Admiral Nagumo, commander of Pearl Harbor Striking Force.
—Japan War History Office

9 Admiral Kusaka, Nagumo's chief of staff and de facto commander of Striking Force.
—Courtesy Admiral Kusaka

10 Commander Fuchida, leader of the first assault wave.
—Courtesy Commander Fuchida

11 Map of entrance to Pearl Harbor hastily drawn by Suguru Suzuki when espionage material he was bringing back from Hawaii was mislaid.
—Courtesy Commander Suzuki

12, 13 Japanese photographer catches first attack on Battleship Row. Bomb from circled plane sent geyser of water towering over ships.
credit for photo 12—National Archives
credit for photo 13—Kyodo Press Service

8

9

10

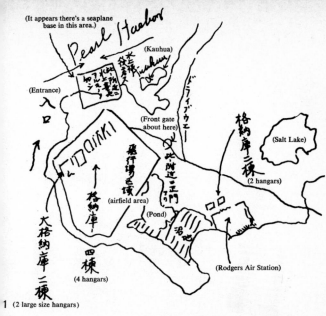

1 (2 large size hangars)

(It appears there's a seaplane base in this area.)

Pearl Harbor

(Kauhua)

(Entrance)

(Front gate about here)

(Salt Lake)

(2 hangars)

(airfield area)

(Pond)

(Rodgers Air Station)

(4 hangars)

2

14

14A

FALL OF SINGAPORE AND THE PHILIPPINES

14 General Yamashita—"the Tiger of Malaya"—who led the successful assault on the "impregnable" fortress of Singapore.
—Japan War History Office

14A Bataan Death March—the end of a tragic ordeal.
—Wide World Photos

15 "God of Operations"—Colonel Masanobu Tsuji, one of the most infuential and controversial officers in the Japanese Army.
—Courtesy Mrs. Tsuji

16 General Manuel Roxas, who became first President of the liberated Philippines, and Colonel Nobuhiko Jimbo, who saved him from execution.
—Courtesy Colonel Jimbo

15

16

17

18

GUADALCANAL

17, 18 Correspondent Gen Nishino, who covered much of Guadalcanal campaign. Nishino took this photograph of General Kawaguchi briefing his officers before the attack on Henderson Field.

credit for photo 18—Courtesy Nishino

19 Twenty-five thousand Japanese lost their lives on Guadalcanal, but 13,000 were saved in a secret withdrawal. —Mainichi

20 Admiral Yamamoto, a few days before he was shot down by American fliers, addressing Japanese pilots about to bomb enemy bases on Guadalcanal. —Mainichi

19

CONFERENCES—1943

21 The first Big Three conference at Teheran—Stalin, Roosevelt
and Churchill. —Wide World Photos

22 The Greater East Asia Conference in Tokyo, presided over by Tojo
with seven countries represented. —Kyodo Press Service

23 The Supreme Command holds a conference at the Imperial Palace
in the presence of the Emperor, April 1943.
—Courtesy Ushio Publishing Co.

24 Unpublished photograph of private **sushi** party in 1944. Many of
the men standing here were later involved in efforts to seek an
early peace. Left to right: Chikuhei Nakajima (former railways
minister. Leader of the **Seiyu Kai**); Mamoru Shigemitsu (Foreign
Minister); General Jiro Minami (former governor of Korea);
Tsuneo Matsudaira (Imperial Household Minister); Admiral Keisuke
Okada (former prime minister); Koki Hirota (former prime minister);
Gisuke Ayukawa (financier); Prince Fumimaro Konoye (former
prime minister); Marquis Koichi Kido (the Lord Keeper of the
Privy Seal); General Kuniaki Koiso (Prime Minister); Admiral
Kantaro Suzuki (President of the Privy Council); Baron Bunkichi Ito
(grandson of Meiji Restoration leader); Admiral Mitsumasa Yonai
(former prime minister and last navy minister).
—Courtesy Marquis Kido

22

23

24

SAIPAN

25, 26 Shizuko Miura, the only army nurse on Saipon, watched Marine landings from the inland heights.

credit for photo 25—Courtesy Mrs. Shizuko Sugano
credit for photo 26—Wide World Photos

25

26

27

28

29

LEYTE

27 General Sosaku Suzuki, commander of all Japanese troops on Leyte and the southern Philippines, who after defeat had a dream of establishing an independent colony on Mindanao.

—Japan War History Office

28 "I shall return." MacArthur lands on Leyte. On his left, wearing pith helmet, is President Sergio Osmeña; just behind him, in helmet, is General Carlos Romulo.

—U.S. Army Photograph

29 The end of Japanese carriers. Rare picture shows **Zuikaku** moments before sinking. Her crew stands at attention singing traditional naval song.

—Courtesy Koichi Narita

IWO JIMA

30 Americans swarm toward Iwo's beaches under heavy fire from
Mount Suribachi.
                                                    —National Archives

31 Iwo's commanding officer—and poet—General Tadamichi
Kuribayashi.
                                            —Courtesy Mrs. Kuribayashi

32 Ensign Toshihiko Ohno, one of the few survivors of the battle.
                                                —Courtesy Ensign Ohno

33 This Japanese soldier lay buried in sand for thirty-six hours,
live grenade in hand, before Marines disarmed him.
                                                —Wide World Photos

31 32

33

34   35

OKINAWA

34 General Mitsuru Ushijima, commander at Okinawa.
—Courtesy Mrs. Sosaku Suzuki

35 General Isamu Cho, Ushijima's aggressive chief of staff.
—Japan War History Office

36 Flamethrowers approach Shuri Castle.   —Wide World Photos

37 Hara-kiri. Ushijima and Cho meet death in their last
headquarters cave.   —U.S. Army Photograph

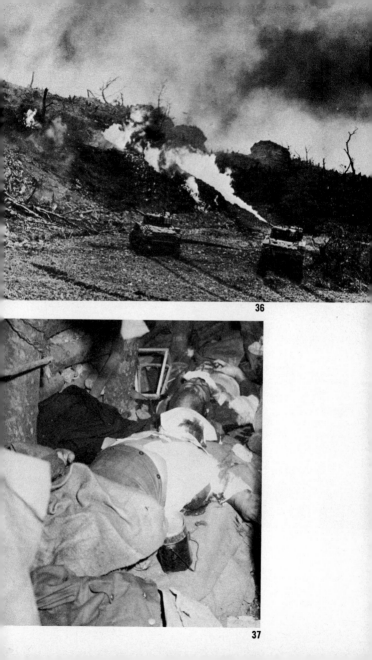

36

37

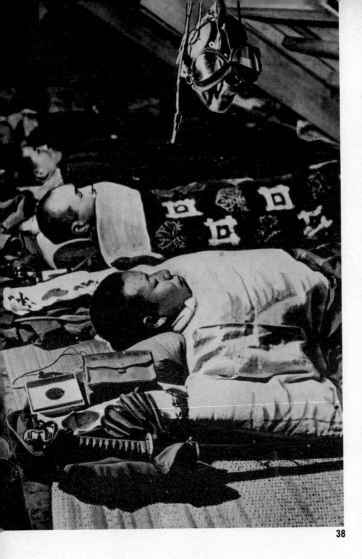

38

KAMIKAZE

38 Kamikaze pilots on eve of their mission.

39 Determined to die, Yasunori Aoki missed his target by yards, crashed into the sea. His bombs failed to detonate and he was rescued against his will.

—Courtesy Ensign Aoki

40 "After I die you'll have to do everything," Aoki wrote to his younger brother just before his mission.

—Courtesy Ensign Aoki

41 Admiral Matome Ugaki, head of all naval **kamikaze** units and Yamamoto's former chief of staff, disappeared on the day of surrender in the last suicide mission of the war.

—Courtesy Captain Yasuji Watanabe

39

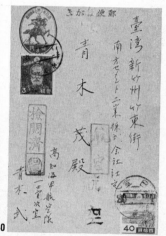

40

41

HOME FRONT

42, 43 Women of Tokyo prepare for air raids. credit for 43—Mainichi
credit for 44—Kyodo Press Service

44 Defenseless Tokyo. B-29 flies unmolested over Diet Building.
—Kyodo Press Service

45 Results of the first fire bombing of Tokyo—March 10, 1945.
One hundred forty thousand died.
—Photo by Koyo Ishikawa in "Documentary of
the Great Tokyo Air Raid"

42   43

44

45

THE BOMB

46 Crew of **Enola Gay** just before leaving Tinian Island with the first atom bomb. In foreground: Major Ferebee, Colonel Tibbets and Captain Van Kirk. —U.S. Air Force Photo

47 News photographer Gonichi Kimura snapped this unique picture two miles from ground zero at Hiroshima. —Courtesy Kimura

48 One hundred thousand died the first day at Hiroshima, and another 100,000 were doomed. —Wide World Photos

49 The center of Hiroshima. —U.S. Air Force Photo

50 Nagasaki. Survivors look for relatives among charred bodies. Stacks of Mitsubishi Steel and Arms Works loom in background. —Mainichi

48

49

50

51

THE PALACE REVOLT

51 The Palace grounds. (1) Ruins of Palace, (2) Imperial Household
Ministry, (3) the **obunko**, temporary house of royal family. Adjacent
to Palace grounds, (4) command post of rebels, Konoye
Division barracks.
—Wide World Photos

52 53 Army Chief of Staff General Yoshijiro Umezu and War Minister
General Korechika Anami sympathized with the dissidents but
refused to join them. —Wide World Photos—Courtesy Colonel
Masahiko Takeshita

54 Major Kenji Hatanaka, idealistic leader of the revolt.
—Courtesy Koichiro Hatanaka

52

53

54

55

56

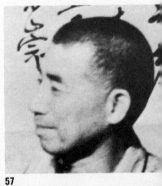

57

58

55 Colonel Masahiko Takeshita, the ranking officer in the revolt and brother-in-law of the War Minister.

—Courtesy Colonel Masahiko Takeshita

56 Colonel Masataka Ida, who gave his reluctant support to Hatanaka.

—Courtesy Colonel Ida

THE END

57 Admiral Takijiro Onishi, originator of **kamikaze** corps. A few hours after this picture was taken, he committed hara-kiri.

—Courtesy Yoshio Kodama

58 All Japan, silent and weeping, listens to the Emperor announce surrender on August 15, 1945.

—Mainichi

59 Surrender on **Missouri.** Foreign Minister Shigemitsu and Army Chief of Staff Umezu head Japanese delegation.

—U.S. Army Photograph

60 The suicide that failed. Former Prime Minister Hideki Tojo shot himself in the chest, barely missing his heart, just before he was to be arrested.

—U.S. Army Photograph

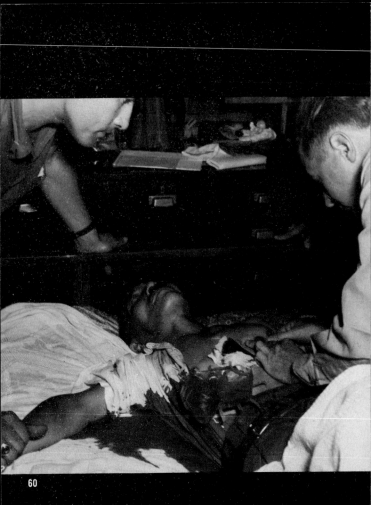

it amused King to see Stalin hopping up from his chair and trotting around the tabe to clink glasses. After dinner Stalin lingered on as if reluctant to let the evening end. Churchill approached him and, equally expansive, said, "England is becoming a shade pinker."

"That's a sign of good health," Stalin replied. "I want to call Mr. Churchill my friend."

"Call me Winston. I call you Joe behind your back."

"No, I want to call you my friend. I'd like to be allowed to call you my good friend."

Churchill was equal to this: "I drink to the proletarian masses!"

"I drink to the Conservative party," said Stalin.

For the Russians, Teheran was largely successful, since they had achieved what they most wanted, a firm date for the second front. The first meeting between Roosevelt and Stalin had also seemed to point the way to closer co-operation in the future. Although Roosevelt had found the Marshal more tough-minded than he had imagined, he was "get-at-able." As the two men parted, Roosevelt said, "We came here with hope and determination. We leave here friends in fact, in spirit, and in purpose."*

Churchill was "well content" with the military solutions reached at Teheran, but not Brooke. "One thing is quite clear," he wrote in his diary, "the more politicians you put together to settle the prosecution of the war, the longer you postpone its conclusion!"

The round of meetings was still not over. The Americans and British returned to Cairo to iron out their own major problem—whether to concentrate almost everything on Operation Overlord or carry on the powerful offensive Roosevelt had promised Chiang Kai-shek.

King and Leahy led those arguing that the promise to the Chinese should not be broken. What if China dropped out of

---

*Six months later Roosevelt told the author Edgar Snow that he had tried his utmost to convince Stalin of America's friendliness and his own good intentions. "In fact the biggest thing I accomplished at Teheran was to get Joe Stalin to see some of my own problems here. I told him, 'You know, I have troubles you don't have at all. You don't have to worry about being re-elected for instance.' ... I also told him something about our press and how to interpret it. 'Don't get hot under the collar,' I said, 'every time Colonel McCormick or Hearst takes a crack at you. They don't represent me or my Administration and they don't represent the majority of the people.' He seemed relieved to hear that."

the war? This would free hundreds of thousands of Japanese troops to fight MacArthur and Nimitz. The British countered that Teheran had changed everthing. Stalin's promise to join in the attack on Japan once Germany was beaten made China much less important for final victory.

On the afternoon of December 5, after more than two days of fruitless discussion, the deadlock was dramatically broken. Roosevelt sent a laconic private message to Churchill: BUCCANEER IS OFF. This was the Bay of Bengal operation, the point of contention. Churchill was so delighted that he phoned Ismay and said cryptically, "He that ruleth his spirit is greater than he that taketh a city."

A message, prepared by Roosevelt and Hopkins, and approved by Churchill, was sent to Chiang Kai-shek:

CONFERENCE WITH STALIN INVOLVES US IN COMBINED GRAND OPERATION ON EUROPEAN CONTINENT IN THE LATE SPRING GIVING FAIR PROSPECT OF TERMINATING WAR WITH GERMANY BY END OF SUMMER OF 1944. THESE OPERATIONS IMPOSE SO LARGE A REQUIREMENT OF HEAVY LANDING CRAFT AS TO MAKE IT IMPRACTICABLE TO DEVOTE A SUFFICIENT NUMBER TO THE AMPHIBIOUS OPERATION IN THE BAY OF BENGAL SIMULTANEOUSLY WITH LAUNCHING OF TARZAN [Burma operation] TO INSURE SUCCESS OF OPERATION. . . .

As 1943 drew to an end, so did the time for talk. Men on the battlefield, not at the conference table, would make the next decisions.

19   To the Marianas

1.

After Guadalcanal, world attention was centered on Europe, where the military action was accelerating. With the fall of Sicily, the drive up the boot of Italy and the surrender of that country by Field Marshal Pietro Badoglio, the Allies ruled the Mediterranean. Germany itself was being pounded from the air, at night by British Bomber Command and during the day by the U. S. Eighth Air Force. The Ruhr was practically destroyed and Hamburg had been leveled by a fire storm.

In Russia, Hitler's Sixth Army had been wiped out at Stalingrad in one of the greatest military debacles of history, and with the help of U. S. Lend-Lease and British aid, the Red Army was already storming west. By October 1943 it had recaptured some 300,000 square miles, including Kharkov, Smolensk and Orel to approach the historic gates of Kiev.

On the other side of the world, Operation Cartwheel—the two-pronged drive of MacArthur and Halsey on Rabaul—was proceeding steadily but sluggishly. These were battles of attrition and though the Japanese contested every phase, their supplies were so limited and they had so little shipping and air support that they were unable to stem the inexorable Allied tide.

Halsey's amphibious force had cleared New Georgia by mid-August. Its defense cost so many planes, ships and troops that Imperial Headquarters finally did what men like Kenryo Sato had been urging for months—ordered a cessation of all further reinforcements to the Solomons; the garrisons of each island would have to hold off the Americans as best they could, for as long as possible, and then withdraw by barge and destroyer. Against tactics born of such desperation, Halsey relentlessly continued up The Slot—to Vella Lavella, to Choiseul and finally to Bougainville, where fourteen thousand Marines landed on the first day of November. It was the last stop before Rabaul.

MacArthur was making even slower progress on New Guinea. Checked in his drive up the east coast on the twin garrisons of Salamaua and Lae, which had been sent only 750 reinforcements and an order to "stand fast," he launched a triple attack—one by ground, one by sea and one by air. While Australian and American infantrymen slogged up toward Salamaua, an amphibious force landed on the coast above Lae, and seventeen hundred parachutists, personally observed by MacArthur, dropped to the west. The parachutists and amphibious troops converged: they captured Lae in eleven days and neutralized Salamaua. MacArthur was at last in position to launch his assault across Dampier Strait to New Britain—and Rabaul.

Operation Cartwheel was moving, but its cost in time was more than expected and gave new weight to a decision made at the end of November in Cairo which was obscured by British-American disagreement on priorities: that the main thrust toward Japan should be through the small islands of the central Pacific. It would lead through the Gilbert and

Marshall islands to the Carolines, and then up toward Japan itself—and would be commanded by Admiral Nimitz.

MacArthur was informed that Rabaul would be neutralized, not taken, and his drive to Tokyo—by way of New Guinea and the Philippines—would proceed as planned but with reduced priorities. But he would not accept relegation to a secondary role. The Central Route, protested MacArthur, was "time-consuming and expensive in our naval power and shipping" and *his* route could be "supported by land-based aircraft which is utterly essential and will immediately cut the enemy lines from Japan to his conquered territory to the southward."

The Joint Chiefs stood firm. The road through the central Pacific was shorter and would make it easier to isolate Japan from her domain in the south. Protracted land battles involving large forces in New Guinea and the Philippines could be avoided. The key battles would be fought on atolls and small islands which the Japanese would have to defend with limited air and ground power. The U. S. Navy, on the other hand, had superiority in carrier-based air power and could easily support landings.

Nimitz' drive had begun with two simultaneous landings in the Gilbert Islands, some two thousand miles southwest of Pearl Harbor. On the morning of November 20, two days before Roosevelt and Churchill met Chiang Kai-shek in Cairo, GI's of the 27th Division waded up the beaches of Makin Atoll after a heavy naval barrage. There were fewer than eight hundred defenders, most of them labor troops, but it took the invaders, trained in a World War I style of combat by overage officers, four days to clear the atoll, at a cost of sixty-six dead.

At the same time, 105 miles to the south, men of the 2nd Marine Division began loading into landing craft and amphtracs (amphibious tractors) off Tarawa. The Marines joked and boasted to keep up their courage. "I should have joined the Boy Scouts," said one. "I just want to spit in a dead Jap's face," said a youngster barely old enough to be out of high school. "Just open his mouth and let him have it."

They faced a much more difficult task than the GI's at Makin. Tarawa Atoll was heavily fortified and held by almost five thousand men, more than half of whom were well-trained combat effectives: the Sasebo 7th Special Landing Force of 1,497 troops led by Commander Takeo Sugai, and the 3rd Special Base Force, a naval landing unit of 1,122 men. The atoll commander, Rear Admiral Keijo Shibasaki, claimed that Tarawa could not be taken by a million men in a hundred years and issued orders "to defend to the last man all vital areas and destroy the enemy at the water's edge."

The defense was centered on Betio in the southwest corner of the atoll, a tiny island a few acres smaller than Monaco. Shaped like a bird, its legs a long jetty, it was protected by a wide shelf of coral. The landing would take place on both sides of the jetty, and the Marines would have to storm a four-foot-high sea wall made of green coconut logs and coral; behind it were well-constructed gun emplacements and trenches.

At dawn the Japanese batteries on Betio opened fire at the approaching armada. The Americans retaliated with three thousand tons of shells. After two and a half hours the entire island was blanketed in flames and it seemed impossible that any human being could have survived the bombardment. From a transport *Time* correspondent Robert Sherrod watched a shell splash near an LST (landing ship, tank). Another sent up a geyser just off his own ship's stern. "My God, what wide shooting!" exclaimed Sherrod, who imagined the shells came from American destroyers. "Those boys need some practice." "You don't think that's our own guns doing that shooting, do you?" a Marine major retorted.

By the time the first three assault waves began slogging ashore the Japanese were out of their shelters manning the sea wall. Their steady rifle and machine-gun fire cut down the Marines, covering the beach with dead and dying who could not be removed in the devastating fusillade. The commander of a platoon of medium tanks refused to grind away over the bodies and ordered his men to back out into the sea and make a detour. Four tanks sank out of sight into potholes, their crews trapped inside; the other two were easy targets for 40-mm. guns.

Shortly after noon 5,000 Marines were ashore, but heavy casualties left them disorganized and vulnerable to night attack. Half of Shibasaki's troops were dead by dusk and his communications had been knocked out by naval gunfire. Consequently, few Japanese infiltrated American lines during the night. The following afternoon, after two more battalions landed, the Marines gained control of most of the island. Admiral Shibasaki was killed in his concrete command post, and his successor radioed Tokyo on November 22: OUR WEAPONS HAVE BEEN DESTROYED AND FROM NOW ON EVERY-

It took four more days before the atoll was completely secured. Almost all the 5,000 defenders were dead; only 17 Japanese and 129 Korean laborers were captured. More than a thousand Americans had died for a few acres of coral, but its capture and that of Makin marked Nimitz' first long stride toward Tokyo.

Ahead lay the Marshalls, 32 island groups and 867 reefs covering more than 400,000 square miles. The original plan had been to take the three most strategic atolls simultaneously but Marine General Holland Smith, after the resistance at Tarawa, considered this too dangerous. Admiral Spruance, the overall invasion commander, agreed. But Nimitz countered with a radical idea that dismayed both Smith and Spruance: leapfrog the first two atolls and assault the third, the heart of the Marshalls, Kwajalein. This was the largest coral atoll in the world, some one hundred islets forming a huge lagoon sixty-six miles long and twenty miles wide.

Spruance and Smith feared that a direct attack on Kwajalein would lay them open to air attack from nearby Japanese bases, but Nimitz persisted. On February 1, 1944, the main island of Kwajalein was subjected to the most concentrated bombardment of the Pacific war. Thirty-six thousand shells from naval vessels and field artillery emplaced on an outlying islet thundered down on Kwajalein. Above the trajectory of shells droned formations of Liberators which released their bombs into the holocaust. The effect was so devastating that one observer reported: "The entire island looked as if it had been picked up to 20,000 feet and then dropped."

The leap into the center of the Marshalls came as a complete surprise to the Japanese. There were 8,500 men on the atoll, but most of them were rear-echelon personnel. Only 2,200 were combat-trained; and they had no defense against American armor. Frustrated officers would beat upon the turrets with swords while their men held grenades to the sides of the tanks until they exploded. They were convinced the Americans had a secret weapon, a device that could detect metal in the dark; every time someone left his hiding place he was killed. Word spread to take off helmets and ground bayonets after dusk. They still were killed; the "secret weapon" was concentrated and steady fire power. It was a hopeless battle for the Japanese but they fought almost to the last man, as at Tarawa. It was a week before the entire atoll was secured and it took the lives of 373 Americans.

Against the advice of his own commanders, Nimitz' success at Kwajalein inspired him to propose yet another bold operation once the Marshalls were secured: a leap of more than twelve hundred miles beyond the Carolines all the way to the Marianas. He envisaged using these islands as a base from which the new B-29 Superfortresses could bomb Japan.

His proposal was attacked from all sides at a joint Army-Navy meeting at Pearl Harbor in January. MacArthur saw it as a further diminution of his own drive to Japan, and his representative, Major General Richard Sutherland, strongly urged that all resources be concentrated instead in the southwest Pacific area. He was supported by Lieutenant General George Kenney, who considered the idea of bombing Japan with Marianas-based B-29's "just a stunt." Even a Navy representative resisted. Rear Admiral Thomas Kinkaid declared that "any talk of the Marianas for a base leaves me cold."

Nimitz was overridden, and emphasis once more shifted to MacArthur's Route to Tokyo. But in Washington, the conclusions of the Pearl Harbor meeting struck Admiral Ernest King "with indignant dismay." He wrote Nimitz: "The idea of rolling up the Japanese along the New Guinea coast, through Halmahera and Mindanao, and up through the Philippines to Luzon, as our major strategic concept, to the exclusion of clearing our Central Pacific line of communications to the Philippines is absurd. Further it is not in accordance with the decisions of the Joint Chiefs of Staff."

Early in February, Sutherland arrived in Washington to advocate MacArthur's case. Without any basis in fact, he told the Joint Chiefs that Nimitz' plans were "relatively weak and slow of progress." MacArthur could be in Mindanao by December if given the resources.

King had no intention of handing over more naval forces to the southwest Pacific theater. With some sarcasm he said that MacArthur had "apparently not accepted" the Cairo decision "and desires a commitment to an advance along a single axis. I do not think that this is a propitious time to change our agreed strategy."

To avoid turning a strategic debate into a personal one, General Marshall suggested that the Joint Strategic Survey Committee study the matter again and report on which route to Japan was preferable. The committee recommendation came back almost immediately: the Central Route should be given priority "with operations in the Southwest Pacific cooperating with and supporting that effort."

MacArthur's role would have been permanently diminished had it not been for the fact that his old antagonist, Marshall, too, was dissatisfied with the committee's conclusions, and after a month's discussion, the Joint Chiefs emerged with a compromise between the central Pacific and southwest Pacific concepts of strategy. On March 12 they issued a directive to Nimitz and MacArthur ordering the former to occupy the Marianas by June 15 and the later to invade Mindanao with the support of the Pacific Fleet exactly five months later.

2.

The new American thrusts had forced Imperial Headquarters to readjust their defense. The desperate scramble of the Army and Navy for appropriations, strategic materials and factories centered on plane production, since both services agreed that the way to victory lay in the air. They agreed to share equally the 45,000 planes to be produced the following year. But a month later, in early January 1944, the Navy requested more than their allotment—26,000 planes.

The Navy's case was persuasive and Tojo acquiesced. "This is too great a problem to settle so quickly," protested his friend and adviser, Kenryo Sato. Until this time the Supreme Command had depended on the Navy to win the Decisive Battle against America on the seas, but now that dream was over. Henceforth the Army would have to play the major role, and the small islands that lay between the advancing Americans and Japan would have to be the "unsinkable carriers," bases for future land battles. The majority of planes, therefore, would have to go to the service that fought these battles, the Army.

Tojo realized that his first decision had been prompted by a desire to keep peace with the Navy. Sato was obviously right and Tojo told him to inform the Navy of the change in priorities. The Navy, in turn, refused to accept the reversed decision. On February 10 the battle was openly joined at a meeting of the Chiefs of Staffs and their advisers at the Palace. Admiral Nagano maintained that the crucial battles with the enemy would still take place at sea. He was challenged by Army Chief of Staff Sugiyama, who had been promoted to field marshal. "If we gave you all the planes you want, would this battle turn the tide of war?"

Nagano bristled. "Of course I can't guarantee anything of the kind! Can *you* guarantee that if we gave you all the planes, you would turn the tide?"

Distracted by a suggestion from Admiral Oka that they all take a break for tea, the antagonists calmed down, but the problem remained unsolved until Sato came up with an ingenious if questionable solution: concentrate production on fighters to the exclusion of bombers. Then an additional 5,000 planes, a total of 50,000 for equal distribution, could be manufactured, only 1,000 shy of the Navy's demand for 26,000 planes. To make up for this deficit, Sato offered 3,500 tons of aluminum. The Navy accepted.

The tempest was over but not the military problems which had aggravated it. The American advance through the central Pacific continued unchecked. On February 17 Nimitz' amphibious force leapfrogged from Kwajalein to the Eniwetok islands at the western limit of the Marshalls, bypassing four atolls where the Japanese had air bases. That same day and the next, American carrier planes also attacked Truk in the Carolines, the home of Combined Fleet, destroying seventy planes on the ground and sinking two auxiliary cruisers, a destroyer, an aircraft ferry, two submarine tenders and twenty-three merchant ships—200,000 tons of shipping in all.

These successive disasters prompted Sato to give Tojo some more unsolicited advice: "We should withdraw to the Philippines, and there gamble on the final decisive battle."

"Is that the opinion of the General Staff?" Tojo asked grimly.

"No, it is my personal opinion."

"Did you consult the General Staff?"

"That's just the point: the General Staff would certainly oppose such a plan. It's my conviction that we should simply override the military." And the first thing to do was abandon the Carolines and the Marianas and fall back to the Philippines.

Tojo got red in the face. "Last year at an imperial conference we made the Marianas and Carolines our last defense line! Do you mean to say that six months later we should give them up without a single fight?"

Sato held his ground. There were only seven airfields in that area and they could easily be neutralized by the Americans before any invasion. But in the Philippines there were

537

hundreds of islands that could be used as bases. "This should be the last battlefield of the war, since if that battle is lost, we won't be able to fight another. That's why we should concentrate all our efforts on one last struggle—and then start a peace offensive." By "peace" he meant to settle for any conditions that would let Japan retain her honor.

Tojo interrupted him. "Don't ever again mention the phrase 'peace offensive.' If you or I ever breathed the words 'wa' or 'wahei' [peace] the morale of our troops would deteriorate."

Sato left, encouraged by the Prime Minister's sympathetic reaction, but his counsel helped lead to an unexpected consequence. Later that evening Tojo suggested to Chief of Staff Sugiyama that he resign. In this "critical situation," Tojo explained, it would be best if he himself concurrently held the posts of war minister and chief of staff.

"That would be a violation of our long tradition," Sugiyama protested. One man shouldn't be responsible for both political and military decisions. The catastrophe at Stalingrad, he pointed out, had resulted from Hitler's concentration of power.

"Führer Hitler was an enlisted man," said Tojo. "I am a general." He assured the marshal that he had been giving as much thought to military affairs as political. "You don't have to worry on that score."

"That's easy to say, but when one man handles two jobs and is torn by a conflict of interest between them, to which does he give the greater importance?" Moreover, it would establish a dangerous precedent for the future.

"In such an unprecedented and widespread war as this, we must take every measure even if it means breaking precedent."

Sugiyama was losing his patience. "If you do this, it will be impossible to maintain order in the Army!"

"That won't happen" was the tight-lipped answer. "If anyone complains, we'll replace him. No objections will be allowed."

The following day, February 21, Tojo relieved Sugiyama as Army Chief of Staff and took the post himself; he also replaced Navy Chief of Staff Nagano with Navy Minister Shigetaro Shimada. The four most important military posts in the nation were now concentrated in the hands of two men.

Sato burst into Tojo's office shouting, "Mr. Prime Minister, what you have done is tremendous!" Tojo was already wearing the braid of the chief of staff. Since becoming prime minister he had discovered that the independence of the Supreme Command was a "big factor" in Japan's military reversals. He was obviously pleased by Sato's reaction and permitted himself a brief smile. "If some of the young officers cause any disturbance about this," he said sternly, "I will not let them get away with it." *Gekokujo* would not be tolerated. "Keep an eye on them."

For the next few hours Sato was engrossed in plans for the last decisive battle in the Philippines. He was interrupted by a phone call from Tojo, who spoke in his new role as chief of staff. "I am going to defend the Marianas and Carolines," he announced curtly.

Tojo's arbitrary consolidation of power, which he and Sato regarded as a curb on the autocratic control of the military, was interpreted by others as a dangerous step toward military dictatorship. Prince Chichibu, the eldest of the Emperor's three brothers, did not believe the same man should be prime minister, war minister and chief of staff. Like Sugiyama, he put this question to Tojo: "What will you do when the General Staff and the War Ministry do not agree on the conduct of war?" Tojo angrily replied in writing: "The most important thing before us at this stage is to achieve victory with all our national resources. So I'll thank you to discuss personal affairs after the war is over. . . . As for the current move, it is only natural that there be much criticism and opposition, since the measure is an unprecedented one. Let us leave it to future historians to determine the right or wrong of this step. Actually, the co-operation between the high command and the government is going very well and there is no trouble at all. My conscience would never let me violate the basic principle of the fundamental character of Japan. If you have any questions on this point, I'll be glad to answer them. If I should ever feel that I am no longer loyal to the Emperor, I will offer my sincere apology and commit hara-kiri in his presence."*

---

*In the Diet the previous year, Tojo had denied that his regime was a dictatorship: "People often refer to this as a dictatorial government, but I should like to make the matter clear . . . The man called Tojo is no more than a single humble subject. I am just the same as you. The sole difference is that I have been given the responsibility of being prime minister. To this extent I am different. It is only when I am exposed to the light of His Majesty that I shine. Were it not for this light, I would be no better than a pebble by the roadside. It is because I enjoy the confidence of His Majesty and occupy my present position that I shine. This puts me in a completely different category from those European rulers who are known as dictators."

The *jushin* (the former premiers) shared Prince Chichibu's concern. To them, moreover, Tojo's leadership was responsible for Japan's plight. They all wanted Tojo removed as prime minister, and two of their number, Prince Konoye and Admiral Okada, went further—his replacement must be a man who would make immediate peace overtures to the Allies. Konoye tried to enlist Marquis Kido in the cause for peace. The Privy Seal was sympathetic but refused to help; privately he thought it would be premature to use his influence on the Emperor.

There were even those in the military working for peace, but for different reasons. The most important was Rear Admiral Sokichi Takagi, a brilliant research expert who had been ordered by Admiral Shimada to conduct a thorough study of the mistakes made in the war as reflected in top-secret files. His analysis of air and shipping losses led him to the inevitable conclusion that Japan could not win the war. Appalled by the extent of the collapse in the Pacific, he saw as the only solution Tojo's dismissal and an immediate quest for peace no matter what the consequences.

Takagi feared that if he submitted this information to Shimada, his own life would be endangered—and the report itself shelved. He met in secret with former Navy Minister Admiral Mitsumasa Yonai and Vice Admiral Shigeyoshi Inoue, both advocates of peace, and told them what he had uncovered. They encouraged him to share his findings with Admiral Okada and others who were in a better position to act. But weeks passed and Tojo still remained in office. Impatient, Takagi assembled half a dozen Navy men he could trust—commanders and captains—and persuaded them that the nation could not survive unless they assassinated Tojo. But how should it be done? Surreptitious inquiries were made to right-wing organizations (experts on assassination). On the basis of their suggestions and personal investigation of Tojo's daily routine, Takagi concluded that an automobile "accident" would ensure success with such a prominent target. The assassins, in three cars, would intercept a Tojo motorcade. One vehicle would crash into Tojo's car, bringing it to a halt; the other two would pull alongside and gun down the Prime Minister with automatic revolvers. The conspirators would all wear uniforms. The others would escape to Formosa in a Navy plane, but Takagi would remain behind and take all the responsibility.*

---

*Another assassination attempt by an elite group of fifty aviation technocrats had already failed. These young men dealt with the

540

Ironically, Tojo himself had begun the search for peace. Before the fall of Singapore he had been involved in an attempt to negotiate with the Allies. On February 12, 1942, he was summoned to the Palace and instructed by the Emperor (at Kido's prompting) "not to miss any opportunity to terminate the war." Tojo sent for the German ambassador, General Eugen Ott, and made him promise not to reveal what he would hear to anyone but Ribbentrop and Hitler: Tojo suggested that Germany and Japan secretly approach the Allies with an offer of peace; he would fly to Berlin to represent the empire personally, if Hitler would send a long-range bomber. The reply from Berlin was polite but lukewarm. Hitler could not take the risk of Tojo crashing in a German plane.

Tojo was discouraged by the German lack of enthusiasm but was not averse to further efforts in the same direction, although he was naïve about how peace might be achieved. On Ambassador Kurusu's return from America later that summer (the Japanese diplomats in Washington were exchanged for Grew and his subordinates), Tojo took him aside at a party given in the diplomat's honor, and in Sugiyama's presence said, "Please arrange to end the war at an early date." Startled by the Prime Minister's "simplicity of mind," Kurusu remarked, "It is easier to start a war than end one."

Japan's fleet and merchant shipping losses were as catastrophic as Takagi's secret report indicated. Most of this

---

research and production of Army planes. Just before Pearl Harbor they had sent an appeal to Tojo to delay war for twenty years, until Japan would be properly prepared to engage a major power. Tojo listened to their arguments in a private meeting and promised to give them two decades to build up the air force.

Consequently, when war came they held Tojo personally responsible. Within six months their fears about the issue of the war were confirmed by technical setbacks: for example, machine tools were losing their precision, and defects in plane design would take years to correct. During the battle for Guadalcanal, Tojo told these technical experts to devise some way to fly planes without gas, suggesting they use "something like air." They laughed aloud until they realized he was serious, then unanimously pledged themselves to a program for peace. They went to Prince Konoye with their demands and later to Tojo himself. The subsequent reprimand incited the fifteen most headstrong to vow to assassinate Tojo. One evening their leader, First Lieutenant Hiroshi Sato, afer drinking too much *sake*, quarreled with their commanding officer and blurted out, "A man like Tojo should be killed." *Kempei* investigated the group, but the only one punished was Sato; he was given a week's confinement on a drunk charge. The ringleaders, however, were all sent to the front.

tonnage had been sent to the bottom by marauding American submarines and little was being done in the Imperial Navy to counter this, the gravest of all threats to Japan's supply lines.

The unpreparedness on the part of the Navy was the result of a combination of tradition and of reluctance to engage in defensive warfare. British naval officers had helped establish the Imperial Navy, which adopted all things English so readily that the Naval Academy at Etajima became a replica of Dartmouth. Bricks were brought from England, and a lock of Lord Nelson's hair enshrined in Memorial Hall. Imitation extended to the galley, and once a day a Western meal, complete with knives, forks and spoons, was served throughout the Navy. In battle, Japanese captains followed British tradition by going down with their sinking ship. More important, the Japanese inherited the British aversion to wage war on commercial vessels, and their submarines were designed to support the fleet and do battle against enemy warships rather than go after defenseless shipping. But such a policy could succeed only if an enemy shared it. The Germans did not, and when their submarines launched devastating raids on British merchantmen in World War I, the British had been forced to retaliate in kind as well as create an efficient antisubmarine service.

The Japanese did neither. They were still using their outmoded, outsized submarines almost exclusively against enemy warships and had virtually ignored antisubmarine warfare; it had little appeal to young officers just starting their careers who wanted more dashing duty. By the fall of 1941 there were but two full-time officers on the Navy General Staff assigned to "rear-line defense"—which included mining, antiaircraft defense and antisubmarine warfare. Operationally such duty was considered as unimportant as it was undesirable.

A single officer, with the derogatory title of "Staff Officer for Training," was responsible for protecting all shipping along six hundred miles of the Honshu coast, in addition to the vast area between Tokyo Bay and Iwo Jima. Moreover, when hostilities broke out there were no provisions for organizing merchant ships into convoys. Most shipmasters wanted to sail alone, anyway, but within six months American submarines had torpedoed so many solo merchantmen that the First Convoy Escort Fleet was established, with headquarters on Formosa. This emergency unit, comprised mostly of overage naval reserve officers, had eight destroyers with which to cover an extensive area. Combined Fleet was reluctant to release any more ships, out of sympathy for destroyer commanders, who detested the monotonous task of herding transports.

By the end of the first year since Pearl Harbor, U. S. submarines had sunk 139 cargo vessels, 560,000 gross tons in all, and at last Imperial Headquarters realized that the war was being lost through an oversight. At home there were pleas for more gasoline, bauxite and other vital production materials. At the front, commanders were begging for food, ammunition and reinforcements. But there weren't enough merchant ships to satisfy anyone's needs, and every week more were going down. It wasn't until March 1943, however, that the Second Convoy Escort Fleet was organized, with headquarters on Saipan. The total resources of both convoy fleets were still pitiful—sixteen destroyers, five coast defense frigates and five torpedo boats.

These stop-gap measures would have been ineffective in any case, but in the meantime the Americans had markedly raised the quality of their own underwater service. Scores of improved submarines were built and manned by well-trained crews; drastically redesigned torpedoes replaced the early, faulty ones, which had occasionally run in a circle and too often had failed to detonate. Accordingly, in September the Japanese suffered a record 172,082 gross-ton loss. The time for drastic measures was long since past, but none were taken until mid-November when Grand Escort Command Headquarters was created. Its commander, Admiral Koshiro Oikawa (who had been navy minister at the time Tojo took over two years before), was given four escort carriers and the 901st Naval Air Group. Unfortunately, all four of the big ships needed extensive repairs and the airmen had no training in antisubmarine tactics. The convoys continued to run haphazardly, each escort-ship commander acting as he thought fit. Losses climbed to 265,068 gross tons in November, but still the government was averse to the adoption of a full-fledged convoy system. Commanders at the front needed supplies too urgently, and small groups of from two to five ships would get there faster. These smaller groups, however, remained easy prey, and the heavy losses continued into the first two months of 1944.

There was no alternative. The "big" convoy system (twenty merchant ships, as compared to Allied convoys of seventy in the Atlantic) finally went into operation early in March. At first it appeared to have wrought a miracle. In the first month, losses dropped drastically. But the elation at Imperial

Headquarters was ill-founded. The U. S. Navy was also implementing a new system and had recalled numerous submarines for training. They would soon be sent out again to launch "wolf pack" raids.

3.

Admiral Togo's epic victory at Tsushima had left future Japanese admirals with an unenviable heritage: the concept of the Decisive Battle, wherein all isues would be settled at one stroke. Unlike his predecessor, the new commander of Combined Fleet, Admiral Mineichi Koga, was cool and conservative—an efficient, plodding officer governed by logic. Yet he too was obsessed by the dream of a battle which would change the course of the war. Being a pragmatist, he was also aware that chances of success were small, but it was Japan's last hope. On March 8 he issued his battle plan, giving it the name of Operation Z. Once the advancing American fleet broke into the Philippine Sea by way of the Marianas or the Palaus or New Guinea, the Combined Fleet would sally forth in full strength. In his efficient, methodical way, he set about concentrating the bulk of Japan's surface force, and near the end of the month gave orders to transfer his headquarters from the battleship *Musashi*, anchored at Palau, to the Philippines.

"Let us go out and die together," he said to his chief of staff, Admiral Shigeru Fukudome, before they flew south. Yamamoto, he added, had died "at exactly the right time" and he "envied him that fact." At nine o'clock on the last day of March they took off separately in two four-engine Kawanishi flying boats and headed due west for the three-hour flight to Mindanao. But before reaching the Philippines, they encountered a storm and Koga's plane disappeared. The fate of Admiral Koga (like that of Amelia Earhart) remains a mystery.* Within a year Combined Fleet had lost two commanders, both while flying near the front.

Fukudome's plane banked to the right to skirt the storm and changed course north toward Manila, but strong head-

---

*There are several theories about Koga's death. One is that he was ambushed, like Yamamoto; U. S. Navy planes shot down his plane and the dying Koga was picked up by an American submarine. There are no available American records of such an ambush or the recovery of the Koga plane. It could have crashed on some island, but it seems far more likely that it was lost at sea, victim of the storm.

winds continued to impede the flying boat's progress and by two o'clock in the morning it was almost out of fuel. The pilot sent word back to Fukudome to prepare for an emergency landing. To the left in the moonlight the admiral could see a long narrow island; it looked like Cebu. During their descent the moon abruptly disappeared from sight; below, the sea was lost in blackness. The pilot became disoriented and lost control. Fukudome, an expert flier himself, groped his way forward, still gripping a briefcase which contained a detailed copy of Operation Z and its cipher system. He reached over the pilot's shoulder and yanked back on the controls to try to bring the bulky flying boat out of its dive. But he pulled too far. The Kawanishi stalled. It fell off on one wing and cartwheeled heavily into the sea.

Fukudome felt water engulf him. He accepted death—the war was lost, anyway—but then he surfaced, still instinctively clinging to the briefcase. The water was bright with flames. He and ten others were free of the wreckage, but the admiral, weighted down by the briefcase, could not stay afloat. He clutched at a seat cushion and started kicking toward the dim shoreline of Cebu. Hour after hour he struggled against the strong current. By dawn he was alone. The others must be far ahead. In the distance Fukudome made out the silhouette of a tall chimney. He recognized the Asano Cement Plant, which was only six miles south of Cebu City, Japanese headquarters for the central Philippines. It was fairly safe territory, even though the island was infested by guerrillas.

He flailed wearily in the water for another hour, close to the limit of his endurance, before he saw several *bancas* (fishing canoes) approaching. He hesitated. Were they guerrillas? He had to chance capture but let the briefcase go. As he was dragged aboard the first *banca,* one of the fishermen— they had seen the flames—caught a glimpse of the slowly sinking briefcase and retrieved it just before it disappeared.

The admiral was taken to Balud along with eight of his comrades; the other two escaped to Japanese headquarters in Cebu City. The captives were delivered to the nearest guerrilla unit, where they told Captian Marcelino Erediano, who had studied at Tokyo Imperial University for a year, that they were unimportant staff officers from Japan on a routine inspection of the area. Erediano, however, noticed that one of them (Fukudome) was treated with considerable deference by the others. Perhaps he was a highranking general? Moreover, the papers in the briefcase with their red TOP SECRET markings were of obvious import. A runner was sent with this information to the commander of all Cebu guerrillas, Lieutenant Colonel James Cushing, an American mining engineer, half Irish, half Mexican. Cushing was an ex-boxer— a hard-drinking, impish individualist. He would have preferred sitting out the war in the mountains with his Filipino wife and child, enjoying life, but the people of Cebu had persuaded him that he alone could unify the quarreling groups of guerrillas on the island.

Cushing immediately radioed MacArthur on his little ATR4A that ten Japanese, including a high-ranking officer, had been captured along with a "whole case" of important documents, some of which looked like a cipher system. The message was picked up by Colonel Wendell Fertig, an engineering officer who had become commander of all guerrillas on Mindanao, and he relayed it to Australia. Here it created such a "tremendous stir" that the Navy offered to divert an operational submarine from its duties as soon as possible and send it to Negros, the island just west of Cebu, to pick up the prisoners and the documents.

Fukudome, his leg injured in the crash, had to be carried on a litter. It took over a week to reach Cushing's mountain hideout in Tupas, ten miles west of Cebu City, and by that time the admiral, under incessant questioning by Erediano, "admitted" that he was Admiral Koga and could even speak some English.

Shortly after Fukudome was delivered to Cushing, Japanese troops from Cebu City, alerted by the two men who had escaped, launched an attack on Tupas. Their commander, Lieutenant Colonel Seito Onishi, threatened to burn down villages and execute civilians in reprisal unless the prisoners were promptly released to him. Cushing retreated farther in the mountains and radioed MacArthur that he could get the documents to Negros but doubted he could deliver Admiral Koga and the other prisoners.

MacArthur replied: ENEMY PRISONERS MUST BE HELD AT ALL COSTS.

It was an impossible order. Cushing had twenty-five men, and Onishi's troops were closing in. He sent the documents to Negros with two runners but informed MacArthur that he would be forced to release "Koga" to avoid continued reprisals. The enraged MacArthur relieved Cushing of command and reduced him to the grade of private.

But "Private" Cushing was still in command, and had to negotiate with Onishi without delay. He asked "Koga" to compose a note requesting Colonel Onishi to refrain from further punitive action in exchange for himself and the others. Fukudome signed the note using Koga's name. It was delivered to Onishi by a civilian, who returned with the colonel's written promise to abide by the proposal. Fukudome was again loaded on a litter. Cushing warmly shook his hand; by now they were friends and even Cushing's fierce mastiff, who bristled at the other Japanese, allowed the admiral to pat him. It was only a moment but it was unique in such a relentless war. An unarmed platoon, led by Lieutenant Pedro Villareal, escorted the prisoners down the mountain path to their freedom.

Fukudome's briefcase found its way to MacArthur via submarine. Its contents were among the most significant enemy documents seized during the war, but Jim Cushing was in disgrace and subject, he imagined with some justification, to worse punishment when MacArthur returned to the Philippines.*

Koga was replaced by Admiral Soemu Toyoda, formerly commander at Yokosuka Naval Base. A brilliant man, he was noted for being so meticulous and sarcastic that more than one subordinate had suffered a nervous breakdown. Moreover, he had been ashore since the start of the war and it was imperative to select for him a chief of staff with broad experience at sea at the highest level. The obvious choice was Admiral Ryunosuke Kusaka, Nagumo's former chief of staff, and now serving under his cousin Admiral Junichi Kusaka at Rabaul. Before leaving Rabaul, he was given a farewell party—a banquet consisting of two cans of sea eel, two slices of broiled eggplant mixed in bean paste, weed soup, and rice boiled with barley. General Imamura contributed half a dozen bottles of *sake*.

---

*Due largely to the efforts of General Courtney Whitney, head of the Allied Intelligence Bureau, Cushing was reinstated. After the war he was awarded a substantial cash bonus for his contributions to victory. It should have been enough money to last Cushing for life in the Islands, but he spent it all in a few months on a series of celebrations that ranged across the Pacific to California. He died in the Philippines twenty years later, beloved by the men who had fought with him, but still a confirmed individualist to the end.

On Cebu there persists the belief that it was Koga who had been held by Cushing, and that he later committed suicide in Manila. The Japanese commander on Cebu, Colonel Onishi, also believed it was Koga he had rescued and that he subsequently committed hara-kiri.

Admiral Fukudome is still alive and spoke of his captivity but was reluctant to go into detail. Most of the information about this event came from Cushing and his comrades.

There was one way to get out of Rabaul—by air—and risk the fate of Yamamoto and Koga. American fighters patrolled overhead almost constantly. For safety, Kusaka's plane took off in the dark, its occupants cheered by a final toast—this time Johnnie Walker Black Label whiskey. At four o'clock the bomber swept low over the harbor, its exhausts lengthened to hide the flames. With dawn their fears of discovery were borne out. A flight of enemy fighters flashed by so close that Kusaka could see the pilots. Inexplicably, the Americans continued on course—without firing a round at Admiral Toyoda's new chief of staff.

The Kusaka plane refueled at Truk and went on to Saipan. Here the admiral held a reunion with Nagumo, who, after Midway and Guadalcanal, had been reduced to commanding a small area fleet. After Rabaul with its Draconian regime, Kusaka was appalled by the meager defenses on such a strategic island and recommended that much more be done. The next morning Kusaka took off for Iwo Jima, where he inspected the little volcanic island during refueling. It was well fortified but lacked sufficient machine guns and artillery. He promised the island commander—Captain Tsunezo Wachi, the secret agent and assistant naval attaché in Mexico City before Pearl Harbor—that he would send more weapons, and wished him a good fight.

Upon arrival at Combined Fleet shore headquarters outside Tokyo, Kusaka's immediate problem was to determine once again where and how the next major battle should be fought. Like his predecessors, Kusaka was imbued with the idea of the Decisive Battle, and inevitably his plan of operation was similar to Koga's. In March the Navy had been drastically reorganized, and now its main force, Vice Admiral Jisaburo Ozawa's First Mobile Fleet, was anchored at Lingga Roads, off Singapore, close to its fuel supply but far from the critical area of the Philippines. Kusaka recalled an old Chinese proverb: "No matter how strong the bow, an arrow in long flight cannot tear the sheerest cloth." It would be necessary to bring the Mobile Fleet forward "in a hop, skip and a jump." The hop would be to Tawi Tawi, one of the southernmost of the Philippine islands; the skip the center of the Philippines; and the jump to the Palaus or Saipan. Kusaka's plan was hand-carried to Toyoda, who was still at Yokosuka. It was approved, and emerged as A-Go (Operation A).

Kusaka recalled the neglected defenses of Saipan, and since the island's strength was essential to the operation, he hounded Army officials who were responsible. Tojo, annoyed by Kusaka's persistence, wrote him: "I personally guarantee with 'a large seal' the defense of Saipan!" The messenger, a colonel, added that the Army *hoped* the Americans would land at Saipan; they would be wiped out.

By the end of April the technical details of A-Go were resolved and a few days later Admiral Toyoda issued the general orders. The "decisive" battle area would be the Palaus, and if the Americans headed straight for the Marianas, they would have to be "lured" south (to save Mobile Fleet fuel and be closer to land air bases), where "a decisive battle with full strength will be opened at a favorable opportunity." The enemy would be "attacked and destroyed for the most part in a day assault." But first the 540 land-based naval planes of the First Air Fleet would destroy "at least one third of the enemy task-force carrier units."

On May 10 Kusaka's "hop, skip and jump" started; Ozawa's Mobile Fleet pulled out of Lingga Roads and headed for Tawi Tawi.

4.

The next American target was Saipan, the most strategic island of the Marianas; Nimitz would be in command. In the meantime MacArthur had already taken another long step toward *his* objective, the Philippines, by jumping all the way from eastern New Guinea to Hollandia, an important harbor area near the northwest end of the island, in an ambitious amphibious operation that completely surprised the 11,000 defenders. The roar of Allied naval guns sent most of the Japanese flying—90 percent were service troops—and the 52,000 invaders had little trouble in clearing the area. At minimal cost MacArthur had secured an excellent air, naval and logistics base. A week after the Mobile Fleet left Lingga Roads he took another stride toward Tokyo—this one a 120-mile lunge farther west to the Sarmi area, which was served by two excellent airfields, with another under construction. There were 14,000 Japanese on hand, but less than half were combat troops and they were caught as unawares as their comrades in Hollandia. They put up little resistance—two Americans were killed on the first day—and MacArthur had another valuable base.

His next objective was Biak, a small island to the west, strategically located in the mouth of New Guinea's largest bay. Biak was forty-five miles long and twenty miles wide, and had three serviceable airstrips which the Japanese considered important enough to defend with 10,000 men. On May 20 the Americans began a week of bombing, but this failed to alert the Japanese commander to the impending invasion, and the 41st Division landed on the island against almost no opposition. The first waves of GI's came ashore at the wrong place but by noon they had established a strong beachhead.

On the Combined Fleet's new flagship, the cruiser *Oyodo*, Toyoda's staff was shaken by the "suddenness" of the Biak landing; it had come on the thirty-ninth anniversary of Tsushima. Kusaka, however, saw it as an opportunity. "If we take it back," he said, "that will draw the Pacific Fleet in sufficiently close so that we can have the Decisive Battle near Palau." His reasoning swayed everyone except the intelligence officer, Commander Chikataka Nakajima, who was of the opinion that MacArthur's landing at Biak was secondary and that the main offensive, completely supported by the Pacific Fleet, would be directed at Saipan. But Kusaka prevailed, and almost overnight a hasty plan to reinforce Biak, Operation KON, was devised.

Nakajima was, of course, right. The three divisions that would land at Saipan in nineteen days—on June 15—had finished arduous training and rehearsed co-ordinated landings in Hawaii; and a flotilla of 110 naval transport vessels, together with an entire division of Liberty ships, was assembling to transport them, along with 7,000 corps and garrison troops, the thirty-two hundred miles to the landing area.

The Marianas, a chain of tropical volcanic islands, were discovered by Magellan in 1521. He was so impressed by the native boats and their rigging that he named them the Islands of the Lateen Sails, but to his less poetic crew they were known as the Islands of the Thieves. In the seventeenth century they were officially renamed to honor Mariana of Austria, widow of Philip IV of Spain, but with the years the Spanish influence waned. America seized Guam, the largest of the islands, during the Spanish-American War. A few months later, in 1899, the harried Spaniards sold the rest of their holdings in the Carolines, Marshalls and Marianas to Germany for some $4,000,000. America could have had the islands, but the McKinley Administration thought they weren't worth that much money.

During World War I the Japanese occupied all these islands, and being on the winning side, were afterward given the mandate over them by the League of Nations. In 1935 they built Aslito Airfield at the southern end of Saipan, and a little later constructed a seaplane base on the west coast and a fighter strip at the northern tip. Some Americans accused Japan of using the island as a military and naval base contrary to the League of Nations Covenant, but there was no more than a handful of troops on the island.*

All native children—they were Chamorros—were required to attend a Japanese school for at least six years, and the brightest boys were encouraged to study at a specialized agricultural training school. Sugar cane was the main crop and production increased under the South Sea Development Company. By the time of Pearl Harbor, Saipan had become a little Tokyo; of its more than thirty thousand people, fewer than four thousand were Chamorros. The island was the length of Manhattan but more than twice its width. Between 1,554-foot Mount Tapotchau in the center and Mount Marpi at the northern end stretched a jagged ridge, pocked with thousands of caves and marked by numerous little peaks and escarpments. This rugged area, as well as the cane fields which covered 70 percent of the island's eighty-five square miles, was ideally suited for defensive warfare.

During the first two years of the war Saipan was nothing but a supply and staging area. Even after the fall of Tarawa and Kwajalein the garrison continued to be little more than a token force, and except for construction of scattered pillboxes, almost nothing was done to fortify the island that was Nimitz' next target.

---

*These American suspicions helped give rise to sensational stories involving the last flight of Amelia Earhart. Miss Earhart and her navigator, Fred Noonan, took off from Lae, New Guinea, on a July morning in 1937, in a twin-engine Lockheed, and disappeared. After the war, rumors persisted that the two had purposely veered off course to spy on military installations on Saipan and had crashed near the seaplane base. They were supposedly imprisoned and then either died of injuries or were executed. Tony Benavente, a police official on Saipan, helped two American officials investigate the case. They interviewed some fifteen men and women (later characterized by Mr. Benavente as "reliable witnesses") who identified the pictures of Earhart and Noonan as "two American prisoners" they had seen in the summer of 1937, and one said he had noticed two blindfolded Caucasians answering descriptions of Earhart and Noonan in the sidecar of a Japanese motorcycle near the seaplane base. A Japanese told him they were American spies who had been picked up offshore.

Nevertheless, there is no conclusive evidence as to the fate of Amelia Earhart, nor is any confirmation on the subject available from official Japanese sources.

On the morning of February 23, 1944, his carrier-based bombers attacked the island's airfields. Civilians heard the firing of their own antiaircraft guns, but where were the Japanese planes? Daily they had flown so low and in such numbers that it was almost impossible to teach school. Seventy-four Japanese planes from Saipan, Tinian and Guam did get into the air, but they couldn't prevent the enemy from destroying 101 planes on the ground. They did manage to shoot down six Americans, but only seven of the seventy-four returned safely to their bases.

On Saipan, quiet life was gone for good. Schools and plants were closed to allow the civilians to build shelters and help construct another airstrip. With work their spirits rose and they regained confidence. But orders came to repatriate old people, women and children to Japan. On March 3 *Amerika-maru* sailed with seventeen hundred passengers, most of them families of officials of the South Sea Development Company or influential citizens. It never reached the homeland. Three days later torpedoes sent it to the bottom. Troop transports bound for the Marianas were also torpedoed, and survivors, arriving in Saipan dejected and without weapons, brought with them the feeling of doom.

In an attempt to stem the succession of American victories in the central Pacific, Imperial Headquarters reorganized the entire command structure of the region and sent Admiral Nagumo to Saipan to command a newly created Central Pacific Area Fleet. Theoretically Nagumo was supreme commander of all forces in the area, Army as well as Navy, but guidelines from Tokyo were so vague that he was virtually a figurehead.

Late in May the 43rd Division, around which the defense of Saipan would be centered, sailed from Japan in two echelons. The first arrived safely, but the second—a convoy which was carrying more than 7,000 troops—was subjected to a series of submarine attacks, and five of the seven transports were sunk. The other two crammed their decks with survivors and continued on. About 5,500 finally reached Saipan with many badly burned or wounded. Few had equipment or weapons. The division was so disorganized that one staff officer, Major Takashi Hirakushi, reported that it would be six months before it could conduct any kind of defense.

Nor were the positions they would defend yet prepared. Lieutenant General Hideyoshi Obata of the 31st Army, who commanded all ground troops in the Marianas from headquarters in Saipan, officially warned Admiral Nagumo. "Specifically," he wrote, "unless the units are supplied with cement, steel reinforcements for cement, barbed wire, lumber, etc., which cannot be obtained in these islands, no matter how many soldiers there are they can do nothing in regard to fortifications but sit around with their arms folded, and the situation is unbearable." The situation now would not improve. Thousands of tons of building materials had already been sunk in transit and no more was on the way.

Time had also run out on the 31,629 defenders (25,469 Army, 6,160 Navy personnel). A massive armada of American ships—535—was converging on Saipan. They carried 127,571 troops, two thirds of them Marines. At sea on June 7, they received word of another mighty assault. On one ship filled with Marines the loudspeaker voice said, "The invasion of France has started. That is all." There was silence. "'Thank God!" someone finally said.

D-Day passed almost unnoticed in Japan. Combined Fleet was preoccupied with Operation KON. The first attempt to reinforce Biak had failed; destroyers and transports were turned back by persistent air attacks. A second attempt by six destroyers was already under way. Near noon of June 8 one of these was sunk by bombers, and the remaining five scuttled back north upon encountering a single American destroyer at midnight.

Admiral Ozawa, commander of the Mobile Fleet, was not as easily intimidated. He radioed Combined Fleet that the airfields of Biak were too valuable to lose and reminded his superiors that another attempt to retake the island "might draw the American Fleet into the anticipated zone of decisive battle and enable us to launch A-Go." Kusaka needed no urging—it was his own plan, after all—and he persuaded Toyoda to let Ozawa make a final endeavor in greater force. KON was strengthened with a light cruiser, six destroyers and the two great battleships, *Musashi* and *Yamato*. On the afternoon of June 10 this redoubtable force left Tawi Tawi for the south.

While Japanese attention was focused on Biak, the Americans were approaching their primary target, Saipan, more than thirteen hundred miles to the northeast. At midday, June 11, they launched a strike of 208 fighters and 8 torpedo bombers against Tinian and Saipan. Ignoring inaccurate antiaircraft fire, they descended on the two islands, which were separated by a narrow channel, strafing and bombing. On Saipan, they left more than a hundred planes smoldering and flames sweeping through the four-foot-high savannah grass on the slopes above Garapan, the largest town on the island.

The whole purpose of Operation KON was suddenly negated. The Marianas were the main target. Combined Fleet suspended KON and ordered its commander to rendezvous with Ozawa in the waters west of Saipan.

Before the two forces met, seven American battleships and eleven destroyers began bombarding Saipan and Tinian. It was June 13, two days before the landing. During the day they expended fifteen thousand 16- and 5-inch shells, but the gun crews had limited experience in shore bombardment, which called for slow, patient adjustment on specific targets, and little damage of military importance was inflicted. Before dawn they were joined by a more practiced fire-support group—eight battleships, six heavy cruisers and five light cruisers. This time the aim was deliberate and accurate.

In Garapan a young volunteer nurse by the name of Shizuko Miura—a tomboy with a round merry face—flinched as the first shells landed. She peered out the window of the first-aid station into the dim light. The Americans were bombarding the town again. As the explosions moved closer she helped transfer those wounded in the earlier shelling to a dugout. With daylight came enemy planes and an even more violent barrage from the ships. It is June 14, Shizuko thought calmly. I have lived for eighteen years and my time to die has come. A shell shook the dugout like an earthquake and knocked her to the ground. She staggered outside. The first-aid station was obliterated. She saw a piece of red metal—it was shrapnel—and, curious, touched it with her finger. It burned her. Planes droned overhead but no one was firing at them. Garapan was aflame. The heat was so intense that she could hardly breathe. She started to make her way through the rubbled streets strewn with bodies.

Offshore two 96-man underwater demolition teams were boldly exploring the reefs south of Garapan. They found no obstacles but their presence helped convince Lieutenant General Yoshitsugu Saito, commander of the 43rd Division, that the invasion was actually at hand and would come on the west coast. He concentrated his troops to meet the attack, shifted his artillery and set up new headquarters on the west coast. Saito was eminently unsuited by nature and training to lead combat troops. He was a stodgy, colorless cavalryman whose previous command had been a horse procurement unit. That his division was chosen as the nucleus of Saipan's defense proved how unimportant the island was considered by Tokyo.

Many of the other troops on Saipan were random units salvaged from sinkings. They were poorly organized, lacked leadership and were without weapons. Admiral Nagumo was the titular head of this haphazard defense force, but he always deferred to General Obata of 31st Army—and *he* was away on an inspection trip of the Palaus, and his chief of staff, Major General Keiji Igeta, was outranked by Saito.

This put the tactical command of the island under the hapless Saito. He was saddled with the philosophy that had governed and depleted the defense against every invasion to date. Tokyo had decreed that as usual, Saipan was to be defended primarily on the beaches, not in depth.

Transports and LST's carrying the 2nd and 4th Marine divisions were drawing close to the west coast of Saipan and would be in position for debarkation the following morning, June 15. On the island they would encounter more than one kind of enemy. As the medical officer of one unit warned: after facing sharks, barracuda, sea snakes, razor-sharp coral, poison fish and giant clams in the surf, they would find worse hazards ashore—leprosy, typhus, filariasis, typhoid and dysentery as well as snakes and giant lizards.

"Sir," one private ventured, "why don't we let the Japs keep the island?"

A more ominous admonition came from a graduate of UCLA, an American girl of Japanese descent who had been visiting a sick aunt in Japan when the war broke out. Nicknamed "Tokyo Rose" by the Americans, she first went on the air as "Ann," short for "announcer," and currently called herself "Orphan Annie, your favorite enemy."

"I've got some swell recordings for you," she was broadcasting, "just in from the States. You'd better enjoy them while you can, because tomorrow at oh-six-hundred you're hitting Saipan . . . and we're ready for you. So, while you're still alive, let's listen to . . ."

The dark ships slowly drew nearer to Saipan, the skies overhead glowing red from burning buildings, grass and woods. Marines on deck could barely make out the formidable silhouette of Mount Tapotchau through the early-morning haze. As the sky lightened, the island—a shadowy purplish land mass—looked like "a great monster rising out of the sea." Charan Kanoa emerged detail by detail; the two divisions would land on a four-mile front centering on the little town. Five miles to the north Garapan, too, took form. There a diversionary force would pretend to land.

Battleships, cruisers and destroyers began the final bombardment at five-thirty. The dug-in defenders along the beaches and on the slopes crouched through the ordeal, prepared to fight to the death. One made a final notation in his diary: "We are waiting with 'Molotov cocktails' and hand grenades ready for the word to rush forward recklessly into the enemy ranks with our swords in our hands. All that worries me is what will happen to Japan after we die."

Twelve minutes later Vice Admiral Richmond Kelly Turner, in command of the Joint Expeditionary Force, issued the order: "Land the Landing Force." Over loudspeakers boomed the chaplains' last prayers and blessings. On *Time* correspondent Robert Sherrod's ship, Chaplain Cunningham was saying, ". . . most of you will return, but some of you will meet the God who made you." A lieutenant colonel named Tompkins turned to Sherrod and remarked, "Perish-the-thought Department!"

Winches lowered boats; hatches were cleared. At seven o'clock the shelling ceased and thirty-four LST's churned up to the line of departure, a little over two miles from shore. The huge bow doors of the bulky vessels yawned open and amphtracs, loaded with Marines, crawled out and began circling in the water like great water bugs. Planes—the first of 155—were already bombing the Charan Kanoa area to keep the beach defenders pinned down; when they left half an hour later the entire shoreline was veiled by clouds of smoke and dust. The bombing was a "thrilling" sight to Sherrod but he wrote in his notebook: "I fear all this smoke and noise does not mean Japs have been killed."

Soon after eight o'clock 719 amphtracs, filled with eight battalions of Marines, started for shore preceded by gunboats and amphibian tanks. Officers passed out chewing gum and warned their men to be ready to discard their heavy cartridge belts in case they had to swim for it.

The four-mile-wide flotilla raked to within eight hundred yards of the shore before a shower of mortar and artillery shells rained down upon the invaders. Eighteen amphibian tanks clambered like crabs over the barrier reef. Behind them several amphtracs were sunk but the rest followed over the reef and into the shallow blue-green lagoon. Dozens of planes coming in low strafed the beach while warships pounded shore defenses for the last time with their 5-inch guns. It was a spectacular sight, organized bedlam.

The landing plan was original. The tanks were to crawl up on the beach and cover the amphtracs, which would transport the troops all the way to high ground. The first wave hit the beach at eight forty-four, and within twenty minutes, more than eight thousand Marines had landed. It was soon evident that all the intense preinvasion bombardment had not silenced the Japanese. Innumerable machine-gun nests and mortar emplacements between the beaches and the ridge opened up a withering fire which did not stop until their crews were blasted to bits. While it lasted it was so accurate that most of the amphtracs had to discharge their load at the edge of the beach. The ones getting through encountered another kind of obstacle: they got bogged down in the sand or were caught in craters and didn't have the power to climb out.

The Marines fought their way slowly into Charan Kanoa. It wasn't made of bamboo and paper as they had imagined, but was a complex of concrete one- and two-story structures covered with bougainvillea in bloom. Each was a little fort. At the center of town they infiltrated past a baseball diamond and grandstand incongruously flanked by a Buddhist temple.

From a flimsy thirty-foot-high observation tower perched on the slopes behind Garapan, Admiral Nagumo watched the invasion. He stood transfixed at the sight of the overwhelming number of ships but turned briefly to Yeoman Noda, who had served as a clerk under Yamamoto until his death, to note that at least four of the battleships he had sunk at Pearl Harbor were back in action. His tone indicated as much admiration as concern.

Not far away, a stray American shell plummeted down on General Saito's staff during an outdoor meeting near the cave that served as his command post. When the smoke cleared, Saito was still sitting unhurt and silent, with his sword stuck in the ground between his spread legs. On both sides men lay sprawled. Half the staff was dead.

But he remained optimistic about the battle itself (although Marines continued to land—twenty thousand during the day—they had suffered two thousand casualties, and only half of the beachhead had been secured) and radioed Tokyo:

AFTER DARK THIS DIVISION WILL LAUNCH A NIGHT ATTACK IN FORCE AND EXPECT TO ANNIHILATE THE ENEMY AT ONE SWOOP.

The men who had to plan the night attack were not as confident. With the division scattered and their own casualties mounting, there were only thirty-six tanks and a thousand infantrymen available to "annihilate the enemy at one swoop."

The operation went wrong from the beginning. Saito was to meet the attack force on a hill above Charan Kanoa to send them off personally, but the Americans, attracted by all the movement toward the assembly point, scattered the general's staff with accurate artillery fire. The tankers waited hour after hour for Saito, who had become separated from his staff in the confusion and darkness. After midnight word came that he had been burned to death in a sugar-cane fire. Major Hirakushi, transformed from public relations officer to commander of the infantry, was relieved of that duty and dispatched to recover the general's body while another officer took charge of the assault. He mounted the first tank, but before it had gone half a mile a shell brought it to a standstill. The remaining tanks clanked down the hill without bothering to wait for the infantrymen. At the bottom they blundered into the swamp east of town and most of them became mired down. The tanks that managed to churn free were finally joined by the panting infantrymen. Officers, swords aloft, led the headlong charge. The Japanese burst into the Marine positions with such vigor that it took a cannonade from 5-inch naval guns and intense machine-gun and rifle fire to stop them. They regrouped and charged again and again. Almost seven hundred died and the American lines were still intact.

Major Hirakushi nearly lost his own life in his attempt to find Saito's body. Incendiary shells made an inferno of a cane field he was crossing and only his sword saved him. Using it as a scythe, he cut a path through to safety. Exhausted, he reached the division command post an hour before dawn. A solitary figure was sitting outside the cave, chin on chest. It was General Saito. "Are you all right, Division Commander?" Hirakushi asked. Saito looked up but made no response.

In a cave overlooking Garapan the nurse Shizuko Miura, who had escaped through the burning town the day before, huddled with other civilians. A soldier peered in with word that more Americans were starting to land just below Garapan, and the tank corps located near the town was moving out to stop them. Shizuko scrambled outside. Her elder

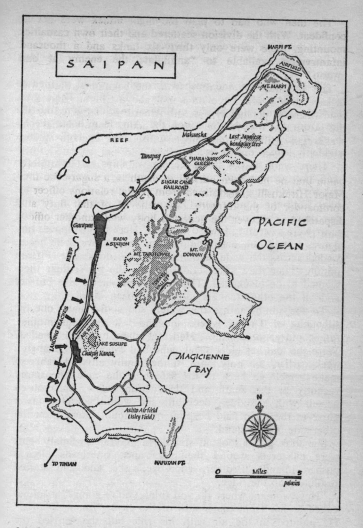

S A I P A N

MARPI PT.

AIRFIELD

MT. MARPI

REEF

Makunsha

Last Japanese headquarters

Tanapag

"HARA-KIRI GULCH"

SUGAR CANE RAILROAD

PACIFIC

OCEAN

Garapan

RADIO STATION

MT. TAPOTCHAU

MT. DONNAY

DEATH VALLEY

LANDING BEACHES

REEF

AIR STRIP

LAKE SUSUPE

Chalan Kanoa

MAGICIENNE BAY

N

Aslito Air field (Isley Field)

TO TINIAN

NAFUTAN PT.

0 — Miles — 5

palacios

brother was in one of the tanks. Below, Garapan was still in flames and through the smoky dawn she saw a ship (it was an LST) approach the reef south of town.

"It's starting!" a soldier shouted. Boats—amphtracs—were disgorging from the mother ship. She watched, almost hypnotized, as the strange craft scuttled over the reef. Angry spits

559

of fire winked from woods along the shore. Tanks rolled out of Garapan and started toward the beach.

"My brother!" Shizuko exclaimed.

"Girl, get back in the cave where it's safe," a soldier warned her.

She ignored him and pushed through a crowd of men to get a better look. The tanks were at the pier. Their guns barked, accompanied by the rattling of machine-gun and rifle fire from the woods. Some of the American boats turned back. Two white hospital ships approached the reef. Flames suddenly leaped out of one.

There were flashes from the big warships far beyond the reef. Then came a series of distant rumbles that were drowned out by shattering explosions from Garapan. The air trembled from the concussions. Enemy planes swept in strafing the shore. The firing from the woods ceased. More landing craft were swarming toward the reef. Here they stopped; tiny figures leaped out, and holding guns high above their heads, waded across the wide lagoon toward the dock area. Fifteen minutes later they were scrambling up the piers; their faces seemed to be blackened. The tanks were silent. Her brother and all the other tankers must have been killed.

To the south, across the water, she could make out the silhouette of Tinian, where she had last seen her mother, father and younger sisters. Had that island too been invaded? Were she and her elder sister, who had evacuated Garapan a week earlier, the only ones in the family alive? Unable to make herself go back to the safety of the cave, she stared vacantly at the death and destruction below. She roused herself with a sudden decision: she would volunteer as a nurse at the main field hospital near Mount Donnay on the other side of the island.

She took a last look at smoldering Garapan. Small boats were clustered around the piers and Americans already pushed inland. "Brother, good-bye," she said and started resolutely up the ridge.

"Hey, woman, where do you think you're going?" a soldier called to her from the mouth of the cave. "Enemy planes!" He pointed in the air with his rifle but she hurried on, ignoring the fighters that swooped down.

Once over the ridge the war seemed far away. She passed a long line of civilians waiting for hardtack. A young woman broke away from the group and embraced her—it was her older sister. Shizuko told her about their brother's death and that she was going to Mount Donnay.

"Bakayaro!" Her brother-in-law was indignant. "You can't go alone to a place where there are only men! Your parents entrusted you to my care. If something happened to you, how could I apologize to them?"

"The rest of the family is dead!" she burst out. "Do you want to be the only one alive?" These fools had not seen the destruction of Garapan, the corpses littering the streets; they still imagined the soldiers would protect them.

She reached the hospital on the slopes of Mount Donnay as the sun was setting. It was a barren field where a vast gathering of wounded men lay on the ground in rows so close together that she could hardly walk between them. Overcome by the stench, she did not notice a middle-aged captain, a surgeon, surveying her through round, thick glasses. "Women can't do anything here," he scolded. "Besides, this is the Army and we can't permit civilians to remain. Go back down the mountain before it gets too dark."

She told him that her father and mother and younger sisters were dead and that she had seen her brother killed in battle at Garapan. The captain walked away but she followed him, pleading. He stopped to talk with another doctor, a young lieutenant, still ignoring her. Finally he motioned to her. "All right," he said sternly, "from now on you are a nurse." He gave her his Red Cross armband and the lieutenant clapped a helmet on her head. "This is the Army, and never act selfishly," said the captain. There were eleven of them to care for all the wounded—three doctors, seven medics and herself. "Obey your commander's order at all times. Many painful and sad things are going to take place. Don't give up and do your best." She looked down at the armband with such obvious pride that the lieutenant gave a little laugh. "She's young and I'm afraid she may become emotional."

Her first duty was holding a flashlight for the little medical team which worked rapidly down a long line of patients. A medic jerked at a protruding piece of shrapnel in one man's back. The patient groaned, fainted. "It's easier when they pass out," the medic told her and yanked again, without success. The captain, the chief surgeon, came over and cut away flesh with a scalpel. The aide tried a third time. Shizuko's hand shook, and the light wavered. "Steady!" said the surgeon as he pulled out a red-and-black piece of shrapnel as big as a fist. Shizuko felt cold sweat under her arms as the surgeon gave the patient an injection. The medic took a mouthful of water and sprayed it on the man's face.

561

The next patient was wounded in the left foot. The surgeon handed her a pair of scissors. "Cut off the trousers," he said. She found a blood-soaked bandage underneath, stuck to the wound as if it were glued. She plucked at it, fearing the man might scream if she pulled too hard.

"Don't hesitate, nurse," said the surgeon sharply. "If you're afraid of a wound and feel so much pity that you can't hurt a patient, you're useless. Here." The patient gritted his teeth. The bandage came free under the surgeon's steady pull and she could see shattered bones. Blood flooded out.

The surgeon examined the wound. "The foot won't be of any use now. We should cut it off." He pricked the foot with the scissors. "Do you feel it?"

"No."

"It's to be expected." He turned to Shizuko. "Nurse, cut off the flesh—and no hesitation."

Nauseated, Shizuko began clipping the loose flesh. The soldier trembled with every tentative swish of the blades, and greasy sweat broke out on his forehead. At last she was finished. The surgeon, who had been watching impatiently, turned to a colleague. "Shall we operate?" he wondered and asked the medic how many anesthetic injections were left. There were but three boxes. "We'll treat him later," the surgeon decided. "Cover the wound, nurse. With the same bandage." She replaced the old blood-stained bandage and the patient was carried to one side.

"This time, nurse, do the whole thing by yourself," said the surgeon. What little confidence she had left vanished. She hoped she'd get someone with a slight wound. A new patient was brought in and the stretcher-bearers smiled at her. She gritted her teeth and somehow got the bandage off for the surgeon's inspection. Each time it was easier. Concerned about the young soldier with the wounded foot, she finally got up her courage to remind the surgeon that he was supposed to operate.

"I completely forgot," he said and ordered the patient carried to the "operating table"—the words themselves made Shizuko's heart beat quickly. The stretcher was placed on two boxes while the medic brought out a plate filled with instruments. First the patient was injected in the back. As soon as the anesthetic took effect the surgeon deftly cut flesh from around the bone with a scalpel that glittered in the light. The medic began hacking with a little saw, scattering the bone in a white powderlike substance. The patient groaned in pain.

"Cheer up! It'll be over in a minute," the medic who was holding the flashlight encouraged him.

Moments later—it seemed like an hour to Shizuko—the bone was severed and the surgeon began trimming away thick pulpy flesh. A stream of red spurted out of the stump. The doctor grabbed at the blood vessel with pincers, but it slipped away and he couldn't find it in the uncertain light. Shizuko could see the blue vessel plainly and pushed forward impatiently, "Doctor, I can pick it up."

Without a word he handed her the pincers. Quickly she plucked up the spurting vessel. The surgeon took the pincers while she bound it tightly with hemp yarn.

"All right," said the surgeon. He put in a few stitches, like an expert seamstress, applied some gauze, bandaged the stump and again injected the patient.

"Thank you very much," said the soldier in a voice as faint as a whisper.

The Marines had done little that day except buttress lines in preparation for a drive across the island. Most of their artillery was ashore, and GI's of the 27th Division were landing. General Saito still had hopes of pushing the Americans back into the sea with the help of tanks and men of a naval Special Landing Force. His first objective was an enemy concentration near the Saipan radio station in the suburbs of Garapan. The attack was set for dusk but the orders were so confusing, the communications so poor, and the problems of terrain so difficult that it wasn't until ten hours later that twenty-five tanks and five hundred men funneled down the ravine leading to the radio station.

The Marines, alerted by the squeak and rattle of armor, called for illumination. Ships lobbed star shells overhead, catching the attackers in the open where they were overwhelmed by a deluge of fire from artillery, mortar, bazooka, rifle and machine gun. Tanks burst into fire, silhouetting others which rumbled out of the shadows. Within an hour most of them were either destroyed or abandoned, but the infantry kept fighting until after dawn. It was no use. The Americans were still in place. They would never be driven into the sea.

The failure of the counterattack was ignored by Tokyo. The Army General Staff, in the name of the Emperor, radioed 31st Army:

BECAUSE THE FATE OF THE JAPANESE EMPIRE DEPENDS ON THE RESULT OF YOUR OPERATION, INSPIRE THE SPIRIT OF THE OFFICERS AND MEN AND TO THE VERY END CONTINUE TO DESTROY THE ENEMY GALLANTLY AND PERSISTENTLY, THUS ASSUAGING THE ANXIETY OF OUR EMPEROR.

General Igeta replied:

HAVE RECEIVED YOUR HONORABLE IMPERIAL WORDS AND WE ARE GRATEFUL FOR BOUNDLESS MAGNANIMITY OF THE IMPERIAL FAVOR. BY BECOMING THE BULWARK OF THE PACIFIC WITH 10,000 DEATHS, WE HOPE TO REQUITE THE IMPERIAL FAVOR.

The Japanese were again committed to a useless fight to the death.

With dawn Shizuko could see that the hospital area was surrounded by rocky little peaks. It was like a stadium with no protection from air raids. There were at least a thousand wounded men on the ground, and the little valley resounded with their constant but subdued chorus of agony. If there is a hell, she thought, this is it.

With two aides holding a large can she went down the lanes of men doling out water. She put a cup to the lips of an inert corporal. He seemed dead. Another patient shook him. "Yoshida, it's water! You wanted it so much. Look, Yoshida, it's a nurse from Japan!" The corporal slowly opened his eyes and groped for her. She grasped his feeble hand tightly and said, "Soldier, I've brought you water. Drink." He mumbled. "He's dreaming of home," his friend explained. The word "home" tightened her throat; then she remembered the admonition about becoming emotional.

She bent over another figure. He had nothing on but a loincloth, and kept his face hidden in his hands. His left eye was black, "as big as a ping-pong ball." It was covered with squirming maggots. The other eye had been gouged out by the worms. Her hands trembled. "Let me treat you, soldier." He remained silent as she picked out the maggots one by one with pincers and dropped them into a can. "My brother was in the Army," she said. "He was a tank man. On June fourth he came to Saipan from Manchuria, and on the sixteenth, near Garapan, he died fighting the enemy. That's why I can't see a soldier without thinking of him as my brother."

"Is that why you came here?" he said in a toneless voice.

She explained why she had become a nurse. Tears flowed out of his terrible left eye. "Thank you."

She started to speak about her family and he painfully fumbled for something tucked under his loincloth. It was a bloodstained picture of a woman in kimono.

"Is this your wife?" The man—his name was Lieutenant Shinoda—nodded. "She's still young."

He told her that he had joined the Army three days after the wedding. "When I was wounded all I could think of was my wife. I wanted to live for her sake. But I shall die . . ."

Shizuko couldn't speak. She resumed plucking out maggots, removing all but those tenaciously clinging to the center of the eyes. To kill these she soaked two wads of gauze in mercurochrome and placed them over his eyes. She applied a bandage and told him she would return. "Help is surely coming. Hold out until then because your wife is waiting for you."

The next day—it was June 18 and the Marines had cut Saipan in two just below Mount Donnay—Shizuko managed to find him a uniform. She changed his eye bandage but discovered that the mercurochrome had done no good. The gauze itself was alive with maggots. He wanted the picture sent back to his wife when he died.

"You won't die. I will surely cure you. And we've heard that reinforcements are coming. Then you can return to the homeland. Keep up your spirits!" To change the subject she talked about her brother and four sisters. She alone was a tomboy and her mother always told her, "Shizuko, behave like a woman." She told Shinoda how lucky he was to have someone waiting back home and how hard the doctors and medics were working to save men like him.

"Nurse, you're really great," said a lively voice. She looked up at a baby-faced second lieutenant. His right arm was in a sling and he had other wounds, but he was in good spirits. "Cheer up!" he told his dejected companions. "How can you call yourselves soldiers and be so downcast? Reinforcements will come in time!" All at once his eyes glistened and he said as if in a dream, "I have a sister in Hokkaido who is about as old as you. For the past two days I've been admiring you and it made me wonder what my sister was doing."

20   "Seven Lives to Repay Our Country!"

1.

Word of American landings on Saipan brought a swift reaction from Admiral Soemu Toyoda. He radioed Admiral Ozawa to "attack the enemy in the Marianas area and annihilate his fleet." Five minutes later Toyoda sent a second message, which repeated Togo's famous words at Tsushima Bay:

THE RISE AND FALL OF IMPERIAL JAPAN DEPENDS ON THIS ONE BATTLE. EVERY MAN SHALL DO HIS UTMOST.

As the Mobile Fleet moved closer to the Marianas, Ozawa and his staff completed plans for the battle. The admiral was tall and stocky. A cool, reticent man, he moved and thought with deliberation. Trained in torpedo warfare, he had assiduously studied carrier tactics and was confident he could beat the Americans, even though he was outnumbered 2 to 1 in flattops. His aircraft had longer range and could attack from as far out as three hundred miles, almost a hundred miles beyond American capabilities. He could also utilize Guam for refueling and rearming in a sort of shuttle operation. Consequently, he could stay out of range of the enemy while attacking; moreover, he would have support from the 500 planes based in the Marianas. Along with his own 473 planes, that should give him as many as Spruance had.

But plans are only as good as the information they are based on and already, unbeknownst to Ozawa, a large portion of the land-based planes had been destroyed by marauding American carrier pilots flying the new Hellcat fighter.* It

---

*On June 4, 1942, a Zero fighter, piloted by Petty Officer Tadayoshi Koga, came in for a forced landing on lonely Akutan Island in the Aleutians. A single enemy machine-gun bullet had severed its pressure-gauge indicator line. Its wheels caught in the tundra and the plane flipped over, breaking Koga's neck. A month later the practically intact Zero was found, and American engineers designed a fighter to send up against it—the F6F Hellcat.

could outclimb and outdive the Zero and was heavily armed. The pilot was protected by heavy armor plating behind, and a thick, bulletproof wind shield ahead. "I love this airplane so much," said one Navy pilot, "that if it could cook I'd marry it".

The pilots themselves were better prepared then their predecessors. Each had at least two years' training and over 300 flying hours, whereas their antagonists were faint copies of those who had fought at Pearl Harbor and Midway. They had six months' training at the most and many had logged few hours in the air. And they were called upon to fly a somewhat improved version of the Zero of Pearl Harbor days that was now so outclassed.

On the afternoon of June 18 one of Ozawa's search planes discovered "an enemy force, including an unknown number of carriers" west of Saipan. Forty miles away from this first sighting another search plane reported "unknown number of carriers, plus ten other ships."

This was Spruance's striking power, Task Force 58, commanded by Vice Admiral Marc Mitscher, who had skippered *Hornet* in the Doolittle raid and the Battle of Midway. He was small, taciturn, hard-bitten. Usually he sat at the after end of his flag bridge in a steel armchair facing the stern, his bald head covered by a duck-billed lobster-man's hat. His was a formidable aggregation, almost twice the size of the Mobile Fleet: seven big carriers, eight light ones, seven battleships, eight heavy cruisers, thirteen light cruisers and sixty-nine destroyers.

Rear Admiral Sueo Obayashi, commander of the three Japanese carriers nearest Mitscher, was tempted to attack at once. The basic principle of air battle was to strike first. After informing Ozawa, he ordered an immediate assault.

Some of his planes were in the air before a message arived from Ozawa requesting all ships to retire and prepare for a massive aerial battle the next morning. Obayashi recovered his planes. "Let's do it properly tomorrow," he told his staff, but privately he feared that such a "golden opportunity" would not present itself again.

It is interesting, and sad, to note that two years had gone by since Colonel Claire Chennault furnished the War Department with complete details of the Zero, along with suggestions for greater maneuverability of the P-40 against the swift Japanese plane—all of which was filed and forgotten. Many an American pilot's life would surely have been saved in the intervening time, as was later indicated by the Hellcat's superiority over the Zero.

Mitscher still had no warning that the Mobile Fleet was approaching. He had been cautioned by Spruance not to sortie in search of the enemy—the main assignment of Task Force 58 was to "cover" Saipan—but when direction-finding apparatus detected Ozawa in the area he told his chief of staff, Captain Arleigh Burke, "It might be a hell of a battle for a while, but I think we can win it," and asked permission by voice radio just before midnight to "come to a westerly course at oh-one-thirty in order to commence treatment of the enemy at oh-five-hundred."

Like Mitscher, Spruance wanted to destroy Ozawa's carriers, yet was bound by definite orders to "capture, occupy and defend Saipan, Tinian and Guam." Allowing Mitscher to be lured away from the Marianas, therefore, would be too much of a "gamble"; he remembered, moreover, how Admiral Togo had waited at Tsushima Strait for the Imperial Russian Fleet to come to him ("We had somewhat the same situation"), and he answered: "Change proposed does not appear advisable.... End run by other [enemy] carrier groups remains possibility and must not be overlooked."

At four-forty-five on June 19 Ozawa again launched search planes, but it was a cloudy, squally morning and it wasn't until seven-thirty that Task Force 58 was finally discovered southwest of Saipan. On the bridge of the flagship—the newly commissioned 33,000-ton 800-foot-long carrier *Taiho*—there was no doubt that this would be a historic day for the Imperial Navy, perhaps another Tsushima. Before the first wave of seventy-one planes took off, flight leaders reported to the bridge vowing to avenge the shame of Midway.

Twenty-six minutes later the second wave—128 planes—lifted from the decks. A dive-bomber pilot, Warrant Officer Akio Komatsu, noticed a torpedo (it had come from the U. S. submarine *Albacore*) plowing directly at *Taiho*. Without hesitation he rammed his stick to the side and forward, and his bomber arced in a suicide dive at the running torpedo. His plane intercepted it a hundred yards short of the carrier. From the bridge Ozawa and his staff watched as plane and torpedo were both destroyed in one thundering geyser. Then they saw the track of another "fish." The big carrier began a turn but the second torpedo smashed into her starboard side. The damage seemed of slight consequence. What could a single hit do to a ship that was "unsinkable"?

Aboard *Oyodo*, the flagship of the Combined Fleet, which

was just weighing anchor at Yokosuka harbor, Vice Admiral Kusaka was not as confident of the day as Ozawa. He had reservations about the Mobile Fleet's long-range attack; it was like a boxer reaching too far out. But he became infected by the optimism around him—the staff gave Ozawa four out of five chances for victory. He started to call his steward to prepare *sake* cups for a celebration, but decided not to tempt fate; he could wait until the first wave had contact with the enemy. Two hours passed without a report. Confidence on the bridge was replaced by uneasiness and then doubt. At last a message arrived: *Taiho* had been "somewhat damaged." Toyoda was silent but the staff exchanged perturbed looks; Kusaka had a sickening premonition that worse news was coming.

At ten o'clock American radar picked up Ozawa's first wave. Mitscher personally sounded the alarm over the radio with a "Hey, Rube!"—the signal for all Hellcats to return to their ships and prepare for battle. By the time the raiders were within seventy-two miles of his flagship, the new *Lexington*, fighters began taking off from her flight deck. The first to see the enemy was Lieutenant Commander C. W. Brewer. He rolled over, and followed by his eleven men, streaked toward the enemy. He blew up a Japanese bomber, blasted the wing off another, then shook off a Zero and set it afire—and moments later gunned down another.

Now Hellcats from three other carriers joined the fight. They viciously ripped into the oncoming Japanese formation, sending at least twenty-five spinning into the sea. The rest pressed on toward the carriers—but encountered a second wave of Hellcats. Sixteen more tumbled down. A single Japanese penetrated the defense line to hit the battleship *South Dakota*.

The second wave was sixty miles from target when a dozen Hellcats from *Essex* swept in on them. Fighters from other carriers quickly closed in and in a few minutes had shot down almost seventy planes. Ozawa's third wave, forty-seven planes, was given the wrong co-ordinates and only twelve were diverted in time to the battle area. Seven of these were shot down. The eighty-four planes of the fourth wave were also misdirected. Six finally reached the carriers but did no damage. The main group, after a futile search for American carriers, jettisoned their bombs and headed for Guam. As they were making their final approach on Orote Field, twenty-seven Hellcats on the prowl hurtled down and destroyed thirty planes—those that landed were so badly shot up that they could not be repaired. In a few hours Ozawa had lost 346 planes while shooting down 15. Japanese naval air power had been crippled, and permanently.

Although not a single American bomb or torpedo had been launched against the Mobile Fleet, it too had been dealt a devastating blow. Just before noon the skipper of the submarine *Cavalla,* Commander Herman J. Kessler, raised his periscope to behold a picture "too good to be true": *Shokaku*—a veteran of Pearl Harbor, Coral Sea and Santa Cruz—was recovering planes. But Kessler couldn't make out what kind of flag she was flying; it might be an American ship. He took another look: *God damn! there was the Rising Sun, big as hell.* He moved in and at 1,000 yards loosed a spread of six torpedoes. Three hit, setting off a series of internal detonations. Flames enveloped the carrier. As her bow settled, water poured through the No. 1 elevator into the hangar. She turned over heavily and sank just after three o'clock.

Taiho, hit by the single torpedo from *Albacore* at the beginning of the battle, had inadvertently become a floating bomb; a damage-control officer had ordered all ventilating ducts opened on the theory that this would clear gasoline fumes. Instead, his action caused the vapors to permeate the ship. Half an hour after *Shokaku* went down, a shuddering explosion wracked *Taiho.* From her bridge the senior staff officer, Captain Toshikazu Ohmae, saw the armored flight deck suddenly "blossom up like Mount Fuji." The hull on the hangar level blew out and the carrier began to settle rapidly.

Ozawa wanted to stay with the ship. He would listen to no one until Ohmae, who had been his close subordinate for years, said, "The battle is still going on and you should remain in command for the final victory." Ozawa silently followed his senior staff officer into a cutter. Fifteen minutes after they had transferred to a cruiser there was a second thunderous detonation. *Taiho* tilted sharply to port and slid into the water stern first.

At Combined Fleet headquarters, aboard *Oyodo,* there was no longer any doubt that A-Go had failed. The staff debated whether the Mobile Fleet should be ordered to fall back at once. Kusaka didn't think the decision should be left up to Ozawa. From personal experience at Midway he knew how difficult it was for a commander to retire on his own from a losing battle. He got Toyoda's approval to dispatch an order to withdraw.

Ozawa had already pulled back to the northwest under cover of darkness to refuel in order to resume the battle the next morning. His opponent, Mitscher, had recovered his planes, and with Spruance's concurrence, started after the Mobile Fleet with three of his four carrier groups. But he headed southwest, the wrong direction, and it wasn't until three-forty the following afternoon that a search plane finally located Ozawa some 275 miles away. Though dusk would fall in a few hours, Mitscher decided to gamble: the target was barely within range of his planes; they would have to strike in the fading light of day; and, finally, try to find their way home in darkness. He turned Task Force 58 into the wind and launched 216 planes. The sun was low as the attacker sighted half a dozen enemy oilers. A few planes peeled off and sank two of these ships while the rest, with orders to concentrate on carriers, fanned out to the northwest.

The clouds above the Mobile Fleet were brilliantly colored in the sunset. Ozawa managed to get seventy-five planes into the air, and these, with the help of antiaircraft fire, knocked down twenty Americans but the others broke through the screen. Bombers hit Ozawa's new flagship, *Zuikàku* (sister ship of *Shokaku*), the light carrier *Chiyoda*, a battleship and a cruiser, but inflicted no serious damage.

Then four torpedo planes from *Belleau Wood* dropped out of the clouds and swept in low on another carrier, *Hiyo*. They were led by Lieutenant (j.g.) George Brown, who had vowed at takeoff to get a carrier no matter what. His plane was set on fire but he came in relentlessly and dropped his torpedo.

At his machine gun in the stern of *Hiyo*, Chief Petty Officer Mitsukuni Oshita heard the cry "Torpedo coming!" He began to count. At 12 he knew the torpedo had missed, and relaxed. An explosion jarred *Hiyo*. Oshita had counted too fast.

A second torpedo rocked the carrier. Fires spread from deck to deck and all power went off. Dead in the water, she began listing to port and the word went out to abandon ship. At the extreme stern, Oshita and a dozen others heard nothing and refused to leave *Hiyo* without a definite order. The ship settled rapidly. Water gurgled up to Oshita's machine gun and he, along with his comrades, started for the rail.

"Wait!" Their commander, a young ensign, drew his sword threateningly. "Sing 'Umi-Yukaba'!" They hurried through the traditional song, but the ensign continued to restrain them with his sword. "Now sing 'the Naval March,'" he ordered. The cowed men sang until the water reached their knees, then broke past the officer and over the side.

Oshita looked back. Fire belched out of the carrier. Spotlighted in the red glare, the ensign clung to the stern rail, sword in hand, still singing. He disappeared as the great bow reared high, and Oshita had to swim desperately to avoid the suction. "The ship is going down!" someone shouted. Oshita turned around. *Hiyo* was sticking up like the finger of a giant. She plunged out of sight with a "horrible sigh" as if, thought Oshita, she were saying, "This is the end."

The long trip home for Mitscher's fliers had turned into a nightmare. Pilot after pilot reported he was running out of gas. "I'm going in while I've still got power. So long," called one. "Where's somebody? I'm lost," radioed a second. Sending out these men had been a daring decision and Mitscher now made another. He ordered the lights on his carriers turned on even though it made them glaring targets for prowling submarines. "The effect on the pilots left behind was magnetic," Lieutenant Commander Robert Winston recalled. "They stood open-mouthed for the sheer audacity of asking the Japs to come and get us. Then a spontaneous cheer went up. To hell with the Japs around us. Our pilots were not to be expendable." Fortunately for the Americans, there were no enemy submarines in the area, and all but thirty-eight of the returning pilots were saved.

The battle was over. Officially it would be known as the Battle of the Philippine Sea, but to Americans who were there it would always be "the Great Marianas Turkey Shoot," a name originated by Commander Paul Buie of *Lexington*. They had sunk three heavy carriers and destroyed 92 percent of Ozawa's carrier planes and 72 percent of his float planes, as well as fifty Guam-based aircraft, a total of 475 or so—at a cost of 2 oilers and 130 planes, including eighty which had splashed near or crashed on their carriers. But the victory was marred by acrid criticism of the man who had engineered it, for not pursuing Ozawa more aggressively. Admiral J. J. ("Jocko") Clark, commander of four carriers in the battle, charged that Raymond Spruance had missed "the chance of the century," and Admiral A. E. Montgomery, who led four other carriers, officially reported that the results "were extremely disappointing to all hands." At naval air headquarters in Pearl Harbor the common complaint was: "This is what comes of placing a nonaviator in command over carriers."

Spruance made no excuses. It would have been "much better and more satisfactory" to have gone after Ozawa's carriers, but he had done what Nimitz wanted—protected Saipan—and in doing so forever after changed the course of war in the Pacific.*

The night after the battle Ozawa dictated a letter of resignation to Admiral Toyoda but the commander in chief of Combined Fleet refused even to read the letter. "I am more responsible for this defeat than Admiral Ozawa," he said, "and I will not accept his resignation."

Admiral Ugaki marked the occasion with another *haiku*:

> *The battle is ended*
> *but the gloomy sky of the rainy season*
> *remains over us.*

2.

The crushing defeat at sea doomed the defenders of Saipan. On the day *Shokaku* and *Taiho* went down, the commander of all American troops on Saipan, Marine General Holland Smith, readied his troops for a final drive up the island. His men had already suffered heavy casualties, particularly from night mortar fire. Marine Captain John A. Magruder watched medics tenderly load corpses into a truck and approached to see if there was anyone he knew. He recognized a youthful, fair-haired replacement and remembered how exuberant he had been upon arrival at the front. A yellow paperback book stuck out of his back pocket—*Our Hearts Were Young and Gay*.

On June 22 two Marine divisions started the offensive to the north while the Army division, the 27th, mopped up the remaining Japanese cut off in the extreme south. The Marine lines were so extended, however, that Smith ordered the 27th Division to take over the center, and the next morning the

---

*When Admiral King landed at Aslito Field shortly after Saipan was secured, his first act was to assure Spruance that he had "done exactly the correct thing with the Fifth Fleet in the Battle of the Philippine Sea, no matter what anyone else might say, especially since he had to remember that the Japanese had another fleet ready in the Inland Sea to pounce upon"—the numerous transports and supply ships that were not yet unloaded.

GI's started up the wooded valley running just east of Mount Tapotchau. It was a narrow gulch not a thousand yards wide, and the remnants of the 136th Regiment of Saito's division looked down on them from cliffs and precipitous hills honeycombed with caves. The GI's, commanded by Major General Ralph Smith, advanced cautiously throughout the day to the annoyance of Holland Smith—his nickname was "Howlin' Mad." He complained to Major General Sanderford Jarman, the senior Army officer on the island, that "if it was not an Army division, and there would be a great cry set up more or less of a political nature," he'd relieve the other Smith on the spot. The leadership of the 27th, he was convinced, stemmed largely "from a gentlemen's club known as the Seventh Regiment, traditionally New York's 'silk stocking' outfit, and likewise a worthy unit, *per se*, with an impeccable reputation for annual balls, banquets and shipshape summer camps."

Ralph Smith acknowledged that his division "was not carrying its full share" and that he was "in no way satisfied with what his regimental commanders had done during the day." He promised Jarman to "personally see to it that the division went forward." Even Smith's presence at the front the following morning did little to move the Army troops up the gorge, which was already known as "Death Valley."

"Howlin' Mad" conferred with Admiral Richmond Turner ("Terrible Turner"), and the two went out to see Spruance on *Indianapolis*. "Ralph Smith has shown that he lacks aggressive spirit," said Smith, "and his division is slowing down our advance. He should be relieved." He suggested that Jarman take over the 27th until another commander was appointed, and Spruance concurred.*

---

*Even before the battle subsided, Lieutenant General Robert C. Richardson, commanding general of all Army forces in the Pacific Ocean Areas, had appointed an all-Army board to investigate the case. It concluded that Holland Smith had authority to relieve Ralph Smith but that the Marine general "was not fully informed regarding conditions in the zone of the 27th Infantry Division" and the relief of the Army Smith "was not justified by the facts."

In Washington, Marshall's deputy, Major General Thomas T. Handy, while admitting that there was some justification for criticizing the GI's for lack of aggressiveness in Death Valley, reported that "Holland Smith's fitness for this command is open to question" because of prejudice against Army personnel and that "bad blood had developed between the Marines and the Army on Saipan" to a dangerous degree. "In my opinion, it would be desirable that both Smiths be ordered out of the Pacific Ocean Area."

A few days after the battle Richardson inflamed more tempers by flying to Saipan to pass out decorations to Army troops without

But a change of commanders made no perceptible difference, and the progress up Death Valley remained painfully slow. The Marines on the right were also stalled, but the 2nd Marine Division on the left fought its way to the top of Mount Tapotchau where the rest of hilly Saipan stretched out to the north like some quiescent monster.

This rugged terrain was about all that stood between the Americans and victory. By nightfall of June 25 there were less than twelve hundred able-bodied men and three tanks left of all Japanese Army front-line units, and General Igeta of the 31st Army was compelled to radio his commander in Guam that Saipan could not be held.

THE FIGHT ON SAIPAN AS THINGS STAND NOW IS PROGRESSING ONE-SIDEDLY, SINCE ALONG WITH THE TREMENDOUS POWER OF HIS BARRAGES, THE ENEMY HOLDS CONTROL OF SEA AND AIR. IN DAYTIME EVEN THE DEPLOYMENT OF UNITS IS VERY DIFFICULT, AND AT NIGHT THE ENEMY CAN MAKE OUT OUR MOVEMENTS WITH EASE BY USING ILLUMINATION SHELLS. MOREOVER, OUR COMMUNICATIONS ARE BECOMING DISRUPTED, AND LIAISON IS BECOMING INCREASINGLY DIFFICULT. DUE TO OUR SERIOUS LACK OF WEAPONS AND EQUIPMENT, ACTIVITY AND CONTROL ARE HINDERED CONSIDERABLY. MOREOVER, WE ARE MENACED BY BRAZENLY LOW-FLYING PLANES, AND THE ENEMY BLASTS AT US FROM ALL SIDES WITH FIERCE NAVAL AND ARTILLERY CROSS FIRE. AS A RESULT, EVEN IF WE REMOVE UNITS FROM THE FRONT LINES AND SEND THEM TO THE REAR, THEIR FIGHTING STRENGTH IS CUT DOWN EVERY DAY. ALSO, THE ENEMY ATTACKS WITH FIERCE CONCENTRATION OF BOMBS AND ARTILLERY. STEP BY STEP HE COMES TOWARD US AND CONCENTRATES HIS FIRE ON US AS WE WITHDRAW, SO THAT WHEREVER WE GO WE ARE QUICKLY SURROUNDED BY FIRE.

---

consulting Nimitz and without approval of Holland Smith. He also reportedly told the Marine commander, "I want you to know you cannot push the Army around the way you have been doing." This was resented not only by Holland Smith but by Spruance and Turner, who vigorously complained to Nimitz of Richardson's "high-handed and irregular actions."

The feud between the two services was taken up by the press. The San Francisco *Examiner*, a Hearst paper, charged that Marine casualties in places like Saipan were excessive, far greater than MacArthur's, and concluded that "the supreme command in the Pacific should, of course, be logically and efficiently entrusted" to him. *Time* and *Life*, Henry Luce's two influential magazines, retaliated with a vigorous defense of Holland Smith, *Time* asserting that "when field commanders hesitate to remove subordinates for fear of interservice contention, battles and lives will be needlessly lost."

But there would be no surrender.

> ... THE POSITIONS ARE TO BE DEFENDED TO THE BITTER END, AND UNLESS HE HAS OTHER ORDERS, EVERY SOLDIER MUST STAND HIS GROUND.

General Saito's report to Tokyo was more emotional:

> ... PLEASE APOLOGIZE DEEPLY TO THE EMPEROR THAT WE CANNOT DO BETTER THAN WE ARE DOING. . . . THERE IS NO HOPE FOR VICTORY IN PLACES WHERE WE DO NOT HAVE CONTROL OF THE AIR AND WE ARE STILL HOPING HERE FOR AERIAL REINFORCEMENTS. . . . PRAYING FOR THE GOOD HEALTH OF THE EMPEROR, WE ALL CRY "BAN-ZAI!"

3.

For Tojo the collapse of Saipan was a political as well as military reverse—a direct threat to his position as prime minister. His popularity had waned as the war situation worsened. Criticism, most of it covert, came from all sides. Prince Chichibu referred to him as "Emperor Tojo." Signs in some Navy offices read: KILL TOJO AND SHIMADA! OUR IMPERIAL COMBINED FLEET IS NOW POWERLESS. PREPARE AT ONCE TO RE-FORM THE CABINET SO WE CAN SEEK PEACE. Among Army intellectuals he was known as *"Jotohei"* ("superior private," the rank above Pfc.) and his administration was labeled "government-by-privates."

Substance was given to this name-calling by the findings of an investigation just concluded by the Army General Staff's own Conduct of War Section. Its chief, Colonel Sei Matsutani, reported that after an exhaustive study by himself, Colonel Sako Tanemura and a major named Hashimoto, there was "now no hope for Japan to reverse the unfavorable war situation. The state of Germany today is about the same as Japan's and grows gradually worse. It is time for us to end the war."

Matsutani took his report to two influential members on the General Staff. The first admitted the validity of the conclusions but forbade Matsutani to release them. The second, equally impressed, refused to allow the colonel to present his case to the Prime Minister. But Matsutani could not be intimidated and brought his findings to Tojo. The colonel expected Tojo to react violently, but he listened quietly, passively. His "sour" face, however, belied his polite demeanor, and within a week the outspoken Matsutani was transferred to China.*

On Saipan General Saito, following orders from 31st Army, once more moved his headquarters, this time to a small cave a mile north of Mount Tapotchau. On June 28 all the military leaders—Nagumo, Saito and Igeta—held a joint staff meeting. Igeta took charge. Except for the former public relations officer, Major Hirakushi, Saito's staff had few suggestions to offer. They crouched listlessly on their haunches; one or two tried to sleep. Saito and Nagumo sat in silence as Igeta outlined a final line of resistance two thirds of the way up the island. They would dig in, from Tanapag in the west to the opposite coast.

There was little reaction. Wearily Saito said that the proposal sounded "all right" to him, and a Navy commander, speaking for Nagumo, said, "We leave it to the Army." The question remained as to how to do it. The troops were dispersed across the northern half of Saipan; there were few lines of communication. Able-bodied men were selected to contact all units. Major Hirakushi set out for Mount Donnay to assemble the remnants of the 136th Regiment. The only soldiers he could find in the area were at the field hospital. He called out for men of the regiment; no one came forward. He reported back to Saito that he could find no troops to build the eastern section of the final line.

Igeta said nothing.

Shizuko had lost all concept of time. On one of her daily visits to Lieutenant Shinoda, a comrade lying nearby began to berate her: "Why didn't you come and see him last night?

---

*In China, Matsutani replaced an even more outspoken colonel, Tsuji, who had just been shipped out to Burma. (His forthright views on Guadalcanal had undoubtedly made him *persona non grata* in Tokyo.) Matsutani never believed there was any connection between his audience with Tojo and his sudden transfer. He had held the China post two years previously and was well qualified for the job.

On the other hand, Colonel Tanemura, who helped with the controversial report and replaced Matsutani as chief of the section, wrote in his "Imperial Headquarters [Army] Diary" on July 3, 1944: "The reason for his transfer is not clear. However, it is believed that his recent outside activities to bring about termination of the war have somehow reached the ears of his superiors, and roused their rage."

Poor Lieutenant Shinoda called for you all through the night and died just an hour ago."

She crouched beside Shinoda's body. There wasn't a maggot on his face. He looked "pale and beautiful." She picked up the photograph of his round-faced wife.

"Couldn't you hear him calling you?" another soldier said in an accusing voice. She couldn't answer. All through the night she had heard voices continuously calling "Nurse!" but it was like "hearing cicadas singing." It was impossible to answer each call.

Yet—she should have recognized Shinoda's urgent voice. She reported his death to one of the medics, who said, "Poor fellow, he had so many maggots that the other patients kicked him until he found this corner off by himself."

Her routine had become a mélange of horrors: the crude toilet filling up with maggots; the dead bodies that rotted and gave off a ghastly phosphorescence at night; the piteous groans and cries of patients; the air raids; the shells shrieking overhead. She had to forget she was a woman in the presence of men stripped naked; she had to forget she was a human being as she amputated arms and legs with a surgical saw and then sewed up the ragged flesh. There was no more anesthesia for operations, and patients would scream until they fainted. The fortunate ones remained unconscious until the operation was over.

In the past few months Prince Konoye had become the confederate of a score of military as well as civilian leaders—among them General Koji Sakai of the General Staff and Admiral Okada—who were disturbed by the course of the war and Tojo's leadership. General Sakai made a clandestine visit to Konoye's suburban home. "To be on the safe side" the general wore civilian clothes. "If Tojo learns what I am about to tell you, I'm sure he will retaliate," he warned. He wanted to impress Konoye that the war should be ended quickly. "Germany still has defensive power, and while the enemy has to fight in both east and west we should take advantage of the situation and enter into negotiations for peace. It will not be to our advantage to wait until Germany is defeated." Tojo could not possibly negotiate such a peace. A new cabinet must be formed.

General Sakai was one of the few liberals in the Army, and Konoye wondered if the Army leadership "could be persuaded to follow this policy."

"At present they don't speak openly but they all think as I

do," the general replied. Matsutani's report had been circulated secretly and a number of Army leaders wanted the Throne informed of its findings.

And after that, what? Konoye wanted to know. How should the Emperor face Tojo with the matter?

"His Majesty should say, 'Despite all efforts by our Army and Navy, the enemy has succeeded in landing on Saipan. What do you think of future operations, Tojo?' He should then ask how they were to meet the requirements of the Army and Navy regarding munitions, planes, ships and oil; about protecting the population from air raids; and what should be done to repel enemy offensives." General Sakai acknowledged that Tojo could answer these questions in several ways—but hoped they would force him "to resign at once."

4.

On June 30 the GI's finally broke through Death Valley ("No one had any tougher job to do," observed Major General Harry Schmidt, commander of the 4th Marine Division), and the entire three-division front was at last connected.

At the Donnay field hospital, a "dying game" order was received. Medics distributed grenades, one for each eight men. The chief surgeon—the captain—climbed up to a little rise at dusk and shouted that "by order of the high command," the field hospital was transferred to a village on the west coast a mile and a half above Tanapag and four miles from the northern tip of Saipan. The vast arena was silent. "All ambulatory patients will accompany me. But to my great sorrow, I must abandon you comrades who cannot walk. Men, die an honorable death as Japanese soldiers."

Shizuko told the captain, "I'm going to stay and kill myself with my patients!"

"You will join us," he said. "That is an order."

All the soldiers wanted to say good-bye and crowded around her. Even those who couldn't walk crawled nearer. There was no need to draw words from them. There was only one subject—home. Each man tried to tell her something about his family. She promised over and over to tell what had happened if she got back to Japan.

One whose jaw had been shot away got her attention. Slavering, he weakly scrawled "Chiba-ken" in the dirt, and then "Takeda." "I understand," she said. "You come from Chiba prefecture and your name is Takeda."

A young officer, his uniform dyed with blood, forced out a few painful words. "You know . . . the song . . . of Kudanzaka?"

"Yes, I like it very much." It was a haunting song about an aged mother from the country taking her dead son's medal to the Yasukuni Shrine in Kudanzaka. She began to sing:

> *"From Ueno Station to Kudanzaka*
> *I get impatient, not knowing my way around.*
> *It has taken me all day, leaning on my cane,*
> *To come and see you, my son, at Kudanzaka.*
>
> *The great* torii [gate] *looming up in the sky*
> *Leads to a magnificent shrine*
> *That enrolls my son among the gods.*
> *Your unworthy mother weeps in her joy.*
>
> *I was a black hen who gave birth to a hawk.*
> *And such good fortune is more than I deserve.*
> *I wanted to show you your Order of the Golden Kite,*
> *And have come to see you, my son, at Kudanzaka."*

She stopped. There was silence except for stifled sobs. "We, too, will go to Yasukuni Shrine!" the young officer exclaimed.

Others joined in: "Let us all go to Yasukuni Shrine together!"

The captain started to lead Shizuko away, along with three hundred patients. Voices followed them: "Thank you, nurse"; "Good-bye, nurse"; "Commander . . . Sergeant . . . nurse . . . thank you all for your kindness."

They reached the end of the field. Shizuko heard a voice cry out, "Good-bye, Mother!" There was a sharp blast—a grenade. She crouched on the ground and flinched as one grenade after another exploded in rapid succession.

The American advance up the island, which begun so laboriously, was now almost unopposed. It had become, as one Marine put it, a "rabbit hunt." This constant pressure had prevented the Japanese from forming their final defensive line across the island, and by July 5 they had been herded into the northern quarter of Saipan.

Japanese headquarters was now on a ridge facing the west coast, a few hundred yards from the new field hospital. The cave overlooked a gulch, already nicknamed "the Valley of Hell." That afternoon Major Hirakushi left the cave to inspect the front lines. They were nonexistent. The men had already retreated on their own before the American drive. Hirakushi's report was greeted by an incredulous silence. Finally General Igeta said, "Tomorrow morning we will begin assembling all remaining troops in the area for the final attack. Let us end this battle."

That evening the headquarters group ate the last of their food—a single can of crab meat and a small rice ball apiece. Hirakushi had been saving two cigarettes which Prince Kaya gave him in Japan as a memento. They were passed from man to man, smoked until they were too small to hold. Hirakushi asked if Igeta and Saito would participate in the final assault. Admiral Nagumo, who had said almost nothing during the long retreat, answered for them: "We three will commit suicide."

Hirakushi wanted to know what would happen to the thousands of civilians who shared the caves with the soldiers and sailors. "There is no longer any distinction between civilians and troops," Saito replied. "It would be better for them to join in the attack with bamboo spears than be captured.* Write out instructions to that effect."

Three hundred sets of Saito's order were mimeographed, but before they could be distributed a messenger arrived from the naval communications cave located several miles to the north. Tokyo ordered the defenders to continue the battle "to gain time"; there was a promise of reinforcements.

The Navy staff officers accepted the order, but the Army would not abandon the last assault. "The arrow has been shot," said one Army man. Another accused the Navy of cowardice. The Navy said it was no time to call names; the Army was disobeying a direct order from Imperial Headquarters.

Nagumo, Igeta and Saito took no part in the argument,

---

*Government propaganda in Japan, portraying Americans and British as "devils," was both widespread and effective. One observer noted in his diary: "I rode a train with a volunteer corps the other day. Their leader lectured, 'Churchill and Roosevelt formed what they called the Atlantic Charter and agreed to kill all Japanese. They made a statement they would kill men and women. We won't let them kill us!' It seems the public believes that the enemy are going to remove the testicles of the Japanese so that they won't have children, or that they will be sent to secluded islands."

which lasted through the night. At dawn, July 6, the shelling and bombing resumed, and a sentry at the mouth of the cave reported that an enemy tank was "peering over" the edge of the cliff above.

Saito, who had been quietly conferring with Nagumo and Igeta, beckoned to Hirakushi. He said the three of them had decided to die at ten o'clock. "Excuse us for going first."

"Do you plan to do it here?"

"Yes, here."

Hirakushi said it would be better to commit suicide privately in a smaller cave nearby. The major left to prepare the new cave while Saito read aloud a farewell message that he wanted conveyed to all Army troops:

"... Our comrades have fallen one after another. Despite the bitterness of defeat, we pledge, 'Seven lives to repay our country.'
... Whether we attack or whether we stay where we are, there is only death. However, in death there is life. We must utilize this opportunity to exalt true Japanese manhood. I will advance with those who remain to deliver still another blow to the American devils, and leave my bones on Saipan as a bulwark of the Pacific.

As it says in the *Senjinkun* [Battle Ethics]: 'I will never suffer the disgrace of being taken alive,' and 'I will offer up the courage of my soul and calmly rejoice in living by the eternal principle.'

Here I pray with you for the eternal life of the Emperor and the welfare of the country and I advance to seek out the enemy.

Follow me."

Hirakushi led the three commanders to the new cave. "What means are you going to use?" he asked.

"We will go through the first step of *seppuku* [cutting open the stomach]," said Saito. "But *seppuku* will take too long, so have an officer stand behind each of us and shoot us in the back of the head." Saito selected Hirakushi. Nagumo requested a naval officer; Igeta didn't express any preference.

Hirakushi returned to the main cave and asked for someone from the Navy to "assist Admiral Nagumo with his suicide." No one answered. Finally a young Army aide said, "Let me do the job." Another Army aide volunteered to shoot Igeta, and the three started back to the suicide cave.

The commanders, all wearing khaki fatigue uniforms, were sitting cross-legged near the mouth of the cave with the diminutive Nagumo in the middle. Hirakushi turned to find some water to wash their faces when he heard a Navy officer call out that his group was heading north alone. Hirakushi started around. The three commanders were lying sprawled on the ground. Behind the bodies stood the two young aides, smoking pistols in hand. The commanders, impatient, had gone ahead without him.

All Hirakushi could do now was burn the bodies and regimental flags. He rounded up men to help, but other officers stopped him—smoke would attract the enemy. Hirakushi agreed to wait until after midnight, just before launching the last attack. The ordeal of the past few days finally took its toll. He collapsed on the floor of the command cave into deep sleep.

It was dark when he woke up. Soldiers and sailors in nondescript uniforms, and armed with rifles, swords and bamboo spears, were assembling outside. They were haphazardly divided into groups and in the moonlight officers began to shepherd them toward the beach. All along the ridge men were filtering down to the narrow coastal plain. At zero hour they would charge independently toward American positions around Tanapag. To Hirakushi the men looked like "spiritless sheep being led to the slaughter," and the officers "guides to the Gates of Hell." Before he left, the major ordered two men to burn the regimental flags and the bodies of the three commanders, then silently led his group, a dozen men, down the steep slope.

More than three thousand Japanese—including civilians like Shizuko's brother-in-law—emerged onto the coastal plain. They left the slope behind littered with thousands upon thousands of empty *sake* and beer bottles.*

Hirakushi and his men reached the shore at four o'clock in the morning on July 7. He stripped and waded into the tepid water to bathe. Rapt, he stared out at the barrier reef, a ghostly shimmering line in the moonlight. Overhead a thick cloud reminded him of a Japanese mother in quilted kimono carrying a baby on her back. As the cloud pulled apart, he conjured up in the lightening sky images of his mother, his wife, his friends. He shook himself free of his fantasy and returned to shore to dress. It felt good to be clean. He was ready to die.

Distant voices were shouting *"Wah! Wah!"*—a Japanese battle cry. There was a crackle of rifle fire from the ridge. The signal to attack! Without waiting for him, his men took off headlong down the beach toward Tanapag. Pistol in one hand (a Taisho with a clip of six shells) and sword in the other, he started after them. He was enveloped by an ex-

---

*Twenty-five years later they still covered the ridge.

plosion and felt as if he were floating right into a huge column of bursting fire. I'm dead, he thought just before the world went black.

At Tanapag the 27th Division had been warned by Holland Smith to expect "an all-out *banzai* attack" along the coast before dawn.* The Japenese swarmed on Tanapag. In the lead half a dozen men held aloft a great red flag, like the vanguard in a dramatic pageant. Behind pressed the fighting troops and then—the most incredible sight of all—hundreds of men with bandaged heads, on crutches, scarcely armed, limping and hobbling.

They swept down the narrow tracks of the sugar-cane railway that skirted the beach and smashed against the 1st and 2nd battalions of the 105th Infantry Regiment like a human tidal wave. It reminded the commander of the 2nd Battalion, Major Edward McCarthy, of a "stampede staged in the old Wild West movies." The Japanese "just kept coming and didn't stop. If you shot one, five more would take his place." They "ran right over" the Americans.

The commander of the 1st Battalion, another Irishman, Lieutenant Colonel William J. O'Brien, stood his ground, an example to his men, a pistol in each hand. Seriously wounded, he fired until his clips were empty, then manned a .50-caliber machine gun until he was killed. The Japanese surged over the two steadfast battalions of GI's (the same ones accused of advancing too slowly up Death Valley), killing or wounding more than 650 of them.

To their right another group of raiders funneled through a winding canyon—soon to be known as "Hara-kiri Gulch"—and hit the 3rd Battalion but these troops were too well emplaced above the gulch and could not be dislodged.

Yeoman Noda, who had served both Yamamoto and Nagumo to the end, was with the large group that overran the Americans on the beach. Shrieking and frenzied, this was hardly a military formation. Suddenly Noda felt as if he had been clouted in the hip with a baseball bat—but there was no pain. He staggered, tried to keep moving but fell—he had been hit by a machine-gun slug. American bodies lay on all sides.** Noda picked up a GI canteen and drank deeply. He tried to struggle to his feet but his right shoe was like lead.

---

*The term *"banzai"* attack was never used by the Japanese.

**Sherrod inspected the scene a few hours later. "The whole area seemed to be a mass of dead bodies, stinking guts and brains."

Unable to bend forward to unlace the shoe, he found an American bayonet and wrenched a stick from the grasp of a dead Japanese. He tied the bayonet to the stick and laboriously hacked at his shoelaces until he could push off the shoe. He still couldn't stand and decided his trouser legs were holding him back. He cut them off but remained as helpless as ever.

He sank back on the sand, resigned. Now the time has come to die, he told himself. In the light of dawn he saw a pool of blood in the sand. To his amazement—his own blood. A few yards away four wounded Japanese were lying on their backs, smoking calmly, as if it were a beach in Japan.

"We're about to die," one of them observed casually and flipped Noda a pack of Hikaris. Noda stretched out on the sand, smoking the cigarette, his mind a blank. He was roused by the soldier who had given him the cigarettes. "Hey, Navy man," he said, "we are about to die. Will you join us?"

Noda held up a grenade. "I have one."

"Excuse us for preceding you."

Noda huddled to avoid grenade shrapnel and shut his eyes. There was a detonation. He looked up and saw four sprawled bodies. How terrible to die by grenade, he thought and was again attracted by the stream of blood flowing from his own body. He considered a tourniquet but changed his mind. It would be better to bleed to death.

He was growing weaker. *I'm only twenty-seven and why should I die here? Whether I live or die won't bring about Japanese victory.* He began remembering things in the past— his school days, catching *dojo* (mudfish). He fainted. The next thing he heard was the chirping of a bird. The landscape was devastated, not a palm tree or bush. Only bodies and ugly craters of sand. If there was no tree, how could it be a bird? What was happening?

There was a mutter of voices speaking a strange language. He felt a kick in the side. He groaned and two Marine corpsmen loaded him onto a stretcher. He saw medics kicking other bodies, Americans as well as Japanese, and just before passing out again he congratulated himself: *If I hadn't been wakened by that bird I would be dead.*

Ahead in Tanapag, Major McCarthy and his surviving officers and noncoms had finally managed to form a perimeter within the village itself. All morning they were pressed slowly back in a vicious house-to-house battle until a platoon of medium tanks rumbled in. Other reinforcements arrived and by late afternoon only isolated little groups of Japanese were alive. The last attack was over.

Just offshore on a white hospital ship, Major Hirakushi was opening his left eye. All he could see was a clean white wall. *I am alive! I have a second life!* He was naked, covered with a blanket. It took some time before he realized his left hand was handcuffed to the bed and that he had been wounded in the head and shoulder. He was so exhausted that it didn't occur to him until later that he, an officer, had disgraced himself by surviving the last assault. All he could think was: *I am alive! I am alive!*

At the new field hospital in the Valley of Hell, Shizuko had crouched in her foxhole throughout the night. In the waxing daylight she noticed movement on the heights above. Dark faces peered through the undergrowth. They were Negro GI's. In her panic she imagined they were gorillas coming down the incline. So the fantastic rumor was true! Americans were using them in battle.

All around her, wounded men had emerged from their dugouts, and turning north, bowed low toward the Imperial Palace. Suddenly strange, raucous music blared from an amplifier—she had never before heard such noise. Its wild disturbing rhythm echoed throughout the entire valley (it was American jazz). The unreality of the scene robbed her of the resolve to kill herself.

The chief surgeon ordered her to give herself up by waving a white handkerchief. She hesitated; the Americans would rape her. "Save yourself!" his assistant, the lieutenant, urged her. As she stood paralyzed at the rim of the foxhole, the Negroes charged forward, lobbing grenades and shouting. All Shizuko could see were their teeth and eyes. The chief surgeon put a pistol to his throat and pulled the trigger. The lieutenant slashed his neck three times with a knife, and collapsed over Shizuko. Warm blood flowed onto her legs. She picked up a hand grenade. She felt cold. *Now I am going to die.* She tried to cry "Mother" but nothing came out. She pulled the safety pin, rapped the grenade against a rock to activate it and threw herself on top of it.

Shizuko heard voices but could not understand them. Cautiously opening her eyes, she discovered that she was in a house. She tried to rise but a young American officer said in Japanese, "You are wounded—don't move."

Shizuko couldn't believe Japanese was coming out of an enemy. Why hadn't she died? She asked for water but the young captain told her she couldn't have any. He poured something out of a can. She tried to drink it but had to spit it out. It was tomato juice and she couldn't stand the taste. He ordered her to finish it and she did. It wasn't death that terrified her, but the Americans. She asked what had happened to the men in the Valley of Hell.

"All died except you," said the officer, an interpreter. He told her that he had studied at a Japanese university and wanted to help her countrymen. "We believe in humanity, even in war." He assured her that many Japanese civilians had survived and were in an internment camp near Charan Kanoa. She didn't believe him. Everybody knew the American devils tore Japanese prisoners apart with tanks. She blurted out that she feared Americans, especially the black ones.

He laughed. "It was Negroes who saved you."

She pleaded with the captain to let her die with her compatriots, and he got permission to take her by truck to Charan Kanoa. As they drove along the coast road in the bright starlight he told her there were many bodies of civilians in the sea. He asked her if she wanted to see them. He ordered the vehicle stopped. With the help of two Negroes he carried her to a cliff. Below, floating bodies clustered the water's edge. One woman had two children lashed to her.

Almost to himself the young officer asked, "Why do Japanese kill themselves like this?" Tears flowed down his cheeks.

Just past midnight they entered Charan Kanoa. To her surprise it was bright with electric lights. Tents sprouted all over. It was a different world. The captain told her this was the camp for Japanese, but she knew it was a trick. She was going to be shot here. Then she saw Japanese children clinging to a wire fence surrounding the tent city. She insisted on getting out, though the captain argued that she should continue to the hospital. "Do you have acquaintances out there? Is that it?"

"There's my mother!" she lied.

She was lifted out of the truck on a stretcher. She insisted on walking and staggered through the gate before she fell. Many friendly hands lifted her up. She was back with her own.

On July 9 at 4:15 P.M., Admiral Turner announced that Saipan was officially secured, and attention turned to neighboring Tinian and Guam. Marines who had once glumly predicted "Golden Gate in '48" were now saying "Home

587

Alive in '45." The battle on Saipan had ended but there remained the onerous and dangerous job of mopping up several thousand stragglers who were hiding in caves. "It means," one cynical Marine commented, "that if you get shot now, you were hit in your own rear areas."

A different but equally difficult task confronted the Americans at the northern tip of the island. There thousands of civilians had gathered and were committing mass suicide rather than surrender. Interpreters and captured Japanese, using public address systems, pleaded with crowds at Marpi Point, which dropped off spectacularly more than a hundred feet to rocky shadows. The fighting was over; safety and food were waiting; the names of those who had already surrendered were read off. Still men threw their children from the cliff and jumped after them; and mothers with babies on their backs would leap into the boiling surf.

There were so many floating bodies that "naval small craft were unable to steer a course without running over them." Lieutenant Emery Cleaves of the minesweeper *Chief* saw the corpse of a nude woman, drowned while giving birth. "The baby's head had entered this world, but that was all of him." Nearby "a small boy of four of five had drowned with his arm firmly clenched around the neck of a Jap soldier; the two bodies rocked crazily in the waves."

Elsewhere on the island families remained hidden from the new conquerors day after day. The Okuyamas—father, mother and four children—found a cave. On the morning of July 17 they were sunbathing on the ledge overlooking the rugged northeast coast, when a soldier from a nearby cave shouted "Enemy!" and pointed above them to the top of the cliff. Fourteen-year-old Ryoko Okuyama, the eldest child, glanced up at four or five big red-faced Americans in camouflage uniforms. They looked so different from the much smaller Japanese soldiers.

The Japanese fired his rifle and the Americans began dropping grenades. The Okuyamas braced themselves against a depression, kicking them off the ledge, but when the missiles continued to fall, the father—a tailor—herded his family down to the bottom of the cliff to another cave. Inside they found a sergeant, an exhausted correspondent from the *Asahi Shimbun*, and an abandoned newborn baby which cried until Mrs. Okuyama picked it up. As the loud American voices came nearer and the sound of gunfire intensified, the baby began to scream. "Quiet it," the sergeant whispered. "Any way!"

Mrs. Okuyama, an attractive woman of thirty-four, tried to nurse the baby but it kept crying. In desperation she put the hem of her jacket over the baby's mouth, and finally stifled the noise. The baby was dead. The sound of machine-gun fire echoed violently in the cave. The voices were just outside. The sergeant handed Okuyama a grenade, held another himself.

Ryoko looked at her father in farewell. Pale and tense, he nodded slightly. The sergeant removed the safety pin of his grenade, so did Okuyama. "We are all going to a nice place together," the mother told four-year-old Yoshitada, the youngest child. He smiled as if it were a game. The two men struck the grenades simultaneously against rocks at their feet. As the fuses hissed, Ryoko thought in rapid succession: Am I going to be a Buddha? Do human beings really have souls? Is there really another world? She felt the cave shake—the concussion had thrown her against the rock wall. Dazed, she heard her little brother give a feeble groan, and she fainted.

She didn't know how long she had remained unconscious. First she saw a vague brightness of red, and as it came into focus she realized it was the open abdomen of the sergeant who was sitting before her, legs crossed, as if asleep. The huge wound was so neat that it reminded her of the human-body exhibit in biology class. The organs, all in place, were "beautiful."

She herself was covered with blood and raw flesh. Appalled, she moved her arms and legs—no pain. She twisted. Still not much pain. Her nine-year-old brother's shirt was blown off. Pieces of shrapnel were sticking in his bare chest, leaving black, burned spots. He was dead. So were her father, little Yoshitada and her six-year-old sister. The flesh had been blown from her sister's head, revealing a skull the color and texture of a transparent candle. Ryoko had a horrifying feeling of loneliness. She was the only one alive. Then she felt something touch her left shoulder.

"Mother, you are alive!"

"I'm dying" was the calm reply. Her mother's legs were shattered and Ryoko ripped strips from a piece of cloth nearby to make bandages.

"It won't work," Mrs. Okuyama said quietly. "I'm going to die. You can't stop the bleeding with something like that."

"But the blood isn't coming out any more!"

"It has all run out," Mrs. Okuyama said. She stared at the bodies of her family. "I'm glad they had a clean death." She turned to Ryoko. "Only you are alive."

"*Okusan, okusan* [Madame]!" It was the *Asahi* man. ~~His agonized voice was almost inaudible.~~ Mother and daughter were astonished to find that someone else had survived. "Kill me. *Okusan*, please."

"I'm dying too," Mrs. Okuyama told him. "My legs are gone. I can't even move. I can't help you."

He looked up slowly; then, writhing in agony, he slammed his head against a jagged rock. He groaned and tried again and again. Finally he was dead.

"After I die you mustn't stay here," Mrs. Okuyama said to her daughter. With darkness she was to leave. "You must live long and follow the path of righteousness with a strong mind." She had written the same words when Ryoko entered middle school.

Mrs. Okuyama painfully unwound a *furoshiki* from her waist—it was filled with money—and tied it tightly around her daughter. "Soon I'll be dead. My vision is getting blurred. I want to lie down. Will you help me?" All the while there was a soft smile on her face. For the first time Ryoko realized how gentle her mother was. How could she ever have feared her?

"My hearing is fading now. Give me your hands." She grasped Ryoko's hands. "I can't talk any more," she said faintly.

"Mother, don't die!"

Mrs. Okuyama smiled and nodded her head. Her lips moved but no sound issued. She was dead.

Almost 22,000 Japanese civilians—two out of three—perished needlessly. And almost the entire garrison—at least 30,000—died.

For the victors the battle was also the most costly to date in the Pacific. Of the 71,000 Americans who had landed on Saipan, 14,111 were killed, wounded or missing in action—more than double the losses at Guadalcanal—but the main bastion protecting Japan's homeland had been seized, and the enemy's carrier-based striking power had been crippled. Even more important, the lowlands of southern Saipan offered the Americans the first site from which massive B-29 bombing raids could be launched at the heart of the Japanese Empire, Tokyo.

PART SIX

The
Decisive Battle

21   **"Let No Heart
Be Faint"**

1.

Never before had a modern Japanese leader gathered to himself so much power. To the world Tojo's position seemed unassailable but in reality his rule was at the point of collapse. Ever since Midway, Imperial Headquarters had refused to acknowledge the growing power of America[*] and the diminishing power of Japan. Shipping losses continued to mount as the American submarine campaign intensified. To the north the Aleutian outposts had been abandoned; to the south, the Solomons and New Guinea had been overrun; and in the central Pacific the defense line—the Marshalls, the Gilberts and finally the Marianas—had collapsed.

At home, production levels were still maintained, but at the expense of extraordinary sacrifices by the people. Not only had many civilian enterprises been converted to war production and more women brought into industry, but teenagers had been added to the labor force. Classroom time was reduced to a minimum and school buildings transformed into military supply depots.

A seven-day workweek was established, with the Sundays so cherished by Japanese "abolished." Trains had become crowded to such an extent that a number of infants were suffocated; trips of more than 100 kilometers required a police permit; diners and sleepers were discontinued. The people's aggression turned on the trains when they were late, now a common occurrence; they stole seat covers and broke windows to get in and out. Consumer goods of every descrip-

---

[*]There were almost a hundred U. S. fleet and escort carriers in the Pacific by late summer of 1944.

tion were drastically curtailed. Food was rationed, clothing was at a premium, coffins had to be used over and over, and there was little gas or charcoal for heating homes. Newspapers were reduced in size, and publication of afternoon editions was suspended; about ten thousand amusement places —including geisha houses—were shut down. Life in Japan, in short, had become drab and onerous. "What kind of a Tokyo has this turned out to be!" lamented comedian Roppa Furukawa in his diary. "Ah, it's no fun being alive any more!"

These extreme austerity measures—coupled with the suspicion that the abandonment of territory, culminating with the fall of Saipan, was more serious than the official communiqués indicated—fostered unrest which centered around Tojo, the symbol of war and peace.

The most outrageous rumors were accepted and passed on: Tojo was using tobacco, whiskey and other loot from the occupied southern areas to bribe members of the Imperial Household Ministry, the board of chamberlains, the *jushin* and privy councilors; he had even paid off the Emperor's brothers—Chichibu and Takamatsu—with automobiles.*

He was ridiculed—behind his back, naturally—for allowing his wife to make public speeches and radio broadcasts and engage in other active efforts to support the war. She was nicknamed *"To Bi-rei,"* a play on the Japanese version of Madame Chiang Kai-shek's name, *"So Bi-rei."* Following the disaster at Saipan, Mrs. Tojo was inundated by anonymous phone calls asking if her husband had committed suicide yet.

There were some who were not willing to leave such a final action up to the Prime Minister himself. In addition to Admiral Sokichi Takagi, whose group was planning to ambush Tojo by machine gun, rebels in the Army also sought his assassination. A major named Tsunoda, recently transferred from China to Imperial Headquarters—together with Tatsukuma Ushijima, president of the Tokyo chapter of *Toa Renmei* (East Asia Federation)—was planning to throw a

---

*These rumors had no basis in fact, but there was some justification for complaints. Tojo did misappropriate power in his utilization of the *kempeitai* to control dissidents. Known pacifists such as Konoye were under strict surveillance, and many citizens had been jailed and a few tortured to death for espousing Christianity or fomenting political opposition. Seigo Nakano, an avowed Nazi, was arrested after making a public speech against Tojo. Soon after his release he committed hara-kiri under such mysterious circumstances that it was commonly believed *kempei* agents had "persuaded" him to kill himself.

The impression was real and caused widespread indignation, but the extent of the repression was exaggerated.

special hydrocyanic bomb at Tojo's car as it slowed on a curve in the Imperial Palace grounds near the Iwaida Bridge. The time was set: the third week of July. But the plot was betrayed by the Emperor's youngest brother, Prince Mikasa, to whom a friend of the conspirators had unintentionally revealed the plan. Instead of giving it his blessing ("Such action was tantamount to rebellion against the Throne") he informed a member of Imperial Headquarters. Ushijima and Tsunoda were arrested by the *kempeitai* and sentenced to death, but as had happened so often in the past, they were given a stay of execution.

Confronted with extensive discontent, Tojo sought advice from the man who had proposed him as prime minister and given his official support through the past months of crisis—the Privy Seal. The counsel Tojo received was as unexpected as it was unwelcome. Kido, finally roused to action by the fall of Saipan, was critical of the recent fusion of power: the two top positions in the Cabinet held by Tojo himself, and the dual role of Admiral Shimada (the Navy Minister-cum-Navy Chief of Staff was regarded by other Navy men as Tojo's *kaban-mochi*—briefcase carrier). "Everyone is concerned about this," said Kido, "and the Emperor himself is extremely annoyed."

Profoundly discomposed, Tojo withdrew without saying a word but returned later in the day. He was willing to re-shuffle the Cabinet but not to surrender his own posts. Kido greeted this compromise with a coolness that seemed hostile to Tojo. He shot to his feet. "There's no sense in talking to you today!" he exclaimed.

He marched out of Kido's office with a slam of the door, but by the time he reached his official residence he had sobered. He told Kenryo Sato, "If Kido has that attitude, it means the Emperor's confidence in me is lost. Therefore I'm giving up the idea of re-forming the Cabinet; instead I will resign."

"It's out of the question to resign at the most critical time of the war!" shouted Sato. All he had to do was replace Shimada with Admiral Yonai; it would appease both the Navy and liberals like Konoye.

But Tojo found it too distasteful to dismiss Shimada, who had supported him so faithfully. Sato quoted the Chinese saying that "in order to attain true justice one should not hesitate to kill one's parents if necessary." "You must 'kill' Shimada no matter how painful it may be. Your obligation to

Shimada is a personal matter. You started this war and you cannot give up in the middle of it."

It was what Tojo himself believed. He summoned Shimada and informed him he would have to resign as navy minister. The admiral was gracious. "I who am leaving can do so with lightened shoulders," he said. "You who stay must continue to bear great responsibilities." He wished Tojo a "good fight" in his coming struggle, and as they shook hands the disciplined Tojo broke down.

The next day, July 17, Shimada submitted his resignation but contrary to Sato's prediction, the liberals were not appeased. Neither was Kido, and after prodding from Konoye, he promised that though major political questions were outside his province, he would report to the Throne the consensus of the *jushin*'s recomendations in reference to Tojo.

Exhilarated, Konoye drove to the home of Baron Hiranuma, where he found two other *jushin*, Admiral Okada and Baron Reijiro Wakatsuki. He told them of Kido's surprising offer. "Now I understand what Kido has been trying to do," Admiral Okada remarked.

By six-thirty all the *jushin* had arrived. Conspiracy was in the air, and after months of ineffectual private complaints, they greeted one another with a sense of purpose. "I should like to draw your attention to the fact that even if the Tojo Cabinet is re-formed," Wakatsuki warned, "the people will not support it."

Admiral Yonai revealed that he had just been "earnestly" invited to join the Cabinet as Shimada's replacement. He had refused, but fully expected Tojo to make a personal appeal and if that failed, go to the Throne for backing. "I have already made up my mind not to accept the offer even if that last step is taken."

Not all the *jushin* wanted Tojo's resignation. General Nobuyuki Abe charged that it was "irresponsible to talk exclusively of knocking down the Cabinet. How can we be sure of getting a better one?"

"Whether the Cabinet is overthrown or not or whether the next one is weak or not is not the point," Hiranuma interjected. The country had reached a crisis and a change of cabinets had to be made—and quickly.

"If I were asked, I wouldn't join the Cabinet," said Hirota, the diplomat who had headed the Cabinet after the 2/26 Incident.

They finally worked out a resolution that pleased everyone but Abe. It read:

The minds and hearts of the people must be infused with new life if the empire is to survive the great problems facing it. All of us in the nation must co-operate and work together. A partial reorganization of the Cabinet will be useless. A powerful new cabinet must be formed that will surge forward unswervingly.

Abe wondered if the results of their meeting shouldn't be passed on to Tojo. The answer was unanimous—No. The resolution was hand-carried to Kido's home. The Privy Seal promised to present it to the Emperor the next morning.

In his office Prime Minister Tojo and Kenryo Sato were pondering Yonai's refusal to join the Cabinet. Sato thought the fault lay with the go-between who had represented Tojo. "Your true intentions haven't yet been gotten across to Yonai," he said. "Let me speak for you direct."

Sato changed to civilian clothes and, unrecognized, slipped by newsmen assigned to the admiral's residence. He pushed his way past the maid, who said her master wasn't in, and fell asleep in the waiting room. An hour later he woke up when Yonai returned from the *jushin* meeting.

Sato tried to impress Yonai that it was essential to save the Cabinet in the middle of war; and his acceptance of a portfolio would accomplish this. Tojo's sole desire was to change the tide of battle. "I can see why you object to his cabinet, but that is merely a personal opinion. At this most critical time I beg you to co-operate with the Tojo Cabinet to overcome our problem."

"I am not an expert in politics." Yonai smiled wryly. "You can see that from my own cabinet. I'm an admiral, not a politician. And I'd like to die an admiral. If you want to use me, make me an adviser to the Navy Minister."

From Yonai's tone it was clear that he could not be persuaded. Sato started back to Tojo's office. He had tried but failed, and now his final advice would negate everything he had previously said. It was two o'clock in the morning, but Tojo was still working in his shirt sleeves, smoke from his ever-present cigarette curling up to the lampshade above his head. Tojo looked up.

"Please resign," said Sato.

Tojo let his breath out in a long sigh. "I will see the Emperor in the morning," he said. "Would you please put in writing what led to my resignation."

As Sato sat down and began to write, he knew in his heart that the war was over, and tears dropped onto the paper.

In the morning, July 18, Tojo—skin sallow, eyes lusterless—told his cabinet in a weary voice that he had decided to resign because of the loss of Saipan. He had hesitated so long only because of the "Badoglio" group in Japan.* The responsibility for Japan's defeat, he added caustically, would have to be borne by the *jushin* and others who had forced him out of office. His shoulders sagged. It was the hottest day of the year. "I must ask you all to resign," he said.

The atmosphere was awkward as each man wrote his resignation. It was ironic that exactly four years earlier Tojo had been chosen war minister.

Stony-faced, Tojo delivered the documents to Kido. The Privy Seal asked whom he would like to succeed him. "I won't say whom I want," Tojo replied with sarcasm. "I imagine the *jushin* have already decided who it will be." Then he started down the long corridor to the Emperor's office to make his last report as prime minister.

The *jushin* had not yet selected his successor but were about to. They met this time in the afternoon—and with Kido as the dominating presence—in the West Room of the Palace. Also present were the Grand Chamberlain and President of the Privy Council Yoshimichi Hara.

General Abe, who had always supported Tojo, wanted the Navy—in the person of Yonai—to form the new cabinet.

"I did take part in politics once," the admiral observed. "And I might try again as navy minister, but I can't become prime minister." Military men had "a one-sided education" and this made them unsuited for such a role. "Politics should be left to politicians."

Konoye appreciated Yonai's idealism but they had to consider the matter from a practical point of view. "'Politics today cannot be carried on without the Army's participation."

Kido and Konoye had long since privately agreed that there should be an interim cabinet before the imperial family became involved. "The bolstering of home defense," Kido retorted, "the increase of Army strength in the homeland, and that of the military police, force us to choose someone from the Army." Wakatsuki acquiesced and so did Yonai. Moments earlier the latter had warned about the dangers of choosing a military man; now he suggested Count Hisaichi

---

*He was referring to the Marshal Pietro Badoglio government, which had surrendered Italy unconditionally to the Allies the previous summer.

Terauchi, who had been promoted to field marshal the year before.

Konoye was willing to accept Terauchi, but not before he had emphasized two points: "First, why did Tojo fall? Of course, it was partially because many unfavorable things were said about him, but also because the Army, unlike the Navy, interferes with every phase of political as well as economic life." This would have to cease. "Second, the nation nowadays seems to be drifting toward a leftist revolution. Everything points in that direction. Losing the war is a dreadful thing, but a revolution is far more dreadful. Once defeated, we may recover in due time, but a leftist revolution would play havoc with the national essence." He wondered if Terauchi could control the dissident elements.

"He is all right," Kido said, "but since he is so far away from here, at the front, it would be difficult to bring him back. We'd better choose someone else."

For a second time Yonai nominated a military man, General Yoshijiro Umezu, the commander of the Kwantung Army who had just been recalled to replace Tojo as chief of staff.

"It's not good to remove him so soon from his new post," objected Kido, who privately thought Umezu would be a poor choice.

Konoye suggested a Navy man, the aged Kantaro Suzuki, who had narrowly escaped death in the 2/26 Incident. "I was with him in the Privy Council," Hara said, "and know him well. He will never accept the offer." Hiranuma's motion of Field Marshal Shunroku Hata, commander in chief in China, got a lukewarm reception.

Again Yonai suggested a general, Kuniaki Koiso. "He's a good man, capable and courageous. I knew him well when he was in my cabinet."

"How does he get along with Army men?" Kido asked.

"Not so badly, I believe," General Abe replied. "He's different from Tojo."

"He's first-rate and devoutly religious," Hiranuma commented.

"I have no objections," said Wakatsuki, "although I don't know him."

Okada thought they were making too hasty a choice, and Konoye supported him. This inspired a lengthy and inconclusive dispute, and in the end they were forced to advise the Emperor to choose one of the three Army men—Terauchi, Hata or Koiso. It was already eight o'clock. They had debated for four hours and it was with a sense of relief that they passed on the responsibility to His Majesty.

Marquis Kido reported immediately to the Emperor, with the suggestion that His Majesty query the Army on Terauchi's availability before making a choice. The answer came from Tojo, who by chance was at the Palace for the installation of his successor, General Umezu. Tojo advised against releasing Terauchi from his post at such a critical time. That left only Hata and Koiso, and the Emperor, after considering Kido's presentations, selected the latter.

During the night Prince Konoye began worrying about Koiso. Would he be able to control the leftists and remain independent of the Army? Perhaps there should be co-premiers, one from the Army, one from the Navy. A combination of Koiso and Yonai, for example. And since Yonai himself had recommended Koiso, it was obvious the two would get along.

The next day he discussed it with Baron Hiranuma, who thought it was a splendid idea. And, more important, so did the Privy Seal. But Yonai remained reluctant. Since he had refused Tojo's invitation to join his cabinet, it would be "improper" now to accept a much more prominent position. But why not navy minister? "I'm confident of handling that post. I'm not ashamed to admit that I might prove to be the best possible navy minister."

Konoye was almost as pleased as if Yonai had accepted co-premiership. With Yonai in the Cabinet, strongly supported by Kido and the Emperor, it would amount to the same thing.

General Koiso arrived from Korea the following afternoon. He was taken directly and without explanation to the waiting room adjoining the Imperial Chamber. Nicknamed "the Tiger of Korea" more for his looks than for his military prowess, he had slanted, catlike eyes, a flat nose and thin lips. He liked *sake* parties and was jovial enough to tolerate another nickname—"Champion Baldhead of Japan." He knew there was a good chance he might be named prime minister and had in his pocket a list of close comrades in Korea for cabinet posts, but his expectations diminished sharply at the entrance of Admiral Yonai. Before he could question Yonai, Kido appeared to usher the two into His Majesty's presence. Who should go first? asked the general, and Kido replied, "Koiso." But the Emperor treated both of them exactly alike. He said they would have to co-operate in forming a new cabinet and warned them not to antagonize Russia.

Yonai was as mystified as Koiso and when the audience was over, he asked Marquis Kido which one was prime minister. "Koiso, of course," said the Privy Seal.

What a strange conversation! Koiso thought. He turned to Yonai. "What office are you going to take? Navy minister?"

"That's the only post I'm capable of filling," the admiral replied.

Tojo's forced resignation gave his wife a sense of relief. Now, at least, the daily hazard of assassination was over. (Coincidentally, Tojo's ally Adolf Hitler had just barely escaped death from a bomb explosion.) Her reasoning was correct. Admiral Takagi, for instance, canceled his plan to gun down Tojo, who had now joined the distinguished purely advisory circle of *jushin*.

2.

Although General MacArthur had been given a target date to invade the Philippines—a preliminary landing at Mindanao to establish airfields, followed three weeks later by a major one at Leyte—the Joint Chiefs had suggested in mid-June that he by-pass the other Philippine islands, including Luzon, and leapfrog all the way from Leyte to Formosa. This would, in effect, eliminate MacArthur's cherished role as Liberator of the Philippines, and his reply was in keeping with his indignation:

... THE PHILIPPINES IS AMERICAN TERRITORY WHERE OUR UNSUPPORTED FORCES WERE DESTROYED BY THE ENEMY. PRACTICALLY ALL OF THE 17,000,000 FILIPINOS REMAIN LOYAL TO THE UNITED STATES AND ARE UNDERGOING THE GREATEST PRIVATION AND SUFFERING BECAUSE WE HAVE NOT BEEN ABLE TO SUPPORT OR SUCCOR THEM. WE HAVE A GREAT NATIONAL OBLIGATION TO DISCHARGE. MOREOVER, IF THE UNITED STATES SHOULD DELIBERATELY BYPASS THE PHILIPPINES, LEAVING OUR PRISONERS, NATIONALS, AND LOYAL FILIPINOS IN ENEMY HANDS WITHOUT AN EFFORT TO RETRIEVE THEM AT EARLIEST MOMENT, WE WOULD INCUR THE GRAVEST PSYCHOLOGICAL REACTION. WE WOULD ADMIT THE TRUTH OF JAPANESE PROPAGANDA TO THE EFFECT THAT WE HAD ABANDONED THE FILIPINOS AND WOULD NOT SHED AMERICAN BLOOD TO REDEEM THEM; WE WOULD UNDOUBTEDLY INCUR THE OPEN HOSTILITY OF THAT PEOPLE; WE WOULD PROBABLY

Marshall replied with a forceful admonition "not to let personal feelings and Philippine politics" overshadow his primary objective, the winning of the war. He asserted that "bypassing" was by no means "synonymous with abandonment." MacArthur, however, was offered the opportunity of reviewing the matter directly with the President. The occasion was to be an unprecedented meeting five weeks hence in Hawaii between Roosevelt, MacArthur and Nimitz. Marshall, Arnold and King were not invited; it was an indication to King that the President, with the Democrats holding their national convention in Chicago, "wished to emphasize his role as Commander in Chief of the Army and Navy."

Roosevelt and his party boarded the heavy cruiser *Baltimore* at San Diego the day after he was nominated for a fourth term. Early in the afternoon of July 26 the cruiser, presidential flag flapping at the main, passed Diamond Head. MacArthur, whose plane had just landed after the long trip from Brisbane, met the President at the pier. The general was still in his winter uniform.

"Douglas," chided Admiral Leahy, a friend for almost forty years, "why don't you wear the right kind of clothes when you come up here to see us?"

"Well, you haven't been where I came from, and it's cold up there in the sky."

The presidential party passed through long lines of soldiers and a cheering crowd to the site of the conference, a palatial private home on Waikiki Beach. There was no longer need to debate priorities of men and matériel, nor was there any question of the success of whatever was to come. After dinner Roosevelt pointed to Mindanao on a map of the Pacific and said, "Douglas, where do we go from here?"

"Leyte, Mr. President, and then Luzon!" MacArthur expounded at length on the advisability of seizing Luzon before invading Formosa. Nimitz made no comment.

The next morning formal talks began in a large living room whose walls were covered with operational maps. Using a long bamboo pointer, MacArthur again urged the occupation of Luzon. This time Nimitz countered, also aided by the pointer, with his own plan for striking directly at Formosa. Roosevelt leaned back in his wheelchair, relishing the lesson in geography. Tactfully he narrowed down the points of disagreement. But his mediation was not necessary. Nimitz, a good listener, finally accepted the validity of MacArthur's argument that national honor and strategy made the liberation of all the Philippines essential before moving on to Formosa.

After lunch MacArthur assured Roosevelt there would be no friction between him and Nimitz. "We see eye to eye, Mr. President," he said. "We understand each other perfectly." Later, as his plane took off for Brisbane, he turned to an aide with a triumphant "We've sold it!"

While the Americans prepared the complex strategy leading up to the Leyte invasion—which was given a definite date, December 20—Imperial Headquarters in Tokyo was attempting to guess their intentions. A "Plan for the Conduct of Future Operations" envisaged attacks on four areas: the Philippines; Formosa and Okinawa; the home islands; and the Kuriles in the north. Though it was given the optimistic name SHO-GO (Operation Victory), it was a plan born of desperation, a series of last-ditch defenses. It was obvious that the Philippines was the next American objective—SHO-1—and it was agreed that this should be made the scene of the Final Decisive Battle both on land and sea.

The question was where and how to meet this challenge and force this confrontation into a genuinely conclusive conflict. It was a problem of geography. The Philippine archipelago, almost 7,100 islands, lay some 500 miles off the mainland of Asia, 230 miles south of Formosa. It extended 1,150 miles from Mindanao due north through the Visayans—the central islands including Cebu and Leyte—to Luzon, the largest and most important island. Only eleven of the islands had an area larger than one thousand square miles and two of these, Mindanao and Luzon, comprised more than two thirds of the total land area. Strategically, however, Leyte—one-thirteenth the size of Mindanao—was equally important. It was in the heart of the archipelago, and its spacious gulf was an invitation to an invasion from the sea.

Southern Army's operations officer wanted to oppose the Americans wherever they landed first—which would be somewhere in the south—before they had a chance to set up bases. But he was overruled by the Army General Staff. It would be impossible to predict exactly where the enemy would strike first. Rather than disperse troops on a number of southern islands, the bulk should be concentrated on Luzon, which had the best roads and could be most easily defended.

The conquest of the Philippines called for combined sea and land operations of a magnitude never before attempted by the United States. MacArthur would lead the assault, but he would have Nimitz' full support. It was the Navy's task to neutralize Japanese air power. The first strike was delivered on September 6 by Vice Admiral Marc Mitscher's Task Force 38. For three days his bombers hit the Palaus, 550 miles due east of Mindanao. Then he shifted the attack to Mindanao itself on September 9 and 10.

These aerial raids spurred Japanese preparations for the defense of the Philippines. In Manila, Field Marshal Terauchi, whose Southern Army was charged with the defense of the vast area from New Guinea to Burma, believed with Tokyo that ground-based planes could sink most of the enemy convoys before they beached. But the local commander of ground troops, Lieutenant General Shigenori Kuroda of the 14th Area Army, argued that the concept was good but you couldn't "fight with concept alone. Words will not sink American ships and that becomes clear when you compare our aircraft with theirs." Japanese air power was negligible and the battle would have to be won on land.

There was even disagreement on how this kind of battle should be fought. "Annihilation at the Beachhead" had been standard operating procedure in all previous invasions. But opposition to this policy was growing. Beach defenses had proved helpless against naval bombardment followed by a determined assault. Imperial Headquarters ordered Terauchi to set up resistance in depth.

The order was passed on to the officer responsible for the defense of Mindanao and the Visayans—Lieutenant General Sosaku Suzuki, who had once been rudely roused out of bed in Malaya by an indignant Colonel Tsuji.* He commanded the 35th Army, the equivalent of a U. S. Army Corps, and had headquarters in Cebu City. The general was described by

---

*"It was the Ishihara-Tsuji clique—the personification of *gekokujo*," General Suzuki told a fellow officer, Major Yoshitaka Horie, after leaving Malaya, "that brought the Japanese Army to this deplorable situation. In Malaya, Tsuji's speech and conduct were often insolent; and there was this problem of inhumane treatment of Chinese merchants, so I advised General Yamashita to punish Tsuji severely and then dismiss him. But he feigned ignorance. I tell you, so long as they [Tsuji, Ishihara, and their like] exert influence on the Army, it can only lead to ruin. Extermination of these poisonous insects should take precedence over all other problems."

his colleagues as a gentle man "of great heart" and "straight as bamboo."

Suzuki not only feared the American invasion would come sooner than his superiors in Tokyo and Manila did (he told his chief of staff to expect a landing about the first of October) but predicted correctly that the enemy would concentrate his attack on Leyte. He placed the 30th Division in northern Mindanao so it could quickly be transferred to Leyte. But immediate events made him doubt his prophecy. On September 10 a message arrived from a naval observation unit that the enemy was landing near Davao on the south coast of Mindanao. Two hours later another report arrived:

AMERICAN MARINES USING AMPHIBIOUS TANKS HAVE LANDED ON SOUTHERN TIP OF SMALL ISLAND LOCATED ACROSS THE BANKS FROM DAVAO.

Suzuki transferred the 30th Division back to the south of Mindanao and alerted Manila. The Fourth Air Army began ferrying planes from New Guinea to the Philippines while Combined Fleet alerted its forces for SHO-1. But there had been no enemy landing. Observers on a hill overlooking the bay had mistaken choppy waves for landing craft.

"Let this mishap be a lesson," Suzuki told his staff. The next time, he trusted, they would not act so precipitately.

Two days later Mitscher resumed his attacks, which would eventually sweep up through the Philippines all the way to Okinawa. Within forty-eight hours, 2,400 sorties had been launched at the Visayans. The damage was so complete and the American casualty rate so minimal that Admiral Halsey, who commanded Third Fleet (which now included most of the ships in Spruance's old Fifth Fleet), asked himself why the Leyte invasion date should not be advanced. He sat in a corner of the bridge of the battleship *New Jersey* and "thought it over." It was really none of his business and might "upset a great many applecarts, possibly all the way up to Mr. Roosevelt and Mr. Churchill," but it might also "cut months off the war."

Halsey summoned his chief of staff, Robert ("Mick") Carney, and his secretary, Harold Stassen, and said, "I'm going to stick my neck out. Send an urgent dispatch to CINCPAC." It recommended cancellation of preliminary operations on Yap, Morotai and Mindanao, and seizure of Leyte "at the earliest possible date." Nimitz forwarded the dispatch to Quebec, where Roosevelt and Churchill were again meeting. The boldness of Halsey's suggestion intrigued them, but they needed MacArthur's blessing.

The general was aboard *Nashville* on his way to Morotai, one of the Spice Islands between New Guinea and Mindanao, the next to the last step on his route to the Philippines, *Nashville* was under radio silence, and the decision rested on MacArthur's chief of staff, General Sutherland, who had remained in New Guinea. He knew his chief would welcome an earlier liberation of the Philippines, so, in MacArthur's name, he radioed Quebec that the invasion of Leyte could take place on October 20, two months ahead of schedule.

On September 15 MacArthur's troops landed unopposed on Morotai while Halsey's were meeting stiff resistance on Pelelieu, one of the Palau islands.* Six days later Mitscher continued his devastating sweeps of the Philippines. Daringly he brought his carriers to within forty miles of the east coast of Luzon to launch four air strikes at the Manila area. The strips at Clark and Nichols fields were plowed up, more than

---

*Pelelieu was defended with such determination that it took a statistical average of 1,589 rounds of heavy and light ammunition to kill each Japanese soldier. American casualties were extremely heavy. In one month of bitter combat, 1,121 Marines were killed.

The Marines were feuding with their own Navy and Army in equal proportions. Just before disembarking for the assault, Marines on correspondent Tom Lea's transport left this notice on the ship's bulletin board in the Ship's Officers Wardroom:

A MESSAGE OF THANKS
From: Marines aboard U.S.S. *Repulsive*
To: Officers and Men aboard U.S.S. *Repulsive*

1. It gives us great pleasure at this time to extend our sincere thanks to all members of the crew for their kind and considerate treatment of Marines during this cruise.
2. We non-combatants realize that the brave and stalwart members of the crew are winning the war in the Pacific. You Navy people even go within ten miles of a Japanese island, thereby risking your precious lives. Oh how courageous you are! Oh how our piles bleed for you.
3. Because of your actions during this voyage it is our heartfelt wish that:
a. The U.S.S. *Repulsive* receives a Jap torpedo immediately after debarkation of all troops.
b. The crew of the U.S.S. *Repulsive* is stranded on Beach Orange Three where Marine units which sailed aboard the ship may repay in some measure the good fellowship extended by the crew and officers during the trip.
4. In conclusion we Marines wish to say to all you dear, dear boys in the Navy: "Bugger you, you bloody bastards!"

two hundred planes destroyed and the shipping in Manila Bay ravaged. Only fifteen U. S. aircraft were lost and no Japanese plane was able to break through the screen protecting Task Force 38.

3.

Now, even in Tokyo, it was clear that the American invasion of the Philippines was imminent. General Kuroda, who had realistically prophesied that Japanese land-based planes could not thwart American sea power, was relieved of his command on the specious grounds that he was "devoting more time to his golf, reading and personal matters than to the execution of his official duties."

His replacement as commander of all ground troops in the Islands was one of the heroes of the early victories, the conqueror of Singapore. After that campaign, General Tomoyuki Yamashita had been sent to Manchuria to train troops. He was not allowed to stop off in Tokyo. This, explained Imperial Headquarters, was to prevent the Russians from learning of his new assignment, but Yamashita, who had been at odds with Tojo for years, was convinced it was just an excuse to get him out of public sight.

On his way south Yamashita told his operations officer, Major Shigeharu Asaeda, who like his chief was impatient for action, that he feared the Philippine campaign was "going to be another Battle of Minatogawa"—one fought by a commander who knew from the beginning he had no chance of victory. But he hid this pessimism from his new staff, and upon arrival at 14th Area Army headquarters at Fort McKinley near Manila on October 6, told them that the fate of Japan rested on the outcome of the battle. Each officer had a "heavy responsibility" to fight resolutely, daringly and with determination to win. "If we all remember this, the Japanese Army must win in the end."

Less than twenty thousand troops—the 16th Division— were garrisoned on the island that was MacArthur's target, Leyte. This unit had landed on the east coast of Luzon on Christmas Eve, 1941, and after participating in the seizure of Manila, fought on Bataan. But the majority of its present complement, including its commander, Lieutenant General Shiro Makino, were replacements who had never before been in battle. In the Japanese Army their reputation was poor;

they were mostly draftees from the Kyoto-Osaka region and were "better businessmen than fighters."

Leyte was wedged between two larger islands, Samar directly to the northeast and Mindanao to the south. In shape it resembled a molar with its roots pointing to Mindanao. On the east coast a fertile plain ran along Leyte Gulf for thirty-five miles. No reefs protected its open sandy beaches, making it a perfect site for landing operations. But a few miles inland MacArthur's men would have to cross a complex of swamps, streams and rice paddies which were almost impassable except by road during the rainy season, which had already begun. The rest of the island was mountainous and heavily wooded, equally difficult to attack or defend. It was infested with small bands of guerrillas, who were in conflict with one another as often as with the Japanese. Their principal value to MacArthur was the reliable information they radioed him about General Makino's defenses.

There were almost a million people on the island, all of them—except for 3,076 Chinese, and a sprinkling of Europeans, Americans and Japanese—placid Visayans who lived by farming and fishing. The principal crops were rice, sugar cane, corn and copra.

At Hollandia as well as at Manus, one of the Admiralty islands two hundred miles north of New Guinea, a vast armada—including battleships, cruisers, small carriers, destroyers, transports, tankers, amphibious craft, minesweepers, salvage tugs and floating drydocks—was preparing to set sail for Leyte. The ships were manned by 50,000 sailors, and the transports and amphibious craft carried 165,000 troops of MacArthur's Sixth Army. The invasion of Leyte would be by far the greatest operation in the Pacific. For the first time all the forces of MacArthur, Nimitz and the overseas bomber commands would be united.

The safe passage of this convoy was still Mitscher's concern and to accomplish this he was to range from the Philippine Sea to the East China Sea and back. Task Force 38, which had already practically eliminated Japanese air power in the Philippines, first steamed a thousand miles north to Okinawa, an island the Japanese considered part of the homeland. Mitscher's 1,396 sorties on October 10 destroyed a hundred planes and considerable shipping, including four cargo vessels, a submarine tender and a dozen torpedo boats.

The admiral swung back south to bomb northern Luzon the following day. Then he reversed course again and just before sunrise on October 12 launched fighters from his four carrier groups at Formosa. Here he met his first serious opposition. Vice Admiral Shigeru Fukudome, commander of the Sixth Base Air Force, sent up 230 fighters to ambush the Americans. Many of his young pilots had learned their combat technology only from films,* but they would probably outnumber the enemy at least 3 to 2.

From his command post Fukudome saw in the distance enemy planes sweep down to his airfields; high above, tiny specks—Zero interceptors—began plummeting toward the Americans. There were flashing explosions and long arching trails of smoke. Fukudome excitedly clapped his hands. "Well done! Well done! A tremendous success!" But the Americans continued to come on in perfect formation. The downed planes were his own. His fighters had been like "so many eggs thrown against the stone wall of the indomitable enemy formation."

Fukudome lost a third of his interceptors in the first strike, and the rest in the second. There was nothing to send up against the third. The Americans resumed their raids the following morning and, unopposed, damaged Formosan air installations more heavily than the previous day. The Japanese retaliated at dusk. Thirty-odd bombers specially designed for night attacks swept out toward Task Force 38, skimming the waves to avoid radar detection. Three dive bombers eluded interceptors and released their bombs at the carrier *Franklin*. Two bombs went wide, but the third exploded on the deck-edge elevator. Fire broke out on the port quarter but was soon extinguished. The heavy cruiser *Canberra* (named after the Australian cruiser sunk in the Battle of Savo) was not so fortunate. A torpedo slammed into her side, ripping a huge hole. Water cascaded in and she came to a dead stop ninety miles from Formosa.

Halsey, on his flagship *New Jersey*, faced a difficult decision. Should he abandon *Canberra* or risk another ship in an attempt to tow her at 4 knots the thirteen hundred miles to Ulithi Atoll in the Carolines? Halsey characteristically took the chance and ordered another cruiser to draw *Canberra* clear. To divert the Japanese he ordered a third and unsched-

---

*The Toho Motion Picture Company constructed a lake in Setagaya and filled it with six-foot models of U. S. warships. Atop a tower a movie camera on a boom took pictures of the vessels from various angles, simulating different speeds of approach. These films were shown as a substitute for flight training in order to save fuel.

uled series of raids on Formosa. In the morning Mitscher sent out three sweeps against Formosan airfields while 109 huge Army Air Force B-29's left their bases deep inside China to hit the Takao area. By dusk, over five hundred Japanese planes had been destroyed in the three-day air battle.

But the surviving Japanese pilots, whose vision of battle had come from a lakeful of models on the Toho film lot, reported the biggest victory in Japanese naval history, and as Halsey's fleet withdrew to strike elsewhere, Admiral Toyoda— at the time in Formosa on an inspection trip—saw this action as confirmation of American disaster. He ordered Fukudome to go after the "remnants" of the Third Fleet with every bomber left. The next day, October 15, Fukudome launched three strikes. One group alone found the enemy, and it was repelled. The following afternoon a flight of 107 aircraft caught up with the retreating Americans. Only three penetrated the fighter screen and one hit the light cruiser *Houston* with a torpedo. Over sixty-five hundred tons of water rushed in and she seemed destined to share the fate of the first *Houston*, destroyed off Java, but damage-control parties kept the leaks in check, and like *Canberra*, she was towed away.

Halsey had not lost a single ship in the sweeps extending from Okinawa to Luzon. Facetiously he radioed Nimitz: THE THIRD FLEET'S SUNKEN AND DAMAGED SHIPS HAVE BEEN SALVAGED AND ARE RETIRING AT HIGH SPEED TOWARD THE ENEMY. He was heading south to support the coming invasion of Leyte.

In Japan neither Combined Fleet nor Imperial Headquarters had any reason to doubt the reports of momentous victories by returning pilots. An official communiqué was issued on October 16 announcing that in the Formosan battle eleven enemy carriers, two battleships, three cruisers and one destroyer or light cruiser had been sunk and almost as many others damaged. In addition, 112 planes had been shot down. It was admitted that 312 Japanese aircraft had not yet "returned" but this was small price for crippling the Third Fleet. The Emperor called for a celebration in Hibiya Park.

To the south a typhoon raged through the Philippines, but by dawn of October 17 the storm had subsided. Through a sea whipped by heavy winds an American attack group—two light cruisers, four destroyers and eight destroyer transports— followed three minesweepers into Leyte Gulf. For twenty minutes one of the cruisers, *Denver,* shelled Suluan, a small island in the mouth of the gulf. Then the 6th Ranger Infantry Battalion debarked from the transports in a driving rain to land unopposed. The Rangers were looking for mine charts in a lighthouse but found none. They disposed of most of the thirty-two-man Japanese garrison, but not before a lookout sent out a radio warning. He so exaggerated the size of the attack group (he reported that "two battleships, two converted aircraft carriers and six destroyers" lay off his island) that their presence created a major alert. Admiral Toyoda, still on Formosa, signaled Admiral Takeo Kurita to bring his formidable First Striking Force up from Singapore, then ordered Ozawa's Mobile Fleet to steam out of the Inland Sea (where it had reorganized after its crushing defeat in the Philippine Sea) and head south toward the Philippines. He also instructed submarines to make for the Leyte area and attack the American fleet. Then he took off for Japan so he could be at Combined Fleet Headquarters once the Decisive Battle started.

But the man in charge of the defense of the Visayans saw the Suluan alert as yet another false report. At Cebu, General Sosaku Suzuki remembered the panic when whitecaps off Mindanao were reported as landing craft. How could the enemy possibly launch an invasion after suffering a greater naval defeat than at Pearl Harbor? His superiors in Manila were just as skeptical; observation pilots had reported seeing nothing in Leyte Gulf through the clouds and rain.

On Leyte itself, General Makino alone feared it was a genuine invasion and ordered an alert—against the advice of his staff, who argued that the American shipping in the mouth of Leyte Gulf was the remnants of the Formosa battle blown south by the typhoon.

October 18 dawned fair, and the Rangers had no trouble landing on Homonhon, an island next to little Suluan. (One of Makino's staff officers flew over the gulf about this time but saw nothing through the fog.) There were no Japanese, no fortifications. Without opposition ("Here we are with all these goddamn bullets and no Japs!") the Rangers accomplished their mission: the erection of a navigation light to guide the convoy. Fifteen miles to the south, other Rangers were swarming ashore at Dinagat, a much bigger island guarding the lower approaches to the gulf. It, too, was uninhabited, and a second navigation light was set up at the tip end, Desolation Point. The convoy would enter the gulf between these two islands.

By noon the entrance to Leyte had been secured. Two

hours later the battleship *Pennsylvania,* along with two cruisers and several destroyers, began to bombard Leyte itself along the gulf. Then underwater teams in landing craft moved in to scout conditions on the beaches. Japanese dug in along the neat rows of coconut trees lining the beach road opened fire, sinking one of the craft. Ignoring the hail of bullets, the other teams went to work and were soon back with a welcome report: the shore was clear of mines and obstacles.

Makino's communications—inadequate to begin with—had been almost completely disrupted by the storm, and he knew none of this. Reassured by the officer who had just flown over the gulf and seen nothing of import, he reported to Suzuki that the American ships sighted earlier in the gulf had probably been looking for refuge from the typhoon.

In Japan this complacency was not shared by Combined Fleet. Just before noon Admiral Toyoda gave the execute to Sho-1, and for the first time his staff revealed to the Army at a combined meeting its detailed plan for an exhaustive battle; the Navy would attack the landing forces in Leyte Gulf with every available ship. This "all-or-nothing" attitude distressed General Kenryo Sato. If the Navy failed, what chance would the Army have in *its* Decisive Battle? "The Combined Fleet belongs not only to the Navy but to the state," Sato pointed out. Its destruction—he used the word "self-destruction"— would leave the homeland open to invasion. "Only the existence of the fleet will make the enemy cautious," he said in a choked voice. "So please, gentlemen, be prudent."

"I am very grateful to know," said Rear Admiral Nakazawa, the Operations Section chief, "that the Combined Fleet is so highly regarded by you Army men." His words were sincere. He pleaded for "a fitting place to die." The Philippines would be the last opportunity. "Please give the Combined Fleet the chance to bloom as flowers of death." His voice faltered. "This is the Navy's earnest request."

Sato could not withstand the tears or the argument. He acceded gracefully. That afternoon the Emperor gave his blessing to Sho-1.

South of the Philippines, scattered over thousands of square miles, the invasion convoy—420 transports and 157 warships—was steaming steadily toward Leyte Gulf. In the van were battleships, cruisers and destroyers of the support and bombardment units, and just before dawn on October 19 they entered the gulf and began shelling the landing beaches.

At the same time carrier planes were striking at every air base on the Visayans. They almost completely destroyed the remaining Japanese air power in the area.

The stage was at last set for the appearance of the gigantic invasion convoy. At eleven o'clock that evening it rendezvoused seventeen miles east of Leyte Gulf and steamed slowly toward the opening, marked by the navigation lights on the islands of Dinagat and Homonhon. Protestant and Catholic services were piped over public address systems, and more than one man had the sinking feeling that he was listening to his own last rites. Up ahead could be heard the muted boom of destroyers lobbing shells onto the landing areas.

In eleven hours the GI's would storm those beaches, and they tried to rest in the stuffy holds. Those who could not sleep counted the slow hours in their bunks or came up on deck in search of fresh air. The ships seemed to be barely moving as they glided through the mouth of the gulf. There was little talk; everyone was too engrossed in his own thoughts and fears. On the left loomed an ominous mass, Dinagat Island, dark except at the tip end, Desolation Point, where a white beacon steadily gleamed.

A GI fell overboard. It was reported over the circuit: "Ships astern keep lookout." Rescue seemed hopeless in the swift-running phosphorescent waters, but twenty minutes later a small craft near the end of the formation sighted the soldier and hauled him aboard.

In the first gray light of October 20—MacArthur had designated it A-Day, since D-Day, to the public, meant June 6, 1944—the dim outline of Leyte materialized. The sun rose behind the convoy, illuminating clear skies overhead. In minutes it was uncomfortably hot. The quiet was shattered abruptly as three battleships opened fire. Gray smoke plumes erupted along Violet and Yellow beaches near Dulag. Twelve minutes later a Japanese observation plane appeared. Ack-ack bursts bloomed on all sides, but the little aircraft moved off unharmed.

At about seven o'clock three other battleships joined in the cannonade, their target White and Red beaches to the north, just below Tacloban, the capital. Within an hour the transports began moving sedately over the glassy water to positions seven miles offshore. The battleships ceased fire to allow cruisers, destroyers and gunboats to move in closer and take up the bombardment. The continuous thunder of guns was suddenly exceeded by an awesome *swoosh* as thousands of rockets shot up simultaneously from the little gunboats. Seconds later there was a thunderous clap. The entire shoreline was "a solid sheet of blinding and exploding flame." When the smoke cleared, those on the transports stared incredulous—where there had been lush jungle growth now lay "a barren, tangled, smoking, dust-covered waste."

At nine forty-five—fifteen minutes before H-hour—the landing craft, which had been jockeying for position as if they were in a sulky race, bored in toward the beaches on a twelve-mile front. In the north the 1st Cavalry Division stormed ashore at White Beach. Sharpshooters knocked snipers out of palm trees with carbines and Garands; concrete pillboxes were dynamited and cavalrymen swept into the coastal highway. To their left the 24th Infantry Division also landed without difficulty—two of their men, one a Filipino, planted the American and Philippine flags on Red Beach—but they ran into nests of resolute Japanese and it took them several hours to reach the road. Farther south the 96th Infantry Division splashed safely ashore at Orange and Blue beaches. Fortunately, most of the artillery located at Catmon Hill, which dominated the region, had been destroyed by the naval bombardment. They pushed inland for almost a mile before they were slowed by marshes and scattered resistance. To their left at the extreme southern end—Violet and Yellow beaches—the 7th Infantry Division, which had seen action at Attu and Kwajalein, encountered the stiffest opposition, but Dulag was captured by noon.

MacArthur watched the landings intently from the bridge of the cruiser *Nashville* until lunch. He reappeared on deck a little before two o'clock, wearing a fresh khaki uniform, sunglasses and marshal's cap. He climbed into a barge loaded with officers and newsmen. It headed for the transport *John Land,* on which Sergio Osmeña, the President of the Philippines since Quezon's death three months earlier, waited along with General Carlos Romulo to be picked up. Romulo hadn't seen MacArthur for two years and eagerly clambered down the rope ladder.

"Carlos, my boy!" MacArthur exclaimed. "Here we are—home!"

Osmeña's affable greeting to MacArthur belied his true feelings. It had taken a personal plea from President Roosevelt to persuade him to return to the Philippines in the shadow of the general. But the exhilaration of the moment overrode personal differences. They were all talking at once. "We're here" was repeated over and over. MacArthur slapped Sutherland on the knee. "Believe it or not," he said with a grin, "we're back."

The barge grounded on Red Beach, some five miles below Tacloban. The ramp flapped down and MacArthur stepped into knee-deep water. He was followed by Osmeña, General George Kenney and the others. The diminutive Romulo, who was wearing new shoes, had difficulty keeping up with MacArthur's long strides.

The shore was encumbered by four damaged landing craft, one still burning, and occasionally the party heard the rattle of machine-gun and rifle fire. Corncob pipe in mouth and armed with an old revolver of his father's which he kept in his back pocket, MacArthur searched a palm grove for the 24th Division commander, Major General Frederick Irving. "This is what I dreamed about," Romulo heard him mutter.

Prone GI's were concentrating fire on something ahead. "Hey, there's General MacArthur," said one.

His buddy didn't even bother to look up. "Oh yeah? And I suppose he's got Eleanor Roosevelt with him."

After a brief chat with General Irving, MacArthur returned to his party. He motioned to Osmeña, put a hand on his shoulder. "Mr. President, how does it feel to be home?" he asked. They sat down on a fallen tree. "As soon as we take Tacloban I am turning the administration over to you. This may be sooner than we planned, things are going so smoothly."

"I am ready whenever you are, General."

They were interrupted by a Signal Corps officer who extended a hand microphone. The "Voice of Freedom" was back on the air. As MacArthur began to talk, his voice charged with emotion and hands trembling, a few drops of rain fell. "People of the Philippines, I have returned. By the grace of Almighty God our forces stand again on Philippine soil . . . At my side is your President, Sergio Osmeña, worthy successor of that great patriot, Manuel Quezon, with members of his cabinet."

In the background, trucks were noisily grinding across the beach, and planes roared overhead. There was an occasional distant boom from ships offshore shelling inland positions. His voice rising, the general called on the people to rally to him in the spirit of Bataan and Corregidor. "As the lines of battle roll forward to bring you within the zone of operations, rise and strike. . . . For your homes and hearths, strike! For future generations of your sons and daughters, strike! In the name of your sacred dead, strike! Let no heart be faint. Let every arm be steeled. The guidance of divine God points the way. Follow in His name to the Holy Grail of righteous victory!"

Osmeña took the microphone. The liberation of the Islands would be a joint enterprise of the Americans and Filipinos, and he urged the populace to co-operate. "We have the word of America that our country, which has been ravaged by war, will be reconstructed and rehabilitated. Steps have already been taken to this end. With the return of normal conditions, law and order will be fully re-established and democratic processes of constitutional government restored."

Romulo also praised the Americans. "You must continue keeping faith with them. You cannot let America down."

Euphoric, MacArthur wandered around the wet grove talking to GI's until an officer nervously said, "Sir, there are snipers over there," and pointed to nearby trees. MacArthur seemed not to hear. He sat down on a log and stared into the distance, at the land he had sworn to liberate.

A few miles to the north, troopers of the 1st Cavalry had reached the outskirts of Tacloban. They dug in, setting up mortars and machine guns in case of a night attack. Instead they were overwhelmed by the liberated. Filipinos crowded past the sentries. There were old people, young mothers with babies; Robert Shaplen of *The New Yorker* saw an aged, wrinkled-faced woman standing, arms outstretched toward the GI's with a beatific smile on her face. She seemed to be in the middle of a dream, too stunned to believe that she was wide awake.

The Americans had a substantial beachhead in the middle of the Philippines along with more than 100,000 tons of cargo. The cost was minimal—forty-nine GI's had died. Roosevelt radioed his congratulations to MacArthur: YOU HAVE THE NATION'S GRATITUDE AND THE NATION'S PRAYERS FOR SUCCESS AS YOU AND YOUR MEN FIGHT YOUR WAY BACK.

The invaders' losses had been light because the defense system had been shattered by the three-day bombardment. Their forward positions destroyed, their ranks thinned by shelling and strafing, the Japanese had fallen back, often leaderless. Few of the units were in communication with Division headquarters. That night Colonel Kanao Kondo of the 22nd Artillery Regiment accused the commander of the 1st Battalion of retreating without orders. Kondo refused to accept the excuse that almost the entire battalion had been killed or wounded, and their guns destroyed. "Why didn't you die?" he raged and ordered the survivors to fight to the end where they stood.

General Makino had no details of the progress of the fighting. On the eve of the invasion he had hastily evacuated his headquarters in Tacloban and was heading inland when the Americans came ashore. He had not yet been able to report what little he knew to his superiors.

At Fort McKinley, Yamashita was trying to evaluate the scanty information from Leyte. Just after ten o'clock his new chief of staff, Lieutenant General Akira Muto, arrived from Sumatra, where he had been "exiled" by Tojo. He was without baggage and wore a grimy uniform—during a bombing at an airfield he had leaped into a muddy ditch to save himself.

Yamashita told him of the invasion. "Very interesting" was his remark. "But where is Leyte?" They were joined by Colonel Ichiji Sugita (Yamashita's interpreter at Singapore), who had just flown in from Tokyo with distressing news for both of them: Imperial Headquarters orderd the 14th Area Army to fight the Decisive Battle on Leyte.

The next day, October 21, MacArthur's four divisions continued to press forward against little resistance. Dulag's airfield was overrun; most of Tacloban was liberated, and a special town meeting was scheduled for the following morning to welcome the victors and to recruit native labor for the Philippine Civil Affairs Unit. Filipinos crowded the market place, ignoring occasional bursts of fire in the outskirts. "We had to obey the Japanese to save our necks," said Saturino Gonzales, a member of the Provincial Board. He spoke to the audience but his words were directed to the Americans— in English. "But there was never any doubt, as you know, what our feelings were beneath. I ask you to consider now what the policies of the American government were like before the Japanese came and how they are to be compared to the Japanese administration. You will now understand the famous democratic ways of the United States."

The next speaker held up a can of K ration. The crowd got the point and cheered in English: "Long live the Americans! Lovely Americans!"

An American colonel told the crowd that the Philippines were theirs: "Your Commonwealth Government will be set up under your own president, President Osmeña. We are going to see that you get food and clothing. We want you to be patient. We need labor. You will get paid for the work you do in Philippine currency and with it you will be able to buy the rice and the other products we will bring. But, by God, you'll do it as free men!"

The *New Yorker* man, Shaplen, doubted that the audience understood everything the colonel said, but their enthusiasm was such that the next speaker, an ex-governor of Leyte, pledged that they would work for the Americans "three hundred and sixty-five days a year, and we will work for nothing."

The colonel's protests were overridden by cries of "Lovely Americans! We will work, we will work!"

In Manila, 340 miles to the northwest, Yamashita was making a final attempt to persuade Field Marshal Terauchi to protest Tokyo's order to make Leyte the site of the conclusive land battle of the Philippines. How could reinforcements break through the American air and submarine blockade around the island? Besides, before sufficient troops and supplies reached Leyte the battle would be over. And was it MacArthur's primary target? Perhaps this was merely a feint before the full-scale invasion of Luzon.

But his arguments came to naught; Terauchi never wavered in his belief that the imminent naval-air counterattack would sink the enemy invasion fleet in Leyte Gulf. The marshal (Muto characterized him as being "in extremely high spirits and optimistic") ordered the 14th Area Army "to totally destroy the enemy on Leyte." Reluctantly Yamashita passed on the order to Suzuki, and promised to send substantial infantry reinforcements to Leyte. Naval support could be expected to reach the island "on the twenty-fourth and twenty-fifth of October."

On Leyte, Makino had been forced to split his 16th Division into the Northern and Southern Leyte Defense Forces. His orders were couched in aggressive prose, but privately he hoped his troops would not collapse before help arrived.

By the next day the Tacloban area was secure enough for the invaders to permit the public appearance of the Allied leaders. Early in the afternoon a Filipino brass band roamed the streets of Tacloban in a weapons carrier; a loudspeaker repeated interminably that MacArthur and Osmeña were coming and there would be ceremonies. Led by the band, an impromptu parade formed and by three o'clock a crowd clustered around the steps of the capitol building.

The MacArthur party disembarked at the old wharf from two PT boats, and with the general in the lead, marched to the capitol. From the steps of the building MacArthur formally announced the establishment of the Philippine Civil Government under President Osmeña and promised to liberate the rest of the Islands. It was a short, unemotional speech, but the fiesta crowd cheered every sentence.

A bugler sounded To the Colors as American and Philippine flags were raised simultaneously. MacArthur shook hands with Osmeña and Romulo. "I and my staff will now retire," he said and started back to the wharf.

22   **The Battle**
of Leyte Gulf

1.

The Mobile Fleet and First Striking Force—the remnants of the Combined Fleet—were approaching the Philippines from the north and west. Vice Admiral Jisaburo Ozawa commanded the Mobile Fleet, whose air power had been shattered in the Marianas and whose remaining planes had proved so ineffectual in the three-day air battle off Formosa. Still, it made a formidable appearance, with the large carrier *Zuikaku,* light carriers *Zuiho, Chitose* and *Chiyoda,* and the battleships *Ise* and *Hyuga,* remodeled into semicarriers. But it was a hollow striking force. There were only 116 planes distributed among the six ships.

The First Striking Force, coming from Singapore, was under the command of Vice Admiral Takeo Kurita. He came from a family of scholars—his father had compiled a distinguished history of Japan—but he was a man of action. He had skippered five destroyers and twice commanded torpedo divisions, then a cruiser division. He had escorted the troops who were to land on Midway, and after participating in the battles around Guadalcanal (including the bombardment of Henderson Field by *Kongo* and *Haruna*), took over the Second Fleet in time to participate in the Battle of the Philippine Sea. His new fleet was strictly a surface force but its fire power was truly redoubtable. It included the two largest and most fearsome battleships in the world, *Musashi* and *Yamato,* as well as five old but serviceable battleships— among them *Haruna,* so often reported sunk, and her sister ship, *Kongo*—eleven heavy cruisers, two light cruisers and nineteen destroyers. The First Striking Force could throw more tons of shells than any fleet afloat.

It arrived at Brunei, Borneo, on October 20 as the Americans were landing on Leyte. Early the next morning Kurita received orders to enter Leyte Gulf at dawn of October 25 and destroy enemy amphibious shipping. Combined Fleet suggested a two-pronged attack: one group would work its way through the confining waters of the Visayans, debouch into the Pacific through San Bernardino Strait, turn south past Samar and enter Leyte Gulf from the east; the other group would break into the gulf from the south through the narrow Surigao Strait between Mindanao and Leyte.

On the long approaches to the battle area, both groups might easily be discovered and ambushed by American submarines and surface units as well as aircraft. Kurita and his staff were willing to accept these perils. What they objected to was the mission as such. They were eager to die in a battle against carriers, but why risk His Majesty's greatest battleships for transports that would already be unloaded? Combined Fleet sympathized with these objections but stood firm. It was too late for any alternative. Kurita, however, was given permission to engage carriers if they came within range.

Kurita decided to bring the major part of his fleet through San Bernardino Strait in order to keep it beyond the range of enemy search planes as long as possible. A detachment of two old battleships and four destroyers under Vice Admiral Teiji Nishimura would take the much shorter southern route. Both groups would enter Leyte Gulf at dawn on the twenty-fifth and converge on the enemy transports and their covering force.

Kurita was resigned to the loss of at least half his ships, but so many of his junior officers openly protested this calculated risk that he abandoned his usual reticence to address his division commanders and their staffs on the deck of the flagship, the heavy cruiser *Atago*. He told them that the war situation was far more critical than they could possibly know. "Would it not be a shame to have the fleet remain intact while our nation perishes? I believe that Imperial Headquarters is giving us a glorious opportunity. You must remember that there are such things as miracles. What man can say that there is no chance for our fleet to turn the tide of war in a Decisive Battle?"

Kurita's words, calm but forceful, were greeted with cries of *"Banzai!"*

At 8 A.M. on October 22, the main body of First Striking Force sortied from Brunei and began steaming northward, followed by the smaller Nishimura detachment, which turned east at the tip of Borneo and headed toward the south entrance to Leyte Gulf, Surigao Strait. The main body continued northeast through the darkness on a zigzag course at 18 knots, skirting the west coast of the long narrow island of Palawan in the 25-mile-wide passage formed by uncharted reefs (aptly called "the Dangerous Ground") and the island itself. In these swift waters near the reefs, two American picket submarines, *Darter* and *Dace,* patrolled the surface side by side. At sixteen minutes past midnight the conning tower of *Darter* reported: "Radar contact, one three one true, thirty thousand yards—contact is doubtful—probably rain cloud."

Rain cloud hell! thought the captain, Commander David McClintock, who was topside. That's the Jap fleet.

The radar operator's report confirmed his guess, and he relayed the information by megaphone to the skipper of *Dace,* Commander Bladen Clagett. "Let's go get them," Clagett called back and both submarines gave chase at flank speed with *Darter* in the lead.

By 4:50 A.M. they had closed the Japanese, and all hands on *Darter* were called to battle stations. At 5:10 she reversed course, submerged. Through the periscope, in the faint light of dawn, McClintock made out a gray mass in the distance. A Japanese column was coming straight at him! He looked to the southeast and saw another column of battleships, cruisers and destroyers several miles away.

The gray vessels bearing down on him grew larger. At 5:25 McClintock identified the lead ship, a heavy cruiser making huge bow waves. It was a beautiful sight and McClintock hoped it was the flagship. All tubes were ready and the range was just under 1,000 yards when the column abruptly zigged to the west, placing the target at a perfect angle. "Fire one!" ordered McClintock. A searchlight on the cruiser signaled. Had she detected the spread of six torpedoes? No, she was holding her course. McClintock took a bearing on the next cruiser.

His first torpedoes were heading for the flagship, *Atago.* On the bridge, Kurita and his chief of staff, Rear Admiral Tomiji Koyanagi, suddenly felt four great tremors in succession. The cruiser began to sink. A destroyer was signaled, and Kurita and his staff swam to it.

On *Dace,* Clagett surveyed the scene through his periscope. "Good Lord," he exclaimed, "it looks like the Fourth of July out there! One is sinking and another is burning. The Japs are firing all over the place. What a show! Stand by for a setup—here they come!" He studied two ships bearing down on him. "Let them pass—they are only cruisers." Behind was a bigger target he mistook for a *Kongo*-class battleship. "Fire one, fire two, fire three, fire four, fire five, fire six," Clagett ordered, and then, "Take her deep, Earl. Let's get the hell out of here!"

They heard the thump of torpedoes striking home and a crackle "like cellophane being crumpled close to our ears." The heavy cruiser *Maya* was breaking up.

Even before Kurita had reached the perilous waters of the central Philippines, he had lost two heavy cruisers, and a third, *Takao,* was in such bad shape that she had to turn back to Borneo. Moreover, his course had been discovered; yet there was nothing to do but continue. At noon he received a message from Combined Fleet which told him what he knew better than anyone else:

IT IS VERY PROBABLE THAT THE ENEMY IS AWARE OF THE FACT THAT WE HAVE CONCENTRATED OUR FORCES . . . HE WILL PROBABLY ACT IN THE FOLLOWING MANNER: (A) CONCENTRATE SUBMARINES IN GREAT STRENGTH IN THE SAN BERNARDINO AND SURIGAO STRAITS AREA. (B) PLAN ATTACKS ON OUR SURFACE FORCES, USING LARGE TYPE PLANES AND TASK FORCES AFTER TOMORROW MORNING. (C) PLAN DECISIVE ACTION BY CONCENTRATING HIS SURFACE STRENGTH IN THE AREA EAST OF SAN BERNARDINO STRAIT AND TACLOBAN WHERE HE HAS HIS TRANSPORT GROUP . . .
AS TO OUR OPERATIONS: (A) EXECUTE OUR ORIGINAL PLAN . . .

2.

By dawn—it was October 24—Kurita was aboard a new flagship, the mighty *Yamato.* His ships were in two circular formations seven miles apart. *Yamato* and her sister ship, *Musashi,* were in the center of the first group, and *Kongo* in the middle of the second. A huge pagodalike tower rose above the deck of *Yamato.* Near the top in the flag bridge was Kurita's headquarters. Just below, in the operations room, his staff was trying to assimilate the fragments of information that were slowly coming in. The First Striking Force went around the southern tip of Mindoro and continued on up into the Sibuyan Sea. The most hazardous part of the trip—a daylight passage following a circumscribed course among numerous islets—not only limited maneuver but was a

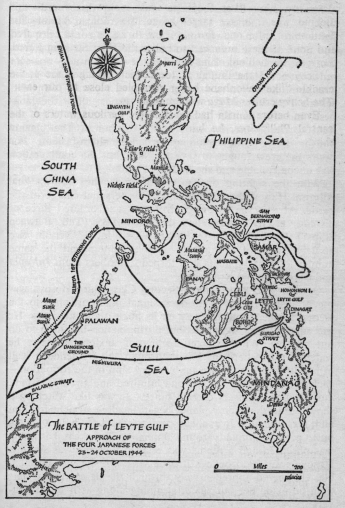

The BATTLE of LEYTE GULF
APPROACH OF
THE FOUR JAPANESE FORCES
23–24 OCTOBER 1944

matchless stalking ground for submarines. But there was no other way to get to San Bernardino Strait, the gateway to the Philippine Sea. Kurita had come to doubt the report that the air engagements off Formosa had crippled American carrier power, but he did not know that Japanese air power in the Philippines had itself been practically annihilated by Halsey and could give him little if any support.

Shortly after 8 A.M. Kurita was again discovered—this time by an American search plane. He radioed Manila for fighter protection. Fewer than a dozen Zeros could be spared and none of these managed to reach the First Striking Force. Every other available land-based plane—180 in all—was sent out to attack Halsey's Third Fleet, which stretched across the Philippine Sea from mid-Luzon to Leyte. Hellcats from Mitscher's Task Force 38 knocked down almost all of the Japanese, but one bomber broke through the screen to hit the light carrier *Princeton* with a 550-lb. bomb. The blazing hangar deck began exploding torpedoes chain-fashion. For hours the crew fought to save the ship, but the conflagration was uncontrollable and she had to be sunk.

With the sighting of Kurita's ships in the Sibuyan Sea, Admiral Halsey characteristically took personal charge of the battle. At 8:37 he by-passed Mitscher and ordered three of his task group commanders direct by TBS (Talk Between Ships:) "Strike! Repeat: Strike! Good luck!" Within two hours the van of this attack—twelve fighters and the same number of dive bombers and torpedo bombers from *Intrepid* and *Cabot*—found Kurita.

On *Musashi,* Petty Officer Second Class Shiro Hosoya was precariously perched in an open signal booth attached to the second bridge, about halfway up its huge island structure. He was supervisor of signalmen but during action had little to do but observe. With a mixed feeling of anxiety and awe he watched the Americans break through the tremendous wall of antiaircraft fire thrown up by every ship in the formation— each battleship had at least one hundred and twenty 25-mm. guns and the cruisers carried ninety. It was like watching a show—until the enemy planes began heading straight for him and for *Yamato.* Just ahead and to the left, half a dozen huge geysers erupted around *Yamato.* The great battleship was obscured and a report was relayed that she was sinking. Hosoya refused to believe it; like *Musashi,* she was unsinkable. He peered apprehensively through the descending waters until he made her out again, steaming along as if on maneuvers.

Suddenly a fountain more than two hundred feet high rose directly in front of Hosoya and drenched the men on deck below. His booth swayed sickeningly as *Musashi* shuddered twice—one from a bomb hit, once from a torpedo. But like her sister, she sailed on serenely as if nothing had happened, evidence that she truly was indestructible. Basically the same as *Yamato*, *Musashi* was better constructed, had superior quarters and was worthy of her nickname, "The Palace." She had been Yamamoto's flagship, then Koga's, and the crew wondered a bit resentfully why Kurita had not chosen to come aboard her for the last battle of the Japanese Navy.

At noon a second attack—twenty-four torpedo planes—swept in toward the two superbattleships. *Musashi* took three more torpedoes but continued on course, all damage under control.

On *Yamato*, which had not yet been hit, Kurita sent another plea for air support, at 1:15 P.M., this to his superior, Admiral Ozawa, as well as to Manila:

WE ARE BEING SUBJECTED TO REPEATED ENEMY CARRIER-BASED AIR ATTACKS. ADVISE IMMEDIATELY OF CONTACTS AND ATTACKS MADE BY YOU ON THE ENEMY.

Fifteen minutes later, twenty-nine planes loomed on the horizon (they were from *Lexington* and *Essex*). To Kurita, the enemy aircraft converging on *Musashi* looked as if they were twice that number.

On *Musashi*'s second bridge Chief Gunnery Officer Koshino was pleading over the voice tube with the captain, Rear Admiral Toshihira Inoguchi, to let him fire the main 18.1-inch guns, the biggest in the world, with a special spray shell called *sanshiki-dan*. "Permission denied," said Inoguchi. A dozen rounds of *sanshiki-dan* could damage a gun's bore; he wanted to save the big guns for the surface battle in Leyte Gulf.

The attackers turned out to be more aggressive than their predecessors. Dive bombers plunged down, accompanied by fighters strafing the decks. The ship became enveloped by water thrown up by near bomb-misses. Then in rapid succession four bombs crashed into *Musashi*. Fragments "like steel popcorn" ricocheted off the bridges. The air was acrid with gunpowder fumes. Another torpedo ripped into the hull.

At last *Musashi* was hurt, and perceptibly. She fell several miles behind *Yamato*, but the executive officer, Captain Kenkichi Kato, who was responsible for damage control, still remained so confident that he didn't think it necessary to report personally to the skipper. The limping ship was, however, affecting the progress of the First Striking Force. Kurita ordered fleet speed reduced to 22 knots so that *Musashi* could keep up, then sent out another request for help.

> FIRST STRIKING FORCE IS ENGAGED IN SEVERE FIGHT IN SIBUYAN SEA. ENEMY AIR ATTACKS ARE EXPECTED TO INCREASE. REQUEST LAND-BASED AIR FORCE AND MOBILE FORCE TO MAKE PROMPT ATTACKS ON ENEMY CARRIER FORCE ESTIMATED TO BE AT LAMON BAY.

Musashi's increased vulnerability gave Chief Gunner Officer Koshino a chance to renew his pleas to use *sanshiki-dan* in the main guns. Admiral Inoguchi argued that the ship was listing, which made it unsafe to fire the guns, but when the executive officer supported Koshino, Inoguchi yielded.

Excitement spread through the ship as the huge guns—the very reason for *Musashi*'s existence—were slowly trained toward the east. Sixty-five planes from *Enterprise* and *Franklin* appeared in the distance. The nine guns roared, the first time they had ever been fired at an enemy. The noise was deafening topside, and belowdecks the ship heaved as if a spread of torpedoes had smashed into her simultaneously. Koshino peered expectantly at the approaching planes but not one was falling into the sea; the formation simply spread out and kept coming.

Only six guns were firing now. The forward turret was silent. One of its guns was jammed with a projectile and the other two could not be elevated higher than 45 degrees. Bombers and torpedo planes swarmed over *Musashi*. From his signal booth Hosoya watched in horror as a line of three torpedoes plowed into the ship's port side, then a bomb exploded into the pagoda structure. Hosoya was knocked to his knees, but almost all those just above him on the command bridge were killed (by chance Inoguchi was at the top of the mast in the observation booth). Seven more torpedoes, bounding like porpoises in the choppy water, smashed one by one into the badly damaged port side.

No one seemed to be in charge of the ship until an order finally came over the voice tube: "First bridge, all killed. Captain will take command from the second bridge." It was Inoguchi, still in the observation tower, and unharmed. There were five more quick explosions, one overhead. The voice from the observation tower was weak: "Captain is wounded. Executive Officer, take command."

Musashi was listing noticeably to port, and on the second bridge Executive Officer Kato ordered the ship leveled by water ballast. Then he leaned out to the signal booth and handed Hosoya a message to transmit to *Yamato,* which was pulling away rapidly.

Electric power was out and Hosoya had to use flags; "*Musashi* capable of cruising at 15 knots. Listing to port about 15 degrees. One bomb hit first bridge, all members killed. Five direct bomb hits and twelve torpedo hits. Captain is alive."

But *Musashi*'s ordeal was not yet over. At 3:20 P.M. the attack was renewed as planes from *Intrepid, Cabot* and *Essex* joined with those still remaining from *Franklin* and *Enterprise.* Kurita's ships continued to throw up a screen of antiaircraft fire but nothing could stop the Americans boring in on *Musashi* for the kill. When they were through, she was left almost helpless, decks awash. The eerie quiet after battle was broken by a shout of "*Banzai!*" from the deck.

"What was that *banzai* for?" Kato yelled down from the second bridge.

"The enemy fleet is destroyed!" a sailor shouted back.

"Who told you that?"

"Chief Gunnery Officer Koshino."

Kato turned back to the bridge. It was just like Koshino to try to keep up the men's morale. The story spread throughout the ship and the crew's fighting spirit remained high despite the seventeen bomb and nineteen torpedo hits. But Kato himself was disconsolate. He informed Inoguchi, who had come down from the observation tower, his left arm in a sling, that the ship was "in no condition to withstand another attack." Hosoya flagged another message to the disappearing Kurita: "Speed six knots, capable of operation. Damage great. What shall we do?"

Musashi was ordered to quit the battle area with a two-destroyer escort. Since leaving Borneo, the First Striking Force had been deprived of the services of a battleship, four heavy cruisers (*Myoko* had just turned back with two damaged shafts) and two destroyers. But the rest of Kurita's fleet continued edging toward the narrows that led to San Bernardino Strait. Just before 4 P.M., however, Kurita had second thoughts. It was still light enough for several more air attacks and it would be impossible to evade them in the channel ahead. They would be trapped. Kurita reversed course and sent a lengthy explanation to Combined Fleet:

... WERE WE TO HAVE FORCED OUR WAY THROUGH AS SCHEDULED UNDER THESE CIRCUMSTANCES, WE WOULD MERELY MAKE OF OURSELVES MEAT FOR THE ENEMY, WITH VERY LITTLE CHANCE OF SUCCESS TO US. IT WAS THEREFORE CONCLUDED THAT OUR BEST COURSE WAS TO RETIRE TEMPORARILY BEYOND RANGE OF HOSTILE PLANES UNTIL FRIENDLY [land-based] PLANES COULD STRIKE A DECISIVE BLOW AGAINST THE ENEMY FORCE.

For an hour Kurita steamed west, but no American planes appeared. Encouraged, he decided to chance the run to San Bernardino Strait, even though there had been no reply to his request for assistance from land-based planes. At 5:15 the First Striking Force reversed course again and began cautiously filing in column between the islands of Masbate and Burias.

On *Musashi,* attempts to level the ship by emergency pumping had failed. Her bow was submerged and she crept along at a few knots. The crew transferred everything movable to the starboard aft section, but the port list grew worse. With the emergency battery-powered signal lamp, Hosoya informed Kurita that *Musashi* was taking on excess water. The answer was:

MUSASHI GO FORWARD OR BACKWARD AT TOP SPEED AND GROUND ON NEAREST ISLAND AND BECOME A LAND BATTERY.

Inoguchi tried to comply, but the listing, sinking ship could only move in circles. He told Hosoya to signal the two escorting destroyers to remove the wounded, but neither acknowledged the message.

"Why don't they come?" Executive Officer Kato fretted and irritably slapped Hosoya on the top of the head. "Try again."

Hosoya repeated the message again and again but there was no reaction. The ship was listing beyond 20 degrees, and as the skies darkened, Inoguchi ordered all men on deck. Ensign Fukujiro Shimoyama, in charge of radio operators, emerged from below with his thirty men, all in spanking clean uniforms. They were appalled at the carnage. Bodies, blasted and mutilated, covered the deck. Shimoyama's men poured gasoline on several hundred thick code books and set them afire. But they burned too slowly; finally Shimoyama had the charred books stowed in canvas bags, weighted with machine guns and tossed overboard.

In the fading light Inoguchi set down his will in a small notebook. It had been a mistake on his part, he wrote, to believe so staunchly in big ships and big guns, and he asked the Emperor and the nation to forgive his errors. He assembled his senior officers and a few petty officers on the second bridge and handed the notebook to Kato. "Give it to the commander of Combined Fleet," he said.

Kato requested permission to go down with the ship. "Damn fool!" Inoguchi muttered. "My responsibility is so great it can't even be compensated by death and I must share the ship's fate, but the executive officer is responsible for taking the crew to safety and getting them aboard a second and third *Musashi* to avenge today's battle." He extended his sword to a youthful ensign. "Thank you for your service. Signal!" Hosoya stepped forward expecting another message but the captain handed him a briefcase containing some money and seven pieces of Toraya sweet bean paste. "Thank you for your service. Do your best to the end."

His last orders to Kato were to save the Emperor's picture, lower the flag and gather all men in the stern for roll call. At about 7:15 P.M. Hosoya supervised the lowering of the flag from the mast as a sailor played the national anthem on a trumpet. The huge flag—an orange sun with sixteen white, sixteen red rays—was reverently tied around the waist of a volunteer, a strong swimmer.

By the time Hosoya and his detail had joined the others in the stern, *Musashi* listed so acutely that ammunition cases and empty shells were clattering down the deck.

"All crew abandon ship," Kato shouted. "You're on your own!"

On the high starboard side Ensign Shimoyama clutched at a rope rail as he pushed the last bag of code books into the sea. The ship took an abrupt lurch to port and the man next to him embraced him, then another hung on to the second man, and another and another, until there was a human chain of ten. Under all this weight the rope snapped and they all tumbled against a hatchway. A second chain of men tobogganed into them, and Shimovama, dazed, gave up trying to save himself. *"Tenno Heika banzai!"* he shouted and left the rest to Fate. The next thing he knew he was in the water with no life belt.

Assistant Paymaster Kiyoshi Takahashi, a youthful ensign, held on to the rail with one hand, still clutching shoes and leggings with the other. He could see some men in the water but hesitated to join them. The ship began rolling on her side. He heard a rumble and saw an avalanche of lumber headed his way. He placed shoes and leggings neatly on the deck, as if he were to return for them later, then vaulted over the rail and scrambled over the ship's exposed bottom toward the keel. As *Musashi* continued to roll he sprinted to keep place, as if on a treadmill. At last he reached the keel and peered down the other side. It was a long drop to the sea but he was a good swimmer. He leaped, bounced off the hull and was unconscious by the time he tumbled into the water.

Hosoya was also running shoeless over razor-sharp barnacles along the bottom of the ship, tring to keep up with her roll. His bare feet were bleeding but he felt no pain. He encountered a gaping black hole. Foaming water rushed in, sucking swimmers back into the bowels of the ship. "Torpedo hole! Follow me!" he shouted and clambered down the steep decline toward the bow. He slipped onto the barnacles, but unaware of the lacerations on his arms and legs, he worked his way to the end of the bow, which was awash. He simply continued on into the water.

Shimoyama, who had been flung safely overboard, after giving up hope, struggled to keep his head above water. A poor swimmer under ideal conditions, he panicked when he heard a monstrous sucking noise. He flailed around and saw the ship falling toward him. He was pulled into the under-tow, and moments later, catapulted to the surface. Half choked, he spat out water but swallowed a mouthful of oil. He was in the middle of a huge slick. He clutched desperately at a piece of lumber and retched.

The good swimmer, Assistant Paymaster Takahashi, who had bounced off the hull, regained consciousness deep under water. Above him glowed a hole of light—too far to be reached. Suddenly a boiling vortex heaved him up. He gasped for air and swam frantically from the undertow. At a distance he turned. *Musashi* was on end, stern in air. In a daze he thought, The ship is standing straight up! He felt the concussion of an underwater explosion. The battleship slid out of sight. All at once there was nothing, not a soul in the strangely calm waters. *I am the only survivor.* He struggled through the viscous oil, collecting bits of flotsam. Then, as if in a dream, he heard distant singing and swam eagerly toward the voices.

Hosoya had also seen *Musashi* sticking up, a black silhouette against the last rays of the sinking sun. Four or five men were clustered at the end of the elevated stern. They seemed to hang on tighter as the great ship plunged. He felt himself being sucked back. There was a gigantic rumble and he flew high in the air. Life seemed to stop as he looked down—almost as if it were happening to someone else—into a great hole in the water far below. He had been gulped and spewed out. Instinctively he rolled into a ball just before splashing back into the sea. Again he was pulled under, into turbulent waters. Still in a fetal-like position, he tumbled around almost unconcerned, with no thought of breathing. Almost too late he realized what was happening and desperately clawed up. At the surface he drew in wonderful air.

The moon lit up the dark sea. There were no voices. He too imagined he was the sole survivor. Someone grabbed him from behind. Hosoya couldn't swim well and purposely sank. The grasping hand let go and when Hosoya surfaced, he was again alone. Then heads began to show up on all sides. He joined a group of men—one was Executive Officer Kato—and they started a search for anything that would float. Hot oil almost a foot deep engulfed them, blackening their faces except for white, swollen mouths and shiny eyes. For an hour Hosoya and Kato clung to the same box. The executive officer began to drowse and Hosoya punched him awake. Someone joked about hitting a superior officer. They sang the national anthem, naval marches and finally popular songs like "Shanghai Gal." After almost four hours, searchlights swept the area and the escort destroyers began picking up survivors. One, however, refused to be rescued. Chief Gunnery Officer Koshino swam away into the darkness.

3.

More than three hundred miles to the north, off Luzon in the Philippine Sea, Ozawa's Mobile Fleet was steaming south. The admiral was to have joined Kurita and Nishimura in the combined attack on Leyte Gulf, but on his way to the battle he had thought of a more effective way to use his four carriers and two semicarriers. He doubted that he could inflict serious damage with only 116 planes. The Mobile Fleet made an impressive appearance, however, and perhaps he could utilize it to draw Halsey's powerful carrier force away from the Leyte area and give Kurita a chance to slip safely through San Bernardino Strait. Ozawa radioed Combined Fleet of his intentions.

The problem had been to make his presence known to Halsey without arousing his suspicions. He did it by launching a strike at *Essex, Lexington* and *Princeton* with seventy-six planes just as Kurita was entering the Sibuyan Sea, moments before the first attack on *Musashi*. It was a hodge-podge collection of almost thirty types of aircraft, but as they took off, the Z flag was raised as it had been twice before in the war—at Pearl Harbor and Midway. The attackers reported hitting two carriers and overflew to Luzon. They had done no damage at all, and moreover, failed in their primary mission. Halsey assumed they were part of the land-based attack on *Princeton* and didn't take the bait. Ozawa, therefore, was forced to send his two semicarriers, *Ise* and *Hyuga,* along with five other ships, farther south as a decoy.

At last American search planes sighted this force, and as Ozawa wanted, this led to the "discovery" at 4:30 P.M. of his main force. He radioed Kurita that the enemy carrier force would probably be drawn north to engage him, thus leaving San Bernardino Strait unguarded. For some reason, the message was never received.

As Ozawa had predicted, this time Halsey fell for the ruse. He knew that the Kurita fleet was steaming toward the gateway to the Philippine Sea, but thought it had been so badly mauled that it "could merely hit and run." Anyway, Admiral Kinkaid's Seventh Fleet, clustered around Leyte Gulf, had more than enough power to destroy Kurita. So why just lie off San Bernardino Strait like a cat at a mousehole and wait for the enemy to strike the first blow? The primary target was Ozawa's carriers. If he destroyed them his future operations "need fear no threat from the sea." Besides, he had no intention of letting Japan's last carrier force escape free, as Spruance had in the Philippine Sea battle; *he* would not be accused of being unaggressive.[*]

Just before 8 P.M. Halsey pointed on a map at Ozawa's position three hundred miles away and told his chief of staff, Robert Carney, "Here's where we're going. Mick, start them north." All that day Halsey had acted as commander of Task Force 38 as well as commander of the entire Third Fleet. In fact, he was leaving Marc Mitscher little to do.

Rear Admiral Carney wrote dispatches ordering all three of Mitscher's available carrier groups to the north. (There was a fourth, recalled from a resupply trip to Ulithi, but it

---

[*]Halsey later told the author Theodore Taylor, "I wish that Spruance had been with Mitscher at Leyte Gulf and I had been with Mitscher in the Battle of the Philippine Sea."

was still hundreds of miles to the east.) Two of these commanders were troubled by the abrupt order. Rear Admiral G. F. Bogan—alarmed by a report that the long-darkened Japanese navigation lights in San Bernardino Strait were lit—personally relayed this disquieting intelligence to one of Halsey's staff officers, who impatiently replied, "Yes, yes, we have that information." Rebuffed, Bogan decided not to recommend that he and Vice Admiral W. A. Lee stay behind with their groups to guard the strait.

"Ching" Lee himself was suspicious of Ozawa and cautioned Halsey that the Japanese carrier force might be a decoy to lure them north. The reply was a curt "Roger." A little later Bogan, too, warned Third Fleet that he was sure Kurita was coming through the strait and got the same answer.

On *Lexington*, Marc Mitscher took Halsey's latest orders to his three task groups to mean that he had been relieved, in effect, as commander of Task Force 38. "Admiral Halsey is in command now," he told his chief of staff, Arleigh Burke, and started for bed.

Commodore Burke was not willing to let it go at this. "We'd better see where that fleet is," he said, and soon word came back that Kurita was "still very much afloat and still moving toward San Bernardino." It was important enough to awaken Mitscher with the suggestion that he urge Halsey to leave two task groups behind to stop Kurita. "Does Admiral Halsey have that report?" Mitscher asked, and when the answer was affirmative, said, "If he wants my advice, he'll ask for it." He rolled over and went back to sleep.

Halsey had not altogether ignored the warnings that Kurita was probably coming through San Bernardino Strait that night. He had already sent out a message that four battleships and a score of cruisers and destroyers "will be formed as Task Force 34" under Admiral Lee to engage Kurita if he appeared. Halsey intended this "merely as a warning," but it was interpreted as an order by Admiral Kinkaid—on his flagship *Wasatch* in Leyte Gulf—who by chance intercepted the message. Assured that Halsey had "set up a plan to guard San Bernardino," Kinkaid no longer worried about Kurita. His concern lay in a different direction. A smaller Japanese surface force—it was Nishimura—was coming up toward him from the south and would probably try to slip through Surigao Strait under cover of darkness and go after the ships massed in Leyte Gulf.

Despite the fact that Kurita had been discovered prematurely and already suffered grievous losses, the plan to disrupt MacArthur's invasion at Leyte Gulf was proceeding better than Combined Fleet had any right to expect. Ozawa had successfully lured Halsey to the north, leaving the strait unguarded and the American commander of shipping in Leyte Gulf complacent. Kurita could still bring more surface fire power than any other fleet in existence, and in the south Nishimura with his seven ships was approaching Surigao Strait on schedule and intact.

Kurita, however, would not be able to keep the rendezvous; the air attacks had delayed him half a day. He radioed Nishimura—on his flagship, *Yamashiro*—to proceed as planned but that he himself would not get to Leyte Gulf until 11 A.M. Nishimura took the news stoically. Like Kurita he was close-mouthed, a seagoing admiral who had never served in the ministry. He was determined to break through Surigao Strait at any cost and die a useful death. (His only son, Teiji, who had graduated at the top of his class at Etajima, had fallen in the Philippines.)

In a van, reconnoitering, was the heavy cruiser *Mogami*, along with three destroyers; they were followed by two old battleships, *Fuso* and *Yamashiro*, and the remaining destroyer, *Shigure*. Just before 11 P.M. *Shigure* sighted three PT boats. On order from Nishimura she turned into them and hit two of the boats. Nishimura radioed Kurita: ADVANCING AS SCHEDULED WHILE DESTROYING ENEMY TORPEDO BOATS.

Nishimura's was not the only Japanese fleet bound for Surigao Strait and the Decisive Battle. Thirty miles behind him came the Second Striking Force, commanded by Vice Admiral Kiyohide Shima. It was an orphan force, despite its impressive appellation, comprising two heavy cruisers, a light cruiser and four destroyers. Originally trained to be the advance guard for Ozawa, it had arbitrarily been placed under Southwest Area Force, headquartered in Manila, and assigned to escort duty. Shima had resisted the order—it would be ignominious to be left out of the coming battle—and his protest to Combined Fleet got him back into action; this time he was to join Kurita in the assault on Leyte Gulf. As he approached the Philippines from the north through the South China Sea, he still did not know exactly what role he would play. Off Lingayen Gulf he got a terse order from the commander of Southwest Area Force to "charge into Leyte Gulf," but again there were no details. A little later, however, a message from Kurita arrived, briefly outlining the joint-attack plan. On his own, Shima decided to follow Nishimura into Surigao Strait; together their two limited forces would be more effective.

Nishimura was informed of Shima's decision but knew nothing more. The two admirals were going into battle, and were from different commands, yet had never communicated with each other. And Nishimura was on radio silence. Acting independently, they would need luck to be able to join forces. As Nishimura neared the strait, PT boats struck again but all their torpedoes missed. The admiral finally radioed that he would go through the narrows between the little island of Panaon and Mindanao—the southern entry to Surigao Strait—at 1:30 A.M.

SEVERAL TORPEDO BOATS SIGHTED BUT ENEMY SITUATION OTHERWISE UNKNOWN.

Still intact, Nishimura steamed through the ten-mile portal on schedule and turned into Surigao Strait itself. Only fifty miles north lay his target—the massed enemy transports.

In the lead were two destroyers, and one mile behind came the flagship, *Yamashiro,* flanked by *Shigure* and another destroyer. Bringing up the rear, six hundred yards apart, were *Fuso* and *Mogami.* Three more PT boats darted out through darkness to launch torpedoes at the destroyers, but Nishimura's luck held. All missed and this time one boat was destroyed.

The moon had set and no wind stirred; the strait was "as calm as a graveyard." It was pleasantly warm on deck, if hot below. Magellan had sailed through these same treacherous waters, now deceptively smooth as glass, from the other direction on March 16, 1521. As if in ominous warning, there were occasional flashes of lightning.

Just ahead, Kinkaid's powerful Seventh Fleet, veiled by darkness, was waiting with apprehension mingled with expectation; no one knew for certain how big the converging Japanese forces were. Aboard the cruiser *Nashville,* General MacArthur refused the captain's request that he disembark. "I have never been able to witness a naval engagement and this is the opportunity of a lifetime. Proceed to the battle area when you wish." Kinkaid invited the general to come aboard his flagship, a transport, but the reply was final: "Transfer from a combatant ship to a noncombatant ship? Never!" The admiral was forced to keep *Nashville* out of the fight.

Tactical command of the action was under Rear Admiral Jesse Oldendorf, and to stop Nishimura and Shima's modest aggregation he had six battleships, four heavy cruisers, four light cruisers and twenty-eight destroyers. Oldendorf was a cheerful man, and reports that his PT boats had scored no hits did not ruffle him. Their main function had been to observe. Soon the Japanese would face destroyers, and then the guns of the cruisers and battleships. At 2:40 A.M. on October 25 a picket destroyer radioed: SKUNK 184 DEGREES, EIGHTEEN MILES.

Nishimura was advancing single file in battle formation. First came the four destroyers, then the two battleships, *Yamashiro* and *Fuso*, and the heavy cruiser *Mogami*. Fifteen minutes later a lookout on the destroyer *Shigure* sighted three ships four miles ahead. The flagship shot up flares, illuminating seven enemy destroyers. They closed fast, and just after 3 A.M. fired twenty-seven torpedoes. One hit *Fuso* and she sheered out to starboard. Five-inch shells were dropping all around the American destroyers, but joined by a second squadron, they came in for another attack.

At 3:20 Shigeru Nishino, captain of *Shigure*, saw phosphorescent wakes "as bright as day" directly ahead. *Shigure* and the other three destroyers heeled over violently, but their attempted evasion came too late. Nishino heard a series of quick explosions. The destroyer just ahead sank with a loud sizzling sound, like a "huge red-hot iron plunged into water"; another was left helplessly adrift and the third limped off.

One of the torpedoes struck a more important target, *Yamashiro*. Nishino heard a calm voice from the flagship say in the clear, "Our ship hit by torpedo. All ships attack!" From what Nishino could see, *Yamashiro*, about a mile and a half away, seemed undamaged. He pulled back to join other ships in a formation attack but could find nothing. What had happened to everyone?

Admiral Nishimura, unaware of the extent of the damage to his fleet, radioed Kurita and Shima from his flagship:

URGENT BATTLE REPORT NUMBER 2. ENEMY TORPEDO BOATS AND DESTROYERS PRESENT ON BOTH SIDES OF NORTHERN ENTRANCE TO SURIGAO STRAIT. TWO OF OUR DESTROYERS TORPEDOED AND DRIFTING, YAMASHIRO SUSTAINED ONE TORPEDO HIT BUT NO IMPEDIMENT TO BATTLE CRUISING.

Eight minutes later, at 3:38 A.M., there was a flash of light to the rear, followed by an awesome rumble. The damaged *Fuso*, nine miles away, had been blown in half. Both ends remained afloat, buring furiously. Twenty minutes later, with a rumble, *Michishio*, the drifting destroyer, also disintegrated.

But Nishimura would not give up. With his remaining three ships, *Yamashiro*, *Mogami* and *Shigure*, he continued north toward Leyte Gulf—and into the leveled guns of the Seventh Fleet. Oldendorf had caught his foe coming bow-on. He had crossed the T, as Nelson had done at Trafalgar and Togo at Tsushima, where more equal forces were involved. At 3:51 the cruisers opened fire followed by the six battleships—all but one had been hit or sunk at Pearl Harbor. This barrage was "the most beautiful sight" the commander of the American destroyer screen had ever witnessed. The blinding streams of tracers arching above his head resembled "a continued stream of lighted railroad cars going over a hill."

Both *Mogami* and *Yamashiro* returned fire even as they recoiled from hit after hit. The heavy cruiser loosed torpedoes at 4:01 A.M. and was soon deluged by shells from destroyers which had closed in. Burning and crippled, she turned back south. *Yamashiro* was also ablaze from stem to stern. At 4:09 the heavy shelling inexplicably stopped. (Oldendorf had got word that he was hitting his own destroyers.) In the hiatus *Yamashiro* too reversed course and started south after *Mogami*, but the flagship was undone. Within ten minutes she capsized and sank, taking with her Nishimura and almost the entire crew.

Thin-skinned *Shigure* was still alive. One shell had ripped through her stern but hundreds of others had missed, sending up an almost constant wall of water on either side. Nishino, benumbed by the deafening roar of battle and the jarring concussions of near misses that had knocked out every precision instrument, saw a large ship in flames to his left. It looked like a huge hunk of red-hot iron; it must be *Fuso*. He ordered right rudder, but there was no response. He brought the destroyer to a stop for repairs.

To the south, just as the first torpedoes were being launched at Nishimura, Shima's Second Striking Force had entered Surigao Strait at 28 knots. Almost immediately Shima's column was set upon by PT boats, which damaged the light cruiser *Abukuma* so severely she had to be left behind. The remaining six ships continued north. They were engulfed in a sudden squall but blindly continued to thread their way through the narrows at the same speed. At 3:25 A.M. the squall ended and Shima, who had not received Nishimura's "Urgent Battle Report Number 2" that his flagship and two destroyers had been torpedoed, ordered the Second Striking Force to go into battle formation with the flagship *Nachi* in the lead, followed by the other heavy cruiser, *Ashigara,* and the four destroyers. Rain spit spasmodically and visibility was poor, but Shima called for more speed. Everyone on *Nachi*'s bridge strained to see ahead. Suddenly there came a blinding blossom of light that seemed to fill the entire strait. Some capital ship had blown up; Shima hoped it was American.

It was *Fuso.*

To encourage Nishimura, Shima said by radiotelephone, "We have arrived at battle site." His column was still bearing down at almost top speed. Ahead, two ships (they were the two sections of *Fuso*) were blazing intensely like "steel-mill flames," and Shima deduced that Nishimura's fleet had been smashed. The Second Striking Force passed to the left of the burning sections, hugging the coast to keep out of the glow.

Through the stationary telescope Shima watched destroyers dart in and out of a smoke screen. His own ships closed on another destroyer to starboard, dead in the water—a Japanese flag on its mast. It flashed out a blue signal: "I am destroyer *Shigure.* Rudder is damaged and under repair."

Nachi plunged into the smoke. In the distance came the deep, slow crump of big guns; the remnants of Nishimura must be ahead and still fighting. The column emerged through the smoke screen, only to face another. To the right was a large ship in flames, but Shima couldn't tell if it was American or Japanese. It was *Mogami.* Shima's radar detected an enemy fleet due north almost six miles. "All ships attack!" he ordered by radiotelephone.

The torpedo officer, Commander Kokichi Mori, suggested that the two heavy cruisers also launch torpedoes from the port. Shima approved, and *Nachi,* followed by *Ashigara,* turned sharply to starboard as the destroyers, which could only fire upon sighting the enemy, spurted straight ahead. Just to the left was *Mogami,* and she appeared to be dead in the water. *Nachi* launched her eight torpedoes, and moved up to hide behind the glare of *Mogami.* But as he approached, Shima saw to his surprise that *Mogami*'s prow had a wake. She was bearing down at almost 8 knots on a collision course. "Hard starboard!" he shouted, but the blazing *Mogami* moved straight at *Nachi* and there was a jarring crunch.

"This is *Mogami!*" someone called from the bridge through a megaphone. "Captain and executive officer killed. Gunnery officer in charge. Steering destroyed. Steering by engine. Sorry."

The two ships drifted slowly as if locked together, then *Nachi* cautiously turned left and the two ships parted, *Mogami* continuing south. The port side of *Nachi*'s prow was gone and engineers reported top speed would be reduced to 20 knots. Shima still wanted to follow his destroyers and attack. "Up ahead the enemy must be waiting for us with open arms," Mori objected. "Nishimura's force is almost totally destroyed. It is obvious that the Second Striking Force will fall into a trap. We may die any time." Besides, they didn't even know what Kurita was doing. "In any case, it's foolish to go ahead now."

There were still two hours left of darkness to hide their withdrawal. Shima's immediate task was to collect the remnants of Nishimura's force as well as his own. The fleeing ships were again harassed by PT boats near the south entrance of the strait. The persistent little craft were fought off, but to the rear a pursuing force of two light cruisers and three destroyers picked off the crippled destroyer *Asagumo*. This ended the surface pursuit, but Shima was not yet out of range of American aircraft. A wave of Avengers found the straggling *Mogami*, and a bomb in the engine room forced her abandonment. (Now only *Shigure* remained of Nishimura's fleet.) Within an hour Shima saw a second wave of Avengers on the horizon. In the radio room Lieutenant (j.g.) Kameda, born in Honolulu, adjusted to the enemy cycle and began broadcasting in English: "Hello, Charley One, hello Charley One. Jap carrier planes attacking us. Abandon your present mission and return to base immediately."

On the bridge Shima watched as the oncoming planes abruptly wheeled and headed back north.*

4.

At almost the same moment that Nishimura prepared to make his foray into Surigao Strait, Kurita edged into San

---

*There is no confirmation of this incident from American sources. It was related by Admiral Shima.

Bernardino Strait two hundred miles to the north. The passage, narrower than Surigao Strait, was difficult for a single ship to navigate even in the daytime because of a stiff 8-knot current. Kurita had to bring a ten-mile column of twenty-two ships through in pitch-dark; all the navigation lights had been turned off.

As Kurita debouched into the Philippine Sea, he expected to encounter attacks from submarines and a sizable surface force. There was not a ship in sight. Expecting discovery momentarily, he placed his ships in night-scouting formation as they skirted the east coast of Samar and headed south for Leyte Gulf.

At 6:27 A.M. the sun rose in a dreary sky, and the order went out to re-form in a circle around *Yamato*. Clouds hung low, occasional gusts of rain swept the ships, and the water was choppy. High in the observation tower of the cruiser *Kumano*, Lieutenant (s.g.) Shigeo Hirayama was dozing at his battle station. Like everyone else in the First Striking Force, he had had almost no sleep in seventy-two hours. He rubbed his eyes hard and searched the horizon. An enemy plane was approaching from the east. It looked like a carrier-based torpedo plane. What was it doing coming straight on?

Its pilot, an ensign named Jensen, on antisubmarine patrol, was as surprised as Hirayama. He started down toward the cruiser in a glide-bomb approach.

Simultaneously observers on *Yamato* sighted four "masts" on the horizon twenty miles to the southeast. They were soon identified as the island structures of carriers. God has come to our assistance! thought Koyanagi. This was a target worthy of their big guns. The younger officers cheered, their cheeks glistening with tears.

It had to be one of Mitscher's four powerful carrier groups. There was no alternative but to attack and Kurita wanted none. His one hope was that this task group was isolated. He closed in, altering his course slightly to 110 degrees, and radioed Combined Fleet:

BY HEAVEN-SENT OPPORTUNITY, WE ARE DASHING TO ATTACK ENEMY CARRIERS. OUR FIRST OBJECTIVE IS TO DESTROY THE FLIGHT DECKS, THEN THE TASK FORCE.

Mitscher's big carriers were far to the north—at Halsey's command—chasing the decoy, Ozawa, and what the Japanese saw was one of the Seventh Fleet's subsidiary forces, Taffy 3, whose function was to provide air cover for the amphibious shipping at Leyte. Commanded by Rear Admiral Clifton A. F. Sprague, it comprised three destroyers and four destroyer escorts, as well as six escort carriers (nicknamed "baby flattops" or "jeeps") holding no more than twenty-eight planes each and with a top speed of 19 knots. Sprague had been caught by surprise; his radar had just detected the enemy.

At 6:58 A.M. the main batteries of *Yamato* bellowed. For the first time the monstrous 3,220-lb. shells were hurled at an enemy surface target from the 70-foot-long barrels. Other ships joined in, as enthusiastic crews, on attack at last, worked their guns in a thundering chorus. Enemy destroyers tried to screen the carriers with smoke, but tiny planes could still be seen taking off from their flight decks "like bees." Kurita ordered General Attack. Breaking formation, all ships closed at optimum speed, and the chase became an unorganized scramble.

Sprague's carriers moved away sluggishly to the east, hastily launching fighters and Avengers armed with bombs. Salvos from the oncoming enemy ships fell closer and closer, sending up pink, green, red, yellow and purple geysers—the projectiles had been loaded with various dyes for identification. Their explosions had a "kind of horrid beauty" for Sprague. At 7:01 A.M. he radioed an appeal in the clear for help. To the south were two similar forces of baby flattops, Taffy 1 and Taffy 2. "Don't be alarmed," shouted the commander of Taffy 2, only thirty miles away. "Remember we're back of you. Don't get excited! Don't do anything rash!"

But these reassurances were meaningless. Sprague knew his ships could not "survive another five minutes of the heavy-caliber fire being received." Just then Taffy 3 was swallowed by a rain squall. It was a brief respite but it gave Sprague time enough to make a hard decision: he would not scatter his force but "pull the enemy out where somebody else could smack him." He turned to the south toward Taffy 2 and its planes; then, at 7:16 A.M., he ordered his three destroyers— *Hoel, Heermann* and *Johnston*—to counterattack. Possibly their sacrifice could buy time. *Johnston* (her captain was a Cherokee, Ernest E. Evans) closed to within 10,000 yards of *Kumano* and launched ten torpedoes. One hit the heavy cruiser, slowing her to 20 knots and putting her out of the battle. But *Johnston* paid for her daring as a trio each of 14- and 6-inch shells tore into her. It was, her senior surviving officer recalled, "like a puppy being smacked by a truck." She somehow remained afloat, her decks and bridge covered with dead.

Hoel was within range of two enemy columns, battleships on the left, cruisers on the right. Her captain, Commander Leon S. Kintberger, started for the big ones. Columns of green-dyed water showered *Hoel*. A shell smashed into the bridge. But the destoyer kept moving in and at 9,000 yards loosed a spread of torpedoes at the leading battleship. Kintberger swung his ship toward the cruisers, but shells knocked out the main engine and jammed the rudder hard right. He could still maneuver the ship by one engine and worked his way broadside of the cruiser column. At 7:35 A.M. his remaining five torpedoes began churning toward *Haguro,* the foremost cruiser.

In the dense smoke *Heermann*, the third destroyer, almost rammed a friendly destroyer escort and barely missed swiping *Hoel*. *Heermann* turned north, and while firing seven torpedoes at *Haguro*, sighted a battleship on the left. It was *Kongo*, which began to concentrate fire on *Heermann*. So did *Haguro* as soon as she had evaded the torpedoes. Two more Japanese battleships bore down on the destroyer, but *Heermann,* outdoing David, pressed the attack on still another adversary, the battleship *Haruna,* which was little more than two miles away. She peppered *Haruna* with 5-inch shells, and after launching her last three torpedoes, scampered away at 8:03 A.M.—miraculously still not hit by anything except shell fragments.

But the damaged *Hoel* was hemmed in by *Kongo* and several heavy cruisers. Hit at least forty times, *Hoel* continued to throw some five hundred shells at the enemy before her remaining engine was knocked out. At 8:30 A.M. she came to a stop, listing to port with one magazine on fire. Only then did Kintberger give the word to abandon ship.

Sprague's six jeep carriers had emerged from the squall in circular formation. Ten miles to the north lay the Japanese battleships, and a little closer to the northeast were four enemy cruisers. These blanketed *Gambier Bay* and *Kalinin Bay* with heavy fire, but the clumsy little carriers managed to evade every salvo. *Kalinin Bay,* however, could not escape the battleships' barrage and was hit fifteen times. Still, damage-control teams working waist-deep in oil and water kept her in formation.

Fighting back with her single 5-inch gun, *Gambier Bay* weaved around, managing to escape any damage for almost half an hour, but at last a shell struck the flight deck. Then a salvo plummeted into the water just off the carrier's port. One shell hit below the water line, flooding the forward engine room. *Gambier Bay* slowed to 11 knots, dropping out of formation.

At 8:30 A.M. Commander Evans, the Cherokee skipper of the already battered destroyer *Johnston*, saw the heavy cruiser *Chikuma* move in for the kill. "Commence firing on the cruiser, Hagen," he told his gunnery officer. "Draw her fire away from *Gambier Bay*."

Johnston limped at 17 knots to within 6,000 yards of *Chikuma* and pumped five shells into her, but she ignored the destroyer. *Heermann*, still sound, joined the attack and forced *Chikuma* to turn some of her guns away from *Gambier Bay*. But it was too late. The carrier began to sink at 8:45 A.M.

Now Evans turned *Johnston* to face the light cruiser *Yahagi* and four destroyers which were converging on the remaining carriers. Evans closed in on *Yahagi*, which was moving into position to torpedo one of the carriers, and discharged such harassing fire with *Johnston*'s 5-inch guns—she made a dozen hits—that the light cruiser was forced to launch her torpedoes prematurely. *Yahagi*'s accompanying destroyers followed suit. Not a carrier was hit, but the Japanese jubilantly reported that "three enemy carriers and one cruiser were enveloped in black smoke and observed to sink, one after another."

Evans, who had pressured the enemy into launching their attack too soon, strutted across the bridge exclaiming, "Now I've seen everything!" But the Japanese had their measure of revenge. Cruisers and destroyers hemmed in *Johnston*. Her crew fought back until the ship was dead in the water and Evans reluctantly had to give the order to abandon her. Of the complement of 327, only 141 were picked up alive. The Cherokee skipper was not among them.

While Sprague's destroyers, aided by the four equally aggressive destroyer escorts, were blunting Kurita's surface attack, carrier planes from Taffy 2 and 3 hit the First Striking Force time and again. Three heavy cruisers—*Suzuya*, *Chikuma* and *Chokai*—sustained such damage that they were forced to retire.

Kurita was unaware that his advance force had been so frustrated; *Yamato*'s last two scout planes had been knocked down and her radiotelephone was out of order. Moreover, it looked from a distance through the smoke as if the advance guard had lost sight of the enemy. "Let's discontinue this chase," Koyanagi advised. "There's still Leyte Gulf to attack." Kurita concurred, and at 9:11 A.M. a message was radioed: RENDEZVOUS, MY COURSE NORTH, SPEED 20.

On the bridge of *Fanshaw Bay*, Sprague heard a signalman yell at 9:25 A.M., "Goddamit, boys, they're getting away!" The surface battle—the last of World War II—was over. Taffy 3 had not only withstood attack from the greatest array of guns afloat as well as a massive torpedo assault but inflicted serious damage on a superior force. For over an hour all was quiet. Then, at 10:50, General Quarters was again sounded on the five surviving jeep carriers. Nine enemy planes were approaching at mast level, so low that radar had failed to pick them up. They climbed to several thousand feet as American fighters tried to intercept them. Five Zero fighters with bombs lashed to their wings emerged from the milling mass and slanted down toward the jeeps. They were led by a recently married lieutenant commander, Yukio Seki. One Zero headed for the bridge of *Kitkun Bay*, its machine guns winking. Onlookers expected it to pull up; instead it drove into the port catwalk, exploded and tumbled on into the sea. Two others roared straight at *Fanshaw Bay*, also with obvious intent to crash into her, only to disintegrate at the last moment. The final two veered off from the heavy fire thrown up by *White Plains*. One, trailing smoke, banked toward *St. Lo* in a right turn as if intending to land, but the pilot pushed the little plane over, slamming it into the flight deck. Fires spread throughout the hangar deck, setting off a chain of violent internal explosions. After having survived the running battle unscathed, *St. Lo* sank.

Her survivors nicknamed the Japanese pilot "devil diver." He was a *kamikaze*. The idea for suicide attacks had recently risen spontaneously among groups of Army and Navy fliers, and several isolated efforts had been made before that day.*

---

*In 1570 a Mongol emperor set sail for Japan with an invasion fleet. It looked as if Japan would easily be conquered, but a typhoon dispersed the Mongol ships. Convinced that the typhoon had been called up by the gods, the Japanese named it *kamikaze*, "divine wind."

The first Navy *kamikaze* was Rear Admiral Masafumi Arima. He took off from Clark Field on October 15, during the Formosa battle, intent on crashing his bomber into a carrier, but was shot down before he reached any American ship. The first *kamikaze* attack, however, had come a month earlier. On the evening of September 12 a group of Army pilots of the 31st Fighter Squadron located on Negros Island decided on their own to launch a suicide attack the following morning. Two were selected—First Lieutenant Takeshi Kosai and a sergeant.

But it was not until Vice Admiral Takijiro Onishi arrived in Luzon—just before the American landing at Leyte—to take command of Fifth Base Air Force and learned he had fewer than a hundred operable planes that the *Kamikaze* Special Attack Corps was officially organized.

"In my opinion," he told his commanders, "there is only one way of channeling our meager strength into maximum efficiency, and that is to organize suicide attack units composed of Zero fighters equipped with 250-kilogram bombs, with each plane to crash-dive into an enemy carrier."

Onishi's proposal was explained to the pilots. "Their eyes shone feverishly in the dimly lit room," reported one commander named Tamai. "Each must have been thinking of this as a chance to avenge comrades who had fallen recently in the fierce Marianas fighting, and at Palau and Yap. Theirs was an enthusiasm that flames naturally in the hearts of youthful men."

Onishi's *kamikaze* group was created specifically to support Kurita's raid on Leyte Gulf, and the first attack had come earlier that morning. Six suicide planes and four escorts took off from Mindanao at 6:30 A.M. and went north. While Taffy 3 was fighting off Kurita, the Special Attack planes came upon Taffy 1. One Zero crashed into *Santee* and another into *Suwannee*, but both of these jeep carriers were soon back in action. Nevertheless, all those who had seen the Japanese boring in with such fatalism were still shaken by the experience. It was a preview of things to come.

5.

It took Kurita almost two hours to collect his scattered forces—reduced from thirty-two ships to fifteen within three days—and again head south in ring formation for Leyte Gulf. The admiral and most of his staff hadn't slept since leaving Brunei and stayed alert by sheer will power. Koyanagi had difficulty moving around the bridge even with the

---

Captain Tatsumaru Sugiyama, one of the fifty aviation experts who had plotted to assassinate Tojo, was in charge of maintenance. He rigged 100-kilogram bombs on two fighter planes, and an hour before dawn the two pilots took off, determined to crash into carriers. They never returned. Apparently they, like Arima, were shot down before reaching a target, since there is no record on September 13 of an enemy plane ramming into an American ship.

help of a cane; he had been hit in the thigh by shrapnel the day before.

Kurita was more certain than ever that he had just encountered one of Halsey's carrier groups (Ozawa's message that he had lured Halsey north never reached First Striking Force). In addition, a report was intercepted—probably from a land-based plane—that a fleet of enemy carriers lay 113 miles north of the mouth of Leyte Gulf. Could they be Halsey's remaining task groups? In any case, Kurita would get no help from Nishimura's detached fleet that was supposed to invade Leyte Gulf from the south; Nishino, on the destroyer *Shigure*, had radioed that his was the only ship left afloat.

About 11:40 A.M. a lookout reported sighting an enemy battleship and several destroyers on the horizon. Kurita gave chase but could find nothing; perhaps the lookout had suffered from a delusion. Then a radio message to the effect that part of Kinkaid's force was making a sortie from Leyte Gulf was intercepted. It appeared likely that most of the transports had escaped. Even those which remained would have had five days to unload.

If Kurita charged into the narrow confines of the gulf to sink these transports, his own ships would be at the mercy of enemy land- and carrier-based planes. The First Striking Force might be wiped out—and for what? A few practically empty transports. This, Kurita reasoned, would be absurd. He decided instead—and he was seconded by Koyanagi and the rest of the staff—to turn north, and with the help of Japanese land-based planes, attack the enemy task force which was located less than a hundred miles away.*

---

*"The destruction of enemy carriers was a kind of obsession with me, and I fell victim to it," Kurita told author Masanori Ito in a unique interview after the war. "As I consider it now, my judgment does not seem to have been sound. Then the decision seemed right, but my mind was extremely fatigued. It should probably be called 'a judgment of exhaustion.' I did not feel tired at the time, but having been under great strain and without sleep for three days and nights, I was drained both physically and mentally."

The admiral refused to be interviewed for this book but consented to let Admiral Koyanagi speak for him. "I think now we should have gone into Leyte Gulf," he said. "So does Admiral Kurita. Then we thought we were doing the best thing but now, with a cool head, I realize we were obsessed by enemy task forces. Just because we got the report—and it turned out to be false—that there was a fleet of enemy carriers nearby, we shouldn't have set out after them."

If Kurita had continued on to Leyte Gulf, he would first have encountered Kinkaid's Seventh Fleet and then undergone a series of air

The entire bridge was electrified by the decision. Forgotten was the ordeal of the past few days, which had left them bone-tired and depressed; it was as if they were going into battle for the first time.

At 12:35 P.M. Kurita sent out a fleet order to reverse course and "engage in decisive battle with the enemy task force which is in position bearing 5 degrees, distant 113 miles from Suluan lighthouse."

The news was greeted on every ship with shouts of *"Banzai!"* The First Striking Force headed north to wage its final battle.

6.

His prey—Task Force 38—was in reality far out of range to the north in its pursuit of Ozawa. Early that morning three American scout planes had discovered the Mobile Force, and by 8 A.M. 180 dive bombers, fighters and torpedo planes had closed in on *Chitose* and *Zuiho*. Only a handful of Japanese fighters came up to intercept. The rest of Ozawa's planes had been sent to the Philippines to save them. Both light carriers were hit by bombs and *Chitose* began to sink. Then a bomb exploded in the forward engine room of the destroyer *Akizuki*, and a torpedo drove into the flagship, *Zuikaku*.

There were no fighters to oppose the second wave. Through heavy flak the thirty-six planes converged on the fourth carrier, *Chiyoda*. Bombs exploded along her deck and, aflame, she assumed a sharp list. Ozawa's flagship could still navigate at 20 knots, but her rudder was damaged and communications were out. Ozawa, who had had to be dragged off the stricken *Taiho* at the Battle of the Philippine Sea, abandoned *Zuikaku* without protest. There was no honor involved. He had accomplished his purpose and given

---

attacks in confined waters. There was considerable shipping in the gulf—including twenty-three LST's and twenty-eight Liberty ships—but what if all these had been sunk? Most of the supplies had been landed, as Kurita has guessed, and there was on shore enough for a month's military operations. MacArthur claimed that loss of these ships would have "placed in jeopardy" the entire invasion. Still aboard were most of the steel landing mats for the airstrips, and without these he could have lost local air superiority temporarily. Also, a naval bombardment on American troops might have wreaked momentary havoc. Nevertheless, it is doubtful that MacArthur's advance would have been delayed more than a week or so.

Kurita his chance to destroy the amphibious shipping in Leyte Gulf.

Halsey's arbitrary actions the day before had left a worried Admiral Kinkaid in the gulf. He tried to confirm his impression that an emergency battle line—the newly created Task Force 34 under Admiral Lee—had been formed in front of San Bernardino Strait, but received no reply for more than two and a half hours. And when Halsey's answer finally arrived it jarred him—Task Force 34 was with the carriers engaging Ozawa!

By this time Kurita's fleet had hit Taffy 3, and Kinkaid replied with a plea for help: URGENTLY NEED BBS [battleships] LEYTE GULF AT ONCE.

Halsey's reaction was one of annoyance. It wasn't his job to protect the Seventh Fleet; he was carrying out a more important mission, attacking the main carrier force of the enemy. The best he could do was order Mitscher's fourth task group, which was still hundreds of miles to the east, to head for Leyte.

In the meantime Kinkaid ("I've had to fight my temper all my life") had sent Halsey another message with details of the powerful force that seemed certain to crush Taffy 3: . . . REQUEST LEE COVER LEYTE AT TOP SPEED X REQUEST FAST CARRIERS MAKE IMMEDIATE STRIKE.

This double request irritated Halsey. He had already done as much as he could and was in the middle of his own battle. Twenty-two minutes later Halsey received still another radio from Kinkaid:

. . . REQUEST IMMEDIATE AIR STRIKE X ALSO REQUEST SUPPORT BY HEAVY SHIPS X MY OBBS [the old battleships which had bombarded Nishimura] LOW IN AMMUNITION.

This was "a new factor, so astonishing" that Halsey found it hard to accept. Why hadn't Kinkaid informed him of this earlier? Halsey replied that he was "still engaging enemy carriers" and had already sent the fourth task group of five carriers and four heavy cruisers to Kinkaid's assistance.

Little more than half an hour later yet another desperate message came from Kinkaid, this one not even in code:

WHERE IS LEE X SEND LEE

In Pearl Harbor, Nimitz was following the trials of Taffy 3, and like Kinkaid, he assumed that Task Force 34 had been detached to guard San Bernardino Strait the previous night. Now he, too, asked Halsey where that phantom task force was. A communications ensign added padding to confuse enemy decoders at the beginning and end of the message:

TURKEY TROTS TO WATER GG FROM CINCPAC . . . X WHERE IS RPT [repeat] WHERE IS TASK FORCE THIRTY-FOUR RR THE WORLD WONDERS

This dispatch reached Halsey's flagship, *New Jersey,* a moment after Kinkaid's message in the clear. The typist, Burton Goldstein, realized that TURKEY TROTS TO WATER was padding and omitted it, but THE WORLD WONDERS, despite the RR which set it off, sounded so plausible that he figured it might be a part of the text itself. So did his superior, a lieutenant, and the message was relayed to the bridge.

Infuriated by the words THE WORLD WONDERS ("as if I had been struck in the face"), Halsey slammed his cap to the deck. Carney grabbed him by the arm and said, "Stop it! What the hell's the matter with you? Pull yourself together!"

Fuming, Halsey showed him the dispatch. How could Chester Nimitz have sent "such an insult"? He ordered one of Mitscher's carrier groups to head south while the other two continued the attacks on Ozawa.

A third strike of more than two hundred planes at 1:10 P.M. set both *Zuikaku* and *Zuiho* afire. The latter steamed off at full speed, but *Zuikaku* gradually heeled over until the flight deck was awash. At 2:07 the big ship, which had survived so many battles, slid under. Mitscher's fourth wave, small like the second, concentrated on *Ise* and *Zuiho*. The rugged converted battleship managed to escape, but *Zuiho*, mortally wounded, was sent under.

It was the end of Ozawa's carriers. Three were at the bottom and the fourth, *Chiyoda,* was dead in the water. Ozawa had decoyed Halsey to the north but the shipping in Leyte Gulf remained intact. His sacrifice had been in vain.

Ten minutes after Kurita made his decision to turn away from Leyte Gulf, he was attacked by seventy fighters and Avengers from Taffy 3. *Tone* and *Nagato* were each hit by bombs but the fleet continued to search for the enemy carriers. Two more air attacks (147 sorties in all from Mitscher's still-distant fourth task group) did no damage, but

Kurita was more certain than ever that his target was close by. All afternoon he pressed the search but found nothing; neither did he hear from Ozawa. By 6 P.M. he had steamed all the way back to San Bernardino Strait. There he patrolled with instructions from Combined Fleet to engage in a night battle if possible.

But the First Striking Force was low on fuel, and since no reports of enemy carriers had come in, Kurita reluctantly ordered a retirement. At 9:25 P.M. the remnants of the once mighty fleet found its way through the dark, dangerous waters of San Bernardino Strait.

The desperate plan to devastate shipping in Leyte Gulf had resulted in catastrophic losses: four carriers, three battleships, six heavy cruisers, three light cruisers and ten destroyers. About 300,000 tons of combat shipping had been sunk, more than a quarter of all Japanese losses since Pearl Harbor. Never again would the Imperial Navy play more than a minor role in the defense of the homeland.

23   The Battle of Breakneck Ridge

1.

Admiral Kurita's defeat on October 25 meant the virtual isolation of the Philippines but General Sosaku Suzuki, who was in charge of the defense of the central islands, had never been more confident. No American had flown over his headquarters island, Cebu, that day—confirmation that enemy air power had been crushed over Formosa. About noon optimistic reports of Kurita's battle off Samar began coming in: a number of American carriers had been sunk; *Yamato* and other battleships were raiding Leyte Gulf.

"General Tomochika," he told his chief of staff, "we are about to step on the center of the stage. There is no greater honor or privilege. We don't even need all the reinforcements they are sending us." Two units were coming from Luzon: the 1st Division would land at Ormoc, on Leyte's west coast, while the 26th Division landed at the port of Carigara, in the north. The two forces would merge and retake Tacloban in ten days.

Of this Suzuki had no doubt: his concern was that MacArthur might try to surrender only his local forces, as Wainwright had done after the fall of Corregidor. "We must demand the capitulation of MacArthur's entire forces, those in New Guinea and other places as well as the troops on Leyte."

Suzuki's "air superiority" would not last long. That night, steel matting for the strips on Leyte was off-loaded but the laying on the following day was hampered by air raids and heavy rains. By nightfall every field was a quagmire. The engineers worked doggedly through the night of the twenty-seventh, and put down the last section on the Tacloban strip soon after dawn in time to welcome P-38's of the Fifth Air Force. One cracked up, but the other thirty-three landed safely.

Under persistent attacks by the U.S. 7th Division, the Japanese had retreated across the coastal plain all the way to Dagami. General Makino ordered the rear guard of his 16th Division to hold the town while the main body fell back to the foothills of the mountain range running down the island.

To the north the U.S. 24th Division was also driving west steadily. Their goal was Jaro, like Dagami at the foothills of the mountains. Held up by stiffening resistance and a river, the first GI's finally broke into the town on October 29 and turned up Highway 2—a twelve-foot-wide road with a crushed-rock and gravel surface—toward Carigara.

Poor communications continued to plague Suzuki. There were only fragmentary reports that the Americans were pushing north. He was, moreover, still ignorant of the debacle at sea. That afternoon Major Shigeharu Asaeda, General Yamashita's operations officer, flew into Cebu from Manila with more good news: the 1st Division would land at Ormoc a few days ahead of schedule, along with a battalion of the 26th Division.

Asaeda did not enlighten Suzuki about the situation confronting him. Suzuki was an able man but too honest and naïve; if he thought he was going to win he would fight much better. Asaeda, therefore, promised Suzuki continued reinforcements that he knew would never be sent, or if sent, could never arrive intact because of America's overwhelming air superiority. Suzuki had no chance to win, but why burden him with the truth? There was a saying: "The blind man fears no snake."

On the morning of November 1, eleven thousand men of the 1st Division left Manila in a driving rainstorm in four large transports escorted by six destroyers and four coastal defense ships. The 1st, also known as Gem Division, was an elite unit established in 1874 which had seen duty in the Sino-Japanese and Russo-Japanese wars. That summer it had been detached from the Kwantung Army and alerted for duty against the Americans. It had gone from northern Manchuria by rail to Shanghai, where it was trained as an emergency force.

En route to Leyte, company commanders explained to their men what lay ahead. On *Takatsu-maru* Lieutenant Minetoshi Yahiro told his platoon leaders that Americans had landed in force on Leyte and one division was heading for Carigara. Gem Division was to stop it. "We have long been preparing for this day. The hour has come when we must use all our training and skills."

Soon after sunset the throbbing noise of the engines stopped and the troops, jammed snugly in tiers of bunks, heard the clatter of chains as anchors plunged down. They had arrived at Ormoc, on Leyte. Orders were shouted; the men, their filthy uniforms crawling with lice, disentangled themselves and started up steep iron ladders to the upper decks out of stifling holds, foul with the stench of bodies.

Corporal Kiyoshi Kamiko, one of Yahiro's squad leaders, gulped in the fresh air. Overhead, stars were bright pinpoints; the sea was calm. He had been a primary-school teacher before being conscripted just after Pearl Harbor. Determined and idealistic, he had enjoyed the years of training in Manchuria, accepting most of the brutalities of noncoms as necessary conditioning. He liked the comradeship of the Army, the feeling that each man depended on the next. Like the other men of Gem Division he was eager to prove himself in battle and do his duty for Japan and the Emperor.

The frightening but exhilarating rumble of distant guns came over the water. To remember the moment, Kamiko looked at his watch in the starlight. It was seven-thirty. Rope ladders tumbled over the sides of the transports, and the men, each weighed down with ninety pounds of equipment, swung awkwardly over the rail. At a flashlight signal from below, Kamiko leaped clumsily into a gently pitching boat. He landed on his back and finally realized why they had been instructed to remove their heavy ammunition belts.

On shore General Tomochika was anxiously observing the landing. He had preceded Suzuki to Leyte, to be greeted by the dismaying report that Makino's entire 16th Division was close to collapse. He stepped forward to meet Lieutenant General Tadasu Kataoka, commander of Gem Division, and his staff. "The First Division," he told them, "will proceed with the greatest possible speed along the Ormoc–Limon–Carigara road [Highway 2] and assemble to the area southeast of Carigara and prepare to attack."

Being a cavalry officer, Kataoka looked for the unexpected. What if they were attacked *before* they reached Carigara in the mountains near Limon?

"Proceed to Carigara," Tomochika answered. The possibility was ridiculous. "There's nothing to worry about."

"Is that so?" Kataoka remarked, but without sarcasm. He asked no more questions.

Yahiro Company settled down in a coconut grove, waiting for the rest of their regiment, the 57th, to come ashore. They began digging *takotsubo* (octopus traps), four and a half feet deep. The dugouts had a lateral scoop at the bottom where a man could huddle during a bombardment. In cross section a *takotsubo* looked like a Christmas stocking.

Sweat stung their eyes, and their shirts were plastered to their backs, but the warm air was preferable to the harsh winds of Manchuria. To the east the sky bloomed a pinkish glow with the unreal dawn of an exotic travel poster. The war seemed far away. Then came a distant buzzing. Someone shouted "Take shelter!" and the men leaped into their holes. The buzzing became a roar. Bombers approached in relentless formation, seeming invincible even when engulfed in black balls of ack-ack explosions.

Bombs from the planes—they were B-24's from Morotai—began to tumble toward the transports, which were still disgorging men and matériel. Zero fighters were suddenly all over the bombers, which continued sedately on course. Three Zeros burst into flames simultaneously, arching toward the ground like comets. A second wave of bombers followed shortly, their silver wings glinting in the sun.

A string of bombs fell in a great parabola toward the transport *Noto-maru*. One bomb disappeared in the smokestack. There was a dull detonation, followed by a chain of muffled blasts. The ship's whistle began to blow mournfully and without stopping. Helpless, Colonel Yoshio Miyauchi, commander of the 57th Regiment, watched the ship he and his troops had just left. He knelt on the beach and prayed, then wandered aimlessly toward the pier. His trucks, horses and most of his ammunition were on the burning ship.

General Tomochika told the dazed colonel to get his men on the road to Carigara as soon as possible. He was to follow a small advance group which had left hours earlier. The division commander, General Kataoka, had already started up Highway 2 with two platoons, and Miyauchi, accompanied by an aide, now set out north on foot to regain his composure.

His regiment didn't start moving out of Ormoc until after midnight. They marched through the night strung out for miles along the narrow highway—unlike their commander, eager for battle. They were unaware of the significance of the sinking of *Noto-maru*.

In the dim light of early dawn—it was November 3—the advance group, under Major Yoshio Imada, was approaching Carigara. It unexpectedly encountered GI's of the 24th Division coming the other way. There was a brief fire fight and Imada retreated into the hills south of Highway 2.

General Kataoka learned about the skirmish just as he and his two platoons reached the heights north of Limon, a village of several score nipa huts where Highway 2 made a precipitous climb over rugged hills, then circled a commanding ridge to the right before descending again to the coast and Carigara. Kataoka ordered Major Imada to attack the advancing Americans; Imada could expect reinforcements, an antitank battalion. Then the general sent back word for Colonel Miyauchi to bring up a small field piece on the double.

This order made no sense to Miyauchi. but he loaded the gun into a truck and climbed aboard to direct operations. As the truck rumbled over the bumpy dirt road, he wondered what good one small piece of artillery would do. At Limon he listened politely to Kataoka explain how he was going to stem the enemy advance down near Carigara. The small gun was positioned to command the road where it made the sharpest turn around the ridge.

All day Miyauchi's 57th Regiment straggled north along the narrow road toward Limon, harassed by American bombing and strafing attacks. More than two hundred men were killed and scores of others were overcome by the intense heat. Darkness when it came offered little relief. Around nine o'clock the men fell out exhausted along the sides of the highway. They were attacked by mosquitoes; those who had not covered their faces before they fell asleep awoke with eyes almost swollen shut, but their eagerness was undiminished as they resumed their march, this time under dark, lowering clouds. Kamiko's battalion was the first to reach Limon, and its commander, Captain Sato, was ordered by Miyauchi to take positions north of the village near the emplaced gun.

On the other side of the mountain range Lieutenant General Walter Krueger, commander of Sixth Army, thought his advance division, the 24th, faced encirclement and annihilation. He knew from aerial observation that a large force of Japanese was marching toward Limon; and he feared the enemy might also land a large amphibious force behind the 24th Division at Carigara. Krueger reacted cautiously. Rather than push forward and take the strategic ridge, breaking through the mountain barrier which as yet was lightly defended, he ordered the 24th Division to halt and prepare to fend off a possible sea invasion in co-operation with the 1st Cavalry Division, which was on its heels.

At dusk Miyauchi's regiment started up the winding road toward the crest of the ridge. An eerie white figure approached. It was a survivor of the 16th Division, swathed in bandages, driven back all the way from Leyte Gulf. He passed silently by. He was followed by more walking wounded, helping one another or hobbling on sticks. Word spread down the ranks that General Makino's division had been annihilated.

Just ahead lay the highest point of Highway 2, where the road bent sharply to the east. The jagged hill mass on the right was covered with shoulder-high cogon grass. It was a natural fortress. Numerous spurs branched off it toward the sea to the northeast and toward the Leyte River Valley to the southwest. In between the steep rises were dense woods.

Here the march stopped. Whispered instructions were passed along to jettison all unnecessary items. The men stuffed their small battle haversacks with hardtack and five grenades each and piled their back packs near the road. Kamiko's company was ordered to take the lead, and his squad led the company—that, he thought proudly, made him the spearhead of Gem Division.

The sky lightened with dramatic suddenness. With the sun came intolerable heat. The air was acrid with powder smoke. The battlefield must be near but the ridge was silent. A rifle cracked. It was quiet again and then Kamiko heard the chirping of birds. The former schoolteacher's heart beat faster. His chest constricted. He turned to his companions. Their eyes were glittering. They had been preparing to fight for three years and were as expectant as he was. An order came up to turn off the road and climb the ridge.

On the other side, GI's were also nearing the top of the ridge. Krueger had ordered the 24th Division to reconnoiter it; the general attack south was to begin in two days.

Kamiko pushed through brush and began the ascent toward the crest. Behind, someone shouted, "Squad Leader Kamiko! Wrong direction!" It was a platoon sergeant. A grenade exploded. The sergeant stumbled, clutching his thigh. Kamiko was showered with debris. A soldier grunted, "I'm hit!" Blinded, Kamiko tripped over him. He forced himself to be calm; gradually he recovered his vision. Geysers of earth erupted on all sides. Grenades lobbed over the crest by the GI's were bounding down the slope like apples spilled from a barrel. Kamiko squirmed toward the sergeant and touched him. He felt warm, sticky blood.

While he was wondering what to do, he heard the hollow thump of mortars, then the deep cough of a machine gun. Bullets whipped through the brush, thumping into bodies and bringing cries of surprise and pain. The first squad was being wiped out without a fight! He fought a paralyzing panic and finally forced himself to shout "Fire!" Rifles crackled. Kamiko looked at his watch. It was exactly ten o'clock on November 5 in the nineteenth year of Showa. It might be his last moment as a human being.

Kamiko fired blindly round after round. He stopped to reload and peered above the brush. There was a thunderous shock, a blinding flash, and darkness. Earth and sand showered him, but he was unhurt. According to the manual, shells from the same gun never landed in the same spot, so he sprang into the newly made crater.

He was immediately joined by two comrades, a light-machine-gun team. They set up their weapon and were about to open fire when mortar rounds began bursting so close that the operator, Ogura, shouted, "It's dangerous here, Squad Leader!" and scrambled out of the hole with his gun.

The entire squad moved laterally, and frantically dug takotsubo among the roots of rotting palm trees. The mortar barrage ceased. Kamiko held up his helmet on a bayonet and a hail of bullets battered the helmet "like a wind-bell." He crouched down again but the firing from the top of the ridge had stopped. He wondered why the GI's, after pinning them down, had fallen back.

Kamiko told his men to eat while they had the chance. They had hardtack but no water. He ordered a man with a

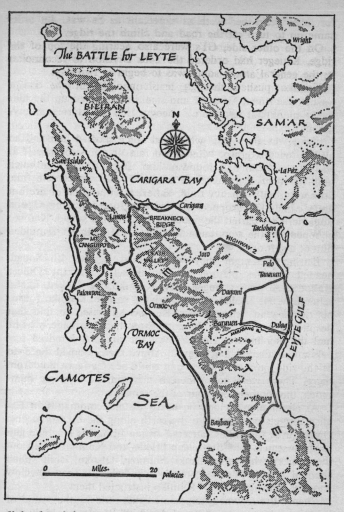

The BATTLE for LEYTE

BILIRAN

SAMAR

Wright

San Isidro

CARIGARA BAY

La Paz

Carigara

LIMON

BREAKNECK
RIDGE

Tacloban

MT.
CANGUIPOT

DEATH
VALLEY

Jaro

HIGHWAY 2

Palo

Tanauan

Dagami

LEYTE GULF

Ormoc

HIGHWAY 2

Palompon

Burauen

MARABANG R.

Dulag

ORMOC
BAY

CAMOTES

SEA

Abuyog

Baybay

0   Miles   20   palacias

slight leg injury to report the situation to the company
commander, Lieutenant Yahiro, then crept along the slope to
make a personal reconnaissance. The other two squads had
been trapped by the mortars and machine guns and only
three men in all were alive. If it hadn't been for Ogura, his
squad too would have been wiped out.

At dusk he gathered his remaining five men and told them

they alone held the hill. He ordered them to collect ammunition, arms and supplies from dead comrades. By midnight they were prepared for the attack that was certain to come at dawn, but their thirst had become unbearable. Kamiko remembered seeing coconut trees somewhere near the crest. He removed all clothing except for his loincloth, tied a washcloth around his head and stealthily crawled up the hill. In the moonlight he found a coconut tree and started shinnying up it.

"Squad Leader!" The whispered voice startled him and he almost lost his grasp. "Get down fast or you'll be shot!" It was Ogura, who had followed him. But Kamiko continued until he reached a cluster of coconuts. He yanked one free, dropped it with a heavy thud. He expected a burst of fire but none came. He dropped ten more before rejoining Ogura. Together they carted the coconuts back to the squad. Kamiko chopped off the tops and distributed the milk. It reminded him of a soft drink.

During the night they were joined by the 4th Squad, headed by the platoon leader himself, Warrant Officer Hakoda. A year younger than Kamiko, he looked like a schoolboy. He apologized for arriving so late. Kamiko roused his own squad before dawn. He was surprised to find that despite the heavy losses, he anticipated battle as eagerly as he had the day before. He surveyed the area. A hundred feet below was winding Highway 2. Above them loomed the crest of the ridge and he guessed one could see Carigara Bay from there. There were now nineteen men on the strategic hummock, the southeastern spur of the range.

At about nine o'clock he heard distant commands in English. Bullets pounded into the earth along the *takotsubo* line. Ogura, eyes "as big as saucers," began firing his machine gun as if possessed. The fire let up briefly and Kamiko called out the names of his men: "Aoki! Shimizu! Otsuka! Ishii!" Each shouted *"Hai!"* (Yes!) from his own hole. "If they get close enough, throw grenades," Kamiko instructed them.

Enemy fire resumed, augmented this time by the sound of heavy machine guns. "Squad Leader!" It was Aoki in the next hole. "The brush is burning!" Smoke swirled across the slope and the crackle of burning cogon grass rose above the din. "Squad Leader!" Aoki again. "The enemy is coming!"

Partially hidden by smoke, the Americans (I Company, 3rd Battalion, 21st Infantry Regiment, 24th Division) had charged over the ridge and were closing in. "Third Squad," Kamiko shouted, "fix bayonets and prepare grenades!" He heard the click of bayonets as he fastened his own and armed his grenades.

"Charge!" screamed the baby-faced Hakoda.

Kamiko was about to relay the order to his own squad, but it didn't make sense. A charge should always be preceded by some kind of covering barrage. Impulsively he yelled, "Third Squad, hold!" The enemy was still screened by the flaming brush. "Target, right oblique!" Kamiko shouted. "Fire!"

Ogura turned his machine gun to the right.

"*Totsugeki!*" It was Hakoda again, urging the 4th Squad to charge into the murderous fire. Hakoda fell and his new sergeant was hit. "Take command," he called out to Kamiko. The Americans were almost upon them. It was all over. Kamiko shouted desperately, "Fire everything you have!"

Suddenly the sky overhead was split with a long screech which was cut off abruptly by an explosion on the slope ahead. Stunned, the infantrymen on both sides stopped shooting. Another big shell landed in front of Kamiko in the midst of advancing Americans. A third shell whined over, plummeting into the enemy's heavy-machine-gun positions. The three rounds had come from a single big Japanese gun just hauled into position.

Kamiko jumped to his feet and shouted, "It's ours!"

Several American machine guns resumed their chattering. A fourth shell exploded. There was silence ahead. This time the enemy machine guns remained silent.

There was no rifle fire from the *takotsubo* on the left and Kamiko crawled over to investigate. Ishii was bent over, head down. "What's the matter?" asked Kamiko and took off Ishii's helmet. His eyes were open but there was a hole the size of a bean in the middle of his forehead. The back of his head was like a burst pomegranate.

Kamiko ground his teeth in anger. Ishii was his best friend—a university man, full of spirit and compassion. He felt heat on his back and whirled around. The wind was driving the grass fire down the slope. Where was the wounded Hakoda? Kamiko began searching to save him from the flames but all he could find was an officer's leather belt, saber and pistol. Had the Americans taken Hakoda prisoner? Machine guns sent him tumbling back to his hole, clutching the platoon leader's possessions.

Aoki called out to him, "Enemy approaching!" Aoki was about to toss a grenade but Kamiko stopped him; the enemy was too far away. Kamiko crawled forward with his own grenades, followed by Ogura. He crouched, ready to stand up and throw—and die. Again a shell—this from a recently positioned four-gun battery—whistled overhead, exploded up the slope.

"Hit! Direct hit!" someone shouted excitedly. "Five or six were blown up!"

Then he heard another voice—that of the company commander, Lieutenant Yahiro! The main force of the company had arrived. Kamiko leaped to his feet. Wiping tears away with the back of one hand, he activated a grenade by slamming it on his helmet and heaved it as far up the hill as he could. His men joined him. There were five quick explosions.

"Charge!" Kamiko shouted. He felt as though nothing could stop him as he hurtled up the charred, smoldering field toward the heavy-machine-gun position with fixed bayonet. Behind pounded his squad. Dead Americans were everywhere, their bodies scorched and swollen; one seemed to be overflowing with yellow grease. Kamiko, followed by eight men, swarmed into the machine-gun emplacement. Gunners had been blown apart; cartridges on their belts were detonating like firecrackers. Every so often one of these explosions set off a grenade. Kamiko was rooted, erect. Amid all this carnage he found himself alive. It was as if he were coming out of a dream. Reality swept over him again; he crouched and once more plunged up toward the crest of the ridge. As he burst over the top he saw spread before him the breathtaking panorama of Carigara Bay. The Americans were scrambling down their side of the ridge; here and there a fleeing figure tumbled haplessly from the fusillade which followed them from the crest.

A single platoon, with the help of a dozen artillery shells, had blunted a determined enemy attack and given the strungout regiment time to reach the front and turn the ridge into a fortress of *takotsubo*, trenches and gun emplacements.

Kamiko remembered how the samurai of the civil-war era took the head of an enemy, and reached for an American officer's helmet. The liner was wet with blood and he hesitated—was it proper for a modern man to take booty? But he still had helmet in hand when he reported to his company commander. Lieutenant Yahiro's face was black with dust and gunpowder, his arm in a sling. He grinned boyishly. "Thank you very much for enduring such hardships," he told Kamiko.

Their battalion commander, Captain Sato, called for the

merits list and wrote on the first page. It was an inimaginable honor for an infantryman, the "dream flower." Usually only fliers and sailors were officially commended. Sato was curious about the American helmet. Kamiko apologized for the blood but the battalion commander put it on, waggling his head several times. "This is light and feels good." Was there one without a bullet hole?

"I'm sure I can find one," Kamiko volunteered.

"If you do, I'll use it."

Yahiro grinned as he hefted an American carbine. "This is light too. I may use it from now on."

That night Kamiko was appointed platoon leader in place of Hakoda. He couldn't sleep; the corpses of comrades lying out front unattended haunted him. From the darkness he heard someone say, "Why do American soldiers die on their backs?" Another voice answered, "The Japanese are well-mannered; even after they've died they hide their private parts." Both laughed.

Just before dawn Kamiko and the two other platoon leaders were ordered to report to the company commander's dugout. Yahiro told them that the rest of their battalion had been ambushed on the way up front and practically wiped out. So their own hummock (it had been renamed Yahiro Hill by Sato in honor of the company) had become the spearhead again—and was isolated. "Reinforcements are sure to come. When the main force of the division arrives, it will be easy to wipe out the enemy. Until then we must defend this position to the end. I hope that each platoon leader will do his best, with resolution, despite the condition of the men."

The Americans who had been forced back resumed their assault on the escarpment—it was nicknamed Breakneck Ridge—with the help of men from the 1st Cavalry Division. This time they attacked on a broader front but still concentrated on the hill where the eighty men of Kamiko's company were waiting, with orders to hold fire. When the GI's were seventy-five yards away, Lieutenant Yahiro shouted "Fire!"

The fusillade of rifle and machine-gun bullets toppled over the enemy "like bowling pins." But the onslaught was stemmed only momentarily. Kamiko grudgingly admired the Americans' ability to advance over the bodies of their comrades, throwing grenades like baseballs. The carnage along the defense line was far worse than the day before, and Kamiko doubted that Yahiro Hill could be held against such determination and firepower. He was impatient with his own single-action Model 38 rifle; it was accurate, but after every shot the five-bullet clip had to be pushed down. He shouted to Ogura to concentrate his machine-gun fire to the right where the American advance was slowing. Perhaps they could be panicked. Grenades, tossed by comrades behind him, flew overhead and bounced toward the enemy. The Americans wavered. One or two turned back and the rest followed pell-mell down the hill.

Yahiro Company had held again, but only twenty-five were alive. The survivors were sent back in relays down to a stream on the other side of Highway 2. They washed their faces in the cool water, filled canteens and ate hardtack. This, Kamiko thought, is the pleasure of nothingness.

The American failure to seize Breakneck Ridge had immediate repercussions. Major General Franklin C. Sibert, commander of X Corps, which included the 24th Infantry and 1st Cavalry divisions, came up front at noon, and without waiting to go through channels, summarily relieved a regimental commander and replaced him with his own intelligence officer, Colonel William J. Verbeck.

Verbeck quickly proved he was one staff officer who was more aggressive than the average line officer. No sooner had he taken command than he sent a company to flank the ridge. It too was pushed back. Undeterred, Verbeck ordered the 2nd Battalion, with Company L attached, to attack the ridge in force the next morning.

November 8 dawned gray. Then the skies darkened dramatically, and rain, whipped by typhoon winds, swept the ridge. Palms bent like bows, and some snapped, others were uprooted. The cogon grass lashed like a turbulent sea. Even so, Verbeck's attack began on schedule. It opened with a heavy-artillery barrage, the boom of cannons competing with the thunder and screaming wind. Infantry moved out through the beating rain, floundering on the muddy slopes. Their maps were inaccurate and it took hours for some units to get into position.

Mortar shells, however had zeroed in on the crest of the ridge. The effect was so devastating that Yahiro ordered the company to fall back to their original *takotsubo* near the highway, and there make the final stand. The men skidded and bumped their way down to holes which were already deep with water but nevertheless offered refuge from the mortar rounds that flew overhead.

Fog engulfed the slope; nothing could be seen beyond ten

yards. As he waited, soaked and miserable, Kamiko re-evaluated the enemy. First, he was no coward; second, he could throw grenades twice as far as the Japanese; third, and most important, he always seemed to be rested. Kamiko's squad was perpetually exhausted; perhaps it was the constant battle without relief, perhaps the lack of food.

There were no mortars to lob shells over the ridge at the approaching Americans, so Yahiro ordered his men to direct steady fire on the crest line of the shrouded ridge. The strategy worked; the display of fire power discouraged the enemy from coming over the top. The defenders regained confidence, but their sense of security was short-lived. To the rear they heard an eerie grinding, thumping noise. An American tank had come around the bend of Highway 2, churning through the morass of mud, its gun spitting out shells. They were surrounded!

Two men scrambled down the hill toward the road, carrying a heavy satchel charge. The men in the *takotsubo* turned and watched the little drama as from an amphitheater until they heard shouts in English near the top of the ridge. "Use grenades!" cried Kamiko and started up the hill followed by his depleted platoon. They tossed grenades over the crest and ran back for more. Three times they scrambled up the slope. With the enemy out of sight, they returned to their holes.

But the Americans returned, as they always did. Kamiko heard something hissing at the rim of his *takotsubo*. An enemy grenade had rolled down the hill and was caught in a tent stake. He looked at Ogura and both shrugged. It was the end. But the grenade fizzled out. Others bounded over the dugouts but exploded after they were past.

On the crest above, a GI leveled his rifle at Kamiko. He crouched in his *takotsubo*, then popped up and fired. The GI fell to the ground, but in his excitement Kamiko pumped three more shells into him. A rifle barrel rose and disappeared like a periscope. It belonged to another GI who was trying to rescue his fallen comrade. Kamiko ran up to the crest and shot him, too; then sprinted back to his hole.

Pfc. Saiji Saito in the next hole leaped forward, following Kamiko's example. At the crest he, too, fired. But instead of retreating, he disappeared on the other side. Why had Saito sacrificed himself so needlessly? Kamiko wondered. Then Saito reappeared like a jack-in-the-box. He swore breathlessly as he leaped into Kamiko's hole, "I hated him so much I had to kick his head off!" Had Saito—a mild youngster who didn't smoke or drink—gone mad? Was this the frenzy of the battlefield Kamiko had read about? And yet, hadn't he himself come close to doing the same thing?

To the rear the American tank—a medium—still moved freely on the road, raking the *takotsubo* from behind with its machine gun and cannon. The two men with the satchel charge sprang out of the ditch and flung the explosive under the tank's tracks. As they leaped back to safety, there was a dull detonation and the tank shuddered. It turned laboriously, however, and retreated around the bend.

Without the tank the American attack faltered and once more the GI's gave up Yahiro Hill. Without hesitation the Japanese clambered up the muddy slope to reoccupy their positions along the crest. This time Kamiko felt no sense of victory. The enemy, who made retreat a tactic, would come back again and again. What did the remnants of Yahiro Company have left to stop them?

Several hundred yards to Kamiko's right on the next hill in the ridge, Sergeant Yoshio Noguchi's platoon had been hurt as badly as Kamiko's by the deadly mortar barrage along the crest. He had two 7.7-mm. machine guns left—his and the one in the next *takotsubo*—but only a few rounds of ammunition.

Crouched in the numbing water up to his waist, Noguchi heard a cry of anguish and the operator of the second gun crawled feebly toward him. Noguchi pulled him in. His right thigh was like "a beehive" gushing blood. His face was pale, drained. The crawling man had attracted steady enemy machine-gun fire. The cogon grass all around Nogushi's *takotsubo* was mowed flat. He cautiously checked on both sides. There was no activity. Apparently he was the last one of his platoon. He was a hardy, experienced soldier, a farm boy who had volunteered for service in 1938. Surrender was out of the question. He put the barrel of his pistol to his temple. He pulled the trigger, but the mechanism was jammed from the mud.

Not twenty-five yards away, Americans in greenish uniforms were coming down his line of *takotsubo*. At each hole they paused with rifles at the ready while two of their number machine-gunned the dead or wounded occupants. The firing grew closer and Noguchi again put pistol to head. Jammed. There was a stuttering rattle of fire a few yards away and Noguchi knew he was next. A branch of palm leaves had been blown by a mortar round to the edge of his hole. With a stick he deftly pulled the palm over the mouth of the *takotsubo*. He pressed flat against the back of his dugout, water up to chin, legs outspread, then pulled the body of the lifeless machine-gun operator in front of him.

The voices were directly overhead. A shiny barrel poked between the leaves. He thought, How well they take care of their weapons. As he plugged his ears with his middle fingers he prayed the bullets would somehow miss him. He felt the concussion from a deafening series of explosions, and scores of bullets churned the water between his legs. The opposite side of the hole collapsed. Noguchi closed his eyes as mud began covering him up to the neck. The palm branch, cut in two, dropped on his head.

The voices moved away and there was a burst of fire in the next hole. Stunned almost beyond thinking, Noguchi felt no pain. Carefully he scraped the mud from his face and opened his eyes. The water in the hole was tinged red. But it was the blood of his human shield.

At last the firing stopped. What were the Americans doing now? With infinite caution he pushed his dead comrade aside and looked out, expecting to see them digging foxholes. They were building something he had never seen before—shallow, rectangular rock forts with canvas roofs.

Noguchi huddled for hours in the bloody water, afraid to make another move until well after dark. At last he painfully got to his feet. All around him were the strange squat shelters; each glowed from a dim light within. He could hear the Americans joking and eating. Cigarette smoke curled invitingly out of the cozy little structures. What kind of soldiers would have lights in the middle of a battlefield?

The lights began going out one by one, and near midnight it started to rain again. Noguchi hoisted himself out of his hole and started crawling away from the one GI he could see was on guard. He came to a wire which seemed to surround the encampment. Some kind of warning device? He crawled under without touching it, and down a steep incline. His legs were so weak and unco-ordinated he had to hold on to vines to keep from falling. At the bottom he found a small stream. He drank on all fours, like a dog. Except for rain, it was the first water he had tasted in days. In the gloom he barely made out scores of bodies—comrades, canteen in hand, had met their death looking for water. In the darkness and rain he could not determine where he was. The battalion command post should be two hundred yards away, but he crawled up and down the draws for more than a mile without finding it. Exhausted, he curled up behind a bush and fell asleep.

He was wakened by voices. Through the brush he saw Americans eating breakfast. In the night he had circled around and around the knob only to climb back up to his starting place. Two GI's headed directly for him. He ducked his head, hoping they wouldn't notice him in the underbrush. Then he felt a stream of fluid splashing against his helmet. One of the Americans was urinating on him. When he looked up, the GI was adjusting his trousers as he ran after his comrades who were already marching off.

Most of Breakneck Ridge, however, still remained in Japanese hands. That morning, after heavy artillery preparation, two soaked battalions of the 24th Division resumed the attack in the driving rain. They advanced but were thrown back by a fresh Japanese battalion. Rain had become as much of a problem to the Americans as the enemy. Their supply route, Highway 2, was a swamp, and engineers were carting up loads of heavy gravel to try to make it passable. Already the GI's were suffering from "immersion foot," similar to the trench foot of Europe: the skin peeled away, leaving raw sores.

The Japanese, too, were afflicted by the endless rain. Using trenching spades, they tried in vain to bail out their *takotsubo*. Kamiko remembered that American knapsacks were waterproof and decided to use one as a bucket. He crawled over to the enemy side of the ridge, found a dead GI—as usual lying face up, mouth open—and took his knapsack. He and Ogura scooped out the water in their hole and passed the knapsack to the next *takotsubo*. Drenched to the skin and cold, they cut off the rubber tubes of gas masks and set them on fire. The smell was nauseating but there was some heat.

Kamiko awoke to another dark dawn—it was November 10. It was nonsense to try to determine one's own deathday, yet he kept doing it. Still he had no fear at all. *"Mei fa tzu!"* he exclaimed—a popular Chinese expression meaning "It is Fate" (similar to *"Que será será"*). There was nothing to do now except enjoy life to its last moment.

The rain increased as American shells plowed into the crest line above them. Under the constant trembling of the earth, the sides of the *takotsubo* began to crumble. It reminded Kamiko of the terrifying earthquake in 1923, which he had never been able to forget. The barrage lifted.

"First platoon, take positions on the ridge line!" Kamiko shouted and charged up the hill, an unrecognizable mass of shell holes. At the top he saw swarms of enemy soldiers halfway up the other side. They seemed numberless (they were two full battalions of the 1st Cavalry Division) and there were only a handful left in Yahiro Company to stop them. He frantically gestured to his men to return to the relative safety of their *takotsubo* down below. He called out a warning as he sped by Yahiro's dugout. He leaped into his hole a moment before bullets swept down the slope. Grenades followed, skipping down into their positions. To the right there was shouting in English. Had the 2nd Platoon been overrun?

Saito yelled, "Out of ammunition!" "Me, too!" another man called. Someone tossed them a few clips in an attempt to divide the remaining ammunition, but it was useless. Driven by anger and frustration, Kamiko plunged out of his *takotsubo,* and followed by three men, churned almost to the top of the hill before lobbing a grenade at the crest. Impulsively—perhaps to frighten the enemy—he shouted in English, "Charge, charge!"

The result was startling. An American rushed over the crest with fixed bayonet and found himself facing Kamiko. The two stared open-mouthed at each other. Neither fired. Then the GI, realizing the order had come from the wrong side, dived back over the crest.

"Company, *tenshin!*" It was the voice of Yahiro's assistant. The word meant literally "turn around and advance" and was a euphemism for "retreat." Yahiro himself repeated the word, then shouted as if in apology, "We will advance later!"

The men of the platoon next to Kamiko's, the 2nd, had never heard the expression before—it had been created recently to cope realistically with the changing tide of war—but the urgency of the command forced them out of their holes, ready to launch the last attack.

"Tenshin! Tenshin!" Yahiro, American carbine in hand, ran out of his *takotsubo* to turn them around.

Kamiko knew the word but had never expected to hear it in battle. Paralyzed, he watched the Americans concentrate their fire on the exposed 2nd Platoon. Yahiro was firing his carbine from the hip. One GI fell. Yahiro picked off another, then was sent spinning to the ground himself. Kamiko helped drag him to a shell hole. Blood spurted from his throat. "Company Commander!" Kamiko pleaded. They held a canteen to Yahiro's mouth. He gulped once, then his head fell lifeless to the side.

Now the fate of the few men left in Yahiro Company was in Kamiko's hands. Retreat was disgraceful; in all their years of training it had been forbidden. They were going to die anyway and should take as many enemy with them as possible. "Throw all the grenades you have left!" he shouted and started up toward the crest, with five men right on his heels. Their unexpected attack caught the Americans momentarily off-guard. They fell back under the rain of grenades. We could win with one machine gun! thought Kamiko. The absurdity of that hope jerked him back to reality. He was leading his men to a meaningless death. "Follow me!" he cried and dodged back down the hill toward Highway 2 with the few survivors of the 2nd Platoon and his own men. He jumped into the ditch by the road, then looked back. Helmeted heads were poking up all along the crest.

There were eleven in the ditch and Kamiko began to lead them down the highway toward Ormoc—along the same stretch of road he had so recently led the entire Gem Division—but the shame of retreat still gnawed at his conscience. Yahiro had ordered them to fall back, yet this withdrawal was his own responsibility—and he had abandoned the body of his commander. He had valued his own life above honor, and the thought tormented him with every step he took to the rear. Then he began to feel defiant: Why die needlessly? It wouldn't help the nation.

He began to feel almost "light of heart." But his euphoria was shattered by the blast of a grenade. It had come from the west, or valley, side of Highway 2. No one was hurt and they broke into a run. How had the enemy outflanked them so fast in such rough terrain? Perhaps it might not even be possible to rejoin the main force.

A few hundred yards down the road they came to a culvert; a stream was running underneath. *Mei fa tzu!* Kamiko reminded himself. The only thing was to do one's best and not worry about the future. They were still alive. They stripped off their foul uniforms. With leggings removed, their bare legs were sickly white, like a bean curd. As they scrubbed their clothes in the stream they began teasing and pushing one another as if they were back in Manchuria; then, clad only in loincloths, lay down unconcerned and before long were asleep.

They were awakened by an ominous staccato. Kamiko jumped up. Above them on the crest of the ridge he could see GI's manning a machine gun. He grabbed his rifle, and while the others snatched up what clothes they could on the run, he emptied his last clips before following them. They were chased by a few mortar rounds which detonated on contact with foliage overhead. Deep within the woods they paused to put on the clothing they had managed to salvage, and circled back to the road.

At a regimental supply depot, Kamiko checked in and the young officer in charge congratulated them for the "great victory" of their battalion. Kamiko stared at him. On the ridge they had been waiting day after day for substantial reinforcements while the 3rd Battalion was being annihilated. Didn't anyone back here at Regiment know what was going on up front?

2.

In Manila, General Yamashita knew at least that Suzuki's troops had encountered stiff opposition at the ridge. He ordered the main thrust diverted from Carigara; instead, Suzuki should turn east off Highway 2 below Limon and strike overland directly across the island to Tacloban. It was a perfunctory order. General Yamashita still questioned the advisability of waging the Decisive Battle on Leyte. It was foolhardy to drain off men and supplies that would be needed so desperately in the battle for Luzon. Moreover, he had reason to believe things were not going too well for Suzuki at Leyte. And had American air and naval power *really* been crippled at Formosa and Leyte?

Field Marshal Terauchi, however, remained unimpressed by these arguments. "We have heard the opinions of Fourteenth Area Army," he said, "but the Leyte operation will continue."

"I fully understand your intention," Yamashita replied. "I will carry it out to a successful end."

Terauchi's confidence came in part from the relative ease with which he had just landed 13,000 men (12,000 of them from the 26th Division) at Ormoc. Moreover, another convoy, carrying 10,000 troops, was approaching Leyte escorted by four destroyers, a minesweeper and a submarine chaser, and screened by three other destroyers.

Early the next morning, November 11, the convoy turned into Ormoc Bay. But at this point Yamashita's suspicion that American air and naval power had not been destroyed was dramatically borne out. Almost two hundred carrier planes from Task Force 38 caught the creeping convoy before it reached the harbor. This first wave concentrated on the six transports, which were hit again and again. The second wave went after the destroyers, and the third swept in, bombing the burning hulks and strafing the men struggling in the water. The slaughter was frightful. At the cost of nine American planes, every transport and four of the destroyers were sunk. Only a few of the 10,000 troops aboard—almost an entire division—managed to swim ashore through the crimson sea.

The catastrophe left Terauchi unchanged, at least outwardly, but it strengthened Yamashita's conviction that Leyte was a lost cause. At the same time he was under orders from Terauchi to continue the operation with vigor. His reservations were reflected in a radio message he sent Suzuki on November 15, which came close to predicting the abandonment of Leyte:

> THE THIRTY-FIFTH ARMY WILL ENDEAVOR TO ACCOMPLISH THE DESTRUCTION OF THE ENEMY ON LEYTE, SETTING AS ITS MINIMUM OBJECTIVE THE DISRUPTION OF THE ENEMY'S USE OF AIR BASES . . .
> IN THE EVENT THAT FURTHER TROOP SHIPMENTS CANNOT BE SENT, LUZON WILL BECOME THE MAIN THEATER OF FUTURE OPERATIONS IN THE PHILIPPINES.

Suzuki, understandably, was confused. Did it mean that the order to launch the main attack across the mountains toward Tacloban was rescinded? He knew the ridge had to be held or the Americans would pour down Highway 2 toward Ormoc. He therefore ordered Kataoka to counterattack. This would hold the ridge line, and moreover, distract American attention from his own drive over the mountains.

U. S. tanks roamed the corkscrew road almost at will. Infantry closed in from three sides, and after bitter hand-to-hand fighting, overran the ridge except for a few spurs at the southeastern end still held by the rearguard of the 57th Regiment of Gem Division. The rest of the regiment withdrew south at night, the weary men keeping together by following the glow of phosphorescent insects rubbed on the back of the man ahead. These men were turned around, and at Suzuki's orders, marched back to retake ground they had just abandoned.

Kamiko found himself back on the ridge—this time at the southern end. He and Aoki had been sent as replacements to Yasuda Company, which was dug in near the top of a rise about the size of Yahiro Hill. Lieutenant Tatsuhide Yasuda was a mild man. "I'm glad you arrived up here safely," he said through tight lips. "The company has been reduced to less than one fourth, so getting you two makes us feel we've got a million on our side." Kamiko was given the 3rd Squad. "We've just dug in and they haven't attacked us yet. But they will come soon. We are glad you are going to die with us."

The chattering of birds wakened Kamiko before dawn. For a moment he thought he was back in the mountains of Chiba. Through the dense foliage he saw something red. Was it some gaudy tropic blossom? No, it was a huge plumed bird that belonged in a zoo. But it was also food. He crawled to his commander's dugout and whispered that he wanted to shoot the bird for food. Lieutenant Yasuda shook his head; one shot would reveal their position. They might as well have fired. The bird, flapping its great ungainly wings, rose noisily like a loaded transport plane and instantly attracted mortar shells that continued spasmodically.

All day Yasuda Company huddled silently in their holes; their food ration was one rice ball for eight men. After dark Yasuda and his three squad leaders crept up to the ridge line. Halfway down the other side a group of Americans was eating out in the open as if it were a picnic grounds. The lieutenant suggested sending down two men to scavenge. Hunger gnawed at them more than fear, and the three squad leaders nodded approval.

Two privates were sent on the suicide mission and all night the company waited anxiously. Once they heard the crump of grenades and the rattle of machine-gun fire; they were certain their comrades had been killed. But at daybreak the two men returned, leaping into Yasuda's dugout with a poncho full of booty, as excited as schoolboys. They had ambushed an American machine-gun position in the dark and scooped up everything they could find. Their plunder turned out to be a few tins of cigarettes and boxes of ammunition that didn't fit their own weapons.

Aoki lit one of the American cigarettes. "Ah, I've forgotten the taste of tobacco," he said after a deep drag. "It makes me dizzy."

That day while enlarging his *takotsubo*, Kamiko caught a lizard. Skinned, it was light pink and reminded him of *megochi*, a fish he used to catch in the sea near his home. Aoki chopped it up with his dagger, boiled the parts in his *hango* until they were white. Kamiko found its taste a cross between fish and chicken. He finished full of vigor, almost as if he had been injected with adrenalin.

At noon Yasuda ordered Kamiko's squad to ascend a

strategic knob a hundred yards to the right and relieve the squad holding it. The knob dominated the area and was constantly under fire. Its capture would compromise the regimental position. All through the afternoon the 3rd Squad kept the enemy at a distance, but the next morning the Americans pressed in close enough to lob grenades. At the height of the attack, the grenade barrage inexplicably stopped.

It was so quiet that Kamiko could hear birds singing—then a strange noise like a blow torch. A cloud of thick black smoke boiled up in front of him. "Flamethrower!" he shouted. He began heaving grenades as far and as fast as possible. At last the flame extinguished. He flopped back exhausted, puzzled about the American withdrawal. A shell landed yards ahead but did not detonate; it buried itself deep into the ground. Kamiko thought it was a dud until the earth erupted in front of him like a volcano. It was the most terrifying thing he had ever experienced; it shattered him as had the earthquake of 1923. He turned to Aoki, his face pale. "They're using some new weapon." (It was actually a delayed fuse.) The earth rumbled time and again, throwing up tons of dirt. To the left, where two men had been hiding in their *takotsubo*, there was now only level ground with three legs protruding. Kamiko felt a hot sting on his arm, then on the foot. They were minor wounds, the only wounds he had suffered in seven full days of suicidal combat. Under protest he was sent to the rear.

His regiment, reduced to less than four hundred men, had disintegrated against relentless American pressure. On November 23, GI's of the 128th Infantry Regiment of the 32nd Division broke through the mountain barrier and into Limon. The Battle of Breakneck Ridge was over. Little remained but pockets of resistance. Two days later General Kataoka ordered the remnants of Gem Division to regroup below Limon near Highway 2.

Kamiko and Aoki hobbled south along the highway. They came to a ravine that stank of death. Thousands of swollen, decomposed bodies were scattered all over the road and in both ditches. At first glance the bodies looked as if they were being attacked by snakes—they were tubes from gas masks. This was "Death Valley." Here, with deadly accuracy, American artillery had caught Japanese troops moving up to the front.

They struck off into the jungle east of the highway. At every stream they found clusters of wounded men lying like corpses, their will to live gone. Kamiko and Aoki pushed on but were obsessed by thoughts of suicide. They met seven other stragglers, led by a Sergeant Hirano, and learned that the Americans had driven a wedge below Breakneck Ridge almost to Highway 2. They would have to fight through the enemy line to rejoin their division. Hunger drove them to raid the first American position they came upon. They fled, arms loaded with GI rations, chased by a volley of rifle fire. What a difference a little food makes! Kamiko thought as he finished a piece of chocolate. They could tolerate their wounds but the lack of food had sapped their morale. If we could eat as much as the Americans, we'd still be up on the ridge fighting, he mused. Victory in battle was simply a case of supply. How could Japan win against such a rich and powerful foe?

They found an American supply parachute and were themselves almost discovered by a column of Negro soldiers carrying boxes. As Kamiko raised his rifle, he was checked by Hirano, who jerked his head. Another column was coming.

"How black they are!" Kamiko whispered; he had never before seen a Negro.

"We're all human beings, but I wonder why they're so different."

"I wonder if they think like Americans?"

"They're Americans too," said Hirano.

They worked their way over a mountain, force-marched all night through a chilling rain; by morning they approached Highway 2, directly behind the enemy front. Kamiko halted the little group. He assured them they would break through; they had food and the Japanese soldier could not be beaten at hand-to-hand combat. "If you have the bad luck to get shot, commit suicide like a man."

They started down toward the highway.

24   Debacle

1.

Organized resistance on Leyte was at the point of collapse but Yamashita in Manila directed General Sosaku Suzuki to concentrate his remaining striking power into a desperation attack (Operation Wa) on American airfields. These nearly established bases were a threat to the entire Philippines as well as the supply route between the homeland and the south—Java, Malaya, Sumatra and Borneo.

There were three major forces on the island. Gem Division had lost more than three quarters of its effectives and at best could only delay the American advance down Highway 2. Makino's 16th Division, after being pushed across the coastal plain, was splintered. Some units were holding ground in the mountains west of Dagami, but the rest were scattered deep inland with the search of food their main occupation; they had been subsisting on raw insects, snails, frogs, lizards, centipedes, roots, grass—and their own sweaty belts.

The third force, the 26th Division, would have to provide the main thrust of Operation Wa. Already the division, except for a battalion detached to protect Ormoc, was moving across the mountain range below Limon in a general attack toward Leyte Gulf. Suzuki ordered them to keep moving southeast, and together with the remnants of the 16th paratroopers flown in from Luzon, attack three airfields near Burauen, a strategic village ten miles west of Dulag, at dawn on December 6.

The hastily conceived plan was compromised from the beginning. First the men of the 26th Division found it difficult to maintain the time schedule set up by Manila; Suzuki asked for a delay of two days, which was denied. Then the operation itself was vitiated by a breakdown in communications.

On December 3 meteorologists predicted an inclement weather front and Suzuki was ordered to postpone the attack for one day. But the message never reached the survivors of the 16th Division, who descended on the airstrip a mile above Burauen as scheduled, just after dawn on December 6. There were now only three hundred of them, their meager force having been further reduced by desertions. They came upon a group of sleeping American engineers bivouacked in the open, and began bayoneting them. The engineers, most of whom had never fired at an enemy, fled except for one of their cooks who killed five Japanese trying to steal food from his kitchen. The raiders held part of the field for several hours, but with no support they were driven back to the woods in the north where they dug in, cursing the paratroopers who had failed to appear.

These seven hundred 'troopers—they came from the 3rd

Parachute Regiment commanded by Lieutenant Colonel Tsunehiro Shirai—were still on Luzon, preparing to board two-engine transports. The first wave of twenty-six transports, with 356 paratroopers aboard, began taking off in mid-afternoon. They grouped and headed south, escorted by fighters. They continued west of Leyte to avoid detection, before circling south of the island and starting up toward Leyte Gulf. The sun was setting as they turned sharply west just below Dulag and followed the Marabang River inland toward Burauen.

They ran into heavy flak, and four planes were destroyed. The others lowered to 750 feet. At six-forty the 'troopers jumped. They were supposed to concentrate at the north field, but because of darkness only Colonel Shirai and sixty others landed at the objective. The main body came down on San Pablo, the strip a mile and a half east of Burauen. They charged, shouting demoniacally in English, "Hello, where are your machine guns?" and "Surrender! Everything is resistless!" Stupefied, Americans watched as the Japanese burned parked planes and ignited gasoline and ammunition dumps.

At the north field, Shirai's force was too small to be effective. It joined the 16th Division infantrymen still hiding in the woods and waited for the second wave of paratroopers. But there would be no second wave; bad weather closed in Leyte again. Nor would there be any help from the 26th Division. A single battalion was within striking range of Burauen, and these exhausted men were intercepted and repulsed by a battalion of the U. S. 11th Airborne Division.

The paratroopers at San Pablo had discovered their mistake, however, and after ravaging that field, struck northwest to join up with Shirai at dawn. Now that he had a respectable force, almost five hundred men, Shirai regrouped. By midmorning he had seized the entire airstrip, and for three days his tenacious men held out against four American battalions. Finally overwhelmed by sheer numbers, the handful of survivors fled into the hills.

While Shirai was mounting his dawn assault on the airstrip at Burauen, an armada of destroyer-transports loaded with an entire American division, the 77th, unexpectedly appeared in Ormoc Bay. The gamble of WA had not only failed but had diverted Suzuki's best troops, the 26th Division, away from the area which was now the target for MacArthur's next strike.

Around six-forty a dozen U. S. destroyers began bombarding the beaches four miles below Ormoc. Landing craft pushed off from the destroyer-transports, and shortly after seven o'clock the first wave of men from "New York's Own" landed unopposed. It was the day of 7's—to the south the 7th Division had already crossed the waist of the island over a supposedly impassable mountain road and was coming up the coast toward Ormoc. The infantrymen were opposed only by the single battalion detached from the 26th Division to protect the city.

Suzuki had erected no obstacles on the beaches—he felt the west coast was protected by the Japanese naval base in Cebu across the narrow Camotes Sea—and was now surrounded. There was little the Japanese could do to cope with the situation. Suzuki instructed the 26th Division, and what was left of the 16th, to about-face and join him at Ormoc. Yamashita expedited the convoys already scheduled for Leyte and in addition ordered five hundred paratroopers of the 4th Parachute Regiment sent to an airfield eight miles above Ormoc near Highway 2. But they didn't arrive until dawn of December 8 and were dropped in the jungle almost five miles north of the target.

Corporal Kiyoshi Kamiko, whose group had just fought its way through the American lines to reach Highway 2, encountered half a dozen of these paratroopers, young, well equipped and eager for battle. Kamiko warned them that they would be outnumbered 10 to 1, but one youngster exclaimed, "My goal is to kill ten before I die!" and then blushed.

His naïveté appalled Kamiko. What right had Imperial Headquarters to send such children out on suicide missions? All the frustrations and doubts of the past few weeks crystallized into a decision that would have seemed treasonable on Yahiro Hill: he would escape to another island. Why die uselessly? He allowed himself to think of Japan, of its beautiful hills and rivers. He would work his way to the west coast with a few trusted companions and steal a native boat. Perhaps they could escape to Borneo. A deep roll of thunder came from the direction of Ormoc. It sounded like enemy artillery. How had the Americans got down there so fast?

Major General Andrew D. Bruce's 77th Division was driving steadily up the west coast toward Ormoc against a congeries of assorted, poorly armed service units commanded by a transportation officer, Colonel Mitsui. His force was dug in on the high ground a few miles below the city and he hoped he could hold out until the 26th Division returned. Other reinforcements were on the way by sea, and on December 9 a battalion of the 30th Division landed at Palompon, a port on the west side of the little peninsula forming Ormoc Bay. It was only fifteen air miles to Ormoc, but thirty-five miles by a winding mountain road, and Bruce's men were already on the outskirts of the city.

The following morning GI's broke through Colonel Mitsui's lines into Ormoc, a mass of choking rubble and blazing buildings. A pall of dark smoke hooded the area. That afternoon General Bruce reported his victory to Corps Commander John R. Hodge, reminding him of a promise made by the commander of the Fifth Air Force:

> . . . WHERE IS THE CASE OF SCOTCH THAT WAS PROMISED BY GENERAL WHITEHEAD FOR THE CAPTURE OF ORMOC. I DON'T DRINK BUT I HAVE AN ASSISTANT DIVISION COMMANDER AND REGIMENTAL COMMANDERS WHO DO . . .

A few hours later Bruce sent another message, referring to the 7th Division which was coming up the west coast road.

> HAVE ROLLED TWO SEVENS IN ORMOC. COME SEVEN COME ELEVEN.

There were still two Japanese convoys en route to Ormoc Bay. One carried 3,000 men of the 8th Division and 900 tons of ammunition and supplies. As the five transports, three destroyers and two submarine chasers, escorted by about thirty fighters, approached the west coast of Leyte the next morning, they were attacked by Marine Corsairs which sank three transports. The remaining ships tried to pick up survivors as they turned in toward Palompon, but 700 men were drowned. Before the fleeing vessels made port, another transport was sunk by Marine and Army planes.

The final convoy—two destroyers and two transports—carried a 400-man naval detachment under Lieutenant Commander Ito, as well as nine amphibious tanks and twenty mortars. It had escaped detection and was still intact as it approached Ormoc several hours after midnight. At this point it was sighted by the destroyer *Coghlan*, which opened fire and sank a destroyer. The transports continued; one anchored near the occupied city and attempted to disembark its troops. The first barge was almost swamped by shells from the shore. "Don't shoot!" the Japanese yelled, unaware that the city was in enemy hands.

The other transport luckily made for the opposite side of the bay, where it unloaded the last reinforcements and supplies that Suzuki would get. Considering that nearly 80 percent of all the vessels dispatched to Leyte had been sunk, it was remarkable that a total of 45,000 troops had made it safely ashore. But their effectiveness was sharply reduced by the fact that little more than 10,000 tons of supplies in all were salvaged.

2.

Although Leyte was not yet lost and Luzon was being fortified for its conclusive battle, Imperial Headquarters ordered preparations expedited for the evacuation of Allied prisoners of war in the Philippines to the homeland. There they could be used as laborers and, possibly, hostages.

Publicly the Japanese had long decried Allied treatment of prisoners while praising their own. Only a few weeks after three of Doolittle's fliers (Lieutenants Dean Hallmark and William Farrow and Sergeant Harold Spatz) were executed—they had been tortured and then given a peremptory trial—the *Nippon Times* condemned the British for the inhuman treatment they were meting out to German prisoners of war.

. . . Needless to say, the Japanese Government, actuated by considerations of humanity, have, up to the present, respected the principles contained in the International Law governing the conduct of war and have done everything in their power with regard to the treatment accorded to the numerous British prisoners of war in their hands.

Americans were depicted as "enjoying life at the various prisoner camps."

On Luzon, at Cabanatuan, several survivors of the Bataan Death March kept secret notebooks whose disclosure would probably have meant summary execution. Colonel James Gillespie, a medical officer, described a new contingent of men marching into the camp:

. . . Inching their way along the road came a ragged formation of dirty, unkempt, unshaven, ragged, half naked forms, pale, bloated, lifeless. They staggered and stumbled, some plodded, others uncertain of their balance and strength lay down only to be urged to continue by the attendants who in many instances were only slightly more able than those they were assisting. Limbs grotesquely swollen to double their size. Faces devoid of expression—form or life. Aged incredibly beyond their years. Bare feet on the stony road. Remnants of ragged gunny sacks as loin cloths. Some stark naked. Bloodshot eyes and cracked lips. Smeared with excreta from their bowels. Thus they came ... to the "end of the road," the strong, young, and alert Americans of the 31st Infantry—the Air Corps and the A.A. The saddest sight indeed it was and may I never see it again.

These prisoners had been forced to eat cats, dogs, baby rats and garbage to remain alive; by now, they had lost an average of fifty-five pounds. In the first year at Cabanatuan, 2,644 of the complement of about 6,500 had died from malaria, dysentery, diphtheria and other diseases. Their deaths, according to Dr. Samuel M. Bloom, a captain, were "directly attributed to neglect of the Japanese, the result of a deliberate policy of starvation and the withholding of medical supplies."

Another diarist, Major Roy L. Bodine, a dentist and a veteran of Bataan, began keeping his clandestine record the day before MacArthur landed on Leyte. It was a day he would never forget; his group was transferred to Manila by truck to Bilibid Prison, where they learned they were simply being staged for shipment to Japan. They dreaded the treatment they might receive in the enemy homeland, but their spirits were lifted by the bombing of the Manila area and the long-awaited news that MacArthur had landed.* On October 28 Dr. Bodine wrote:

That added to the bombing makes us hope that the Nips won't be able to get us out of here.
Every day they have rumors of us leaving in 2 or 3 days, but keep putting it off. We hope and pray constantly that they can't. Really "Sweating it Out."

Bodine's hopes were never realized. On December 12, all patients were given a cursory examination. The food improved, and soap and toilet paper were issued—sure signs they were about to leave. "If MacArthur gets this close and then lets us go, will really be mad," wrote Bodine.

The next morning he and 1,618 other prisoners filed down Quezon Avenue and past the walled city. Filipinos lined the

*At the prison camp in nearby Santo Tomás University this information came in an underground news bulletin with the words: "Better Leyte than never."

sidewalks to watch the sad procession; many surreptitiously gave the V sign. Luneta Park was crammed with hastily erected barracks but the Gran Luna section, where Bodine had lived as a boy (his father had been an Army dentist), was unchanged. As they approached the dock area he saw the effects of the recent American bombing, and out in the bay were at least forty hulks.

At Pier 7 the prisoners began filing aboard a 15,000-ton luxury liner built just before the war for the tourist trade, *Oryoku-maru*.* With grim amusement Major Adrianus J. van Oosten, who had survived a dozen jungle battles on Bataan, watched MacArthur's shiny Packard, hoisted in a cargo net, career against the side of the hold, smashing its fenders. Lieutenant Colonel Curtis Beecher, a Marine, who recalled coming alongside the same pier back in 1929 on his return from duty in China, was herded along with seven hundred other prisoners into the dungeonlike forward hold; its previous occupants had been horses. In a few minutes the air was dead and hot and their uniforms became soaked with perspiration.

The Bodine group—three hundred Army and Navy medics and civilians—was packed amidships, three decks down. Eight buckets of rice and pans of fish were lowered after dark. The liner began to move. It steamed around Bataan into the Subic Bay and continued on a northern course. Suddenly, alerted to some danger ahead, it turned back and anchored in the protective waters below Olongapo. The prisoners sat hunched in the dark, their minds churning. A couple of years more in Japan, Bodine thought, or a watery grave from subs and planes.

---

*Seven weeks earlier a 5,000-ton freighter loaded with 1,805 prisoners from the Philippines had been torpedoed in the South China Sea (probably by the U. S. submarine *Shark II*). Five Americans survived, including Sergeant Calvin Graef and Corporal Donald Meyer, and they only by a remarkable series of coincidences: after hanging on to wreckage all night, they found a lifeboat containing a keg of fresh water; while fixing the rudder, they discovered a small compartment containing a sealed tin of hardtack; a box floated alongside which just happened to hold pulleys and rigging that exactly fitted their boat; finally, a pole someone had retrieved hours earlier turned out to be their mast. Just as they were about to raise the sail a Japanese destroyer approached to within a hundred yards but for some reason passed by without firing her machine guns. Even so, they probably would not have made it safely to China if fortune had not continued to favor them. After two days of sailing they were picked up by Chinese fishermen in a junk who landed them on the only area along the coast held by Chiang Kai-shek.

The condition of the seven hundred men massed in the forehold was already intolerable. The only ventilation came through a small hatch. A few pails had been tossed down to them for human waste. These were quickly filled and the hold reeked from urine and feces scattered on the deck. From the darkness came a shriek, "Oh, my God!" A man urinated into his canteen and drank the liquid. Colonel Beecher thought of the Black Hole of Calcutta; reading about it had made little impression but now he knew how horrible it must have been. An inhuman noise rose over the sighs and moans, which sounded to Major van Oosten like the gobbling of turkeys. Suddenly the sound was repeated quite close-by; the man next to him began to babble. In the shaft of starlight from the hatch, Van Oosten could see that his neighbor was losing consciousness. His puffed whitish tongue wagged between drooping lips. His eyes were glazed, unseeing. He slumped over. He was dead.

In the afterhold the other six hundred men were experiencing the same hell. They had been given a skimpy meal of rice and fish but no water. Most of them had unthinkingly emptied their canteens during the hot march through the streets. They began fanning the air in unison with mess kits but it made no difference. The men stripped in the ovenlike heat. In the darkness they shouted for water. But the guards ignored them; their own comrades had come to the Philippines in the same holds, if not as crowded. The prisoners' exertions slowly exhausted the oxygen from the air. One man, suffocating, toppled over silently with incredible restraint, but others, gasping for breath, thrashed about wildly before collapsing. A dozen, crazed by thirst, went berserk; they slashed at the throats and wrists of companions to suck blood. The panic turned the hold into bedlam. To Major Virgil McCollum, another veteran of Bataan, it was "the most horrible experience imaginable and probably unprecedented in the annals of civilization." As the dim light of dawn filtered through the hatch, several score bodies lay lifeless—suffocated or murdered.

From topside the men heard excited shouting. There was the bark of antiaircraft guns, and shards of glass showered through the hatches. Bombs pummeled the ship and machine-gun bullets clattered noisily along the decks above. In the afterhold, prisoners clawed up ladders, terrified lest they be trapped below, but were driven back by guards firing down into their midst. The bombers returned at half-hour intervals.

Amidships, Major Bodine and two friends, Captain John Hudgins and Major Bob Nelson, pushed into a little storeroom to escape stray bullets which were ricocheting through the hatch above. It was stifling but a refuge—that is, unless a bomb or torpedo made a direct hit. Bodine was a Catholic, and with death so close he prayed continuously. He said the rosary and repeated all the prayers he knew, and above the deafening clamor of shrapnel and bullets against iron, he heard Hudgins saying over and over, "Jesus save us." Packed in the little room they found it impossible to stay awake during the lull between attacks. They jerked from sleep whenever a new raid started and began drowsily mumbling another prayer.

Those in the forward hold faced another night of horror. There were shouts of "Quiet!" and "At ease!" but as the temperature reached 110 degrees, riot again erupted. It was the "worst and most brutal period" of Colonel Beecher's life. All around him men were going mad. They collided with one another in the dark, slipping and falling in the feces; the sick were trampled; wild, deadly fights erupted. Men dropped to their knees like animals to lap up sewage running in open drains.

In the rear, Major McCollum forced his way to the hull and licked the steel plates where a little moisture had condensed. The pandemonium was even worse than the first night. "Many men lost their minds," a colonel later wrote in his official report, "and crawled about in the absolute darkness armed with knives, attempting to kill people in order to drink their blood or armed with canteens filled with urine and swinging them in the dark. The hold was so crowded and everyone so interlocked with one another that the only movement possible was over the heads and bodies of others."

At about four o'clock in the morning an interpreter announced to the prisoners amidships that they were going ashore at dawn and could take along pants, shirt, canteen and mess kit—if they wanted shoes they'd have to carry them. The men crammed as much as possible in their pockets, and in the dark pawed through musette bags for their most valuable possessions. Bodine put his wife's rosary around his neck on top of his own, and slung his shoes over his shoulders. At the last moment he remembered his notebook and shoved it inside his shirt. What he most regretted leaving behind was his dental instruments. He had carried them all through the battles on Bataan, on the Death March and into several camps.

Shortly after dawn the first twenty-five men, including five wounded, started up the ladder. The interpreter was back in a few minutes calling for another group of twenty-five. As they started up the ladder the interpreter frenziedly waved them back: "Many planes! Many planes!"

A bomb crashed into the rear of *Oryoku-maru*. The blast hurled shrapnel through the afthold. Superstructure tumbled down the hatchway, pinning screaming men. Flames swept through the wreckage. More than a hundred of the trapped prisoners were dead; 150 were dying.

In the forehold, the strongest scaled the forty-foot ladder and opened the hatch covers. Nearby they discovered sacks of raw sugar and dropped several to those below. Van Oosten wolfed down a handful of sugar. Miraculously he seemed to feel a charge of energy and mounted the ladder, something he was certain he could not have done a moment before. On deck, Japanese killed by the strafing and bombing were shrouded in straw rice sacks and piled in a long row five bodies high. Van Oosten leaped over the side. The cool water was invigorating and he swam toward shore. The exercise, after two cramped days, abruptly loosed his bowels.

A guard shouted down to the Bodine group, "All go home, speedo!" Topside Bodine saw a beach a quarter of a mile away—Olongapo. Hundreds of men, Japanese and Americans, were already in the water, struggling to reach land. There were shouts to those standing indecisively at the rails that the ship was going down. Bodine tossed a piece of four-by-four overboard and jumped after it. Halfway, he looked back. The luxury liner looked like a scrap heap. Four American planes came in low. One peeled off as if to strafe, but the men in the water waved frantically and with a waggle of the wings it zoomed off. Bodine decided to swim back to help the others. He noticed a dangling rope ladder and impulsively started to climb up to get the clothes he had discarded on deck. He didn't realize how weak he was until he began pulling himself up. On deck he made a bundle of his shirt, an old Filipino hat and a pair of shoes. He tied it to a 3-inch-shell crate, which he threw over the side, and jumped again.

The 1,300 surviving prisoners were shepherded to a fenced-in tennis court, where they huddled on the concrete in the sun.

3.

That morning, December 15, MacArthur took a long stride toward Luzon. At seven-thirty two of his regimental combat teams landed without opposition on Mindoro, a few miles below Luzon, and by late afternoon had pushed seven miles inland.

General Yamashita had no intention of wasting troops on the defense of Mindoro—the garrison numbered only a thousand—nor did he intend to dispatch any more reinforcements to Leyte. On December 22 he radioed his decision to Suzuki's headquarters at Cebu City:

REDEPLOY YOUR TROOPS TO FIGHT EXTENDED HOLDING ACTION IN AREAS OF YOUR CHOICE. SELECT AREAS SUCH AS BACALOD ON NEGROS WHICH ARE HIGHLY SUITABLE FOR SELF-SUSTAINING ACTION. THIS MESSAGE RELIEVES YOU OF YOUR ASSIGNED MISSION.

The message would not reach Suzuki himself until three days later, but he had already ordered the remnants of the 35th Army to assemble near Palompon.

Besides Suzuki, the individual most distraught by the abandonment of Leyte was perhaps Prime Minister Kuniaki Koiso. On November 8 he had publicly committed his government to victory on Leyte. In a radio broadcast to the nation he compared Leyte with the Battle of Tennozan in 1582, which had decided the issue of who was to rule Japan. Koiso had in effect guaranteed that if Japan won on Leyte, she would win the war. He learned of the decision to abandon Leyte at a particularly awkward moment—when he was on his way to an audience with the Emperor. His Majesty asked immediately how the Prime Minister was going to explain the loss of Leyte to the people after equating it with the Battle of Tennozan. Unstrung, Koiso mumbled that he would make the best of the situation, but he knew that only some miracle could save his cabinet.

Suzuki's order to congregate in the Palompon area was thwarted by a surprise move by General Bruce's force on Christmas morning, which forced Suzuki and his staff to flee up the west coast of Leyte toward the mountains near San Isidro. They evacuated Palompon just before a reinforced battalion of the U. S. 77th Division approached the port itself from the sea in amphtracs and LCM's (landing craft, mechanized). The area was bombarded by 155-mm. guns located a dozen miles inland, and a barrage by mortar boats preceded the landing itself. At seven-twenty the first wave reached shore without opposition and had seized the town by noon. General Bruce radioed his corps commander:

THE 77TH INFANTRY DIVISION'S CHRISTMAS CONTRIBUTION TO THE LEYTE CAMPAIGN IS THE CAPTURE OF PALOMPON, THE LAST MAIN PORT OF THE ENEMY. WE ARE ALL GRATEFUL TO THE ALMIGHTY ON THIS BIRTHDAY OF THE SON AND ON THE SEASON OF THE FEAST OF LIGHTS.

In the afternoon MacArthur announced that the Leyte campaign was over "except for minor mopping-up operations." He turned over this last phase to Eighth Army so that Krueger's Sixth Army could prepare for the invasion of Luzon.

On Christmas night Kiyoshi Kamiko and three companions reached a beach a few miles from Suzuki's temporary headquarters. As the sounds of battle in Palompon subsided, they heard incongruous paeans of "Peace on earth, good will to men." GI's were playing Christmas carols in the hills above.

Kamiko and his comrades had fought their way to the coast through marauding bands of guerrillas and over almost impassable terrain, ranging from quicksand and swamps to precipitous ravines. (Aoki and Sergeant Hirano had become separated from the group, which at times comprised as many as fifty.) More than once their resolve to escape the island had wavered. Only hours earlier, conscience-stricken at the thought of desertion, they had left one of their party who was wounded and started down the beach toward Palompon to help defend the city. They were intercepted by a retreating Japanese officer who turned them around and ordered them to follow his unit. As they neared the coconut grove where their wounded comrade, Tokoro, lay hidden, Kamiko and his group fell behind, determined once more to escape.

In the dark they found a *banca* and rigged it with a sail they made from a tent. They loaded the little outrigger with rifles, canteens and coconuts, and clambered in.

"What about Tokoro?" someone asked under his breath.

Nakamura, a fisherman on whom they depended for navigation, warned that five would be too many, but Kamiko was against abandoning the wounded man. A voice interrupted their whispered argument: "Group Leader, I'm staying here." Tokoro was sitting on the beach a few yards away. "It's best for me."

"Group Leader, I'm staying too." Nakamura jumped out of the boat. Another man followed.

Kamiko wearily beached the stern of the *banca* and joined the others who were sitting silently with Tokoro. Finally Tokoro said he was sorry for all the trouble he had caused and hobbled off.

"The boat is too small even for the four of us," Nakamura muttered. "We can't reach another island in this thing."

"You knew that from the beginning!" Kamiko shouted. "You say you want to die on land and you *don't* want to die at sea! It doesn't matter where you die. The question is which choice offers the best chance of survival."

The others remained hunched in a tight circle on the sand, staring at the slender *banca*, which was tossing in the waves.

There was a shot. It was Tokoro. "What a pity," someone said, and another, "It's better he did that than drown."

This pushed Kamiko over the edge. He grabbed a grenade from his knapsack. "Let's follow Tokoro!" he cried. "We can't live until tomorrow. So, as you say, let's die on land. We've lived together, let's all die together! Everybody bring heads close!" He activated the grenade. In four seconds it would explode.

Nakamura lurched back. "I'll go!" he shouted.

Kamiko tossed the grenade back over his shoulder just before it detonated. He leaped to his feet. "Well, let's go!"

The *banca* sailed slowly out of the inlet in the moonlight. Nakamura, so reluctant on shore, was a new man as he deftly guided the boat toward Cebu. Abruptly the moonlight was cut off and something cold slapped his cheek. Rain. Dark clouds swirled ominously. Nakamura looked up, then said, "Let's return."

"We're at sea, Nakamura, and determined to die," said Kamiko. "So keep going."

The fragile outrigger tossed erratically. Nakamura clung stony-faced to the tiller as the others bailed with their canteens. A dark shape materialized in front of them with a roar—it must be a speedboat transporting 35th Army headquarters to Cebu. They shouted and waved but the craft droned past. It was an American PT boat.

Just before dawn the rain stopped and the sun rose on a calmed sea. All around them were small, bare rock islets. To the south, out of the morning light, emerged the vague outline of a large island. It had to be Cebu, their first goal. Nakamura changed course, and with the wind behind it, the little *banca* cut through the water as fast as a bicycle at top speed.

Kamiko began to sing his favorite song, one he had taught his pupils:

> *"From a far-off island whose name I don't know*
> *A coconut comes floating.*
> *How many months have you been tossing on the waves*
> *Far from the shores of your native island?*
>
> *I think about tides far away*
> *And wonder when I will return to my native land."*

4.

General Suzuki had chosen to concentrate the remnants of his forces, more than ten thousand troops, on a rugged, heavily forested 1,200-foot mountain on the west coast between Palompon and San Isidro called Canguipot. Its eastern and western slopes were rocky, making it a natural fortress. Every day stragglers from the 1st Division and 68th Brigade arrived exhausted at Mount Canguipot, but those left of the 16th and 26th divisions were pinned down near Highway 2.

Many of these men had no intention of trying to reach Suzuki's position even if they could disengage themselves. Like Kamiko, they could not avoid the logic that it was senseless to die on Leyte in such circumstances. In the mountains north of Ormoc between Highway 2 and the west coast Lieutenant General Shimpei Fukue, on his own, was planning to escape from the island with his depleted 102nd Division, which had played an insignificant role in the fighting. Already fifty of his men had left by boat.

On the night of December 29, Suzuki received the first message from Fukue in more than a week: the 102nd Division was marching to the coast, where it would set sail in small boats for Cebu. The action was unprecedented in Suzuki's experience and only with difficulty was he dissuaded from court-martialing Fukue summarily. Instead he ordered the 102nd Division to remain in place; Fukue himself was to report at once at Army headquarters with his chief of staff.

But even this direct order was ignored. Fukue's answer—

composed by his chief of staff, a colonel named Wada—was as infuriating as the original decision to desert: "We appreciate the efforts of the Army but at the present time we are very occupied preparing for evacuation. The division commander and chief of staff are consequently unable to report to Army headquarters."

On New Year's Eve, Fukue had the effrontery to ask Suzuki to facilitate his insubordination: "All boats that were prepared for the retreat were destroyed by American planes on the night of the 30th, thus delaying our departure. Would it be possible for you to send an armored craft to aid the departure of the division commander?" Fukue and his staff, like Kamiko, managed to get across the Camotes Sea by *banca*. In Cebu City the general was relieved of his command by order of Suzuki. He accepted Suzuki's instruction to remain on the island of Cebu; there was nowhere else to go.

On Leyte, Mount Canguipot was being prepared for a long siege. Large quantities of provisions were purchased from local farmers and augmented by fern, grass and wild spinach. Salt was separated from sea water. Suzuki's plan as far as Leyte was concerned was to tie up as many enemy troops as possible, but he too was coming to doubt the usefulness of such a sacrifice. Realistically, how long could he expect Mount Canguipot to hold out? One determined assault would overrun it. Almost a hundred men were dying of starvation every day. How was that helping the empire? Moreover, Yamashita had long since given him permission to evacuate.

It was a wrenching decision for a samurai; only a week before, he would never have imagined he'd make it. Gem Division would be the first to leave. On the night of January 12, 1945, General Kataoka and his headquarters set off in three launches, safely reaching Cebu soon after dawn. In the next week 743 men—all that remained of the elite Gem Division—reached Cebu with four heavy machine guns, eleven light ones and five grenade launchers. But as Lieutenant General Robert Eichelberger's Eighth Army closed in on Suzuki, continued evacuation became almost impossible.

Except for sixteen weeks of tedious mopping up, the fighting was over. The 70,000 Japanese who came to defend Leyte against 250,000 well-armed Americans had fought as well as could be expected. They wounded 12,000 GI's and killed 3,500, but only about 5,000—one in thirteen—would live to see Japan. It was a decisive battle—for the Americans. They had destroyed an entire army and permanently crippled Japan's remaining air force and fleet. The homeland itself now lay exposed, except for two island fortresses—Iwo Jima and Okinawa.

PART SEVEN

Beyond
the Bitter End

25   **"Our**
          Golden Opportunity"

1.

A relatively unpublicized war was going on in China and Burma that was frustrating and miserable for all sides—there were more than two—as well as the hundreds of millions of civilians trapped in the turmoil. Fought over a tremendous area, it was an ideological and geographical nightmare.

The British had been humiliatingly expelled from Burma in early 1942, and their attempts to return had met with limited success; forays by the Americans and Chinese into the Japanese-occupied territory had been equally inconclusive. But by the end of 1944 insatiable ambition had brought the Japanese to the point of disaster in Burma. Their dream was to topple India, that insecure pedestal of British imperialism, with the help of Chandra Bose's Indian National Army. The initial stepping stone was Imphal, a strategic city fifty miles west of the Burmese border. Not only was it the gateway to India but its occupation would be of inestimable propaganda value and an inspiration to all anti-imperialists.

For many months the Japanese military leadership in Burma, champing under orders to remain on the defensive, had been requesting an invasion of India. These appeals, and those of Chandra Bose, were heeded at last: early in 1944 Imperial Headquarters ordered the 15th Army to invest "the vital areas of northeastern India in the vicinity of Imphal." Its commander, Lieutenant General Renya Mutaguchi, regarded the capture of Imphal as the first in a series of deep thrusts into India. He had been brought to this view by an enemy, Brigadier Orde Charles Wingate, a messianic figure whose Chindits* had been harassing the Japanese commanders of Burma in a number of unorthodox stabs far behind the lines. Although opposed to earlier plans to invade India, Mutaguchi had been impressed by Wingate's raids. If an Englishman could bring troops through dense jungle and over mountains, so could he, and in far greater force. But leading a group of specially trained guerrillas over such terrain was one thing; leading an entire army was another.

Colonel Tadashi Katakura, Mutaguchi's operations officer, appreciated the obstacles: there were formidable rivers and rugged mountains to traverse; moreover, 15th Army was not logistically prepared to carry out such a long, arduous campaign with its present shortage of food, ammunition and medical supplies. Katakura forcefully pressed his misgivings—he had lost none of his bluntness since being shot in the neck during the 2/26 Incident for opposing the rebels—but Mutaguchi could not be persuaded to change the plans.

On March 8, 1944, three reinforced Japanese divisions and a division of Bose's I.N.A.—155,000 troops in all—crossed the Chindwin River and struck out across the mountains separating the two countries. On Indian soil Bose's men fell to their knees to kiss their native earth. Shouting *"Jai Hind! Jai Hind!,"* they pushed ahead toward Kohima, a city eighty miles north of Imphal, astride the British supply route. There they would turn south and march to Imphal, followed by the 31st Division after it had subdued Kohima. The other two Japanese divisions headed straight for Imphal.

The most proficient ground commander in the Far East, Lieutenant General William J. Slim of the British-Indian Fourteenth Army, had surmised that Mutaguchi would strike at Imphal—with perhaps a single brigade diverted to Kohima—and awaited the battle in a "rather complacent mood." His plan was to let the Japanese advance to the edge of the Imphal Plain, and when they were "committed in assaults on our prepared positions," to counterattack in full force and destroy them.

"My heart sank," he later wrote, when he learned that the enemy—two divisions strong—was attacking Kohima. This not only placed an important garrison city in jeopardy but threatened his army's sole supply base and railhead at Dimapur, which lay about thirty miles to the northwest. He ordered immediate reinforcements. "As I struggled hard to

---

*A mispronunciation of *chinthe,* Burmese for "lion."

redress my errors and to speed by rail and air these reinforcements I knew that all depended on the steadfastness of the troops already meeting the first impetus of attack. If they could hold until help arrived, all would be well; if not we were near disaster." What Slim feared above all was that the Japanese would by-pass Kohima and move on the railroad. An emergency line was set up on Kohima Ridge to block the road to Dimapur. Men were "scraped up" from the local administrative forces; five hundred convalescents were armed and put in the line.

But the commander of the 31st Division, Lieutenant General Kotoku Sato, directed all his forces at Kohima, where the defenders resisted so stubbornly—they were driven onto a single hill—that the Indian National Army troops alone turned south toward Imphal. On the steep hillsides south and west of that city, the other two Japanese divisions were already erecting a formidable system of earth-and-log bunkers, preparatory to launching their combined attack.

On April 18 the commander of the Indian force reported the unbelievable news that the road down to Imphal was lightly defended; his advance units were "only a stone's throw away" from the city itself. Victory was imminent; Bose had bales of new currency ready for circulation. But his dream was shattered when Sato, who had found more than he had bargained for at Kohima, refused to follow to Imphal. Instead he arbitrarily ordered his men to prepare to return to Burma; he had verbal permission (it was not meant to be taken literally) to withdraw if he weren't resupplied with food and ammunition by mid-April.

Bose was furious—without Sato backing their spearhead, the I.N.A. troops could never break through to Imphal. He was sure it was a plot of 15th Army and accused the Japanese of purposely depriving Indians of winning the first significant victory in their own country. Mutaguchi was equally furious with Sato (and relieved him of his command), but no explanation satisfied Bose.

The Japanese at Imphal were ready to attack, and asked Bose to deliver a radio broadcast on the Emperor's birthday, offering him Imphal as a present. Bose was insulted. Perversely he now opposed any invasion of India that was not led by I.N.A. He argued that the appearance of Indian troops would spark revolts throughout the nation, whereas Japanese invaders would only bring thousands of Indians to the side of the British.

The altercation gave General Slim a double advantage: it

divided the enemy and provided time for substantial reinforcements to reach the Imphal area by rail and air. The Japanese were converging on the city from six roads, but the defenders, with strong air support, held at every point. The debilitating battle continued inconclusively week after week. Both Japanese divisional commanders became convinced it would be impossible to storm Imphal, and one even began withdrawing troops without orders.

Vice Chief of the Army General Staff Hikosaburo Hata—accompanied by Colonel Sugita and other staff officers—arrived at the front to investigate; they returned to Tokyo with disheartening conclusions for Tojo: "There is little probability that the Imperial operation will succeed."

Tojo turned on Hata, accusing him of defeatism. The Prime Minister had counted on the success of Operation U to divert the public's attention from the startling loss of the Marshalls in the Pacific. He was so beside himself with frustration that his sarcasm also seemed to include Prince Mikasa, the Emperor's brother, who sat directly in front of Hata, and a chill came over the room. Hata remained silent. "If I'd been Hata," Colonel Tanemura wrote in his Diary, "I'd have ripped off my staff insignia and fought him."

On June 5 Mutaguchi met with his superior, General Masakazu Kawabe, Burma Area Army commander. Mutaguchi had already been obliged to dismiss all three of his division commanders—something unheard of in the history of the Japanese Army (one for incompetence, one for illness, and the third for refusing to obey orders) and it was on the tip of his tongue to declare that the time had come to suspend Operation U. But he could not speak. "I was hoping," Mutaguchi later recalled, "that General Kawabe would perceive in silence what was in my heart."

Kawabe was not that perceptive. "The destiny of Subhas Chandra Bose was mine as well as his," he wrote in his memoirs. "Therefore I had to assist Mutaguchi by all means in my power. I kept telling myself so."

The day following this meeting the British won back Kohima, after sixty-four days of some of the most bitter fighting of the war. A force of Japanese and Indians still held the road to Imphal, but within two weeks the British had smashed through and started to aid their harassed comrades in Imphal.

Mutaguchi's problems were aggravated by the arrival of the monsoon. Ceaseless rains poured down, washing out the jungle trails back to Burma. Only one of his three divisions had brought adequate food supplies; the others had to subsist on grass, potatoes, snails, lizards, snakes—anything they could get their hands on, including monkeys.

Mutaguchi still could not bring himself to ask Kawabe for permission to withdraw but came close to it by inference. "If operations are to be suspended and the army is to go over to the defensive," he wrote, "it is advisable that the army be withdrawn to the line running from the high ground on the right bank of the Chindwin River through the high ground to the northwest of Mawlaik to the Tiddim area."

Kawabe's reply appeared uncompromising: he expected the 15th Army to do its duty "zealously" and fight harder. But his senior staff officer was already en route to Manila with a request for Field Marshal Terauchi to suspend the operation. Terauchi approved but word did not reach Mutaguchi until July 9. Four days later the troops began retreating toward the Chindwin River. On the long trek back over the mountains in the pounding rain, men fought one another for food. Thousands of sick and wounded fell out of the march and killed themselves with grenades. The paths were seas of mud and when a man stumbled he became half buried in slime; shoes were stolen from those struggling feebly to extricate themselves. Light machine guns, rifles, helmets, gas masks—anything useless—littered the trails. Only the will to live propelled the survivors; the men hobbled along with improvised canes, and those who lasted out a day's march huddled together for sleep that rarely came because of the constant downpour. Many drowned, too feeble to raise their heads above the rising water, and the Chindwin River itself, their goal, claimed the lives of hundreds more in its swollen waters.

In all, 65,000 men died—more than two and a half times the number lost on Guadalcanal, and about as many as fell on Leyte. Mutaguchi, his chief of staff and senior staff officers were relieved of their posts, as were Kawabe and his chief of staff. The command shake-up and the destruction of the 15th Army infected every other unit in Burma, and by the end of the year Japanese rule was at the point of collapse.

2.

In China, that tangled, multi-sided war continued to be a source of frustration to everyone concerned except the Communists. The Japanese had conquered a vast area in eastern China but were no nearer to a final solution in their agonizingly long war in that enigmatic country. Though they occupied one important city after another, it was like tunneling in the sand; the Nanking puppet government of Wang Ching-wei was unable to consolidate the victories after the Japanese troops moved on. The Japanese dominated the coast, rivers, railroads, and highways, but in the expanses between, another struggle was going on among the Chinese themselves. Chiang Kai-shek was fighting Mao Tse-tung's armies for control while the war lords sided with whatever group was winning.

China bred dissension. Lieutenant General Joseph W. ("Vinegar Joe") Stilwell, commander of all American forces in China, remained at incessant odds with "Old Leatherface" Chennault, commander of 14th Air Force, an outgrowth of the American Volunteer Group, the Flying Tigers. Their argument most often focused on the policies of the man Stilwell derisively called "Peanut"—Chiang. In a series of vituperative messages to Washington, Stilwell charged that the aid sent to China was being criminally wasted by the Kuomintang; moreover, its armies were expending as little matériel as possible against the Japanese, since "Peanut" was bent on saving men and supplies for the postwar confrontation with Mao.

This, in large part, was true. Since the second Cairo Conference, when Chiang felt his vital interests were betrayed by Roosevelt under the influence of Churchill, the Nationalist troops had been waging passive warfare against Japan. In some sectors there had been virtual truce between the Kuomintang and the Japanese for over two years. A Chinese officer at an air base in Hupeh, for example, defended his refusal to shoot at passing Japanese aircraft with the excuse that if his men did so, "the Japs would be angry and would take revenge and return and bomb the city and do a lot of damage." Another of Chiang's officers argued that it was unnecessary for the Chinese "to take up an offensive against the Japs because soon the United States will surround Japan and then the Japs will have to retreat without fighting, and so it is better to leave them alone, and get along as best we can as we are."

Although Stilwell's indignation was justified, he failed to appreciate the fact that the Kuomintang forces were more than paying for Lend-Lease assistance by tying up almost a million Japanese troops who might otherwise be used against MacArthur and Nimitz. Accordingly, Chiang not only resented Stilwell's attitude but felt he had been taken in by American Communist propaganda, which labeled the Generalissimo a fascist and pictured Mao as an agrarian reformer, not a genuine Communist. "In the mistaken belief that the Chinese Communist forces, if placed under his [Stilwell's] command, would obey his orders and wholeheartedly fight the Japanese," Chiang wrote, "he assured me that the Government could safely re-equip them on the same basis as the Government forces and set them free for combat against the Japanese from where they were being held down by the Government's blockade. Moreover, the Government, he pointed out, could thus also release its forces immobilized on blockade duty for redeployment against the common enemy. ... Stilwell's subsequent disagreement with me was entirely brought about by the machinations of the Communists and their fellow-travelers. It almost caused the disruption of Sino-American military co-operation in the China-Burma Theater of War."

Chennault subscribed to this assessment as well as the allegation that Stilwell was spending too much time playing soldier in Burma, where he would disappear in the jungle for weeks, rifle in hand. By now the two American commanders were barely on speaking terms. A staunch advocate of ground warfare, "Vinegar Joe" thought Chennault's idea of fighting the war in China's skies was ridiculous. Wars were won on the ground. For months the two had been battling over supplies to 14th U. S. Air Force. In frustration, Chennault wrote personal letters to Roosevelt complaining he had not been given the tools promised him; nevertheless, his B-24's and fighters had provided the only bright spot in China with their effective raids on Japanese shipping and lines of communications.

Like Stilwell, though to a lesser degree, Roosevelt was becoming impatient with the Nationalists, and like Stilwell, he was primarily concerned with Burma. In early 1944 he urged Chiang and Stilwell to launch a major offensive across the Salween River into Burma. Chiang questioned the priority of such a campaign; he was far more worried about the Japanese in China. His reluctance drew stronger demands for action from Roosevelt—but still without result. The sudden thrust by Mutaguchi across the Indian border toward Imphal ended the debate as far as Roosevelt was concerned. On April 3 he radioed Chiang an implied threat to cut off Lend-Lease aid unless a Kuomintang army attacked down the Burma Road in the near future:

. . . TO ME THE TIME IS RIPE FOR ELEMENTS OF YOUR SEVENTY-FIRST ARMY GROUP TO ADVANCE WITHOUT FURTHER DELAY AND SEIZE THE TENGCHUNG-LUNGLING AREAS. A SHELL OF A DIVISION OPPOSES YOU ON THE SALWEEN. YOUR ADVANCE TO THE WEST CANNOT HELP BUT SUCCEED. TO TAKE ADVANTAGE OF JUST SUCH AN OPPORTUNITY, WE HAVE, DURING THE PAST YEAR, BEEN EQUIPPING AND TRAINING YOUR YOKE FORCE [the Yunnan divisions]. IF THEY ARE NOT TO BE USED IN THE COMMON CAUSE OUR MOST STRENUOUS AND EXTENSIVE EFFORTS TO FLY IN EQUIPMENT AND TO FURNISH INSTRUCTUAL PERSONNEL HAVE NOT BEEN JUSTIFIED . . .

Chiang Kai-shek did not formally reply to this message but within two weeks War Minister and Chief of Staff, General Ho Ying-chin, approved an assault across the Salween. Chennault, who also served as Chief of Staff of the Chinese Air Force, saw a far greater threat in China itself. He warned Chiang that the Japanese were about to launch an offensive on American air bases lying southeast of the Nationalist capital, Chungking. "Under the circumstances, therefore," he wrote, "it is necessary to inform your Excellency that the combined air forces in China, excluding the VLR [B-29] project, may not be able to withstand the expected Japanese air offensive and will certainly be unable to afford air support to the Chinese ground forces over the areas and on the scale desired. In order to put the air forces on a footing to accomplish these missions, drastic measures to provide them with adequate supplies and adequate strength must be taken. As the Japanese threat appears to be immediate, such measures should be taken without further delay."

He sent a similar warning to Stilwell, who replied that the threat to Imphal took precedence in the China-Burma-India theater and, therefore, Chennault's 14th Air Force must accept reductions in supplies; it would "simply have to cut" its operation. Chennault was infuriated. A week earlier he had written Stilwell that he was convinced the security of China as a base for future military operations against Japan was at stake:

. . . Since the Japanese no longer have the men and material to spare for rice raids or training exercises, it seems to me that they must now mean business. The whole logic of their situation points to this conclusion. They must make ready for eventual abandonment of their more extended commitments in order to try to hold on an interior line. To do this they must somehow neutralize the

Allied China base on their flank and protect Formosa, the key to their inner defenses. The urgency of doing this has been immeasurably increased by the prospect of B-29 operations against Formosa and the Japanese Islands, which alone would be sufficient to provoke a violent reaction. . . .

At the same time he made another personal appeal to Roosevelt; an attack in eastern China was imminent and he doubted it could be withstood.

I wish I could tell you that I have no fear of the outcome. I expect the Chinese forces to make the strongest resistance they can. We shall do our best to give them, by means of airpower, a margin over the Japanese. But owing to the concentration of our resources on fighting in Burma little has been done to strengthen the Chinese armies and for the same reason the 14th Air Force is still operating on a shoe string. If we were even a little stronger I should not be worried. Since men, equipment and supplies are still very short I can say to you that we will fight very hard.

I am the more concerned since the shrewdest Chinese leaders I have consulted are convinced that any Japanese success within China will touch off violent new price rises and probably political unrest with inevitable effects on the energy of the Chinese resistance. I note a mood of discouragement among the more influential Chinese.

Chennault's assessment of Japanese intentions was accurate. Tokyo had already ordered the commander of the China Expeditionary Army to occupy the eastern China airfields and the three important railroads in the area. The operation, named ICHI-GO, was divided into two phases. The first would disperse the Chinese forces, "particularly the Nationalists," between the Yellow River and the Yangtze, and secure the rail lines from Peking to Hankow. After that, eleven divisions with several others in reserve would cross the Yangtze and continue southwest, seizing first Changsha, and Hengyang in Hunan Province, then Kweilin, Liuchow and Nanning in Kwangsi Province. Capture of this last city would neutralize two important 14th Air Force fields.

ICHI-GO was preceded by an intensive propaganda campaign aimed at alienating China from her Western allies and lowering the morale of the Kuomintang troops. Bales of pamphlets proclaimed that Japan's enemy was the American-British force, not Chiang's army, and her objective was the establishment of a new China. If the Chinese offered no resistance they would be treated as friends. Japanese troops, moreover, were given strict orders to cease burning, looting and raping; they were to "treat the local inhabitants with kindness and respect." The men were taught a new marching song:

> Taking loving care of trees and grass,
> The Japanese troops march through Hunan Province.
> How kind their hearts are!
> Behold, the clouds there and rivers here
> Appear just as they are in our homeland.
> These sights impress our soldiers' manly breasts.
> With worn shoes they plod onward,
> Blood streams onto the soil;
> Let us defend this forest and that mountain with our blood.
> Our enemies are Anglo-Americans, the white-faced demons.

ICHI-GO began on the night of April 17. The 37th Division crossed the Yellow River as Mutaguchi's men were investing Kohima. Yet, curiously, there was no co-ordination or co-operation between the two operations. That same day Stilwell told Chennault that his primary mission was the defense of the B-29 fields at Chengtu, "even at the expense of shipping strikes and support of the Chinese ground forces." Chennault wanted to throw all his planes against the oncoming Japanese. Defending Chengtu, he radioed Stilwell, presented no immediate problem, since it lay west of Chungking. Confronted with the imminent collapse of eastern China, Stilwell gave Chennault permission to use the P-47's assigned to the defense of Chengtu, and ordered B-24's of the 380th Bombardment Group to deliver fuel to the 14th Air Force.

But the additional air support hardly slowed the Japanese advance. The Chinese armies in the area had deteriorated after almost four years of inactivity. Chennault saw his failure as a predictable result of Stilwell's policies, and reported to him that he had been handicapped by "lack of tonnage for aviation supplies and a general disbelief in Japanese offensive plans."

Suspecting that Chennault was preparing a case against him, Stilwell penned a long, bitter analysis of their old antagonism:*

Chennault has assured the Generalissimo that air power is the answer. He has told him that if the 14th AF is supported, he can effectively prevent a Jap invasion. Now he realizes it can't be

---

*It was found in Stilwell's file clipped to a radio message dated May 14, 1944.

done, and he is trying to prepare an out for himself by claiming that with a *little more,* which we won't give him, he can still do it. He tries to duck the consequences of having sold the wrong bill of goods, and put the blame on those who pointed out the danger long ago and tried to apply the remedy.

He has failed to damage the Jap supply line. He has not caused any Jap withdrawals. On the contrary, our preparations have done exactly what I prophesied, i.e., drawn a Jap reaction, which he now acknowledges the ground forces can't handle, even with the total air support he asked for and got.

Unimpressed by the attack of 72,000 Nationalist troops into Burma in mid-May, Stilwell officially continued his complaints against Chiang. He finally forced the issue in a radio to Marshall:

CKS WILL SQUEEZE OUT OF US EVERYTHING HE CAN GET TO MAKE US PAY FOR THE PRIVILEGE OF GETTING AT JAPAN THROUGH CHINA. HE WILL DO NOTHING TO HELP UNLESS FORCED INTO IT. NO MATTER HOW MUCH WE MAY BLAME ANY OF THE CHINESE GOVERNMENT AGENCIES FOR OBSTRUCTION, THE ULTIMATE RESPONSIBILITY RESTS SQUARELY ON THE SHOULDERS OF THE G-MO. IF HE IS WHAT HE CLAIMS TO BE, HE MUST ACCEPT THE RESPONSIBILITY. . . .

SO WITH THE CHINESE THE CHOICE SEEMS TO BE TO GET REALISTIC AND INSIST ON A QUID PRO QUO, OR ELSE RESTRICT OUR EFFORT IN CHINA TO MAINTAINING WHAT AMERICAN AVIATION WE CAN. THE LATTER COURSE ALLOWS CKS TO WELSH ON HIS AGREEMENTS. IT ALSO LAYS THE ULTIMATE BURDEN OF FIGHTING THE JAP ARMY ON THE U.S.A. I CONTEND THAT ULTIMATELY THE JAP ARMY MUST BE FOUGHT ON THE MAINLAND OF ASIA. IF YOU DO NOT BELIEVE THIS, AND THINK THAT JAPAN CAN BE DEFEATED BY OTHER MEANS, THEN THE PROPER COURSE MAY WELL BE TO CUT OUR EFFORT HERE TO THE A.T.C. AND THE MAINTENANCE OF WHATEVER AIR FORCE YOU CONSIDER SUITABLE IN CHINA. . . .

I REQUEST YOUR DECISION. IS MY MISSION CHANGED, OR SHALL I GO AHEAD AS BEFORE?

Washington's answer jolted Stillwell, and made official a policy which had been brewing for some time. It had been decided, Marshall replied, that operations in China and Southeast Asia would be determined by the contribution they made to campaigns in the central and southwest Pacific.

... JAPAN SHOULD BE DEFEATED WITHOUT UNDERTAKING A MAJOR CAMPAIGN AGAINST HER ON THE MAINLAND OF ASIA IF HER DEFEAT CAN BE ACCOMPLISHED IN THIS MANNER. SUBSEQUENT OPERATIONS AGAINST THE JAPANESE GROUND ARMY IN ASIA SHOULD THEN BE IN THE NATURE OF A MOPPING-UP OPERATION. ...

Henceforth China would be, primarily, an air base from which to bomb the Japanese mainland with B-29's. The idea for the Superfortress had been inspired by fears in 1939 that England would be overwhelmed, and there would be no air bases in Europe to attack Germany. It was a monstrous plane, dwarfing the B-17. It was 99 feet long and almost 28 feet high, with a wingspan of more than 141 feet. But it was sleek, its skin flush-riveted, and could cruise at more than 350 miles an hour at an altitude of 38,000 feet and carry four tons of bombs for 3,500 miles. From the beginning its builders had been plagued by engine trouble. An experimental model caught fire in the air, crashed and killed the entire crew. It wasn't until the summer of 1943 that the first production model took to the air—and this one, in fact, was full of "bugs."

The Marianas had been selected as the eventual base for mounting B-29 raids on Japan, but as long as these islands were in Japanese hands, Air Force planners decided to launch the first raids from China in spite of the formidable logistics problem. All fuel and supplies had to be hauled by air from India over the Hump—the Himalayas—to the four airfields in Chengtu which were still under construction. Moreover, the 4,000-mile round trip from Chengtu to Tokyo reduced the bomb-load capacity.

The B-29's were given their first test in combat before leaving India. It was a relatively short mission, but it dramatized the operational difficulties which beset the new bomber. On June 5, 1944, ninety-eight Superfortresses took off to bomb Bangkok. One crashed immediately, fourteen aborted and several others never reached the target. The remainder approached Bangkok in ragged formation. Two planes crashed on the way home, two ditched into the Bay of Bengal and forty-two landed at the wrong bases. But the mission was deemed an "operational success"; the B-29's were ready for Japan.

On June 15, ninety-two Superfortresses left for Chengtu, where they would refuel before the final long leg to Japan.

Seventy-nine of the planes reached the staging area, but only sixty-eight got back into the air that afternoon. Of those, one crashed on takeoff and four others turned back because of mechanical failure. The first B-29 reached the target—the Imperial Iron and Steel Works at Yawata on the island of Kyushu—just before midnight, Chinese time. Flak was heavy and several fighters came up to intercept, but of the bombers that made it to Yawata, only six were lightly damaged. The bombing itself was a failure—a single missile hit the Imperial works—but the effect on the Japanese was indelible. The war had at last reached the homeland.

In eastern China, Japanese troops were at the gates of Changsha. The fall of this great city three days later created panic in Chungking; the War Ministry ordered the execution of several field commanders. Two Japanese divisions, the 116th and 68th, were already driving down toward Hengyang, a hundred miles farther south. They seized an adjoining airfield on June 26, and two days later assailed the walled city itself. Surrender was expected momentarily, when Major General Fong Hsien-chueh, commander of the Chinese 10th Army, confounded the Japanese and surprised the Americans by making a determined stand. His troops—supported by Chennault's fighters and bombers, which made hazardous night attacks on enemy supply convoys—flung back the Japanese day after day.

Low on food and ammunition, the invaders withdrew within a fortnight. At Kweilin, which would have been the city next in the path of the Japanese drive, victory celebrations lasted for a week, its streets acrid from the interminable explosions of firecrackers. Merchants inundated American airmen at the Kweilin base with ivory, jade, silk and lacquerware.

The Japanese were soon back in force, however, with forty thousand fresh troops. General Fong resumed his dogged defense of Hengyang, but Chiang Kai-shek no longer supported him; for some reason he distrusted Fong's superior, Marshal Hseuh Yo. The Generalissimo ordered suspension of all Chinese and American supplies to the besieged city.

Chennault turned to an old antagonist for help. He radioed Stilwell a request for permission to fly guns and ammunition to Fong. Stilwell's headquarters replied noncommittally that the proposition was being given "best treatment in this shop," but took no action. Chennault sent another request, for 500 tons. This time the answer was definite:

IN VIEW LOCATION HSEUH YO'S FORCES, HIS MISSION, RAPIDLY CHANGING SITUATION, CHINESE MISUSE OF EQUIPMENT THEY HAVE AND IMPROPER EMPLOYMENT OF THEIR FORCES, YOUR PROPOSAL TO FLY 500 TONS OF SMALL ARMS AND AMMUNITION WOULD BE WASTE OF EFFORT. ENTIRE AMERICAN EFFORT SHOULD BE CONTINUED FROM THE AIR.

Several weeks later Hengyang fell. But Chennault's 14th Air Force continued attacking the Japanese supply lines and forced the enemy to postpone their assault on Kweilin for a month.

If China—whose role in the war had been diminished—collapsed, it would release 820,000 Japanese troops. Consequently, Roosevelt dispatched a personal representative to Chungking with orders to keep China in the war by unifying all Chinese military forces, including those of the Communists, against Japan. He selected a civilian, elevated to the rank of major general, Patrick J. Hurley, a successful corporation lawyer who had been Secretary of War under President Herbert Hoover. He was hearty and affable, and had won Roosevelt's confidence by the way he had carried out wartime diplomatic missions to Russia and the Middle East.

Hurley was en route to China, via Moscow, when V. M. Molotov, Commissar of Foreign Affairs, told him that Russia wanted to be friends with Nationalist China. Hadn't he, Molotov, personally brought about the release of Chiang after the Young Marshal kidnapped him in 1936? How could China blame Russia for her own internal dissension? The Soviet Union had no interest in the Chinese Communists—they were Communists in name only. America should try to help the Chinese people improve their economy, and to unify Mao's and Chiang's armies.

Hurley, who saw life in simplistic terms, took almost everything Molotov said at face value. In Chungking he told the Generalissimo that he needn't worry about the Chinese Communists' being controlled from Russia—wasn't it obvious that they weren't really Communists at all?

Chiang was unconvinced; he had read Mao's articles and speeches. Nor could Hurley persuade Chiang to place Stilwell in command of all Chinese armed forces, as Marshall had so long been demanding. On September 25 the Generalissimo sent Hurley an *aide-mémoire* stating that his recent experiences had clearly shown him that General Stilwell was "unfitted for the vast, complex and delicate duties which the new command will entail. Almost from the moment of his arrival in China, he showed his disregard for that mutual confidence and respect which are essential to the successful collaboration of allied forces ... Last October, I intended to ask for his recall, but when General Stilwell solemnly promised that in the future he would unreservedly obey my orders and would give me no further cause for disappointment, I withdrew my request. Unhappily, General Stilwell's solemn promise has never been implemented. . . ." Chiang promised to support any qualified replacement.

Stilwell radioed Marshall that the *aide-mémoire* was a tissue of false statements and that Chiang had "no intention of instituting any real democratic reforms or of forming a united front with the Communists."

Marshall forwarded this rejoinder to Roosevelt, whose disenchantment with the Generalissimo was evident in the reply he sent Chungking on October 5:

... THE GROUND SITUATION IN CHINA HAS SO DETERIORATED SINCE MY ORIGINAL PROPOSAL THAT I NOW AM INCLINED TO FEEL THAT THE UNITED STATES GOVERNMENT SHOULD NOT ASSUME THE RESPONSIBILITY INVOLVED IN PLACING AN AMERICAN OFFICER IN COMMAND OF YOUR GROUND FORCES THROUGHOUT CHINA. . . .

Chiang in turn, tried to blame Stilwell—and Roosevelt indirectly—for the collapse in eastern China. In another *aide-mémoire* to Hurley, he charged that the disaster had been occasioned by Stilwell's insistence on an offensive in northern Burma.

... As I had feared, the Japanese took advantage of the opportunity thus offered to launch an offensive within China attacking first in Honan and then in Hunan. Owing to the Burma campaign, no adequately trained and equipped reinforcements were available for these war areas ... The forces brought to bear by the Japanese in their offensive in east China were six times as great as those confronting General Stilwell in north Burma, and the consequences of defeat were certain to outweigh in China all results of victory in the north Burma campaign. Yet General Stilwell exhibited complete indifference to the outcome in east China; so much so that in the critical days of the east China operations, he consistently refused to release Lend Lease munitions already available in Yunnan for use in the East China fighting. . . .

In short, we have taken Myitkyina [Burma] but we have lost

almost all east China, and in this General Stilwell cannot be absolved of grave responsibility. . . .

He took issue with the President's derogatory refusal to appoint an American commander of Chinese forces.

I am wholly confident that if the President replaces General Stilwell with a qualified American officer, we can work together to reverse the present trend and achieve a vital contribution to the final victory.

Hurley had hoped he would conciliate Stilwell and Chiang, but now he was certain that this was impossible and that Stilwell must leave China. He radioed Roosevelt:

... MY OPINION IS THAT IF YOU SUSTAIN STILWELL IN THIS CONTROVERSY, YOU WILL LOSE CHIANG KAI-SHEK AND POSSIBLY YOU WILL LOSE CHINA WITH HIM.

For a week the fate of the China-Burma-India theater hung in the balance as both Stilwell and Hurley bombarded Washington with conflicting advice. Finally, on October 18 (two days before MacArthur landed at Leyte), Roosevelt radioed Chiang that he was recalling Stilwell but would not appoint an American to command the Chinese forces. He did promise to send Major General Albert C. Wedemeyer, to be the Generalissimo's new Chief of Staff and to command all U. S. forces in China.

With Stilwell gone, the affable Hurley could devote his full attention to the unique problem of uniting Mao and Chiang. On November 7, against the advice of Chiang, whom he called "Mr. Shek," he flew to the Communist capital of Yenan, where his idea was already being promoted; every American official and visiting journalist had been assured by Communist spokesmen that what China needed was a coalition government based on democratic principles. The mustachioed Hurley arrived, chest loaded with medals, impressing the onlookers with his flowing mane of white hair and ramrod carriage. In a booming voice he lectured Mao Tse-tung (he pronounced it "moose dung"), Chou En-lai and their aides on five points of possible accord with the Kuomintang. The Communists were startled by his manner, but responded with nods and smiles. That evening at an elaborate banquet he astounded his sedate hosts. After toasts to Stalin, Roosevelt and Churchill, he stood up and let loose a wild Indian war whoop. John K. Emmerson and other Foreign

Service experts tried to explain that it was just a quaint old American custom signifying good wishes to all.

Whatever the Communists thought, they accepted Hurley's statement with minor revisions. The five points called for unification of all military forces in China "for the immediate defeat of Japan and the reconstruction of China." The Chungking government was "to be reorganized into a coalition National Government embracing representatives of all anti-Japanese parties and non-partisan political bodies. A new democratic policy providing for reform in military, political, economic and cultural affairs shall be promulgated and made effective." The coalition regime would support the principles of Sun Yat-sen and set up a "government of the people, for the people and by the people," which would "establish justice, freedom of conscience, freedom of press, freedom of speech, freedom of assembly and association, the right to petition the government for the redress of grievances, the right of writ of habeas corpus and the right of residence." There was nothing in the document that any admirer of the Declaration of Independence would not have approved, including two additional phrases, borrowed from President Roosevelt—freedom from fear and freedom from want.

Hurley—now known as "Little Whiskers" to the Communists—flew back to Chungking with Chou En-lai, imagining that his mission was accomplished. How could anybody possibly object to such "innocuous" and noble sentiments? Molotov was right. The Chinese Reds were ersatz Communists; the Russians would never have reconciled such liberal policies with their own authoritarian practices.

Chungking greeted the document with derision, and its sponsor with a new nickname, "The Second Big Wind." "The Communists have sold you a bill of goods," T. V. Soong said to Hurley. "Never will the National Government grant the Communist request." Soong knew his brother-in-law; Chiang told Hurley that the agreement would lead to Communist domination of the coalition government. Nor could he accept Hurley's assurance that America would guarantee his position as President and Generalissimo. The coalition would be regarded by the Chinese as total defeat for the Kuomintang.

Hurley persisted in his belief that the most divergent views could be brought together by good will and persuaded the Chungking leaders to draw up a counterproposal. This stipulated that Communist forces be accepted into the Nationalist Army and that the Communist party be legalized; Mao, however, was to turn over control of his troops to the

National Military Council. It subscribed to Sun Yat-sen's principles and guaranteed the various freedoms and civil liberties, "subject only to the specific needs of security in the effective prosecution of the war against Japan."

Hurley passed along this proposal to Yenan, hoping it might be acceptable. It was not. Chou En-lai felt betrayed and replied that the Communists could find no common basis in Chiang's proposition; the Yenan government would have to be accepted as an equal in a genuine coalition government.

On October 31 General Wedemeyer arrived to replace the controversial Stilwell. The strategic situation in the Pacific had altered with the crushing American naval victories off Leyte, and with the possibility that Stalin would send sixty divisions against Japan three months after Germany was defeated. But it was still important to keep Chiang's armies in the field so they could continue to tie up masses of Japanese troops. Wedemeyer radioed Marshall that the military situation was worsening; Kweilin and its airfield would soon be lost, and Kunming, the capital of Yunnan Province, would undoubtedly be the next target.

There had been some changes in the Japanese command as well. In September, General Yasuji Okamura took over the China Expeditionary Army, and although his command was vast, he took personal charge of the 6th Area Army, which was in the midst of Operation ICHI. Its aim, however, was by no means as ambitious as Wedemeyer feared; Tokyo had no intention of driving as far west as Chungking. The acquisition of more Chinese territory held no attraction; the eastern China air bases did. Their seizure would prevent long-range bombing raids on the last outposts in the Pacific and the homeland.

Kweilin and Liuchow fell. Almost alone Chennault put up effective resistance with his B-25's and fighters. To do so, he did not hesitate to use any means to divert supplies from the B-29 project, which he derided as the last chance of the "bomber radicals" to prove the Douhet theory of unescorted, high-altitude bombing. The results of the B-29 raids seemed to bear out Chennault's belief that it was "a grandiose and foolish concept." After the first disappointing attack on Japan, the big bombers hit Kyushu four more times, as well as Manchuria and Palembang on Sumatra. Each raid was as ineffective as the first.

Replacement of the commander of the China B-29's by

Major General Curtis LeMay—an aggressive, resourceful leader whose Third Bombardment Division had performed brilliantly against Germany—made little difference. He found he had inherited an "utterly impossible situation" in China as well as "the buggiest damn airplane that ever came down the pike." He set up a new maintenance system, tried to teach the crews to bomb in formation, as the B-17's had done in Europe. Despite his vigorous efforts, a series of raids on Manchuria, Formosa, Rangoon, Singapore and Kyushu accomplished so little that he himself was forced to admit that his Superfortresses had not yet "made much of a splash in the war."*

3.

In the Marianas the B-29 program was also experiencing difficulties. Beset by tropical downpours that made Saipan roads impassable, engineers had not yet completed the first 8,500-foot strip at Isley (formerly Aslito) Field when the first B-29, *Joltin' Josie the Pacific Pioneer,* piloted by Brigadier General Heywood ("Possum") Hansell, touched down on October 12, 1944.

"The thrill that went through all was almost electric in effect" as the great plane rolled to a halt, one witness reported. According to *Brief,* the magazine for AAF personnel in the Pacific: "The war just about stopped dead in its tracks the day *Joltin' Josie* arrived . . . The first of the B-29s had been inspected by every big gear and ogled from afar by every small fry for 5,000 miles. She was a sensation."

A few days later Brigadier General Emmett ("Rosie") O'Donnell—a B-17 veteran of the first frustrating days of war in the Philippines—arrived to open the 73rd Bombardment Wing headquarters and set up intensive unit training. After half a dozen missions over Truk and Iwo Jima, the tiny volcanic island almost halfway to Tokyo, O'Connell's fliers were ready to strike at the Japanese capital.

The plan was an open secret, and on the morning of

---

*The U. S. Strategic Bombing Survey later concluded that attacks launched by the B-29's based in China "did not warrant diversion of the effort entailed and that the aviation gas and supplies used by B-29's might have been more profitably allocated to expansion of tactical and shipping operations of the 14th Air Force." The 800 tons of bombs they dropped were of "insufficient weight and accuracy to produce significant results."

November 17 hundreds of vehicles converged on Isley Field. Twenty-four war correspondents and an array of still photographers and newsreel cameramen were on hand. As "Rosie" O'Donnell climbed into his B-29, dozens of flash bulbs exploded. But rain that persisted for days forced postponements until the morning of November 24.

At six-fifteen the first plane, *Dauntless Dotty*, with O'Donnell at the controls, rumbled and roared down the long runway. The wheels of the silver plane hugged the black top to its end—and onto the short coral extension. At the last moment *Dauntless Dotty* heaved up, just skimming the sea, and made a slow turn toward Tokyo. There were 110 B-29's behind her. En route, seventeen were forced back. An undercast almost obscured the target—the Nakajima airplane-engine plant at Musashino ten miles northwest of the Imperial Palace—and as the unescorted planes, swept by a 120-knot tailwind, roared over at about 445 miles an hour, they unloaded their bombs at altitudes of from 27,000 to 32,000 feet. Only forty-eight bombs, including three duds, hit the plant complex, causing slight damage; the rest blasted dock and crowded urban areas. More than a hundred assorted fighters came up to intercept the Superfortresses; one bomber was knocked down, and that by a damaged Zero whose pilot deliberately rammed into its tail.

Three days later the 73rd Wing returned. This time the engine plant was completely hidden by clouds, and the sixty-two B-29's had to go after secondary targets. Unsuccessful as these first two strikes were, they chilled Imperial Headquarters as well as the public. Important factories would not always be protected by a cloud cover, and there seemed to be no effective defense against the B-29. Already the foundations of Japan's basic industry had been undermined by persistent American submarine and air attacks on shipping. There was little crude oil for the refineries; no coke or ore for the steel mills; and the munitions plants were short of steel and aluminum. The economy could not endure continued B-29 attacks. They would somehow have to be contained.

Until such time, emergency measures would have to be taken to protect a ship which had become a source of pride and a symbol of hope to the entire nation. Combined Fleet ordered *Shinano*, sister ship of the super-battleships *Yamato* and *Musashi*, to flee Tokyo Bay for the relative safety of the Inland Sea. She had been converted into the world's largest carrier, and many navy-yard workmen were still aboard the recently launched 68,000-ton ship. Driven by 200,000-h.p. turbines, she hurriedly got underway in the late afternoon on November 28, and steamed south with her untrained crew, escorted by three destroyers.

An armored flight deck, an island, and hangar and storage spaces had been grafted onto the basic structure. *Shinano* was a seagoing armadillo, encircled at the water line by an eight-inch main belt of armor; great armored bulges below the water line reduced the effectiveness of any torpedo hit. Deadly fumes could not be drawn through the ventilating system, as they had on *Taiho*. Fire hazard had been further reduced by the elimination of wooden structures, the use of a special fire-resistant paint and the installation of a revolutionary foam extinguisher system. To fend off air attacks there were sixteen 5-inch high-angle guns, as well as one hundred and forty 24-mm. antiaircraft machine guns and a dozen multiple-rocket launchers.

Theoretically, *Shinano* was the most impregnable carrier ever launched, but there were naval engineers who privately regarded her as an ill-conceived and too hastily constructed monstrosity which was neither battleship nor carrier.

A hundred miles south of Tokyo the American submarine *Archerfish* was looking for a target. Her primary mission was to rescue crews of B-29's forced to ditch in the area, but the day's air strike had been scrubbed and *Archerfish* was free to leave her assigned station. The most likely hunting ground, decided Skipper Joseph F. Enright, was off Tokyo Bay. At 8:48 P.M., radar detected a target to the north. Through binoculars Enright made out in the moonlight a long, low shape nine miles away. It looked like a tanker. *Archerfish* headed toward the target to make a surface attack from the starboard beam. As they drew closer, Enright identified it as a carrier with three escorts. He decided to try to get ahead of the flattop, submerge and attack. He ordered course reversed and maximum speed from the four big 16-cylinder engines.

Shinano was making 18 knots, the same as *Archerfish*, but zigzagging reduced her speed enough for the stalker to move up slowly. At midnight, however, *Shinano* picked up speed and the submarine gradually fell behind. Three hours later the carrier abruptly swung around directly toward *Archerfish*. Enright waited for a few minutes to make sure it was in fact a base-course change. He ordered the bridge cleared and the diving alarm sounded. *Archerfish* slipped beneath the waves.

"Up periscope," Enright ordered. He grasped the handles and stared ahead. "I see him," he finally said. He asked the distance to the track.

"Five-five-oh yards" was the almost instantaneous answer from the executive, "Bobo" Bobczynski.

"Left full rudder. Left to course zero-nine-zero." Enright asked Plot how much time.

"He'll be here in two minutes."

Enright spun the periscope to scan the area. "Down 'scope!" he called. "Escort passing overhead!" The periscope lowered just in time to avoid a destroyer churning above them. Enright raised the periscope again on the bearing generated by the fire-control computer. It was perfect—right on the mark. At 3:17 A.M. Enright said "Fire!" The range was 1,400 yards, just forward of the carrier's beam. At eight-second intervals six torpedoes headed toward the target, running "hot, straight, and normal."

Enright watched the first two "fish" hit, then swung the periscope around to check destroyers. They were converging on *Archerfish*. "Take her down," he said.

Lookouts on *Shinano* stared helplessly as these two torpedoes, and two more, ripped into the big carrier. Captain Toshio Abe was not alarmed. Four hits were nothing; *Musashi*, basically of the same design, had taken nineteen torpedoes and many bombs before going down. He ordered the ship continued on course at 18 knots.

Musashi had indeed taken far more damage, but her veteran crew was responsible for her extended survival. Abe's inexperienced damage control teams, hampered by the rough seas, could not stop the flow of water. Some of the compartments, moreover, lacked watertight doors. Abe could have grounded the ship or made it into port, but he held course and speed throughout the night. By dawn it was apparent even to those with blind faith in *Shinano* that she was mortally wounded. Abe reduced speed but it was too late. At 10:18 A.M., November 29, with the huge carrier listing sharply, Abe gave the order to abandon ship. Half an hour later, without having fired a gun or launched a plane, *Shinano* sank with a deafening rumble, taking with her Abe and five hundred shipmates.

The following week Japan's constant natural nemesis, the earthquake, struck the Nagoya area on Honshu Island. Its massive tremors left a long section of the rail bed in ruin, crippled a number of munitions plants and obliterated a factory in Toyohashi producing precision instruments. At the same time destruction from the air increased in effectiveness. In December, B-29's from Saipan bombed the Mitsubishi Aircraft Engine Works at Nagoya three times with such accuracy that the Japanese were forced to start moving equipment to underground sites.

4.

On January 9, 1945—the same day Superfortresses returned to Tokyo for the sixth time, and for the sixth time were ineffectual—General Krueger's Sixth Army invaded Luzon. They landed at Lingayen Gulf on the same beaches that Homma had stormed little more than three years earlier. They were expected, but there was almost no opposition and it was obvious by nightfall that General Yamashita had no intention of seriously contesting the landing. There was some concern on the part of American intelligence and operations officers that they were being drawn into a trap, but January 10 also proved to be an easy day and by dusk advance units had pushed eight miles inland. Within a week XIV Corps on the right had advanced thirty miles, losing thirty men. On the left, I Corps was making almost as good progress at the cost of 220 American casualties.

That night Yamashita finally launched a counterattack, a one-division operation designed to give him time to withdraw supplies and men to the north. He would give up the entire Central Plains–Manila Bay area and make his stand in the rugged mountains of North Luzon, where the terrain would give the defenders the advantage. It would be a battle of attrition, far from the Decisive Battle proclaimed so often.

The Japanese people, however, were told that the enemy had been lured into just such a battle on Luzon. But the reality of the situation was impossible to ignore completely, and on January 21 Prime Minister Koiso was obliged to make a rare admission to the Diet. He acknowledged that "the military developments in the Pacific theater are in a state which does not necessarily admit of optimism. However, the greatly extended supply lines of the enemy on all fronts are exposed to our attacks and in this fact, I believe, is to be found our golden opportunity to grasp victory.

"Now indeed is the time for us, the one hundred million, to give vent to our flaming ardor, and following in the footsteps of the valiant men of the Special Attack Corps, demonstrate even more spirit of sure victory in the field of production."

Imperial Headquarters was still intent on transporting prisoners of war from the Philippines to the homeland despite the sinking of two prison ships. Dr. Bodine, Major Virgil McCollum and the other survivors of *Oryoku-maru* were at sea again en route to Japan. They had left Lingayen Gulf just after Christmas in two groups—a thousand on a large freighter, *Enoura-maru,* and 236, including Bodine, on a smaller ship, *Brazil-maru.*

Major McCollum was aboard the bigger ship; sixteen prisoners died in the crowded holds on the way to Takao, Formosa—the first leg of the trip to Japan. For days the two ships remained in the harbor. It was getting cold. The threadbare parts of summer uniforms worn during the swim from the sinking *Oryoku-maru,* or thin cotton shirts and trousers issued to many who had reached shore naked, gave little protection. After a week of seemingly endless misery the men from the smaller ship were loaded onto *Enoura-maru.*

McCollum and Bodine were in the afthold with more than seven hundred others. It was seventy feet wide, ninety feet long, Halfway up one side of the vast chamber stretched a balcony. Here the Americans segregated their sick. Urine and feces dripped down from the balcony onto those below. There was little food and almost no water. The death rate rose to over ten a day.

On January 9—as General Krueger's troops came ashore at Lingayen Gulf—the prisoners heard the roar of American bombers sweeping in low. A deafening explosion rocked the ship. Bodine saw sparks fly as fragments burst through the hold. His left arm burned and he knew he was hit. He hunkered down as low as he could. At least fifteen were killed by the blast, and scores wounded.

In the forward hold, Marine Colonel Beecher was putting a spoon of rice to his mouth when slugs of metal whistled past him, burying themselves into a nearby stanchion. Heavy wooden hatch covers and steel beams cascaded onto the prisoners. Holes miraculously appeared in the side of the ship—"it was like a sieve." Dazed, Beecher shook himself. He felt nothing, then remembered from World War I that one felt no pain at the moment of being wounded. But how could he not be hit? The dead were everywhere. One corner was piled with bodies, mangled and bloody.

The carnage was indescribable. More than half of the five

hundred men in the hold were killed outright. For the wounded, shrieking in pain, there was no medicine, no dressings. Nor was there any answer from topside to pleas for help. In the darkness, panic and hysteria gripped the survivors. Three of the eight field officers were dead, crushed by a single beam. "Van, you and me were not worth living," one officer remarked to Major van Oosten, "but Bob Roberts got killed. He had so much to live for and so much to do."

For two days, with little water or food, and no medical assistance, the survivors existed in a hell none would ever forget. It was like a scene from Dante's Inferno as wraithlike figures wandered dazed in the dark, stinking hull among the piles of corpses. It was not uncommon to find a man sitting on a body as he ate his pitiful meal. Finally a small Japanese medical party descended into the holds. They treated the minor cases but ignored the seriously wounded, who were "dying like flies." The dead were removed—some five hundred of them—and barged ashore for cremation.

On the afternoon of January 13 the prisoners were transferred to *Brazil-maru*. It sailed at dawn, and the next two weeks seemed to McCollum "an eternity of horror." The once-a-day ration barely kept the prisoners alive; if they were lucky, four men got a level mess kit of rice, and six men shared a canteen cup of water. The winter cold, as they proceeded north, added to their misery. They tried to keep warm by lying down spoon fashion under straw mats, "hugging each other for BTUs to keep alive." When the position became too painful a man would yell "Shift!" and the group rolled simultaneously to the other hip. Sometimes a neighbor would not turn—he was dead.

Snow fell through the open hatches, and scores of men who had survived wounds, dysentery and starvation froze to death. Sometimes life could be bought from the guards—a West Point class ring would bring an empty rice sack as a blanket—but death was becoming commonplace. When the shout "Roll out your dead!" went up in the morning, often thirty or more bodies were collected. The victims all looked alike: macabre mannikins with teeth exposed in a snarl between drawn lips, ribs almost bursting, sunken eyes, pipe-stem legs and arms.

In a primal urge to survive, men would jerk mats off those too weak or sick to cling to them; they fought one another like dogs over scraps of food. The prisoners were saved from chaos by the example set by a handful of officers and the three chaplains—a Lutheran, another Protestant named

713

Nagle, and a Catholic, Father Cummings. In the end these three, worn by their exhaustive efforts, sacrificed their lives for the others.

Hardest to endure was the increasing scarcity of water, sometimes a spoonful or so a day, sometimes none. January 24 Bodine described in his diary how he and several others stole out of the hold at night to get water condensed in the cylinders of the ship's deck engines.

. . . Finally got a half canteen and drank a cupful but got beaten with gun butt three times. Black as spades and little can be seen. Guard huddles in a little shack. If I'd been alone I'd been OK but others kept drawing his attention to me. It's a good way to get shot but worth it. Later in AM got kicked around trying to get Irons some snow from dirty deck . . . Not so many deaths last night. My bowels loosened up and had first movement since Friday. We have lost so much fat that sphincter has nothing to work on and even with formed stools can't control movements. Amount of filth in and out of clothes indescribable. Snowing rather hard this AM and temperature close to freezing. Keep praying it's our last day. We do need warmth, water, food and cleanliness. . . .

Three days later he wrote:

. . . Coldest night we've had. No chow now or no water in AM but chow small amount in PM. Suffered agony all night. Father Cummings died. Kowalski gone; I am the only one left from my foot locker group. About 40 men died last night not buried. Hope ends soon. . . .

Bodine kept dreaming of waterfalls, springs and lemonade, and wakened by the bitter cold, made plans to live on a houseboat or in a house trailer or bungalow and keep a few turkeys and ducks.

On the night of January 29 the ship docked at Moji, on Kyushu Island in Japan, and the prisoners were given a physical test—the insertion of a rectal thermometer in the anus. At dawn they were lined up topside in the freezing wind and sleet to receive new clothing—shoes, wool trousers, padded jackets, socks and long cotton underwear. Those near the head of the line got the complete issue, but they had to pay a price. They were compelled to strip in the numbing cold, and with icy water from the decks running over their bare feet, they clumsily tried to dress. Guards beat them with sticks to hurry them up.

Bodine, near the end of the line, got nothing—and his

shoes had just been confiscated. As he started off the ship supporting a weak comrade, both were sprayed with Lysol. They were marched through driving wet snow to an empty, unheated warehouse near the pier, where Bodine traded his broken mess-kit knife for an old pair of shoes, and was able to fill his canteen with ice-cold water from a barrel outside a window. He was issued his first square meal in more than two and a half years: a cup of steamed rice, several spoonfuls of salted fish, a large crawfish, a few slices of salted radishes, a piece of something that was peppery, and fruit that tasted like pineapple.

Six more prisoners died in the cold warehouse. Of the 1,619 who had left Manila on *Oryoku-maru*, 450 were left, and at least a hundred of these would soon die. The survivors had got water and one good meal but there was still an overriding question: What next?

5.

The same question, but in a larger sense, was about to be asked at Yalta, a seaside resort in the Crimea, where the Big Three would determine the future face not only of Europe but of the Far East as well. On January 23, just before Roosevelt left Washington, the Joint Chiefs of Staff formally advised him that Russia's entry into the war against Japan was vital to the interests of the United States. It was Marshall's opinion, as well as MacArthur's, that conquest of the 700,000-man elite Kwantung Army in Manchuria without Soviet help would cost the lives of hundreds of thousands of Americans.* A few U. S. naval intelligence experts—Captain

---

*On March 23, 1955, MacArthur charged that his views had not been sought at the Yalta Conference, and that if they had he "would most emphatically have recommended against bringing the Soviet into the Pacific war at that late date." In February 1945 he gave three listeners the opposite impression. After his conversation with MacArthur, Brigadier General George Lincoln reported: "Concerning over-all plan, General MacArthur considers it essential that maximum number of Jap divisions be engaged and pinned down on Asiatic mainland before United States forces strike Japan proper." Colonel Paul L. Freeman, Jr., recorded: "He emphatically stated that we must not invade Japan proper unless the Russian Army is previously committed to action in Manchuria." And the new Secretary of the Navy, James V. Forrestal, wrote in his diary: "He said he felt that our strength should be reserved for use in the Japanese mainland, on the plain of Tokyo, and that this cou'd not be done without the assurance that the Japanese would be heavily engaged by the Russians in Manchuria."

Ellis Zacharias and his staff—shrewdly guessed that this Kwantung Army existed primarily on paper, since the cream of the troops had already been transferred to Leyte and other threatened sectors. But they were not heeded.

Three days later Foreign Secretary Anthony Eden sent Churchill a note from Moscow warning him to beware of the political demands which the Russians would probably make as their price for attacking Manchuria.

. . . There may perhaps be little argument about a Russian claim to recover possession of South Sakhalin which was ceded to Japan by the Treaty of Portsmouth in 1905. The Americans may look more closely at any claim to take the Kuriles. But a most difficult issue is likely to arise over Manchuria and Korea. We do not yet know what Russia's requirements are likely to be, but our conformity with the Cairo Declaration, for which we ourselves share responsibility, will be closely scrutinized by the Chinese, the Americans and others; and it is possible that these requirements can only be satisfied at the expense of incessant friction with the Chinese who may receive American support and expect ours also.

At all events there is here a potential cauldron of international dispute. It seems advisable therefore, at this stage, to go warily and to avoid anything like commitments or encouragement to Russia.

The conference opened on February 4, and its first concern was postwar Europe. The plenary meetings were lively, often heated, with Roosevelt again playing the mediator between Churchill and Stalin. The British somewhat resented Roosevelt's self-appointed role as umpire, and a few were outspoken about what they considered his appalling ignorance of the history of eastern Europe. Eden felt that Roosevelt's wish "to make it plain to Stalin that the United States was not 'ganging up' with Britain against Russia" was leading to "some confusion in Anglo-American relations which profited the Russians." Roosevelt admittedly was a consummate politician who could clearly see an immediate objective, but "his long-range vision was not quite sure." A. H. Birse, Churchill's interpreter, thought Roosevelt looked worn out. "The former self-confidence and firmness of tone, so evident at Teheran, seemed to have gone. His voice was that of a man weary in spirit . . . The good-humoured, benevolent uncle had become a shadow of his former self."

The relationship between the President and Churchill remained close, intimate as between two brothers and with the mixed feelings of brothers. Roosevelt had risked his political future to send Lend-Lease aid to Churchill in 1940 when Britain was in mortal peril—but continued to lecture his senior on the immorality of colonialism. "I believe you are trying to do away with the British Empire," Churchill once told him in private. Of this there was no doubt. "The colonial system means war," Roosevelt had confided to his son Elliott. "Exploit the resources of an India, a Burma, a Java; take all the wealth out of those countries, but never put anything back into them, things like education, decent standard of living, minimum health requirements—all you're doing is negating the value of a kind of organizational structure for peace before it begins."

On February 8 the American Chiefs of Staff were at last to take up their main concern—the war in the Pacific. They met with the Soviet Chiefs of Staff at the palace of Prince Yusupov, who assassinated Rasputin, to settle military problems in the Far East and in particular to determine what steps Russia should take once war with Japan was declared.

Six miles away at Livadia Palace, Roosevelt's headquarters, the President was cautiously approaching the same question with Stalin in the presence of Foreign Commissar Molotov, Averell Harriman and two interpreters. Livadia, built in Italian Renaissance style during Czar Nicholas' reign, was an imposing structure of honey-colored plaster trimmed with white marble. It stood more than 150 feet above the Black Sea, looking out on both water and precipitous mountains.

Roosevelt remarked that he favored intensive bombing of Japan by B-29's, thus obviating actual invasion of the homeland. Stalin interrupted him. "I'd like to discuss," he said without preamble, "the political conditions under which the U.S.S.R. would enter the war against Japan."

Roosevelt had a ready answer. There would be no difficulty, he said, regarding Russia's getting the southern half of Sakhalin Island and the Kurile Islands as a quid pro quo. As for giving the Soviets a warm-water port in the Far East, what about leasing Dairen from the Chinese or making it a free port? Stalin was noncommittal. Instead he asked for something more—use of the Manchurian railways. Roosevelt could see no harm in that, and suggested that they be leased under Russian operation or under a joint Russian-Chinese commission.

This satisfied Stalin but he said a bit threateningly, "If these conditions are not met, it would be difficult for me and Molotov to explain to the Soviet people why Russia was entering a war against Japan, a country with which they had no great trouble."

"I haven't had an opportunity to talk to Marshal Chiang Kai-shek," said Roosevelt. "One of the difficulties in speaking with the Chinese is that anything said to them is broadcast to the world in twenty-four hours."

Stalin agreed that it wasn't yet necessary to speak to the Chinese. "Regarding the question of a warm-water port, we won't be difficult; I won't object to an internationalized free port."

They began a candid discussion of China's internal problems. America, said Roosevelt, had been attempting to keep China alive. "China will remain alive," Stalin remarked with a little smile, but he thought it strange that the Kuomintang and Communists could not maintain a united front against the Japanese.

Roosevelt replied that Wedemeyer and Hurley were making better progress than their predecessors in uniting Chungking and Yenan. The blame for the breach lay more with the Kuomintang and Chungking than with the so-called Communists.

The talk switched to Korea, and Roosevelt confidentially remarked that although he personally felt it wasn't necessary to invite the British to take part in the trusteeship of that country, they might resent not being asked.

"They most certainly would be offended," said Stalin with his feral grin. "In fact, the Prime Minister might kill us." Then to everyone's surprise he said agreeably, "I think the British should be invited."

The next morning at eleven o'clock the Combined Chiefs discussed their final military report, agreeing that for planning purposes the earliest date to expect the defeat of Germany was July 1, 1945, and the latest, December 31, 1945. The fall of Japan was set at eighteen months after the collapse of Germany.

That afternoon Roosevelt, Stalin, Churchill and their principal advisers assembled in the courtyard of Livadia Palace to be photographed. As soon as they returned to the ballroom—the site of all the plenary meetings—the new Secretary of State, Edward Stettinius, Jr., began reading the plan the three foreign ministers had drawn up that morning for dealing with territorial trusteeships in the United Nations. Before he could finish, Churchill testily cried out that he hadn't agreed to a single word of the report. "I have not been consulted nor heard the subject until now!" He was so agitated that his horn-rimmed glasses slipped to the end of his nose. "Under no circumstances will I ever consent to the fumbling fingers of forty or fifty nations prying into the life's existence of the British Empire! As long as I am Prime Minister I shall never yield a scrap of Britain's heritage!"

The following afternoon, February 10, Ambassador Harriman met Molotov at Yusupov Palace. The American ambassador was handed an English translation of the U.S.S.R.'s political conditions for going to war with Japan: the status quo was to be preserved in Outer Mongolia, and territory seized by Japan after the war in 1904-5—principally the southern part of Sakhalin Island, Port Arthur and Dairen—must be returned. Stalin also demanded control of the Manchurian railways and the Kurile Islands. In return Russia, besides declaring war on Japan, would conclude a pact of friendship and alliance with Chiang.

Harriman thought there were three amendments the President "would wish to make before accepting." Dairen and Port Arthur would have to be free ports, and the Manchurian railways operated by a joint Sino-Soviet commission. "In addition, I feel sure that the President wouldn't wish to dispose of these two matters in which China is interested, without concurrence of Generalissimo Chiang Kai-shek."

At Livadia, Harriman showed Roosevelt the draft of Stalin's proposal together with the amendments he himself had brought up. Assured he was acting in the best interests of America, the President approved the amendments, and asked the ambassador to resubmit them to Molotov.

The warm relationship between Stalin and Roosevelt, begun at Teheran, continued at Yalta until that afternoon when Churchill announced he had been "practically instructed" by his government not to mention figures in the matter of reparations, and Roosevelt said he too was afraid the mention of the specific amount (Stalin had brought up the figure of $20,000,000,000, with half going to Russia) would make many Americans think of reparations solely in terms of dollars and cents.

It seemed to Stalin that Roosevelt was ganging up with Churchill against him, and he became visibly angry. Though the matter was hastily smoothed over, Stalin was apparently so concerned by his own flare of hostility that he took Harriman aside as soon as they recessed for tea to tell him that he was prepared to meet the President halfway on the agreement to join the war against Japan. "I'm entirely willing to have Dairen a free port under international control," he said. "But Port Arthur is different. It's to be a Russian naval base and therefore Russia requires a lease."

"Why don't you discuss this matter at once with the President?" Harriman suggested, and before long Stalin and Roosevelt were huddled together conferring in hushed voices, their brief rift healed. They reached complete agreement. The only question now was how and when to tell Chiang of the accord. The President wondered if Stalin wished to take up these matters with T. V. Soong in Moscow or if he would rather that he, Roosevelt, take them up directly with the Generalissimo.

I am an interested party, said Stalin. It would be better if the President did it. When should the subject be discussed with the Generalissimo? asked Roosevelt, sensitive to the problem of secrecy. I'll let you know when I'm prepared to have this done, said Stalin, who wanted to have twenty-five more divisions in the Far East before informing Chiang Kai-shek. At that point Churchill joined them and they did not continue the discussion.

The Prime Minister did not learn of the agreement until the next morning. He was about to sign it when Eden, who was appalled by what he had just read, stopped him. In the presence of Stalin and Roosevelt the Foreign Secretary branded the agreement "a discreditable byproduct of the conference." Churchill rebuffed him; British prestige in the Orient would suffer if he followed Eden's advice. He defiantly added his signature to the accord.

A few hours later the Yalta Conference ended. At the final luncheon there was a general feeling of relief that everything had gone so well. Roosevelt was in high spirits. His cherished Declaration on Liberated Europe, the promise of self-determination for these nations, was accepted, and Stalin had agreed in writing to enter the war against Japan two or three months after the fall of Germany.*

There was an aura of quiet satisfaction among the Americans. To Ambassador Harriman it was a solid diplomatic

---

*Several weeks after the conference, Roosevelt summoned the American journalist and author Edgar Snow to the White House. "I got along absolutely splendidly with Stalin this time," said the President. "I feel I finally got to know the man and like him." He waved aside Snow's reservations "with airy optimism," while admitting that the Russians obviously were "going to do things in their own way in areas they occupy." Roosevelt seemed confident that future problems could be settled by mutual compromise. "I got the impression," he said, "that the Russians are now fully satisfied and that we can work out everything together. I am convinced we are going to get along."

success. Stalin had agreed to support Chiang Kai-shek and recognize the sovereignty of the Chinese Nationalist government over Manchuria. Harry Hopkins was sure that this was the dawn of a new day for everyone. The first victory of the peace had been won with the Russians proving they could be reasonable and far-seeing.

Some of the British, however, had serious reservations, particularly about the fate of Poland; Roosevelt's health had been an adverse factor of the meetings and had led him into serious errors. But it was he alone who had promoted—in the face of a reluctant Stalin and dubious Churchill—the most lasting achievement of the conference, formation of the United Nations Organization.

The conditions of Stalin's agreement to fight Japan were known only to a few. If they had been circulated there would undoubtedly have been objections over Roosevelt and Churchill's promise that the Soviet claims for territory in the Far East "shall be unquestionably fulfilled after Japan has been defeated." Russia had, in effect, been bribed to do something she wanted very much to do. She would run no risk at all and suffer little cost in blood and matériel in attacking a beleaguered Japan once Germany was crushed. Moreover, the spoils of war—in particular the occupation of Manchuria—were a far greater inducement to join the assault than the secret pledges won from the West.

26   "Like Hell with the Fire Out"

1.

Several weeks before the landings at Leyte, the Joint Chiefs of Staff were persuaded—at the urgent request of Raymond Spruance and three Army generals—to proceed to Japan by way of Iwo Jima rather than Formosa. The immediate beneficiary was the Air Force. Iwo Jima was 625 miles north of Saipan and 660 miles south of Tokyo: a perfect halfway house for the VLR (Very Long Range) bombing project. Crippled Superfortresses could use it in emergencies, and from there the shorter-range P-51 Mustangs could escort the B-29's all the way to Japan.

Japanese resistance on Leyte forced a postponement of the Iwo Jima invasion, first to February 3 and then to February 19. The soft-spoken Spruance, veteran of Midway and the Marianas, was named overall commander, while Richmond Kelly Turner, who had learned so much at Guadalcanal, was made Joint Expeditionary Force commander. It was to be an all-Marine operation with "Howlin' Mad" Smith as commander of Expeditionary Troops. He in turn selected Major General Harry Schmidt to command the Landing Force, three divisions. The two assigned to hit the beaches on D-day, the 4th and 5th, began arduous amphibious exercises in Hawaii, while the 3rd, the reserve, trained on Guam.

From the sea Iwo Jima (Sulphur Island) resembled a half-submerged whale but from the air it looked like a fat porkchop. Its most distinctive feature was an extinct volcano at the narrow (southern) end. Only 556 feet in height, it seemed more imposing, jutting as it did straight up from the sea. This was Mount Suribachi, Japanese for "cone-shaped bowl."

The island was nearly five miles long and two and a half miles wide—a third the area of Manhattan. Though its volcano was inactive, the entire island seemed to be alive with jets of steam and boiling sulphur pits. The combination of coastal cliffs and rugged Suribachi gave the appearance of another Rock of Gibraltar. Yet habitants had the queasy feeling that the island might disappear any minute into the ocean.

The fat northern part of the triangular island was a plateau some 350 feet high with inaccessible rocky shores, but at the narrow end toward Suribachi there were wide stretches suitable for amphibious landings. The beach to the east was the one selected for the Marines to assault, but what looked like black sand was volcanic ash and cinders, so light that a heavy man could sink to his knees. While the sterile soil provided little natural cover on the windswept beaches and plateau, the little hills and valleys surrounding the table-land were dense with jungle growth.

Iwo was one in a chain of islands hanging like a loose necklace from the entrance of Tokyo Bay to within three hundred miles of the Marianas: first the Izu Islands, then the Bonins, and finally the Volcanoes—three islets in a north–south line, with Iwo in the center.

The Bonins were first settled in 1830 when two New Englanders, a Genoese and twenty-five Hawaiians landed at Chichi Jima, not quite two hundred miles north of Iwo. Twenty-three years later Commodore Perry visited Chichi and took possession of it for the United States, with intent to make it a provisioning station for American naval ships and mail steamers. But President Franklin Pierce repudiated his action, and in 1861 Japan, claiming that the Prince of Ogasawara had discovered the Bonins in 1593, annexed them all.

An Englishman, Gore by name, came upon the Volcanoes in 1673 and gave Sulphur Island its name. Next a Russian explorer arrived, in 1805, but neither of these men thought the Volcanoes were worth colonizing, and it wasn't until eight decades later that the first settlers—they were Japanese—landed on Iwo. Like all the other islands in the chain it was placed under the jurisdiction of the Tokyo Prefectural Government to be administered as a part of the homeland.

By the middle of the 1930's there were almost eleven hundred colonists, living in flimsy, one-storied Japanese-style homes. The main village, Motoyama, was located a little north of the exact center of the island near the sulphur pits. Vegetables, bananas, pineapples, papayas, sugar cane and grain were grown for local consumption but the economy was based on a sugar mill and a sulphur refinery. The sugar mill did so badly that it was converted into processing medical herbs. There were two schools run by seven teachers, the Taihei-ken inn, and a bar serviced by three girls. Six times a year ships brought supplies, visitors, and news from Japan.

Of the entire chain, Iwo alone was suitable for airfields, but for years the Imperial Navy paid little attention to it except for installing radio and weather stations. In 1940 the Mabuchi Construction Company began an airfield with two strips almost a mile long near the foot of Mount Suribachi. The following spring a Navy lieutenant arrived with ninety-three men to start erecting gun positions. Two thousand civilian laborers poured onto the island.

It was not until early 1944 when the Marshalls were invaded that the island, along with Formosa, received the full attention of Imperial Headquarters. First Commander Tsunezo Wachi, the former assistant naval attaché (and secret agent) in Mexico, landed with a garrison of more than five thousand sailors. Then work commenced on a second airfield on the central plateau, and by the end of May the Army had a garrison of 5,170, thirteen artillery pieces and more than two hundred machine guns; the Navy had fourteen coast defense guns, a dozen heavy pieces and one hundred and fifty 25-mm. machine guns for antiaircraft defense. But there was

Lieutenant General Tadamichi Kuribayashi arrived in June to set up headquarters for the 109th Division and assume overall command, he found a divided community.

The Japanese had divined American intentions long before they were conceived. "The entire Army and the nation will depend on you for the defense of that key island," Tojo had told the fifty-three-year-old Kuribayashi. Japanese estimates of American aims seemed to be confirmed a fortnight after Kuribayashi's arrival. Fifty-one carrier planes—intent only on neutralizing the island's air power—knocked down sixty-six interceptors and then bombed Iwo almost at will.

The raid was sobering to Kuribayashi. Nevertheless, he put on a show of confidence to his subordinates. "When the enemy comes here, we can contain him," he told a newly arrived major, Yoshitaka Horie, over whiskey, "and then our Combined Fleet will come to slap his face. That is to say, our role here is a massive containing action."

Horie knew more about the Navy than most Navy men; he had worked for a year to try to improve the convoy system. "General," he said, "there is no longer any Combined Fleet. Some scattered naval forces remain, but they have no striking power. Haven't you been informed of the results of A-Go?" He described the devastating defeat off the Marianas ten days earlier.

The general accused him of being intoxicated. "This island is under the jurisdiction of the city of Tokyo!"

"When I saw this island from the air today," Horie replied, "I thought the best thing to do would be to sink it to the bottom of the sea." It could be done with enough explosives.

"You're drunk," Kuribayashi reiterated, but with less conviction. In the morning he took Horie to the beach at the foot of Suribachi. He threw himself on the black sand as if he had just stormed ashore. "This beach is wide," he said and pointed to the adjoining airstrip. "Yes, the enemy must land here. They have no alternative." For the next two hours Kuribayashi compelled Horie, who had been wounded in China, to fling himself down all over the airfield, a target while the general "shot" him time and again with a walking stick. Horie thought he had the mind of a squad leader; it was easy to believe the derogatory stories of the general's obsession with details.

But Kuribayashi must have been impressed with Horie—or at least with the information he seemed to possess. He insisted that the major come to dinner again. They resumed their drinking, and all of a sudden Horie found himself talking about the disaster at Midway, and the pitiful state of convoy escort operations. Kuribayashi, his mind in a turmoil, tried to disparage what Horie said, and called him "a walking encyclopedia." But this resistance made Horie more persuasive. The general's face grew pale as the major disclosed the Combined Fleet's retreat from Truk to Palau, and then to the Philippines.

"The nineteenth of June [the Marianas Turkey Shoot] marked the death of Combined Fleet and Japan," said the major, his eyes glistening with tears. He tried to clear his throat. "If we could each kill ten enemies before dying, the world would realize it was really we who won the war!"

"Ah," sighed Kuribayashi, "I didn't know any of this."

"Personally I am reconciled to dying." Horie drew out a packet of potassium cyanide. Sobered, the two men sat in silence.

Kuribayashi ordered the evacuation of civilians and accelerated the program to build underground defenses in the porous volcanic rocks. He had decided to defend the island in depth rather than concentrate his efforts on annihilating the enemy on the beaches, and by midsummer Iwo was undermined with tunnels and caves. Reinforcements swelled the Army complement to 7,350 men. The Navy grew to 2,300 and received a new commander, Rear Admiral Toshinosuke Ichimaru, an experienced pilot who still limped from the crash of an experimental plane in 1926. His new combat command had inspired him to poetry:.

> Let me fall like a flower petal.
> May enemy bombs be directed at me, and enemy shells
> Mark me as their target.
>
> I go, never to return.
> Turning my head, I see the majestic mountain [Fuji-san].
> May His Majesty live as long.

On August 10 Major Horie, who was now stationed on Chichi Jima, returned to Iwo to establish an emergency supply transportation system. He brought with him as gifts for 109th Division headquarters two bottles of water—there wasn't a spring on the island—and some vegetables. Kuribayashi was sitting on his porch in a relaxed mood, even though twenty-eight light tanks had recently been sunk in transit. Most of the 145th Infantry Regiment had arrived safely, and he was pleased to find them well trained. But at dinner, after several tumblers of whiskey, he complained that he couldn't depend on his staff. There had been a growing resistance to his radical tactical plan of defense. "They react slowly to everything, and I can't restrain my impatience." What was the situation on Chichi Jima?

There were many overage officers there. One lieutenant colonel, past sixty, had asked Horie, "Why dig so many caves? We're all going to die, anyway."

"Japan has reached the end of the road," Kuribayashi reflected and poured the major another glass of whiskey.

The general's irritation with his staff embarrassed Horie the next day at the traditional morning ceremony in front of Division headquarters. After everyone had turned toward the Imperial Palace and bowed, the adjutant began reading communiqués. Kuribayashi interrupted the recital to criticize his chief of staff, Colonel Shizuichi Hori, for his bristling mustache. Later that morning Major Horie visited the headquarters of the largest unit in the 109th Division, the five-thousand-man 2nd Mixed Brigade, and was buttonholed by its commander, Major General Kotau Osuga, and the colonel with the offending mustache. For twenty minutes the two complained of Kuribayashi's arbitrary insistence on leaving the beaches undefended. That meant giving up Airfield No. 1, the only airstrip long enough for bombers.

Major Horie realized that he was largely to blame for the difference of opinion. Ignorant of the great naval defeat on June 19, these officers were still confident that the Combined Fleet would steam to their aid once the battle was joined. But he said nothing. It was not safe to tell everyone the truth.

Admiral Ichimaru was equally opposed to Kuribayashi's plan, and that afternoon he and three other naval officers confronted the general in Horie's presence. Commander Hijiri Urabe of the Third Air Fleet made it clear that he was conveying the opinions of the Navy General Staff, not his own. "The Navy wants to build pillboxes around Chidori [Airfield No. 1] and is ready to send about three hundred twenty-five-millimeter machine guns as well as the necessary building materials. The enemy can land only near Chidori. Therefore, if we defend it with pillboxes in depth, Iwo Jima will be impregnable."

It was the visitor from Chichi Jima who responded, not Kuribayashi. "How long did our guns last along the beaches at Saipan and Guam? Will you please show me just how

against hundreds of naval guns and aircraft is futile. The lessons we learned at Saipan, Guam and Tinian have taught us beyond any doubt that the best defense is to snipe at the enemy from caves. We must realize we can't defend a beach." Besides, Major Horie added, the enemy's big naval guns could blow up any pillbox. "Under the circumstances, how long could we hold out on Iwo Jima?" He suggested that Navy guns and materials be utilized to strengthen the defenses of Mount Suribachi and the Motoyama area.

"I agree with Major Horie," said Kuribayashi curtly.

Urabe asked the general to reconsider, then turned to Horie with a forced smile. "I'm particularly surprised that Major Horie, who has always been considered friendly to the Navy, opposes me."

"If I hadn't read the battle reports from Guadalcanal, Saipan and Guam, I might have agreed with the Navy without hesitation. Now my conscience doesn't permit me to do so."

Kuribayashi remained opposed to strong defense of the beaches, but he needed the Navy's co-operation as well as their supplies and weapons, particularly dynamite, cement and machine guns. The next morning he suggested a compromise: the Navy could use half of the material for beach pillboxes if the remainder went to the Army. Commander Urabe more than welcomed the suggestion. "Yesterday I promised to send you enough building material for three hundred pillboxes," he said. "As soon as I return to Japan I will make every effort to get enough for three hundred and fifty."

Kuribayashi summoned all his commanders and formally announced his battle plan: they were neither to fire at landing craft nor to oppose the landing on the beaches without orders. Once the enemy pushed inland five hundred yards, automatic weapons near the airfield as well as artillery on Suribachi and the Motoyama plateau area would open up. General Osuga and Colonel Hori still contravened Kuribayashi but he overrode them. "Once the enemy invades the island," Kuribayashi said, "every man will resist until the end, making his position his tomb. Every man will do his best to kill ten enemy soldiers."

The garrison of 21,000 troops—14,000 Army, 7,000 Navy—was distributed into five sectors with 1,860 men assigned to Mount Suribachi, where they would fight independently, delaying the enemy as long as possible. Numerous caves had been dug into the slopes facing the beaches, their en-

angled as protection against blasts and flamethrowers. Inside the mountain, work was almost completed on a vast storied gallery—complete with steam, water, electricity and plastered walls.

The rest of the island was studded with thick-walled pill-boxes. Many had additional protection: fifty-foot piles of sand. Big Navy coast guns were sited to enfilade the beaches,

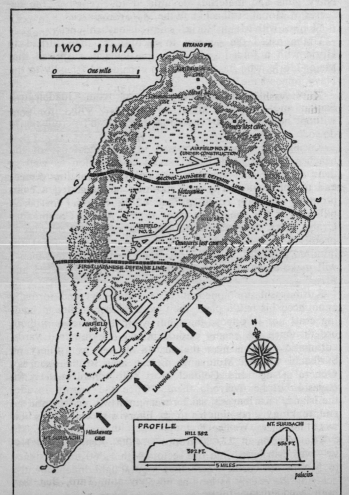

IWO JIMA

0   One mile   1

KITANO PT.

Kuribayashi cave

Communications cave

Nishi *cave*

Ohno's last cave

AIRFIELD NO. 3
(UNDER CONSTRUCTION)

SECOND JAPANESE DEFENSE LINE

Motoyama

PLATEAU AREA

AIRFIELD NO. 2

HILL 382

Omagari's last cave

FIRST JAPANESE DEFENSE LINE

AIRFIELD NO. 1

LANDING BEACHES

N

MT. SURIBACHI

Hinikawa's cave

PROFILE

HILL 382   MT. SURIBACHI

392 FT.   556 FT.

5 MILES

palacios

and antiaircraft guns were emplaced so that it would take a direct hit to destroy them.

The northern part of the island was a rabbit warren of natural and man-made caves; they were labyrinths of chambers and connecting tunnels, vented at the top for steam and sulphur fumes to escape. One, Brigade headquarters, located near Motoyama, could hold 2,000 troops; it was seventy-five feet deep and had a dozen entrances.

The first main line of defense—a network of dug-in positions for artillery, light machine guns and even buried tanks—ran along the southern edge of the plateau between the two airfields. A second line ran just beyond the second airfield through Motoyama.

Kuribayashi wrote home regularly. He chided his wife for visiting so much, and his eldest daughter, Yoko, for poor spelling and penmanship. When Mrs. Kuribayashi complained that life in Tokyo was getting unbearable, he pointed out that Iwo Jima was much worse.

. . . Our sole source of supply is rain water. I have a cup of water to wash my face—actually, my eyes only, then Lieutenant Fujita [his aide] uses the water. After he is through with it, I keep it for toilet purposes. The soldiers, in general, don't even have that much. Every day, after I've inspected defense positions, I dream in vain of drinking a cup of cool water. There are a lot of flies. Also many cockroaches crawl all over us. They are very dirty. Fortunately, there are no snakes or poisonous reptiles.

On September 12 he started preparing her for what he knew was coming.

. . . The enemy may land on this island soon. Once they do, we must follow the fate of those on Attu and Saipan.

Our officers and men know about "Death" very well. I am sorry to end my life here, fighting the United States of America but I want to defend this island as long as possible and to delay the enemy air raids on Tokyo.

Ah! You have worked well for a long time as my wife and the mother of my three children. Your life will become harder and more precarious. Watch out for your health and live long. The future of our children will not be easy either. Please take care of them after my death.

He also warned Yoko and his only son, Taro, that they both faced a dismal future.

. . . The enemy landing on my island is merely a question of time. If the defense of this island fails, then Tokyo will be raided day and night. It is beyond words to describe the chaos, terror, heavy damage and confusion of an air raid. Those who live idly in Tokyo can't even imagine what it's like. Therefore, in case of a raid, the most important thing is to keep the family together. Anyone cut off from the family can die on the roadside. This actually happened in the great Kanto earthquake of 1923. You must work for your family with your mother as the central figure.

Regardless of school regulations, you must protect your home first. You don't have to obey the regulations scrupulously because the situation will be too serious to worry about the safety of a schoolhouse. Suppose you tried to go to your school to save it and your own home was destroyed and your mother killed? What would you do then? You must share the fate of your mother.

To begin with, once Tokyo is raided it means that Iwo Jima has been taken by the enemy. It means your father is dead. In other words you—fatherless brother and sister—must depend on your mother. It's pitiful enough to be fatherless children but what happens if you lose your mother? And from now on you must reconcile yourselves to living without a father.

A little later he wrote Taro a separate letter underlining his duties as the only son.

. . . The life of your father is like a flicker of flame in the wind. It is apparent your father will have the same fate as the commanders of Saipan, Tinian and Guam. There is no possibility of my survival. Therefore, you must be the central figure of our family and help Mother. Until now you have been a boy brought up in a hothouse. When I was in Tokyo I tried to give you a kind of Spartan training but perhaps you didn't realize it was done with a father's real love. In the future, you may understand.

He advised Taro to read, study, quit smoking, avoid drinking, joke at home to keep everyone in good spirits, and use both sides of a page without indentations or spaces when writing future letters.

By the end of November the underground fortifications and batteries—some eight hundred guns in all—were ready for battle. Airfield No. 2 was operational and construction was initiated on a third strip, another mile to the north. Kuribayashi had also rid himself of dissent within his own staff. He relieved his outspoken chief of staff, the mustachioed Colonel Hori, and the commander of the 2nd Mixed Brigade, General Osuga, and sent them both to an underground hospital on the island "to regain their health."

On January 21, 1945, Kuribayashi told his wife to stop praying for his return. He was destined to die on Iwo:

. . . I don't care where my grave is located. My ashes will not be returned home and my soul will remain with you and the children. Live as long as possible and please take care of the children.

He also admonished his brother to protect him from publicity.

. . . Please put a stone on my grave with these simple words: "Tomb of Lieutenant General Tadamichi Kuribayashi." Don't let any newspapermen or magazine writers play me up in their stories. . . . I would like my name kept clean even after my death.

2.

For six weeks Iwo Jima had been bombed daily by B-24's from the Marianas with occasional help from Superfortresses. But the most intensive attacks came from the sea, and by February 15, warships had bombarded the little island with 21,926 shells. Remarkably, there were relatively few casualties; the defenders had moved underground. The following dawn six battleships, four heavy cruisers and a light cruiser arrived off Mount Suribachi. Destroyers and destroyer escorts darted in front of them, and a dozen jeep carriers ("baby flattops"), fifty miles south of the island, sent out combat air and antisubmarine patrols.

The correspondent and author John P. Marquand (who had not only won a Pulitzer prize for *The Late George Apley* but created a famous Oriental detective, Mr. Moto) wrote that it would have been hard to mistake Iwo "for anything but a Japanese island, for it had the faint delicate colors of a painting on a scroll of silk."

The battleships and cruisers began the initial bombardment. The shelling "turned out to be a slow, careful probing for almost invisible targets, with long dull intervals between the firing." It reminded Marquand of "the weaving and feinting of a fighter watching for an opening early in the first round. To put it another way, our task force was like a group of big-game hunters surrounding a slightly wounded but dangerous animal. They were approaching him slowly and respectfully, endeavoring to gauge his strength and at the same time to tempt him into action."

Except for a few unauthorized rounds, the Japanese held their fire. Then an overcast settled over the island like a protective cloak, and though the bombardment continued spasmodically until late afternoon, the damage was negligible.

To the north, the homeland itself was under attack from the sea. Planes from Mitscher's Task Force 58, which had boldly closed to within sixty miles of the mainland, were striking at plants near Tokyo producing aircraft frames and engines. The next morning, February 17, his bombers went after the Musashino plants, already the target of B-29's. Just before noon, however, the weather closed in, and Mitscher headed back toward Iwo Jima to back up the landing forces, cheered by the results of his foray, particularly the showing against the Japanese air defense: 341 enemy planes had reportedly been shot down and 190 destroyed on the ground, at the cost of only 49 aircraft.

At Iwo Jima the weather had improved and visibility was good. Minesweepers 750 yards from shore drew scattered fire from the island, and the heavy cruiser *Pensacola* moved in to help. This target proved too tempting for one battery commander. His guns hit the cruiser six times before she retired with 17 dead and 120 wounded. Destroyers closed in to cover gunboats armed with rockets which were a thousand yards offshore. Speedboats loaded with frogmen passed through this line.

The Japanese were shaken, as much by the enemy's nonchalance as by his display of power. Popular music floated across the water, as if from a group of people on an excursion, and they could see American sailors with towels around their necks gawking at the island like tourists. Kuribayashi had no longer any doubt that this was the landing. At 10:35 A.M. he ordered several batteries to open up on the gunboats, which retaliated with their rockets. This, in turn, brought on a barrage from big guns hidden at the foot of Mount Suribachi and at the northern end of Iwo. Several gunboats were hit, and planes laid a smoke screen while destroyers fired white phosphorus shells. The speedboats, which had continued undeterred toward the island, arced sharply near the shore line, and about a hundred frogmen flopped into the surf. They found no underwater or beach obstacles and a single mine, which was detonated.

At Airfield No. 2 there were two operable Zero fighters, armed with 60-kilogram bombs, concealed in a concrete revetment. Their pilots had been ordered to ram the largest ship they could reach, but one of them balked. "You're going to die, anyway," said a friend. The pilot insisted that his head hurt. His commander turned to a group of pilots and asked for a volunteer. One hoisted himself into the plane. The camouflage was whipped off, and the two Zeros taxied smartly from the revetment onto the strip. They managed to get into the air, but as they skimmed over Suribachi both were caught in the artillery fire and tumbled into the sea.

The second day of bombardment ended, and Kuribayashi, thinking he had repulsed a landing, radioed of his success to Tokyo. Admiral Toyoda of Combined Fleet sent his congratulations to Admiral Ichimaru:

DESPITE VERY POWERFUL ENEMY BOMBINGS AND SHELL-INGS, YOUR UNIT AT IWO COOLLY JUDGED THE ENEMY INTENTIONS AND FOILED THE FIRST LANDING ATTEMPT AND SERENELY AWAITS THE NEXT ONE, DETERMINED TO HOLD IWO AT ANY COST. I AM GREATLY ELATED TO KNOW THAT, AND I WISH YOU TO CONTINUE TO MAINTAIN HIGH MORALE AND REPULSE THE ENEMY, NO MATTER HOW IN-TENSE HIS ATTACKS, AND SAFEGUARD THE OUTER DEFENS-ES OF OUR HOMELAND.

The two-day shelling caused few casualties but had uncovered Kuribayashi's hidden batteries and the extent of his defenses, enabling the Americans to revise effectively their bombardment pattern for the final day. Fire would be concentrated on the area around the southeast beach, the one the Marines would storm.

The morning sky was cloudy with bursts of rain. "Close beach and get going," ordered the commander of the Gunfire and Covering Force at 7:45 A.M. For the first time the shelling was devastating; photos indicated that half the pillboxes and most of the blockhouses on the beach had been torn from their foundations.

That evening the Marines of the 4th and 5th divisions, who had left Saipan on LST's and transports on February 15 and 16, filed their way through the chow lines, checked their gear, packs and weapons. There was no apparent tension or edginess. Everyone looked the same as the day before.

In his cabin on the command ship, Eldorado, "Howlin' Mad" Smith was reading the Bible. His men would suffer severe casualties when they hit the beach in a few hours. He was a Methodist but he wore a St. Christopher's medal blessed by the Pope. Several weeks earlier he had written to Lieutenant General Alexander Vandegrift, who was now Commandant of the Marine Corps, that he felt taking a fortress like Iwo Jima wasn't worth the heavy casualties his men would suffer.

. . . On two separate occasions I protested that naval gunfire is insufficient, with the result that it has been increased to some extent, but not enough, in my opinion, to suffice. I can only go so far.

We have done all we could to get ready . . . and I believe it will be successful, but the thought of the probable casualties causes me extreme unhappiness . . . would to God that something might happen to cancel the operation altogether.

At 3:30 A.M. on D-day—February 19—the Marines had steak for breakfast. By the time they moved out on deck to the debarkation nets it was light, and through the mist they saw, looking lonely and abandoned, the island of Iwo. Mount Suribachi disappeared ominously into a low cloud.

John Marquand was atop the air lookout station on his ship. Iwo Jima had "never looked more aesthetically ugly . . . or more completely Japanese. Its silhouette was like a sea monster with the little dead volcano for the head, and the beach area for the neck, and all the rest of it with its scrubby, brown cliffs for the body. It also had the minute, fussy compactness of those miniature Japanese gardens. Its stones and rocks were like those contorted, wind-scoured, water-worn boulders which the Japanese love to collect as landscape decorations."

The transports and landing craft jockeyed over the calm waters toward their disembarkment positions. At 6:40 A.M. seven battleships, four heavy and four light cruisers began the heaviest pre–H-hour naval bombardment of the war. Five minutes later nine gunboats—LCI(R)'s—showered the Motoyama plateau with rockets while other gunboats—LCI(M)'s—pumped mortar rounds into the slopes of Suribachi. At 8:03 the bombardment let up to allow 120 carrier planes to blanket the southeast beach, Suribachi and Airfield No. 1 with rockets, napalm and explosive bombs. They climbed away as abruptly as they had appeared and the shelling resumed. This time ten destroyers joined in. The island seemed to shimmer through the burgeoning pall of dust and smoke. More planes swooped down, hosing the black sands with streams of bullets. It was the most "terrify ing" bombardment the correspondent Robert Sherrod had ever witnessed. "Though I've seen this many times," he recorded in his notebook, "I can't help thinking, 'Nobody can live through this.' But I know better."

Huddled in their pillboxes, blockhouses and caves, the Japanese endured the concussions, fingers jammed into their ears. Their final instructions from Kuribayashi had been explicit:

Above all else, we shall dedicate ourselves and our entire strength to the defense of this island.

We shall grasp grenades, charge enemy tanks and destroy them.

We shall infiltrate into the midst of the enemy and annihilate them.

With every salvo we will, without fail, kill the enemy.

Each man will make it his duty to kill ten of the enemy before dying.

Until we are destroyed to the last man, we shall harass the enemy by guerrilla tactics.

From the mouth of his cave on Suribachi, Pfc. Kiyomi Hirakawa—a former government official—watched entranced as the vast flotilla of enemy ships waddled into place. How systematic and beautiful! he thought. It was the massed equipment that awed him, not the enemy himself. He knew all about the American fighting man from propaganda lectures and pamphlets. "They call themselves brave soldiers," read one such pamphlet entitled *The Psychology of the Individual American*, "yet they have no desire for the glory of their ancestors or posterity, nor for the glory of the family name. They as individuals want to be known as brave and to be given publicity. They are people who love adventure and danger. There are accounts of Americans who tried to go over Niagara Falls in a barrel. . . . They fear death, but being individualists, they do not think much about what will happen hereafter. Rather, when doing something adventurous, they are not afraid to die. They are expert liars. They are taken in by flattery and propaganda. Their desires are very materialistic. They go into battle with no spiritual incentive, and rely on material superiority."

The LST's, loaded with the first five assault waves, moved into final position 5,500 yards offshore. Slogans like "*Too Late to Worry*" were scrawled on the ramps. These lowered ponderously, and amphtracs began popping out into the sea ("It's like all the cats in the world having kittens," Marquand observed to a petty officer) and skittering toward Iwo. The first wave of sixty-nine amphtracs, each carrying some twenty men, climbed onto the beach at 9:02 A.M., two hours after H-hour, and began to crawl forward. Twenty yards inland they encountered a steep terrace fifteen feet high in places. The amphtracs churned vigorously through the black volcanic ash, which was as loose as sugar, but only a few breasted the terrace. The others disgorged their occupants at its base, where the heavily laden men sank over their ankles in the black sand. They struggled forward through sporadic rifle fire and desultory rounds of mortar. Perhaps enemy strength had been exaggerated or the massive bombardment had driven the Japanese underground.

But once the Marines heaved themselves up the collapsing terrace, they were met by machine-gun and rifle fire from concealed pillboxes, blockhouses and caves. Mortar shells flew over their heads, crashing around amphtracs heading toward shore. Marines blown into the sea tried to swim to the beach but their heavy packs pulled them below the surface.

The 5th Division, going into action for the first time, was spewing onto the beaches on the left. One regimental combat team, the 28th, moved doggedly toward Mount Suribachi. Its job was to cut across the 700-yard-wide neck of sand to the other side of the island, isolate the volcano and storm up it while another team, the 27th, attacked the southern end of Airfield No. 1.

On the right flank two regiments of the 4th Division were to help seize the airfield and then the ridge guarding the Motoyama plateau. It was the first battle for Private Allen R. Matthews, a combat correspondent, and on the amphtrac he felt immortal, indestructible. He could picture himself grieving over the death of a friend—never a friend grieving over him. But as he scrambled onto the beach, mechanically chewing gum, his mind in a turmoil, he told himself, Run run run, get off the beach, don't hole up on the beach unless it's absolutely necessary because they're sighting on the beach and they'll get you sure as hell ... get off the beach and run. But he couldn't. He staggered under the weight of equipment and sank into the sand. He heard nothing of the thunder of battle, but something compelled him to look to the rear. The sand spouted like a geyser of black water. His mouth was so dry that his chewing gum stuck to his teeth and tongue. He lurched forward trying to spit it out but bits clung to his lip

All around, men were running and stumbling in a nightmare silence. They seemed to have no weapons, no uniforms, no faces. Suddenly he heard a noise. "Co-o—orpsman!" wailed a vaice in pain and terror. "Oh, co-o-orpsman!" Marines weren't supposed to cry out like that. It came from a man sitting in a shallow depression in the terrace; he was inert, like a statue. On the left, three men were heaped oddly. They had to be dead.

Frenzied, Matthews pumped his legs into the soft ash of the sheer terrace, awkwardly holding his rifle aloft to keep sand out of the breech. At last he was on top. He started for a shell crater but wallowed helplessly in the sand. What a fine target I am! he thought. He fell again, and rolled weakly into a hole. He swallowed for saliva but his swollen tongue scraped dryly against his palate. He retched and at last saliva flowed. He surveyed the scene. Now he was a veteran; he knew he too might be killed.

The first walking wounded were reporting to regimental aid stations. One, his jaw hanging by threads of flesh, suffered himself to be bandaged but refused to be evacuated. He tried to talk, then knelt and wrote something in the volcanic ash. The words filled in immediately. He scuffed the sand disgustedly and allowed himself to be led away.

The first tanks lumbered ashore at 9:30 A.M. They floundered in the soft ash. Some managed to climb over the terrace, but more were trapped and knocked out systematically by antitank guns. The 4th Division in particular had been counting on their support, and its drive toward the airfield was painfully slow. Caught in murderous cross fire from innumerable pillboxes and blockhouses, its troops had to subdue each one with demolitions and flamethrowers.

Second Lieutenant Benjamin Roselle, Jr., didn't land until 1 P.M. with his naval gunfire liaison team. Burdened with radio gear, they struggled up the terrace at the extreme right end of the battle line. Roselle's left foot was almost blown off by a mortar round. His men put a tourniquet on his leg while he cracked jokes. Another mortar shell landed on them, killing two of his men and peppering Roselle's good leg with shrapnel. He was left with one man, and the two of them hugged the ground until a third round detonated just above them. Roselle was hit again, this time in the shoulder. The enlisted man's right leg was blown off, and he silently crawled down the terrace, the stump dragging behind him. All by himself now, Roselle could think of nothing but his mother walking up from the shoreline toward the terrace. Roselle felt himself lifted—and dropped. He didn't care. He glanced at his watch just as shrapnel ripped through his wrist. The watch was gone; in its place was a gaping red hole. This is what it feels like to be crucified, he thought.

To the Americans on the beach the fire seemed intense, but Kuribayashi's gunners were still firing with restraint, and many batteries up the island were not firing at all. Ammunition was husbanded; every round had to count. In his first radio report to Tokyo the general cited the commander of a platoon of antitank guns for knocking out more than twenty enemy tanks before succumbing, and requested that he be promoted posthumously to captain. He praised two other antitank commanders, an infantry officer and the entire 145th Infantry Regiment. He also reported that company funds totaling 120,000 yen were "hereby donated to the National Treasury"—the money had been burned.

By dusk thirty thousand Marines were ashore. Five hundred and sixty-six had been killed or were dying of wounds. The rest were crowded into a small beachhead, 4,400 yards long and 1,100 yards at its deepest point. They had failed to reach the first day's objectives and were digging in for the expected counterattack. But Kuribayashi was as careful of his men as he was of his ammunition. Unlike the commander at Saipan, he was not going to waste troops in futile night charges. He did something far more effective: ordered harassing mortar and artillery fire.

Throughout the night Marine ammunition dumps were detonated one by one with mystifying accuracy, as if there had been an observer within American lines. Finally a Marine heard a low clicking sound coming from the hulk of a beached Japanese transport. With a few comrades, the Marine crept up to the derelict. He made out a ghostly figure inside—a Japanese with a radio transmitter strapped on his back. Although his death brought a sharp decrease in Japanese artillery accuracy, the beach area was so crowded that casualties continued to be severe. Neither could anything stop the havoc wrought by rockets screaming out of the dark night. They were not conventional missiles. Japanese naval aviation ordnance men had somehow found a way to convert 60- and 250-kilogram bombs into rockets, launching them electrically along slanted wooden ramps. The "rocket" flew up the 45-degree incline, arched some 2,000 yards in the general direction of enemy positions and exploded on contact.

"The first night on Iwo Jima can only be described as a nightmare in hell," wrote Sherrod. By dawn dead littered the black sand. Nowhere in the Pacific had he seen such badly mangled bodies; legs and arms lay fifty feet from torsos. A light rain was falling. It was cold. The naval bombardment started at 7:40 A.M., an hour later than on D-day. After fifty minutes the Marines attacked. On the left, at the base of Suribachi, the going was arduous; the 28th had made little more than two hundred yards by dark even with the help of artillery, half-tracks, and supplementary shelling by destroyers which approached within 250 yards of land.

On the right the 4th Division broke through to Airfield No. 1, then pivoted north and encountered Kuribayashi's first major defense line. Throughout the long day of combat, dogs brought ashore by their Marine masters roamed the beach. One named George was already a veteran of two previous landings. Another, a feisty fox terrier, contemptuous of the nerve-shattering explosions on all sides, romped with a live grenade, rolling it around, flinging it in the air. He carried it to a foxhole, scattering its occupants. He trotted after them, refusing orders to drop it. Finally he obeyed, but as soon as a Marine reached for the grenade he would playfully snatch it up again. They tempted him with food but he wanted to play. The men threw sticks to distract him; he wouldn't abandon his new toy. Finally someone thought of ignoring him. After a few minutes the fox terrier abandoned the grenade; it was retrieved and the battle against the Japanese resumed.

After dark the bomb-rockets again hurled into the closely packed Marines. During a lull the men crouching in Sherrod's shell hole felt the earth jar under them, followed by a weird noise like "someone banging on the radiator in the apartment below." It was probably a mild tremor, but no one jeered when a sergeant said, "Oh, my God, the Japs are digging underneath us now."

3.

On the third day, February 21, the naval bombardment once more commenced at 7:40 A.M., and again the Marines launched attacks fifty minutes later with close support from carrier planes. By early afternoon the 28th Marines had blasted through formidable stone and concrete defenses, almost to the base of Suribachi. The general attack to the north also started well, particularly on the extreme left, where tanks could maneuver. Here the 5th Division pushed ahead 1,000 yards. On the right, the 4th Division encountered rugged terrain and heavier fire, and made half that distance.

At dusk the Japanese struck from the air for the first time. Five *kamikaze* based near Tokyo broke through the fighter screen around *Saratoga*, which lay thirty-five miles off Iwo Jima. The first two suicide planes were set afire but kept boring in. They skipped off the water and into the carrier. The remaining three smashed directly into *Saratoga* and exploded. Before the blazes were brought under control, five more planes appeared. Four were shot down, but the fifth dropped a bomb that tore a 25-foot hole in the flight deck. The badly damaged *Saratoga* was compelled to start directly back to America for extensive repairs. A few miles away a single *kamikaze* started fires on the jeep carrier *Bismarck Sea* which could not be contained. Blazing from stem to stern, she plunged to the bottom a few minutes after midnight.

That evening's "Home and Empire" broadcast in Tokyo mentioned the landings of enemy soldiers on Iwo Jima, and spoke of their leaders with uncharacteristic admiration:

"This man Turner is called and known as the 'Alligator' in the American Navy.* He is associated with this name because his work is very similar to that of an alligator, which lives both on land and in the water. Also, the true nature of an alligator is that once he bites into something he will not let go. Turner's nature is also like this.

"Spruance, with a powerful offensive spirit, and Turner, with excellent determinative power, have led their men to a point where they are indeed close to the mainland, but they find themselves in a dilemma, as they are unable to either advance or retreat.

"This man Turner, who has been responsible for the death of so many of our precious men, shall not return home alive—he must not, and will not. This is one of the many things we can do to put to rest the many souls of those who have paid the supreme sacrifice."

The steady, cold rain continued throughout February 22 as the Marines tightened their hold on "Hotrocks," code name

---

*Admiral Turner was never nicknamed "Alligator." The Japanese apparently got the name from the V Amphibious Corps shoulder patch.

for Suribachi, completely surrounding the volcano except for a 400-yard stretch on the west coast. The Japanese commander, Colonel Kanehiko Atsuji, informed Kuribayashi by radio that his casualties were heavy:

> NOW ENEMY IS BURNING US WITH FLAMETHROWERS. IF WE REMAIN IN OUR POSITIONS WE SHALL BE EXTERMINATED. WE WOULD LIKE TO GO OUT FOR THE FINAL ATTACK.

Suicidal attacks had dominated Japanese military philosophy since Guadalcanal, to the enemy's advantage. Kuribayashi curtly replied:

> I HAD ASSUMED CHIDORI [Airfield No. 1] WOULD BE OVERRUN QUICKLY BY THE ENEMY BUT WHAT HAS HAPPENED TO MAKE MOUNT SURIBACHI FALL WITHIN THREE DAYS?

The next morning the Marines resumed the assault on the battered volcano, edging up its sheer sides in the face of concentrated fire. Where the defenders ran short of ammunition, they rolled rocks down the steep inclines. Pillboxes and underground galleries were seized. Marines bellied into smaller caves, knives in teeth, to eliminate the enemy in close combat. First Lieutenant Harold Schrier and forty men neared the summit. He had an American flag and instructions from Lieutenant Colonel Chandler Johnson, his battalion commander, to place it "on top of the hill." At about 10:15 A.M. they reached the rim of the crater, which was blanketed with dead Japanese. At the lip they were momentarily pinned down by a burst of fire from a small group on the other side. During this skirmish, somebody found a long piece of pipe. The flag—it was 54 by 28 inches—was secured to one end, and at 10:20 Lieutenant Schrier and five men, including an Indian, Louis Charlo, raised the Stars and Stripes. A photographer from *Leatherneck* magazine began taking pictures, but a sixteen-year-old, Pfc. James Robeson, disparaged his entreaty to pose: "Hollywood Marines!" Two Japanese charged from a cave, one with a grenade, the other with drawn sword. Robeson shot the latter. The other lobbed his grenade at the photographer, who leaped into the crater and tumbled down fifty feet with his camera. It was smashed but the pictures were intact.

From the beach area below, the small flag was barely

visible. Men in foxholes cheered and punched one another. There were tears. Ship's whistles and horns screeched. Fortuitously James Forrestal, who had become Secretary of the Navy after the death of Frank Knox, was coming ashore with "Howlin' Mad" Smith. "Holland," Forrestal said gravely, "the raising of that flag on Suribachi means a Marine Corps for the next five hundred years."

Colonel Johnson, who had sent up the flag, turned to his adjutant: "Some son of a bitch is going to want that flag but he's not going to get it." He ordered the original brought down, and another put in its place. A much larger flag from an LST was attached to the pipe at noon. Joe Rosenthal, who had photographed the landings at Pelelieu and Guam for the Associated Press, had arrived too late for the initial flag raising. He almost missed the second in his frantic efforts to pile up stones so he could get a better vantage point. As the chubby photographer balanced himself atop his rock heap, six men started to swing up the flagpole. Rosenthal barely had time to get the shot; other photographers began suggesting different poses. One Marine stood under the waving flag, then three. Finally twenty were persuaded to yell and brandish their rifles. This was the only picture Rosenthal thought might rate a wirephoto; he sent off his film packs to Guam for routine processing.

The Marines attacking north heard the news from the beachmaster. "Mount Suribachi is ours!" he announced over the loudspeaker used to direct the unloading operations. "The American flag has been raised over it by the Fifth Marine Division. Fine work, men." The exhausted fighters took time out to turn toward the flag fluttering on top of the volcano. The loudspeaker continued, "We have only 2,630 yards to go to secure the island."

"Only," someone grunted, "only . . ."

That afternoon General Harry Schmidt came ashore, ready to direct the Landing Force, the largest body of Marines to fight under a single command, three full divisions. He met with the commanders of the 4th and 5th divisions; it was agreed that the reserve division, the 3rd, which had come ashore, would drive directly up the middle toward Airfield No. 2, with the 4th on the right and the 5th on the left. Sherrod asked General Schmidt how long the campaign would last. "Five more days after today," Schmidt replied. "I said last week it would take ten days and I haven't changed my mind."

The first line of Japanese defenses was giving way, but more than twenty-five infiltration teams charged suicidally into the Marine positions, against Kuribayashi's orders, and were wiped out to the man. Just to the rear, however, in the center of Iwo, Airfield No. 2 was heavily fortified with hundreds of pillboxes and concealed batteries. For two days it withstood almost constant pounding by ships, planes, artillery and tanks. Now it was up to the infantry of the reserve division—two battalions of the 21st Regiment. "We have got to get that field today," the commander of the 3rd Battalion told his men on Saturday, February 24. At 9:30 A.M., behind a rolling artillery barrage, the two battalions launched themselves at the seemingly impregnable positions. It was one of the most resolute charges since Pickett's at Gettysburg. The Marines flung themselves at pillboxes with grenades and bayonets. When weapons became clogged by volcanic ash, they closed the enemy with rifle butts, picks—even entrenching tools.

The Japanese—the remnants of the 145th Regiment—would not retreat, and the carnage on both sides was awesome. In minutes a Marine company lost four of its officers, but the two battalions swept onto the airfield. Beyond, the terrain changed from volcanic dunes to "a wild, barren stretch of rocky ridges, cut into crags, chasms, and gulleys." It reminded Sergeant Alvin Josephy, a combat correspondent, of "the Bad Lands of the American West—or, as some-one said, like hell with the fire out." From one of the ridges, a frenzied horde of Japanese poured out, flinging back the Marines, who re-formed and charged at the ridge again. For an hour and a half the two opponents battled savagely with bayonets and grenades. When it was all over, one third of the island was American.

By nightfall on Sunday the Marines had wrested most of the airfield from the Japanese and pressed on yard by yard toward Motoyama village. Kuribayashi radioed Tokyo that after one week of combat, front-line troops had averaged 50 percent losses, and most of the machine guns and 60 percent of the big guns had been destroyed.

The first picture Rosenthal had taken—the one snapped quickly as the large flag was being hoisted on Suribachi—would become the most famous picture of the war. It reached the United States in time to make the Sunday papers, where it was featured on the front page, including that of the *New York Times.* Its dramatic composition was unforgettable, symbolizing simultaneously heroism, suffering and accomplishment.*

On Monday, the Marines went into battle under clear skies for the first time since the landing. But by noon the inevitable rain resumed, and the three-division attack slowly pushd forward until advance units of the 4th Division reached a formidable rise, Hill 382, to the right of Motoyama, where they were driven off by rockets and mortar rounds. The 4th pressed on the following morning, five battalions abreast. The vicious hand-to-hand fighting continued, bringing the division's daily casualties up to 792.

All along the line Marines suffered heavily, but morale remained high. Humorous signs proliferated in caves and were posted beside foxholes:

SURIBACHI HEIGHTS REALTY COMPANY
OCEAN VIEW
COOL BREEZES
FREE FIREWORKS NIGHTLY!

COOK WANTED

ICHIMOTO'S INN
UNDER NEW MANAGEMENT
SOON AVAILABLE TO PERSONNEL
OF THE U. S. ARMY (WE HOPE)

NOTICE: THIS FOXHOLE IS PRIVATELY OWNED
AND WAS NOT CONSTRUCTED WITH THE

---

*Three of the six Marines in the picture were to die on Iwo Jima. The others were brought back to America to help spur the Seventh War Loan Drive. One, an Indian named Ira Hayes, could not cope with the publicity. "He was a helluva good fighting man, but he wasn't the kind of guy you send on a bond tour," wrote Technical Sergeant Keyes Beech, who accompanied the three men on the tour. "He was terribly, terribly shy and ill at ease. As a defense against his own insecurity, he drank like a fish whenever he could sneak away. Maybe Hayes would have been a lush without the bond tour—but the bond tour helped. If we ever get into another war I'm going to campaign against bond tours. . . . What we used to ask ourselves, in the few minutes of privacy we had on tour, was why the hell it was necessary for us to go around on a vaudeville act to persuade a bunch of fat cats who had grown rich in the war to invest in a sure thing. . . ." During the tour Hayes made one speech from the heart. This was to the National Congress of American Indians. With tears in his eyes he told them that good things were coming out of the war and that "white men are gonna understand Indians better, and it's gonna be a better world." He died an alcoholic in 1955.

The mounting casualties also revived the altercation between the Army and the Marine Corps which had first
surfaced in the press during the battle for Saipan. The San
Francisco *Examiner*, a Hearst paper, declared in a front-page
editorial on February 27 that there was "awesome evidence
in the situation that the attacking American forces are paying
heavily for the island, perhaps too heavily," and that they
were "in danger of being worn out before they ever reach
the really critical Japanese areas." The editorial went on to
praise MacArthur as America's best and most successful
strategist:

He wins all his objectives.
He outwits and outmaneuvers and outguesses and outthinks the
Japanese.
HE SAVES THE LIVES OF HIS OWN MEN, not only for the
future and vital operations that must be fought before Japan is
defeated, but for their own safe return to their families and loved
ones in the American homeland after the peace is won.
It is our good fortune to have such a strategist as General Mac-
Arthur in the Pacific War.
Why do we not USE him more, and indeed, why do we not give
him supreme command in the Pacific war, and utilize to the utmost
his rare military genius of winning important battles without the
excessive loss of precious American lives?

Marine policy was defended the following day by another
San Francisco paper, the *Chronicle*:

The recapture of the Philippines remains competent, energetic,
and immensely heartening to the American people. We are proud
of that job.
To slur the United States Marines in one type of operation,
however, to draw odious comparisons between theirs and the type
of operations conducted by General MacArthur is to raise a sinister
fantasy. To hint that the Marines die fast and move slowly on Iwo
Jima because Marine and Naval leadership in that assault is incompetent is an attempt at a damnable swindle of the American people.
The *Chronicle* does not propose to engage in controversy over
the relative merits of our fighting forces in the various theaters of
war. But neither does the *Chronicle* propose to remain mute when
the United States Marines, or any force on the world battle line, is
butchered at home to make a Roman holiday.

The War Department itself was searching for ways to reduce casualties on all fronts. The most controversial had already been suggested to Admiral Nimitz by General Marshall's office, which had previously made similar recommendations for the European theater of operations: the use of poison gas. There were large quantities on hand. Nimitz pondered its employment on Iwo Jima but concluded that "the United States should not be the first to violate the Geneva Convention."*

General Schmidt's prediction that the battle would be over in ten days was clearly overoptimistic. The Japanese still held more than half of the island. By early afternoon of the tenth day, however, the 3rd Division broke through the second Kuribayashi line, flooding into the rubble that once was the village of Motoyama. On the right the men of the 4th Division had nearly surrounded Hill 382, but it took them two more days to secure it.

That morning—it was Saturday, March 3—the first plane set down on Airfield No. 1's dirt strip, which Seabees had repaired and lengthened to 3,000 feet during the fighting. It was a Navy C-47 hospital plane from the Marianas with medical supplies and mail. A woman, Barbara Finch of Reuters, stepped out amid exploding shells. "How the hell did you get here?" a Marine shouted, and she was pushed in a tent, then under a jeep. She was hustled back aboard the plane, which lumbered down the runway on its return to Saipan. The second plane to arrive was a Curtiss R5C carrying 2½ tons of mortar ammunition.

While the battle still raged, one of its primary aims was fulfilled. On Sunday a B-29 in distress heaved in sight; it was *Dinah Might*, which had dropped its payload on Tokyo. She was almost out of gas and the fuel selector valve would not switch to the auxiliary tanks. First Lieutenant Fred Malo dragged the field twice, then brought in the huge craft. She

---

*Stanley P. Lovell of the Office of Strategic Services was sent to Pearl Harbor in late June 1944 to discuss the matter with Admiral Nimitz. When Lovell returned to Washington he learned that the proposal had been disapproved by the White House: "All prior endorsements denied—Franklin D. Roosevelt, Commander-in-Chief." Unexpected opposition had also come from London. The British, who had at first recommended the utilization of gas against certain objectives, now resolutely disfavored its use against Germany; they feared Hitler would retaliate against England. The quote from Admiral Nimitz came in an interview shortly before his death. It concluded with a

careened down the runway in a huge cloud of dust, sheering off a telephone pole with one wing and slamming to a stop just before she ran out of space. Faulty valve fixed, *Dinah Might* lifted off for Saipan, her eleven-man crew evangelists for the Marine Corps. (Six weeks later Malo and all but one of the crew would die—some over Kawasaki, Japan, and some on a takeoff crash at Tinian.) Admiral Spruance was watching with satisfaction from his quarter-deck on *Indianapolis*; it justified his urgent request to occupy the island.

That morning Kuribayashi relayed a rambling report to the Army Vice Chief of Staff through the radio station at Chichi Jima. Its length was mute testimony to his fear that it might be his last message.

. . . OUR FORCES ARE MAKING EVERY EFFORT TO ANNIHILATE THE ENEMY. BUT WE HAVE ALREADY LOST MOST GUNS AND TANKS AND TWO-THIRDS OF OFFICERS. WE MAY HAVE SOME DIFFICULTIES IN FUTURE ENGAGEMENTS. SINCE OUR HEADQUARTERS AND COMMUNICATION CENTER ARE NOW EXPOSED TO THE ENEMY'S FRONT LINE, WE FEAR WE MAY BE CUT OFF FROM TOKYO. OF COURSE, SOME STRONGPOINTS MAY BE ABLE TO FIGHT DELAYING BATTLES FOR SEVERAL MORE DAYS. EVEN IF THE STRONGPOINTS FALL, WE HOPE THE SURVIVORS WILL CONTINUE TO FIGHT TO THE END . . . WE ARE SORRY INDEED WE COULD NOT HAVE DEFENDED THE ISLAND SUCCESSFULLY. NOW I, KURIBAYASHI, BELIEVE THAT THE ENEMY WILL INVADE JAPAN PROPER FROM THIS ISLAND . . . I AM VERY SORRY BECAUSE I CAN IMAGINE THE SCENES OF DISASTER IN OUR EMPIRE. HOWEVER, I COMFORT MYSELF A LITTLE, SEEING MY OFFICERS AND MEN DIE WITHOUT REGRET AFTER STRUGGLING IN THIS INCH-BY-INCH BATTLE AGAINST AN OVERWHELMING ENEMY WITH MANY TANKS AND BEING EXPOSED TO INDESCRIBABLE BOMBARDMENTS. ALTHOUGH MY OWN DEATH APPROACHES, I CALMLY PRAY TO GOD FOR A GOOD FUTURE FOR MY MOTHERLAND. SINCE THERE MAY BE A GREAT CHANGE IN THE BATTLE SITUATION AND TELEGRAPHIC COMMUNICATIONS MAY BE CUT, I WOULD LIKE NOW TO APOLOGIZE TO MY SENIOR AND FELLOW OFFICERS FOR NOT BEING STRONG ENOUGH TO STOP THE ENEMY INVASION.

He recalled the glory of ancient days; how the Mongols who took Eki and Tsushima islands were repelled on the shores of Kyushu.

. . . BELIEVING THAT MY MOTHERLAND WILL NEVER GO DOWN IN RUIN, MY SOUL WILL ALWAYS ASSAULT THE

DASTARDLY ENEMY AND DEFEND THE LANDS OF THE EM-
PIRE FOREVER.
PLEASE NOTE OUR BATTLE REPORTS AND REMARKS SENT
BY TELEGRAPH. IF THEY HELP MODIFY FUTURE MILITARY
TACTICS AND TRAINING PLANS I SHALL BE VERY PLEASED.
. . .
FINALLY I HEREBY THANK MY SENIOR AND FELLOW
OFFICERS AGAIN FOR THEIR KIND HELP DURING MY LIFE.
I WOULD LIKE TO ADD THAT WE CO-OPERATED WELL
WITH OUR NAVY UNTIL THE LAST MOMENT.
                                    GOOD-BYE, T. KURIBAYASHI

Japanese resistance continued stronger than the Americans
had expected, though there was little co-ordination among
Kuribayashi's units. Desperate measures were taken to stop
American flamethrowing tanks: volunteers strapped explosives on their backs and became living booby traps as they
lay concealed in the path of the advancing vehicles. Their
situation seemed so hopeless to Major General Sadasue Senda, who had replaced the troublesome Osuga as commander
of the 2nd Mixed Brigade, that he signaled Kuribayashi for
permission to launch a final general attack. Kuribayashi angrily ordered him to hold his positions; leaving the caves
would merely hasten the collapse of Iwo. But Senda, who
had fought against the Russians in Manchuria, proved to be
even more mutinous than Osuga. On the evening of March 8
he summoned his officers to his sweltering command cave, a
deep labyrinth which reeked of sulphur. There, in the 120-de-
gree heat, he read out instructions for a general attack: a
barrage of howitzers, rockets and mortars at six o'clock the
next evening would precede a mass assault south toward
Mount Suribachi; the Navy would support the attack on both
flanks. "I will always be at the head of the troops," Senda
declared. They passed around a single cup of water, to seal
the order with a toast. Senda thanked them. "Let us all
meet again at Yasukuni Shrine in Tokyo."

The transmittal of his order to Navy headquarters, a mile
away was by word of mouth, which led to a misinterpreta-
tion: that the attack would take place that night—since Pearl
Harbor, the eighth of every month had a special significance.
In the darkness almost fifteen hundred Navy men from
various units started stealthily toward the line of departure
armed with bamboo spears, rifles, grenades and a few light
machine guns.

Lieutenant (s.g.) Satoru Omagari—in charge of the
former "jet propulsion" rocket unit that had raised such

havoc in the first days of fighting—led his 140 men out of their 75-foot-deep cave. He had orders to bring them to the Navy Cemetery, between airfields No. 2 and No. 3, where they would consolidate with other units. Harassed by sporadic mortar and artillery fire, and often lost in the unfamiliar terrain, Omagari arrived with fifteen men. In the sandy little valley there was chaos; more than a thousand men, hopelessly disorganized, milled around in the dark. At midnight the mob was started south toward the front-line positions of the 4th Division. They were to work cautiously through the cratered area, but undisciplined cries of *"Banzai!"* alerted the enemy. An almost instantaneous display of star-shell flares exposed the attackers. Mortar rounds threw up geysers of earth and ash. At least eight hundred men died.

The troops in Omagari's area were pinned down by machine guns. For an hour they crouched in shell holes or behind rocks awaiting the opportunity to steal back into their caves. But Omagari was not ready to give up. With several hundred men he began searching for an Army officer to lead them. He found the cave headquarters of an Army unit, the 26th Tank Regiment, but no one seemed to know anything about a general attack. The hot-blooded Omagari accused them of shirking, and almost came to blows with a captain. The argument brought out the commander's adjutant, a major. He said there would be no attack. Kuribayashi had countermanded Senda's order.

The commander himself, Lieutenant Colonel Takeichi Nishi, joined them. He was a baron from a distinguished family, and Japan's best-known horseman. In the 1932 Olympics in Los Angeles he and his horse, Uranus, had won first prize in the individual jumping event. He invited Omagari and his men to stay on as replacements, but Omagari still refused to believe the attack was canceled. He visualized his Navy comrades retaking Suribachi without him. The battle-weary Nishi was tolerant. "If one wants to die," he said, "he can do it any time. It is only fifty meters to the American positions."

Omagari impetuously left the cave, but by the time he had marshaled his men he realized it was too late to join the general attack. Downcast, he returned and offered his men to Nishi. But Omagari rejected cave warfare for himself. He volunteered to make himself a human bomb and throw himself under the treads of an enemy tank. He was promised his turn would come in a few days.

The following afternoon a patrol from the 3rd Marine Division reached the northeastern end of the island. The men washed their faces in the sea and cavorted barefoot in the surf. They brought back a canteen of salt water, and as proof that the Japanese forces had been split in two, it was sent to General Schmidt with the inscription "For inspection, not consumption." As far as Schmidt was concerned the battle was over, and he informed the Navy that he no longer needed carrier planes for close support. Admiral Turner was already on his way back to Guam.

General Kuribayashi had prevented the launching of a full fledged general attack, but Senda, who had initiated the idea, could not be restrained. Gathering all the forces in his immediate area that night, and with a grenade in each hand, he led the charge. Around his forehead was a white band emblazoned with the Rising Sun. The attack was as futile as Kuribayashi had predicted. Almost every man died, including Senda.

By March 11 the Japanese were backed into small areas, one on the northeastern end of the island and the other on the northwest coast, where Kuribayashi and Admiral Ichimaru still held out in their deep caves while the remnants of their commands continued a suicidal defense. In the tankers' cave, not far away, Omagari waited for darkness before setting out on his final mission. After midnight he left the cave with a box of dynamite on his back. He found five bodies near a gully—a logical route of advance for American tanks—and worked his way into the stinking pile, smearing his uniform and face with blood, and draping himself with entrails. Who will be using my guts tomorrow? he wondered.

All through the day he waited, perspiring in the sun, for the clank of an enemy tank. The smell was nauseating. Huge bluebottle flies hovered overhead like buzzards. Why couldn't the end come at once and cleanly? Scenes from his childhood and treacherous thoughts interrupted his wish for death. Was this what he had been educated and trained for? He and his generation had been reared only for war to believe it was beautiful and glorious to die for the Emperor. Was lying among the dead covered with stinking guts beautiful? He had revered the forty-seven *ronin*, under the impression that they exemplified the inherent characteristics of the Japanese. If so, why had he and his comrades been bombarded with propaganda designed to make them seek death in battle?

With darkness he crept back to his cave. He tried to clean

himself, but the stench of death clung tenaciously. He was irresistibly drawn back to the battlefield, where he spent another day among the corpses, agonizing over the meaning of life as a Japanese. Again no tank appeared, and by nightfall he returned to the cave robbed of most of his illusions. He was sure of but one thing: never again would he venture out as a human bomb.

Across the island in the other pocket, Navy Lieutenant Toshihiko Ohno and his men had been driven from place to place by the advancing Americans. Ohno had commanded an antiaircraft battery of fifty-four men, but now only five were left. In some ways Ohno, who was six feet tall and slender, was more like a young American officer fresh from OCS than a typical Japanese officer. A recent college graduate, sensitive and gentle of manner, he seemed unsuited to command men, but under fire he had matured. He and his men were huddled in a pillbox about eleven feet square. The entrance was blocked and they had crawled through the gunport. They were sprawled on the concrete floor, sleeping off a feast; they had found two cases of hardtack and candy, three large bags of sugar, and a ten-gallon can half filled with water.

A noise awakened Ohno. Through the porthole he saw a Marine helmet. As he drew his pistol, the helmet disappeared. There was a hissing noise, and a grenade bounded off the floor. Someone leaped in front of Ohno and tossed a blanket over the grenade just before it detonated. It exploded upward and no one was hit. Dazed, Ohno did not at first comprehend that a bundle of dynamite sticks had just been shoved into the porthole. He snatched the smoldering blanket and used it to force the dynamite to the rear of the porthole. He leaped back, hugged the wall and shouted a warning. Everyone stuck thumbs in ears, middle fingers on noses and last two fingers over mouths. "*Tenno Heika banzai!*" he said to himself and visualized his wife and mother. "I'm ready . . ." The pillbox seemed to rise three feet in the air. It was as if his body were being pressed together by some unearthly force. He heard himself cry out, "Ahhh!"

The pillbox swirled with smoke. "Are you all right?" he asked his men. All but an enlisted man named Kitagata replied. Through a hole where the ventilator had blown out, a shaft of light illuminated Kitagata. His head was bleeding and sand peppered his skin. He moaned. A shadow interposed the foggy shaft of light; a Marine was peering down. Ohno clamped a hand over Kitagata's mouth. The shadow withdrew and someone outside shouted, "Let's go!" They were safe for the moment.

4.

On March 14 a small group of Marine officers and men stood at attention around an incinerated Japanese bunker. A colonel representing Admiral Nimitz read a proclamation:

". . . United States forces under my command have occupied this and other of the Volcano Islands. All powers of government of the Japanese Empire in these islands so occupied are hereby suspended. All powers of government are vested in me as military governor and will be exercised by subordinate commanders under my direction. . . ."

Three privates atop the bunker attached the flag to an eighty-foot pole, and as a bugler sounded Colors, raised it. There was little conversation after the ceremony. "Howlin' Mad" Smith, his eyes glistening, turned to his aide: "This was the toughest yet." In the past twenty-four days, seven Marines had won the Medal of Honor by throwing themselves on grenades to save their comrades. "Among the Americans who served on Iwo Island," Nimitz later wrote, "uncommon valor was a common virtue."

Deep underground, not far away, there was another flag ceremony. General Kuribayashi ordered the banner of the 145th Regiment burned to prevent it from falling into enemy hands. Two days later the regiment no longer existed, neither did the 2nd Mixed Brigade. At 5:35 P.M. Kuribayashi radioed Tokyo what he once more thought would be his farewell message:

THE BATTLE IS APPROACHING ITS END.
SINCE THE ENEMY'S LANDING, EVEN THE GODS WOULD WEEP AT THE BRAVERY OF THE OFFICERS AND MEN UNDER MY COMMAND.
IN PARTICULAR, I AM PLEASED THAT OUR TROOPS WITH EMPTY HANDS CARRIED OUT A SERIES OF DESPERATE FIGHTS AGAINST AN ENEMY POSSESSING OVERWHELMING MATERIAL SUPERIORITY ON LAND, SEA AND AIR.
HOWEVER, MY MEN DIED ONE BY ONE AND I REGRET VERY MUCH THAT I HAVE ALLOWED THE ENEMY TO OCCUPY A PIECE OF JAPANESE TERRITORY.
NOW THERE IS NO MORE AMMUNITION, NO MORE WATER.

ALL THE SURVIVORS WILL ENGAGE IN A GENERAL AT-
TACK.
AS I THINK OF MY DEBT OF GRATITUDE TO MY COUNTRY, I
HAVE NO REGRETS.
UNLESS THIS ISLAND IS RETAKEN, I BELIEVE JAPAN CAN
NEVER BE SAFE. I SINCERELY HOPE MY SOUL WILL SPEAR-
HEAD A FUTURE ATTACK.
PRAYING TO GOD FOR THE FINAL VICTORY AND SAFETY OF
OUR MOTHERLAND, LET ME SAY "SAYONARA" EVERLAST-
INGLY. . . .

He ended with three of his poems:

WITHOUT AMMUNITION
IT IS SAD FOR ME TO LEAVE THIS WORLD,
HAVING FAILED TO ACHIEVE MY IMPORTANT MISSION
FOR THE MOTHERLAND.

I COULD NEVER ROT IN THE FIELDS
UNLESS MY SOUL TOOK VENGEANCE
MAY I TAKE UP ARMS, EVEN UNTO THE SEVENTH
LIFE.

I WORRY OVER WHAT JAPAN'S FUTURE WILL BE
WHEN WEEDS COVER THIS ISLAND.

It seemed that Kuribayashi was ready, at last, for the
general attack. His final order was simple:

1. The battle is approaching its ultimate phase.
2. Our garrison will make a general attack aganst the enemy tonight. Starting time will be 0001 hours, 18 March, 1945.
3. . . . Everyone will fight to the death. No man will be concerned about his life.
4. I will always be at the head of our troops.

During the day code books and other secret documents
were burned in the Navy headquarters cave. Just before dusk
Admiral Ichimaru summoned his able-bodied men, about
sixty at the most, to a large chamber sixty-five yards beneath
the surface. "To date," he said, "you have overcome any and
all difficulties, obeyed my orders and fought gallantly against
an enemy with overwhelming supplies. The loss of this island
means that Yankee military boots will soon tread on our
motherland. However, you are warriors of Japan. Don't be
too anxious to die. Live in high spirits, kill as many enemies
as possible and fight for your seventh life. Thank you."
His senior staff officer, Commander Takeji Mase, stepped

forward and in a loud voice read a letter from the admiral to President Roosevelt. It charged Roosevelt with vilifying Japan by calling her "a yellow peril, a bloodthirsty nation, and a protoplasm of the military clique." America was responsible for starting the war, not Japan. "Judging from your actions, the white races—especially you Anglo-Saxons—are monopolizing the fruits of the world at the expense of the colored races. . . . Why is it that you, an already flourishing nation, nip in the bud the movement for freedom of the suppressed nations of the East? All we want is for you to return to the East that which belongs to the East." Nor could the admiral comprehend how Roosevelt dared criticize Hitler's program while co-operating with the Soviet Union, whose principal aim was the socialization of the world. "If only brute force decides who rules the world, war will go on endlessly and there will never be universal peace or happiness. When you achieve your barbaric world monopoly, remember the failure of your predecessor, President Wilson, at the height of his power."

The letter was placed in the stomach band of the communications officer, and an English version* was entrusted to Lieutenant Commander Kunio Akada.

Half an hour before midnight Admiral Ichimaru, leaving almost a hundred wounded behind, went out of the cave with his sixty men. They were immediately overwhelmed by a maelstrom of American artillery, mortar and machine-gun fire.

Kuribayashi left his cave about the same time with almost five hundred troops. But most of them had no weapons and he had no intention of leading a final charge. He merely moved a short distance to the north to a safer cave. They were joined just before dawn by a dozen survivors of the futile Navy assault. Among them was Admiral Ichimaru.

Colonel Nishi had never received the general-attack order, nor did he know the assault had never amounted to anything. As far as he was concerned the battle was not over, and the following night he started north to attack Marines positioned near a large rock overlooking the beach. He carried a whip, the one he had used in the Olympics, and in his breast pocket was a lock of Uranus' mane. At the foot of the rock Nishi and two hundred men, including Omagari, were pinned down

---

*It was found by the Americans and is now in the museum of the U. S. Naval Academy at Annapolis. The complete text is reproduced in the Notes.

by heavy fire. Dawn exposed them to a devastating rain of grenades. In the uproar Omagari heard Nishi call "Assemble!" and crept toward his position with forty others. Nishi said they were in a "hornet's nest," and they would have to find refuge in the caves along the beach.

On Chichi Jima, Major Horie had been unable to make radio contact with Iwo since the night of Kuribayashi's transfer to the new cave. On the morning of March 23, after five days, the silence was broken by a flood of messages. The operator on Iwo Jima was inexplicably on the air again with a backlog of terminal reports which came through without pause. Horie read them choked with emotion. Kuribayashi described the fighting; enemy invitations to surrender (by loudspeaker) were greated with derision; they continued the assault despite the fact that they had been out of food and water for five days.

... BUT OUR FIGHTING SPIRIT STILL RUNS HIGH. WE ARE GOING TO FIGHT RESOLUTELY TO THE END.

There was silence. It was Kuribayashi's last dispatch, but just before dusk, after almost twenty minutes' silence, the radio crackled again with the operator's final message. This time it was in the clear.

ALL OFFICERS AND MEN OF CHICHI JIMA, FAREWELL.

It was all over except for a final *banzai* charge three days later by a group of approximately 350 Army and Navy men, including 40 *battotai* (a group carrying swords). Out of the rocky gorges on the northwestern tip of the island they crawled half naked, like cavemen, to sweep down in a frenzy over anything in their path. Their wild assault surprised an Air Force and Seabee encampment. A Marine pioneer battalion, hastily summoned, drove into the melee, but it took an entire day of fierce hand-to-hand fighting before two thirds were slaughtered and the rest dispersed.

Early the next morning, March 27, General Kuribayashi, who had been wounded while moving to another refuge, came to the mouth of his cave with a staff officer, Colonel Kaneji Nakane. Kuribayashi faced north toward the Imperial Palace, knelt and solemnly bowed three times. He stabbed himself in the abdomen and bowed his head. Nakane raised his sword and brought it down on the general's neck. He buried the body with the help of a sergeant and crawled back into the cave to inform Colonel Tadashi Takaishi, Kuribayashi's chief of staff, and Admiral Ichimaru what had happened; then he returned with Takaishi to the scene of Kuribayashi's death. The two men shot themselves.

That evening just before eleven o'clock Ichimaru, followed by ten men, also emerged into the open. A volley of machine-gun fire cut down the admiral and two officers behind him.

The Battle of Iwo Jima had cost the lives of 4,554 Marines and 363 Navy men, the greatest American toll in World War II, considering the length of the battle and the number of men involved. Of the 21,000 defenders, little more than 3,000 were alive. Of these, 216 had become prisoners of war. The others remained huddled in their sweltering, sulphuric caves like hunted animals—hungry, thirsty, desperate and bewildered. For all but a few, the only prospect ahead was death.

27   The Flowers of Edo

1.

About a year before Pearl Harbor the Japanese government had ordered the civilian population to form groups of "neighborhood societies" for the purpose of controlling the rationing and air-defense programs. Each unit comprised about a dozen families, and by now the system had wrought a drastic change in the traditional Japanese family structure. Hardship had forced families to depend more on neighbors than on close relatives, who might live miles away. Everyone, whether high born or low, took part in community air-raid drills, relaying water pails and carrying stretchers, lumber and sand. Democracy extended to food and other rationed necessities, such as clothing: women wore *mompei* (loose baggy slacks), and all men the drab khaki "national uniform." Children had taken naturally to the idea of sharing everything alike, and grownups were learning that only through co-operation could they survive.

There was a slogan, "We are all equals," which took on a

new significance late in 1944 when the bombing intensified. Night raids, usually aimed at residental sections, invoked more fear than the daytime attacks. On a food-buying trip in the country, Mrs. Sumie Seo Mishima could even stop and admire the spectacle of the approaching Bees—the popular name for Superfortresses: "In the eastern sky loomed a flight, another flight and yet another of B-29's ... Trailing white streamers of exhaust gas, they sailed in perfect formation through the blue-gold sky ... like shawls of pearly fish riding through the seas of the universe." This esthetic meditation was quickly shattered when the graceful-looking fish dropped their eggs. "The process of splashing the earth with showers of incendiary bullets in rhythmic rumbles of ocean breakers, and hurling heavy bombs, each pounding with a fatal thud into the depths of the globe, was repeated by each flight of planes. On almost every raid, it seemed to us, the American planes brought over new kinds of bombs and shells, which behaved differently in sound effects from those used the last time. The unaccustomed noises intensified the terrors and thrills of each new invasion."

It was an unusually cold winter and some homes had to suffer broken water pipes for months before they were repaired. The novelist Jun Takami noted in his diary that in some homes "where the upstairs toilet pipes had burst and the water poured downstairs, the people had to use umbrellas in the house, and when the water froze on the floor they were able to ice-skate on it."

Fear gave birth to new superstitions: if you ate rice balls with scallions inside, and cooked with red beans, you would never be hit by a bomb. Better yet, if you ate only scallions for breakfast you were sure not to be hit, but after a while there was an added fillip: you had to let someone else know about this trick—along the lines of the chain-letter principle —otherwise it wouldn't work. Another superstition originated when a couple who miraculously survived a close bomb hit found two dead goldfish nearby. They thought the goldfish had died for them, so they put the fish in their family Buddhist shrine and worshiped them. When word of what had happened spread and people had found it difficult to obtain live goldfish, porcelain goldfish were manufactured in quantity and sold at exorbitant prices.

Although the bombing raids had wrought drastic changes in the lives of the people in the Japanese homeland, their primary purpose—to obliterate all production facilities—had not been achieved. "This outfit has been getting a lot of publicity without having really accomplished a hell of a lot in bombing results," Curtis LeMay complained to Lieutenant Colonel St. Clair McKelway, his public relations officer, on March 6. LeMay had taken over B-29 operations in the Marianas six weeks earlier. He was glad to be out of China, with its insuperable problem of supply, but continued to be plagued by operational failures and mediocre results. The strategic bombing program, principally utilizing high explosives, which had devastated Germany with its concentrated industrial complexes, had done little to slow production in Japan, where two thirds of the industry was dispersed in homes and small factories manned by thirty workers or less.

LeMay hit upon a radical scheme for his planes: to go in low at night, stripped of most armament to increase the payload, and scatter incendiary bombs onto the tinderbox targets over a wide area. Two days later, without consulting Washington, he had field orders cut for a strike of B-29's. At briefing the following morning, March 9, the crews were informed they would attack Tokyo that night at low altitudes —from 5,000 to 8,000 feet. Their reaction of protest was audible. All guns except tail cannons would be removed; the announcement shocked the men to silence. It was suicide.

At 5:36 P.M. the first B-29 rolled down the runway of North Field on Guam and thundered into the sultry air. Fifty seconds later another was airborne, and another and another. One plane couldn't get up enough speed; its brakes were frozen and couldn't be released. Friction turned the landing gear white-hot and the brake fluid burst into flame. When the wheels melted, the gear collapsed. In a shower of sparks the huge craft slithered on its belly, careened off the runway and smashed into the coral beyond with a fearsome explosion.

At 6:15 P.M., B-29's from Tinian and Saipan began joining the elephantine procession in the air. The 333 bombers droned northward. Up ahead against the dark horizon an eruption of explosions appeared—Iwo Jima, where General Senda was about to lead the remnants of the 2nd Mixed Brigade and assorted naval units in his futile general attack. The big planes bounced in the low-level turbulence, but as they neared Tokyo the weather improved. The men, like knights getting into armor, pulled on bulky flak suits and heavy steel helmets, then peered ahead for the glow of fires to be set momentarily by the pathfinders.

Back on Guam, General LeMay paced the floor. If the raid worked the way he hoped, the war could be shortened. He would immediately inaugurate a series of similar raids all over Japan. The slaughter of civilians would be unprecedented, but Japan's industry had to be destroyed. If not, it would take an invasion to end the conflict and that might cost the lives of half a million Americans, perhaps a million.

A new moon cast a dim light but stars shone brightly over Tokyo. At midnight the pathfinders located their aiming points and prepared to mark out the heart of Tokyo with napalm-filled M47 bombs. This three-by-four-mile downtown section was once the gayest, liveliest area in the Orient, but now there was little traffic and most of the shops and theaters were boarded up. Nevertheless, 750,000 low-income workers existed in this congested city-within-a-city that was never asleep. Thousands of home factories were in constant operation.

With its profusion of wooden buildings Tokyo had continually been victim of massive fires from the time it was called Edo. These conflagrations became such an integral part of city life that they were given the poetic name "Flowers of Edo." Despite eventual modernization of the fire-fighting system, there was no guard against disaster by fire. In 1923, following the great earthquake, fire razed most of the city. Two years later Tokyo was devastated again, as it was a third time in 1932.

There were now 8,100 trained firemen and 1,117 pieces of equipment scattered throughout the city, with static water tanks for emergency use. Still, this army of firefighters was not adequate to cover the 213 square miles of the metropolitan area, particularly in time of war. The downtown section remained the most vulnerable. Few fire lanes had been cut through its crowded buildings; they would be ready in a year or two, city officials had promised.

The siren howling around midnight on March 9 sounded just the same as dozens of other alerts. Since previous raids on the city had done little damage, there didn't seem to be any cause for alarm; Radio Tokyo reported that enemy bombers were circling above the seaport of Choshi, fifty miles northeast of the capital, and that there was no immediate danger.

The pathfinders had not yet been discovered in their low sweep toward the unwary city at better than 300 miles an hour. The first two planes, crossing paths over the target, released their strings of bombs in perfect unison at 12:15 A.M.

One hundred feet above the ground the M47 missiles split apart, scattering two-foot-long napalm sticks which burst into flame on impact, spreading jellied fire. In minutes a blazing X was etched in downtown Tokyo. Ten more pathfinders roared in to drop their napalm on the X. Then came the main force, three wings, in orderly but random formation, at altitudes varying from 4,900 to 9,200 feet. Searchlights poked frantically at the raiders, and puffs of antiaircraft fire detonated without effect. There was no fighter opposition.

Whipped by a stiffening wind, the fires spread rapidly as succeeding bombers fanned out toward the residential areas to unload their thousands of sticks of napalm. Flame fed upon flame, creating a sweeping conflagration. Huge balls of fire leaped from building to building with hurricane force, creating an incandescent tidal wave exceeding 1,800 degrees Fahrenheit.

Those on the ground were momentarily paralyzed by the awesome sight of the planes blanketing them like huge dragons—greenish from searchlight beams, crimson from the glare below. From the Bunkyo-ku residential district overlooking the center of the blaze, seventeen-year-old Susumu Takahashi watched clusters of bombs—they would soon be nicknamed Molotov Breadbaskets—flower over Tokyo Imperial University. He was a student at Showa Medical College, and after the air-raid alarm he had remained in the house to study for exams while the rest of the family went into the shelter. From the dull-red sky, pieces of flaming debris floated down all around Takahashi. A blaze erupted on the roof of the house and he started slapping at it with a "fire swatter"—strips of rags attached to the end of a long pole. The next house exploded into flames like a gas-filled oven. He ran to his room to pick up three books—he was still going to take the exam the next day—then looked for the family memorial tablets at their private Buddhist shrine. They were gone; his mother must have taken them earlier. He grabbed a silver-and-gold Buddha and carefully selected the best antiques—ivory figures. Out of habit, he pulled the door shut, buried the antiques in the family shelter (it was empty, the others had fled) and started up the street. To the right everything was ablaze. He ran to a main road on the left where a fire engine stood helpless, its hoses slack, surrounded by flaming buildings. There was no water.

The only way to safety was a bridge across the Kanda River but it lay beyond a wall of fire. A group of people huddled in the street, staring at the flames as if hypnotized.

Charred trees and telephone poles were scattered across the road like matchsticks. The firemen shouted to make for the bridge—or die. Young Takahashi led the way, leaping over tree trunks that burned like logs in a mammoth fireplace. The others followed in single file. He was blinded by the intense light and gasped for breath. He stumbled, at the end of his endurance. Then through the roiling smoke he made out the concrete bridge, crowded with squatting people. He was safe.

Takahashi had struggled through the fringe of the conflagration. The Sekimuras lived less than two miles from the center of the fiery X. When they first saw flames near the Tokyo Station, they bundled up their four children in quilted hooded fire capes and joined a stream of people heading for one of the branches of the Sumida River. Walking through crisply burned debris that was beginning to fall like black snow reminded Mrs. Sekimura of the fires after the great earthquake of 1923, when she was twelve. The sight of bombs bursting open overhead "like bunches of bananas" entranced rather than terrified her.

They pushed their way across the bridge to escape the roaring blaze that was pursuing them "like a wild animal." A strong wind sucked into the flames swept a stinging storm of pebbles into their faces. They turned, backs to the gale, and plodded slowly away from the conflagration, fascinated at the sight of oil drums rocketing through the roof of a cable factory near the river and exploding into balls of fire a hundred feet in the air.

The center of Tokyo was as incandescent as the sun. Billowing clouds of smoke surged up, illuminated below by orange flames. Thousands crouched terrified in their wooden shelters, where they would be roasted alive, but most of those in the doomed area tried to flee—to the great Buddhist temple in Asakusa, which became their tomb, or, like the Sekimuras, toward the eleven steel bridges spanning the winding Sumida River. For a while these were escape routes, but the flames, too, crossed the river and then there was no escape for those lagging behind.

"The red glow that spread over the southeastern horizon quickly bulged up and filled the entire sky," Mrs. Sumie Mishima observed, "so that even where we were, on the opposite edge of the city, an eerie pink light settled on the earth and clearly lit up the deep-lined faces of the awestruck people. The burning seemed to go on all the night."

The tremendous thermals of heat buffeted the B-29's overhead, tossing some of them several thousand feet upward in the air. Far above, the plane carrying LeMay's chief of staff, Brigadier General Thomas Powers, cruised back and forth. He photographed the conflagration, and reported to LeMay that Tokyo was an inferno. The crews in the last waves could smell the stench of burned flesh; some men vomited. Bombing in Europe had seemed antiseptic from the air; here it was a nauseating reality.

At dawn young Takahashi looked down on the smoldering city from his vantage point in Tokyo Medical-Dental College. The center of the capital was flat wasteland except for stone statues, concrete pillars and walls, steel frames, and a scattering of telephone poles, their ends smoking like tapers. It's gone, he thought.

Mrs. Sekimura, baby on her back, set out to try to recover the belongings she had buried in the ground. The bridge was clogged with the bodies of those who had been trapped. The river itself, almost evaporated, was choked with swollen corpses and household possessions. On the other side, heat still radiating from the ground made the brisk March day feel like early summer. The places she had known most of her life had vanished. All she could recognize was the cable factory; it was twisted and deformed like melted candy. There were bodies everywhere. Some were naked, black; a few were oddly upright, crouched as if trying to run; some were clasping hands in prayer; others seated as if in contemplation. One man's head had shrunk to the size of a grapefruit. Dead covered with straw were piled high in schoolyards. The stink of death permeated the air.

At last she found the ashes of her home but the ground was too hot to dig. She looked around carefully, since it was almost impossible to buy even a piece of paper or a pair of chopsticks; if the loss of a teapot was tragic, the loss of one's possessions meant a reversion to animal life. All she could save was a *kama* for cooking rice; she picked it up with a stick so it wouldn't scorch her hands. Curiously, the sight of so much death left her untouched. She walked mechanically by the corpses of neighbors, unable to shed a tear. There were the mother and daughter who lived across the street. They were completely black except for white rings around the eyes; and they had always been so neat. Dazed, she passed the hospital and its emergency pool of water. It was filled with layer upon layer of sprawling bodies. A man stopped her and remarked that he had been in that human heap. "Everyone else is dead," he said in a toneless voice. "Miraculously I didn't even get hurt."

People poked at the layers of bodies with long sticks in search of relatives. Money spilled out of an old woman's *obi* and stuck to her wet body. Nobody reached for it. Through the gutted wall of a geisha house spilled hundreds of colorful silk kimonos. Mrs. Sekimura lifted the filmy garments tenderly in her hands; they were so expensive. What a shame such material was ruined. Not far away legs protruded awkwardly from the rubble.

Everywhere she encountered corpses in agonized positions—mothers trying to shield charred babies; husbands and wives welded together by the heat in a final embrace. Other survivors had returned and in charcoal were scrawling public messages to their loved ones on walls and sidewalks.

Sixteen square miles of Tokyo had been burned to the ground and city officials later estimated that there were 130,000 dead, almost the same carnage as at Dresden.*

The next night LeMay sent 313 bombers with napalm to Nagoya, the empire's third largest city. Massive incendiary raids on Osaka and Kobe followed in rapid succession. Within a week, forty-five square miles of crucial industrial areas had been incinerated. There could be no doubt that LeMay's new tactics would soon crush Japan's capacity to wage effective warfare. But more was being destroyed than Japanese military power. In the process a multitude of defenseless civilians had already been killed.

Americans' attitude toward bombing had undergone a complete reversal since their sincere revulsion against the indiscriminate murder of civilians in Spanish cities and in China. At the outbreak of war in Europe, Roosevelt, reflecting the humanitarian ethics of his countrymen, dispatched messages to all belligerents urging them to refrain from the "inhuman barbarism" of bombing civilians. Even after Pearl Harbor, leaders of American air power emphasized daylight precision bombing, aimed at the destruction of selected military targets. But gradually the efficacy of this program was not borne out, and areas of bombing were enlarged to include the destruction of anything that sustained the enemy's war effort, including, if necessary, the populace itself. It was a policy which went largely unspoken and unrecorded but it seemed clear that the entire enemy population, at home as well as at the front, would have to be brutalized before it could be forced to surrender.

*The Japan War History office calculated that 72,489 died.

Public opinion accepted this metamorphosis with only an occasional outburst of moral concern. By 1945 almost every American agreed that Japan and Germany deserved every bomb that fell on their countries. *Time* magazine, for example, described LeMay's fire bombings of Tokyo as "a dream come true" which proved that "properly kindled, Japanese cities will burn like autumn leaves."

Americans in particular had little sympathy for an enemy which had attacked Pearl Harbor without warning and perpetrated such atrocities as the Bataan Death March. It was, consequently, the rare voice which spoke out in the name of humanity for the hundreds of thousands of mutilated and cremated civilians. *America*, the Jesuit weekly, doubted that mass raids squared "either with God's law or the nobility of our cause." An English pamphlet entitled *Massacre by Death* was distributed in the United States with a special introduction endorsed by twenty-eight prominent American educators and clergymen such as Harry Emerson Fosdick and Oswald Garrison Villard; it urged the readers to "examine their hearts" regarding their participation in the "carnival of death." America, including most of its clergy, rejected such exhortations. "God has given us the weapons," retorted one clergyman in the letter section of the *New York Times*; "let us use them." What was criminal in Coventry, Rotterdam, Warsaw and London had become heroic in Hamburg, Dresden, Osaka and Tokyo.

2.

Japan's last important outposts of resistance in the Philippines and Burma were in jeopardy. On Luzon, MacArthur's men had retaken Bataan and Corregidor. Nothing better illustrated the difference between the two foes than their defenses of the tiny, tadpole-shaped island. The Americans had resisted for twelve hours before Wainwright felt that further fighting was meaningless. Three years later the 5,000 Japanese defenders fought for eleven days against an aggressive, overwhelming parachute and amphibious assault. All except 20 died. Strategically it made little difference whether they had fought for eleven days or eleven hours.

MacArthur was in a sentimental mood when he journeyed to The Rock by PT boat. "Gentlemen," he said, "it has been a long way back." On the shattered remnants of the outpost he gave the order to raise the American flag. "Hoist the colors and let no enemy ever haul them down." After the ceremony he inspected the ruins. "This is atonement," he said.

Unlike Corregidor, Manila was not to have been defended at all. Yamashita moved all except security troops out of the city, but no sooner had they left than Rear Admiral Sanji Iwabuchi reoccupied Manila with 16,000 sailors. Iwabuchi had orders from his superior, Vice Admiral Denshichi Okochi, to destroy all port facilities and naval storehouses. Once there, Iwabuchi commandeered the 3,750 Army security troops, and against Yamashita's specific order, turned the city into a battlefield. By the time the Americans secured it on March 4, the capital was rubble and thousands of civilians had died, many as the result of atrocities committed by the Japanese.*

But the Philippines were far from cleared. Yamashita had 170,000 well-fed, well-armed troops. Most of them defended the northern redoubt under his direct command, but there were large groups holding out in the mountains east and northeast of Manila and in the Zambales Mountains near Clark Field. Theirs was not to be the long-sought Decisive

---

*Like General Homma, Yamashita was tried, convicted and executed on MacArthur's orders. The atrocities committed in Manila weighed heavily against him despite the fact that he had ordered the city evacuated by all troops. The trial was conducted as hastily as Homma's. MacArthur radioed from Tokyo that he doubted the need of the defense "for more time" and "urged" that the tribunal be concluded with dispatch. There was no question but that the verdict would be guilty, nor could MacArthur find any "mitigating circumstances" in his review of the case. "The proceedings were guided by that rationale of all judicial purpose—to ascertain the full truth unshackled by any artificialities of narrow method or technical arbitrariness. The results are above challenge."

But two Associate Justices of the Supreme Court condemned the findings. Frank Murphy declared that the "spirit of revenge and retribution, masked in formal legal procedure for purposes of dealing with a fallen enemy commander, can do more lasting harm than all of the atrocities giving rise to that spirit." Wiley Rutledge said it "was no trial in the tradition of the common law and the Constitution," and quoted Thomas Paine: "He that would make his own liberty secure must guard even his enemy from oppression; for if he violates this duty he establishes a precedent that will reach himself."

President Truman refused to commute the sentence to life imprisonment and Yamashita was hanged on February 23, 1946, in Los Baños, a town thirty-five miles south of Manila. He was "calm and stoical." His last words were: "I will pray for the Emperor's long life and his prosperity forever!"

"We have been unjust, hypocritical, and vindictive," said Yamashita's chief counsel, Captain Adolf Reel, Jr. "We have defeated our enemies on the battlefield, but we have let their spirit triumph in our hearts."

Battle but rather one of attrition. Yamashita's role was to delay MacArthur, and in the process, kill as many Americans as possible.

The GI's, incited by the deplorable state of American civilian and military prisoners at the Santo Tomás prison, set out to annihilate Yamashita's men with renewed vehemence. Posters urged them to have no mercy on the "yellow bastards." Even without such incitement, the attitude of many American soldiers toward the Japanese led to excesses. In his *Wartime Diaries*, Charles Lindbergh, who toured the Pacific wrote: "Our men think nothing of shooting a Japanese prisoner or a soldier attempting to surrender. They treat the Jap with less respect than they would give an animal, and these acts are condoned by almost everyone. We claim to be fighting for civilization, but the more I see of this war in the Pacific the less right I think we have to claim to be civilized. In fact, I am not sure that our record in this respect stands so much higher than the Japs'."

The racial implications extended even to the victims of the Japanese—the Filipino civilians—who were disparagingly referred to as "flips" or "gooks."

There would be no battle of attrition in Burma. The British had followed the Japanese survivors of Imphal across the mountains into Burma and across the Chindwin River. On the day MacArthur's troops landed at Lingayen Gulf, January 9, they launched an offensive toward Mandalay and the heart of Burma. Still drained by the Imphal disaster, the Japanese could do little to impede the British sweep south.

Ba Maw knew the war was lost and he began preparing for the postwar armed struggle to evict the British from his country. He would have to find ways to keep alive the spirit of freedom among the Burmese, coupled with a continuing hatred for the British raj. He set up a Supreme Defence Council to mobilize war activities among his people. "This is the final battle in our long struggle with British imperialism," he told them. "We have fought it three times before and lost, and so became a subject race for generations. We must now fight and win this fourth and final round with the help of Japan, for if we lose again we shall be slaves for a very long time more."

Ba Maw was successful in implanting a lasting antagonism toward the British but could not slow their drive. On March 9 they entered Mandalay, capturing the Obo railway station and Mandalay Hill, then continued south toward the capital, Rangoon.

Important as the Philippines and Burma once seemed to the Japanese military leaders, they could not escape the inevitable logic that the empire's last hope lay in the successful defense of a relatively small island just 350 miles south of the homeland—Okinawa. Admiral Tomioka, for example, believed the enemy could be beaten there with an all-out effort, and this victory would give Japan six months to negotiate a peace which would guarantee the continuing rule of the Emperor.

The fall of Leyte and Iwo Jima had left General Koiso's Cabinet at the point of collapse. Koiso had purposely been installed as interim premier, and from his first day in office his course had been uncertain. With all the prestige of his position but without genuine support from any faction, Koiso exerted almost no influence on the prosecution of the war and none at all on the subterranean efforts for peace. Unlike Tojo, he did not represent the militarists, many of whom regarded him with suspicion. Nor was he privy to the continuous and complex maneuvers of the peace groups.

Concern over the future of the nation under such leadership was so acute that the Emperor summoned Marquis Kido and suggested that it might be necessary for him to consult the former prime ministers concerning the deteriorating war situation. Only once before, on the eve of the war itself, had the Emperor convened the *jushin* to discuss anything except the selection of a new premier.

Kido had the *jushin* brought to the Emperor's office one at a time, lest the military become suspicious if they appeared as a group. It would also make it easier for each man to speak freely. But except for Konoye's, their advice was vague and poorly thought through, or simply an emotional appeal to continue the fight with determination. Konoye's appraisal was a closely reasoned, if misguided, examination of the political and military abyss into which Japan would fall unless peace were concluded shortly. His opinions were expressed in an eight-page *Memorial to the Throne*, written in his own hand with Japanese brush and read aloud to the Emperor. It is doubtful that any subject other than Konoye would have dared present such a frank evaluation directly to His Majesty. Like almost everything else concerning Konoye it was an anomaly—objective and subjective, practical and impractical. Starting with a courageous pronouncement ("Regrettable though it is, I believe that Japan has already lost the war"), he made a charge based solely on his own growing paranoia toward Communism ("The greatest danger to maintenance of Japan's imperial system comes not from defeat itself but from the threat of a Communist revolution"). Then, in an attempt to prove that Japan was about to be seized by native Reds, he accurately foresaw the course of Marxism in eastern Europe and Korea. His next historical assessment, however, was again faulted by his fixed idea: the Manchurian Incident, the China Incident and the Greater East Asian War, too, had been "a scheme consciously plotted" by Army radicals, themselves puppets of right-wing civilian extremists who were "simply Communists clothed in national essence, secretly intending to bring about a Communist revolution."

Like so many intellectuals who lean far left in their youth and grow conservative with age, Konoye saw the Red menace everywhere. He charged that those who were sponsoring the slogan "One Hundred Million Die Together" had done so at the instigation of "Communists who are trying to throw the country into confusion and bring about a revolution." Moreover, some Army leaders were so infused with pro-Soviet sentiment that they were "urging an alliance with Russia at any cost while others were calling for co-operation with Mao."

Yet the conclusion that he drew from these fanciful accusations was inescapable logic: peace could only be negotiated if the militarists ("Although they know they cannot win the war, I believe they will fight to the death in order to save face") were circumvented. "Thus if the tree is severed at the roots, its leaves and branches will wither and die." His recommendation for dealing with the die-hard militarists, however, was unrealistic, though desirable: eliminate them by a coup d'état, and then negotiate directly with America and Britain.

All its inconsistencies notwithstanding, the rambling *Memorial* stimulated both the Emperor and his chief adviser. Unlike his fellow *jushin,* Konoye had uncovered the core of the problem, and while his solution was impractical, it would eventually be transformed into an efficacious plan for peace by the pragmatic Kido.

Prime Minister Koiso's personal desire to end the war favorably was not curbed by the lack of confidence shown in him by the pacifists and militarists. Perversely, he saw peace with Chiang Kai-shek as the key to honorable negotiations with America and Britain. Moreover, his choice for go-between was a man known throughout the Far East as an intriguer, Miao Pin. An official of the Nanking puppet regime, he claimed to be in secret radio communication with the Chungking government. Koiso's own foreign minister and his most knowledgeable adviser on China, Mamoru Shigemitsu, warned that the notorious Miao was merely trying to promote his own ambitions. "To believe in his mediatory role," Shigemitsu later wrote, "was childish naïveté and betrayal of ignorance of Chinese politics."

Koiso would not listen and persuaded his war minister, Field Marshal Sugiyama, to bring Miao to Japan on a military plane. At the airport near Tokyo, Miao ignored the Prime Minister, who had invited him, and insisted on being driven directly to a meeting with a member of the royal family, Prince Higashikuni, where he tried to ingratiate himself with the Emperor. But His Majesty found such intrigue as distasteful as had Koiso's Cabinet. Miao returned ignominiously to China—subsequently to be executed by Chiang—and with him disappeared Koiso's last hope of remaining in power.

28   The Last Sortie

1.

Extending south from Japan and curving toward Formosa for 790 miles like a long tail was a chain of some 140 islands, the Ryukyus. In the middle of this archipelago lay the last important bastion guarding the homeland, Okinawa. An elongated island about sixty miles from north to south, and only two miles wide near the middle, it was an ideal staging area for invasion of Japan with its flat waist for airfields and two deep-water bays suitable for naval bases. Its climate was subtropical, moderated by the Kuroshio (the Gulf Stream of the Pacific) and the Ogasawara Current. Humidity was high all year round; rainfall was heavy and erratic with a single day's downpour occasionally equaling a month's average. From May to November two typhoons a month swept over the island.

Okinawa was a crossroads of the Orient, lying almost equidistant from Japan, China and Formosa, and had been influenced by all three as well as by the islands of the South Pacific. In 1372 it was taken over as a tributary by the founder of the Ming Dynasty. Two centuries later Japanese from Kyushu ravaged the island but allowed its inhabitants to continue sending tribute to China. This unique dual subservience existed until 1875, when Hirohito's grandfather dispatched an invasion force which took complete control of the Ryukyus. Four years later Emperor Meiji formally annexed the archipelago, made Japanese the official language and replaced Okinawa's king with a governor. As a colony the 450,000 people of Okinawa—the majority crammed into the southern, more habitable section of the island—continued to live as they had for centuries, scratching out a meager living predominantly as farmers.

This neglect notwithstanding, Okinawa had by the outbreak of war with the West become an integral part of the empire, and was represented in the Diet as one of Japan's forty-seven prefectures. Technically its inhabitants were first-class citizens, but most mainlanders did not consider them their social equals. The Okinawans, with their mixed heritage, regarded themselves as Japanese and were as loyal to the Emperor as any Tokyo resident, though most of them still practiced Chinese ancestor worship, and their *chichi* (protective household gods in the form of fantastic lions) were as much Chinese as Japanese. Only in Okinawa did colorful porcelain *chichi*, in myriad poses and sizes, cling to the tile roofs, ready to strike down any unfriendly intruder.

For the first three years of the Pacific war, fewer than 600 troops were stationed in the Ryukyus, and it wasn't until April 1, 1944, that the 32nd Army, three full divisions and a brigade, was activated on Okinawa. At the end of the year it was significantly weakened by the transfer of the elite 9th Division to Formosa, but the Army commander—Lieutenant General Mitsuru Ushijima, a quiet and competent officer who had recently been commandant of the Military Academy—still had a sizable force: the 24th Division from Manchuria comprised 14,000 men, including several thousand Okinawan conscripts; the 62nd Division, 12,000 troops, mainly infantrymen, who had fought in China; and the 5,000 men of the 44th Independent Mixed Brigade. There was also a single tank regiment of fourteen medium and thirteen light tanks, and various artillery units with a respectable number of 22-mm. machine cannon, 75-mm. guns, 150-mm. howitzers and 81-mm. mortars, as well as twenty-four huge 320-mm. spigot mortars which belched out 675-lb. shells.

In addition, Ushijima could count on two shipping-engineer regiments, a variety of service units and 20,000 members of the *Boeitai,* a home guard unit of Okinawans burning with ardor to serve their Emperor.

The withdrawal of the 9th Division forced Ushijima to formulate a new defense plan that would utilize his remaining men to the best advantage. He was almost certain that the enemy would land on the west coast just below the waist of the island along the spacious Hagushi beaches, so he concentrated his men in the south. He also began converting as many naval and service troops into front-line soldiers as possible. From sea-raiding battalions, formed to man suicide boats, he extracted 5,500 foot soldiers, and though they were poorly trained and equipped, they were eager to fight on land. Another 10,000 naval personnel were organized into a force commanded by an admiral. To free more military personnel for combat, 3,900 Okinawans were temporarily assigned to the 32nd Army as labor troops; 600 students became messengers, orderlies and communication assistants at the various headquarters. One group of enthusiastic high school students was trained to fight; 750 of them were formed into special Blood and Iron for the Emperor duty units and trained to infiltrate enemy lines and carry on guerrilla warfare.

Just above Okinawa's two largest cities, Naha and Shuri, the terrain was ideal for defense, and it was here that Ushijima erected a defense line in depth, a series of concentric fortresses, facing north and extending across the island. Numerous caves, blockhouses, and gun emplacements were carved into the ridges and hills connected by a complex system of tunnels. Even the Chinese lyre-shaped tombs which dotted the countryside were transformed into pillboxes, over the objections of the older Okinawans. As at Iwo Jima, Ushijima would let the enemy land and engage him only from prepared positions. By March more than 100,000 defenders, including the *Boeitai,* were in place. The two most experienced divisions manned the main defense line, while the third division and the 44th Independent Mixed Brigade were positioned at the southern end of Okinawa as insurance against any landing in that area. The northern half of the island was given mere token defense—two battalions.

Ushijima had correctly foreseen American plans. They would come ashore at the Hagushi beaches, although there would be a decoy landing in the south. "Iceberg" was to be a joint Army-Navy operation under the overall command of Admiral Spruance, who had opposed the invasion of Formosa. An Army general, Simon Bolivar Buckner, Jr.—another opponent of Formosa—would lead all the ground troops.

His father, one of the Confederacy's first generals, had escaped from a Union prison. The son was a Spartan and went to extreme limits to prove it. During the Aleutian campaign he had slept on a thin mattress with a sheet for cover; he trained himself to read without glasses by squinting his eyes. His Tenth Army was made up of six combat-experienced divisions, half Army, half Marine. The Army trained and rehearsed on Espíritu Santo and Leyte, while the Marines used Guadalcanal. The task of transporting the assault force of 183,000 troops and 747,000 measurement tons of cargo to the battlefield was formidable. Four hundred and thirty assault transports would have to be loaded at eleven different ports, ranging from Seattle to Leyte.

The first step, on March 24, was the capture of the Keramas, a group of small mountainous islands fifteen miles west of Naha. There were but 750 defenders to contend with, and they scattered for the hills and caves. It was obvious before dusk that the islands would soon provide a seaplane base and a fleet anchorage.

That same day a systematic naval bombardment of Okinawa began. A week later frogmen worked openly along the Hagushi beaches, clearing debris and detonating mines, while Japanese onshore watched in admiration mixed with frustration, holding fire as instructed. The climax of the bombardment came on March 31. When it ceased Rear Admiral W. H. P. Blandy, in charge of all preliminary operations, announced that the preparation was "sufficient for a successful landing." At this point, 27,226 rounds of 5-inch or larger-caliber shells had carpeted Okinawa. The effect appeared devastating but the main line of defense was still almost intact. Just before dawn on April 1, Easter Sunday, the crash of naval gunfire again wakened Ushijima's men. Those along the west coast peered out of their shelters at an awesome sight: 1,300 ships massed offshore.

It was L-(for Love) day. At eight o'clock landing craft packed with helmeted assault troops started for the beaches; LST's disgorged their armored amphibians and amphibian tractors also loaded with men and equipment. There was almost no opposition as two Army and two Marine divisions poured ashore during the morning. "This is hard to believe," wrote Robert Sherrod. "I've already lived longer than I thought I would," remarked one infantryman of the 7th Division as he reached the top of a hill. He spoke for everyone. By night more than 60,000 Americans were ashore in a beachhead not quite three miles long and a mile in depth. Except for the uncontested Guadalcanal landing, it was the least costly of any major invasion—twenty-eight dead, twenty-seven missing. "We were on Okinawa an hour and a half after H-hour, without being shot at, and hadn't even gotten our feet wet," reported the GI's favorite correspondent, Ernie Pyle. Okinawa was a piece of cake.

Tenth Army moved swiftly on all fronts, meeting some resistance around the airfield from a *Boeitai* unit, and before the end of the second day the Kadena strip was not only cleared but repaired for emergency landings. On the third day the Marines, who had swung north, spanned the narrow waist of the island. Okinawa was cut in two. The Army divisions going south continued to meet desultory resistance. At the commanding village of Shimabuku they were confronted by a pair of Japanese—trembling old men who bowed repeatedly. One was the headman, the other was Councilman Shosei Kima, a teacher. Kima had persuaded the 1,300 villagers to remain in their homes rather than flee into the countryside and risk starvation.

"You American gentleman!" Kima called out. "Me Okinawan Christian!"

The Americans warily covered the two Okinawans with their weapons. There was a tense wait of several minutes until a Nisei interpreter, Thomas Higa, arrived. "*Sensei* [Teacher]!," he shouted, seizing Kima's hand. "Kima-*sensei*, don't you remember me? My name is Taro Higa. I was one of your pupils in elementary school."

All that day the Americans pushed deeper into the island to the north and south. Where was the enemy? Lieutenant Colonel James Brown of the 12th Marine Regiment, sent a note to the divisional supply officer: "Colonel, please send us a dead Jap. A lot of my men have never seen one. We'll bury him for you."

2.

Without support from any quarter, Prime Minister Koiso's regime was doomed. Nevertheless, he continued to make frantic if futile attempts to save his cabinet. He confused the Emperor by first suggesting a drastic reorganization of it and a moment later offering to resign; he took the same proposal of reorganization to Kido, who reacted coolly; downcast, he returned to His Majesty, who, embarrassed by Koiso's flounderings, said, "Study the matter carefully."

It was a polite suggestion to step down but Koiso continued to insinuate himself. He told Prince Higashikuni he could "properly carry on the war" if he were reinstated on the active list; then he could be appointed war minister. He complained that the Army had repeatedly turned down his request to replace War Minister Sugiyama, and he was going to take the matter direct to the Emperor. Again His Majesty was noncommittal.

Koiso had exhausted every means left to save his government. Piqued, he told Kido on the afternoon of April 4 that he was going to resign the following day. The most important function of the Privy Seal was to select a new premier. By tradition Kido would first have convened the *jushin* and asked for their opinions before advising the Emperor. This time, however, a preliminary investigation had to be made at once, to ensure the selection of a man who would work for peace, yet be acceptable to the Army.

It was an exceptional step but one that had the full approval of His Majesty. On April 5, as Koiso was presenting his formal resignation to the Emperor, Marquis Kido sounded out each of the four military leaders separately. He suggested that it was perhaps time to form "an Imperial Headquarters or Conduct of War cabinet," in which the prime minister, necessarily a military man, would control not only the affairs of state but the Supreme Command. Both Army Chief of Staff Umezu and War Minister Sugiyama were cool to such a cabinet. Umezu acknowledged that the battle on Okinawa was going badly but that Japan "must be prepared to fight to the end." Sugiyama was just as pessimistic, yet held out the hope that once Russia defeated Germany she might advise her allies to make peace with Japan. Navy Chief of Staff Koshiro Oikawa was uncertain about the outcome of the war—he doubted that even a victory on Okinawa would end it; the enemy would simply attack again.

The testimony of these three indicated to Kido that the high command had privately come to realize that the war could not be won. As for the fourth man, Navy Minister Yonai's secret advocacy of peace was, of course, well known to the marquis. Besides, the minister had found a suitable candidate for the premiership: Admiral Kantaro Suzuki. The suggestion seemed ideal to Kido. The former Grand Chamberlain was a "large-scale" man, whom His Majesty affectionately called *oyaji* (old man).

Later that afternoon, at five o'clock, the *jushin*—except Baron Wakatsuki, whose train was late—assembled in the

Imperial Chamber to select a premier. They were joined by Kido and the new head of the Privy Council,* who was fortuitously the Privy Seal's choice for prime minister—Admiral Suzuki. In Tojo's first session as a *jushin*, he was alert and aggressive, making it obvious from the first that he would reject any peace candidate. His fellow *jushin* all opposed him but not overtly. For fear of alerting the militarists, they could not risk an open clash.

"Koiso's resignation states that the affairs of the state as well as the Supreme Command need revision," Tojo began. "What does this mean?" It was as much a challenge as a question.

"Prime Minister Koiso doesn't give any special explanations," Kido replied.

"It is not desirable to have many changes of government during the war," Tojo said belligerently. "The next cabinet must be the last one! Now, there are two schools of thought in this nation: one that we should fight till the end to secure the future of the country; the other to bring peace speedily even at the expense of unconditional surrender. I believe we must first settle this point."

"The next cabinet must consider a wide variety of subjects," said Admiral Keisuke Okada, who like Suzuki (his private choice for prime minister) had had such a narrow escape during the 2/26 Incident. "This is the cabinet on whose shoulders will rest the destiny of our nation until the end, and which will marshal the entire strength of the nation. Questions such as peace and war cannot be determined here."

There was an uneasy pause and two of the civilians—Hiranuma and Hirota—attempted to placate Tojo. Both asserted, tongue in cheek, that the war must be fought to the end. The *jushin* began debating the requisites of the future prime minister but without naming any one person. At last, after an hour, it was President of the Privy Council Suzuki who suggested that one of the *jushin* themselves accept the post. "Since the physical strain is so great, I should like to ask Prince Konoye, the youngest in the group, to come forward."

Konoye declined; he was too compromised by the mistakes and commitments of his three past governments. Hiranuma agreed that Konoye was unacceptable on these grounds, reiterated (for Tojo's benefit) that the war must be prose-

---

*Yoshimichi Hara had died in 1944.

cuted vigorously, and then proposed the favorite candidate of Kido and Okada—Admiral Suzuki. The response was enthusiastic.

"I agree," said Konoye.

"Very good idea," said Wakatsuki, who had arrived out of breath and apologetic. "We couldn't make a better choice."

Suzuki himself objected; he had promised his family he would not accept the post. "I think I told Admiral Okada once that if a military man goes into politics, he would only lead the nation to defeat. This is proved by the fall of Rome, the eclipse of the Kaiser and the fate of the Romanovs. Because of this principle, I cannot accept the honor. Besides, I am hard of hearing."

Hiranuma begged him to reconsider. "The public trusts your honest and loyal character."

It was difficult even for Tojo to disapprove of Suzuki—he was a devout Taoist, free of ambition; he came from a solid military background; his brother was a respected general—but he lacked one vital qualification. Tojo began by praising the admiral but challenged his tenet that the military should avoid politics. "The enemy is getting impatient. He will try a bold strategy; he is likely to attempt landing somewhere on Japan proper. Home defense will then become a vital matter. The government and the high command must be fused into one. Therefore the premier must be a soldier on the active list." He proposed Field Marshal Shunroku Hata.

Kido restrained himself. "What is your opinion, Mr. Hirota?"

"We must have someone from the Army or Navy who can control and lead them."

"Your opinion, please, Admiral Okada?"

Okada refused to endorse anyone except Suzuki, who had been summarily rejected by Tojo. "I know of no one," he said, "so I can say nothing."

Kido acknowledged that the homeland would soon be a battlefield and the new cabinet would need the full confidence of the nation. But there he parted company with Tojo. "Personally," he said, "I hope that His Excellency Suzuki will rise to the occasion." He turned directly to Tojo. "We must look at the situation in a wider perspective than yours."

Tojo glared at Kido. Until now he had curbed his bitterness toward the Privy Seal, whom he blamed for his own downfall. "Be very careful, otherwise I'm afraid the Army will *soppo o muku* [turn its head away]! If it does, the new cabinet will fall."

The phrase infuriated rather than intimidated Kido. "It is very serious to have the Army turn its head away from us," he said. "Do you yourself feel that way?"

"I can't say that I don't."

Kido stood his ground. "The atmosphere at this meeting is really quite antimilitaristic. Perhaps the people will turn their heads away from the Army!"

Tojo's threatening posture also provoked Okada to action. "At a time as critical as this," he exclaimed indignantly, "how dare a man who once accepted the imperial command to be premier say that the Army might turn its head away!"

Tojo realized he had gone too far. "I'm sorry," he said. "I take back what I just said. I meant to say that the Army will find such a choice disagreeable."

Tojo was isolated. The whole trend of the meeting had turned against him.

"Keeping all this in mind," Kido summed up, "I will present my views to the Emperor and ask for his decision." A few minutes later, at eight o'clock, the meeting was adjourned, and the members filed to a nearby room for dinner. Before they were through, Kido asked Suzuki to return with him to the conference room. "If you form a government," Kido told him, "we would have to ask you to carry out extremely important tasks." Once more Suzuki demurred; he didn't think he was fit for the job and he lacked confidence.

Kido persisted. The times were too perilous to decline on the grounds that a military man should not become involved in politics. "It is beyond that, Admiral. We must recommend someone to the Emperor whom he trusts implicitly."

Suzuki capitulated. "If the Emperor orders me to form a new cabinet, I will do it," he said. There was no emotion, not a trace of reluctance in his voice. At ten o'clock the seventy-eight-year-old admiral, his back bowed with age, entered the Emperor's study. His Majesty, who was alone except for Grand Chamberlain Hisanori Fujita, said simply, "I order you to form a cabinet." He omitted the traditional admonitions and conditions.

"I am very pleased to be so honored by His Majesty's offer but I beg to decline as I did at the *jushin* meeting held late this afternoon." Within an hour he had changed his mind twice. "I am merely His Majesty's humble naval officer and have had no experience in political affairs. Further, I have no political opinions. My motto has been to abide by the adage of Emperor Meiji to the effect that military men should never interfere in politics. Therefore, begging His Majesty's pardon, I must refrain from accepting His Majesty's offer."

The Emperor smiled understandingly. "I know, Suzuki, what you're trying to say and appreciate your position, but at this critical moment there is no one but you for this task. That is why I have asked you."

As he slowly backed away, Suzuki said, "With His Majesty's permission, I wish to think it over fully," but the Emperor's sincerity had already decided him to once more change his mind. As a result of more than seven years' service as Grand Chamberlain, he had also interpreted correctly the unspoken words of His Majesty: to end the conflict as soon as possible.*

3.

That evening on the Inland Sea, farewell parties enlivened the superbattleship *Yamato* and nine other ships of the Second Fleet. Its commander, Vice Admiral Seiichi Ito, had been ordered by Admiral Soemu Toyoda, commander of Combined Fleet, to lead these remnants against enemy vessels anchored off Okinawa. Toyoda informed all commanders in Combined Fleet of the suicide sortie:

THE FATE OF OUR EMPIRE TRULY RESTS UPON THIS ONE ACTION. I HAVE CALLED FOR THE ORGANIZATION OF A SURFACE SPECIAL ATTACK UNIT FOR A BREAKTHROUGH OPERATION OF UNRIVALED BRAVERY SO THAT THE POWER OF THE IMPERIAL NAVY MAY BE FELT IN THIS ONE ACTION IN ORDER THAT THE BRILLIANT TRADITION OF THE IMPERIAL NAVY'S SURFACE FORCES MAY BE EXALTED AND OUR GLORY HANDED DOWN TO POSTERITY. EACH UNIT, REGARDLESS OF WHETHER OR NOT IT IS A SPECIAL ATTACK UNIT, WILL HARDEN ITS RESOLVE TO FIGHT GLORIOUSLY TO THE DEATH TO COMPLETELY DESTROY THE ENEMY FLEET, THEREBY ESTABLISHING FIRMLY AN ETERNAL FOUNDATION FOR THE EMPIRE.**

---

*The Emperor was equally sensitive to Suzuki's aims. After the war he told Kido's chief secretary, Marquis Yasumasa Matsudaira, "I was aware of Suzuki's sentiments from the very beginning of his appointment as premier, and likewise I was convinced that Suzuki understood my sentiments. Consequently I was in no hurry at the time to express to him my desires for peace."

**After the war Admiral Toyoda said, "I knew very well what the fate would be of warships without air cover, and that the probability of success was very slight. Nevertheless, we had to do everything to help our troops at Okinawa."

The party Rear Admiral Keizo Komura gave for commanding officers of his Second Destroyer Squadron aboard his flagship, the light cruiser *Yahagi*, was boisterous. Each ship had taken on just enough fuel for a one-way trip, but knowledge of this and the certainty of their death seemed to free the officers from care. Komura and Captain Tameichi Hara, skipper of *Yahagi*, left their comrades singing the fraternal "Doki no Sakura" and went on an impromptu tour of the ship. In the sailors' quarters they found men sleeping peacefully in their hammocks. In an engine room a machinist's mate sweating diligently over a generator told Hara, "I changed watches with my buddy who likes to drink." He wanted to be absolutely sure there would be no power failure at Okinawa.

Hara clambered topside, overwhelmed with emotion and alcohol. He felt tremendously happy as he clung to a post for support. *"Nippon banzai!"* he yelled, tears streaming down his cheeks. *"Yahagi banzai! Nippon banzai!"*

Vice Admiral Ryunosuke Kusaka, Toyoda's chief of staff, veteran of Pearl Harbor, Midway and the carrier battles off Guadalcanal, had vehemently opposed the suicide sortie of the Second Fleet; *Yamato* could be used to better advantage in the battle for the mainland. But he was the one selected to fly to the Inland Sea on the morning of April 6 (the fleet would depart that evening for its rendezvous with destiny) to explain personally the significance of the mission. Ito understood; he wanted advice on one matter. "What should I do if we are so badly damaged on the way that we can't proceed?"

Kusaka could not help him. "You'll have to decide that for yourself." They drank a last cup of *sake*.

"I see," said Ito. "Please do not be uneasy about me. My mind is calm. I have no regrets and am leaving willingly." He asked Kusaka to address his senior officers. Kusaka told them it was Combined Fleet's last chance as well as the nation's. They must break through the American naval force off Okinawa and ground their ships on the island. *Yamato*'s big guns—their range was 25 miles—could devastate the enemy positions.

There were private doubts but no one voiced them. The captain of *Yamato*, however—Rear Admiral Kosaku Ariga— was eager. With a perpetual grin, he slapped his stomach every time Kusaka made a point. Captain Hara wrote his family that he was going on a surface attack mission:

. . . It is a great responsibility as well as a great honor to be skipper of a ship in this sortie to Okinawa. Know that I am happy and proud of this opportunity. Be proud of me. Farewell.

Extra supplies were off-loaded from the ships. The sick as well as the midshipmen were compelled to disembark against their will. The sun shone through the mist as the fleet weighed anchor at 3 P.M. Hara's cruiser, *Yahagi*, got under way first, followed by four detroyers, and finally *Yamato* with four more destroyers.

As the ten-ship column slowly proceeded south through the Inland Sea, the first of ten mass air raids was launched against ships clustered off Okinawa. For almost four hours, 341 bombers dropped their explosives in conventional style while 355 *kamikaze* plummeted down on the Americans. By dark three destroyers, an LST and two ammunition ships had been sunk, and ten other ships heavily damaged.

On *Yamato*, Admiral Ito was elated by reports that thirty enemy ships had been seen going down, while another twenty were afire. Overhead Kusaka followed the column in a floatplane as far as his fuel would allow, then waved an arm in farewell as the little plane banked away. That evening *Yahagi*'s thousand-man crew assembled on her deck to hear Captain Hara read a final message from Admiral Toyoda exhorting them to fight to the end—the fate of the nation rested "on this operation." As the shouts of *"Banzai!"* subsided, Hara added practical strictures of his own, which scandalized most of the crew: "Our mission appears suicidal, and it is. But I wish to emphasize that suicide is not the objective. The objective is victory. You are not sheep whipped to a sacrificial altar. . . . Once this ship is crippled or sunk, do not hesitate to save yourselves for the next fight. There will be other battles. You are not to commit suicide. You are to beat the enemy!"

This time there were no *banzai*. A perturbed lieutenant broke the silence: he had been taught at the Academy to die with his ship. Hara understood his concern. "In feudal times," he said, "lives were wasted cheaply, but we are in the twentieth century. The code of *bushido* says that a warrior lives in such a way that he is always prepared to die." But this didn't mean that their lives should be forfeited meaninglessly. "We are to win this war and not think of dying." He called on them to turn the tide of battle. There was a spontaneous cheer for the Emperor and *Yahagi*.

At 8 P.M. the Second Fleet cautiously picked its way

through the mines of Bungo Strait and sortied into the Pacific. Ito ordered a course at 20 knots down the coast of Kyushu. (His column had already been sighted by two American submarines.) At dawn the ten ships entered the open sea below the island. They shifted into a ring formation with *Yamato* in the center, and began zigzagging south toward Okinawa at 24 knots. The last escort planes turned back, and as the coast of Kyushu dropped out of sight, the fleet was alone.

Rain from low leaden clouds swept the Japanese ships at 8 A.M. An hour later one of the destroyers, *Asashimo*, dropped out of the ring, signaling that she was having engine trouble but would try to make repairs. Before long she too was out of sight. Slowly the overcast broke and at 11:30 a seaplane appeared about ten miles to the east. It was American. Then came a warning from an island lookout station ahead that 250 enemy planes were winging south.

Admiral Spruance, still in command of Fifth Fleet, had told Marc Mitscher, Task Force 58, to let the enemy ships continue south, leaving them to the guns of surface units, but Mitscher wanted this opportunity to demonstrate once and for all that his airmen could sink the most formidable ship afloat; naval airmen claimed that they had sunk *Musashi* in the Philippines, but submarines could possibly have done it. The unexpected appearance of *Yamato*, her sister ship, "provided a clean-cut chance to prove, if proof was needed, aircraft superiority."

Mitscher sent off planes from Task Groups 58.1 and 58.2, then turned to his chief of staff. "Inform Admiral Spruance that I propose to attack the *Yamato* sortie group at 1200 unless otherwise directed." The message to Spruance read: "Will you take them or shall I?" Spruance scribbled on his message blank: "You take them."

On *Yahagi*'s bridge, shortly after noon, Admiral Komura saw the approaching planes first. "Here they come!" he exclaimed to Captain Hara. Rapidly the ships opened formation as crews scrambled to battle stations. The fleet was abruptly blanketed by a rain squall, but only for ten minutes. A lookout on *Yahagi* called out, "Planes on port bow!"

Hara turned. Planes, more than forty of them, were diving out of a low thick cloud. *Yamato*'s 150 antiaircraft and machine guns hesitated momentarily, then the sky erupted with black puffs, crisscrossed by tracers. But the Americans burst through this wall of flak. Two bombs crashed near

781

Yamato's mainmast. A torpedo ripped into the battleship's port side.

The 8,500-ton *Yahagi* heeled sharply in the rain to avoid the resolute assault, but at 12:45 P.M. she staggered from a bomb. Almost immediately a momentous shudder ran through the ship; a torpedo had plunged into her port side just below the waterline. The cruiser coasted to a stop, helpless and dead in the water, as a second group of attackers dropped out of the clouds. A bomb detonated on the forecastle, another in the stern; a torpedo rammed into the starboard bow. *Yahagi* vibrated violently, as if, thought Hara, she were made of paper.

The planes climbing away through patches of clear sky seemed almost cocky, and in the abrupt, unearthly quiet, Hara surveyed his wrecked cruiser in dismay. Admiral Komura wanted to transfer to one of the destroyers and continue on to Okinawa. The destroyer *Isokaze* was signaled to come alongside to take on survivors, but as she slowly closed, the hapless destroyer was caught by a second wave of planes bursting through a cloud. *Yahagi*, too, was raked by machine-gun bullets. Komura refused to escape in a cutter. He would die on *Yahagi* rather than on some nameless little boat.

A few miles away the twisted decks of *Yamato* were jammed with butchered bodies, a tangle of intestines, limbs, torsos. Blood coursed down the scuppers. The sides of the battleship had buckled and she had slowed to 18 knots. But Admiral Ariga kept her on course to Okinawa. At 1:35 P.M. a third wave—it looked like 150 planes—swept in, concentrating on the damaged port side. *Yamato* heeled and swerved, but two more torpedoes—the fifth and sixth—drove into the left side while seven or more bombs exploded on the center deck. Machine-gun bullets swept the ship "like rain," annihilating half of the antiaircraft gun crews. Steering was damaged and the list increased to 15 degrees.

At 1:50 the officer supervising water control phoned the bridge: "We have reached maximum water level. To prevent further listing we must flood the starboard engine rooms." This meant cutting speed to 9 knots, but the commander of air defense had been pleading for half an hour to correct the listing so he could fire his guns. The executive officer, Captain Jiro Nomura, hesitated but a moment. "Flood the engine rooms," he said.

Slowly the battleship began to level. Then another torpedo hit the port and the listing resumed. At 2 P.M. *Yamato* took her eighth torpedo, this one on the starboard side. An urgent call came from the emergency steering room: "Too much water here. We can no longer steer—" The steering commander's voice was cut off.

"Bring the ship north!" Admiral Ariga shouted. Traditionally a dead man was faced north; Ariga wanted to do the same for the dying *Yamato*. But the men in the emergency steering room had drowned at their posts, and the ship began circling slowly to port, out of control, just as the fourth wave appeared. The temporary hospital on the bow was obliterated. Three more torpedoes knifed into the hulk. Listing increased to 18 degrees; speed slowed to 7 knots.

The cruiser *Yahagi* was rapidly settling, her decks already awash. She had absorbed thirteen bombs and seven torpedoes. Everywhere he looked Captain Hara saw destroyers either sinking or in flames. Two seemed unharmed and they were darting protectively around *Yamato*. Admiral Komura felt water creeping up his legs. He glanced at his watch—it was 2:05. Just then he was sucked under. He knew it was the end of his life but he remained conscious, engulfed in swirling water, for what seemed an eternity before he shot to the surface. As he paddled through the oily water he saw a black-faced man. It was Hara. At the crest of a wave Hara got a glimpse of *Yamato* six-odd miles away. Planes swarmed around her like gnats. But she was moving, a beautiful sight!

On *Yamato*'s bridge Executive Officer Nomura noticed red lights flash on the warning board. He approached to see where the danger was. Half a dozen lights glowed—gun turret No. 1 and at least five ammunition storerooms. Were they going to have a chain explosion? Of the 1,170 rounds for the big guns, 3 had been fired. If the remaining shells detonated, the "unsinkable" *Yamato* would burst at the seams. A backup warning device began its ominous buzzing, then another and another and another. He heard Ariga shout at him, "Can't we pump water into the ammunition rooms?" and his voice seemed to be "tearing his throat." It was impossible. The water control command post was destroyed. Nomura waited for the explosion that would obliterate them all. He thought with a measure of satisfaction, Well, that's all right. It will be a samurai's hara-kiri.

Shortly after 2:15 P.M. the twelfth torpedo struck the port side, as if, Nomura thought, "we had received the *coup de grâce*." If the order to abandon ship wasn't given without delay, the crew would be lost. But no instructions came from Admiral Ariga. Nomura lurched up the narrow spiral staircase to the second bridge, where he could survey the ship. Normally the top deck was twenty-five feet above water level; the port side of the deck was awash. It was incongruous to see men sitting at the bow smoking and eating hardtack. Inexplicably, Nomura was annoyed at their nonchalance.

Towering water columns geysered on either side of the ship. Nomura's eyes swept the superstructure. Something was missing. The flag! He took another look; the mast itself was gone. Were the pictures of the Emperor and Empress safe? During a battle they were kept in the main gun command post, the most armored place aboard ship. Nomura phoned the gun commander and learned he had locked himself in his cabin with the pictures lest they float away when the ship sank.

With *Yamato* listing more than 30 degrees, Nomura phoned Ariga. "The end is near," he said. It was time for the entire crew to come topside. Ariga, in turn, informed Admiral Ito over the voice tube that there was no longer any prospect of correcting the list.

"Fleet Commander, your person is valuable. Please leave the ship with the crew. I alone will remain." Ariga gave orders to assemble on the upper deck, then phoned Nomura, who was still on the second bridge. "Executive Officer," he said hoarsely, "leave the ship immediately and report the details of the action to Combined Fleet." Nomura's protest was curtly ignored by Ariga. "I'm remaining with the ship. Be sure to get home alive."

"Captain," Nomura insisted, "I'm staying with you."

"Executive Officer, that is an order." He hung up and told a crewman to lash him to the compass post. Sailors started tying each other to the bridge binnacle. "What are you doing?" Ariga shouted angrily. "You young men jump in and swim for it."

Ito refused to leave the ship too. He shook hands with Chief of Staff Morishita, and while his staff looked on "with ten thousand feelings," the admiral balanced his way along the listing deck, opened the door of a spiral staircase and disappeared. His aide made a move to follow but Morishita shouted, "*Baka!* Young men should live to serve the Emperor!"

At 2:25 P.M. the listing increased rapidly until the great ship was rolling on her beam ends. Cries of *"Banzai!"* were drowned out by the rush of water. *Yamato* was on one side, like a foundered whale. Lights blacked out as gun wreckage, ammunition, pieces of bodies slid inexorably into the sea. Men struggled up the almost vertical deck, slipping on their comrades' blood. At the top they clambered over the starboard rail, where they clustered on the side of the ship.

Executive Officer Nomura felt himself being pulled under water by a titanic force. In the clear sea he saw other men "dancing about" in the whirlpool. Below was a bottomless dark blue. The light above diminished. Close to death, he felt his sense of awareness becoming unexpectedly clear. He tumbled deeper and deeper in agony. Bright red flashes shot through the water. A series of concussions slammed him like battering rams. It was as if "heaven and earth were blowing up." The ammunition was exploding under water. Nomura was propelled to the surface. Balls of fire arched across the waves. He rolled over on his back and floated. The end of *Yamato*, he thought; the end of the Imperial Navy.

Aboard the destroyer *Yukikaze* its captain, Commander Tochigi Terauchi, watched in despair as *Yamato*—it stood for "Japan"—rolled over and disappeared. He signaled Captain Masayoshi Yoshida, the new senior officer of the fleet, who was aboard the destroyer *Fuyutsuki:* "Recommend we proceed with mission."

"Pick up survivors and then we will decide course of action" was the answer.

Yukikaze's torpedo officer wanted to lower a cutter for survivors but Terauchi stopped him. "This is no ordinary mission," he shouted. "This is a suicide attack. Even with *Yamato* gone we should continue." He signaled Yoshida again, requesting reconsideration, then ordered his men to pick up survivors but only those who could be used in the attack. "Ignore the wounded!"*

Those in the water faced a double hazard—abandonment and bullets from strafing American planes which systematically stitched a pattern of death across the battle area. Hara watched in wonder as a flying boat skimmed the surface and settled to taxi speed nearby. It churned toward a patch of water dyed green. An American pilot scrambled out of a life raft into the plane, and as it heaved out of the sea like an aged goose, Hara felt envious.

It was hours later, near dusk, when Hara himself, along with Admiral Komura and other survivors of *Yahagi*, was finally picked up by the destroyer *Hatsushimo*. Komura took

---

Yamato had a crew of 3,332, of whom 269 survived.

time to clean his oily face and put on a borrowed uniform before he wrote out a message for Combined Fleet: "We are now heading for Okinawa." His entire fleet consisted of two sound destroyers; two other destroyers had survived and both of them were limping back to Japan. But before Komura's message could be transmitted, Combined Fleet canceled the entire Okinawa mission. *Hatsushimo* reversed course for home. It was Komura who had sent the first planes over Pearl Harbor—the search planes from *Chikuma*—and he had survived the last sortie of the Japanese Navy. He had seen the beginning and the end. "I've had enough," he muttered.

4.

In Tokyo that night Hajime Suzuki, the only son of the next prime minister, could not sleep. His father, who had miraculously survived the 2/26 Incident (the bullet that had pierced his heart was still lodged in his back), undoubtedly faced danger from radical young officers again. But Hajime was no longer a child and felt he should become his father's shield. Early the next morning Hajime told Suzuki that he would quit his job at the Agriculture Ministry and become his personal secretary. "Don't accompany me to death," said the admiral. "I have come a long way but you still have far to go." Hajime could not be dissuaded—personal aspirations would be meaningless in a defeated Japan.

Suzuki summoned Admiral Keisuke Okada to his house and asked him to serve as munitions minister in the new cabinet. Okada was as appalled by the suggestion (he had been retired from the Navy for seven years and remained anathema to the radical officers) as he was by the confusion in the Suzuki household. The admiral was surrounded by well-meaning amateurs who could hardly use a telephone properly, let alone help him select a cabinet. Okada phoned his son-in-law, Hisatsune Sakomizu, who had spirited him out of the Prime Minister's (Okada's) official residence in 1936. "I am now at Admiral Suzuki's, helping him form a cabinet," he began. Sakomizu, with his shrewd grasp of both politics and the military, was "the only one" who could prevent Suzuki from making disastrous mistakes. Within the hour Sakomizu left his post at the Finance Ministry to become cabinet secretary.

Suzuki's greatest strength was a conviction that he was best qualified to end the war, but he had not yet made up his mind how to go about it. If he announced such a "defeatist" policy, even to his cabinet, he would be forced out of office or assassinated. For a while he would have to play *haragei* (the "stomach game"), that is, to dissemble, to support the war while seeking peace. As a result, Konoye refused a cabinet post when Suzuki would not give any assurance that he would "work for peace." On the other hand, he was quick to promise Marshal Sugiyama that he would carry on the war to its ultimate end, and moreover, told reporters, "Now is the time for every one of the hundred million people to cast away what holds them down and to become the glorious shields for the defense of the national structure. I, of course, will deal with the national administration and am prepared to fall as the spearhead of you, the people. I ask you, the people, to manifest a new fighting power with the courageous and furious will to drive ahead over my body, and thus to put the Imperial Mind at ease."

At the time, Suzuki did not reveal his stratagem to anyone, but his son, Hajime, intuitively understood his father and informed close friends, in a written announcement, of his true intentions.

The Cabinet was invested on April 7, though the most significant position, that of foreign minister, had not been filled. The other selections had been based on advice by fellow *jushin* and Sakomizu, but after considerable thought Suzuki's preference for the man who would have to engineer peace negotiations was Shigenori Togo. Investigation indicated that Togo, who had held the post at the time of Pearl Harbor, had opposed going to war and later resigned in opposition to Tojo's "dictatorial and high-handed policies."

Togo was rusticating in Karuizawa, the favorite resort town of diplomats near the Japanese Alps, when he got a phone call from a go-between—the governor of Nagano Prefecture—transmitting Suzuki's offer. Togo's reply was blunt: Not until he had discussed the matter with the new Prime Minister and "reached an agreement of views." He would not return to public life unless he had a free hand. In Tokyo, however, he found Suzuki unwilling to abandon *haragei*, even in a confidential conversation with someone who shared his own views. "I assume you took office with some definite things in mind," Togo told him in his heavy Kyushu accent, "since it will be anything but easy to manage the affairs of state now, with the war effort in its last throes."

Suzuki's answer could not have alienated Togo more: "I

think that we can still carry on the war for another two or three years."

Togo declined the post. "Even if I felt able to accept the grave responsibility of our diplomacy, the Prime Minister and I would be unable to co-operate effectively so long as we held divergent views on the prospects for the war."

But the matter did not end there. Too many others saw Togo as an advocate for peace and each in turn brought pressure upon him. Within twenty-four hours he was importuned by half a dozen leaders, including two *jushin* and the Emperor's chief adviser. Admiral Okada, for instance, argued that Suzuki's policy was not "necessarily rigid" and Togo could "help mold it," and Okada's son-in-law, Sakomizu, excused Suzuki: it would have been too hazardous for him to speak of an early peace at their initial meeting. "Such language, coming from one in the Prime Minister's position and in those circumstances, might have had undesirable repercussions."

Togo could not understand such circuity. If Suzuki had agreed with him about peace, why couldn't he have let him know in their private conversation? If Suzuki did not even trust the man he wanted as foreign minister, how could they possibly co-operate in the critical days ahead?

The next appeal came from the office of the Privy Seal. Matsudaira, Kido's chief secretary, revealed that the Emperor himself was hoping the war would end. This concerted effort brought Togo a second time to Suzuki, who now realized he must be more candid. "So far as the outcome of the war is concerned," he told Togo, "your views are quite satisfactory to me. And as to diplomacy, you shall have a free hand."

Togo remained reluctant. He demanded assurance that the Cabinet would support peace negotiations if a study showed that the war could not be continued for three more years at least. Suzuki dropped all pretense. Without qualification he accepted Togo's condition. To the rest of the world, however, the admiral continued *haragei*, pretending to be as dedicated to a fight to the bitter end as a Tojo.

5.

After a week on Okinawa, the two American Army divisions pressing south had still encountered nothing but enemy outposts and were far ahead of schedule.

Admiral Turner was so confident that he radioed Nimitz at noon on April 8:

I MAY BE CRAZY BUT IT LOOKS LIKE THE JAPS HAVE QUIT THE WAR, AT LEAST IN THIS SECTION.

DELETE ALL AFTER "CRAZY" was Nimitz' sardonic reply. The Army troops were about to encounter the formidable defense system above Shuri. Here the island was four miles wide, a series of rolling limestone hills pocked with natural caves, dotted with burial tombs and broken by terraces, escarpments and ravines. Since the hills ran generally from east to west, the Americans faced successive natural lines of defense.

That afternoon, persistent enemy fire brought Buckner's east flank to a complete halt while his west flank was delayed by a hill mass extending east for a thousand yards from the coast to Highway 5, a road running through the middle of the defense system all the way down to Shuri. This land elevation was Kakazu Ridge, two hills connected by a saddle. It didn't look like much of an obstacle, for it was neither high nor jagged, merely a squat hump covered with grass, brush and small trees.

But this chunky, ugly hill was one of the keys of the Shuri defense, and when the Americans stormed up to its crest on the morning of April 9 they were met by a spirited defense. By late afternoon, out of ammunition and their ranks decimated, they fell back. The next two days were a bloody stalemate as the Americans on both flanks repeatedly attacked and were thrown back.

It was the battle Ushijima wanted, but being on the defense rankled his impatient subordinates; they had persuaded him, against his better judgment, to approve a six-battalion assault the following night, April 12, in conjunction with another mass *kamikaze* raid. The 22nd Regiment (of the 62nd Division) would attack on the left, and on the evening of the eleventh its commander, Lieutenant Colonel Masaru Yoshida, who had been in Okinawa less than a month, assembled his officers to outline the mission. "You will be traveling in darkness over bad roads and under heavy shelling; the secrecy of our plans must be maintained to the last. March in a sinuous 'eel line.' Although you are going to an unfamiliar place, do not make any noise when you arrive, but dig *takotsubo* in hard ground and camouflage them skillfully by dawn tomorrow."

It was raining heavily as the men, toting 110-lb. packs, started toward the front on the muddy roads.

Early the following morning 185 *kamikaze*, accompanied by 150 fighters and 45 torpedo planes, began assaulting the ships around Okinawa. Then came 8 two-engine bombers; underneath them hung a new weapon, the *oka* (cherry blossom) bomb. Powered by three booster rockets, this one-way glider looked like a torpedo with small wings, and the pilot could dive its ton of tri-nitro-anisol explosives at more than 500 knots.* The new suicide weapon was nicknamed *baka*

---

*There were other suicidal measures, but all were relatively unsuccessful. Miniature submarines, which received so much publicity, were involved in six verified raids: Pearl Harbor; Sydney Harbor, May 31, 1942; the Guadalcanal area, November 23 and December 7, 1942; off Madagascar, May 31, 1942; and west of the Mindanao Sea, January 5, 1945. Twenty-eight submariners died and insignificant damage was inflicted. A new two-man submarine, *Kairyu* (Sea Dragon), with a range of 250 miles and a payload of two aviation-type torpedoes, was in production. By the end of the war there were 230, but not one was used.

Another notable failure was the *kaiten* (turn toward Heaven), a human torpedo which was brought close to the target on the deck of a conventional submarine. An early model penetrated the Ulithi lagoon and sank the oiler *Mississinewa* carrying 400,000 gallons of aviation gas. This success spurred improvements, and the final *kaiten* model was fifty-four feet long and carried a warhead of 3,000 pounds of high explosives. Such a charge, the inventors claimed, could sink any warship afloat, and a submarine carrying four *kaiten* on its back could approach a U. S. anchorage and sink four large ships in a single attack. That was the prophecy and hope. Hundreds of *kaiten* were launched against Allied vessels but they sent only one more to the bottom, the merchant vessel *Canada Victory*. The destroyer escort, *Underhill*, was hit by a *kaiten*, then sunk accidentally by friendly forces. Almost nine hundred Japanese died in the *kaiten* program.

Equally futile was Operation Flying Elephant, an ambitious program to launch thousands of large hydrogen balloons, equipped with incendiary bombs, against the heavily wooded northwest section of the United States. Over Japan the balloons would be caught up in the jet stream at 33,000 feet and travel eastward at 120 miles an hour, reaching Washington, Oregon or Montana in approximately forty-eight hours. The balloons, which had a lifting power of 300 kilograms at sea level, were manufactured in a number of Tokyo movie theaters and a *sumo* stadium by a work force of paperhangers, schoolgirls and women from the *iromachi* (red-light districts). The balloons were fashioned out of rice paper strengthened with *konnyaku* (devil's-tongue root, an important ingredient in sukiyaki); the entire *konnyaku* crop was requisitioned. Each balloon required 600 strips of paper, pasted together to form a sphere. Several million workers were involved in the production of 10,000 balloons. On November 1, 1944, the commanders of the launching sites in Chiba, Ibaraki and Fukushima prefectures were ordered to "initiate the attacks on North America!" A staff officer was dispatched

("stupid") bomb by the Americans, but it didn't lessen the terror it spread instantly throughout the fleet. At about 2:45 P.M. one dropped from the belly of its mother ship and arrowed into the destroyer *Mannert L. Abele*, which had just been staggered by a *kamikaze* hit. The ship jackknifed in two and sank almost instantly. Another *oka* exploded on the destroyer *Stanly*. In the meantime, *kamikaze* and conventional planes sank *LCS(L)-33* and damaged a battleship, three destroyers and eight other ships.

The assault on the ground was less successful. It opened with a concentrated artillery and mortar barrage, which lifted at midnight. Japanese infantrymen began infiltrating into the American positions, but the glare of NGF star shells caught them in the open and within an hour the counterattack faltered. For the first time Warrant Officer Kaname Imai of the 22nd Regiment, the son of a Shinto priest, heard the word "retreat" from his battalion commander. He repeated it, but his men stood uncomprehending. "After me!" called Imai and started trotting forward as if on the attack. His men followed and so did several other platoons, as he swung back to the rear.

In Warm Springs, Georgia, it was still April 12. After lunch President Roosevelt sat for a water-color portrait at the clapboard cottage called the Little White House, two miles from the Warm Springs Foundation. At 1:15 P.M. he closed his eyes and said quietly, "I have a terrific headache." He slumped over unconscious.

Dr. James Paullin, former president of the American Medical Association, arrived, after a two-hour race over back roads, to find the President "in a cold sweat, ashy gray and breathing with difficulty." His pulse was barely perceptible and four minutes later his heart sounds disappeared completely. Dr. Paullin gave him an intracardiac dose of adrenalin. The President's heart beat a few times, then stopped forever. It was 3:55 P.M.

The Nazis looked upon his death as a last-minute reprieve from defeat. "Fate has laid low your greatest enemy. God has not abandoned us," Goebbels feverishly told Hitler over the phone. "Twice he has saved you from savage assassins. Death, which the enemy aimed at you in 1939 and 1944, has

---

to the Ise Shrine to pray for success. In the next six months 9,300 balloons were released into the jet stream. The results were disappointing: a few minor forest fires were started in the Pacific Northwest.

now struck down our most dangerous enemy. It is a miracle!"

Japan's new leader, on the other hand, did not rejoice. Prime Minister Suzuki broadcast his condolences to the American people, expressing his "profound sympathy" over the loss of a man who was responsible for the "Americans' advantageous position today."* Japanese propagandists did take advantage of the situation, however, to promote a story that Roosevelt had died in anguish—and altered his last words from "I have a terrific headache" to "I have made a terrific mistake."

Otherwise little attention was devoted to Roosevelt's death except on editorial pages. "It is Heaven's punishment," said the *Mainichi*. "As the incarnation of American imperialism, he has had a cursed influence on the whole of mankind." The *Asahi Shimbun* quoted Admiral Nomura, who had worked so hard for peace in Washington, as saying, "This may be a foolish thing, but I had a dream four or five days ago. I was at the White House and when I went into Roosevelt's room there was a coffin there. The adjutant pointed to the coffin and told me Roosevelt was in there. This dream has come true. But no matter who dies, the American war drive will undergo no change and we must be determined to fight it out to the finish."

The news reached Okinawa at dawn on the thirteenth. "Attention! Attention! All hands!" loudspeakers blasted on American ships. "President Roosevelt is dead. Repeat, our Supreme Commander, President Roosevelt, is dead." There was shock amounting to disbelief, and Admiral Turner was compelled to issue official confirmation. Beyond the grief loomed new concerns. Would his death affect the conduct of the war? Would his successor, Harry Truman, also demand unconditional surrender?

Japanese Army propagandists on Okinawa, taking a cue from the homeland, printed leaflets which linked the President's demise with the fate of the Americans on the island.

We must express our deep regret over the death of President Roosevelt. The "American Tragedy" is now raised here at Okinawa with his death. You must have seen 70% of your CVs [aircraft carriers] and 73% of your Bs [battleships] sink or be damaged causing 150,000 casualties. Not only the late President but anyone

---

*Suzuki's broadcast was not reported in the Japanese press, and even his son knew nothing of it until after the war.

else would die in the excess of worry to hear such an annihilative damage. The dreadful loss that led your late leader to death will make you orphans of this island. The Japanese special attack corps will sink your vessels to the last destroyer. You will witness it realized in the near future.

One GI looked up from the leaflet as blasts of gunfire from American ships reverberated from Nakagusuku Bay and exclaimed, "Where the hell do they think that stuff's coming from?"

Few Japanese shared Goebbels' illusion that Roosevelt's death presaged a turn in the tide of war. Territories they had conquered in the first months of the conflict had been retaken or were falling. Nowhere was this more evident than in the Philippines. Yamashita still held his northern redoubt, but MacArthur was firmly entrenched on western Mindanao and was preparing a full-scale sweep across the island.

General Sosaku Suzuki had been forced to abandon Leyte to join the 743 men who had already been evacuated to Cebu. Almost all of the 12,000 or so left behind, including General Makino of the 16th Division, were fated to die—by starvation, suicide or at the hands of the enemy. Americans had already landed on Cebu by the time Suzuki reached the capital, and he decided to chance the perilous trip to Mindanao, where there were almost two full divisions of able-bodied troops as well as 12,000 Japanese civilians. Why not gather all these people in the mountains northwest of Davao? There they would be able to fight off the enemy indefinitely, and moreover, establish a self-sufficient society, intermarrying with the natives. It would be a paradise with absolutely no discrimination. His enthusiasm was shared by General Tomochika, his chief of staff. Between them they drew up a constitution and picked a temporary name for the "dream nation"—the Suzuki Kingdom.

"In case I die en route," Suzuki told Tomochika just before they embarked in five *bancas* on April 10, "you must take my place as Thirty-fifth Army commander and carry on our project." He memorialized the ordeal they faced with a poem:

> Do not starve to death,
> Go into the fields;
> Even though we die bravely,
> It will not stop the forward advance,
> For I am the commander,
> And fortunately I am still able to serve;
> Give me many glories.

It took six days for the little flotilla, often beset by storms, to reach southern Negros. With dark they set out on the last long lap, across the open water to Mindanao. There was no wind and the tide ran against them, but resolute paddling brought them to the main current. All but Suzuki's boat were swept into the Mindanao Sea, and by ten o'clock they were far ahead out of sight. Exhausted, Suzuki and his companions could no longer best the current, and their *banca* drifted back toward Negros. In the morning an American plane discovered them near a lighthouse.

"Jump!" cried the general's aide, First Lieutenant Tokujo Watano, and leaped over the side. But Suzuki remained in the *banca*. As bullets ripped up the water toward the dugout, Watano saw his general, sword in hand, lean over as if committing hara-kiri. It was the end of Suzuki and of his dream kingdom.*

29   The Iron Typhoon

1.

On the day of Roosevelt's death Kantaro Suzuki's Cabinet authorized the organization of a Volunteer Army of men from fifteen to fifty-five and women from seventeen to forty-five for the mainland battle. Newspapers continued to write confidently of Okinawa, whose fall would necessitate the use of the volunteers. "The enemy did the very thing we expected when we were working out the details of our plans for dealing with him," said a retired admiral named Endo. "The strategy under which we have allowed the enemy to invade the Okinawan islands has much in common with the strategy of fighting with our backs to the wall. We could not resort to this strategy unless we were fully conscious of our power to thrust at the enemy's vitals while letting him thrust at our less vital parts."

But General Ushijima's 32nd Army had already been dealt a more grievous wound. In two weeks of fighting, almost seven thousand of its best troops had fallen, and although the

---

*Only Tomochika's boat reached Mindanao, and shortly the island was dominated by MacArthur. "What started as a dream," Tomochika later remarked, "ended in a nightmare."

Shuri line was holding, Marines had overrun the northern half of the island—which was defended by two battalions—except for Motobu Peninsula. On April 16 they seized Yaetake, a rugged 1,200-foot peak which dominated the peninsula, after an arduous three-day struggle, virtually ending the campaign in northern Okinawa.

A few miles west of the peninsula lay Ie Shima, an oval-shaped island five miles long, flat except for an extinct volcano which rose dramatically 600 feet near the center where the last Japanese troops in the area were garrisoned. Occupation of the island was assigned to the Army, and at eight o'clock that same morning, after a naval bombardment, GI's clambered over the high dunes toward the airfield, the main objective of the invasion. On their approach to the volcano they encountered a maze of tunnels, bunkers, caves and spider holes. From these positions the outnumbered garrison, buttressed by hundreds of civilian volunteers, gave the 77th Division the toughest opposition yet.

Ernie Pyle temporarily left the Marines on Okinawa to be with the GI's, for whom he had a special affinity. On April 18 he was on his way up front in a jeep with a regimental commander when the road was swept by machine-gun bullets. Pyle, a frail little man, leaped into a ditch. As he raised his head to get a look, he was hit in the temple. He died instantly and was buried nearby.*

Back on Okinawa the Marines sat around that evening reciting favorite passages from his columns. "It seems a shame such a big guy had to get it on such a lousy little island," said a corporal. They checked his bedroll, which he had left behind. It contained a single personal item—a chain of colored sea shells. They wrapped it and forwarded it to Pyle's widow, "That Girl."

North of the Shuri line the Army had been readying a general attack on its defense system. "It is going to be really tough," predicted Major General John Hodge, commander of XXIV Corps. "There are sixty-five to seventy thousand fighting Japs holed up in the south end of the island, and I

---

*Today a monument marks the place. It reads: "At this spot the 77th Infantry Division lost a buddy, Ernie Pyle, 18 April 1945." "More than any other man," President Truman eulogized, "he became the spokesman of the ordinary American in arms doing so many extraordinary things."

see no way to get them out except blast them out yard by yard."

The Navy was brought in to help. At five-forty the next morning six battleships, six cruisers and eight destroyers began bombarding the five-mile defense complex extending across the island. Twenty minutes later, twenty-seven battalions of artillery—324 pieces in all—sounded off, digging up front-line positions before lifting 500 yards to the rear. At six-thirty the artillery lowered, splattering the front lines for another ten minutes. It was the greatest single concentration of artillery in Pacific warfare—19,000 shells.

The artillery elevated once more while assault platoons of two divisions, the 7th in the east and the 96th in the center, rushed forward. Fifty minutes later another division, the 27th, assaulted Kakazu Ridge on the west end of the line.

Incredibly, the unprecedented bombardment left the Japanese relatively intact, and though all three units attacked aggressively, all three were thrown back. Casualties were high, particularly in the 27th Division sector, where twenty-two tanks were destroyed in futile charges against formidable Kakazu Ridge. By late afternoon XXIV Corps had lost 720 dead, wounded and missing. During the next four days the two divisions on the flanks made negligible gains in slow, grinding advances, but the GI's of the 96th did manage to drive forward more than 1,000 yards—only to face the heart of the Shuri defenses, a rugged little escarpment that stuck up like a segment of the Great Wall of China. This was Maeda Ridge, which, with its forbidding sheer cliffs, proved to be a fortress in fact as well as in appearance. The GI's were promptly repelled. General Buckner, the Tenth Army commander, rejected a proposal to make an amphibious landing behind the Japanese lines: the reefs in the south were too dangerous, the beaches inadequate for supplies, and any beachhead could be contained by the multitude of Japanese in the area.

Buckner's reasoning was logical—but incorrect. Much as Ushijima feared such a maneuver ("It would bring a prompt end to the fighting"), he was compelled to transfer his rear-guard division north to beef up the Shuri line. These replacements began marching up front at night, and by the evening of April 25 most of them were in position to relieve the casualty-ridden defenders. They arrived in time to face the brunt of a renewed American attack on Maeda. It too failed. One company of the 96th Division scaled up to the top at a prohibitive cost of eighteen casualties in minutes.

Another company formed a human chain to breast the ridge, but the three key men at the top were cut down by machine-gun bullets.

To their left, at the eastern terminus of Maeda, GI's gained the tops of two rolling hills and caught more than five hundred Japanese out in the open at the very moment when American tanks and armored flamethrowers rolled up High-

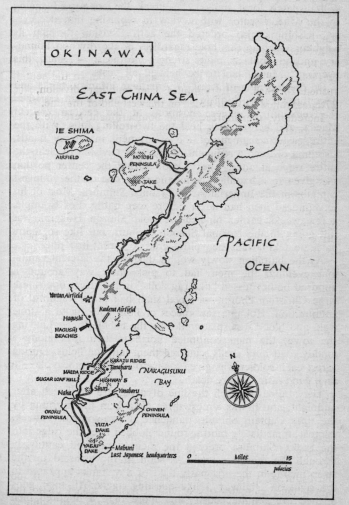

way 5, which curved around the end of the ridge. The cross fire annihilated the Japanese.

Fearing that the enemy might break through in force and come up behind the escarpment, Ushijima sent a curt directive to 62nd Division: "The enemy with troops following tanks has been advancing into the southern and eastern sectors of Maeda since about 1300. The 62nd Division will dispatch local units . . . attack the enemy advancing in the Maeda sector with a view to repulsing him decisively." Ushijima also ordered the 24th Division to help its neighbors seal up this hole regardless of the division boundary and to "put its main strength northeast of Shuri this evening." Maeda had to be held at all costs.

On the morning of April 27 American infantry, tanks and flamethrowers, working in close co-operation, again assaulted the remaining Japanese positions at the eastern end of Maeda, and before dusk held the two rolling hills. With the entire eastern segment of the escarpment in enemy hands, Ushijima ordered a regiment of the 24th Division to clear the entire ridge at once. The task of seizing the center portion was given to a battalion commanded by one of the youngest captains in the Imperial Army, Tsuneo Shimura. Most of his six hundred men had never before seen battle. For example, a few weeks earlier nineteen-year-old Shuzen Hokama was still going to the Normal School in Shuri, but like so many patriotic Okinawans he volunteered for front-line duty.

As the battalion slowly wound through the ancient capital that evening, the men had to pick their way around a hundred bodies tossed "like rag dolls" in the street opposite a large Christian church—a naval shell had hit a wagonful of ammunition. Hokama saw pieces of flesh sticking to a stone wall, and blood was splattered over the cobblestones. Leaving the town, the men continued north in two files along a muddy road until shells scattered them into the fields. During a rest each soldier was given a slice of canned pineapple—"a final good taste" before death.

They failed to reach the line of departure until well after midnight, and it was almost three o'clock in the morning by the time Captain Shimura launched a two-company attack. Almost immediately mortar rounds lobbed over the ridge into the ranks. Shimura ordered the men to proceed cautiously through the mortar screen. As soon as they started up the steep incline in the first pasty light of day, tanks appeared to the right on Highway 5 like questing tigers. All their guns opened fire simultaneously, and more than a hundred men were killed in the first moments. The survivors took cover in Chinese tombs and rude air shelters, or behind rocks. Shimura and seven others found safety in a tomb, where they hid for the rest of the day.

The tanks finally departed with the last rays of sunlight. Shimura emerged to find one third of his men dead, but Regiment still insisted that he take the cliffs that night. He marked his back with white strips and led his men forward along a dry streambed. Halfway up the incline he stumbled across a camouflaged opening. Crouched inside the cave were fifty men—the remnants of the Kaya Detachment. Armed only with a few rifles, they had been driven off the escarpment. Shimura's entrance was greeted with exclamations and tears. Colonel Kaya embraced Shimura with relief. "From now on I'm leaving everything up to you," he said. He wouldn't discuss the battle or what he knew of the enemy's positions; instead he proffered a cup of *sake,* which the captain refused.

Shimura left the cave in disgust and brought his men to the lip of the crest. They remained hidden until dawn, when they suddenly launched grenades, and under cover of fire from light machine guns burst over the edge, screeching and brandishing their glistening bayonets. Their momentum carried them to the summit of the ridge, a jutting piece of limestone that resembled a castle turret—it had already been nicknamed "Needle Rock" by the GI's. Here they overran the handful of Americans at the center of the escarpment, and then spread out along a front of two hundred yards, positioning themselves behind rocks or in small caves. Their quick success was due as much to their élan as to the debilitating struggle that had seesawed along the ridge for four days. The American units facing them had been reduced to about 40 percent combat efficiency, and some platoons were down to half a dozen men.

The fighting near the west coast was not as fierce as that on the escarpment but had been almost as costly to both sides. The next day, April 30, the 1st Marine Division began relieving the 27th Infantry Division, which had suffered 2,661 casualties in less than two weeks. Down the line of Marines slouching ahead the word was passed: "Doggies coming back." The Marines straightened up and smartly raised weapons to their shoulders. But the GI's (to one Marine they looked "dirty and dispirited, turned into zombies") ignored their parading replacements. A passing Marine made a sarcastic remark but was silenced by his comrades; perhaps they would come out the same way—those who survived.

Fresh Army troops were also moved up to Maeda Ridge. Time and again GI's, carrying satchel charges, scaled the heights with ropes and grapnels but were repeatedly driven back by the Japanese, who emerged from an intricate network of caves. Shimura held his positions near Needle Rock against a dozen resolute assaults, and his defense was so impressive that Regiment ordered him to go on the attack himself. That night he was to retake the first rolling hummock to his right, called Satan Hill by the Japanese. He sent the 5th Company. The men reached the hill soon after midnight and sent up flares to signal that they had taken the objective. But since they could not dig *takotsubo* in the rocky soil, they were caught unprotected at first light and were annihilated to the last man.

The enemy soldiers had been on the island for a month and their number had grown to 170,000. Okinawa had been transformed into a Little America. Roads had been widened and improved—to accommodate the tens of thousands of vehicles that swarmed ashore—supply dumps set up, antiaircraft guns emplaced, and phone service established linking all Army and Navy installations.

The Japanese, who had been taught to despise the Americans, were impressed by their rational way of fighting. They were dressed sensibly, had endless quantities of ammunition and food, and seemed to turn war into an adventure. Even the enemy's tattoos intrigued the Japanese.

In a cave a hundred feet beneath the ancient Shuri Castle, where Commodore Perry had been received in state by the King of Okinawa almost a century before, Ushijima's chief of staff, Lieutenant General Isamu Cho, vociferously demanded another all-out counterattack. He was a hearty man who smoked and drank to excess. His Army career—like that of Tsuji—had been studded with acts of *gekokujo*. He had participated in the abortive Brocade Flag Revolution of 1931. Afterward he was transferred to Manchuria, where his penchant for intrigue prolonged the border fighting with Russia at Changkufeng in 1938. His temper was short, and it was not unusual for him to slap his orderly, his aide or a junior officer in a line unit. Now arguing with Ushijima, he brandished his long cigarette holder as if it were a weapon.

Ushijima listened politely. He often exhibited such deference that it made those around him uneasy—with the exception of Cho, whose present belligerence had been aggravated by the *sake* they had all consumed in the past hour. Ushijima's reservations were supported only by his operations officer, who alone debated Cho's repeated demands for a decisive strike. Colonel Hiromichi Yahara—a grim-faced man with the nickname "Sobersides"—refused to be intimidated. "To take the offensive with inferior forces against overwhelmingly superior enemy forces is reckless and will lead to early defeat." Moreover, he went on, they would have to attack an enemy which held commanding ground. The sensible course was to continue current operations. He thought annihilation was inevitable, but invaluable time could be won for Imperial Headquarters by a strategic holding action. A counterattack would at best inflict light casualties on the enemy, and thousands of His Majesty's troops would be sacrificed in vain. But the Japanese instinct to attack when cornered was irrepressible. The commander of the 62nd Division sprang to his feet and aggressively backed Cho, as did the other division and brigade commanders who had been frustrated by the defensive tactics forced upon them. With misgivings, Ushijima ordered the offensive to begin in two days.

It was a complicated and ambitious plan—co-ordinated with another massive *kamikaze* attack on shipping and supported by tactical bombers—to drive a wedge five miles north into the American lines. Two regiments, their way cleared by a heavy artillery barrage, would start the assault east of Highway 5 while a third stormed down from Maeda Ridge, and with considerable tank support press on along the highway to the heights beyond. The 44th Independent Mixed Brigade would follow for half a mile before turning left toward the west coast. To mislead the enemy there would also be two amphibious landings behind the American lines, one on the west coast and the other on the east coast.

At dusk on May 3, artillery began to pound enemy frontline positions, and *kamikaze* planes struck at U. S. shipping, sinking the destroyer *Little* and *LSM-195*, and damaging four other ships. Just after midnight an attack by sixty conventional bombers on Tenth Army's rear areas coincided with the two amphibious forces' advance up the coasts in barges. The western unit mistakenly landed near a Marine company. Alerted by shouts of *"Banzai!"* the Marines turned on the surprised Japanese a murderous mortar barrage and concentrated machine-gun and rifle fire. The few who escaped were hunted down and killed. The sole captive was a carrier pigeon. It was released carrying a typical Marine taunt: "We are returning your pigeon. Sorry we cannot return your demolition engineers." The amphibious force plowing up the east coast was sighted by a naval patrol which illuminated the area with star shells. Most of the barges were destroyed, and the score of men who made it to shore were eliminated.

An hour before dawn the Japanese artillery barrage reached a deafening climax which continued for half an hour. Then two red flares shot up: the signal to attack. Japanese infantrymen surged forward pell-mell. On the right, two thousand were soon caught in the open terrain by American artillery. Those who survived tried to forge ahead but were systematically picked off on the exposed flatland.

The successful outcome of the assault in the center was dependent on armored support. But since accurate enemy artillery fire had immobilized all the medium tanks, no more than nine light ones managed to pull behind the spearhead, Captain Koichi Ito's 600-man battalion. Ito's troops pierced the American lines in the predawn gloom but were pinned down by automatic weapons fire. The nine tanks tried to close up but artillery found their range one by one. Ito decided to go on without tank support and led his scattered battalion toward the first objective, a hill mass one mile northeast of Maeda near the town of Tanabaru.

Fragmentary reports reaching 32nd Army headquarters later in the morning claimed impressive victories and touched off celebrations in the cave under the wreckage of Shuri Castle. However, no one but Ito had made a substantial breakthrough, and he was ordered to assault the hill above Tanabaru that night. With his men he pushed ahead along either side of Highway 5 until they were blocked by enemy shells. Since Ito now had armored support—the tanks had come up under cover of darkness—he was able to continue. Six tanks were destroyed during the fierce fire fights that followed, but Ito and his men covered the long, arduous mile through the American lines to Tanabaru. He mined the road running through town and by dawn had set up a perimeter defense on the slope of the hill. Then he radioed in the clear—his code men were dead—that he and almost 450 of his troops had reached the objective. He was ordered to stay in place.

By noon of May 5 it was obvious even to the blustery Cho that the counterattack, which he had fathered, had failed. Now he saw no hope at all for Okinawa; defeat was certain.

Ito was still lodged above Tanabaru but he was under

constant pressure from all sides. During the day a hundred more of his detachment had been killed by flamethrowers, mortars and grenades. The next morning the American assaults continued and were repulsed by sacrificial measures. There were now fewer than 150 of the 600 men who had started the offensive, and Ito was preparing himself for death when a message wrapped around a rock hurtled into his *takotsubo*. It was from his radioman: an order had just been received to fall back. On taking leave of the wounded, he distributed grenades among them before he assembled his able-bodied men at the foot of the hill. At midnight they moved south in the darkness but the one mile of enemy territory took its toll. Only Ito and a dozen others broke through.

The Japanese had struck with every resource they could muster but were easily crushed by Hodge's XXIV Corps. The success coincided with a much more significant achievement. At high noon on May 8 every American artillery piece and naval gun fired three volleys—Germany had surrendered.

Defeating the Japanese in an open, wasteful charge was one thing, but dislodging them from dug-in defenses was devastating. Maeda Ridge had turned into a bloody version of "King of the Hill," with first one side holding the crest and then the other. One GI battalion, the 1st of the 307th Infantry Regiment, lost more than half its men in eight days, including eight company commanders in a thirty-six-hour period.

The Japanese losses were far more grievous. Young Captain Shimura, for example, had once had 600 men on the ridge line; now there were fewer than 150 left and most of them were severely wounded. Still he refused to withdraw on order; he wanted to die where most of his men had been killed. Regiment insisted that he was to fall back, and a staff officer of the 24th Division sent a personal message in code with the argument that he would "find other suitable battlefields to die on." Shimura told his men of the order but he was going to remain as a guerrilla. "Those who wish to stay with me, can. We'll stick it out here on this ridge until we die." Some of the men went underground and the rest withdrew, leaving Maeda Ridge to the Americans.

With the fall of Maeda the American offensive slowly ground forward all across the island. Two full Marine divisions (III Amphibious Corps) now held the western flank: after an arduous battle the 6th had seized Sugar Loaf Hill, the western anchor of the entire defense line, less than a mile from Shuri, and the 1st Division, which had been in battle since Guadalcanal, advanced through Wana Draw, a narrow, rocky passage leading to the center of the former capital. Farther east, all the way to the coast, the three divisions of XXIV Corps, advancing slowly, captured Chocolate Drop, Flattop and other hills just east of Shuri. By dusk on May 21 the city itself was invested from three sides but as darkness overtook the fighting, so did torrential rains. Wana Draw became a swamp. Tanks and amphibian tractors churned helplessly in mud. All along the front, foxholes carved out of the clay slopes began to disintegrate, and those on lower ground had to be bailed constantly like leaky boats. For almost a full week the downpour continued. Little food could be brought up front; sleep in the constant deluge was impossible; the dead could not be buried and were left to decompose.

The respite granted him by the rain notwithstanding, General Ushijima decided to abandon Shuri. More than sixty thousand of his troops had been killed in the bloody defense of the city. The 62nd and 24th divisions and the 44th Independent Mixed Brigade—the heart of his army—had been shattered by relentless enemy naval gunfire, artillery fire and bombings, as well as infantry and tank assaults. He overrode protests against any retreat, however localized, on the grounds that an attempt to make a stand at Shuri would accelerate the fall of Okinawa.

2.

In the May issue of the commercial magazine *Jitsugyo-no-Nippon*, Rear Admiral Etsuzo Kurihara wrote:

Some people favor the method of letting the enemy cut our skin while we cut the enemy's body, and of letting him cut our body while we cut his bone. I am opposed to such a calculating strategy. Rather, I am in favor of letting the enemy cut our bone while we cut the enemy's bone. Each Japanese can do this. This method will give rise to a great tenacity among our people. This is the tactics of our Special Attack Corps.

Kamikaze tactics had been tried against the Americans since the battle for Leyte Gulf, but at Okinawa they became an integral part of the defense. Since the Easter landing six massive *kamikaze* attacks, involving more than fifteen hundred planes, had been loosed at the hundreds of American vessels concentrated around the island. Several hundred of these planes had careened through dense flak and exploded on their targets, sending to the bottom almost a score of American ships and seriously damaging some twenty-five others. Grim as the figures were, they did not tell the true story of death, terror and heroism on either side. It was blood-curdling to watch a plane aim relentlessly at your ship, its pilot resolved to blast you and himself to hell.

The seventh *kamikaze* raid, on May 25, co-ordinated with Ushijima's withdrawal from Shuri and was preceded by a suicide unit of saboteurs which was brought by five bombers to Yontan Airfield in central Okinawa. Four of the two-engine planes were shot down, but the fifth made a belly-landing on the field. Americans watched incredulous as its occupants disgorged and scattered to the flight line lobbing grenades and incendiaries into parked planes. Seven aircraft were destroyed, twenty-six others damaged, and two fuel dumps containing 70,000 gallons of gasoline set ablaze before the raiders were killed.

Offshore, *kamikaze* were already sweeping in toward the transport area, and in the next twelve hours 176 Special Attack planes bored in on their targets. They sank *LSM-135* and the destroyer escort *Bates*. Four other ships had to be scuttled, scrapped or decommissioned as a result of damage.

The fanaticism of these fliers was frightening to Americans in its finality, yet "there was a hypnotic fascination to a sight so alien to our Western philosophy," Vice Admiral C. R. Brown observed. "We watched each plunging *kamikaze* with the detached horror of one witnessing a terrible spectacle rather than as the intended victim. We forgot self for the moment as we groped hopelessly for the thought of that other man up there." Out of this almost morbid fascination came a welter of theories and rumors: *kamikaze* fliers went into battle like priests in hooded robes; they were drugged; they had to be chained to their cockpits; they were an elite group trained from youth for suicide. They were, in fact, average young Japanese who were volunteers. Their goal was to die a meaningful death and they were convinced that the Special Attack system was the best possible way to overcome Japan's inferior productivity vis-à-vis America. One man could damage or sink a carrier or battleship and take a thousand enemies with him.

Ensign Yasunori Aoki, born in Tokyo twenty-two years earlier, believed in their slogan: "One plane, one warship."

His love of nature had led him to Agricultural and Forestry College on Formosa. Faced with conscription, he joined the Imperial Navy "for its glamor," learned to fly, and by early 1945 was an instructor at Kochi on the island of Shikoku. There, volunteers were sought for the Special Attack Corps. Each flier, instructor as well as student, was told to write his name on a piece of paper. Those who wished to volunteer would place a circle above their name; those who declined a triangle. There was no coercion and several unhesitatingly drew triangles, but Aoki felt it would be cowardly. Besides, since no one would survive the war, he preferred to die as a flier; he might even sink a ship.

The volunteers were trained to skim the water at 30 feet, then climb and fire at a control tower. They flew the *Shiragiku* (White Chrysanthemum), a slow, bulky, two-seat trainer. Aoki, as commander of his plane, became its navigator, although, in his opinion, one was not needed; but without a superior in the second seat, perhaps the pilot would be tempted to turn back.

The weeks went by quickly. The training was absorbing and the mission itself was so far in the future that it seemed unreal. But once the training ended, Aoki began to realize that he was under sentence of death; the sense of doom grew as the planes were remodeled for the mission. An extra fuel tank was lashed inside the cabin, and a 250-kilogram bomb fixed to either wing. As he surveyed his own aircraft Aoki could not help thinking, This is the plane that is going to take me on a one-way trip.

On May 25 his group was transferred to Kanoya on Kyushu, a staging area for the last flight to Okinawa. The finality of his fate overwhelmed him. His comrades' appearance of serenity gave him a feeling of inferiority. At dusk Aoki watched a flight of *kamikaze* leave for Okinawa—his own group was next. He returned disconsolate to the barracks, an elementary school, where he found to his amazement half a dozen men who he thought had just taken off. Their refusal to go assuaged his own burden of shame; he could never be *that* cowardly.

The following noon he was lying in the grass watching the planes of his group being wheeled out and prepared for the mission. Suddenly the ground around him erupted; the Americans were bombing the base. Aoki didn't move. It made no difference if he was killed, he told himself; he hoped he would live in a more peaceful time in his reincarnation. But as he sauntered back to the barracks, life, which had seemed too cheap moments before, became more precious than ever. An extra day of living would be priceless; even an extra hour, a minute, a second. He stopped to watch the antics of a fly. "How lucky you are to be alive," he said aloud. After supper the group gathered for a briefing on next day's mission. Each crew was to pick its own altitude and course. The majority chose to take an indirect course to the east or west. Aoki suggested going to Okinawa direct. His pilot, a seventeen-year-old named Yokoyama, was agreeable.

They went to bed early and Aoki awoke, composed, just before dawn. I'm all right! he thought. May 27, his last day on earth, was brilliant and clear, and he felt extraordinarily refreshed and keen. He had already put aside fingernail clippings and a lock of hair for his family. Now he wrote postcards to each of his parents, his four younger sisters and his younger brother. "Our divine country will not be destroyed," he told them, and then prayed that Japan would survive total defeat.

Late that afternoon his group was given a ceremonial supper. An administrative officer proposed a toast. Aoki downed his *sake* in one gulp before noticing that his drinking friends sipped theirs. A newsreel cameraman asked the young men to pose. They donned their leather helmets decorated with the emblem of the Rising Sun; a few banded their helmets with *hachimaki*. Linking arms, they sang lustily "Doki no Sakura" ("Class of Cherry Blossoms").

At final inspection a captain stopped in front of Aoki and wondered why his face was crimson. "Don't you feel well?" It was merely the *sake*, explained Aoki. "If you don't feel well," said the captain solicitously, "you can stay behind and join a later group."

"I'm all right, sir."

The fifteen crews piled into a truck and were followed by well-wishers. At the field they incongruously slipped into life jackets emblazoned with large Rising Suns. Aoki's pockets were empty except for a picture of his family and two small wooden *omamori*, Buddhist good luck charms, which he hoped would help him achieve his mission.

Just before dusk there was a farewell ceremony conducted by a rear admiral. During his speech Aoki heard a group of staff officers at the side chatting and laughing. He bitterly resented their treating such an occasion so casually. Their chief instructor solemnly wished them success. "There is an observation post on Okinawa that will confirm the results of your mission," he said. "Tonight there is a full moon. It will be watching you, so you won't be alone. I will join you later; please wait for me." The thirty men shed tears unashamedly. They knew he wished he were going with them, and were grateful that a fellow airman had prevented their last moments on earth from being commonplace.

As the fifteen planes taxied into position, there was a flutter of handkerchiefs, caps and flags from the little crowd along the runway. Over the roar of the engines Aoki heard someone shouting, "Aoki! Aoki!" He turned in his seat. There behind the plane, chasing after him, gesticulating and weeping, was one of the pilots who had refused to take off on the previous flight. Aoki felt embarrassed and resentful; it was like being pursued by a woman. But he smiled and called out, "Follow us!" as the old trainer gathered speed and lifted off the field. Its climb prolonged the fading sunset. How beautiful! Aoki thought.

At 3,000 feet the young pilot took a course almost directly south for Tori Shima (Bird Island), which lay sixty miles west of Okinawa. Here they would turn left straight for the transport area. Ahead a single plane was veering off on its indirect course. Below was a green light marking Sada Point. This was the last light in the homeland and Aoki watched it intently until it vanished. He peered down at a small island. Streaks of white smoke curled up. Some housewife was cooking dinner for her family. He couldn't help thinking, You're living and I am going to die.

A layer of clouds forced Yokoyama to descend to 2,200 feet, but the air was so turbulent underneath that he lowered to 1,000 feet. They droned on monotonously hour after hour. The estimated time of arrival at Bird Island passed. Aoki motioned Yokoyama to continue and rechecked his watch. It was eleven-thirty. The attack was scheduled to start at midnight; they would never make it on time. After five minutes he ordered Yokoyama to turn east and start his descent. Aoki scattered tinfoil to jam enemy radar, then pulled a toggle which set the propellers on the two bombs spinning. The bombs were now armed and would explode on contact. The cloud cover above had become scattered and Aoki saw the reflection of the moon in the water. There was a flash of lightning. Another. No, some enemy ship was shooting at them. Yokoyama pulled the trainer up to 300 feet; Aoki strained to see the ship but was blinded by the angry flash of antiaircraft fire perhaps no more than a mile away. It would take a minute to reach the ship, and the ack-ack fire was becoming more accurate.

"Break right!" he ordered.

Bright streaks of fire stitched toward them. Tracers! There was a roar, and what looked like a Grumman flashed by. *Shimatta*, he thought—damn it! There was not so much as a pistol to fight it off, and if Yokoyama tried to turn away he would present an easier target. Aoki pulled open his canopy, raised himself and looked around. The Grumman was gone. He told the pilot to head back toward Okinawa. Almost immediately they came upon a destroyer cruising unconcerned in front of them in a southerly direction. "Dive!" Aoki shouted. Yokoyama had been trained to dive counterclockwise to avoid crashing into any friendly plane but now he would have to go in clockwise, something he had never done before.

Not a shot came up from the destroyer as they approached from the stern. Aoki was still out of his seat, arms crossed on the canopy, chin on arms, staring fixedly at the destroyer. He was serene as he waited for the explosion of oblivion. They were now so close that even if the American fired it would be too late. He was content; his death would be meaningful.

Neither he nor Yokoyama said a word as the lumbering old trainer roared toward the destroyer. There was a crash as they hit the water. Aoki found himself still in the plane—by a double coincidence still alive. Since Yokoyama had never before stalked a moving target, it had managed to pull out from under him. But why hadn't the bombs exploded on contact?

"*Buntaicho* [Commander], come over here!" Yokoyama was standing on top of the settling plane. Aoki heaved himself out of the cockpit just before the aircraft plunged nose first beneath the waves, and inflated the life jacket that had seemed so pointless. They were alone in the darkness—no ships, no planes.

"What shall we do?" asked Yokoyama.

Having already forsaken life, Aoki found it difficult to answer. He felt no joy whatsoever at being alive. At dawn they could distinguish a strip of land in the distance. It must be Okinawa. Aoki suggested that they swim for it, but they were cut off by an enemy destroyer. They lay motionless in the water as if dead, their arms locked together. As the destroyer pulled alongside they closed their eyes and opened their mouths. A grappling hook caught Yokoyama's trouser leg. "Kick it off!" Aoki shouted but the pilot couldn't shake loose and was hauled in like a fish, with Aoki still clutching his arm. Aoki started up the rope dangling over the side of the ship; he was caught now but would escape or commit suicide later.

"You're climbing up!" Yokoyama exclaimed, incredulous.

On deck they refused cigarettes and bread. Yokoyama glared at Aoki with resentment. They were transferred to a larger ship, and once it became obvious that escape was impossible, Aoki demonstrated to his pilot how to commit suicide by biting the tongue and choking on the blood. With tongue extended, Aoki punched his chin again and again. For all the pain, there was very little blood. Then he tried to strangle himself with a thick strand of twisted string. A guard rushed in as he was blacking out. He concluded that it was his fate to live and became a model prisoner.*

3.

On the eve of Aoki's suicidal mission, General Ushijima began withdrawing his headquarters from Shuri, along with what was left of the 62nd Division and the 27th Tank Regiment, leaving a defense shell out front. The heavy rain covered the retreat but made it a trial, particularly for the walking wounded. They had had no medicine and almost no food or water since evacuation from the front. In small groups those who could stand moved off into the drenching rain, shepherded by young Okinawan nurses who had recently attended the Normal School, and hanging onto ropes for guidance in the darkness.

The movement in the enemy rear area was not discovered by the Americans for another twenty-four hours. Then artillery and naval support ships began interdicting roads and junctions. The following day, May 27, General Buckner dispatched new instructions to III and XXIV Corps:

Indications point to possible enemy retirement to new defensive positions with possible counteroffensive against our forces threatening his flank. Initiate without delay strong and unrelenting pressure to ascertain probable intentions and keep him off balance. Enemy

---

*When Aoki returned to Japan in late 1946, he was greeted by his uncle, a lieutenant general, with joy and understanding—and for the first time Aoki was glad to be alive. "I've had two lives," he later said. "Now every moment is precious."

must not repeat not be permitted to establish himself securely on new position with only nominal interference.

Aggressive combat patrols probed along the entire Shuri front, but the shell protecting the retreat held and patrols reported there was no indication of Japanese withdrawal. Tenth Army intelligence concurred: "It now looks as though the Japanese thinks holding the line around north of Shuri is his best bet. . . . It is probable that we will gradually surround the Shuri position."

The Army predicted a siege, but the Marines would not wait. The 1st Division stormed Shuri Ridge on May 29 and found it lightly defended. They swept on to the ruins of the castle. Here the defense stiffened, but that evening the Tenth Army intelligence officer re-evaluated the situation: he was now certain that the "enemy was holding the Shuri lines with a shell, and that the bulk of the troops were elsewhere."

Behind a curtain of almost constant rain, Ushijima had escaped with most of his forces and had established new headquarters nine miles due south of Shuri Castle in a cliffside cave overlooking the rugged coast of the island. But the withdrawal had been costly to the Okinawans. In panic, hordes of civilians had fled south behind the troops and had been slaughtered by shells and bombs. Thousands were left dead along the quagmire roads.

On the last day of May, Marines and GI's cautiously entered the former capital from two sides. Shuri lay in ruins, ravaged by mortars, 1,000-lb. bombs and almost two hundred rounds of artillery and naval gunfire. Only two structures— the concrete Normal School and the Methodist church— remained. Buried in the smoldering rubble were hundreds of civilians and their scattered possessions. The stench of rotting flesh penetrated the sharp odor of smoke.

Shuri Castle itself, which it had taken ten thousand laborers eight years to construct, was almost completely demolished by naval shells. Its massive ramparts were toppled like a child's play blocks. Two large bronze bells, battered by shell fire, were at least recognizable. On them was inscribed:

. . . Behold! What is a bell? A bell is that which sounds far, wide and high. It is a precious Buddhist instrument, bringing order to the daily routine of the monk. . . .

It will always toll on time, to herald the approaching darkness or the hour of dawn. It will startle the indolent into activity that will restore honor to his name. And how will the bell sound? It will echo far and wide like a peal of thunder, but with utmost purity. And sinful men, hearing the bell, will be saved.

General Buckner was jubilant that the enemy had abandoned the formidable defense system. "Ushijima missed the boat on his withdrawal from the Shuri line," he told his staff that evening. "It's all over now but cleaning up pockets of resistance. This doesn't mean there won't be still fighting but the Japanese won't be able to organize another line."

However, Ushijima had found another natural barrier six miles below Shuri. It was a coral escarpment—dominated by two adjoining hills, Yuza-dake and Yaeju-dake—which transversed most of the southern tip of Okinawa like a huge wall. It was loftier and more rugged than Maeda Ridge. Here, backs to the sea, the Japanese would make their last stand.

On June 1 the Americans began to close in. Progress was slow as they slogged forward through ankle-deep mud. Thick cloud formations blanketed the lowlands stretching below the formidable barrier as the flanks fanned out to seize the peninsula on either side. The one to the east, Chinen, was lightly defended, but Oroku Peninsula, which jutted out just below Naha, was held by two thousand Navy troops. Under orders from Ushijima, they had abandoned their installations on the peninsula, after destroying most of their equipment and heavy weapons, and moved south; but there, below the new natural defense line, they found civilians occupying most of the caves they were supposed to fortify. Rather than force out the Okinawans, as the Army was doing, they returned to the peninsula, where, with small arms, they held off aggressive Marine amphibious and land attacks.

At long last, on June 5, the rain ended but it had left its mark. The approaches to the Yuza-Yaeju wall were a morass of soft clay through which American tanks could not negotiate. It was not until June 10 that the 96th Division launched an assault on Yaeju, renamed "the Big Apple" by the GI's. It took two days of concentrated artillery fire and intense close combat for one regiment to establish firm positions on the northern slope of the Big Apple.

Ushijima had almost no artillery to keep the foe at bay; nor did his infantry reinforcements. slowed by poor communications, arrive in time. The Americans consolidated each gain before the Japanese could counterattack effectively, and by midnight on June 13 the entire eastern half of the ridge line had begun to collapse.

The stubborn sailors on Oroku Peninsula had also succumbed at last to Marines of the 6th Division, but the savage struggle had cost the Americans 1,608 casualties. On June 15 the bodies of Rear Admiral Minoru Ota, the Japanese commander, and five of his staff were found in his subterranean headquarters. They were sprawled, throats cut, on an elevated platform covered with blood-soaked mattresses.

Almost a thousand Japanese were being killed every day as the battle fragmented into a series of fierce contests for caves. That same evening Colonel Hitoshi Kanayama, commander of the 27th Regiment of the 7th Division, gathered his officers and noncoms in his command cave. From a small dais he announced that Division was to launch a general attack at dawn. But he could not obey the order. There were fewer than a hundred men left in his regiment and he imagined other units were just as depleted. It was impossible to carry on organized warfare any longer.

Kanayama poured gasoline on the regimental flag and touched a match to it. As the standard flared up, he said, "During the past three months you men have gone through unspeakable hardships. I thank you all for having fought so well. I am now dissolving the regiment. You will act on your own. Those who wish to return to the homeland are free to make the attempt. I am going to die here, but you are not to share my responsibility."

These words left his subordinates bewildered; they resented being left on their own. Drawing a dagger, Kanayama gazed at his men and again admonished them not to "follow" him. Purposefully and without sound he slashed his abdomen in the ritual pattern. As the blood pumped out, his head fell forward. His adjutant, Captain Sato, brought his raised sword down sharply, severing Kanayama's head. Then Sato shot himself. Another officer, a first lieutenant named Adachi, drew his pistol. "*Tenno Heika banzai!*" he cried out before he pulled the trigger.

4.

The fighting had degenerated into a cruel hunt as the Americans went after their entombed prey with grenades, satchel charges and flamethrowers. By June 17, Ushijima's 32nd Army was dazed and shattered. Discipline had evaporated. Survivors committed acts that would have been unthinkable a few days before: they challenged their officers;

fought like savages in their caves for food and water; murdered and raped civilians.

In Headquarters cave, deep within a craggy, precipitous cliff near the tip of the island, General Ushijima stoically waited for the end. It was a long cave, near the top of the cliff, with one end facing the sea more than two hundred feet below, and the other overlooking the village of Mabuni—and the approaching enemy. Ushijima had just finished reading a surrender appeal from Buckner which had been dropped behind the lines:

The forces under your command have fought bravely and well, and your infantry tactics have merited the respect of your opponents. . . . Like myself, you are an infantry general long schooled and practiced in infantry warfare. . . . I believe, therefore, that you understand as clearly as I, that the destruction of all Japanese resistance on the island is merely a matter of days. . . .

While this bid for surrender brought a faint smile to Ushijima's face, Cho broke into derisive, almost uncontrollable laughter—how could a samurai even consider such a proposal? The rapidly deteriorating situation had wrought a disturbing transformation in Cho. Ushijima would lie thoughtfully on his cot, reading or writing poetry, but Cho paced the cave like a caged animal, often grabbing his sword as if he had just seen an enemy.

Ushijima remained himself. He was particularly considerate to the young Okinawan students who served as his personal aides; he patted them paternally on the head and questioned them about their families. His sense of humor was sharpened by adversity. Once when Cho strode up to the end of the cave facing Mabuni and urinated into the wind, Ushijima said with a laugh, "You'd better hurry. Your thing is too big a target for the enemy."

At noon on June 18 his opponent, Simon Bolivar Buckner, roamed far forward to observe a fresh unit of Marines moving into battle. He watched for an hour; then as he started down from his observation post, a Japanese shell exploded directly overhead. A fragment shattered a mound of coral, and freakishly, one jagged piece of coral flew up and embedded itself in the general's chest. Ten minutes later he died.

Ushijima's last order written from the cave urged his men "to fight to the last and die for the eternal cause of loyalty to the Emperor," but not in a suicide charge. He instructed survivors of the 32nd Army to filter through enemy lines in civilian clothes and join the small band of guerrillas in the north of the island. With darkness the first groups tried to get through but were detected. The area was illuminated by flares and star shells, and those who weren't killed immediately were forced to go to ground again.

At noon the following day an explosion rocked the north entrance of Ushijima's cave. American tanks had approached Mabuni and were firing directly on cave openings in the hill rising below the village. Jinsai Higa, an Okinawan who had served in New Guinea before illness forced him to return to Naha, was giving Ushijima a haircut. Cho approached the general as the barber was putting away his utensils, and said, "Thank you very much." What for? asked Ushijima. "You took my advice when I didn't think you would. You let me have my way on the counterattack."

"I thought it would be easier that way," Ushijima replied. "It was always my policy to leave decisions up to my subordinates."

"At one time I thought of committing hara-kiri if you didn't approve of my plan," Cho said gruffly. "But you let me do it—and with a smile. You made it so easy for me and I want to thank you before we part in this world."

Civilians and soldiers alike faced extermination in the hundreds of caves that honeycombed the southern tip of the island. Two miles west of Ushijima's headquarters a group of Okinawan student nurses—turned out of their hospital when it was disbanded—had found refuge with scores of civilians in an underground cave. Nobuko Yamashiro was only seventeen. She was trying desperately to save her dying sister, Yoshiko, also a nurse. But there was no food or water in the cave and she was afraid to venture outside. The nurses had been driven from cave to cave, and on the evening of the eighteenth were ordered by soldiers to move once again—to find "a safer refuge" farther south.

Resentful and weary, the nurses started up the ladder leading to the cave opening. A shout of "Enemy attack!" was cut off by the rattle of firing. Blue sparks showered those on the ladder. Gas! Acrid smoke billowed into the cave. Choking and blinded, the occupants groped toward the ladder. Nobuko gagged as if something clutched her throat. She cried out painfully for her sister. Hell must be like this, she thought. Grenades exploded thunderously. Then there was silence.

"Now we are all going to die," said a calm masculine voice. "Let us sing 'Umi Yukaba.'" As they tried to sing their favorite patriotic song Nobuko fainted. She came to with a strange sense of euphoria; never before had she wakened with such a wonderful feeling of well-being. She struggled to get up from the floor, but her body weighed too much. Why? People were moaning all around her; she must be wounded too. Her left thigh and neck began to throb, and she discovered that she had been hit by shrapnel.

She tried again and again to rise. Where was her sister? Fighting an overpowering desire to sleep, she commanded herself to stay awake; she knew she would die if she succumbed. She pulled up her legs, and in a fetal position rolled over on her knees. Crawling among the bodies sprawled on the cave floor, she began examining them carefully one by one. At the foot of the ladder she looked up. An American soldier stood silhouetted against a startlingly blue sky. She stifled a cough and crept back into the blackness to continue the agonizing search. When she found her sister at the rear of the cave she was dead.

Amplified pleas to surrender from tanks and from boats cruising offshore were far more effective than they had been at Saipan and Iwo Jima. Masses of civilians and a substantial number of soldiers abandoned their subterranean hiding places. Before nightfall more than four thousand Okinawans and eight hundred military had surrendered. The soldiers came out, as they had been instructed, stripped to their loincloths. One marched up to the lines of the 7th Infantry Division, saber in hand. He stood stiffly at attention, saluted and handed over his weapon to Sergeant Alvin Hannah. Another carried two small dictionaries—one English–Japanese, the other Japanese–English. After a bit of sampling he exclaimed cheerfully, "Me vanquished, miserable, dishonorable, depraved."

As Ushijima radioed his farewell message to Imperial Headquarters on the evening of June 21, Cho was composing one of his own which he hoped could be delivered by hand. "Our strategy, tactics and methods were all utilized to the utmost and we fought valiantly, but they had little effect against the superior material strength of the enemy," he wrote, adding that he was departing this life "without regret, fear, shame or obligations."

Their last duties completed, the two generals now readied themselves for death. A grim-faced Colonel Yahara asked

Ushijima for permission to commit suicide. The general gently but firmly refused the request. "If you die there will be no one left who knows the truth about the battle of Okinawa. Bear the temporary shame but endure it. This is an order of your Army commander."

Soon after sunrise on June 22 Ushijima asked Higa to give him the final ritual haircut. His sense of humor had not deserted him. As the barber revolved him from side to side, Ushijima joked, "I'm a human rotary machine." By noon the Americans had occupied the upper part of the cave. After a few hours the general opened a can of pineapple—the last food in the cave—and shared it with anyone, soldier or civilian, who happened to pass by.

Late in the afternoon Ushijima and Cho kneeled ceremoniously side by side. Cho deliberately lowered his head so as to expose his neck. Captain Sakaguchi, a fifth-grade *kendo* expert, brought down his sword, but his injured right hand wavered and the blade did not go deeply enough. Sergeant Kyushu Fujita seized the sword and severed the spinal column.

"The Okinawans must resent me," Ushijima said regretfully as he bared his abdomen and stoically cut himself. His spinal cord was severed and seven of his staff, using pistols, committed mass suicide.

The same day at Tenth Army headquarters near the Kadena airfield, representatives of Tenth Army, the two corps and the divisions stood at attention as the band played "The Star-Spangled Banner." The color guard raised the Stars and Stripes, denoting that the island of Okinawa was secure.

But for thousands of Japanese soldiers and civilians, still hiding from the Americans, the ordeal was far from over. Thirteen-year-old Shigeru Kinjo crept out of the cave where his family had found shelter and got his first close glimpse of the enemy. They were naked from the waist up, hairy like animals. It is the end, thought Shigeru. He discredited the enemy leaflets claiming that no prisoners would be killed; they would have their noses and ears cut off. Back in the cave he rejoined the family, which sat huddled in a close circle. Someone activated a grenade against a rock and threw it in their midst. Shigeru thought the world had exploded. He heard his sister mutter something, then her death rattle.

"I'm not dead," said a voice and then, pleadingly, "Explode another!"

A second detonation rocked the little cave. Pieces of flesh

struck Shigeru. Still a few survived but no one suggested a third grenade. Someone did propose that they cut their arteries and bleed to death, but no one acted. They remained apathetically in the cave all night. In the morning a voice shouted in English, "Come out!" Almost immediately a can tumbled into the cave spewing white smoke. Two more tear gas canisters exploded. Suffocating, Shigeru crawled out into the open, both legs bleeding profusely. He felt himself being lifted onto a soldier's back. At the village of Makabe the enemy soldier (a Marine) lowered Shigeru and opened a can of clams. It had a Japanese label but the boy was certain the clams were poisoned and refused to eat them. The soldier said something, then cut Shigeru two bamboo canes, and as the youngster hobbled toward a collecting station he wondered, When will the murdering begin?

A mile to the northwest the Americans had been trying to clear a multilevel labyrinthian cave with smoke bombs for more than a week. At least three hundred soldiers and eight hundred civilians were bottled inside. Petty Officer Shikichi Miyagi had escaped from Oroku Peninsula after Admiral Ota's death to find his wife Betty, a Hawaiian, and had succeeded. Now the smoke became so suffocating that Miyagi—one of the most celebrated karate experts in Okinawa, the home of karate—toted his unconscious wife piggyback deep into the cave through hip-high mud.

The mud became a stream and soon water was up to Miyagi's shoulders. The water revived Betty, and when Miyagi could no longer touch bottom he gave her the glowing candle that was guiding them and swam through the water with the collar of her dress in his teeth. Every few yards he lowered his feet to rest but they sank into gummy mud and he flailed frantically to keep head above water. The nightmare seemed endless—he had no idea how long—until his feet touched solid ground and he could relieve his tortured muscles. Together the Miyagis pulled themselves onto a bank. Then they noticed a cold breeze—there had to be an entrance nearby—and saw a light ahead. It was a candle in the center of half a dozen civilians.

The ordeal left them with one conviction: they would rather die on the surface in the sunlight than smother in the dark. At the entrance they heard American voices. Betty shouted "Hello!" and said that she was from Hawaii and that her older brother was with her.

"We've come to save you," someone shouted back. "Come out!"

They emerged from the cave and found themselves in a cul-de-sac, twenty feet deep. Above them a circle of rifles rimmed its lips. Ropes tumbled down, followed by a dozen Marines hand over hand. Instead of being killed the Miyagis were hauled swiftly to the top. They could scarcely believe what was happening. Americans, smiling broadly, pressed K rations, water and cigarettes on them. A lieutenant pumped Miyagi's hand. Marines embraced them, rubbed cheeks with them, and then began bringing cans of gasoline to the cave mouth. Miyagi tried to stop them. Gesturing excitedly, he explained that the burning gasoline would kill not only the Japanese soldiers in the higher lateral but the civilians in the lower level as well. He volunteered to go back into the cave and bring out the civilians. Clad in brand-new Marine fatigues, he fought his way into the cave past armed Japanese guards, and persuaded all eight hundred civilians to surrender.

Farther south, at the very end of the island in thorny brush near the shoreline, thirteen Okinawan student nurses led by Seizen Nakasone, an instructor at the Normal School, were preparing for suicide that night—thousands of civilians had already killed themselves with grenades, motivated in equal proportion by a desire to die as true Japanese and by fear of the enemy. The girls sat in a circle singing "Sayonara," a haunting song composed by their young music teacher. In a turmoil Nakasone went off by himself to sort out his thoughts. How futile to die with nobody knowing anything about it! The dew on the trees shone in the moonlight, beautiful and mysterious.

At dawn he noticed Americans in green fatigues stealthily approaching. These were the Anglo-Saxon devils, yet he no longer feared them. Why should he and the girls kill themselves? He hastened to his students and found them huddling in a tight circle.

"Nakasone-sensei, is it all right to die now?" asked one who held a grenade. From the first she had urged suicide.

Nakasone asked them to wait—he was hoping to stall them until the Americans arrived. Two of the youngest girls whimpered for their mothers and were allowed to leave the circle. Again the girl with the grenade asked if the time had come. Again Nakasone said to wait. He started toward the beach to intercept the enemy. One GI wrote "Food—Water" on a piece of paper. Nakasone, followed by the GI's, returned to the girls and tried to convince them that the Americans, who began to close in, wouldn't harm them in any way. But they remained terrified of the "foreign devils" until they noticed one soldier cradling a rifle in one arm and a baby in the other and crooning repeatedly, "Don't cry, baby." One by one the girls left the circle—all except the resolute girl with the grenade. Nakasone wrenched it from her hand. She raced to the beach and flung herself into the water. Soldiers dragged her out, bleeding from coral cuts and still struggling. Nakasone, imagining he was the only Okinawan man who had surrendered, stifled his sense of shame. At least he had saved his students.

But Nakasone was far from alone. In the next week at least 3,000 soldiers and labor troops heeded the pleas of Petty Officer Miyagi and other Japanese volunteers like him who time and again went deep into the earth to save their comrades. Those who refused were trapped in their caves by flamethrowers and demolitions, and during the same period, 9,000 military were exterminated.

On July 2 the Okinawan campaign was officially declared ended. In almost exactly three months Americans had lost 12,520 GI's, Marines and sailors, dead or missing. It was their greatest toll in the Pacific.

The Japanese lost 110,000 troops. In addition, civilian casualties reached unprecedented proportions. Caught between two armies, approximately 75,000 innocent men, women and children died. And their sacrifice was in vain. Japan had lost the last major battle she could fight outside the homeland itself.

30   The Stragglers

1.

Even with the mainland threatened, millions of troops continued to occupy large segments of the crumbling Japanese Empire. The bastion at Rabaul, long by-passed, still stood, and the horde of soldiers in China controlled most of that country. But the men in Burma, the Philippines and the leapfrogged islands of the Pacific were lost to Japan. Few would ever return to the homeland. Those who did not commit hara-kiri or die in a last suicidal charge were abandoned, sick and starving, living from day to day, driven by the will to survive.

Corporal Kiyoshi Kamiko, the former schoolteacher, was one of these. Since sailing away from Leyte in a *banca*, he had escaped capture and death a dozen times. By April he had reached Negros, the large island west of Cebu, but before he could resume his voyage to freedom, he was conscripted by an Army unit and forced to help man a defense against the Americans who had recently landed. Kamiko, however, had not given up his dream of a new life on Borneo and persuaded six others to desert and come with him. He promoted himself to sergeant, and on the morning of April 30 led the way into the dense jungle toward the southwest coast. But each rugged mountain was succeeded by another, and for a month they had no food other than snails and crabs. There was little relief from poisonous insects except urine applied to the swollen areas, and when they were asleep, leeches crept into their eyeballs and began sucking blood. They stuck painfully until, big as marbles and black with blood, they fell off. The men ate them; nothing went to waste in the jungle.

Food became an obsession, and they remembered a story about a cook serving his unit soup made from an executed Filipino. "The thought of eating human flesh is disgusting," someone remarked. "But I understand it tastes very good as long as you don't know it."

"'When a man is really starving," said a recruit named Yabuki, "he'll eat anything." Had Yabuki ever eaten human flesh? "No, I haven't, but I worked in a crematorium on Hokkaido and there a man soon lost the feeling that he was handling human flesh. If you're squeamish you can't be a cremator. One day an ordinary fellow came to me secretly and asked for burned brains." What for? "I understand they're very beneficial if you're sick."

The conversation repelled Kamiko and he feared Yabuki might get the idea of eating Mayama, a tubercular recruit who was so thin that his puttees kept slipping down his legs. One night Kamiko overheard Yabuki whisper, "Anyway, he'll soon die," and on wakening discovered that both Yabuki's and Mayama's beds of leaves were empty. Kamiko found them at a stream. Mayama was drying his skeleton frame after a bath while Yabuki, crouched behind a rock with drawn sword, watched him like a hunter would his prey. Kamiko shouted a warning and the commotion brought the others. Yabuki, his eyes gleaming strangely, dropped his sword and exclaimed, "Forgive me!" Kamiko beat him savagely until his hands were raw. Yabuki submitted docilely, finally toppling back, his face covered with blood.

On their continued march Yabuki tried to rationalize what he had done. Mayama, he argued, was dying from tuberculosis but could not kill himself. "It would not be murder if I killed him. I would only be helping him to die sooner." Then he added, "What nonsense just to let his body rot! It would please the spirit of Mayama that his body was used to save his hungry comrades."

That night Kamiko dreamed he was attending a funeral on a warm spring day with larks flying in the sky. "Do you want to bury him or cremate him?" asked a young man wearing *montsuki*, a ceremonial garment. It was Usui, a pale, poetic recruit.

"Please let me do it if you are going to cremate him," said a man in work clothes—Yabuki.

"The enemy will discover us by the fire," warned the head of the village—another member of the troup, Nakao. A middle-aged woman, attended by girls, said, "Let us now prepare the meal." They made a soup that tasted like *satsuma-jiru* (a soy bean soup with pork and vegetables). "Very good," said the woman.

"Yes, of course," said one of the girls, "the meat is Mayama."

"So? This is Mayama?" asked another girl and laughed merrily. "How nice."

It was all so pleasant and natural that in the morning Kamiko felt happier than he had since landing on Negros. He wondered why, until he vaguely remembered having had a delightful dream. Even after he realized that he had dreamed of eating Mayama, the sense of well-being continued. He felt no distaste, not the slightest sense of guilt, and in the days to follow he found himself muttering as he marched, "I want to eat Mayama. I want to eat Mayama."

They crossed another mountain. At the foot they forded a swollen river. The feeble Mayama was swept away, but clung to a rock with his last strength and was saved by the others. They encountered an insane Japanese soldier lurking near ten dead comrades. Beyond were empty U.S. foxholes filled with abandoned equipment. They put on American uniforms and shoes, and retrieved a box of K rations, "a gift of the gods." They also found four kinds of cigarettes—Camel, Lucky Strike, Chesterfield and Philip Morris—proof, thought Kamiko, that they had "rejoined the human race."

Within a mile they came to a village where they were ambushed by guerrillas—fourteen thousand Filipinos under Lieutenant Colonel Salvador Abcede had controlled two thirds of the island since the beginning of the year. The Japanese were backed up against a river. Cornered, they leaped into the rushing water. Mayama struggled weakly in the current until his head finally disappeared. Downstream Kamiko and the others emerged on the opposite bank and scrambled up a steep hill. Behind them almost three hundred guerrillas fanned out in pursuit. But at the top of the hill the Japanese were trapped again. Filipinos astride buffaloes closed in on them from another rise, shooting and shouting. There was a burst of machine-pistol fire. Three men fell and two of them begged Kamiko—who had the only rifle—to kill them. They didn't want to die at the hands of the enemy.

"I'll avenge you and then die with you!" Kamiko crouched behind a fallen tree. He had three grenades. He would toss two and save the last for himself. One of the wounded men, Nakajima, again pleaded with Kamiko to shoot him. He called out that he wanted to help him, but since Nakajima lay hidden in the tall grass, Kamiko couldn't see where he was without exposing himself. Nakajima managed to raise himself in a sitting position, and Kamiko saw him point to his forehead with one finger. Kimiko took aim, closed his eyes and fired.

The buffaloes thundered toward the crest. In one moment I will be dead, thought Kamiko. Twenty-four years old ... never had a woman . . . Kiyoshi Kamiko will have disappeared . . . Mother, forgive me.

"You missed!" Kamiko could hardly believe his ears; it was Nakajima's voice. "Shoot me again!" But before Kamiko could pull the trigger, dismounted guerrillas swarmed over Nakajima.

Guerrillas were lurching behind a bush above Kamiko. They shouted to their comrades below that they had discovered another one. The leader of the main group—a big man wearing a panama hat—rushed forward, a rifle with fixed bayonet in his left hand.

Kamiko saw his mother's face. He suddenly got up and aimed at the big man who was lunging at him. Startled, the Filipino tried to shift his gun to his right hand. Kamiko hesitated—the man was so close and suddenly so helpless— then fired. A bright red blotch instantly stained the guerrilla's shirt. He staggered and collapsed.

All at once there was silence. Kamiko looked around him.

There wasn't a Filipino in sight. (According to Nakao, who watched hidden in the grass, the three men directly behind the big Filipino were simultaneously bowled over, apparently all felled by Kamiko's single bullet. The other guerrillas panicked "at the fantastic sight" and disappeared.) Kamiko, who never dreamt he would survive the skirmish, hastily collected the three grenades and the bullets he had placed on the grass and leaped over the bush. There was a crackle of gunfire as bullets whizzed by like angry bees. But he scrambled safely up the hill, rifle cradled in arms. At the top there was a ravine. Without hesitation he leaped into space. He bounced like a ball but still clung to the rifle. Stunned, he hid behind fallen trees just as curious faces poked over the edge of the ravine. One Filipino started down on a thick vine but gave up halfway.

Utterly exhausted, Kamiko fell asleep. He woke with a bright full moon shining down on him. He climbed up the ravine. The hillside was empty. He found a field of onions and ate a dozen before he dozed off again.

Crazed by fatigue and attacks of malaria, he followed a highway that seemed to lead to the coast until he dropped from exhaustion. He was wakened by the deafening roar of trucks—U. S. vehicles going in the opposite direction. Now he knew he was heading for the coast and Borneo, but he lost track of the days. He was so weak he could hardly put one foot in front of the other. He made hazy plans to ambush an American truck for K rations with his last grenade, and rehearsed killing himself with his rifle by pushing the trigger with his toe. But no truck passed and he fell asleep.

He heard a voice saying as from a great distance, "It's a Japanese soldier. He's dead." He wanted his rifle but couldn't move. His head throbbed and he was getting fainter. He knew he was dying. "Mother, *sayonara,*" he mumbled. A moment later (in fact, it was days) he saw stars shining and heard the buzz of conversation. Someone—a man in uniform—was speaking Japanese but Kamiko couldn't make out the words because of the clamor of locusts. Gradually he realized that the sound of locusts was in his own head and that the stars were rays of sunlight coming through holes in a tent. The tent was American and so was the soldier. Kamiko knew he was captured, and that his dream of Borneo was also an illusion.*

---

*Kamiko and Nakao survived. So, incredibly, did Mayama. Soon

There were more stragglers concentrated per square mile on Iwo Jima than on any other island in the Pacific. When Iwo Jima was officially declared secure in mid-March, Marines estimated there were not more than three hundred Japanese left alive in the caves; there were close to three thousand. Those who finally emerged after dark to prowl for provisions and safer caves found an unrecognizable landscape. Seven thousand Seabees had laid down twenty miles of roads, erected extensive housing, built breakwaters and piers, and levelled the central plateau near Motoyama to make a 10,000-foot runway, the longest in the Pacific. Scavengers often crossed paths at night without exchanging a word, but when the new moon shone (a time of sentiment to the Japanese) they would reminisce furtively about home, family and food—and finally wonder how they would die: hara-kiri or a suicide attack.

Escape from Iwo Jima was virtually impossible but there were those with the audacity to try. Ohno, the young Navy lieutenant who had escaped apparent death by dynamite in a pillbox, was one of these; he still had visions of becoming a trader or diplomat. By April 2 he had improvised a compass by magnetizing a wax needle with the magnet in a telephone receiver, and with four others collected enough material for a raft—eighteen-foot planks, empty water drums, one half of an American pup tent for a sail and the other half torn in strips, for rope—and laboriously buried it in the sand so it could hastily be assembled on the first moonless night. Hopefully they would sail north at six knots and in twelve hours catch the *Kuroshio,* which swept up past Japan.

On the first completely overcast night they hastened to the beach with their supply of food and water, and began building the raft. They estimated it would take two hours, but by the time they had erected the mast and attached the shelter half it was midnight. Too late, said Kitagata, formerly a fisherman from Hokkaido, who would navigate. Moreover,

---

after publication of his book, *I Did Not Die on Leyte,* in 1965, Kamiko encountered Mayama on a street in Tokyo. When Kamiko revealed that another of their group had survived, Mayama recoiled in fright. He said, however, that he had never been afraid of being eaten by Kamiko. "Because," he explained, "you were a teacher."

the waves were running high. He held back until Ohno drew his sword and threatened to kill him.

Kicking energetically, the five men managed to propel the bulky craft through six-foot-high breakers, coming in at long regular intervals. Thirty yards offshore a towering breaker smashed into the raft. Ohno found himself alone and thrashed desperately. Another breaker crashed down; he was torn away and knocked out. He came to on the beach. Kitagata was staring down at him almost accusingly. One of the men was sprawled in the wreckage of the raft; his skull was split open. The survivors buried him in the sand and returned disconsolately to their cave, all hope of escape gone.

In a cave at the base of Mount Suribachi, the last twenty-two survivors of that battle had withstood everything. Neither flamethrowers nor burning gasoline had been able to dislodge them, but when sea water came gushing at them from hoses, they were forced to surface. Private Kiyomi Hirakawa was next to the last in line and the exit caved in before he was half out. He flailed for his life through the sand but was held back by the last man clutching his legs. Hirakawa was wrenched to safety by those already out, and as he vainly burrowed for the man below, they disappeared up the beach. Hirakawa patiently waited until dawn, but only five of his comrades returned. They had been ambushed by the enemy. Four of them went underground again but the fifth man and Hirakawa decided to stay in the fresh air and terminate their nightmare existence with a grenade.

The sunrise was beautiful, the ocean a deep green, the grass glistening with dew. They found a cigarette butt dropped by some GI—the Army had just taken over from the Marines. They lit it with a book of U. S. matches and hunkered down behind a rock sharing puffs. Not twenty yards away GI's began issuing from tents to wash and brush their teeth, and noticed the smoke curling from behind the rock. The two Japanese were signaled to come out. They didn't move; they wanted at least one American to draw closer so they could all die with the single grenade.

Several GI's approached cautiously and flipped two lighted cigarettes near the rock. Hirakawa retrieved his—the first whole cigarette he had seen in more than a month. Two packs landed at their feet. Certain they would die at any moment, the two stragglers frantically smoked one after another. Two apples bounced to the base of the rock. Hirakawa, already dizzy from the cigarettes, devoured his but couldn't taste it.

An American started to move slowly toward them with a couple of beer bottles. This is the last treat before death, thought Hirakawa, and reached for his grenade. The GI stopped fifteen feet away. He put down the bottles and tipped his hand to pantomime drinking. He was too far away to be killed by the grenade. The two Japanese moved forward but the GI stepped back. Hirakawa put the bottle to his mouth. It was water! Ambrosia after the sulphurous drippings they had subsisted on in the cave.

While the two stood indecisively savoring the water, a Japanese cadet in American uniform arrived breathless. He told them that the entire garrison on Iwo Jima had been listed as dead in Japan. "Why should we die twice?" the youngster reasoned. "It doesn't make sense."

Life had suddenly become possible for Hirakawa. I'm "dead" already, he rationalized, and now have the chance for a second existence, almost like reincarnation.

The two men surrendered. They were given a shower and clean fatigues, and they watched incredulous as an American doctor tenderly dressed a Japanese enlisted man's leg, allowing blood and pus to stain his own uniform. No Japanese doctor would ever do that, thought Hirakawa. How could he fear Americans after that? What a waste, those terrible months in the cave, he thought. Why did so many of us die so needlessly?

Misfortune still plagued Lieutenant Ohno. Two of his men—Yamakage and Matsudo—had left one evening for food and ammunition but never returned, and he was alone with Kitagata. For endless hours they endured a solitary confinement in their cave, punctuated occasionally by jarring explosions of grenades tossed at random by patrolling GI's. The two fugitives were so close to Seabee work parties that they could hear jazz music piped over a loudspeaker, and once it seemed they would surely be discovered by Americans gossiping overhead when Kitagata farted.

One unrealistic hope sustained them: there would be a major Japanese counterattack from the sea on May 27, Navy Day. That morning they celebrated with the last of their stolen food—a can of ham and eggs and fruit punch—and confidently waited hour after hour for the arrival of the Combined Fleet. As the sky darkened, so did their spirits. They brooded for two days and then impulsively left their cave armed with three grenades apiece and a determination to make their own deaths as costly as possible. The darkened island seemed deserted until they intercepted two wandering GI's, who fled before Ohno could activate the first grenade— the two "GI's" were his own men, Yamakage and Matsudo.

They returned discouraged to their cave and slept. Ohno was alerted by a hissing. Grenade! He seized a blanket and was only half covered before it exploded. At first he thought he was unharmed, then he saw that his clothes were smoldering. A phosphorus grenade had showered him with burning red specks. He brushed at them frantically; bits stuck under his fingernails. In agony he dug his inflamed fingers into the ground. A package of dynamite tumbled through the cave entrance. The two men were thrown to the dirt by the thumping concussion. Through the clearing smoke they saw the entrance blasted wide open. Ohno, sword in one hand and grenade in the other, started forward. Kitagata seized him. "Useless," he whispered.

The throaty rumble of a motor and clanging gears preced- ed an avalanche of earth. Then everything was dark. They had been sealed in by a bulldozer. They crept back to an emergency exit and at dusk once more came to the surface with their six grenades. A complex of tents had magically mushroomed nearby and Kitagata thought grenades were not sufficient for a "proper" assault. He wanted to search for land mines buried during the battle. After five hours they were still empty-handed. Now Kitagata refused to attack altogether, but Ohno remained resolved to end it all that night. "You need only one grenade to kill yourself," he said. "Give me the other two."

Kitagata refused even that. Cowering in the predawn fog, Ohno smeared himself with stolen toothpaste and Lux soap so he would smell like an American. As he hung a necklace of three grenades around his neck he said, "We'll meet at Yasukuni Shrine." He began crawling toward the barbed-wire fence enclosing the tents. Near the gate he reached for his sword but it had slipped out of its scabbard; he cursed himself for not carrying it in his teeth like a movie com- mando.

In the dim light he was confident he could deceive the sentry with his "Yankee odor." But there was no guard to fool. He picked up a stone to activate the grenades and made for the largest tent, one enclosed by screen. He peered inside—a mess hall. Creeping to the next tent, he cautiously rolled up a canvas side. A man, bare to the waist, was lying on a cot a few feet away sleepily scratching his hairy chest. Ohno struck the grenade and waited for the hiss. The fuse apparently had deteriorated after several months in damp caves. He tried a second. This one hissed briefly but fizzled out.

He tied the two duds to the third grenade and tried to activate it. Again nothing happened. Tears of vexation came to his eyes. There were no weapons in the tent, not even a trenching tool. What kind of soldiers were these? It was growing lighter now and he slipped into another tent. Two of the four field cots were occupied—but no guns. Someone approached, whistling a tune. Ohno ducked behind an empty cot just before the whistler, a tall, heavyset man, stalked into the tent. He went directly to Ohno's cot and started making it. Certain he had been discovered, Ohno sprang to his feet—a scraggy apparition with Medusa hair. The big American plunged out of the tent with a shrill scream. The two men on the cots leaped at Ohno and clung to him until the whistler returned with half a dozen armed men. At bay, waiting to be shot, Ohno asked the whistler in stumbling English for his name—it would be an interesting tale to tell in Heaven. The big man, his face still drained, reluctantly mumbled "Bill." The other GI's burst into laughter. One of them said, "Please," and casually motioned Ohno to follow. Inexplicably Ohno felt as if he had found new friends. He turned to Bill and said, "How is Gary Cooper?"*

Not far from where Ohno was enjoying hotcakes and coffee, Lieutenant Satoru Omagari, who had spent two full days trying to blow himself up along with an American tank, again failed to kill himself—this time he thrust a pistol into his mouth and pulled the trigger. There was an empty click. He had long since given his troops permission to surrender, but few had done so. It would have meant eternal disgrace to a man's family, and he himself would become a *musekimono* (an outcast), one whose name was erased from the census register of his town or village. Legally he ceased to exist and the only way to get employment would be to move away and assume a false name.

Even Omagari allowed himself to contemplate surrender,

---

*On November 30, 1946, ashes marked with Ohno's name were delivered to his father. That same day, Ohno himself arrived home after almost a year and a half of imprisonment in Hawaii. "What a remarkable day!" exclaimed the father as they bowed. "Suddenly I have two sons."

but as an officer he knew that such an act could be punishable by death after the war. Driven from hiding place to hiding place by the Americans, he decided to return with his men to the Navy Aviation cave, whose occupants guarded its entrances against Japanese as well as Americans: their *hikocho* (squadron leader), a lieutenant, and his staff refused to share the spacious cave and its plentiful supply of food and water with anyone.

Now at night Omagari and his men nevertheless surprised the guards at one entrance and broke in. There were at least 150 sailors in the rambling cave and they pressed around the interlopers, curious about what was going on above—few of them had seen daylight in the past two months. They were being terrorized by the *hikocho*'s regime; enlisted men were sent out systematically on assault missions and not allowed to return lest they "draw enemy attention to the cave." They wanted Omagari to help rid them of their commander. Perhaps he would encourage the lieutenant to steal an American plane for escape from the island—a plan the *hikocho* was tentatively considering.

He talked eagerly of his plan to the newcomers, and Omagari's encouragement sounded so genuine that the lieutenant and four of his followers left the cave to find a plane. Their departure was celebrated with song, *sake* and whiskey, but the revelry was interrupted by a commotion near the rear entrance. The *hikocho*'s party was clamoring to get back in—they had quickly discovered that it was impossible to approach the flight line. They were blocked by an irate group of enlisted men. "You yourself made the rule that once a man left, he couldn't return," one of them shouted.

As their new senior officer, Omagari told the sailors, as he had previously told his own men, that they were on their own. Life in the cave became relaxed with the evaporation of military discipline. In the intense heat the men reverted to nakedness, but the officers did retain a measure of dignity by wearing their loincloths.

Within days the cave was discovered by the Americans. Grenades and smoke bombs drove the occupants into its deepest recesses. As the attacks intensified, a large group decided to flee the island by raft. Everyone was captured almost immediately, and several were released so they could return to the cave to persuade their comrades to surrender. Their appeals failed and the assaults continued. Omagari was singled out by loudspeaker: "I want to talk with you. Will you come out?" It was a fellow officer, but Omagari ignored him. An American took the microphone and announced that the cave would be flooded the next day.

The sailors refused to believe that there was enough water on the island for such an operation. "Let them pour it in," someone boasted. "We'll drink it!" As sea water was pumped into the cave the men scrambled to lateral tunnels which were slightly higher. Then with a crump, fire raced across the torrent; gasoline had been poured on top of the water and ignited. Only those who had retreated to the highest lateral survived.

The following day a yellowish beam probed the smoke-filled cavern. Omagari fumbled for a light machine gun, then saw it was one of his own petty officers with a flashlight. He was wearing an American uniform. Two more Japanese, also in GI fatigues, came forward. They had cigarettes. They had been treated well by the enemy and said there were many Japanese prisoners, including a major. Then they left to allow their countrymen to make their own decision. No one spoke until a sailor said, "I think I'll leave too."

"If you want to live," said Omagari, "surrender." One by one the men excused themselves with formal bows and filed out of the cave. Finally Omagari was left with an old friend, Ensign Kakuta, who was severely wounded.

"What shall we do?" Omagari asked him.

Kakuta was delirious and raved like a madman until Omagari suggested that they die at once together. "I don't want to die," Kakuta replied in a flash of sanity.

Neither did Omagari. But he couldn't turn himself over naked to the enemy. He found a bolt of cotton loincloth material, and taking leave of Kakuta, crept out of the cave, pistol in hand. Half a dozen Americans, grinning broadly, came toward him. A baby-faced first lieutenant stretched out his hand.

"Wait," Omagari said in Japanese. "I am an officer and must be clothed before I greet you." He modestly turned his back, ripped off six feet of material and adroitly fashioned himself a loincloth. Then he too extended a hand.

He remained composed until after he had showered, then he broke down. It was the first time he had ever wept. He refused to talk and had no appetite. After supper the other prisoners riotously celebrated their resurrection with bawdy songs. He decried their behavior, and his depression increased to the point where he no longer wanted to live. He vowed that when he returned to the cave in the morning to bring out Kakuta, he would kill himself.

He made the mistake of confiding his plan to a fellow officer, who informed the Americans. Omagari was put under restraint. Like Yasunori Aoki, the *kamikaze* flier, he bit his tongue to choke on his own blood. He too failed. Then he tried to strangle himself with his bare hands, but each attempt became feebler. It was weeks before he finally accepted the degradation of surrender.

But hundreds of other stragglers on Iwo Jima could not yet bring themselves to consider surrender. Nor could they bring themselves to commit hara-kiri. They continued to hide beneath the crust of the little island, like dead souls on a distant planet. Among them were Ohno's two men—Yamakage and Matsudo. Six years later they were the last of the Iwo Jima garrison to surrender.*

---

*They held out until 1951. Yamakage returned to Iwo Jima with Stuart Griffin, a historian at Tachikawa Air Base and later columnist for the *Mainichi*. They had come to find the diary Yamakage insisted he had kept for five years. The two men methodically searched Yamakage's last cave, and finding nothing, Griffin expressed doubt that there had ever been a diary. That evening Yamakage disappeared to continue the quest for the notebook. In the morning he returned dejected, with torn hands.

Just before their plane was to leave, Griffin and Yamakage were driven to the summit of Mount Suribachi to take pictures. At the crest Yamakage started trotting with eyes on the ground. He paused, turned and slowly walked back. Then he again loped toward the edge of the cliff overlooking the sea. He picked up speed, threw both arms in the air, shouted something and jumped. Griffin ran to the edge of the cliff. There was a drop of twenty yards to a rocky ledge covered with sand, and he saw an indentation as if something had hit it. Out of sight, a hundred yards below on another ledge, lay the body of Yamakage.

He and Matsudo were by no means the last stragglers in the Pacific to surrender. In the next six years men were found all the way from Saipan to Mindoro. Two soldiers on Guam surrendered almost sixteen years after the liberation of that island. Perhaps there are more to come; they have been reported in the Philippines, New Guinea and Guadalcanal.

PART EIGHT

"One Hundred Million Die Together"

31   In Quest
of Peace

1.

The American landing on Okinawa coincided with the final convulsions of the Third Reich. While Count Folke Bernadotte risked his life on trips to and from Germany to arrange peace in Europe through Gestapo chief Heinrich Himmler, other Swedes were endeavoring to bring an end to the war in the Pacific through various channels, some of them spurious.

Widar Bagge, the Swedish minister to Japan, was approached by Mamoru Shigemitsu, foreign minister in the Koiso Cabinet, with a suggestion that Sweden intercede on Japan's behalf with the United States. It came to nothing because of opposition from Shigemitsu's successor, Shigenori Togo, who was convinced that a much more influential go-between than Sweden could be found.

A private effort was introduced by another Bernadotte, Prince Carl, grandnephew of the King of Sweden, and Eric Erickson, a shipbroker who had business ties with Japan. The two urged Major General Makoto Onodera, the Japanese military attaché in Stockholm, to seek peace through Sweden. On his part Prince Carl would request the King to send "a confidential, friendly letter to the Emperor of Japan suggesting peace be negotiated as soon as possible."

Prince Carl also informed the Swedish Foreign Minister, Christian Günther, of the plan. Günther was not at all pleased, since it by-passed the regular channel, Bagge, and he protested to the Japanese minister in Stockholm. Presently General Onodera received a peremptory cable from Tokyo:

JAPAN'S POLICY IS TO FIGHT TO THE END, BUT WE HAVE

INFORMATION THAT SOMEONE IS CONDUCTING A PEACE MOVE IN NORTHERN EUROPE. YOU ARE TO INVESTIGATE THE MATTER AND REPORT YOUR FINDINGS.

There were also two peace efforts of a more substantial nature being mounted in Switzerland. Both involved Allen W. Dulles, OSS representative for the area of Germany, southeastern Europe and parts of France and Italy with headquarters in Berne. The first was initiated by a German, Dr. Fritz Hack, a man of mystery who could have come out of a spy novel. He was a friend of Japan who felt it had been "stupid" for Japan to start the war. He enlisted the aid of Commander Yoshiro Fujimura, the naval attaché in Berne, who had come to realize that Japan had no chance of victory and felt that it was his duty to help bring peace no matter what the personal risk. They were joined by two other Japanese—Shigeyoshi Tsuyama, the European representative of the Osaka Shipping Line, and Shintaro Ryu, the European correspondent of the *Asahi Shimbun.*

The four conspirators held a series of clandestine meetings with representatives of Dulles and convinced them of their own political reliability. Moreover, they had access to a Navy Type 94 code machine with which they could communicate directly with Navy Headquarters in Japan without having to go through diplomatic channels. On May 3 Dr. Hack was informed by the Dulles office that the U. S. State Department authorized the commencement of direct peace negotiations with the Fujimura group.

The self-appointed peacemakers painstakingly composed a message addressed to Navy Minister Yonai and the new Chief of Staff, Admiral Soemu Toyoda, informing them that Dulles had offered to act as mediator and described him as "a leading political figure of America who has long associated with Lippmann and Stettinius, and especially enjoys the confidence of President Roosevelt and is directly connected with the President." They had confused Dulles with his brother, John Foster, but did accurately state that Dulles had been "guiding the American political warfare for nearly all of Europe with Switzerland as his base, and particularly noteworthy is the fact that it was largely through his efforts that separate peace was effected with North Italy in early May." Instructions were "requested immediately."

Near midnight on May 8, the day of Germany's surrender, Fujimura and Tsuyama cautiously entered the darkened legation building, and with the aid of a flashlight, climbed up to the code room on the third floor. First Tsuyama set the machine for the proper date and hour, then he began typing the message in romanized Japanese. The machine automatically transmitted this in code.

In the next eight days, six more telegrams were secretly dispatched reporting Germany's surrender and the plans to move American and British units from Europe to the Far East, along with the admonition to seek peace before it was too late. After thirteen days of silence from Navy Headquarters, the conspirators sent another telegram to Yonai and Toyoda urgently requesting an early reply to the first message, since the United States was "pressing" them for an answer. It came two days later and was signed by the Naval Affairs Bureau chief:

... THE PRINCIPAL POINT OF YOUR NEGOTIATION WITH MR. DULLES FULLY UNDERSTOOD, BUT THERE ARE CERTAIN POINTS WHICH INDICATE AN ENEMY PLOT, THEREFORE WE ADVISE YOU TO BE VERY CAUTIOUS.

Incredulous, the Fujimura group saw the answer as a subterfuge. They in turn requested concrete evidence of "enemy machinations" and insisted that the Dulles agency was a reliable political organ directly connected with the President.

MR. DULLES AND ALL OTHERS ARE EXPECTING A SINCERE REPLY FROM JAPAN. EVEN IF WE CONCEDE A GREAT DEAL AND ADMIT IT TO BE AN ENEMY PLOT, WOULD IT NOT BE MORE ADVANTAGEOUS TO AVOID THE SAD PLIGHT OF GER-MANY WHICH LOST EVERYTHING? ARE THERE ANY MEANS WHICH PROVIDE BETTER CONDITIONS THAN THIS FOR JAPAN AT PRESENT?

Navy Headquarters did not reply. Nor did they so much as acknowledge continued requests for action. They had not ignored the flood of messages from Switzerland. In fact, these had created violent disagreement among the naval leaders. Three men were strongly in favor of accepting the Dulles proposal—the Chief of Operations, the head of the Naval Affairs Bureau, and Admiral Sokichi Takagi (erstwhile plotter to kill Tojo), who offered to fly to Switzerland to open negotiations. But Chief of Staff Toyoda, as well as the rest of his staff, was strongly opposed. The Dulles proposal was either a "trial balloon to sound out Japan's fighting spirit or a plot to lower morale."

The lack of response from Tokyo drove Fujimura to

extremes. He volunteered to fly to Japan to explain in person the importance of Dulles' position in establishing a reliable high-level contact between the two belligerents. Dulles, however, feared that such a journey would compromise the negotiations and suggested that the Japanese send a fully authorized representative to Switzerland. America would guarantee safe air transportation. Fujimura transmitted this promising offer directly to Yonai in words so strong that they verged on the insulting.

Yonai was at last spurred to action. He took the proposal to the Foreign Minister. Wtih some trepidation—Togo too knew little about Dulles—he asked Yonai to explore the proposal more thoroughly, and the admiral dispatched a message to Berne that seemed to give approval:

> YOUR POINT IS FULLY UNDERSTOOD. THE PAPERS RELAT-
> ING TO THE AFFAIR HAVE BEEN REFERRED TO THE FOR-
> EIGN MINISTER AND YOU ARE REQUESTED TO TAKE PROPER
> MEASURES IN CLOSE CO-OPERATION WITH THE MINISTER
> AND OTHER PERSONS CONCERNED AT YOUR PLACE.

Despite the vague phraseology, this was the first encouragement the conspirators had received from Tokyo, although it meant that negotiations were now in the hands of the Foreign Ministry. But their enthusiasm began to dim as days passed without receipt of specific instructions from either Togo or Yonai on how to proceed. This procrastination had a similar effect on the Americans. It seemed increasingly apparent either that the men they were dealing with in Switzerland had little influence or that Tokyo had no interest in pursuing negotiations through Dulles. Togo's silence, however, was due to another cause. The Navy's reservations had become too strong; Admiral Toyoda had grown more convinced than ever that Fujimura ("only a commander in the Navy," at that) was the victim of American duplicity. Moreover, the Japanese leaders were already considering opening a channel to negotiations in a completely different direction.

While Japan searched hesitatingly for peace, her cities were being reduced to ashes. LeMay's campaign to destroy the homeland's industrial centers had reached a cataclysmic climax. Nagoya was a ruined city, and 34.2 square miles of Tokyo had been incinerated in four devastating raids, after which the usual greeting between friends was simply, "Not burned out yet?"—nothing else seemed to matter. On May

23, in the afternoon, 562 B-29's headed back to lay waste the area along the west side of Tokyo harbor that included residential as well as industrial communities. Pilots had been instructed to avoid the Palace, "since the Emperor of Japan is not at present a liability and may later become an asset." Another five square miles were destroyed that night. Thirty-six hours later 502 Superfortresses returned to hit the heart of Tokyo with 3,262 tons of incendiaries.

Once again a fire storm seared the capital, and by dawn 16.8 square miles of the financial, commercial and government district lay in ruins, including the detention house of Tokyo Army Prison. Among the tens of thousands of incinerated victims were sixty-two imprisoned Allied airmen. The uncontrollable flames reached the Imperial Palace. Flying debris leaped the moat, setting brushwood fires which spread to several buildings, including the Palace itself. Twenty-eight members of the staff died, but the Emperor and Empress were safe in their underground shelter. Because of the bombings, they now resided in the *obunko* (the imperial library), a long one-story building fronted by a row of imposing pillars half a mile from the Palace in the imperial garden. It was connected by a long tunnel to the *obunko* annex, an underground complex. Outside the Palace walls, the pavilions of the Dowager Empress, the Crown Prince and other royal personages were completely destroyed, as were the Foreign Ministry, the Prime Minister's official residence, and the Navy Department and Greater East Asia Department buildings.

More than half of the sprawling city was gutted, a wasteland like Nagoya. Radio Tokyo had often broadcast an overoptimistic ditty, which now seemed more irrelevant than ever:

> *Why should we be afraid of air raids?*
> *The big sky is protected with iron defenses.*
> *For young and old it is time to stand up;*
> *We are loaded with the honor of defending the*
> *   homeland.*
> *Come on, enemy planes! Come on many times!*

During the attack the Bees had buzzed the skyline of Tokyo with impunity, since the antiaircraft guns had long since ceased to operate, and deafened the ears of the people with their "thundering boom." This time the incendiaries, descending in "hissing and rattling bundles," set fire to the Mishimas' house. It burned slowly because it was filled with books. Poking in the embers, Mrs. Sumie Mishima found "layers upon layers of ashes of different colors. The Chinese books of the Sung and the Ming dynasty, with their softly creamed paper and beautiful wood-printed scripts, had turned into glistening snow-white powder of the finest quality imaginable. . . . The modern books produced coarse ashes in various shades of dingy gray." Mrs. Mishima put the white ashes in a broken jar, and her family found them "the cleanest possible toothpowder."

Four nights later LeMay turned to nearby Yokohama, the nation's fifth largest city; after the 517 raiders left, 85 percent of the metropolitan area was in flames. With the Tokyo–Yokohama area in ruins, the B-29's concentrated on Osaka and Kobe, and within two weeks both cities had been eliminated as targets. More than a hundred square miles of the principal cities were obliterated; Phase I of LeMay's Urban Area Program was accomplished. Two million buildings— almost one third of all construction—were razed, and at least thirteen million people left homeless.

2.

Even before Tokyo's second catastrophic fire storm, Prime Minister Suzuki had instructed Cabinet Secretary Sakomizu to make a confidential study of Japan's resources to see whether the nation could possibly continue the war. A special investigatory bureau was set up which included military and civilian experts from the Cabinet Planning Board, the Foreign, Finance and Munitions ministries, and the Army and Navy.

Their findings revealed that the situation was more critical than anyone had realized. Every aspect of Japanese life, civilian as well as military, was affected by the lack of basic raw materials. Steel production was less than 100,000 tons per month, two thirds below the official estimate. Similarly, aircraft production had dropped to a third of its quota because of shortages in aluminum and bauxite, and lack of coal had curtailed munitions production by 50 percent. Shipping was down to 1,000,000 tons, and the entire transportation system was crippled by fuel shortages and lack of manpower to handle cargo. The Sakomizu report predicted that in weeks there would be no rail transportation between cities, construction of steel ships would end and the chemical industry would collapse.

In a desperate attempt to replenish diminishing oil reserves, ersatz aviation fuel was being made from pine trees,* and since the population was faced with the specter of starvation—the rice harvest was the smallest since 1905—the government devised a plan to convert acorns into food. "The entire people will be called upon to give their aid. Schoolchildren and evacuees in particular will be enjoined to collect the maximum goal of five million *koku* [5.2 bushels] of acorns." The official daily food ration—when it could be obtained—had fallen below 1,500 calories, two thirds of the minimum Japanese standard. Those in the cities suffered most, and millions went into the country each Sunday to barter kimonos, jewelry, furniture, anything of value, for sweet potatoes, vegetables, and fruit.

The Sakomizu report was released to a newly inaugurated "inner cabinet" officially titled the Supreme Council for the Conduct of the War but commonly called the Big Six, since it was comprised of the Prime Minister, the Foreign Minister and the four military chiefs. The implications of the report were unassailable, and on May 12, at a meeting of the Big Six, Admiral Yonai made a suggestion that could have caused his expulsion a week earlier. He proposed that they ask Russia to mediate a settlement of the war. Togo, who was as anxious to negotiate a peace as anyone else in the room, snapped that Yonai didn't know much about Russia if he imagined she would really help Japan. Suzuki, however, could see no reason why they shouldn't at least sound out the Soviets.

The forbidden subject of peace was at last out in the open, but one of the military men apprehensively suggested that they keep their discussions within the confines of the room—lest the morale of the armed forces be "seriously shaken." In this conspiratorial atmosphere they candidly discussed possible mediation by Switzerland, Sweden, China or the Vatican and concluded that these channels would undoubtedly end in the Allies' demand for unconditional surrender. General Yoshijiro Umezu, the Army Chief of Staff, saw the Soviet Union

---

*The pine root oil project required a work force of millions to grub out the pine roots, as well as more than 37,000 small distillation units, producing 3 to 4 gallons of crude oil per day. Production eventually reached 70,000 barrels a month, but the process of refining was so difficult that little more than 3,000 barrels of aviation gasoline were produced by the end of the war.

with its power and prestige as the best possible go-between for Japan. General Korechika Anami, the War Minister, concurred: the Soviets would prefer a strong Japan to emerge from the war as a buffer between their Asian possessions and the United States.

The undiplomatic Togo accused them of being unrealistic. "The matter of Japan must have been discussed at the Yalta Conference," he said, "so it is probably hopeless to try and get the Soviets on our side now. Judging from past Russian actions [recently he had told Sakomizu, "The Soviet Union is not to be trusted"], I think it's even going to be difficult to keep her from joining the war. It would be better, in my opinion, to negotiate directly with the United States for a cease-fire."

But Suzuki, who was still playing *haragei,* backed the generals. "Stalin seems to be like Saigo,* and I believe he will make every effort on our behalf if we ask him." Togo, who was from Kyushu, saw no similarity but when it became evident that the Army was willing to negotiate through Russia alone, he agreed to write up a draft memorandum to that effect. He presented it to the Big Six on May 14:

It should be clearly made known to Russia that she owes her victory over Germany to Japan, since we remained neutral, and that it would be to the advantage of the Soviets to help Japan maintain her international position, since they may have the United States as an enemy in the future.

The memorandum warned that Russia, having achieved her victory over Germany, might demand a price "much beyond our imagination," and Japan should be prepared to give up Port Arthur, Dairen, the railways in South Manchuria and the northern portions of the Kuriles.

Togo expected opposition from the military at the prospect of giving up so much territory, but the Big Six approved the draft unanimously and instructed him to initiate negotiations. Togo reckoned that the straightest line to Moscow would go through a former premier and foreign minister, Koki Hirota, who had many ties with diplomats of the Soviet Union. Togo asked him to sound out the Soviet ambassador, Yakov Malik, who was staying at Gohra, a resort town in the Hakone area, a two-hour drive from Tokyo.

---

*The samurai hero from Kyushu who arranged with rebel troops a peaceable transfer of the city of Edo in 1867.

Hirota was to try to convince Malik to reverse the recent Soviet decision not to extend their Neutrality Pact,* and ask for help in ending the war. The devastating May 25 fire bombing of Tokyo delayed Hirota's departure, and it was not until June 3 that he finally reached Gohra. That evening he strolled around the mountain village like any other vacationer and stopped, as if by chance, at the Gohra Hotel, a comfortable European-type establishment, to chat with Malik.

"It is very fortunate that Japan and the Soviet Union have not exchanged blows in this war," Hirota said affably, and congratulated Malik on his country's victory over Hitler. He assured Malik that the Japanese people earnestly desired friendly relations with both the Soviet Union and China. Malik was guarded—he implied that there were those in Japan who showed considerable antagonism to the Soviet Union—but he did invite Hirota to dinner at the hotel the next evening.

Over the table Hirota concentrated on Japan's desire to resuscitate the Neutrality Pact. "Japan wishes to promote friendly relations with the Soviet Union even before it terminates. That's why we are currently trying to figure out how to go about it."

Malik replied that Russia had consistently maintained a peaceful policy but that her distrust of Japan was based on the many belligerent acts of the past and the anti-Soviet feeling in Japan.

Hirota pointed out that there was "an increasing number of people who are beginning to understand the attitude of the U.S.S.R. ... Japan wishes to find means to maintain peace with the Soviet Union for a long time to come." When Malik wondered if this was simply Hirota's personal opinion, the answer was: "I want you to know that what I just told you reflects the attitude of the Imperial Government as well as the people."

---

*On April 5, 1945, the Soviet government had announced that it could not renew its pact with Japan because the situation had "basically altered" since it was signed. *A Short History of the U.S.S.R.* states that the pact "ran out on April 5, 1945." It did not terminate until April 13, 1946, and according to its terms, a full year's notice had to be given if either party did not wish to renew it. Unaware of the secret provisions in the Yalta agreement, the Japanese felt assured of a twelve-month period of grace, during which time they might get the Russians to sign a new pact. Perhaps the Soviet historians made a mistake; perhaps they were attempting to obscure the fact that when Russia declared war on Japan on August 8, 1945, she was violating a treaty.

Malik pondered this for a moment, then said he wanted a few days to think the matter over before giving an answer. Hirota was encouraged; he had dealt with the Russians before and knew they were inherently cautious. He reported to Togo that "the atmosphere of the talks was friendly, that the Russian side responded satisfactorily and the conversations looked hopeful."

But hopes for a negotiated peace were dashed the following morning—it was June 6—at another Big Six meeting when Togo was handed a document composed by the Supreme Command entitled *The Fundamental Policy to be Followed Henceforth in the Conduct of the War*. It demanded an official reaffirmation of carrying the war to its ultimate conclusion:

With a faith born of eternal loyalty as our inspiration, we shall—thanks to the advantages of our terrain and the unity of our nation—prosecute the war to the biter end in order to uphold our *kokutai* [national essence], protect the imperial land and achieve our goals of conquest.

There followed a list of steps that would have to be taken, including all-out preparations for defense of the mainland and organization of a national volunteer army. Togo read on in consternation. No one had consulted him about this. If accepted, it ensured Japan's destruction. Ironically, Sakomizu's devastating report was attached, and items from it had been quoted out of context with the ostensible purpose of giving weight to the Supreme Command's position.

Togo stood up painfully—he had been suffering from pernicious anemia for five years. "Going through these items," he said, waving the Sakomizu report, "I can find no reason for continuing the war. As far as I can see, there is no relation between your draft proposal and the detailed items submitted." He ridiculed all the Supreme Command's theories, including the one that the nearer the battlefield came to Japan, the more advantageous it would be. And what about the strained will of the hard-pressed people?

At this Admiral Toyoda lost his composure. "Even if the Japanese people are weary of the war, we must fight to the last man!"

General Anami was furious. "If we cannot fulfill our responsibility as advisers to the Throne," he exclaimed, "we should offer our sincere apologies by committing hara-kiri!"

Another hour passed. Without any support Togo could no

longer delay the decision, and the resolution to fight to the end was passed. On his way out, Togo confronted Admiral Yonai. "I expected support from you today," he complained, "but I got none."

Two days later, on June 8, an imperial conference was convened to present the Supreme Council's resolution to the Emperor for his approval. It was held in the Imperial Household Ministry because of fire damage to the Palace. In attendance, besides the Emperor, were the Big Six, President of the Privy Council Hiranuma, the Munitions Minister, the Agriculture and Forestry Minister, and four secretaries including Sakomizu.

Unprepared for what he was hearing, the Emperor sat silent on his dais "with a grave look on his face." Togo alone expressed reservations but they were muted, apparently out of consideration for His Majesty, and at the conclusion of the stilted discussion, even he did not respond to Suzuki's request for summary opinions on the new policy. "Well, then," said the Prime Minister, "I conclude that no one has any particular objection to the plan."

The thirteen members rose, bowed to the Emperor and backed out of the room. As the Emperor emerged from the meeting Marquis Kido was puzzled by the concern on his face and wondered why. "They have made this decision," His Majesty replied and showed the Privy Seal a copy of the new policy. It was as great a surprise to Kido as it had been to Togo, and it undermined his faith in Suzuki. Now it was apparent that he could no longer depend on the aging Prime Minister, even with the support of Togo, to take the initiative for peace. As confidential adviser to the Throne, tradition required Kido to remain above politics. In the past he had circumvented this restriction indirectly, but now somehow he had to take positive action.

The problem seemed insoluble. All that afternoon and into the night he searched for a solution. Ideally the initiative should come from the Army, whose power could thwart other peace movements. The solution was inescapable: there was one source no one could oppose—the Throne. Kido decided to confront the Emperor with candor. He felt that in the crisis, such an unprecedented approach was necessary to persuade His Majesty to end the war by personal intervention. At last the Privy Seal dropped off to sleep.

In the morning he marshaled his arguments in a paper entitled *Tentative Plan to Cope with the Situation*. At 1:30

P.M. he presented himself to the Emperor. "Under the circumstances," he said, "I consider any peace move almost impossible, but I will, with His Majesty's gracious permission, try to address myself to the problem. These are my ideas."

The Emperor studied the document. The first four paragraphs summed up the situation: reports on production indicated that it was unlikely war could be waged by the end of the year; further, the devastation wrought by the bombings, aggravated by the growing food shortage, would create serious unrest throughout the nation.

5. Based on the above, I believe Japan must resolutely move toward a resumption of peace by terminating hostilities. How shall this objective be attained? That is the question which calls for cautious study.

6. It is almost certain, in the light of various announcements, speeches and articles made public by the enemy in their peace offensive, that the enemy's main object is to overthrow the so-called *gumbatsu*, that is, military clique.

7. Although it is customary to start negotiations with a proposal of peace from the military, followed by negotiations on the part of the government, this would be almost impossible at the present stage in Japan's current condition. Moreover, if we wait for a more favorable opportunity, it may be too late. Then Japan would share Germany's fate and her minimum demands—the security of the royal family and retention of our national essence—might not even be met.

8. Exceptional and unprecedented measures have to be taken—and we do so with awe and trepidation—but I believe the only possible course is to ask His Majesty to intervene for the sake of the people and initiate termination of hostilities in the following manner:

9. Start negotiations with an intermediary power with His Majesty's personal message. . . .

10. The message should cite the Imperial Rescript on the Declaration of War [December 8, 1941] and emphasize His Majesty's constant desire for peace and his decision to end the war—bearing the unbearable in view of the heavy damages we have sustained in the war—on reasonable terms. The minimum peace terms are:

Honorable peace (this may, inevitably, be the minimum term)

If guarantee is obtained that the Pacific be truly pacific . . . Japan will renounce her right of occupation and claim of leadership for all occupied areas, provided that the nations and peoples therein attain their independence.

The Japanese armed forces in these occupied areas will be withdrawn by Japan on her own accord. . . .

11. As for armament limitation, Japan must be prepared to meet demands for a pretty heavy reduction. We must be contented with minimum armament for national defense.

This is my personal opinion, candidly expressed. It contains only the essential points.

The Emperor appeared to be "greatly satisfied" by what he read, and Kido asked permission to discuss the proposal with the Prime Minister and other leaders; he would need the support of key men in the Cabinet before the Emperor could be openly involved. His Majesty approved: "Do it at once."

Kido, however, felt it was wiser to wait for a few days. The Diet was in session and the entire Cabinet was too involved in politics. On the morning of June 13, the final day of the proceedings, Kido intercepted Suzuki on his way to the Diet Building. He briefly outlined his peace plan and got a promise from Suzuki to return as soon as the Diet was adjourned.

In the meantime Kido talked to Admiral Yonai. He was the only one of the four military chiefs the Privy Seal was sure would not betray the peace plan. He asked the admiral to read the proposal. Yonai reacted with his usual caution. "Of course, very good idea," he said with restrained enthusiasm, "but I wonder how the Prime Minister really feels about the war?"

So did Kido.

The object of their conjecture was just rising from his seat to address the House of Peers and House of Representatives. Suzuki was far more committed to peace then he had indicated to Kido, and was about to prove it in public. He began by referring to a speech he had made in San Francisco twenty-seven years before when he commanded the training fleet. His listeners, who were prepared to indulge the reminiscences of an old man, were shocked by the point he was making.

"The gist of my speech was: 'Japan is not warlike. She is the most peace-loving nation in the world. There is no reason why she and the United States should come to war, but if they do, the conflict will be a long one and end disastrously. The Pacific Ocean, as the name suggests, should be the Sea of Peace with no troop transports permitted on its surface.

However, if such an unhappy event should come to pass, both sides will be meted out punishment by the gods.' "*

A wave of indignation swept the vast hall. The word "peace" and the desirability to achieve it had been publicly proclaimed by the head of the government, and the effect was not mitigated by Suzuki's concluding exhortation that the nation must fight to the end and that unconditional surrender would mean the ruin of the Japanese race. As he turned from the podium the hostility erupted into boos, threatening gestures, and cries of "Down with the Suzuki Cabinet!" One Diet member, however, elbowed his way to Cabinet Secretary Sakomizu. "Now I understand what the Prime Minister means in his heart," he said tearfully. "Please continue!"

If Suzuki heard the jeers, he ignored them as he absently waved at the audience. Forcing his way through the pressing crowd, he started for the Imperial Household Ministry to make the traditional report to the Emperor. Then he proceeded down the corridor to Kido's office, where he read the Privy Seal's unique plan in its entirety. Suzuki promised to do everything he could to further its aims, but like Yonai, he seemed to have some reservations: "I wonder what Admiral Yonai thinks about all this?"

"Yonai said the same thing about you," Kido told him. This struck Suzuki as comical, but Kido was perturbed. How was it that at such a critical point in the war neither the Prime Minister nor his Navy Minister knew what the other "had in his stomach"?

Suzuki's pledge to help Kido did not alter his public stance. At a press conference the following morning he spoke like a militarist. "If our hundred million people fight with the resolve to sacrifice their lives, I believe it is not at all impossible to attain the great goal of preserving the essence of Japan. . . . None of our fighting men can understand how it is that Germany, with such a large army left, was not able to hold out until the end. In quantities of arms and supplies, we may not compare favorably with the enemy, but our determination as we stand on the firing line is peculiar to us alone.

---

*Suzuki had submitted the speech to his cabinet two days earlier and was urged to eliminate the phrase "Sea of Peace," and the reference to retribution; the Americans alone should be punished by the gods. But Suzuki ignored both suggestions. He told his son just before the Diet session that there would be no point in making a speech with such deletions; he hoped that the United States would take his words as a subtle peace feeler.

With this formidable strength we must fight to the end, the entire population uniting as one body."

Kido now summoned the third member of the Cabinet whose support was vital, Foreign Minister Togo. The Privy Seal did not show him the written proposal but confided to him that the Emperor was deeply disturbed by the decision presented to him at the latest imperial conference. Togo pointed out to him that he had opposed the suicidal Army plan at the Big Six meeting.

"I know," said Kido. "I have some ideas of my own about peace and I need your help." He indicated that the Emperor might possibly make a public statement calling for peace.

Togo was ready to do anything he could, and said he would be extremely gratified "if the Emperor were to say now that we should work to end the war without delay, for there could be no greater aid to the attainment of my purpose than such words from the Throne."

It was not Kido's intention to involve the other three military chiefs, but on impulse one day he found himself telling War Minister Anami about his proposal. It happened as a result of Anami's casual remark as he left the Privy Seal's office: "I hear you're resigning. Is it true?"

Perhaps the fact that they had once been very intimate— Anami was military aide to the Emperor when Kido was chief secretary to the Privy Seal—led Kido to say, "I'm not resigning, but if I tell you what's on my mind you may ask me to resign."

"What is it?" Anami wanted to know.

Kido revealed the entire peace plan and the part the Throne would play in it. His instinct was sound. Anami was not antagonistic; in fact, he "agreed in principle" with the Privy Seal's line of action. He had considerable reservations, however, about its timing. It would be more advantageous, he pointed out, for Japan to sue for peace "after the United States has sustained heavy losses in the Mainland Beach Operation."

Then Kido belittled the fact that thousands of planes had been collected to be thrown against the invaders. "When they are gone, what will you do?" Since Japan did not have more strength than to destroy one third of the American landing force, it would be better to come to terms before the invasion. Anami recognized the authority of Kido's tactical conclusions—his own secret files*—and although he would not support the Kido plan, he promised not to oppose it "too vigorously" before the Big Six.

The unexpected opportunity to sound out Anami had been "assistance from Heaven." Now Kido felt he had the backing he needed to confront the Supreme Council. On June 22 the Emperor, at the instigation of his Privy Seal, abruptly summoned the Big Six to the *obunko* annex. He signified the unique informality of the occasion by speaking first. "This is not an imperial command," he said simply, "but merely a discussion. At the last meeting of the Supreme Council it was decided to adopt a new policy and prepare the homeland for defense. But now I have deemed it necessary to consider a move toward peace, an unprecedented one, and I ask you to take steps at once to realize my wish." General Umezu and Admiral Toyoda, the two men Kido had not consulted, were staggered.

The Emperor asked if they had considered initiating negotiations. He already knew the answer—Togo had privately kept him informed. Suzuki struggled to his feet and allowed as how the government had given thought to negotiations. Togo gave a full account of Hirota's conversations with Malik.

"When will an envoy be sent to the Soviet Union?" the Emperor asked. "Is there any chance of success?"

Togo estimated that envoys would probably arrive in Moscow before mid-July. He warned, however, that Japan would no doubt be forced to make numerous concessions to Stalin.

The Emperor turned to the two Army representatives, who had remained silent. Anami kept his word to Kido: he did not object to any attempt "to save the situation," but expressed his fear that it would be construed as a sign of weakness if Japan appeared too anxious to end the war. Army Chief of Staff Umezu, on the other hand, was openly distressed: any proposal of peace would have incalculable

---

*Top-secret information was often channeled to Kido and other proponents of peace by a special group of influential aides who were endeavoring to reform the Big Six into a peace body. The group was composed of Colonel Sei Matsutani, Suzuki's first secretary; Toshikazu Kase, Togo's secretary; Marquis Yasumasa Matsudaira, Kido's aide and secretary; and the redoubtable Admiral Takagi, who represented Yonai. These four conferred frequently, occasionally changing the meeting place to prevent being tracked down by the *kempeitai*. Their favorite rendezvous was a secluded room in the Diet Building.

impact at home and abroad and should be "treated with the utmost caution."

"Does treating the proposal 'with the utmost caution' imply acting only after having struck another blow at the enemy?" the Emperor asked. Umezu said no. "It is all very well to be cautious, but if we are too cautious we will miss our opportunity."

"Well, the sooner the better, then," Umezu conceded.

It was the first palpable step toward peace.

On June 24 Hirota, at Togo's bidding, once more visited Malik. This time Hirota abandoned the language of diplomacy and made a direct request to have the moribund Neutrality Pact superseded. Malik remained evasive however; there was no need for another pact, he said, since the previous one was still in effect.

In desperation, Hirota offered rubber, tin, lead and tungsten in exchange for oil. "If the Soviet Army and the Japanese Navy were to join forces," he said, "Japan and the Soviet Union together would become the strongest force in the world!"

Understandably, Malik was not impressed; the bulk of the Imperial Navy was resting on the bottom of the sea. He replied that Russia didn't have enough oil for her own needs. Brusquely he questioned the necessity for further meetings unless Japan came up with some "concrete plan."

In less than a week Hirota returned with one in writing: in return for a new nonaggression treaty and oil, Japan promised to give Manchuria her independence and relinquish her fishing concessions in Soviet waters. Malik remained noncommittal; he would get back to Hirota when he got an answer from Moscow. Then he asked if it was true that Japan and America were conducting peace negotiations in Sweden.

"Of course not," Hirota exclaimed. Japan would surely consult the Soviet Union before engaging in any negotiations at all.

Hirota's ingenuous answer was close to the truth: Japan had turned down two offers to negotiate in Sweden, and the Fujimura channel in Berne had been abandoned as well. But a new, more prestigious peace venture was getting under way in Switzerland. It was inspired by a remark made by Lieutenant General Seigo Okamoto, the military attaché, to two Japanese bankers—Kojiro Kitamura and Kan Yoshimura, officials of the Bank for International Settlements in Basel. "Japan intends to fight to the end," he had told them.

"However, she can't fight an extended war, and if there is any peace move on the part of the Americans, I would like to negotiate with them."

Such words from a general in such a sensitive position had an electrifying effect on the two civilians. Perhaps it was possible, after all, to save Japan from total ruin? But how could the militarists back home be persuaded to countenance these negotiations?

"Chief of Staff Umezu and I are very close friends," Okamoto said confidently. "In the Nomonhan Incident [on the Manchurian border in 1938] he was my Army commander. So he will listen to what I say."

The bankers agreed to "sound out" the Americans. But who was there with sufficient prestige to act as go-between? They settled on Per Jacobsson, a director of their bank and known for his proficiency as a negotiator in international disputes. Like so many Swedes before him, Jacobsson was responsive. He was well thought of by the Americans, and easily made direct contact with a Dulles operative.

Jacobsson told the two bankers that the Americans fully appreciated the respect in which the royal family was held by the Japanese; that was why they had sedulously avoided bombing the Imperial Palace. The conditions for any peace talks would, of course, have to be unconditional surrender. Yoshimura objected to the term even in a purely military sense. It was better than continuing a hopeless war, argued Jacobsson. The Kaiser's surrender in 1918 had prevented Germany from being totally occupied, as it was now, and had, furthermore, led to the retention of the German government. It was likely that both the Constitution and the Throne could be saved even after unconditional surrender.

On July 10 Jacobsson was back talking to the Americans, this time to Gero von S. Gaevernitz, Dulles' German-born second-in-command who had masterminded the surrender of all German forces in Italy. Gaevernitz re-emphasized the necessity for unconditional surrender but also held out hope that the Japanese might be able to retain their Emperor. No, the latter item could not be put in writing. The only ones who could do that were President Truman and Churchill. It would take weeks.

"Could not Allen Dulles tell what his [own] impression is?" asked Jacobsson.

"He would not be authorized to do so."

"Have you never done or said anything without authorization?"

Gaevernitz conceded the possibility. "But suppose Allen Dulles made such a statement and suppose a leakage occurred in Tokyo. The result might be that Dulles could no longer be used by the State Department." Instead Gaevernitz proposed that Jacobsson exaggerate a bit and tell the Japanese that he was "in direct contact with the Americans responsible for these surrender negotiations." He added that in his opinion "these talks ought not to be carried on with anybody else than those present. No other Americans. If the Japanese approached the U. S. Military Attaché that would only muddle matters. He might not want to go on with the talks. And no Swiss."

Now the next step was up to the Japanese. But General Okamoto, whose words had instigated the conspiracy, refused to involve Tokyo until he was assured of the fate of the royal family and the Constitution. These restrictions did not discourage Jacobsson. He had just received word from the Americans that in a few days he was to meet Dulles himself in Germany, and confident of his own powers of persuasion, he felt he might persuade Dulles to allay Okamoto's fears.

While these scattered efforts went on, the Japanese militarists completed their final plans for suicidal defense of the homeland—Operation Decision (KETSU-GO). More than ten thousand planes—most of them hastily converted trainers—had been collected. Two thirds of these would be thrown into the battle for Kyushu; the rest would be reserved to repel any landing near Tokyo. In the face of the bloody lessons of Tarawa and Saipan, the plan was to crush the Americans on the beaches with fifty-three infantry divisions and twenty-five brigades—a total of 2,350,000 troops. These would be backed by almost 4,000,000 Army and Navy civilian employees, a special garrison force of 250,000, and a 28,000,000 civilian militia. This last mammoth force would evolve from the national volunteer military service law for men from fifteen to sixty and women from seventeen to forty-five which had been unanimously passed at the final Diet session. The military spokesmen, whose impressive testimony had ensured passage of the bill, later showed Suzuki and his cabinet a display of the weapons that would be used by the volunteers: muzzle-loading rifles and bamboo sticks cut into spears stacked beside bows and arrows from feudal times.

3.

The negotiations initiated by the Japanese government itself were being ignored. A week had gone by and Moscow had not replied to Hirota's overtures. It was the Emperor who lost his patience, and he sent for Prime Minister Suzuki on July 7. "It will not do to miss the opportunity of exploring the Soviet Union's real intentions," he said. Couldn't Russia be asked directly to mediate? Why not dispatch the special envoy with a personal message from the Throne?

Konoye was the Emperor's obvious choice for such a mission. He was summoned to Tokyo on July 12 from his summer home in Karuizawa. Dressed as a commoner in simple khakis—the national civilian uniform—he waited with mixed emotions in the *obunko* for the Emperor to ascend from his underground office. His Majesty's appearance was unsettling—he looked pale, exhausted and ill-groomed. Contrary to court protocol, the two were alone. Kido's hope that this would encourage frankness was borne out by Konoye's reply to the question: What did the former prime minister think should be done about the war? "The people are tired of war," Konoye replied candidly. "They all wish His Majesty would condescend to act in their behalf and do something to relieve their plight. There are even those who say His Majesty is to blame. It is necessary to end the war as soon as possible."

The Emperor told him to make preparations to leave for Moscow. Though Konoye was privately opposed to relying on Russia as go-between, he was willing to take any step to rectify his past mistakes. He brought up the occasion of the signing of the Tripartite Pact, when the Emperor had warned him that it would eventually lead to war with Britain and America. "At that time," Konoye went on, "His Majesty graciously told me I would have to share the consequences with him, the good things as well as the bad. Now if it is the imperial command"—he was choked with emotion—"I am prepared to risk my life for His Majesty's sake."

As soon as Konoye left, the Emperor was rejoined by Kido. He turned to the Privy Seal and said with satisfaction, "This time he appears to be resolute."

Even as the Emperor was sounding out Konoye, Ambassador Naotake Sato in Moscow was advised of the prince's imminent arrival:

HIS MAJESTY IS EXTREMELY ANXIOUS TO TERMINATE THE WAR AS SOON AS POSSIBLE, BEING DEEPLY CONCERNED THAT ANY FURTHER CONTINUATION OF HOSTILITIES WILL ONLY AGGRAVATE THE UNTOLD MISERIES OF THE MILLIONS UPON MILLIONS OF INNOCENT MEN AND WOMEN IN THE COUNTRIES AT WAR. SHOULD, HOWEVER, THE UNITED STATES AND GREAT BRITAIN INSIST ON UNCONDITIONAL SURRENDER, JAPAN WOULD BE FORCED TO FIGHT TO THE BITTER END WITH ALL HER MIGHT IN ORDER TO VINDICATE HER HONOR AND SAFEGUARD HER NATIONAL EXISTENCE, WHICH, TO OUR INTENSE REGRET, WOULD ENTAIL FUR-THER BLOODSHED. OUR GOVERNMENT THEREFORE DESIRES TO NEGOTIATE FOR A SPEEDY RESTORATION OF PEACE, PROMPTED AS WE SINCERELY ARE BY SOLICITUDE FOR THE WELFARE OF MANKIND. FOR THIS PURPOSE PRINCE KONOYE WILL PROCEED TO MOSCOW WITH A PERSONAL MESSAGE FROM THE EMPEROR AND IT IS REQUESTED THAT THE SOVIET GOVERNMENT KINDLY PROVIDE HIM WITH TRAVEL FACILITIES.

Sato knew the Russians well enough to doubt that anything good would come of this maneuver; at one time he had spent almost nine years in St. Petersburg and had been ambassador in Moscow since early 1942. In what way, he reasoned, would the Soviets profit from a speedy end to the war in the Pacific? Molotov had shown no interest in the Hirota-Malik conversations. Why would he be interested now? His assessment was confirmed as soon as he phoned the Kremlin and requested an appointment with the Foreign Commissar. Molotov was about to leave for an Allied conference in Germany and was too busy. Would Deputy Commissar Alexander Lozovsky do?

Lozovsky (his real name was A. S. Dridso) was as uncooperative as Malik had been with Hirota. He politely side-stepped every attempt Sato made to get prompt approval for Konoye's visit. The most Lozovsky would say was that a reply would take at least several days.

Sato cabled a report to Togo, with the caustic observation that if Konoye was merely coming to enunciate "previous abstractions, lacking in concreteness," he had better stay home, and the following day added some unpalatable advice:

... A PEACE TREATY BY NEGOTIATION IS SOMETHING WHICH CANNOT WIN THE SUPPORT OF THE SOVIET UNION. IN THE FINAL ANALYSIS, IF OUR COUNTRY TRULY DESIRES TO TERMINATE THE WAR, WE HAVE NO ALTERNATIVE BUT TO ACCEPT UNCONDITIONAL SURRENDER OR SOMETHING VERY CLOSE TO IT.

The question of Japan's surrender was also being pursued by Per Jacobsson and Allen Dulles in Germany. The OSS now had headquarters at Wiesbaden in a champagne factory that once supplied wine to Himmler. The stench was so penetrating, however, that Jacobsson's meeting with Dulles and Gaevernitz took place in their billets, a snug two-story stucco house.

Dulles' primary concern was whether the Japanese negotiators were sincere. Jacobsson was certain that they were and that the peace party in Japan was doing its best, but Dulles remained suspicious. "Isn't this perhaps a trick of the war party to strengthen morale? To try to show how unreasonable the Americans are?"

Jacobsson resented the implication that he was an accessory to a deception. He curtly conceded that he did not have Dulles' experience in negotiating but that he had a reputation for being trustworthy. "I even persuaded De Valera to negotiate with the British in 1935-37."

They argued for hours in stifling heat and retired with nothing resolved. At breakfast Jacobsson renewed his appeal to maintain the Throne—the crux, he felt, of the negotiations. The position of the Emperor should depend solely on how he conducted himself. He could disassociate himself from the military, and if he then came out with a peace move, something could be worked out. This way the American public would be able to distinguish between the royal family and the war clique.

Dulles could not, even by inference, commit his government to such a policy. If, however, the Emperor took the lead in effectuating a surrender and removed Japanese troops from foreign soil, Americans would be more prone to let him continue to reign. It was merely an opinion but one from a man of position, and Dulles' parting words emphasized his sincerity. "We very much appreciate that you have come here," he told Jacobsson. "Don't think we do not." Then he made a phone call to Potsdam, a city just west of Berlin, where President Truman and his advisers had just arrived to meet with Churchill and Stalin in the final conference of the war.

"That Was Not
Any Decision That
You Had to Worry About"

1.

On the morning of July 15, *Augusta*, the cruiser that had brought Roosevelt to his historic meeting with Churchill off Newfoundland to promulgate the Atlantic Charter, docked at Antwerp with Harry S. Truman. A little after noon he was aboard the presidential plane, *The Sacred Cow*, bound for Potsdam and the meeting code-named "Terminal."

War had forced an uneasy alliance between capitalism and Communism, and the advent of peace exposed the underlying antagonisms between East and West. The union forged at Yalta was already disintegrating. Stalin had broken his promise to honor the Declaration of Liberated Europe by attempting to communize all territory liberated by the Red Army in eastern Europe. He himself suspected the West of plotting behind his back: witness the "anti-Soviet" negotiations recently concluded by the Dulles group in North Italy.

There was no doubt how the new President intended to handle the Russians. Molotov had already found his frankness disconcerting. "The United States is prepared to carry out loyally all the agreements reached at Yalta and only asks that the Soviet government do the same," he had told the Foreign Commissar at their first meeting in Washington. "But I want it clearly understood that this can be only on a basis of the mutual observation of agreements and not on the basis of a one-way street."

"I have never been talked to like that in my life!" Molotov exclaimed angrily.

"Carry out your agreements, and you won't get talked to like that," said Truman.

Truman's goals for "Terminal" were clear. He wanted to establish just political and economic principles for the occupation of Germany, enforce the Declaration on Liberated Europe (particularly in reference to Poland) and solve the reparations problem. All of these would be on the agenda of the plenary sessions. But termination of the war in Asia would require equal though unofficial attention. To Truman, this "most urgent" problem at Potsdam could not be settled around the formal conference table but required a private encounter with Stalin. At the behest of Marshall and MacArthur he was to insinuate the Soviets into the war against Japan as soon as possible. He was to do this even with the secret knowledge that an atomic bomb would soon be tested in New Mexico.

He had brought with him a draft declaration calling on the Japanese to surrender. It had been instigated by a diplomat who had strived to prevent war, Joseph Grew. Appalled by reports of the fire bombings in Tokyo, he had called on Truman on May 29 (he was Acting Secretary of State while Stettinius attended the United Nations conference in San Francisco) with the plea that the President issue a proclamation informing the Japanese that unconditional surrender did not mean the end of the imperial system. Without such assurance, he said, it was doubtful that the Japanese would ever surrender. He was supported by Far Eastern experts in the State Department, such as Eugene Dooman, Joseph Ballantine and Professor George Blakeslee.

"I've already given thought to the matter," Truman replied, "and it seems to me a sound idea." He wanted Ambassador Grew to consult the Joint Chiefs and the Secretaries of War and Navy before a final decision was made.

Stimson and Forrestal "liked the idea," and so did Marshall, but the Chief of Staff feared that a public proclamation "at this time would be premature." Stimson thought the wording would depend on the successful testing of the atom bomb. The Secretary of War had become increasingly preoccupied over the use of the bomb. He headed a group of prominent civilians known as the Interim Committee which included three noted scientists and which had been set up to advise the President on the political, military and scientific questions that the unleashing of atomic energy would raise. He put his conclusions to the committee, which met two days later with General Marshall and a four-man advisory Scientific Panel. "Gentlemen," he said, "it is our responsibility to recommend action that may turn the course of civilization. In our hands we expect soon to have a weapon of wholly unprecedented destructive power. Today's prime fact is war. Our great task is to bring this war to a prompt and successful conclusion. We may assume that our new weapon puts in our hands overwhelming power. It is our obligation to use this power with the best wisdom we can command. To us now the matter of first importance is how our use of this new weapon will appear in the long view of history."

One of the Scientific Panel members, Dr. J. Robert Oppenheimer, the physicist responsible for the design and testing of the bomb, estimated that a single atomic explosion would probably kill twenty thousand people. The mention of this figure appalled Stimson. The objective, he interjected, should be military destruction, not the lives of civilians. For example, Kyoto, one of the cities on a list of targets, should not be bombed; it was a cultural center and its shrines were revered. His knowledge of the ancient city was fortuitous; recently the son of a friend, a student of the Orient, had told him at length of the charms of Kyoto.

There was no question in General Marshall's mind that the bomb should be used to end the war quickly and save American lives, but he did not want to use the prestige of his office to influence the committee. He said that he hoped the bomb would not have to be dropped; it would prematurely reveal to the Soviets the new power America possessed and diminish its deterrent effect in the postwar world.

When they adjourned for lunch Dr. Arthur Holly Compton, another of the consulting scientists, turned to Stimson on his left and asked if some nonmilitary demonstration couldn't be arranged to impress the Japanese. The possibility was debated at the table. If an isolated place in Japan were announced in advance, the plane carrying the bomb might be shot down. Moreover, what if the demonstration bomb didn't work? Innumerable things could go wrong. And if a test were made on neutral ground, the Japanese leaders might think it was faked. The conclusion was that the bomb should be used as soon as possible "against such a target as to make clear its devastating strength"—without warning.

The three scientists on the Interim Committee—Vannevar Bush, James B. Conant and Karl Compton—concurred but a number of other scientists working on the bomb were dismayed at their recommendation. They were led by Dr. James Franck, a refugee from Germany and a Nobel-prize physicist. He and seven other well-known scientists submitted a report to the committee:

. . . If the United States were to be the first to release this new means of indiscriminate destruction upon mankind, she would sacrifice public support throughout the world, precipitate the race for armaments, and prejudice the possibility of reaching an international agreement on the future control of such weapons.

Much more favorable conditions for the eventual achievement of such an agreement could be created if nuclear bombs were first revealed to the world by demonstration in an appropriately selected uninhabited area. . . .

After a long, searching weekend at the Los Alamos Scientific Laboratory in New Mexico, Arthur Compton, Oppenheimer and the other two members of the Scientific Panel—Ernest Lawrence and Enrico Fermi—drew up their answer to the Franck Report. "Our hearts were heavy," Compton recalled, "as on June 16 we turned in this report to the Interim Committee."

. . . Those who advocate a purely technical demonstration would wish to outlaw the use of atomic weapons and have feared that if we use the weapons now our position in future negotiations will be prejudiced. Others emphasize the opportunity of saving American lives by immediate military use and believe that such use will improve the international prospects, in that they are more concerned with the prevention of war than with the elimination of this special weapon.

We find ourselves closer to these latter views: we can propose no technical demonstration likely to bring an end to the war; we see no acceptable alternative to direct military use.*

In Washington, Stimson and the Assistant Secretary of War, John J. McCloy, were preparing for a crucial meeting with the Joint Chiefs of Staff and the President to determine whether to blockade and bomb Japan into submission or whether to land on the main islands. McCloy opposed both plans. For weeks he and Grew had privately discussed the future of Japan and had come to the same conclusion: that she should be offered an honorable surrender. McCloy had promised to use his influence on Stimson and now said, "We should have our heads examined if we don't consider a political solution." America had command of the sea and air and, in addition, possessed the atomic bomb. Japan should be allowed to keep the Emperor on a constitutional basis and also have access to but not control over vital raw materials.

---

*In an address at Notre Dame University on February 6, 1967, Dr. Edward Teller voiced regret over this decision: "We could have exploded the bomb over Tokyo at a safe altitude and done nothing more than shake the windows. We could have demonstrated in a wonderful way that man's technical ingenuity can stop a most horrible war."

The President, McCloy went on, should send the Emperor, or the Suzuki government, a personal message outlining this offer, with the threat that if it was not accepted the United States would have no alternative but to employ a new weapon, the atomic bomb, on Japan. Such a procedure would probably bring about the end of the war without further casualties, and if not, America would be in a better moral position if she had to use the bomb. As McCloy spelled out the form and substance of the proposal, Stimson was in apparent agreement saying he thought it a statesmanlike way to proceed and would advocate it at the meeting. On Sunday evening, however, he phoned McCloy. "Jack," he said, "I'm not up to going to that meeting tomorrow." He was plagued with one of his migraine headaches. "I'll arrange with the White House to have you take my place."

Just before three-thirty on Monday, June 18, McCloy arrived at the conference room in the White House. The President's chief of staff, Admiral Leahy, was there, along with two of the Joint Chiefs—King and Marshall—but Arnold was represented by Lieutenant General Ira C. Eaker. Then Stimson, looking worn and in pain, entered. He had dragged himself out of bed.

Truman called for opinions from each, beginning with Marshall. The Army Chief of Staff insisted that there was no choice but to invade the main islands. The initial landing, on the island of Kyushu on November 1, would involve 766,700 troops. Losses would be heavy, but air power alone, he said, was simply not enough to conquer Japan. Speaking for the Air Force, Eaker confirmed this judgment; the air arm had not been able to subdue the Germans. Admiral King also supported Marshall.

To McCloy's chagrin, Stimson nodded assent. However, he also suggested that some alternatives should be explored. "I do think that there is a large submerged class in Japan who do not favor the present war and whose full opinion and influence have not yet been felt ... I feel something should be done to arouse them and to develop any possible influence they might have before it becomes necessary to come to grips with them." But he said nothing about the message to the Emperor which he had indicated to McCloy he would propose.

Truman turned to Leahy. The admiral, blunt as always, denounced Roosevelt's Casablanca formula. "I do not agree with those who say that unless we obtain the unconditional surrender of the Japanese that we will have lost the war. I fear no menace from Japan in the foreseeable future, even if we are unsuccessful in forcing unconditional surrender. What I do fear is that our insistence on unconditional surrender will only result in making the Japanese more desperate and thereby increase our casualty lists. I don't think this is at all necessary."

Truman didn't believe the public was ready to accept relaxation of the demand for unconditional surrender. As for the Kyushu operation—and here McCloy thought he sounded somewhat reluctant—he said that he was "quite sure that the Joint Chiefs should proceed." But they were not to invade the main island of Honshu without consulting him. Nor did he want matters to have progressed to such an extent that he "would have no alternative" but to approve such an invasion.

With that, the meeting was apparently over and the conferees, in a resigned mood, started to get to their feet. The President stopped them. "No one is leaving this meeting without committing himself. McCloy, you haven't said anything. What is your view?"

McCloy looked at Stimson questioningly. Stimson nodded. McCloy repeated what he had told the Secretary of War, including the sentence "We should have our heads examined if we don't consider a political solution." Admiral King glared at him, but Truman was impressed. "Well, this is just what I wanted considered," he said. "Spell out the message you think we should send."

Verbally McCloy composed a message to the Emperor promising continuation of the imperial regime and ending with a threat to use the atomic bomb. The last two words had an electrifying effect. McCloy "sensed the chills that ran up and down the spines" of his listeners. Everyone in the room knew about the bomb, but it was such a secret that except in private conversations, it was rarely mentioned.

Truman said that the use of the atomic bomb was a "good possibility," as if the subject had never before been brought up at a formal meeting he had attended. He asked everyone to remain in the room; it was time the matter was placed on the table. The talk concentrated on the feasibility of the bomb itself and on the question of whether the Japanese should be warned before it was used. Although there was considerable discussion about the unpredictability of the bomb—"How do we know it will go off?" . . . "It would be a great fiasco if it did not work" . . . "What would happen if we gave the warning and it would not work?"—everyone seemed to take for granted that it would be dropped if necessary. Without any formal statement, the decision to use the bomb had, in essence, just been confirmed. Truman told McCloy to "give further thought to this message but don't mention the bomb at this stage."

Sobered by the finality of the moment, Stimson left the meeting more resolved than ever to see that Japan was given a realistic chance to surrender. With the help of Grew and Forrestal he began marshaling all arguments in favor of warning Japan before the bomb was used. Concurrently McCloy, Dooman and Ballantine set to work on the text of a declaration to the Japanese outlining surrender terms, to be issued jointly by America, Britain and China. Paragraph 12 contained the sole exception to unconditional surrender and the one most vital to the Japanese—the possibility of retention of the Emperor:

The occupying forces of the Allies shall be withdrawn from Japan as soon as these objectives have been accomplished and there has been established in accordance with the freely expressed will of the Japanese people a peacefully inclined and responsible government. This may include a constitutional monarchy under the present dynasty if the peace-loving nations can be convinced of the genuine determination of such a government to follow policies of peace which will render impossible the future development of aggressive militarism in Japan.

On Monday morning, July 2, Truman gave general approval to the declaration, but James F. Byrnes, the new Secretary of State, questioned the last sentence of Paragraph 12. So did Cordell Hull. It sounded "too much like appeasement," he advised Byrnes. "The Emperor and the ruling classes must be stripped of all extraordinary privileges and placed on a level before the law of everybody else." Public opinion coincided with this view. In a recent Gallup poll one third had favored executing Hirohito, and 37 percent wanted him put on trial, imprisoned for life or executed. Only 7 percent believed he should be left alone or used as a puppet.

On the way to Potsdam aboard *Augusta*, the President and Byrnes made the final decision to eliminate the controversial sentence. At the same time Truman privately re-examined the decision to use the bomb. There had been no doubt among the leaders of the Allies, including Churchill, that the bomb should be dropped once it was ready. In a sense Truman's decision was inevitable. "As far as I was concerned," General Leslie Groves, overseer of the Manhattan Project, later wrote, "his decision was one of noninterference—basically, a decision not to upset the existing plans." Nevertheless, one man would have to push the button and that was the President, and Truman now accepted the responsibility with confidence. After all, it was purely a military weapon, he reasoned, and it had to be used.*

2.

The actual site of the conference was a pleasant town surrounded by woods on the outskirts of Potsdam. Almost totally untouched by the war, Babelsberg had been a summer resort and the playground of Germany's movie colony. It reminded Major General John Deane, head of the U. S. Military Mission in Moscow, of a ghost city. On Sunday, July 15, Truman was installed in a three-story stucco house, once the home of a movie producer now in a Russian labor battalion. Located on Griebnitz Lake, "the Little White House," as it was nicknamed, was surrounded by groves of trees and an elegant garden which, like the house, showed signs of neglect. Churchill was billeted nearby in similar seedy splendor; Stalin was a mile away.

The conference, scheduled to open on Monday, July 16, was postponed until the next day because Stalin had suffered a slight heart attack. The one question about the bomb that remained—would it work?—was answered Monday evening at seven-thirty by a cable from Washington addressed to Stimson:

---

*To a question posed in an interview by the author in 1958 that the decision must have come only after considerable soul-searching, President Truman replied, "Hell, no, I made it like"—he snapped his fingers—"that!"

A year later, on April 28, 1959, he told a seminar at Columbia University, "The atom bomb was no 'great decision.' It was used in the war, and for your information, there were more people killed by fire bombs in Tokyo than dropping of the atom bombs accounted for. It was merely another powerful weapon in the arsenal of righteousness. The dropping of the two bombs stopped the war, saved millions of lives. It is just the same as artillery on our side. Napoleon said that victory is always on the side of the artillery. It was a purely military decision to end the war."

At the end of the seminar, a student again pressed him. "That was not any decision that you had to worry about," the President retorted. "It was just the same as getting a bigger gun than the other fellow had to win the war and that's what it was used for. Nothing else but an artillery weapon."

OPERATED ON THIS MORNING. DIAGNOSIS NOT YET COMPLETE BUT RESULTS SEEM SATISFACTORY AND ALREADY EXCEED EXPECTATIONS. LOCAL PRESS RELEASE NECESSARY AS INTEREST EXTENDS GREAT DISTANCE. DR. GROVES PLEASED. HE RETURNS [to Washington] TOMORROW. I WILL KEEP YOU POSTED.

The atomic bomb had been successfully exploded in Alamogordo, New Mexico. Groves and his deputy, Brigadier General Thomas Farrell, had watched the explosion from a distance of ten thousand yards. Awed by the stupendous blast Farrell exclaimed, "The war is over!" "Yes, it is over," said Groves, "as soon as we drop one or two on Japan!"

Stimson cabled back: I SEND MY WARMEST CONGRATULATIONS TO THE DOCTOR AND HIS CONSULTANT. The timing could not have been better as far as the President was concerned. The following noon Generalissimo Stalin (he had just been given the new title) arrived at the Little White House with Molotov and his interpreter, Pavlov.

Stalin chatted amiably for a few moments with Truman and Byrnes, then brought up the subject that was foremost in the President's mind: the war in the Pacific. He confided that the Japanese had requested him to mediate a peace but he had made no definite reply, since they were not ready to accept unconditional surrender. Both Truman and Byrnes knew every detail of the Japanese overture—the messages flying between Togo and Sato had been intercepted and decoded—but they pretended they were hearing it for the first time. Unprompted, Stalin announced that the Red Army would be prepared to attack early in August. The only obstacle was settlement of minor matters with Chiang Kai-shek, such as disposition of Dairen.

Dairen should be maintained as an open port, said Truman. If we get control of it, Stalin replied reassuringly, it will be. At lunch Stalin was expansive. He praised the wine. It was a propitious observation: when the Filipino waiter whipped the towel from the bottle, a California label came into view.

The first plenary session opened at ten past five in Cecilienhof Palace, one-time residence of Crown Prince Wilhelm and recently used as an army hospital. Beautifully furnished, the spacious two-story brownstone building on the lake reminded General Deane of an estate in Newport or Grosse Pointe.

The conferees settled around an imposing oaken table in the palace reception room which was decorated with the flags of the three nations. At Stalin's suggestion Truman (Churchill's interpreter thought he looked like a "polite but determined Chairman of a Board Meeting") took the chair. The initial discussions focused on Europe's postwar problems. Afterward at his quarters Churchill confided to Lord Moran, "Stalin is very amiable but he is opening his mouth very wide." He noted that the Generalissimo had switched to cigars, perhaps after the heart attack. "He says he prefers them to cigarettes. If he is photographed smoking a cigar with me everybody will say it is my influence. I said so to him." Moran asked the Prime Minister if he thought Truman had real ability. "I should think he has. At any rate, he is a man of immense determination. He takes no notice of delicate ground, he just plants his foot firmly on it." In illustration he stamped both bare feet solidly on the floor.

A few hours later Stimson received another report from the Interim Committee:

> DOCTOR HAS JUST RETURNED MOST ENTHUSIASTIC AND CONFIDENT THAT THE LITTLE BOY IS AS HUSKY AS HIS BIG BROTHER. THE LIGHT IN HIS EYES DISCERNIBLE FROM HERE TO HIGHHOLD [Stimson's home on Long Island] AND I COULD HAVE HEARD HIS SCREAMS FROM HERE TO MY FARM.

The officers decoding this coy subterfuge figured the seventy-seven-year-old Stimson had become a father and wondered if the conference would adjourn for a day to celebrate. "The little boy" was, of course, the plutonium bomb just exploded in New Mexico and "his big brother" the untested uranium gun-type bomb that would be dropped on Japan.

Success at Alamogordo had aggravated the distress of scores of scientists who had made it possible. Dr. Leo Szilard (like Dr. Franck, a refugee from the Nazis) submitted a petition to the Interim Committee drawn up by himself and signed by fifty-seven Chicago scientists. It urged that the Japanese be given suitable warning and the opportunity to surrender.*

---

*Szilard had gone much further in an early draft of this petition, calling for an outright ban on the use of atomic bombs: "Once they were introduced as an instrument of war it would be difficult to resist the temptation of putting them to such use. . . . Thus a nation which sets the precedent of using these newly liberated forces of nature for purposes of destruction may have to bear the responsibility of opening the door to an era of devastation on an unimaginable scale."
Few of his colleagues would endorse this draft on the grounds that if

At lunch on Wednesday, Truman sounded out Churchill on the question of apprising the Russians about the bomb. Churchill suggested that if Truman was "resolved to tell," he should explain that he had been waiting for the successful test. Then he would have an answer to the question, Why did you not tell us this before? Churchill also offered other advice. The phrase "unconditional surrender" bothered him; it could lead to tremendous loss of American lives. Couldn't it be expressed in another way so that the Allies got "all the essentials for future peace and security, and yet left the Japanese some show of saving their military honour and some assurance of their national existence, after they had complied with all safeguards necessary for the conqueror."

"I don't think the Japanese have any honor after Pearl Harbor," Truman retorted. "At any rate they have something for which they are ready to face certain death in very large numbers, and this may not be so important to us as to them."

That afternoon Truman met with Stalin. The President made no mention of the bomb, but Stalin had a secret to confide that was already known to Truman. The Generalissimo showed him the Emperor's confidential message requesting that Prince Konoye be received as an emissary of peace. Stalin wondered if he shouldn't ignore it; the U.S.S.R. would "eventually" declare war on Japan.

Innocently Truman told him to do what he thought best. Stalin suggested he "lull" the Japanese to sleep: what if he told the Japanese government that the message was so vague about Konoye's visit that he couldn't give a concrete reply?

So it was that Molotov's deputy in Moscow, Alexander Lozovsky, after keeping Ambassador Sato waiting for five days, at last sent him a confidential letter: the Emperor's proposal was so vague and Prince Konoye's mission so unclear that his government did not feel it could reply definitely to either question. Sato followed up his report to Tokyo with a plea to accept peace on any terms as long as the Emperor remained on the throne:

I REALIZE THAT IT IS A GREAT CRIME TO DARE TO MAKE SUCH STATEMENTS, KNOWING THEY ARE CONTRARY TO

---

the bomb was not used they would be guilty of allowing the war to drag on and the slaughter to continue. Others completely disagreed with Szilard and countered with their own petitions. One such concluded: "In short, are we to go on shedding American blood when we have available a means to speedy victory? No! If we can save even a handful of American lives, then let us use this weapon—now!"

THE VIEWS OF THE GOVERNMENT. THE REASON FOR DOING SO HOWEVER, IS THAT I BELIEVE THAT THE ONLY POLICY FOR OUR NATION'S SALVATION MUST COINCIDE WITH THESE IDEAS.

But his superiors back home were not yet ready to go that far, and if they had, the Americans would have given no formal assurance regarding the Emperor.

In Switzerland, however, Per Jacobsson was more determined than ever to open a channel for negotiations. He had finally succeeded in overcoming General Okamoto's reluctance to trust any American promises not in writing—by sophistry: the Americans had broken their written promises after World War I; now they were refusing to put promises in writing because they intended to keep their word. It appealed to Oriental logic and General Okamoto agreed to cable Tokyo a "strong recommendation" to end the war.

As a result of Okamoto's positive action Allen Dulles flew to Potsdam to give Stimson a firsthand report of the Japanese overtures. Dulles did not expect an immediate response, nor did he get it. He was satisfied, nevertheless, that the very real possibility of negotiations through Okamoto had been pointed out to "authoritative American quarters in a timely and, I believe, effective method." But the American leaders, now in possession of the ultimate weapon, were already determined to accept nothing short of unconditional surrender, and were no longer capable of considering negotiations even as the most peace-minded Japanese saw them.*

---

*This hardened position was belied on July 18 in a startling letter to the editor which appeared in the Washington *Post* signed "An Observer." The writer proclaimed that American military law, based upon historical precedents, clearly specified that conquest or occupation did not affect the sovereignty of a defeated nation. Its suggestion that the United States was open to negotiations through regular diplomatic channels created a minor furor in the capital. Knowledgeable reporters interpreted it as an official trial balloon. They had been privately informed, indeed, that it was the work of Ellis Zacharias, a maverick Navy captain and head of Op-16-W, a secret naval operational intelligence agency concerned mainly with psychological warfare. As an "official spokesman," Zacharias had for some time been assuring the Japanese by radio that unconditional surrender was largely a military term and did not mean the end of Japan's way of life. But the writer of the letter was actually one of his assistants, Ladislas Farago, who had spontaneously, on his own, decided to mitigate the unconditional surrender formula. Zacharias, when he learned of his subordinate's enterprise, approved of it and, moreover, repeated the advice to the Japanese in a subsequent broadcast.

On July 21 Stimson read aloud to Truman and Byrnes a detailed report from eyewitnesses describing the awesome spectacle at Alamogordo. Both were "immensely pleased" and Truman was "tremendously pepped up." The following morning Stimson brought the report to Churchill, who was exhilarated. The Prime Minister leaned forward. "Stimson, what was gunpowder?" he asked rhetorically, brandishing his cigar. "Trivial. What was electricity? Meaningless. This atomic bomb is the Second Coming in wrath." Suddenly he remembered something amusing. "Now I know what happened to Truman yesterday. I couldn't understand it. When he got to the meeting after having read this report he was a changed man. He told the Russians just where they got off and generally bossed the whole meeting." His excitement went beyond the scientific triumph. It would no longer be necessary to invade Japan. "Now all this nightmare picture had vanished," he later wrote. "In its place was the vision—fair and bright indeed it seemed—of the end of the whole war in one or two violent shocks. . . . Moreover, we should not need the Russians."

As far as Churchill and Truman were concerned, the decision to drop the bomb had been made. But three American military men continued to debate the issue. Beyond his moral reservations, Admiral Leahy suspected that the scientists and others in the program wanted to use the bomb "because of the vast sums that had been spent on the project." General "Hap" Arnold claimed that conventional bombing alone could end the war, even in the face of Marshall's insistence that it was either the bomb or a costly invasion. General Dwight Eisenhower also took vehement issue with Marshall's conclusion. He told Stimson privately that Japan was already defeated. Dropping the bomb was "completely unnecessary." Moreover, America should avoid rousing world condemnation by using a weapon which, in his opinion, "was no longer mandatory as a measure to save American lives."

On the evening of July 23, Churchill was host at a banquet. Many of the innumerable toasts and speeches were drowned out by the Royal Air Force Band. Mischievous, Churchill whispered to Leahy that it was his retaliation for being "bored to tears" by classical music at the Truman and Stalin banquets.

The President said he hoped he had been fair at the conference and would endeavor to be so in the future. Stalin immediately got to his feet. "Honesty adorns the man," he said and spoke at length in praise of Truman. King leaned over to Moran and whispered, "Watch the President. This is all new to him, but he can take it. He is a more typical American than Roosevelt, and he will do a good job, not only for the United States but for the whole world."

The toasts became more effusive. Churchill addressed the Soviet leader as Stalin the Great, and he in turn startled his listeners with "Here's to our next meeting in Tokyo!" After dessert Stalin began moving methodically around the big table collecting autographs on his menu.

Socially the banquet was an unqualified success, but the morning after revived doubts about the continuing unity of the Big Three. Field-Marshal Brooke, now Lord Alanbrooke, glumly noted in his diary: "One fact that stands out more clearly than any other is that nothing is ever settled!" The Big Three were no longer drawn together by the bonds of a common cause.

Truman's morning began with the news that the bomb should be ready by August 4-5, almost certainly no later than August 10. Before lunch he reviewed the final report of the Combined Chiefs, who recommended that Russia be brought into the war as soon as possible in order to eventuate the earliest possible surrender of Japan. This conclusion was a reflection of their conservative attitude toward an untried weapon. Secretary of State Byrnes, however, had no misgivings. Like Churchill, he saw the bomb as a means to end the war. It made Russia's entry, which would surely complicate the postwar settlements in Asia, unnecessary. At lunch he was so persuasive that Truman agreed that while Stalin had to be informed of the bomb, he should be told in a casual way. Otherwise the Generalissimo might realize its full import and move into Manchuria against the Japanese before the date he had promised—"early in August."*

After adjournment of the plenary that afternoon, Truman singled out Stalin and offhandedly mentioned, without using the words "nuclear" or "atomic," that America had "a new weapon of unusual destructive force." Just as casually Stalin

---

*Within two hours the Combined Chiefs of Staff would hear General Alexei E. Antonov, Chief of Staff of the Red Army, announce that "Soviet troops were now being concentrated in the Far East and would be ready to commence operations against Japan in the last half of August. The actual date, however, would depend upon the result of conferences with Chinese representatives which had not yet been completed."

replied that he was glad to hear it and hoped the Americans would make "good use of it against the Japanese."*

Churchill, who shared Byrnes's desire to keep Russia out of Asia, sidled up to Truman. "How did it go?" he asked conspiratorially.

"He never asked a question."

Within twenty-four hours the operational order to drop the first atomic bomb was on its way to General Carl A. ("Tooey") Spaatz, the new commander of the Strategic Air Forces:

The 509 Composite Group, 20th Air Force will deliver its first special bomb as soon as weather will permit visual bombing after about 3 August 1945 on one of the targets: Hiroshima, Kokura, Niigata and Nagasaki. To carry military and civilian scientific personnel from the War Department to observe and record the effects of the explosion of the bomb, additional aircraft will accompany the airplane carrying the bomb. The observing planes will stay several miles distant from the point of impact of the bomb. . . .

A day later the heavy cruiser *Indianapolis* dropped anchor a thousand yards off Tinian Island in the Marianas. Numerous small craft swarmed around the warship, and high-ranking officers of all services climbed aboard to watch the unloading of its top-secret cargo, a metal cylinder about eighteen inches in diameter and two feet high—the heart of the first practical atomic bomb. It weighed several hundred pounds and contained U-235, a derivation of uranium metal, shielded by lead. The momentous occasion was marred by a slight miscalculation. The wire on the winch lowering the cylinder to an LCT was six feet short and the onlookers—GI's and brass alike—jeered the sailors. But at last the ticklish job was over and the U-235 was safely ashore. *Indianapolis'* grave responsibility was over.**

---

*In 1946 Alexander Werth, war correspondent in the Soviet Union for the Sunday *Times* of London, asked Molotov if the Soviets had been told about the bomb at Potsdam. Molotov looked startled, thought for a moment and then said: "It's a tricky subject, and the real answer to your question is both Yes and No. We were told of a 'super-bomb,' of a bomb 'the like of which had never been seen'; but the word *atom* was not used."

**Less than four days later *Indianapolis* was hit by three torpedoes from the submarine *I-58*, skippered by Lieutenant Commander Mochitsura Hashimoto. She sank in twelve minutes. There were no lifeboats and few life rafts. Incredibly, *Indianapolis* was not missed for almost four days and, consequently, only 316 of her crew of 1,196 were

On July 25 the opposition Labour party challenged Churchill's leadership at the polls for the first time since the war began. Churchill flew home, and though still confident his Conservative party would get a substantial majority in the election, he carried with him a feeling of foreboding. "I dreamed that life was over," he told Moran. "I saw—it was very vivid—my dead body under a white sheet on a table in an empty room. I recognized my bare feet projecting from under the sheet. It was very life-like." Then he added, "Perhaps this is the end." He went to bed still confident of victory but was wakened "with a sharp stab of almost physical pain." He was suddenly convinced he was beaten and thought: "The power to shape the future would be denied me. The knowledge and experience I had gathered, the authority and goodwill I had gained in so many countries, would vanish."

By noon on the twenty-sixth it was obvious that the Labour party would win; Clement Attlee would be the new Prime Minister and return to Potsdam in his stead. "It may be a blessing in disguise," said Mrs. Churchill at luncheon.

"At the moment it seems quite effectively disguised."

The bomb was on Tinian, the orders for its use were cut. Now all that remained was to dispatch the final warning to Japan, the Potsdam Proclamation.* On the day of Churchill's defeat, President Truman ordered the Office of War Information in Washington to beam the message in the open to Japan. It threatened "the utter destruction of the Japanese homeland" unless Japan surrendered unconditionally, but made no mention of the atomic bomb; nor did it contain the controversial paragraph about retaining the Emperor. It limited Japanese sovereignty to the four main islands, but did promise that the Japanese would not be "enslaved as a race or destroyed as a nation" and would be allowed "to maintain such industries as will sustain her economy" and permitted access to raw materials. Moreover, the occupying forces would be withdrawn as soon as a new order was established and there were convincing proof that Japan's war-making capabilities were destroyed.

---

rescued. It was the most controversial sea disaster in American naval history.

*The State Department makes a distinction between the Potsdam Proclamation (the July 26 document demanding that Japan surrender unconditionally) and the Potsdam Declaration (the Allied policy statement concerning Europe), although both are usually referred to as "the declaration."

China and Britain had approved the proclamation, but not until that night was it shown to the Russians, who were understandably surprised and annoyed. Molotov immediately got on the phone with a request that the release of the declaration be postponed for a few days. Too late, Byrnes replied apologetically, it has already been issued. He hurriedly added, "I deemed it inappropriate to consult the Soviet Union about the document when your government was not at war with Japan."

Japanese monitors picked up the broadcast of the proclamation on the morning of July 27, Tokyo time. Togo's first reaction was that "it was evidently not a dictate of unconditional surrender." Perhaps the Emperor's personal desire for peace had become known to the Allies and moderated their attitude. There were, of course, some ambiguities but it was clearly desirable to enter into negotiations with the Allies for clarification and "revision—even if it should be slight—of disadvantageous points in the declaration." He reported at once to the Emperor urging that the ultimatum be "treated with the utmost circumspection, both domestically and internationally." He worried particularly about what might happen if Japan let it be known that she intended to reject it. In subsequent reports to the Big Six and then to the entire Cabinet, Togo recommended the same course as he had outlined to the Emperor. Admiral Toyoda countered that they should issue a statement at once proclaiming that "the government regarded the declaration as absurd and would not consider it."

Prime Minister Suzuki supported Togo, but everyone agreed that the proclamation had to be announced in the newspapers. The military wanted an official rejection to accompany the press release, but Suzuki suggested that they ignore the ultimatum. A compromise was reached: they would allow the papers to publish an expurgated version, without comment or criticism.

In the morning, however, several newspapers disregarded instructions and did editorialize, much to the discomfort of the Foreign Ministry. The *Mainichi* headlined the story LAUGHABLE MATTER and the *Asahi Shimbun* declared: "Since the joint declaration of American, Britain and Chungking is a thing of no great moment, it will merely serve to re-enhance the government's resolve to carry the war forward unfalteringly to a successful conclusion!"

Togo thought the military were responsible—the editors would never have had the courage to defy the government on their own—and they countered his accusation with renewed insistence that the declaration be refuted in definite terms. Once more a compromise was reached: the Prime Minister would read a statement belittling the Allied terms without rejecting them. At four o'clock Suzuki told reporters, "The Potsdam Proclamation, in my opinion, is just a rehash of the Cairo Declaration, and the government therefore does not consider it of great importance. We must *mokusatsu* it." The word means literally "kill with silence" but as Suzuki later told his son, he intended it to stand for the English phrase "No comment," for which there is no Japanese equivalent. Americans, however, understandably applied the dictionary meanings: "ignore" and "treat with silent contempt." On July 30 the *New York Times* headline read: JAPAN OFFICIALLY TURNS DOWN ALLIED SURRENDER ULTIMATUM.

The use of the atom bomb was inevitable, but for the Americans a question still remained: Would the Russians declare war *before* the bomb brought about a quick Japanese surrender? Only days before, General Antonov had postponed Soviet entry until "the last half of August." Now, after issue of the proclamation, Molotov pressed for a letter formally inviting Russian participation in the war. Truman stalled for forty-eight hours but finally, on the last day of July, sent Stalin the draft of an ambiguous invitation stating that "it would be proper for the Soviet Union to indicate its willingness to consult and cooperate with other great powers now at war with Japan with a view to joint action on behalf of the community of nations to maintain peace and security."

In a covering note, which attempted to shift the onus of the initiative on the Russians, Truman said he would send them a formal, signed copy after Stalin had reached an agreement with Chiang Kai-shek. "If you decide to use it, it will be all right. However, if you decide to issue a statement basing your action on other ground or for any other reason prefer not to use this letter, it will be satisfactory to me. I leave it to your good judgment."

"Terminal" was over. Truman, Attlee and Stalin publicly expressed their gratification, but there was an underlying atmosphere of weariness and disappointment. Truman, suspicious of Russian motives, privately resolved not to allow them "any part in the control of Japan" or to reveal anything about the bomb until there was some agreement on control and inspection. "You never saw such pig-headed people as are the Russians," he wrote his mother. "I hope I never have to hold another conference with them—but, of course, I will."

Leahy was proud of the way Truman had stood up to Stalin, particularly in refusing to be "bulldozed into any reparations agreement that would repeat the history of World War I," but continued Soviet objections to proposals important to the future peace of Europe had left the admiral with "serious doubts that any peace treaties acceptable to our government could be negotiated." Byrnes too was dissatisfied. The concessions won from Stalin depended on the Russians' carrying out their part of the bargain, and by this time Byrnes had "little confidence in their pledges."

"Terminal" had offered a unique opportunity to the victors of the war to further order and justice in a world torn by conflict for a decade. Instead, however, it created new conflicts for the post-war world.

3.

In Moscow, Ambassador Sato once more tried to convince Tokyo that the U.S.S.R. had no intention of intervening on Japan's behalf:

. . . I BELIEVE THAT STALIN FEELS THAT THERE IS ABSOLUTELY NO NECESSITY FOR MAKING A VOLUNTARY AGREEMENT WITH JAPAN. ON THIS POINT I SEE A SERIOUS DISCREPANCY BETWEEN YOUR VIEW AND THE ACTUAL STATE OF AFFAIRS.

But the Japanese leaders could not face the truth. They seemed immobilized by a common wishful conviction that the Soviet Union would come to the assistance of Japan. Even the pragmatic Kido expected a favorable reply once Molotov and Stalin returned to Moscow. Togo continued to press Sato:

. . . IT IS REQUESTED THAT FURTHER EFFORTS BE EXERTED TO SOMEHOW MAKE THE SOVIET UNION ENTHUSIASTIC OVER THE SPECIAL ENVOY. . . . SINCE THE LOSS OF ONE DAY RELATIVE TO THIS PRESENT MATTER MAY RESULT IN A THOUSAND YEARS OF REGRET, IT IS REQUESTED THAT YOU IMMEDIATELY HAVE A TALK WITH MOLOTOV. . . .

While the Japanese waited hopefully for Russia to solve their problems, the first atomic bomb was ready for delivery, waiting only for good weather, and others were en route. Rather than explore peace with a Japan that desperately sought it, American leaders were resolved to bring a summary end to the war—and avenge the humiliation of Pearl Harbor as well as the countless atrocities committed throughout the Pacific—with a weapon already weighted with controversy.

The bomb was assembled in an air-conditioned bomb hut on Tinian on the first day of August. It was ten feet long and twenty-eight inches in diameter, and except for its size, resembled an ordinary bomb.

The men who would drop it, the 509th Group, had been training under such secrecy that only their commander, Colonel Paul W. Tibbets, Jr., knew what their mission was to be. Their area was surrounded by barbed-wire fences and protected by machine guns. A general needed a pass to enter.

For all the stringent security measures, the 509th seemed to be doing very little. Occasionally they flew off in threes to dump a single bomb on enemy territory. They were derided by the other outfits on the island. One anonymous satirist wrote:

> Into the air the secret rose,
> Where they're going, nobody knows.
> Tomorrow they'll return again,
> But we'll never know where they've been.
> Don't ask us about results or such,
> Unless you want to get in Dutch.
> But take it from one who is sure of the score,
> The 509th is winning the war.

On the morning of August 5, the weather was forecast as favorable for takeoff after midnight. The previous night Captain William Parsons, a Navy ordnance expert who was responsible for arming the bomb, had witnessed four B-29's crash in succession on takeoff. He told General Thomas Farrell, in command of the secret project, that if the plane carrying the bomb failed to get into the air safely, an atomic explosion might be set off that would ravage the entire island.

"We will just have to pray that it doesn't happen."

"Well, if I made the final assembly of that bomb after we left the island, that couldn't happen." Farrell asked if he had ever before assembled a bomb under these conditions. "No, but I've got all day to try it."

"Go ahead and try it."

Late in the afternoon the bomb, scrawled with rude crayoned messages for the Emperor, was rolled out of its air-conditioned building into the glaring sunlight and transferred to the bomb bay of a B-29 named *Enola Gay* after Colonel Tibbets' mother. At dusk Parsons climbed into the stifling fuselage. Squatting beside the bomb, he practiced the final assembly hour after hour.

"For God's sake, man," said Farrell when he saw Parsons' bleeding hands, "let me loan you a pair of pigskin gloves. They're thin ones."

"I wouldn't dare. I've got to feel the touch."

At 7:17 P.M. Farrell radioed Groves: JUDGE [Parsons] TO LOAD BOMB AFTER TAKEOFF. . . . Shortly after 10 P.M. six crews were summoned to a Quonset assembly hut for briefing. Soberly they watched Tibbets stride up to a platform. "Tonight is the night we have all been waiting for," he said. "Our long months of training are to be put to the test. We will soon know if we have been successful or failed. Upon our efforts tonight it is possible that history will be made." They were to drop a bomb containing a destructive force equivalent to 20,000 tons of TNT. (The crew of *Enola Gay* had been told three days earlier what they would carry.) "Because this bomb is so powerful, we must use different tactics from those we have employed when using ordinary bombs." He explained that three weather planes would take off first and cover the three selected cities so the target could be changed at the last minute. An hour later *Enola Gay*, followed by two escort planes with scientific and photographic equipment, would leave. All three would rendezvous over Iwo Jima a few minutes after dawn.

At a final midnight briefing each man was issued a pair of adjustable arc welder's goggles to protect his eyes from the intense flash of the explosion. The crews bowed their heads in awed silence absorbing the words of Chaplain William Downey, a husky twenty-seven-year-old Lutheran: ". . . We pray Thee that the end of the war may come soon, and that once more we may know peace on earth. May the men who fly this night be kept safe in Thy care, and may they be returned safely to us. . . ."

The men solemnly filed into the mess hall for preflight supper, and were handed menus embellished with GI humor:

> *Look! Real eggs ("How da ya want them?")*
> *Rolled oats ("Why?")*
> *Milk ("No fishing")*

> *Sausage ("We think it's pork")*
> *Apple butter ("Looks like axle grease")*
> *Butter ("Yep, it's out of again")*
> *Coffee ("Saniflush")*
> *Bread ("Someone get a toaster")*

After the three weather planes lifted off into the night at 1:37 A.M., a crowd of well-wishers and photographers gathered around *Enola Gay*, and scores of flashbulbs popped, causing some apprehension that Japanese guerrillas in the hills might radio Tokyo that something extraordinary was taking place.

Enola Gay and her two escorts taxied to their runways. From the North Field control tower William Laurence, science editor of the *New York Times* and the sole newspaperman covering the story, watched intently, at General Farrell's side, as *Enola Gay* slowly rumbled down the runway. She accelerated to 180 miles an hour, but burdened by her extra weight, seemed earthbound. The onlookers, remembering the four Superfortresses that had crashed the night before, strained to help lift the plane into the air.

Tibbets was holding the nose down to build up speed but his co-pilot, Captain Robert A. Lewis, thought it was "gobbling a little too much runway," and began to put back pressure on the wheel. At last, with only a few yards of the oiled coral left, the huge aircraft soared up into the darkness.

In the tower, General Farrell turned to a Navy officer. "I never saw a plane use that much runway," he said. "I thought Tibbets was never going to pull it off."

It was exactly 2:45 A.M., August 6. It would be a day to remember.

33   **Hiroshima**

1.

Once *Enola Gay* had climbed to 4,000 feet, Captain Parsons lowered himself into the bomb bay and while his assistant, First Lieutenant Morris Jeppson, a Mormon, illuminated the bomb with a flashlight, he cautiously inserted the explosive detonating charge through the bomb's tail. It was almost half an hour before Parsons said, "Okay, that'll do it."

Jeppson removed a green plug from the bomb, replacing it with a red one. The electrical circuit was completed; the bomb was ready to be dropped. In the rear compartment Tibbets tried to sleep—he had been awake for twenty-four hours—but it was impossible, and after fifteen minutes he started to crawl back through the narrow thirty-foot tube that led to the front compartment. The tail gunner, Staff Sergeant George R. Caron, in a Brooklyn Dodgers baseball cap, held him back. "Say, Colonel," he asked, "are we splitting atoms today?"

"You're pretty close, Bob."

Tibbets relieved his co-pilot. Lewis left the cockpit for a snack and noticed little green lights on a black box. He asked Parsons "what the hell" they meant. They indicated that the bomb was okay; red lights meant trouble.

Tibbets watched Mount Suribachi, scarred from battle, slowly rise out of the sea in the dawn light. He moved the throttles forward and *Enola Gay* began to climb. It was 4:52 A.M. In minutes the plane had reached 9,000 feet, where she was joined by her two escorts. Below on Iwo Jima—the emergency stand-by base—awaited Tibbets' security chief, Major William Uanna. Tibbets called him by voice radio: "Bud, we are proceeding to target."

Tibbets picked up the intercom and told everyone to remain at his station until the bombing was over. Once Japan was sighted, he said, their conversation would be recorded. "This is for history, so watch your language. We're carrying the first atomic bomb."

Most of the crew had never heard the word "atomic" before. Its very sound was chilling.

Their primary target was Hiroshima on the southeast coast of Honshu, Japan's principal island. From this, the empire's eighth largest city, 120,000 civilians had been evacuated to the countryside, but 245,000 still remained. The city was almost unscarred by the war. Like the people of Dresden before them, the citizens of Hiroshima felt that their city was to be spared, though it was headquarters of 2nd General Army and was an important military port of embarkation. Their reasons for hope of immunity ranged from the naïve to the preposterous: they were exempt because they had numerous relatives in the United States; their city, like Kyoto, was so beautiful that the Americans wanted it as a residential area after the war; President Truman's mother lived nearby. They had taken little notice of 720,000 leaflets fluttering from the sky two days before, warning them that their city among others would be obliterated unless Japan surrendered at once. At 7:09 A.M. (an hour earlier than Tinian time), sirens blasted for a long minute. It was the third air-raid warning since midnight and few took to the shelters. The latest alert had been set off by *Straight Flush*, a weather plane bearing a cartoon of a Japanese soldier being flushed down a toilet. It was on the same course that Tibbets would take if the weather conditions at Hiroshima were favorable enough. If not, Tibbets would be sent to Kokura or Nagasaki.

From the distance Hiroshima appeared to be blanketed by an undercast, but by the time *Straight Flush* reached the bombing point the observer-bombardier, First Lieutenant Kenneth Wey, could see Hiroshima clearly through his bomb-sight. It was flat and consisted of six long slender islands lying in the delta of the Ota River. From 32,000 feet the city resembled the fingers of a deformed hand. On the southern tips docks jutted into the beautiful Inland Sea. The delta itself was rimmed by small mountains.

At 7:25 *Straight Flush* turned back toward its base, Tinian, harassed by scattered flak that burst far short of the target. The pilot, Major Claude Eatherly,* ordered the radio operator to send out the following message: "Low clouds, 1 to $3/10$ths. Middle cloud amount, 1 to $3/10$ths. Advice: Bomb primary."

Enola Gay had just reached its bombing height of almost 32,000 feet, and Co-pilot Lewis noted in the log he was writing at the request of *New York Times* correspondent William Laurence: "Well, folks, it won't be long."

Tibbets was informed of Eatherly's message and turned to his navigator, Captain Theodore ("Dutch") Van Kirk: "It's Hiroshima." At 7:50 (their watches read 8:50) the big aircraft reached Shikoku Island. Just beyond was Honshu— and Hiroshima. The crew hurriedly strapped on their flak suits. The radar and IFF (Identification, Friend or Foe)

---

*After the war Major Eatherly was exploited by a number of "Ban the Bomb" groups which claimed he was a martyr, an "American Dreyfus," jailed and hounded because of expressed guilt for his part in the Hiroshima bombing. A rash of books and articles made numerous false claims (at least one of which originated with Eatherly himself): that he personally selected Hiroshima as a target; that he was given the D.F.C.; that he flew through the bomb cloud at Hiroshima; that he commanded the bombing of Hiroshima; that he participated in the bombing of Nagasaki.

were switched off. The ship remained on autopilot. Parsons sent word up front that the lights were still green, then crawled forward to the cockpit where he looked over Tibbets' shoulder through a large opening in the clouds. A sprawling city lay below. "Do you agree that's the target?" Tibbets asked.

"Yes," said Parsons with a nod.

It was 8:09 A.M. "We are about to start the bomb run," Tibbets announced over the intercom. "Put on your goggles and place them up on your forehead. When the countdown starts, pull the goggles over your eyes and leave them there until after the flash."

Lewis added another line to his log, the only in-flight record of the mission: "There will be a short intermission while we bomb our target."

The instrument plane, *The Great Artiste*, dropped back 1,000 yards. The other escort, *Number 91*, began circling to mark time and position itself for photographs.

Enola Gay's bombardier, Major Thomas Ferebee, was leaning forward, left eye pressed to the Norden bombsight, his mustache flaring to either side. At 8:13 plus thirty seconds Tibbets said, "It's yours." Ferebee's bombsight required flight corrections in autopilot as the Superfortress headed west 31,600 feet over Hiroshima at a ground speed of approximately 285 miles an hour. The clouds had scattered and Ferebee could clearly distinguish what was already so familiar from target photographs—the seven tributaries of the Ota River which formed the six islands. The aiming point, the center of Aioi Bridge, crept to the cross hairs of the bombsight.

"I've got it," he said. In forty-five seconds he sent the bombing radio-tone signal through the intercom. The crew pulled down their dark glasses—all except the two pilots and Ferebee, who could not have seen through the bombsight with them.

At 8:15 plus seventeen seconds the plane's bomb-bay doors automatically swung open. The release of the bomb was timed electrically through the bombsight according to the information Ferebee fed into it. His finger was at a toggle button ready to push if the bomb failed to release. The radio tone stopped abruptly and he watched the elongated missile drop bottom first, flip over and hurtle nose down on Hiroshima. Nine thousand pounds lighter, the plane lunged upward. Tibbets banked violently to the right until he had come around more than 150 degrees, then nosed down to pick up speed.

The bomb-bay doors of *The Great Artiste* gaped open and three packs tumbled out. Almost immediately each one flowered into a parachute; dangling below was a cylinder resembling a fire extinguisher—it was a transmitter sending back data.

Tibbets ordered everyone to "make sure those goggles are on." The bomb was set to detonate in forty-three seconds, and at thirty-five he slipped on his own glasses.

Hiroshima was serene and so was the sky above it as the people continued on their daily routine. Those who noticed the three parachutes imagined that the plane had been hit and that the crew was bailing out or that more propaganda leaflets had been jettisoned. One man, remembering how the last leaflets had shimmered down in the sun, thought, The Americans have brought us some more beautiful things.

Several hundred yards north of Aioi Bridge (Ferebee's target), Private Shigeru Shimoyama, a recent draftee, looked up and idly peered through his thick glasses at one of the drifting chutes. He was standing outside his barracks, a huge wooden structure once a warehouse. He had been in Hiroshima four days and was already "bored to death." He wished he were back in Tokyo making school notebooks. All at once a pinkish light burst in the sky like a cosmic flash bulb.

Clocks all over Hiroshima were fixed forever at 8:15.

The bomb exploded 660 yards from the ground into a fireball almost 110 yards in diameter. Those directly below heard nothing, nor could they later agree what color the *pika* (lightning) flash was—blue, pink, reddish, dark-brown, yellow or purple.

The heat emanating from the fireball lasted a fraction of a second but was so intense (almost 300,000 degrees Centigrade) that it melted the surface of granite within a thousand yards of the hypocenter, or ground zero—directly under the burst. Roof tiles softened and changed in color from black to olive or brown. All over the center of the city numerous silhouettes were imprinted on walls. On Yorozuyo Bridge ten people left permanent outlines of themselves on the railing and the tar-paved surface.

Moments later came an unearthly concussion that obliterated all but a few solid, earthquake-proof buildings within two miles. Ferebee had been almost on target, little more than 300 yards off the intended drop point.

Private Shimoyama was 550 yards north of ground zero. He was not directly exposed to the *pika* flash or his life would have been puffed out, but the blast hurled him into the vast barnlike warehouse, driving him into the collapsing roof beam where five long nails in his back held him suspended several feet off the ground. His glasses were still intact.

Five hundred yards farther north Captain Hideo Sematoo, a company commander, had just cantered up to his office and was removing his riding boots. The building fell on top of him and ignited. He thought of the seven years he had fought in Manchuria, China, Singapore, Malaya and New Guinea. How miserable to be burned to death rather than die in battle! *"Tenno Heika banzai!"* he shouted. As the flames reached for him, the wreckage above him was pulled away and he wrenched himself free. Nauseated, he looked at an eerie yellow sky. The ground was flat as far as he could see. Everything was gone—towering Hiroshima Castle and 2nd General Army headquarters. Instinctively he stumbled and crawled toward the main branch of the Ota River. There, crowded along the banks, were hundreds of dazed patients and nurses from the Army Hospital. Their hair was burned off, their skin charred a dark brown. He felt chilly.

A thousand yards on the other side of the hypocenter, Mrs. Yasuko Nukushina was trapped in the ruins of the family *sake* store. Her first thought was of her four-year-old daughter, Ikuko, who was playing outside somewhere. Unaccountably, she heard Ikuko's voice beside her: "I'm afraid, Mama." She told the child they were buried and would die there. Her own words made her claw desperately at the wreckage. She was a slight woman, four feet six inches tall, but in her frenzy she broke free into the yard. All around was devastation. She somehow felt responsible; "her" bomb had also destroyed the neighborhood. People drifted by expressionless and silent like sleepwalkers in tattered, smoldering clothing. It was a parade of wraiths, an evocation of a Buddhist hell. She watched mesmerized until someone touched her. Grasping Ikuko's hand, she joined the procession. In her confusion she had the illusion that vast numbers of planes were roaring over the city, dropping bomb after bomb without cessation.

Fourteen hundred yards east of ground zero at the presbytery of the only Catholic church in the city, Father Superior Hugo Lassalle, a German, had heard a plane overhead. He went to the window. The empty sky flared yellow—and the ceiling dropped. Cut and bleeding, Father Lassalle found his way to the street. It was dark. The entire city was covered by a blanket of dust. With another German priest he began searching through the rubble for residents of the mission.

Half a dozen blocks south, fifteen-year-old Michiko Yamaoka had just left home for work at the telephone office. She remembered "a magnesium flash," then a faraway voice calling "Michiko!" Her mother. "I'm here," she answered but didn't know where that was. She couldn't see—she must be blind! She heard her mother shout, "My daughter is buried under there!" Another voice, a man's, advised the mother to escape the flames sweeping down the street. Michiko begged her mother to save herself and heard running steps diminish to silence. She was going to die. Then came a shaft of light as concrete blocks were pushed aside by soldiers. Her mother was bleeding profusely, one arm skewered by a piece of wood. She ordered Michiko to escape. She herself was staying to rescue two relatives under the ruins of their house.

Michiko moved through a nightmare world—past charred bodies—a crying baby sealed behind the twisted iron bars of a collapsed reinforced-concrete building. She saw someone she knew and called out.

"Who are you?" the other girl asked.

"Michiko."

The friend stared at her. "Your nose and eyebrows are gone!"

Michiko felt her face. It was so swollen that her nose seemed to have disappeared.

In the same area, 350 young girls from the Girls Commercial School had been working in an empty lot, clearing an evacuated area. They wore blue *mompei* and jackets but no hats or fire hoods, and those who turned, curious, toward the *pika*—almost 300 of them—were instantly doomed. Twelve-year-old Miyoko Matsubara's instinct was to bury her face in her arms. She regained consciousness in unimaginable desolation—no people, no buildings—only limitless rubble. Where were her *mompei*? All she had around her waist was a white cloth belt and it was on fire. (Everyone wearing dark clothing who was exposed to the *pika* suffered primary thermal burns but the cruel flash reflected harmlessly off white material.) She started to beat out the flames with her right hand but to her horror she saw strips of skin, her skin, dangling from it.

Mrs. Tomita had given birth to a baby girl that morning.

Together with her husband, Torao, she was admiring their newborn daughter, Hiroko, when an intense light filled the window. Mrs. Tomita remembered a whooshing noise before losing consciousness. She came to on the floor. Her husband was gone. The baby in her little red dress was lying on top of the sewing machine—alive but unnaturally silent. Mrs. Tomita wrapped diapers tightly around her distended stomach—the midwife had told her to move as little as possible—and walked out into the street with the baby. Torao was hysterically digging in the ruins for their other two children. He found the elder daughter still alive, but her brother was hopelessly buried somewhere under the mass. There was a shout that more planes were on the way and the family sought shelter in a ditch trickling with foul water.

Less than a mile south of ground zero the main building of Hiroshima University stood intact amid the devastation. The hands of its huge clock, which faced the campus, had stopped at 8:15. But the bomb, which had stilled so many other clocks and watches at that time, had nothing to do with it; several days previously it had stopped prophetically at that catastrophic moment.

Two student nurses, who were ill in bed at a wooden dormitory of the Red Cross Hospital across the street, neither saw nor heard the bomb. Their first sensation was that their lungs were collapsing. Kyoko Sato crawled out of the caved-in building into a maelstrom of dust. A muffled call, "Sato san!" led her to her friend, whom she pried loose from the debris. Together they tried to cross the highway to report to the hospital but couldn't penetrate the solid stream of silent humanity moving away from the city, half naked and bleeding but without hysteria, not even tears. The unreality of it was terrifying.

Dr. Fumio Shigeto, head of internal medicine at the hospital, never reached his office that morning. On his way to work, he was waiting for a trolley at the end of a long line which bent around the corner of the Hiroshima railway station, 2,000 yards east of the hypocenter. The flash seemed to turn a group of girls ahead of him white, almost invisible. An incendiary bomb! As he dropped to the sidewalk, covering eyes and ears, a heavy slate slammed into his back. Whirls of smoke blotted out the sun. In the darkness he groped blindly to reach shelter before the next wave of attackers came on. Fearing poison gas, he covered his mouth with a handkerchief.

A breeze from the east gradually cleared the area as

though it were dawn, revealing an incredible scene: the buildings in front of the station were collapsed, flattened; half-naked and smoldering bodies covered the ground. Of the people at the trolley stop he alone, the last one in line, was unhurt, protected by the corner of the station building. Dr. Shigeto started for the hospital but was stopped by an impenetrable wall of advancing flames. He turned and ran for open space—toward an Army drill ground behind the station. He saw scores of survivors milling around, crying hysterically, and to ease the pain of their burns they extended their arms from which dangled long curls of skin.

A nurse approached him; he must be a doctor because he carried a black bag and had a trim little mustache. She begged him to help another doctor and his wife lying on the ground. His first thought was: What if this mob of desperate people discovers I am a physician? He couldn't help them all. "Please treat my wife first," said the injured doctor, who was bleeding profusely. Shigeto gave the woman a camphor shot for shock, followed by another injection to stop the bleeding. He rearranged the bandages the nurse had applied and then turned to the other wounded, treating them until he ran out of medicine and supplies. There was nothing else he could do. He fled toward the hills.

2.

Enola Gay's crew members saw a pinpoint of purplish red light miles below them instantly expand into a ball of purple fire. This exploded into a chaotic mass of flames and clouds emanating smoke rings of fog. A white column of smoke emerged from the purple clouds, rising rapidly to 10,000 feet, where it bloomed into an immense mushroom which seethed turbulently as it continued to almost 50,000 feet.

A shock wave rocked *Enola Gay*. Tibbets thought it was antiaircraft fire and shouted "Flak!" Parsons yelled that it was shock and added, "We're in the clear now." Co-pilot Lewis cast a backward glance at the flash, even though he had removed his dark glasses seconds before the explosion to look at the instrument panel. Ferebee had become so fascinated by the long trajectory of the bomb that he forgot to pull down his goggles. It was as if a photographer's flash bulb had gone off in his face. Tibbets swept off his goggles, scanned the panel and banked the ship back toward Hiroshima to observe the results.

"Holy Moses, what a mess!" Sergeant Caron, the tail gunner, exclaimed over the intercom.

"My God," said Lewis, "what have we done?" He jotted the words "My God!" in his log. It looked as if Hiroshima had been "torn apart," and made him feel as if they were "Buck Rogers twenty-fifth-century warriors."

The navigator, "Dutch" Van Kirk, was stunned at first, next filled with pride and finally relieved that it was all over. There were cheers over the intercom; it meant the end of the war. Then the crew began to think of the people on the ground.

Tibbets ordered the radio operator to send a message in the clear that the primary target had been bombed visually with good results. Parsons sent another, this one in code:

RESULTS CLEAR CUT, SUCCESSFUL IN ALL RESPECTS. VISIBLE EFFECTS GREATER THAN TRINITY [the test at Alamogordo]. CONDITIONS NORMAL IN AIRPLANE FOLLOWING DELIVERY, PROCEEDING TO PAPACY [Tinian]. . . .

A few miles away the scientists in *The Great Artiste* were glued to their blast-recording gear. In the photo plane Dr. Bernard Waldman, a physicist from Notre Dame, was in the bombardier's seat, operating a special high-speed movie camera he had brought from America. There hadn't been time to test it in the air. He had counted to forty after the bomb dropped and turned on the camera. As the plane banked away First Lieutenant Russell Gackenbach, the navigator, also snapped a series of pictures with his pocket camera.

On the ground, two and a half miles south of the hypocenter, former news photographer Gonichi Kimura was working outside a stable for the Army when he saw a strong flash to his left and simultaneously felt a searing blast of heat. At first he thought the Hiroshima Gas Company's tank had exploded, but since he soon discovered that it was still standing, he felt intuitively that some special bomb must have been dropped and decided to take pictures as soon as he could get to his camera, which was stored in the warehouse nearby. By the time he had crawled through the wreckage of the stable, the narrow white column of smoke from the bomb had changed to pink and the top started to swell, making it look like a mushroom, and it kept growing massively.

At the warehouse Kimura found all the windows shattered from the blast, and there was so much broken glass on the floor where his camera was kept that he could not even step inside, but he managed to stretch in and pull the drawer open. The trees outside the warehouse were in the way, so he returned to the stable to take his first pictures of the atomic cloud—"indeed, a gruesome sight"—which was now covering most of the sky. Fires which had broken out in the western part of the city were spreading rapidly, and he finished his roll of film from the roof of a factory.* Kimura escaped the bomb without injury, but he never saw his wife again—he had left her at home after breakfast that morning.

Those near the hypocenter never heard the explosion of the bomb. With distance, the noise grew perceptible, then shattering. From three miles it sounded like the rumbling of unworldly thunder; at four miles it was a distant moan which grew into a jarring boom. Near the port of Kure, twelve miles to the southeast, Tadahiko Kitayama thought a nearby ammunition dump had detonated, and several miles offshore, salvagers attempting to raise the four-man submarine *Koryu*, which was stuck in the bottom mud, heard a deafening "thunderbolt" clap. Moments later they noticed a B-29 coming from the direction of Hiroshima.

For a quarter of an hour the atmosphere above Hiroshima was churned by cosmic forces. Then huge drops of rain began to plummet down. The rising cloud column had carried moisture sufficiently high for water vapor to condense, and stained by radioactive dust, fall in large drops. The "black rain," weird and almost supernatural, horrified the survivors. Was it some kind of poisonous oil that would stick to the skin and slowly kill them? It pelted down on the half-naked people, leaving gray streaks on their bodies, releasing in many of them a sense of awareness of the unimaginable disaster that had been visited on Hiroshima. Mrs. Tomita tried to protect her two-hour-old baby, but little Hiroko was soaked by the fallout. She still had not uttered a sound since the blast.**

---

*Kimura developed the films himself at home. They were overexposed but usable, and one is reprinted in the picture section of this book. Waldman's film was ruined when it was processed in the well-equipped photo laboratory at Tinian. The equipment had to be kept at 70 degrees but the refrigeration unit malfunctioned, subjecting the film to excessive heat stripping the emulsion. The pictures in Lieutenant Gackenbach's little camera were excellent.

**Miraculously the entire family, except for the boy who was never found, survived with few ill effects. Hiroko was nicknamed "Pikako" (little *pika*), and grew to be an attractive, healthy young woman—a

The deadly rain, which had changed into a foggy, yellowish drizzle, spread to the northwest. Almost none fell on the area to the east where the fires were more intense, and Dr. Yoshimasa Matsuzaka, a skin specialist and head of the city's civil defense, was trying to bring some order out of chaos. Ignoring his own wounds, he put on his civil defense uniform which his wife had rescued from the wreckage of his office, and leaning on his son, marched toward the East District police station holding high a Rising Sun flag on a long stick. The sight of the determined little procession extending first-aid treatment—Mrs. Matsuzaka and three nurses brought up the rear—calmed the people. The group set up a first-aid station in front of the police headquarters—it was 1,200 yards from the hypocenter—and long lines of injured and burned began to form outside the shell of the station house.

From his destroyed home less than half a mile away the police chief, Shiroku Tanabe, was desperately trying to get to the station. But he was impeded by thousands of refugees (they looked "as if they had crawled out of a pool of blood") streaming away from ground zero. By the time Tanabe reached the station house, it had caught fire. He took command and organized a bucket brigade to a nearby "fire pool." Though half the building was ablaze, Dr. Matsuzaka and his indomitable first-aid team continued to treat the injured and to urge them to seek refuge outside the city.

All over town, charcoal braziers full of hot coals (housewives had been preparing breakfast) ignited the tinderbox rubble. These thousands of small fires were whipped into fury by a cyclonic wind that was sucked in toward the hypocenter with such force that large trees were uprooted. Blasts of flame—they could have come from monster blowtorches—erratically ripped off corrugated roofs as if they were cardboard, blasted houses apart and twisted metal bridges. Telephone poles ignited explosively.

Near the site of Hiroshima Castle four men staggered though the burning streets with a massive portrait of the Emperor; they had rescued it from the inferno of the 2nd General Army communications center and were trying to get it safely out of the city. At the sight of the picture, lines of apathetic refugees broke into cries of "The Emperor's portrait!" The burned and bleeding saluted or bowed low. Those

---

local tennis champion. The Tomitas rebuilt on the ruins of their former home.

unable to get to their feet clasped hands in prayer. As the picture was trundled through Asano Sentei Park to a waiting boat moored on the river, towering pine trees flamed into torches. Wounded soldiers on the banks, waiting to be rescued, struggled to attention and saluted as the boat headed upstream for safety through a shower of flaming debris.

Their commander, General Fujii, was incinerated in the first minutes at his quarters near the castle but Private Shigeru Shimoyama, who was closer to ground zero, was still alive even after being impaled on the spikes of a roof beam. He painfully pulled himself free from the spikes, and using his head as a battering ram, relentlessly slammed at the roof, blinded by streams of blood, until he broke through. Thick stifling clouds of dust swirled about him, but he could tell that some irresistible force had swept across the city like the hand of a vengeful giant. At the river he watched scores of wounded making the long frantic leap from its banks. What did they think they were doing? The surface of the water was covered with carmine scum. From blood? Shimoyama kept telling himself to remain calm. He was no stranger to disaster; he had almost been killed in the earthquake of '23, the Doolittle raid and the Tokyo fire bombing of April 13. He started up the river against the wind; it would help keep the fires behind him.

Directly in his path was a cavalry horse standing alone. It was pink; the blast had seared off its skin. It looked at him pleadingly and followed with a few faltering steps. The pitiful sight fascinated Shimoyama, and he had to force himself to press on (he would dream about the pink horse for years afterward). Half a dozen other soldiers were also purposefully following the bank north, but it was as if each man was solitary, preoccupied with his own survival. Civilians, some almost naked, tried to keep up with them, but as the dull rumble of flames behind grew louder, the soldiers quickened their pace, leaving the others far behind.

Several miles upstream Shimoyama forded the river where the water only came up to his neck. As he proceeded into the suburbs where the havoc of the bomb had not reached, he was obsessed by one thought—that it was an atomic bomb. He must get home and see his daughter before he died of the effects. In 1943 a brother-in-law of his had informed him that the Japanese were working on one and for the past few days, oddly, there had been so much talk in his barracks about such a bomb that if a man lost his temper someone would say, "He's like an atomic bomb." He passed scores of high school girls, horribly burned, sprawling on either side of the road. Long strips of skin hung in ribbons from their faces, arms and legs. They reached out in supplication for water. But what could he do? Farther up the road, villagers were laying sliced cucumbers on the burns of other survivors and carrying those most seriously hurt to first-aid stations in vegetable carts.

The first fragmentary reports that came into Tokyo indicated simply that Hiroshima had suffered an unprecedented disaster. Imperial Headquarters could not raise the 2nd General Army communications center for fuller details.

Marquis Kido immediately informed the Emperor that Hiroshima had been laid waste by some secret weapon. "Under these circumstances we must bow to the inevitable," said His Majesty. He could not hide his anguish. "No matter what happens to me, we must put an end to this war as soon as possible. This tragedy must not be repeated." But both agreed that the psychological moment had not yet come for the Emperor to take personal action.

In the dying light of dusk the fires began to subside and from a distance Hiroshima looked peaceful, like the gigantic encampment of a quiescent army on the plain. And high overhead, stars appeared startlingly bright against the darkening sky. The flow out of the city had been reversed as the first trickle of help entered from the outside.

Dr. Shigeto of the Red Cross Hospital, who had fled the holocaust, was back. Going from one first-aid station to another, he was told that water was harmful for those suffering burns. On the contrary, he announced, it flushed the poison from burns out of the system. He had signs put up: YOU MAY GIVE WATER. DR. SHIGETO, VICE DIRECTOR, RED CROSS HOSPITAL.

As he penetrated deeper into the ravaged city, he found his way blocked by smoldering rubble. Although there seemed to be no passable road, he saw to his astonishment a large charcoal-burning truck come rumbling out of the smoke, its cab crowded with men. He recognized the driver, a *sake* manufacturer from his suburb. He had braved the inferno to carry emergency food and *sake* to his customers, but found their stores burned down. Shigeto started past the truck. "There's not a living soul in there!" the driver called out. "Not an animal. What use is a doctor?" Shigeto was forcibly lifted into the truck.

The doctor had to borrow a bicycle to cover the last mile

home. He came unexpectedly upon a woman, a baby on her back, wandering on the dark road. When she saw him she began to weep hysterically. It was his wife, and in his memory, she had already placed a burning candle on the family Buddhist shrine.

Outside the city, first-aid stations were powerless to help the hundreds dying every hour. Seven-year-old Shizuko Iura was close to death but no one had heard her cry or complain. She continually asked for water, which her mother gave her against the advice of attendants. Why not ease her dying? "Father [he was a sailor on some Pacific island] is far away from home in a dangerous place," Shizuko said as if she saw him in a vision. "Please stay alive, Mother. If both us die, he will be very lonely." She mentioned the names of all her friends and relatives. When she came to her grandparents she added, "They were good to me." She cried "Papa, Papa!" and died.

That day perhaps 100,000 human beings perished in Hiroshima, and an equal number were dying from burns, injuries and a disease of the atomic age, radiation poisoning.*

3.

At 2:58 P.M., local time, *Enola Gay* touched down on Tinian's North Field. Several hundred officers and men rushed to surround the aircraft as the crew emerged. General "Tooey" Spaatz strode up and pinned a D.S.C. on Tibbets, who embarrassedly poked his pipe up a coverall sleeve as he stood at attention. The crew was interrogated in the officers club, a Quonset hut, over lemonade laced with bourbon. An intelligence officer asked Navigator Van Kirk for the exact drop time. He replied, "At 091517K"—seventeen seconds past schedule.

"Why were you late?"

Everyone laughed. General Farrell left the interrogation to

---

*Professor Shogo Nagaoka, the first curator of the Peace Memorial in Hiroshima, concluded that at least 200,000 died as a result of the bomb. This figure was corroborated by Drs. Naomi Shohno and K. Sakuma after an extensive study.

Twenty-two of the victims were American prisoners of war, and included several women. This was revealed to a Japanese newspaper in July 1970 by Hiroshi Yanagida, a *kempei* warrant officer, who had guarded the Americans. There were twenty-three prisoners in all. The twenty-third, a young soldier, was pulled out of the rubble alive, but he was killed by an angry mob of Japanese survivors.

send his first full report (an earlier bulletin had been transmitted based on the initial reports radioed from *Enola Gay*) to General Groves:

... FLASH NOT SO BLINDING AS TRINITY BECAUSE OF BRIGHT SUNLIGHT. FIRST THERE WAS A BALL OF FIRE CHANGING IN A FEW SECONDS TO PURPLE CLOUDS AND FLAMES BOILING AND SWIRLING UPWARD. FLASH OBSERVED JUST AFTER AIRPLANE ROLLED OUT OF TURN. ALL AGREED LIGHT WAS INTENSELY BRIGHT. ...

ENTIRE CITY EXCEPT OUTERMOST ENDS OF DOCK AREAS WAS COVERED WITH A DARK GRAY DUST LAYER WHICH JOINED THE CLOUD COLUMN. IT WAS EXTREMELY TURBULENT WITH FLASHES OF FIRE VISIBLE IN THE DUST. ESTIMATED DIAMETER OF THIS DUST LAYER IS AT LEAST THREE MILES. ONE OBSERVER STATED IT LOOKED AS THOUGH WHOLE TOWN WAS BEING TORN APART WITH COLUMNS OF DUST RISING OUT OF VALLEYS APPROACHING THE TOWN. DUE TO DUST VISUAL OBSERVATIONS OF STRUCTURAL DAMAGE COULD NOT BE MADE.

JUDGE [Parsons] AND OTHER OBSERVERS FELT THIS STRIKE WAS TREMENDOUS AND AWESOME EVEN IN COMPARISON WITH TR [Trinity]. ITS EFFECTS MAY BE ATTRIBUTED BY THE JAPANESE TO A HUGE METEOR.

In Washington, Groves had received the preliminary message just before midnight, August 5. Because of the hour he did not awaken General Marshall; he went to sleep in his office to be on hand when the more detailed report came in. It arrived at 4:15 A.M., and three and a half hours later Chief of Staff Marshall transmitted the information by scrambler telephone to Stimson at his home on Long Island. The Secretary of War agreed that Truman's prepared statement concerning the bomb should be released to the press that morning.

It announced that a revolutionary bomb had been dropped on Hiroshima, which was described as an important Army base. "It is an atomic bomb. It is a harnessing of the basic power of the universe. The force from which the sun draws its power has been loosed against those who brought war to the Far East." America was prepared to obliterate all Japanese factories, docks, communications. "It was to spare the Japanese people from utter destruction that the ultimatum of July 26 was issued at Potsdam. Their leaders promptly rejected that ultimatum. If they do not now accept our terms, they may expect a rain of ruin from the air, the like of which has never been seen on this earth."

Truman was aboard *Augusta* on his way home from Potsdam. Army Captain Franklin Graham interrupted the President at lunch in the after mess hall to hand him a short dispatch from Stimson saying that the "big bomb" had been dropped on Hiroshima, apparently with success. Truman looked up. "Captain Graham," he remarked, "this is the greatest thing in history," and lapsed into silence. Within minutes another message arrived. It quoted the report from Parsons that the results had been "clear cut, successful in all respects."

Truman had kept the first dispatch to himself. Now he brusquely shoved his chair back and strode over to Byrnes at a nearby table. "It's time to get on home!" he said cryptically. He picked up a fork and rapped it sharply against a glass. The room went silent and he told the sailors about the new weapon. The President left for the officers wardroom, the cheers of the enlisted men following him down the companionway. "Keep your seats, gentlemen," he told the startled officers. "We have just dropped a bomb on Japan which has more power than twenty thousand tons of TNT. It was an overwhelming success. We won the gamble!"

At his home in Tokyo, Cabinet Secretary Sakomizu was in bed half asleep when the Domei News Agency phoned about the Truman announcement. The words "atomic bomb" brought him wide awake. He was shocked, but realized at the same time that this was the "golden opportunity" to end the war. No nation could defend itself against atomic bombs. It wouldn't be necessary to blame the military or the munitions makers for losing the war. He picked up the phone to call the Prime Minister.

34   . . . and Nagasaki

1.

In Hiroshima the mysterious effects of radiation were making themselves known at dawn on August 7. Shogo Nagaoka, formerly a geologist at the university, was trying to get through the rubble to the campus. A recent draftee, he had deserted his Army unit out of concern for the fate of the university and had been traveling for hours. He could hardly fathom the endless devastation. At the Gokoku Shrine near the hypocenter he slumped exhausted at the foot of a stone lantern. He felt a stinging sensation—it was radiation—and sprang to his feet. Then he noticed a strange silhouette on the lantern and that some of its surface was melted. An awful and sudden realization came to him: an atomic bomb! Japan had to surrender at once.

At scores of aid stations doctors were mystified. Their patients' symptoms were so bizarre that it was suspected an acrid poison gas had been used to spread bacillary dysentery. Some victims were scorched on just one side of the face; oddly, some had the shadow of a nose or ear stenciled on their cheek. Like Nagaoka, Dr. Shigeto of the Red Cross Hospital had heard of atomic energy and guessed that the victims were suffering from primary radiation. He checked the walls of the hospital with a simple X-ray indicator. The count was so low, however, that he concluded it was safe to remain.

The aftereffects were unpredictable. Private Shimoyama, one of those closest to ground zero, had been near-sighted before the *pika*. Now as he peered through his glasses everything seemed slightly blurred to him. Was he going blind? When he finally removed his glasses he discovered that he had regained perfect vision. But his hair was falling out and he was suffering from the same sickness that had struck thousands of others. First they felt nauseated and vomited; diarrhea and fever followed. Other reactions were erratic. Some victims were covered with brilliant spots—red, green-yellow, black and purple—and lived; others whose bodies had no apparent marks died abruptly. One man escaped with a slightly burned hand and ignored it until he began vomiting blood. He put his injured hand in water for relief and "something strange and bluish came out of it, like smoke."

Terror of the unknown, intensified by vague feelings of guilt and shame, swept over the survivors: they were alive because they had ignored pleas of relatives and neighbors for help and left them trapped in burning wreckage. The anguished voices of those who had died kept haunting them. Parents who had lost children blamed themselves, and children who had lost parents felt this was punishment for some wrongdoing. The tragedy had cruelly shattered the intricate and intimate structure of Japanese family life.

In Tokyo the Army's fanatic reluctance to accept the responsibility of surrender led them to question the significance of the complete destruction of a major city. They saw no merit in Foreign Minister Togo's suggestion that Japan accept the Potsdam Proclamation even when he pointed out with logic that the bomb "drastically alters the whole military situation and offers the military ample grounds for ending the war."

"Such a move is uncalled for," War Minister Anami countered. "Furthermore, we do not yet know if the bomb was atomic." They only had Truman's word for it. It might be a trick. Dr. Yoshio Nishina, the nation's leading nuclear scientist, should be sent at once to investigate Hiroshima.

As Dr. Nishina and Lieutenant General Seizo Arisue, chief of Intelligence, were about to board a plane at Tachikawa Air Base, an air-raid siren began its banshee howl. Arisue ordered Dr. Nishina to wait until the All Clear sounded, but he and several subordinates took off immediately. Their plane arrived over Hiroshima just before dusk. The general had seen many cities laid waste by fire bombings—usually there was smoldering debris, smoke from emergency kitchens and some signs of human activity—but below him stretched a lifeless desert. No smoke, no fires, nothing. There wasn't a street in sight.

The pilot turned and shouted, "Sir, this is supposed to be Hiroshima. What should we do?"

"Land!"

The plane touched down on a sod strip near the harbor. As Arisue descended he noticed that the grass, a strange clay color, was leaning toward the Inland Sea; it looked as if it had been pressed by some giant hot iron. The party was met by a lieutenant colonel who saluted smartly. The left half of his face was severely burned, the right half untouched. Arisue was taken by motorboat to Army Maritime Transport Command. At the dock he was greeted by Lieutenant General Hideo Baba, a friend since the Military Academy, who reported that there was no water or electricity in Hiroshima. The two generals sat in the open at a long wooden table lit by candles. Baba had difficulty controlling his voice. He described how his daughter had perished on her way to high school. "Not my daughter alone, but thousands of other innocent children were massacred. This new bomb is satanic, too atrocious and horrible to use." He covered his face with his hands.

Arisue put his arm around his friend. "Please remember that we are military men," he finally said. Baba apologized for breaking down. He told Arisue that there was "a persistent rumor" that the Americans were going to drop another of the new bombs on Tokyo.*

People were returning to the city in ever-increasing numbers. Work groups began collecting bodies and incinerating them with whatever wood they could find. The stench was nauseating, somewhat like broiled sardines, but some of the workers had developed a perverse craving for the smell; it actually stimulated their appetites.

Dr. Nishina's plane arrived over Hiroshima the following afternoon. He surveyed the city and instantly concluded that an atomic bomb alone could have wreaked such havoc. He informed General Arisue that it had been a uranium-type bomb similar to the one he was trying to develop. Should he continue work on his bomb?

Arisue didn't answer.

The destruction of Hiroshima made Japan's unrealistic hope for negotiated peace through the good offices of the Soviet Union more urgent than ever. Togo cabled Ambassador Sato in Moscow:

THE SITUATION IS BECOMING SO ACUTE THAT WE MUST HAVE CLARIFICATION OF THE SOVIET ATTITUDE AS SOON AS POSSIBLE. PLEASE MAKE FURTHER EFFORTS TO OBTAIN A REPLY IMMEDIATELY.

In the afternoon on August 8 the ambassador requested an immediate audience with Molotov, who had been avoiding him for several weeks. He was granted an appointment at eight that evening but moments later he was inexplicably asked to move up the meeting to five o'clock. Sato forced himself to remain calm as he entered the rambling Kremlin complex a few minutes before five. He was ushered into

---

*The fear that Tokyo was to be the next atomic target was "confirmed" the following night by a captured American fighter pilot downed near Osaka. Lieutenant Marcus McDilda didn't have the slightest idea what atomic energy was until an interrogator, a general, jabbed the tip of a sword into the American's lip and threatened to cut off his head. McDilda obliged. In his Florida drawl he described how atoms were split into pluses and minuses, which were then separated by a lead shield encased in a box thirty-six feet long and twenty-four feet wide. When the box was dropped from a plane, the lead shield melted and the pluses and minuses reunited with a monstrous explosion that could lay waste an entire city. Awed, his inquisitors wanted to know the next target. McDilda thought quickly. "I believe Kyoto and Tokyo. Tokyo is supposed to be bombed in the next few days."

Molotov's study, but before he could greet the Foreign Commissar in Russian as was his custom, Molotov cut him off with a wave of the hand. "I have here, in the name of the Soviet Union, a notification to the Japanese government which I wish to communicate to you."

Sato's instinct told him this was a declaration of war. Although he'd been expecting it, the reality of it was a blow. Molotov left his desk and sat down at the head of a long table. Sato was directed to a chair at the other end. With set expression Molotov began to read a document:

"After the defeat and capitulation of Hitlerite Germany, Japan remained the only great power which still stands for the continuation of the war.

"The demand of the three powers, the United States, Great Britain and China, of July 26 for the unconditional surrender of the Japanese armed forces was rejected by Japan. Thus the proposal made by the Japanese Government to the Soviet Union for mediation in the Far East has lost all foundation.

"Taking into account the refusal of Japan to capitulate, the Allies approached the Soviet Government with a proposal to join the war against Japanese aggression and thus shorten the duration of the war, reduce the number of casualties and contribute toward the most speedy restoration of peace.

"True to its obligation as an Ally, the Soviet Government has accepted the proposal of the Allies and has joined in the declaration of the Allied powers of July 26.

"The Soviet Government considers that this policy is the only means able to bring peace nearer, to free the people from further sacrifice and suffering and to give the Japanese people the opportunity of avoiding the danger of destruction suffered by Germany after her refusal to accept unconditional surrender.

"In view of the above, the Soviet Government declares that from tomorrow, that is from August 9, the Soviet Union will consider herself in a state of war against Japan."

Controlling his agitation, Ambassador Sato politely expressed regret that the Soviet Union was breaking a nonaggression pact almost a year before it expired. Now, as a favor, could he cable the information to his government? Molotov emerged from behind the impersonal façade: Sato could send any cables he wished, and in code. He said he personally regretted what had happened. "I have been quite satisfied with your actions as Japanese ambassador the past few years and am pleased that we two could maintain good relations between our governments until today in spite of the difficulties facing us."

"I am grateful for the good will and hospitality of your government," Sato replied in halting Russian, "which has enabled me to stay in Moscow during this difficult time. It is indeed a sad thing that we shall have to part as enemies. But this cannot be helped. At any rate, let us part with a handshake. It may be the last one."

They shook hands, but almost immediately the telephones at the Japanese embassy were disconnected and all radio equipment confiscated. Sato wrote out a message in plain Japanese text and sent it to the cable office.

2.

The bombing of Hiroshima had undoubtedly inspired the Russians to advance their timetable to enter the war, but for months 1,600,000 troops under the command of Marshal A. M. Vasilievsky had been assembling along the Manchurian border. They faced a Kwantung Army, half their size, which had been stripped of all armor and antitank guns, and whose average efficiency was not quite 30 percent of a prewar front-line unit.

Two hours after Molotov read the declaration of war to Sato, two Soviet armies crossed into Manchuria from the west. At the same time another army, based in Vladivostok, invaded from the east. Roads were muddy and streams overflowed their banks from a day-long downpour, but the three great Russian columns converged inexorably on Tsitsihar, Taonan and the cosmopolitan city of Harbin.

Shortly after his meeting with Sato, Molotov informed Ambassador Averell Harriman that war with Japan would start at midnight. The Soviet Union had decided to honor its pledge to the day to enter the Pacific war three months after the defeat of Germany.

Later in the evening Harriman and George Kennan found Stalin in a talkative mood. He announced that the first Soviet units had already advanced ten or twelve kilometers into Manchuria. "Who would have thought that things would have progressed so far by this time!" he exulted.

Harriman asked him what effect the atomic bomb would have on the Japanese. Stalin was confident that the enemy was looking for any pretext to form a new government that could arrange a surrender. Harriman's reminder of how fortunate the Soviets were to be on the side that had developed the bomb set Stalin off on an affable discussion of atomic energy. He seemed undisturbed that the allies had scored a scientific triumph. There was no hint that the previous day he had summoned five of Russia's foremost nuclear scientists to the Kremlin and ordered them to develop their own bomb as soon as possible regardless of cost; he had put Lavrenti P. Beria, General Commissar of State Security and the most feared man in the Soviet Union, in overall charge of the project.

It was understandable that Americans as a whole regarded the atomic bomb primarily as a deliverance from four costly years of war. A few, however, saw beyond the common exultance. Admiral Leahy thought it was an inhuman weapon to use on a people that was already defeated and ready to surrender, and that Americans "had adopted an ethical standard common to the barbarians of the Dark Ages."*

Stimson also remained gravely concerned. That afternoon he had showed the President a photo which graphically illustrated the "total destruction" of Hiroshima. He said they must make every effort to persuade Japan to surrender as quickly as possible, and success depended largely on the manner in which the Japanese were approached. "When you punish your dog," he said, "you don't keep souring on him all day after the punishment is over; if you want to keep his affection, punishment takes care of itself. In the same way with Japan. They naturally are a smiling people and we have to get on those terms with them. . . ."

But Truman was not prepared to go beyond the Potsdam Proclamation. He was not unmoved by the photo of Hiroshima, and recognized "the terrible responsibility such destruction placed upon us here and himself." At the same time, a second atomic bomb would have to be used presently. No top-level meeting had been convened to discuss the necessity of a second bomb, no attempt made to determine if the first bomb or Russian entry into the conflict had quickened Japan's intent to surrender. If there were any moral com-

---

*In his dissenting, and largely ignored, opinion at the Tokyo Tribunal, Justice Radhabinad Pal of India declared that "if any indiscriminate destruction of civilian life and property is still illegitimate in warfare, then, in the Pacific war, the decision to use the atom bomb is the only near approach to the directives of the German Emperor during the first World War and of the Nazi leaders during the second World War. Nothing like this could be traced to the credit of the present accused."

punctions felt by anyone of influence, except Stimson, they were not expressed to the President; and he felt none. He was ready to drop two bombs, three—and more, if it meant saving American lives.

On Guam, thirty-two copies of orders for the second raid were mimeographed. The decision on how and when to use subsequent bombs was now in the hands of the Joint Chiefs of Staff. Takeoff time would be early the next morning, August 9. There were two possible targets, both on the island of Kyushu: the primary was "Kokura Arsenal and City," and the secondary, "Nagasaki Urban Area."

On nearby Saipan, sixteen million leaflets designed to persuade the Japanese to surrender were being turned out by the Office of War Information printing plant. The very first propaganda had been ineffective. Obsolete, archaic phrases were used; drawings showed Japanese men wearing kimono left side over right like women, and pictured chopsticks placed one on each side of a plate like a knife and fork; the Japanese characters were often ludicrously inept: "freedom of speech" became "freedom of words," and "freedom of want"—"freedom from desire." But these mistakes had been rectified, and since the beginning of the year American leaflets had made an impact on the population. The present one, in particular, would have an indelible effect on public morale:

TO THE JAPANESE PEOPLE

America asks that you take immediate heed of what we say on this leaflet.

We are in possession of the most destructive explosive ever devised by man. A single one of our newly developed atomic bombs is actually the equivalent in explosive power to what 2,000 of our giant B-29s can carry on a single mission. This awful fact is one for you to ponder and we solemnly assure you that it is grimly accurate.

We have just begun to use this weapon against your homeland. If you still have any doubt, make inquiry as to what happened to Hiroshima when just one atomic bomb fell on that city.

Before using this bomb to destroy every resource of the military by which they are prolonging this useless war, we ask that you now petition the Emperor to end the war. Our President has outlined for you the thirteen consequences of an honorable surrender. We urge that you accept these consequences and begin work of building a new, better and peace-loving Japan.

You should take steps now to cease military resistance. Otherwise, we shall resolutely employ this bomb and all our other superior weapons to promptly and forcefully end the war.

Evacuate your cities now!

Even before the pamphlets were delivered, newspapers in Japan were warning that "new-type" bombs had been used at Hiroshima which "should not be made light of." The enemy, said the *Nippon Times*, now appeared to be "intent on killing and wounding as many innocent people as possible due to his urgent desire to end the war speedily." An editorial titled "A Moral Outrage Against Humanity" revealed that the new bomb possessed "unprecedented power. Not only was the greater part of the city wiped out, but an extraordinary proportion of the inhabitants have been either killed or wounded."

On the afternoon of August 8 Major Charles ("Chuck") Sweeney, who had piloted the instrument plane *Great Artiste* over Hiroshima, was informed that he was to drop the second bomb, using another aircraft. Unlike the bomb used at Hiroshima, this was a spherical plutonium missile, ten feet eight inches long and five feet in diameter, called "Fat Man" after Churchill. Colonel Tibbets told Sweeney and his crew that "Fat Man" would make the first bomb obsolete. He wished them luck.

For their mission Sweeney and his crew would use *Bock's Car*, while her regular pilot, Captain Frederick Bock, Jr., would fly the instrument plane.* *The Great Artiste* was unofficially being prepared for an unscheduled double role: three young scientists—Luis Alvarez, Philip Morrison and Robert Serber—were attaching a personal appeal, signed by them, to the canisters which would be parachuted over the target to gather data. Each envelope was addressed to Professor Ryokichi Sagane, a Japanese nuclear scientist whom all of them had known and worked with in the thirties at the University of California Radiation Laboratory.

---

*This last-minute switch of planes was to confuse historians. By mistake the official communiqué announced that *The Great Artiste* had dropped the bomb and this was incorporated in most accounts, including several written by eyewitnesses. The error was discovered in 1946 when plans were made to retire *The Great Artiste*, because of her historical role, and it was learned that the serial number of the plane carrying the bomb was different.

To: Prof. R. Sagane.
From: Three of your former scientific colleagues during your stay in the United States.

We are sending this as a personal message to urge that you use your influence as a reputable nuclear physicist, to convince the Japanese General Staff of the terrible consequences which will be suffered by your people if you continue in this war.

You have known for several years that an atomic bomb could be built if a nation were willing to pay the enormous cost of preparing the necessary material. Now that you have seen that we have constructed the production plants, there can be no doubt in your mind, that all the output of these factories, working 24 hours a day, will be exploded on your homeland.

Within the space of three weeks, we have proof-fired one bomb in the American desert, exploded one in Hiroshima, and fired the third this morning.

We implore you to confirm these facts to your leaders, and to do your utmost to stop the destruction and waste of life which can only result in the total annihilation of all your cities if continued. As scientists, we deplore the use to which a beautiful discovery has been put, but we can assure you that unless Japan surrenders at once, this rain of atomic bombs will increase manyfold in fury.*

At 3:49 A.M. *Bock's Car* rumbled down the long runway. Unlike the first bomb, "Fat Man" could not be assembled in flight and was fully armed at takeoff. The B-29's ground run seemed interminable but its nose finally lifted, and lumbering off to the north in the darkness, it was closely followed by *The Great Artiste* and the photograph plane.

The mission seemed jinxed from the start. Sweeney discovered that the fuel selector to the 600 gallons of gas in his bomb-bay tank was inoperative. With that reserve unavailable, *Bock's Car*'s range was dangerously restricted, but Sweeney decided to keep going. At 8:09 A.M. Tokyo time, one minute ahead of schedule, a small island appeared ahead through a break in the clouds. It was Yakushima, off the

---

*Professor Sagane did not read the letter until after the war. Had he received it immediately he would have tried to persuade a group of influential scientists to join him in a protest, but the letter was deliberately kept from him. The day after the bombing one of his former students, a naval officer, informed him with visible agitation that a letter from several Americans, addressed to the professor, had just been turned over to the Navy. However, an Army officer instructed Professor Sagane to discount any rumor he might hear that the Navy had found a letter "about the atom bomb" because there was no such letter.

south coast of Kyushu, where *Bock's Car* was to rendezvous with her escorts.

Three minutes later another B-29 loomed out of the clouds. It was *The Great Artiste*. The two planes circled for forty-five minutes but the photograph plane did not appear. "The hell with it," Sweeney told his co-pilot. "We can't wait any longer." He waggled his wings and headed for the primary target. Kokura, a port on the northeast coast of Kyushu, was reported clearly visible. But the city turned out to be partially obscured by smoke and haze, and Bombardier Kermit Beahan, who had been ordered to make a visual drop, could not find the aiming point. He called back to Sweeney, "We'll have to make another run."

"Pilot to crew," Sweeney announced. "No drop. Repeat. No drop." He banked sharply and they came in for a second attempt. Captain Beahan squinted into the rubber eyepiece of the Norden MK 15 bombsight. All he could see was dense smoke. "I can't pick up the aiming point," he said.

"No drop," Sweeney told him. "Repeat. No drop."

They came in from the east. Here, too, Kokura was hidden. The flight engineer reported that fuel was "getting critical," with just about enough to get them back to Iwo Jima. "Roger," Sweeney acknowledged, but turned to the weaponeer—the officer in charge of "Fat Man," Commander Frederick Ashworth—and said, "We'll go on to secondary target, if you agree." The Navy man nodded. "Proceeding to Nagasaki," Sweeney told the crew and turned southwest. The Nagasaki weather plane had reported only two-tenths cloud cover over the city.

Nagasaki, a city of 200,000, spread over precipitous hills, like San Francisco. Its bay faced the East China Sea. It was a fabled port of spectacular beauty, particularly now, for a touch of autumn had come early and many of the trees were brilliant with reddish browns and yellows. The center of town fronted the bay which was formed by the Urakami River flowing into it from the north. With the centuries, Nagasaki had expanded from this nucleus into several valleys, including the one fashioned by the river which had become an industrial complex employing 90 percent of the city's labor force.

In 1571 the Portuguese had helped build it from a fishing village into Japan's chief port for foreign trade, and introduced tobacco, firearms and Christianity. The new faith became so widespread that the government took brutal steps to repress it. All missionaries were either killed or forced to leave the country, but in the seventeenth century 37,000 of their followers rebelled against religious persecution. They rallied around a castle near Nagasaki, and with the help of guns on a few Dutch vessels, held off the armies of the central government for three months before being slaughtered almost to a man.

Their faith survived, however, and Nagasaki remained the most Europeanized, the most Christian city in Japan, a harmonious blend of the cultures of East and West with its numerous Christian churches and schools, hundreds of Western-type houses, and such tourist attractions as Glover's Mansion, the legendary home of Madame Butterfly overlooking the harbor.

Shigeyoshi Morimoto was on his way home to Nagasaki, a nervous and shaken man. Only three days before, he had miraculously escaped death in Hiroshima, where he had been working for the past months making antiaircraft kites for the Army. He had been shopping for paint brushes less than 900 yards from ground zero when the bomb exploded, and the wreckage of the flimsy store protected him from the *pika*. He had fled the city, along with three assistants, in a coal car bound for Nagasaki and safety. All night long they talked compulsively about "the bomb." Had Japan been punished by some supernatural force for attacking Pearl Harbor? By the time the freight train made its steep, dramatic descent into the Nagasaki terminal, Morimoto had an unshakable premonition that the bomb would follow him to his own home. He had to warn his wife. As he approached his shop, which was in the center of town, it was almost 11 A.M.

Misfortune continued to dog *Bock's Car*. As it neared the target it encountered deteriorating weather. The cloud cover over Nagasaki would probably be nine-tenths. Sweeney told Commander Ashworth that with the reduced fuel they couldn't make more than one pass and suggested dropping "Fat Man" by radar. Ashworth hesitated; he was supposed to jettison the bomb into the ocean if he couldn't find the target visually. What a waste that would be, he thought, and decided to disobey orders. "Go ahead and drop it by radar," he told Sweeney, "if you can't do it visually."

The drop point, chosen for maximum devastation of the city, was on high ground near Morimoto's kite shop. An explosion here should wipe out the center of town, the port area and reach up into the factories of the Urakami Valley. Nagasaki appeared on the radar scope at 11 A.M. Bombar-

dier Beahan shouted to Sweeney, "I've got it. I see the city."
So he would be able to bomb visually, after all. Through a
break in the cloud cover he could see the oval rim of an outdoor stadium on the banks of the Urakami River. It was
almost two miles northwest of the scheduled hypocenter but
would have to do. He trained his cross hairs on the stadium,
and seconds later, at 11:01 A.M. the plane lurched upward.

"Bombs away," Beahan reported over the intercom, then
corrected himself, "Bomb away."

Morimoto, the kite maker, was breathlessly telling his wife
that a terrible bomb had been dropped on Hiroshima and
that he feared Nagasaki would be next. He began to describe
the *pika*: "First there is a great blue flash—" A blinding blue
flash cut off his words. He flung back a trap door in the floor
and shoved his wife and infant son into their shelter. As he
pulled down the heavy lid there was a terrifying tremor, like
an earthquake.

If there had been no clouds overhead, the Morimoto shop,
directly under the original drop point, would have been
obliterated but the bomb exploded several hundred yards
northeast of the stadium and the river, almost exactly between the Mitsubishi Steel and Arms Works and the Mitsubishi Torpedo Factory.

Hajime Iwanaga, who would be fourteen the next day, was
bathing in the Urakami River near the torpedo factory. He
saw a black object (it was an instrument canister) drop from
a plane and burst into a parachute. He called out "Friendly
plane!" to a comrade and exuberantly ducked his face in the
water as the *pika* flashed. Seconds later he emerged into a
blinding world. Something warm clung to his left shoulder. It
was yellowish. Mystified, he touched it and saw skin come
off. He splashed toward the bank as the sky darkened ominously, and was reaching for his clothes when two dark-green
spheres, the size of baseballs, streaked at him. One struck his
shirt, set it afire, and disintegrated. As he clambered up the
bank he heard a comrade in the river shriek in agony,
"Mother!" Huge raindrops pummeled him for a moment.

Taeko Fukabori, a year older, was helping pump water out
of a large natural cave which served as a public air-raid
shelter. She was hurled into the mud and remembered hearing how people had been buried alive in a bomb raid the week
before at the shipyards. Terrified, she groped her way toward
the exit. Outside (the cave was less than 200 yards from
ground zero) she found herself right in hell. Bodies of workers at the entrance were so charred that she could not

distinguish their backs from their fronts. A person without hair and blackened body—it was impossible to tell if it was man or woman—walked by, seemingly oblivious, with only a burning string around the waist.

Taeko started up the eastern slope of the valley to get home to her mother. A soldier stopped her and said that direction was impassable. She followed him across the railroad tracks to the river, unaware that the right side of her face and her right shoulder were burned. Inexplicably, she was suddenly certain that her family on the hill was safe.

Further up the slope, adjacent to the municipal prison and less than 275 yards from the hypocenter, twelve-year-old Kazuko Tokai had crawled into the small, unfinished family shelter to rest. Two feet of dirt above it saved her from the *pika*. She felt an indescribable sensation on her body and heard a crackling noise like the sizzling of broiling steak. She crawled outside, into darkness. Confused—she thought that it was night—and unable to feel or smell a thing, she began walking aimlessly.

As the dust cleared, Kazuko found herself at a crumbled wall—all that was left of Urakami Prison. She turned around to get back home. The house had disappeared. Kazuko freed her mother, who was buried under tiles, and together they located Mr. Tokai in the rubble. His skin came off like a glove as they pulled him out.

Near the top of the slope in a seventy-bed tuberculosis sanatorium—1,500 yards from ground zero—Dr. Tatsuichiro Akizuki was inserting a long needle into the side of a male patient when he heard an eerie noise, as if a huge plane were roaring down at them. It was going to hit the hospital! "Drop on the floor!" he yelled. He withdrew the needle and plunged to the floor. There was a white flash and debris rained on him. He struggled to his feet, unharmed. The air was filled with choking dust from pulverized plaster.

He feared all the patients on the second and third floors were dead, and he started for the staircase with one of the nurses. Patients were coming down, frightened but only superficially wounded. Through a window he saw yellow smoke in Urakami Valley. The cathedral was on fire: so was the vocational high school. The sky was red and a murky yellow. He was drawn outside to the garden. Eggplant leaves and potato plants were smoldering. It had to be similar to the bomb used at Hiroshima. The president of Nagasaki Medical College had seen the wreckage in that city, and just the day before, had excitedly described it at a student-faculty meeting.

At the bottom of the valley Hachiro Kosasa had gone into the storehouse of the torpedo factory to get some metal material when he sensed something vaguely odd. He turned and saw the windows aglow with colored lights—a gas tank must have exploded. He dropped to the floor as the ceiling collapsed. Unaware of deep cuts in his head, legs and thigh, he staggered toward the plant infirmary, but it was gone. In the twilight gloom people milled around helplessly. His instinct was to escape, try to get home. Weak from loss of blood, he tied his legging around his thigh as a tourniquet, and driven by fear that his body might not be found by relatives and given a proper funeral, he headed south toward the Mitsubishi Steel and Arms Works. Soon his leg no longer supported him and he continued the journey on hands and knees.

At the steel works, which stretched for almost a mile down to the railroad station, sixteen-year-old Etsuko Obata had started a new job that morning filing machine parts on the second floor. The concussion knocked her unconscious; when she came to, she found herself suspended in wreckage six feet above the ground floor. She was carried to a truck bound for the University Hospital up on the eastern slope, but fires forced the "ambulance" to detour south, toward the station. This avenue too became blocked by spreading fires, and the patients were instructed to get out and walk. Etsuko lowered herself painfully onto the highway. The sun looked big and red, burning red. She tried to crawl under the truck for shelter but couldn't. Incongruously, there was a heavy shower, the raindrops hissing into the fires and hot earth.

Overhead, the crews in the two B-29's saw "a giant ball of fire rise as though from the bowels of the earth, belching forth enormous white smoke rings." Correspondent William Laurence in *The Great Artiste* watched a fiery column shoot two miles into the sky. He began scribbling frantically as the pillar of fire became "a living thing, a new species of being, born right before incredulous eyes." A giant mushroom billowed at the top, even more alive than the towering pillar. It seethed and boiled in white fury like a thousand geysers. In seconds it broke free from the stem and a smaller mushroom took its place. It was, Laurence thought, like a decapitated monster growing a new head.

In *Bock's Car* the rear gunner shouted over the intercom to Sweeney, "Major, let's get the hell out of here!"

As Sweeney swung the plane away from the terrible sight, Co-pilot Albury called to the bombardier, "Well, Bea, there's a hundred thousand Japs you just killed."

Beahan didn't answer.

The men began to unbend from the tension. While removing their cumbersome flak suits they shouted congratulations to one another, and the radio operator sent Sweeney's first report back to Tinian:

BOMBED NAGASAKI 090158Z VISUALLY WITH NO FIGHTER OPPOSITION AND NO FLAK. RESULTS "TECHNICALLY SUCCESSFUL" BUT OTHER FACTORS INVOLVED MAKE CONFERENCE NECESSARY BEFORE TAKING FURTHER STEPS. VISIBLE EFFECTS ABOUT EQUAL TO HIROSHIMA. TROUBLE IN AIRPLANE FOLLOWING DELIVERY REQUIRES US TO PROCEED TO OKINAWA. FUEL ONLY TO GET TO OKINAWA.

The victims of Nagasaki were not all Japanese. A work party of Allied prisoners at the Steel and Arms Works was caught in the blast and a number of them died. A POW camp a mile away was badly damaged and no one would ever know how many perished. Even forty miles away at the Senryu Camp, Dr. Julien M. Goodman, a surgeon captured on Bataan, felt the concussion. There was a deep rumble, followed by a blast of air. The earth trembled. Within moments there was another tremor, and an Australian physician, Dr. John Higgin, remarked, "This must be the beginning of a great naval barrage." The shock waves and tremors continued for almost five minutes. The inexplicable phenomenon transformed the camp. The prisoners were called into the mess hall and informed that no more work details would be sent to the coal-mine shafts.

A Japanese seaplane was heading directly for Nagasaki through clouds at 10,000 feet. Ten minutes earlier a report had come in to the naval air base at Sasebo of a "great bombing" on nearby Nagasaki, and the pilot, a twenty-year-old cadet, had made an unauthorized takeoff to investigate. Cadet Nobukazu Komatsu had heard Truman's announcement about Hiroshima by short wave. Perhaps this, too, was an atomic bomb.

The plane broke out of the clouds and was confronted by a huge column of black smoke. At the top "like the head of a monster," was a massive, swelling ball changing colors kaleidoscopically. Drawing closer, Komatsu realized that the colors were an illusion caused by the sun's rays. He started circling around the cloud; everything below was obscured. He shouted to his two companions, "Let's cut into the cloud!"

It was like an oven. Komatsu slid open the cockpit window and extended his gloved hand—it was like plunging his arm into live steam. He jerked it back, slammed the window shut, and found his glove covered with "sticky dust." One of his comrades cried out; Chief Petty Officer Umeda was vomiting. The darkness and heat intensified. The third man, Cadet Tomimura, opened his window for relief. A blast of heat swept into his face. He screamed and shut the window just before the seaplane burst into sunlight again. Their faces were covered with grayish dust.

His head throbbing, and fighting nausea, Komatsu descended in circles. Below, Nagasaki was a mass of flames and dark billowing clouds. He reduced power to go lower for pictures but the heat forced him to turn toward the bay. There he would land in the harbor and continue to explore the city on foot.*

3.

Ambassador Sato's report to Tokyo that the Soviet Union had declared war was never transmitted, Molotov's promise notwithstanding. The Russians themselves, hours later, broadcast the news. It was monitored by the radio room of the Foreign Ministry before dawn that morning, while *Bock's Car* was still hundreds of miles from Nagasaki. Smashed was Togo's last tenuous hope for negotiations through the U.S.S.R., which he had pressed so hard, despite a conviction that it was hopeless. Japan had been stabbed in the back without warning—he was as indignant as Cordell Hull had been on Pearl Harbor day. He took the information personally to Prime Minister Suzuki, berating him for his failure to call an emergency meeting of the Big Six the previous day. Togo's anger was unnecessary. This time Suzuki did not argue or play with words; his reaction was simple and straightforward. "Let us end the war," he said. But first he wanted to make certain that the Emperor would approve an

---

*Umeda died of leukemia two years later; Tomimura also died of leukemia in 1964; Komatsu still suffers from anemia.

immediate surrender, At the *obunko* he found his Majesty agreeable to acceptance of any terms that would lead to peace.

With this assurance Suzuki called to order an emergency meeting of the Big Six. It was 11 A.M., one minute before 'Fat Man" fell on Nagasaki. "Under the present circumstances," Suzuki began, "I have concluded that our only alternative is to accept the Potsdam Proclamation and terminate the war. I would like to hear your opinions on this."

No one spoke.

"Why are you all so silent?" asked Admiral Yonai. "We won't accomplish a thing unless we speak frankly."

The other three military men resented Yonai's willingness to discuss surrender, yet the Russian invasion of Manchuria had shaken them more than the bombing of Hiroshima.*

An officer entered the room with the report that a second atomic bomb had been dropped. This disquieting news, coupled with that from Manchuria, brought the pent-up resentment of Anami, Umezu and Toyoda into the open. They knew in their hearts that surrender was inevitable but adamantly refused to accept the Potsdam Proclamation even if the Emperor was allowed to reign. They insisted, in addition, that war criminals be tried by the Japanese themselves, that the Army be demobilized by Japanese officers, and that the occupation force be limited.

Togo impatiently tried to make them acknowledge the reality of the situation. With Japan so close to collapse, the Allies would undoubtedly reject such stipulations and the entire effort for peace would be endangered. Could the military offer any hope of victory? War Minister Anami could not, but he still wanted Japan to fight one more great battle—on the mainland. Could you keep the enemy from landing? Togo persisted.

"With luck we will be able to repulse the invaders before they land," Umezu answered. "At any rate, I can say with confidence that we will be able to destroy the major part of an invading force. That is, we will be able to inflict extremely heavy damage on the enemy."

---

*After the war Admiral Toyoda said, "I believe the Russian participation in the war against Japan rather than the atom bombs did more to hasten the surrender." The official British history, *The War Against Japan,* supports this contention: ". . . for it brought home to all members of the Supreme Council the realization that the last hope of a negotiated peace had gone and there was no alternative but to accept the Allied terms sooner or later."

Togo pressed him: What difference would that make? The enemy would simply launch a second or third assault if necessary. There was nothing to do but sue for peace with a minimum of counterdemands. After three hours the issue remained unresolved. Suzuki adjourned the meeting and reported its inconclusive results to Marquis Kido. "There is but one solution," he told the Privy Seal. "We must ask the Emperor to make the decision."

It was a bold suggestion; powerful though the Emperor was, his role did not encompass initiation of policy. But Kido also realized that only an extraordinary act of the Throne could save Japan. Without hesitation the Privy Seal explained the situation to the Emperor. His Majesty, too, saw the necessity for defying tradition.

The Cabinet meeting that afternoon did no more to settle the issue than the Big Six had that morning. The military again lined up against the civilians—all except Yonai, who maintained that nothing could be gained by continuing the war. "Therefore we must forget about 'face' and surrender as quickly as possible, and begin to consider at once how best to preserve the country."

His words incensed his fellow officers. Anami had difficulty in containing his animosity. "That we will inflict severe losses on the enemy when he invades Japan is certain," he said, "and it is not impossible to reverse the situation and pull victory out of defeat." Furthermore, Army units in the field would not submit to demobilization. "Our men will simply refuse to lay down their arms. They know they are forbidden to surrender. There is really no alternative for us but to continue the war."

Four civilian ministers—Agriculture, Commerce, Transportation and Munitions—differed. The people were on the verge of exhaustion; the rice crop was the poorest in years, the country no longer had the strength to fight.

Anami interrupted impatiently. "Everyone understands all that, but we must fight to the end no matter how great the odds against us!"

At the mouth of the Urakami River the globular gas tank near the railroad station lifted into the air like monstrous fireballs, crashed back to earth and shot up again. Drum cans rocketed much higher. Just to the north, survivors were dazedly working their way from ground zero. A naked man, expressionless, was carrying a boy with entrails spilling from is stomach. A cat, its hair burned kinky, was licking intestines hanging from a horse.

Midori Nishida was a messenger girl at the Steel and Arms Works whose hair had been set afire by the *pika*. She sought to escape across the Ohashi railroad bridge just above the stadium, unaware that she was heading into the center of destruction. The ties had burned out and she inched across, balancing on the twisted rails. The river below was filled with bodies. The buttocks of one woman near the bank were blown up like balloons. Nearby a black-and-white cow covered with raw spots of pink was placidly lapping water.

At one point Midori almost fell and asked for help from a girl coming the other way. It was a classmate, but Midori's scorched appearance frightened her; she burst into tears and refused to touch Midori. Resentfully Midori edged her way to the east bank. She passed a charred naked man standing like a statue with arms and legs spread apart. He was dead. Beyond she saw bales of charcoal. She was almost on them before she realized they were human beings. Their faces were huge and round as if pumped up with gas. There were no buildings, only flat, smoldering rubble. Near the hypocenter she encountered someone else from her class, a boy. He didn't recognize her until she spoke. "Are you really Nishida-*san*?" he said.

All around them, agonized voices pleaded for help. Midori felt irresistibly drawn to them and in panic fled back toward the river. With her new companion she picked her way south along the bank until they found a place shallow enough to ford. They passed a mother and daughter seated on a scorched *futon*. The girl was leaning forward, dead, her head drooping in the water. The mother stared at her blankly. Why didn't she pull her daughter out of the water? Midori wondered and continued south past the Steel and Arms Works, unaware that the soles of her sneakers were burned through.

As twilight began to obscure the visual horror of Nagasaki, thousands of survivors were unable to leave the blasted area because of wounds or inertia. Little Kazuko Tokai, whose scanty earth refuge 275 yards from ground zero had saved her from injury, was huddled with her mother and father in an empty public shelter near the ruins of their home. Just before the stars appeared, Kazuko's father died. Her mother's voice became hoarse and barely discernible. "Don't die!" Kazuko begged in the darkness. There was no answer, nor could Kazuko rouse her. She, too, was dead. The girl waited. She heard no sound from anywhere in the vast nothingness. I'm the only one left alive, she thought.*

35   "To Bear the Unbearable"

1.

In Tokyo that evening the Cabinet continued the fruitless debate. As spokesman for the militarists, Anami seemed as adamant as ever, but Sakomizu suspected that the War Minister was playing his own game of *haragei*. If Anami really meant what he said, all he had to do was resign and the Cabinet would be dissolved—whoever followed would have to be subservient to the militarists. Just before eleven Prime Minister Suzuki, who had scrupulously avoided getting involved in the argument, adjourned the meeting. It was clear that the Cabinet itself was unable to reach a decision. Now the last recourse was to call upon the Emperor.

Minutes later in his private office the Prime Minister instructed Sakomizu to arrange for an immediate imperial conference. First it would be necessary to obtain the *kakuban* (handwritten seal) of the Army and Navy Chiefs of Staff. With foresight Sakomizu had already persuaded Admiral Toyoda and General Umezu to put their seals on a request for the meeting—he had told them, quite reasonably, that it might have to be called at a moment's notice. The two officers had assumed that a conference with the Emperor would be held only if a unanimous decision was reached. Sakomizu did not ask Umezu or Toyoda for confirmation of their approval, since he knew they would not give it. Nor did he inform his chief that he had acquired the seals under provisional circumstances.

Within the hour the puzzled conferees—they had been summoned hastily without full explanation—began arriving singly at the *obunko*. They stepped out of their cars in the bright moonlight and were escorted by one of the chamber

---

*Americans put the death toll at 35,000; the officials of Nagasaki, 74,800.

lains down a steep, mat-lined stairway to the long tunnel which led to the *obunko* annex, the imperial underground complex. Built into the side of a hill, it consisted of half a dozen rooms, the largest a conference chamber, poorly ventilated, sweltering. It was spare and gloomy with a ceiling supported by steel beams, and walls paneled in dark wood.

In addition to the Big Six—along with four secretaries, including the ubiquitous Sakomizu—the aged Baron Hiranuma, President of the Privy Council, had been summoned. In the anteroom their anger and confusion focused on Sakomizu. Toyoda, Umezu and two military secretaries pressed around him, their swords clanging ominously, and accused him of obtaining their *kaki ban* under false pretenses.

The Cabinet Secretary could not calm them even when forced to lie: "We are not going to make any decision at this conference." He escaped his accusers only when the conferees were instructed to take their seats in the conference room at two long parallel tables. At the head of the tables on a dais was a much smaller one covered with gold-lined brocade behind which was a chair and a six-panel gilt screen.

At ten minutes before midnight the Emperor entered. He appeared tired and concerned. He lowered himself heavily into the chair on the dais. The conferees bowed and sat down, avoiding looking directly at him. Several of the older men began coughing, increasing the feeling of uneasiness. At Suzuki's request, Sakomizu read the Potsdam Proclamation. The disturbing words stuck in his throat.

Suzuki briefly reviewed the recent debates in the Supreme Council and Cabinet, and then called on each member of the Big Six in turn for a statement. Despite the oppressive heat Togo was self-possessed. He quietly declared that the Potsdam Proclamation should be accepted at once so long as *kokutai*, the national essence, could be maintained. Admiral Yonai was just as contained. "I agree with Foreign Minister Togo," he said evenly.

His unequivocal concurrence enraged War Minister Anami, the next in line. "I oppose the opinions of the Foreign Minister!" he exclaimed. The Army could not agree to surrender unless the Allies allowed Japan to demobilize her own troops, try her own war criminals and limit the occupation force. "If not, we must continue fighting with courage and find life in death." His cheeks glistened with tears and his voice became strident as he pleaded for a last decisive battle in the homeland. "I am quite sure we could inflict great casualties on the enemy, and even if we fail in the attempt, our hundred million people are ready to die for honor, glorifying the deeds of the Japanese race in recorded history!"

The shaven-headed Umezu got to his feet. It would be unthinkable, he announced sternly, to surrender unconditionally after so many brave men had died for the Emperor.

Admiral Toyoda should have been the next to speak but Suzuki, seemingly confused but perhaps by design, asked Baron Hiranuma for his opinion. Anami and Umezu eyed him suspiciously—he might be well known as an ultranationalist, but like most of the *jushin*, he was probably a "Badoglio" —as he posed a series of pointed questions ending with one which called for a direct answer from the military: Could they continue the war?

Umezu assured him that further atomic attacks could be stemmed by antiaircraft measures. "We have been preserving our strength for future operations," he said, "and we expect to counterattack in time."

The legalistic Hiranuma appeared unimpressed. He agreed more or less with Togo, but he said they should negotiate with the Allies for the Army's demands. He turned to the Emperor. "In accordance with the legacy of His Imperial Forefathers, His Imperial Majesty is also responsible for preventing unrest in the nation. I should like to ask His Majesty to make his decision with this point in mind." The crusty old man sat down.

When Toyoda finally spoke he tried to re-emphasize the militarist position, but his conclusions were ambiguous: "We cannot say that final victory is a sure thing, but at the same time we do not believe that we will be completely defeated."

For more than two hours the old arguments had been repeated almost word for word. As Toyoda finished, Suzuki again got to his feet, slowly and deliberately. It appeared to Sakomizu that he was at last going to reveal the convictions he had repressed so long. What he said, however, astonished his listeners even more: "We have been discussing this matter many hours without reaching a conclusion. The situation is indeed serious, but not a moment has been spent in vain. We have no precedent—and I find it difficult to do—but with the greatest reverence I must now ask the Emperor to express his wishes."

He turned toward his ruler. He asked that the Emperor decide whether Japan should accept the Potsdam Proclamation outright or demand the conditions the Army wanted,

Unaccountably, he stepped away from his chair toward His Majesty. There were gasps.

"Mr. Prime Minister!" Anami exclaimed, but Suzuki seemed not to hear him and advanced to the foot of the Emperor's small podium, his large shoulders bent with age. He stopped and bowed very low. With an understanding nod His Majesty bid Suzuki to sit down. The old man couldn't catch the words and cupped a hand to his left ear. The Emperor beckoned him to return to his place.

As soon as Suzuki was seated the Emperor himself got to his feet. His voice, usually expressionless, was noticeably strained. "I have given serious thought to the situation prevailing at home and abroad and have concluded that continuing the war means destruction for the nation and a prolongation of bloodshed and cruelty in the world." The others listened with heads bowed. "I cannot bear to see my innocent people suffer any longer. Ending the war is the only way to restore world peace and to relieve the nation from the terrible distress with which it is burdened." He paused.

Sakomizu glanced at His Majesty, who was gazing thoughtfully at the ceiling as he wiped his glasses with a white-gloved thumb. The Cabinet Secretary felt tears flooding his eyes. The conferees were no longer sitting stiffly in their chairs but had thrown themselves forward—some arms outstretched, prostrate on the tables, sobbing unashamedly. By now the Emperor had regained his composure. He resumed speaking in a voice choked with emotion but was again forced to stop. Sakomizu wanted to cry out, "We now all understand His Majesty's wishes. Please do not condescend to say another word."

"It pains me," the Emperor was saying, "to think of those who served me so faithfully, the soldiers and sailors who have been killed or wounded in far-off battles, the families who have lost all their worldly goods—and often their lives as well—in the air raids at home. It goes without saying that it is unbearable for me to see the brave and loyal fighting men of Japan disarmed. It is equally unbearable that others who have rendered me devoted service should now be punished as instigators of the war. Nevertheless, the time has come when we must bear the unbearable. When I recall the feelings of my Imperial Grandsire, the Emperor Meiji, at the time of the Triple Intervention [by Russia, Germany and France in 1895], I swallow my own tears and give my sanction to the proposal to accept the Allied proclamation on the basis outlined by the Foreign Minister."*

He had finished. Suzuki stood up, as did the others. "I have respectfully listened to His Majesty's gracious words," he said.

The Emperor started to reply but instead nodded. Slowly, as if burdened with some intolerable weight, he left the room.

"His majesty's decision," said Suzuki, "should now be made the unanimous decision of this conference." Of course, it had not been a decision in the Western sense, merely an expression of his wish. But to a loyal Japanese—and all eleven men in the room were that—his wish was tantamount to a command. The minutes of the meeting were recorded, and the conferees, still shaken by the Emperor's anguish, began affixing their signatures, thus approving acceptance of the Potsdam Proclamation with the proviso that the Allies recognize the lawful status of the Emperor.

All but Baron Hiranuma. As usual something bothered him; he objected to the phrasing of the stipulation "the status of our Emperor is one ordained by God." He was adamant that the exact wording of the Constitution—"the supreme power of the Emperor"—be substituted.

Hiranuma added his signature at two-thirty. The momentous meeting was over and the military had approved what amounted to unconditional surrender. But in the absence of His Majesty, their frustration and sense of betrayal were directed at Suzuki. "You didn't keep your promise, Mr. Prime Minister!" shouted Lieutenant General Masao Yoshizumi, who had sat as a secretary. "Are you happy now?"

Anami stepped between them.

There was one more formality—approval by the entire Cabinet. It was convened at once at Suzuki's home, where the ministers also drafted identical notes to each of the Allies accepting the Potsdam Proclamation "with the understanding

---

*In his talk with Grand Chamberlain Fujita in January 1946, the Emperor pointed out the difference between the decisions to start the war and end it, and how it affected his role as emperor. "At the time of surrender, there was no prospect of agreement no matter how many discussions they [the Big Six] had. In addition to the intense bombings, we had suffered atomic bombs, and the ravages of war were suddenly accelerated. Lastly, when Suzuki asked me, at the imperial conference, which of the two views should be taken, I was given the opportunity to express my own free will for the first time without violating anybody else's authority or responsibilities. . . ."

that the said declaration does not compromise any demand which prejudices the prerogatives of His Majesty as a Sovereign Ruler."*

It had been a long evening. Suzuki went upstairs to bed. Sakomizu didn't leave but slumped down in an armchair and was soon asleep. The others wearily headed home through the dark, quiet streets of Tokyo. Everyone but Togo. Debilitated by pernicious anemia, he was probably the most exhausted of all. Light was just faintly coming from the east as his car stopped at the makeshift Foreign Ministry, where he wanted to record the Emperor's words which burned in his mind. He dictated them to his unofficial secretary, his son-in-law Fumihiko Togo, who, despite the family ties, remained in awe of the old man. He had rarely seen him exhibit any emotion, but as Togo recited what His Majesty had said his eyes filled with tears.

August 10 dawned hot and muggy in Tokyo. At Army Headquarters on Ichigaya Heights more than fifty officers of the War Ministry waited in an air-raid shelter for the appearance of General Anami. The emergency summons of so many important officers aroused lively speculation. Was the War Minister going to announce the merger of the Army and Navy? Was it something about the atomic bomb or was he going to report on last night's imperial conference?

At nine-thirty Anami, flanked by two high-ranking officers, strode down the long tunnel from the Headquarters building and into the bunker. As he mounted a little platform, riding crop in right hand, the audience clustered about him in a semicircle. Quietly he said that last night's imperial conference had decided to accept the Potsdam Proclamation.

Incredulous, several shouted "No!" Anami held up his hands for quiet. "I do not know what excuse I can offer," he said, "but since it is the wish of His Majesty that we accept the Potsdam Proclamation there is nothing that can be done." He told them of the Army's minimum demands and regretted he had been unable to get them accepted. He promised, however, to make another attempt, and he asked for their help to keep order in the Army whatever happened.

---

*The wording in English was imprecise. Later Shunichi Matsumoto, Vice Minister to Togo, called it misleading. It should have read: "We accept the Potsdam Proclamation. We understand that this acceptance does not affect the position of the Imperial Household."

"You individual feelings and those of the men under you must be disregarded."

A major stepped forward. "What about the duty of the military to protect the nation?"

Ordinarily a gentle man, Anami brandished his crop at the major. "If anybody disobeys Anami's order, he will have to cut Anami down!"

Lieutenant Colonel Masao Inaba of the Military Affairs Bureau approached the general with a plan to keep order in the Army. "Regardless of whether we end the war or not," he said, "we must send out instructions to keep fighting, particularly with the Soviet troops advancing in Manchuria."

"Write it out," said Anami.

It still remained for the Cabinet to decide how much the public should be told. The military was unwilling to reveal the Emperor's decision for fear it would immediately undermine Japan's will to fight and bring chaos. A compromise was reached: they would merely issue a vague statement that would help prepare the people for surrender. It was composed by Kainan Shimomura, President of the Information Board, and his staff. It boasted of victories, condemned the new bomb as ruthless and barbarous, and warned that the enemy was about to invade the homeland. The last paragraph alone gave an indication that the public was about to face an unprecedented situation:

In truth, we must recognize that we are now beset with the worst possible situation. Just as the government is exerting its utmost efforts to defend the homeland, safeguard *kokutai*, and preserve the honor of the nation, so too must the people rise to the occasion and overcome all manner of difficulties in order to protect the national essence of their empire.

On the other hand, there was no hint at all of surrender in Inaba's instructions to the officers and men of the Army, to fight the holy war to the end:

We are determined to fight resolutely, although we may have to chew grass, eat dirt and sleep in the fields. It is our belief that there is life in death. This is the spirit of the great Nanko, who wanted to be reborn seven times in order to serve the country, or the indomitable spirit of Tokimune, who refused to be swayed and pressed on vigorously with the work of crushing the Mongolian horde.

Shortly after Inaba sent the message to the War Minister for approval, two perturbed lieutenant colonels—one a press officer, the other Masahiko Takeshita, Anami's brother-in-law—burst into Inaba's office with the information that the Cabinet was about to issue a statement hinting at surrender. Since this would create confusion among the troops, they must broadcast Inaba's exhortation at once. Inaba turned his wastebasket upside down and retrieved a crumpled sheet of paper, the original draft of his statement. Because it was in Anami's name he hesitated releasing it without the War Minister's approval. But the two colonels convinced him there was no time, and copies of the instructions were sent immediately to all local radio stations and newspapers.

The two conflicting statements, issued almost simultaneously, baffled the editors and station managers and forced Togo to take precipitous action. Anami's statement would undoubtedly lead the Allies to believe that Japan was resolved to continue hostilities. The formal notes informing the Allies of Japan's willingness to surrender were being processed through sluggish diplomatic channels, and a few hours' delay might mean a third atomic bomb. Why not send out the official note immediately as a news story? There was a good possibility some military censor, if he recognized the contents of the message, might hold it up. To circumvent this it was decided to transmit the Japanese proposal in English in Morse code. By the time the censors translated the message, it would hopefully, be too late.

Saiji Hasegawa, foreign news editor of Domei, agreed to accept the hazardous assignment of relaying the message. He put it on the transmitters at 8 P.M. beamed first to the United States, then to Europe. He waited tensely, praying that its contents would not be monitored.

Almost at that moment the streets of Tokyo were disrupted with a rash of exploding grenades. The Army dissidents, including Colonel Inaba, hoped to create a disturbance that would necessitate the proclamation of martial law throughout the city. With Tokyo under military control, the Emperor might be influenced to change his mind and continue the war. But the city, so inured to bombings, ignored the fitful explosions.

In Nagasaki leaflets fluttered down on the razed city, tardily warning its citizens to evacuate.

2.

On the other side of the world it was still the morning of August 10. At 7:33 A.M. the Morse code message sent out by Hasegawa—providentially the Japanese Army censors hadn't bothered to check it—was picked up by American monitors. President Truman summoned Leahy, Byrnes, Stimson and Forrestal to his office and read them the message. Since it was from an unofficial source, he asked them each in turn if it could be considered as an acceptance of the Potsdam Proclamation. If so, should they let the Emperor continue to reign? For weeks a number of influential men, including Harry Hopkins, Archibald MacLeish and Dean Acheson, had been urging abolishment of the imperial system.

But three of his four advisers in the room opposed such drastic counsel. To the ailing Stimson, retention of the Emperor was a practical matter. He pointed out that the Allies would need Hirohito's help to effect the surrender of the scattered Japanese armies. "Something like this use of the Emperor must be made in order to save us from a score of bloody Iwo Jimas and Okinawas all over China and the New Netherlands." Leahy had "no feelings about little Hirohito" but supported Stimson.

Byrnes, however, was against retreating "from our demand for unconditional surrender. That demand was presented to Japan before the use of the bomb and before the Soviet Union was a belligerent. If any conditions are to be accepted, I want the United States and not Japan to state the conditions." Forrestal countered that the Japanese could be reassured "by an affirmative statement on our part in which we could see to it that the language of surrender accorded fully with our intent and view."

Japan's offer to surrender aggravated Stimson's concern over the continued loss of life. He proposed that they call a bombing halt—carrier-based planes and B-29's from the Marianas were still blasting Japanese cities; there were growing misgivings in America over the use of the atomic bomb. "We must remember," Forrestal added, "that this nation will have to bear the focus of the hatred by the Japanese."

Truman remained noncommittal. He decided to wait until the official surrender came through diplomatic channels, but he ordered Byrnes to start drafting an answer at once. The Secretary of State weighed every word, aware that he spoke for Russia, China and Great Britain as well as his own country. Shortly before noon he was informed that the Swiss embassy had just received the official Japanese offer to surrender. As soon as this message arrived he personally brought it, along with his draft to Japan, to the White House. Truman called an emergency meeting of the Cabinet and at 2 P.M. began reading Byrnes's reply. Stimson was pleased by its conciliatory tone (". . . it was a pretty wise and careful statement and stood a better chance of being accepted than a more outspoken one"). It stated that from the moment of surrender, the authority of the Emperor and the Japanese government to rule the state would be subject to the Supreme Commander of the Allied Powers and that the ultimate form of government of Japan would be established by the freely expressed will of the Japanese people. Everyone agreed that this should reassure the Japanese about the future position of their Emperor without compromising the basic principle of unconditional surrender.

First, however, the message to Tokyo had to be approved by the Allies, and copies were cabled to the U.S. ambassadors in London, Moscow and Chungking with a request that they secure quick compliance.

Admiral King sent word of the negotiations to Nimitz at Pearl Harbor, and recalling the first alert dispatched by the Navy ten days before the "day of infamy," his message began: THIS IS A PEACE WARNING. . . .

The more General Anami reviewed the events of the past thirty-six hours, the more resentful he grew toward Suzuki and Togo. As he drove to his office on the morning of August 11, after archery practice in his garden, he grumbled about the Prime Minister to his secretary, Colonel Saburo Hayashi. The appearance in his office of half a dozen disgruntled officers—including his sister's husband, Colonel Takeshita—elicited more specific complaints: the imperial conference had been so impromptu that Togo alone had been prepared to present his proposal to the Emperor; and why was Baron Hiranuma at the meeting? Anami left the impression that the conferees had been maneuvered into approving surrender.

These accusations were vaguely expressed but they encouraged the dissidents to commit another act of *gekokujo*, and a score of them gathered secretly in the War Ministry itself to plan a coup. Takeshita, as senior officer, warned them that what they were doing was punishable by death. First, he suggested, they must isolate the Emperor from those urging him to seek peace. Then they would enlist Anami to advise the Emperor to continue the war. A hard-fought Decisive Battle on the mainland could inflict such losses on the Americans that an honorable peace might be arranged. If not, they would carry on the war as guerrillas in the mountains.

The conspirators took up the plan enthusiastically. They would use the troops stationed in Tokyo to surround the Palace grounds. They would cut the lines of communication and occupy broadcasting stations, newspapers and key government buildings. Then they would arrest the "Badoglios" like Suzuki, Togo and Kido.

Takeshita was confident that Anami would eventually join them and, in turn, bring Umezu. Then the two local commanders, Lieutenant General Takeshi Mori of the Konoye Division and General Shizuichi Tanaka of Eastern District Army, would have to co-operate. With the Army Chief of Staff and the War Minister supporting the coup, they would not fail—as had the small group of officers who briefly seized Tokyo in 1936. It would, in essence, be an Army operation. They would be acting lawfully under its highest commanders for the good of the nation.

This concept of legality was a perversion of the teachings of Professor Kiyoshi Hiraizumi, who had incalculable influence over the officer corps. In 1926, at the age of thirty-one, he became an assistant professor at Tokyo Imperial University. His main interest was Japanese history, his main purpose to preserve the spirit of the leaders of the Meiji period. When Communism began sweeping the campus he countered by establishing his Green-Green School.* The essence of his teaching was that each nation has its own tradition, history and morality and other nations should respect the differences. He taught that Japanese society was based on complete loyalty and obedience to parents, nation and Emperor, and Green-Green evolved into an ultranationalist school with Shinto as its bone, Confucianism as its flesh and *bushido* as its blood.

---

*The name was inspired by a line from a poem written by a Chinese patriot just before his execution by Mongol raiders: "Evergreens in the snow are even greener." That is, the man under fire who remains "green" is truly pure.

Hiraizumi was a slender, mild little man who looked what he was, a professor of history, but in his first lecture at the Military Academy he made a dramatic entrance, striding up to the platform with a sword. He put it aside and spoke softly, never using his hands or contorting his face for effect. Somehow he electrified every young officer in that audience and each succeeding audience with his burning sincerity. What they heard about the Imperial Way and their country so imbued them with the spirit of self-sacrifice to Emperor and country that his sayings were often on the lips of those going off on *kamikaze* missions.

High-rnking officers remained his disciples. While he was prime minister, Tojo often sought his advice and Anami still held him in the highest regard. Takeshita and others in the conspiracy had attended the Green-Green School and believed they were now acting out what Hiraizumi preached. Wouldn't unconditional surrender destroy *Yamato damashii* and *kokutai*? Consequently, it was perfectly proper to defy the Emperor's decision for peace, since it was a mistaken and ill-advised judgment. In fact, true faithfulness to the Throne made temporary disobedience to the Emperor imperative.

3.

With one exception the Allies immediately accepted Byrnes's proposed reply to Japan. The Soviet government was "skeptical" about the Japanese offer: Molotov found it neither unconditional nor concrete. Therefore, the Red Army was continuing its advance into Manchuria.

Harriman, however, pressed for a quick answer and Molotov complied—with one proviso: "The Soviet Government also considers that, in case of an affirmative reply from the Japanese Government, the Allied Powers should reach an agreement on the candidacy or candidacies for representation of the Allied High Command to which the Japanese Emperor and the Japanese Government are to be subordinated."

Harriman "took firm exception" to this stipulation; his government would never agree to it. He was not even exactly sure what it meant. Molotov explained that the High Command in the Far East should consist of two people, an American and a Russian general.

Harriman's reaction was sharp and unequivocal. The United States had carried the main burden of the Pacific war for four years and by doing so had kept Japan off Russia's back. The Soviets had been in the war two days. Therefore it was unthinkable that the Supreme Command should be anyone other than an American. Molotov answered heatedly but Harriman remained firm; he would send the suggestion to Washington but he knew that it would be unacceptable.

Harriman returned to his office still angry. He was called to the phone. It was M. Pavlov, Molotov's secretary, who said that the Foreign Commissar had checked with Stalin and that there had been a misunderstanding: "consultation" had been intended, but not necessarily "approval." Harriman again warned that the words "or candidacies" would not be acceptable in Washington. A few minutes later Pavlov called again to say that Stalin was agreeable to deletion of the offending words and would confirm it in writing.

With peace so imminent, Forrestal and Stimson once more tried to persuade President Truman to cease all air and naval action against Japan as a humane gesture. Truman would not hear of it. Pressure, he said, should be maintained so the Japanese wouldn't be encouraged to request further concessions. He did promise to suspend further atomic missions unless Tokyo's reply was unsatisfactory. Two more atomic bombs were ready on Tinian, and drops were tentatively scheduled for August 13 and 16. General Spaatz acknowledged that battered Tokyo was too poor a target for a conventional bombing, and he was still eager to drop an atomic bomb on the capital.*

While the Byrnes reply was officially being processed through Switzerland, it was also being broadcast to the Orient by short wave from San Francisco for its propaganda effect on the Japanese civilian population. The man who had clandestinely transmitted Japan's answer to the Potsdam Proclamation, Saiji Hasegawa of Domei, was informed by a monitoring station of the Allied counterproposal just after midnight of the eleventh. He notified the Foreign Ministry and then phoned his close friend Sakomizu. The sleepy Cabinet Secretary was anxious to know what it said. "We don't have the complete text yet," Hasegawa replied, "but it doesn't look too good."

For more than two hours Sakomizu waited impatiently until the full English text was delivered to him:

_____

*There was a persistent rumor abroad in Tokyo that the capital was going to be hit by an atom bomb on August 13.

With regard to the Japanese Government's message accepting the terms of the Potsdam proclamation but containing the statement, "with the understanding that the said declaration does not comprise any demand which prejudices the prerogatives of His Majesty as a sovereign ruler," our position is as follows:

From the moment of surrender, the authority of the Emperor and the Japanese Government to rule the state shall be subject to the Supreme Commander of the Allied powers, who will take such steps as he deems proper to effectuate the surrender terms.

The Emperor will be required to authorize and ensure the signature by the Government of Japan and the Japanese Imperial General Headquarters of the surrender terms necessary to carry out the provisions of the Potsdam Declaration, and shall issue his commands to all the Japanese military, naval and air authorities and to all the forces under their control wherever located to cease active operations and to surrender their arms, and to issue such other orders as the Supreme Commander may require to give effect to the surrender terms.

Immediately upon the surrender the Japanese Government shall transport prisoners of war and civilian internees to places of safety, as directed, where they can quickly be placed aboard Allied transports.

The ultimate form of the Government of Japan shall, in accordance with the Potsdam Declaration, be established by the freely expressed will of the Japanese people.

The armed forces of the Allied Powers will remain in Japan until the purposes set forth in the Potsdam Declaration are achieved.

It wasn't as negative as Hasegawa had indicated. The Allies didn't reject outright the Japanese demand to retain the Emperor, but his ultimate fate was not indicated and this *would* give the war party grounds to reject the entire proposal. Sakomizu was joined by Vice Foreign Minister Matsumoto, who had raced through the streets of Tokyo. His face fell as he read the note.

Its vagueness regarding the national essence was compounded by two typographical errors in the fifth paragraph. Byrnes had written "The ultimate form of government of Japan," but the monitor had transcribed it to read "The ultimate form of the Government of Japan." Did the capitol *G* refer exclusively to civilian administration, or did it include the Emperor? And was there any particular connotation to "the"? Matsumoto took the optimistic view that "the Government" excluded His Majesty; the best thing to do was "gulp down" the note as a whole lest the militarists break it into parts that could be disputed interminably. While Matsumoto took his recommendation to Togo, Sakomizu headed for Suzuki's home. The old Prime Minister listened to the new proposal and the reasoning, then said gravely, "In any case, we must end the war."

At the *obunko*, Kido explained the problems the note presented to the Emperor. "That's all beside the point," said His Majesty. "It would be useless if the people didn't want an emperor. I think it's perfectly all right to leave the matter up to the people." His serenity was like "a blow on the head" to Kido. What had concerned the Privy Seal so much had evaporated under the Emperor's absolute confidence in his subjects.

Sakomizu's fears about the reaction of the military were justified. The Army and Navy Chiefs of Staff saw in the Byrnes reply ample excuse to continue the war and were the first—even before Togo—to reach the Emperor with their objections.

His Majesty indicated their conclusions were premature; no formal Allied answer had yet been received. "We will be sure to study it after it arrives," he said, putting them off. "We can probably make another inquiry about those points still in doubt."

But he himself had already reached a conclusion. He advised Togo, who arrived at the *obunko* two hours later, that the Allied proposal was satisfactory and should be accepted. His reaction was as welcome to Suzuki as it had been to Togo, but eventual acceptance of Allied terms was far from assured. The phrasing regarding the Emperor disturbed conservatives like Baron Hiranuma, whose anxiety about *kokutai* brought him to Suzuki's home. First he strenuously objected to the statement that "the authority of the Emperor and the Japanese Government to rule the state shall be subject to the Supreme Commander of the Allied powers." The words "subject to" he translated as slavery. He also took exception to the paragraph declaring that the ultimate form of government be established by the people. That was unbearable. The Emperor was a deity and could not be subject to the will of the populace.

That afternoon the full Cabinet met to discuss the Byrnes reply. Togo saw no reason not to accept it. Paragraph 2 left the position of His Majesty unimpaired in principle and paragraph 5 allowed the people of Japan to select their own form of government. "It is impossible," he argued, "to conceive that the overwhelming loyal majority of our people would not wish to preserve our traditional system." Moreover, if they demanded revisions in the phraseology it was quite likely that those among the Allies antagonistic to the imperial system might demand the abolition of the imperial house.

But General Anami (moments before, he had been cornered in his own office by the young dissidents who demanded that the proposal be rejected: "If you cannot bring that about, you should commit hara-kiri!") stood firm and was supported in his resistance by Hiranuma and two other civilians under the baron's influence, the Interior and Justice ministers. There were others who sided with Togo, but Admiral Yonai alone spoke out. After more than an hour's unproductive debate Suzuki—who had remained silent, reluctant perhaps to stand against such formidable opposition—finally said, "If disarmament is forced upon us, we have no alternative but to continue the war."

The outspoken Togo, incredulous at Suzuki's vacillation, managed to control his temper. He had to find some way to postpone the decision. "Inasmuch as the official reply of the Allies has not yet arrived," he said (as the Emperor had said before him), "we had better continue our discussion after receipt of it." There was no objection. Togo followed Suzuki into his private office, berating him. What a time to bring up the question of disarmament! he shouted. "Unless we are resigned to rupture of the negotiations for peace, there is no alternative to acceptance of their reply as it stands," he said. Wasn't the Prime Minister aware that the Emperor wanted the war ended and that the question at issue involved the very existence of the imperial house? "If you persist in this attitude, I may have to report independently to the Throne!"

Togo returned to his own office more depressed than angry. He told Matsumoto that he might have to resign. The Vice Minister begged him to do nothing hastily. "Although a formal reply from the Allies is expected at any moment," he suggested, "why don't we pretend it didn't arrive until tomorrow morning.* Tonight, please go home and rest." Scarcely listening, Togo nodded consent and dejectedly started for his car. He had to inform Marquis Kido of Suzuki's "betrayal."

The Privy Seal phoned Suzuki's office and requested his

---

*The message from Washington, routed through Berne, arrived at the Foreign Ministry moments later, at 6:40 P.M., but the Telegraph Section chief, following Matsumoto's instructions, postdated it 7:40 A.M., August 13, and kept it in his basket.

presence. He was informed that the Prime Minister was not available but would report to the Imperial Household Ministry as soon as he was free. An hour passed, two, and Kido's anxiety grew. Finally, at 9:30 P.M., Suzuki arrived, grumbling about the "Hiranuma crowd" who were setting themselves up as guardians of *kokutai*.

"I don't intend belittling the argument of those who are anxious to jealously guard the national essence," said Kido, "but on the basis of careful study, the Foreign Minister assures us that there is nothing objectionable in the paragraph in question. . . . Should we turn down the Potsdam Proclamation at this stage and should the war be continued, a million innocent Japanese would die from bombings and starvation." Suzuki's defensive posture relaxed, and Kido continued, "If we bring about peace now, four or five of us may be assassinated but it would be worth it. Without wavering or hesitation, let us carry out the policy to accept the Potsdam Proclamation!"

"Let us do it!" Suzuki suddenly exclaimed.

In the Cabinet meeting General Anami had been unequivocally opposed to acceptance of the Allied proposal but privately he was beset by doubt. How could he go against the will of the Emperor? Like the dissidents who had accosted him that afternoon, he believed the honorable course for Japan was to continue the war, but with His Majesty's permission. Perhaps he could persuade Prince Mikasa to help change his brother's mind. With his secretary, Colonel Hayashi, he drove to the shelter that had become the prince's home after his palace was destroyed.

Anami was disconcerted by Mikasa's hostile reception. He was aware there had been an imperial family meeting that afternoon but not that Mikasa, as well as all the other princes of the blood, had pledged their support to the Emperor in his decision. Hastily Anami added that he was anxious to forestall headstrong younger officers who opposed surrender.

"Since the Manchurian Incident the Army has at times acted not quite in accordance with the imperial wish," said the prince. "It is most improper that you should still want to continue the war when things have reached this stage." Chastened, Anami departed, leaving Mikasa wondering how such a responsible officer could ignore His Majesty's instructions. Was this feeling prevalent at Army Headquarters? Later several Army staff officers called on Prince Mikasa. One happened to be an old schoolmate, and they talked in the garden outside the shelter. When Mikasa told his friend about Anami's request, he asked why the prince didn't speak to the Emperor. His booming voice and argumentative manner gave Mikasa the impression that he was being threatened. Their raised voices alarmed the princess, who was in the shelter, and made her fear for her husband's safety.

Shaken by Mikasa's reaction, the staff officer tried to placate the prince: Anami could control the unruly officers; moreover, the Army would remain a disciplined force under the War Minister's leadership. "There is no need to be concerned about a rebellion."

Anami could not fall asleep. Long after midnight he awakened his secretary and sent him to his staunchest ally, the Army Chief of Staff, with a suggestion that General Umezu ask Field Marshal Shunroku Hata to intercede with the Emperor on behalf of the Army's senior officers. "You must forgive me," Umezu told Hayashi as he paced the floor, "but I now favor acceptance of the Potsdam Proclamation."

Even after Umezu's dramatic change of heart, Anami made yet another private attempt to sway the Emperor. Early in the morning—it was August 13—he unceremoniously interrupted the Privy Seal's breakfast, literally "bounding" into the room. Kido had never seen him so distraught. Words poured out of him. The Allied terms would destroy the soul of Japan. There should be a final Decisive Battle. "Couldn't you just once more request the Emperor to reconsider acceptance of the note?"

"I cannot do that," Kido replied. He disputed Anami's charge that leaving the choice of government up to the people would mark the end of the national essence. He went further. "Supposing the Emperor does change his mind, rescind the peace proposal of the tenth, and issue a proclamation for a final Decisive Battle?" The Allied powers would undoubtedly regard His Majesty as a fool or a lunatic. "It would be unbearable to subject him to such insults."

Anami got control of himself. "I understand how you feel," he said. "In your position, you must protect the Emperor."

"The Army is very powerful," said Kido with sympathy, "and you will have a difficult job to keep it under control."

Anami forced a smile. "You have no idea what it's like in the War Ministry." They shook hands.

At 9 A.M. the Big Six continued the debate which the

Cabinet had been unable to resolve the previous day. The session was still deadlocked when a phone call from the *obunko* interrupted proceedings. The Emperor had been informed of Anami's emotional visit to Kido and now he wanted to see the two Chiefs of Staff, Umezu and Toyoda.

Negotiations were under way to end the war, the Emperor told them, and in his oblique manner implied that he wanted as little bloodshed as possible until a decision was made. He asked what air operations would be conducted during the negotiations. Umezu replied they would only fire when fired upon. The Emperor nodded approval.

The two officers bowed themselves out and returned to the Big Six conference. If the Emperor had summoned them for the dual purpose of saving lives and influencing the debate, it had no immediate effect on the deliberations of the Big Six. However, that afternoon at the Cabinet meeting the majority of members now favored acceptance of the Allied demands; moreover, the leader of the opposition, General Anami, purposefully let it be known privately, in a typically Japanese roundabout way, that he was not as adamant as he appeared.

He pushed away from the conference table and signaled Sakomizu to follow him into the next room, where he phoned the chief of the Military Affairs Bureau, the short-tempered General Masao Yoshizumi. "I'm at the Cabinet meeting," said Anami, "and every one of the ministers is being brought over to your views. So all of you people stay where you are until I get back." Sakomizu was mystified. The situation was just the opposite. Anami winked. "I am right here with the Cabinet Secretary," Anami continued, "and if you want you can speak to him directly about how things are going in the meeting." Suddenly Sakomizu understood. Anami was playing *haragei* to quiet his rebellious insubordinates at Army Headquarters.

But Anami's words, which were intended to forestall the dissidents, had the opposite effect. The Cabinet meeting was dramatically disrupted at 3:45 P.M. A messenger brought in a copy of an Army communiqué which would be released by newspapers and radio stations in fifteen minutes: "The Army, upon receipt of a newly issued imperial command, has renewed offensive action against the United States, the United Kingdom, the Soviet Union and China."

"I don't know anything about this!" Anami exclaimed. He immediately phoned Umezu, who had left earlier to return to Army Headquarters. The Chief of Staff was as outraged as

Anami. An imperial command needed approval of both the War Ministry and the General Staff, and neither he nor Anami had given it. It must have been approved by his deputy and Anami's deputy despite the War Minister's specific instructions by phone to General Yoshizumi to do nothing. Umezu issued an order to quash the communiqué and it was stopped minutes before it was to be broadcast.

The meeting resumed, but Anami had momentarily lost interest in the proceedings. Even as the two civilians who also opposed immediate surrender—the Interior and Justice ministers—almost alone persisted in demands for better terms, the War Minister seemed perturbed and lost in reverie.

"Byrnes's reply," Togo insisted, "unquestionably represents the least common denominator of the terms of the several Allies, and it is imperative that we accept them as they now stand, if we are to bring about peace for the sake of the reconstruction of Japan and the welfare of the human race."

Another quibble over semantics resulted. Exasperated, Suzuki broke in. "Are the military leaders intent on upsetting our efforts to terminate the war by deliberately grumbling over Byrnes's reply? Why can't we interpret it as we see it?" They must make a final decision. A number of ministers had refrained from expressing their opinions and now he wanted each one to speak out clearly. He pointed at the Justice Minister. He, of course, agreed with Anami and Toyoda, as did the Interior Minister. Several were reluctant to take a positive position—as Suzuki himself had been—but he questioned them testily until all but one approved surrender. Now Suzuki too had to declare himself.

"I have made up my mind," he said, "to end the war at this critical moment in compliance with the wishes of the Emperor. On examining the Allied reply, I found some points that seemed unacceptable but when I carefully perused them I discovered that the United States had no ill will toward us in laying out these conditions, and I feel they have no intention of changing the status of the Emperor. I believe I must end the war as desired by His Majesty, so I will fully report to the Throne what we have discussed here, and ask for his final decision."

There was no question what the decision would be. But Anami, whose position made him personally responsible for the outcome of the war, was torn by conflicting loyalties and unable to accept the inevitable. After the Cabinet was dismissed he followed Suzuki to his office, where a naval doctor was waiting to see the Prime Minister. "Won't you please give me two more days before calling another imperial conference?" Anami asked.

"I'm sorry," replied Suzuki. "This is our golden opportunity and we must seize it at once." After Anami left, the Prime Minister turned to the doctor. "If we delay," he said, "the Russians may occupy Hokkaido as well as Manchuria, Korea and Sakhalin Island. That would deal this country a fatal blow. We must act now while the negotiations are confined primarily to the United States."

"But General Anami might kill himself."

"I know," said Suzuki. "I am sorry."

The emerging leader of the conspirators was not Anami's brother-in-law, Colonel Takeshita, but an officer he outranked, Major Kenji Hatanaka. Hantanaka outwardly appeared to be the antithesis of a revolutionary. He was quiet, studious and modest, but his unshakable dedication to *kokutai* and his unwillingness to compromise gave him unchallenged authority. Anami's support remained the key to success, since every level of command would trust him, and that evening the conspirators had been invited to meet with him at his residence. Twice before, Hatanaka had arranged go-betweens to enlist Anami in the conspiracy. First he thought he had persuaded Takeshita to intercede with his brother-in-law, but the colonel's reluctance to use his privileged position proved too strong. Next he asked Professor Hiraizumi, whose philosophy of national honor permeated Army Headquarters, to speak to the War Minister, although Hiraizumi had written him a letter requesting that he and the other rebels "refrain from acting rashly at their own discretion" and be guided instead by Anami. Hatanaka, always an optimist, hoped that the professor would advise Anami to join the plot but, in fact Hiraizumi was going to urge him to obey the Emperor implicitly. Hatanaka personally escorted Hiraizumi to the anteroom of the War Minister, but the professor never got to see him. After a long wait he was informed that Anami was in conference at the Palace and would not be back for some time.

At 8 P.M.—the August night was still and muggy—the inner circle of conspirators crowded into Anami's modest one-story wooden house, now serving as official residence after the fire bombings. Hatanaka first wanted to alienate the general from those advocating surrender and reported the rumor that the "Badoglios" were planning to assassinate him. Anami, amused, smiled tolerantly. Nor did the plan for the coup itself seem to impress him: Kido, Suzuki, Togo and Yonai were to be imprisoned, martial law proclaimed and the Palace isolated. To accomplish all this, four generals—Anami, Umezu, Tanaka and Mori—would have to cooperate. Anami ignored the treasonous nature of the plan but faulted the staff work. For instance, how were they going to handle communications?

Takeshita persisted. "We must carry out the plan!" he exclaimed. Besides, it had to be before the imperial conference formally agreed to accept the Byrnes note. Anami's noncommittal manner left the conspirators unsure of his intentions. Colonel Okikatsu Arao was discouraged, but Takeshita would not give up.

In order not to antagonize the group, Anami promised to use his influence "first thing in the morning" with Umezu—who he knew had already resolved to support the Emperor. But the young officers wanted more immediate action. This time Anami put them off by agreeing to see one of their number, Colonel Arao, at midnight when, he implied, he might give the coup fuller consideration. As he accompanied them to the porch, he called out solicitously. "Be careful! You may be under surveillance. You had better return in separate groups instead of all together."

Takeshita waited with his brother-in-law until the others had left. Was Anami going to join them? asked the colonel, presuming on their relationship. "One cannot reveal one's true thoughts in the presence of such a large group," answered the general. He said no more, but Takeshita departed with renewed optimism.

The Army and Navy Chiefs of Staff—Umezu and Toyoda—had not felt direct pressure from the conspirators but were unable to repress resurgent qualms about accepting unconditional surrender. They called Foreign Minister Togo from a dinner party for a private meeting in the underground conference room of the Prime Minister's official residence. But Togo remained unwilling to consider any last-minute stipulations. He repeated time and again, "Impossible!" There was a hubbub outside and Sakomizu, who had arranged the meeting, apologetically ushered in Admiral Onishi, organizer of the *kamikaze* corps. He approached Admiral Toyoda and in a choking voice confessed that he had just begged Prince Takamatsu to ask his brother to continue the war. But he had of course been no more successful than Anami had been with Prince Mikasa. Instead Takamatsu said, "You military people have already lost the Emperor's confidence!" Onishi's eyes brimmed with tears. "We must submit a plan to gain victory to His Majesty and ask him to reconsider his decision. We must throw ourselves headlong into the plan and make it come true. If we are prepared to sacrifice twenty million Japanese lives in a 'special attack' effort, victory will be ours!" His impassioned appeal brought no response and he turned, desperate, to Togo.

"If we had any realistic hope of victory no one would for a moment think of accepting the Potsdam Proclamation," said the Foreign Minister. "But winning one battle will not win the war for us."

Air-raid sirens began screeching. It was an excuse for Togo to adjourn the meeting. As he drove home through the blacked-out streets he ruminated on what Onishi had said about sacrificing twenty million lives. The final decision for peace had to be reached the next day. "We could bear anything," he later wrote, "if it promised a return; the arrows and bamboo spears of which the military men were prattling promised none."

36   The Palace Revolt

1.

As the sky east of Tokyo began to lighten on August 14 a lone B-29, high overhead, droned toward the center of the city disgorging a trail of missiles. One by one they burst, releasing clouds of fluttering pamphlets. The text had been hastily drafted in Washington by the Office of War Information, translated into Japanese characters and radiophotoed to Saipan.

TO THE JAPANESE PEOPLE

These American planes are not dropping bombs on you today. They are dropping leaflets instead because the Japanese Government has offered to surrender, and every Japanese has a right to know the terms of that offer and the reply made to it by the United States Government on behalf of itself, the British, the Chinese, and the Russians. Your government now has a chance to end the war immediately.

The Japanese conditional acceptance of the Potsdam Proclamation was quoted, as well as Byrnes's reply.

Marquis Kido took one of the pamphlets, which had landed on the Palace grounds, to the *obunko*. He told the Emperor that if they fell into the hands of the troops who knew nothing of the negotiations, they could cause an uprising. His Majesty should convoke an imperial conference without delay so he could inform the councilors of his determined desire to end the war immediately.

The Emperor glanced through the leaflet and instructed his Privy Seal to find Suzuki at once. Fortunately the Prime Minister was already in the anteroom. Under the circumstances, Suzuki said, it would take too much time to obtain the seals of the two Chiefs of Staff; instead, he would have to request the Emperor to take the unprecedented step of mustering the imperial conference on his own authority. Kido saw the necessity of this emergency measure. Moreover, he decided that another unprecedented step was called for: he would accompany Suzuki when he saw the Emperor. Never before had the Privy Seal been present at a private audience between Prime Minister and Emperor. His Majesty not only agreed to call the meeting at 10:30 A.M. but went much further. If there was a deadlock he would "command" the Cabinet to accept the terms of the Byrnes note.

That morning Anami was again urged to take a stand regarding the conspiracy. At his midnight meeting with Colonel Arao he had hedged to such a degree that his secretary, Colonel Hayashi, who had advised him to be frank with Arao, said curtly, "From the way you just talked I couldn't tell if you were for their plan or not." Now, with the coup hours away, the rebels descended on Anami at Army Headquarters with demands for his immediate assistance. Once more Anami could not bring himself to give them a straight no; he left them in his office with the excuse that he had to sound out the Army Chief of Staff.

Umezu was in no such state of indecision. He told Anami that it would be sacrilege to employ armed troops on the Palace grounds. On the way back to his own office Anami was intercepted by the conspirators. He could no longer avoid the issue. "After discussing the matter with the Chief of Staff," he said, "I've decided not to support your action." He refused to discuss it further and summarily strode out of the building, where a car was waiting to take him to the

Prime Minister's underground conference room for a Cabinet meeting.*

It had hardly begun before it was announced that they were to transfer en masse to the *obunko* annex for an emergency imperial conference, the first fully attended meeting with the Emperor since the historic one of December 1, 1941. They were not even given time to change into formal clothes; the Munitions Minister, for example, had to borrow a necktie from an Imperial Household staff official and have it tied by the Welfare Minister. For the second time in five days the military had been maneuvered into a confrontation they were not prepared for, and Suzuki bore the brunt of their resentment.

As they filed into the restricted underground conference room they saw that the tables had been removed and replaced by two long rows of chairs to accept their increased number. They waited uneasily in the steaming and claustrophobic chamber. At about 10:50 the Emperor, dressed in Army uniform and wearing white gloves, entered with General Hasunuma, his chief military aide-de-camp.

Suzuki apologized to the Emperor for the fact that his cabinet had not unanimously approved acceptance of the Byrnes note. He indicated the three principal dissenters— Toyoda, Umezu and Anami—and asked them to state their arguments directly to His Majesty. Umezu called for a continuance of the war. If surrender meant the end of the national essence, then the entire nation should be sacrificed in a final battle. His words were echoed by Admiral Toyoda. Anami, whose emotions constricted his voice, wanted to fight on unless the Allies definitely promised to guarantee the Emperor's safety. There was still a chance to win, and if not, at least the war could be ended on better terms.

The Emperor waited but no one else got to his feet. Finally he nodded. "If there are no more opinions," he said, "I will express mine. I want you all to agree with my conclusions. I have listened carefully to all of the arguments opposing Japan's acceptance of the Allied reply as it stands, but my own view has not changed. I have studied internal as well as international conditions and have come to the conclusion that we cannot continue the war any longer." His gloved hand brushed tears from his cheeks. The sight unnerved several of the conferees, who were unable to stifle sobs. "I

---

*During air raids and alerts, Cabinet meetings were held in a safer place, the Telephone Operations office in the Akasaka section.

have studied the Allied reply and concluded that it virtually acknowledges the position of our note sent a few days ago. I find it quite acceptable. Some seem to question the Allied motives in regard to the supreme power of the Emperor, but I agree with the Foreign Minister. I do not believe the note was written to subvert our *kokutai*. I realize full well how difficult it will be for the loyal officers and men of the Army and Navy to surrender their arms to the enemy and see their country occupied, and perhaps stand accused of being war criminals." His voice broke and he stopped momentarily. "So many died in battle and their families still suffer. . . . I think of all these with such sympathy." Again he raised glove to cheek. "All these feelings are so hard to bear, but I cannot let my subjects suffer any longer. I wish to save the people at the risk of my own life. If the war continues our entire nation will be laid waste, hundreds of thousands more will die. I cannot endure this, and the decision I must now make is like the one made by Emperor Meiji at the time of the Triple Intervention when he bore the unbearable and endured the unendurable. Now I must do it and together we must all unite to rebuild Japan into a peaceful country." He paused again. Two of the ministers had collapsed uncontrollably to the floor.

"It is my desire that all of you, my ministers of state, bow to my wishes and accept the Allied reply forthwith. The people know nothing about this situation and will be surprised to hear of my sudden decision. I am ready to do anything. If it is for the good of the people I am willing to make a broadcast. I will go anywhere to persuade the officers and men of the Army and Navy to lay down their arms. It is my desire that the Cabinet at once draw up an imperial rescript to end the war."

In their anguish and grief the conferees clung to each other. Suzuki struggled to his feet, apologized again, stepped in front of the dais and bowed. The Emperor rose and wearily headed for the door.

Just before Umezu left Army Headquarters for the meeting, two of the conspirators had burst into his office and berated him. In an attempt at conciliation he told them that he didn't "absolutely" disapprove of the coup. They started headlong down the hallway to Colonel Takeshita's office. "Umezu is going along with us!" one of them shouted. Anami had to be advised of this development at once and Takeshita drove to the Prime Minister's. He discovered to his consternation that the Cabinet meeting had been interrupted for an emergency conference with the Emperor. At the Palace grounds he was forced to wait at the Imperial Household Ministry, and then, after an interminable interval, was informed that everyone had returned to the Prime Minister's underground chambers to resume the Cabinet meeting. At the Prime Minister's he again had to wait. The Cabinet was having lunch.

When the meal was over, General Anami headed for the men's room followed by his secretary. The War Minister was unnaturally animated. "We have just received information," he exclaimed to Colonel Hayashi, "that the United States fleet is outside Tokyo Bay! What do you think about attacking them with everything we have?" Hayashi became exasperated with War Minister Anami's continued vacillation. It was as though he had not attended the imperial conference. "It won't do," he said. "In the first place it's only a rumor that the U. S. fleet is outside Tokyo Bay. Secondly, the Emperor has just demanded an end to the war."

A man of deep convictions, Anami was emotionally torn by his capacity to see the merits of the facts on all sides. He decided to return to Army Headquarters for a few minutes before the Cabinet meeting reconvened, and face the conspirators. As he passed through the anteroom he ran into his waiting brother-in-law. "General Umezu has changed his mind!" Takeshita burst out.

Anami's face brightened. "Is that so?" he said with quickened interest. Then, remembering that it was all over, he added dejectedly, "But everything has already been decided."

The colonel pleaded with him to use his influence at the Cabinet meeting, but Anami shook his head. "Then at least resign from the Cabinet," Takeshita persisted. If he did, the Suzuki government would be dissolved and could not terminate the war.

"Get me some ink," Anami said with renewed enthusiasm. "I will write my resignation." But again he changed his mind—peace was inevitable whether he left the Cabinet or not "And if I resign," he added, "I will never again see the Emperor."

Anami found his office at Ichigaya Heights occupied by at least fifteen conspirators. There was no pretense left in the War Minister. "A council in the imperial presence has just been held," he said, "and the Emperor has finally decided to end the war." His apology for not meeting their expectations was acknowledged by an embarrassed silence. "The entire

Army must act in complete accord with this decision," he said. "Japan will face difficult times, but no matter how arduous life becomes, I ask you to do your utmost to preserve the national essence."

A lieutenant colonel, Masataka Ida, challenged him. Why had he changed his mind?

General Anami closed his eyes, remembering the harrowing experience that morning in the *obunko* annex. "I could not oppose the decision once His Majesty made it." He told them that the Emperor, with tears in his eyes, had turned to him expressly and said, "Anami, I understand it is particularly difficult for you, but you must bear it!" He gazed at the bitter faces around him but this time made no attempt to mollify them. "The decision stands and must be obeyed," he said with dignity and determination. "Those who are dissatisfied will have to cut me down first!"

Clearly, there was nothing more to be said. Major Hatanaka broke down. Tears coursed down his cheeks and he sobbed. Anami was moved, but without a word he turned and left the room. The others followed him out one by one, heads bowed.

Anami returned to a Cabinet meeting which was more subdued than any in memory. Suzuki had reprimanded his ministers for twice forcing the Emperor to make the decision for peace; it was an affront to His Majesty. There was no rebuttal to his harsh words. Bowing to the Emperor's will, each of the fifteen ministers signed the document accepting the Potsdam Proclamation unconditionally.

One crucial problem remained: How should the decision be presented to the nation? President of the Information Board Kainan Shimomura suggested that the Emperor broadcast an imperial rescript. It was distasteful, but words about capitulation would be believed only if they came from his mouth. The Cabinet unanimously agreed, with one proviso: it would be presumptuous to ask His Majesty to speak directly to his subjects over the airwaves. It should be a recording.

2.

The rumor Anami had heard that an American fleet lay off Tokyo Bay swept through Army Headquarters. Enemy troops were preparing to land; paratroopers were about to drop on all important airports. Panicked officers hauled files to the courtyard and set fire to classified documents. A colonel from Okinawa, brandishing his two-handed dress sword, charged into the office which translated English-language broadcasts and newspapers. He accused the translators of promulgating defeatism. Slashing his sword at them, he shouted, "You deserve to die for misleading us!" but he was overcome with tears and left abruptly, slamming the door.

General Takeshi Mori, commander of the Konoye Division, which guarded the Palace grounds, loosed his frustrations on the chief of Intelligence. He stormed into General Seizo Arisue's office shouting, "Kill yourself! I'll commit hara-kiri after I see you dead!" Arisue reminded him it was his duty to guard the Emperor. "That is my business. I'll defend His Majesty. Then I'll kill you!" Shaken, Arisue walked over to the office of the Chief of Operations, General Shuichi Miyazaki, who also had been threatened by Mori. "He was out of his mind," said Arisue.

Discipline was disintegrating on all levels. *Kempei* noncoms assigned to the building had deserted, taking clothing and food with them; junior officers insulted their superiors; some senior officers closeted themselves behind their doors with whiskey and *sake*. Disruption had one positive effect: it unified the Army leaders. Anami, Umezu, Hata and Sugiyama all put their seals to a terse declaration which amounted to a credo: "The Army will act in accord with the imperial decision to the last." All section chiefs were instructed to report to Conference Room I, where War Minister Anami would address them.

At 3:30 P.M. Anami climbed a small platform. "The Emperor has decided to end the war," he told the standing audience. "It is, therefore, proper that we abide by the imperial wish. His Majesty is confident that the *kokutai* will be maintained and he has expressed that conviction to the field marshals. Difficulties lie ahead for all of us, but you officers must face the fact that death does not absolve you from your duty. You must stay alive, even if it means eating grass and sleeping on thorns and rocks."

Anami's speech destroyed the possibility of any coup involving high-ranking officers. Only the unshakable Major Hatanaka and several die-hard comrades remained resolved to act. Moreover, they still had a good chance of seizing the Palace grounds; two majors of General Mori's division—one was Tojo's son-in-law Hidemasa Koga—still espoused their cause. There was one new objective, however, of the highest

940

priority. They would have to intercept the recording the Emperor was to make before it was delivered to the NHK (Japan Broadcasting Corporation) Building.

All afternoon Hatanaka had been bicycling around Tokyo in the sweltering heat, attempting to revitalize the conspiracy. His obsession led him to the sixth floor of the Dai Ichi Insurance Building, where General Shizuichi Tanaka, commander of Eastern District Army, had a suite. Unannounced, he strode into the general's private office. Tanaka ordered him to get out. The general's fury left Hatanaka speechless. He saluted smartly, whirled around and left.

His resolution had not dissipated, however, and he pedaled back to Ichigaya Heights to re-enlist those who had abandoned the conspiracy. First he went to Colonel Ida; the solution, Ida had decided, after hearing Anami's pronouncement, was for the leading officers at Army Headquarters to commit mass suicide in apology to the Emperor and the nation—but few were willing to join him.

Hatanaka asked Ida to follow him up to the roof, where they could talk freely. He had "something important" to say: he planned to occupy the Palace grounds that night. "Most of the battalion and company commanders of the Konoye Division have already agreed," he said persuasively.

"It won't work," Ida replied. "The Emperor has already made his decision. And what about the commander of the Konoye Division?"

"I'm not sure of Mori," Hatanaka conceded, "but we must bring him in somehow." Ida doubted that General Mori could be won over. "I know, but that can't stop me. The Emperor himself probably is not sure whether accepting the Potsdam Proclamation will mean maintenance of the national essence. How can we obey the Emperor's order when we're fifty percent uncertain of its outcome?" Any Japanese having such doubts, he rationalized, and not rising up in this most critical time of history, would leave a stain on national honor. "That's why I must test this by acting now. If the coup d'état fails, it will prove that the Emperor's decision was correct. If it succeeds, then it will prove that I was right. I must do something. I can't just sit and wait."

Ida could not go along with this reasoning, but he admired Hatanaka for risking his life for an ideal. "If you're serious about it, go ahead," he said. "I can't stop you."

But Hatanaka wanted more than approval. "I would appreciate your help." Ida said he would have to think it over, but he had no intention of changing his mind.

On the stairway Hatanaka encountered Colonel Masao Inaba, who had written the unauthorized exhortation to the troops to go on fighting. Inaba would not even pretend he would consider supporting the new conspiracy. "The Cabinet has already signed the surrender document," he said, "and the Emperor is going to broadcast tomorrow. It's useless. Give it up."

Exactly what the Emperor would say in this broadcast—the imperial rescript—was still being debated by the Cabinet. Anami could not tolerate the phrase "the war situation is growing more unfavorable for us every day." How could he endorse such a statement? It would brand all the communiqués from Imperial Headquarters as lies. Besides, they hadn't yet lost the war.

Yonai confronted him with the catastrophic losses of Burma and Okinawa, and another lengthy argument was averted by Sakomizu, who diplomatically suggested that they change the wording to read "the war situation has developed not necessarily to Japan's advantage."

During a recess Anami returned to his residence near the Diet Building to change into dress uniform for the ceremonious signing of the document. As he was about to leave the little house, Field Marshal Shunroku Hata and former Prime Minister Tojo appeared. It was obvious that after the surrender they would all be tried as war criminals, and Tojo wanted everyone to testify that they had fought a defensive war. Hata had a different request: he wanted to give up the rank of field marshal.

As the Cabinet worked to approve the final wording of the rescript, two officials at the Household Ministry were making copies with brush; one would be the official document, another would be used by the Emperor at the recording. His Majesty was shown the finished version and requested five minor changes. It would take several hours to make new copies, since the rescript contained about eight hundred characters.* Instead the copyists wrote the alterations on slips of paper that were pasted to the original. Then came a phone call from the Prime Minister's—another change, the one requested by Anami. This was followed by the frustrating discovery that a clause had been omitted from one of the copies.

---

*The final draft of the rescript had 815 characters. By coincidence it was to be broadcast on 8/15, that is, August 15.

At last, at 8:30 P.M., the Emperor, in the presence of Prime Minister Suzuki, signed the patchwork document and affixed his seal. Still the formal surrender to the Allies could not be transmitted until the entire Cabinet had signed it. It took almost an hour and a half to collect all the signatures. At about 11 P.M. the last man, the Transportation Minister, arrived at the Prime Minister's conference room and signed. Surrender was official. A secretary phoned the Foreign Ministry and identical cables in English were sent to the Japanese legations in Switzerland and Sweden. The ministers in those countries were instructed to transmit the following message to the United States, Great Britain, the Soviet Union and China:

With reference to the Japanese Government's note of August 10 regarding their acceptance of the provisions of the Potsdam declaration and the reply of the Governments of the United States, Great Britain, the Soviet Union, and China sent by American Secretary of State Byrnes under the date of August 11, the Japanese Government have the honor to communicate to the Governments of the four powers as follows:

1. His Majesty the Emperor has issued an Imperial rescript regarding Japan's acceptance of the provisions of the Potsdam declaration.

2. His Majesty the Emperor is prepared to authorize and ensure the signature of his government and the Imperial General Headquarters of the necessary terms for carrying out the provisions of the Potsdam declaration. His Majesty is also prepared to issue his commands to all the military, naval, and air authorities of Japan and all the forces under their control wherever located to cease active operations, to surrender arms and to issue such other orders as may be required by the Supreme Commander of the Allied Forces for the execution of the above-mentioned terms.

The Cabinet ministers sat numb around the table. There were no more decisions to make. Suzuki got up and left the room. Anami, in his full uniform, rose and approached his old antagonist, Togo. He squared his shoulders and said in a dignified tone, "I have seen the Foreign Minister's draft of the communication to the Allied powers regarding the occupation and disarmament, and I am grateful beyond description. Had I known that the matter would be dealt with in that way, I should not have felt it necessary to speak so zealously at the imperial conference."

Togo thought this was being overly polite and replied rather stiffly that he had always been sympathetic to the conditions for surrender proposed by the military.

Anami buckled on his sword, and with cap under his arm he entered Suzuki's private office. He saluted the Prime Minister. "Ever since the peace talk started, I have given you a great deal of trouble and I am here to express my regrets. What I did was only so that our *kokutai* could be maintained—that was all. I hope you understand this and I deeply apologize."

"I am fully aware of that," said Suzuki and went up to Anami, who was blinking the tears from his eyes. He grasped the general's hand. "But Anami-*san*, please rest assured that the Imperial Household will always be blessed by peace, for His Majesty always prayed for peace at the spring and autumn festivals of his imperial ancestors."

3.

In the Household Ministry a four-man crew from NHK had been waiting since midafternoon to record the Emperor's announcement of surrender. Daitaro Arakawa, the director of engineering at NHK, had set up equipment in adjoining rooms on the second floor. Only once before had His Majesty's voice been recorded; on December 2, 1928, through an acoustical freak, NHK microphones had inadvertently picked up the young Emperor's voice fifty yards away when he was reading a rescript to the Army.

At 11:30 P.M. the Emperor was escorted to the microphone, which stood in front of two gold-foiled screens. Chamberlain Yasuhide Toda, whose voice somewhat resembled the Emperor's, said a few words into the microphone so the engineers could judge how to modulate the volume for His Majesty.

"How loudly shall I speak?" the Emperor asked.

President of the Information Board Shimomura said that his ordinary voice, which was loud, would be adequate. But the Emperor unconsciously lowered his voice as he spoke the words in the unique, imperial language:

"TO OUR GOOD AND LOYAL SUBJECTS

"After pondering deeply the general trends of the world and the actual conditions obtaining in Our Empire today, We have decided to effect a settlement of the present situation by resorting to an extraordinary measure.

"We have ordered Our Government to communicate to the Governments of the United States, Great Britain, China and the

Soviet Union that Our Empire accepts the provisions of their Joint Declaration.

"To strive for the common prosperity and happiness of all nations, as well as the security and well-being of Our subjects, is the solemn obligation which has been handed down by Our Imperial Ancestors, and which We lay close to heart. Indeed, We declared war on America and Britain out of Our sincere desire to ensure Japan's self-preservation and the stabilization of East Asia, it being far from Our thought either to infringe upon the sovereignty of other nations or to embark upon territorial aggrandizement. But now the war has lasted for nearly four years. Despite the best that has been done by everyone—the gallant fighting of military and naval forces, the diligence and assiduity of Our servants of the State and the devoted service of Our one hundred million people—the war situation has developed not necessarily to Japan's advantage, while the general trends of the world have all turned against her interest. Moreover, the enemy has begun to employ a new and most cruel bomb, the power of which to do damage is indeed incalculable, taking the toll of many innocent lives. Should We continue to fight, it would not only result in an ultimate collapse and obliteration of the Japanese nation, but also it would lead to the total extinction of human civilization. Such being the case, how are We to save the millions of Our subjects; or to atone Ourselves before the hallowed spirits of Our Imperial Ancestors? This is the reason why We have ordered the acceptance of the provisions of the Joint Declaration of the Powers.

"We cannot but express the deepest sense of regret to our allied nations of East Asia, who have consistently co-operated with the Empire toward the emancipation of East Asia. The thought of those officers and men as well as others who have fallen in the fields of battle, those who died at their posts of duty, or those who met with untimely death and all their bereaved families, pains Our heart night and day. The welfare of the wounded and the war-sufferers, and of those who have lost their homes and livelihood, are the objects of Our profound solicitude. The hardships and sufferings to which Our nation is to be subject hereafter will certainly be great. We are keenly aware of the inmost feelings of all ye, Our subjects. However, it is according to the dictate of time and fate that We have resolved to pave the way for a grand peace for all the generations to come by enduring the unendurable and suffering what is insufferable.

"Having been able to safeguard and maintain the structure of the Imperial State, We are always with ye, Our good and loyal subjects, relying upon your sincerity and integrity. Beware most strictly of any outbursts of emotion which may engender needless complications, or any fraternal contention and strife which may create confusion, lead ye astray and cause ye to lose the confidence of the world. Let the entire nation continue as one family from generation to generation, ever firm in its faith of the imperishableness of its divine land, and mindful of its heavy burden of responsibilities, and the long road before it. Unite your total strength to be devoted to the construction for the future. Cultivate the ways of rectitude; foster nobility of spirit; and work with resolution so as ye may enhance the innate glory of the Imperial State and keep pace with the progress of the world."

His Majesty turned and said, "Was it all right?" An engineer in the other room embarrassedly replied that he was sorry but a few words were not clear. The Emperor, who was showing increased interest in the proceedings, knew he had stuttered several times and said he wanted to do it again. This time his voice was pitched too high and he skipped a character. "I'm willing to make another," he said obligingly, but it was thought that this would be "too great an ordeal" for him.

It was decided that the second version would be the official one, and the first used only in an emergency. The two sets of two 10-inch disks each were carefully placed in separate cardboard containers, then put in a cotton bag that someone found in the room. Now the problem was: Where would be the safest place to keep them? The obvious place— the radio station—would be vulnerable in case there was any truth to the rumor about an uprising; the Household Ministry would be more secure. Consequently, the records were locked in a small safe on the second floor.

These precautions were well taken. The Palace grounds were about to be sealed from the outside world by rebel troops, and already a general had been assassinated. Rebuffed at Army Headquarters, Hatanaka had gone to Colonel Toyojiro Haga, commander of the Second Regiment of the Konoye Division, and by swearing that Generals Anami, Umezu, Tanaka and Mori had joined the conspiracy, won his reluctant support. Then Hatanaka bicycled back to Ichigaya Heights, where he awakened Colonel Ida—for the past week many officers had been sleeping at Army Headquarters. Again Hatanaka grossly exaggerated his backing: "The regimental commanders of Konoye Division have all agreed to come in with us! The only one left to convince is the division commander." He doubted that Mori would listen to him (the general had been one of his instructors at the War College and still regarded him as a "student"), but Ida, as a lieutenant colonel, might be heeded. Hatanaka swore that if Mori refused to join them, he would abandon his entire plan.

Ida still endorsed the purpose of the revolt, and he convinced himself that he should go along with Hatanaka. If General Mori could be persuaded to join them, he assured himself, that "would help to prove we were right." Moreover, if trouble started, Ida would be on hand to stop it.

On bicycles the two men followed the dark streets to the Konoye Division barracks, which were located just outside the Palace compound only a few hundred yards from the *obunko*. A flat tire prevented them from reaching Mori's office until 11 P.M. and the general had just left to inspect the grounds. Even when Mori returned they were kept waiting in the orderly room; the general was visiting with his brother-in-law, Lieutenant Colonel Michinori Shiraishi. Shortly after midnight Hatanaka impatiently stood up. "Never mind about his visitor," he said. "Let's go in and see Mori." Ida followed him to the general's office. At the door Hatanaka stopped. "You go in by yourself," he said. At the same time he would try to re-enlist Colonel Takeshita's help with his brother-in-law. He left Ida so exasperated that he almost returned to Army Headquarters. But Ida knocked at the door and entered.

General Mori (a scholarly, solemn man with the appropriate nickname *Osho-san*, "head monk") had berated two generals that afternoon at Army Headquarters for their part in losing the war. He greeted Ida affably, and without asking why he had come, began a philosophic monologue on life and religion. It was half an hour before Ida could find an appropriate opening. Ordinarily, he said, a loyal Japanese obeyed any order of the Emperor, such obedience was a virtue. But today it was the duty of the loyal subject to advise His Majesty to reconsider his decision. "It is not true loyalty to the Emperor to obey him blindly." Mori listened perturbed, but with growing interest. Ida pressed him. "If you are absolutely convinced that the Allies have guaranteed to maintain the national essence, then obey the Emperor, but if you are uncertain, shouldn't you so advise His Majesty?" But it would be too late unless the recording His Majesty made was seized. He urged Mori to mobilize the Konoye Division at once.

"I'm not sure what is right," Mori said dubiously. "I would like to go to Meiji Shrine, where I can cleanse myself of all impure thoughts. Then I can tell who is correct—you or me." Colonel Kazuo Mizutani, the general's chief of staff, entered. "You came in at the right moment," said Mori and turned to Ida, who was dripping with nervous perspiration. "Ask him what he thinks."

947

Mizutani suggested that they talk in his office while the general changed clothes to go to the shrine. In the corridor they encountered Major Hatanaka—thanks to his persuasiveness, Colonel Takeshita had agreed to see Anami once more—and several other conspirators.

Ida said that he and General Mori were going to the Meiji Shrine, but first he had to see Colonel Mizutani for a moment.

"This is all a waste of time!" Hatanaka exclaimed irritably.

It wouldn't take long; Ida ordered Hatanaka to wait in Mori's office.

But Hatanaka was in no mood for delay. Impatience had brought him to the point of recklessness. In fact, he was ready to cut Mori down if he rejected them. He strode into Mori's office, followed by several other aggressive sympathizers. Ignoring military courtesy, Hatanaka abruptly asked—rather, insisted—that the general join them. But Mori would not be rushed; he would decide only after he had visited the shrine.

His procrastination was intolerable. Captain Shigetaro Uehara, of the Air Academy, advanced on him with drawn sword. Colonel Shiraishi lunged to shield his brother-in-law, General Mori. Uehara struck him down. Another rebel officer, a major, slashed viciously at the prone Shiraishi, almost beheading him. Uehara's impulsive attack unleashed the pent-up emotions of days of frustration. Hatanaka leveled his pistol at Mori and pulled the trigger. The general collapsed into the blood flowing from Shiraishi's body and died.

Ida and Mizutani heard the shot and a clattering of feet. They ran into the corridor. There was Hatanaka, his face drained, pistol still in hand. Instantly Ida guessed what had happened. "*Bakayaro!*" he shouted. Why couldn't Hatanaka have waited; Mori might have joined them after he had visited the Meiji Shrine.

"I did it because there was no time left," Hatanaka muttered. "I'm sorry." He bowed his head but he had lost none of his determination. He begged Ida to make another appeal to General Tanaka. With Mori dead, the division was now under his command.

Ida had reluctantly accompanied Hatanaka to the Konoye Division to prevent violence, but now that the worst had happened he had become in effect, an accessory to assassination, committed to a course he had resisted. With Mori's death, serious opposition to the coup within the Konoye Division was eliminated and its troops would shortly occupy

948

the Palace grounds. Accompanied by an almost hysterical Colonel Mizutani, Ida speeded by staff car to the Dai Ichi Building, headquarters of Eastern District Army. Mizutani rushed into Tanaka's inner office while Ida, without mentioning Mori's murder, requested Tanaka's chief of staff, Major General Tatsuhiko Takashima, to cooperate with the rebels. Takashima's reaction seemed almost one of embarrassment—it was like "jumping from fire into ice water"—and Ida's too-easily-won confidence evaporated.

The phone rang. It was Major Koga, Tojo's son-in-law, reporting that the Konoye Division had just revolted and would never surrender. Eastern District Army must join them. General Takashima went into Tanaka's private office, leaving Ida with one of the staff officers with whom he continued to argue. But the staff officer maintained that there was not the slightest possibility that General Tanaka would oppose the Emperor. His certainty brought Ida back to reality. Soberly he said, "I will do my best to withdraw the troops before dawn."

An order had already been issued to regimental commanders of the Konoye Division—it bore General Mori's seal but it had been placed there by Hatanaka. The instructions, actually written by Major Koga, directed the troops to occupy the Palace grounds, thus "protecting" the Emperor and *kokutai*; one company was sent to the NHK Building to control what was broadcast. Contingents totaling more than a thousand men cordoned the Palace grounds. The majority, as in the 2/26 uprising, had no idea that they were acting as insurgents. In appearance all that seemed to be taking place was an emergency reinforcement of the permanent guard posts. Within minutes all of the great gates clanged shut and the Emperor was isolated from the outside.

Nor was anyone, no matter what his rank, allowed to leave the grounds without Hatanaka's permission. Inside the Imperial Household Ministry, the Emperor had finished his recording, and President Shimomura and the NHK crew drove away. As their cars approached the Sakashita Gate, barely a hundred yards away, soldiers with fixed bayonets halted them. One peered into the first car. He had been alerted to look for the President of the Information Board. Shimomura's secretary acknowledged who they were and the entire contingent was taken under escort to a small wooden guardhouse for interrogation. One of the group disclosed that the recording had been turned over to a chamberlain for safekeeping. A search party was sent to the Imperial Household Ministry.

On the fourth floor of the ministry Kido was routed from his cot by Chamberlain Yasuhide Toda. The Privy Seal had been kept half awake by a succession of noises—air-raid sirens, the thud of bombs in the distance,* announcement from the loudspeaker in the hall reporting damage, and most recently the crunch of marching feet on gravel.

Toda informed him that rebel soldiers were in the building looking for Kido and the recording, and that the *obunko* itself was surrounded. The Privy Seal remained calm. "I expected something like this," he said. "The Army is *shoganai yatsu* [damn foolish]." Since Kido's appearance was little known outside Palace circles, Toda suggested that he move to the court physician's night-duty quarters, where he could pose as a doctor. No sooner was Kido stretched out on the doctor's bed than he began brooding about how humiliating it would be to be killed while hiding like Kira in *The Forty-seven Ronin*. He returned to his office, where he hastily collected his most secret documents, tore them to bits and flushed them down the toilet.

He was interrupted by another plea to seek sanctuary. Chamberlain Yoshihiro Tokugawa importuned him to join the Imperial Household Minister in a storage room in the basement. The clatter of soldiers' boots echoed down the corridor and Kido allowed himself to be led down a dark staircase.

Chamberlain Toda, who thought he had left Kido safely in the physician's office, now tried to make his way on foot to the *obunko* to alert the court staff; all phone connections had been severed. He feared that the short cut to the *obunko*, a small tunnel, would be guarded, and as he started on a circuitous route, half a dozen soldiers appeared out of the darkness. Toda explained he was a chamberlain, but the commanding officer was unimpressed. Shoving a pistol in his chest, he said, "Go back; the road is blocked."

Toda returned to the ministry. At the entrance he ran into Tokugawa, and together they started back for the *obunko*, this time by way of the tunnel. As expected, there were sentries guarding the other end, but there was no officer in charge. Imperiously they announced that they were chamber-

---

*During the day, 821 Superfortresses had left the Marianas to bomb the Tokyo area. General Spaatz had wanted "as big a finale as possible."

lains on duty, and were allowed to pass. At the *obunko* they aroused the court ladies but instructed them not to awaken the royal family. Tokugawa, a short man, tried to pull down the iron shutters over the windows, but they were so rusty that it required several husky bodyguards to finish the job. As he and Toda started back to the Household Ministry a second lieutenant called out to halt, but they broke into a run and escaped.

The main entrance of the ministry was now guarded by a heavy-machine-gun crew and they entered separately by side doors. On the second floor Toda was apprehended by rebel soldiers with bayonets who were escorting a bound prisoner, an NHK official.

"Who are you?" one of the soldiers asked.

"I am a chamberlain," Toda replied.

The soldier turned to his prisoner. "Did you give the records to this chamberlain?"

"No, it was a much taller man with a big nose."

The man he had given them to was Tokugawa, who in fact was smaller. Shortly after re-entering the ministry, Tokugawa had been caught by the second lieutenant who had tried to stop him near the *obunko*. He ordered soldiers to take the chamberlain to the guardhouse.

But Tokugawa, whose ancestors had once ruled Japan for more than 250 years, haughtily refused to go. "If you have any business with me," he said, "I'll discuss it here." Two other rebel officers were attracted by the altercation. "Cut him down!" one of them shouted. "It won't do you any good to kill me," said Tokugawa with dignity.

"I wouldn't rust my sword on you," the second lieutenant sneered, but obviously he was impressed by Tokugawa's bearing and tried to justify the coup. It had been necessary, he said, to occupy the Palace grounds because the Emperor's advisers had misled him. "Those men are *keshikaran* [outrageous]!" Tokugawa merely stared at him. Incensed, the lieutenant yelled, "Don't you have the Japanese spirit?"

"I am a chamberlain," Tokugawa said proudly. "You are not the ones defending the country. To defend our nation, everyone has to co-operate."

A noncom slapped Tokugawa's face so hard that his glasses were knocked awry and hung on one ear. Tokugawa called to a Palace policeman (the small police force had been powerless to resist the rebels openly), "Get in touch with the aides-de-camp!" The second lieutenant seized the policeman, but Tokugawa, who acted as though he were in charge, stopped him with an indignant "He's on duty." The policeman was released. Another rebel officer politely asked Tokugawa the way to the Privy Seal's office.

Tokugawa gave the directions but added. "I doubt that you'll find him there." Then he turned and strode away. No one tried to stop him. He went into the office of the Emperor's military aides.

"They're like madmen," warned Admiral Toshihisa Nakamura, the Emperor's naval aide. "Be careful." He wanted to know where Kido really was.

"I'm not disclosing to anyone where he is," said Tokugawa. He could not trust any senior officer who merely secluded himself in an office during such an emergency. "Rest assured he's safe."

Major Hatanaka had succeeded in isolating the Emperor, but his recording could not be found. Moreover, Colonel Ida, whom he had sent on a vital mission, was back with a disconcerting report: there would be no help from the outside. "Eastern District Army won't go along," he said. In fact, Ida himself no longer thought the coup was feasible. "Once the men of the Konoye Division discover that their commander has been killed, they'll refuse to continue. If you try to force this thing through, there will be chaos. There's no other alternative: withdraw all troops before dawn." Hatanaka tried to interrupt, but Ida held up his hand. "Face the facts; the coup has failed, but if you pull out all the troops quickly the people will never know what happened." It would all pass like "a midsummer night's dream."

Hatanaka's face sagged. "I understand," he said.

"I'm going to report what has happened to the War Minister," Ida went on. Would Hatanaka promise to withdraw the troops? Hatanaka nodded. But the effect of Ida's reasoning dissipated with his departure, and Hatanaka's spirit of revolt flared as bright as ever. He returned to the control point of the uprising, the Konoye barracks, where Colonel Haga, commander of the 2nd Regiment, was growing suspicious of Mori's prolonged absence. Hatanaka tried to parry the colonel's questions but Major Koga could no longer remain silent. He confessed to his superior that Mori was dead and urged him to take command of the division.

How did Mori die? demanded Colonel Haga. Neither Hatanaka nor Koga professed to know. Perturbed as he was, Colonel Haga would have continued his reluctant alliance with the dissidents but for a phone call that moment from

Eastern District Army headquarters. Tanaka's chief of staff, General Takashima, wanted to know exactly what was going on in the Palace grounds. Haga could not give specific answers and handed the phone to Hatanaka.

"This is Major Hatanaka, Your Excellency," he said in a trembling voice. "Please understand our ardor."

It was lucky that Takashima had reached the ringleader. He remembered Hatanaka from the War College as a bright, naïve idealist, and decided "to admonish him gently and reason with him rather than order or reprimand him." He said he understood how the dissidents felt, but the Emperor had issued his order and Eastern Army* was going to obey it. "Do not use any force now that there's no prospect of success. It will only cause further needless sacrifices. . . . In Japan it is both pragmatic and highly moral to obey His Majesty's order." He paused. "Did I get through to you?"

Everything Ida had just predicted was materializing. Hatanaka's voice broke. "I understand very well, Your Excellency. I'd like to think it over. I have one more request. Please give us ten minutes to broadcast before His Majesty goes on the air." He wanted to tell the people why the young officers had revolted.

Takashima said that would be "irresolution," and as many lives as possible should be saved. "We have reached the point where the final outcome cannot be changed. Hatanaka, do you understand me?" There was no answer. Then Takashima heard a faint sobbing.

Even hearing one side of the conversation confirmed Haga's suspicions. He raged at Hatanaka and Koga for claiming support of Eastern District Army, and he too ordered them to end the rebellion at once or they would have to kill him.

As he had before when forcefully confronted, Hatanaka verbally capitulated but privately had not given up. He was all set to pursue a new tactic. He would prevent the Emperor's broadcast at the NHK Building, which was occupied by his troops, and instead make a personal plea to the nation himself.

Colonel Takeshita found War Minister Anami at his modest residence near the Diet Building. He had come as much

---

*General Tanaka commanded two units simultaneously, Eastern District Army and 12th Army Group. Together they were popularly known as Eastern Army.

out of fear that his brother-in-law might take his life as to fulfill his promise on behalf of the dissidents. Anami was sitting at a table in the living room writing his will. To one side a bed of mats was laid out. Over it hung a canopy of mosquito netting. The general hastily folded the document and said somewhat accusingly, "What do you want?"

Takeshita could see he was preparing himself for death. It was pointless to talk of the uprising, so he chatted inconsequentially with Anami for some time over *sake*. Finally the general said casually, "I'm thinking of killing myself tonight."

"It may be proper for you to commit suicide," Takeshita replied, "but it doesn't have to be tonight, does it?"

Anami seemed relieved. "I thought you would try to talk me out of it. I'm pleased you approve." He showed Takeshita the will, which was dated August 14. "The fourteenth is the anniversary of the death of my father and the twenty first is the date my son was killed in action. I debated which date I should pick, but the twenty first is too late. I could not bear to hear the Emperor's broadcast tomorrow."

They talked about personal matters until two in the morning, when a distant volley of gunfire in the direction of the Palace grounds reminded Takeshita of his promise to Hatanaka. He outlined the latest rebel plan.* But Anami was preoccupied with his own death—as far as he was concerned the coup was a foregone failure. In another attempt to delay his brother-in-law, Takeshita questioned whether he could perform the disembowelment ritual of *seppuku* with so much *sake* in him.

"I have a fifth-degree rank in *kendo*, so I won't fail," he said confidently. "*Sake* makes you bleed more profusely. That way you are certain of dying. Should anything go wrong, I want you to assist me." He stripped to the waist and wrapped a band of white cotton around his belly. But the preparations

---

*Hatanaka was not the only officer who had planned an insurrection. Some forty men, led by the commander of the Yokohama Guard, drove up to Tokyo to assassinate the "Badoglios" in the government. They barricaded the Prime Minister's office just before dawn on August 15. They had hoped to trap Suzuki and other ministers inside, but the Prime Minister was asleep at home. The rebels set fire to the empty building and headed for the Suzuki house. The Suzukis escaped in car—it had to be pushed to get started—just before the rebels arrived. Again the would-be assassins became arsonists and at gunpoint prevented firemen from saving the house. Frustrated, the gang headed for Baron Hiranuma's residence, which they also set afire. The aged baron, leaving his false teeth behind, escaped through a garden gate, the one one not covered by his pursuers.

for the ceremony were suspended by the arrival of Colonel Ida, who had come to inform the War Minister about Hatanaka. But he said nothing, not wishing to "upset" a man about to commit suicide.

"Come in," said Anami. "I am getting ready to die." Did Ida approve?

"I think it would be *kekko* [fine]," Ida told the War Minister, and added that not only had he himself advocated mass suicide, but Anami's example would end all confusion in the Army and terminate any other plots. Ida bowed his head and held back his tears. "I will accompany you shortly," he said.

Anami reached over and slapped Ida's cheek sharply. "It's enough with me; you must not die!" he said and enfolded him in a long embrace. Both men broke down. "Don't die," said Anami in little more than a whisper. "I depend on you for the future of Japan. Do you understand?"

"Yes, sir, I understand." But Ida still intended to kill himself.

"Let's have a farewell drink," Anami suggested, suddenly cheerful. As the three men sipped *sake* they were again interrupted, this time by Colonel Hayashi, who appeared with the general's jacket draped over his arm. He said brusquely, "General, you are urgently requested at the ministry. We should leave immediately."

Annoyed, Anami turned and said, "You make too much noise. Get out!"

The three resumed their drinking. Anami showed Ida two scrolls. One was signed "War Minister Korechika Anami" and read:

> *Believing in the eternity of our Divine Land,*
> *with my death I apologize to the Emperor*
> *for the great crime.*

The other was a *waka*, a thirty-one-syllable poem:

> *Having received great favors from the Emperor,*
> *I do not have even half a word to leave*
> *in the hour of my death.*

"General, it will soon be dawn," Takeshita reminded him.

"I will go now," said Anami. "Farewell."

As soon as Colonel Ida had bowed himself out of the room, Anami once more asked Takeshita to give him the *coup de grâce* if he failed to kill himself. He placed his uniform neatly in an alcove, embraced his brother-in-law and made a final request—that the uniform be put on his body.

There was yet another interruption, around four o'clock. Lieutenant General Sanji Okido, chief of the *kempeitai*, had come to see the War Minister. Anami told Takeshita to handle the matter. He moved off the straw mat to the corridor and sat cross-legged facing the Imperial Palace. According to the etiquette of *seppuku*, if he stained the tatami with his blood it meant that he considered himself blameless. He deliberately thrust the dagger deep into his abdomen, then slashed twice—to the right and straight up. This was *kappuku*, so excruciatingly painful that few could force themselves to do it. He sat erect as the blood flowed onto the floor and soaked the two scrolls at his side. He heard someone approach, and called out loudly, "Who's that?"

It was Hayashi. Anami groaned and his secretary rushed back to the reception room to get Takeshita. "Tell my sister he's committed hara-kiri," said Takeshita. In the corridor he found the general leaning forward slightly, a dripping dagger in his right hand; with the left he was searching for the jugular vein. Suddenly he plunged the dagger into his throat. Curiously, almost no blood flowed from the wound and Takeshita said, "Can I assist you?"

"*Muyo* [No need]," Anami grunted. "Go away."

Takeshita withdrew, but the general's groans made him go back. "Are you in pain?" he asked. Anami was unconscious. Takeshita picked up the dagger and drove it all the way into the nape of his neck. He draped Anami's coat, heavy with medals, over the dying man.

4.

It was now early morning, another sultry day, August 15. Troops still occupied the Palace grounds; the original orders had not yet been rescinded.

At 6:15 Chamberlain Toda once more tried to regain entrance to the *obunko*, but this time he was unsuccessful. A young officer had orders to let no one in, whoever he was. Toda pretended he had to escort the Emperor to safety, since the air-raid alert was still on, but to no avail. He was finally allowed to pass through on orders of an older officer who reasoned that since the rebels might have to invade the *obunko* en masse to search for the recording which had still not been located, what difference would it make if a single man entered now?

Inside, Toda informed Grand Chamberlain Hisanori Fujita that the insurgents might break in at any moment and that there would probably be a hand-to-hand fight. They had to awaken the Emperor. At 6:40 he appeared in his dressing gown. The events of the previous evening distressed him. "Don't they understand my true intentions yet?" There were tears in his eyes. "Assemble all the Konoye Division officers and men and I will talk to them myself."

A mild-mannered chamberlain, Yasuya Mitsui, was selected to go through the cordon and contact the military. He had not gone fifty yards before an elderly officer stopped him with the question, "Are you a chamberlain?"

It was General Tanaka. A man of culture and a strict disciplinarian, he had gone to Oxford and had once, like Tojo, commanded the *kempeitai* in the Kwantung Army. He had come in person to restore order; he had already arrested one of the majors in the conspiracy and had commanded Colonel Haga to withdraw all his men to their original stations.

"Don't be afraid," he said to the chamberlain. He bowed and extended a large calling card; Mitsui brought out his own. The two bowed again. "I'm sorry for causing so much trouble," said the general. "Within the hour everything will be under control. Please don't worry. All the troops will be withdrawn."* The chamberlain unceremoniously sprinted back to the *obunko*.

Major Hatanaka had been in personal control of the NHK Building for two hours. At gunpoint he had ordered Morio Tateno, who was about to broadcast the early-morning news, to give him the microphone so he could talk to the nation. Tateno invented several excuses: an imminent air raid made it impossible to transmit without permission from Eastern District Army; in addition, it would take time to inform local stations to stand by for a national hookup.

Tateno went into the control room and asked for a line to

---

*On the evening of August 24, wearing full uniform, Tanaka shot himself at his desk. Previously he had told General Takashima that the revolt had little to do with his decision to take his own life. It was primarily because he felt responsible for the burning of the Imperial Palace and the lives lost in the Tokyo fire raids. He had to apologize to the Emperor. He said that no one else in the Eastern District Army should commit suicide: "I will take the responsibility for everyone."

General Tanaka's office. The engineer understood the ruse. He began talking into the dead phone whose line had already been cut by the rebels. He pretended he couldn't get through. Hatanaka waited, resigned, but one of his lieutenants, irritated by the continued delay, jabbed at the engineer with his pistol and threatened to shoot if he didn't hurry. Hatanaka intervened. "I have to convey my feelings to the people," he told Tateno. It was more of a supplication than a demand. He held out a fistful of papers scrawled in pencil. Tateno read the first characters: "Our unit has been defending the palace. . . ."

Tateno asked them to be patient. "We are doing our best to contact Eastern District Army." The charade was cut short by the ringing of another phone in the booth. The engineer listened for a moment and looked uncertainly at Tateno. It was Eastern District Army and they wanted to talk to "the officer in the studio."

Hatanaka took the phone and listened passively. He had gone back on his word to give up the revolt and now faced a direct order to desist. Still, he pleaded for the opportunity to make a final explanation to the public, but it was obvious to Tateno that the request was denied. Dejected, Hatanaka put down the receiver. It was all over.

At 7:21 A.M. Tateno made a special announcement to the nation: "At noon today the Emperor will broadcast his rescript. Let us all respectfully listen to the voice of the Emperor. Electric power will be transmitted to those areas not served during daylight hours. The public shall be given access to radio sets in all plants, railroad stations and government offices. The broadcast will be heard at noon today." The circle is complete, Tateno thought. At the same microphone on the morning of December 8, 1941 he had made the first announcement that war had begun.

The organized opposition to surrender was over, but numerous intransigent individuals and groups remained ready to give up their lives to prevent it. The Palace staff feared that there would be another attempt to destroy the Emperor's recording. Even getting the disks from the safe on the second floor through the Household Ministry to the courtyard was risky. One set, stamped COPY, was placed in a square lacquer box bearing the imperial crest and carried ostentatiously through the dark labyrinthian corridors by a ministry official, Motohiko Kakei. The other set, stamped ORIGINAL, was put in the lunch bag of a chamberlain who slung it over his shoulder. Both messengers reached the ground floor safely,

Then Kakei wrapped the lacquer box in a purple *furoshiki* and set out for the studio in a Palace limousine. The lunch bag was handed over to another official, who was driven off in a metropolitan police car. The copy was delivered without incident to the stand-by studio in the basement of the NHK Building. The ORIGINAL set was taken to the office of the chairman of NHK, where it was locked in a safe.

With the arrival of *kempei*, sent as a result of Hatanaka's phone conversation with Eastern District Army, all the rebels left the NHK Building without protest. Hatanaka did not return to Army Headquarters. His one thought was to prove his sincerity and bring his violent actions to a proper close. With one companion who had remained steadfast from the beginning, Lieutenant Colonel Jiro Shiizaki, he gravitated toward the spacious plaza in front of the Imperial Palace. Here, in a last futile gesture, they passed out leaflets calling on the people to prevent the surrender. At 11:20 A.M. Hatanaka drew the pistol that had killed General Mori and fired a bullet into his own forehead. Shiizaki thrust a sword into his middle, then put a pistol to his head and pulled the trigger.

In Hatanaka's pocket a poem was found:

> *I have nothing to regret*
> *now that the dark clouds have disappeared*
> *from the reign of the Emperor.*

The broadcast, even without the presence of His Majesty, was ceremonial. Studio 8 was crowded with NHK staff members as well as official witnesses from the Cabinet, the Information Board, the Household Ministry and the Army. At almost the same moment that Hatanaka killed himself, the chairman of NHK took the records marked ORIGINAL out of his safe. It was suggested that they be tested, but would it be respectful to the Emperor? The consensus was that it would be wise to rehearse to avoid any mishaps.

The Emperor's voice roused a *kempei* lieutenant who was standing outside Studio 8. Drawing his sword, he shouted, "If this is a surrender broadcast, I will kill every one of you!" He was seized by an Army lieutenant and herded off by guards.

Inside the studio Chokugen Wada, Japan's most popular announcer, sat pale and tense at a table behind a microphone, watching the second hand of a clock sweep around to join the other hand at twelve. At exactly noon he said, "This will be a broadcast of the gravest importance. Will all listeners please rise. His Majesty the Emperor will now read his imperial rescript to the people of Japan. We respectfully transmit his voice."

After the reverent strains of the national anthem, "Kimigayo," ended, there was a pause followed by the voice that few had heard: "To Our Good and Loyal Subjects: After pondering deeply the general trends of the world and the actual conditions obtaining in Our Empire today, We have decided to effect a settlement of the present situation by resorting to an extraordinary measure. . . ."

37   The Voice
of the Crane

1.

An entire nation listened attentively, awed by the high-pitched, almost unreal voice. The strange imperial language, coupled with poor reception, allowed few of His Majesty's subjects to understand exactly what he was saying. It was evident only that a surrender, or something equally catastrophic had occurred.

"Cultivate the ways of rectitude; foster nobility of spirit; and work with resolution so as ye may enhance the innate glory of the Imperial State and keep pace with the progress of the world."

There was silence. The listeners, who had stood or kneeled quietly, faces contorted, could no longer hold their emotions. Millions wept, perhaps more people simultaneously than at any other moment in the world's history. Yet underlying the humiliation and sorrow was an undeniable sense of relief. The terrible burden of years of war, death and destruction was at last over.

At the *obunko* the Emperor had intently followed his own words on a prewar RCA radio. At the Household Ministry, Kido reacted with mixed emotions, secretly triumphant that what he had been striving for so diligently was finally achieved.

In a dingy auditorium at Army Headquarters hundreds of officers, including General Umezu—resplendent in dress uni-

960

forms, complete with white gloves, decorations and swords—still stood at attention, tears coursing down their cheeks. But for some officers the war was not yet over. Not far from Tokyo at Atsugi Air Base, Navy Captain Yasuna Kozono, commander of the 302nd Air Group, climbed to a platform near the runway to address his pilots. The order to surrender, he said, meant the end of the national essence, and to obey it would be treason. Join me and destroy the enemy, he cried. Scores, inflamed by his words, shouted back, *"Banzai!"* And at Oita Air Base on northeastern Kyushu, Admiral Matome Ugaki, Yamamoto's former chief of staff and now commander of all naval *kamikaze* units, was equally resolved to die fighting. He felt responsible for Yamamoto's death—he could not forget the sight of his chief plunging to his doom—and had recently written to Captain Watanabe: "I must pay for it." The Emperor's words increased his shame. Now more than ever it was his duty to follow all those Special Attack men he had sent off to die.

The Voice of the Crane* reached troops thousands of miles from the homeland, as far away as Harbin, Manchuria. Tomomi Yamato, a staff officer, was chagrined to discover that the voice of the man who was more than mortal wavered with hesitancy. How could he have bowed so many times in the direction of the Imperial Palace? But infected by the sobs around him, he could not stifle his own. Out of habit he turned toward the imperial crest above the door of the headquarters building and made his last salute as a Japanese soldier. Then he put on civilian clothes to avoid capture by the approaching Soviets.

On Okinawa, Captain Tsuneo Shimura, the battalion commander whose troops had held Maeda Ridge so stubbornly, was still fighting as a guerrilla. He was trying to steal an American vehicle in order to break through to the north when the sky above was suddenly filled with tracers. It was beautiful, like fireworks, and he thought for a moment it was the Japanese counterattack he had dreamed of. But scouts returned with a report of an American victory celebration. They were drinking beer and shooting in the air. What new disaster had befallen Japan?

Words alone, even the Emperor's, could not bring an abrupt end to the emotions war had engendered for more

---

*The crane is the symbol for the Emperor or the Throne, in the same manner that the Crown is synonymous with the reigning monarch in England.

than four years. In Fukuoka, on the island of Kyushu, some sixteen captured B-29 crewmen were trucked to a hill near a crematorium where eight of their comrades had been beheaded four days earlier. The Americans were forced to strip and then were led one by one into the woods and executed.

No reply to Japan's offer to surrender had yet been received from America, but Navy units were ordered to cease fire before midnight. The Army, however, was reluctant to proceed without a formal reply from Washington. At the last Suzuki Cabinet meeting that afternoon it was learned that it would take twelve days to notify troops isolated in New Guinea and the Philippines. The Allies had to be advised of this communication problem.

Suzuki said he was ashamed that he had "troubled His Majesty twice for his august decision." Now, however, it was necessary to form a new cabinet as soon as possible. Shortly before three o'clock Suzuki tendered the resignation of his entire cabinet to the Emperor. For the last time Kido, at the behest of the Emperor, was requested to select a new prime minister. In consultation with the *jushin* he had already decided that Prince Higashikuni was the best choice. The prince, however, had discouraged such overtures; politics had financially ruined his father. He was, moreover, a man of rare independence. When he was a second lieutenant at the War College he declined an invitation to attend a dinner given by Emperor Meiji; he quarreled with the crown prince (later Emperor Taisho); and he had to be persuaded by a field marshal to retain his membership in the royal family. A few years later he married the Emperor Meiji's daughter, Princess Toshiko, but he still aspired, above all else, to be a private and free citizen.

But today the Emperor approved of Kido's selection—as a member of the royal family, his uncle-in-law was above politics and immune to attack.

"As I told you last night," Prince Higashikuni informed Kido's emissary, "I had no intention whatever of accepting the premiership. But in these circumstances and with the situation so perilous, I believe I will think it over."

At Oita Air Base on Kyushu, Admiral Ugaki was preparing for the final *kamikaze* mission of his command. In his diary he called for vengeance:

There are many cases which have brought Japan to this situation. I must assume responsibility. However, to take a broad view, the main cause was the difference in strength between the two nations [Japan and America]. I hope that not only military men but the whole Japanese people will endure hardships, stir up the *Yamato* spirit and do their utmost to rebuild the nation so that Japan can have her revenge in the future. I, too, have made up my mind to serve our country forever with the spirit of Masahige Kusunoki.

Ugaki arrived at the airfield in a uniform stripped of all insignia, carrying a pair of binoculars and a short samurai sword given him by Yamamoto. The plan was for a three-plane strike, but eleven small bombers were on the ramp. Ugaki mounted a small platform and asked the assembled fliers if they were "all so willing to die with me"? Every hand shot up. He climbed into the cockpit behind the pilot of the leading plane. Warrant Officer Akiyoshi Endo, whom he had replaced, protested, "You've taken my seat!"

"I have relieved you," said Ugaki with the suggestion of a smile. Undeterred, Endo scrambled up and tried to wedge himself in beside the admiral. Ugaki good-naturedly moved over.

Four of the bombers had to turn back because of engine trouble but the rest continued on toward Okinawa. At 7:24 P.M. Endo radioed back an impassioned farewell message from Ugaki:

I alone am to blame for our failure to defend the homeland and destroy the arrogant enemy. The valiant efforts of all officers and men of my command during the past six months have been greatly appreciated.

I am going to make an attack at Okinawa, where my men have fallen like cherry blossoms. There I will crash into and destroy the conceited enemy in the true spirit of *bushido*, with firm conviction and faith in the eternity of Imperial Japan.

I trust that the members of all units under my command will understand my motives, will overcome all hardships of the future and will strive for the reconstruction of our great homeland, that it may survive forever.

Long live His Imperial Majesty the Emperor!

Minutes later Endo advised that the plane was diving toward a target.*

The bodies of Anami and the two rebel leaders, Hatanaka and Shiizaki, were brought to a building adjoining Army

---

*This was the last report of the seven planes. Curiously, there is no U. S. record of any *kamikaze* attack on that date.

Headquarters for memorial services. Hundreds of mourners filed by to honor them, particularly Anami, who had given his life to bring order to the nation.

Early that evening Colonel Ida, Hatanaka's reluctant ally, came to pay his respects. He had written his will and said farewell to his wife. In his office next door he lay down to prepare himself spiritually for death. When all was quiet he rose and walked down the darkened dorridor to Anami's office. Here, as was fitting, he would commit suicide. At the door a major named Sakai called to him.

"What are you doing here, Sakai?"

"What about you?"

"Never mind," Ida told him. "Just leave me alone."

Sakai said that he had been ordered to "keep an eye on" the colonel. "If you want to die, you'll have to kill me first."

Ida was annoyed. "Can't you understand the feelings of a samurai?" But Sakai persisted and their argument dissipated Ida's resolve. When one misses the time for hara-kiri, he thought ruefully, it is gone forever.

They returned to Ida's office, where they stretched out on adjoining cots and talked for hours. In the morning Ida was awakened by a macabre request. His wife and her father (his name was Ida and he had adopted his son-in-law) had come to claim the body. Awkwardly Ida tried to explain what had happened, but on his wife's face appeared an inquiring look as if she were asking: Why are you still alive?

In another section of Tokyo the creator of the *kamikaze* corps, Admiral Takijiro Onishi, lay mortally wounded by his own hand in his home. He sent for his associate and friend, Yoshio Kodama, whose sword he had borrowed the night before. Kodama found Onishi still conscious, though he had slit his abdomen and stabbed himself in the chest and throat. He seized Kodama's hand. "What I want to tell you is written in my will on the top of the desk. There's also a letter to my wife; she is in the country." He smiled faintly. "I thought your sword was sharper. It didn't cut very well."

The weapon was on the floor, and Kodama picked it up. "Your Excellency," he whispered, "I will go with you."

"*Bakayaro!*" Onishi shouted in a surprisingly strong voice. "What would you gain by dying now? Instead— There is another letter on my desk. Take it to Atsugi Air Base at once and bring those headstrong men under control. That will do more good for Japan than dying here." His forehead was covered with perspiration and he gasped for words. "Many of the nationalists will rise up. Stop them!"

Kodama found the letter on the desk. In it the man who a few days before had pleaded with Admiral Toyoda and Foreign Minister Togo to sacrifice twenty million lives in a final defense of the homeland apologized for his failure to bring victory. He wanted the young people of Japan to find a moral in his death. "To be reckless is only to aid the enemy. You must abide by the spirit of the Emperor's decision with utmost perseverance. Do not forget your rightful pride in being Japanese. You are the treasure of the nation. With all the fervor of spirit of the Special Attackers, strive for the welfare of Japan and for peace throughout the world."

Beside the letter was a *haiku*, Onishi's last poem:

> *Refreshed.*
> *I feel like the clear moon*
> *after a storm.*

Kodama turned back to the admiral, who was vomiting blood, and begged Onishi to stay alive until he brought back his wife—it would take about five hours. Onishi smiled wanly. "Is there anything more stupid than a military man committing suicide and then prolonging death just to wait for his wife?" He reached for Kodama's hand. *"Sayonara."*

2.

The knowledge that he was the Emperor's "personal choice" for prime minister made it almost impossible for Prince Higashikuni to refuse. "I can't think of my own welfare in this critical situation," he resignedly told Kido on the morning of August 16, "and if I can be of any service to the country I shall be pleased to accept the post." Before making up his mind, however, he wanted to know what the current situation was.

Kido informed him that General MacArthur required a liaison officer representing the Japanese government sent to Manila promptly. "So it is expedient to form a cabinet as soon as possible. At the present time we have no means to deal with the Americans, and the Allies might regard any delay with suspicion and make our situation even more difficult." The previous night's attempted coup made it necessary to select someone respected by the Army. "If you do not accept the post, you will cause His Majesty great anxiety."

Higashikuni pondered: it would be onerous to lead a

defeated nation, but he knew he could control the riotous acts of dissident Army men through colleagues in the service—he held the rank of general—and once Japan's future was settled, he could step down. "I will humbly accept the imperial order to form a cabinet," he said.

Before noon a note accepting the Japanese surrender offer arrived from Washington and Imperial Headquarters issued orders to all Army and Navy units to cease hostilities. In addition, the Emperor instructed three members of his family to tour overseas commands and reassure the troops that he had made the decision to surrender of his own free will. Prince Tsunenori Takeda, a lieutenant colonel, would cover the forces in Korea and Manchuria; Prince Yasuhiko Asaka, a colonel, the China Expeditionary Army and the China Area Fleet; and Prince Haruhito Kanin, son of the former Army Chief of Staff, Shanghai, Canton, Saigon, Singapore, Indochina and Nanking. The three men left Haneda Airport in identical white twin-engine Mitsubishi Ki-57 Army transports.

Overt acts of rebellion still plagued the homeland itself. The pilots at Atsugi Air Base dropped thousands of leaflets on the Tokyo area accusing the *jushin* and the Suzuki government of misleading the Emperor. Their leader, Captain Kozono, remained firm even when confronted by an admiral. He charged that the Emperor must be insane to surrender; the war had to continue. But the mutiny collapsed. That night the distraught Kozono began raving about Amaterasu, the Sun Goddess, and had to be restrained. Injected with morphine, he was placed in a strait jacket and taken to a naval hospital.

The spirit of rebellion also permeated Oita Air Base, whence Admiral Ugaki had taken off on Japan's last *kamikaze* mission. Ugaki's replacement, Admiral Ryunosuke Kusaka, veteran of Pearl Harbor and Midway, summoned all senior officers; a group of younger officers crowded into the room, uninvited and belligerent. Kusaka said he knew there were some among them who, out of patriotism, thought the war should continue—but "as long as my eyes are black [i.e., as long as he lived] I will not tolerate any rash action." Those intent on revolt would first have to "cut me to pieces." He closed his eyes expecting to be killed. For what seemed an eternity there was silence. Then Kusaka heard sobbing and opened his eyes.

"Your speech has cooled our heads," one of the young officers admitted. He and several others promised to control their men. Kusaka glanced around the room. "How about you older officers? Do any of you disagree with me?" No one spoke up. "If anyone changes his mind, come and see me any time. I have no guards at night. It's very hot and I shall sleep naked [unprotected]."

That night he was awakened by a voice shouting, *"Chokan! Chokan!"* (Commander in chief!). It was a feverish commander with a drawn pistol and sword. He had just "had a revelation": unless Japan waged the final battle she would have no future. "According to God, you are the only one to lead us."

Kusaka looked at him levelly. "You believe in God's prophecy but I cannot—perhaps I haven't had enough religious training. In any case, the Emperor himself ordered me to carry out these duties and I cannot trust in God, only myself." He sensed that time itself would take care of the young man's problem and suggested that he fly up to Tokyo and report this revelation to the commander of Combined Fleet, the Navy Minister and the Prime Minister.*

The new Prime Minister lay awake that night burdened by his unwanted responsibility. Prince Higashikuni recalled a long-forgotten incident twenty-five years before in France. He had told an aged fortuneteller that he was a simple painter, but she looked up from his palm and said, "It is a lie. You will become prime minister of Japan." With a laugh he admitted that he was a prince and an officer. "In Japan, members of the royal family and Army men as a rule are not allowed to become politicians. So how can I become prime minister?"

"Japan will have a revolution or some great trouble and you will become prime minister."

At eleven o'clock the next morning, August 17, he presented his suggestions for Cabinet ministers to the Emperor. Yonai alone retained his post. Togo had declined to stay on as foreign minister and would be succeeded by his predecessor, Mamoru Shigemitsu. Prince Konoye was to be a minister without portfolio. Those and the other choices were agreeable to His Majesty.

The new government's first task was to send a mission to Manila to arrange with General MacArthur for the surrender

---

*The commander was received by Admirals Ozawa and Yonai. Before seeing Higashikuni, he sat down on a bench to rest and dropped off to sleep. He awakened too late for his appointment and reasoned, "It must have been God's will that I fell asleep," and that he had misinterpreted the revelation.

of Japanese troops in the field. The man selected to lead it was Lieutenant General Torashiro Kawabe, Umezu's deputy. Since there was still fear that rebel pilots might intercept the delegation, elaborate precautions were taken. A little after dawn on August 19 the sixteen members arrived at Haneda Airport, where they boarded several small planes. After a few minutes over Tokyo Bay they descended for a landing at Kisarazu Air Base. Here two war-weary and bullet-punctured, cigar-shaped Mitsubishi bombers—the type known as "Bettys" to the Allies—were waiting. In accordance with instructions from MacArthur they had been painted white and marked with large green crosses.

Only after the delegates were on board did the pilots open sealed orders: their destination was Ie Shima, the tiny island where Ernie Pyle had died. Together the Bettys droned south. Over Kyushu the anxious delegates watched a formation of planes heading straight for them. But they had American markings, and the passengers relaxed as two bombers and a dozen fighters surrounded them protectively. The Japanese planes radioed the password: "Bataan," and the reassuring reply was, "We are Bataan's watchdog. Follow us." For an hour and a half the incongruous group continued over the South China Sea until Ie Shima's peak heaved in sight. The first bomber landed smoothly on the Birch airstrip, but the pilot of the second forgot to lower his handing flaps. The plane flared nearly over the runway but landed jarringly on the coral. It taxied uncertainly to its parking position. As soon as the delegates appeared, hundreds of GI's and Navy men pressed round them, snapping pictures.

The sixteen Japanese transferred to an American plane, a four-engine C-54, where they were given box lunches. Two GI's passed out cups of orange juice. Katsuo Okazaki, the ranking Foreign Ministry representative, ordered his secretary by hand signals to tip the American $10 apiece.

The C-54 arrived at Nichols Field shortly before dusk. General Kawabe led the group across the ramp to the nearest American, Colonel Sidney Mashbir, chief of MacArthur's staff of translators. As Mashbir saluted he saw Okazaki come toward him with extended hand—they were prewar acquaintances. Mashbir swung up his right fist with thumb up as an informal greeting; to avoid the onus of shaking hands with an enemy he had practiced this gesture twenty times in front of a mirror. The colonel then escorted the delegation to Major General Charles Willoughby, head of MacArthur's Intelligence Division. Thousands of soldiers, civilians and newsmen closed in, and the clicking of cameras seemed to Okazaki "like machine guns fired at strange animals."

Willoughby shared his car with Kawabe and on the way into Manila affably asked what language he would prefer to converse in. Kawabe suggested German—coincidentally it was Willoughby's native language. Their rapport was immediate, and to Kawabe, unexpected.

Curious groups had gathered along the narrow streets leading to Dewey Boulevard. GI's hollered *"Banzai!"* goodnaturedly, but the Filipinos were hostile. There were shouts of *"Baka!"* Rocks were thrown; they bounced off the cars while the Japanese pointedly looked straight ahead.

As soon as they had settled in the Rosario Apartments, a two-story building near the Manila Hotel, they were served a turkey dinner, which they remembered "with relish" years later. Afterward they were shuttled to City Hall, where they were escorted to seats at a large conference table facing their American counterparts. Kawabe sat directly opposite MacArthur's chief of staff, Sutherland, who read out General Order Number One. It enumerated the authorities to which the scattered Japanese armed forces would surrender. Those in China, Formosa and northern Indochina would capitulate to Chiang Kai-shek, while those in Manchuria, southern Sakhalin and northern Korea would surrender to the Russians. All other forces would be taken over by the British and Americans. Formal surrender would take place on an American warship in Tokyo Bay in early September. Japanese delegates were ordered to reveal the placement of all troops and ships, the location of airfields, submarine and *kaiten* bases, ammunition dumps and minefields.

The next morning the conference reconvened. Sutherland handed Kawabe a draft of the *Instrument of Surrender* to be issued by the Emperor. Kawabe dropped it on the table, then picked it up gingerly as if, an American naval officer observed, it were deadly poison. He thrust it at his aide, Second Lieutenant Sadao Otake, a graduate of New York University, where he was called Roy, and said *"Yakuse!"* (Translate!).

The first words—"I, Hirohito, Emperor of Japan"—made Otake turn pale. The Emperor never used the word *watakushi* for "I," but one that was his alone, *Chin*—the royal "We." Kawabe listened to the translation with folded arms and eyes closed tight as if in pain, and at the word *owari* (the end), he slapped the table and said *"Shimai!"* (Finished!).

Mashbir, an expert on Japan, realized how offensive the bald words written for the Emperor were to the Japanese—it was obvious that they were "dying right there in their chairs." At the Rosario, while the delegates were packing for the return to Japan, he and Willoughby tried to reassure Kawabe and Okazaki. "I am sure," Mashbir said in Japanese, "that it's not the intention of the Supreme Commander to degrade or debase your Emperor in the eyes of your people." He told them to disregard the wording of the declaration—he would take up the matter personally with General MacArthur. He advised them to draw it up themselves "in the normal form of an imperial rescript and ending in the approved and customary manner." Mashbir explained to Willoughby what he had promised the Japanese. The general couldn't understand why the Japanese were so upset.

"General Willoughby," Okazaki said in English, "it is of the utmost importance. It is impossible for me to explain to you how important it really is!"

As the delegation was leaving the Rosario, Otake introduced himself to a Nisei standing guard. The guard, in turn, said his name was Takamura. In America, Otake had married a Nisei of the same name. "Do you have a sister named Etsuyo?" he asked. The guard nodded and Otake said, "I'm her husband." They shook hands. "Look me up in Japan," Otake said to his brother-in-law as the car drove off.

General Sutherland agreed that Mashbir had acted properly in permitting the Japanese to reword the document but wanted him to explain it to MacArthur. The commander in chief put his arm around the colonel's shoulder and said, "Mashbir, you handled that exactly right. As a matter of fact, I have no desire whatever to debase him [the Emperor] in the eyes of his own people." Orderly government could best be maintained through Hirohito. He wondered if His Majesty would call on him in Tokyo. "If he does, it will be the first time that a Japanese emperor ever called on anyone won't it?"

"Yes, sir, it will be, and I'm sure that he'll do exactly that."

At Ie Shima the delegates discovered that one of the Mitsubishis was unable to take off for Japan. Otake ridiculed the possibility of sabotage expressed by several delegates—was the plane that had pancaked coming in. Kawabe, Okazaki and six others boarded the other bomber and settled down for the long flight home. Okazaki began dictating memorandum to a junior official, Harumi Takeuchi (who would later become ambassador to the Philippines). But General Kawabe sat preoccupied, marveling at the respect they had been shown by the Americans. "If human beings were to sincerely exercise justice and humanity in their relations with one another," he later wrote, "the horrors of war in all likelihood could be avoided, and even if a war unfortunately broke out, the victor would not become arrogant and the suffering of the losers would be alleviated immediately. A truly great cultural nation is the first requisite."

In the darkness following sunset, cold air whistled in through bullet holes in the fuselage. The passengers began drinking whiskey to keep warm and eventually fell asleep. At about eleven they were awakened by the pilot. A fuel tank had sprung a leak and they were heading for the nearest land. If they didn't make it, the bomber would float only briefly. They were to put on life jackets.

Their overriding concern was the documents—the Americans might interpret their loss as a ruse to delay the surrender formalities. The papers were entrusted to Okazaki, an athlete who had represented Japan in the 1924 Olympics in Paris.

The engines began missing and the plane descended. Through the window Takeuchi saw the sea just below shimmering in the moonlight. He tried to tie his life jacket but his fingers were too cold. Silently everyone except Okazaki put his hands against the seat in front of him and lowered his head. Okazaki was clutching the precious papers with both hands. The bomber bounced into the sea, water spraying over the windows. It skipped like a flat sone until it hit something and stopped abruptly.

Oil cans tumbled over Takeuchi and he heard someone say, "We are all right." He felt something sticky on his face. He thought it was blood, but it was oil. The pilot unlatched a side door. Whitecaps lashed against the plane, and Takeuchi hoped he could make it out before they sank. Then he realized that, incongruously, the pilot was standing in water up to his knees.

Okazaki, dazed from a blow on his forehead, stumbled out of the aircraft on his own and waded ashore. Ahead, in the moonlight, was Mount Fuji.

3.

The United States was having more trouble with her allies than with Japan. Stalin wanted a greater share of the spoils of war. In a cable to Truman he proposed that the Japanese on the Kuriles, which had been "awarded" to the Soviets at Yalta, as well as those on the top half of Hokkaido, the northernmost home island, be surrendered to the Russian Far East commander.

... THIS LATTER PROPOSAL HAS A SPECIAL MEANING FOR THE RUSSIAN PUBLIC OPINION. AS IT IS KNOWN, THE JAPANESE IN 1919-1921 HELD UNDER OCCUPATION OF THEIR TROOPS THE WHOLE SOVIET FAR EAST. THE RUSSIAN PUBLIC OPINION WOULD BE SERIOUSLY OFFENDED IF THE RUSSIAN TROOPS WOULD NOT HAVE AN OCCUPATION REGION IN SOME PART OF THE JAPANESE PROPER TERRITORY.
GREATLY I WISH THAT MY MODEST SUGGESTIONS AS STATED ABOVE WOULD NOT MEET ANY OBJECTIONS.

Rankled, Truman replied that while he could go along with the Kurile proposal, he would like it to be understood that America wanted an air base on one of the Kurile islands. About Hokkaido, however, he was adamant; present arrangements for the surrender of the Japanese on all four of the main islands must stand.

Stalin, in turn, was indignant. Two days later, on August 22, he replied that he "did not expect such an answer" regarding Hokkaido; and nothing had been mentioned at Yalta about a permanent American air base in the Kuriles.

... DEMANDS OF SUCH A NATURE ARE USUALLY LAID BEFORE EITHER A CONQUERED STATE, OR SUCH AN ALLIED STATE WHICH IS IN NO POSITION TO DEFEND WITH ITS OWN MEANS CERTAIN PARTS OF ITS TERRITORY AND, IN VIEW OF THIS, EXPRESSES READINESS TO GRANT ITS ALLY AN APPROPRIATE BASE. I DO NOT BELIEVE THAT THE SOVIET UNION COULD BE INCLUDED AMONG SUCH STATES ... AS YOUR MESSAGE DOES NOT STATE ANY MOTIVES FOR A DEMAND TO GRANT A PERMANENT BASE I HAVE TO TELL YOU FRANKLY THAT NEITHER I NOR MY COLLEAGUES UNDERSTAND WHAT CIRCUMSTANCES PROMPTED SUCH A DEMAND TO BE MADE OF THE SOVIET UNION.

Truman's "first inclination was to let this message with its strong undercurrent of antagonism go unanswered," but he reconsidered and terminated the altercation with the explanation that the United States merely wanted a temporary base in the Kuriles for emergency use during the occupation of Japan.

The question of China, however, was not so easily resolved. Four days before the Japanese accepted the Potsdam Proclamation, Chu Teh, commanding general of the Communist forces, announced falsely that Japan had surrendered unconditionally and ordered Red units to occupy whatever towns and cities they could. Chiang Kai-shek charged that this was "an abrupt and illegal action" and ordered Chu Teh to desist from independent movement against the Japanese. The Communist radio thereupon branded Chiang a fascist. "We want to announce to our three great allies, the people of China and the world that the Chungking High Command cannot represent the Chinese people and the Chinese troops which really oppose the Japanese. The Chinese people demand that anti-Japanese troops in liberated China under Commander in Chief Chu Teh have the right to send their representatives directly to participate in accepting a Japanese surrender by the Allies."

Red Chinese plans for postwar domination were hobbled by their ideological comrades in Moscow. On the day before Japan's surrender, Molotov signed accords with Nationalist China. It was an affront that would plague Soviet-Red China rapport for decades.

In the meantime Russia was intent on establishing herself on the Asian mainland in force. The Red Army had already seized much of Manchuria against almost no opposition from the weakened Kwantung Army. Each occupied city was plundered. Tons of wheat, flour, rice, kaoliang (grain sorghum) and soybeans were shipped back to the Soviet Union along with machinery, rolling stock, paper, printing machines, photographic and electric equipment. Chairs, desks, telephones, typewriters were cleared from every office. Carloads of broken furniture and countless crates of broken glass were dispatched westward as if junk itself were a treasure to the Soviets.

The Japanese prisoners of war were stripped of all valubles, including the gold fillings in their teeth. Rape, pillage and murder became commonplace, but these atrocities were not inspired by hatred or vengeance. The conquerors, like their predecessors Attila and his Huns, were enjoying the looty of war.

The unreasoning spirit to resist capitulation did not die with Hatanaka and Ugaki. Late in the afternoon of August 22, ten young men with white bands around their foreheads, calling themselves the *Sonjo Gigun* (the Righteous Group for Upholding Imperial Rule and Driving Out Foreigners), occupied Atago Hill, within sight of the American embassy. With pistols and grenades they threatened a cordon of police sent to disperse them. In the pouring rain they linked arms and sang the national anthem. Three times they shouted *"Tenno Heika banzai!"* And then there was a multiple roar as five grenades exploded almost simultaneously. Everyone lay dead. Their leader had left a note of farewell: "The cicada rain falls in vain on defeated hills and streams." A few days later the wives of three of the dead rebels climbed to the top of Atago Hill and also attempted suicide. Two died. In a wave of self-destruction, eleven transport officers belonging to a Buddhist sect killed themselves in front of the Imperial Palace, and fourteen students committed hara-kiri at the Yoyogi parade grounds.

Other rebels continued sporadic attacks on communication centers. The NHK station at Kawaguchi was briefly occupied by a major and sixty-six soldiers from a communication school; some forty civilians, including ten women, seized the broadcasting station in Matsui and then attacked the post office, a power station, the local newspaper and the prefectural government office.

The announcement that American forces would shortly occupy the country invoked new fears and unrest. Wild rumors made the population panicky: the Chinese were landing at Osaka; thousands of American soldiers were already looting and raping in Yokohama. Girls and family treasures were evacuated to the country or the mountains. Newspapers ran columns of advice on how to get along with the American troops. Women were told: "Don't go out at all in the evening. Keep watches and other valuables at home. When in danger of being raped, show the most dignified attitude. Don't yield. Cry for help." They were cautioned to avoid "provocative acts" such as smoking or going without socks. Some factories issued poison capsules for women workers.

Soon after dawn on August 28, forty-five C-47's approached Mount Fuji with the American advance party, commanded by Colonel Charles Tench, a member of MacArthur's staff. At Atsugi Air Base the lead plane taxied to a stop and the first conqueror ever to step on Japanese soil emerged in the person of Colonel Tench. From the edge of the ramp a mob of shouting Japanese headed for him, and for a moment he thought he was about to be cut down by fanatics. Then he noticed a small reception party near the plane. A short officer stepped forward and announced that he was Lieutenant General Seizo Arisue.* As the two walked toward a tent in the reception area, Japanese cameramen and U. S. Signal Corps photographers recorded almost every step. In the tent Colonel Tench went pale when Arisue offered him orange punch. To show it wasn't poisoned the general drained a glass of it before Tench hesitantly took a sip.

Within forty-eight hours Atsugi was occupied in force by the 11th Airborne Division, whose four-engine transports touched down every two minutes for hours. No sooner was the air base secured than another C-54 appeared in the distance. It was *Bataan*, with General of the Army Douglas MacArthur on board. He was discussing the fate of Japan with his Military Secretary, Brigadier General Bonner Fellers, who had visited the country numerous times. "It's very simple," said MacArthur. "We'll use the instrumentality of the Japanese government to implement the occupation." Among other things, he was going to give Japanese women the right to vote.

"The Japanese men won't like it."

"I don't care. I want to discredit the military. Women don't want war."

---

*Two hours earlier, three blue American fighter planes had hurtled down at Atsugi. One dropped a large tube. Arisue stood paralyzed and watched it tumble down, fearing it had been dropped by radical Americans who wanted to continue the war. The tube landed on the grass without exploding. When it was gingerly brought to Arisue, he noticed a cap at one end. The cap was unscrewed, thus "deactivating" the missile; inside, there was a rolled cloth. It was a fifteen-foot banner:

WELCOME U. S. ARMY
U. S. Navy

A note requested the Navy's banner be attached to the side of a hangar where MacArthur's officers would see it on disembarking. Arisue, "afraid to allow anything that might cause ill feeling and trouble," ordered it hidden.

975

The big transport touched down at 2:19 P.M. MacArthur, the first to leave the plane, paused at the top of the ladder and Fellers heard him mutter, "This is the payoff." He lit his corncob and descended, pipe clenched between teeth. General Robert Eichelberger, who had preceded him by a few hours, came up to him and they shook hands. "Bob," said MacArthur, grinning broadly, "from Melbourne to Tokyo is a long way, but this seems to be the end of the road."

A line of dilapidated cars was waiting to take the MacArthur group to temporary headquarters in Yokohama. At the head of the column was a red fire engine, which reminded General Courtney Whitney of the Toonerville Trolley. It lunged forward with a startling explosion, and the motorcade clanged and crawled the fifteen miles to Yokohama. The entire length of the road was lined with almost thirty thousand Japanese soldiers, who stood on guard, their backs to MacArthur.

The Americans were quartered at the New Grand Hotel, a luxury establishment erected after the earthquake of 1923. At dinner Whitney warned his chief that the steak might be poisoned, but MacArthur laughed and brushed it off with "No one can live forever." Later that evening he told his staff, which had congregated in his room, "Boys, this is the greatest adventure in military history. Here we sit in the enemy's country with only a handful of troops, looking down the throats of nineteen fully armed divisions and seventy million fanatics. One false move and the Alamo would look like a Sunday-school picnic!"

The following day Lieutenant General Jonathan W. Wainwright was flown in from a POW camp in Manchuria. When MacArthur, who was having dinner, heard that Wainwright was in the lobby, he immediately went downstairs to greet the most famous survivor of Bataan. The officer who had lost through surrender more troops than any other American commander stood haggard and aged far beyond his years. His hair was snow-white, his uniform hung loose on his skeletal frame and he supported himself with a cane. He tried to smile. MacArthur embraced him but Wainwright was unable to speak. "Well, Skinny," said MacArthur with emotion, putting his hands on the other man's shoulders.

Wainwright got out one choked word, "General." While photographers took pictures, he found his voice: he believed he was in disgrace for surrendering the Philippines.* But

---

*In his *Reminiscences*, MacArthur states that he was "shocked" to

MacArthur reassured him; Wainwright could have anything he wanted.

"General, the only thing I want now is command of a corps," Wainwright said huskily. "That is what I wanted right in the beginning."

"Why, Jim, your old corps is yours when you want it."

Only a token occupation force was sent to ravaged Tokyo. The newsmen who accompanied it wanted above all to interview Tokyo Rose. She was finally located by correspondents Harry Brundige and Clark Lee through a Japanese newsman named Yamashita who brought her to the Imperial Hotel on the morning of September 1. She wore slacks and her hair was in pigtails. With her was a solemn young Portuguese-Japanese.

"This is Iva Ikuko Toguri, your Tokyo Rose. And this is her husband, Philip d'Aquino."

"Are you really Tokyo Rose?" Brundige asked.

"The one and only," she said with a smile.

Brundige offered her $2,000 for an exclusive first-person story for *Cosmopolitan* magazine which he would ghost-write, with the proviso, however, that she stay away from all other correspondents—as well as Army Intelligence and the CIC—until the story appeared. She agreed, and Brundige tapped out seventeen pages of notes on his portable typewriter. What emerged was the ironic story of an intelligent, scholarly young woman with a degree in zoology from UCLA who had sold out the country she loved for the country she hated—for $6.60 a month—because the alternative to propaganda broadcasting was work in a munitions factory.

After graduation from UCLA, Iva had gone to Japan, under protest, to see her mother's sister who was ill—her mother was too sick to make the trip. She found she disliked almost everything about Japan, including rice and her relatives, but before she could go back home the war broke out. She supported herself as a secretary, which led to a job as typist with the Japanese Broadcasting Corporation. At the behest of an American Army captain—an ex-radio commentator who had himself been persuaded to return to his old trade, for the other side—she agreed to make fifteen-minute

___

ind this out, apparently forgetting the messages he sent Marshall in 942 about Wainwright, including one which declared he believed his uccessor had "temporarily become unbalanced."

daily broadcasts to the Allied soldiers. In her capacity as disk jockey she met and became friends with American POW's who were broadcasting propaganda for the Japanese. (They were subsequently pardoned because they had been forced to it under "immediate threat of death or bodily harm.") Iva used to bring food, medicine, cigarettes—whatever she could scrape up for the prisoners. "It was manna from heaven," she said later, "to be among people who thought and felt as I did."

The editor of *Cosmopolitan*, however, was astounded that Brundige had negotiated with a traitor and by return cable demanded an explanation. Disgusted, Brundige turned over his scoop to Lee. He submitted his own version to the International News Service, which released it at once.*

5.

At Navy Secretary Forrestal's instigation, the formal surrender ceremonies took place on the battleship *Missouri* in Tokyo Bay on September 2, just three days after MacArthur's arrival. Truman was particularly pleased by the choice. *Missouri*, one of the four largest battleships in the world, had been named after his own state and christened by his daughter, Margaret.

On September 1 Commander Horace Bird, *Missouri*'s gunnery officer, conducted a dress rehearsal on the ship's deck. He gathered three hundred sailors to represent the dignitaries. Everything went smoothly until the band began the "Admiral's March," signaling Nimitz' arrival. "Nimitz" did not appear. The admiral's stand-in, a burly chief boatswain's mate nicknamed "Two-Gut," was immobilized by his role. He stood transfixed, scratching his head. "I'll be damned!" he said in an awed voice. "Me an admiral!"

The next morning Commander Bird watched the dawn

---

*Mrs. D'Aquino was arrested on a charge of treason. At the grand jury session in September 1948 Lee and Brundige "poured it on the Army captain who taught Rose her broadcasting business"—to them, he was guiltier than she was—and the jury demanded an indictment for the captain as well as Tokyo Rose. Informed that the captain was not under the jurisdiction of the court, the jury refused to charge her. When the prosecution assured the jury that the captain would also be brought to justice, Iva was indicted. She was tried, convicted as a traitor, sentenced to ten years in prison and fined $10,000. The captain was never tried; he was promoted to major.

with disappointment. It was cool and gray. At about 7:30 a destroyer lay to, and correspondents from all over the world clambered aboard the battleship. Each was given a position, but the intimidated Japanese alone remained in place. The Russians were particularly obstreperous, roaming around the ship "like wild men."

For the Americans the moment brought back vivid memories. Robert Trumbull of the *New York Times* would never forget the hectic morning in Pearl Harbor when he worked for a Honolulu paper, nor would Webley Edwards, in charge of the pool broadcast on *Missouri*, who had announced by radio from Honolulu on December 7, "This is the real McCoy!"

Destroyers pulled alongside *Missouri*, discharging Allied generals and admirals including Halsey, Helfrich, Turner, Percival, Stilwell, Wainwright, Spaatz, Kenney and Eichelberger. At 8:05 Nimitz was piped aboard, followed shortly by MacArthur. There was so much excitement that the arrival of the two senior American officers went generally unnoticed. Commander Bird rushed ahead of them calling out, "Gentlemen, General MacArthur and Admiral Nimitz are approaching." Bird was ignored. In desperation he shouted, "Attention, all hands!" As one the assembled admirals and generals snapped to attention. In the immediate silence, waves could be heard lapping around the water line.

Now the destroyer *Lansdowne*, named after the commander of the dirigible *Shenandoah*, appeared with the eleven Japanese delegates. There had been a controversy about who would lead the Japanese. It was intolerable to think that Prime Minister Higashikuni, a member of the royal family, should be subjected to such humiliation, and Prince Konoye, who had risked his life for two years for peace, could not bring himself to face the shame of the moment. The onerous responsibility fell on the new foreign minister, Shigemitsu, who regarded it as "a painful but profitable task," and was honored that the Emperor had entrusted him with it. Army Chief of Staff Umezu was there under duress; it had taken a personal appeal from His Majesty. Navy Chief of Staff Toyoda ordered his operations officer, Admiral Tomioka, to take his place. "You lost the war," he said, "so you go"; Tomioka acquiesced but had already made up his mind to commit hara-kiri after the ceremonies.

The Japanese delegates were not even sure of protocol once they were on board. Should they salute, bow, shake hands or smile? Their adviser, Colonel Mashbir, had told the military to salute; the civilians should merely take off their hats and bow. "And I suggest that all of you wear a *shiran kao* [nonchalant face]."

Mashbir started up *Missouri*'s gangway at exactly 8:55, followed by a Japanese civilian in a tall silk hat, cutaway and ascot. He was laboriously pulling himself up, groaning with every step. It was Foreign Minister Shigemitsu, whose left leg had been blown off by an assassin's bomb in Shanghai years before. His new artificial limb caused him excruciating agony. Bird, watching from above, expected the grim-faced general behind the man in the silk hat to give him a hand—it was Umezu, who regarded Shigemitsu as a detestable "Badoglio" and refused to take notice of his plight. Bird himself stepped down to offer a hand. Shigemitsu shook his head but then stiffly allowed the American to assist him momentarily.

Shigemitsu's painful progress across the quarter-deck to the ladder leading to the ceremony deck made him the center of attraction. An American correspondent noted that the onlookers watched him "with savage satisfaction." Shigemitsu shook off Bird's further offer of assistance and awkwardly mounted the ladder, his face a mask.

Once the Japanese were in place, the entire company came to attention for the invocation by the ship's chaplain. They remained at attention while a record of "The Star-Spangled Banner" was played over amplifiers. In the long uneasy pause that followed, Toshikazu Kase (previously Matsuoka's and now the new Foreign Minister's secretary) discovered several miniature Rising Suns painted on a nearby bulkhead, apparently to indicate destroyed Japanese planes or submarines. As he counted them, Kase's throat constricted. Beside him Admiral Tomioka was consumed by wonder and anger—wonder that the Americans showed no sign of contempt for the Japanese and anger at the presence of the Soviet delegates; they were part Asian, yet they had ignored Japan's plea to act as peacemaker and then stabbed her in the back in Manchuria.*

---

*On the same day Generalissimo Stalin made an important radio broadcast to the Russian people. He said they had a special account to settle with Japan ever since she seized southern Sakhalin and strengthened her grip on the Kuriles in 1904.

"But the defeat of the Russian troops in 1904 during the Russo-Japanese War left bitter memories with our people. It was a dark stain on our country's honor. Our people waited with

General MacArthur appeared, walking briskly with Nimitz and Halsey across the deck to a table covered with documents. The British had offered one used at the Battle of Jutland, but since it was too small, Bird had substituted a battered mess table covered with a coffee-stained green felt cloth; the documents had been arranged to hide the stains. Wainwright and Percival stepped to MacArthur's side behind the table.

"We are gathered here," MacArthur said, "representatives of the major warring powers, to conclude a solemn agreement whereby peace may be restored. The issues, involving divergent ideals and ideologies, have been determined on the battlefields of the world and hence are not for our discussion or our debate. Nor is it for us here to meet, representing as we do a majority of the peoples of the earth, in a spirit of distrust, malice or hatred. But rather it is for us, both victors and vanquished, to rise to that higher dignity which alone benefits the sacred purposes we are about to serve, committing all our people unreservedly to faithful compliance with the understanding they are here formally to assume."

Tomioka was impressed by the absence of rancor or retribution in MacArthur's words. General Yatsuji Nagai, who had accompanied Matsuoka to Berlin and Moscow, couldn't take his eyes away from MacArthur. How young-looking and fit he was in contrast to Umezu! Had the psychological impact of losing the war prematurely aged the Chief of Staff? Colonel Ichiji Sugita, who had interpreted at an earlier surrender ceremony, stared fixedly at another Allied officer, General Percival. Their eyes met and held, both apparently remembering the painful scene at the Ford factory in Singapore.

"It is my earnest hope," MacArthur continued, "—indeed the hope of all mankind—that from this solemn occasion a better world shall emerge out of the blood and carnage of the past, a world founded upon faith and understanding, a world dedicated to the dignity of man and the fulfillment of his most cherished wish for freedom, tolerance and justice."

Almost as if on cue the clouds parted, and in the distance the peak of Mount Fuji sparkled in the sun. MacArthur indicated a chair at the opposite side of the table. Shigemitsu

confidence for the day when Japan would suffer defeat and the stain could be wiped out. We of the older generation have been waiting for this day for forty years. Now it is here. Today Japan has conceded her defeat and signed the documents of unconditional surrender. . . ."

limped forward and sat down. He fumbled uncertainly with his hat, gloves and cane, giving the impression of stalling. Halsey wanted to slap him and say, "Sign, damn you! Sign!" MacArthur, however, realized that Shigemitsu was confused, and turning to his chief of staff, said sharply, "Sutherland, show him where to sign." Shigemitsu signed. Next Umezu marched forward stiffly, and without bothering to sit down, scrawled his name. Using separate pens, MacArthur now signed as Supreme Commander of the Allied Powers. Then in turn Nimitz and the other allies signed for their respective countries: General Hsu Yung-chang for China, Admiral Sir Bruce Fraser for the United Kingdom, Lieutenant General K. Derevyanko for the Soviet Union, General Sir Thomas Blamey for Australia, Colonel L. Moore-Gosgrove for Canada, General Jacques Leclerc for France, Admiral C. E. L. Helfrich for the Netherlands and Air Vice-Marshal Sir L. M. Isitt for New Zealand.

The dignity of the occasion was marred briefly by an inebriated delegate—it was not an American—who obtrusively began making faces at the Japanese. Shigemitsu stared him down and without expression slowly and deliberately put on his top hat. The other Japanese civilians followed suit. Perhaps it was a coincidence, thought Mashbir, but it struck him as an effective example of Oriental subtlety.

The last signatures were inscribed and MacArthur again addressed the assemblage. "Let us pray," he said, "that peace now be restored to the world and that God will preserve it always. These proceedings are now closed." He walked over to Halsey and put his arm around his shoulders. Bird was close by and thought he heard MacArthur say, "Bill, where in the hell are those airplanes?" As if in answer came a rumble in the distance. Thousands of carrier planes and B-29's swept over *Missouri* in an inspiring exhibition.

MacArthur left the ceremony deck for another microphone which would broadcast his message to America. "Today the guns are silent," he said. "A great tragedy has ended. A great victory has been won. The skies no longer rain death—the seas bear only commerce—men everywhere walk upright in the sunlight. The entire world is quietly at peace. The holy mission has been completed. . . .

"A new era is upon us. Even the lesson of victory itself brings with it profound concern, both for our future security, and the survival of civilization. . . . Military alliances, balances of power, leagues of nations, all in turn failed, leaving the only path to be by way of the crucible of war. . . .

"The utter destructiveness of war now blots out this alternative. We have had our last chance. If we do not devise some greater and more equitable system, Armageddon will be at our door. . . ."

MacArthur's words were in a very real sense a pledge that the United States would treat the fallen enemy with understanding and compassion. And throughout Japan itself, the populace was beginning to recover from the anguish of an almost intolerable fate. "If we allow the pain and humility to breed within us the dark thoughts of future revenge," the *Nippon Times* advised its readers in words that were meant to be inspiring and proved to be prophetic, "our spirit will be warped and perverted into a morbidly base design. . . . But if we use this pain and this humiliation as a spur to self-reflection and reform, and if we make this self-reflection and reform the motive force for a great constructive effort, there is nothing to stop us from building, out of the ashes of our defeat, a magnificent new Japan free from the dross of the old which is now gone, a new Japan which will vindicate our pride by winning the respect of the world."

Epilogue

1.

Six days after the ceremonies on *Missouri*, MacArthur came to Tokyo. At noon, on September 8, he strode to the terrace of the U. S. embassy, where an honor guard from the 1st Cavalry Division was attaching a historic flag to the halyards of the flagpole. "General Eichelberger," he said sonorously, "have our country's flag unfurled, and in Tokyo's sun let it wave its full glory as a symbol of hope for the oppressed and as a harbinger of victory for the right." To the sound of bugles the flag, which had flown over the Capitol Building in Washington on Pearl Harbor day, climbed up the staff.

If the reality of MacArthur the Conqueror's arrival, accentuated by the American colors which waved humiliatingly within sight of the Imperial Palace, was fairly incomprehensible to the Japanese people in all its implications, the defeat was intolerable to the military, who were directly responsible for the failure to stop the enemy. Moreover, many of them expected to stand trial, and within three days MacArthur issued orders for the arrest of the first forty alleged war criminals.

There was one name on the list which was recognized by everyone—Hideki Tojo. Almost immediately Tojo's modest home in Setagaya was besieged by correspondents and photographers. They crowded before the stone walls which fronted the house. Confined in his office, Tojo sat writing at a large desk. The room was dominated by a full-length portrait of the former premier in full military regalia. On another wall hung a tiger skin sent by an admirer from Malaya.

The crowd outside continued to grow while newsmen pushed into the garden itself, and by midafternoon the crush had become so overwhelming that Tojo told his wife to get out of the house at once with their maid; the children had already been evacuated to Kyushu. Mrs. Tojo was reluctant to go. "Take care of yourself," she said, fearing he might commit suicide. "Please, take care of yourself," she repeated and bowed. His answer was a noncommittal grunt.

She left by the back door with the maid. They circled around the wall and came up the street toward the driveway. Ahead was a confused mass of cars and people. The crowd blocked any view of her home, so she entered the garden of the house across the street which was on a slight rise. It belonged to a doctor named Suzuki who had earlier marked Tojo's chest with charcoal to indicate the location of his heart. Over the wall she could see that American soldiers—they were MP's—had already surrounded her house. An officer shouted, "Tell this yellow bastard we've waited long enough. Bring him out!" Suddenly she heard a muffled shot and the soldiers began breaking into the house. Even from across the street she recognized the sound of splintering wood. It was 4:17 P.M.

Major Paul Kraus and the arresting party, followed by George Jones, a reporter for the *New York Times*, broke into the office. Tojo, his jacket off, stood wavering beside an easy chair. Blood stained his shirt. In his right hand he still held a .32-caliber Colt, which now confronted the intruders.

"Don't shoot!" Kraus called out.

Tojo gave no indication that he had heard, but the gun clattered to the floor and he collapsed into the chair. He motioned to a Japanese police guard who had followed the Americans into the office and asked for water. He emptied the glass in a few gulps and wanted more.

In the garden across the road Mrs. Tojo knelt, repeating a Buddhist prayer. She imagined his agony and tried to prepare herself for the moment the Americans would bring out his body. Instead an ambulance appeared and a Japanese doctor rushed into the house.

At 4:29 Tojo's lips moved. Two Japanese interpreters, who accompanied the press, began to record his words. "I am very sorry it is taking me so long to die," he murmured. His face was contorted in pain but those of the Americans staring down at him showed no sympathy. "The Greater East Asian war was justified and righteous," he said. "I am very sorry for the nation and all the races of the Greater Asiatic powers. I would not like to be judged before a conqueror's court. I wait for the righteous judgment of history." His voice grew stronger but his words were not always distinct. "I wished to commit suicide but sometimes that fails." His bullet had entered almost exactly where Dr. Suzuki had marked his chest, but it had just missed his heart.

As medics transferred him to a divan, Tojo whispered, "I did not shoot myself in the head, because I wanted the people to recognize my features and know I was dead." He was taken to the 48th Evacuation Hospital in Yokohama, and in the evening General Eichelberger came to his bedside. Tojo opened his eyes and tried to bow. "I am dying," he said. "I am sorry to have given General Eichelberger so much trouble."

"Do you mean tonight or the last few years?"

"Tonight. I want General Eichelberger to have my new saber."

Tojo lived to stand trial as a major war criminal;* but the

---

*Near the end of the tedious proceedings, which took place at the Army Headquarters building on Ichigaya Heights, Tojo and Yoshio Kodama watched two American planes from the exercise yard of Sugamo Prison. "Kodama," the general said, "this trial will be meaningful only if there is no more war. As you see above, they are practicing to go against the Russians. By the time the trial ends there will be uneasy relations between the Soviets and the United States. If there is another war, a war crimes trial like this is really meaningless."

On November 12, 1948, Tojo was sentenced to death. In prison he had become a changed man. Religion now dominated his life and he was nicknamed *Tera-kozo* ("the Buddhist priestling"). A few hours before his execution he told Dr. Shinsho Hanayama, a Buddhist priest and one of the prison chaplains, that he had much to be thankful for: his body would soon become part of the soil of Japan; his death would be not only an apology to the Japanese but a move toward peace and the rebuilding of Japan. He said it was time that he died, since he had few teeth left, his eyes were failing and his memory was poor. And it was better to die than spend the rest of his days in prison, the victim of worldly passions. Finally, it was joyful to die in the knowledge that he would be reborn in Amida's paradise. He had even developed a sense of humor. With a grin he held up a Cannon washcloth and said, "Kannon-sama [the Buddhist Goddess of Mercy] has finally appeared."

In his final testament Tojo called on the Americans not to alienate the feelings of the Japanese or infect them with Communism. Japan had been the sole bulwark in Asia against Communism, and now Manchuria was becoming a base for the communization of the continent. The Americans had also divided Korea, which he prophesied would lead to great trouble in the future.

He apologized for the atrocities committed by the Japanese military and urged the American military to show compassion and repentance toward the civilians of Japan, who had suffered so grievously from indiscriminate air attacks and the two atomic bombs. He predicted that a third world war was bound to break out because of the conflicting interests of the United States and the Soviet Union, and since the battlefields would be Japan, China and Korea, it was the responsibility of the Americans to protect a helpless Japan.

The testament closed with two poems:

987

following morning Marshal Sugiyama was more accurate in his aim. He shot himself in the heart at his office. When his wife learned of his death, she followed the example of the wife of General Maresuke Nogi, who had led all troops in the Russo-Japanese War and later killed himself in apology for the death of his men. She knelt before a Buddhist shrine in her room, drank a thimbleful of cyanide and fell on a small dagger.

Trial at the hands of the victors was anathema to the Japanese leaders, but it was particularly repugnant to an aristocrat like Prince Konoye with his inordinate sense of pride. He too preferred death to such humiliation. Facetiously he told a friend, "I'm a lazybones and I might find life in prison easy and carefree"—for thirty years he had never even carried a wallet nor squeezed a wet washcloth when he took a bath—"but I could never stand the shame of being called a war criminal."

The night before Konoye was to leave for Sugamo Prison his younger son, Michitaka,* searched his father's bedroom for weapons or poison. Although he found nothing, he was still worried, so before going to bed, he returned to his father's room. They talked at length about the China Incident, the negotiations with America, and the heavy responsibility Konoye felt toward the Emperor and the people. Michitaka thought his father should record these personal feelings. Konoye wrote for some time with a pencil—there was no writing brush available—then handed the script to his son. "This is not worded properly," he said, "but it expresses how I feel right now."

Michitaka sensed that these might be their last moments

Although I now depart,
I shall return to this land,
as I have yet to repay
my debt to my country.

It is time for farewell.
I shall wait beneath the moss,
until the flowers are fragrant again
in the islands of Yamato [Japan].

He walked up the thirteen steps to the gallows with dignity. Just after midnight on December 22, the trap was sprung.

*Konoye's eldest son, Fumitaka (called "Butch" at Princeton) had been captured by the Russians in Manchuria. He died in a prison camp not far from Moscow.

together. "For a long time I've only given you trouble and failed to be filial to you. I apologize."

Konoye rebuffed the overture. "What does 'to be filial' mean?" he asked and turned away. They sat in silence. Finally Michitaka said, "It is quite late now. Please go to sleep." He hesitated. "You will leave tomorrow?"

Konoye did not reply, but Michitaka continued to gaze at him entreatingly. Konoye returned the look as if saying, his son thought, "Why do you still ask me such a question? I was under the impression that you understood everything." Michitaka had never before seen such a "strange, distasteful" expression on his father's face, and for the first time he perceived his intention to die.

"If you need anything during the night, please call me," Michitaka said. "I'll be in the next room."

Just before dawn Michitaka managed to fall asleep but was soon awakened by his mother's excited voice. He tried to get up but was momentarily paralyzed. He remained seated, eyes closed, body trembling. At last he rose and entered his father's bedroom. Konoye was stretched out, looking calm and serene, as if sleeping. There was no sign of anguish on his patrician face. He was dead. A brownish bottle, empty, lay beside his pillow.

Americans considered Japan's titular leader, the Emperor, along with Tojo, to be the one most responsible for the war. Now he was even being reviled by some of the liberated Japanese press, who branded him a lecher as well as a warmonger. There were demonstrations outside MacArthur's headquarters advocating his removal. The Supreme Commander ignored these and similar demands from the Russians and segments of the American and Australian press. To bring the Emperor to trial would provoke guerrilla warfare throughout the nation and perpetuate a military government.

MacArthur was more than determined to treat the Emperor with respect—against the advice of his own staff, who wanted him summoned peremptorily to Allied headquarters as a show of power. "To do so," the general said, "would be to outrage the feelings of the Japanese people and make a martyr of the Emperor in their eyes. No, I shall wait and in time the Emperor will voluntarily come to see me. In this case, the patience of the East rather than the haste of the West will best serve our purpose."

The soundness of MacArthur's intuition was borne out. Two weeks after Tojo's attempted suicide, the Emperor himself requested an interview. Wearing cutaway, striped trousers, button shoes and top hat, he drove up to the American embassy with Grand Chamberlain Fujita. He stepped out of his ancient limousine and was greeted by a salute from General Fellers. As Fellers' hand came down, the Emperor seized it. A young Japanese interpreter explained that His Majesty was pleased to see the general.

"I am honored to meet you," Fellers replied. "Come in and meet General MacArthur." The Emperor nervously allowed himself to be escorted into the embassy by Fellers and up the spacious staircase to MacArthur's office on the second floor.

To put His Majesty at ease MacArthur mentioned that he had been presented to his father, Emperor Taisho, after the Russo-Japanese War, then thoughtfully dismissed everyone except his interpreter. They sat down before an open fire, unaware that the general's wife and young son, Arthur, were peering out at them from behind the red curtains. The general extended an American cigarette, which His Majesty took with thanks, his hands trembling while MacArthur lit it.

Kido's last advice to the Emperor before he left for the embassy had been not to assume any responsibility for the war, but now he did just that. "I come to you, General MacArthur, to offer myself to the judgment of the powers you represent as the one to bear sole responsibility for every political and military decision made and action taken by my people in the conduct of this war."

MacArthur was moved, as he later described the scene, "to the marrow of my bones. He was an Emperor by inherent birth, but in that instant I knew I faced the First Gentleman of Japan in his own right."

2.

World War II was over, but it had left in its wake more problems than it had solved. Asia, in the throes of an extensive revolt, was discarding the shackles of Western domination. Warfare would be transformed from a global conflict into fragmented nationalist struggles of liberation.

Ironically, one of Japan's most cherished war aims was being achieved. Asia was at last freeing itself from the white man. Great Britain had already lost Burma and was being pried loose from India. In the Dutch East Indies, Achmed Sukarno and Mohammed Hatti, who had supported the Japanese during the conflict, were mounting an irresistible independence movement.

In China the war had settled the contest for supremacy between the Communists and the Western-dominated Kuomintang. With the extensive destruction of property and loss of capital, Nationalist industry was at a standstill. Prices were more than two thousand times the level of 1937; on the foreign exchange the Chinese currency had dropped more than 70 percent in value within a month of Japan's surrender. Inflation had practically wiped out China's middle class and left intellectuals disillusioned. Beset by such difficulties, the Nationalists could not answer the needs of the people, and unlike the Communists, they were not willing to divide the land. For better or for worse—and it could not be much worse for the common man—China's only hope was Mao.

Land reform was also the keystone of the new government of Indochina. During the war the Viet Minh (Independence League), led by Ho Chi Minh, a Communist, fought the French and Japanese with the sympathy and support of Great Britain and the United States, to emerge as the dominant nationalist movement in the country. Peace brought the abdication of the playboy emperor, Bao Dai, and the Viet Minh proclaimed a new nation, the Republic of Vietnam, with a Declaration of Independence borrowed from America. But the United States, which had pledged independence for Indochina during the war, had already changed her policy. On August 24, 1945, President Truman informed General de Gaulle that he favored the return of Indochina to France. In the republic's first election, in January 1946, the Viet Minh won a majority in the new assembly, but French troops in the country, with the help of reinforcements from France shipped in American transports, seized Saigon, and Bao Dai was eventually restored as ruler. Puppet monarchies were also established in Cambodia and Laos, and all these governments were recognized by the United States.

American support of French colonialism indicated that her leaders intended to follow Britain's antiquated East of Suez policy—self-determination for nations of Europe but not for Asia—convinced that Asians did not know what was best for themselves and world security. America still had not learned that she had spent her blood and treasure to help win two disparate wars: one against Fascism in Europe, and the other against Asian aspirations. And the course of world history was irrevocably determined for the next two, three, perhaps four decades.

Several months after the war an aged woodman, his face deeply creased by the years, stopped in front of the Dai Ichi Building, MacArthur's new headquarters. Strapped to his back was a towering bundle of kindling. First he bowed low to MacArthur's standard, then he turned and bowed just as low to the Imperial Palace on the other side of the plaza. American bystanders watched with perplexed amusement as if he were a living paradox of the inscrutable Orient. But the Japanese who saw him understood. He was acknowledging without reservations the temporal power of today's *shogun* while revering what was eternal across the avenue.

終り

Acknowledgments

This book could not have been written without the co-operation of hundreds of people in Asia, Europe and the United States, particularly those who permitted themselves to be interviewed. Libraries contributed immeasurably to the book: the National Archives and Records Service, Alexandria, Virginia (Wilbur Nigh and Lois Aldridge); the National Archives (John E. Taylor); the Library of Congress; the main branch of the New York Public Library; the Danbury (Connecticut) Public Library; the Diet Library in Tokyo; the Library of the U. S. Embassy Annex in Tokyo (Mrs. Yuji Yamamoto); the Houghton Library, Harvard University (Marte Shaw and W. H. Bond); the Yale University Library (Judith A. Schiff); and the Franklin D. Roosevelt Library (Elizabeth Drewry, William Stewart, Jerome Deyo, Robert Parks, Mrs. Anne Morris and Joseph Marshall).

Numerous agencies, organizations and individuals made substantial contributions to this book:

The United States: Lieutenant Colonel Gerald M. Holland, Lieutenant Commander Herbert C. Prendergast and Anna Urband of the Magazine and Book Branch, Office of the Assistant Secretary of Defense; Betty Sprigg, Audio-Visual Division, Directorate for Defense Information; Roland F. Gill, Historical Reference Section Headquarters, Marine Corps; Brigadier General Hal C. Pattison, Judge Israel Wice, Charles B. MacDonald, Charles Romanus, Detmar H. Finke and Hannah Zeidlik of the Office of the Chief of Military History, Department of the Army; the Departments of Navy and Air Force; Arthur G. Kogan, Historical Division of the Department of State; six fellow authors: Michael Erlanger, Walter Lord, Martin Blumenson, Ladislas Farago, Tom Mahoney and Tom Coffey; my two typists, Isabelle Bates and Helen Toland; my special research assistant, Dale P. Harper; Myron Land and Robert Meskill of *Look* magazine; Colonel Ray M. O'Day, *Chit Chat*; Professor John McV. Haight, Jr., Lehigh University; James O. Wade, World Publishing Company; Japan National Tourist Organization, New York City; William Henry Chamberlin; Pearl Buck; John J. McCloy; Mark Wohlfeld; Major Robert C. Mikesh; Virgil O. McCollum; Jean Colbert, WTIC, Hartford, Connecticut; Marty Allen; Captain Joseph W. Enright; Dr. Roy L. Bodine, Jr.; and Jean Ennis, Cynthia Humber, Elizabeth Kapuster, Sono Rosenberg, Anthony Wimpfheimer, Donald Klopfer and Bennett Cerf of Random House, Inc.

Germany: The late Gero von S. Gaevernitz; and Karola Gillich, my German representative.

Guadalcanal: Brian D. Hackman, J. C. Glover and Dominic Otuana of the Geological Survey Department, British Solomon Islands.

Philippines: Aurelio Repato; C. Bohannon; J. A. Villamor; Eduardo Montilla; and Secretary of Foreign Affairs Carlos Romulo.

Okinawa: Dr. Samuel Mukaida, Samuel H. Kitamura and Joseph S. Evans, Jr., of Public Affairs Department, U. S. Civil Administration of the Ryukyu Islands; and Eikichi Yamazato.

Thailand: Sol Sanders, the *U. S. News and World Report.*

Iwo Jima: A. B. Truax, the U. S. Coast Guard; and U. S. Air Force.

Republic of China: James Wei, director of the Government Information Office.

Guam: Rear Admiral Horace V. Bird.

Hawaii: Colonel James Sunderman and Major Mart Smith, U. S. Air Force; and Captain W. J. Holmes.

Saipan: Tony Benavente; and the civilian pilot who flew me throughout the Marianas.

Tinian: Henry Fleming.

Malaya: Abdul Majid bin Ithman.

New Guinea: John Robertson.

Japan

Tokyo: Prince Takahito Mikasa; Ambassador Edwin O. Reischauer, John Emmerson and George Saito of the U. S. Embassy; Colonels Susumu Nishiura and Hiroshi Fukushige, Lieutenant Colonels Yutaka Fujita and Masao Inaba, Commander Kengo Tominaga, Kazue Ohtani, Kenji Koyama and Captain Masanori Odagiri of the Japan Self-Defense Force War History Office; Rear Admiral Sadatoshi Tomioka, Historical Research Institute; Robert Trumbull, the *New York Times;* Denroku Sakai, the *Asahi Shimbun;* Tatsuo Shibata, editor-in-chief of the *Mainichi Daily News;* Shinji Hasegawa, director of the *Japan Times;* Kyo Naruse, president of Hara Shobo; Lewis Bush and Hiroshi Niino, NHK; John Rich, NBC; Ernest Richter, managing editor, *Pacific Stars and Stripes;* Dr. Kazutaka Watanabe, New Family Center; Taro Fukuda, Japan Public Relations, Inc.; Tomohiko Ushiba, former private secretary to Prince Konoye; Mrs. Fumimaro Konoye, widow of Prince Konoye; Toshio Katsube, Tokyo Fuji Co.;

Kazuaki Arichi of the Foreign Ministry; Captain Sadae Ikeda, who arranged interviews with survivors of *Musashi;* Yoshimichi Itagawa, who arranged interviews with veterans in Hokkaido; Koichi Narita, who, together with Kiyoshi Kamiko, arranged trip to Leyte; Commander Suguru Suzuki; Mrs. Junko Kawabe, widow of General Masakazu Kawabe; Mrs. Yoshii Kuribayashi, widow of General Tadamichi Kuribayashi; Mrs. Haruko Ichimaru, eldest daughter of the late Admiral Toshinosuke Ichimaru; Mrs. Yoshie Onishi, widow of Admiral Takijiro Onishi; Yoshio Kodama; Captain Atsushi Oi of the Air-Sea Technical Research Association; Mrs. Sadako Fushimi, widow of Prince Hiroyoshi Fushimi; Mrs. Toyoko Dantani, widow of Sergeant Minoru Dantani (Iwo Jima); Petty Officer Iwao Matsumoto and Sergeant Shinya Ryumae, veterans of Iwo Jima; Lieutenant Colonel Shigeharu Asaeda; Major Iwao Takahashi, son-in-law of the late General Sosaku Suzuki; Mrs. Chitose Tsuji, widow of Colonel Masanobu Tsuji; Seizo Yamanaka, Mannesmann Aktiengesellschaft liaison office in Japan; Yoichi Nagata; Den Oshima; Motoji Tokushima; Keizaburo Matsumoto; Beiji Yamamoto; Mrs. Kimiko Matsumura; Toshio Haneda; Mrs. Keiko Ohtake; and the following translators: Kanji Motai, Tsuneo Oki, Toshio Nagasaki, Kiichiro Kumano and Toshihiko Kasahara.

Oiso: Marquis Koichi Kodo, who arranged interviews with a number of officials in the Imperial Household Ministry and made numerous suggestions.

Hiroshima: Shogo Nagaoka, co-ordinator and guide; Mrs. Barbara Reynolds, Hiroshima Friendship Center; Mayor Shinzo Hamai; Masao Niide, chief of the Foreign Affairs Section, City Hall; Seigo Wada, Municipal Government, who arranged a number of interviews.

Nagasaki: Shogo Nagaoka, co-ordinator and guide; Deputy Mayor Kaoru Naruse; Mayor Tsutomu Tagawa, Toshiyuki Hayama and Sunao Tanaka, who arranged a number of interviews.

Osaka: Gen Nishino, the *Mainichi.*

Kyoto: Dr. Yoichi Misaki, who arranged interviews with survivors of the 16th Division and Koichiro Hatanaka.

Matsuyama: Toyoshige Miyoshi.

Hokkaido: Daisuke Kuriga, who arranged research interviews.

Kure: Shinji Chiba, who arranged trips to Kure, Etajima, Iwakuni and Hashirajima; and Captain Arashi Kamimura, commander, Educational Troops, Maritime Defense Agency, Kure.

Etajima: Admiral Toshihiko Tomita, Superintendent of Naval Academy; and Seizo Okamura, curator of Naval Academy Gallery.

Iwakuni: Colonel Hideo Nakamura, commanding officer, Iwakuni Air Base, Japan Self-Defense Force; Lieutenant William M. Bokholt, Marine Corps Air Station; Hajime Takahashi, harbor master, Iwakuni; Mrs. Yoshiko Kugiya, proprietress of Kugiman Inn.

Hashirajima: Hisaro Fujimoto; Tsutae Fujiyama; and Isamu Horimoto.

Yokusuka: Vice Admiral Nobuo Fukuchi, commandant, Memorial Battleship *Mikasa;* Rear Admiral Frank L. Johnson, Captain Tom Dwyer and Douglas Wada, U. S. Naval Forces in Japan. Mr. Wada arranged a number of special interviews and acted as interpreter.

Finally I would like to thank six people who contributed most outstandingly to the book: my chief assistant and interpreter, my wife Toshiko; my two representatives in Japan, Tokiji Matsumura and Major Yoshitaka Horie; my copyeditor, Mrs. Barbara Willson, not only for correcting mistakes but for suggesting innumerable improvements in style and content; my agent, Paul Revere Reynolds, who gave me the idea for this project and was a constant source of encouragement throughout the five years it took to complete it; and my editor, Robert Loomis, who labored so diligently with me for more than sixteen months on the final draft that the finished manuscript could properly be called a collaboration.

Sources

A. Interviews

(Rank at time of action)

Lieutenant Heijiro Abe, Pearl Harbor and Midway (2 interviews)
Valeriano Abello, Leyte
Yasuharu Agarie, Okinawa
Dr. Tatsuichiro Akizuki, Nagasaki
Zoilo Andrade, Leyte
Ensign Yasunori Aoki, *kamikaze* flier (3 interviews)
Antonio Aquino, Bataan
Daitaro Arakawa, NHK
General Sadao Araki*
Colonel Okikatsu Arao, Palace revolt
Major Shigeharu Asaeda, Tsuji's assistant (4 interviews)
Lieutenant (j.g.) Wahei Asami, *Musashi*
Yoshinori Ataka, Hiroshima
Prime Minister Clement Attlee*
Tony Benavente, Saipan
Admiral Thomas Binford, Battle of Java Sea
Commander Horace V. Bird, *Missouri*
Admiral C. C. Bloch, Pearl Harbor
General Clifford Bluemel, Bataan
Paul C. Blum, peace move in Switzerland
Major Roy L. Bodine, Jr., prisoner of war
C. T. R. Bohannan, Philippines
Charles Bohlen, Yalta and Potsdam (2 interviews)
Ordnanceman 3rd Class Donald Briggs, Pearl Harbor
Corporal Durward Brooks, Clark Field
Lewis Bush, British prisoner of war
Captain Richard Carmichael, Pearl Harbor
Corporal Roy Castleberry, Bataan
Chen Cheng,* Minister of War, Nationalist China
Shinji Chiba, navigation instructor
Dr. Shigeko Chihara, Okinawa
Colonel Jim Cushing,* Cebu
Hisaji Dai, Hiroshima

---

*deceased

Hiroaki Daido, Hiroshima

Sergeant Dwayne Davis, Clark Field

Major James P. S. Devereux, Wake Island

General Akio Doi, Soviet expert (3 interviews)

Eugene Hoffman Dooman, adviser to Ambassador Grew*

Allen Dulles*

Hideo Edo, Mitsui Real Estate Co., Ltd. (2 interviews)

Private George E. Elliott, Jr., Pearl Harbor

John Kenneth Emmerson, consular staff in Yenan

Mrs. Tsuyako Eshima, Nagasaki

Ramon Esperas, Leyte

Admiral Frank Jack Fletcher

Hisaro Fujimoto, Hashirajima

Commander Yoshiro Fujimura, peace move in Switzerland (2 interviews)

Colonel Nobuo Fujisawa, aviation maintenance officer

Lieutenant Yoshimi Fujiwara, Iwo Jima

Tsutae Fujiyama, Hashirajima

Taeko Fukabori, Nagasaki (Mrs. Furukawa)

Captain Nobuo Fukuchi, Personnel Bureau, Navy Ministry

Admiral Shigeru Fukudome

Commander Shizuo Fukui, naval construction expert

George A. Furness, IMTFE counsel

First Sergeant Noboru Furukawa, Leyte (2 interviews)

Gero von S. Gaevernitz,* peace move in Switzerland

Jesse Gaines, Pearl Harbor

Lieutenant Wilmer Earl Gallaher, Midway

Commander Minoru Genda, Pearl Harbor and Midway (2 interviews)

Stuart Griffin, Iwo Jima

J. C. Glover, Guadalcanal

Vicente Guerrero, Saipan

Brian D. Hackman, Guadalcanal

Colonel Tatsuo Haki, Bataan

Ryuji Hamai, Hiroshima

Shinzo Hamai,* mayor of Hiroshima (2 interviews)

W. Averell Harriman, U. S. ambassador to Moscow

Saiji Hasegawa, Domei

Shinichi Hasegawa, Yonosuke Matsuoka's secretary

Colonel Takushiro Hattori,* Army General Staff (3 interviews)

Toshiyuki Hayama, Nagasaki

Mrs. Matsuyo Hayashi, Hiroshima

Colonel Saburo Hayashi, Palace revolt

Tosaku Hayashiya, Tokyo fire bombing, May 25, 1945

Jinsai Higa, General Ushijima's barber

Professor Kiyoshi Hiraizumi, teacher of the Imperial Way (2 interviews)

---

*deceased

Private Kiyomi Hirakawa, Iwo Jima
Lieutenant Colonel Takashi Hirakushi, Saipan (2 interviews)
Lieutenant (s.g.) Shigeo Hirayama, Battle of Leyte Gulf
Matao Hisatomi, correspondent on Leyte
General Ho Ying-chin, Chief of Staff, Chinese Nationalist Army
Private Shuzen Hokama, Okinawa (2 interviews)
Admiral Ernest Holtzworth, Pearl Harbor
Jiro Homma, peace move in Sweden
Major Yoshitaka Horie, Iwo Jima, etc. (4 interviews)
Naoki Hoshino, Tojo Cabinet (3 interviews)
Morisada Hosokawa, Prince Konoye's secretary and son-in-law
Petty Officer Shiro Hosoya, *Musashi* (2 interviews)
Lieutenant Colonel Masataka Ida, Palace revolt (2 interviews)
Major Einosuke Iemura, Guadalcanal
Tsuyako Iju, Okinawa
Captain Sadae Ikeda, *Musashi* (2 interviews)
Lieutenant Haruki Iki, sinking of *Repulse*
Professor Seiji Imabori, Hiroshima
Warrant Officer Kaname Imai, Okinawa
Colonel Takeo Imai, Marco Polo Bridge incident and Bataan (2 interviews)
General Hitoshi Imamura,* Java and Guadalcanal
Major Kumao Imoto, Army General Staff and Guadalcanal (2 interviews)
Lieutenant Colonel Masao Inaba, Palace revolt (2 interviews)
Sergeant Kenichi Inagaki, Leyte (2 interviews)
Dr. Masaru Inaoka, Iwo Jima
Genji Inoue, Leyte
Sukemasa Irie, Chamberlain to the Emperor
Ryoichi Ishizaki, Leyte
Yoshimichi Itagawa, The Wounded Soldiers' Association of Japan
Captain Koichi Ito, Okinawa
Colonel Tsuneo Ito, War History Office
Pfc. Waichi Ito, Leyte (2 interviews)
Commander Haruki Itoh, Guadalcanal
Mrs. Fukiko Iura, Hiroshima
Colonel Hideo Iwakuro, peace negotiations in Washingon (3 interviews)
Mrs. Chiyo Iwamiya, proprietress of Iwamiya Inn, Mitsukue, Shikoku
Hajime Iwanaga, Nagasaki
Rikuro Iwata, student factory worker
Tomoko Iwata, student factory worker
Miyoko Jahana, Okinawa (Mrs. Toguchi)
Colonel Nobuhiko Jimbo, Philippines (2 interviews)
General Albert Jones,* Bataan
Hideko Kakinohana, Okinawa (Mrs. Yoshimura)

---

*deceased

Corporal Kiyoshi Kamiko, Leyte (3 interviews)
Shinichi Kamimura, chief, Chinese Section, Foreign Ministry, Marco Polo incident
Lieutenant Hisamichi Kano, Philippines
Osanaga Kanroji, High Priest, the Meiji Shrine
Toshikazu Kase, assistant to Matsuoka and Togo
Colonel Tadashi Katakura, 2/26 Incident, Burma, etc. (5 interviews)
Captain Kenkichi Kato, *Musashi*
Toshio Katsube, Tokyo fire bombing, March 10, 1945
Seigo Kawasaki, Okinawa (2 interviews)
Okinori Kaya, Tojo Cabinet (3 interviews)
Marquis Koichi Kido (4 interviews)
Gonichi Kumura, Hiroshima
Ikuko Kimura, employed by Shigenori Togo
Shigeru Kinjo, Okinawa
Kojiro Kitamura, peace move in Switzerland
Tadahiko Kitayama, Hiroshima, etc. (2 interviews)
Shunzo Kobayashi, Matsuoka's defense counsel at IMTFE
Yoshio Kodama, associate of Tsuji, Onishi, etc. (4 interviews)
Keizo Kohno, Burma
Yuichiro Kominami, Tokyo fire bombing, March 10, 1945
Captain Keizo Komura, Pearl Harbor to Okinawa (2 interviews)
Michitaka Konoye, younger son of Prince Konoye (2 interviews)
General Haruo Konuma, Guadalcanal (3 interviews)
Hachiro Kosasa, Nagasaki (2 interviews)
Mrs. Hachiro Kosasa, Nagasaki
Lieutenant Commander Choichi Koyama, *Hatsuyuki*
Admiral Tomiji Koyanagi, Guadalcanal, Marianas and Leyte (2 interviews)
Sachiko Kuda, Okinawa (Mrs. Omi)
Mrs. Yoshiko Kugiya, proprietress of Kugiman Inn
Lieutenant (s.g.) Kazutoshi Kuhara, Pearl Harbor, etc.
Captain Hiromu Kumano, Imphal campaign
Daisuke Kuriga, Sakhalin
Pfc. Noboru Kuriyama, Okinawa
Mrs. Saburo Kurusu
Admiral Jinichi Kusaka, commander, Southeast Area Fleet
Admiral Ryunosuke Kusaka (6 interviews)
Father Hugo Lassalle (Makibi Enomiya), Hiroshima
Yeoman C. O. Lines, Pearl Harbor
Tokuzo Makiminato, Okinawa
Toraichi Masuda, Leyte
Tsuneo Mataba, naval salvage expert
Miyoko Matsubara, Hiroshima
Shigeharu Matsumoto, managing editor of Domei
Lieutenant Hirata Matsumura, Pearl Harbor
Cadet Hisashi Matsumura, information on prisoners of war
Kenichiro Matsuoka, son of Yosuke Matsuoka

Colonel Sei Matsutani, Army General Staff
Dr. Yoshimasa Matsuzaka, Hiroshima
John J. McCloy, The Assistant Secretary of War
Yates McDaniel, Singapore
Prince Mikasa
Admiral Gunichi Mikawa, Battle of Savo Island
Dr. Yoichi Misaki, Leyte (2 interviews)
Shizuko Miura, Saipan (Mrs. Sugano)
Petty Officer Shikichi Miyagi, Okinawa (3 interviews)
Shuji Miyahara, student mobilization
Mieko Miyahira, Okinawa
Colonel Yoshio Miyauchi, Leyte
Commander Kazunari Miyo, Navy General Staff (2 interviews)
Eduardo Montilla, Leyte
Captain Joseph Moore, Clark Field
Chiematsu Mori, Shikoku
Lieutenant (j.g.) Juzo Mori, Pearl Harbor
Shigeyoshi Morimoto, Nagasaki
Mrs. Shigeyoshi Morimoto, Nagasaki
Pfc. Hiroshi Morishima, Leyte (2 interviews)
Professor Ichiro Moritaki, Hiroshima
Dr. Tadashi Moriya, Leyte
Colonel William Morse, Philippines
Baron Yonosuke (Ian) Mutsu, Domei
General Yatsuji Nagai, Matsuoka trip to Germany, and *Missouri* (2 interviews)
Professor Shogo Nagaoka, Hiroshima and Nagasaki (3 interviews)
Captain Ko Nagasawa,* Java Sea, Coral Sea and Midway (2 interviews)
Lieutenant (s.g.) Masanao Naito, *Musashi*
Chomei Nakachi, Okinawa
Fumihiko Nakajima, Marianas
Pfc. Hideichi Nakamura, Leyte (2 interviews)
Yukio Nakamura, secret service agent, Marco Polo Bridge incident
Seizen Nakasone, Okinawa
General Akira Nara,* Bataan (2 interviews)
Kaoru Naruse, Nagasaki (2 interviews)
Ricardo P. Negru, Leyte
Hiroshi Niino, NHK (2 interviews)
Fleet Admiral Chester Nimitz*
Ambassador Haruhiko Nishi, Foreign Minister Togo's deputy (2 interviews)
Midori Nishida, Nagasaki
Masao Nishikawa, Leyte
Sergeant Kunio Nishimura, Leyte (2 interviews)
Gen Nishino, Guadalcanal (5 interviews)
Commander Shigeru Nishino, Battle of Surigao Strait

---

*deceased

Colonel Susumu Nashiura, secretary to Tojo (2 interviews)
Zenso Noborikawa, Okinawa
Yeoman Second Class Mitsuharu Noda, *Yamato* and Saipan
First Lieutenant Sajibei Noguchi, Imphal campaign
Sergeant Yoshio Noguchi, Leyte (3 interviews)
Admiral Kichisaburo Nomura,* ambassador to the United States
Admiral Naokuni Nomura, German-Japanese military cooperation
Mrs. Fumiko Nozaki, Okinawa
Shinichi Nozaki, Okinawa
Mrs. Yasuko Nukushina, Hiroshima
Etsuko Obata, Nagasaki
Admiral Sueo Obayashi, Battle of the Philippine Sea
Mikio Ogawa, Leyte
Kiwamu Ogiwara, Matsuoka's *shosei*
Captain Toshikazu Ohmae, Battle of the Philippine Sea, etc. (2 interviews)
Ensign Toshihiko Ohno, Iwo Jima (4 interviews)
Captain Atsushi Oi, naval expert
Seizo Okamura, curator of Naval Gallery, Etajima
Pfc. Kazuyuki Okumura, Leyte
Ryoko Okuyama, Saipan (Mrs. Miura)
Ensign Satoru Omagari, Iwo Jima (4 interviews)
Yeoman Heijiro Omi, Admiral Yamamoto's chief orderly (interviews)
Kunio Ono, Hiroshima
Takeshi Ono, Manchuria
General Makoto Onodera, peace move in Sweden
Yoshiko Ooganeku, Okinawa (Mrs. Kitashiro)
Colonel Adrianus van Oosten, prisoner of war
Tokuo Ootowa, Hiroshima
Chosei Osato, Okinawa
General Hiroshi Oshima, Japanese ambassador to Germany
Chief Petty Officer Mitsukuni Oshita, sinking of *Hiyo*
Sergio Osmeña, President of the Philippines
Masahide Ota, Okinawa
Lieutenant Sadao (Roy) Otake, surrender mission to Manila
Sayao Otsuka, midget-submarine training
General Eugen Ott, German ambassador to Japan
Dominic Otuana, Guadalcanal
Second Lieutenant Robert Overstreet, Pearl Harbor
Jose S. Pangelinan, Saipan
Joe Price, Leyte
Robert Price, Leyte
Vicente Quintero, Leyte (2 interviews)
Ambassador Edwin O. Reischauer
First Lieutenant John Rich, Saipan and Iwo Jima (2 interviews)

---

*deceased

Admiral Francis Rockwell, Philippines
General Carlos Romulo, MacArthur's staff (2 interviews)
Shintaro Ryu,* peace move in Switzerland
Manuel Sablan, Saipan
Sheriff Mariano Sablan, Saipan
Mayor Vicente D. Sablan, Saipan
Dr. Ryokichi Sagane,* Nagasaki
Pfc. Koichi Saijo, Okinawa (2 interviews)
Petty Officer Haruyoshi Saima, Battle of Cape Esperance
Ensign Kazuo Sakamaki, Pearl Harbor
Joe Sakisat, Saipan
Hisatsune Sakomizu, secretary to Prime Ministers Okada and
    Suzuki (2 interviews)
Tomie Sanada, Hiroshima (Mrs. Fujii)
General Sadamu Sanagi, Philippines
Colonel Fabian Sanchez, Cebu
Commander Naohiro Sata, Pearl Harbor
General Kenryo Sato, adviser to Tojo (7 interviews)
Kyoko Sato, Hiroshima (Mrs. Heiya Yamamoto)
Naotake Sato, Japanese ambassador to Russia (2 interviews)
General Shozaburo Sato, 2/26 Incident
Petty Officer Taro Sato, *Musashi*
Captain Manuel Segura, Cebu
Emi Sekimura, Tokyo fire bombing, March 10, 1945 (Mrs. Seo)
Mrs. Yoshie Sekumura, Toyo fire bombing, March 10, 1945
Captain Hideo Sematoo, Hiroshima
Tatsuo Shibata, editor-in-chief, the *Mainichi Daily News*
Pfc. Toshio Shida, Okinawa
Lieutenant Yoshio Shiga, Pearl Harbor and Battle of the Santa
    Cruz Islands (3 interviews)
Dr. Fumio Shigeto, Hiroshima
Admiral Kiyohide Shima, Battle of Surigao Strait (3 interviews)
Ensign Fukujiro Shimoyama, *Musashi*
Private Shigeru Shimoyama, Hiroshima (5 interviews)
Captain Tsuneo Shimura, Okinawa (2 interviews)
Cesario Sipaco, Leyte
John H. Skeen, Jr., General Homma's defense counsel
Sturmbannführer (Major) Otto Skorzeny, Teheran
Admiral W. W. Smith, Pearl Harbor
Admiral Raymond Spruance*
Admiral Harold Stark
Kamekichi Sugimoto, Nagasaki
Major Mitsuo Suginoo, Guadalcanal
Colonel Ichiji Sugita, Singapore and *Missouri* (2 interviews)
Captain Tatsumaru Sugiyama, aviation officers' plot against Tojo,
    etc. (2 interviews)
Captain Eijiro Suzuki, Pearl Harbor (2 interviews)

---

*deceased

Hajime Suzuki, son of Prime Minister Suzuki
Commander Suguru Suzuki, Pearl Harbor
Pfc. Tadashi Suzuki, Guadalcanal
General Teiichi Suzuki, President of the Cabinet Planning Board
(2 interviews)
Admiral Sokichi Takagi, Navy Ministry
Hachiro Takahashi, Burma
Lieutenant (s.g.) Katsusaku Takahashi, sinking of *Repulse*
Ensign Kiyoshi Takahashi, *Musashi*
Dr. Shingo Takahashi, Leyte
Dr. Susumu Takahashi, Tokyo fire bombing, March 10, 1945
Chiyo Takamori, Hiroshima (Mrs. Takeuchi)
General Tatsuhiko Takashima, chief of staff to General Seiichi
Tanaka
Lieutenant Colonel Masahiko Takeshita, Palace revolt (2 inter-
views)
Harumi Takeuchi, peace mission to Manila
Shiroku Tanabe, Hiroshima
Commander Yahachi Tanabe, Midway
Lieutenant Commander Tomonobu Tanaka, sinking of *Soryu*
Morio Tateno, NHK announcer
Nobuyuki Tateno, Japanese literature
Corporal Shinjiro Terasaki, Leyte (2 interviews)
Commander Masamichi Terauchi, *Yukikaze*
Yasuhide Toda, Chamberlain to the Emperor
Junji Togashi, *Mainichi* reporter
Fumihiko Togo, son-in-law and adopted son of Shigenori Togo
Mrs. Hideki Tojo (2 interviews)
Hitoshi Tokai, Nagasaki
Kazuko Tokai, Nagasaki (Mrs. Tanaka)
Yoshihiro Tokugawa, Chamberlain to the Emperor
Captain Sadatoshi Tomioka, Naval General Staff (5 interviews)
Admiral Toshihiko Tomita, Etajima
Mrs. Yoshiko Tomita, Hiroshima
General Yoshiharu Tomochika, Leyte (2 interviews)
Chief Petty Officer Hisao Tomokane, *Shimakaze*
Commander Shukichi Toshikawa, Battle of Java Sea
Staff Sergeant Frank Trammell,* Clark Field
Colonel Jesse Traywick, Jr., Philippines
President Harry S. Truman
Robert Trumbull, Pearl Harbor and *Missouri* (2 interviews)
Sadako Tsutsumimachi, Hiroshima (Mrs. Tochida)
Seiyu Uema, Okinawa
Takeshi Usami, Grand Steward of the Imperial Household
Tomohiko Ushiba, Prince Konoye's secretary (2 interviews)
General Takaji Wachi, C/S Generals Homma and Yamashita
Captain Tsunezo Wachi, Mexico and Iwo Jima

---

*deceased

etty Officer Tadashi Wada, *kamikaze* pilot trainee

Vang Chia-yu, Nationalist China Ministry of Information

General Wang Shu-ming, Flying Tigers

Commander Yasuji Watanabe,* on Yamamoto's staff (3 interviews)

econd Lieutenant William Welch, Pearl Harbor

Kiichiro Yamada, Leyte (2 interviews)

adahiro Yamada, Leyte

Taro Yamada, naval ordnance expert

enji Yamaguchi, Nagasaki

Major Chikuro Yamamoto, Guadalcanal

Lieutenant (s.g.) Heiya Yamamoto, *Akizuki*

Mrs. Makiko Yamamoto, widow of Commander Yuji Yamamoto

Lieutenant (s.g.) Masahide Yamamoto, Guadalcanal sea battles

Michiko Yamaoka, Hiroshima

Nobuko Yamashiro, Okinawa (Mrs. Oshiro)

Zikichi Yamazato, Okinawa

Kayo Yasuo, Okinawa

Major Jesus Ybanez, Cebu

Shigeru Yoshida,* Japanese ambassador to Great Britain

Shozaburo Yoshida, Rabaul (3 interviews)

Ensign Takeo Yoshikawa, Pearl Harbor

Hajime Yukimune, Hiroshima

B. Documents, Records and Reports

Foreign Relations of the United States: Diplomatic Papers. The Far East: 1931, Vol. III; 1932, Vols. III and IV; 1933, Vol. III; 1934, Vol. III; 1935, Vol. III; 1936, Vol. VI; 1937, Vols. III and IV; 1938, Vols. III and IV; 1939, Vols. III and IV; 1940, Vol. IV; 1941, Vols. III and IV. Washington: Department of State, 1946-1956.

Papers Relating to the Foreign Relations of the United States: Japan, 1931–1941. 2 vols. Washington: Department of State, 1943.

Peace and War: United States Foreign Policy, 1931–1941. Washington: Department of State, 1946.

International Military Tribunal for the Far East, Dissenting Judgement (Justice Radhabinad Pal). Calcutta: Sanyal, 1953.

International Military Tribunal for the Far East. *Interrogations* (listed in Notes).

apan Defense Agency. Archives of the War History Office. Unpublished manuscripts and records which are the source of the series of histories being written by the War History Office.

apan International Politics Association. "Records of the Meetings

---

*deceased

of the Liaison and Imperial Conferences." Compiled by Dr
Jun Tsunoda, and others. Published in 7 vols. by Asal
Shimbun, Tokyo, in 1962-1963, under the title *The Road t*
the Pacific War.

Japan Ministry of Foreign Affairs. Archives and Document
Section. "The Circumstances relating to the Termination o
the War and Relative Historical Materials." Unpublishe
manuscript and materials. Published version: *Historical Rec*
ords of the Surrender. 2 vols. Tokyo: Shimbun Gekkan, 1952

————. *Chronological Tables and Major Documents pertaining t*
Japan's Foreign Relations. 2 volumes. Tokyo: Nihon Kokusa
Rengo Kyokai, 1955.

————. Archives 1868-1945, microfilmed for the Library o
Congress, 1949-1951. Compiled by Cecil H. Uyehara. Wash
ington: Photoduplication Service, Library of Congress, 1954.

Japanese monographs and studies. U.S. Department of the Army
Office, Chief of Military History Archives (listed in Notes)

The NHK File on the Emperor's recording and the Palace revolt

Pearl Harbor Attack. Hearings before the Joint Committee on th
Investigation of the Pearl Harbor Attack, Congress of th
United States, Seventy-ninth Congress. Washington: U.S. Gov
ernment Printing Office, 1946.

Takashima, Tatsuhiko. "Notes," a report by Major General Ta
tsuhiko Takashima. Unpublished.

U.S. Strategic Bombing Survey (USSBS). *The Effects of Strategi*
Bombing on Japanese Morale. Washington: U.S. Governmen
Printing Office, 1947.

————. *Interrogations of Japanese Officers, Navy.* Unpublished.

————. *Interrogations of Japanese Officials.* 2 vols. Washington
U.S. Government Printing Office, 1946.

————. *Japan's Struggle to End the War.* Washington: U.S
Government Printing Office, 1946.

C. *Official Histories*

AUSTRALIA

Wigmore, Lionel. *The Japanese Thrust.* Canberra: Australian Wa
Memorial, 1957.

GREAT BRITAIN

History of the Second World War (United Kingdom Military
Series). London, Her Majesty's Stationery Office:

Ehrman, John. *Grand Strategy*, Vol. VI. 1956.
Gwyer, John M.A., and J.R.M. Butler. *Grand Strategy,* Vol. III
Part 1, 1964.

Kirby, Woodburn S. *The War against Japan,* Vols. I and V. 1957 and 1969.

JAPAN

Defense Agency, War History Office. *Advance Operations into Malaya.* Tokyo: Asagumo Shimbun, 1966.

UNITED STATES

Department of the Air Force. *The Army Air Forces in World War II:*

Craven, W.F., and J.L. Cate, eds. Vol. IV, *The Pacific—Guadalcanal to Saipan;* Vol. V, *The Pacific—Matterhorn to Nagasaki.* University of Chicago Press, 1950 and 1953.

Department of the Army. Publications of the Office of the Chief of Military History. Washington, U.S. Government Printing Office:

Appleman, Roy E., James M. Burns, Russell A. Gugeler and John Stevens. *Okinawa: The Last Battle.* 1948.
Cannon, M. Hamlin. *Leyte: The Return to the Philippines.* 1954.
Conn, Stetson, Rose C. Engelman and Byron Fairchild. *Guarding the United States and Its Outposts.* 1964.
Crowl, Philip A. *Campaign in the Marianas.* 1960.
———, and Edmund G. Love. *Seizure of the Gilberts and Marshalls.* 1960.
Greenfield, Kent Roberts, ed. *Command Decisions.* New York: Harcourt, 1959.
Matloff, Maurice. *Strategic Planning for Coalition Warfare: 1943–1944.* 1959.
———, and Edwin M. Snell. *Strategic Planning for Coalition Warfare: 1941–1942.* 1953.
Miller, John, Jr., *Guadalcanal: The First Offensive.* 1949.
Morton, Louis. *The Fall of the Philippines.* 1953.
———, *Strategy and Command: The First Two Years.* 1962.
Romanus, Charles F., and Riley Sunderland. *Stilwell's Command Problems.* 1956.
———. *Stilwell's Mission to China.* 1953.
———. *Time Runs Out in CBI.* 1959.
Smith, Robert Ross. *The Approach to the Philippines.* 1953.
———. *Triumph in the Philippines.* 1963.
Watson, Mark Skinner. *Chief of Staff: Prewar Plans and Preparations: 1941–1942.* 1950.
Williams, Mary H., compiler. *Chronology: 1941–1945.* 1960.

Department of the Navy

Marine Corps. Washington, U.S. Government Printing Office for Historical Branch, Marine Corps:

Bartley, Lt. Col. Whitman S. *Iwo Jima: Amphibious Epic.* 1954.

Hoffman, Major Carl W. *Saipan: The Beginning of the End.* 1950.

Hough, Lieutenant Colonel Frank O., Major Verle E. Ludwig, and Henry I. Shaw, Jr. *Pearl Harbor to Guadalcanal.* 1958.

Nichols, Major Charles S., Jr., and Henry I. Shaw, Jr. *Okinawa: Victory in the Pacific.* 1955.

Zimmerman, Major John L. *The Guadalcanal Campaign.* 1949.

Navy. Boston, Little, Brown:

Morison, Samuel Eliot. *History of the United States Naval Operations in World War II.* Vol. III. *The Rising Sun in the Pacific,* 1948; Vol. IV, *Coral Sea, Midway and Submarine Actions,* 1949; Vol. V, *Struggle for Guadalcanal,* 1949; Vol. VI, *Breaking the Bismarcks Barrier,* 1950; Vol. VII, *Aleutians, Gilberts and Marshalls,* 1951; Vol. VIII, *New Guinea and the Marianas,* 1953; Vol. XII, *Leyte,* 1958; Vol. XIII, *The Liberation of the Philippines,* 1959; Vol. XVI, *Victory in the Pacific,* 1960.

D. Newspaper and Magazine Articles (listed in Notes)

E. Biographies, Diaries, Memoirs, Studies of History

Academy of Sciences of the U.S.S.R., Institute of History. *A Short History of the U.S.S.R.,* Part II. A. Samsonov, ed. Moscow: Progress Publishers, 1965.

Adams, Henry H. *1942: The Year That Doomed the Axis.* New York: McKay, 1967.

Agawa, Hiroyuki. *Isoroku Yamamoto.* Tokyo: Shincho Sha, 1966

Alperovitz, Gar. *Atomic Diplomacy: Hiroshima and Potsdam* New York: Simon & Schuster, 1965.

Arnold, H. H. *Global Mission.* New York: Harper, 1949.

Attiwell, Kenneth. *Fortress.* Garden City, N.Y.: Doubleday, 1960

Attlee, Clement R. *As It Happened.* New York: Viking, 1954.

————, and Frances Williams. *Twilight of Empire: Memoirs o Prime Minister Clement Attlee.* New York: Barnes, 1962.

Baker, Richard Terrill. *Darkness of the Sun.* New York: Abingdon Cokesbury, 1947.

Ba Maw. *Breakthrough in Burma.* New Haven: Yale Universit Press, 1968.

Barbey, Daniel E. *MacArthur's Amphibious Navy.* Annapolis Md.: U.S. Naval Institute, 1969.

Beach, Edward L. *Submarine.* New York: Holt, 1952.

Beard, Charles A. *President Roosevelt and the Coming of th War.* New Haven: Yale University Press, 1948.

Belote, James H., and William M. *Corregidor: The Saga of a Fortress.* New York: Harper, 1967.

Benedict, Ruth. *The Chrysanthemum and the Sword.* Boston: Houghton Miffin, 1946.

Bennett, Henry Gordon. *Why Singapore Fell.* Sydney: Angus & Robertson, 1944.

Birse, A. H. *Memoirs of an Interpreter.* London: Michael Joseph, 1967.

Bisson, T. A. *Japan in China.* New York: Macmillan, 1938.

Blum, John Morton. *From the Diaries of Henry Morgenthau, Jr.,* Vol. II, *Years of Urgency, 1938–1941;* Vol. III, *Years of War, 1941–1945.* Boston: Houghton Mifflin, 1965 and 1967.

Bodine, Major Roy L., Jr. *Jap POW Diary.* Unpublished.

Bosworth, Allan R. *America's Concentration Camps.* New York: Norton, 1967.

Brooks, Lester. *Behind Japan's Surrender.* New York: McGraw-Hill, 1968.

Browne, Cecil. *From Suez to Singapore.* New York: Random House, 1942.

Bryant, Arthur. *Triumph in the West.* New York: Doubleday, 1959.

———. *The Turn of the Tide* (the diaries of Lord Alanbrooke). New York: Doubleday, 1957.

Burtness, Paul S., and Warren Ober, eds. *The Puzzle of Pearl Harbor.* Evanston, Ill.: Row, Peterson, 1962.

Busch, Noel F. *The Emperor's Sword.* New York: Funk & Wagnalls, 1969.

Bush, Lewis. *Clutch of Circumstance.* Tokyo: Okuyama, 1956.

———. *Japanalia, A Concise Cyclopedia.* Tokyo: Tokyo News Service, 1965.

Butow, Robert J. C. *Japan's Decision to Surrender.* Stanford University Press, 1954.

———. *Tojo and the Coming of the War.* Princeton University Press, 1961.

Byas, Hugh. *Government by Assassination.* New York: Harper, 1958.

Byrnes, James F. *All in One Lifetime.* New York: Harper, 1958.

———. *Speaking Frankly.* New York: Harper, 1947.

Bywater, Hector C. *The Great Pacific War.* London: Constable, 1925.

Caidin, Martin. *A Torch to the Enemy.* New York: Ballantine, 1960.

Chamberlin, William Henry. *Japan over Asia.* Garden City, N.Y.: Blue Ribbon, 1942.

Chen Cheng. *Outline of the Course of Eight Years of Resistance.* Unpublished.

Chennault, Claire Lee. *Way of a Fighter*. New York: Putnam, 1949.

Chiang Kai-shek. *Soviet Russia in China*. New York: Farrar, Straus, 1958.

Chinnock, Frank W. *Nagasaki: The Forgotten Bomb*. New York: World, 1969.

Churchill, Winston S. *The Second World War*, Vol. III, *The Grand Alliance;* Vol. IV, *The Hinge of Fate;* Vol. V, *Closing the Ring;* Vol. VI, *Triumph and Tragedy*. Boston: Houghton Mifflin, 1950, 1951 and 1953.

Ciano, Count Galeazzo. *Ciano's Diaries, 1939–1943*. Hugh Gibson, editor. Introduction by Sumner Welles. New York: Doubleday, 1946.

Clarke, Hugh, and Takeo Yamashita. *To Sydney by Stealth*. London: Horwitz, 1966.

Cohen, Jerome B. *Japan's Economy in War and Reconstruction*. University of Minnesota Press, 1949.

Compton, Arthur Holly. *Atomic Quest*. New York: Oxford University Press, 1956.

Cordero, Colonel V. N. *My Experiences during the War with Japan*. Privately printed.

Craig, William. *The Fall of Japan*. New York: Dial, 1967.

Crowley, James B. *Japan's Quest for Autonomy*. Princeton University Press, 1966.

Davis, Burke. *Get Yamamoto*. New York: Random House, 1969.

———. *Marine!* Boston: Little, Brown, 1962.

Davis, Kenneth S. *Experience of War*. Garden City, N.Y.: Doubleday, 1965.

Deakin, F. W., and G. R. Storry. *The Case of Richard Sorge*. New York: Harper, 1966.

Deane, John R. *The Strange Alliance*. New York: Viking, 1947.

Dunn, Frederick S. *Peace-Making and the Settlement with Japan*. Princeton University Press, 1963.

Dyess, William. *The Dyess Story*. New York: Putnam, 1942.

Eden, Anthony. *The Memoirs of Anthony Eden*, Vol. III, *The Reckoning*. Boston: Houghton Mifflin, 1965.

Edmonds, Walter D. *They Fought with What They Had*. Boston: Little, Brown, 1951.

Eichelberger, Robert L. *Our Jungle Road to Tokyo*. New York: Viking, 1950.

Falk, Stanley L. *Bataan: The March of Death*. New York: Norton, 1962.

———. *Decision at Leyte*. New York: Norton, 1966.

Farago, Ladislas. *The Broken Seal*. New York: Random House, 1967.

———. *Burn after Reading*. New York: Walker, 1961.

Feis, Herbert. *Between War and Peace*. Princeton University Press, 1960.

———. *The China Tangle*. Princeton University Press, 1953.

———. *Contest over Japan*. New York: Norton, 1968.

———. *Japan Subdued*. Princeton University Press, 1961.

———. *The Road to Pearl Harbor*. Princeton University Press, 1950.

Feldt, Eric A. *The Coast Watchers*. New York: Oxford University Press, 1946.

Fitzgerald, C. P. *The Birth of Communist China*. Baltimore, Md.: Penguin, 1964.

Forrestal, E. P. *Admiral Raymond A. Spruance, USN: A Study in Command*. Washington: U.S. Government Printing Office, 1966.

Forrestal, James. *The Forrestal Diaries*. Walter Millis, ed. New York: Viking, 1951.

Friedlander, Saul. *Prelude to Downfall: Hitler and the United States, 1939–1941*. New York: Knopf, 1967.

Fuchida, Mitsuo, and Masatake Okumiya. *Midway, The Battle That Doomed Japan*. Annapolis, Md.: U.S. Naval Institute, 1955.

Garfield, Brian W. *The Thousand-Mile War: World War II in Alaska and the Aleutians*. Garden City, N.Y.: Doubleday, 1969.

Glines, Carroll V. *Doolittle's Tokyo Raiders*. New York: Van Nostrand, 1964.

Grew, Joseph C. *The Diary of Joseph C. Grew* and *The Papers of Joseph C. Grew*. Cambridge: Houghton Library, Harvard University.

———. *Ten Years in Japan*. New York: Simon & Schuster, 1944.

———. *Turbulent Era*. 2 vols. Boston: Houghton Mifflin, 1952.

Gunnison, Arch. *So Sorry, No Peace*. New York: Viking, 1944.

Halsey, William F., and J. Bryan III. *Admiral Halsey's Story*. New York: McGraw-Hill, 1947.

Hara, Tameichi, Fred Saito and Roger Pineau. *Japanese Destroyer Captain*. New York: Ballantine, 1961.

Hashimoto, Mochitsura. *Sunk*. New York: Holt, 1954.

Hattori, Takushiro. *The Complete History of the Greater East Asia War*. Tokyo: Hara Shobo, 1966.

Hearn, Lafcadio. *Japan: An Interpretation*. New York: Grosset & Dunlap, 1904.

Heinrichs, Waldo H., Jr. *American Ambassador: Joseph C. Grew and the Development of the U.S. Diplomatic Tradition*. Boston: Little, Brown, 1966.

Hersey, John. *Hiroshima*. New York: Knopf, 1946.

Hewlett, Richard G., and Oscar E. Anderson, Jr. *The New World*. University Park, Pa.: The Pennsylvania State University Press, 1962.

Higashikuni, Prince Toshihiko. *The War Diary of a Member of the Royal Family*. Tokyo: Nihon Shuho Sha, 1957.

Holmes, W. J. *Undersea Victory*. Garden City, N.Y.: Doubleday, 1966.

Homma, Masaharu. *The Diary of Masaharu Homma*. Unpublished.

Horie, Yoshitaka. *End of the Ogasawara Army Corps*. Compiled by Major Horie for the Association of Veterans of the Ogasawara Corps. Tokyo: Hara Shobo, 1969.

————. *Fighting Spirit—Iwo Jima*. Tokyo: Kobun Sha, 1965.

Hosokawa, Morisada. *Information Never Reached the Emperor*. 2 vols. Tokyo: Dokosha Isobe Shobo, 1953.

Hsu Kai-yu. *Chou En-lai*. Garden City, N.Y.: Doubleday, 1968.

Huie, William Bradford. *The Hero of Iwo Jima*. New York: New American Library, 1962.

————. *The Hiroshima Pilot*. New York: Putnam, 1964.

Hull, Cordell. *The Memoirs of Cordell Hull*. 2 vols. New York: Macmillan, 1948.

Hunt, Frazier. *MacArthur and the War against Japan*. New York: Scribner, 1944.

Ike, Nobutaka. *Japan's Decision for War: Liaison and Imperial Conference Records, March-December, 1941*. Stanford University Press, 1967.

Ind, Allison. *Allied Intelligence Bureau*. New York: McKay, 1958.

Inoguchi, Rikihei, Tadashi Nakajima and Roger Pineau. *The Divine Wind*. Annapolis, Md.: U.S. Naval Institute, 1958.

Iriye, Akira. *Across the Pacific*. New York: Harcourt, 1967.

————. *After Imperialism*. Cambridge: Harvard University Press, 1965.

Ismay, Hastings Lionel. *The Memoirs of General Lord Ismay*. New York: Viking, 1960.

Ito, Masanori. *The End of the Imperial Japanese Navy*. New York: Norton, 1962.

Ito, Masashi. *The Emperor's Last Soldiers*. New York: Coward-McCann, 1967.

James, David H. *The Rise and Fall of the Japanese Empire*. London: Allen & Unwin, 1951.

Johnston, Stanley. *Queen of the Flat-Tops*. New York: Dutton, 1942.

Jones, E. Stanley. *A Song of Ascents*. Nashville, Tenn.: Abingdon Press, 1968.

Joya, Mock. *Things Japanese*. Tokyo: Tokyo News Service, 1958.

Jucker-Fleetwood, Erin E., ed. *The Per Jacobsson Mediations*. Basle: Basle Centre for Economic and Financial Research.

Kahn, David. *The Code-Breakers*. New York: Macmillan, 1967

Kahn, E. J., Jr. *The Stragglers*. New York: Random House, 1962

Kamiko, Kiyoshi. *I Didn't Die on Leyte*. Tokyo: Shuppan Kyodo Sha, 1966.

Karig, Walter, and others. *Battle Report*, Vol. I, *Pearl Harbor to Coral Sea*; Vol. IV, *The End of an Empire*. New York: Rinehart, 1944 and 1948.

Kase, Toshikazu. *Journey to the Missouri*. New Haven: Yale University Press, 1950.

Kato, Masuo. *The Lost War*. New York: Knopf, 1946.

Kennan, George F. *Memoirs, 1925–1950*. Boston: Little, Brown, 1967.

Kenney, George C. *General Kenney Reports*. New York: Duell, Sloan & Pearce, 1949.

Kido, Koichi. *Diary of Koichi Kido*. 2 vols. Tokyo: Tokyo University Press, 1966.

————. *The Relevant Documents of Koichi Kido*. Compiled by the Society for the Study of the Kido Diary. Tokyo: Tokyo University Press, 1966.

King, Ernest J., and Walter Muir Whitehill. *Fleet Admiral King*. London: Eyre & Spottiswoode, 1953.

Kiyosawa, Kiyoshi, and others. *Diaries in Darkness*. Tokyo: Shuei Sha, 1966.

Knebel, Fletcher, and Charles W. Bailey II. *No High Ground*. New York: Harper, 1960.

Kodama, Yoshio. *I Was Defeated*. Japan: Radiopress, 1959.

Kolko, Gabriel. *The Politics of War*. New York: Random House, 1968.

Konoye, Fumimaro. *The Konoye Diary*. Compiled by Kyodo Press. Tokyo: Kyodo Press, 1968.

————. *My Efforts towards Peace*. Tokyo: Nippon Dempo Tsushinsha, 1946.

Koyanagi, Tomiji. *The Kurita Fleet*. Tokyo: Ushio Shobo, 1956.

Kurzman, Dan. *Kishi and Japan*. New York: Obolensky, 1960.

Kusaka, Ryunosuke. *The Combined Fleet: Memoirs of Former Chief of Staff Kusaka*. Tokyo: Mainichi Shimbun, 1952.

Lamont, Lansing. *Day of Trinity*. New York: Atheneum, 1965.

Langer, William L., and S. Everett Gleason. *The Undeclared War*. New York: Harper, 1953.

Laurence, William L. *Dawn over Zero*. New York: Knopf, 1946.

Leahy, William D. *I Was There*. New York: Whittlesey, 1950.

Leckie, Robert. *Challenge for the Pacific*. Garden City, N.Y.: Doubleday, 1965.

LeMay, Curtis E., with MacKinlay Kantor. *Mission with LeMay: My Story*. Garden City, N.Y.: Doubleday, 1965.

Lifton, Robert Jay. *Death in Life: Survivors of Hiroshima*. New York: Random House, 1968.

Lockwood, Charles A., and Hans Christian Adamson. *Battles of the Philippine Sea*. New York: Crowell, 1967.

Lord, Walter. *Day of Infamy*. New York: Holt, 1957.

————. *Incredible Victory*. New York: Harper, 1967.

Lu, David J. *From the Marco Polo Bridge to Pearl Harbor*. Washington: Public Affairs Press, 1961.

MacArthur, Douglas. *Reminiscences*. New York: McGraw-Hill, 1964.

Mallaby, George. *From My Level*. New York: Atheneum, 1965.

Marquand, John P. *Thirty Years*. Boston: Little, Brown, 1945.

Mashbir, Sidney Forrester. *I Was an American Spy*. New York: Vantage, 1953.

Matthews, Allen R. *The Assault*. New York: Simon & Schuster, 1947.

Miller, Thomas G., Jr. *The Cactus Air Force*. New York: Harper, 1969.

Mishima, Sumie. *The Broader Way*. New York: John Day, 1953.

Moorad, George. *Lost Peace in China*. New York: Dutton, 1949.

Moore, Frederick. *With Japan's Leaders*. New York: Scribner, 1942.

Moran, Lord (Sir Charles Wilson). *Churchill: Taken from the Diaries of Lord Moran*. Boston: Houghton Mifflin, 1966.

Myers, Hugh H. *Prisoner of War, World War II*. Metropolitan Press.

Naeve, Virginia, ed. *Friends of the Hibakusha*. Denver, Colo.: Swallow, 1964.

Nakasone, Seizen. *Tragedy of Okinawa*. Tokyo: Kacho Shobo, 1951.

Neumann, William L. *America Encounters Japan: From Perry to MacArthur*. Baltimore: The Johns Hopkins Press, 1963.

Newcomb, Richard F. *Abandon Ship!* New York: Holt, 1958.

————. *Iwo Jima*. New York: Holt, 1965.

————. *Savo*. New York: Rinehart, 1961.

Nishino, Gen. *Isle of Death: Guadalcanal*. Tokyo: Masu Shobo, 1956.

Nomura, Jiro. *Sea of Lamentation*. Tokyo: Yomiuri Shimbun, 1967.

Ogata, Sadako N. *Defiance in Manchuria*. Berkeley: University of California Press, 1964.

Okumiya, Masatake, and Jiro Horikoshi, with Martin Caidin. *Zero*. New York: Dutton, 1956.

Okuyama, Ryoko. *Left Alive on Saipan, the Island of Suicide*. Tokyo: Hara Shobo, 1967.

Omura, Bunji. *The Last Genro*. Philadelphia: Lippincott, 1938.

Pacific War Research Society. *Japan's Longest Day*. Tokyo and Palo Alto, Calif.: Kodansha International, 1968.

Peffer, Nathaniel. *The Far East*. Ann Arbor: University of Michigan Press, 1958.

Pogue, Forrest C. *George C. Marshall: Ordeal and Hope*. New York: Viking, 1966.

Potter, E. B., and Chester W. Nimitz, eds. *The Great Sea War*. Englewood Cliffs, N.J.: Prentice-Hall, 1960.

Prange, Gordon. *Tora, Tora, Tora*. Tokyo: Reader's Digest of Japan, 1966.

Rappaport, Armin. *Henry L. Simpson and Japan, 1931–1933*. University of Chicago Press, 1963.

Reischauer, Edwin O. *Japan Past and Present*. Rev. ed. New York: Knopf, 1964.

Romulo, Carlos. *I Saw the Fall of the Philippines*. New York: Doubleday, Doran, 1943.

Roosevelt, Eleanor. *This I Remember*. New York: Harper, 1949.

Roosevelt, Elliott. *As He Saw It*. New York: Duell, Sloan & Pearce, 1946.

Roosevelt, Franklin D. *Papers*. Franklin D. Roosevelt Library, Hyde Park, N.Y.

Saito, Dr. Yoshie. *Deceived History: An Inside Account of Matsuoka and in the Tripartite Pact*. Tokyo: Yomiuri Shimbun, 1955.

Sakai, Saburo, with Martin Caidin and Fred Saito. *Samurai!* New York: Dutton, 1957.

Sakomizu, Hisatsune. *The Prime Minister's Official Residence under Machine-Gun Fire*. Tokyo: Kobun Sha, 1965.

Sansom, G.B. *The Western World and Japan*. New York: Knopf, 1951.

Sato, Kenryo. *The Greater East Asia War Memoirs*. Tokyo: Tokuma Shoten, 1966.

Sato, Naotake. *My Eighty Years Reminiscences*. Tokyo: Jiji Press, 1964.

Schroeder, Paul W. *The Axis Alliance and Japanese-American Relations, 1941*. Ithaca: Cornell University Press, 1958.

Seward, Jack. *Hara-kiri*. Rutland, Vt., and Tokyo: Tuttle, 1968.

Sherman, Frederick C. *Combat Command*. New York: Dutton, 1950.

Sherrod, Robert. *Tarawa*. New York: Duell, Sloan & Pearce, 1944.

Sherwood, Robert E. *Roosevelt and Hopkins*. New York: Harper, 1948.

Shigemitsu, Mamoru. *Japan and Her Destiny*. New York: Dutton, 1958.

Shimomura, Kainan. *Notes on the Termination of the War*. Tokyo: Kamakura Bunko, 1948.

Shirer, William L. *The Rise and Fall of the Third Reich*. New York: Simon & Schuster, 1960.

Slim, William J. *Defeat into Victory*. New York: McKay, 1961.

Smith, S. E., compiler & ed. *The United States Marine Corps in World War II*. New York: Random House, 1969.

———. compiler & ed. *The United States Navy in World War II*. New York: Morrow, 1966.

Snell, John L., ed. *The Meaning of Yalta*. Baton Rouge: Louisiana State University Press, 1956.

Snow, Edgar. *Red Star over China*. New York: Random House, 1938.

Stafford, Edward P. *The Big E*. New York: Random House, 1962.

Stimson, Henry L. *The Diary of Henry L. Stimson* and *The Papers of Henry L. Stimson*. New Haven: Yale University Library.

———, and McGeorge Bundy. *On Active Service in Peace and War*. New York: Harper, 1947.

Storry, Richard. *The Double Patriots*. Boston: Houghton Mifflin, 1957.

Sugano, Shizuko. *The End at Saipan*. Tokyo: Shuppan Kyodo Sha, 1959.

Sugiyama, Gen. *Notes of Field Marshal Sugiyama*. Compiled by the Army General Staff. Tokyo: Hara Shobo, 1967.

The Biography of Kantaro Suzuki. Compilation Committee for the Biography of Kantaro Suzuki. Tokyo: Privately printed, 1960.

Suzuki, Takeshi. *Sun over the Raging Seas*. Compilation Committee of Confidential Documents concerning Prime Minister Suzuki. Tokyo: Privately printed, 1960.

Takagi, Sokichi. *History of Naval Battles in the Pacific*. Tokyo: Iwanami Shoten, 1949.

————. *Memoir of the Termination of the War*. Tokyo: Kobundo, 1948.

Takahashi, H. *A History of the Minami Organization*. Unpublished.

Takahashi, Masaye. *The 2/26 Incident*. Tokyo: Chuo Koron Sha, 1965.

Takami, Jun. *Diary of Jun Takami*. Tokyo: Keiso Shobo, 1964.

Takeshita, Masahiko. Diary of Lieutenant Colonel Masahiko Takeshita. Unpublished.

Taleja, Thaddeus. *Climax at Midway*. New York: Norton, 1960.

Tanemura, Sako. *Secret Diary of Imperial Headquarters*. Tokyo: Diamond Sha, 1952.

Tansill, Charles Callan. *Back Door to War*. Chicago: Regnery, 1952.

Tarling, Nicholas. *Southeast Asia, Past and Present*. Melbourne: Cheshire, 1966.

Taylor, Theodore. *The Magnificent Mitscher*. New York: Norton, 1960.

Terasaki, Gwen. *Bridge to the Sun*. Chapel Hill: University of North Carolina Press, 1957.

Terasaki, Ryuji. *Navy Spirit: Life of Commander Jisaburo Ozawa*. Tokyo: Tokuma Shoten, 1967.

Togo, Shigenori. *The Cause of Japan*. New York: Simon & Schuster, 1956.

Toland, John. *But Not in Shame*. New York: Random House, 1961.

————. *The Flying Tigers*. New York: Random House, 1963.

————. *The Last 100 Days*. New York: Random House, 1966.

Tolischus, Otto D. *Tokyo Record*. New York: Reynal & Hitchcock, 1943.

Tomioka, Sadatoshi. *The Outbreak and Termination of the War*. Tokyo: Mainichi Shimbun, 1968.

Trefousse, Hans Louis. *What Happened at Pearl Harbor?* New York: Twayne, 1958.

Tregaskis, Richard. *Guadalcanal Diary*. New York: Random House, 1943.

Truman, Harry S. *Memoirs*, Vol. I, *Years of Decisions*. Garden City, N.Y.: Doubleday, 1955.

Tsuji, Masanobu. *Guadalcanal*. Tamba-shi, Nara: Yotoku Sha, 1950.

————. *Singapore: The Japanese Version*. New York: St. Martin's, 1960.

Ueda, Toshio, ed. *Treatise on the Termination of the Pacific War*. Compiled by Japan Diplomatic Association. Tokyo: Tokyo University Press, 1958.

Ugaki, Matome. *Record of Sea Battles: Diary of the Late Vice Admiral Matome Ugaki*. 2 vols. Compiled by Rear Admirals Kanji Ogawa and Toshiyuki Yokoi. Tokyo: Nippon Shuppan Kyodo, 1952-1953.

Ulam, Adam B. *Expansion and Coexistence*. New York: Praeger, 1968.

United States Marine Corps Combat Correspondents. *Semper fidelis: The U.S. Marines in the Pacific, 1942–1945*. Edited and arranged by Patrick O'Sheel and Gene Cook. New York: Sloane, 1947.

Uno, Kazumaro. *Corregidor: Isle of Delusion*. Privately printed.

Vandegrift, A. A. *Once a Marine: The Memoirs of General A. A. Vandegrift*. As told to Robert A. Asprey. New York: Norton, 1964.

Van Slyke, Lyman P., ed. *The Chinese Communist Movement: A Report of the United States War Department, July 1945*. Stanford University Press, 1968.

Wainwright, Johathan. *General Wainwright's Story*. Garden City, N.Y.: Doubleday, 1946.

Weller, George A. *Singapore Is Silent*. New York: Harcourt, 1943.

Werth, Alexander. *Russia at War, 1941–1945*. New York: Dutton, 1964.

White, Theodore H., and Annalee Jacoby. *Thunder out of China*. New York: Sloane, 1946.

White, W. L. *They Were Expendable*. Boston: Little, Brown, 1942.

Whitney, Courtney. *MacArthur: His Rendezvous with History*. New York: Knopf, 1956.

Willoughby, Charles A. *Shanghai Conspiracy*. New York: Dutton, 1952.

Wohlstetter, Roberta. *Pearl Harbor: Warning and Decision*. Stanford University Press, 1962.

Yabe, Teiji. *Fumimaro Konoye*. 2 vols. Compilation-Publication Society of the Biography of Fumimaro Konoye. Tokyo: Privately printed, 1951-1952.

Yamamoto, Kumaichi. *Memoirs of the Greater East Asia War*. Manuscripts left by the late Kumaichi Yamamoto. Japan: Privately printed, 1964.

Yamamoto, Tomomi. *Four Years in Hell*. Japan: Asian Publications, 1952.

Yanaga, Chitoshi. *Japanese People and Politics*. New York: Wiley, 1956.

Yokota, Yutaka, with Joseph D. Harrington. *The Kaiten Weapon.* New York: Ballantine, 1962.

Yoshida, Shigeru. *The Yoshida Memoirs.* Boston: Houghton Mifflin, 1962.

Young, Arthur N. *China and the Helping Hand 1937–1945.* Cambridge: Harvard University Press, 1963.

Notes

The main sources for each chapter are listed below with explanatory details. The books which proved of overall value, and which will not be referred to again, are: *Record of Sea Battles: Diary of the Late Vice Admiral Matome Ugaki*, compiled by Rear Admirals Kanji Ogawa and Toshiyuki Yokoi; *Outbreak and Termination of the War*, by Sadatoshi Tomioka; *Japan and Her Destiny*, by Mamoru Shigemitsu; *Roosevelt and Hopkins*, by Robert E. Sherwood; *A Collection of War Memoirs and Notes*, compiled by the Japanese Foreign Ministry; *The Combined Fleet: Memoirs of Former Chief of Staff Kusaka*, by Admiral Ryunosuke Kusaka; *Secret Diary of Imperial Headquarters*, by Colonel Sako Tanemura; *The Complete History of the Greater Asia War*, by Colonel Takushiro Hattori; *Greater East Asia War Memoirs*, by General Kenryo Sato; *Japanalia: A Concise Cyclopedia*, by Lewis Bush; *Things Japanese*, by Mock Joya; *The Sugiyama Notes*, compiled by the Army General Staff; and *The Diary of Koichi Kido*. The last book is the unexpurgated edition of the diary and runs from January 1, 1930, through December 15, 1945; it was published in 1966 along with *Relevant Documents of Koichi Kido*. An English translation of the diary is being prepared by Robert J. C. Butow and will be invaluable to historians and students of the Pacific war. The version of *The Kido Diary* used at the International Military Tribunal for the Far East (hereafter referred to as IMTFE) was not only incomplete but inaccurately translated.

1. Gekokujo

The events leading up to the 2/26 Incident are based on interviews with Naoki Hoshino, Yoshio Kodama, Generals Teiichi Suzuki, Kenryo Sato, Sadao Araki and Akio Doi, and the following books: *Defiance in Manchuria*, by Sadako N. Ogata; *After Imperialism* and *Across the Pacific*, by Akira Iriye; *From the Marco Polo Bridge to Pearl Harbor*, by David J. Lu; *Japan in China*, by T. A. Bisson; *I Was Defeated*, by Yoshio Kodama; *Government by Assassination*, by Hugh Byas; *Japan over Asia*, by William Henry Chamberlin; and *The Double Patriots*, by Richard Storry.

The 2/26 Incident: interviews with Hisatsune Sakomizu, Marquis Koichi Kido, Generals Tadashi Katakura,* Sadao Araki, Kenryo Sato and Shozaburo Sato; correspondence with William Henry Chamberlin; "Witness to the 2/26 Assassination," by Y. Arima in the *Weekly Shincho* magazine; *The Prime Minister's Official Residence under Machine-Gun Fire,* by Hisatsune Sakomizu; *The Biography of Kantaro Suzuki;* BYAS; STORRY; CHAMBERLIN; *The Last Genro,* by Bunji Omura; *The 2/26 Incident,* by Masaye Takahashi; and secret report, "An Account of Major Katakura's Accident in the 2/26 Incident," by General Tadashi Katakura.

Information on the Emperor comes from interviews with his youngest brother (Prince Mikasa); Marquis Kido; Junji Togashi; Chamberlains Sukemasa Irie, Yoshihiro Tokugawa and Yasuhide Toda; and Osanaga Kanroji, one of His Majesty's instructors and currently High Priest of the Meiji Shrine.

Material on Sorge is based on an interview with Tomohiko Ushiba; *Shanghai Conspiracy,* by Charles A. Willoughby; and *The Case of Richard Sorge,* by F. W. Deakin and G. R. Storry.

2. To the Marco Polo Bridge

Interviews with Arashi Kamimura, Yukio Nakamura, Generals Sadao Araki, Akio Doi, Kenryo Sato, Teiichi Suzuki, Ho Yingchin and Takeo Imai; articles in the April 15, 1952, issue of *The Reporter* by Charles Wertenbaker and in the May 1963 issue of the *Journal of Asian Studies* by James B. Crowley; IMTFE, *Dissenting Judgement* (Justice R. A. Pal); OGATA; *Red Star over China,* by Edgar Snow; CHAMBERLIN, *Soviet Russia in China,* by Chiang Kai-shek; *The Birth of Communist China,* by C. P. Fitzgerald; *Chou En-lai,* by Hsu Kai-yu; *The Chinese Communist Movement: A Report of the U. S. War Department, July 1945,* edited by Lyman P. Van Slyke; KODAMA; *Lost Peace in China,* by George Moorad; BISSON; *Japan's Quest for Autonomy,* by James B. Crowley; and *A Short History of the U.S.S.R.,* Part II, compiled by the Academy of Sciences of the U.S.S.R., Institute of History.

Eight books were used throughout Chapters 2 to 7: *With Japan's Leaders,* by Frederick Moore; *American Ambassador,* by Waldo H. Heinrichs, Jr.; *The Road to Pearl Harbor,* by Herbert Feis; LU; *Turbulent Era* and *Ten Years in Japan,* by Joseph C. Grew; and *Tojo and the Coming of the War,* by Robert J. C. Butow, an accurate and objective study of the events leading to Pearl Harbor based primarily on Japanese sources.

Both Chinese Communist and Kuomintang sources put the date of the signing of the Communist-Kuomintang agreement at July 15, 1937, but the Central Chinese Communist Party of Inner

---

*Throughout the Notes, the highest military rank attained will be given; Major Katakura, for example, became a general. Enlisted ranks are omitted.

Mongolia announced several years ago that the original document had been found in Mongolia and was dated July 5.

3. "Then the War Will Be a Desperate One"

Early relations between Japan and the United States: cited material; and *America Encounters Japan: From Perry to MacArthur*, by William L. Neumann.

Differences between East and West: unpublished articles by Dr. Kazutaka Watanabe.

Matsuoka: interviews with Kenichiro Matsuoka, Kiwamu Ogiwara, Toshikazu Kase, Shunzo Kobayashi and General Yatsuji Nagai; *Yosuke Matsuoka*, by T. Furukaki; *Deceived History: An Inside Account of Matsuoka and the Tripartite Pact*, by Dr. Yoshie Saito.

Iwakuro mission: interviews with Major General Hideo Iwakuro; "Fight for Peace," by General Iwakuro, in the August 1966 issue of *Bungei-Shunju;* "Taking Part in the Japan–U. S. Negotiations," a pamphlet by General Iwakuro; and *The Broken Seal*, by Ladislas Farago.

Negotiations between Japan and the United States (which extend to Chapters 4, 5 and 7): interviews with Eugene Dooman; Generals Hiroshi Oshima, Kenryo Sato and Teiichi Suzuki; Michitaka Konoye; Tomohiko Ushiba; Zenjun Hirose; Colonel Susumu Nishiura; Naoki Hoshino; and Marquis Kido; "Germany and Pearl Harbor," by Hans Louis Trefousse, in the *Far Eastern Quarterly;* *Fumimaro Konoye*, by Teiji Yabe; the Konoye Family Book (privately printed); *My Efforts Towards Peace*, by Fumimaro Konoye; *Memoirs of the Greater East Asia War*, by Kumaichi Yamamoto; *The War Diary of a Member of the Royal Family*, by Prince Higashikuni; *The Axis Alliance and Japanese-American Relations, 1941*, by Paul W. Schroeder; *The Diary of Joseph C. Grew* and the Grew Papers (courtesy of the Houghton Library, Harvard University); *The Diary of Henry L. Stimson* and the Stimson Papers (courtesy of the Yale University Library); *Peace and War: United States Foreign Policy 1931–1941*, compiled by U. S. Department of State; *The Undeclared War*, by William L. Langer and S. Everett Gleason; *Foreign Relations of the United States* (hereafter referred to as FRUS), *1940*, Vol. IV, *The Far East*; FRUS, *1941*, Vol. IV, *The Far East*; FRUS, *Japan 1931–1941*, Vols. I and II; *The Memoirs of Cordell Hull*, Vol. II; *On Active Service in Peace and War*, by Henry L. Stimson and McGeorge Bundy; *The Cause of Japan*, by Shigenori Togo; *President Roosevelt and the Coming of War*, by Charles A. Beard; *Back Door to War*, by Charles Callan Tansill; NEUMANN; *From the Diaries of Henry Morgenthau, Jr.*, Vol. II, *Years of Urgency 1938-1941*, by John Morton Blum; *Japanese People and Politics*, by Chitoshi Yanaga; *Prelude to Downfall: Hitler and the United States 1939–1941*, by Saul Friedlander; and IMTFE . . . JUSTICE R. A. PAL.

The dialogue in the liaison and imperial conferences was reconstructed from recollections of those attending and on detailed official notes found in the War History Office Archives of the Japan Defense Agency by a group of scholars headed by Dr. Jun Tsunoda of the National Diet Library. These notes were published as a supplementary volume to the *Asahi Shimbun's* seven-volume work *The Road to the Pacific War*. The records of sixty-two of these conferences, held between March and December in 1941, were translated into English by Nobutaka Ike, professor of political science at Stanford University, and published under the title *Japan's Decision for War*.

4. "Go Back to Blank Paper"

See Notes for Chapter 3. Material also based on interviews with Eugene Dooman; Tomohiko Ushiba; Okinori Kaya; Admiral Kichisaburo Nomura; Marquis Kido; Naoki Hoshino; Generals Hideo Iwakuro, Kenryo Sato and Teiichi Suzuki; Shigeharu Matsumoto; Yoshio Kodama; Mrs. Hideki Tojo; and Prince Konoye's mistress; the Papers of President Roosevelt, at the Franklin D. Roosevelt Library, Hyde Park; "The Hull-Nomura Conversations: A Fundamental Misconception," by Robert J. C. Butow, in the *American Historical Review* (July 1960); KODAMA; *Kishi and Japan*, by Dan Kurzman; and *Tokyo Record*, by Otto D. Tolischus.

The cable from Ambassador Grew to Secretary of State Hull on September 29, 1941, is a paraphrase by the State Department of the original text.

5. The Fatal Note

See Notes for Chapter 3. There were also interviews with Marquis Kido; Tomohiko Ushiba; Naoki Hoshino; Okinori Kaya; Mrs. Saburo Kurusu; Admiral Kichisaburo Nomura; Generals Kenryo Sato, Hiroshi Oshima and Teiichi Suzuki; and Ambassador Haruhiko Nishi, who brought to my attention the errors made in the American translations of Japanese diplomatic messages. The footnote on page 163 is based on "How Stimson Meant to 'Maneuver' the Japanese," by Richard N. Current, in the *Mississippi Historical Review* (June 1953).

6. Operation Z

Interviews with Admirals Ryunosuke Kusaka, Shigeru Fukudome and Sadatoshi Tomioka; Captains Naohiro Sata, Yasuji Watanabe, Tsunezo Wachi, Kazunari Miyo, Atsushi Oi and Eijiro Suzuki; Commanders Heijiro Abe, Yoshio Shiga and Suguru Suzuki; Lieutenant Juzo Mori; Ensign Takeo Yoshikawa; Mitsuharu Noda, Heijiro Omi, Yoshio Kodama, Sayao Otsuka; Mrs. Chiyo Iwamiya; Generals Kenryo Sato, Minoru Genda; and Admiral Sadamu Sanagi; Colonels Kumao Imoto and Takushiro Hattori; Lieutenant Colonel Shigeharu Asaeda; letter from Carl S. Sipple to Walter Lord (February 28, 1957); "The Combined Fleet and My Memoirs of the Navy," a magazine article by Heijiro Omi; "The Inside Story of the Pearl Harbor Plan," by Robert E. Ward, in *U. S. Naval Institute Proceedings*—hereafter referred to as USNIP (December 1951); "Combined Fleet Secret Operations Order No. 1"; *Tora, Tora, Tora,* by Gorden Prange (published in Japan in 1966); *The Great Pacific War,* by Hector C. Bywater; *Isoroku Yamamoto,* by Hiroyuki Agawa; *Get Yamamoto,* by Burke Davis; *Day of Infamy,* by Walter Lord; *The End of the Imperial Japanese Navy,* by Masanori Ito; *The Emperor's Sword,* by Noel F. Busch; FARAGO; *Singapore: The Japanese Version,* by Masanobu Tsuji; *History of United States Naval Operations in World War II,* Vol. III, *The Rising Sun in the Pacific,* by Samuel Eliot Morison; *The Fall of the Philippines,* by Louis Morton; DEAKIN & STORRY; and WILLOUGHBY.

7. "This War May Come Quicker Than Anyone Dreams"

See Notes for Chapter 3. There were also interviews with Admirals Ryunosuke Kusaka, Keizo Komura, Kazutoshi Kuhara, Sadatoshi Tomioka, Kichisaburo Nomura, Gunichi Mikawa and Harold Stark; Captains Yasuji Watanabe, Naohiro Sata and Kazunari Miyo; Commanders Yoshio Shiga, Hirata Matsumura, Saguru Suzuki, Heijiro Abe; Lieutenant Juzo Mori; Ensign Takeo Yoshikawa; Heijiro Omi, Mitsuharu Noda; Generals Minoru Genda, Kenryo Sato, Teiichi Suzuki and Hiroshi Oshima; Colonel Kumao Imoto; Lieutenant Colonel Shigeharu Asaeda; Frank Trammell; George Elliott, Jr.; Ambassador Haruhiko Nishi; Ikuko Kimura; Fumihiko Togo; Mrs. Saburo Kurusu; the late Bernard Baruch; Mrs. Yoshiko Kugiya; Marquis Kido; Naoki Hoshino; Okinori Kaya; United States Strategic Bombing Survey (hereafter referred to as USSBS) Navy interrogation #29 (Captain M. Fuchida); "Political Survey Prior to Outbreak of War," a report by Admiral Sadatoshi Tomioka; IMTFE documents #1079 (Kazuji Kameyama) and #2597 (Tateki Shirao); an interview with Vice Admiral Frank E. Beatty in the *National Review* (December 13, 1966); *The Lost War,* by Masuo Kato; *A Song of Ascents,* by E. Stanley Jones; PRANGE; *Bridge to the Sun,* by Gwen Terasaki; FARAGO; LORD; TOLISCHUS; ITO; *The War against Japan,* Vol. I, by Major-General S. Woodburn Kirby; *Grand Strategy,* Vol. III, Part I, by J. M. A. Gwyer and J. R. M. Butler *Chief of Staff Prewar Plans and Preparations,* by Mark S. Watson; MORTON; MORISON, *The Rising Sun; What Happened at Pearl Harbor?,* by Hans Louis Trefousse; *Pearl Harbor: Warning and Decision,* by Roberta Wohlstetter; TSUJI; *Sunk,* by Mochitsura Hashimoto; *The Puzzle of Pearl Harbor,* by Paul S. Burtness and Warren U. Ober; and *But Not in Shame,* by John Toland. The last book was also used throughout Chapters 8 to 13.

The rare conversation between Grand Chamberlain Fujita and the Emperor appears in *Sun over the Raging Seas,* the Suzuki Family Book, which was privately printed in 1969. Chamberlain

Fujita revealed this information because he felt he would soon die and wanted it recorded for posterity.

8. "I Shall Never Look Back"

Interviews with Admirals Chester Nimitz, C. C. Bloch, Ernest Holtzworth, W. W. Smith, Harold Stark, Kichisaburo Nomura, Keizo Komura, Gunichi Mikawa, Ryunosuke Kusaka and Sadatoshi Tomioka; Captains Yasuji Watanabe, Eijiro Suzuki, Kazunari Miyo and Naohiro Sata; Commanders Heijiro Abe, Hirata Matsumura and Yoshio Shiga; Lieutenant Juzo Mori; Ensigns Takeo Yoshikawa and Kazuo Sakamaki; Generals Minoru Genda, Joseph H. Moore and Richard Carmichael; Colonels Susumu Nishiura, Takushiro Hattori, William Morse and William Welch; Lieutenant Colonel Shigeharu Asaeda; and Major Durward Brooks; Lieutenant Robert Overstreet; Heijiro Omi; Mitsuharu Noda; Jesse Gaines; C. O. Lines; Donald Briggs; Dwaine Davis; Baron Ian Mutsu; Marquis Kido; Robert Trumbull; Okinori Kaya; Morio Tateno; Yates McDaniel. Also USSBS Navy interrogations #6 and #29 (Captain M. Fuchida); memorandum by Ferdinand Mayor on his conversation with Kurusu on December 7, 1941; "Records of the Meeting of the Inquiry Committee of the Privy Council, December 8, 1941"; article on Pearl Harbor by Robert Trumbull in the *New York Times Magazine* (December 4, 1966); PRANGE; LORD; KATO; TSUJI; *Way of a Fighter.* by Claire Lee Chennault; *The Flying Tigers,* by John Toland; *The Second World War,* Vol. III, *The Grand Alliance,* by Winston Churchill; MORISON, *The Rising Sun*; WOHLSTETTER; TREFOUSSE; *Ciano's Diaries*; MORTON; *This I Remember,* by Eleanor Roosevelt; *As He Saw It,* by Elliott Roosevelt; *They Fought with What They Had,* by Walter D. Edmonds; and BURTNESS & OBER.

9. "The Formidable Years That Lie Before Us"

Interviews with President Sergio Osmeña; Generals Hiroshi Oshima, James Devereux and Carlos Romulo; Admirals Chester Nimitz and Ryunosuke Kusaka; Captains Tsunezo Wachi and Masamichi Fujita; Commanders Katsusaku Takahashi and Choichi Koyama; Lieutenants Haruki Iki and Sadao Takai; and Carl Mydans; "Japanese Victory: The Sinking of Force Z," by David Mason, in *History of the Second World War* magazine, Vol. II, No. 13; IMTFE document #4002 (General Oshima); *The Turn of the Tide,* by Arthur Bryant; *From Suez to Singapore,* by Cecil Browne; GWYER & BUTLER; KIRBY; *Samurai,* by Saburo Sakai; *The Memoirs of Anthony Eden,* Vol. III, *The Reckoning; The Rise and Fall of the Third Reich,* by William L. Shirer; CHURCHILL; *Churchill: Taken from the Diaries of Lord Moran; Strategic Planning for Coalition Warfare: 1941–1942,* by Maurice Matloff and Edwin M. Snell; and *So Sorry, No Peace,* by Arch Gunnison.

10. "For a Wasted Hope and Sure Defeat"

Interviews with Carl Mydans; Generals Akira Nara, Takeo Imai and Ichiji Sugita; Colonels Kumao Imoto and Susumu Nishiura; Antonio Aquino, President Sergio Osmeña; Lieutenant Colonel Shigeharu Asaeda; Admirals Sadatoshi Tomioka and T. H. Binford; Captains Ko Nagasawa and Kazunari Miyo; Commander Shukichi Toshikawa; correspondence with Admiral C. E. L. Helfrich; "Operations of Malaya Campaign, from 8th December, 1941, to 15th February, 1942," official report by Lieutenant-General A. E. Percival; "Japanese Victory: The Conquest of Malaya," by Arthur Swinson, in *History of the Second World War* magazine, Vol. VI, No. 11; "Malayan Campaign," a report by Shigeharu Asaeda; "Statement on the Malayan Campaign," by General Tomoyuki Yamashita at his trial in Manila; *Battle Report: Pearl Harbor to Coral Sea*, by Walter Karig, and others; *The Rise and Fall of the Japanese Empire*, by David H. James; *Fortress*, by Kenneth Attiwell; *Singapore Is Silent*, by George Weller; CHURCHILL, Vol. IV, *The Hinge of Fate*; *Why Singapore Fell*, by H. G. Bennett; TSUJI; KIRBY; *The Japanese Thrust*, by Lionel Wigmore; *George C. Marshall: Ordeal and Hope*, by Forrest C. Pogue; MORISON, *The Rising Sun*; MORTON; *Doolittle's Tokyo Raiders*, by Carroll V. Glines; and *MacArthur and the War Against Japan*, by Frazier Hunt.

Stories filed by Japanese reporters praising Colonel Takechi for his crossing of Mount Natib were approved by General Nara. He never revealed the facts—not until 1960, and then, he told me, "only because I went to Amherst and you went to Williams."

11. "To Show Them Mercy Is to Prolong the War"

Interviews with Generals Albert M. Jones, Clifford Bluemel, Takeo Imai, Akira Nara and Carlos Romulo; Colonels Susumu Nishiura, Takushiro Hattori, Kumao Imoto and Nobuhiko Jimbo; Antonio Aquino; Roy Castleberry and numerous survivors of the Bataan Death March; correspondence with Captain John Bulkeley and Mark Wohlfeld; "A Strange Order Received at the Bataan Battle Front," an unpublished article by Lieutenant General Takeo Imai; "Dawn of the Philippines," privately printed pamphlet by Nobuhiko Jimbo; "Bataan Death March," doctoral thesis of Stanley Lawrence Falk; the Homma Diary (unpublished); documents for the defense at General Homma's trial; MORTON; *I Saw the Fall of the Philippines*, by Carlos Romulo; *MacArthur: His Rendezvous with History*, by Courtney Whitney; *They Were Expendable*, by W. L. White; *The Dyess Story*, by William Dyess; and *General Wainwright's Story*, by Jonathan M. Wainwright.

12. "But Not in Shame"

Interviews with General Takaji Wachi; Colonels Jesse T. Traywick, Jr., Nobuhiko Jimbo, Susumu Nishiura and Takushiro Hattori; Admiral Sadatoshi Tomioka; Captains Yasuji Watanabe and Kazunari Miyo; Lieutenant Hisamichi Kano; John H. Skeen, Jr.;

Gen Nishino and Heijiro Omi; THE HOMMA DIARY; the Homma documents; "Corregidor—A Name, A Symbol, A Tradition," by Colonel William C. Braly, in the *Coast Artillery Journal* (July-August 1947); POGUE; *Corregidor: Isle of Delusion*, by Kazumaro Uno; *Corregidor: The Saga of a Fortress*, by James H. and William M. Belote; WAINWRIGHT; and HUNT.

In *But Not in Shame* I concluded that the atrocities committed on the Death March had not been "purposefully planned and executed." Colonel Ray O'Day, one of the survivors of the march, took issue with me after publication of the book and put me in touch with Colonel Nobuhiko Jimbo. With new information from Colonel Jimbo and Gen Nishino I approached commanders on Bataan such as General Imai and received corroboration of Colonel O'Day's charges.

13. The Tide Turns

Interviews with Admirals Ryunosuke Kusaka, Frank Jack Fletcher, Chester Nimitz, Raymond Spruance, Keizo Komura, Sadatoshi Tomioka; Captains Ko Nagasawa, Kazunari Miyo, Yasuji Watanabe; Commanders Yahachi Tanabe, Heijiro Abe and Yoshio Shiga; Lieutenant Wilmer Earl Gallaher; Ensign Kazuo Sakamaki; General Minoru Genda; Colonels Susumu Nishiura and Takushiro Hattori; Mitsuharu Noda and Heijiro Omi; USSBS Navy interrogations #39 (Captain H. Ohara), #4 (Captain Taijiro Aoki) and #1 (Captain Takahisa Amagai); "I Sank the *Yorktown* at Midway," by Yahachi Tanabe, with Joseph D. Harrington, in USNIP (May 1963); "Never a Battle Like Midway," by J. Bryan III in the *Saturday Evening Post* (March 26, 1949); "Torpedo Squadron 8," in *Life* (August 31, 1942); *Incredible Victory*, by Walter Lord; *Admiral Raymond A. Spruance, USN: A Study in Command*, by Vice Admiral E. P. Forrestal; *Climax at Midway*, by Thaddeus Taleja; *Midway—The Battle That Doomed Japan*, by Mitsuo Fuchida and Masatake Okumiya; ITO; *Combat Command*, by Admiral Frederick C. Sherman; *Queen of the Flat-Tops*, by Stanley Johnston; MORISON, Vol. IV, *Coral Sea, Midway and Submarine Actions*; and *The Code-Breakers*, by David Kahn.

In my version of the Battle of Midway in *But Not in Shame*, Gallaher and McClusky attack *Akagi*, while Best attacks *Soryu* and Leslie goes after *Kaga*. This account was based on interviews and after-action reports, but since then Walter Lord, while researching *Incredible Victory*, became convinced that the American fliers, who had only fragmentary information about the Japanese carriers, were mistaken. Mr. Lord's conclusions, I believe, are correct. Incidentally, Mr. Lord and I interviewed several naval men in Japan simultaneously in 1966 and later exchanged notes.

14. Operation Shoestring

Interviews with Admirals Gunichi Mikawa and Sadatoshi Tomioka; Commander Haruki Itoh; General Haruo Konuma; Colonel Kumao Imoto; Haruyoshi Saima; Brian Hackman; J. C.

Glover; and Gen Nishino; "A Brief History of Geological and Geophysical Investigations in the British Solomon Islands 1881-1961," a report by J. C. Glover; *Guadalcanal Diary*, by Richard Tregaskis; *The Coast Watchers*, by Eric A. Feldt; SAKAI; and POGUE.

The following books were used throughout Chapters 14 to 17: *Isle of Death: Guadalcanal*, by Gen Nishino; *The Guadalcanal Campaign*, by Major John L. Zimmerman, USMCR; *Pearl Harbor to Guadalcanal*, by Lieutenant Colonel Frank O. Hough, USMCR, Major Verle E. Ludwig, USMC, and Henry I. Shaw, Jr.; *The Great Sea War*, edited by E. B. Potter and Fleet Admiral Chester W. Nimitz; *Semper Fidelis*, by Marine Corps combat correspondents (hereafter referred to as SEMPER FIDELIS); *1942: The Year that Doomed the Axis*, by Henry H. Adams; MORISON, Vol. V, *The Struggle for Guadalcanal*; *Guadalcanal: The First Offensive*, by John Miller, Jr.; *Savo*, by Richard F. Newcomb; *The Big E*, by Edward P. Stafford; *Once a Marine: The Memoirs of General A. A. Vandegrift, U.S.M.C.*, as told to Robert B. Asprey; *Challenge for the Pacific*, by Robert Leckie; *The Army Air Forces in World War II*, Vol. IV, *The Pacific: Guadalcanal to Saipan*, edited by Wesley F. Craven and James L. Cate; ITO; *The United States Navy in World War II* and *The United States Marine Corps in World War II*, compiled and edited by S. E. Smith.

15. Green Hell

See Notes for Chapter 14. Additional sources were interviews with General Haruo Konuma and Gen Nishino; "Guadalcanal," by Koji Mori, in the *Mainichi* (August 5, 1967); *Guadalcanal*, by Masanobu Tsuji.

According to Brian Hackman, who recently mapped Guadalcanal for the British Solomon Islands Protectorate, two rivers near Henderson Field are spelled incorrectly by U. S. Army and Marine historians: "Matanikau" and "Lunga" should be Mataniko and Lungga.

The Japanese operation to retake Guadalcanal was called KA. Some Western historians have assumed this stood for "Guadalcanal," in the mistaken belief that it was the first syllable of the Japanese for "Guadalcanal." *Ka* is merely a letter in the Japanese alphabet.

16. "I Deserve Ten Thousand Deaths"

See Notes for Chapter 14. Also, interviews with Gen Nishino; Generals Haruo Konuma and Hitoshi Imamura; Admirals Keizo Komura, Ryunosuke Kusaka, Jinichi Kusaka, Sadatoshi Tomioka and Tomiji Koyanagi; Captains Ko Nagasawa, Toshikazu Ohmae and Masahide Yamamoto; and Commander Yoshio Shiga; USSBS Navy interrogation #16 (Commander Masatake Okumiya); "Japan's Losing Struggle for Guadalcanal," by Vice Admiral Raizo Tanaka, with the assistance of Roger Pineau, in USNIP

(August 1956); TSUJI, *Guadalcanal; The Cactus Air Force*, by Thomas G. Miller, Jr.; *Admiral Halsey's Story*, by Fleet Admiral William F. Halsey and J. Bryan III; *Marine! The Life of Lieutenant General Lewis B. (Chesty) Puller*, by Burke Davis.

17. The End

See Notes for Chapter 14. Also, interviews with Gen Nishino; Generals Kenryo Sato, Hitoshi Imamura, Chikuro Yamamoto, Haruo Konuma and Teiichi Suzuki; Colonels Kumao Imoto, Mitsuo Suginoo and Susumu Nishiura; Major Einosuke Iemura; and Captain Masahide Yamamoto; Admirals Tomiji Koyanagi and Sadatoshi Tomioka; Captain Yasuji Watanabe; Commander Haruki Itoh; and Tadashi Suzuki; USSBS Navy interrogation #33 (Lieutenant Commander Horishi Tokuno); "Miraculous Total Evacuation of Japanese Troops from Guadalcanal," unpublished article by Haruki Itoh; "The Retreat from Guadalcanal," a memorandum by Rear Admiral Tomiji Koyanagi; IMTFE documents #62081 and #55452 (Colonel Joichiro Sanada); TSUJI, *Guadalcanal; General Kenney Reports*, by George C. Kenney; and *Our Jungle Road to Tokyo*, by Robert L. Eichelberger.

To avoid standing trial as a war criminal, Colonel Tsuji went underground in Thailand, immediately after the surrender, disguised as a Buddhist priest. He made his way secretly to Japan and hid for thirty months with friends such as Yoshio Kodama. He surfaced when the tribunals ended, and in September 1952 was elected to the Diet from the first district in Ishikawa Prefecture. He was re-elected in 1956 but resigned three years later to run for the House of Councilors, to which he was elected. As he was taking his seat General Kawaguchi shouted at him, "Tsuji-*san*, you are not qualified to represent the people. Have shame!" Kawaguchi had been feuding with Tsuji ever since his emergence. "I can't bear to see a man of such complete immorality writing best sellers, riding high and becoming *nouveau riche*," he told Gen Nishino. "My patience is running out." The two antagonists finally had a face-to-face debate before a capacity audience at Town Hall in Kanazawa. Kawaguchi not only accused Tsuji of lying about the Guadalcanal campaign but charged him with atrocities against prisoners in Singapore and the Philippines. Tsuji denied the accusations but admitted he had erred in calling Kawaguchi a coward for leaving his troops on Guadalcanal; he had not known the facts when he made the charge.

In 1961 the Japanese government sent Tsuji to Southeast Asia to investigate the political and military situation. He arrived in Bangkok on April 4 and continued on to Laos where he vanished. Several months later it was reported that Tsuji had entered Red China, and in December the Japanese Red Cross requested the Red Chinese Red Cross to locate him. He never was found and his mysterious disappearance has resulted in numerous sensational rumors: he was working for the Communists; he was working against the Communists; he was in the Middle East; he was in

Japan incognito. Mrs. Chitose Tsuji believes her husband is dead, but Shigeharu Asaeda—who had accompanied him on numerous postwar trips to interview Nasser, Mao, Chou En-lai, and other Asian and Middle East leaders—reports there is a slight possibility that he is in a Red Chinese prison.

18. Of Mice and Men

Interviews with Generals Hitoshi Imamura, Hideo Iwakuro and Kenryo Sato; Admirals Jinichi Kusaka and Ryunosuke Kusaka; Captains Atsushi Oi and Yasuji Watanabe; Hachiro Takahasi; Major Yoshitaka Horie; and Yoshio Kodama; "Fragments from F.D.R.," by Edgar Snow, in *Monthly Review* (March 1957); "The Social Perception of Skin Color in Japan," by Hiroshi Wagatsuma, in *Daedalus* (Spring 1967); letter from Pearl Buck to Mrs. Roosevelt, December 12, 1941 (in the Franklin D. Roosevelt Library); "The Race Barrier That Must Be Destroyed," by Pearl Buck, in the *New York Times Magazine* (May 31, 1942); Elmer Davis letter (Franklin D. Roosevelt Library); "I Shot Down Yamamoto," by Colonel Thomas Lanphier, Jr., in *Reader's Digest* (January 1967); "Why Japan's Anti-Submarine Warfare Failed," by Captain Atsushi Oi, in USNIP (June 1952); *Guarding the United States and Its Outposts*, by Stetson Conn, Rose C. Engelman and Byron Fairchild; *Strategy and Command: The First Two Years*, by Louis Morton; *Strategic Planning for Coalition Warfare: 1943-1944*, by Maurice Matloff; *America's Concentration Camps*, by Allan R. Bosworth; *A History of the Minami Organization*, by Hachiro Takahashi; *Memoirs of an Interpreter*, by A. H. Birse; *I Was There*, by Fleet Admiral William D. Leahy; KENNEY; DAVIS, *Get Yamamoto; Fleet Admiral King*, by Ernest J. King and Walter Muir Whitehill; *The Thousand-Mile War: World War II in Alaska and the Aleutians*, by Brian W. Garfield; MORISON, Vol. VII, *Aleutians, Gilberts and Marshalls; Seizure of the Gilberts and Marshalls*, by Philip A. Crowl and Edmund G. Love; MORISON, Vol. VIII, *New Guinea and the Marianas; Global Mission*, by H. H. Arnold; HALSEY & BRYAN; KODAMA; *Southeast Asia, Past and Present*, by Nicholas Tarling; *Breakthrough in Burma*, by Ba Maw; EDEN; LORD MORAN; *The Memoirs of General Lord Ismay; Triumph in the West*, by Arthur Bryant; CHURCHILL, HINGE OF FATE, and Vol. V, *Closing the Ring*.

19. To the Marianas

Saipan: interviews with Shizuko (Miura) Sugano, Mitsuharu Noda, Mariano Sablan, Mañuel Sablan, Joe Sakisat, John Rich, Vicente Guerrero, Tony Benavente, Jose Pangelinan and Colonel Takashi Hirakushi; *The End at Saipan*, by Shizuko (Miura) Sugano; *Campaign in the Marianas*, by Philip A. Crowl; SMITH, *U. S. Marine Corps*; SEMPER FIDELIS; MORISON, *New Guinea and the Marianas*; and *Saipan: The Beginning of the End*, by Major Carl W. Hoffmann, USMC.

The Koga case: interviews with Jim Cushing, Admiral Shigeru

Fukudome, Colonel Fabian Sanchez, Major Jesus Ybanez, Captain Manuel Segura and Mrs. Yuji Yamamoto; "The Capture of Admiral Koga," a newspaper article by Gregorio M. Mercado; *Allied Intelligence Bureau*, by Colonel Allison Ind.

Miscellaneous: interviews with Generals Kenryo Sato and Eugen Ott; Admirals Jinichi Kusaka, Ryunosuke Kusaka and Sokichi Takagi; Major Yoshitaka Horie; Captain Tsunezo Wachi; Marquis Kido; Yoshio Kodama; and Hideo Edo; "The Failure of the Japanese Convoy Escort," by Yoshitaka Horie, in USNIP (October 1956); article by George Sansom in *International Affairs* (October 1948); MATLOFF; FORRESTAL; *Tarawa*, by Robert Sherrod; CROWL & LOVE; *History of Naval Battles in the Pacific*, by Admiral Sokichi Takagi; *Undersea Victory*, by W. J. Holmes; *Japan's Economy in War and Reconstruction*, by Jerome B. Cohen; and *The Diary of Fumimaro Konoye*. The last book is a secret diary kept by Prince Konoye from June 21, 1944, through July 24, 1944, while under surveillance by the *kempeitai*. He dictated the entries to his secretary, Fukumatsu Ueno, who kept the document (a thick university notebook) with him at all times because of its explosive contents—at the time, Prince Konoye was plotting to overthrow Tojo and end the war. While escaping from a fire bombing in Tokyo in April 1945, Uemo lost the diary and it was presumed to have burned. According to Konoye's mistress, the prince (who had once said that all diaries were useless) wept when he learned of the loss.

In October 1967 the notebook was found among the effects of a man who had just died; there was no connection between him and Ueno, or Prince Konoye. The handwriting was authenticated as Ueno's, and the diary was returned to the Konoye family; it is now at the Yomei Library in Kyoto. In 1968 the diary was published in Tokyo by Kyoto Press.

As the war progressed, Tojo became increasingly convinced that the independence of the Supreme Command was contributing to Japan's military reverses. After the war he told interrogators, "I am not saying that the independence of the Supreme Command is a bad thing. There are some good points about it too; for example, being able to conduct operations without political interference. It was a good thing in 1890, when the Constitution was established for the High Command to be untrammeled, but these days, when the influence of a single action is felt around the world, a certain amount of control by the political authority is necessary. However, under the Japanese system it was impossible."

20. "Seven Lives to Repay Our Country!"
Battle of the Philippine Sea: interviews with Admirals Sueo Obayashi and Ryunosuke Kusaka; Captains Toshikazu Ohmae and Shigeo Hirayama; and Mitsukuni Oshita; USSBS Navy interrogations #9 (Vice Admiral Takeo Kurita) and #3 (Vice Admiral

Jisaburo Ozawa); "The Shokakus," by Hajime Fukaya, in USNIP (June 1952); *The Magnificent Mitscher*, by Theodore Taylor; FORRESTAL; *Battles of the Philippine Sea*, by Charles A. Lockwood and Hans Christian Adamson; GARFIELD; KING & WHITEHILL; MORISON, *New Guinea and the Marianas*; and POTTER & NIMITZ.

Saipan: interviews with Shizuko (Miura) Sugano, Ryoko Okuyama, John Rich, Mitsuharu Noda and Colonel Takashi Hirakushi; "A Lone Survivor at Saipan—Isle of Death," by Ryoko Okuyama, in *Fujin Koron* (December 1966), and *Left Alive on Saipan, the Island of Suicide*, by the same author; SUGANO; CROWL; SEMPER FIDELIS; SMITH, *U. S. Marine Corps*; CRAVEN & CATE; HOFFMANN.

Miscellaneous: interview with Marquis Kido; THE KONOYE DIARY; and *Information Never Reached the Emperor*, by Morisada Hosokawa.

21. "Let No Heart Be Faint"

Leyte: interviews with President Sergio Osmeña; Generals Carlos Romulo and Yoshiharu Tomochika; Admiral Ryunosuke Kusaka; Lieutenant Colonel Shigeharu Asaeda; Eduardo Montilla, Bob Price, Joe Price, Cesario Sipaco, Valeriano Abello, Vicente Quintero, and the following members of the 16th Division: Waichi Ito, Shinjiro Terasaki, Sadahiro Yamada, Kiichiro Yamada, Kazuyuki Okumura, Hideichi Nakamura, Noboru Furukawa, Dr. Yoichi Misaki, Kunio Nishimura and Hiroshi Morishima; "The True Facts of the Leyte Operation," a monograph by Major General Yoshiharu Tomochika; "Souvenir Program on the 13th Anniversary Celebration Leyte Landing of the American Forces of Liberation," compiled by the Tacloban Lions Club; "Lovely Americans," by Robert Shaplen, in *The New Yorker* (November 28, 1944); "35th Army Operations, 1944–1945" (official report); *Command Decisions*, prepared by Office of the Chief of Military History; TAYLOR; MATLOFF; HALSEY & BRYAN; KING & WHITEHILL; *End of the Ogasawara Army Corps*, compiled by Yoshitaka Horie, and others; *The Approach to the Philippines*, by Robert Ross Smith; *Leyte: The Return to the Philippines*, by M. Hamlin Cannon; *Decision at Leyte*, by Stanley L. Falk; *Reminiscences*, by General Douglas MacArthur; and *MacArthur's Amphibious Navy*, by Daniel E. Barbey.

Miscellaneous: interviews with Prince Mikasa, Prime Minister Shigeru Yoshida, Marquis Kido. General Kenryo Sato, Admirals Naokumi Nomura and Sokichi Takagi, Colonel Sei Matsutani, Morisada Hosokawa, and Mrs. Hideki Tojo; "Strategic Aspects of the Battle off Formosa," by Vice Admiral Shigeru Fukudome, in USNIP (December 1952); IMTFE documents #58228 and #53405 (Admiral Keisuke Okada); *Memoir of the Termination of the War*, by Sokichi Takagi; *The History of the Great Rightists*, by Bokusui Arakara; HOSOKAWA; THE KONOYE DIARY; *Diaries in Darkness* (diaries of civilians), compiled by Kiyoshi Kayosawa, and others; and COHEN.

22. The Battle of Leyte Gulf

Interviews with Admirals Tomiji Koyanagi, Kiyohide Shima, Keizo Komura and Ryunosuke Kusaka; Captains Toshikazu Ohmae and Tatsumaru Sugiyama; Shigeo Hirayama, Kenkichi Kato and Sadae Ikeda; Commander Shigeru Nishino; Lieutenants Heiya Yamamoto, Wahei Asami and Masanao Naito; Ensign Fukujiro Shimoyama; Kiyoshi Takahashi, Shiro Hosoya, Taro Sito and Hisao Tomokane; "The Japs Had Us on the Ropes," by Rear Admiral C. A. F. Sprague and Lieutenant Philip H. Gustafson, in *American* magazine (April 1945); "With Kurita in the Battle for Leyte Gulf," by Rear Admiral Tomiji Koyanagi, in USNIP (February 1953); "Battle Stations Submerged," by Lieutenant Commander R. C. Benitez, *loc. cit.*; USSBS Navy interrogations #69 (Rear Admiral Chikai Matsuda), #58 (Commander Kokichi Mori), #55 (Vice Admiral Jisaburo Ozawa), #41 (Commander Tonosuke Otani), #35 (Rear Admiral Tomiji Koyanagi) #9 (Vice Admiral Takeo Kurita); *The Kurita Fleet*, by Tomiji Koyanagi; MORISON, Vol. XII, *Leyte*; ITO; *The Divine Wind*, by Rikihei Inoguchi, Tadashi Nakajima and Roger Pineau; FALK, *Leyte*; LOCKWOOD & ADAMSON; TAYLOR; HALSEY & BRYAN; and *Battle Report: The End of an Empire*, by Walter Karig, and others.

23. The Battle of Breakneck Ridge

Interviews with Generals Tomochika and Miyauchi; Lieutenant Colonel Shigeharu Asaeda; Kiyoshi Kamiko, Yoshio Noguchi, Noboru Furukawa and Hiroshi Morishima; "Staff Studies of the Japanese 35th Army on Leyte," by Colonel Toshii Watanabe; "Operations of the 1st Japanese Division on Leyte," a report by Colonel Junkichi Okabayashi; TOMOCHIKA, "Leyte Operation"; *I Didn't Die on Leyte*, by Kiyoshi Kamiko; FALK, *Leyte*; and CANNON.

In August 1966 I accompanied a Japanese party (fifty survivors and relatives of soldiers who had died) to Leyte. The survivors collected the remains of comrades who had fallen, and the entire party conducted a number of Shinto memorial services at the battle sites. Kamiko and Noguchi re-enacted their battle experiences on Breakneck Ridge.

24. Debacle

Leyte: interviews with Generals Yoshiharu Tomochika and Yoshio Miyauchi; Captain Arashi Kamimura; Koyoshi Kamiko, Yoshio Noguchi, Hiroshi Morishima, Noboru Furukawa, Eduardo R. Bugho (and other members of the 4th Leyte Warfare Guerilla Brigade), Ricardo P. Negru and Zoilo Andrade; two reports: "The Relief of Lieutenant General Shimpei Fukue of His Command of the 102nd Division" and "35th Army Operations, 1944-1945."

Prisoners of war: correspondence with Calvin Graef, Donald Meyer, Colonel James O. Gillespie, Colonel Curtis Beecher; Lieutenant Colonels Virgil O. McCollum and Adrianus J. van

Oosten, and Major Roy L. Bodine, Jr.; "Notebook" of Colonel James O. Gillespie; "Five Came Back," by Gene Weeks, in *Hence* (July-August-September 1946); an address, "Medical Experience in Japanese Prison Camp," delivered by Major Samuel M. Bloom at Mount Sinai Hospital, New York, on May 15, 1945; *Jap POW Diary* (unpublished), by Major R. L. Bodine, Jr.; "Hell Ships," unpublished article by A. J. van Oosten; official report by Lieutenant Colonel O. O. Wilson; *Prisoner of War, World War II*, by Hugh H. Myers; and *My Experiences during the War with Japan* (privately printed), by Colonel V. N. Cordero.

25. "Our Golden Opportunity"

Burma: interviews with Generals Hideo Iwakuro and Tadashi Katakura; and Captain Hiromu Kumano and Sajibei Noguchi; "Retreat to the Chindwin," by General Iwaichi Fujiwara, in *History of the Second World War* magazine, Vol. 5, No. 10; *Defeat into Victory*, by General William J. Slim; BA MAW.

China: interviews with John Emmerson and Vice President Chen Cheng; "Propaganda Used against China by the China Expeditionary Army during ICHI-Go [Operation Ichi]," a report by Lieutenant Colonel Tadao Inoue; CHENNAULT; The Stilwell Papers; *Thunder out of China*, by Theodore H. White and Annalee Jacoby; *Outline of the Course of Eight Years of Resistance* (unpublished), by Chen Cheng; *Stilwell's Mission to China, Stilwell's Command Problems* and *Time Runs Out in CBI*, by Charles F. Romanus and Riley Sunderland; *The China Tangle*, by Herbert Feis; *China and the Helping Hand 1937-1945*, by Arthur N. Young; FITZGERALD; VAN SLYKE; HSU KAI-YU; and CHIANG KAI-SHEK.

Prisoners of war: see Notes for Chapter 24.

Yalta: interviews with Ambassador W. Averell Harriman and Charles Bohlen; SNOW, "Fragments from F.D.R."; *The Last 100 Days*, by John Toland; FRUS, *The Conferences at Malta and Yalta 1945*; KING & WHITEHILL; EDEN; *The Meaning of Yalta*, by John N. Snell, and others; LEAHY; and BIRSE.

Miscellaneous: interviews with General Yoshiharu Tomochika, and with Shizuo Fukui; correspondence with Captain John F. Enright; "Statement on the Philippine Operations in 1944-1945," by General Tomoyuki Yamashita at his trial; "*Shinano:* The Jinx Carrier," by Lynn Lucius Moore, in USNIP (February 1953); THE KONOYE DIARY; HOSOKAWA; *Mission with LeMay*, by General Curtis E. LeMay, with MacKinlay Kantor; *Triumph in the Philippines*, by Robert Ross Smith; and *Submarine*, by Edward L. Beach.

26. "Like Hell with the Fire Out"

Interviews with Major Yoshitaka Horie, Captain Tsunezo Wachi, Dr. Masaru Inaoka, John Rich, Toshihiko Ohno, Satoru Omagari, Kiyomi Hirakawa and Yoshimi Fujiwara; a series of interviews conducted by Major Horie for this book in 1970; "Translation of Diary Found on Dead Japanese Officer on Iwo

Jima" by a patrol from C Company, 147th Infantry, March 27, 1945; "A Japanese Remembers Iwo Jima," by Toshihiko Ohno, in the *New York Times Magazine* (February 14, 1965); "Iwo Jima," by Yasuo Kato in *Jiji Shimpo* (February 18, 1952); "Prisoners of War," article by Yoshitaka Hori; *Fighting Spirit—Iwo Jima* (unpublished), by Yoshitaka Horie; HORIE, *End of the Ogasawara;* SEMPER FIDELIS; *Iwo Jima: Amphibious Epic,* by Lieutenant Colonel Whitman S. Bartley; *Iwo Jima,* by Richard F. Newcomb; *The Hero of Iwo Jima,* by William Bradford Huie; MORISON, Vol. XV, *Victory in the Pacific;* VANDEGRIFT (with ASPREY); *Thirty Years,* by John P. Marquand; and *The Assault,* by Allen R. Matthews.

The letter Rear Admiral Toshinosuke Ichimaru addressed to President Roosevelt was found by a Marine in a cave in the northern part of the island. It is now in the museum of the U. S. Naval Academy in Annapolis. It is reprinted here in full:

Rear Admiral T. Ichimaru of the Japanese Navy sends this note to Roosevelt. I have one word to give you upon the termination of this battle.

Approximately a century has elapsed since Nippon, after Commodore Perry's entry to Shimoda, became widely affiliated with the countries of the world. During this period of intercourse, Nippon has met with many national crises, as well as the undesired Sino-Japanese War, Russo-Japanese War, the World War, the Manchurian Incident, and the China Incident. Nippon is now, unfortunately, in a state of open conflict with your country. Judging Nippon from just this side of the screen, you may slander our nation as a yellow peril, or a blood-thirsty nation, or maybe a protoplasm of military clique.

Though you may use the surprise attack on Pearl Harbor as your primary material for propaganda, I believe you, of all persons, know best that you left Nippon no other method in order to save herself from self-destruction.

His Imperial Highness, as clearly shown in the "Rescript of the Founder of the Empire" "Yosei" (Justice), "Choki" (Sagacity) and "Sekkei" (Benevolence), contained in the above three-fold doctrine, rules in the realization of "Hakko-ichiu" (the universe under His Sacred Rule) in His Gracious mind.

The realization of which means the habitation of their respective fatherlands under their own customs and traditions, thus insuring the everlasting peace of the world.

Emperor Meiji's "The four seas of the world that are united in brotherhood will know no high waves nor wind" (composed during the Russo-Japanese War), won the appraisal of your uncle, Theodore Roosevelt, as you yourself know.

We, the Nippon-jin, though may follow all lines of trade, it is through our each walk of life that we support the Imperial doctrine. We, the soldiers of the Imperial Fighting Force take up arms to further the above stated "doctrine."

Though we, at the time, are externally taken by your air raids and shelling, backed by your material superiority, spiritually we are burning with delight and enjoying the peace of mind.

This peacefulness of mind, the common universal stigma of the Nippon-jin burning with fervour in the upholding of the Imperial Doctrine may be impossible for you and Churchill to understand. I hereupon pitying your spiritual feebleness pen a word or two.

Judging from your actions, white races, especially you Anglo-Saxons at the sacrifice of the coloured races, are monopolizing the fruits of the world.

In order to attain this end, countless machinations were used to cajole the yellow races, and to finally deprive them of any strength. Nippon in retaliation to your imperialism tried to free the oriental nations from your punitive bonds, only to be faced by your dogged opposition. You now consider your once friendly Nippon a harmful existence to your luscious plan, a bunch of barbarians that must be exterminated. The completion of this Greater East Asia War will bring about the birth of the East Asia Co-Prosperity Area, this in turn will in the near future result in the everlasting peace of the world, if of course, it is not hampered upon by your unending imperialism.

Why is it that you, an already flourishing nation, nip in bud the movement for the freedom of the suppressed nations of the East. It is no other than to return to the East that which belongs to the East.

It is beyond our contemplation when we try to understand your stinted narrowness. The existence of the East Asia Co-Prosperity sphere does not in anyway encroach upon your safety as a nation; on the contrary, will act as a pillar of world peace insuring the happiness of the world. His Imperial Majesty's true aim is no other than the attainment of this everlasting peace.

Studying the condition of the never ending racial struggle resulting from mutual misunderstanding of the European countries, it is not difficult to feel the need of the everlasting universal peace.

Present Hitler's crusade of "His Fatherland" is brought about by no other than the stupidity of holding only Germany, the loser of the World War, solely responsible for the 1914-1918 calamity and the deprivation of German's re-establishment.

It is beyond my imagination of how you can slander Hitler's program and at the same time cooperate with Stalin's "Soviet Russia" which has as its principle aim the "socialization" of the world at large.

If only the brute force decides the ruler of the world, fighting will everlastingly be repeated, and never will the world know peace nor happiness.

Upon the attainment of your barbaric world monopoly, never forget to retain in your mind the failure of your predecessor President Wilson at his heights.

27. The Flowers of Edo

Interviews with Rikuro Iwata, Emi Sekimura, Yoshie Sekimura, Tosaku Hayashiya, Yuichiro Kominami and Susumu Takahashi; USSBS Navy interrogation #28 (Major Hiroshi Toga); KIYOSAWA; *The Diary of Jun Takami; The Broader Way*, by Sumie Mishima; LeMay (with KANTOR); *A Torch to the Enemy*, by Martin Caidin; CRAVEN & CATE, Vol. V, *The Pacific: Matterhorn to Nagasaki*; SMITH, *Triumph*; PRINCE HIGASHIKUNI; HOSOKAWA; and BA MAW.

28. The Last Sortie

The last sortie: interviews with Admirals Keizo Komura and Ryunosuke Kusaka; Commander Tochigi Terauchi; and Lieutenant Akira Yunoki; "Okinawa Area Naval Operations," Japanese Monograph #83 (OCMH); USSBS Navy interrogation #32 (Commander T. Miyamoto); *Sea of Lamentation*, by Captain Jiro Nomura; FORRESTAL; ITO; and *Japanese Destroyer Captain*, by Captain Tameichi Hara.

Okinawa: interviews with Admiral Sadatoshi Tomioka; Colonels Tsuneo Ito, Tsuneo Shimura, and Koichi Ito; Warrant Officer Kaname Imai; Dr. Shigeko Chihara; Shuzen Hokama, Hisashi Matsumura, Shikichi Miyagi, Mrs. Fumiko Nozaki and Zenso Noborikawa; "Okinawa: A Key to the Western Pacific," by Hyman Kublin, in USNIP (December 1954); "Unexpected Meeting of Teacher and Pupil of Opposite Sides Saves 1,300 Villagers," in the *Okinawa Times* (June 22, 1963); *Okinawa: The Last Battle*, by Roy E. Appleman, James M. Burns, Russell A. Gugeler and John Stevens; MORISON, *Victory; and Okinawa: Victory in the Pacific*, by Major Charles S. Nichols, Jr., USMC, and Henry I. Shaw, Jr.

Miscellaneous: interviews with Morisada Hosokawa, Marquis Kido, Hajime Suzuki, Hisatsune Sakomizu and General Yoshiharu Tomochika; letter from Mamoru Shigemitsu to Gordon W. Prange, February 5, 1950, concerning resignation of the Koiso Cabinet and the Miao Pin affair; IMTFE documents #55127 (Baron Kiichiro Hiranuma), #61636 (Yasumasa Matsudaira) and #55906 (Kuniaki Koiso); "Operation 'Flying Elephant.' " by Mitsutoshi Kondo in *This Is Japan* (1966 edition); *The Kaiten Weapon*, by Yutaka Yokota (with Joseph D. Harrington); HOSOKAWA; PRINCE HIGASHIKUNI; and TOGO.

29. The Iron Typhoon

Interviews with Colonels Tsuneo Shimura, Tsuneo Ito and Koichi Ito; Warrant Officer Kaname Imai; Nobuko Yamashiro,

Toshio Shida, Jinsai Higa, Eikichi Yamazato, Seigo Kawasaki, Masahide Ota, Mieko Miyahira, Shikichi Miyagi, Sachiko Kuda, Hideko Yoshimura, Chosei Osato, Seizu Uema, Tokuzo Makiminato, Chomei Nabachi, Tsuyako Iju, Shinichi Nozaki, Shuzen Hokama, Miyoko Toguchi, Yoshiko Kitashiro, Noburo Kuriyama, Yasuharu Agarie, Shigeru Kinjo, Seizen Nakasone, Yasuo Kayo, Koichi Saijo and Yasunori Aoki; *The Operations of the 7th Infantry Division in Okinawa*, a unit history prepared by Historical Division, U. S. War Department Special Staff; NICHOLS & SHAW; APPLEMAN; INOGUCHI; and *Tragedy of Okinawa*, by Seizen Nakasone.

There is a question about the time of death of Generals Ushijima and Cho. The account in *Okinawa: The Last Battle*, the most authoritative book on the battle, is based on information from a prisoner who heard it from other prisoners. It claims that the suicides occurred at 4 A.M., June 22. Higa, who still lives in Okinawa, testified that he gave Ushijima a haircut four hours later. Higa learned of the suicides from Kuzono's orderly, *Jotohei* Kimura, who witnessed them. Higa returned to the command cave and saw the bodies "lying around like tuna fish." There is another story that Ushijima and Cho committed suicide on a ledge outside the cave. But the bodies were found by Americans inside the cave. See photograph in picture section.

30. The Stragglers

Interviews with Kiyoshi Kamiko, Masaru Inaoka, Toshihiko Ohno, Satoru Omagari and Stewart Griffin; KAMIKO; *The Emperor's Last Soldiers*, by Masashi Ito; and *The Stragglers*, by E. J. Kahn, Jr.

Colonel Nishi's body was never found. Some survivors believe he was wounded in a charge on Airfield No. 2, and after telling his aide to turn him toward the Imperial Palace, shot himself in the head; others claim he died on the north beach. The Baroness Nishi prefers to believe the latter; it would be insupportable to imagine his body "run over" by innumerable American bombers.

31. In Quest of Peace

Interviews with Admirals Sadatoshi Tomioka and Sokichi Takagi, Ambassador Naotake Sato, Gero von S. Gaevernitz, Allen Dulles, Paul Blum, Yoshiro Fujimura, Shintaro Ryu, General Makato Onodera, Kojiro Kitamura, Jiro Homma, Hajime Suzuki, Hisatsune Sakomizu, Marquis Kido and Prime Minister Shigeru Yoshida; "Unmaterialized Peace Movement in Sweden Now Exceedingly Regretted," unpublished article by General Makoto Onodera; "The Japanese Peace Effort in Sweden," unpublished article by General Onodera; "The Mysterious Dr. Hack," by Gero von S. Gaelvernitz, in *Frankfurter Allgemeine Zeitung* (August 31, 1965); IMTFE documents #61477 (Suemasa Okamoto), #64118 (Yoshiro Fujimura), #54483 (Shigenori Togo), #61978 (Vice Admiral Zenshiro Hoshina), and #61338 (General Masao Yoshizumi); *The Per Jacobsson Mediation*, edited by Erin E. Jucker-Fleetwood; *Japanese-U.S.S.R. Diplomatic Negotiations*, compiled by Research Department, Japanese Foreign Ministry; *Journey to the Missouri*, by Toshikazu Kase; *The Yoshida Memoirs*, by Shigeru Yoshida; MORISON, *Victory;* LeMAY (with KANTOR); and *Russia at War*, by Alexander Werth.

The following books were used in Chapters 31 through 36: *Japan's Decision to Surrender*, by Robert J. C. Butow; *Behind Japan's Surrender*, by Lester Brooks; *The Fall of Japan*, by William Craig; HOSOKAWA; CRAVEN & CATE, *Matterhorn to Nagasaki;* SAKOMIZU; SUZUKI BIOGRAPHY; *Historical Records on the Surrender*, 2 vols., compiled by the Japanese Foreign Ministry; and *Notes on the Termination of the War*, by Kainan Shimomura.

According to the *History of the Great Patriotic War of the Soviet Union*, there had been peace-feelers before Hirota approached Malik. "First of all, two private persons approached the Russians on behalf of the Japanese Government—Mr. Mijakawa, the Japanese Consul General in Harbin, and Mr. Tanakamuru, fishing magnate.

"On March 4 [1945], the same Tanakamuru called on Mr. J. Malik, the Soviet Ambassador in Tokyo, saying that neither Japan nor the United States could start speaking of peace. A 'divine outside force' was necessary to bring about a peace settlement, and the Soviet Union could play that role.

"After the formation of the Suzuki Government, these peace-feelers became even more explicit. Foreign Minister Togo asked Mr. Malik on April 20 to arrange for him a meeting with Mr. Molotov."

In 1953 Allen Dulles told Fujimura that if the Japanese had accepted the Fujimura-Dulles proposal, the "present tragedy in Korea" could have been avoided. "The history of the world," he said, "would have been different."

32. "That Was Not Any Decision That You Had to Worry About"
Interviews with President Harry S. Truman, Ambassador Charles Bohlen, Eugene Dooman, John J. McCloy, Prime Minister Clement Attlee, Allen Dulles, Ladislas Farago, Ambassador Naotake Sato, Marquis Kido, Hajime Suzuki and Saiji Hasegawa; "The Decision to Use the Atomic Bomb," by Henry L. Stimson, in *Harper's* (February 1947); correspondence with John J. McCloy, Major Robert Lewis and Colonel Thomas W. Ferebee; GREW, *Turbulent Era;* HEINRICHS; BIRSE; *The Strange Alliance*, by John R. Deane; TOLAND, *Last 100 Days; My Eighty Years Reminiscences*, by Naotake Sato; JUCKER-FLEETWOOD; *Year of Decisions*, by Harry S. Truman; *Speaking Frankly* and *All in One Lifetime*, by James F. Byrnes; *The* [James] *Forrestal Diaries*, edited by Walter Mellis; LEAHY; OCMH, *Command Decisions: Japan Subdued*, and *Between War and Peace*, by Herbert Feis; STIMSON

& BUNDY; THE STIMSON DIARY; *Burn after Reading*, by Ladislas Farago; *The New World*, by Richard G. Hewlett and Oscar E. Anderson, Jr.; *Atomic Diplomacy: Hiroshima and Potsdam*, by Gar Alperovitz; *Day of Trinity*, by Lansing Lamont; *Atomic Quest*, by Arthur Holly Compton; *Abandon Ship!*, by Richard F. Newcomb; *Dawn over Zero*, by William L. Laurence; WERTH; *Experience of War*, by Kenneth S. Davis; CHURCHILL, Vol. VI, *Triumph and Tragedy*; LORD MORAN; *Twilight of Empire: Memoirs of Prime Minister Clement Attlee*, as set down by Frances Williams; *As It Happened*, by Clement R. Attlee; *Memoirs*, by George F. Kennan; and GRAND STRATEGY, Vol. VI, y John Ehrman. IMTFE document #503 (Shigenori Togo) was used for Chapters 32 to 36.

Late in July 1945 the Zacharias office in Washington proposed bold plan to send General Oshima, who had recently been captured in southern Germany, to Tokyo on a secret mission of peace. The party—to be led by a hero of adventure movies, Douglas Fairbanks, Jr.—would proceed to Japan by submarine. Forrestal and Admiral King approved the mission but were overridden by others close to Truman.

3. Hiroshima

Interviews with Kyoko Sato, Michiko Yamaoka, Hiroaki Daido, Mrs. Fukiko Iura, Mayor Shinzo Hamai. Dr. Fumio Shigeto, Sadako Tsutsumachi, Shiroku Tanabe, Tomie Fujii, Hisaji Dai, Syuji Hamai, Tadahiko Kitayama, Mrs. Matsuyo Hayashi, Ryo Fukumaru, Yoshinori Ataka, Tokuo Ootowa, Chiyo Takamori, Mrs. Yasuko Nukushina, Dr. Yoshimasa Matsuzaka, Shogo Nagaoka, Kunio Ono, Gonichi Kimura, Captain Hideo Sematoo, Mrs. Yoshiko Tomita, Father Hugo Lassalle (Makibi Enomiya), Kiyoko Matsubara, Shigeru Shimoyama, Tsuneo Mataba and Dr. Bernard Waldman; correspondence with Major Robert Lewis and Colonel Thomas W. Ferebee; "Dr. Teller Urges More Explosive Use," by Roger Birdsell, in the South Bend *Tribune* February 7, 1967); "Story of the Atomic Bomb," unpublished article by Dr. Ryokichi Sagane; "Delayed Effects Occurring within the First Decade after Exposure of Young Individuals to the Hiroshima Atomic Bomb" (Atomic Bomb Casualty Commission Pamphlet), by Robert W. Miller, M.D.; "Determination of the Burst Point and Hypocenter of the Atomic Bomb in Hiroshima" (ABCC), by Edward T. Arakawa and Shogo Nagaoka; *Hiroshima*, by John Hersey; *Hiroshima Pilot*, by William Bradford Huie; TRUMAN; and THE STIMSON DIARY.

The following pamphlets and books were used for Chapters 33 and 34: "Residual Radiation in Hiroshima and Nagasaki" (ABCC), by Edward T. Arakawa; "Actual Facts of the A-Bomb Disaster" (ABBC), by Drs. Naomi Shohno, Yukio Fujimoto and Akashi Nakamura; "Human Radiation Effects" (ABCC), by Drs. Kenneth G. Johnson and Antonio Cicco; "Geological Study of Damages Caused by Atomic Bombs in Hiroshima and Nagasaki"

(ABCC), by T. Watanabe, S. Nagaoka, and others; *No High Ground*, by Fletcher Knebel and Charles W. Bailey II; *Friends of the Hibakusha*, edited by Virginia Naeve; LAURENCE; *Death in Life*, by Robert Jay Lifton; and FEIS, *Japan Subdued*.

34. . . . and Nagasaki

Interviews with Shogo Nagaoka, H. Yukimune, Professor Seiji Imabori, Dr. Tatsuichiro Akizuki, Etsuko Obata, Hachiro Kosasa, Dr. Ryokichi Sagane, Kaoru Naruse, Kamekichi Sugimoto, Hitoshi Tokai, Kazuko Tokai, Shigeyoshi Morimoto, Toshiyuki Hayama, Senji Yamaguchi, Hajime Iwanaga, Mayor Tsutomu Tagawa, Taeko Fukakori, Midori Nishida, Hajime Suzuki, Marquis Kido, Ambassador Naotake Sato, Hisatsune Sakomizu, Tomio Yamamoto, Saiji Hasegawa and Admiral Sadatoshi Tomioka; "Notes on the Nagasaki Atom Bomb," unpublished article by Yoshiko Araki; "Unforgettable Evacuation," unpublished article by Yoshiko Kato; "Record of Operations against Soviet Russia," Japanese Monograph #155 (OCMH); correspondence with Dr. Julien M. Goodman; and *Nagasaki, The Forgotten Bomb*, by Frank W. Chinnock, the only full-length account of the Nagasaki bombing.

Shogo Nagaoka, with nine children and little money, dedicated his life to the study of the atomic bombings. He was forced to sell most of the family possessions, including his wife's kimonos. It was he who set up the museum in Hiroshima's Park of Peace and was its first curator.

35. "To Bear the Unbearable"

Interviews with Professor Kiyoshi Hiraizumi; Prince Mikasa; Marquis Kido; Admiral Sadatoshi Tomioka; General Masahiko Takeshita; Colonels Saburo Hayashi, Masao Inaba and Okikatsu Arao; Fumihiko Togo; Hajime Suzuki; and Saiji Hasegawa; IMTFE documents #57670 (Admiral Soemu Toyoda), #60745 (Yasumasa Matsudaira), #61883 (General Yatsuji Nagai), #61636 (Yasumasa Matsudaira), #62049 ("The Unpublished Record on Termination of the War, Kept by the Japanese Navy General Staff"), #61481 (Shunichi Matsumoto), #61475 (Marquis Kido), #53437 (Admiral Zenshiro Hoshina), #59496 (Colonel Makoto Tsukamoto), #55127 (Kiichiro Hiranuma); "The Reason Why the Affair Happened," unpublished article by Colonel Masataka Ida; *The Takeshita Diary* (unpublished), by Masahiko Takeshita; KING & WHITEHILL; THE FORRESTAL DIARIES; BYRNES; *One Lifetime* and *Speaking Frankly*; TRUMAN; THE GREW DIARY; THE STIMSON DIARY; *Treatise on the Termination of the Pacific War*, compiled by the Japan Diplomatic Association; general editor, T. Ueda.

36. The Palace Revolt

Interviews with Marquis Kido; Professor Kiyoshi Hiraizumi; General Tatsuhiko Takashima; and Colonels Masahiko Takeshita, Saburo Hayashi, Masao Inaba, Okikatsu Arao and Masataka Ida;

Hajime Suzuki; Morio Tateno; Daitaro Arakawa; and Chamberlains Yoshihiro Tokugawa and Yasuhide Toda; IMTFE documents #61978 (Admiral Zenshiro Hoshina), #56367 and #50025A (Masahiko Takeshita), #61338 (General Masao Yoshizumi); "Notes," a report by General Tatsuhiko Takashima; "Anami," an unpublished article by Colonel Masataka Ida; "Army Minister General Korechika Anami," a speech delivered at the Defense Training School on November 11, 1964, by General Masahiko Takeshita; *Hara-kiri*, by Jack Seward; documents from the NHK File on the Palace revolt; and KIRBY, *The War against Japan*, Vol. V.

37. The Voice of the Crane

Interviews with Generals Bonner Fellers, Yatsuji Nagai, Masahiko Takeshita and Ichiji Sugita; Admirals Horace V. Bird, Sadatoshi Tomioka and Ryunosuke Kusaka; Colonels Tsuneo Shimura and Masataka Ida; Baron Ian Mutsu; Ambassador Harumi Takeuchi; Roy Otake; Takeshi Ono; Robert Trumbull; Yoshio Kodama; Marquis Kido; IMTFE document #50025A (Masahiko Takeshita); IDA, "Anami"; "Welcome U. S. Army Signed U. S. Navy," by Hal Drake, in *Pacific Stars and Stripes;* "The End of World War II," unpublished article by Rear Admiral Horace V. Bird; an article on Tokyo Rose by Harry T. Brundige, in *American Mercury* (January 1954); "An Account of the Honorable Deaths of the Righteous Army for the Cause of Reverence for the Emperor and Expulsion of Foreigners: Twelve Patriots and Patriotesses of Atago Hill," article by Katsuichi Ohba; "Going down to Manila," article by Katsuo Okazaki; "The Emperor's Courier," unpublished article by Robert C. Mikesh; *Four Years in Hell*, by Tomomi Yamamoto; MACARTHUR; EICHELBERGER; *I Was an American Spy*, by Sidney Forrester Mashbir; WHITE & JACOBY; documents from the NHK File; PRINCE HIGASHIKUNI; NOGUCHI; TRUMAN; FEIS, *China Tangle;* VAN SLYKE; KASE; MORISON, *Victory;* and KATO.

Admiral Tomioka was so impressed by MacArthur's speech at the surrender ceremonies that his resolve to commit hara-kiri weakened. Moreover, one of his former teachers urged him to live so he could write an objective history of the war; no one else, he said, was as qualified. With the help of Admiral Yonai, Tomioka collected important documents—including the original rescripts of the Emperor—which had been ordered destroyed, and hid them. He wanted to preserve them as proof "that the millions who had died had done so for the Emperor; otherwise their souls would never be comforted." Since then he has devoted his life to the history of the Pacific war and is currently head of the Historical Research Institute in Tokyo. The Emperor's rescripts and many other high-echelon documents are still in his library.

Epilogue

Interviews with Michitaka Konoye, Marquis Kido, Mrs. Hideki Tojo and General Bonner Fellers; Tojo story by George E.

Jones, in the *New York Times* (September 12, 1945); "Tragedy in Vietnam," by Frederick L. Schuman in *The Berkshire Review* (Spring 1968); BUTOW, *Tojo;* EICHELBERGER; YOUNG; *The Politics of War*, by Gabriel Kolko; and FEIS, *Contest.*

Index

1056

1068

1070